Keeping the Republic

POWER AND CITIZENSHIP IN AMERICAN POLITICS

THE ESSENTIALS

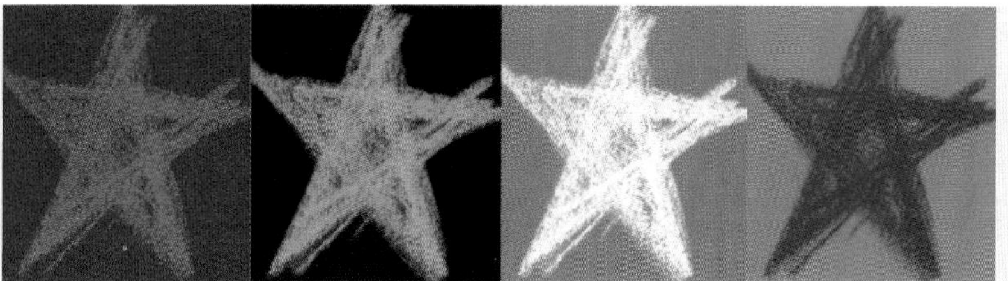

THIRD EDITION

Christine Barbour, Indiana University

Gerald C. Wright, Indiana University

with

Matthew J. Streb, Northern Illinois University

Michael R. Wolf, Indiana University–Purdue University Fort Wayne

A Division of Congressional Quarterly Inc.
Washington, D.C.

CQ Press
1255 22nd Street, NW, Suite 400
Washington, DC 20037

Phone: 202-729-1900; toll-free, 1-866-427-7737 (1-866-4CQ-PRESS)

Web: www.cqpress.com

Cover and interior design and composition: Naylor Design, Inc.

⊗ The paper used in this publication exceeds the requirements of the American National Standard for Information Sciences—Permanence of Paper for Printed Library Materials, ANSI Z39.48-1992.

Printed and bound in the United States of America

09 08 07 06 05 1 2 3 4 5

Library of Congress Cataloging-in-Publication Data

Barbour, Christine
Keeping the republic: power and citizenship in American politics/Christine Barbour, Gerald C. Wright; with Matthew J. Streb [and] Michael R. Wolf.—3rd ed. [abridged]
p. cm.
ISBN 1-933116-00-5 (alk. paper)
1. United States—Politics and government—Textbooks. I. Wright, Gerald C. II. Streb, Matthew J. (Matthew Justin). III. Wolf, Michael R. IV. Title.

JK276.B372 2006
320.473—dc22 2005027937

We dedicate this book with love to our moms, Patti Barbour and Doris Wright,

To the memory of our dads, John Barbour and Gerry Wright,

To our kids, Andrea and Darrin, Monica and Michael,

To our granddaughters, Amelia, Elena, and Paloma,

And to each other.

ABOUT THE AUTHORS

Christine Barbour teaches in the political science department and the Honors College at Indiana University, where she has become increasingly interested in how teachers of large classes can maximize what their students learn. At Indiana, Professor Barbour has been a Lilly Fellow, working on a project to increase student retention in large introductory courses, and a member of the Freshman Learning Project, a university-wide effort to improve the first-year undergraduate experience. She has served on the *New York Times* College Advisory Board, working with other educators to develop ways to integrate newspaper reading into the undergraduate curriculum. She has won several teaching honors, with two awarded by her students meaning the most to her: the Indiana University Student Alumni Association Award for Outstanding Faculty (1995–1996) and the Indiana University Chapter of the Society of Professional Journalists Brown Derby Award (1997). When not teaching or writing textbooks, Professor Barbour enjoys playing with her five dogs, traveling with her coauthor, and writing about food. She writes a food column for the *Herald Times* of Bloomington and is a coauthor of *Indiana Cooks!* (2005). She is currently working on a book about local politics, development, and the fishing industry in Apalachicola, Florida.

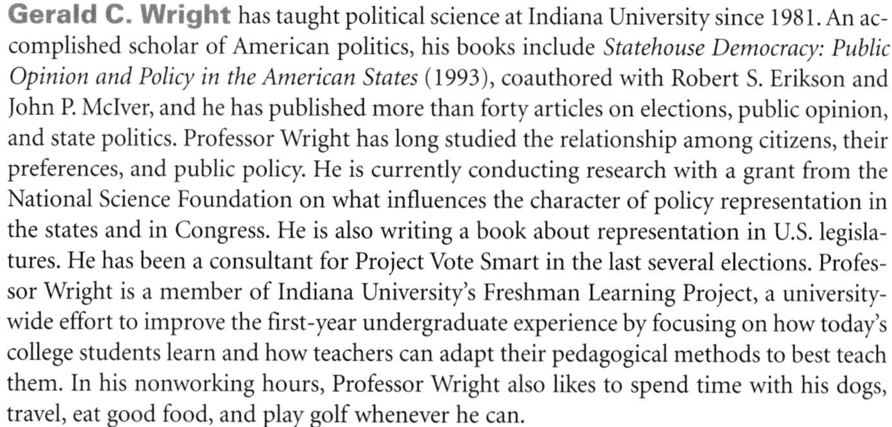

Gerald C. Wright has taught political science at Indiana University since 1981. An accomplished scholar of American politics, his books include *Statehouse Democracy: Public Opinion and Policy in the American States* (1993), coauthored with Robert S. Erikson and John P. McIver, and he has published more than forty articles on elections, public opinion, and state politics. Professor Wright has long studied the relationship among citizens, their preferences, and public policy. He is currently conducting research with a grant from the National Science Foundation on what influences the character of policy representation in the states and in Congress. He is also writing a book about representation in U.S. legislatures. He has been a consultant for Project Vote Smart in the last several elections. Professor Wright is a member of Indiana University's Freshman Learning Project, a university-wide effort to improve the first-year undergraduate experience by focusing on how today's college students learn and how teachers can adapt their pedagogical methods to best teach them. In his nonworking hours, Professor Wright also likes to spend time with his dogs, travel, eat good food, and play golf whenever he can.

With Matthew J. Streb and Michael R. Wolf. Streb is assistant professor in the political science department at Northern Illinois University. He is the author of *The New Electoral Politics of Race* (2002) and the editor or coeditor of *Polls and Politics* (2004), *Clued in to Politics: A Critical Thinking Reader on American Government* (2004), and *Law and Election Politics* (2005). He specializes and teaches in the areas of parties, elections, polling and public opinion, Congress, civil rights movements, and research methods. Wolf is assistant professor in the political science department at Indiana University–Purdue University Fort Wayne. He specializes in and teaches courses on Congress, voting behavior, and comparative electoral behavior.

BRIEF CONTENTS

NON
à la Constitution
au gouvernement
à Chirac

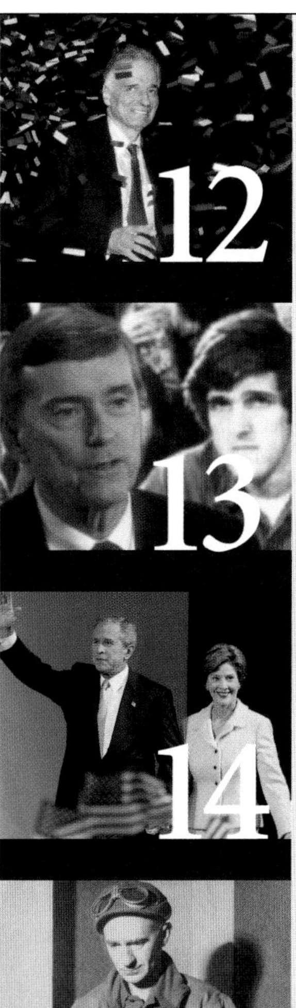

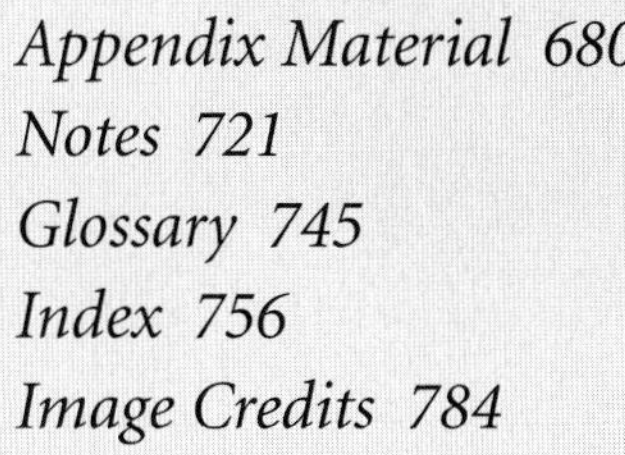

CONTENTS

3

4

5

NOT A
CRIME
RACIAL JUSTICE COALITION
6

Referendum et manif le soir
NON
à la Constitution
au gouvernement
à Chirac

12

KEN CORDIER
P.O.W. Dec. 1966 - Mar. 1973
www.swiftvets.com
13

PREFACE

When one of us was a freshman journalism major in college, more years ago now than she cares to remember, she took an introduction to American politics course—mostly because the other courses she wanted were already full. But the class was a revelation. The teacher was terrific, the textbook provocative, and the final paper assignment an eye opener. "As Benjamin Franklin was leaving Independence Hall," the assignment read, "he was stopped by a woman who asked, 'What have you created?' Franklin replied, 'A Republic, Madam, if you can keep it.' " Had we succeeded in keeping our republic? Had we been given a democracy in the first place? These questions sparked the imagination. With the writing of an impassioned freshman essay about the limits and possibilities of American democracy, a lifetime love affair with politics was born. If we have one goal in writing this textbook, it is to share the excitement of discovering humankind's capacity to find innovative solutions to those problems that arise from our efforts to live together on a planet too small, with resources too scarce, and with saintliness in too short a supply. In this book we honor the human capacity to manage our collective lives with peace, and even, at times, dignity. And in particular, we celebrate the American political system and the founders' extraordinary contribution to the possibilities of human governance.

WHERE WE ARE GOING

Between the two of us, we have been teaching American politics for more than half a century. We have used a lot of textbooks in that time. Some of them have been too difficult for introductory students (although we have enjoyed them as political scientists!), and others have tried excessively to accommodate the beginning student and have ended up being too light in their coverage of basic information. When we had to scramble to find enough details to write reasonable exam questions, we knew that the effort to write an accessible textbook had gone too far. We wanted our students to have the best and most complete treatment of the American political system we could find, presented in a way that would catch their imagination, be easy to understand, and engage them in the system they were learning about.

This book is the result of that desire. It covers essential topics with clear explanations, but it is also a thematic book, intended to guide students through a wealth of material and to help them make sense of the content both academically and personally. To that end we develop two themes that run throughout every chapter: an analytic theme to assist students in organizing the details and connect them to the larger ideas and concepts of American politics and an evaluative theme to help them find personal meaning in the American political system and develop standards for making judgments about how well the system works. Taken together, these themes provide students a framework on which to hang the myriad complexities of American politics.

The analytic theme we chose is a classic in political science: politics is a struggle over limited power and resources, as gripping as a sporting event in its final minutes, but much more vital. The rules guiding that struggle influence who will win and who will lose, so that often the struggles with the most at stake are over the rule-making itself. In short, and in the words of a very famous political scientist, *politics is about who gets what and how they get it.* To illustrate this theme, we begin and end every chapter with a feature called *What's at Stake?* that poses a question about what people want from politics—what they are struggling to get and how the rules affect who gets it. At the end of every major chapter section, we stop to revisit Harold Laswell's definition in context and ask *Who, What, How?* This periodic analytic summary helps solidify the conceptual work of the book and gives students a sturdy framework within which to organize the facts and other empirical information we want them to learn.

For the evaluative theme, we focus on the "who" in the formulation of "who gets what and how." Who are the country's citizens? What are the ways they engage in political life? In order to "keep" a republic, citizens must shoulder responsibilities as well as exercise their rights. We challenge students to view democratic participation among the diverse population as the price of maintaining liberty.

Our citizenship theme has three dimensions. First, in our *Profiles in Citizenship* feature, present in every chapter, we introduce students to important figures in American politics and ask the subjects why they are involved in public service or some aspect of political life. Based on personal interviews with these people, the profiles model republic-keeping behavior for students, helping them to see what is expected of them as members of a democratic polity. We unabashedly feel that a primary goal of teaching introductory politics is not only to create good scholars but also to create good citizens. Second, at the end of nearly every chapter, the feature *The Citizens and . . .* provides a critical view of what citizens can or cannot do in American politics, evaluating how democratic various aspects of the American system actually are and what possibilities exist for change. Third, we premise this book on the belief that the skills that make good students and good academics are the same skills that make good citizens: the ability to think critically about and process new information and the ability to be actively engaged in one's subject. Accordingly, in our *Consider the Source* feature, we help students examine critically all the various kinds of political information they are bombarded with—from information in textbooks like this one, to information from the media or the Internet, to information from their congressperson or political party.

HOW WE GET THERE

In many ways this book follows the same path that most American politics texts do: there are chapters on all the subjects that instructors scramble to cover in a short amount of time. But in keeping with our goal of making the enormous amount of material here more accessible to our students, we have made some changes to the typical format. After our introductory chapter, we have included a chapter not found in every book: "American Citizens and Political Culture." Given our emphasis on citizens, this chapter is key; it covers the history and legal status of citizens and immigrants in America and the ideas and beliefs that unite us as Americans as well as the ideas that divide us politically. This chapter introduces an innovative feature called *Who Are We?* which describes through graphs and charts just who we Americans are and where we come from, what we believe, how educated we are, and how much money we make. This recurring feature aims at exploding stereotypes and providing questions to lead students to think critically about the political consequences of America's demographic profile. To guide students in understanding just what the numbers and figures mean, the *Consider the Source* feature in chapter 2 teaches some basic skills for statistical analysis.

Another chapter that breaks with tradition is chapter 4, "Federalism and the U.S. Constitution," which provides an analytic and comparative study of the basic rules governing this country—highlighted up front because of our emphasis on the *how* of American politics. This chapter covers the essential elements of the Constitution: federalism, the three branches, separation of powers and checks and balances, and amendability. In each case we examine the rules the founders provided, look at the alternatives they might have chosen, and ask what difference the rules make to who wins and who loses in America. This chapter is explicitly comparative. For each rule change considered, we look at a country that does things differently. We drive home early the idea that understanding the rules is crucial to understanding how and to whose advantage the system works. Throughout the text we look carefully at alternatives to our system of government as manifested in other countries—and among the fifty states.

Because of the prominence we give to rules—and to institutions—this book covers Congress, the presidency, the bureaucracy, and the courts before looking at public opinion, parties, interest groups, voting, and the media—the inputs or processes of politics that are shaped by those rules. While this approach may seem counterintuitive to instructors who have logged many miles teaching it the other way around, we have found that it is not counterintuitive to students, who have an easier time grasping the notion that the rules make a difference when they are presented with those rules in the first half of the course. We have, however, taken care to write the chapters so that they will fit into any organizational framework.

We have long believed that teaching is a two-way street, and we welcome comments, criticisms, or just a pleasant chat about politics or pedagogy. You can email us directly at barbour@indiana.edu and wright1@indiana.edu, or write to us at the Department of Political Science, Indiana University, Bloomington, IN 47405.

WHAT'S NEW IN THE THIRD EDITION

The political world changes daily and we make every effort to capture the dramatic events that have occurred in the world. As we write this preface, the country struggles to rebuild New Orleans, to reassess the federal government's ability to handle disasters, to come to terms with our role in Iraq, and to choose a new member of the Supreme Court. Our job as your textbook authors is to make sense of those changes within the framework that we believe helps students interpret and understand American politics.

Accordingly, we've provided major updates and current examples throughout the text. Graphs in every chapter have been revised to reflect the newest data available, and more than two-thirds of the photographs have been replaced with new, current images.

Writing the third edition also gave us an opportunity to revise and improve some of the pedagogical features to make them more useful and pertinent to both instructors and students.

- We've moved our old *Keeping the Republic* boxes to our Web site to make room for *Profiles in Citizenship*—a feature that models civic involvement for students through interviews with public figures like Condoleezza Rice, James Carville, Sandra Day O'Connor, Newt Gingrich, Rahm Emanuel, Christine Todd Whitman, Russell Feingold, Bill Maher, and eleven others. By engaging students with these individuals' stories we hope to spur their imaginations into action.
- New *What's at Stake?* features examine such topics as the role of 527 groups in the 2004 election, the redistricting in Texas that sent Democratic state legislators heading for the hills, the struggle over executive privilege that emerged during John Bolton's confirmation hearings as ambassador to the United Nations, the prospects for a constitutional amendment allowing for a foreign-born president, the implementation of the No Child Left Behind Act, the growing national debt, rising gas prices and drilling in ANWR, and the waging of preventive war in the Middle East. In all, we have replaced or significantly updated more than half of the *What's at Stake?* chapter openers.
- We streamlined our *Who, What, How* chapter breaks by removing the old file-tab graphics and bulleted lists. Now the breaks flow into the narrative of the chapter but still give students a chance to stop and reflect on what they have read through the lens of the book's themes.
- In chapter 1 we have clarified the book's approach, and explicitly tied the skills of analysis and evaluation to the themes of power and citizenship. A diagram on page 26 shows students clearly how these skills and themes fit together under the general goal of critical thinking about American politics.

SUPPLEMENTS

We know how important good resources can be in the teaching of American government. Our goal has been to create resources that not only support but also enhance the text's themes and features. Matthew Streb and Michael Wolf, intimately familiar with the book's goals and approach as well as with the revisions in this edition, have put together a comprehensive package to address instructors' teaching needs.

- Our **Test Bank** has more than 1,400 test questions, separated into factual and conceptual multiple choice, short answer, fill-in-the-blank, and short essay questions to help you create exams. The test bank is available in Word and WordPerfect format, as well as fully loaded in *CQP Test Writer*—a flexible and easy-to-use test-generation software that allows you to build and customize exams.
- **PowerPoint Lecture Slides** provide an outline for each chapter, highlighting key concepts and leaving plenty of room for adaptability.
- The **Instructor's Manual** includes chapter overviews, lecture starters, class activities, and discussion questions, all of which provide the backbone for lectures and

in-class discussions while pointing to ways the power and citizenship themes can be further developed.

- All of the book's **Figures, Tables, and Maps**, in full color, are available as both PowerPoint slides and PDFs, so that you can easily teach with them in the classroom. The publisher will also provide a set of acetates upon request. Please contact James Headley at jheadley@cqpress.com.
- **"Clicker" Slides** are available for those instructors who use these new student response systems. This set of additional slides provides a unique way to help track participation, gauge comprehension, and instantly poll student opinion.
- The **Instructor's Resource Web Page** (at republic.cqpress.com) takes the book's material further with a wealth of additional resources including tables and figures not found in the book, syllabi, sample classroom assignments, and a new on-line teaching forum that we hope will foster an active users' community so that you may find and share tips with your colleagues. The idea is to pass on secrets of success, offer solutions to problems, and benefit from the variety of your peers' classroom experiences.
- A free six-month subscription to ***CQ Weekly*** is available through CQ Press to instructors who adopt *Keeping the Republic* (subject to minimum quantities). We use *CQ Weekly* to stay up to date on current developments and we know many of our colleagues do as well. This is a useful source to animate your lectures with topical and insightful analysis from the same magazine that informs politicians and policymakers in Washington.

Because students need help outside the classroom as well, we provide a companion Web site at **republic.cqpress.com**. Matthew Streb and Michael Wolf have prepared a wealth of materials to help students master each chapter's learning objectives, vocabulary, and basic and conceptual information.

- Our **KTRblog** will provide news postings about twice a week, connecting current events to the book's themes and topics.
- A **Study** section offers summaries and learning objectives that encapsulate the most important facts and concepts of each chapter.
- Practice **Quizzes** allow students to work through approximately twenty multiple choice questions per chapter and receive immediate results, both by question type (e.g., conceptual, factual, and vocabulary) and by chapter section so that they can effectively gauge their comprehension. If you would like to track your students' online work, you can have them email their quiz results directly to you.
- **Flashcards** are a handy way for students to review the book's key terms. They can also mark terms they would like to return to as well as shuffle and reset their cards.
- Web-based **Exercises** provide activities that encourage students to apply information, concepts, and principles from the text in a series of interactive questions.
- An **Explore** section has annotated Web links to facilitate further research, as well as the *Keeping the Republic* boxes from previous editions that point students to where they can get involved in the political process.
- Our **Take a Position** feature builds on particular issues or controversies covered in

the text, leading students through the critical thinking process so that they can build a balanced, well-argued position on current events. For example, launching from the *Consider the Source* in chapter 3, students take a position on whether history should be taught from a traditional or multicultural perspective. The *What's at Stake?* in chapter 11 is the starting point for students to address whether the United States should have national referenda.

ACKNOWLEDGMENTS

The Africans say that it takes a village to raise a child—it is certainly true that it takes one to write a textbook! We could not have done it without a community of family, friends, colleagues, students, reviewers, and editors, who supported us, nagged us, maddened us, and kept us on our toes. Not only is this a better book because of their help and support, but it would not have been a book at all without them.

On the family front, we thank our parents, our kids, and our siblings (and our nephews and nieces!!) who have hung in there with us even when they thought we were nuts (and even when they were right). Our friends, old and new, have all listened to endless progress reports (and reports of no progress at all) and cheered the small victories with us. Sharing slow food with fast friends has kept us sane, and we especially thank Bob and Kathleen, as always, Pat and Julia, Fenton and Rich, Dave and Krissy, David and Scott, Ronnie and Evan, and Russ and Connie. Thanks also to John Bond for his long friendship and good book advice. On the home front we are forever grateful for the unconditional love and support, not to mention occasional intellectual revelation (Hobbes was wrong: it is not a dog-eat-dog world after all!), offered up gladly by Daphne, Gina, Zoë, Ginger, Bandon, and Maggie. (Though we lost Max, Clio, and Spook along the way, they were among our earliest and strongest supporters and we miss them still.) And we are so very thankful to Pam Stogsdill and Tammy Blunck for looking after us and keeping the whole lot in order.

Colleagues now or once in the Political Science Department at Indiana University have given us invaluable help on details beyond our ken: Yvette Alex Assensoh, Jack Bielasiak, Doris Burton, Ted Carmines, Dana Chabot, Mike Ensley, Chuck Epp, Judy Failer, Russ Hanson, Margie Hershey, Bobbi Herzberg, Virginia Hettinger, Jeff Isaac, Burt Monroe, Lin Ostrom, Rich Pacelle, Karen Rasler, Leroy Rieselbach, Jean Robinson, Steve Sanders, Pat Sellers, and John Williams. IU colleagues from other schools and departments have been terrific: Trevor Brown, Dave Weaver, and Cleve Wilhoit from the Journalism School, Bill McGregor and Roger Parks from the School of Public and Environmental Affairs, John Patrick from the School of Education, and Julia Lamber and Pat Bande from the Law School have all helped out on substantive matters. Many IU folks have made an immeasurable contribution by raising our consciousness about teaching to new levels: Joan Middendorf, David Pace, Laura Plummer, Tine Reimers, Ray Smith, and Samuel Thompson, as well as all the Freshman Learning Project people. Dwayne Schau, James Russell, Bob Goelhert, Fenton Martin, and all the librarians in the Government Publications section of our library have done yeoman service for us. We are also grateful to colleagues from other institutions: Joe Aistrup, Shaun Bowler, Bob Brown, Tom Carsey, Kisuk Cho, E. J. Dionne, Todd Donovan, Bob Erikson, David Hobbs, Kathleen Knight, David Lee, David McCuan, John McIver, Dick Merriman, Glenn Parker, Denise Scheberle, John Sislin, Dorald Stoltz, and Linda Streb. Rich Pacelle and Robert Sahr were particularly helpful.

Special thanks to all our students, undergraduate and graduate, past and present, who inspired us to write this book in the first place. Many students helped us in more concrete ways, working tirelessly as research assistants, writing boxed features, and putting together the material at the end of the chapters. Now colleagues at other universities, Tom Carsey, Dave Holian, Tracy Osborn, Brian Schaffner, and Jon Winburn all helped keep us going. Mike Wagner and Jessica Gerrity, still at IU, were also super helpful on this edition. We are also grateful to Hugh Aprile, Liz Bevers, Christopher McCollough, Rachel Shelton, Jim Trilling, and Kevin Willhite for their help early in the project.

Thanks also to Mike Stull, for taking us seriously in the first place, to Jean Woy, for the vision that helped shape the book, and to our early development editors, Ann West and Ann Kirby-Payne. Ann West in particular was a friend, a support, and a fabulous editor. We will love her forever.

We have also benefited tremendously from the help of the folks at Project Vote Smart and the many outstanding political scientists around the country who have provided critical reviews of the manuscript at every step of the way. We'd like to thank the following people who took time away from their own work to critique and make suggestions for the improvement of ours. They include all the candy reviewers—Sheldon Appleton, Paul Babbitt, Harry Bralley, Scott Brown, Peter Carlson, David Holian, Carol Humphrey, Glen Hunt, Marilyn Mote-Yale, and Craig Ortsey—and also:

Danny M. Adkison, *Oklahoma State University*
Ellen Andersen, *Indiana University–Purdue University Indianapolis*
Sheldon Appleton, *Oakland University*
Kevin Bailey, *Texas House of Rep., District 140*
David C. Benford, *Tarrant County College*
Jeffrey A. Bosworth, *Mansfield University*
Ralph Edward Bradford, *University of Central Florida*
James Bromeland, *Winona State University*
Robert D. Brown, *University of Mississippi*
Scott E. Buchanan, *Gordon College*
John F. Burke, *University of St. Thomas*
Anne Marie Cammisa, *Suffolk University*
Francis Carleton, *University of Wisconsin at Green Bay*
Jennifer B. Clark, *South Texas Community College*
Renee Cramer, *California State University, Long Beach*
Paul Davis, *Truckee Meadows Community College*
Christine L. Day, *University of New Orleans*
Robert E. DiClerico, *West Virginia University*
Robert L. Dion, *University of Evansville*
Victoria Farrar-Myers, *University of Texas at Arlington*
Femi Ferreira, *Hutchinson Community College*
Phillip Gianos, *California State University, Fullerton*
Dana K. Glencross, *Oklahoma City Community College*
Eugene Goss, *El Camino College*
Victoria Hammond, *Austin Community College*
Patrick J. Haney, *Miami University*
Charles A. Hantz, *Danville Area Community College*
Roberta Herzberg, *Utah State University, Logan*
David Holian, *University of North Carolina at Greensboro*
Ronald J. Hrebenar, *University of Utah*

Tseggai Isaac, *University of Missouri–Rolla*
William G. Jacoby, *Michigan State University*
W. Lee Johnston, *University of North Carolina Wilmington*
Kelechi A. Kalu, *University of Northern Colorado*
Joshua Kaplan, *University of Notre Dame*
John D. Kay, *Santa Barbara City College*
Kendra A. King, *University of Georgia*
Bernard D. Kolasa, *University of Nebraska at Omaha*
John F. Kozlowicz, *University of Wisconsin–Whitewater*
Lisa Langenbach, *Middle Tennessee State University*
Ted Lewis, *Collin County Community College*
Brad Lockerbie, *University of Georgia*
Paul M. Lucko, *Angelina College*
Vincent N. Mancini, *Delaware County Community College*
Ursula G. McGraw, *Coastal Bend College*
Tim McKeown, *University of North Carolina at Chapel Hill*
Sam Wescoat McKinstry, *East Tennessee State University*
Lauri McNown, *University of Colorado at Boulder*
Lawrence Miller, *Collin County Community College*
Maureen F. Moakley, *University of Rhode Island*
Theodore R. Mosch, *University of Tennessee at Martin*
Melinda A. Mueller, *Eastern Illinois University*
David Nice, *Washington State University*
James A. Norris, *Texas A&M International University*
Richard Pacelle, *Georgia Southern University*
George E. Pippin, *Jones County Junior College*
David Robinson, *University of Houston–Downtown*
Dario Albert Rozas, *Milwaukee Area Technical College*
Robert C. Sahr, *Oregon State University*
Denise Scheberle, *University of Wisconsin at Green Bay*
Thomas A. Schmeling, *Rhode Island College*
Paul Scracic, *Youngstown State University*
Todd Shaw, *University of South Carolina*
Daniel M. Shea, *Allegheny College*
Neil Snortland, *University of Arkansas at Little Rock*
Michael W. Sonnleitner, *Portland Community College*
Robert E. Sterken Jr., *University of Texas at Tyler*
Ruth Ann Strickland, *Appalachian State University*
Tom Sweeney, *North Central College*
Richard S. Unruh, *Fresno Pacific University*
Lynn Vacca, *Lambuth University*
Jan P. Vermeer, *Nebraska Wesleyan University*
Molly Waite, *William Rainey Harper College*
Matt Wetstein, *San Joaquin Delta College*
Lois Duke Whitaker, *Georgia Southern University*
Cheryl Wilf, *Kutztown University*
David E. Woodard, *Concordia University*
David J. Zimny, *Los Medanos College*

In this edition we are also incredibly indebted to the busy public servants who made the *Profiles in Citizenship* possible. We are gratified and humbled that they believed in the project enough to give us their valuable time. Deep appreciation to

Tiffany Benjamin, Esmeralda Santiago, Newt Gingrich, Lissa Morgenthaler-Jones, Bill Maher, Ward Connerly, Russ Feingold, Condoleezza Rice, Coleen Rowley, Sandra Day O'Connor, Andrew Kohut, Rahm Emanuel, Wayne Pacelle, James Carville, Markos Moulitsas, Jason West, Christine Todd Whitman, Mitch Daniels, and Lee Hamilton. Thanks, also, to Todd Walters at Kenyon College, and to Andrea Parmenter for her quick and careful transcriptions of the interviews.

There are three people in particular without whom this edition would never have seen the light of day. Pat Haney has provided the nuts and bolts of the foreign policy chapter since the first edition. Pat has been a cheerful, tireless collaborator for more than ten years now, and we are so grateful to him. Matthew Streb and Michael Wolf have also been involved with this book since its inception, first serving as research assistants while they were in grad school and then stepping up to the bat to help us get this edition out quickly. We thank them from the bottom of our hearts for everything they contributed, and we are especially grateful to Page and Logan and Beth and Ray, who made most of the sacrifice. Matt and Mike would like to thank Marjorie Campbell, Patrick Furlong, Katie Jones, and Craig Ortsey for their help.

Finally, it is our great privilege to acknowledge and thank all the people at CQ Press who believed in this book and made this edition possible. In this day and age of huge publishing conglomerates, it has been such a pleasure to work with a small committed team who are dedicated to top-quality work. Brenda Carter's vision of the Press and our place in it is inspiring and exciting; Charisse Kiino earned our instant gratitude for so thoroughly and immediately "getting" what this book is about. They have both worked tirelessly with us on decisions big and small, and we have relied heavily on their good sense, their wisdom, and their patience. Too old to keep his hours, we had nevertheless long heard of the legendary James Headley—and we are thrilled that he is now on our side; likewise, thanks to Alan Barber, Amanda Bednarz, Michael Dunaway, Linda Trygar, Kyle Kovacevich, Jennifer Schroeder, Brendan McCarthy, and Brendon Kelly. For putting this beautiful book together and drawing your attention to it, we thank the folks on the production, editorial, and marketing teams: Steve Pazdan, Paul Pressau, Margot Ziperman, Ann Davies, Anne Stewart, Colleen Ganey, Dwain Smith, Bonnie Erickson, Erin Long, and Stephanie Grow. We are indebted to everyone who made such a heroic effort to get this book out under a tight deadline, but special mention goes to Debra Naylor, who not only designed this gorgeous book but also fit the text to the design with an unerring eye, and to Lorna Notsch, our extraordinary project editor who held the whole thing together so well, working impossible hours and remaining unfailingly cheerful in the face of last-minute challenges. Thanks, also, to Amy Marks for her gentle but thorough copyediting.

We learned a long time ago that the efforts of the authors on a project like this are dwarfed by the labors of the development editor. We have been extraordinarily lucky through the years to have had top-notch DEs on this book, and against all odds our luck has held on this edition. Michael Kerns has been unflagging and good natured and highly professional—his excellent book sense is second only to his knack for soothing volatile authors. In our demanding production schedule the brunt of the work fell on his shoulders and he bore it with grace. Michael, we thank you.

Christine Barbour
Gerald C. Wright

TO THE STUDENT

SUGGESTIONS ON HOW TO READ THIS TEXTBOOK

1. As they say in Chicago about voting, do it **early and often**. If you open the book for the first time the night before the exam, you will not learn much from it and it won't help your grade. Start reading the chapters in conjunction with the lectures, and reread them all at least once before the exam. A minimum of two readings is necessary for a decent education and a decent grade.

2. Read the **chapter outlines!** There is a wealth of information in the outlines and in all the chapter headings. They tell you what we think is important, what our basic argument is, and how all the material fits together. Often, chapter subheadings list elements of an argument that may show up on a quiz. Be alert to these clues.

3. **Read actively!** Constantly ask yourself: What does this mean? Why is this important? How do these different facts fit together? What are the broad arguments here? How does this material relate to class lectures? How does it relate to the broad themes of the class? When you stop asking these questions you are merely moving your eyes over the page and that is a waste of time. This is especially true of the *What's at Stake?* vignettes at the beginning of each chapter (and the follow-up at the chapter's end). Try to keep the themes and questions posed in the *What's at Stake?* vignette alive as you read the chapter so that you can make the important connections to the material being covered.

4. **Highlight or take notes**. Some people prefer highlighting because it's quicker than taking notes, but others think that writing down the most important points helps in remembering them later on. Whichever method you choose (and you must choose one), be sure you're doing it properly! The point of both methods is to make sure that you interact with the material and learn it instead of just passively watching it pass before your eyes—and that you have in some way indicated the most important points so that you do not need to read the entire chapter your second time through.

   Highlighting. Highlight with a pen or marker that enables you to read what's on the page. Do not highlight too much. An entirely yellow page will not give you any clues about what is important. Read each paragraph and ask yourself: What is the basic idea of this paragraph? Highlight that. Avoid highlighting all the examples and illustrations. You should be able to recall them on your own when you see the main idea. Beware of highlighting too little. If whole pages go by with no marking, you are probably not highlighting enough.

Outlining. Again, the key is to write down enough, but not too much. Recopying a chapter written by someone else is deadly boring—and a waste of time. Go for key ideas, terms, and arguments.

5. Don't be afraid to **write in your book**. Even if you choose to outline instead of highlight, make notes to yourself in the margins of your book, pointing out cross-references, connections, ideas, and examples. Especially note tie-ins to the lectures, or summaries of broad arguments.

6. Read and reread the ***Who, What, How*** **summaries** at the end of each chapter section. These will help you digest the material just covered and get you ready to go on to the next section.

7. Note all **key terms**, including those that appear in chapter headings. Be sure you understand the definition and significance, and write the significance in the margin of your book!

8. Do not skip **charts, graphs, pictures, or other illustrations**! These things are there for a purpose, because they convey crucial information or illustrate a point in the text. After you read a chart or graph, make a note in the margin about what it means. Pay special attention to the *Who Are We?* features. These graphs and tables offer you a glimpse of the people of the United States—our ethnic backgrounds, our income and education, our representatives in government—that will enhance your understanding of American government and how demographic changes are likely to affect policy in the future.

9. Do not skip the ***Consider the Source*** **boxes**, the ***Profiles in Citizenship*** **boxes**, or the other boxes in the book. They are not filler! The *Consider the Source* boxes provide advice on becoming a critical consumer of the many varieties of political information that come your way. They list questions to ask yourself about the articles you read, the campaign ads and movies you see, and the graphs you study, among other things. The *Profiles in Citizenship* boxes highlight the achievements of a political actor pertinent to that chapter's focus. They model citizen participation and can serve as a beacon for your own political power long after you've completed your American government course. The other boxes, like the "Madame President?" box on page 358, may highlight an important trend or focus on an example of something discussed in the text. They'll often give you another angle from which to understand the chapter themes.

10. Make use of the **chapter ending material**. The final section of each chapter, called *The Citizens and . . .* addresses your role as a citizen in the context of the chapter topics. When you've finished the chapter, be sure to read the *Summary.* Like the *Who, What, How* summaries, the end-of-chapter summaries will help put the chapter's information in perspective, summarizing the major points made in each chapter section. Then test yourself with the practice quiz. The answers, along with fifteen other questions per chapter, can be found on the companion Web site at republic.cqpress.com. Use the flashcards on the site to test how well you know the chapter's vocabulary. All the Web material is there to ensure you've mastered the chapter's topics and can point to areas you need to study further.

Keeping the Republic

What was up in 2004? Traditionally, American voters aged 18–29 are among the least likely to vote, in contrast to older citizens (demonstrating against the privatization of Social Security, below), who are much more politically active—and more likely to get what they want from the political system as a consequence. But in 2004, college-aged voters across the country turned out in record numbers. Students at Ohio's Kenyon College, showing real determination to have their voices heard, waited in the rain for up to ten hours to vote (right). Does the 2004 election herald a lasting change, or was it just a blip?

POLITICS: WHO GETS WHAT, AND HOW?

1

WHAT'S AT STAKE?

For me, the experience is one I will never forget," says Kenyon College student Todd Walters. "Some people say they will never forget where they were when they heard the news about Kennedy being shot, well this was one of those moments for me." [1]

What was the earthshaking, once-in-a-lifetime event that is seared into Walters's memory? Surprising as it may seem, it was not a national tragedy or a personal triumph but something younger people are not even supposed to care very much about. It was his first vote in a presidential election.

It took Walters seven and a half long hours of waiting in line to cast that vote on November 2, 2004. His roommate waited for ten. For Walters and his fellow students, that election became an exercise not only in democracy but also in patience, commitment, and determination to show that they could make a difference.

Long waits to vote were not uncommon in Ohio in 2004. One of the so-called battleground states where the electoral votes were hotly contested and voter registration drives had been wildly successful; in many precincts there were not enough voting machines to handle the crowds of new voters. Many voters around the state tired of waiting or had to leave to go to work or cope with families.

But at tiny Kenyon College, in Gambier, Ohio, students persevered. Campus groups had done such an excellent job getting students registered at Kenyon that the two voting machines that normally handled the campus turnout of a few hundred had to handle thousands instead.

And so they waited. As the day wore on, members of political parties brought the young voters snacks and bottled water and students took turns standing in for each other so they could get brief respites from the tedium of waiting in line. Those who'd had the good fortune or sense to vote early went to the dining hall and returned with trays of food for those still waiting. The president of the college excused their absences from class and the administration extended the deadline for spring registration, due to end that day. New friendships were forged as the students stood in line, suffused with a sense of camaraderie and purpose.

Exhausted, some students gave up and went home, but most stayed, and in the end they voted. The last Kenyon students finally left the polling place just before dawn the next day, weary but triumphant at having accomplished what they came for.

The Kenyon students were not the only college-aged voters to break records that day. When the exit poll results came out, the leaders of MTV's Rock the Vote, America Coming Together, MoveOn.org, and other groups monitoring the youth turnout were jubilant. While young people were the same percentage of the electorate (18 percent) that they had been in 2000, the electorate as a whole had turned out in numbers much greater than normal, and young voters had kept pace. Turnout of voters aged eighteen to twenty-nine was 51.6 percent overall (up from 42.3 percent in 2000), and in the battleground states it was 64.4 percent, up 13 points from the previous presidential election.

These statistics would surely have given considerable peace of mind to Benjamin Franklin, who was keenly aware of the importance of popular attention to the political process. In 1787, when asked by a woman what he and other founders of the Constitution had created, he answered: "A Republic, Madam, if you can keep it." But ever since eighteen year olds had been given the vote in 1972, their voting turnout had been low, their efforts to keep the republic distinctly lackluster.

Young people have generally been less interested in politics than their elders, and less informed. In one 2002 survey, only 51 percent of those aged eighteen to twenty-five could name Dick Cheney as vice president of the United States and only 45 percent said they were interested in local politics, fewer than any other age group.[2] One writer, noting that Americans of all ages expressed increasingly high levels of distrust in government and dislike for politics, sounded the dire warning that "a nation that hates politics will not long thrive as a democracy." [3]

For those who believe that political engagement is essential to the prosperity of democracy, a critical question is whether 2004 constitutes a lasting change in young people's political attitudes. Perhaps it was a fluke, a one-time thing, tied to vague rumors about an impending draft to support the Iraqi war, or to an unusually close election, or to extraordinary get-out-the-vote efforts made by the political parties and other activist groups. Is young people's political involvement really such a big deal, or is concern about keeping the republic just an idiosyncrasy of long-deceased founders and hyperactive political science professors? What is really at stake for American democracy in the issue of youthful engagement in the political system? We will be able to address this question better after we explore the meaning of politics and the difference it makes in our lives. *

Have you got grand ambitions for your life? Do you want a powerful position in business, influence in high places, money to make things happen? Perhaps you would like to make a difference in the world, heal the sick, fight for peace, feed the poor. Or maybe all you want from life is a good education, a well-paying job, a comfortable home, and a safe, prosperous, contented existence. Think politics has nothing to do with any of those things? Think again.

The things that make those goals attainable—a strong national defense, education loans or tax deductions for tuition money, economic prosperity, full employment, favorable mortgage rates, policies that let us take time off from work to have kids, secure streets and neighborhoods, cheap and efficient public transportation—are all influenced by or are the products of politics.

Yet, if you listen to the news, politics may seem like one long campaign commercial: eternal bickering and finger-pointing by people who are feathering their nests and those of their cronies at the expense of the voters. Politics, which we would like to think of as a noble and even morally elevated activity, takes on all the worst characteristics of the business world, where we expect people to take advantage of each other and pursue their own private interests. Can this really be the heritage of Thomas Jefferson and Abraham Lincoln? Can this be the "world's greatest democracy" at work?

In this chapter we get to the heart of what politics is, how it relates to other concepts such as power, government, rules, economics, and citizenship. We propose that politics can best be understood as the struggle over who gets power and resources in society. Politics produces winners and losers, and much of the reason it can look so ugly is that people fight desperately not to be losers.

Contrary to their depictions in the media, and maybe even in our own minds, the people who are doing that desperate fighting are not some special breed of people who are different—more corrupt or self-interested or greedy—from the rest of us. They *are* us—whether they are officials in Washington or mayors of small towns, corporate CEOs or representatives of labor unions, local cops or soldiers in the Middle East, church-goers or atheists, doctors or lawyers, shopkeepers or consumers, professors or students, they are the people that in a democracy we call *citizens.*

As we will see, it is the beauty of a democracy that all the people, including the everyday people like us, get to fight for what they want. Not everyone can win, of course, and many never come close. But the people who pay attention and who learn how the rules work can begin to use those rules to increase their chances of getting what they want, whether it is a lower personal tax bill, greater pollution controls, a more aggressive foreign policy, safer streets, a better educated population, or more public parks. If they become very skilled citizens, they can even begin to change the rules so that they can fight more easily for the kind of society they think is important, and so that people like them are more likely to end up winners in the high-stakes game we call politics.

The government our founders created for us gives us a remarkable playing field on which to engage in that game. Like any other politicians, the designers of the American system were caught up in the struggle for power and resources, and in the desire to write laws that would maximize the chances that they, and people like them, would be winners in the new system. Regardless of their motivations, they crafted a government remarkable for its ability to generate compromise and stability, and also for its potential to realize freedom and prosperity for its citizens.

To help you better understand the system they gave us and our place in it, in this chapter you will learn

- the meaning of "politics"
- the varieties of political systems and the roles they endorse for the individuals who live in them
- the historical origins of American democracy
- the goals and concerns of the founders as they created the American system
- the components of critical thinking and how the themes of power and citizenship will serve as our framework for understanding American politics

WHAT IS POLITICS?

Over two thousand years ago, the Greek philosopher Aristotle said that we are political animals, and political animals we seem destined to remain. The truth is that politics is a fundamental and complex human activity. In some ways it is our capacity to be political—to cooperate, bargain, and compromise—that helps distinguish us from all the other animals out there. While it may have its baser moments—Watergate, White House interns, and Enron come to mind—politics also allows us to reach more exalted heights than we could ever achieve alone—from the dedication of a new public library, to the dismantling of the Berlin Wall, to the establishment of democratic elections in Iraq.

Since this book is about politics in all its glory as well as its shame, we need to begin with a clear definition. One of the most famous definitions, put forth by the well-known political scientist Harold Lasswell, is still one of the best, and we will use it to frame our discussion throughout this book. Lasswell defined **politics** as "who gets what when and how."[4] Politics is a way of determining, without recourse to violence, who gets power and resources in society, and how they get them. **Power** is the ability to get other people to do what you want them to do. The resources in question here might be governmental jobs, tax revenues, laws that help you get your way, or public policies that work to your advantage.

politics who gets what, when, and how; a process of determining how power and resources are distributed in a society without recourse to violence

power the ability to get other people to do what you want

social order a particular view of how we ought to organize and live our collective lives; who should get what

The tools of politics are compromise and cooperation, discussion and debate, even, sometimes, bribery and deceit. Politics is the process through which we try to arrange our collective lives in some kind of **social order** so that we can live without crashing into each other at every turn, and to provide ourselves with goods and services we could not obtain alone. But politics is also about getting your own way. Your own way may be a noble goal for society or pure self-interest, but the struggle you engage in is a political struggle. Because politics is about power and other scarce resources, there will always be winners and losers in politics. If everybody could always get his or her own way, politics would disappear. It is because we cannot always get what we want that politics exists.

What would a world without politics be like? There would be no resolution or compromise between conflicting interests, because those are certainly political activities. There would be no agreements struck, bargains made, or alliances formed. Unless there were enough of every valued resource to go around, or unless the world were big enough that we could live our lives without coming into contact with other human beings, life would be constant conflict—what the philosopher Thomas Hobbes (1588–1679) called a "war of all against all." Individuals, unable to cooperate with one another (because cooperation is essentially political), would have no option but to resort to brute force to settle disputes and allocate resources.

Our capacity to be political saves us from that fate. We do have the ability to persuade, cajole, bargain, promise, compromise, and cooperate. We do have the ability to agree on what principles should guide our handling of power and other scarce resources and to live our collective lives according to those principles. Because there are many potential theories about how to manage power—who should have it, how it should be used, how it should be transferred—agreement on which principles are **legitimate**, or accepted as "right," can break down. When agreement on what is legitimate fails, violence often takes its place. Indeed, the human history of warfare attests to the fragility of political life.

Putting Their Heads Together
Republican senator John McCain of Arizona and Democratic senator Edward Kennedy of Massachusetts confer over prescription drug legislation. Even though their parties are frequently at odds on substantive policy issues, the kind of cooperation they exhibit here is in line with the Senate's long tradition of deference and courtesy among members. Such diplomacy might strike some observers as archaic and phony given how much is at stake in the policy outcomes they debate, but it serves an important purpose—limiting hostilities and enabling members to reach the compromises that make democratic government possible.

Although one characteristic of government is that it has a monopoly on the legitimate use of force, politics means that we have alternatives, that bloodshed is not the only way of dealing with human conflict. Interestingly, the word *politics* comes from the Greek word *polis,* meaning "city-state." Similarly, the word *civilization* comes from the Latin word *civitas,* meaning "city" or "state." Thus, our Western notions of politics and civilization share similar roots, all tied up with what it means to live a shared public life.

legitimate accepted as "right" or proper

POLITICS AND GOVERNMENT

Although the words *politics* and *government* are sometimes used interchangeably, they really refer to different things. Politics is a process or an activity through which power and resources are gained and lost. **Government**, on the other hand, is a system or organization for exercising authority over a body of people.

government a system or organization for exercising authority over a body of people

American *politics* is what happens in the halls of Congress, on the campaign trail, at Washington cocktail parties, and in neighborhood association meetings. It is the making of promises, deals, and laws. American *government* is the Constitution and the institutions set up by the Constitution for the exercise of authority by the American people, over the American people.

Authority is power that citizens view as legitimate, or "right"—power that we have implicitly consented to. You can think of it this way: As children, we probably did

authority power that is recognized as legitimate

as our parents told us or submitted to their punishment if we didn't because we recognized their authority over us. As we became adults, we started to claim that they had less authority over us, that we could do what we wanted. We no longer saw their power as wholly legitimate or appropriate. Governments exercise authority because people recognize them as legitimate even if they often do not like doing what they are told (paying taxes, for instance). When governments cease to be regarded as legitimate, the result may be revolution or civil war, unless the state is powerful enough to suppress all opposition.

RULES AND INSTITUTIONS

Government is shaped by the process of politics, but it in turn provides the rules and institutions that shape the way politics continues to operate. The rules and institutions of government have a profound effect on how power is distributed and who wins and loses in the political arena. Life is different in other countries not only because they speak different languages and eat different foods but also because their governments establish rules that cause life to be lived in different ways.

rules directives that specify how resources will be distributed or what procedures govern collective activity

Rules can be thought of as the *how,* in the definition "who gets what, and *how.*" They are directives that determine how resources are allocated and how collective action takes place—that is, they determine how we try to get the things we want. We can do it violently, or we can do it politically, according to the rules. Those rules can provide for a single dictator, for a king, for rule by God's representative on earth or by the rich, for rule by a majority of the people, or for any other arrangement. The point of the rules is to provide some framework for us to solve without violence the problems that are generated by our collective lives.

Because the rules we choose can influence which people will get what they want most often, understanding the rules is crucial to understanding politics. Consider for a moment the impact a change of rules would have on the outcome of the sport of basketball, for instance. What if the average height of the players could be no more than 5′10″? What if the baskets were lowered? What if foul shots counted for two points rather than one? Basketball would be a very different game, and the teams recruited would look quite unlike the teams we now cheer for. So it is with governments and politics: change the people who are allowed to vote or the length of time a person can serve in office, and the political process and the potential winners and losers change drastically.

institutions organizations in which governmental power is exercised

We can think of **institutions** as the *where* of the political struggle, though Lasswell didn't include a "where" component in his definition. They are the organizations where governmental power is exercised. In the United States, our rules provide for the institutions of a representative democracy, that is, rule by the elected representatives of the people, and for a federal political system. Our Constitution lays the foundation for the institutions of Congress, the presidency, the courts, and the bureaucracy as a stage on which the drama of politics plays itself out. Other systems might call for different institutions, perhaps an all-powerful parliament, or a monarch, or even a committee of rulers.

These complicated systems of rules and institutions do not appear out of thin air. They are carefully designed by the founders of different systems to create the kinds of society they think will be stable and prosperous, but also where people like themselves are likely to be winners. Remember that not only the rules but also the institutions we choose influence who most easily and most often get their own way.

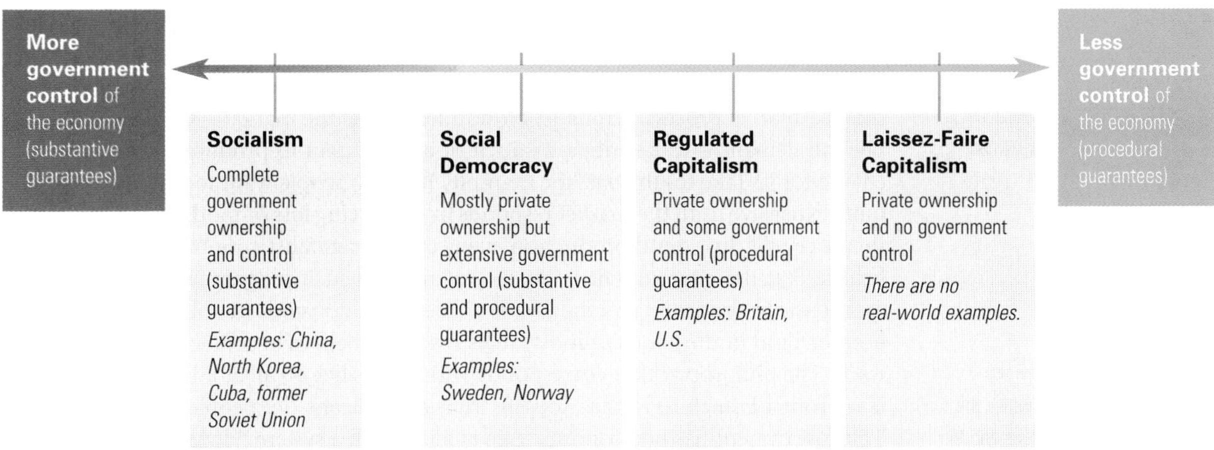

FIGURE 1.1
A Comparison of Economic Systems
Economic systems are largely defined by the degree to which government owns the means by which material resources are produced (e.g., factories and industry) and controls economic decision making. On a scale ranging from socialism—complete government ownership and control of the economy (on the left)—to laissez-faire capitalism—complete individual ownership and control of the economy (on the right)—social democracies would be located in the center. These hybrid systems are characterized by mostly private ownership of the means of production but considerable government control over economic decisions.

POLITICS AND ECONOMICS

In addition to distinguishing between politics and government, and rules and institutions, we must also figure out where economics fits into the scheme of things. Whereas politics is concerned with the distribution of power and resources in society, **economics** is concerned specifically with the production and distribution of society's wealth—material goods like bread, toothpaste, and housing, and services like medical care, education, and entertainment.

economics production and distribution of a society's material resources and services

Because both politics and economics focus on the distribution of society's resources, political and economic questions often get confused in contemporary life. Questions about how to pay for government, about government's role in the economy, and about whether government or the private sector should provide certain services have political and economic dimensions. Because there are no clear-cut distinctions here, it can be difficult to keep these terms straight.

The sources of the words *politics* and *economics* suggest that their meanings were once more distinct than they are today. We already saw that the Greek source of the word *political* was *polis,* or "city-state," the basic political unit of ancient Greece. For the free male citizens of the city-state of Athens (by no means the majority of the inhabitants), politics was a prestigious and jealously restricted activity. However, the public, political world of Athens was possible only because a whole class of people (slaves and women) existed to support the private world, the *oikonomia,* or "household." This early division of the world into the political and the economic clearly separated the two realms. Political life was public, and economic life was private. Today, that distinction is not nearly so simple. What is public and private now depends on what is controlled by government. The various forms of economic systems are shown in Figure 1.1.

capitalist economy an economic system in which the market determines production, distribution, and price decisions and property is privately owned

Capitalism In a pure **capitalist economy**, all the means that are used to produce material resources (industry, business, and land, for instance) are privately owned, and decisions about production and distribution are left to individuals operating through the free-market process. Capitalist economies rely on the market—the process of supply and demand—to decide how much of a given item to produce or how much to charge for it. Take toothpaste, for example. If many people want toothpaste, it will be quite expensive until the market responds by producing lots of toothpaste, whereupon the price will drop until production evens out. In capitalist countries, people do not believe that the government is capable of making such judgments (like how much toothpaste to produce), and they want to keep such decisions out of the hands of government and in the hands of individuals who they believe know best about what they want. The philosophy that corresponds with this belief is called **laissez-faire capitalism**, from a French term that, loosely translated, means "let people do as they wish." The government has no economic role at all in such a system. However, no economic system today maintains a purely unregulated form of capitalism, with the government completely uninvolved.

laissez-faire capitalism an economic system in which the market makes all decisions and the government plays no role

regulated capitalism a market system in which the government intervenes to protect rights and make procedural guarantees

procedural guarantees government assurance that the rules will work smoothly and treat everyone fairly, with no promise of particular outcomes

Like most other countries today, the United States has a system of **regulated capitalism**. It maintains a capitalist economy and individual freedom from government interference remains the norm, but it allows government to step in and regulate the economy to guarantee individual rights and to provide **procedural guarantees** that the rules will work smoothly and fairly. Although in theory the market ought to provide everything that people need and want, and should regulate itself as well, sometimes the market breaks down, or fails. In regulated capitalism, the government steps in to try to fix it.

Markets have cycles: periods of growth are often followed by periods of slowdown or recession. Individuals and businesses look to government for protection from these cyclical effects—for example, when Franklin Roosevelt created the Works Progress Administration to get Americans back to work during the Great Depression, and when the Federal Reserve Bank lowered interest rates to stimulate the economy during the recession early in the first George W. Bush administration. Government may also act to ensure the safety of the consumer public and of working people or to encourage fair business practices (like prevention of monopolies), or to provide goods and services that people have no incentive to produce themselves.

Highways, streetlights, libraries, museums, schools, social security, national defense, and a clean environment are some examples of the goods and services that many people are unable or unwilling to produce privately. Consequently, government undertakes to provide these things (with money provided by taxpayers) and, in doing so, becomes not only a political but an economic actor as well. To the extent that government gets involved in a capitalist economy, we move away from laissez-faire to regulated capitalism.

socialist economy an economic system in which the state determines production, distribution, and price decisions and property is government owned

Socialism In a **socialist economy** like that of the former Soviet Union (based loosely on the ideas of German economist Karl Marx), economic decisions are made not by individuals through the market but rather by politicians, based on their judgment of what society needs. Rather than allowing the market to determine the proper distribution of material resources, politicians decide what the distribution ought to be and then create economic policy to bring that outcome about. In other words, they do not emphasize procedural guarantees of fair rules and process, but rather **substantive guarantees** of what they believe to be fair outcomes.

substantive guarantees government assurance of particular outcomes or results

According to the basic values of a socialist or communist system (although there are some theoretical differences between the two, they are similar for our purposes here), it is unjust for some people to own more property than others and to have power over them because of it. Consequently, the theory goes, the state or society—not corporations or individuals—should own the property (like land, factories, and corporations). In such systems, the public and private spheres overlap, and politics controls the distribution of all resources. The societies that have tried to put these theories into practice have ended up with very repressive political systems, but Marx hoped that eventually socialism would evolve to a point where each individual had control over his or her own life—a radical form of democracy.

No Small Undertaking
If the U.S. Postal Service only kept its biggest and most profitable routes open, small rural sites like this one in Bradley, Michigan, would probably be shut down. Government control ensures that mail delivery is widespread and relatively inexpensive, getting your letters to icy outposts in Alaska or the swamps of Florida for less than 40 cents.

Many theories hold that socialism is possible only after a revolution that thoroughly overthrows the old system to make way for new values and institutions. This is what happened in Russia in 1917 and in China in the 1940s. Since the socialist economies of the former Soviet Union and eastern Europe have fallen apart, socialism has been left with few supporters, although some nations, like China, North Korea, and Cuba, still claim allegiance to it.

Social Democracy Some countries in western Europe, especially the Scandinavian nations of Norway, Denmark, and Sweden, have developed hybrid economic systems. As noted in Figure 1.1, these systems represent something of a middle ground between socialist and capitalist systems. Primarily capitalist, in that they believe most property can be privately held, proponents of **social democracy** nonetheless argue that the values of equality promoted by socialism are attractive and can be brought about by democratic reform rather than revolution. Believing that the economy does not have to be owned by the state for its effects to be controlled by the state, social democratic countries attempt to strike a difficult balance between providing substantive guarantees of fair outcomes and procedural guarantees of fair rules.

social democracy a hybrid system combining a capitalist economy and a government that supports equality

Since World War II, the citizens of many western European nations have elected social democrats to office, where they have enacted policies to bring about more equality—for instance, the elimination of poverty and unemployment, better housing, and adequate health care for all. Even where social democratic governments are voted out of office, such programs have proved so popular that it is often difficult for new leaders to alter them.

VARIETIES OF POLITICAL SYSTEMS AND THE CONCEPT OF CITIZENSHIP

Just as there are different kinds of economic systems, there are different sorts of political systems, based on different ideas about who should have power and what the social order should be—that is, how much public regulation there should be over individual behavior. For our purposes, we can divide political systems into two types: those in which the government has the power to impose a particular social order, deciding how individuals ought to behave, and those in which individuals exercise personal power over most of their own behavior and ultimately over government as well.

Figure 1.2 offers a comparison of these systems. The first type of system, called authoritarian government, potentially has total power over its subjects; the second type, nonauthoritarian government, permits citizens to limit the state's power by claiming

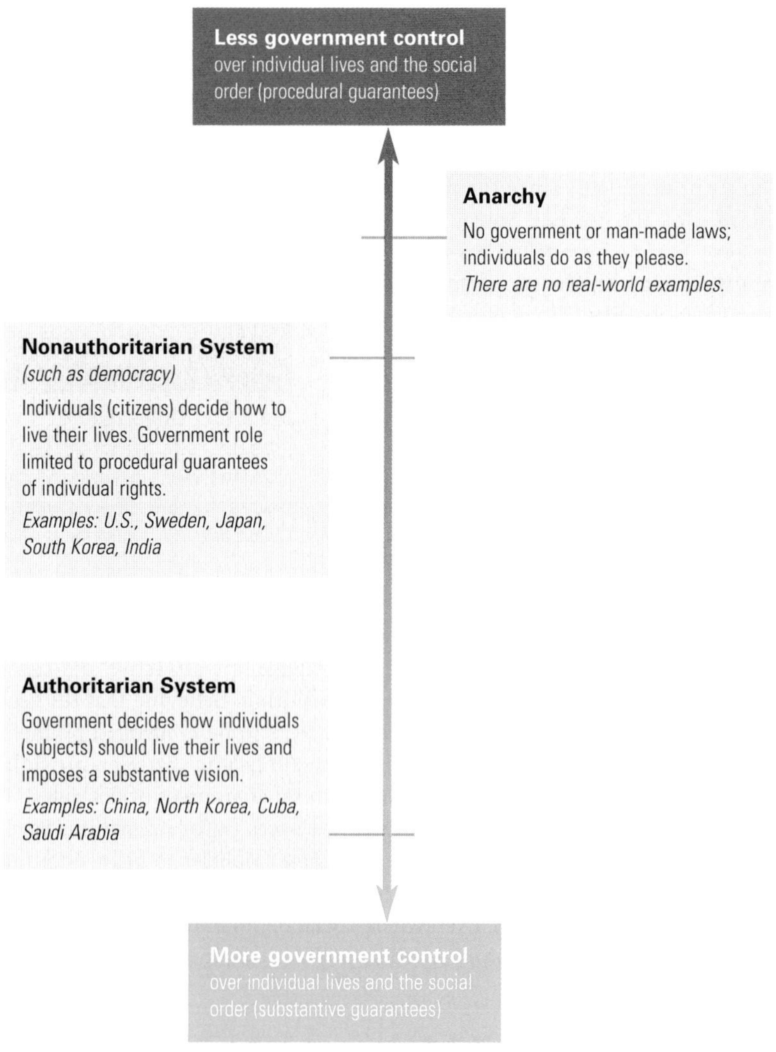

FIGURE 1.2
A Comparison of Political Systems
Political systems are defined by the extent to which individual citizens or governments decide what the social order should look like, that is, how people should live their collective, noneconomic lives. Except for anarchies, every system allots a role to government to regulate individual behavior, for example, to prohibit murder, rape, and theft. But beyond such basic regulation, they differ radically on who gets to determine how individuals live their lives, and whether government's role is simply to provide procedural guarantees that protect individuals' rights to make their own decisions or to provide a much more substantive view of how individuals should behave.

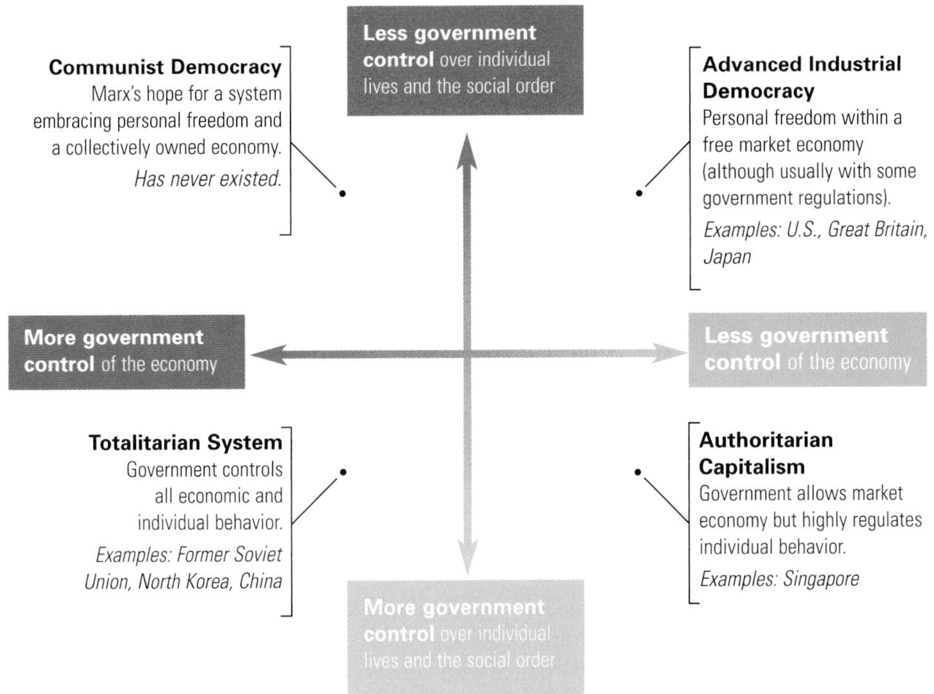

FIGURE 1.3
Political and Economic Systems Political systems work in conjunction with economic systems, but government control over the economy does not necessarily translate into tight control over the social order. We have identified four possible combinations of these systems signified by the labeled points in each quadrant. These points are approximate, however, and some nations cannot be so easily classified. Sweden is an advanced industrial democracy by most measures, for instance, but because of its commitment to substantive economic values, it would be located much closer to the vertical axis.

rights that the government must protect. Another way to think about this, to use the terminology we introduced in the previous section, is that in authoritarian systems, government makes substantive decisions about how people ought to live their lives; in nonauthoritarian systems, government merely guarantees that there are fair rules and leaves the rest to individual control. Sometimes governments that exercise substantive decision making in the economic realm also do so with respect to the social order. But, as Figure 1.3 shows, there are several possible combinations of economic and political systems.

AUTHORITARIAN SYSTEMS

Authoritarian governments give ultimate power to the state rather than to the people to decide how they ought to live their lives. By "authoritarian governments," we usually mean those in which the people cannot effectively claim rights against the state; where the state chooses to exercise its power, the people have no choice but to submit to its will. Such a government may be **totalitarian**; that is, as in the earlier example of the former Soviet Union, it may exercise its power over every part of society—economic, social, political, and moral—leaving little or no private realm for individuals.

authoritarian governments systems in which the state holds all power over the social order

totalitarian government a system in which absolute power is exercised over every aspect of life

An authoritarian state may also limit its own power. In such cases, it may deny individuals rights in those spheres where it chooses to act, but it may leave large areas of society, such as a capitalist economy, free from governmental interference. Singapore is an example of this type of authoritarian capitalism; people have considerable economic freedom, but stringent social regulations limit their noneconomic behavior. When American teenager Michael Fay was caught vandalizing cars in Singapore in

1994, the government there sentenced him to be caned. In the United States, people have rights that prevent cruel and unusual punishment like caning, but in Singapore, Fay had no such rights and had to submit to the government's will.

Often authoritarian governments pay lip service to the people, but when push comes to shove, as it usually does in such states, the people have no effective power against the government. Again, to use the terminology we introduced earlier, government does not provide guarantees of fair processes for individuals; it guarantees a substantive vision of what life will be like—what individuals will believe, how they will act, what they will choose.

Authoritarian governments can take various forms:

monarchy an authoritarian government with power vested in a king or queen

- A **monarchy** vests the ultimate power in one person (the king or queen), believing either that God or some other higher power has designated that person a divine representative on earth, or that the person's birth, wealth, or even knowledge entitles him or her to the supreme position. A monarchy is not necessarily authoritarian (for instance, in the British constitutional monarchy, Parliament and not the monarch is sovereign), but it is when the king or queen holds the ultimate power.
- Some forms of authoritarian government give God or other divinities a more direct line of power. In a **theocracy**, God is the sovereign, speaking through the voice of an earthly appointee such as a pope or a prophet. For example, a fundamentalist Islamic leader governs Iran, a country where every element of the legal system and culture is in strict concordance with conservative Islamic principles.
- In a **fascist government**, the state is sovereign. Nazi Germany and Italy under Mussolini are examples of states run by dictators for the greater glory not of themselves or God but of the state.
- Sovereignty may be vested in a party or group within a state, often called **oligarchy** (government by the few). The authoritarian regimes of the former Soviet Union were run by the powerful Communist Party.

theocracy an authoritarian government that claims to draw its power from divine or religious authority

fascist government an authoritarian government in which policy is made for the ultimate glory of the state

oligarchy rule by a small group of elites

NONAUTHORITARIAN SYSTEMS

anarchy the absence of government and laws

In nonauthoritarian systems, ultimate power rests with the individuals to make decisions concerning their lives. The most extreme form of nonauthoritarianism is called **anarchy**. Anarchists would do away with government and laws altogether. People advocate anarchy because they value the freedom to do whatever they want more than they value the order and security that governments provide by forbidding or regulating certain kinds of behavior. Few people are true anarchists, however. While anarchy may sound attractive in theory, the inherent difficulties of the position make it hard to practice. For instance, how could you even organize a revolution to get rid of government without some rules about who is to do what and how decisions are to be made?

democracy government that vests power in the people

Democracy A less extreme form of nonauthoritarian government, and one much more familiar to us, is **democracy** (from the Greek *demos,* meaning "people"). In democracies, government is not external to the people, as it is authoritarian systems; in a fundamental sense, government is the people. Recognizing that collective life usually calls for some restrictions on what individuals may do (laws forbidding murder, for instance, or theft), democracies nevertheless try to maximize freedom for the individuals who live under them. Although they generally make decisions through some sort of majority rule, democracies still provide procedural guarantees to preserve individual rights—usually protections of due process and minority rights. This means that if individuals living in a democracy feel their rights have been violated, they have the right to ask government to remedy the situation.

Democracies are based on the principle of **popular sovereignty**; that is, there is no power higher than the people and, in the United States, the document establishing their authority, the Constitution. The central idea here is that no government is considered legitimate unless the governed consent to it, and people are not truly free unless they live under a law of their own making. The people of many Western countries have found this idea persuasive enough to found their governments on it. In recent years, especially since the mid-1980s, democracy has been spreading rapidly through the rest of the world as the preferred form of government. No longer the primary province of industrialized Western nations, attempts at democratic governance now extend into Asia, Latin America, Africa, eastern Europe, and the republics of the former Soviet Union. There are many varieties of democracy other than our own. Some democracies make the legislature (the representatives of the people) the most important authority; some retain a monarch with limited powers; some hold referenda at the national level to get direct feedback on how the people want them to act on specific issues.

popular sovereignty the concept that the citizens are the ultimate source of political power

Theories of Democracy Generally, as we indicated, democracies hold that the will of the majority should prevail. This is misleadingly simple, however. Some theories of democracy hold that all the people should agree on political decisions. This rule of unanimity makes decision making very slow, and sometimes impossible, since everyone has to be persuaded to agree. Even when majority rule is the norm, there are many ways of calculating the majority. Is it 50 percent plus one? Two-thirds? Three-fourths? Decision making grows increasingly difficult the greater the number of people who are required to agree. And, of course, majority rule brings with it the problem of minority rights. If the majority gets its way, what happens to the rights of those who disagree? Democratic theorists have tried to grapple with these problems in various ways, none of them entirely satisfactory to all people:

- Theorists of **elite democracy** propose that democracy is merely a system of choosing among competing leaders; for the average citizen, input ends after the leader is chosen.[5] Some proponents of this view believe that actual political decisions are made not by elected officials but by the elite in business, the military, the media, and education. In this view, elections are merely symbolic—to perpetuate the illusion that citizens have consented to their government. Elite theorists may claim that participation is important, if not for self-rule, then because people should at least feel as if they are making a difference. Otherwise they have no stake in the political system.
- Advocates of **pluralist democracy** argue that what is important is not so much individual participation but membership in groups that participate in government decision making on their members' behalf.[6] As a way of trying to influence a system that gives them only limited voice, citizens join groups of people with whom they share an interest, such as labor unions, professional associations, and environmental or business groups. These groups represent their members' interests and try to influence government to enact policy that carries out the group's will. Some pluralists argue that individual citizens have little effective power and that only when they are organized into groups are they truly a force for government to reckon with.

elite democracy a theory of democracy that limits the citizens' role to choosing among competing leaders

pluralist democracy a theory of democracy that holds that citizen membership in groups is the key to political power

participatory democracy a theory of democracy that holds that citizens should actively and directly control all aspects of their lives

- Supporters of **participatory democracy** claim that more than consent or majority rule in making governmental decisions is needed. Individuals have the right to control all the circumstances of their lives, and direct democratic participation should take place not only in government but in industry, education, and community affairs as well.[7] For advocates of this view, democracy is more than a way to make decisions: it is a way of life, an end in itself.

THE ROLE OF THE PEOPLE

So far we have given a good deal of attention to the latter parts of Lasswell's definition of politics. But easily as important as the *what* and the *how* in Laswell's formulation is the *who*. Underlying the different political theories we have looked at are fundamental differences in the powers and opportunities possessed by everyday people.

subjects individuals who are obliged to submit to a government authority against which they have no rights

The People as Subjects In authoritarian systems, the people are **subjects** of their government. They possess no rights that protect them from that government; they must do whatever the government says or face the consequences, without any other recourse. They have obligations to the state but no rights or privileges to offset those obligations. They may be winners or losers in government decisions, but they have very little control over which it may be.

Spreading Democracy
Following the overthrow of Saddam Hussein's authoritarian regime in Iraq, the United States installed a provisional government meant to rule the country until popular elections established a government of the people's choice. In January 2005, Iraqis had the chance for their voices to be heard, dipping their fingers in purple ink as a mark that they had voted but making them easy targets for insurgents who threatened to kill those who had participated in the election. Indeed, insurgents killed at least twenty-eight Iraqis on election day, making the act of flaunting their ink-stained fingers truly an act of civic courage.

citizens members of a political community having both rights and responsibilities

The People as Citizens Everyday people in democratic systems have a potentially powerful role to play. They are more than mere subjects; they are **citizens**, or members of a political community with rights as well as obligations. Democratic theory says that power is drawn from the people, that the people are sovereign, that they must consent to be governed, and that their government must respond to their will. In practical terms, this may not seem to mean much, since not consenting doesn't necessarily give us the right to disobey government. It does give us the option of leaving, however, and seeking a more congenial set of rules elsewhere. Subjects of authoritarian governments rarely have this freedom.

In democratic systems, the rules of government can provide for all sorts of

Tiffany Benjamin

How do you get to be a delegate to the Democratic National Convention when you are only twenty years old? According to Tiffany Benjamin, all it takes is a dare from a friend, the willingness to take a risk, and a little bit of luck. She doesn't mention that it also takes some uncommon guts and determination, but that's clearly the case.

". . .it was a cool party. So I decided I would stay."

Tiffany was an undergraduate at Indiana University when she and a friend decided it would be a kick to go to the 2000 Democratic National Convention in Los Angeles, where Al Gore would receive the nomination for president. They were both active in the Democratic Party on campus, so both got emails from the party outlining the steps to winning one of the coveted spots at the national convention.

The chances of getting elected were tiny, they knew, but they badly wanted to go to L.A. "I'll do this if you'll do it," Tiffany told her friend. And he said, "Okay, I dare you," and she said, "I dare *you*," and she went and got all her forms filled in and sent them out on the very last possible day, only to find that her friend had chickened out. "I couldn't do it," he told her. "I was too afraid."

Afraid? If Tiffany's ever heard the word, she doesn't let on. First, she headed off to the Democratic National Convention (yes, she won election as an alternate at-large delegate, only to step into the shoes of a delegate who couldn't go). She had a blast, as she knew she would. Cameras followed her around as one of the youngest delegates, and she attended party after party, meeting famous politicians, listening to speeches, and becoming more deeply inspired with the ideas of these people who believe in the same things she believes in, and who fight for the same things she fights for.

Then it was back to Bloomington for her senior year and a summer as an international exchange student in Mauritius--a tiny country in the middle of the Indian Ocean--before heading off to Harvard Law School.

Maybe Tiffany's intrepid stance toward life in general (and political life in particular) is a self-protective byproduct of growing up with a Republican dad and a Democratic mom (divorced since she was a baby). Eventually she decided her views were closer to the Democrats'. Looking for activities to get involved in when she arrived at Indiana University, she saw a mass flier advertising a party meeting and went. "And I kind of clicked with some of the people, and it was a cool party. So I decided I would stay."

Stay she did. Tiffany threw herself into the business of politics, active on campus but also volunteering to work on campaigns, starting with John Hamilton's effort to win Indiana's 8th congressional district in 2000. "That was the best experience for me ever, even though we lost. . . . I felt like my views were getting lost, and the issues I really cared about were getting lost." It galvanized her. "From then on I just got severely, actively involved."

And that's where she has been ever since. Reflecting back as a freshly minted lawyer about to move to Washington, D.C., to begin a new career, Tiffany's deep, abrupt chuckle is as contagious and engaging as ever, her eyes just as wickedly full of irony and fun, but there is a core of underlying seriousness that wasn't there before. Working as a student public defender with adult clients and juveniles caught up in the courts, seeing what happens to people who cannot get the system to work for them, has only strengthened the resolve to make a difference that she discovered as a freshman while she was looking for ways to make some friends on campus.

Advice on doing the impossible (like getting to a nominating convention in 2008):

Don't be afraid of anything. Listen to yourself first, because a million people told me I wasn't going to get there. And another thing is, don't take it too seriously. And be sure to have a lot of fun.

On keeping the republic:

Get involved. And that doesn't just mean vote, and it doesn't just mean go to a political party meeting. It means find out what the issues are, think about how you feel about those issues, and then *do* something. . . . Whatever you do, it does absolutely make a difference. Even if you think it doesn't matter, you will be impressed in the ways that, ten years from now, someone will come up to you and tell you that what you did mattered.

Source: Tiffany Benjamin spoke with Christine Barbour in March 2005.

different roles for citizens. At a minimum, citizens can usually vote in periodic and free elections. They may be able to run for office, subject to certain conditions, like age or residence. They can support candidates for office, organize political groups or parties, attend meetings, write letters to officials or the press, march in protest or support of various causes, even speak out on street corners.

Theoretically, democracies are ruled by "the people," but different democracies have at times been very selective about whom they count as citizens. Beginning with our days as colonists, Americans have excluded many groups of people from citizenship: people of the "wrong" religion, income bracket, race, ethnic group, lifestyle, and gender have all been excluded from enjoying the full rights of colonial or U.S. citizenship at different times. In fact, American history is the story of those various groups fighting to be included as citizens. Just because a system is called a democracy is no guarantee that all or even most of its residents possess the status of citizen.

Citizen Rights and Responsibilities Citizens in democratic systems are said to possess certain rights or areas where government cannot infringe on their freedom. Just what these rights are varies in different democracies, but they usually include freedoms of speech and the press, the right to assemble, and certain legal protections guaranteeing fair treatment in the criminal justice system. Almost all of these rights are designed to allow citizens to criticize their government openly without threat of retribution by that government.

Citizens of democracies also possess obligations or responsibilities to the public realm. They have the obligation to obey the law, for instance, once they have consented to the government (even if that consent amounts only to not leaving); they may also have the obligation to pay taxes, serve in the military, or sit on juries. Some theorists argue that virtuous citizens should put community interests ahead of personal interests. A less extreme version of this view holds that while citizens may go about their own business and pursue their own interests, they must continue to pay attention to their government. Participating in its decisions is the price of maintaining their own liberty and, by extension, the liberty of the whole. Should citizens abdicate this role by tuning out to public life, the safeguards of democracy can disappear, to be replaced with the trappings of authoritarian government. There is nothing automatic about democracy. If left unattended by nonvigilant citizens, the freedoms of democracy can be lost to an all-powerful state, and citizens can become transformed into subjects of the government they failed to keep in check.

ORIGINS OF DEMOCRACY IN AMERICA

Government in the United States is the product of particular decisions the founders made about the who, what, and how of American politics. There was nothing inevitable about those decisions, and had they decided otherwise, our system would look very different indeed.

Given the world in which the founders lived, democracy was not an obvious choice for them, and many scholars argue that in some respects the system they created is not really very democratic. We can see this more clearly if we understand the intellectual heritage of the early Americans, the historical experience, and the theories about government that informed them.

THE ANCIENT GREEK EXPERIENCE

The heyday of democracy, of course, was ancient Athens, from about 500 to 300 B.C. Even Athenian democracy, as we have already indicated, was a pretty selective business. To be sure, it was rule by "the people," but "the people" was defined narrowly to exclude women, slaves, youth, and resident aliens. Athenian democracy was not built on values of equality, even of opportunity, except for the 10 percent of the population defined as citizens. With its limited number of citizens and its small area of only one thousand square miles, Athens was a participatory democracy in which all citizens could gather in one place to vote on political matters. While this privileged group indulged its passion for public activity, the vast majority of residents was required to do all the work to support them. We can see parallels to early American democracy, which restricted participation in political affairs to a relatively small number of white men.

POLITICS IN THE MIDDLE AGES

Limited as Athenian democracy was, it was positively wide open compared to most of the forms of government that existed during the Middle Ages, from roughly A.D. 600 to 1500. During this period, monarchs gradually consolidated their power over their subjects, and some even challenged the greatest political power of the time, the Catholic Church. Some earthly rulers claimed to take their authority from God, in a principle called the **divine right of kings**. Privileged groups in society like the clergy or the nobles had some rights, but ordinary individuals were quite powerless politically. Subjects of authoritarian governments and an authoritarian church, they had obligations to their rulers but no rights they could claim as their own. If a ruler is installed by divine mandate, who, after all, has any rights against God? Education was restricted, and most people in the Middle Ages were dependent on political and ecclesiastical leaders for protection and information, as well as salvation.

divine right of kings the principle that earthly rulers receive their authority from God

THE PROTESTANT REFORMATION AND THE ENLIGHTENMENT

Between 1500 and 1700, important changes took place in the ways that people thought about politics and their political leaders. The **Protestant Reformation** led the way in the 1500s, claiming essentially that individuals could pray directly to God and receive salvation on faith alone, without the church's involvement. In fact, Martin Luther, the German priest who spearheaded the Reformation, argued that the whole complex structure of the medieval church could be dispensed with. His ideas spread and were embraced by a number of European monarchs, leading to a split between Catholic and Protestant countries. Where the church was seen as unnecessary, it lost political as well as religious clout, and its decline paved the way for new ideas about the world.

Protestant Reformation the break from the Roman Catholic Church in the 1500s by those who believed in direct access to God and salvation by faith

Those new ideas came with the **Enlightenment** period of the late 1600s and 1700s, when ideas about science and the possibilities of knowledge began to blow away the shadows and cobwebs of medieval superstition. A new and refreshing understanding of human beings and their place in the natural world, based on human reasoning, took hold. Enlightenment philosophy said that human beings were not at the mercy of a world they could not understand, but rather they could learn the secrets of nature and, with education as their tool, harness the world to do their bidding.

Enlightenment a philosophical movement (1600s–1700s) that emphasized human reason, scientific examination, and industrial progress

Not only did scientific and economic development take off, but philosophers applied the intoxicating new theories about the potential of knowledge to the political world. Thomas Hobbes (who slightly preceded the Enlightenment) and John Locke, two English philosophers, came up with theories about how government should be established that discredited divine right. Governments are born not because God ordains them, but because life without government was "solitary, poor, nasty, brutish, and short" in Hobbes's words, and "inconvenient" in Locke's. The foundation of government was reason, not faith, and reason leads people to consent to being governed because they are better off that way.

The idea of citizenship that was born in the Enlightenment constituted another break with the past. People have freedom and rights before government exists, declared Locke. When they decide they are better off with government than without it, they enter into a **social contract**, giving up a few of those rights in exchange for the protection of the rest of their rights by a government established by the majority. If that government fails to protect their rights, then it has broken the contract and the people are free to form a new government, or not, as they please. But the key element here is that for authority to be legitimate, citizens must *consent* to it.

social contract the notion that society is based on an agreement between government and the governed in which people agree to give up some rights in exchange for the protection of others

These ideas were not exactly democratic, but they were much closer than what had come before. Nowhere did Locke suggest that all people ought to participate in politics, or that people are necessarily equal. In fact, he was concerned mostly with the preservation of private property, suggesting that only property owners would have cause to be bothered with government because only they have something concrete to lose.

CITIZENSHIP IN AMERICA

For our purposes, the most important thing about John Locke is that he was writing at the same time the American founders were thinking about how to build a new government. Locke particularly influenced the writings of James Madison, a major author of our Constitution. Madison, as we will see, was worried about a system that was too democratic.

THE DANGERS OF DEMOCRACY

Enthusiastic popular participation under the government established by the Articles of Confederation—the document that tied the colonies together before the Constitution was drafted—almost ended the new government before it began. Like Locke, Madison thought government had a duty to protect property, and if people who didn't have property could get involved in politics, they might not care about protecting the property of others. Worse, they might form "factions," groups pursuing their own self-interests rather than the public interest, and even try to get some of that property for themselves. So Madison rejected notions of "pure democracy," in which all citizens would have direct power to control government, and opted instead for what he called a "republic."

A **republic**, according to Madison, differs from a democracy mainly in that it employs representation and can work in a large state. Most theorists agree that democracy is impossible in practice if there are a lot of citizens and all have to be heard from. But we do not march to Washington or phone our legislator every time we want to register a political preference. Instead, we choose representatives—members of the

republic a government in which decisions are made through representatives of the people

House of Representatives, senators, and the president—to represent our views for us. Madison thought this would be a safer system than direct participation (all of us crowding into town halls or the Capitol) because public passions would be cooled off by the process. You might be furious about health care costs when you vote for your senator, but he or she will represent your views with less anger. The founders hoped that the representatives would be older, wealthier, and wiser than the average American, and they would be better able to make cool and rational decisions.

MADISON'S VISION OF CITIZENSHIP

The notion of citizenship that emerges from Madison's writings is not a very flattering one for the average American, and it is important to note that it is not the only ideal of citizenship in the American political tradition. Madison's low expectations of the American public were a reaction to an earlier tradition that had put great faith in the ability of democratic man to put the interests of the community ahead of his own, to act with what scholars call "republican virtue." According to this idea, a virtuous citizen could be trusted with the most serious of political decisions because if he (women were not citizens at that time, of course) were properly educated and kept from the influence of scandal and corruption, he would be willing to sacrifice his own advancement for the sake of the whole. His decisions would be guided not by his self-interest but by his public-interested spirit. At the time of the founding, hope was strong that although the court of the British monarch had become corrupt beyond redemption, America was still a land where virtue could triumph over greed. In fact, for many people this was a crucial argument for American independence: severing the ties would prevent that corruption from creeping across the Atlantic and would allow the new country to keep its virtuous political nature free from the British taint.[8]

When democratic rules that relied on the virtue, or public interestedness, of the American citizen were put into effect, however, especially in the days immediately after independence, these expectations seemed to be doomed. Instead of acting for the good of the community, Americans seemed to be just as self-interested as the British had been. When given nearly free rein to rule themselves, they had no trouble remembering the rights of citizenship but ignored the responsibilities that come with it. They passed laws in state legislatures that canceled debts and contracts and otherwise worked to the advantage of the poor majority of farmers and debtors—and that seriously threatened the economic and political stability of the more well-to-do. It was in this context of national disappointment that Madison devised his notion of the republic. Since people had proved, so he thought, not to be activated by virtue, then a government must be designed that would produce virtuous results, regardless of the character of the citizens who participated in it.

AMERICAN CITIZENSHIP TODAY

Today two competing views of citizenship still exist in the United States. One, echoing Madison, sees human nature as self-interested and holds that individual participation in government should be limited, that "too much" democracy is a bad thing. The second view continues to put its faith in the citizen's ability to act virtuously, not just for his or her own good but for the common good. President John F. Kennedy movingly evoked such a view in his inaugural address in 1960, when he urged Americans to "ask

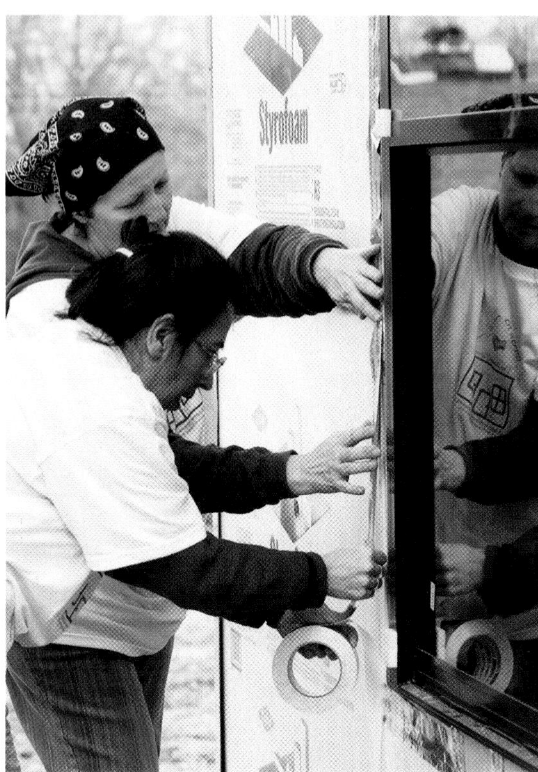

Building a Foundation to the Common Good
Public-interested citizenship can take many forms. To combat homelessness and substandard housing, volunteers for Habitat for Humanity join together with future homeowners to build low-cost homes, which are then sold to the homeowners at no profit. The volunteers shown here are working on a joint project between the Muslim and Jewish communities in Tyler, Texas, to help strengthen ties between the two groups. Habitat for Humanity builds nearly six thousand homes for low-income families in the United States, and almost twenty thousand internationally, each year.

not what your country can do for you—ask what you can do for your country." These views of citizenship have coexisted throughout our history. Especially in times of crisis such as war or national tragedy, the second view of individual sacrifice for the public good has seemed more prominent. In the wake of September 11, 2001, citizens freely gave their time and money to help their fellow countrypeople and were more willing to join the military and volunteer for community service. At other times, and particularly at the national level of politics, the dominant view of citizenship has appeared to be one of self-interested actors going about their own business with little regard for the public good. When observers claim, as they often do today, that there is a crisis of American citizenship, they usually mean that civic virtue is taking second place to self-interest as a guiding principle of citizenship.

These two notions of citizenship do not necessarily have to be at loggerheads, however. Where self-interest and public spirit meet in democratic practice is in the process of deliberation, collectively considering and evaluating goals and ideals for communal life and action. Individuals bring their own agendas and interests, but in the process of discussing them with others holding different views, parties can find common ground and turn it into a base for collective action. Conflict can erupt too, of course, but the process of deliberation at least creates a forum from which the possibility of consensus might emerge. Scholar and journalist E. J. Dionne reflects on this possibility: "At the heart of republicanism [remember that this is not a reference to our modern parties] is the belief that self-government is not a drab necessity but a joy to be treasured. It is the view that politics is not simply a grubby confrontation of competing interests but an arena in which citizens can learn from each other and discover an 'enlightened self-interest' in common." Despite evidence of a growing American disaffection for politics, Dionne hopes that Americans will find again the "joy" in self-governance because, he warns, "A nation that hates politics will not long thrive as a democracy." [9]

HOW TO USE THE THEMES AND FEATURES IN THIS BOOK

Our primary goal in this book is to get you thinking critically about American politics. Critical thinking is a crucial skill to learn no matter what training your major or career plans call for. As we discuss in the *Consider the Source* box in this chapter, **critical thinking** is the analysis and evaluation of ideas and arguments based on reason and evidence—it means digging deep into what you read and what you hear and asking tough questions. Critical thinking is what all good scholars do, and it is also what savvy citizens do.

critical thinking analysis and evaluation of ideas and arguments based on reason and evidence

Thinking Like a Political Scientist

This book is an introduction to American politics and, in a way, it is also an introduction to political science. Political science is not exactly the same kind of science as biology or geology. Not only is it difficult to put our subjects (people and political systems) under a microscope to observe their behavior, but we are somewhat limited in our ability to test our theories. We cannot replay World War II in order to test our ideas about what caused it, for example. A further problem is our subjectivity; we are the phenomena under investigation, and so we may have stronger feelings about our research and our findings than we would, say, about cells and rocks.

These difficulties do not make a science of politics impossible, but they do mean we must proceed with caution. Even among political scientists there is disagreement about whether a rigorous science of the political world is a reasonable goal. What we can agree on is that it is possible to advance our understanding of politics beyond mere guessing or debates about political preferences. Although we use many methods in our work (statistical analysis, mathematical modeling, case studies, and philosophical reasoning, to name only a few), what political scientists have in common is an emphasis on *critical thinking* about politics.

Critical thinking means challenging the conclusions of others, asking why or why not, turning the accepted wisdom upside down, and exploring alternative interpretations. It means considering the sources of information—not accepting an explanation just because someone in authority offers it, or because you have always been told that it is the true explanation, but because you have independently discovered that there are good reasons for accepting it. You may emerge from reading this textbook with the same ideas about politics that you have always had; it is not our goal to change your mind. But as a critical thinker, you will be able to back up your old ideas with new and persuasive arguments of your own, or to move beyond your current ideas to see politics in a new light.

Critical thinking sounds like work and it sounds like faultfinding—two potentially unpleasant activities. While it may be hard work at first (what skill worth having isn't difficult to begin with?), in fact, what we mean by critical thinking has nothing to do with faultfinding or being negative. *Critical* in this case means careful evaluation, vigilant judgment. It means being wary of the surface appearance of what we hear and read, and digging deeper, looking for the subtext—what a person means and intends, whether that person has evidence for his or her conclusions, what the political implications of those conclusions really are.

Becoming adept at critical thinking has a number of benefits:

- We learn to be good democratic citizens. Critical thinking helps us sort through the barrage of information that regularly assails us, and it teaches us to process this information thoughtfully. Critical awareness of what our leaders are doing and the ability to understand and evaluate what they tell us is the lifeblood of democratic government.
- We are better able to hold our own in political (or other) arguments: we think more logically and clearly, we are more persuasive, and we impress people with our grasp of reason and fact. There is not a career in the world that is not enhanced by critical thinking skills.
- We become much better students. The skills of the critical thinker are not just the skills of the good citizen; they are the skills of the scholar. When we read critically we figure out what is important quickly and easily, we know what questions to ask to tease out more meaning, we can decide whether what we are reading is worth our time, and we know what to take with us and what to discard.

Although it may sound a little dull and dusty, critical thinking can be a vital and enjoyable activity. When we are good at it, it empowers and liberates us. We are not at the mercy of others' conclusions and decisions. We can evaluate facts and arguments for ourselves, turning conventional wisdom upside down and exploring the world of ideas with confidence.

How Does One Learn to Think Critically?

The trick to learning how to think critically is to do it. It helps to have a model to follow, however, and we provide one below. The focus of critical thinking here is

(continued on next page)

understanding political argument. *Argument* in this case refers not to a confrontation or a fight, but rather to a political contention, based on a set of assumptions, supported by evidence, leading to a clear, well-developed conclusion with consequences for how we understand the world.

Critical thinking involves constantly asking questions about the arguments we read about: who has created it, what is the basic case and what values underlie it, what evidence is used to back up it up, what conclusions are drawn, and what difference does the whole thing make. To help you remember the questions to ask, we have used a mnemonic device that creates an acronym from the five major steps of critical thinking. Until asking these questions becomes second nature, thinking of them as CLUES to critical thinking about American politics will help you keep them in mind as you read.

This is what CLUES stands for:

Consider the source and the audience

Lay out the argument and the underlying values and assumptions

Uncover the evidence

Evaluate the conclusion

Sort out the political implications

We'll investigate each of these steps in a little more depth.

Consider the source and the audience

Who wrote the argument in question? Where did the item appear? What audience is it directed toward? What do the author or publisher need to do to attract and keep the audience? How might that affect content?

If the person is a mainstream journalist, he or she probably has a reputation as an objective reporter to preserve, and will at least make an honest attempt to provide unbiased information. Even so, knowing the actual news source will help you nail that down. Even in a reputable national paper like the *New York Times* or the *Wall Street Journal*, if the item comes from the editorial pages, you can count on it having an ideological point of view—usually (but not exclusively) liberal in the case of the *Times*, conservative in the case of the *Wall Street Journal*. Opinion magazines will have even more blatant points of view. Readers go to those sources looking for a particular perspective, and that may affect the reliability of the information you find.

Lay out the argument and the underlying values and assumptions

What basic argument does the author want to make? What assumptions about the world does he or she hold? What values about what is important and what government should do? Are all the important terms clearly defined?

As Figure 1.4 illustrates, our analytic and evaluative tasks in this book focus on the twin themes of power and citizenship. We have adopted the classic definition of politics proposed by the late political scientist Harold Lasswell that politics is "who gets what when and how." We simplify his understanding by dropping the *when* and focusing on politics as the struggle by citizens over who gets power and resources in society and how they get them.

analysis understanding how something works by breaking it down into its component parts

Lasswell's definition of politics gives us a framework of **analysis** for this book; that is, it outlines how we will break down politics into its component parts in order to understand it. Analysis helps us understand how something works, much like taking a car apart and putting it back together again helps us understand how it runs. Lasswell's definition provides a very strong analytic framework because it focuses our attention on questions we can ask to figure out what is going on in politics.

Accordingly, in this book, we will analyze American politics in terms of three sets of questions:

If these things aren't clear, the author may be unclear him or herself. There is a lot of sloppy thinking out there, and being able to identify it and discard it is very valuable. Often we are intimidated by a smart-sounding argument, only to discover on closer examination that it just doesn't hold up. A more insidious case occurs when the author is trying to obscure the point in order to get you to sign on to something you might not otherwise accept. If the argument, values, and assumptions are not perfectly clear and up front, there may be a hidden agenda you should know about. You don't want to be persuaded by someone who claims to be an advocate for democracy, only to find out that democracy means something completely different to him or her than it does to you.

Uncover the evidence

Has the author done basic research to back up his or her argument with facts and evidence?

Good arguments cannot be based on gut feelings, rumor, or wishful thinking. They should be based on hard evidence, either empirical, verifiable observations about the world or solid, logical reasoning. If the argument is worth being held, it should be able to stand up to rigorous examination and the author should be able to defend it on these grounds. If the evidence or logic is missing, the argument can usually be dismissed.

Evaluate the conclusion

Is the argument successful? Does it convince you? Why or why not? Does it change your mind about any beliefs you held previously? Does accepting this argument require you to rethink any of your other beliefs?

Conclusions should follow logically from the assumptions and values of an argument, if solid evidence and reasoning supports it. What is the conclusion here? What is the author asking you to accept as the product of his or her argument? Does it make sense to you? Do you "buy it?" If you do, does it fit with your other ideas or do you need to refine what you previously thought? Have you learned from this argument, or have you merely had your own beliefs reinforced?

Sort out the political implications

What is the political significance of this argument? What difference does it make to your understanding of the way the political world works? How does it affect who gets what scarce resources and how they get them? How does it affect who wins in the political process and who loses?

Political news is valuable if it means something. If it doesn't, it may entertain you, but essentially it wastes your time if it claims to be something more than entertainment. Make the information you get prove its importance, and if it doesn't, find a different news source to rely on.

Source: Adapted from the authors' "Preface to the Student," in Christine Barbour and Matthew J. Streb, *Clued in to Politics: A Critical Thinking Reader in American Government* (Boston: Houghton Mifflin, 2004).

- **Who** are the parties involved? What resources, powers, and rights do they bring to the struggle?
- **What** do they have at stake? What do they stand to win or lose? Is it power, influence, position, policy, or values?
- **How** do the rules shape the outcome? Where do the rules come from? What strategies or tactics do the political actors employ to use the rules to get what they want?

If you know who is involved in a political situation, what is at stake, and how (under what rules) the conflict over resources will eventually be resolved, you will have a pretty good grasp of what is going on, and you will probably be able to figure out new situations, even when your days of taking a course in American government are far behind you. To get you in the habit of asking those questions, we have designed several features in this text explicitly to reinforce them.

As you found at the start of your reading, each chapter opens with a *What's at Stake?* feature that analyzes a political situation in terms of what various groups of

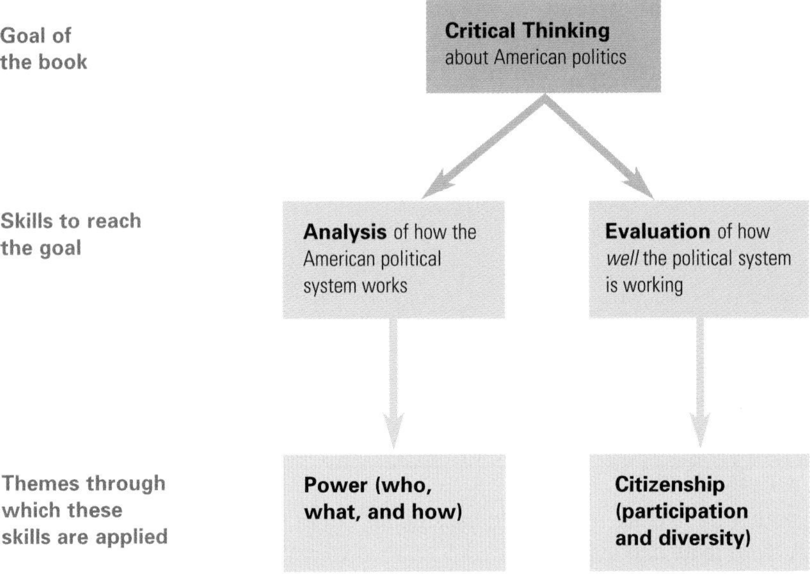

FIGURE 1.4
Themes and Goal of this Book

citizens stand to win or lose. Each chapter ends with a *What's at Stake Revisited* feature, where we return to the issues raised in the introduction, once you have the substantive material of the chapter under your belt. We will also focus our analysis along the way by closing each major chapter section with a *Who, What, How* feature that will explicitly address these questions and concisely summarize what you have learned. We reinforce the task of analysis with a *Consider the Source* feature in each chapter that discusses ways you can improve your critical thinking skills by analyzing (that is, taking apart) different kinds of sources of information about politics. Finally, toward the end of every chapter we provide a *Thinking Outside the Box* box that helps you take the analysis one step further: What if the rules or the actors or the stakes were different? What would be the impact on American politics? How would it work differently?

As political scientists, however, we not only want to understand *how* the system works, we also want to assess *how well* it works. A second task of critical thinking is **evaluation**, or seeing how well something measures up according to a standard or principle. We could choose any number of standards by which to evaluate American politics, but the most relevant, for most of us, is the principle of democracy and the role of citizens.

evaluation assessing how well something works or performs according to a particular standard or yardstick

We can draw on the two traditions of self-interested and public-interested citizenship we have discussed to evaluate the powers, opportunities, and challenges presented to American citizens by the system of government under which they live. In addition to the two competing threads of citizenship in America, we can also look at the kinds of action that citizens engage in and whether they take advantage of the options that are available to them. For instance, citizen action might be restricted by the rules, or by popular interest, to merely choosing between competing candidates for office, as in the model of *elite democracy* described earlier. Alternatively, the rules of the system might encourage citizens to band together in groups to get what they want, as they do in *pluralist democracy.* Or the system might be open and offer highly motivated citizens a variety of opportunities to get involved, as they do in *participatory democracy.* American democracy has elements of all three of these models, and one way to evaluate citizenship in America is to look at what opportunities for each type of participation exist and whether citizens take advantage of them.

To evaluate how democratic the United States is, we will look at the changing concept and practice of citizenship in this country with respect to the subject matter of most chapters in a section called *The Citizens and. . . .* In that section we will look at citizenship from many angles, considering such questions as: What role do "the people" have in American politics? How has that role expanded or diminished over time? What kinds of political participation do the rules of American politics (formal and informal) allow, encourage, or require citizens to take? What kinds of political participation are discouraged, limited, or forbidden? Do citizens take advantage of the opportunities for political action that the rules provide them? How do they react to the rules that limit their participation? How do citizens in different times exercise their rights and responsibilities? What do citizens need to do to "keep" the republic? How democratic is the United States?

To put all this in perspective, each chapter includes two other features that give you a more concrete idea of what citizen participation might mean on a personal level. *Profiles in Citizenship* introduce you to individuals who have committed a good part of their lives to public service and focus on what citizenship means to those people and what inspired them to take on a public role. *Who Are We?* provides some demographic data to bring the diversity of the American citizenry front and center and highlight the difficulties inherent in uniting into a single nation individuals and groups with such different and often conflicting interests.

We have outlined seven features that recur throughout this book. Remember that each is designed to help you to think critically about American politics either by analyzing power in terms of who gets what, and how, or by evaluating citizenship to determine how well we are keeping Benjamin Franklin's mandate to keep the republic. And remember that further exploration of the book's themes is always available on the text web site at republic.cqpress.com.

WHAT'S AT STAKE REVISITED

We began this chapter by asking whether youthful engagement in politics is really a matter of great importance, and what might be at stake in the question of whether the gains in youth vote we saw in 2004 turn out to be permanent. Since then we have covered a lot of ground, arguing that politics is fundamental to human life and in fact makes life easier for us by giving us a nonviolent way to resolve disputes. We pointed out that politics is a method by which power and resources get distributed in society: politics is who gets what, and how they get it. Citizens who are aware and involved stand a much greater chance of getting what they want from the system than do those who check out or turn away. One clear consequence when young people disregard politics, then, is that they are less likely to get what they want from the political system. This is in fact exactly what happens.

continued

WHAT'S AT STAKE REVISITED *(continued)*

There are also consequences for the system as a whole. Democracy is neither inevitable nor self-sustaining. As we will see in this book, the American system is a work of political genius that in many ways takes us as we are. It can accommodate the self-interested citizen, at least some of the time, but it depends for its continued existence on the presence of public-interested citizens as well.

Ironically, the absence of a public-interested spirit among us can be damaging to our own self-interest. People who pay attention to politics learn to use the rules of the system to get the things they want. Many college students complained that the 2000 election, with its focus on prescription drug coverage for the elderly and the financial solvency of Social Security, was "not about them" or the issues they cared about. A glance at voter turnout statistics tells us why: older people vote in far greater numbers than do young people. By not participating, young people ensure that they are not a force that politicians have to reckon with.

The increased youth vote in 2004, however, makes it likely that politicians will not soon risk ignoring the areas of government action that matter to young people. "Young voters are back, and politicians will ignore them at their peril," one political science professor told the *Boston Globe.* "I'm convinced that we've turned the corner and that young Americans will continue to be important players in the electoral process."[10]

We always rely on government to provide some things—good schools, safe neighborhoods, well-maintained roads, a stable economy—but in times of war or other national crisis, government looms even larger in our lives. We depend on it to protect us, our families, our homes, and our livelihoods. At that point, our failure to be able to use the system to get the things we value becomes far more critical. Consider one issue that has affected many generations of young people during wartime: the draft. From 1948 to 1973, young American men were drafted into compulsory military service. Although the draft ended in 1973, President Carter made it mandatory for men aged eighteen to twenty-five to register with the Selective Service; failure to do so can be punished with a $250,000 fine and five years in jail, and offenders cannot get student loans or government jobs. While there are no current plans to reinstate the draft, officials moved fast after September 11, 2001, to fill vacancies on Selective Service or draft boards around the country.[11] Before the 2004 election, rumors flew fast and furiously that the Iraq war, almost universally believed to need more manpower, would require a draft.[12] Young people can hardly claim that that issue is "not about them."

But it is not just young people who have a stake in their own indifference to politics. All American citizens are at risk, for in a very real sense, the future of the American republic is in the hands of those who are just today learning to keep it. As we have argued in this chapter, keeping the republic requires constant vigilance and critical citizenship. As we proceed through this introduction to American politics, remember what you have at stake in becoming an educated citizen of the U.S. government.

Thinking Outside the Box

- Do subjects enjoy any advantages that citizens don't have?
- When, if ever, should individuals be asked to sacrifice their own good for that of their country?
- Why does critical thinking feel like so much more work than "regular thinking?"

To Sum Up

KEY TERMS
republic.cqpress.com

analysis (p. 24)
anarchy (p. 14)
authoritarian governments (p. 13)
authority (p. 7)
capitalist economy (p. 10)
citizens (p. 16)
critical thinking (p. 22)
democracy (p. 14)
divine right of kings (p. 19)
economics (p. 9)
elite democracy (p. 15)
Enlightenment (p. 19)
evaluation (p. 26)
fascist government (p. 14)
government (p. 7)
institutions (p. 8)
laissez-faire capitalism (p. 10)
legitimate (p. 7)
monarchy (p. 14)
oligarchy (p. 14)
participatory democracy (p. 16)
pluralist democracy (p. 15)
politics (p. 6)
popular sovereignty (p. 15)
power (p. 6)
procedural guarantees (p. 10)
Protestant Reformation (p. 19)
regulated capitalism (p. 10)
republic (p. 19)
rules (p. 8)
social contract (p. 19)
social democracy (p. 11)
socialist economy (p. 10)
social order (p. 6)
subjects (p. 16)
substantive guarantees (p. 11)
theocracy (p. 14)
totalitarian government (p. 13)

Key terms, chapter summaries, practice quizzes, Internet links, and other study aids are available on the companion Web site at: republic.cqpress.com.

SUMMARY
republic.cqpress.com

- Politics may appear to be a grubby, greedy pursuit, filled with scandal and back-room dealing. In fact, despite its shortcomings and sometimes shabby reputation, politics is an essential means for resolving differences and determining how power and resources are distributed in society. Politics is about who gets power and resources in society—and how they get them.
- Government, a product of the political process, is the system established for exercising authority over a group of people. In America, the government is embodied in the Constitution and the institutions set up by the Constitution. The Constitution represents the compromises and deals made by the founders on a number of fundamental issues, including how best to divide governing power.
- Politics establishes the rules and institutions that shape how power is distributed in political interactions. The most fundamental rules of our political system are those that define and empower our political institutions and the way these institutions interact with each other and with individual citizens.
- Government is shaped not only by politics but also by economics, which is concerned specifically with the distribution of wealth and society's resources. The United States has a regulated capitalist economy, which means that property is owned privately and decisions about the production of goods and the distribution of wealth are left to marketplace forces with some governmental control.
- Political systems dictate how power is distributed among leaders and citizens, and these systems take many forms. Authoritarian systems give ultimate power to the state; nonauthoritarian systems, like democracy, place power largely in the hands of the people. Democracy is based on the principle of popular sovereignty, giving the people the ultimate power to govern. The meaning of citizenship is key to the definition of democracy, and citizens are believed to have rights protecting them from government as well as responsibilities to the public realm.
- The meaning of American democracy can be traced to the time of the nation's founding. During that period, two competing views of citizenship emerged. The first view, articulated by James Madison, sees the citizen as fundamentally self-interested; this view led the founders to fear too much citizen participation in government. The second view puts faith in citizens' ability to act for the common good, to put their obligation to the public ahead of their own self-interest. Both views are still alive and well today, and we can see evidence of both sentiments at work in political life.
- In this book we'll look at two ways of thinking critically about American politics: analyzing how our American political system works and evaluating how well it works. We will rely on two underlying themes to pursue this course. The first is the assumption that all political events and situations can be examined by looking at who the actors are, what they have to win or lose, and how the rules shape the way political actors engage in their struggle. This analytic framework should provide us with a clear understanding of how power functions in our system. Examining who gets what they want and how they achieve it in political outcomes highlights the

second theme of this text: how diverse citizens participate in political life in order to improve their own individual situations *and* promote the interests of the community at large. We will carefully evaluate citizenship as a means to determine how well the American system is working.

PRACTICE QUIZ

republic.cqpress.com

1. In the definition of politics we have discussed, rules can be thought of as the

a. who.

b. what.

c. how.

d. where.

e. when.

2. Which of the following systems is based on substantive guarantees?

a. Regulated capitalism

b. Laissez faire

c. Socialism

d. Anarchy

e. Democracy

3. The two competing views of U.S. citizenship incorporate

a. authority and subjecthood.

b. public interest and private interest.

c. virtue and vice.

d. tolerance and bigotry.

e. democracy and republicanism.

4. Which of the following is true regarding ancient Greek (Athenian) democracy?

a. It became the model copied in its entirety in the Articles of Confederation.

b. It established a republic in which representatives were chosen to voice the people's wishes.

c. It was a participatory democracy, but only a small percentage of the people were citizens.

d. It was the first system in which slaves were given the right to vote.

e. It became the model copied in its entirety in the Constitution.

5. Which of the following is NOT associated with Locke's argument about a social contract?

a. For governmental authority to be legitimate, citizens must consent to it.

b. People give government legitimacy by deciding it is better to be governed than not.

c. People enter into a social contract, agreeing to give up certain rights for the protection of others.

d. If government fails to protect citizens' rights, then people are free to form a new government

e. The divine right of kings should provide the legitimacy of any government.

SUGGESTED RESOURCES

republic.cqpress.com

Books

Dionne, E. J., Jr. 1991. *Why Americans Hate Politics.* New York: Simon & Schuster. Why do Americans "hate" politics? Dionne argues that partisan politics make it impossible for politicians to solve the very problems they promise the voters they'll address.

Hobbes, Thomas. 1996. *Leviathan.* Edited by Richard Tuck. Cambridge Texts in the History of Political Thought. New York: Cambridge University Press. Writing in 1651, English philosopher Thomas Hobbes described a state of nature in which life is "solitary, poor, nasty, brutish, and short." His analysis of society and power explains why citizens agree to be ruled by a powerful state: to preserve peace and security.

Jamieson, Kathleen Hall. 2000. *Everything You Think You Know About Politics . . . and Why You're Wrong.* New York: Basic Books. In a collection of essays, Jamieson uses political fact rather than personal opinions to dispel a variety of myths regarding American politics.

Lasswell, Harold. 1936. *Politics: Who Gets What, When, and How.* New York: McGraw-Hill. Lasswell's classic work on politics, originally published in 1911, lays out the definition of *politics* that is used throughout this textbook.

Locke, John. 1952. *Second Treatise on Government.* With Introduction by Thomas P. Peardon. Indianapolis, Ind.: Bobbs-Merrill. Here you'll find Locke's influential ideas about natural rights, consent, the social contract, and the legitimacy of revolting against a government that breaks the contract.

Putnam, Robert D. 2000. *Bowling Alone: The Collapse and Revival of American Community.* New York: Simon & Schuster. In this influential book, Putnam argues that Americans have become increasingly disconnected from the societal bonds that hold its culture together.

Rosenthal, Alan, Burdett A. Loomis, John R. Hibbing, and Karl T. Kurtz. 2003. *Republic on Trial: The Case for Representative Democracy.* Washington, D.C.: CQ Press. This short work by four noted political scientists lays out the case for why a representative democracy works better than any conceivable alternative.

Tocqueville, Alexis de. 1945. *Democracy in America.* Edited by Phillips Bradley. New York: Vintage Books. An intricate and extremely interesting report on American politics and culture as described by a visiting Frenchman during the nineteenth century.

Web Sites

American Political Science Association. www.apsanet.org. This Web site of the leading professional organization for the study of political science offers excellent information on the study of political science, careers in the field, and its many publications.

FirstGov.com. Official information resource for the U.S. federal government, providing easy access to all on-line government resources.

Internet Public Library. www.ipl.org. The Internet Public Library, hosted by the University of Michigan, is a gateway to countless online sources. Look for the government and political science categories.

SpeakOut.com. This site, managed by an on-line opinion research company, provides a way for visitors to participate in on-line polls, send messages to public officials, and sign petitions on issues they care about.

Movies

***Erin Brockovich.* 2000.** A woman down on her luck manages to find a job as a legal assistant and by connecting with others works toward the good of the community by exposing a power company that has been dumping toxic waste and poisoning a community. This popular film exposes what's at stake when an everyday citizen takes an interest and gets involved.

***Lord of the Flies.* 1963.** A group of schoolboys are shipwrecked on an uninhabited island and turn into savages for their own survival. While the movie (based on William Golding's 1954 novel) is chilling, it provides an excellent illustration of what life would be like without a ruling government.

***Nineteen Eighty-Four.* 1984.** This adaptation of George Orwell's classic novel depicts a totalitarian society in which the government controls all aspects of life.

Some Americans believe that all government services should be provided in English only. These activists in Denver, Colorado, hold signs demanding "English for Our Children" in local schools. Across the country, similar efforts clash with the belief that government should ensure equal rights to residents in areas with high numbers of non-English speakers by offering multilingual signs and forms. The registrar of voters in San Jose, California, has signs in English, Spanish, Vietnamese, and Chinese.

AMERICAN CITIZENS AND POLITICAL CULTURE

2

WHAT'S AT STAKE?

Let's test your knowledge of some basic American trivia. Is our national bird the eagle, or the turkey? (It's the eagle, adopted by Congress in 1782.) How about the national flower: the daffodil, or the rose? (The rose was declared our "national floral emblem" in 1986.) What's our official song: "America, The Beautiful" or "The Star Spangled Banner?" ("The Star Spangled Banner" became our national anthem in 1931.) Doing okay so far? Try this one: is the official language of the United States of America called American or English? Stumped? Don't worry, it's a trick question. The United States has no official language at all.

No official language? Such a fact seems jarring on its face. Don't nations need an official language to hold them together and to provide for a common culture? Isn't language at least as important a symbol of national unity and pride as a bird, a flower, or a song?

Supporters of a movement called "Official English" answer an emphatic "yes," and they are working hard to make it happen. To them Official English means that, except in matters of public safety, English should be the only language sanctioned and used by the government—not only for official business in Congress, the courts, and the executive branch but also on driver's license applications, ballots, applications for federal aid, and tax forms.

They argue that immigrants are better off when they learn English, so they should be forced to do so as fast as they can by being immersed in it, an approach their opponents call "sink or swim." They say bilingual education merely postpones the moment that immigrant children are assimilated into American culture, and that printing paperwork in multiple languages is costly to taxpayers and sends a signal to immigrants that it is not important that they learn English. Accordingly, they actively support legislation, or even an amendment to the Constitution, that would make English the official tongue of the United States.

Their opponents advocate a concept they call "English Plus." They hold that while English is and should remain the primary language in the United States, the languages that immigrants bring with them are a valuable resource that should be preserved. They say further that the guarantee of equal rights in the Constitution means that until people do learn English, they have a right to language assistance to give them equal access to American society.

National policy today comes closest to the English Plus model. Public schools must teach students in a language that they can understand while they are learning English, and official documents are printed in a variety of languages (driver's license exams are given in forty-three languages, for example, voting ballots are printed in twenty-eight, and instructions for the 2000 census were printed in fifty). In 2000 President Bill Clinton gave the movement some teeth, when he signed Executive Order 13166, which requires that federally funded programs be accessible to those with limited proficiency in English.

Supporters of English Plus say that, while not perfect, the system works. Although well over three hundred different languages are spoken in the United States, census figures say that 92 percent of the country's residents claim to speak English very well. Meanwhile, the ethnic diversity and traditions that immigrants cherish are preserved and honored, and the civil rights of all are protected. They say that their opponents, whom they call "English Only" advocates, are anti-immigrant and even racist.

Official English supporters, on the other hand, contend that the system is very broken indeed, and that English is in danger of losing its status as the primary national language, as more and more immigrants hold on to their own languages and cultures. They say that their opponents take political correctness too far or that they are un-American.

What is it about the idea of a national language that elicits such vigorous fighting and name-calling? Why is it so much more controversial than the effort to name our favored flora, fauna, or music? What is really at stake in the debate over whether English ought to be named the official language of the United States? *

Over the years, American schoolchildren have grown up hearing two conflicting stories about who we are as a nation. The first, that we are a melting pot, implies that the United States is a vast cauldron into which go many cultures and ethnicities, all of which are boiled down into some sort of homogenized American stew. The other story, that we are a multicultural nation, tells us that each cultural, ethnic, and religious identity should be preserved and celebrated, lest its distinctive nature be lost. Reality, as is often the case, falls somewhere in between these two competing images of the American people.

The rich diversity of the American people is one of the United States's greatest strengths, combining talents, tradition, culture, and custom from every corner of the world. But our diversity, far from being uniformly celebrated, has also contributed to some of the nation's deepest conflicts. We cannot possibly understand the drama that is American politics without an in-depth look at who the actors are: the *who* in many ways shapes the *what* and *how* of politics.

To help you better understand the *who* in American politics, in this chapter you will learn about

- our roots as immigrants and the role of immigration in American politics
- demographic trends that help us see what Americans are like in terms of crucial variables like age, race, income level, and education, and the ways these trends affect American political life
- American political beliefs—those that pull us together as a nation and those that drive us into partisan divisions

WHO ARE WE?

Our politics—what we want from government and how we try to get it—stems from who we are. Who Americans are—where they have come from and what they have brought with them, what their lives look like and how they spend their time and money, what they believe and how they act on those beliefs—helps determine what they choose to fight for politically and how they elect to carry out the fight. It is critically important, as we approach the study of American politics, that we understand who American citizens are: where their roots lie, what their lives are like, and what sorts of things they need and value.

Since we cannot, of course, meet all the Americans who are out there, we settle for the next best thing: we use statistics to tell us the relevant things about a large and unwieldy population. Throughout this book, we use statistics, in the form of charts and graphs, to examine the demographic trends that shape our national culture—political and otherwise—in a feature called *Who Are We?* We'll use this information not only to understand better who we are but also to consider how the characteristics, habits, and lives of real people relate to the political issues that shape our society. (Be sure to read "*Consider the Source:* How to Be a Critical Reader of Charts and Graphs" on page 43, for a discussion on the uses and limits of statistics in politics. It will serve you well as you read this book.)

In "*Who Are We?* The American People" on the next page, you will see that our population is gradually aging; older people demand more money for pensions and nursing home care, and they compete for scarce resources with younger families, who want better schools and health care for children. You will see that the white population in the United States will soon be outnumbered by ethnic and racial minority populations that traditionally support affirmative action and other policies (less popular with whites) designed to raise them up from the lower end of the socioeconomic scale. Our population is in constant flux, and every change in the makeup of the people brings a change in what we try to get from government and how we try to get it.

As you look at these depictions of the American people and American life, try to imagine the political problems that arise from such incredible diversity. How can a government represent the interests of people with such varied backgrounds, needs, and preferences? How does who we are affect what we want and how we go about getting it?

The American People

Who we are, and who we, as Americans, will be in the future influences the types of demands we make on government, how much attention these demands will receive, and the government's ability to meet them. Over the next fifty years, the American population will become older; the most economically productive groups will decline as a percentage of the population. What do fewer workers and more dependents mean for the government's ability to get the revenues necessary to pay for the benefits and services citizens want? In addition, the racial and ethnic balance in the population will change as the white majority shrinks. Whose concerns are likely to get more attention from public officials in the future?

The Aging of America, 2000 to 2050: More dependents, fewer working Americans.

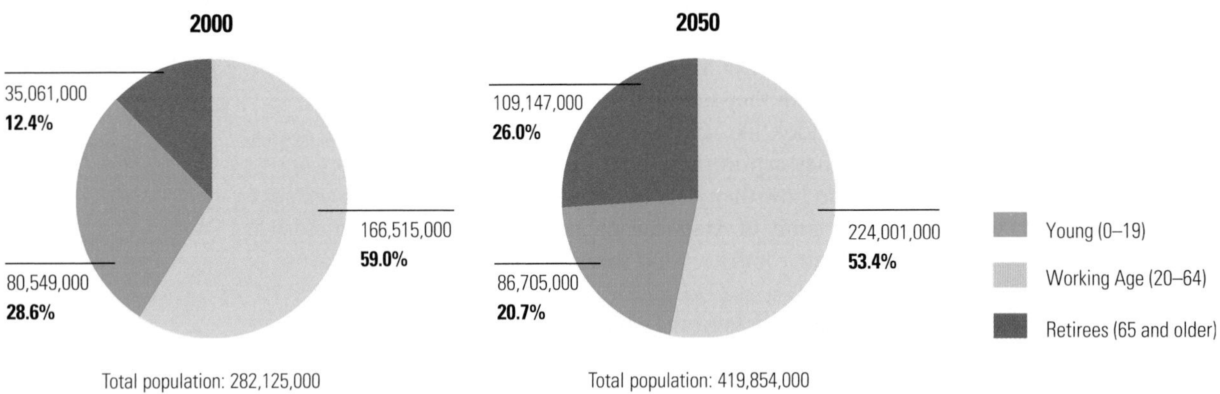

Source: U.S. Census Bureau, "U.S. Interim Projections by Age, Sex, Race, and Hispanic Origin," March 18, 2004, www.census.gov/ipc/www/usinterimproj/.

The U.S. Population by Race and Hispanic Origin, 2000 to 2050: The white majority is shrinking.

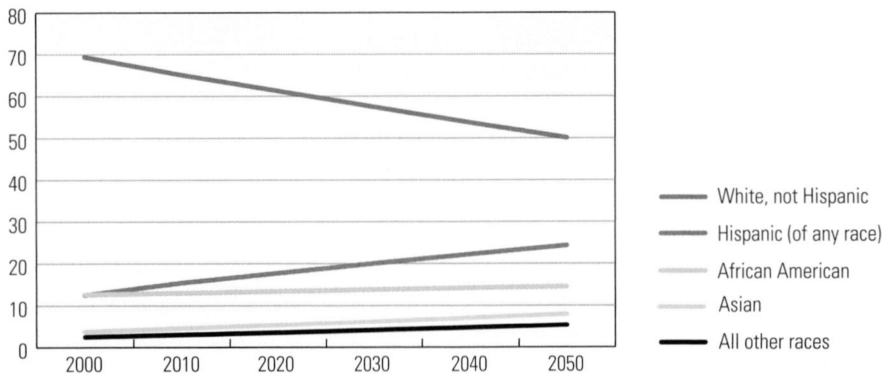

Note: All other races includes American Indian and Alaska Native alone, Native Hawaiian and Other Pacific Islander alone, and Two or More Races. Race and Hispanic origin are two separate concepts; people who identify their origin as Hispanic may be of any race.

Source: U.S. Census Bureau, "U.S. Interim Projections by Age, Sex, Race, and Hispanic Origin," March 14, 2004, www.census.gov/ipc/www/usinterimproj/.

WHERE DO WE COME FROM?

In Chapter 1, we said that citizenship exacts obligations from individuals and also confers rights on them and that the American concept of citizenship contains both self-interested and public-spirited elements. But citizenship is not only a normative concept—that is, a prescription for how governments ought to treat residents and how those residents ought to act; it is also a very precise legal status. A fundamental element of democracy is not just the careful specification of the rights and obligations of citizenship but also an equally careful legal description of just who is a citizen and how that status can be acquired by immigrants who choose to switch their allegiance to a new country. In this section we look at the legal definition of American citizenship and at the long history of immigration that has shaped our body politic.

AMERICAN CITIZENSHIP

American citizens are usually born, not made. If you are born in any of the fifty states or in most of America's overseas territories, such as Puerto Rico or Guam, you are an American citizen, whether your parents are Americans or not. This follows the principle of international law called *jus soli,* which means literally "the right of the soil." The exceptions to this rule in the United States are children born to foreign diplomats serving in the United States and children born on foreign ships in U.S. waters. These children would not be considered U.S. citizens. According to another legal principle, *jus sanguinis* ("the right by blood"), if you are born outside the United States to American parents, you are also an American citizen (or you can become one if you are adopted by American parents). Interestingly, if you are born in the United States but one of your parents holds citizenship in another country, depending on that country's laws, you may be able to hold dual citizenship. Most countries, including the United States, require that a child with dual citizenship declare allegiance to one country on turning age eighteen. It is worth noting that requirements for U.S. citizenship, particularly as they affect people born outside the country, have changed frequently over time.

So far, citizenship seems relatively straightforward. But as we know, the United States since its birth has been a nation of **immigrants**, people who are citizens or subjects of another country who come here to live and work. The feature "*Who Are We?* Where We Come From" helps us to understand some characteristics of the foreign-born population of the United States. Today there are strict limitations on the numbers of immigrants who may legally enter the country. There are also strict rules governing the criteria for entry. If immigrants come here legally on permanent resident visas—that is, if they follow the rules and regulations of the U.S. Citizenship and Immigration Services (USCIS)—they may be eligible to apply for citizenship through a process called **naturalization**.

immigrants citizens or subjects of one country who move to another country to live or work

naturalization the legal process of acquiring citizenship for someone who has not acquired it by birth

Where We Come From

America has always been a land of immigrants. In the twenty-first century, most new arrivals are coming from Latin America, especially Mexico, as well as from different countries in Asia, while the waves of immigration that brought white Europeans to America over the past two centuries have slowed to a relative trickle. What different demands does immigration put on a democratic political system? What support services do immigrants need, and how do citizens respond to providing those services? What role does a common language play in forming a national identity?

Percentage of the U.S. Population That is Foreign Born, 1900 to 2000: Major loosening of immigration policy in 1965 and 1986 has increased the immigrant population.

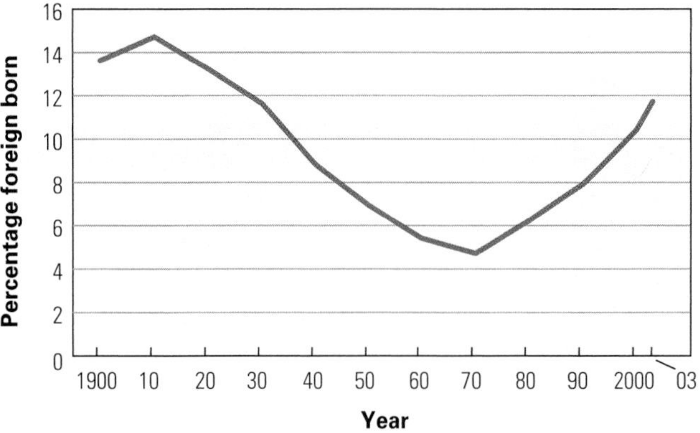

Note: Data from the Current Population Survey include the civilian noninstitutionalized population plus Armed Forces living off post or with their families on post.

Source: U.S. Census Bureau, Current Population Reports, "Profile of the Foreign-Born Population in the United States: 2000," Figure 1-1, December 2001; 2003 data calculated from U.S. Census Bureau, "Foreign-Born Population of the United States," Table 1-1.

Country of Origin for Today's Foreign-Born Americans: More than 31,107,000 Americans were born outside the United States.

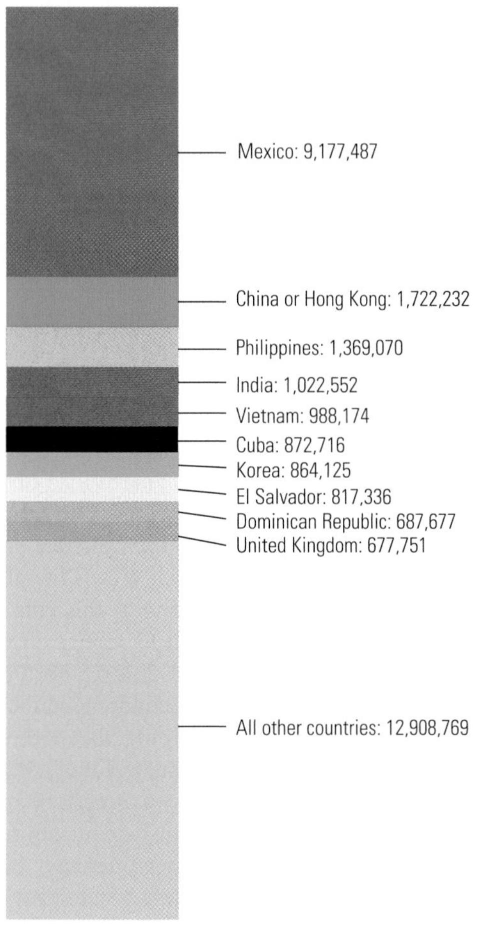

Source: U.S. Census Bureau, Census 2000 Summary File 3 (SF3) Sample Data.

NONIMMIGRANTS

asylum protection or sanctuary, especially from political persecution

refugees individuals who flee an area or country because of persecution on the basis of race, nationality, religion, group membership, or political opinion

Many people who come to the United States do not come as legal permanent residents. The UCSIS refers to these people as nonimmigrants. Some arrive seeking **asylum**, or protection. These are political **refugees**, who are allowed into the United States if they face or are threatened with persecution because of their race, religion, nationality, membership in a particular social group, or political opinions. Not everyone who feels threatened is given legal refugee status, however; the USCIS requires that the fear of persecution be "well founded," and it is itself the final judge of a well-founded fear. Refugees may become legal permanent residents after they have lived here continuously for one year (although there are annual limits on the number who

The Languages We Speak: The top twenty-five.

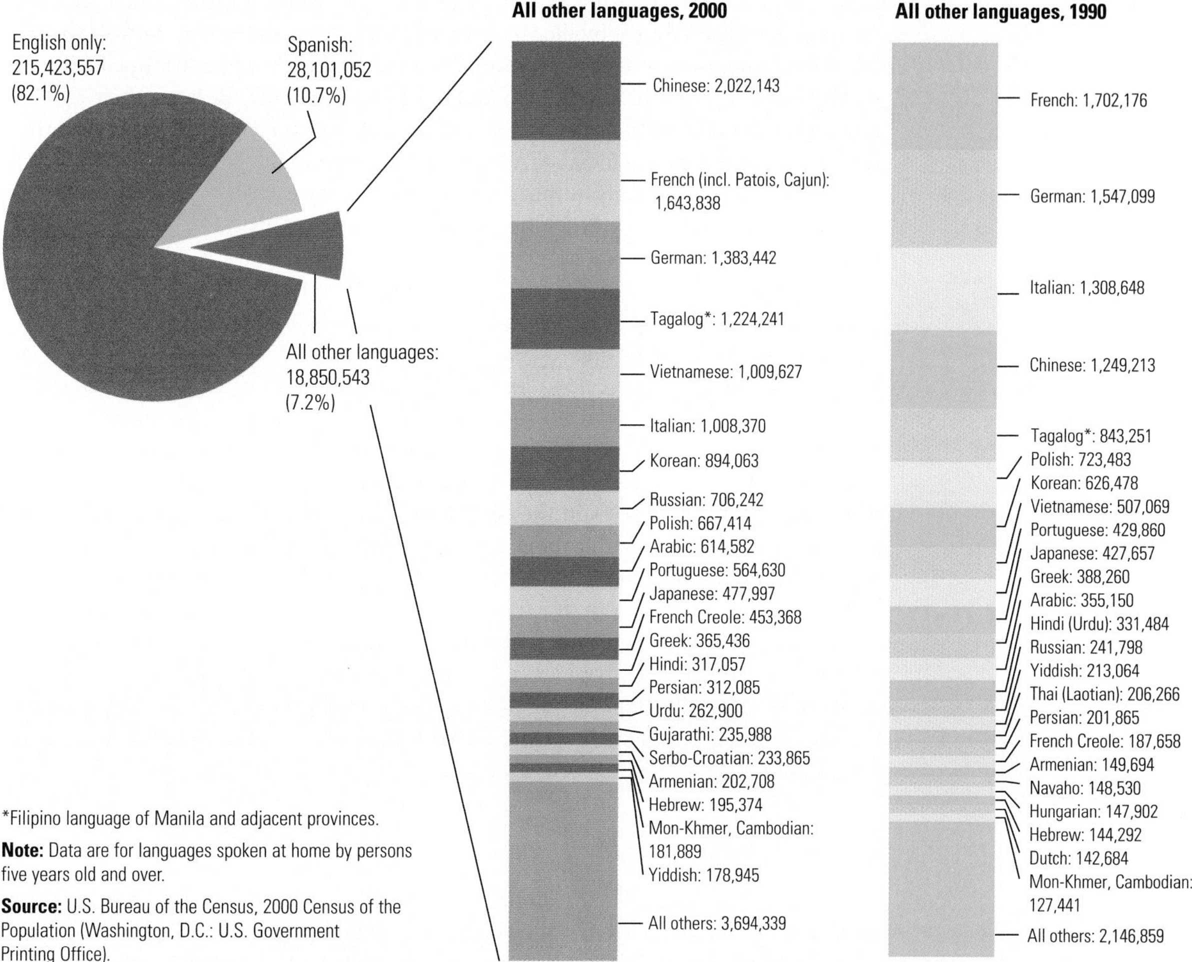

*Filipino language of Manila and adjacent provinces.

Note: Data are for languages spoken at home by persons five years old and over.

Source: U.S. Bureau of the Census, 2000 Census of the Population (Washington, D.C.: U.S. Government Printing Office).

may do so), at which time they can begin accumulating the in-residence time required to become a citizen, if they wish to.

Other people who may come to the United States legally but without official permanent resident status include visitors, foreign government officials, students, international representatives, temporary workers, members of foreign media, and exchange visitors. These people are expected to return to their home countries and not take up permanent residence in the United States.

Illegal immigrants have arrived here by avoiding the USCIS regulations, usually because they would not qualify for one reason or another. American laws have become increasingly harsh with respect to illegal immigrants, but people continue to come anyway. Many illegal immigrants act like "citizens," obeying the laws, paying taxes, and sending their children to school. Nonetheless, some areas of the country, particularly those near the Mexican-American border, like Texas and California, often have serious problems brought on by illegal immigration. Even with border controls to regulate the number of new arrivals, communities can find themselves swamped with new residents, often poor and unskilled, looking for a better life. Because their children must be educated and they themselves may be entitled to receive social services, they can pose a significant financial burden on those communities without necessarily increasing the available funds. Although many illegals pay taxes, many also work off the books, meaning they do not contribute to the tax base. Furthermore, most income taxes are federal, and federal money is distributed back to states and localities to fund social services based on the population count in the census. Since illegal immigrants are understandably reluctant to come forward to be counted, their communities are typically underfunded in that respect as well.

Just because a person is not a legal permanent resident of the United States does not mean that he or she has no rights and responsibilities here, any more than the fact that our traveling in another country means that we have no rights and obligations there. Immigrants enjoy some rights, primarily legal protections. Not only are they entitled to due process in the courts (guarantee of a fair trial, right to a lawyer, and so on), but the U.S. Supreme Court has ruled that it is illegal to discriminate against immigrants in the United States.[1] Nevertheless, their rights are limited; they cannot, for instance, vote in our national elections (although some localities, in the hopes of integrating immigrants into their communities, allow them to vote in local elections[2]) or decide to live here permanently without permission (which may or may not be granted). In addition, immigrants, even legal ones, are subject to the decisions of the USCIS, which is empowered by Congress to exercise authority in immigration matters.

U.S. IMMIGRATION POLICY

Immigration law is made by Congress (with the approval of the president) and implemented by a federal agency, the USCIS. The 1996 Illegal Immigration Reform and Immigrant Responsibility Act had granted the agency, then known as the Immigration and Naturalization Service (INS), considerable power to make nonappealable decisions at the border that can result in the deportation of an immigrant who may have quite innocently violated an INS rule and who then cannot reenter the country for five years. In the wake of September 11, 2001, new legislation took the INS out of the Department of Justice, where it was formerly located, renamed it the U.S. Citizenship and Immigration Services, and placed it under the jurisdiction of the newly formed Department of Homeland Security.

While many people in a country may be motivated by generosity or humanitarian concerns in the immigration policies they promote, the nation's leaders are also obligated to do what is in the country's best interest. In general, nations want to admit immigrants who will make that country better off. Thus, even when we open our doors to refugees from foreign wars or persecution, there are generally limits on how many may come in. Since September 11, as evidenced by the fact that the USCIS is now part of the Department of Homeland Security, security issues have come to play a central role in deciding who may enter the country.

Taking the Oath
Navy sailor Maria Palacios, a native of Mexico, takes the oath of allegiance to the United States along with two hundred other marines and sailors in a U.S. naturalization ceremony at Camp Pendleton near San Diego, California on January 30, 2004. While native-born Americans rarely think about their status as citizens, naturalized immigrants must pledge their allegiance to their new nation, renounce their former home, and vow to "support and defend the Constitution and laws of the United States of America against all enemies," which this woman did by enlisting in the military before she'd even become a citizen.

Reasons for Controlling Immigration No country, not even the huge United States, can manage to absorb every discontented or threatened global resident who wants a better or safer life. Every job given to an immigrant means one less job for an American citizen, and jobs are just the sort of scarce resource over which political battles are fought. If times are good and unemployment is low, newcomers may not be a problem, but when the economy hits hard times, immigration can be a bitter issue for jobless Americans. Immigrants, especially the very young and the very old, are also large consumers of social services and community resources. Immigrants do contribute to the economy by their labor and their taxes, but they are disproportionately distributed throughout the population, and so some areas find their social service systems more burdened than others.

Nations typically want to admit immigrants who can do things the country's citizens are unable or unwilling to do. During and after World War II, when the United States wanted to develop a rocket program, German scientists with the necessary expertise were desirable immigrants. When the Soviet Union fell in 1991, we became concerned that former Soviets familiar with Moscow's weapons of mass destruction and other defense technology might be lured to work in countries we considered to be our enemies, so in 1992 Congress passed a special law making it easier for such scientists and their families to immigrate to the United States. At times in our history when our labor force was insufficient for the demands of industrialization and railroad building and when western states wanted larger populations, immigrants were welcomed. Today, immigration law allows for temporary workers to come to work in agriculture when our own labor force falls short or is unwilling to work for low wages. As a rule, however, immigrants are expected to be skilled and financially stable so that they do not become a burden on the American social services system. Remember that politics is about how power and resources are distributed in society; whether government services go to legal citizens or illegal immigrants is a hotly contested issue.

At times, motivated by cultural stereotypes, global events, and domestic economic circumstances, Americans have decided that we have allowed "enough" immigrants to settle here, or that we are admitting too many of the "wrong" kind of immigrants, and we have encouraged politicians to enact restrictions. From 1882 to 1943, legislation outlawed Chinese immigration because westerners saw it as an economic and cultural threat. Reacting to the large numbers of southern and eastern Europeans who began flooding into the country in the very late 1800s and early 1900s, legislation in the 1920s limited immigration by individual nationalities to a small percentage of the total number of immigrants already in residence from each country. This quota system favored the northern and western nationalities, seen as more desirable immigrants, who had arrived in larger numbers earlier, allowing Great Britain and Ireland to send 65,721 immigrants yearly, for instance, but Italy only 5,802.[3]

Immigration Law Today Congress abolished the existing immigration quota system in 1965 with the Immigration and Nationality Act. This act doubled the number of people allowed to enter the country, set limits on immigration from the Western Hemisphere, and made it easier for families to join members who had already immigrated. More open borders meant immigration was increasingly harder to control. Reacting to the waves of illegal immigrants who entered the country in the 1970s and 1980s, Congress passed the Immigration Reform and Control Act in 1986, granting amnesty to illegals who had entered before 1982 and attempting to tighten controls on those who came after. Although this law included sanctions for those who hired illegal immigrants, people continued to cross the border illegally from Mexico looking for work. Two laws passed in the mid-1990s have also had an important effect on immigration. The welfare reform act passed by Congress and signed by President Clinton in 1996 reduced or eliminated many of the social services that could be received by legal immigrants, many of whom had lived, worked, and paid taxes in this country for some time. This caused a boom in naturalization applications, as many of these people became citizens to escape the restrictions. Most of the restrictions were removed by law within two years in any case. The second effort in the 1990s to limit immigration was the 1996 law, mentioned earlier, that strengthened the power of the INS. The overall impact of this law has been to reduce the practical rights that immigrants and visitors to this country can claim: would-be immigrants can find themselves deported (or sent home) before they can use the courts to protect their rights.

Despite the trend of tightening immigration laws, President George W. Bush indicated early in his first administration that he was considering giving amnesty—freedom from punishment, including deportation—to the estimated three to four million Mexicans living illegally in the United States. Conservatives in Bush's own party, long known for their opposition to looser immigration laws, and advocates for immigrants

How to Be a Critical Reader of Charts and Graphs

When we talk about American politics, we frequently talk about large numbers—of people, of votes, of incomes, of ages, of policy preferences or opinions. Political scientist and graphics expert Edward R. Tufte says, "Often the most effective way to describe, explore, and summarize a set of numbers—even a very large set—is to look at pictures of those numbers."[1] Charts, graphs, and other visual depictions of numbers and numerical relationships have an advantage over words in that they can, at their best, give the viewer "the greatest number of ideas in the shortest time with the least ink in the smallest space."[2]

To those for whom numbers pose no difficulties, graphs and charts are a welcome insight into how those numbers are organized and related. For the rest of us, charts and graphs may signal a potential nightmare of numerical relationships that make the inside of our heads itch and tempt us to skip them altogether. Unfortunately, being statistically illiterate in the modern world is just slightly less disastrous than being unable to read words and sentences. Numbers, statistics, and data are the currency of modern economics and business, they are part and parcel of any science, and they make the computer world tick. It may be comfortable to ignore graphs and charts, but it is ultimately damaging to your job prospects, your pocketbook, and your peace of mind. To get the statistically challenged through this course in American politics and to sharpen the skills of those of you who are not afflicted with a math block, we provide some brief definitions and rules for the critical interpretation of charts and graphs, and we offer some advice on how to avoid being hoodwinked by those who use statistical figures carelessly or unscrupulously.

Data and Statistics

Political scientists, in fact all scientists, are focused on their **data**, or the empirical results of their research. Your data are what you find out, and they become the evidence to support your theories about how the world works. When those data are in numerical or quantitative terms, like how many people say they voted for Democrats or Republicans, or how much of the federal budget is devoted to various programs like welfare and education, or how much money candidates spend on their elections, the result can look like one gigantic, unorganized mass of numbers.

To help bring order to the chaos of the data they amass, scientists use statistical analysis. While a statistic is a numerical fact, such as the population of the United States, **statistics** is the science of collecting, organizing, and interpreting numerical data. At its simplest, it allows us to calculate the **mean**, or average, of a bunch of numbers, and to see how far individual data points fall away from, or **deviate** from, the mean. So, for instance, instead of having to deal with income figures for all Americans, we can talk about the average income, and we can compare average incomes for different groups, as we do in the figure on page 53, and make intelligent observations about the distribution of income in the United States. When we do this, the numbers are no longer an incoherent mass, but they start to take on some shape and organization, and we can talk about them in a useful way.

Calculating means, and deviations from the means, is only the tip of the statistical iceberg; advanced statistical techniques can allow us to discern complicated patterns over time, to look at the way that different political characteristics change in relation to each other, and to see what kinds of political and economic factors seem to explain different political phenomena best. We use statistics to compare groups and characteristics of groups with one another and over time. We use statistics to discern relationships among characteristics that we might not otherwise be able to see. And we use statistics to look at the distribution of characteristics across a population, and to see how a part relates to the whole group. Although statistics can be used in almost any discipline, from economics to medicine, it is interesting to note that the word comes from the Latin for "state" or"government." Statistics might have been tailor-made for investigating political puzzles.

Displaying the Data

Once they have gathered their data and begun to analyze them, scientists need a way to show other people what they have found. It is here that a picture can often be worth a thousand words. There are many ways to graphically display numerical data and the relationship among them; here are a few of the most common, all of which you are likely to run into, not only in this book but also in newspapers, magazines, and reports for stockholders:

- **Tables** are perhaps the simplest way to display data, and we use many tables in this book. In a table, information is arranged in columns (going down) and in rows (going across). To read information presented in this way, look carefully at the title or caption to see what the table is about. Read the column headings,

(continued on next page)

and then follow the information along the rows. The information might be purely descriptive (what is the population of this state?), or you might be able to compare the different rows (which states have the highest average income or educational achievements?). Sometimes tables provide information that can be compared within each row (how does the state's average income compare to its poverty rate or educational level?).

- **Pie charts** are a way of showing how some parts fit into the whole. In a pie chart, each wedge is a certain percentage (or so many hundredths) of the whole pie (which is 100 percent). So, for example, the top pie charts on page 36 allow us to see the population of the United States, broken down by age group—young (19 and under), working age (20–64) or retirees (65 and older.) Seeing this information graphically gives us a clearer idea of the relationship of the parts and their relative sizes than we would get simply from reading the information in words. Pie charts are also used to compare these relationships over time. The pie charts on page 36 show the sizes of different age groups today, and what they are projected to be in the 2050. We can clearly see that the percentage of the working age population will shrink relative to the size of the number of retirees and we can speculate about what the political implications of such changes will be. As recent debates about Social Security make clear, for instance, the money for the Social Security benefits paid to current retirees comes from current workers. The changing age distribution means relatively fewer workers will have to pay for the benefits of a growing number of retired people. (Another way of conveying the same information in multiple pie charts is with a stacked bar chart, which is much like a pie chart, except that the space is a rectangle instead of a circle and it is divided into sections instead of wedges. When these sections are stacked, as they are on pages 38 and 39, comparisons are easy.)

- **Bar charts** are designed to allow you to compare two categories of things with each other: for example, groups of people (ages, gender, races), states, regions, or units of time. One set is plotted along the horizontal axis, the other on the vertical axis. The first graph on page 53 is a bar chart. To get the maximum amount of information from a bar chart, read the title carefully, and be sure you understand what is being measured on each axis. Note the relationship between the two. Did it change at some point? What happened then to make that occur?

- **Line graphs** are related to bar charts, except that points are plotted to show up as a continuous line instead of a series of steps. In a line graph you can find a value on the vertical axis for every value on the horizontal axis. In a bar chart you want to make individual comparisons of the columns to each other, but in a line graph, you want your eye to sweep from one end of the graph to the other, to note broad trends and patterns. Frequently the variable on the horizontal axis is time, and the graph traces some other variable, perhaps age or number of immigrants or average income, across time. The left-hand graph on page 38, marking changes in the foreign-born population over time, is a line graph. The different colored lines in the right-hand graph on page 53 allow us to look at changes in several behaviors over the same time frame. We know for instance that since 1973 time spent at work is on the rise, while leisure time has declined.

What to Watch Out for

Charts and graphs are obviously a boon to our ability to communicate information about large numbers, but there are also hidden pitfalls. Statistics, like any other kind of information, are open to manipulation and distortion. The hazards only seem to be greater when it comes to statistics because, since so few of us understand them or look critically at graphic displays, the mistakes and deceptions escape scrutiny more frequently than do those perpetrated in words.

Professor Tufte tells us that "graphical excellence begins with telling the truth about data."[3] To tell the truth about the data, the graph must display the data without distortion. Some common distortions of display include the following:

- **Altering the baseline.** Normally, the numbers that go up the vertical axis begin at zero and move up at regularly scheduled intervals. The real relationship between the numbers on each axis can be disguised, however, if the baseline is not zero—especially if it is below zero. All the bars or data points will seem to be positive because they are above the baseline, but in fact they may be negative.

- **Changing the units of analysis, and comparison.** Note the first example on page 45, where yearly payments to travel agents for 1976 and 1977 are compared in a bar chart to *half* a year's payment for 1978. It looks as if there has been an abrupt decline in commissions in 1978, but that impression is an attempt to mislead, gleaned only by careful attention to the graph.

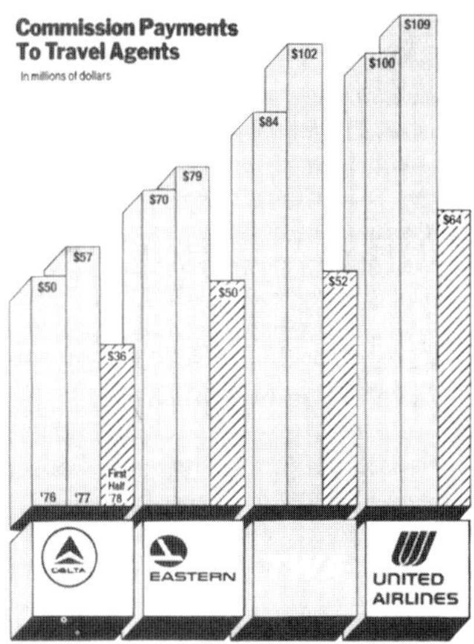

Source: *The New York Times,* 8 August 1978, D-1. Copyright ©1978 by *The New York Times.* Reprinted by permission

- **Using averages or means when they are misleading.** The mean, calculated by adding up a series of values and dividing by the number of values, generally gives us a good mid-range estimate. However, sometimes the outlying values, the ones at the top or bottom, are so far from the middle that the mean is too high or too low to represent the middle. When this happens, we often prefer to use the **median**, calculated by arranging all the values numerically and then finding the one that is actually in the physical middle. For example, the income distribution in the United States is such that a relatively few billionaires make far more money than everyone else. When we calculate the national mean income, these high incomes at the top give us an artificially high picture of the salary a typical American makes. The median will give us a far more accurate picture of the middle-income range than the mean. The use of the mean is usually fine, but we need to be alert to those occasions when it can disguise an uneven distribution.
- **Not using constant dollars.** Dollar values cannot be compared over time because inflation means that a dollar today buys far less than it did, say, fifty years ago. For an accurate comparison, we need to use constant dollars, that is, dollars that have been adjusted for changing price levels over time. When graphs show the difference in money spent or earned over time, they usually do not adjust the figures for inflation. If a chart shows the growth of the minimum wage over time, it would seem at first glance as if legislation has steadily increased the legal minimum wage over time. In fact, however, the purchasing power of the dollar has declined over time, and the minimum wage in constant dollars, adjusted for inflation, has actually been *declining* since its height in the 1970s, despite its apparent growth.
- **Not showing populations as a percentage of the base.** Often charts and graphs will show a growth in the numbers of a group without relating the group to the population as a whole. For instance, a graph that shows the percentage of blacks on welfare over time may be useful information, but it would be more useful when put into the context of their percentage of the total people on welfare. Not showing populations as parts of the whole is only one way in which graphs remove data from context. Always ask yourself if some crucial information is missing that would help you understand the data better.
- **Implying causality where none exists.** As this Solar Radiation and Stock Prices example shows, graphs can put together any pieces of information and imply that one causes the other. Causality, however, is very difficult to show, and generally the best we can do is to show that two things are correlated. Beware of cause-and-effect claims.

1. Edward R. Tufte, *The Visual Display of Quantitative Information* (Cheshire, Conn.: Graphics Press, 1983), 9.
2. Tufte, 51.
3. Tufte, 53.

Solar Radiation and Stock Prices

A. New York stock prices (Barron's average). B. Solar Radiation, inverted, and C. London stock prices, all by months, 1929 (after Garcia-Mata and Shaffner).

Source: Edwin R. Dewey and Edwin F. Dakin, *Cycles: The Science of Prediction* (New York, 1947), 144.

from other nations, immediately howled. Bush backed down. Days later, the White House reported that its real interest was in an expanded guest worker program, in which workers could enter the country from Mexico to work temporarily in industries that needed low-wage labor. Some of these guest workers would be able to "earn" the right to become permanent residents and citizens by working and paying taxes. In addition, illegal immigrants already here might be able to earn their own legalization through similar means. Furthermore, Bush hinted that he might be amenable to expanding the program to groups other than Mexicans. These plans were put on hold in the aftermath of the tougher enforcement of immigration laws and heightened scrutiny of immigrants that followed September 11, 2001, but Bush revived his call for a guest worker program immediately after the 2004 election. He claimed it would help fill jobs Americans were unwilling to take and bolster homeland security by providing a record of who was in the United States. Democrats and moderate Republican legislators like Arizona senator John McCain hailed the proposals, but again, conservatives vowed to block passage of any such legislation, demanding instead new laws to crack down on illegal immigrants.

WHO, WHAT, HOW Immigration and citizenship are issues in which the political and humanitarian stakes are very high. For non-Americans who are threatened or impoverished in their native countries, the stakes are sanctuary, prosperity, and improved quality of life, which they seek to gain through acquiring asylum or by becoming legal or illegal immigrants.

People who are already American citizens have a stake here as well. At issue is the desire to be sensitive to humanitarian concerns, as well as to fill gaps in the nation's pool of workers and skills, and to meet the needs of current citizens. These often conflicting goals are turned into law by policy makers in Congress and the White House, and their solutions are implemented by the bureaucracy of the USCIS.

WHAT WE BELIEVE: THE IDEAS THAT UNITE US

Making a single nation out of such a diverse people is no easy feat. It is possible only because, despite all our differences, Americans share some fundamental attitudes and beliefs about how the world works and how it should work. These ideas, our political culture, pull us together, and, indeed, provide a framework in which we can also disagree politically without resorting to violence and civil war.

political culture the broad pattern of ideas, beliefs, and values about citizens and government held by a population

values central ideas, principles, or standards that most people agree are important

Political culture refers to the general political orientation or disposition of a nation—the shared values and beliefs about the nature of the political world that give us a common language in which to discuss and debate political ideas. **Values** are ideals or principles that most people agree are important, even though they may disagree on exactly how the value—such as "equality" or "freedom"—ought to be defined. Often we take our own culture so much for granted that we aren't even aware of it, and thus we can have trouble seeing it as clearly as someone who was not raised in it. For that reason, it is often easier to see our own political culture by contrasting it to another.

Political culture is shared, although certainly some individuals find themselves at odds with it. When we say, "Americans think. . .," we mean that most Americans hold those views, not that there is unanimous agreement on them. Political culture is handed down from generation to generation, through families, schools, communities, literature, churches and synagogues, and so on, helping to provide stability for the nation by ensuring that a majority of citizens are well grounded in and committed to the basic values that sustain it. We will talk about the process through which values are transferred in Chapter 11, "Public Opinion."

FAITH IN RULES AND INDIVIDUALS

In American political culture, our expectations of government focus on rules and processes rather than on results; for example, we want government to guarantee a fair playing field but not to guarantee equal outcomes for all the players. In addition, we believe that individuals are responsible for their own welfare and that what is good for them is good for society as a whole. Our insistence on fair rules, as we saw in Chapter 1, is an emphasis on **procedural guarantees**, while the belief in the primacy of the individual citizen is called **individualism**. American culture is not wholly procedural and individualistic—indeed, differences on these matters constitute some of the major partisan divisions in American politics—but it tends to be more so than are most other nations.

procedural guarantees government assurance that the rules will work smoothly and treat everyone fairly, with no promise of particular outcomes

individualism belief that what is good for society is based on what is good for individuals

To illustrate this point, we can compare American culture to the more social democratic cultures of Scandinavia, such as Sweden, Denmark, and Norway. In many ways, the United States and the countries in Scandinavia are more similar than they are different: they are all capitalist democracies, and they essentially agree that individuals ought to make most of the decisions about their own lives. Recall our comparison of political and economic systems from Chapter 1; the United States and Scandinavia, which reject substantial governmental control of both the social order and the economy, would all fit into the upper-right quadrant of Figure 1.3, along with other advanced industrial democracies like Japan and Great Britain.

They do differ in some important ways, however. While all advanced industrial democracies repudiate the wholehearted substantive guarantees of communism, the Scandinavian countries have a greater tolerance for some substantive economic policy than does the more procedural United States. We will explore these differences here in more detail so that we can better understand what American culture supports and what it does not.

Procedural Guarantees As we have noted, when we say that American political culture is procedural, we mean that Americans generally prefer government to guarantee fair processes—such as a free market to distribute goods, majority rule to make decisions, due process to determine guilt and innocence—rather than specific outcomes. The social democratic countries of Sweden, Norway, and Denmark, however, as we saw in Chapter 1, believe that government should actively seek to realize the values of equality—perhaps to guarantee a certain quality of life to all citizens or to increase equality of income. Government can then be evaluated by how well it produces those substantive outcomes, not just on how well it guarantees fair processes.

While American politics does set some substantive goals for public policy, Americans are generally more comfortable ensuring that things are done in a fair and proper way, and trusting that the outcomes will be good ones because the rules are fair. Although the American government does get involved in social programs and welfare, it aims more at helping individuals get on their feet so that they can participate in the market (fair procedures) rather than at cleaning up slums or eliminating poverty (substantive goals).

Individualism The individualistic nature of American political culture means that individuals, not government or society, are seen as responsible for their own well-being. This contrasts with a collectivist point of view, which holds that what is good for society may not be the same as what is in the interest of individuals.

Thus, our politics revolves around the belief that individuals are usually the best judges of what is good for them; we assume that what is good for society will automatically follow. For contrast, let's look again at Sweden, a democratic capitalist country like the United States, but one with a more collectivist political culture. At one time, Sweden had a policy that held down the wages of workers so that more profitable and less profitable industries would be more equal, and society, according to the Swedish view, would be better off. Americans would reject this policy as violating their belief in individualism (and proceduralism as well). American government rarely asks citizens to make major economic sacrifices for the public good, although individuals often do so privately and voluntarily. Where Americans are asked to make economic sacrifices, like paying taxes, they are unpopular and more modest than in most other countries. A collective interest that supersedes individual interests is generally invoked in the United States only in times of war or national crisis. This echoes the two American notions of self-interested and public-interested citizenship we discussed in Chapter 1.

CORE AMERICAN VALUES: DEMOCRACY, FREEDOM, AND EQUALITY

We can see our American procedural and individualistic perspective when we examine the different meanings of three core American values: democracy, freedom, and equality.

Democracy Democracy in America, as we have seen, means representative democracy, based on consent and majority rule. Basically, American democracy is a procedure to make political decisions, to choose political leaders, and to select policies for the nation. It is seen as a fundamentally just or fair way of making decisions because every individual who cares to participate is heard in the process, and all interests are considered. We don't reject a democratically made decision because it is not fair; it is fair precisely *because* it is democratically made. Democracy is valued primarily not for the way it makes citizens feel, or the effects it has on them, but for the decisions it produces. Americans see democracy as the appropriate procedure for making public decisions—that is, decisions about government—but generally not for decisions in the private realm. Rarely do employees have a binding vote on company policy, for example, as they do in some Scandinavian countries.

Freedom Americans also put a very high premium on the value of freedom, defined as freedom for the individual from restraint by the state. This view of freedom is procedural in the sense that it guarantees that no unfair restrictions will be put in the way of your pursuit of what you want, but it does not promise you any help in achieving those things. For instance, when Americans say, "We are all free to get a job," we mean that no discriminatory laws or other legal barriers are stopping us from applying for any particular position; a substantive view of freedom would ensure us the training to get a job so that our freedom meant a positive opportunity, not just the absence of restraint.

Americans have an extraordinary commitment to procedural freedom, perhaps because our values were forged during the Enlightenment when liberty was a guiding principle. This commitment can be seen nowhere so clearly as in the Bill of Rights, the first ten amendments to the U.S. Constitution, which guarantee our basic civil liberties, the areas where government cannot interfere with individual action. Those civil liberties include freedom of speech and expression, freedom of belief, freedom of the press, and the right to assemble, just to name a few. (See Chapter 5, "Fundamental American Liberties," for a complete discussion of these rights.)

But Americans also believe in economic freedom, the freedom to participate in the marketplace, to acquire money and property, and to do with those resources pretty much as we please. Americans believe that it is government's job to protect our property, not to take it away or regulate our use of it too heavily. Our commitment to individualism is apparent here too. Even if society as a whole would be better off if we paid off the federal debt (the amount our government owes from spending more than it brings in), our individualistic view of economic freedom means that Americans have one of the lowest tax rates in the industrialized world (see Figure 2.1). This reflects our national tendency in normal times to emphasize the rights of citizenship over its obligations.

Equality A third central value in American political culture is equality. Of all the values we hold dear, equality is probably the one we cast most clearly in procedural versus substantive terms. Equality in America means equality of treatment, of access, of opportunity, not equality of result. People should have equal access to run the race, but we don't expect them all to finish in the same place. Thus, we believe in political equality (one person, one vote) and equality before the law—that the law shouldn't make unreasonable distinctions among people the basis for treating them differently, and that all people should have equal access to the legal system.

One problem the courts have faced is deciding what counts as a reasonable distinction. Can the law justifiably discriminate between—that is, treat differently—men and women, minorities and white Protestants, rich and poor, young and old? When the rules treat people differently, even if the goal is to make them more equal in the long run, many Americans get very upset. Witness how controversial affirmative action policies are in this country. The point of such policies is to allow special opportunities to members of groups that have been discriminated against in the past, in order to remedy the long-term effects of that discrimination. For many Americans, such policies violate our commitment to procedural solutions. They wonder how treating people unequally can be fair.

WHO, WHAT, HOW To live as a nation, citizens need to share a view of who they are and what their world should be like. If they have no common culture, they fragment and break apart, like the divided peoples of Ireland and the former Yugoslavia. Political cultures provide coherence and national unity to citizens who may be very different in other ways.

Americans achieve national unity through a political culture based on procedural and individualistic visions of democracy, freedom, and equality.

FIGURE 2.1
U.S. Tax Burden Compared to Other Countries

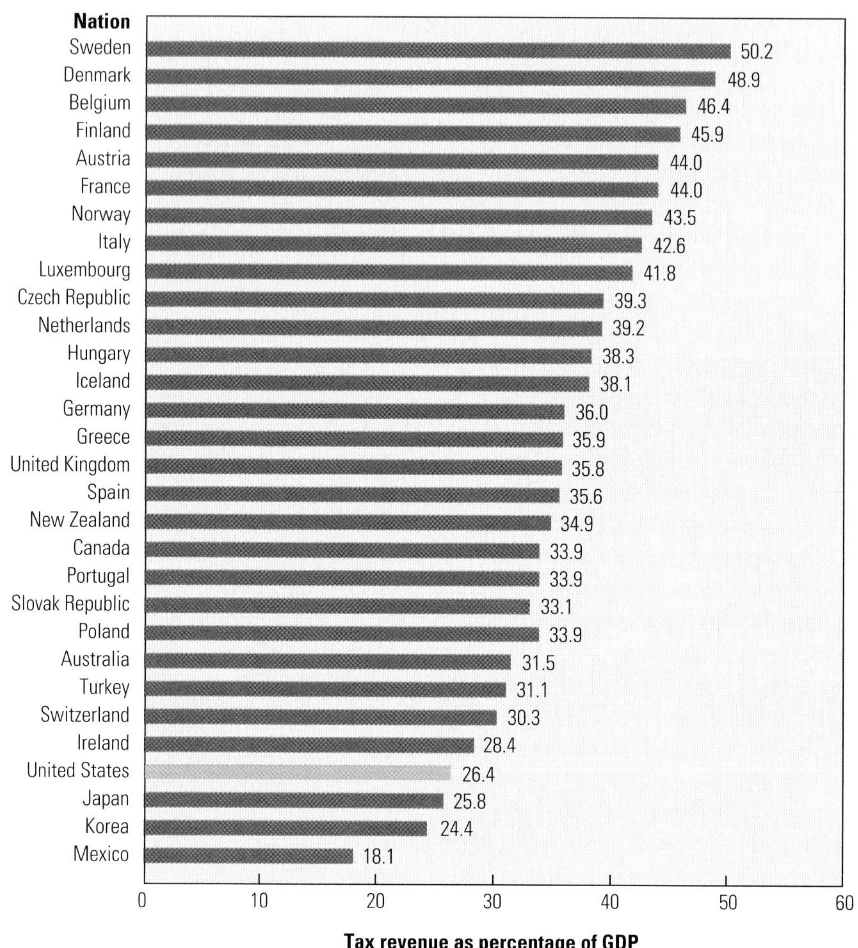

Note: Data refer to the general government sector, which is a consolidation for central, state and local governments plus social security. Non-tax receipts consist of property income (including dividends and other transfers from public enterprises), fees, charges, sales, fines, capital transfers received by the general government, etc.

Source: OECD, http:/www.oecd.org/dataoecd/5/51/2483816.xls, Annex Table 26.

WHAT WE BELIEVE: THE IDEAS THAT DIVIDE US

Most Americans are united in their commitment at some level to a political culture based on proceduralism and individualism and to the key values of democracy, freedom, and equality. This shared political culture gives us a common political language, a way to talk about politics that keeps us united even though we may disagree about many specific ideas and issues.

That's a good thing since, human nature being what it is, it is entirely likely that we will disagree about politics, and disagree often. Although Americans have much in common, there are over 250 million of us and the *Who Are We?* features graphically demonstrates how dramatically different we are in terms of our religious, educational, geographic, and professional backgrounds. We have different interests, different beliefs, different prejudices, different hopes and dreams.

With all that diversity we are bound to have a variety of beliefs and opinions about politics, the economy, and society that help us make sense of our world, but that can divide us into opposing camps. These camps, or different belief systems, are called **ideologies**. Sharing a political culture doesn't mean we don't have ideological differences, but it gives us a common language in which to debate, and resolve our differences, and a set of boundaries that keep those differences from getting out of hand.

ideologies sets of beliefs about politics and society that help people make sense of their world

In fact, because we share that political culture, our range of debate in the United States is fairly narrow compared with the ideological spectrum of many countries. We have no successful communist or socialist parties here, for instance, because the ideologies on which those parties are founded seem to most Americans to push the limits of procedural and individualistic culture too far, especially in the economic realm. The two main ideological camps in the United States are the liberals (associated, since the 1930s, with the Democratic Party) and the conservatives (with the Republicans), with many Americans falling somewhere in between. But because we are all part of American political culture, we are still procedural and individualistic, still believe in democracy, freedom, and equality, even if we are also liberals or conservatives.

There are lots of different ways of characterizing American ideologies. In general terms, we can say that **conservatives** tend to be in favor of traditional social values, distrust government action except in matters of national security, are slow to advocate change, and place a priority on the maintenance of social order. **Liberals**, in contrast, value the possibilities of progress and change, trust government, look for innovations as answers to social problems, and focus on the expansion of individual rights and expression. For a more rigorous understanding of ideology in America we can focus on the two main ideological dimensions of economics and social order issues.

conservatives people who generally favor limited government and are cautious about change

liberals people who generally favor government action and view change as progress

THE ECONOMIC DIMENSION

Traditionally, we have understood ideology to be centered on differences in economic views, much like those located on our economic continuum in Chapter 1 (see Figure 1.1). Based on these economic ideological dimensions, we often say that the liberals who advocate a large role for government in regulating the economy are on the far left, and those conservatives who advocate minimal government control are on the far right. Because we lack any widespread radical socialist traditions in the United States, both American liberals and conservatives are found on the right side of the broader economic continuum we discussed in Chapter 1.

Since the Great Depression in the 1930s and Roosevelt's New Deal (a set of government policies designed to get the economy moving and to protect citizens from the worst effects of the Depression), American conservatives and liberals have taken the following positions with respect to government and the economy. Conservatives, reflecting a belief that government is not to be trusted with too much power and is, in any case, not a competent economic actor, and that private property is sacrosanct and should remain wholly private, have reacted against the increasing role of the government in the American economy. Liberals, in contrast, arguing that the economic market cannot regulate itself and, left alone, is susceptible to such ailments as depressions and recessions, have a much more positive view of government and the good it can

Who is Getting How Much

Almost everyone would like more money. These figures tell us who is earning it and who is not. While men make more than women on average, and non-Hispanic whites earn more than Hispanics and African Americans, the biggest differences emerge among education levels. Since higher education is so clearly linked to economic success, should access to higher education be more open? How large should the gap between America's richest and poorest people be?

The Rich Get Richer: The income gap is getting wider.

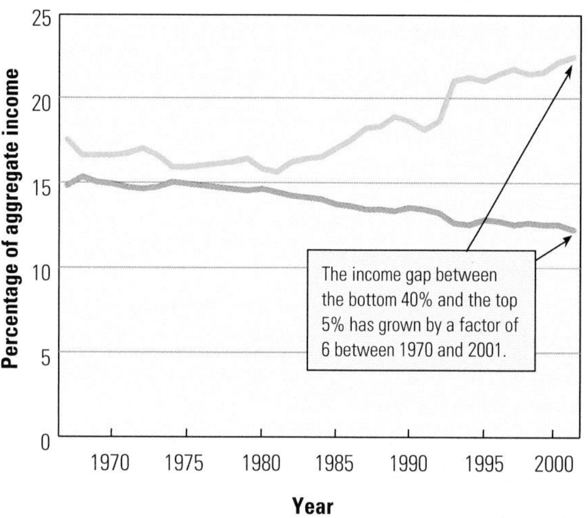

Source: U.S Census Bureau, Current Population Survey, Table IE-3, "Household Shares of Aggregate Income by Fifths of the Income Distribution: 1967 to 2001," May 14, 2004.

Work Time vs. Leisure Time: Americans are working longer hours.

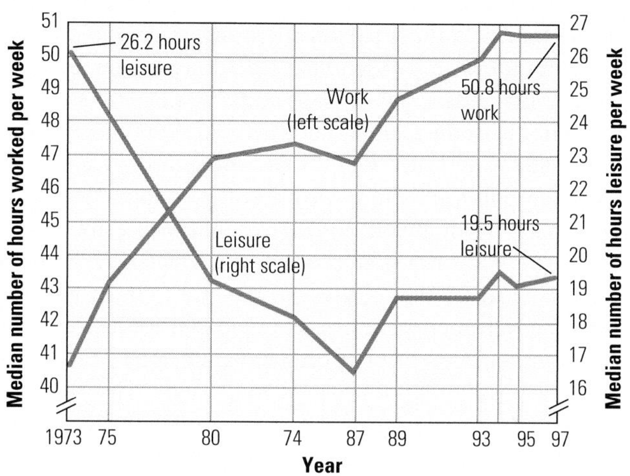

Note: Work includes working for pay, keeping house, and going to school.

Source: Louis Harris & Associates.

do in addressing economic and social problems. Typically, conservatives have tended to be wealthier, upper-class Americans, whereas liberals have been more likely to be lower-paid blue-collar workers. See "*Who Are We?* Who Is Getting How Much" to see how much American incomes vary.

THE SOCIAL ORDER DIMENSION

In the 1980s and 1990s, another ideological dimension became prominent in the United States. Perhaps because, as some researchers have argued, most people are able to meet their basic economic needs and more people than ever before are identifying themselves as middle class, many Americans began to focus less on economic questions and more on issues of morality and quality of life. The new ideological dimension, which is analogous to the social order dimension we discussed in Chapter 1, divides people on the question of how much government control there should be over the moral and social order—whether government's role is limited to protecting

The Size of Our Paychecks: Income Level by Gender, Race, and Education Level

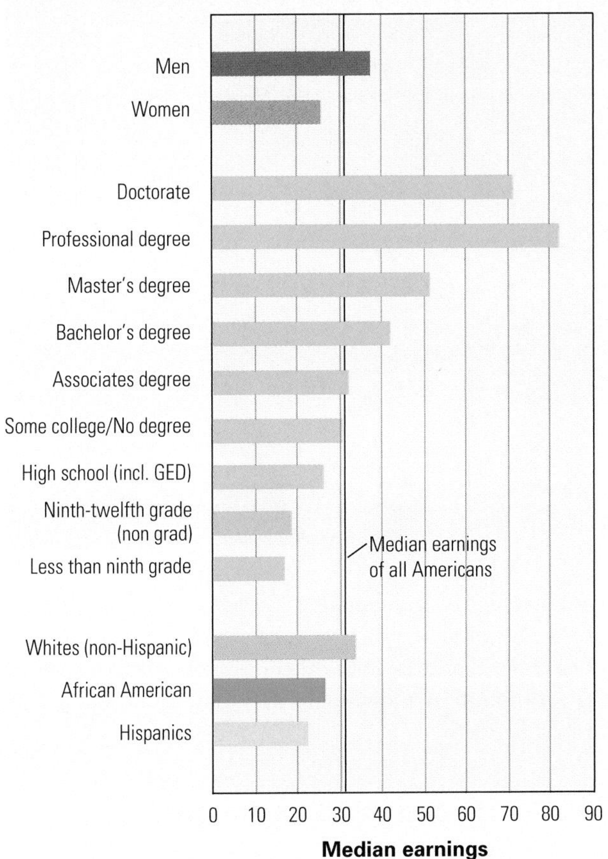

Note: For persons aged 25 and older.

Source: U.S. Census Bureau, Annual Demographic Survey, Table PINC-03, "Educational Attainment—People 25 Years Old and Over, by Total Money Earnings in 2003, Work Experience in 2003, Age, Race, Hispanic Origin and Sex."

Enrollment in Higher Education: More and more Americans are going to college.

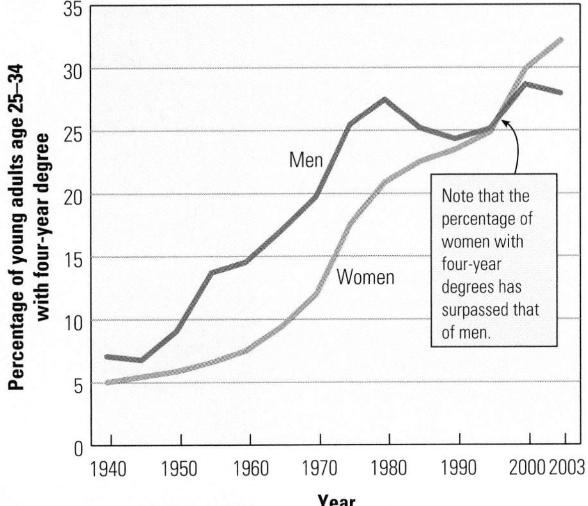

Source: Calculated by the authors from U.S. Census Bureau, Table A-1, "Years of School Completed by People 25 Years and Over, by Age and Sex: Selected Years 1940 to 2003," June 29, 2004.

individual rights and providing procedural guarantees of equality and due process, or whether the government should be involved in making more substantive judgments about how people should live their lives.

While few people in the United States want to go so far as to create a social order that makes all moral and political decisions for its subjects, there are some who hold that it is the state's job to create and protect a preferred social order, although visions of what that preferred order should be may differ. A conservative view of the preferred social order usually includes an emphasis on religion in public life (prayer in school, public posting of religious documents like the Ten Commandments), a rejection of abortion and physician-assisted suicide, promotion of traditional family values (including a rejection of gay marriage and other gay rights), and censorship of materials that promote alternative visions of the social order. Conservatives are not the only ones who seek to tell individuals how to live their lives, however. There is also a newer, more liberal vision of the social order that prescribes an expanded government role to regulate individual lives to achieve different substantive ends—the preservation of the

Across the Great Divide Valley Pentecostal Church in Caldwell, Idaho, joined other churches in the area in using these signs to show support for installing a Ten Commandments monument at the Idaho Statehouse. The U.S. Constitution guarantees a separation of church and state, but many conservative Christians support such religious symbols in public buildings. Despite high-profile cases, like the removal of a similar monument from the Alabama Supreme Court building in summer 2003, some still see it as the government's role to enforce a moralistic social order.

environment, for instance (laws that require individuals to recycle or that tax gasoline to encourage conservation), or the creation of a sense of community based on equality and protection of minorities (rules that urge political correctness, and censorship of pornography), or even the promotion of individual safety (laws promoting gun control, seat belts, and motorcycle helmets).

THE RELATIONSHIP BETWEEN THE TWO IDEOLOGICAL DIMENSIONS

economic liberals those who favor an expanded government role in the economy but a limited role in the social order

Clearly, this social order ideological dimension does not dovetail neatly with the more traditional liberal and conservative orientations toward government action. Figure 2.2 shows some of the ideological positions that are yielded by these two dimensions, though note that what this figure shows is a detail of the broader political spectrum we saw in Chapter 1 and is focused on the narrower spectrum commonly found in an advanced industrial democracy. For instance, **economic liberals**, who are willing to allow government to make substantive decisions about the economy, tend to embrace the top procedural individualistic position on the social order dimension, and so they fall into the upper-left quadrant of the figure. Some economic policies they favor are job training and housing subsidies for the poor, taxation to support social programs, and affirmative action to ensure that opportunities for economic success are truly equal. As far as government regulation of individuals' private lives, however, these liberals favor a hands-off stance, preferring individuals to have maximum freedom over their noneconomic affairs. While they are willing to let government regulate such behaviors as murder, rape, and theft, they believe that most moral issues (such as abortion and the right to die) are questions of individual responsibility.

economic conservatives those who favor a strictly procedural government role in the economy and the social order

Economic conservatives share their liberal counterparts' reluctance to allow government interference in people's private lives, but they combine this with a conviction that government should limit involvement in the economy as well. In the upper-right quadrant of the figure, these economic conservatives prefer government to limit its

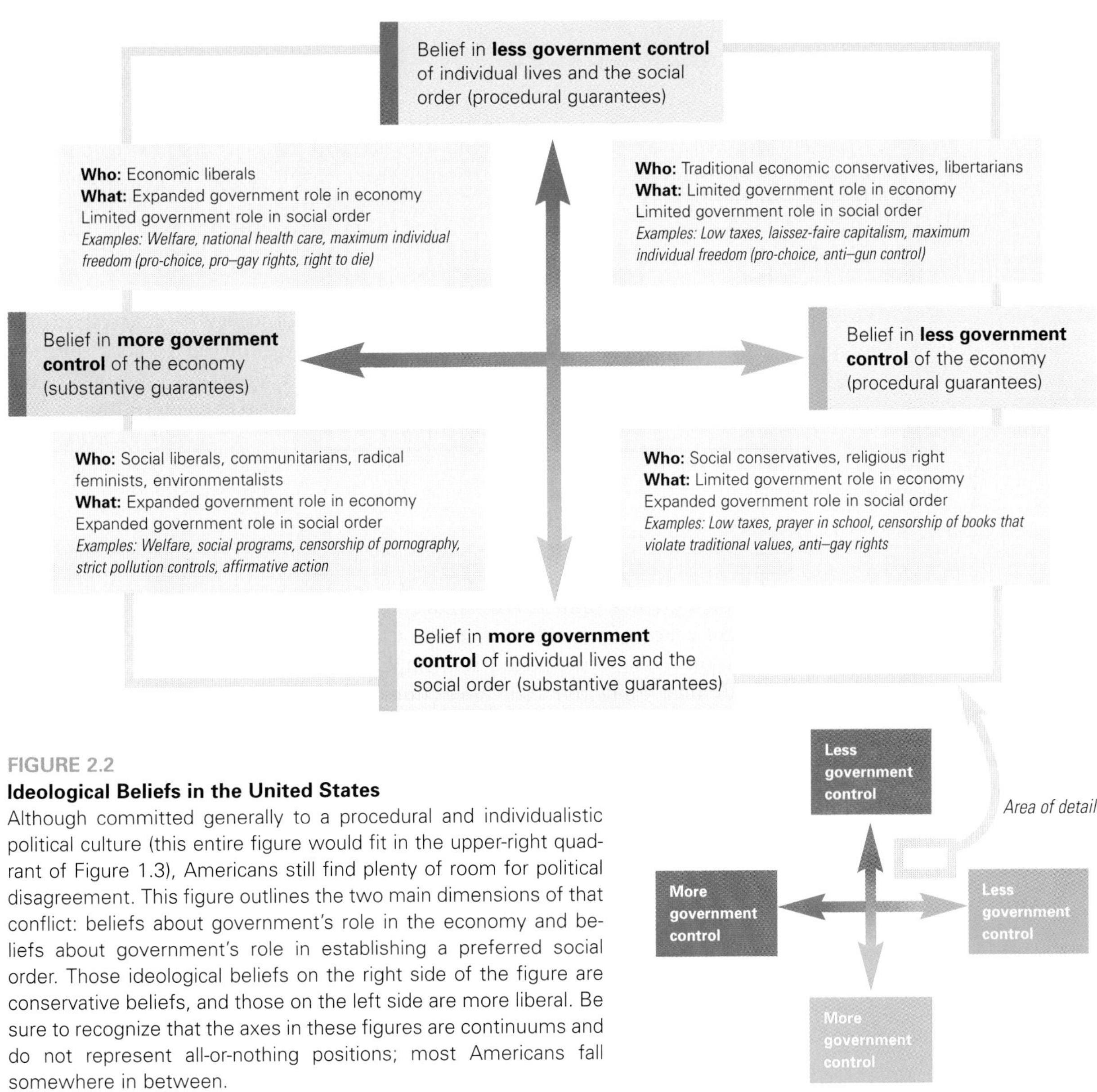

FIGURE 2.2
Ideological Beliefs in the United States
Although committed generally to a procedural and individualistic political culture (this entire figure would fit in the upper-right quadrant of Figure 1.3), Americans still find plenty of room for political disagreement. This figure outlines the two main dimensions of that conflict: beliefs about government's role in the economy and beliefs about government's role in establishing a preferred social order. Those ideological beliefs on the right side of the figure are conservative beliefs, and those on the left side are more liberal. Be sure to recognize that the axes in these figures are continuums and do not represent all-or-nothing positions; most Americans fall somewhere in between.

role in economic decision making to regulation of the market (like changing interest rates and cutting taxes to end recessions), elimination of "unfair" trade practices, (like monopolies), and provision of some public goods, (like highways and national defense). The most extreme holders of these views are called **libertarians**, people who believe that only minimal government action in any sphere is acceptable.

libertarians those who favor a minimal government role in any sphere

In the lower-left quadrant of the figure, people tend to favor a substantive government role in achieving a more equal distribution of material resources (such as welfare programs and health care for the poor) but want that equality carried into the social order as well. They are willing, at least to some extent, to allow government to regulate individual behavior to create what they see as a better society. While they continue to want the freedom to make individual moral choices that economic liberals want, **social liberals** are happy to see some government action to realize a substantive vision of what society should be like. This liberal vision is forward looking and adaptive to changing social roles and technological progress. It seeks to regulate the effects of that progress, protecting the physical environment and individual well-being from the hazards of modern life.

social liberals those who favor greater control of the economy and the social order to bring about greater equality and to regulate the effects of progress

communitarians those who favor a strong substantive government role in the economy and the social order in order to realize their vision of a community of equals

social conservatives those who endorse limited government control of the economy but considerable government intervention to realize a traditional social order; based on religious values and hierarchy rather than equality

The most extreme adherents of social liberalism are sometimes called **communitarians** for their strong commitment to a community based on radical equality of all people. It is a collectivist, community-based vision that holds that individuals should be expected to make some sacrifices for the betterment of society. Because collectivism is not very popular in the American individualist culture, strong adherents to this view are relatively few in number. Many economic liberals, however, pick up some of the policy prescriptions of social liberals, like environmentalism and gun control.

To the right of them, and below economic conservatives on the figure, are **social conservatives**. These people share economic conservatives' views on limited government involvement in the economy, but with less force and perhaps for different reasons (in fact, many social conservatives, as members of the working class, were once New Deal liberals). Their primary concern is with their vision of the moral tone of life, not economics, and it does not seem incongruous to them that they should want a limited economic role for government while requiring that politicians enact a fairly substantive set of laws to create a particular moral order. Their vision of that order includes an emphasis on fundamentalist religious values and traditional family roles, and a rejection of change or diversity that it sees as destructive of the preferred social order. It seeks to protect people's moral character rather than their physical or economic well-being, and embraces a notion of community that emphasizes a hierarchical order (everyone in his or her proper place) rather than equality for all.

WHERE DO WE FIT IN?

Many people, indeed most of us, might find it difficult to identify ourselves as simply "liberal" or "conservative," because we consider ourselves liberal on some issues, conservative on others. The framework in Figure 2.3 allows us to see ourselves and major groups in society as we might line up if we distinguish between economic and social-moral values. We can see, for instance, the real spatial distance that lies between (1) *the religious right* (as social conservatives are known), who are very conservative on political and moral issues but who were once part of the coalition of southern blue-collar workers who supported FDR on the New Deal; (2) *traditional Republicans,* who are very conservative on economic issues but often more libertarian on political and moral issues, wanting government to guarantee procedural fairness and keep the peace, but otherwise to leave them alone; and (3) *moderate Republicans,* who are far less conservative economically and morally. No wonder President Bush has his work cut out for him holding the different factions of his party together.

Similarly, the Democrats must try to respond to the *economic liberals* in the party, very procedural on most political and moral issues (barring affirmative action) but relatively (for Americans) substantive on economic concerns, to *social liberals,* substantive on both economic and social issues, and to newer groups, like the *Democratic*

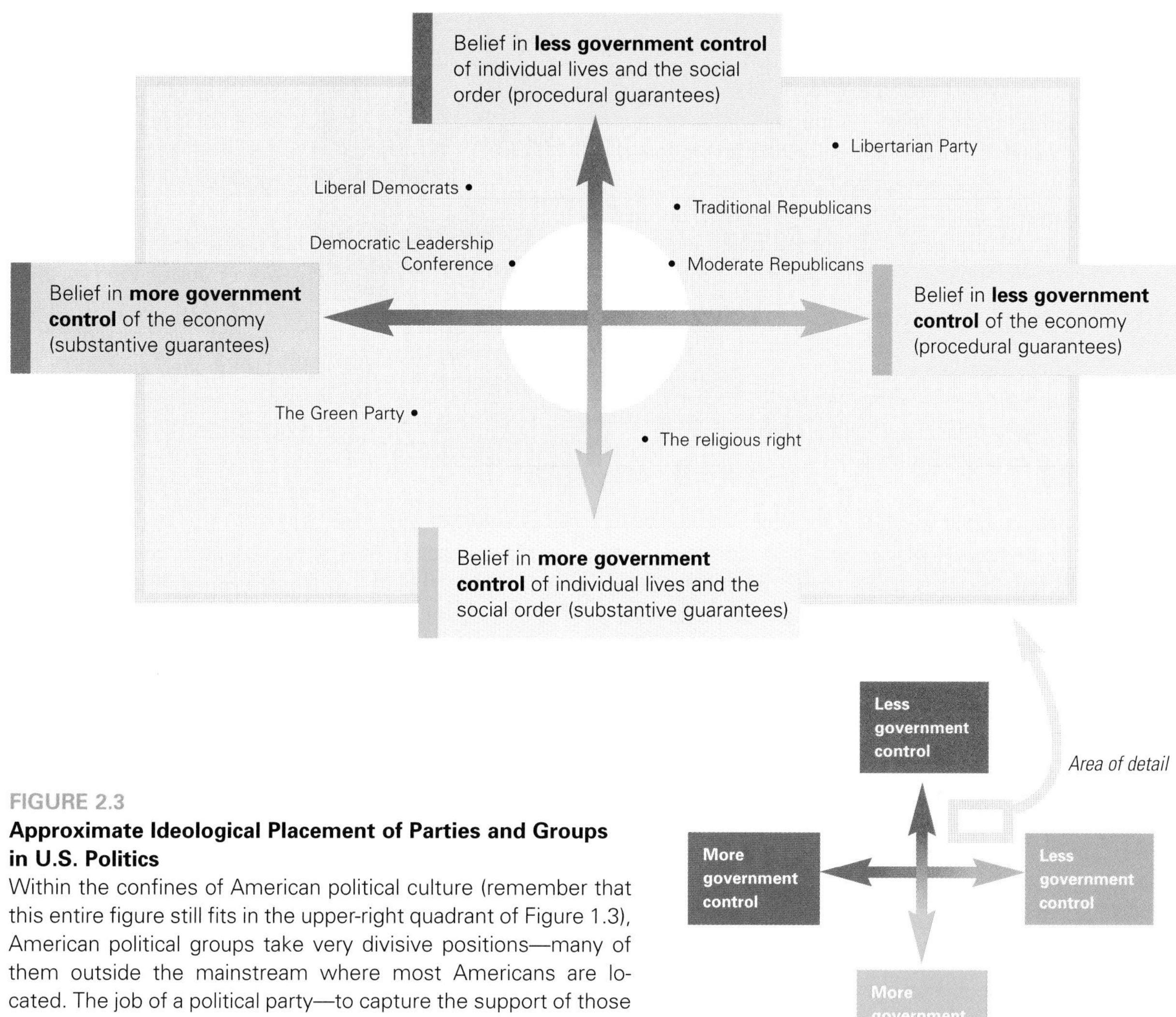

FIGURE 2.3
Approximate Ideological Placement of Parties and Groups in U.S. Politics
Within the confines of American political culture (remember that this entire figure still fits in the upper-right quadrant of Figure 1.3), American political groups take very divisive positions—many of them outside the mainstream where most Americans are located. The job of a political party—to capture the support of those groups without losing the Americans in the middle—can be a tough one.

Leadership Conference (DLC), that are fairly procedural on political and moral issues but not very substantive on economic matters at all. It was President Clinton, as a DLC founder, who helped move his party closer to the mainstream from a position that, we can see in Figure 2.3, is clearly out of alignment with the position taken by most Americans. Ironically, in the 2000 election, Al Gore's commitment to the DLC position left him vulnerable to attack from Ralph Nader, who, as a representative of the Green Party, came from the lower-left quadrant. This position does not draw huge numbers of supporters, but in an election as close as the one in 2000, it probably drew sufficient support from Gore to cost him the election. In 2004, Democratic candidate John Kerry did not have to worry as much about appealing to voters in that lower-left quadrant since many of them disliked George W. Bush so much that they were

Profiles in Citizenship

Esmeralda Santiago

The weird thing about meeting a person whose memoirs you have read is that you know the intimate details of her life, and yet you don't know her at all. She's an old friend and a stranger, at once familiar and unknown.

But Esmeralda Santiago's voice is as warm as her writing, lilting with the echoes of her Puerto Rican childhood, curling around you, drawing you in. Welcomed into her home, offered a cup of tea, you don't stay a stranger for long. Santiago's fast grin dissolves into a rich, delicious chuckle, her huge brown eyes crinkle up, her soft dark hair, laced with silver, waves back from a face gently lined with a life generously lived.

"The minute that I realized that I would not be silenced, then I knew I had to speak."

It's an amazing journey she has made from the metal shack in Macun with the rude privy out back, where ripe, luscious guavas hang from the trees, free for the picking, to the tony hills of suburban New York, where the houses look like mansions and the indoor plumbing is elegant but the imported guavas in the grocery store are hard and expensive. It's an immigrant's journey that has taken every bit of strength and pluck and intelligence she could muster, and it has left her suspended between two cultures, at home in both, but belonging entirely to neither.

Sitting in her bright, light dining room, she describes how this cultural odyssey has shaped her allegiances. "When I talk about my community—depending on who's listening—they respond to different things. And so if I say 'my community' in a roomful of Latinos they think I'm speaking about Puerto Ricans and if I'm in a roomful of women they think I'm talking about women, and of course in Westchester County they think I'm talking about Westchester."

Like all Puerto Ricans, she is an American citizen, but her faint accent and exotic beauty make it clear she is not "from here." But when she goes back to Puerto Rico, a place that means home even though she left when she was thirteen, she is not from there either. On the island she has been told that she is too American—that her accent is not right, her personality too assertive.

And so, in a voice that belongs to all immigrants, she says, "It's a constant flux of—Where is my culture? Which culture do I belong to? Which is my community? Who am I representing now? And is there a point at which I represent just me? And who is that person? That's why I write memoirs. To answer those questions."

willing to vote for a candidate they did not completely agree with in order to try to oust Bush from office.

WHO, WHAT, HOW Although most Americans share a political culture, deep political differences can remain about whose view of government should prevail and who should benefit from its actions. These differences have traditionally centered on government's economic role but increasingly also involve views on establishing a preferred social order, and on what the preferred social order should be. Generally in the United States, ideologies go by the umbrella labels "liberalism" and "conservatism," although many differences exist even within these broad perspectives. Ideological conflict can be very contentious since what is at stake are fundamental views of what the political world ought to look like.

And it is why her memoirs resonate so thoroughly with so many people who themselves have launched a new life in a new place, while not entirely releasing their grip on the old.

In all her communities, Santiago has become a voice for those who cannot speak for themselves. She says, "I think it comes from having to accompany my mother to the welfare office where I saw that somebody had to help these people, you know. And I would go there with my mother, but we would frequently spend the whole day because there were no translators for the other women and men there and so I would be the translator. I would be this little fifteen year old with really broken English, but I was the only one who could be an intermediary, and I think that that experience is one that I still live. I really feel like I'm out there speaking for people who, for whatever reasons, are not able to do that."

So today she is actively involved in issues she cares about, ranging from the protection of battered women, to the artistic development of adolescents, to the support of public libraries. Of the latter, she says, it is essential for the survival of democracy in an information age that there be places where people can go to get "the knowledge of the world" without having to spend the grocery money to get it. "That, to me," she says, "is democracy."

On why she speaks out:

With gifts comes responsibility. If you have a gift, it's not just a gift. If you're a painter, then it's not just a talent that you have. You have the responsibility to then express the soul of a people—of your community, whatever that community is. And for me, the minute that I realized that I would not be silenced, then I knew I had to speak. It was really that simple. I couldn't sleep, I couldn't look at myself in the mirror if I didn't speak about these things. . . . No matter what the personal cost and no matter what other people think. . . . I want to let *them* lose sleep over it [*laughs*]. I would like that better. I love it when I get calls the next day, saying, "I was up all night thinking about what you said yesterday," and I'm going "Oh, good!" [*laughs*].

On the American founders and the job of keeping the republic:

Well, we forget about them. They're these old guys in funny costumes. We don't think of them as great thinkers and people who had a passion. . . . I mean they were humanists. They were not [just] creating a government, they were creating a community. We go back to that word . . . and they saw this as a community of people, of human beings, and that to me is what a country is. It's not the institutions; it's the people living there.

[Students] have to stop thinking about patriotism in terms of the country, the nation. . . . They have to think of it in terms of the guy sitting next to them. *Patria* is the people who make up a country. When it all changed for me was when I had to help somebody. . . . That's when I became patriotic. Because that human being needed help. And I could give it.

Source: Esmeralda Santiago talked with Christine Barbour and Gerald Wright on March 25, 2005.

THE CITIZENS AND AMERICAN POLITICAL BELIEFS

One of the core values of American political culture is democracy, an ideal that unites citizens—both those who are born here as well as more newly minted naturalized citizens—in the activity of self-governance. The American notion of democracy is a procedural one, a representative democracy valued for making decisions in which all voices are heard. It doesn't ask much of us except that we pay attention to the news of the day and come together periodically and vote to elect our public officials.

Keeping in mind that Madison's "republican government" was not meant to be a "pure" democracy, it is interesting to note that it has grown more democratic in some ways in the past two hundred years. For one thing, more people can participate now—such as women and African Americans—and, since eighteen year olds won the right to vote, the electorate is younger than ever before. But in many ways government remains removed from "the people," even if the definition of "the people" has expanded over time. While more people *can* participate in American politics, the truth is that not very many *do.* American turnout rates (the percentages of people who go to the polls and vote on election days) are abysmally low compared to other Western industrialized democracies, and surveys show that many Americans are apathetic toward politics. Even in 2004, a year of unusually high turnout, only 59 percent of eligible voters cast a vote.

How does American democracy work with such low rates of participation or interest on the part of the citizenry? One theory, based on the elite notion of democracy described in Chapter 1, claims that it doesn't really matter whether people participate in politics because all important decisions are made by elites—leaders in business, politics, education, the military, and the media. People don't vote because their votes don't really matter.

Drawing on the pluralist theory of democracy, another explanation claims that Americans don't need to participate individually because their views are represented in government sufficiently through their membership in various groups. For instance, a citizen may be a member of an environmental group, a professional association or labor union, a parent-teacher organization, a veterans' group, a church, or a political party. While that citizen may not bother to vote on Election Day, his or her voice is nonetheless heard because all the groups to which he or she belongs have political influence.

But some educators and social scientists argue that falling levels of involvement, interest, and trust in politics are not something to be explained and dismissed with complacency, but instead signal a true civic crisis in American politics. They see a swing from the community-minded citizens of republican virtue to the self-interested citizens of Madisonian theory so severe that the fabric of American political life is threatened. These scholars argue that democracies can survive only with the support and vigilance of citizens, and that American citizens are so disengaged as the new century begins as to put democracy itself in danger. They would place the responsibility for low levels of participation in the United States not just on the system but also on the citizens themselves for not availing themselves of the opportunities for engagement that exist.

For instance, Benjamin Barber, discussing the tendency of Americans to take their freedoms for granted and to assume that since they were born free they will naturally remain free, says that citizenship is the "price of liberty." [4] For all the importance of presidents and senators and justices in the American political system, it is the people, the citizens, who are entrusted with "keeping the republic." The founders did not have great expectations of the citizens of the new country, and they feared the ravages of mob rule if there were "too much" democracy, but they knew well that the ultimate safeguards of free government are free citizens. Government whose citizens abdicate their role is government whose freedom, fragile at the best of times, is in jeopardy. We live in an age of overwhelming cynicism about and distrust in government. One manifestation of that cynicism and distrust is that citizens are opting out of government participation, not only not voting but not even paying attention.

While the question of how democratic the United States is may seem to be largely an academic one—that is, one that has little or no relevance to your personal life—it is really a question of who has the power, who is likely to be a winner in the political process. Looked at this way, the question has quite a lot to do with your life, especially as government starts to make more demands on you and you on it. Are you likely to be a winner or a loser? Are you going to get what you want from the political system? How much power do people like you have to get their way in government?

WHAT'S AT STAKE REVISITED

America has been a polyglot country since its founding (as early as 1664 there were eighteen languages spoken on the island of Manhattan alone), but although some states passed "English-only" laws, especially in the 1800s, there has been little national enthusiasm for endorsing an "official" language until recently. Since it has been obvious to all that, despite the influx of immigrants, it is necessary to speak English to succeed in the United States, the goal of most language policy in the United States has traditionally been to accommodate those who are less than proficient.

But for groups like ProEnglish, U.S. English, Inc., and English First, the efforts at accommodation have gotten out of hand. They argue that the goal of language policy should not be the promotion or celebration of diversity but rather assimilation of immigrants into the mainstream, and their motives range from the desire to "protect English" to the belief that immigrants will be better off if less assistance in their native tongues is provided.

Since 1981, members of Congress have regularly introduced legislation to make English the country's official language, most recently in the 108th Congress (2002–2004). Although the bills have not yet passed into law, advocates remain hopeful. State-level efforts have been successful in about half the states, and the Republican gains in the 2004 congressional elections gave new heart to Official English groups, who expect conservative advocates to reintroduce the legislation. It is not clear that such legislation would be signed into law even were it to pass: as governor of Texas, President Bush was a strong supporter of English Plus.

On its surface, the debate between Official English and English Plus supporters seems to be about issues such as whether bilingual education "works" or how much it costs to print ballots in many languages. A casual observer could be forgiven for thinking that the issue is just about which means to use to pursue an agreed-upon end—a cost-effective improvement in the quality of life of immigrants.

But what is really at stake here is something much deeper than pedagogy or fiscal discipline as means to an end. Truthfully, there is no agreed-upon end, and for many the welfare of immigrants is really secondary to the primary conflict with which we opened this chapter—a conflict between a vision of the United States as a melting pot in which all cultures are boiled into a homogenized "American culture," or as a crazy salad, where all the ingredients keep their own separate and distinct identities. What is at stake in the debate over an official language is a view of an America based on assimilation versus one based on multiculturalism.

These two competing visions can be located on either end of the social order ideological dimension that we discussed earlier in this chapter (see Figure 2.3). Many English Plus advocates tend to be at the top of the social order axis on this issue, believing in less government control over individual lives and more procedural guarantees to allow individuals to decide how to live their own lives. These people see the

continued

Thinking Outside the Box

- Should it be possible to lose one's citizenship under any circumstances?
- Do ideological differences strengthen or weaken a political culture?
- Does it matter to the success of a democracy if relatively few people take an active political role (by paying attention, voting, exchanging political views, etc.)?

WHAT'S AT STAKE REVISITED *(continued)*

issue as one of equal rights and access, a fundamentally procedural issue. Both moderate liberals and traditional conservatives fit into this group, which is why the Official English movement is opposed by such strange bedfellows as President Bush, former President Clinton, and the libertarian American Civil Liberties Union.

It is at the substantive end of the social order dimension that the debate gets more complex and interesting from a political point of view, since there are supporters of English Plus in the lower-left quadrant of Figure 2.3 and supporters of Official English in the lower-right quadrant. These two groups are not just arguing about rights for immigrants but rather are debating the very nature of the America they want to live in.

On the left is a view of America as multicultural, a thriving marketplace of cultures, beliefs, languages, traditions, all recognizably American, but retaining some of the distinctive immigrant heritage they brought to this country. Such an America is eclectic and diverse, tolerant and open. By its nature it is always changing and evolving. It views the other side's vision as being hidebound and stagnant, and fundamentally unjust to the cultures whose distinguishing characteristics it would see subsumed into a homogenized white European Christian "Americanism."

On the right is a vision of America that is more resistant to change, where traditional values from the nation's predominantly Christian heritage form the backbone of the country, and immigrants, no matter what their origins, are expected to assimilate to those values as they become part of American culture. Such a vision sees a multicultural America as a threat to American life. This is a substantive vision of America bound by the values of stability, order, and conformity.

Given the fundamental differences in how they view America, the two lower quadrants in American culture are bound to clash on the subject of English as an official language. Each side would like to convince the public that they differ only on approaches to solving a particular problem, when in fact many of them disagree on what the problem is to be solved. And, of course, the issue is complicated by the fact that for many Americans in the upper ideological quadrants the debate really is about different means to the end of improving immigrants' lives.

With so many deeply held convictions at stake, this issue is unlikely to be resolved any time soon but it serves to illustrate how ideologically complicated some issues can be in American political culture. Such complexity is difficult to sort out, but unless we take the time to do so, we may never be clear on what is really at stake in American politics.

To Sum Up

KEY TERMS

republic.cqpress.com

asylum (p. 38)
communitarians (p. 56)
conservatives (p. 51)
economic conservatives (p. 54)
economic liberals (p. 54)
ideologies (p. 51)
immigrants (p. 37)
individualism (p. 47)
liberals (p. 51)
libertarians (p. 55)
naturalization (p. 37)
political culture (p. 46)
procedural guarantees (p. 47)
refugees (p. 38)
social conservatives (p. 56)
social liberals (p. 56)
values (p. 46)

Key terms, chapter summaries, practice quizzes, Internet links, and other study aids are available on the companion Web site at: republic.cqpress.com.

SUMMARY

republic.cqpress.com

- U.S. immigrants are citizens or subjects of another country who come here to live and work. To become full citizens, they must undergo naturalization by fulfilling requirements designated by the U.S. Citizenship and Immigration Services.
- In recent years, the influx of illegal immigrants, particularly in the southwestern states, has occupied national debate. Advocates of strict immigration policy complain that illegal aliens consume government services without paying taxes. Opponents of these policies support the provision of basic services for people who, like our ancestors, are escaping hardship and hoping for a better future. Congress, with the president's approval, makes immigration law, but these rules change frequently.
- Americans share common values and beliefs about how the world should work that allow us to be a nation despite our diversity.
- The American political culture is described as both procedural and individualistic. Because we focus more on fair rules than on the outcomes of those rules, our culture has a procedural nature. In addition, our individualistic nature means that we assume that individuals know what is best for them and that individuals, not government or society, are responsible for their own well-being.
- Democracy, freedom, and equality are three central American values. Generally, Americans acknowledge democracy as the most appropriate way to make public decisions. We value freedom *for* the individual *from* government restraint, and we value equality of opportunity rather than equality of result.
- While the range of ideological debate is fairly narrow in America when compared to other countries, there exists an ideological division among economic liberals, social liberals, economic conservatives, and social conservatives based largely on attitudes toward government control of the economy and of the social order.
- America's growing political apathy is well documented. Yet despite abysmal voting rates, the country continues to function, a fact that may be explained by several theories. However, many people claim that such apathy may indeed signal a crisis of democracy.

PRACTICE QUIZ

republic.cqpress.com

1. If immigrants follow the rules and regulations of the U.S. Citizenship and Immigration Services, they may apply for citizenship through the process of

a. immigration substantiation.
b. initiation.
c. initialization.
d. dual citizenship.
e. naturalization.

2. According to the first "Who Are We?" feature in this chapter, which of the following statements is correct concerning projections of the American population between now and 2050?

a. As a percentage of the total population, whites continue to grow at a faster pace than do ethnic or racial majorities.

b. By 2050 the number of retirees will diminish by half.

c. By 2050, African Americans are projected to be twice the number of Hispanics in the U.S. population.

d. By 2050, white Americans will make up only slightly more than half of the total U.S. population.

e. Hispanics remain the slowest growing ethnic group in the United States.

3. Which of the following is NOT one of the core values that make up American political culture?

a. Democracy

b. Freedom

c. Libertarianism

d. Equality

e. All of the above are core values in American political culture.

4. Which of the following terms refers to the sets of beliefs about politics and society that help people make sense of their world?

a. Political culture

b. Political ideology

c. Democracy

d. Liberalism

e. Social conservatism

5. The phrase "we want government to guarantee a fair playing field but not to guarantee equal outcomes for all the players" best reflects

a. the importance Americans place on individualism and procedural guarantees in their political culture.

b. the enduring idea that immigration to the United States is completely open to all immigrants, no matter their country of origination.

c. the main contention between conservatives and liberals in American ideological debates.

d. the reason we are not a very diverse nation.

e. issues we believe in but that divide us.

SUGGESTED RESOURCES

republic.cqpress.com

Books

DeLaet, Debra L. 2000. *U.S. Immigration Policy in an Age of Rights.* Westport, Conn.: Praeger. A historical discussion of the development of immigration policy.

Schlesinger, Arthur, Jr. 1991. *The Disuniting of America.* Knoxville, Tenn.: Whittle. One of America's greatest characteristics is its multicultural makeup. Schlesinger, one of America's most prominent historians, warns us about the problems also associated with multiculturalism.

Schreuder, Sally Abel. 1995. *How to Become a United States Citizen: A Step-by-Step Guidebook for Self-Instruction.* 5th ed. Occidental, Calif.: Nolo Press-Occidental. Ever wonder what it would take to become a U.S. citizen if you were not born one? This book provides all of the interesting details.

Schudson, Michael. 1998. *The Good Citizen: A History of American Civil Life.* New York: Free Press. A provocative analysis of how this country's definition of what makes "a good citizen" has changed over time. Schudson believes we expect too much from our citizens.

Smith, Rogers M. 1997. *Civic Ideals: Conflicting Visions of Citizenship in U.S. History.* New Haven: Yale University Press. A comprehensive and troubling look at the ways in which citizens have been denied basic citizenship rights from the colonial period to the Progressive era.

Suro, Roberto. 1998. *Strangers Among Us: Latino Lives in America.* New York: Vintage Books. Suro, a *Washington Post* staff writer, takes a sensitive look into the lives and struggles of Latino immigrants in the United States.

White, John Kenneth. 2003. *The Values Divide: American Politics and Culture in Transition.* New York: Chatham House. A study of the role that values play in American public and private life. White argues that the values divide in America was responsible for the close 2000 presidential election.

Two excellent sources for statistics on just about every facet of American life are ***The New York Times Almanac*** and ***The Wall Street Journal Almanac.***

Web Sites

FedStats. www.fedstats.gov. This portal to all statistics produced by the federal government is searchable by agency or topic.

U.S. Census Bureau. www.census.gov. An extremely valuable site with vast amounts of data—current, historical, and future projections—on the American people and businesses.

U.S. Citizenship and Immigration Services. www.uscis.gov. A rich resource, this page contains immigration statistics, reports, and information on immigration and naturalization law.

Movies

Ellis Island. Produced for the History Channel, this thorough and moving documentary chronicles the experiences endured by the more than twelve million immigrants who passed through New York's Ellis Island en route to their new lives in America.

***In America.* 2002.** A moving portrait of an Irish immigrant family in New York struggling to make ends meet and find their place in a chaotic new city.

***Moscow on the Hudson.* 1984.** Robin Williams plays a musician in a Russian circus who defects—in the middle of New York City's Bloomingdale's—and struggles with the American way of life.

***The Terminal.* 2004.** A man traveling from his eastern European country to New York finds that his home country disintegrated, and as a man without a country, he becomes trapped in a loophole in the Department of Homeland Security's immigration policies.

We celebrate the Boston Tea Party (right) as a strike for freedom and a more democratic government, but for the British, the American revolutionaries were extremists using terror and destruction to accomplish their ends. Timothy McVeigh (below)—the American executed for the 1993 bombing of the federal office building in Oklahoma City—argued that he too was a revolutionary acting against what he saw as an evil and corrupt government. Are the tactics of terrorists ever justified?

POLITICS OF THE AMERICAN FOUNDING

3

WHAT'S AT STAKE?

Timothy McVeigh saw himself as a soldier in a righteous war. Furious, in 1992, when federal agents raided the home of white separatists in Ruby Ridge, Idaho, and again in 1993, when seventy-six people died in a federal siege of the Waco, Texas, compound of religious extremists, fearful and outraged that the government might take away his beloved guns, McVeigh, once a U.S. Army gunner in the Persian Gulf War, declared war on the United States itself.

McVeigh signaled the start of that war on the morning of April 19, 1995, by blowing up the Murrah Federal Building in Oklahoma City. Two years to the day after Waco and on the 218th anniversary of the day that shots fired at Lexington and Concord launched the American Revolution, McVeigh parked a truck loaded with explosives in front of the Murrah Building, and lit a detonator fuse. One hundred and sixty-eight people died in the blast. McVeigh described the nineteen dead children as "collateral damage"; his only regret, he said, was that he "didn't knock the building down." Insisting to the end that "one man's terrorist is another man's freedom fighter," McVeigh was executed in 2001 by the very government he sought to defeat.

McVeigh's claim to be protecting the U.S. Constitution against the U.S. government itself puts him in the company of thousands of American militia members, everyday men and women who say that they are the ideological heirs of the American Revolution. They liken themselves to the colonial Sons of Liberty who rejected the authority of the British government and took it upon themselves to enforce the laws they thought were just. The Sons of Liberty instigated the Boston Massacre and the Boston Tea Party, historical events that we celebrate as patriotic but that would be considered treason or terrorism if they took place today.

Today's so-called Patriot groups claim that the federal government has become as tyrannical as the British government ever was, that it deprives citizens of their liberty and overregulates their everyday lives. They go so far as to claim that federal authority is illegitimate. Militia members reject a variety of federal laws, from those limiting the weapons that individual citizens can own, to those imposing taxes on income, to those requiring the registration of motor vehicles. They maintain that government should stay out of individual lives, providing security at the national level perhaps, but allowing citizens to regulate and protect their own lives.

Some militias go even further. Many militia members are convinced, for instance, that the United Nations is seeking to take over the United States (and that top U.S. officials are letting this happen). Others blend their quests for individual liberty with rigid requirements about who should enjoy that liberty. White supremacist or anti-Semitic groups aim at achieving an all-white continent or see Jewish collaboration behind ominous plots to destroy America.

Although there are some indications that militia membership is down in the wake of the negative publicity surrounding the Oklahoma City bombing, estimates still put the number of Patriot groups around the country at almost two hundred.[1] These groups base their claim to legitimate existence on the Second Amendment of the Constitution, which reads, "A well regulated Militia, being necessary to the security of a free State, the right of the people to keep and bear Arms, shall not be infringed." Members of state militias, and other groups like them, take this amendment literally and absolutely, as did Timothy McVeigh.

The federal government has reacted strongly to limit the threat presented by state militias and others who believe that its authority is not legitimate. Partly in response to the Oklahoma City bombing, Congress passed an antiterrorism bill signed by President Bill Clinton in 1996 that would make it easier for federal agencies to monitor the activities of such groups. Those powers were broadened in the wake of the September 11, 2001, attack on the United States by foreign terrorists, and the anthrax attacks on the U.S. mail that followed. President George W. Bush gave the Department of Homeland Security a broad mandate to combat terrorism, including the homegrown variety.

Is the federal government responding appropriately to these threats? Are these groups, as they claim, the embodiment of revolutionary patriotism? Do they support the Constitution, or sabotage it? Think about these questions as you read this chapter on the founding of the United States. Think about the consequences and implications of revolutionary activity then and now. We return to the question of what's at stake for American politics in the militia movement at the end of the chapter. *

From the moment students start coloring in pictures of grateful Pilgrims and cutting out construction paper turkeys in grade school, the founding of the United States is a recurring focus of American education, and with good reason. Democratic societies, as we saw in the first chapter, rely on the consent of their citizens to maintain lawful behavior and public order. A commitment to the rules and the goals of the American system requires that we feel good about that system. What better way to stir up good feelings and patriotism than by recounting thrilling stories of bravery and derring-do on the part of selfless heroes dedicated to the cause of American liberty? We celebrate the Fourth of July with fireworks and parades, displaying publicly our commitment to American values and our belief that our country is special, in the same way that other nations celebrate their origins all over the world. Bastille Day (July 14) in France, May 17 in Norway, October 1 in China, July 6 in Malawi, Africa—all are days on which people rally together to celebrate their common past and their hopes for the future.

Of course people feel real pride in their countries and of course many nations, not only our own, do have amazing stories to tell about their earliest days. But as political scientists, we must separate myth from reality. For us, the founding of the United States is central not because it inspires warm feelings of patriotism but because it can teach us about American politics, the struggles for power that forged the political system that continues to shape our collective struggles today.

The history of the American founding has been told from many points of view. You are probably most familiar with this account: The early colonists escaped to America to avoid religious persecution in Europe. Having arrived on the shores of the New World, they built communities that allowed them to practice their religions in peace and to govern themselves as free people. When the tyrannical British king made unreasonable demands on the colonists, they had no choice but to protect their liberty by going to war and by establishing a new government of their own.

But sound historical evidence suggests that the story is more complicated, and more interesting, than that. A closer look shows that the early Americans were complex beings with economic and political agendas as well as religious and philosophical motives. After much struggle among themselves, the majority of Americans decided that those agendas could be better and more profitably carried out if they broke their ties with England.[2]

Just because a controversial event like the founding is recounted by historians or political scientists one or two hundred years after it happens does not guarantee that there is common agreement on what actually took place. People write history not from a position of absolute truth but from particular points of view. When we read a historical account, as critical thinkers we need to ask probing questions: Who is telling the story? What point of view is being represented? What values and priorities lie behind it? If I accept this interpretation, what else will I have to accept? (See "*Consider the Source:* Reading Your Textbook With a Critical Eye.")

In this chapter we talk a lot about history—the history of the American founding and the creation of the Constitution. Like all other authors, we have a particular point of view that affects how we tell the story. True to the first basic theme of this book, we are interested in power and politics. We want to understand American government in terms of who the winners and losers are likely to be. It makes sense for us to begin by looking at the founding to see who the winners and losers were then. We are also interested in how rules and institutions make it more likely that some people will win and others lose. Certainly an examination of the early debates about rules and institutions will help us understand that. Finally, because we are interested in winners and losers, we are interested in understanding how people come to be defined as players in the system in the first place, the focus of the second theme of this book—citizenship. It was during the founding that many of the initial decisions were made about who "We, the people" would actually be. Specifically, in this chapter, you will learn about

- the battle of colonial powers for control of America
- the process of settlement by the English
- the break with England and the Revolution
- the initial attempt at American government: the Articles of Confederation
- the Constitutional Convention
- the ratification of the Constitution
- the role of everyday citizens in the founding

Consider the Source

Reading Your Textbook With a Critical Eye

Consider these two passages describing the same familiar event: Christopher Columbus's arrival in the Americas.[1]

From a 1947 textbook:

> At last the rulers of Spain gave Columbus three small ships, and he sailed away to the west across the Atlantic Ocean. His sailors became frightened. They were sure the ships would come to the edge of the world and just fall off into space. The sailors were ready to throw their captain into the ocean and turn around and go back. Then, at last they all saw the land ahead. They saw low green shores with tall palm trees swaying in the wind. Columbus had found the New World. This happened on October 12, 1492. It was a great day for Christopher Columbus—and for the whole world as well.

And from a 1991 text:

> When Columbus stepped ashore on Guanahani Island in October 1492, he planted the Spanish flag in the sand and claimed the land as a possession of Ferdinand and Isabella. He did so despite the obvious fact that the island already belonged to someone else—the "Indians" who gathered on the beach to gaze with wonder at the strangers who had suddenly arrived in three great, white-winged canoes. He gave no thought to the rights of the local inhabitants. Nearly every later explorer—French, English, Dutch and all the others as well as the Spanish—thoughtlessly dismissed the people they encountered. What we like to think of as the discovery of America was actually the invasion and conquest of America.

Which one of these passages is "true"? The first was the conventional textbook wisdom through the 1950s and 1960s in America. The latter reflects a growing criticism that traditional American history has been told from the perspective of history's "winners," largely white middle-class males of European background. Together they highlight the point that history *does* vary depending on who is telling it, and when they are telling it, and even to whom they are telling it. The telling of history is a potent political act, as one recent study explains, citing George Orwell's *1984* that "who controls the past controls the future."[2] What this means to you is that the critical vigilance we have urged you to apply to all the information that regularly bombards you should be applied to your textbooks as well. And yes, that means *this* textbook too.

There is some truth to the idea that history is written by the winners, but it is also true that the winners change over time. If history was once securely in the hands of the white European male, it is now the battleground of a cultural war between those who believe the old way of telling (and teaching) history was accurate, and those who believe it left out the considerable achievements of women and minorities and masked some of the less admirable episodes of our past in order to glorify our heritage.[3] For instance, one author in the 1990s studied twelve high school history textbooks and documented areas where he felt the "history" was inaccurate or misleading. His criticism includes claims that history textbooks create heroic figures by emphasizing the positive aspects of their lives and ignoring their less admirable traits; that they create myths about the American founding that glorify Anglo-European settlers at the expense of the Native Americans and Spanish setters who were already here; that they virtually ignore racism and its opponents, minimizing its deep and lasting effects on our culture; that they neglect the recent past; and that they idealize progress and the exceptional role America plays in the world, skipping over very real problems and issues of concern.[4]

The battle over textbook content had reached a peak with the publication of the National History Standards, written under a bipartisan effort initiated by President George H. W. Bush in 1989. The objective was to ensure that all high school students would be exposed to a common core of scholarship in a variety of subjects. Bipartisanship quickly dissolved when the standards were published. Emphasizing a view of American history that went beyond the usual European orientation, the standards focused less on traditional historical personalities and achievements and more on issues, conflicts, and the effort to get students to question traditional assumptions about our past. They were quickly accused of undervaluing white male historical figures in favor of minorities and women, of engaging in "quota history," in which people were discussed because of their demographic fit rather than their substantive contribution, of celebrating non-Western players in American history but ignoring their atrocities, and of pushing a liberal ideological agenda that favored the interests of feminists and multiculturalists.[5] Counting mentions of various topics in the index of the standards, a critic pointed out that the Seneca Indians' constitution was mentioned nine times, but Paul Revere's ride not at all. The United States Senate resolved 99–1 to denounce the standards for showing too little respect for the contributions of Western civilization. Ultimately revised to recapture some of the traditional themes of American history and to be less prescriptive, the stan-

dards are now influencing the writing of new high school history textbooks.

The question of bias in textbooks is not reserved for history books. We state in Chapters 1 and 3 that this textbook itself has a point of view, an interest in highlighting the issues of power and citizenship, and in focusing on the impact of the rules in American politics. In addition, we take a multicultural approach. While we do not ignore or disparage the achievements of the traditional heroes of American history, we do not think that their outstanding political accomplishments warrant ignoring the contributions, also substantial, of people who have not traditionally been politically powerful.

The fact that all textbooks have some sort of bias means you must be as critically careful in what you accept from textbook authors as you are (or should be) in what you accept from any other scholars or newspaper writers or other media commentators. Apply the rules of critical thinking discussed in Chapter 1. In addition, here are some specific questions you can ask yourself about your textbooks:

1. **Who are the authors?** Do they have a particular point of view (that is, do they promote particular values or ideas)? What is it? Are any points of view left out of the story they tell? Whose? How might this influence the book's content? (Clues to an author's orientation can often be found in the preface or the introduction, where the author tells you what has motivated him or her to write the book. Ironically, this is the section most readers skip.)
2. **Who is the audience of the book?** If it is a big, colorful book, it is probably aimed at a wide market. If so, what is that likely to say about its content? If it is a smaller book with a tighter focus, what sorts of people is it trying to appeal to? Why did your teacher or school select this book?
3. **What kinds of evidence does the book provide?** If it backs up an argument with plenty of facts from reputable sources, then perhaps its claims are true, even if they are surprising or unfamiliar to you. On the other hand, if the book is telling you things that you have always assumed to be true but does not offer factual support, what might that say to you? What kinds of counterevidence could be provided? Do the authors make an effort to cover both sides of an issue or controversy? Read footnotes, and if something troubles you, locate the primary source (the one the authors relied on) and read it yourself.
4. **What are the book's conclusions?** Do they cause you to look at a subject in a new way? Are they surprising? Exciting? Troublesome? What is the source of your reaction? Is it intellectual, or emotional? What caused you to react this way?
5. **How would your friends or classmates react to your book's arguments?** What does your professor have to say about them? As you analyze your textbook, asking the questions we have listed here, discuss some of the issues that arise with your colleagues. Their perspective might strengthen your convictions, or they might even change your mind. Coworkers can prove to be one of your chief assets in life. Take advantage of what they have to offer.

1. These two passages were cited in a chart accompanying Sam Dillon, "Schools Growing Harsher in Scrutiny of Columbus," *New York Times,* October 12, 1992, 4, web version. The first paragraph is from Merlin M. Ames, *My Country* (Sacramento: California State Department of Education, 1947); the second is from John A. Garraty, *The Story of America* (New York: Holt Rinehart Winston, Harcourt Brace Jovanovich, 1991).
2. Laura Hein and Mark Seldon, eds., *Censoring History: Citizenship and Memory in Japan, Germany, and the United States* (Armonk, N.Y.: M. E. Sharpe, 2000).
3. Frances Fitzgerald, *America Revised* (New York: Vintage Books, 1979).
4. James W. Loewen, *Lies My Teacher Told Me* (New York: New Press, 1995).
5. John Fonte, "History on Trial: Culture and the Teaching of the Past" (book reviews), *National Review,* November 10, 1997.

THE FIRST BATTLES FOR AMERICA

America was a battlefield—both political and military—long before the Revolution. Not only did nature confront the colonists with brutal winters, harsh droughts, disease, and other unanticipated disasters, but also the New World was already inhabited before the British settlers arrived, both by Native Americans and by Spanish and French colonists.

Every American schoolchild learns that the Americas were occupied by native inhabitants. The native American Indians (so named because Columbus thought on his arrival in America that he had found a new route to India) were themselves a diverse group of people. Their different cultural traditions led them to react to the newcomers in different ways. Many of them initially helped the Europeans overcome the rigors of life in the New World. But cultural differences between the Indians and the Europeans, and the latter's conviction that their beliefs and practices were superior to Indian ways, made the relationship between the two unpredictable. Some Indians engaged in political dealings with the Europeans, forming military coalitions (partnerships), trade alliances, and other arrangements. Others were more hostile, particularly in the face of the European assumption that the New World was theirs to subdue and exploit. Many Indians, in some of America's more shameful historical moments, were treated brutally and pushed out of their homelands.

FIGURE 3.1
European Colonies in the New World Around 1600

Source: Carol Berkin et al., *Making America,* 2d ed. (Boston: Houghton Mifflin, 1999). Copyright © 1999 by Houghton Mifflin Company. Reprinted with permission.

Some of the earliest political struggles were not between settlers and mother country but between mother countries themselves, competing for the rights to America's rich resources. The ancestors of many of the 21 million Spanish-speaking people in America today were living in what is now New Mexico, California, Colorado, and Texas, for instance, before very many people were speaking English in America at all. Had political conditions been different for Spain and England in the seventeenth century, this book might well be written in Spanish, and English speakers would constitute the minority today.

Spain in the sixteenth century seemed to be well on its way to owning the New World. Spanish explorers had laid claim to both eastern and western North America as well as key parts of Central and South America (see Figure 3.1). But Spain was not able to hold on to its advantageous position. In international politics—that is, politics between nations rather than within a single nation—nations rarely consent to be governed by a higher authority. Each nation usually believes that it is sovereign and submits to no power higher than its own. When it comes to resolving disputes among nations in the absence of effective law, the strongest wins.

The monarchs of England liked the idea of getting a piece of the treasure that was being exported regularly from the Americas. Spain and England were already in conflict in Europe, and Spain was vulnerable. Its military resources were becoming exhausted, its economy was ailing, its manufacturing and commerce were not keeping pace with British advances, and its population, so necessary for building colonies across the ocean, was decreasing. As the Spanish Empire declined, the British Empire prospered. The English defeat of the Spanish Armada in 1588 further weakened Spain's position. Although the British had signed several treaties agreeing to stay out of Spain's business in the New World, Spain was not powerful enough to enforce those treaties.

WHO, WHAT, HOW The political actors in North America during the earliest period of European settlement—the British, Spanish, French, and the American Indians—had perhaps more at stake than they knew. Whoever won the battle for North America would put their stamp on the globe in a major way.

The tactics and rules that the different colonists used to establish or maintain their presence in North America came from the full range of human possibility: from politics, with its bargaining, negotiation, and compromise; from economics, with the establishment of trade; and from military power and violence. But as is usually the case when competing nations recognize no common framework of rules, the battle for control of America came down to a military one.

THE ENGLISH SETTLERS

Declaring that they had a legitimate right to colonize unoccupied territory, the British set about inhabiting the American eastern coast. After some initial false starts in Virginia, the English settled at Jamestown, Virginia, in 1607, and began a series of successful efforts at colonization. Despite treaties, Spanish spies, intrigue with Native Americans, and occasional military action, Britain edged Spain out of the colonial picture in eastern America. Had Spain been able to enforce the treaties Britain had signed, or had it been able to form a more constant and productive alliance with France, it might have been able to reverse its fortunes. In due time the English would have to fend off the Dutch and the French as well, but by the late 1700s the eastern seaboard colonies were heavily English (see Figure 3.2). Though Spain maintained its presence in the West and the Southwest, those territories did not figure in American politics until much later.

REASONS FOR LEAVING ENGLAND

Many British subjects were eager and willing to try their luck across the Atlantic. They came to America to make their fortunes, to practice their religions without interference, to become landowners—to take advantage of a host of opportunities that England, still struggling out of the straightjacket of **feudalism**, could not offer. *Feudalism* rested on a rigid social and political hierarchy based on the ownership of land, but land ownership was restricted to the very few. Individuals lived out their lives in the class to which they were born; it was unheard of to work one's way up from peasant to landowner.

feudalism a hierarchical political and economic system based on the ownership of land by the few

Religious practice was similarly limited. Henry VIII's break with the Catholic Church in 1533 resulted in the establishment of the reformed Church of England. But

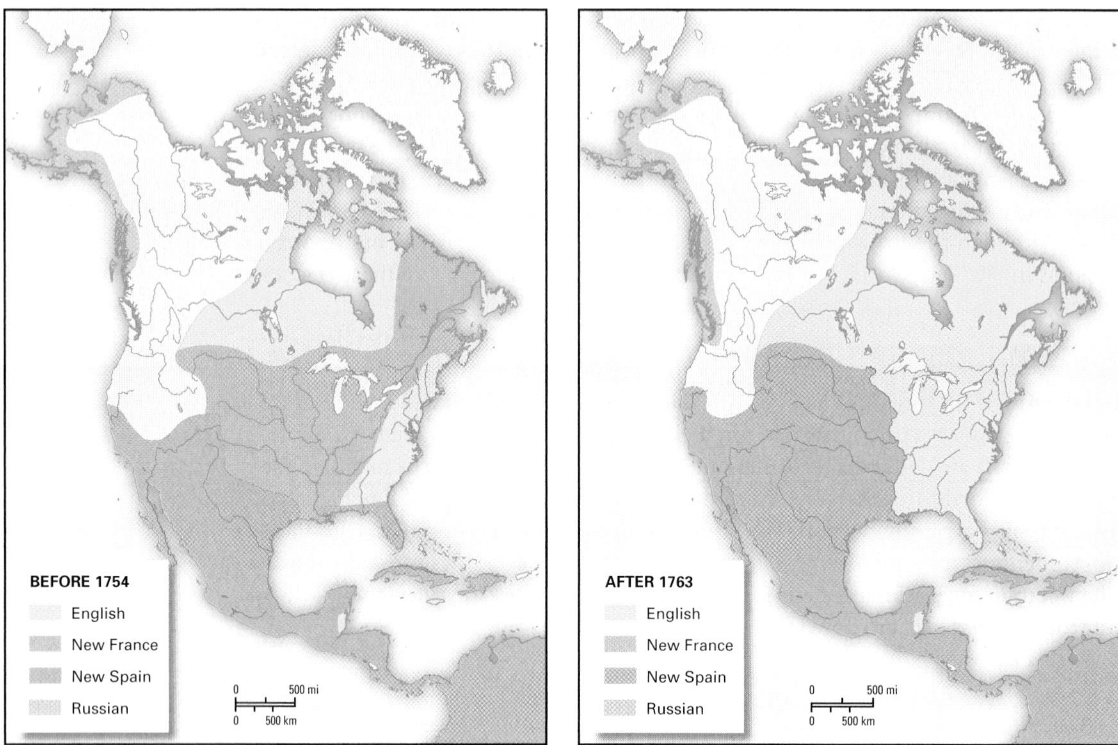

FIGURE 3.2 **Gradual Dominance of Great Britain in the New World in the 1700s**

Source: Mary Beth Norton et al., *A People and a Nation,* 6th ed. (Boston: Houghton Mifflin, 2001). Copyright © 2001 by Houghton Mifflin Company. Reprinted with permission.

Puritans a Protestant religious sect that sought to reform the Church of England in the sixteenth and seventeenth centuries

on the European continent, under the influence of the German theologian Martin Luther and the French theologian John Calvin, Protestant religious reform was even more radical. English sects like the **Puritans** chafed under the rules of the Church of England and wanted more reform in the Protestant style, limiting church membership to the people they thought God had chosen, and emphasizing the morally upright life.

Life in England in the 1600s was on the brink of major change. Within the century, political thinkers would begin to reject the idea that monarchs ruled through divine right, would favor increasing the power of Parliament at the expense of the king, and would promote the idea that individuals were not merely subjects but citizens, with rights that government could not violate. Civil war and revolution in England would give teeth to these fresh ideas. The new philosophy, a product of the Enlightenment, was open to religious tolerance, giving rise to more reformist and separatist sects. Commerce and trade would create the beginnings of a new middle class with financial power independent of the landed class of feudalism, a class that would blossom with the rise of industry in the 1700s.

But in the early 1600s, settlers came to America in part because England seemed resistant to change. It would be a mistake to think, however, that the colonists, having been repressed in England, came to America hoping to achieve liberty for all people. The colonists emigrated in order to practice their religions freely (but not necessarily to let others practice theirs), to own land, to engage in trade, to avoid debtors' prison. England also had a national interest in sending colonists to America. Under the economic system of mercantilism, nations competed for the world's resources through trade, and colonies were a primary source of raw materials for manufacturing. Entrepreneurs often supported colonization as an investment, and the government issued charters to companies, giving them the right to settle land as English colonies.

POLITICAL PARTICIPATION IN THE COLONIES

It shouldn't surprise us, therefore, to find that the settlers often created communities that were in some ways as restrictive and repressive as the ones they had left behind in England. The difference, of course, was that *they* were now the ones doing the repressing rather than the ones being repressed. In other ways, life in America was more open than life in Britain. Land was widely available. Although much of it was inhabited by Native Americans, the Indians believed in communal or shared use of property. The Europeans arrived with notions of private property and the sophisticated weaponry to defend the land they claimed. Some colonies set up systems of self-rule, with representative assemblies such as Virginia's House of Burgesses, Maryland's House of Delegates, and the town meetings of the northern colonies. Though they had governors, often appointed by the king, at least until the late 1600s the colonies were left largely, though not exclusively, to their own devices.

Clearly, while the colonies offered more opportunities than did life in Britain, they also continued many of the injustices that some colonists had hoped to escape. A useful way to understand who had power in the colonies is to look at the rules regulating political participation—that is, who was allowed to vote in colonial law-making bodies, who wasn't, and why. Each colony set its own voting rules, based on such factors as property, religion, gender, and race

Property Qualifications for Voting Although voting laws varied in England by locality as well, there they had in common an emphasis on property-holding requirements. Very simply, conventional British wisdom held that if you didn't own property, you were unlikely to take a serious interest in government (whose job was largely to protect property, after all), and you were equally unlikely to share the values and virtues attached to rural life, which formed the core of British upper-class culture.

The colonists tended to subscribe to this same view of government and property, but they did not rush to impose property qualifications for the vote. Jamestown, Virginia, for instance, had no property requirement for political participation in its early years, going so far as to permit even servants to vote. Gradually all the colonies began to require of voters some degree of property ownership or, later, tax-paying status. This requirement did not exclude as many people from voting in America as in England since property owning was so much more widespread among the settlers.

Religious Qualifications for Voting More pervasive than property-owning or tax-paying requirements, at least in the earliest days of colonial government, were moral or religious qualifications. The northern colonies especially were concerned about keeping the ungodly out of government. Early voting laws in Massachusetts, for instance, denied the vote to people who were not members of the Puritans' church. Remember, these were the same settlers who had fled England because *their* religious freedom was being denied. By 1640 this practice effectively prevented three-fourths of the Massachusetts population from having any political power. Even though the requirements were loosened somewhat in 1660, by royal order from King Charles II, they remained extremely restrictive.[3] Finally, in 1691, the religious diversity in Massachusetts created sufficient pressure to separate church and government, and Massachusetts moved into line with Virginia and the other colonies that based an individual's political rights on his wealth rather than his character.

Women and Colonial Politics We used the pronoun *his* in the preceding section because generally colonial voting was reserved for males. There was, however, some slippage in this practice. Women weren't officially excluded from political participation in America until the Revolution. Until then, as in England, they occasionally could exercise the vote when they satisfied the property requirement and when there were no voting males in their households. In some localities, widows particularly, or daughters who had inherited a parent's property, could vote or participate in church meetings (which sometimes amounted to the same thing). Some colonies allowed women to vote, whereas others, notably Pennsylvania, Delaware, Virginia, Georgia, New York, and South Carolina, excluded them, at least for some period of time.[4]

In some cases women were able to get involved in local politics, or even at the colony level, if they had property or were acting for a man who had had to abdicate his role. William Penn's wife, Hannah, for instance, took over the administration of Pennsylvania when Penn was disabled by a stroke. Women's participation was not the rule, however, and there were clear limits to the colonists' acceptance of it.

slavery the ownership, for forced labor, of one people by another

African Americans and the Institution of Slavery Before **slavery** took hold as an American institution at the end of the 1600s, Africans were subjected to the same laws and codes of behavior as Europeans living in America. The record shows cases of blacks buying themselves out of temporary servitude, amassing property, even owning servants of their own and enjoying the same legal status as whites.[5]

But the colonies required tremendous amounts of cheap labor to produce the raw materials and goods needed for trade with England under the mercantilist system.

A Small Oversight
Although the men who drafted the New Jersey constitution were careful to specify that only property holders could vote, they forgot to explicitly exclude women. Therefore, beginning in 1776, female property holders were eligible to vote in New Jersey, until the "error" was corrected in 1807. A century passed before the state once again gave women the right to vote.

The answer to the problem of cheap, plentiful labor was not far away. Black slaves had been the backbone of the sugar plantations in the Caribbean since the 1500s, and when English people from the Caribbean island of Barbados settled South Carolina in 1670, they brought the institution of slavery with them. Slavery proved economically profitable even in the more commercial areas of New England, but it utterly transformed the tobacco plantations of Maryland and Virginia. By the time of the Revolution, almost 200,000 Africans lived in Maryland and Virginia alone.[6]

Slavery was illegal under British law so, borrowing from the Caribbean settlements, the colonists developed their own legal framework to regulate the institution. Naturally the legal system could not treat whites and blacks alike when it permitted one race to own the other. The rights of blacks were gradually stripped away. In the 1640s, Maryland denied blacks the right to bear arms. A 1669 Virginia law declared that if a slave "should chance to die" when resisting his or her master or the master's agent, it would not be a felony—a crime that legally required malice—because no one would destroy his own property with malice. Most politically damaging, by the 1680s free blacks were forbidden to own property, the only access to political power that colonial society recognized.[7]

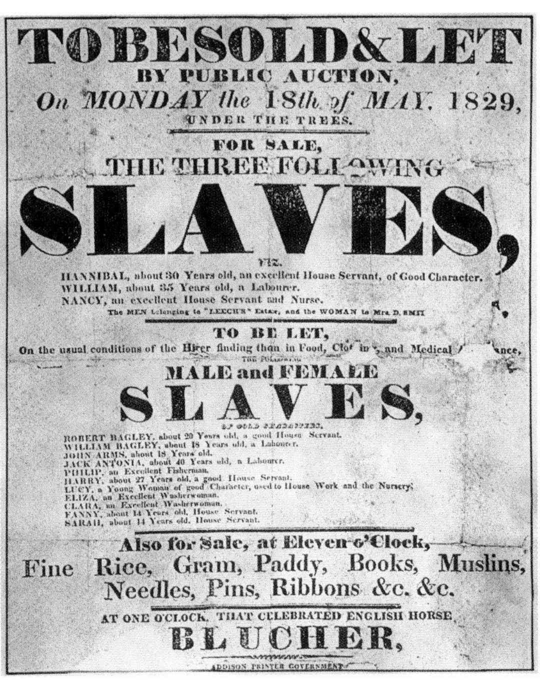

Tragic Cargo
The profitability of tobacco in Virginia, then cotton in Alabama and Mississippi, demanded new sources of cheap labor. As a result, approximately 275,000 enslaved Africans were shipped to the American colonies during the eighteenth century. Typically, between 10 and 30 percent perished during the passage. Once they arrived they were sold in auctions, alongside rice, books, horses, and other goods.

Reasons for these legal changes are not hard to find. Slavery cannot work if slaves are not dependent, defenseless, and dominated by the fear of death. Otherwise they could simply walk away from it. Also, an institution as dehumanizing as slavery requires some justification that enables slaveholders to live with themselves, especially in the Enlightenment era, when words like "natural rights" and "liberty" were on everyone's tongue. It was said that the Africans were childlike, lazy, and undisciplined and that they needed the supervision of slaveowners. The worse slaves were treated, the more their humanity was denied. Racism, the belief that one race is superior to another, undoubtedly existed before slavery was well established in America, but the institution of slavery made it a part of American political culture. We discuss the issue of race in American politics in more detail in Chapter 6.

WHO, WHAT, HOW The English colonists wanted, first and foremost, to find new opportunities in America. But those opportunities were not available to all. Religious and property qualifications for the vote, and the exclusion of women and blacks from political life, meant that the colonial leaders did not feel that simply living in a place or obeying the laws or even paying taxes carried with it the right to participate in government. Following the rigid British social hierarchy, they wanted rules to ensure that the "right kind" of people could participate, people who could be depended on to make the kind of rules that would ensure their status and maintain the established order. The danger of expanding the vote, of course, is that the new majority might want something very different from what the old majority wanted.

THE SPLIT FROM ENGLAND

Both England and America accepted as perfectly normal the relationships of colonial power that initially bound them together. Americans, as colonists, were obliged to make England their primary trading partner, and all goods they traded to other countries had to pass through Britain, where a tax was collected on them. The benefits of being a colony, however, including financial support by British corporations, military defense by the British Army and Navy, and a secure market for their agricultural products, usually outweighed any burdens of colonial obligation. Eventually the relationship started to sour as the colonists developed an identity as Americans rather than as transplanted English people, and as the British became a more intrusive political presence. Even then, they searched painstakingly for a way to fix the relationship before they decided to eliminate it altogether. Revolution was not an idea that occurred readily to either side.

BRITISH ATTEMPTS TO GAIN CONTROL OF THE COLONIES

French and Indian War
a war fought between France and England, and allied Indians, from 1754 to 1763; resulted in France's expulsion from New World

Whether the British government had actually become oppressive in the years before 1776 is open to interpretation. Certainly the colonists thought so. Britain was deeply in debt, having won the **French and Indian War**, which effectively forced the French out of North America and the Spanish to vacate Florida and retreat west of the Mississippi. The war, fought to defend the British colonies and colonists in America, turned into a major and expensive conflict across the Atlantic as well. Britain, having done its protective duty as a colonial power and having taxed British citizens heavily to finance the war, turned to its colonies to help pay for their defense. It chose to do that by levying taxes on the colonies and by attempting to enforce more strictly the trade laws that would increase British profits from American resources.

The irony is that, with the British victory in the war, the colonies were largely free of Spanish, French, and Indian threat. No longer in need of British protection, they could afford to resist British efforts to make them help pay for it.[8] The series of acts the British passed infuriated the colonists. The Sugar Act of 1764, which imposed customs taxes, or duties, on sugar, was seen as unfair and unduly burdensome in a depressed postwar economy, and the Stamp Act of 1765 incited protests and demonstrations throughout the colonies. Similar to a tax in effect in Great Britain for nearly a century, it required that a tax be paid, in scarce British currency, on every piece of printed matter in the colonies, including newspapers, legal documents, and even playing cards. The colonists claimed that the law was an infringement on their liberty and a violation of their rights not to be taxed without their consent. Continued protests and political changes in England resulted in the repeal of the Stamp Act in 1766. The Townshend Acts of 1767, taxing goods imported from England such as paper, glass, and tea, followed by the Tea Act of 1773, were seen by the colonists as intolerable violations of their rights. To show their displeasure they hurled 342 chests of tea into Boston Harbor in the infamous Boston Tea Party. Britain responded by passing the Coercive Acts of 1774, designed to punish the citizens of Massachusetts. In the process, Parliament sowed the seeds that would blossom into revolution in just a few years.

CHANGING IDEAS ABOUT POLITICS

The American reluctance to cooperate with Britain was reinforced by the colonists' changing worldview. Philosophical ideas that were fermenting in England and the European Enlightenment as a whole, especially those of John Locke, were finding a natural home in America. Bernard Bailyn, a scholar of early American history, says that American thinking challenged and broke with British ideology on the interpretation of three major concepts: representation, constitution, and sovereignty.[9]

With respect to representation, Americans came to believe that elected representatives should do precisely what the people who elected them told them to do. This was very different from the British notion of "virtual representation," in which the representative followed his conscience, acting in the best interests of the country as a whole and thus, by definition, of the citizens who lived there. The colonists also began to understand the notion of a constitution as a specific grant of powers to and limitations on government, including Parliament itself. This was in turn directly connected to the notion of sovereignty. For the British, the sovereign authority was Parliament, which established the rule of law and constitutional principles. But the colonists held fast to the principle of **popular sovereignty**; that is, the ultimate authority, the power to govern, belonged in the hands of the people.

popular sovereignty the concept that the citizens are the ultimate source of political power

These philosophical changes meant that any British colonial authority had begun to seem illegitimate to many of the colonists. Much has been made in American schoolbooks about the colonists' defiant rejection of British taxation without representation. The British had offered Americans representation in Parliament, however, and they had rejected it in the assemblies of South Carolina and Virginia.[10] It wasn't just taxation the colonists objected to; it was the British Parliament itself.

Some loyalists to the Crown continued to support British authority because they were involved in British administration of the colonies, because they had commercial ties to Britain, because they believed that America still needed British military protection, or because they were committed to the notion of monarchy. For the rest of the colonists, however, it became harder and harder to recognize British power over them as legitimate authority.

REVOLUTION

From the moment that the unpopularly taxed tea plunged into Boston Harbor in December 1773, it became apparent that the Americans were not going to settle down and behave like proper and orthodox colonists. Even before the Tea Party, mobs in many towns were demonstrating and

Political Spin, Colonial Style
A series of brawls between British troops and local workers reached a climax on March 5, 1770, in what became known as the Boston Massacre. Five colonists were killed, including Crispus Attucks, a black sailor and former slave. Sam Adams, organizer of the Sons of Liberty, and Paul Revere, whose etching of the event is seen here, were both effective propagandists and elevated the skirmish into a brave struggle for freedom.

rioting against British control. Calling themselves the Sons of Liberty, and under the guidance of the eccentric Samuel Adams, cousin to the future president John Adams, rebellious colonists routinely caused extensive damage and, in early 1770, provoked the so-called Boston Massacre, an attack by British soldiers that left six civilians dead and further inflamed popular sentiments.

By the time of the Boston Tea Party, also incited by the Sons of Liberty, passions were at a fever pitch. The American patriots called a meeting in Philadelphia in September 1774. Known as the First Continental Congress, the meeting declared the Coercive Acts void, announced a plan to stop trade with England, and called for a second meeting in May 1775. Before they could meet again, in the early spring of 1775, the king's army went marching to arrest Samuel Adams and another patriot, John Hancock, and to discover the hiding place of the colonists' weapons. Roused by the silversmith Paul Revere, Americans in Lexington and Concord fired the first shots of rebellion at the British, and revolution was truly under way.

THE DECLARATION OF INDEPENDENCE

"Common Sense" 1776 pamphlet by Thomas Paine that persuaded many Americans to support the Revolutionary cause

Even in the midst of war, the colonists did not at first clearly articulate a desire for independence from England. But publication of the pamphlet **"Common Sense,"** written by the English-born Thomas Paine, turned their old ideas upside-down. Paine called for the rejection of the king, for independence, and for republican government, and his passionate writing crystallized the thinking of the colonial leaders.[11]

In 1776, at the direction of a committee of the Continental Congress, thirty-four-year-old Thomas Jefferson sat down to write a declaration of independence from England. His training as a lawyer at the College of William and Mary, and his service as a representative in the Virginia House of Burgesses, helped prepare him for his task, but he had an impressive intellect in any case. President John Kennedy once announced to a group of Nobel Prize winners he was entertaining that they were "the most extraordinary collection of talents that has ever gathered at the White House, with the possible exception of when Thomas Jefferson dined alone." [12] A testimony to Jefferson's capabilities is the strategically brilliant document that he produced.

Declaration of Independence the political document that dissolved the colonial ties between the United States and Britain

The **Declaration of Independence** is first and foremost a political document. Having decided to make the break from England, the American founders had to convince themselves, their fellow colonists, and the rest of the world that they were doing the right thing. Revolutions are generally frowned on politically, unless the revolutionaries can convince the world that they have particularly good and legitimate reasons for their actions. Other national leaders don't like them because they upset the status quo and give ideas to the politically discontent in their own countries. In addition, revolutionaries face the problem of justifying *their* revolution, but no other ones. After all, they presumably intend to set up a new government after the revolution, and they don't want people revolting against *it*. The story told to justify a revolution has to guard against setting off a chain reaction. The Declaration of Independence admirably performs all these tasks.

Jefferson did not have to hunt farther than the writing of John Locke for a good reason for his revolution. Recall from Chapter 1 that Locke said that government is based on a contract between the rulers and the ruled. The ruled agree to obey the laws as long as the rulers protect their basic rights to life, liberty, and property. If the rulers fail to do that, they break the contract and the ruled are free to set up another government. This is exactly what the second paragraph of the Declaration of Independence says, except that Jefferson changed "property" to "the pursuit of happiness," perhaps to garner the support of those Americans who didn't own enough property to worry about. Having established that the breaking of the social contract was a good reason for revolution, Jefferson could justify the American Revolution if he could show that Britain had broken such a contract by violating the colonists' rights.

Consequently, he spelled out all the things that King George III had allegedly done to breach the social contract. Turn to the Declaration in the Appendix of this book and notice the extensive list of grievances against the king. For twenty-seven paragraphs, Jefferson documented just how badly the monarch had treated the colonists. Note, however, that many of the things the colonists complained of were the normal acts of a colonial power. No one had told the king that he was a party to a Lockean contract, so it isn't surprising that he violated it at every turn. Furthermore, some of the things he was blamed for were the acts of Parliament, not of the king at all. Perhaps because the colonists intended to have some sort of parliament of their own, or perhaps, as some scholars have argued, because they simply did not recognize Parliament's authority over them, George III was the sole focus of their wrath and resentment. But the clear goal of the document was to so thoroughly discredit George III that this revolution became inevitable in the eyes of every American, and the world.

"... THAT ALL MEN ARE CREATED EQUAL"

The Declaration of Independence begins with a proud statement of the equality of all men. Since so much of this document relies heavily on Locke, and since clearly the colonists did *not* mean that all men are created equal, it is worth turning to Locke for some help in seeing exactly what they did mean. In his most famous work, *A Second Treatise on Government,* Locke wrote,

> Though I have said above that all men are by nature equal, I cannot be supposed to understand all sorts of equality. Age or virtue may give men a just precedency. Excellency of parts and merit may place others above the common level. Birth may subject some, and alliance or benefits others, to pay an observance to those whom nature, gratitude, or other respects may have made it due.[13]

Men are equal in a natural sense, said Locke, but society quickly establishes many dimensions on which they may be unequal. A particularly sticky point for Locke's ideas on equality is his treatment of slavery, which he did not endorse but ultimately failed to condemn. Here too our founders would have been in agreement with him.

Their ambivalence about slavery and equality can be seen in a passage that Jefferson included in the original draft of the Declaration, as part of the political indictment of George III. He wrote:

> He [George III] has waged cruel war against human nature itself, violating its most sacred rights of life and liberty in the persons of a distant people who never offended him, captivating and carrying them into slavery in another hemisphere or to incur miserable death in their transportation thither.[14]

Blaming King George for the institution of slavery, and including it on a list of behaviors so horrible that they justify revolution, was an amazing act on the part of a man who not only owned slaves himself, but was writing on behalf of many other slave owners. His action shows just how politically confusing and morally ambiguous the issue was at that time. Reflecting the political realities of the time, the passage was eventually deleted.

African Americans and the Revolution The Revolution was a mixed blessing for American slaves. On the one hand, many slaves won their freedom as a result of the war: Slavery was outlawed north of Maryland, and many slaves in the Upper South also were freed. The British offered freedom in exchange for service in the British army, although the conditions they provided were not always a great improvement over enslavement. The abolitionist, or antislavery, movement gathered steam in some northern cities, expressing moral and constitutional objections to the institution of slavery. Whereas before the Revolution only about 5 percent of American blacks were free, the number grew tremendously with the coming of war.[15]

Many African Americans served in the war. There were probably about twelve blacks in the first battle at Lexington and Concord, in Massachusetts. The South feared the idea of arming slaves, for obvious reasons, but by the time Congress began to fix troop quotas for each state, southerners were drafting slaves to serve in their masters' places.

In the aftermath of war, however, African Americans did not find their lot greatly improved, despite the ringing rhetoric of equality that fed the Revolution. The economic profitability of slave labor still existed in the South, and slaves continued to be imported from Africa in large numbers. The explanatory myth—that all men were created equal but that blacks weren't quite men and thus could be treated unequally—spread throughout the new country, making even free blacks unwelcome in many communities. By 1786 New Jersey prohibited free blacks from entering the state, and within twenty years, northern states had started passing laws specifically denying free blacks the right to vote.[16]

Native Americans and the Revolution Native Americans were another group the founders did not consider to be prospective citizens. The European view of the Indians had always been that they were a simple, inferior people. Their communal property holding, their nonmonarchical political systems, their divisions of labor between women working in the fields and men hunting for game, all struck the colonists as naive and primitive. Pushed farther and farther west by land-hungry colonists, the Indians were actively hostile to the American cause in the Revolution. Knowing this, the British hoped to gain their allegiance in the war. But the colonists, having asked in vain for the Indians to stay out of what they called a "family quarrel," were able to suppress early on the Indians' attempts to get revenge for their treatment at the hands of the settlers.[17] There was certainly no suggestion that the claim of equality at the beginning of the Declaration of Independence might include the peoples who had lived on the continent for centuries before the white man arrived.

Women and the Revolution Neither was there any question that "all men" might somehow be a generic term for human beings that would include women. Politically the Revolution proved to be a step backward for women: It was after the war that states began specifically to prohibit women, even those with property, from voting.[18] That doesn't mean, however, that women did not get involved in the war effort. Within the constraints of society, they contributed what they could to the American cause. They boycotted tea and other British imports, sewed flags, made bandages and clothing, nursed and housed soldiers, and collected money to support the Continental Army.

Politics Makes Strange Bedfellows
Sometimes the only thing political allies have in common is an enemy. Mohawk chief Thayendanegea, also known by the English name Joseph Brant, believed Iroquois lands would be lost if the colonists won independence. He arranged an Iroquois alliance with the British, defeating colonial forces in upper New York. The losing American general retaliated by burning forty Indian villages. After the Revolution, as Thayendanegea feared, his people were forced to relocate to Canada.

Not Just a Man's War
Deborah Sampson, a soldier under George Washington's command, was one of a small number of women who disguised themselves and fought as males in the Revolutionary War. After the war, she was dishonorably discharged when it was discovered that she was a woman. It took ten years of effort and the intervention of Washington himself, but Sampson eventually became the first woman to receive a soldier's pension in the U.S. Army.

Under the name Daughters of Liberty, women in many towns met publicly to discuss the events of the day, spinning and weaving to make the colonies less dependent on imported cotton and woolens from England, and drinking herbal tea instead of tea that was taxed by the British. Some women moved beyond such mild patriotic activities to outright political behavior, writing pamphlets urging independence, spying on enemy troops, carrying messages, and even, in isolated instances, fighting on the battlefields.[19]

Men's understanding of women's place in early American politics is nicely put by Thomas Jefferson, writing from Europe to a woman in America in 1788:

> But our good ladies, I trust, have been too wise to wrinkle their foreheads with politics. They are contented to soothe & calm the minds of their husbands returning ruffled from political debate. They have the good sense to value domestic happiness above all others. There is no part of the earth where so much of this is enjoyed as in America.[20]

Women's role with respect to politics is plain: they may be wise and prudent, but their proper sphere is the domestic, not the political, world. They are almost "too good" for politics, representing peace and serenity, moral happiness rather than political dissension, the values of the home over the values of the state. This explanation provides a flattering reason for keeping women in "their place," while allowing men to reign in the world of politics.

WHO, WHAT, HOW By the mid-1700s the interests of the British and the colonists were clearly beginning to separate. If the colonists had played by the rules of imperial politics, England would have been content. It would have taxed the colonies to pay its war debts, but it also would have continued to protect them and rule benignly from across the sea.

The colonial leaders, however, changed the rules. Rejecting British authority, they established new rules based on Enlightenment thought. Then they used impassioned rhetoric and inspiring theory to engage the rest of the colonists in their rebellion. Finally, they used revolution to sever their ties with England.

While the Revolution dramatically changed American fortunes, not everyone's life was altered for the good by political independence. Many of those who were not enfranchised before the war—slaves and free blacks, American Indians, and women—remained powerless afterward, and in some cases, voting rules became even more restrictive.

THE ARTICLES OF CONFEDERATION

constitution the rules that establish a government

Articles of Confederation the first constitution of the United States (1777) creating an association of states with weak central government

In 1777 the Continental Congress met to try to come up with a framework or constitution for the new government. We use the word *constitution* in this country almost as if it could refer only to one specific document. In truth, a **constitution** is any establishment of rules that "constitutes"—that is, makes up—a government. It may be written, as in our case, or unwritten, as in Great Britain's. One constitution can endure for over two hundred years, as ours has, or it can change quite frequently, as the French constitution has. What's important about a constitution is that it sets up a government, the rules and institutions for running a nation. As we have said before, those rules have direct consequences for how politics works in a given country, who the winners are and who the losers will be.

The **Articles of Confederation**, our first constitution, created the kind of government the founders, fresh from their colonial experience, preferred. The rules set up by the Articles of Confederation show the states' jealousy of their own power. Having just won their independence from one large national power, the last thing they wanted to do was create another. They were also extremely wary of one another, and much of the debate over the Articles of Confederation reflected wide concern that the rules not give any states preferential treatment. (See the Appendix for the text of the Articles of Confederation.)

The Articles established a "firm league of friendship" among the thirteen American states, but they did not empower a central government to act effectively on behalf of those states. The Articles were ultimately replaced because, without a strong central government, they were unable to provide the economic and political stability that the founders wanted. Even so, under this set of rules, some people were better off, and some problems, namely the resolution of boundary disputes and the political organization of new territories, were handled extremely well.

THE PROVISIONS OF THE ARTICLES

The government set up by the Articles was called a **confederation** because it established a system in which each state would retain almost all of its own power to do what it wanted. In other words, in a confederation, each state is sovereign, and the central government has only the job of running the collective business of the states. It has no independent source of power and resources for its operations. Another characteristic of a confederation is that, because it is founded on state sovereignty (authority), it says nothing about individuals. It creates neither rights nor obligations for individual citizens, leaving such matters to be handled by state constitutions.

confederation a government in which independent states unite for common purpose, but retain their own sovereignty

Under the Articles of Confederation, Congress had many formal powers, including the power to establish and direct the armed forces, to decide matters of war and peace, to coin money, and to enter into treaties. However, its powers were quite limited; for example, while Congress controlled the armed forces, it had no power to draft soldiers or to tax citizens to pay for its military needs. Its inability to tax put Congress—and the central government as a whole—at the mercy of the states. The government could ask, but it was up to the states to contribute or not as they chose. Furthermore, Congress lacked the ability to regulate commerce between states, and between states and foreign powers. It could not establish a common and stable monetary system. In essence, the Articles allowed the states to be thirteen independent units, printing their own currencies, setting their own tariffs, and establishing their own laws with regard to financial and political matters. In every critical case—national security, national economic prosperity, and the general welfare—the United States government had to rely on the voluntary goodwill and cooperation of the state governments. That meant that the success of the new nation depended on what went on in state legislatures around the country.

SOME WINNERS, SOME LOSERS

The era of American history following the Revolution was dubbed "this critical period" by John Quincy Adams, nephew of patriot Samuel Adams, and future president of the country. During this time, while the states were under the weak union of the Articles, the future of the United States was very much up in the air. The lack of an effective central government meant that the country had difficulty conducting business with other countries and enforcing harmonious trade relations and treaties. Domestic politics was equally difficult. Economic conditions following the war were poor. Many people owed money and could not pay their debts. State taxes were high and the economy was depressed, offering farmers few opportunities to sell their produce, for example, and hindering those with commercial interests from conducting business as they had before the war.

The radical poverty of some Americans seemed particularly unjust to those hardest hit, especially in light of the rhetoric of the Revolution about equality for all. Having used "equality" as a rallying cry during the war, the founders were afterward faced with a population that wanted to take equality seriously and eliminate the differences that existed between men.[21]

One of the ways this passion for equality manifested itself was in some of the state legislatures, where laws were passed to ease the burden of debtors and farmers. Often the focus of the laws was property, but rather than preserving property, as Lockean theory said laws should do, these laws frequently were designed to confiscate or redistribute property instead. The have-nots in society, and the people acting on their behalf, were using the law to redress what they saw as injustices in early American life. To relieve postwar suffering, they printed paper money, seized property, and suspended "the ordinary means for the recovery of debts."[22] In other words, in those states, people with debts and mortgages could legally escape or postpone paying the money they owed. With so much economic insecurity, naturally those who owned property would not continue to invest and lend money. The Articles of Confederation, in their effort to preserve power for the states, had provided for no checks or limitations on state legislatures. In fact, such action would have been seen under the Articles as infringing on the sovereignty of the states.

popular tyranny the unrestrained power of the people

Shays's Rebellion a grassroots uprising (1787) by armed Massachusetts farmers protesting foreclosures

The political elite in the new country started to grumble about **popular tyranny**. In a monarchy, one feared the unrestrained power of the king, but perhaps in a republican government one had to fear the unrestrained power of the people. The final straw was **Shays's Rebellion**. Massachusetts was a state whose legislature, dominated by wealthy and secure citizens, had not taken measures to aid the debt-ridden population. In an effort to keep their land from foreclosure (seizure by those to whom they owed money), a mob of angry musket-wielding farmers from western Massachusetts, led by a former officer of the Continental Army, Daniel Shays, stormed a federal armory in Springfield that housed 450 tons of military supplies in January 1787. The mob was turned back after a violent clash with state militia, but the attack frightened and embarrassed the leaders of the United States, who feared that the rebellion foreshadowed the failure of their grand experiment in self-governance. In their minds, it underscored the importance of discovering what James Madison would call "a republican remedy for those diseases most incident to republican government."[23] In other words, the leaders had to find a way to contain and limit the will of the people in a government that was to be based on the will of the people. If the rules of government were not producing the "right" winners and losers, then the rules would have to be changed before the elite lost the power to change them.

WHO, WHAT, HOW The fledgling states had an enormous amount at stake as they forged their new government after the Revolution. Perceiving that alarming abuses of power by the British king had come from a strong national government, they were determined to limit the central power of the new nation. The solution was to form a "firm league of friendship" among the several states but to keep the power of any central institutions as weak as possible.

With widespread land ownership possible and with the need for popular support, most farmers and artisans enjoyed the status of citizenship. Given easy access to the state legislatures under the Articles of Confederation, they were able to use the rules of the new political system to take the edge off the economic hardships they were facing.

But the same rules that made it so easy for the new citizens to influence their state governments made it more difficult for the political and economic leaders of the former colonies to protect their own economic security. In their eyes, new rules were needed that would remove government from the rough-and-ready hands of the farmers and protect it from what they saw as unreasonable demands.

THE CONSTITUTIONAL CONVENTION

Even before Shays and his men attacked the Springfield armory, delegates from key states had met in Annapolis, Maryland, to discuss the nation's commercial weaknesses. There they adopted a proposal to have each state send delegates to a national convention to be held in Philadelphia in May 1787. The purpose of the meeting would be to make the national government strong enough to handle the demands of united action.

The Philadelphia Convention was authorized to try to fix the Articles of Confederation, but it was clear that many of the fifty-five state delegates who gathered in May were not interested in saving the existing framework at all. Many of the delegates represented the elite of American society, and thus they were among those being most injured under the terms of the Articles. When it became apparent that the **Constitutional Convention** was replacing, not revising, the Articles, some delegates refused to attend, declaring that such a convention was outside the Articles of Confederation and therefore illegal—in fact, it was treason. The convention was in essence overthrowing the government.

Constitutional Convention the assembly of fifty-five delegates in the summer of 1787 to recast the Articles of Confederation; the result was the U.S. Constitution

"AN ASSEMBLY OF DEMIGODS"

When Thomas Jefferson, unable to attend the convention because he was on a diplomatic mission to Europe, heard about the Philadelphia meeting, he called it "an assembly of demigods."[24] Certainly the delegates were among the most educated, powerful, and wealthy citizens of the new country. Some leading figures were absent. Not only was Jefferson in Paris, but John Adams was also in Europe. Samuel Adams had not been elected but had declared his general disapproval of the "unconstitutional" undertaking, as had Patrick Henry, another hotheaded revolutionary patriot and advocate of states' rights. But there was George Washington, from Virginia, the general who had led American troops to victory in the Revolution. Also from Virginia were George Mason, Edmund Randolph, and James Madison, the sickly and diminutive but brilliant politician who would make a greater imprint on the final Constitution than all the other delegates combined. Other delegates were also impressive: eighty-one-year-old Benjamin Franklin, as mentally astute as ever, if increasingly feeble in body; Gouverneur Morris from Pennsylvania; and Alexander Hamilton among the New Yorkers.

These delegates represented the very cream of American society. They were well educated in an age when most of the population was not, about 50 percent having gone to schools like Harvard, William and Mary, Columbia (called King's College until 1784), and other institutions that are still at the top of the educational hierarchy. They were also wealthy; they were lawyers, land speculators, merchants, planters, and investors. Even though they were, on the whole, a young group (over half were under forty, and James Madison just thirty-six), they were politically experienced. Many had been active in Revolutionary politics, and they were well read in the political theories of the day, like the ideas of Enlightenment thinker John Locke.

This impressive gathering met through a sweltering Philadelphia summer to reconstruct the foundations of American government. The heat and humidity were heightened because the windows of Convention Hall were kept closed against listening ears and, consequently, the possibility of a cooling breeze. So serious was the convention about secrecy that when a delegate found a copy of one of the major proposals,

Demigods at Work
The fifty-five men assembled in Philadelphia in 1787, now revered as the founders of a nation, represented the colonies' monied and educated elite. They met in complete secrecy, armed guards at the doors, for fear their disagreements, if made public, could be used against them by those opposed to a strong national government. The U.S. Constitution, produced by these men, has survived more than two hundred years.

apparently dropped by another delegate, he turned it over to presiding officer George Washington. Washington took the entire convention to task for its carelessness and threw the document on the table, saying, "Let him who owns it take it." No one dared.[25] We owe most of what we know about the convention today to the notes of James Madison, which he insisted not be published until after the deaths of all the convention delegates.[26]

HOW STRONG A CENTRAL GOVERNMENT?

As the delegates had hoped, the debates at the Constitutional Convention produced a very different system of rules than that established by the Articles of Confederation. Many of these rules were compromises that emerged as the conflicting interests brought by delegates to the convention were resolved.

Imagine that you face the delegates' challenge—to construct a new government from scratch. You can create all the rules, arrange all the institutions, just to your liking. The only hitch is that you have other delegates to work with. Delegate A, for instance, is a merchant with a lot of property; he has big plans for a strong government that can ensure secure conditions for conducting business and can adequately protect property. Delegate B is a planter. In Delegate B's experience, big governments are dangerous. Big governments are removed from the people, and it is easy for corruption to take root when people can't keep a close eye on what their officials are doing. People like Delegate B think that they do better when power is broken up and localized and there is no strong central government. In fact, Delegate B would prefer a government like that provided by the Articles of Confederation. How do you reconcile these two very different agendas?

The solution adopted under the Articles of Confederation had basically favored Delegate B's position. The new Constitution, given the profiles of the delegates in attendance, was moving strongly in favor of Delegate A's position. Naturally the agreement of all those who followed Delegate B would be important in ratifying, or getting approval for, the final Constitution, so their concerns could not be ignored. The compromise chosen by the founders at the Constitutional Convention was called federalism. Unlike a confederation, in which the states retain the ultimate power over the whole, **federalism** gives the central government its own source of power, in this case the Constitution of the people of the United States. But unlike a unitary system, which we discuss in Chapter 4, federalism also gives independent power to the states.

federalism a political system in which power is divided between the central and regional units

Compared to how they fared under the Articles of Confederation, the advocates of states' rights were losers under the new Constitution, but they were better off than they might have been. The states could have had *all* their power stripped away. The economic elite, people like Delegate A, were clear winners under the new rules. This proved to be one of the central issues during the ratification debates. Those who sided with the federalism alternative, who mostly resembled Delegate A, came to be known as **Federalists**. The people like Delegate B, who continued to hold onto the strong state–weak central government option, were called **Anti-Federalists**. We will return to them shortly.

Federalists supporters of the Constitution, who favored a strong central government

Anti-Federalists advocates of states' rights who opposed the Constitution

LARGE STATES, SMALL STATES

Once the convention delegates agreed that federalism would provide the framework of the new government, they had to decide how to allot power among the states. Should all states count the same in decision making, or should the larger states have more power than the smaller ones? The rules chosen here could have a crucial impact on the politics of the country. If small states and large states had equal amounts of power in national government, residents of large states such as Virginia, Massachusetts, and New York would effectively have less voice in the government than would residents of small states, like New Jersey and Rhode Island, since they would have proportionately less influence on how their power was wielded. If power were allocated on the basis of size, however, the importance of the small states would be reduced.

Two plans were offered by convention delegates to resolve this issue. The first, the **Virginia Plan**, was created by James Madison and presented at the convention by Edmund Randolph. The Virginia Plan represented the preference of the large, more populous states. This plan proposed that the country would have a strong national government, run by a bicameral (two-house) legislature. One house would be elected directly by the people, one indirectly by a combination of the state legislatures and the popularly elected national house. But the numbers of representatives would be determined by the taxes paid by the residents of the state, which would reflect the free population in the state. In other words, large states would have more representatives in both houses of the legislature, and national law and policy would be weighted heavily in their favor. Just three large states, Virginia, Massachusetts, and Pennsylvania, would be able to form a majority and carry national legislation their way. The Virginia Plan also called for a single executive, to see that the laws were carried out, and a national

Virginia Plan a proposal at the Constitutional Convention that congressional representation be based on population, thus favoring the large states judiciary, both appointed by the legislature, and it gave the national government power to override state laws.

A different plan, presented by William Paterson of New Jersey, was designed by the smaller states to offer the convention an alternative that would better protect their interests. The **New Jersey Plan** amounted to a reinforcement, not a replacement, of the Articles of Confederation. It provided for a multiperson executive, so that no one person could possess too much power, and for congressional acts to be the "supreme law of the land." Most significantly, however, the Congress was much like the one that had existed under the Articles. In a unicameral (one-house) legislature, each state got only one vote. The delegates would be chosen by state legislatures. The powers of Congress were stronger than under the Articles, but the national government was still dependent on the states for some of its funding. The large states disliked this plan because small states together could block what the larger states wanted, even though the larger states had more people and contributed more revenue.

New Jersey Plan a proposal at the Constitutional Convention that congressional representation be equal, thus favoring the small states

The prospects for a new government could have foundered on this issue. The stuffy heat of the closed Convention Hall shortened the tempers of the weary delegates, and frustration made compromise difficult. Each side had too much to lose by yielding to the other's plan. The solution finally arrived at was politics at its best. The **Great Compromise** kept much of the framework of the Virginia Plan. It was a strong federal structure headed by a central government with sufficient power to tax its citizens, regulate commerce, conduct foreign affairs, organize the military, and exercise other central powers. It called for a single executive and a national judicial system. The compromise that allowed the smaller states to live with it involved the composition of the legislature. Like the Virginia Plan, it provided for two houses. The House of Representatives would be based on state population, giving the large states the extra clout they felt they deserved, but in the Senate each state had two votes. This gave the smaller states relatively much more power in the Senate than in the House of Representatives. Members of the House of Representatives would be elected directly by the people, members of the Senate by the state legislatures. Thus the government would be directly binding on the people as well as on the states. A key to the compromise was that most legislation would need the approval of both houses, so that neither large states nor small states could hold the entire government hostage to their wishes. The smaller states were sufficiently happy with this plan that most of them voted to approve, or ratify, the Constitution quickly and easily. See Table 3.1 for a comparison of the Constitution with the Articles of Confederation and the different plans for reform.

Great Compromise the constitutional solution to congressional representation: equal votes in the Senate, votes by population in the House

NORTH AND SOUTH

The compromise reconciling the large and small states was not the only one crafted by the delegates. The northern and the southern states, which is to say the non–slave-owning and the slave-owning states, were at odds over how population was to be determined for purposes of representation in the House of Representatives. The southern states wanted to count slaves as part of their populations when determining how many representatives they got, even though they had no intention of letting the slaves vote. Including slaves would give them more representatives and, thus, more power in the House. For exactly that reason, the northern states said that if slaves could not vote, they should not be counted. The compromise, also a triumph of politics if not humanity, is known as the **Three-fifths Compromise**. It was based

Three-fifths Compromise the formula for counting five slaves as three people for purposes of representation that reconciled northern and southern factions at the Constitutional Convention

TABLE 3.1 **Distribution of Powers Under the Articles of Confederation, the New Jersey and Virginia Plans, and the U.S. Constitution**

KEY QUESTIONS	ARTICLES OF CONFEDERATION	NEW JERSEY PLAN	VIRGINIA PLAN	THE CONSTITUTION
Who is sovereign?	States	States	People	People
What law is supreme?	State law	State law	National law	National law
What kind of legislature; what is the basis for representation?	Unicameral legislature; equal votes for all states	Unicameral legislature; one vote per state	Bicameral legislature; representation in both houses based on population	Bicameral legislature; equal votes in Senate, representation by population in House
How are laws passed?	Two-thirds vote to pass important measures	Extraordinary majority to pass measures	Majority decision making	Simple majority vote in Congress, presidential veto
What powers are given to Congress?	No congressional power to levy taxes, regulate commerce	Congressional power to regulate commerce and tax	Congressional power to regulate commerce and tax	Congressional power to regulate commerce and tax
What kind of executive is there?	No executive branch; laws executed by congressional committee	Multiple executive	No restriction on strong single executive	Strong executive
What kind of judiciary is there?	No federal court system	No federal court system	National judiciary	Federal court system
How can the document be changed?	All states required to approve amendments	Unanimous approval of amendments by states	Popular ratification	Amendment process less difficult

on a formula developed by the Confederation Congress in 1763 to allocate tax assessments among the states. According to this compromise, for representation purposes, each slave would count as three-fifths of a person, every five slaves counting as three people. Interestingly, the actual language in the Constitution is a good deal cagier than this. It says that representatives and taxes shall be determined according to population, figured "by adding to the whole Number of free Persons, including those bound to Service for a Term of Years, and excluding Indians not taxed, three fifths of *all other persons.*"

The issue of slavery was divisive enough for the early Americans that the most politically safe approach was not to mention it explicitly at all and thus to avoid having to endorse or condemn it. Implicitly, of course, their silence had the effect of letting slavery continue. Article I, Section 9, of the Constitution, in similarly vague language, allows that "The Migration or Importation of such Persons as any of the States now existing shall think proper to admit, shall not be prohibited by Congress prior to the Year one thousand eight hundred and eight, but a Tax or duty may be imposed on such Importation, not exceeding ten dollars for each Person." Even more damning, Article IV, Section 2, obliquely provides for the return of runaway slaves: "No Person held to Service or Labour in one State under the Laws thereof, escaping into another, shall, in Consequence of any Law or Regulation therein, be discharged from such Service or Labour, but shall be delivered up on Claim of the Party to whom such Service or Labour may be due." The word *slavery* does not appear in the Constitution until it is expressly outlawed in the Thirteenth Amendment, passed in December 1865, over eighty years after the writing of the Constitution.

WHO, WHAT, HOW Not only the political and economic elite but also the everyday citizens who did not attend the Constitutional Convention stood to gain or lose dramatically from the proceedings. What was at stake that summer were the very rules that would provide the framework for so many political battles in the future.

Differences clearly existed among the founding elites. Those representing large states, of course, wanted rules that would give their states more power, based on their larger population, tax base, and size. Representatives of small states, on the other hand, wanted rules that would give the states equal power, so that they would not be squashed by the large states. North and South also differed on the rules: The North wanted representation to be based on the population of free citizens, while the South wanted to include slaves in the population count. The Great Compromise and the Three-fifths Compromise solved both disagreements.

Finally, the people at the convention were divided along another dimension as well. The Federalists sought to create a strong central government more resistant to the whims of popular opinion. Opposing them, the Anti-Federalists wanted a decentralized government, closer to the control of the people. It was the Federalists who controlled the agenda at the Convention and who ultimately determined the structure of the new government.

RATIFICATION

ratification the process through which a proposal is formally approved and adopted by vote

For the Constitution to become the law of the land, it had to go through the process of **ratification**—being voted on and approved by state conventions in at least nine of the states. As it happens, the Constitution was eventually ratified by all thirteen states, but not until some major political battles had been fought.

FEDERALISTS VERSUS ANTI-FEDERALISTS

Those in favor of ratification called themselves the Federalists. The Federalists, like Delegate A in our hypothetical constitution-building scenario, were mostly men with a considerable economic stake in the new nation. Having fared poorly under the Articles, they were certain that if America were to grow as an economic and world power, it needed to be the kind of country people with property would want to invest in. Security and order were key values, as was popular control. The Federalists thought people like themselves should be in charge of the government, although some of them did not object to an expanded suffrage if government had enough built-in protections. Mostly, these students of the Enlightenment were convinced that a good government could be designed if the underlying principles of human behavior were known. If people were ambitious and tended toward corruption, then government should make use of those characteristics to produce good outcomes.

The Anti-Federalists, on the other hand, rejected the notion that ambition and corruption were inevitable parts of human nature. If government could be kept small and local, and popular scrutiny truly vigilant, then Americans could live happy and contented lives without getting involved in the seamier side of politics. If America did not stray from its rural roots and values, it could permanently avoid the creeping corruption that they believed threatened it. The Articles of Confederation were more attractive to the Anti-Federalists than was the Constitution because they did not call for a strong central government that, tucked away from the voters' eyes, could become a hotbed of political intrigue. Instead, the Articles vested power in the state governments, which could be more easily watched and controlled.

Writing under various aliases as well as their own names, the Federalists and Anti-Federalists fired arguments back and forth in pamphlets and newspaper editorials, aimed at persuading undecided Americans to come out for or against the Constitution. The Federalists were far more aggressive and organized in their "media blitz," hitting New York newspapers with a series of eloquent editorials published under the pen name Publius, but really written by Alexander Hamilton, James Madison, and John Jay. These essays were bound and distributed in other states where the ratification struggle was close. Known as ***The Federalist Papers***, they are one of the main texts on early American politics today. In response, the Anti-Federalists published essays written under such names as Cato, Brutus, and The Federal Farmer.[27]

The Federalist Papers a series of essays written in support of the Constitution to build support for its ratification

THE FEDERALIST PAPERS

There were eighty-five essays written by Publius. These essays are clever, they are well thought out and logical, but they are also tricky and persuasive examples of the hard sell. Two of the most important of the essays, numbers 10 and 51, are reprinted in the Appendix of this book. Their archaic language makes *The Federalist Papers* generally difficult reading for contemporary students. However, the arguments in support of the Constitution are laid out so beautifully that taking the trouble to read them is worthwhile. It would be a good idea to turn to them and read them carefully now.

In *Federalist* No. 10, Madison tried to convince Americans that a large country was no more likely to succumb to the effects of special interests than a small one (preferred by the Anti-Federalists). He explained that the greatest danger to a republic came from **factions**—what we might call interest groups. Factions are groups of people motivated by a common interest, but one different from the interest of the country as a whole. Farmers, for instance, have an interest in keeping food prices high, even though that would make most Americans worse off. Businesspeople prefer high import duties on foreign goods, even though they make both foreign and domestic goods more expensive for the rest of us. Factions are not a particular problem when they constitute a minority of the population because they are offset by majority rule. They become problematic, however, when they are a majority. Factions usually have economic roots, the most basic being between the haves and have-nots in society. One of the majority factions that worried Madison was the mass of propertyless people whose behavior was so threatening to property holders under the Articles of Confederation.

factions groups of citizens united by some common passion or interest and opposed to the rights of other citizens or to the interests of the whole community

To control the *causes* of factions would be to infringe on individual liberty. But Madison believed that the *effects* of factions were easily managed in a large republic. First of all, representation would dilute the effects of factions, and it was in this essay that Madison made his famous distinction between "pure democracy" and a "republic." In addition, if the territory were sufficiently large, factions would be neutralized because there would be so many of them that no one would be likely to become a majority. Furthermore, it would be difficult for people who shared common interests to find one another if some lived in South Carolina, for instance, and others lived in New Hampshire. Clearly Madison never anticipated the invention of the fax machine or the Internet. We discuss Madison's argument about factions again in Chapter 13 when we take up the topic of interest groups. In the meantime, however, notice how Madison relied on mechanical elements of politics (size and representation) to remedy a flaw in human nature (the tendency to form divisive factions). This is typical of the Federalists' approach to government, and reflects the importance of institutions as well as rules in bringing about desired outcomes in politics.

We see the same emphasis on mechanical solutions to political problems in *Federalist* No. 51. Here Madison argued that the institutions proposed in the Constitution would lead to neither corruption nor tyranny. The solution was the principles of checks and balances and separation of powers. We discuss these at length in Chapter 4, but it is worth looking at Madison's interesting explanation of why such checks work. Again building his case on a potential defect of human character, he said, "Ambition must be made to counteract ambition." [28] If men tend to be ambitious, give two ambitious men the job of watching over each other, and neither will let the other have an advantage.

The eighty-fourth *Federalist Paper* was written by Hamilton. It doesn't reflect great principles, but it is interesting politically because it failed dismally. The Constitution was ratified in spite of it, not because of it. In this essay, Hamilton argued that a **Bill of Rights**—a listing of the protections against government infringement of individual rights guaranteed to citizens by government itself—was not necessary in a constitution.

Bill of Rights a summary of citizen rights guaranteed and protected by a government; added to the Constitution as its first ten amendments in order to achieve ratification

The original draft of the Constitution contained no Bill of Rights. Some state constitutions had them, and so the Federalists argued that a federal Bill of Rights would be redundant. Moreover, the limited government set up by the federal Constitution didn't have the power to infringe on individual rights anyway, and many of the rights that would be included in a Bill of Rights were already in the body of the text. To the Anti-Federalists, already afraid of the invasive power of the national government, this omission was more appalling than any other aspect of the Constitution.

Hamilton argued that a Bill of Rights was unnecessary, even dangerous. As it stood, Hamilton said, the national government didn't have the power to interfere with citizens' lives in many ways, and any interference at all would be suspect. But if the Constitution were prefaced with a list of things government could *not* do to individuals, then government would assume it had the power to do anything that wasn't expressly forbidden. Therefore, government, instead of being unlikely to trespass on its citizens' rights, would be more likely to do so with a Bill of Rights than without. This argument was so unpersuasive to Americans at that time that the Federalists were forced to give in to Anti-Federalist pressure during the ratification process. The price of ratification exacted by several states was the Bill of Rights, really a Bill of "Limits" on the federal government, added to the Constitution as the first ten amendments. We look at those limits in detail in Chapter 5, on fundamental American liberties.

THE FINAL VOTE

The smaller states, gratified by the compromise that gave them equal representation in the Senate, and believing they would be better off as part of a strong nation, ratified the Constitution quickly. The vote was unanimous in Delaware, New Jersey, and Georgia. In Connecticut (128–40) and Pennsylvania (46–23), the convention votes, though not unanimous, were strongly in favor of the Constitution. This may have helped to tip the balance for Massachusetts, voting much more closely to ratify (187–168). Maryland (63–11) and South Carolina (149–73) voted in favor of ratification in the spring of 1788, leaving only one more state to supply the requisite nine to make the Constitution law.

The battles in the remaining states were much tighter. When the Virginia convention met in June 1788, the Federalists felt that it could provide the decisive vote and threw much of their effort into securing passage. Madison and his Federalist colleagues debated with such Anti-Federalist advocates as George Mason and Patrick Henry, promising as they had in Massachusetts to support a Bill of Rights. Virginia ratified the Constitution by the narrow margin of 89 to 79, preceded by a few days by New Hampshire, voting 57 to 47. Establishment of the Constitution as the law of the land was ensured with approval of ten states. New York also narrowly passed the Constitution, 30 to 27, but North Carolina defeated it (193–75) and Rhode Island, which had not sent delegates to the Constitutional Convention, refused to call a state convention to put it to the vote. Later both North Carolina and Rhode Island voted to ratify and join the union, in November 1789 and May 1790, respectively.[29] Figure 3.3 summarizes the voting on the Constitution.

Again we can see how important rules are in determining outcomes. The Articles of Confederation had required the approval of all the states. Had the Constitutional

FIGURE 3.3 **Ratification of the Constitution**

STATE	DATE OF RATIFICATION	VOTE IN CONVENTION	RANK IN POPULATION
1. Delaware	Dec. 7, 1787	30 to 0	13
2. Pennsylvania	Dec. 12, 1787	46 to 23	3
3. New Jersey	Dec. 18, 1787	38 to 0	9
4. Georgia	Jan. 2, 1788	26 to 0	11
5. Connecticut	Jan. 9, 1788	128 to 40	8
6. Massachusetts (including Maine)	Feb. 7, 1788	187 to 168	2
7. Maryland	Apr. 28, 1788	63 to 11	6
8. South Carolina	May 23, 1788	149 to 73	7
9. New Hampshire	June 21, 1788	57 to 47	10
10. Virginia	June 26, 1788	89 to 79	1
11. New York	July 26, 1788	30 to 27	5
12. North Carolina	Nov. 21, 1789	194 to 77	4
13. Rhode Island	May 29, 1790	34 to 32	12

Profiles in Citizenship

Newt Gingrich

History is anything but dull when it comes from the mouth of the man who has made so much of it. Newt Gingrich is the architect of the Contract With America, a document that helped propel the Republicans into the majority in Congress in 1994 for the first time in forty years, and made him Speaker of the U.S. House of Representatives from 1995 to 1998. As you will see in Chapter 7, his ideas and the policies they generated still inform the terms of political debate in this country a decade later.

"The primary breakthroughs have all been historic. It was the Greeks discovering the concept of self-governance, it was the Romans creating the objective sense of law. . . ."

But sitting at his desk at the American Enterprise Institute, with his distinguished gray head tilted slightly as he listens to a question, his fingertips pressed lightly together as he thinks over the answer, it is hard to forget that long before he revolutionized American politics in the 1990s, Newt Gingrich was a history professor at Western Georgia College. For the last six years he has resumed the work of a scholar in the rarified atmosphere of the American Enterprise Institute, a conservative Washington think tank, where, in addition to being a media commentator and advisor to his party, he can play with ideas and talk to other smart people to his heart's content.

Clearly life as an intellectual suits him. Does it mean Gingrich has given up politics for good? Maybe, but maybe not. The media have had a field day speculating on the possibility that he'll run for president in 2008. He hasn't said yes, but then he hasn't said no, either. It's hard to imagine that all that energy and creativity and leadership potential aren't going to run for *something.* His recent book, *Winning the Future*, a vigorous, conservative strategy for the remaking of America, certainly hints at his intention to stay active in public life.

It seems to be part of who he is. When he was as young as ten years old, he was flexing his civic muscles by petitioning the Harrisburg (Pennsylvania) City Council to build a zoo. They didn't, but only, he claims with a smile, because his military family moved away before he could persuade them. Given his extraordinary record of public achievement since, it is a good bet he'd have gotten his zoo if the Gingrich family had stayed put.

But they did not. Throughout his junior high years the Gingriches lived in a number of post–World War II European cities—gracious, civilized cities-turned-battlefields that still bore the scars of combat. There was no pretending that the atrocities of war "couldn't happen there"; they had happened, and it was apparent to

Convention chosen a similar rule of unanimity, the Constitution may very well have been defeated. Recognizing that unanimous approval was not probable, however, the Federalists decided to require ratification by only nine of the thirteen, making adoption of the Constitution far more likely.

WHO, WHAT, HOW The fight over ratification of the Constitution had not only the actual form of government at stake but also a deep philosophical difference about the nature of human beings and the possibilities of republican government. The Federalists favored the new Constitution. For the Anti-Federalists, the Constitution seemed to present innumerable opportunities for corruption to fester. Knowing they had lost the battle for public opinion and for votes, they made the attachment of a Bill of Rights a condition of their acquiescence.

Gingrich that they could happen at home, too, if serious steps weren't taken. He says, "Out of all that experience I concluded that citizenship was central to our freedom and our safety, and that having civilian leaders who thought about it every day was central to our survival. I spent the summer of 1958 praying about it, and then in August of 1958 [when he was 15] I decided to do what I've been doing ever since."

What he does—the short answer—is to study history and glean from it insights about human motivation and behavior, and then use those historical insights to make things happen today. He is committed to crafting new ideas out of old lessons, leading his fellow citizens on a mission he believes will restore the country to fundamental principles.

Ask him to explain just why it's important to study history and he pauses so long you wonder if he's forgotten the question or perhaps thinks it's so obvious that he won't deign to give it an answer. But no, he's just assembling his thoughts; you can almost hear the clicks and whirls of the processors. He opens his mouth and gracefully constructed sentences tumble out, fully formed. No umms, no stumbles, just perfect, elegant prose. Here's what he says:

On why students should study history:

> If you've never run out of gas, you may not understand why filling your gas tank matters. And if you've never had your brakes fail, you may not care about having your brakes checked. And if you've never slid on an icy road, you may not understand why learning to drive on ice really matters. For citizens, if you haven't lived in a bombed-out city like Beirut or Baghdad, if you haven't seen a genocidal massacre like Rwanda, if you haven't been in a situation where people were starving to death, like Calcutta, you may not understand why you ought to study history. Because your life is good and it's easy and it's soft.
>
> But for most of the history of the human race, most people, most of the time, have lived as slaves or as subjects to other people. And they lived lives that were short and desperate and where they had very little hope. And the primary breakthroughs have all been historic. It was the Greeks discovering the concept of self-governance, it was the Romans creating the objective sense of law, it was the Jewish tradition of being endowed by God—those came together and fused in Britain with the Magna Carta, and created a sense of rights that we take for granted every day. Because we have several hundred years of history protecting us. And the morning that history disappears, there's no reason to believe we'll be any better than Beirut or Baghdad.

On keeping the republic:

> Be responsible, live out your responsibilities as a citizen, dedicate some amount of your time every day or every week to knowing what is going on in the world, be active in campaigns, and if nobody is worthy of your support, run yourself. . . . The whole notion of civil society [is] doing something as a volunteer, doing something, helping your fellow American, being involved with human beings. America only works as an organic society. . . . We're the most stunningly voluntaristic society in the world. And so if voluntarism dries up, in some ways America dries up.

Source: Newt Gingrich talked with Christine Barbour on March 21, 2005.

THE CITIZENS AND THE FOUNDING

As we said at the beginning of this chapter, there are different stories to be told about the American founding. We did not want to fall into the oversimplification trap, portraying the founding as a headlong rush to liberty on the part of an oppressed people. Politics is always a good deal more complicated than that, and this is a book about politics. We also wanted to avoid telling a story that errs on the other end of one-sidedness, depicting the American founding as an elite-driven period of history, in which the political, economic, and religious leaders decided they were better off without English rule, inspired the masses to revolt, and then created a Constitution that established rules that benefited people like themselves. Neither of these stories is entirely untrue, but they obscure two very important points.

COMPETING ELITES

The first point is that there was not just one "elite" group at work during the founding period. Although political and economic leaders might have acted together over the matter of the break with England (and even then, important elites remained loyal to Britain), once the business of independence was settled, it was clear that competing elite groups existed: leaders of big states and small states, leaders of the northern and southern states, merchant elites and agricultural elites, elites who found their security in a strong national government and those who found it in decentralized power. The power struggle between all those adversaries resulted in the compromises that form the framework of our government today.

THE RISE OF THE "ORDINARY" CITIZEN

The second point is that not all the actors during the founding period were among the top tier of political, economic, and religious leadership. Just because the Revolution and the government-building that followed it were not the product of ordinary citizens zealous for liberty does not mean that ordinary citizens had nothing to do with it.

Citizenship as we know it today was a fledgling creation at the time of the founding. The British had not been citizens of the English government but subjects of the English Crown. There is a world of difference between a subject and a citizen, as we pointed out in Chapter 1. The subject has a personal tie to the monarch; the citizen has a legal tie to a national territory. The subject has obligations; the citizen has both obligations and rights. One writer identifies three elements of American citizenship that were accepted in principle (though hard to put into practice) after the Revolution: (1) Citizenship should rest on consent, (2) there should not be grades or levels of citizenship, and (3) citizenship should confer equal rights on all citizens.[30] The source for these new ideas about citizenship was Enlightenment thinking. We have seen in the ideas of John Locke the concept of the social contract—that citizenship is the product of a contractual agreement between rulers and ruled that makes obeying the law contingent on having one's rights protected by the state.

These new ideas were not all equally easy to put into practice. The notion of citizenship based on consent was relatively straightforward. In a way, the Declaration of Independence constituted a withdrawal of colonial consent to be ruled by George III, and the ratification of the Constitution was a collective consent to the new government. It was more difficult for Americans to work out how to avoid different levels of citizenship and to confer equal rights on all citizens.

In the European tradition, people born into different orders of society (based largely on their families' ownership of land) had, if not different levels of citizenship, then different social and political status. In America, the abundance of land meant that people who in Europe would have been at the bottom of the social and political order were catapulted into the landowner class and were thus eligible to be citizens in the new republic. Under the Articles of Confederation especially, Americans embraced this new definition of mass citizenship, but their experience during the critical period led the founders to mistrust it profoundly. To some extent, the writing of the Constitution was about reining in the power of the citizens, checking and balancing the power of the people as well as the power of the government.

The second factor of the new definition of citizenship that was hard for the early Americans to practice was the notion that citizenship conferred equal rights. Here principle clashed with profound prejudice. We saw throughout this chapter that the rights of citizenship were systematically denied to Native Americans, to African Americans, and to women. The ideals of citizenship that were born during the founding are truly innovative and inspiring, but they were unavailable in practice to a major portion of the population for well over a hundred years. While it is conventional today to be appalled at the failure of the founders to practice the principles of equality they preached, and certainly that failure *is* appalling in light of today's values, we should remember that the whole project of citizenship was new to the founders and that in many ways they were far more democratic than any who had come before them. One of our tasks in this book will be to trace the evolving concept and practice of American citizenship, as the conferral of equal rights so majestically proclaimed in the Declaration slowly becomes reality for all Americans.

WHAT'S AT STAKE REVISITED

Having read the history of Revolutionary America, what would you say is at stake in the modern militia movement? The existence of state militias and similar groups poses a troubling dilemma for the federal government. On the one hand, the purpose of government is to protect our rights, and the Constitution surely guarantees Americans freedom of speech and assembly. On the other hand, government must hold the monopoly on the legitimate use of force in society or it will fall, just as the British government fell to the American colonies. If groups are allowed to amass weapons and forcibly resist or even attack U.S. law enforcers, then they constitute "mini-governments," or competing centers of authority, and life for citizens becomes chaotic and dangerous.

The American system was designed to be relatively responsive to the wishes of the American public. Citizens can get involved, they can vote, run for office, change the laws, and amend the Constitution. By permitting these legitimate ways of affecting American politics, the founders hoped to prevent the rise of such groups as the militia. They intended to create a society characterized by political stability, not by revolution, which is why Jefferson's Declaration of Independence is so careful to point out that revolutions should occur only when there is no alternative course of action.

Thinking Outside the Box

- Are there any circumstances in which it would be justifiable for groups in the United States to rebel against the federal government today?
- How would American politics be different today if we had retained the Articles of Confederation instead of adopting the Constitution?
- Would we have more freedoms today, or fewer, without the Bill of Rights?

Some militia members reject the idea of working through the system; they say, as did Timothy McVeigh, that they consider themselves at war with the federal government. We call disregard for the law at the individual level "crime," at the group level "terrorism" or "insurrection," and at the majority level "revolution." It is the job of any government worth its salt to prevent all three kinds of activities. Thus, it is not the existence or the beliefs but the *activities* of the militia groups that government seeks to control.

What is at stake in the state militia movement are the very issues of legitimate government authority and the rights of individual citizens. It is very difficult to draw the line between the protection of individual rights and the exercise of government authority. In a democracy, we want to respect the rights of all citizens, but this respect can be thwarted when a small number of individuals reject the rules of the game agreed on by the vast majority.

To Sum Up

KEY TERMS
republic.cqpress.com

Anti-Federalists (p. 89)
Articles of Confederation (p. 84)
Bill of Rights (p. 94)
"Common Sense" (p. 80)
confederation (p. 85)
constitution (p. 84)
Constitutional Convention (p. 87)
Declaration of Independence (p. 80)
factions (p. 93)
federalism (p. 89)
The Federalist Papers (p. 93)
Federalists (p. 89)
feudalism (p. 73)
French and Indian War (p. 78)
Great Compromise (p. 90)
New Jersey Plan (p. 90)
popular sovereignty (p. 79)
popular tyranny (p. 86)
Puritans (p. 74)
ratification (p. 92)
Shays's Rebellion (p. 86)
slavery (p. 76)
Three-fifths Compromise (p. 90)
Virginia Plan (p. 89)

Key terms, chapter summaries, practice quizzes, Internet links, and other study aids are available on the companion Web site at: republic.cqpress.com.

SUMMARY
republic.cqpress.com

- The politics of the American founding shaped the political compromises embodied in the Constitution. This in turn defines the institutions and many of the rules that do much to determine the winners and losers in political struggles today.
- The battle for America involved a number of different groups, including American Indians, the Spanish, the French, and the British colonists. The English settlers came for many reasons, including religious and economic, but then duplicated many of the politically restrictive practices in the colonies that they had sought to escape in England. These included restrictions on political participation and a narrow definition of citizenship.
- The Revolution was caused by many factors, including British attempts to get the colonies to pay for the costs of the wars fought to protect them.
- The pressures from the Crown for additional taxes coincided with new ideas about the proper role of government among colonial elites. These ideas are embodied in Jefferson's politically masterful writing of the Declaration of Independence.
- The government under the Articles of Confederation granted too much power to the states, which in a number of cases came to serve the interests of farmers and debtors. The Constitutional Convention was called to design a government with stronger centralized powers that would overcome the weaknesses elites perceived in the Articles.
- The new Constitution was derived from a number of key compromises: Federalism was set as a principle to allocate power to both the central government and the states; the Great Compromise allocated power in the new national legislature; and the Three-fifths Compromise provided a political solution to the problem of counting slaves in the southern states for purposes of representation in the House of Representatives.
- The politics of ratification of the Constitution provides a lesson in the marriage between practical politics and political principle. *The Federalist Papers* served as political propaganda to convince citizens to favor ratification, and they serve today as a record of the reasoning behind many of the elements of our Constitution.

PRACTICE QUIZ

republic.cqpress.com

1. Britain established its dominance over the colonies by

a. winning the French and Indian War.
b. winning the War of the Roses.
c. winning the Spanish-American War.
d. legal agreements such as the Mayflower Compact.
e. constant intimidation of the colonists.

2. The significance of *Common Sense* was that it

a. provided a persuasive argument for taxation without representation.
b. convinced the founders to eliminate property rights for voting.
c. articulated the idea that the British monarch was the legitimate ruler of the colonies.
d. convinced many people that revolution was necessary.
e. was the first document to argue that slavery had no place in the colonies.

3. The government created by the Articles of Confederation is described in this chapter as

a. the first grant of national power in the United States.
b. an association of states with a weak central government.
c. presidential government.
d. the "great American Parliament."
e. no more democratic than when the colonies were under British rule.

4. Which of the following was missing from the original draft of the Constitution?

a. A listing of the protections against government infringement of individual rights
b. National treaty power
c. A provision for the return of fugitive slaves
d. Power of the national government to coin money or levy taxes
e. Presidential veto power

5. According to this chapter, the politics of the American founding was

a. dominated solely by elites.
b. quite contentious, and the founders were rarely able to compromise.
c. influenced both by the views of competing elites and a new notion of citizenship.
d. unique because ordinary citizens played a leading role in creating the Constitution.
e. surprisingly not contentious, and little disagreement existed over the development of the new government.

SUGGESTED RESOURCES

republic.cqpress.com

Books

Bailyn, Bernard. 1967. *The Ideological Origins of the American Revolution.* Cambridge, Mass.: Belknap Press. An exceptionally detailed account of the pamphlets and other writings that convinced the thirteen colonies to revolt from Mother England.

Beard, Charles A. 1913. *An Economic Interpretation of the Constitution of the United States.* New York: Free Press. Beard argues that the framers of the Constitution were really more concerned about protecting their own interests than about guarding the strength of the nation.

Berkin, Carol. 2005. *Revolutionary Mothers: Women in the Struggle for America's Independence.* New York: Knopf. A thorough historical account of the many roles women played during the struggle for independence, from boycotting household goods produced by the British and managing farms to fundraising and inciting sentiments through propaganda.

Loewen, James W. 1995. *Lies My Teacher Told Me: Everything Your American History Textbook Got Wrong.* New York: New Press. A stimulating book even for those who find history boring; Loewen explains why some of what you read in your high school history class may have been just plain wrong!

McCullough, David. 2001. *John Adams.* New York: Simon & Schuster. A thorough and intimate portrait of the American patriot, a man not fond of politics who nonetheless played an integral role in the shaping of the American government.

Paine, Thomas. 1953. *Common Sense and Other Political Writings.* Indianapolis, Ind.: Bobbs-Merrill. Paine's writing may have been the most influential document in persuading the colonists to revolt against the English monarchy.

West, Thomas G. 1997. *Vindicating the Founders: Race, Sex, Class, and Justice in the Origins of America.* Lanham, Md.: Rowman & Littlefield. A provocative account of the beliefs of our founding fathers that refutes those who argue that our founders were really hypocrites who did not live by the words "all men are created equal."

Wood, Gordon S. 1998. *The Creation of the American Republic, 1776–1787.* Chapel Hill: University of North Carolina Press. The most comprehensive and respected source available on political thought during the early development of the United States.

Web Sites

American Memory. memory.loc.gov. The Library of Congress's American Memory collection is a gateway to numerous historical topics—such as African American, American Indian, and women's history; immigration; religion; maps; and more.

The Federalist Papers Online. www.mcs.net/~knautzr/fed/fedpaper.html. A guide to all of *The Federalist Papers,* with links to other important constitutional documents.

National Archives and Records Administration. www.archives.gov. See the original Declaration of Independence, the U.S. Constitution, the Bill of Rights, and countless other historical documents and records on this site.

National Constitution Center. www.constitutioncenter.org. The Web site for this center has educational resources, an interactive Constitution, a constitutional timeline, and other information on the historical context of this founding document.

Movies

***1776.* 1972.** A musical comedy about the signing of the Declaration of Independence.

***Liberty! The American Revolution.* 1998.** The acclaimed PBS documentary covers the political maneuverings of the American War for Independence in six episodes. Dramatic readings of historical letters and documents breathe life into this compelling series.

***The Patriot.* 2000.** Mel Gibson plays a veteran of the French and Indian War who reluctantly joins the fight for independence against the British in the Revolution after one son is killed and another is captured by the enemy.

Arnold Schwarzenegger was greeted with great enthusiasm at the 2004 Republican National Convention (right). Many in the GOP held out hope that the U.S. Constitution will be amended to allow a foreign-born citizen, such as Schwarzenegger, to become president. Others believe amendments should be considered only under extraordinary circumstances so that the U.S. Constitution does not bulk up like some state constitutions. Alabama currently leads the pack; its unwieldy constitution has more than 770 amendments.

FEDERALISM AND THE U.S. CONSTITUTION

4

WHAT'S AT STAKE?

The Terminator for president? Is this a joke? It's a little hard to tell, because in the "Amend for Arnold" campaign, everyone seems to be having a pretty good time. There is plenty of media glitz—web sites and commercials and television talk shows—and all the standard campaign paraphernalia like buttons and printed T-shirts. Prominent everywhere are the poised and cheerful advocates, the politician's familiar smiling face.

But the effort to make it possible for Arnold Schwarzenegger to run for president of the United States is a very serious business—it is all about altering that most fundamental of American political documents, the U.S. Constitution. The goal of the "Amend for Arnold" campaign is to change the provision in Article II of the Constitution that states

> No person except a natural-born citizen, or a citizen of the United States, at the time of the adoption of this Constitution, shall be eligible to the office of President; neither shall any person be eligible to that office who shall not have attained to the age of thirty-five years, and been fourteen years a resident within the United States.

Arnold Schwarzenegger was born in Austria and is a naturalized, not a natural-born American. In fact, he has kept his feet in both camps, retaining citizenship status in his native Austria alongside the U.S. citizenship he acquired in 1983. And therein lies the rub.

In more ways than most of us, Arnold Schwarzenegger is living the American dream. He has ridden hard work and good luck to the heights of success. He is an award-winning bodybuilder, a B-movie actor extraordinaire, and a millionaire who is married to Maria Shriver, a member of the famous Kennedy clan. In 2003, as part of an unusual recall election, he was able to bypass a grueling primary battle to step, seemingly effortlessly, into the California governor's mansion. But even though he may seem to have it all, Arnold can never dream the dream of young natural-born American children everywhere—because of Article II, he cannot grow up to be president.

Unless, that is, the "Amend for Arnold" movement is a success. The brainchild of California businesswoman Lissa Morgenthaler-Jones, "Amend for Arnold" is a nationwide campaign to support a constitutional amendment to allow naturalized citizens to become president if they have lived in this country for twenty years. Not only would Republicans like Schwarzenegger benefit from the amendment's passage but also Democrats like Michigan governor Jennifer Granholm, who was born in Canada.

Nonetheless, many observers see the amendment as part of a direct effort to make Schwarzenegger president and they hate it. In response to the "Amend for Arnold" campaign (amendforarnold.com), Austin-based radio host Alex Smith has launched a rival campaign, "Americans Against Arnold" (arnoldexposed.com), declaring that Schwarzenegger's personal history (including accusations of sexual harassment and statements of admiration for Hitler) make him unfit to be president.

The Arnold Amendment, introduced in the Senate in 2004 as the "Equal Right to Govern Amendment" by Schwarzenegger's friend Utah senator Orrin Hatch did not come up for a vote, but it will be reintroduced in both the Senate and the House in 2005. Other less Arnold-friendly versions of the amendment have been discussed—one putting the minimum length of citizenship at thirty-five years, one specifying that the law would not take effect for ten years from the point of ratification, and still another precluding a person (such as Arnold) who holds dual citizenship from becoming president.

Much of the substantive debate over changing the natural-born requirement for president focuses on two positions. On the one side are people who fear, as did the founders when they wrote the Constitution, that a person under foreign influence could be groomed to run for president and subvert the national interest, or that someone with divided loyalties could not always be trusted to support the United States. On the other side are those who argue that to exclude non–native-born Americans from the presidency is to discriminate against immigrants and to deny the country the opportunity to take advantage of a large pool of talent.

But others oppose the amendment not on its merits, because they dislike Arnold or believe that all presidents should be natural-born citizens, but because they are wary of altering the Constitution without great cause. Amending the Constitution, they say, should be approached with immense caution.

What is bothering this last group of people? Why the extra caution and wariness in the matter of changing this founding document? What is at stake in amending the Constitution of the United States? *

Imagine that you are playing Monopoly but you've lost the rule book. You and your friends decide to play anyway and make up the rules as you go along. Even though the game still looks like Monopoly, and you're using the Monopoly board, and the money, and the game pieces, and the little houses and hotels, if you aren't following the official Monopoly rules, you aren't really playing Monopoly.

In the same way, imagine that America becomes afflicted with a sort of collective amnesia so that all the provisions of the Constitution are forgotten. Or perhaps the whole country gets fed up with politics as usual in America and votes to replace our Constitution with, say, the French Constitution. Even if we kept all our old politicians, and the White House and the Capitol, and the streets of Washington, what went on there would no longer be recognizable as American politics. What is distinctive about any political system is not just the people or the buildings, but also the rules and the ideas that lie behind them and give them life and meaning.

In politics, as in games, rules are crucial. The rules set up the institutions and the procedures that are the heart of the political system, and these institutions and procedures help determine who the winners and losers in politics will be, what outcomes will result, and how resources will be distributed. Political rules are themselves the product of a political process, as we saw in Chapter 3. Rules do not drop from the sky, all written and ready to be implemented. Instead they are created by human beings, determined to establish procedures that will help them, and people like them, get what they want from the system. If you change the rules, you change the people who will be advantaged and disadvantaged by those rules.

The founders were not in agreement about the sorts of rules that should be the base of American government. Instead they were feeling their way, weighing historical experience against contemporary reality. They had to craft new rules to achieve their goal of a government whose authority comes from the people but whose power was limited so as to preserve the liberty of those people. The questions that consumed them may surprise us. We know about the debate over how much power should belong to the national government and how much to the states. But discussions ranged far beyond issues of federalism versus states' rights. How should laws be made, and by whom? Should the British Parliament be a model for the new legislature, with the

CALVIN AND HOBBES © 1990 Watterson. Dist. by UNIVERSAL PRESS SYNDICATE. Reprinted with permission. All rights reserved.

"lords" represented in one house and the "common people" in the other? Or should there even be two houses at all? What about the executive? Should it be a king, as in England? Should it be just one person, or should several people serve as executive at the same time? How much power should the executive have, and how should he or they be chosen? And what role would the courts play? How could all these institutions be designed so that no one could become powerful enough to destroy the others? How could the system change with the times and yet still provide for stable governance?

Their answers to those questions are contained in the official rule book for who gets what, and how, in America, which is of course the Constitution. In Chapter 3 we talked about the political forces that produced the Constitution, the preferences of various groups for certain rules, and the compromises these groups evolved to get the document passed. In this chapter we look at the Constitution from the inside. Since rules are so important in producing certain kinds of outcomes in the political system, it is essential that we understand not only what the rules provide for, but also what the choice of those rules means, what other kinds of rules exist that the founders did *not* choose, and what outcomes the founders rejected by not choosing those alternative rules.

Scholars spend whole lifetimes studying the Constitution. We can't achieve their level of detail here, but fortunately we don't need to. To familiarize you with some key issues that all constitution builders have to deal with, in this chapter you will learn about

- what institutions the founders created to perform the three main tasks of governing: making the laws, executing the laws, and adjudicating the laws
- the constitutional relationship among those institutions
- how the founders resolved constitutionally the issue of relations between regional units (states, in our case) and national government
- the flexibility the founders built into the Constitution to change with the times

The best way to understand these issues is to look at the founders' concerns, the constitutional provisions they established, the alternatives they might have chosen, and how their choice affects who gets what, and how, in American politics.

THE THREE BRANCHES OF GOVERNMENT

All governments must have the power to do three things: (1) legislate, or make the laws; (2) administer, or execute the laws; and (3) adjudicate, or interpret the laws. The kinds of institutions they create to manage those powers vary widely. Because of our system of separation of powers, which we discuss later in this chapter, separate branches of government handle the legislative, executive, and judicial powers. Article I of the Constitution sets up Congress, our legislature; Article II establishes the presidency, our executive; and Article III outlines the federal court system, our judiciary.

THE LEGISLATIVE BRANCH

Legislative power is lawmaking power. Laws can be created by a single ruler or by a political party, they can be divined from natural or religious principles, or they can be made by the citizens who will have to obey the laws or by representatives working on their behalf. Most countries that claim to be democratic choose the last method of lawmaking. The body of government that makes laws is called the **legislature**. Legislatures themselves can be set up in different ways: they can have one or two chambers, or houses; members can be elected, appointed, or hereditary; and if elected, they can be chosen by the people directly or by some other body. A variety of electoral rules can apply. The U.S. Congress is a **bicameral legislature**, meaning there are two chambers, and the legislators are elected directly by the people for terms of two or six years, depending on the house.

legislature the body of government that makes laws

bicameral legislature legislature with two chambers

The Case for Representation In *Federalist* No. 10, James Madison argued that American laws should be made by representatives of the people rather than by the people themselves. He rejected what he called "pure democracies," small political systems in which the citizens make and administer their own laws. Instead Madison recommended a **republic**, a system in which a larger number of citizens delegate, or assign, the tasks of governing to a smaller body. A republic claims two advantages: the dangers of factions are reduced, and the people running the government are presumably the best equipped to do so. Representation, said Madison, helps to "refine and enlarge the public views by passing them through the medium of a chosen body of citizens," distinguished by their wisdom, patriotism, and love of justice.[1]

republic a government in which decisions are made through representatives of the people

Of course, Americans were already long accustomed to the idea of representation. All the states had legislatures. The Articles of Confederation had provided for representation as well, and even Britain had representation of a sort in Parliament.

What Does the Constitution Say? Article I sets out the framework of the legislative branch of government. Since the founders expected the legislature to be the most important part of the new government, they spent the most time specifying its composition, the qualifications for membership, its powers, and its limitations.

The best known part of Article I is the famous Section 8, which spells out the specific powers of Congress (Table 4.1). This list is followed by the provision that Congress can do anything "necessary and proper" to carry out its duties. The Supreme Court has interpreted this clause so broadly that there are few effective restrictions on what Congress can do.

The House of Representatives, where representation is based on population, was intended to be truly the representative of all the people, the "voice of the common man," as it were. To be elected to the House, a candidate need be only twenty-five years old and a citizen for seven years. Since House terms last two years, members run for reelection often and can be ousted fairly easily, according to public whim. The founders intended this office to be accessible to and easily influenced by citizens and to reflect frequent changes in public opinion.

The Senate is another matter. Candidates have to be at least thirty years old and citizens for nine years—older, wiser, and, the founders hoped, more stable than the representatives in the House. Because senatorial terms last for six years, senators are not so easily swayed by changes in public sentiment. In addition, senators were originally elected not directly by the people, but by members of their state legislatures. Election by state legislators, themselves already a "refinement" of the general public, would ensure that senators were a higher caliber of citizen: more in tune with "the commercial and monied interest," as

TABLE 4.1
Powers of Congress

PART OF CONSTITUTION	POWERS
Article I, Section 8	Collect taxes
	Regulate commerce
	Coin and regulate money
	Establish post offices/roads
	Declare war
	Raise and manage armed services
	Make laws

Massachusetts delegate Elbridge Gerry put it at the Constitutional Convention.[2] The Senate would thus be a more aristocratic body, that is, it would look more like the British House of Lords, where members are admitted on the basis of their birth or achievement, not by election.

Possible Alternatives: A Unicameral Legislature? The Congress we have is not the only Congress the founders could have given us. Instead of establishing the House of Representatives and the Senate, for instance, they could have established one legislative chamber only, what we call a **unicameral legislature**. Many countries today have unicameral legislatures—Malta, New Zealand, Denmark, Sweden, Spain, Israel, North Korea, Kuwait, Syria, Malawi, and Cameroon, to name a few. And while most of the fifty United States have followed the national example with bicameral state legislatures, Nebraska has chosen a unicameral, nonpartisan legislature.

unicameral legislature a legislature with one chamber

Proponents of such institutions claim that lawmaking is faster and more efficient when laws are debated and voted on in only one chamber. They say such laws are also more responsive to changes in public opinion, which at least theoretically is a good thing in a democracy.

On the national level, a unicameral system can help encourage citizens to feel a sense of identity with their government, since it implies that the whole country shares the same fundamental interests and can thus be represented by a single body. Originally in Europe, governments had different legislative chambers to represent different social classes or estates in society. We can see the remnants of this system in the British Parliament, whose upper chamber is called the House of Lords, and lower, the House of Commons, or the common people. The French once had five houses in their legislature, and the Swedish four. As countries become more democratic, that is, as their governments become more representative of the people as a whole and not of social classes, the legislatures become more streamlined. Sweden eventually moved to two legislative houses, and in 1971 it adopted a unicameral legislature. France now has two. Britain still has the Lords and the Commons, but increasing democratization has

It Just Keeps Going . . . and Going . . .
Speaker of the House Dennis Hastert, at the podium, administers the oath to members at the opening of the 109th Congress in 2005. The U.S. Congress is the oldest democratic legislative body in the world, still fulfilling the functions originally spelled out by the Constitution. For more than 215 years this document has shaped the rules by which American politics operate.

meant less legislative power for the House of Lords, which now can only delay, not block, laws made by the House of Commons.[3] In that sense, the fewer chambers a legislature has, the more representative it is of the people as a whole.

A unicameral system has several clear disadvantages, however. For one thing, such a system makes it difficult for the legislature to represent more than one set of interests. Although the United States did not have the feudal history of Europe, with its remnants of nobility and commons, it was still a country with frequently conflicting economic interests, as politics under the Articles of Confederation had made painfully evident. Our founders preferred bicameralism in part because the two houses could represent different interests in society—the people's interests in the House and the more elite interests in the Senate.

In addition to providing for representation of different interests, another advantage of a bicameral legislature was its ability to represent the different levels of the federal government in the legislative process. Typically, federal governments that preserve a bicameral structure do so with the intention of having the "people" represented in one house and the individual regions, in our case the states, in another. In the United States, representation in the House is based on the state's population, and representation in the Senate is based simply on statehood, with each state getting two votes. The fact that the senators used to be elected by the state legislatures reinforces the *federal* aspect of this arrangement. In the German *Bundesrat,* the members are chosen by the governments of each state.

A final reason the founders were convinced that bicameralism was better for the young republic than unicameralism is that they believed the more they divided the power of government into smaller units, the safer the government would be from those who would abuse its power. Two legislative chambers would keep a watch over each other and check their tendencies to get out of hand. The quick legislative responsiveness of a unicameral legislature can have some drawbacks. Changes in public opinion are often only temporary, and perhaps a society in a calmer moment would not want the laws to be changed so hastily. Rapid-response lawmaking can also result in excessive amounts of legislation, creating a legal system that confuses and baffles the citizenry. When asked by Thomas Jefferson, who had been in France during the Constitutional Convention, why the delegates had adopted a bicameral legislature, George Washington explained that just as one would pour one's coffee into the saucer to cool it off (a common practice of the day), "we pour legislation into the senatorial saucer to cool it." As Professor Richard Fenno points out, legislation has as often been cooled by pouring it into the House of Representatives. Each chamber has served to cool the passions of the other; this requirement that laws be passed twice has helped keep the American legislature in check.[4]

THE EXECUTIVE BRANCH

The **executive** is the part of government that "executes" the laws, or sees they are carried out. Although technically executives serve in an administrative role, many end up with some decision-making or legislative power as well. National executives are the leaders of their countries, and they participate, with varying amounts of power, in making laws and policies. That role can range from the U.S. president, who, while not a part of the legislature itself, can propose, encourage, and veto legislation, to European prime ministers, who are part of the legislature and may have, as in the British case, the power to dissolve the entire legislature and call a new election.

executive the branch of government responsible for putting laws into effect

Fears of the Founders That the Articles of Confederation provided for no executive power at all was a testimony to the founders' conviction that such a power threatened their liberty. The chaos that resulted under the Articles, however, made it clear that a stronger government was called for—not only a stronger legislature but a stronger executive as well. The constitutional debates reveal that many of the founders were haunted by the idea that they might inadvertently reestablish that same tyrannical power over themselves that they had escaped only recently with the Revolution. The central controversies focused on whether the executive should be more than one person, whether he should be able to seek reelection as many times as he wanted, and whether he should be elected directly by the people or indirectly by the legislature.

The founders were divided. On one side were those like Alexander Hamilton who insisted that only a vigorous executive could provide the stability necessary to preserve liberty. Hamilton recommended an executive appointed for life so that he would be independent of the political process. Others, like Edmund Randolph of Virginia, were unwilling to entertain the notion of a single executive, let alone one chosen for life. Randolph proposed instead three executives, representing various regions of the country, as a safer repository of power.[5]

Those fearing a strong executive believed its power could be limited by dividing it among several officeholders, but they eventually lost to those who believed there should be a single president. The issue of whether the executive should be allowed to run for reelection for an unlimited number of terms got tangled up with the question of just how the president was to be elected. If, as some founders argued, he were chosen by Congress rather than by the people, then he should be limited to one term. Since he would be dependent on Congress for his power, he might fail to provide an adequate check on that body, perhaps currying favor with Congress in order to be chosen for additional terms.

On the other hand, the founders had no great trust in "the people," as we have seen, so popular election of the president was considered highly suspect, even though it would free the executive from dependence on Congress and allow him to be elected for multiple terms. Alexander Hamilton wanted to go so far as to have the president serve for life, thereby eliminating the problem of being dependent on Congress *or* on the popular will.

That these diverse ideas were resolved and consensus was achieved is one of the marvels of the American founding. The final provision of presidential authority was neither as powerful as Hamilton's kinglike lifetime executive nor as constrained as Randolph's multiple executive. Still it was a much stronger office than many of the founders, particularly the Anti-Federalists, wanted.

What Does the Constitution Say? The solution finally chosen by the founders is a complicated one, but it satisfies all the concerns raised at the convention. The president, a single executive, would serve an unlimited number of four-year terms. (A constitutional amendment in 1951 limited the president to two elected terms.) But in addition, the president would be chosen neither by Congress nor directly by the people. Instead the Constitution provides for his selection by an intermediary body called the **electoral college**. Citizens vote not for the presidential candidates, but for a slate of electors, who cast their votes for the candidates about six weeks after the general election. The founders believed that this procedure would ensure a president elected by well-informed delegates who, having no other lawmaking power, could not be bribed

electoral college an intermediary body that elects the president or otherwise influenced by candidates. We will say more about how this process works in Chapter 14, on elections.

Article II of the Constitution establishes the executive. The four sections of that article make the following provisions:

- Section 1 sets out the four-year term and the manner of election (that is, the details of the electoral college). It also provides for the qualifications for office: that the president must be a natural-born citizen of the United States, at least thirty-five years old, and a resident of the United States for at least fourteen years. The vice president serves if the president cannot, and Congress can make laws about the succession if the vice president is incapacitated.
- Section 2 establishes the powers of the chief executive. He is commander-in-chief of the armed forces and of the state militias when they are serving the nation, and he has the power to grant pardons for offenses against the United States. With the advice and consent of two-thirds of the Senate, the president can make treaties, and with a simple majority vote of the Senate the president can appoint ambassadors, ministers, consuls, Supreme Court justices, and other U.S. officials whose appointments are not otherwise provided for.
- Section 3 says that the president will periodically tell Congress how the country is doing (the State of the Union address given every January) and will propose to them those measures he thinks appropriate and necessary. Under extraordinary circumstances the president calls Congress into session or, if the two houses of Congress cannot agree on when to end their sessions, may adjourn them. The president also receives ambassadors and public officials, executes the laws, and commissions all officers of the United States.
- Section 4 specifies that the president, vice president, and other civil officers of the United States (such as Supreme Court justices) can be impeached, tried, and convicted for "treason, bribery, or other high crimes and misdemeanors."

Possible Alternatives: A Parliamentary System? As the debates over the American executive clearly show, many options were open to the founders as they designed the executive office. They chose what is referred to today as a **presidential system**, in which a leader is chosen independently of the legislature to serve a fixed term of office that is unaffected by the success or failure of the legislature. The principal alternative to a presidential system among contemporary democracies is called a **parliamentary system**, in which the executive is a member of the legislature, chosen by the legislators themselves, not by a separate national election. When the founders briefly considered the consequences of having a president chosen by Congress, they were discussing something like a parliamentary system. The fundamental difference between a parliamentary system and a presidential system is that in the former the legislature and the executive are merged, but in the latter they are separate. In parliamentary systems the executive is accountable to the legislature, but in a presidential system he or she is independent.

presidential system
government in which the executive is chosen independently of the legislature and the two branches are separate

parliamentary system
government in which the executive is chosen by the legislature from among its members and the two branches are merged

Generally speaking, the executive or prime minister in a parliamentary system is the chosen leader of the majority party in the legislature. This would be roughly equivalent to allowing the majority party in the House of Representatives to install its leader, the Speaker of the House, as the national executive. What is striking about the parliamentary system is that most of the citizens of the country never vote for the

No Diplomatic Immunity from Scrutiny
The U.S. Constitution spells out the president's power to appoint officials to a number of posts, but the Senate has to approve the nominees. President Bush nominated John Bolton to be the U.S. ambassador to the United Nations in 2005, but Senate Democrats, questioning Bolton's commitment to the mission of the U.N. and his temperament, blocked his confirmation. When Congress adjourned, Bush used what is called a recess appointment to appoint Bolton. The recess appointment enabled Bush to circumvent the Senate, but it expires at the end of the current Congress, in January 2007.

national leader. Only members of the prime minister's legislative district actually cast a vote for him or her. If the parliament does not think the prime minister is doing a good job, it can replace him or her without consulting the voters of the country.

This process is very different from the American provision for impeachment of the president for criminal activity. Parliaments can remove executives for reasons of political or ideological disagreement. Although there may be political disagreement over the grounds for impeachment in the American case, as there was in the impeachment of President Bill Clinton, there must be at least an allegation of criminal activity, which need not exist for removal in a parliamentary system. (If the United States had a parliamentary system, then a legislative vote of "no confidence" could have ousted the president at the beginning of the process.) Consequently the executive in a parliamentary system is dependent on the legislature and cannot provide any effective check if the legislature abuses its power. In Germany's parliamentary government, an independent court can restrain the legislature and keep it within the bounds of the constitution, but the British system has no check at all. The upper house of Parliament, the House of Lords, is the highest court and even it cannot declare an act of the House of Commons unconstitutional. The French system is a curious hybrid. It is parliamentary since the prime minister is chosen from the majority party in the legislature, but there is *also* a strong president who is independent of the legislature. Because the French split the executive functions, there is an executive check on the legislature, even though it is a parliamentary system.

Politics in a parliamentary system is very different than it is in a presidential system. Leadership is clearly more concentrated. Because the prime minister usually chooses his or her cabinet from the legislature, the executive and legislative truly overlap. It is much easier for a prime minister to get his or her programs and laws passed by the legislature because, under normal circumstances, he or she already has the party votes to pass them. If the party has a serious loss of faith or "confidence" in the prime minister, it can force the prime minister out of office. Thus the prime minister has a strong incentive to cooperate with the legislature. In some cases, like the British, the prime minister has some countervailing clout of his or her own. The British prime minister has the power to call parliamentary elections at will within a five-year period and consequently can jeopardize the jobs of members of parliament, or at least threaten to do so. This does not necessarily result in more frequent elections in Britain than in the United States with its fixed elections (from 1900 to 2004 Britain held twenty-seven general elections to the United States's twenty-four), but it does mean the prime minister can time the elections to take place when the party's fortunes are high. One result of this close relationship between executive and legislative is that the ties of political party membership seem to be stronger in a parliamentary system, in which a party's domination of national politics depends on block voting along party lines. As we will see in Chapter 12, *party discipline,* as this is called, is much reduced in the U.S. system.

THE JUDICIAL BRANCH

Judicial power is the power to interpret the laws and to judge whether the laws have been broken. Naturally, by establishing how a given law is to be understood, the courts (the agents of judicial power) end up making law as well. Our constitutional provisions for the establishment of the judiciary are brief and vague; much of the American federal judiciary under the Supreme Court is left to Congress to arrange. But the founders left plenty of clues as to how they felt about judicial power in their debates and their writings, particularly in *The Federalist Papers.*

judicial power the power to interpret laws and judge whether a law has been broken

The "Least Dangerous" Branch In *Federalist* No. 78, Hamilton made clear his view that the judiciary was the least threatening branch of power. The executive and the legislature might endanger liberty, but not so the judiciary. Hamilton said that as long as government functions are separate from one another (that is, as long as the judiciary is not part of the executive or the legislature) then the judiciary "will always be the least dangerous to the political rights of the Constitution; because it has the least capacity to annoy or injure them." The executive "holds the sword," and the legislature "commands the purse." The judiciary, controlling neither sword nor purse, neither "strength nor wealth of the society," has neither "FORCE nor WILL but merely judgment." [6]

Although the founders were not particularly worried, then, that the judiciary would be too powerful, they did want to be sure it would not be too political—that is, caught up in the fray of competing interests and influence. The only federal court they discussed in much detail was the Supreme Court, but the justices of that Court were to be appointed for life, provided they maintain "good behavior," in part to preserve them from politics. Once appointed they need not be concerned with seeking the favor of the legislature, the executive, or the people. Instead of trying to do what is popular, they can concentrate on doing what is just, or constitutional.

Even though the founders wanted to keep the Court out of politics, they did make it possible for the justices to get involved when they considered it necessary. The practice of judicial review is introduced through the back door, first mentioned by Hamilton in *Federalist* No. 78 and then institutionalized by the Supreme Court itself, with Chief Justice John Marshall's 1803 ruling in *Marbury v. Madison,* a dispute over presidential appointments. **Judicial review** allows the Supreme Court to rule that an act of Congress or the executive branch (or of a state or local government) is unconstitutional, that is, that it runs afoul of constitutional principles. This review process is not an automatic part of lawmaking; the Court does not examine every law that Congress passes or every executive order to be sure that it does not violate the Constitution. Rather, if a law is challenged as unconstitutional by an individual or group, and if it is appealed all the way to the Supreme Court, then the justices may decide to rule on it.

judicial review power of the Supreme Court to rule on the constitutionality of laws

This remarkable grant of power to the "least dangerous" branch to nullify legislation is *not* itself in the Constitution. In *Federalist* No. 78, Hamilton argued that it was consistent with the Constitution, however. In response to critics who objected that such a practice would place the unelected Court in a superior position to the elected representatives of the people, Hamilton wrote that, on the contrary, it raised the people, as authors of the Constitution, over the government as a whole. Thus, judicial review enhanced democracy rather than diminished it.

In 1803 Marshall agreed. As the nation's highest law, the Constitution set the limits on what is acceptable legislation. As the interpreter of the Constitution, it is the

Supreme Court's duty to determine when laws fall outside those limits. Interestingly, this gigantic grant of power to the Court was made by the Court itself and remains unchallenged by the other branches. The irony is that the sort of empire-building the founders hoped to avoid appears in the branch they took the least care to safeguard. We return to *Marbury v. Madison* and judicial review in Chapter 10, on the court system.

What Does the Constitution Say? Article III of the Constitution is very short. It says that the judicial power of the United States is to be "vested in one Supreme Court, and in such inferior courts as the Congress may from time to time ordain and establish," and that judges serve as long as they demonstrate "good behavior." It also explains that the Supreme Court has original jurisdiction in some types of cases and appellate jurisdiction in others. That is, in some cases the Supreme Court is the only Court that can rule; much more often, inferior courts try cases, but their rulings can be appealed to the Supreme Court. Article III provides for jury trials in all criminal cases except impeachment, and it defines the practice of and punishment for acts of treason. Because the Constitution is so silent on the role of the courts in America, that role has been left to be defined by Congress and, in some cases, by the courts themselves.

legislative supremacy an alternative to judicial review, the acceptance of legislative acts as the final law of the land

Possible Alternatives: Legislative Supremacy? Clearly one alternative to judicial review is to allow the legislature's laws to stand unchallenged. This system of **legislative supremacy** underlies British politics. The British have no written constitution. Acts of Parliament are the final law of the land and cannot be reviewed or struck down by the courts. They become part of the general collection of acts, laws, traditions, and court cases that make up the British "unwritten constitution." Our Court is thus more powerful, and our legislature correspondingly less powerful, than the same institutions in the British system. We are accustomed to believing that judicial review is an important limitation on Congress and a protection of individual liberty. Britain is not remarkably behind the United States, however, in terms of either legislative tyranny or human rights. Think about how much difference judicial review really makes, especially if you consider the experience of a country like Japan, where judicial review usually results in upholding government behavior *over* individual rights and liberties.[7]

Yet another alternative to our system would be to give judicial review *more* teeth. The German Constitutional Court also reviews legislation to determine if it fits with the German Basic Law, but it does not need to wait for cases to come to it on appeal. National and state executives, the lower house of the legislature (the *Bundestag*), or even citizens can ask the German high court to determine whether a law is constitutional. Like the U.S. Supreme Court, the Constitutional Court is flooded with far more cases than it can accept and must pick and choose the issues on which it will rule.

WHO, WHAT, HOW The founders' goal was to devise a legislature, an executive, and a judiciary that would correct the flaws of the Articles of Confederation while balancing the rights and powers of citizens against the need for the government to be secure from abuse and corruption. The means they employed were unusual—they had the unique opportunity to write the rule book, the Constitution, from scratch, constrained only by the necessity of gaining the approval of sufficient states to allow the Constitution to be ratified and thus seen as legitimate.

SEPARATION OF POWERS AND CHECKS AND BALANCES

separation of powers the institutional arrangement that assigns judicial, executive, and legislative powers to different persons or groups, thereby limiting the powers of each

Separation of powers means that the legislature, the executive, and the judicial powers are not exercised by the same person or group of people, lest they abuse the considerable amount of power they hold. We are indebted to the French Enlightenment philosopher the Baron de Montesquieu for explaining this notion. In his massive book *The Spirit of the Laws,* Montesquieu wrote that liberty could be threatened only if the same group who enacted tyrannical laws also executed them. He said, "There would be an end of everything, were the same man or the same body, whether of nobles or of the people, to exercise those three powers, that of enacting laws, that of executing the public resolutions, and of trying the causes of individuals."[8] Putting all political power into one set of hands is like putting all our eggs in one basket. If the person or body of people entrusted with all the power becomes corrupt or dictatorial, the whole system will go bad. If, on the other hand, power is divided so that each branch is in separate hands, one may go bad while leaving the other two intact. The principle of separation of powers gives each of the branches authority over its own domain.

checks and balances the principle that allows each branch of government to exercise some form of control over the others

A complementary principle, **checks and balances**, allows each of the branches to police the others, checking any abuses and balancing the powers of government. The purpose of this additional authority is to ensure that no branch can exercise power tyrannically. In our case, the president can veto an act of Congress, Congress can override a veto, the Supreme Court can declare a law of Congress unconstitutional, Congress can, with the help of the states, amend the Constitution itself, and so on. Figure 4.1 illustrates these relationships.

REPUBLICAN REMEDIES

In *Federalist* No. 51, James Madison wrote, "If men were angels, no government would be necessary. If angels were to govern men, neither external nor internal controls on government would be necessary."[9] Alas, we are not angels, nor are we governed by angels. Since human nature is flawed and humans are sometimes ambitious, greedy, and corruptible, precautions must be taken to create a government that will make use of human nature, not be destroyed by it. A republic, which offers so many opportunities to so many people to take advantage of political power, requires special controls; the job, according to Madison, was to find a "republican remedy for those diseases most incident to republican government."[10] He said, "In framing a government which is to be administered by men over men, the great difficulty is this: you must first enable the government to control the governed; and in the next place oblige it to control itself."[11] The founders used separation of powers and checks and balances to oblige government to control itself, to impose internal limitations on government power in order to safeguard the liberty of the people.

The founders were generally supportive of separation of powers, some form of which appeared in all the state governments. Not so readily accepted was the notion of checks and balances, that once power was separated, it should be somehow shared. Having carefully kept the executive from taking on a legislative role, the founders were reluctant, for example, to give the president veto power.

In *Federalist* No. 47, Madison explained the relationship of separation of powers to checks and balances. Rather than damaging the protection offered by separation of

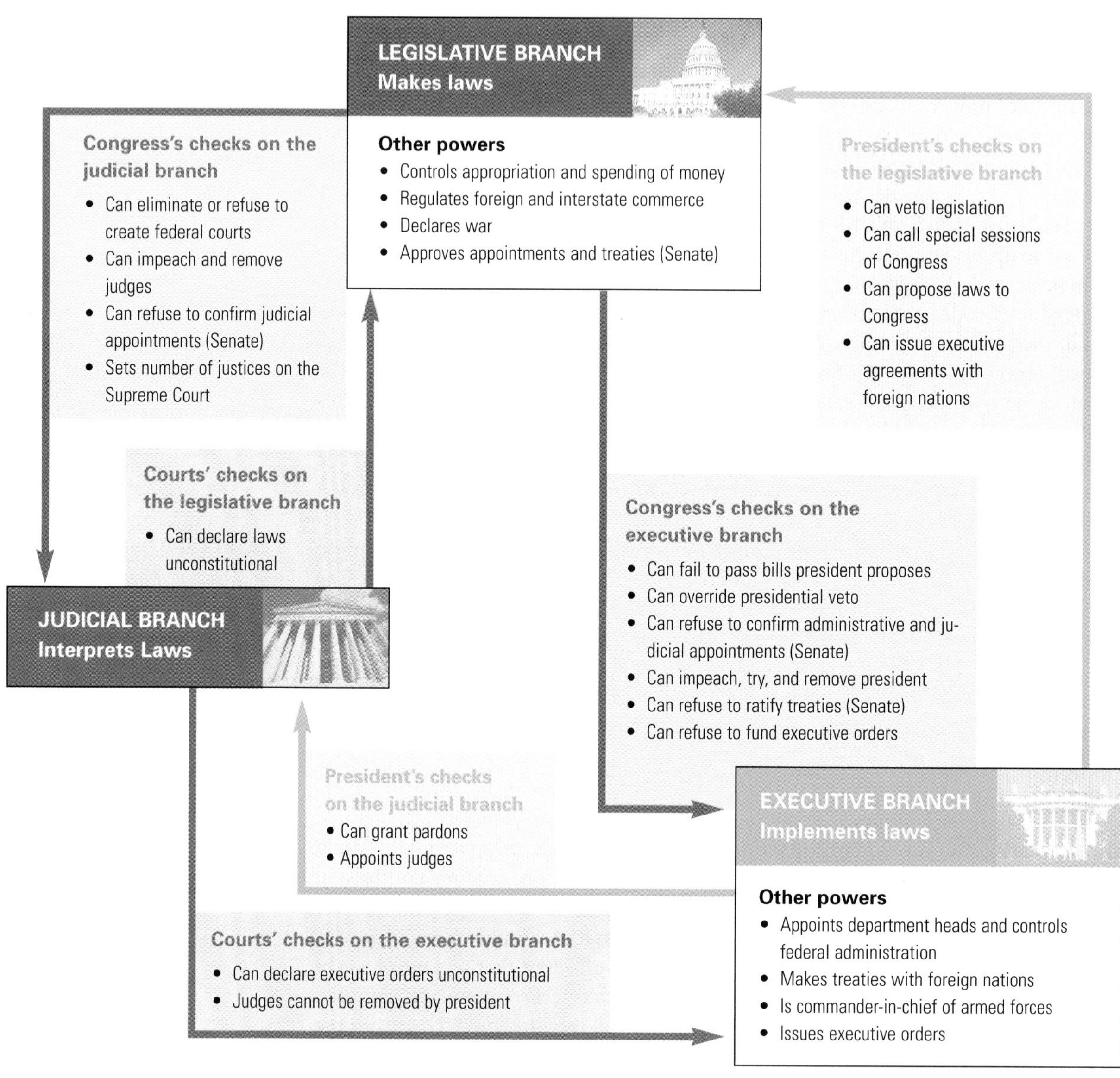

FIGURE 4.1
Separation of Powers and Checks and Balances

powers, sharing some control over each branch reinforced security because no branch could wield its power without some check. The trick was to give people in each branch an interest in controlling the behavior of the others. This is how human nature, flawed though it might be, could be used to limit the abuses of power. As Madison put it, in *Federalist* No. 51: "Ambition must be made to counteract ambition." [12] Thus, there was no danger in sharing some control over the branches because jealous humans would always be looking over their shoulders for potential abuses.

WHAT DOES THE CONSTITUTION SAY?

The Constitution establishes separation of powers with articles setting up a different institution for each branch of government. We have already examined Article I, establishing Congress as the legislature; Article II, establishing the president as the executive; and Article III, outlining the court system. Checks and balances are provided by clauses within each of those articles.

- Article I sets up a bicameral legislature. Because both houses must agree on all legislation, each can check the other. Article I also describes the presidential veto, with which the president can check Congress, and the override provision, by which two-thirds of Congress can check the president. Congress can also use impeachment to check abuses of the executive or judicial branch.
- Article II empowers the president to execute the laws and to share some legislative function by "recommending laws." He has some checks on the judiciary through his power to appoint judges, but his appointment power is checked by the requirement that a majority of the Senate must confirm his choices. The president can also check the judiciary by granting pardons. The president is commander-in-chief of the armed forces, but his ability to exercise his authority is checked by the Article I provision that only Congress can declare war.
- Article III creates the Supreme Court. The Court's ruling in the case of *Marbury v. Madison* fills in some of the gaps in this vague article by establishing judicial review, a true check on the legislative and executive branches. The Congress can countercheck judicial review by amending the Constitution (with the help of the states).

The Constitution wisely ensures that no branch of the government can act independently of the others, yet none is wholly dependent on the others either. This approach results in a structure of separation of powers and checks and balances that is distinctively American.

POSSIBLE ALTERNATIVES: FUSION OF POWERS?

An alternative way to deal with the different branches of government is to fuse rather than separate them. We have already discussed what this might look like when we compared a parliamentary system with a presidential system. A parliamentary system involves a clear **fusion of powers**. Because the components of government are not separate, no formal internal checks can curb the use of power. That is not to say that the flaws in human nature might not still encourage members of the government to keep a jealous eye on one another, but no deliberate mechanism exists to bring these checks into being. In a democracy, external checks may still be provided by the people, through either the ballet box or public opinion polls. Where the government is not freely and popularly elected, or, more rarely these days, when all the components are fused into a single monarch, even the checks of popular control are missing.

fusion of powers an alternative to separation of powers, combining or blending branches of government

WHO, WHAT, HOW The founders wanted, for themselves and the public, a government that would not succumb to the worst of human nature. The viability and stability of the American system would be jeopardized if they could not find a way to tame the jealousy, greed, and ambition that might threaten the new republic. The remedy they chose to preserve the American Constitution from its own leaders and citizens is the set of rules called separation of powers and checks and balances. Whether the founders were right or wrong about human nature, the principles of government they established have been remarkably effective at guaranteeing the long-term survival of the American system.

FEDERALISM

Federalism, as we said in Chapter 3, is a political system in which authority is divided between different levels of government. In the United States, federalism refers to the relationship between the national government (also frequently, but confusingly, called the *federal* government) and the states. Each level has some power independent of the other levels so that no level is entirely dependent on another for its existence. For the founders, federalism was a compromise in the bitter dispute between those who wanted stronger state governments and those who preferred a stronger national government. Both sides knew that the rules dividing power between the states and the federal government were crucial to determining who would be the winners and losers in the new country.

Today the effects of federalism are all around us. We pay income taxes to the national government, which parcels out the money to the states, under certain conditions, to be spent on programs such as welfare, highways, and education. In most states, local schools are funded by local property taxes and run by local school boards (local governments are created under the authority of the state), and state universities are supported by state taxes and influenced by the state legislatures. Even so, both state and local governments are subject to national legislation, such as the requirement that schools be open to students of all races, and both can be affected by national decisions about funding various programs. Sometimes the lines of responsibility can be extremely unclear. Witness the simultaneous presence in many areas of city police, county police, state police, and, at the national level, the Federal Bureau of Investigation (FBI), all coordinated, for some purposes, by the national Department of Homeland Security.

Even when a given responsibility lies at the state level, the national government frequently finds a way to enforce its will. For instance, it is up to the states to decide on the minimum drinking age for their citizens. In the 1970s, many states required people to be only eighteen or nineteen before they could legally buy alcohol; today all the states have a uniform drinking age of twenty-one. The change came about because interest groups persuaded officials in the federal, that is national, government that the higher age would lead to fewer alcohol-related highway accidents and greater public safety. The federal government couldn't pass a law setting a nationwide drinking age of twenty-one, but it could control the flow of highway money to the states. By withholding 5 percent of federal highway funds, which every state wants and needs, until a state raised the drinking age to twenty-one, Congress prevailed. Similar congressional pressure led states to lower the legal standard for drunk driving to a 0.08 percent blood alcohol level by the fall of 2003.[13] These examples show how the relations between levels of government work when neither level can directly force the other to do what it wants.

WHAT DOES THE CONSTITUTION SAY?

No single section of the Constitution deals with federalism. Instead the provisions dividing up power between the states and the national government appear throughout the Constitution. Local government is not mentioned in the Constitution at all, because it is completely under the jurisdiction of the states. Most of the Constitution is concerned with establishing the powers of the national government. Since Congress is the main lawmaking arm of the national government, many of the powers of the national government are the powers of Congress. The strongest statement of national power is a list of the **enumerated powers of Congress** (Article I, Section 8). This list is followed by a clause that gives Congress the power to make all laws that are "necessary and proper" to carry out its powers. The **necessary and proper clause** (also called the "elastic clause" because the Supreme Court has interpreted it broadly) has been used to justify giving Congress many powers never mentioned in the Constitution. National power is also based on the **supremacy clause** of Article VI, which says that the Constitution and laws made in accordance with it are "the supreme law of the land." This means that when national and state laws conflict, the national laws will be followed. The Constitution also sets some limitations on the national government. Article I, Section 9, lists some specific powers not granted to Congress, and the Bill of Rights (the first ten amendments to the Constitution) limits the power of the national government over individuals.

enumerated powers of Congress congressional powers specifically named in the Constitution (Article 1, Section 8)

necessary and proper clause constitutional authorization for Congress to make any law required to carry out its powers

supremacy clause constitutional declaration (Article VI) that the Constitution and laws made under its provisions are the supreme law of the land

The Constitution says considerably less about the powers granted to the states. The Tenth Amendment says that all powers not given to the national government are reserved for the states, although, as we will soon see, the Court's interpretation of the necessary and proper clause as elastic makes it difficult to see which powers are withheld from the national government. The states are given the power to approve the Constitution itself and any amendments to it. The Constitution also limits state powers. Article I, Section 10, denies the states certain powers, mostly the kinds they possessed under the Articles of Confederation. The Fourteenth Amendment limits the power of the states over individual liberties, essentially a Bill of Rights that protects individuals from state action, since the first ten amendments apply only to the national government.

What these constitutional provisions mean is that the line between the national government and the state governments is not clearly drawn. We can see from Figure 4.2 that the Constitution designates specific powers as national, state, or concurrent. **Concurrent powers** are those that both levels of government may exercise. But the federal relationship is a good deal more complex than this figure would lead us to believe. The Supreme Court has become crucial to establishing the exact limits of such provisions as the necessary and proper clause, the supremacy clause, the Tenth Amendment, and the Fourteenth Amendment. Its interpretation has changed over time, especially as historical demands have forced the Court to think about federalism in new ways.

concurrent powers powers that are shared by both the federal and state governments

TWO VIEWS OF FEDERALISM

Political scientists have also changed the way they think about federalism. For many years the prevailing theory was known as **dual federalism**, basically arguing that the relationship between the two levels of government was like a layer cake. That is, the national and state governments were to be understood as two self-contained layers,

dual federalism the federal system under which the national and state governments were responsible for separate policy areas

NATIONAL POWERS	CONCURRENT POWERS	STATE POWERS
• Admit new states into the Union • Coin money • Conduct foreign affairs • Declare war • Establish courts inferior to the Supreme Court • Make laws that are necessary for carrying out the powers vested by the Constitution • Raise and maintain armies, navies • Regulate commerce with foreign nations and among the states	• Borrow and spend money for the general welfare • Charter and regulate banks; charter corporations • Collect taxes • Establish courts • Establish highways • Pass and enforce laws • Take private property for public purposes, with just compensation	**Powers reserved to the states** • Conduct elections and determine voter qualifications • Establish local governments • Maintain militia (National Guard) • Provide for public health, safety, and morals • Ratify amendments to the federal Constitution • Regulate intrastate commerce **States expressly prohibited from:** • Abridging the privileges or immunities of citizens or denying due process and equal protection of the laws (14th Amendment) • Coining money • Entering into treaties • Keeping troops or navies • Levying import or export taxes on goods • Making war

FIGURE 4.2
The Constitutional Division of Powers Between the National Government and the States

each essentially separate from the other and carrying out its functions independently. In its own area of power, each level was supreme. Dual federalism reflects the formal distribution of powers in the Constitution, and perhaps it was an accurate portrayal of the judicial interpretation of the federal system for our first hundred years or so.

But this theory was criticized for not realistically describing the way the federal relationship was evolving in the twentieth century. It certainly did not take into account the changes brought about by the New Deal. The layer cake image was replaced by a new bakery metaphor. According to the new theory of **cooperative federalism**, rather than being two distinct layers, the national and state levels were swirled together like the chocolate and vanilla batter in a marble cake.[14] National and state powers were interdependent, and each level required the cooperation of the other to get things done. In fact, federalism came to be seen by political scientists as a partnership, but one in which the dominant partner was, more often than not, the national government.

cooperative federalism the federal system under which the national and state governments share responsibilities for most domestic policy areas

POSSIBLE ALTERNATIVES TO FEDERALISM

The federal system was not the only alternative available to our founders for organizing the relationship between the central government and the states. In fact, as we know, it wasn't even their first choice as a framework for government. The Articles of Confederation, which preceded the Constitution, handled the relationship quite differently. We can look at federalism as a compromise system that borrows some attributes from a unitary system and some from a confederal system, as shown in Figure 4.3. Had the founders chosen either of these alternatives, American government would look very different today.

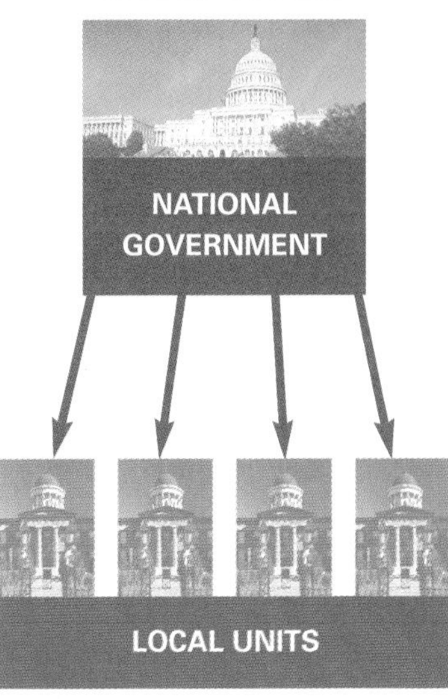

FIGURE 4.3

The Division and Flow of Power in Confederal, Federal, and Unitary Systems of Government

In a confederal system the local units hold all the powers, and the central government is dependent on those units for its existence. In a federal system the flow of power goes in both directions: power is shared, with both the central and local governments holding some powers independent of the other. In a unitary system the central government ultimately has all the power, and the local units are dependent on it.

Unitary Systems In a **unitary system** the central government ultimately has all the power. Local units (states or counties) may have some power at some times, but basically they are dependent on the central unit, which can alter or even abolish them. Many contemporary countries have unitary systems, among them Britain, France, Japan, Denmark, Norway, Sweden, Hungary, and the Philippines.

unitary system government in which all power is centralized

Politics in Britain, for example, works very differently from politics in the United States, partly due to the different rules that organize central and local government. Most important decisions are made in London, from foreign policy to housing policy—even the details of what ought to be included in the school curriculum. Even local taxes are determined centrally. When Margaret Thatcher, the former British prime minister, believed that some municipal units in London were not supportive of her government's policies, she simply dissolved the administrative units. Similarly, in 1972, when the legislature in Northern Ireland (a part of Great Britain) could not resolve its religious conflicts, the central government suspended the local lawmaking body and ruled Northern Ireland from London. These actions are tantamount to a Republican president dissolving a Democratic state that disagreed with his policies, or the national government suspending the state legislature in Alabama during the days of segregation and running the state from Washington. Such an arrangement has been impossible in the United States except during the chaotic state of emergency following the Civil War. What is commonplace under a unitary system is unimaginable under our federal rules.

Confederal Systems Confederal systems provide an equally sharp contrast to federal systems, even though the names sound quite similar. In **confederal systems** the local units hold all the power, and the central government is dependent on them for its

confederal systems governments in which local units hold all the power existence. The local units remain sovereign, and the central government has only as much power as those units allow it to have. Examples of confederal systems include America under the Articles of Confederation and associations such as the United Nations and the European Union, twenty-five European nations that have joined economic and political forces. The European Union has been experiencing problems much like ours after the Revolutionary War, debating whether it ought to move in a federal direction. Some of the nations involved, jealous of their sovereignty, have been reluctant. See the box, "A European Constitution?"

WHAT DIFFERENCE DOES FEDERALISM MAKE?

That our founders settled on federalism, rather than a unitary or a confederal system, makes a great deal of difference to American politics. Federalism gave the founders a government that could take effective action, restore economic stability, and regulate disputes among the states, while still allowing the states considerable autonomy. Several specific consequences deserve discussion.

Effects on State Politics The federal relationship has an impact on state politics by placing the states in competition with each other for scarce resources. For example, consider the so-called race to the bottom that some observers and academics fear results when states have discretion over benefit levels and eligibility requirements for social programs such as welfare. The concern is that the states will cut benefits because they worry that being more generous than neighboring states will cause poor people to move into their states. That is, some policymakers fear that if they don't cut payments, their states will become "welfare magnets." When benefits and program requirements are set by the national government, states have fewer incentives to cut benefits in the race to the bottom.[15]

A second consequence of competition among the states is their competition for industry. "Smokestack chasing" happens as states bid against one another to get industries to locate within their borders by providing them with property and corporate income tax breaks, loan financing, and educational training for workers, and by assuming the costs of roads, sewers, and other infrastructure that new industries would otherwise have to pay for themselves. For instance, in the early 1980s, Tennessee outbid other states for a Nissan automobile plant by paying roughly $11,000 per job. After that, the stakes became increasingly higher so that, in 1993, Alabama "won" a thirty-five-state race to grab the Mercedes-Benz sport utility vehicle plant with an incentive plan that cost the state around $200,000 for each of the expected 1,500 jobs.[16]

More recently, as economic experts have concluded that these bidding wars benefit the industries much more than they do the states, the states have developed other strategies for economic development.[17] Nevertheless, the states don't seem able to kick the smokestack-chasing habit entirely, as evident in Florida's 2004 use of federal money intended to relieve the states' fiscal burdens to lure a large biotech firm to Palm Beach County.[18]

Effects on Citizens Federalism also makes a difference in the lives of citizens. It provides real power at levels of government that are close to the citizens. Citizens can thus have access to officials and processes of government that they could not have if there

A European Constitution?

As small, individual countries, the nations of Europe are not very formidable economically, politically, or militarily. Since their days of empire ended, their relative power internationally has shrunk while the power of the United States (ironically a former colony itself) has grown by leaps. Hoping to take a leaf out of the founders' book by banding together, several European nations have experimented with various collective arrangements, most recently the European Union (EU), which was formed out of the earlier European Community in 1992.

Although the previous organizations created after World War II were considerably smaller in size and scope, today's EU has expanded to include Austria, Belgium, Cyprus, the Czech Republic, Denmark, Estonia, Finland, France, Germany, Greece, Hungary, Ireland, Italy, Latvia, Lithuania, Luxembourg, Malta, the Netherlands, Poland, Portugal, Slovakia, Slovenia, Spain, Sweden, and the United Kingdom and will likely welcome several new member states within a few years. Most share a common currency (the euro), a common economic market, and a central bank, as well as a popularly elected parliament, a court with extensive powers over the national courts and legal systems, and the beginnings of a common army.

The ultimate purpose of the EU has always been controversial. The basic question faced by its members has been whether the organization should aspire to become a pan-European superstate (a "United States of Europe") or whether it should confine itself to strictly economic matters. In earlier years, some of its less enthusiastic members, notably Britain, waged a campaign against political integration and "federalism," which they called the "f-word." Instead, the member states retained considerable sovereignty (the ability to do what they want) politically, if not economically, and could exercise a veto on many political, economic, and social issues of mutual concern. This was similar in spirit, if not in form, to the United States under the Articles of Confederation.

More recently, representatives of the twenty-five EU member nations negotiated a "constitutional treaty" to govern the organization. Completed in June 2004 and currently in the process of ratification, the purpose of this document is to create "a new world superpower" to rival the stature and authority of the United States. The process of negotiating the EU constitutional treaty has required EU member-state politicians to tackle the issue of political integration head-on. When their goals were only to form an economic union, a confederal system was sufficient. But as those goals progressed from strictly economic to political and military, some politicians have begun to argue that stronger central power is necessary, especially if the EU is to speak with a single voice in foreign and military affairs. The new constitutional treaty recognizes that fact with a more federal system, creating the position of EU foreign minister and giving the EU the ability to sign international treaties on behalf of all of its member states for the first time.

That those goals remain highly controversial was demonstrated by the fact that the first two nations to hold referenda on the new constitution, France and the Netherlands, defeated it. In the more than fifty years since efforts at European integration began, the trend has been toward increasing power at the central level, but these negative votes may force the EU to change course. If the constitutional treaty or a similar document is someday ratified, it is the federalists who will be able to claim victory, much as they did in Philadelphia more than two hundred years ago. If not, it is the European anti-federalists who will have won the day.

Source: "A Difficult Birth," *Economist,* June 26, 2004, 53–54; "What It All Means," *Economist,* June 26, 2004. 54.

were just one distant, effective unit. Federalism also enhances the power of interest groups in that it provides a variety of government levels at which different groups can try to gain political advantage. Often a group that is not successful at one level can try again at another and "shop" for institutions or agencies that are more receptive to its requests. The states vary considerably in their political ideologies and thus in the policies they are likely to adopt. (See "*Who Are We?* How We Differ From State to State.") For example, African Americans were unable to achieve significant political influence in the South as long as the southern states, with their segregationist traditions, were allowed to control access to the voting booths. When the national government stepped in to stop segregation with the Civil Rights Act of 1964, the balance of power began to become less lopsided. Conversely, when women were unable to get the vote at the national level, they turned their attention to the states, and won their suffrage there first. Today we see the effects of group power most clearly in the area of the environment. Without the action of the federal government, many of the states in the American West would adopt much more lenient rules for use of federal lands for grazing, farming, and oil exploration, all of which can be quite profitable for them. Although environmentalists have little clout in places like Utah or Alaska, they are far more influential in Washington, D.C., where policy is currently made.

Increased Flexibility Federalism gives government considerable flexibility to preserve local standards and to respond to local needs—that is, to solve problems at the levels at which they occur. Examples include local traffic laws, community school policies, and city and county housing codes. Federalism also allows experimentation with public policy. If all laws and policies need not be uniform across the country, then different states may try different solutions to common problems and share the results of their experiments. For instance, in 1993, policymakers in Georgia, hoping to stem the loss of their brightest young people to out-of-state colleges and universities, developed a way to fund higher education that would make going to school in Georgia more attractive. Using funds from the state lottery, Georgia's Hope Scholarships pay for tuition, mandatory fees, and a book allowance for any Georgia resident who completes high school with a "B" average, a program that one close observer calls "probably the most successful public initiative in Georgia history." The program has been so successful that other states, including Florida, Kentucky, Nevada, Maryland, and Texas, have adopted versions tailored to meet their own particular needs.[19]

The flexibility that federalism offers states has disadvantages as well. Where policies are made and enforced locally, all economies of scale are lost. Many functions are also repeated across the country as states locally administer national programs. Making and enforcing laws can be troublesome as well under federalism. Different penalties for the same crime can make it difficult to gauge the consequences of one's behavior across states. For example, being caught with an ounce of marijuana will get an offender a $5,000 fine and up to five years in jail in Florida, but in California it draws only a $100 fine, and in Massachusetts a first-time offender gets probation.[20] Most problematic is the fact that federalism permits, even encourages, local prejudices to find their way into law. To the degree that states have more rather than less power, the uniform enforcement of civil rights cannot be guaranteed. Gay Americans, for example, do not have the same rights in all localities of the United States today.

But even though federalism is not a perfect system, overall it has proved to be a flexible and effective compromise for American government. The United States is not the only nation with a federal system, although other countries may distribute power

How We Differ From State to State

Population growth varies from state to state, as do the political ideologies that influence voting patterns. As these two maps show, the fastest-growing states are by and large conservative (based on public opinion polls that correlate highly with the policies that officials in those states enact). Bearing in mind that population growth is reflected in the electoral college and in the number of congressional seats each state holds, how might these trends affect national elections?

Regional Ideologies and Population Growth, by State:

Political ideology in the states

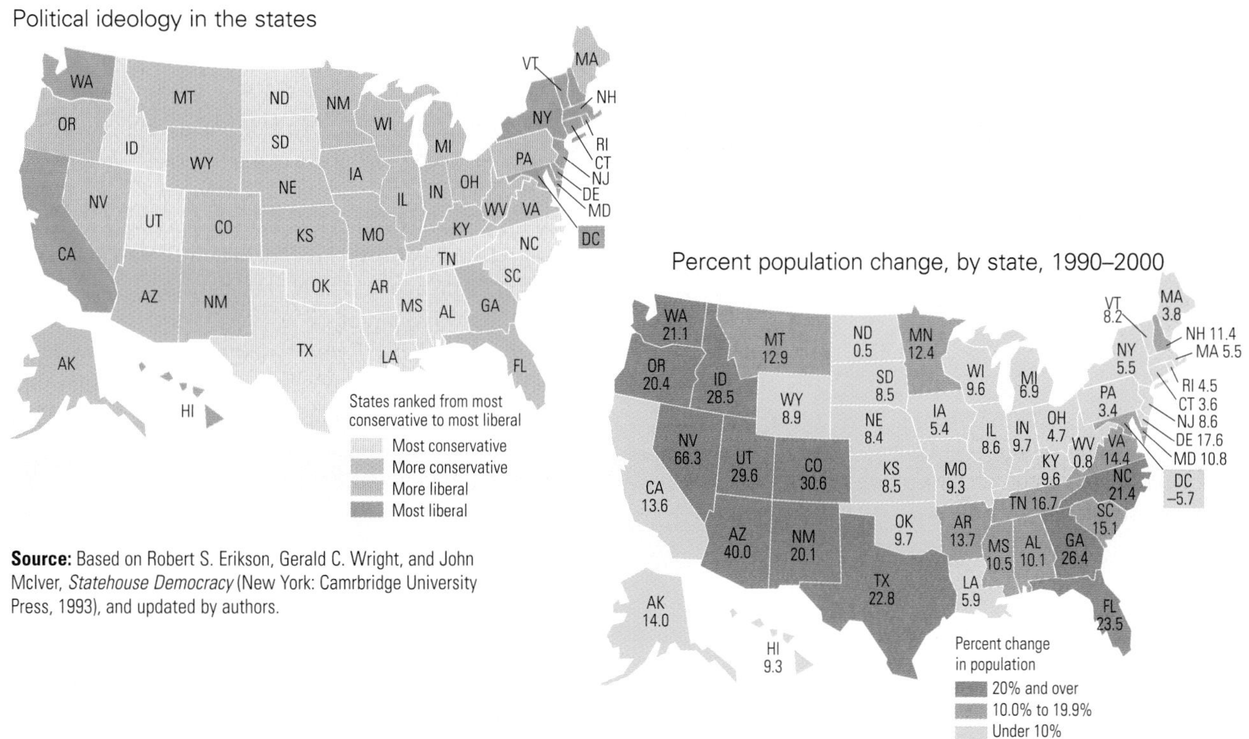

Source: Based on Robert S. Erikson, Gerald C. Wright, and John McIver, *Statehouse Democracy* (New York: Camrbridge University Press, 1993), and updated by authors.

Source: U.S. Bureau of the Census, *Statistical Abstracts of the United States, 2004–2005.* www.census.gov/prod/2004pubs/04statab/pop.pdf. Table 18.

among their various units differently than we do. Germany, Canada, Mexico, Australia, and Switzerland are all examples of federal systems.

THE CHANGING BALANCE: AMERICAN FEDERALISM OVER TIME

Although the Constitution provides for both national powers and state powers (as well as some shared powers), several factors have caused the balance between the two to change considerably since it was written. First, because of the founders' disagreement over how power should be distributed in the new country, the final wording

Consider the Source

How to Read the Op-Ed Pages With a Critical Eye

"All the news that's fit to print," proclaims the banner of the *New York Times*. But news isn't the only thing you'll find in what readers fondly refer to as "the old gray lady." Some of the most informative, entertaining, and, frequently, infuriating "news" printed in the *New York Times*—and most other newspapers today—can be found in the op-ed pages, where opinion pieces, editorials, and letters to the editor reign supreme. Often the last two inside pages of the first section, the op-ed pages need to be read differently from the rest of the paper. Writers of the standard news pages try to be objective, and while their values and beliefs may sneak in, they attempt to keep their opinion's influence on their work to a minimum.

Writers on the op-ed pages, in contrast, flaunt their opinions, proudly display their biases, and make value-laden claims with abandon. This can make for fascinating reading, and can help you to formulate your own opinions, if you know what you are reading. Op-ed writers include:

- **The newspaper's editorial board**—editors employed by the paper who take stands on public matters, recommend courses of action to officials, and endorse candidates for office. On the whole, editorial boards are more conservative than liberal (for example, they have endorsed Republican presidential candidates far more often than they have endorsed Democrats)—but they often reflect the ideological tendencies of their reader base. The editors of the *New York Times,* which is read by a liberal urban population, take stances that are on the more liberal side, while the *Wall Street Journal,* subscribed to by the national business community, is more conservative. *USA Today,* which aspires to a broad national circulation, attempts to be more moderate in its outlook.
- **Columnists**—writers employed by the paper or by a news syndicate (whose work is distributed to many newspapers) who analyze current events from their personal ideological point of view. Columnists can be liberal, like Ellen Goodman (*Boston Globe*) and Molly Ivins (*Fort Worth Star-Telegram*), or conservative, like David Brooks (*New York Times*), George Will (*Washington Post*), and Robert Novak (nationally syndicated). The *Washington Post*'s E. J. Dionne and David Broder, and the *New York Times*'s Maureen Dowd, are all cogent observers and critics of the political scene who defy precise placement on an ideological scale. While their values tend toward the liberal, they are equally hard on both parties.

about national and state powers was kept vague intentionally, which probably helped the Constitution get ratified. Because it wasn't clear how much power the different levels held, it has been possible ever since for both ardent Federalists and states' rights advocates to find support for their positions in the document.

Another factor that has caused the balance of national and state power to shift over time has to do with the role given to the Supreme Court to step in and interpret what it thinks the Constitution really means when conflict exists over which level of government should have the final say on a given issue. Those interpretations have varied along with the people sitting on the Court and with historical circumstances.

The circumstances themselves have helped to alter the balance of state and national power over time. The context of American life is periodically transformed through major events such as the end of slavery and the Civil war, the process of industrialization and the growth of big business, the economic collapse of the Great Depression in the 1930s, world wars (both hot and cold) followed by the fall of communism in the 1980s, and the devastating terrorist attacks of September 11, 2001. With these events come shifts in the demands made of the different levels of government. When we talk about federalism in the United States, we are talking about specific constitutional rules and provisions, but we are also talking about a continuously changing context in which those rules are understood.

- **Guest columnists**—ranging from the country's elite in the *New York Times* to everyday Americans in *USA Today*—who expound their views on a wide range of issues.
- **Readers of the newspaper**—who write letters to the editor, responding either to points of news coverage in the newspaper or to other items on the op-ed pages.

Here are some questions to ask yourself as you read the op-ed section of the newspaper:

- **Who is the author?** What do you know about him or her? As you get used to reading certain newspaper editorial pages and columnists you will know what to expect from them. Guest columnists are harder to gauge. The paper should tell you who they are, but you can always do further research on the web or elsewhere. Figure out how the author's job or achievements might influence his or her views.
- **What are the values underlying the piece you are reading?** Does the author make his or her values clear? If not, can you figure out what they are from the things the person writes? Unless you know the values that motivate an author, it is difficult to judge fairly what he or she has to say, and it can be difficult not to be hoodwinked as well.
- **Is the author building an argument?** If so, are the premises or assumptions that the author makes clear? Does the author cite adequate evidence to back up his or her points? Does the argument make sense? Notice that these are versions of the same questions we set out as guides to critical thinking in Chapter 1. Always think critically when you are reading an op-ed piece, or you are in danger of taking someone's opinions and preferences as fact!
- **What kinds of literary devices does the author use that you might not find in a straight news story?** Opinion writers, especially columnists, might use sarcasm or irony to expose what they see as the absurdities of politics or political figures, and they might even invent fictional characters. What is the point of these literary devices? Are they effective?
- **Has the author persuaded you?** Why or why not? Has the author shown you how to look at a familiar situation in a new light, or has he or she merely reinforced your own opinions? Do you feel inspired to write a letter to the editor on the subject? If so, do it!

Two trends are apparent when we examine American federalism throughout our history. One is that American government in general is growing in size, at both the state and national levels. We make many more demands of government than did, say, the citizens of George Washington's time, or Abraham Lincoln's, and the apparatus to satisfy those demands has grown accordingly. But within that overall growth, a second trend has been the gradual strengthening of the national government at the expense of the states.

The increase in the size of government shouldn't surprise us. One indisputable truth about the United States is that, over the years, it has gotten bigger, more industrialized, more urban, and more technical. As the country has grown, so have our expectations of what the government will do for us. We want to be protected from the fluctuations of the market, from natural disasters, from terrorists, from unfair business practices, and from unsafe foods and drugs. We want government to protect our "rights," but our concept of those rights has expanded beyond the first ten amendments to the Constitution to include things like economic security in old age, a minimum standard of living for all citizens, a safe interstate highway system, and crime-free neighborhoods. These new demands and expectations create larger government at all levels but particularly at the national level, where the resources and will to accomplish such broad policy goals are more likely to exist.

"If All You Have Is a Hammer, Everything Looks Like a Nail"
Republican Representative Tom Delay of Texas, known in Washington as the "Hammer," was one of the prime advocates for pushing the federal government to intervene in the case of a brain-damaged Florida woman, Terri Schiavo, kept alive by a feeding tube. Such issues are traditionally addressed by the states. Although Republicans are generally held to favor leaving decisions to the states whenever possible, they increasingly look to the federal government to solve problems as they tighten their hold on the reigns of national power and can better control the outcomes there.

Traditionally, liberals have preferred to rely on a strong central government to solve many social problems that the states have not solved, such as discrimination and poverty. Conservatives have tended to believe that "big government" causes more problems than it solves. Like the Anti-Federalists at the founding, they have preferred to see power and government services located at the state or local level, closer to the people being governed. In the last few years, however, since Republicans have held the reins of power in both the legislative and executive branches, the conservative distaste for big government has waned somewhat as they have been the ones dictating the actions of that government. President Bush's "No Child Left Behind Act," for instance, took away many of the prerogatives of local school districts to decide whether to engage in regular testing of students, and yet it enjoyed the support of many conservatives. Some Republicans themselves have noted that, once they come to Washington, conservatives can be "as bad as liberals" about enforcing the national will on states.[21]

The growth of the national government's power over the states can be traced by looking at four moments in our national history: the early judicial decisions of Chief Justice John Marshall, the Civil War, the New Deal, and the civil rights movement and the expanded use of the Fourteenth Amendment from the 1950s through the 1970s. Since the late 1970s, we have seen increasing opposition to the growth of what is called "big government" on the part of citizens and officials alike, but most of the efforts to cut it back in size and to restore power to the states have been mixed.

John Marshall: Strengthening the Constitutional Powers of the National Government
John Marshall, the third chief justice of the U.S. Supreme Court (1801–1835), was a man of decidedly Federalist views. His rulings did much to strengthen the power of the national government both during his lifetime and after. The 1819 case of ***McCulloch v. Maryland*** set the tone. In resolving this dispute about whether Congress had the power to charter a bank and whether the state of Maryland had the power to tax that bank, Marshall had plenty of scope for exercising his preference for a strong national government. Congress did have the power, he ruled, even though the Constitu-

McCulloch v. Maryland
Supreme Court ruling (1819) confirming the supremacy of national over state government

tion didn't spell it out, because Congress was empowered to do whatever was necessary and proper to fulfill its constitutional obligations.

Marshall did not interpret the word *necessary* to mean "absolutely essential," but rather he took a looser view, holding that Congress had the power to do whatever was "appropriate" to execute its powers. If that meant chartering a bank, then the necessary and proper clause could be stretched to include chartering a bank. Furthermore, Maryland could not tax the federal bank because "the power to tax involves the power to destroy." [22] If Maryland could tax the federal bank, that would imply the state had the power to destroy the bank, making Maryland supreme over the national government and violating the Constitution's supremacy clause, which makes the national government supreme.

Marshall continued this theme in ***Gibbons v. Ogden*** in 1824.[23] In deciding that New York did not have the right to create a steamboat monopoly on the Hudson River, Marshall focused on the part of Article I, Section 8, that allows Congress to regulate commerce "among the several states." He interpreted commerce very broadly to include almost any kind of business, creating a justification for a national government that could freely regulate business and that was dominant over the states.

Gibbons v. Ogden Supreme Court ruling (1824) establishing national authority over interstate business

Gibbons v. Ogden did not immediately establish national authority over business. Business interests were far too strong to meekly accept government authority, and subsequent Court decisions recognized that strength and a prevailing public philosophy of laissez-faire. The national government's power in general was limited by cases such as *Cooley v. Board of Wardens of Port of Philadelphia* (1851),[24] which gave the states greater power to regulate commerce if local interests outweigh national interests, and *Dred Scott v. Sanford* (1857),[25] which held that Congress did not have the power to outlaw slavery in the territories.

The Civil War: National Domination of the States The Civil War represented a giant step in the direction of a stronger national government. The war itself was fought for a variety of reasons. Besides the issue of slavery and the conflicting economic and cultural interests of the North and South, the war was fought to resolve the question of national versus state supremacy. When the national government, dominated by the northern states, passed legislation that would have furthered northern interests, the southern states tried to invoke the doctrine of nullification. **Nullification** was the idea that states could render national laws null if they disagreed with them, but the national government never recognized this doctrine. The southern states also seceded, or withdrew from the United States, as a way of rejecting national authority, but the Union's victory in the ensuing war decisively showed that states did not retain their sovereignty under the Constitution.

nullification declaration by a state that a federal law is void within its borders

The New Deal: National Power Over Business The Civil War did not settle the question of the proper balance of power between national government and business interests. In the years following the war, the courts struck down both state and national laws regulating business. For example, *Pollock v. Farmer's Loan and Trust Company* (1895) held that the federal income tax was unconstitutional[26] (until it was legalized by the Sixteenth Amendment to the Constitution in 1913). *Lochner v. New York* (1905) said that states could not regulate working hours for bakers.[27] This ruling was used as the basis for rejecting state and national regulation of business until the middle of the New Deal in the 1930s. *Hammer v. Dagenhart* (1918) said that national laws prohibiting child labor were outside Congress's power to regulate commerce and therefore were unconstitutional.[28]

Throughout the early years of Franklin Roosevelt's New Deal, designed amid the devastation of the Great Depression of the 1930s to recapture economic stability through economic regulations, the Supreme Court maintained its antiregulation stance. But the president berated the Court for striking down his programs, and public opinion backed the New Deal and Roosevelt himself against the interests of big business. Eventually the Court had a change of heart. Once established as constitutional, New Deal policies redefined the purpose of American government and thus the scope of both national and state powers. The relationship between the nation and the states became more cooperative as the government became employer, provider, and insurer of millions of Americans in times of hardship. Our social security system was born during the New Deal, as were many other national programs designed to get America back to work and back on its feet. A sharper contrast to the laissez-faire policies of the turn of the century can hardly be imagined.

Civil Rights: National Protection Against State Abuse The national government picked up a host of new roles as American society became more complex, including that of guarantor of individual rights against state abuse. The Fourteenth Amendment to the Constitution was passed after the Civil War to make sure southern states extended all the protections of the Constitution to the newly freed slaves. In the 1950s and 1960s the Supreme Court used the amendment to strike down a variety of state laws that maintained segregated, or separate, facilities for whites and African Americans, from railway cars to classrooms. By the 1970s the Court's interpretation of the Fourteenth Amendment had expanded, allowing it to declare unconstitutional many state laws that it said deprived state citizens of their rights as U.S. citizens. For instance, the Court ruled that states had to guarantee those accused of state crimes the same protections that the Bill of Rights guaranteed those accused of federal crimes. As we will see in more detail in Chapter 5, the Fourteenth Amendment has come to be a means for severely limiting the states' powers over their own citizens.

Selling a New Deal
This highly partisan contemporary cartoon shows President Franklin Roosevelt cheerfully steering the American ship of state toward economic recovery, unswayed by selfish big-business barons. New Deal programs ushered in a greatly expanded role for the national government.

The trend toward increased national power has not put an end to the debate over federalism, however. In the 1970s and 1980s, Presidents Richard Nixon and Ronald Reagan tried hard to return some responsibilities to the states, mainly by giving them more control over how they spend federal money. In the next section, we look at recent efforts to alter the balance of federal power in favor of the states.

THE POLITICS OF CONTEMPORARY FEDERALISM

Clearly, federalism is a continually renegotiated compromise between advocates of strong national government on the one hand and advocates of state power on the other. From the 1970s through the end of the twentieth century, however, frustration over the size of the national government's deficit (the result of spending more money than is brought in) and ideological changes, particularly the election of Republican majorities in Congress, has fed a **devolution** movement, an effort to give more power and responsibility back to the states. How far this movement toward devolution will go is not yet clear, but naturally, as the state-federal relationship changes, so do the arenas in which citizens and their leaders make the decisions that become government policy. Such a fundamental shift usually means changes in the probable winners and losers of American politics.

devolution the transfer of powers and responsibilities from the federal government to the states

Beginning with *Marbury v. Madison*, the Supreme Court gradually interpreted the Constitution in ways that gave the national government more power relative to the states. More recently, however, a majority on the Court has moved to adopt a much stronger states' rights position. In 1995, for example, the Court ruled that Congress took its constitutional authority to regulate interstate commerce too far when it made laws about how far from a schoolyard a person carrying a gun had to stay.[29] In *Printz v. United States* (1997), the Court struck down part of the Brady Bill, a federal gun control law that required state law enforcement officers to conduct background checks of prospective gun purchasers, because it compelled state employees to administer a federal program, essentially making them agents of the federal government.[30] In cases following *Printz*, the Court continued to limit the powers of Congress, holding, for instance, that Congress has overstepped its constitutional bounds when it allows citizens to sue the states for violating federal laws like age discrimination laws or when it protects the right of state employees to sue for overtime pay or for patent holders to sue the states for patent infringement.[31]

Even when the Supreme Court's decisions give the federal government greater latitude in exercising its powers, the states are still responsible for the policies that most affect our lives. For instance, the states retain primary responsibility for everything from education to regulation of funeral parlors, from licensing physicians to building roads and telling us how fast we can drive on them. Most questions of contemporary federalism involve the national government trying to influence how the states and localities go about providing the goods and services and regulating the behaviors that have traditionally been within their jurisdictions.

Why should the national government care so much about what the states do? Congress wants to make policies that influence or control the states for several reasons. First, from a Congress member's perspective, it is easier to solve many social and economic problems at the national level. Pervasive problems such as race discrimination or air and water pollution do not affect just the populations of individual states. When a political problem does not stop at the state border, it can be easier to conceive of solutions that cross the border as well; such solutions require national coordination. In some instances, national problem solving involves redistributing resources from one state or region to another, which individual states, on their own, would be unwilling or unable to do.

Second, members of Congress frequently want to control policymakers in their states so that their constituents will see them as the deliverers of resources and good things and will reward their generosity and political skill at the polls. After the expansion of the federal government's role during the New Deal, the Democratic Party maintained a majority in Congress by becoming known as the party that delivered economic benefits to various socioeconomic groups and geographic areas of the country.[32] Since the 1970s, members of Congress have used the promise of local benefits to convince voters to support them. Incumbents have embraced their roles as representatives who can deliver highways, parks, welfare benefits, urban renewal, and assistance to farmers, ranchers, miners, educators, and just about everyone else. Doing well by constituents gets incumbents reelected.[33]

Third, sometimes members of Congress prefer to adopt national legislation to preempt what states may be doing or planning to do. In some cases they might object to state laws, as Congress did when it passed civil rights legislation against the strong preferences of the southern states. In other cases they might enact legislation to prevent states from making fifty different regulatory laws for the same product. Here they are being sensitive to the wishes of corporations and businesses—generally large contributors to politicians—to have a single set of laws governing their activities. If Congress makes a set of nationally binding regulations, a business does not have to incur the expense of altering its product or service to meet different state standards.

To deliver on their promises, national politicians must have the cooperation of the states. Although some policies, such as Social Security, can be administered easily at the national level, others, such as changing educational policy or altering the drinking age, remain under state authority and cannot be legislated in Washington. Federal policymakers face one of their biggest challenges in this regard: how to get the states to do what federal officials have decided they should do.

Let's take the question of mathematics education as an example. Assume that members of Congress have decided that we face a "math crisis" and that more math training needs to take place in our high schools for the nation to remain competitive in the world economy of the twenty-first century. How will they get the education policymakers—that is, the states—to go along with them? One sure way to influence math education would be for the federal government to build and staff a system of "federal schools." Then it could have any kind of a curriculum it wanted. But doing so would be enormously expensive and wasteful, because the states and localities already have schools and already teach math in them. The more efficient alternative would be to try to influence how the states and localities teach more math. Here Congress would face the same challenges it does with respect to other policy areas such as health, occupational safety, transportation, and welfare. When Congress wants to act in these areas, it has to find ways to work with the states and localities.

Congressional Strategies for Influencing State Policy Congress has essentially two resources to work with when it comes to influencing the states to do what it wants: authority and money. As we can see in Table 4.2, combinations of these resources yield four possibilities. The winners and losers in the political process will change depending on which option Congress chooses.

TABLE 4.2 How the National Government Influences the States

OPTION	RULES	FEDERAL FUNDS?	CHARACTER OF THE NATIONAL/STATE RELATIONSHIP
Option One: No National Government Influence	Few or no rules	No	States have autonomy and pay for their own programs. Results in high diversity of policies, including inequality. Promotes state competition and its outcomes. Calls for congressional and presidential restraint in exercising their powers.
Option Two: Categorical Grants	Strict rules and regulations	Yes	Good for congressional credit taking. Ensures state compliance and policy uniformity. Heavy federal regulatory burden ("red tape"). National policy requirements may not be appropriate for local conditions.
Option Three: Block Grants	Broad grants of power within program areas	Yes	Greater state flexibility, program economy. State politicians love money without "strings." Greater program innovation. Undermines congressional credit taking. Grants become highly vulnerable to federal budget cuts. Leads to policy diversity and inequality, meeting state rather than national goals.
Option Four: Unfunded Mandates	Specific rules and compliance obligations	No	Very cheap for the federal government. Easy way for members of Congress to garner favor. States complain about unfairness and burdensome regulations. Undermines state cooperation.

- *Option One: No National Government Influence.* In the period of dual federalism, the federal government left most domestic policy decisions to the states. Precollege education is a good example: the federal government did not provide instructions to the states about curriculum goals (let alone math training), nor did it provide the funds for education. The combination of no instructions and no funding (first row in Table 4.2) yields the outcome of no national government influence. This means the states organized education as they wished. To follow our math example, the outcome of no national government influence would be that some states might concentrate on math, whereas others might emphasize a different educational issue. Such policy differences are a natural outcome of a situation in which the states, rather than the federal government, have more power.

- *Option Two: Categorical Grants.* In our example, Congress might decide that the nation's long-run economic health depends on massive improvements in high school mathematics education. "No national government influence" is clearly not an option here. Congress could pass a resolution declaring its desire for better math education in high school, but if it wants results, it would have to put some teeth in its "request." If Congress really wants to effect a change, it would have to provide instructions and an incentive for the states to improve math education.

  The most popular tool Congress has devised for this purpose is the **categorical grant** (see the second row in Table 4.2), which provides very detailed instructions, regulations, and compliance requirements for the states (and sometimes for local governments as well) in specific policy areas. If a state complies with the requirements, federal money is released for those specified purposes. If a state doesn't comply with the detailed provisions of the categorical grant, it doesn't

categorical grant federal funds provided for a specific purpose, restricted by detailed instructions, regulations, and compliance standards get the money. In many cases the states have to provide some funding themselves. They might, for instance, have to match the amount contributed by the federal government.

In our example, the federal government could pass a math education act that would provide funds on a per-pupil basis for math education in the high schools. The bill might set standards for certain performance or testing levels, requirements for teacher certification in advanced math education training, and perhaps specific goals for decreasing the gender and racial gaps in math performance. School districts and state school boards would have to document their compliance in order to receive their funds.

The states, like most governments, never have enough money to meet all their citizens' demands, so categorical grants can look very attractive, at least on the surface. The grants can be refused, but most of the time they are welcomed. In fact, over time state and local governments have become so dependent on federal grants that these subsidies now make up 25 percent of all state and local spending.[34] Thus the categorical grant has become a powerful tool of the federal government in getting the states to do what it wants.

Categorical grants are responsible for the large growth in federal influence on the states. Use of the grants blossomed in the 1960s and 1970s, primarily because they are very attractive to Congress. Members of Congress receive credit for sponsoring specific grant programs, which in turn help establish members as national policy leaders, building their reputations with their constituents for bringing "home" federal money. Also, because senators and House members are backed by coalitions of various interest groups, specific program requirements are a way to ensure that a policy does what members (and their backers) want—even in states where local political leaders prefer a different course. By contrast, state politicians hate the requirements and all the paperwork that go with reporting compliance with federal regulations. States and localities also frequently argue that federal regulations prevent them from doing a good job. They want the money, but they also want more flexibility.

- *Option Three: Block Grants.* Conservatives have long chafed at the detailed, Washington-centered nature of categorical grants. State politicians understandably want the maximum amount of freedom possible. They want to control their own destinies, not just carry out political deals made in Washington, and they want to please the coalitions of interests and voters that put them in power in the states. Thus they argue for maintaining federal funding but with fewer regulations. Their preferred policy tool, the **block grant** (seen in the third row of Table 4.2), combines broad (rather than detailed) program requirements and regulations with funding from the federal treasury. Block grants give the states considerable freedom in using the funds in broad policy areas.

block grant federal funds provided for a broad purpose, unrestricted by detailed requirements and regulations

To continue our math education example, the federal government might provide the states with a lump-sum block grant and instructions to spend it on education as each state sees fit. If Congress demanded that the money be spent on math education and insisted on other conditions, then the grant would start to look more like a categorical grant and less like a block grant. With an education block grant, members of Congress could not count on their math education problem being solved on a national basis unless it coincidentally resulted from the individual decisions in fifty states and innumerable localities.

One extreme and short-lived form of the block grant in the 1970s was President Richard Nixon's proposal to give money to the states and localities with no strings attached in the form of General Revenue Sharing (GRS)—not in place of categorical grants, but largely in addition to existing programs. GRS was immensely popular with the governors and mayors, but it never had great congressional backing because members of Congress could neither take credit for nor control how lower governments were spending these federal funds. Congress did not object when, in 1986, President Ronald Reagan suggested abolishing GRS as a way of reducing the deficit.[35]

Less extreme versions of the block grant were pushed by Republican presidents Nixon, Reagan, and Gerald Ford. However, the largest and most significant block grant was instituted under Democratic president Bill Clinton in 1996 with the passage of the welfare reform act. This reform changed a categorical grant program called Aid to Families with Dependent Children (AFDC) to a welfare block grant to the states, Temporary Assistance to Needy Families (TANF).

AFDC had allowed Washington to set the terms for cash aid to poor families with children, to fund the program with the states, and to require that the states administer the program according to federal specifications. In place for thirty years, AFDC had proved to have many unintended consequences, and even supporters of welfare in general agreed that the old program needed revamping.

Under TANF, the states have greater leeway in defining many of the rules of their welfare programs, such as qualifications and work requirements. The states do not get a blank check, however; they must continue to spend at certain levels and to adopt some federal provisions, such as the limits on how long a person can stay on welfare. TANF has ended welfare as an entitlement. Under AFDC, all families who qualified were guaranteed benefits—just as people who qualify for Social Security are assured coverage. This guarantee is not part of TANF. If the states run short of money—for example, if the economy slows down—families that might otherwise qualify may not receive welfare benefits. Such decisions, and their repercussions, are left to the individual states.

Congress has generally resisted the block grant approach for both policy and political reasons. In policy terms, many members of Congress fear that the states will do what they want instead of what Congress intends. One member characterized the idea of putting federal money into block grants as "pouring money down a rat hole." [36] That is, members are concerned that the states will not do a good job without regulations. And because it is impossible to control how the states deal with particular problems under block grants, a number of important differences, or inequalities, exist in how the state programs are run.

Congress also has political objections to block grants, which may be even more important to its members than their policy concerns. When federal funds are not attached to specific programs, they lose their electoral appeal for members of Congress, as the members can no longer take credit for the programs. From a representative's standpoint, it does not make political sense to take the heat for taxing people's income, only to turn those funds over in block grants so that governors and mayors get the credit for how the money is spent. In addition, interest groups contribute millions of dollars to congressional campaigns when members of Congress have control over program specifics. If Congress allows the states to assume that control, interest groups have less incentive to make congressional campaign contributions. As a result, the tendency has been to place more conditions on block grants with each annual congressional appropriation.[37]

Categorical grants remain the predominant form of federal aid, amounting to about 80 percent of all aid to state and local governments. The change from AFDC to TANF was an important milestone in welfare policy, but Congress has not yet continued this approach in other policy areas.

unfunded mandate a federal order that states operate and pay for a program created at the national level

- *Option Four: Unfunded Mandates.* The politics of federalism yields one more strategy, shown in the bottom row of Table 4.2. When the federal government issues an **unfunded mandate**, it imposes specific policy requirements on the states but does not provide a way to pay for those activities. Here Congress either threatens criminal or civil penalties or promises to cut off other, often unrelated, federal funds if the states do not comply with its directions. A good example of an unfunded mandate is the Americans with Disabilities Act of 1990, which requires states to guarantee access for the physically disabled to all public buildings and programs. The University of Missouri, for instance, spent $15 million on one hundred different construction projects to make its campus accessible. Although the goals of the act are popular, the provision of federal requirements without federal funding remains highly controversial.

  In terms of our math education example, the national government might say to the states that at least 45 percent of the students enrolled in advanced high school math courses be female, and, if that quota is not met, the states stand to lose 5 percent of their sewage treatment funds. This requirement could be set with no new federal funding for education at all.

  Unfunded mandates became more attractive to members of Congress in the era of the ballooning national deficit.[38] Whereas Congress passed unfunded mandates

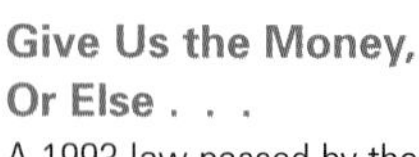

Give Us the Money, Or Else . . .
A 1993 law passed by the U.S. Congress mandated that local law enforcement officers conduct background checks on gun purchasers. The law did not, however, provide any funding to local governments enabling them to implement the restrictions. While the Supreme Court's ruling in *Printz v. United States,* which overturned the law, did not explicitly mention "unfunded mandates," many commentators viewed the absence of funding as a major downfall of the legislation.

only eleven times from 1931 through the 1960s, it passed fifty-two such mandates in the 1970s and 1980s, a trend that continued into the 1990s.[39] Congress can please interest groups and particular citizen groups by passing such laws, but the laws infuriate state politicians, who have to come up with the money to pay for them. In 1987, South Dakota challenged the law tying federal highway funds to a minimum drinking age, arguing that Congress had exceeded its spending powers. The Supreme Court ruled in favor of the federal government.[40]

President Clinton, working with the Republican majorities in Congress, pushed through the Unfunded Mandate Act of 1995, which promised to reimburse the states for expensive unfunded mandates or to pass a separate law acknowledging the cost of an unfunded mandate. This act has limited congressional efforts to pass "good laws" that cost the U.S. Treasury nothing. However, because Congress can define what the states see as an unfunded mandate in several different ways—as a simple "clarification of legislative intent," for example—Congress has continued to push some policy costs on to the states.[41] President Bush's "No Child Left Behind Act," for instance, requires extensive testing at the local level and intervention for failing students and schools. The states argue that the program is underfunded and thus constitutes a major unfunded mandate.[42]

The Move Toward Devolution As we mentioned earlier, from the 1980s at least until the terrorist attacks in the fall of 2001, there had been a good deal of momentum toward devolution, or giving power back to the states. This momentum has come from three sources. First, the states themselves have enthusiastically embraced the opportunity to chart their own courses. Health care reform in Oregon and welfare reform in Wisconsin attest to the creative fervor that can be released when states are given rein to innovate policy solutions for themselves.

Second, Congress has also supported the devolution movement, albeit with mixed feelings. Federal budget difficulties from the 1990s to the present generate significant pressure to economize, and the Republican majority in Congress through much of this time has reinforced the movement toward more block grants and fewer federal restrictions and financial grants. As we have seen, however, the ideological predilection of Republicans for state control has been tempered by the desire of members of Congress to claim power and policy success for themselves and their reelection efforts. The third source of the momentum toward devolution has been the Supreme Court, which under Chief Justice William Rehnquist has supported the move toward states' rights with a series of rulings that have cut away the ability of the federal government to impose its will on the states. For instance, in the 1997 case *Printz v. United States,* as we saw earlier, the Court overturned part of the Brady Bill, which required, among other things, that local law enforcement officials conduct background checks on prospective gun purchasers.[43] This ruling, with other decisions, appeared to be putting teeth back into the Tenth Amendment, which had been largely lost in the balance of previous Court decisions that had tilted toward national power.[44]

The current status of devolution seems to be a contradictory mix of rhetoric about returning power to the states and new national initiatives (and program requirements) in areas such as Medicaid, welfare, law enforcement, and education. Although Congress talks about devolution, it often gives in to electoral pressure to try new national solutions to salient problems.

One odd halfway strategy that has unfolded is for the federal government to create national policy but to grant "waivers" from federal regulations so that the states can experiment with different policies. Notice, however, that with waivers, the federal government retains all the power; the conditional leeway it gives the states should not be confused with real power at the state level. The advantage is that some of the states may develop new programs that work better than the old federal programs. If this happens and it serves congressional interests, the federal government may pressure the rest of the states to adopt the successful program. Indeed, state innovations are one of the prime justifications for federalism. Justice Louis Brandeis called the states our "laboratories of democracy," in which many different solutions to societal problems can be tried.

Advocates for the national government and advocates for the states are engaged in a constant struggle for more power, and they have been since the days of the Articles of Confederation. To get more power for the national government, advocates have relied on cooperative federalism, which gives the federal government a role in domestic policy, and on the rules of categorical grants and unfunded mandates, which maximize national power with minimal state input. States, by contrast, benefited more from dual federalism, under which the federal role was confined largely to foreign affairs. Since the advent of cooperative federalism, the states have favored policies in which the power of the federal government is limited. The process of devolution has meant more block grants and fewer categorical grants and unfunded mandates.

Devolution and the Bush Administration President George W. Bush's contribution to the devolution effort has been somewhat ambiguous. As a Republican governor, he was strongly committed ideologically to a smaller national government, yet many of his policies, even before September 11, 2001, required a substantial federal role. Under fire from conservatives in the early days of his administration for betraying his campaign pledge to restore states' rights, he was in the process of preparing an executive order to bolster those rights when the terrorist attacks took place.

Since that time, ideological and political pressure to devolve powers to the states has been countered by what is perceived to be an urgent need to tighten national defenses at home and abroad—an activity that by definition can be undertaken only by the national government. If that federal role is undertaken successfully, national sentiment toward the government is also likely to change: indeed, levels of trust in the federal government rose immediately after the September 11 attacks. Such sentiment may very well be reflected in state, congressional, and court decisions, and the progress toward devolution may slow or halt.

The fate of devolution is also unclear under the Bush administration for another reason—one that reflects a curious tension in modern conservative thought. As we saw in Chapter 2, while traditional conservatives believe that the federal government should have a limited role in most aspects of American lives, more recent social conservatives are willing to see the national government take on a more substantive role in order to achieve social or moral goals of which they approve.

Consequently, for instance, in November 2001, Bush's first attorney general, John Ashcroft, challenged an Oregon assisted suicide law, declaring that Oregon doctors who prescribed federally regulated medications to help their patients end their lives in accordance with that law would lose their licenses to prescribe federally regulated medicine, essentially ending their medical careers. Arguing that Ashcroft's interference in a state matter was unwarranted, Oregon went to court and the Supreme Court will hear this case in 2005.

Similarly, in early 2005, Republicans in Congress passed a law, signed by President Bush, to allow federal courts to review the case of Terri Schiavo, a woman in a persistent vegetative state whose husband had gone through the Florida state courts to have her feeding tube removed. The federal courts, including the Supreme Court, refused to hear the case. Such actions suggest that the commitment of social conservatives to states' rights is more pragmatic than principled: when they believe that their moral goals can be best met at the state level, they applaud state efforts; when they believe they are most likely to win at the national level, they support federal action. In doing so, they incite criticism from more traditional states' rights advocates. Whether the Bush administration can resolve this tension remains to be seen.

WHO, WHAT, HOW Where decisions are made—in Washington, D.C., or in the state capitals—makes a big difference in who gets what, and how they get it. The compromise of federalism as it appears in the Constitution, and as it has been interpreted by the Supreme Court, allows the nation, the states, and the citizens to get political benefits that would not be possible under either a unitary or a confederal system, but the balance of power has swung back and forth over the years, with the states, the federal government, and now the states again appearing to be the overall winners. Much of the current battle is fought in the halls of Congress, where states pull for a dual federalist interpretation that would give them block grants and devolution, and the national government holds out for a cooperative federalism in which it can award categorical grants and exact unfunded mandates.

AMENDABILITY

If a constitution is a rule book, then its capacity to be changed over time is critical to its remaining a viable political document. A rigid constitution runs the risk of ceasing to seem legitimate to citizens who have no prospect of changing the rules according to shifting political realities and visions of the public good. A constitution that is too easily revised, on the other hand, can be seen as no more than a political tool in the hands of the strongest interests in society. A final feature of the U.S. Constitution that deserves mention in this chapter is its **amendability**—that is, the founders' provision for a method of amendment, or change, that allows the Constitution to grow and adapt to new circumstances. In fact, they provided for two methods: the formal amendment process outlined in the Constitution, and an informal process that results from the vagueness of the document and the evolution of the role of the courts.

amendability the provision for the Constitution to be changed, so as to adapt to new circumstances

In the more than two hundred years since the U.S. Constitution was written, almost 9,750 amendments have been introduced, but it has been formally amended only 27 times. We have passed amendments to expand the protections of civil liberties and rights—to protect freedom of speech and religion, to provide guarantees against abuses of the criminal justice system, to guarantee citizenship rights to African Americans, and to extend the right to vote to blacks, women, and 18 year olds.

We have also passed amendments on more mechanical matters—to tinker with the rules of the political institutions the Constitution sets up in order to better control the outcomes. To that end, we have made senatorial elections direct, we have limited a president to two terms in office, and we have provided for a succession if the president is unable to serve out his term.

On at least one occasion we have also used the Constitution to make a policy that could more easily have been made through normal legislative channels. With the rat-

Lissa Morgenthaler-Jones

At first she thought Arnold Schwarzenegger was just a muscle-bound moron, but five minutes after meeting him, Lissa Morgenthaler-Jones changed her mind. "You could go all the way to the White House," she remembers thinking. "You are that good."

The trouble is, Schwarzenegger can't get to the White House. He was born in Austria, and when it comes to running for president, the U.S. Constitution says only natural-born Americans need apply. His ineligibility strikes Morgenthaler-Jones as profoundly unfair. Her solution? Amend for Arnold, of course.

"You can start by saying I got tired of yelling at the television set."

When most of us want to change the world, we might think of voting, or writing a letter to our congressperson, or, if we are feeling really committed and energetic, maybe marching in protest. But trying to amend the Constitution? Who does that?

Evidently Morgenthaler-Jones does. Sitting in her sunny office in Menlo Park, California, with giant posters of Schwarzenegger on the walls and Amend for Arnold T-shirts and buttons tacked up everywhere, she reflects on how this got started. Raised by moderate Republicans, she was frustrated by watching the party move ever more to the right. "I want someone strong enough to hold the center," she says, "and that is the single biggest reason I got into this. . . . You can start by saying I got tired of yelling at the television set."

Maybe moving from yelling at the TV to amending the Constitution seems reasonable to this retired biotech mutual fund manager because she comes from a long line of political activists who go after what they want. In 1946, despising the candidate for the Senate in Pennsylvania, her grandmother decided to run against him. She lost but was offered a post in the governor's cabinet, a mere quarter-century after women had been given the right to vote. Not much later, in 1952, Morgenthaler-Jones's mom decided to storm the Iowa caucuses with her friends to get her candidate, Eisenhower, nominated for the presidency. She ended up going to the Republican national convention. And Morgenthaler-Jones's venture capitalist dad is no political slouch either. He was instrumental in getting legislation passed in 1978 to reduce the capital gains tax—a move that helped spur the growth of Silicon Valley and made a lot of people a lot of money.

Her family's activism sent a powerful message. "I watched my father while I was in college, flying back and forth and back and forth, testifying in Washington. And it made an impact on me. . . . So yes, I have a model for what happens when you stand up and say 'let's do this.' And then people start coming to you because they had the same idea and they wanted to do it and now they know where we can all rally."

"Let's do this" could be the family motto—the question she asks herself about amending the Constitution is not "*if*" or "*whether*," but "*how* am I going to get this done?" But amending the Constitution is hard, we remind Morgenthaler-Jones. "It's supposed to be hard," she says. "And thank God for it, because otherwise the Constitution would be as ugly and overladen as one of our California spending bills." Still, hard doesn't intimidate her. Although her conversation is scattershot—she speeds through a host of topics ranging from renewable energy, to California politics, to the latest book she has read—when it comes to her political strategy she is focused and determined.

It will take her, she estimates, about six years—six years of fundraising, forming alliances, lobbying Congress, and educating the public. Already Amendus.org is running commercials ("You cannot choose the land of your birth," Morgenthaler-Jones's sultry voice intones on the commercial, "You *can* choose the land you love.") Will she succeed? She certainly hopes so, but most important to her is meeting the challenge to get this done. Here are some of her thoughts:

On going for a long shot:

If I'm on the side that is fighting for right, I don't care if I spend my entire life tilting at that windmill. The women who tried to get the Nineteenth Amendment passed lived and died knowing they would not get to see what they fought all their lives for. I can tilt this windmill.

On keeping the republic:

Hang on to your patience and never, never, never give up. My father calls it constant vigilance and he applies it to everything. It's the training of the soldier. If you want to make change you have to be extremely realistic about what can be done in what time frame.

Source: Lissa Morgenthaler-Jones spoke with Christine Barbour and Gerald Wright on March 31, 2005.

Sisters in Protest
The Equal Rights Amendment to the Constitution had a simple primary provision: "Equality of rights under the law shall not be denied or abridged by the United States or by any state on account of sex." The amendment was introduced in every Congress from 1923 until it passed in 1972, but it ultimately failed just three states short of the required three-quarters of the states needed for ratification. Even without the amendment, times have changed. Notice that at this late-1970s rally for the ERA in Springfield, Illinois, all of the protesters are women—and all of the reporters are men. Would we see these clear gender differences if such a protest were held today?

ification of the Eighteenth Amendment in 1919 we instituted Prohibition, making the production and sale of alcohol illegal. When our national views on temperance changed, we repealed the amendment in 1933, having to pass a new amendment to do so.

But the Constitution can be changed in more subtle ways by the Supreme Court without an amendment ever being passed. In the name of interpreting the Constitution, for example, the Supreme Court has extended many of the Bill of Rights protections to state citizens via the Fourteenth Amendment, permitted the national government to regulate business, prohibited child labor, and extended equal protection of the laws to women. In some cases, amendments had earlier been introduced to accomplish these goals but failed to be ratified (like the child labor amendment and the Equal Rights Amendment), and sometimes the Court has simply decided to interpret the Constitution in a new way. Judicial interpretation is at times quite controversial. Many scholars and politicians believe that the literal word of the founders should be adhered to, while others claim that the founders could not have anticipated all the opportunities and pitfalls of modern life and that the Constitution should be understood to be a flexible or "living" document. We return to this controversy when we look more closely at the courts in Chapter 10.

WHAT DOES THE CONSTITUTION SAY?

The Constitution is silent on the subject of judicial interpretation, but in part because it is so silent, especially in Article III, the courts have been able to evolve their own role. On the other hand, Article V spells out in detail the rather confusing procedures for officially amending the Constitution. These procedures are federal; that is, they require the involvement and approval of the states as well as the national government. The procedures boil down to this: Amendments may be proposed either by a two-thirds vote of the House and the Senate or, when two-thirds of the states request it, by a constitutional convention. Amendments must be approved either by the legislatures of three-fourths of the states or by conventions of three-fourths of the states. (See Figure 4.4.) Two interesting qualifications are contained in Article V. No amendment affecting slavery could be made before 1808, and no amendment can deprive a state of its equal vote in the Senate without that state's consent. We can easily imagine the North-South and large state–small state conflicts that produced those compromises.

POSSIBLE ALTERNATIVES: MAKING THE CONSTITUTION EASIER OR HARDER TO AMEND

The fifty states provide some interesting examples of alternative rules for amending constitutions. Compared to the national government, some states make it harder to amend their own constitutions. For instance, twelve states require that the amendment pass in more than one session of the legislature, that is, in successive years.

Rules can also make it much easier to amend constitutions. Some states require only simple legislative majorities (50 percent plus one) to propose amendments, and unlike the national Constitution, some states give their citizens a substantial role in the process through mechanisms called referenda and initiatives, which we discuss in the next section. The method by which an amendment is proposed can affect the success of the amendment itself. For instance, amendments limiting the number of terms legislators can serve have been passed in several states with the citizen-controlled initiative, but they have not fared well in states that depend on state legislatures to propose amendments. With opinion polls showing large public majorities favoring term limits, we can safely assume that term limits for Congress would pass much faster if the U.S. Constitution had a provision for a national constitutional initiative. Congress has proven, not surprisingly, reluctant to put restrictions on congressional careers.

One problem with making it too easy to amend a constitution is that public opinion can be fickle, and we might not always want the constitution to respond too hastily to changes in public whim. A second problem is that where amendments can be made

FIGURE 4.4 **Amending the Constitution**

An amendment may be proposed by either...

A two-thirds vote in both houses of Congress

...or...

A national convention called by Congress at the request of two-thirds of state legislatures

An amendment may be approved by either...

Legislatures in three-fourths of states

...or...

Ratifying conventions in three-fourths of states

Used 26 times

Used 1 time

Never used

Never used

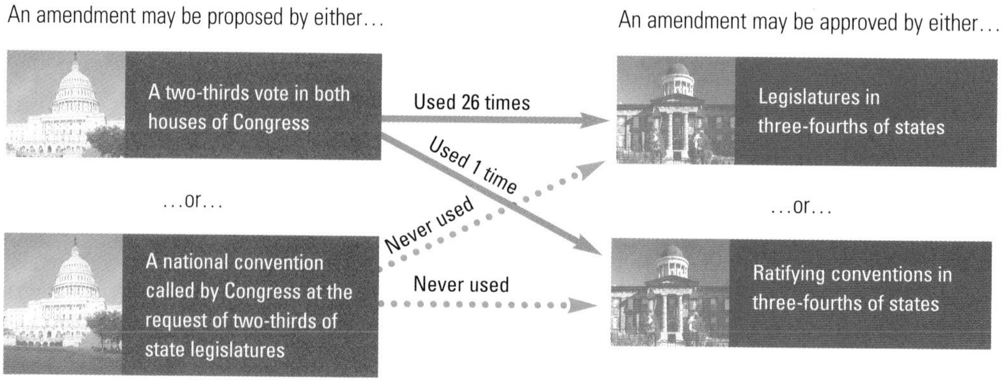

easily, special interests push for amendments that give them tax breaks or other protections. Constitutional status of their special treatment protects those interests from having to periodically justify that treatment to the public and the legislature.

Finally, where constitutions can be amended more easily, they are amended more frequently. The initiative process in California permits relatively easy translation of citizen concerns into constitutional issues. Compared to just 27 amendments of our national Constitution, California's constitution has been amended 480 times with everything from putting a cap on taxes, to limiting legislative terms, to withholding public services from illegal immigrants. Such matters would be the subject of ordinary legislation in states where amending is more difficult and thus would not have "higher law" status. Some critics feel that the fundamental importance of a constitution is trivialized by cluttering it up with many additions that could be dealt with in other ways.

Two good reasons, then, why the U.S. Constitution has weathered the passing of time so well are (1) it is not too detailed and explicit, and (2) its amendment procedure, in Madison's words, "guards equally against that extreme facility, which would render the Constitution too mutable; and the extreme difficulty, which might perpetuate its discovered faults." [45]

WHO, WHAT, HOW The founders and the American public had an enormous stake in a Constitution that would survive. The founders had their own reputations as nation-builders at stake, but they and the public also badly wanted their new experiment in self-governance to prove successful, to validate the Enlightenment view of the world. For the Constitution to survive, it had to be able to change, but to change judiciously. The amendment process provided in the Constitution allows for just such change. But occasionally this process is too slow for what the courts consider justice, and they use their broad powers to interpret the existing words of the Constitution in light of the changed circumstances of the modern day. That is, they focus not so much on what the founders meant at the time, but on what they would intend if they were alive today. The founders would have been as mixed in support of this practice as are contemporary scholars. Perhaps the focus of so many critical eyes on the Court has served as an informal check on this power.

THE CITIZENS AND THE CONSTITUTION

Remember Benjamin Franklin's reply to the woman who asked him what he and his colleagues had created? "A Republic, Madam, if you can keep it." In fact, however, the Constitution assigns citizens only the slimmest of roles in keeping the republic. The founders wrote a constitution that in many respects profoundly limits citizen participation.

The political role available to "the people" moved from "subject" to "citizen" with the writing of the Constitution, and especially with the addition of the Bill of Rights, but the citizen's political options were narrow. It is true that he could vote if he met the tight restrictions that the states might require. His role as voter, however, was and is confined to choosing among competing political elites, in the case of the Senate or the presidential electors, or among competing people like himself who are running for the House, but who will themselves be constrained once in power by a system of checks and balances and the necessity of running for reelection in two years.

The Constitution is not a participatory document. It does not create a democratic society in which individuals take an active part in their own governance. The national political system is remote from most individuals, as the Anti-Federalists claimed it would be, and the opportunities to get involved in it are few and costly in terms of time, energy, and money. In fact, the founders preferred it that way. They did not trust human beings, either to know their own best interests or to handle power without being corrupted. They wanted popular power to serve as a potential check on the elected leaders, but they wanted to impose strict checks on popular power as well, to prevent disturbances like Shays's Rebellion from springing up to threaten the system. The Constitution was the republic's insurance policy against chaos and instability.

But in two crucial ways the Constitution does enhance opportunities for participation. First, because it creates a federal system, participation can flourish at the state and local levels even while it remains limited at the national level. We will see that a variety of less formal options are available to citizens, but three of the formal mechanisms of direct democracy at the state level deserve special mention: the initiative, the referendum, and the recall.

initiative citizen petitions to place a proposal or constitutional amendment on the ballot, to be adopted or rejected by majority vote, bypassing the legislature

With the **initiative**, citizens can force a constitutional amendment or state law to be placed on the ballot. This is accomplished by getting a sufficient number of signatures on petitions, typically between 3 and 15 percent of those voting in the last election for governor. Once on the ballot, an initiative is adopted with a majority vote and becomes law, *completely bypassing the state legislature.* About half of the states have provisions for the initiative, and in California it has become the principal way to make significant changes to state law.

referendum an election in which a bill passed by the state legislature is submitted to voters for approval

The **referendum** is an election in which bills passed by the state legislatures are submitted to the voters for their approval. In most states, constitutional amendments have to be submitted for a referendum vote, and in some states questions of taxation do also. A number of the states allow citizens to call for a referendum (by petition) on controversial laws passed by the state legislature, and in many cases the state legislatures themselves can ask for a referendum on matters they believe the voters should decide directly. Referenda are often very complicated and difficult to understand, but they can have large consequences for the citizens who must decipher them and vote on them.

recall elections votes to remove elected officials from office

Recall elections are a way for citizens to remove elected officials from office before their terms are up. These too require petitions, usually with more signatures than are needed for an initiative (frequently 25 percent of the electorate). Statewide recalls are infrequent, but some are quite notable, like the one that removed Gray Davis as governor of California in 2003, clearing the way for Arnold Schwarzenegger's election.

The record of these three measures of direct democracy is mixed. They do enhance opportunities for individuals to participate, and they give citizens more control over what their government does. However, many citizens do not take advantage of these opportunities, leaving greater power concentrated in the hands of those who do. Furthermore, many of the details of lawmaking can be complicated and hard to understand without careful study—something most citizens don't have time to give them. As a result, the people who do vote can be misled or manipulated by complex or obscure wording and it is hard for them to know exactly what they are voting on. Finally, direct democracy, by eliminating the checks the founders thought important, makes government more responsive to short-term fluctuations in public opinion, sometimes denying politicians the necessary time to take a long-term approach to problem solving and policymaking.

A second way that the Constitution enhances opportunities for citizen participation, even though it makes such activity difficult at the national level, is by providing political stability. It is precisely because the Constitution has protected the United States from the kind of chaos and instability that existed under the Articles of Confederation that citizens have the luxury of developing a host of citizenship roles that are not prescribed in the Constitution. Citizens participate in local government, on school boards and in parent-teacher organizations, in charitable groups, and in service organizations. They volunteer in congressional and presidential election campaigns, they run for office, and they serve as magistrates. They circulate petitions, take part in fundraising drives, and participate in neighborhood associations. They file lawsuits, they belong to interest groups, and they march in parades and demonstrations. They read papers and watch the news, they call in to radio talk shows, and they write letters to the editor. They surf political sites on the Internet and register their opinions through web site polling.

In twenty-first-century America, the opportunities for community, local, and state participation are only likely to increase, and this at a time when the Internet brings even the national government closer to many homes. All of these activities are acts of citizenship, albeit a kind of citizenship on which the Constitution is silent. Our founding document does not endorse a role for citizens, other than that of watchful voter, but it creates a political environment in which a variety of forms of civic participation can flourish.

WHAT'S AT STAKE REVISITED

As we have seen, Americans are famously cautious about amending their Constitution. It has been amended only twenty-seven times in its entire history, and ten of those happened in one fell swoop when the Bill of Rights was adopted. So when it comes to the issue of whether to amend the Constitution to allow foreign-born citizens to become president, many people argue that we need to continue to be careful about adding another amendment. What is really at stake in all this caution?

Many of the arguments about whether to amend the Constitution to allow foreign-born Americans to be president concern whether this is an urgent problem that really needs solving through what one editorial called "the drastic remedy of a constitutional overhaul." [46] Opponents warn about cluttering the Constitution with unnecessary amendments, which might have the effect of making us less cautious about new amendments in the future, setting us on what another editorial called a "slippery slope" of constitutional change.[47] Their fear is that the founding document comes to be seen as a bloated instrument of party politics and loses its legitimacy as an impartial rule book—the disinterested guarantor of our procedural rights as Americans.

In the end, worry about amendments other than this particular one is probably what causes many people to oppose the Arnold Amendment. Although the

continued

WHAT'S AT STAKE REVISITED *(continued)*

amendment would be one of the more mechanical rule-changing kinds of amendments that on its face, at least, does not seem to promise radical change for American life, many other amendments on the current agenda are all about freedoms and values. These other amendments tap into our deep ideological differences on whether government should be in the substantive business of telling us how to live our lives or should merely confine itself to providing procedural guarantees.

For instance, many recent calls to amend the Constitution have focused on banning abortion, banning gay marriage, banning flag burning, or permitting prayer in school. For the most part, people split into partisan camps in their support of or opposition to those amendments. Democrats tend to oppose such amendments, believing they curtail fundamental individual rights, and Republicans tend to support them, claiming that they promote important traditional values.

But one can go even further in drawing partisan lines around this issue. Democrats, in general, as liberals who believe that change is inevitable and probably a good thing, are more willing to see the Constitution as a flexible, living document that can be continually altered in small, nonpermanent ways by judicial interpretation. Republicans, on the other hand, share, for the most part, the conservative suspicion of change and a belief that the words of the founders ought not to be tampered with by unelected judges. They are willing to change the Constitution, and even to change it in deep and fundamental ways, but they prefer to do it by amendment.

So what is at stake in the issue of constitutional amendment is really a contest between two basic ideological views about change, the role of the courts, and even about whether government should have more procedural or substantive control over how we live our lives. The founders made it difficult to amend the Constitution precisely to avoid having it used as a pawn in partisan politics. The Arnold Amendment, while in the long run not clearly a partisan issue, ends up viewed with suspicion all the same.

Thinking Outside the Box

- Are there any advantages to living under Calvinball rules?
- Which really *is* the least dangerous branch of the federal government?
- What would the U.S. government be like today if states had the power of nullification?

To Sum Up

KEY TERMS

republic.cqpress.com

amendability (p. 141)
bicameral legislature (p. 109)
block grant (p. 136)
categorical grant (p. 135)
checks and balances (p. 117)
concurrent powers (p. 121)
confederal systems (p. 123)
cooperative federalism (p. 122)
devolution (p. 133)
dual federalism (p. 121)
electoral college (p. 112)
enumerated powers of Congress (p. 121)
executive (p. 111)
fusion of powers (p. 119)
Gibbons v. Ogden (p. 131)
initiative (p. 146)
judicial power (p. 115)
judicial review (p. 115)
legislative supremacy (p. 116)
legislature (p. 109)
McCulloch v. Maryland (p. 130)
necessary and proper clause (p. 121)
nullification (p. 131)
parliamentary system (p. 113)
presidential system (p. 113)
recall election (p. 146)
referendum (p. 146)
republic (p. 109)
separation of powers (p. 117)
supremacy clause (p. 121)
unfunded mandate (p. 138)
unicameral legislature (p. 110)
unitary system (p. 123)

Key terms, chapter summaries, practice quizzes, Internet links, and other study aids are available on the companion Web site at: republic.cqpress.com.

SUMMARY

republic.cqpress.com

- The Constitution is the rule book of American politics. The great decisions and compromises of the founding were really about the allocation of power among the branches of the government, between the national and state governments, and between government and citizens.
- Congress is given broad lawmaking responsibilities in the Constitution. It is composed of two houses, the House of Representatives and the Senate, each with different qualifications, terms of office, and constituencies. Having two houses of the legislature that are constitutionally separated from the president means that more interests are involved in policymaking and that it takes longer to get things done in the United States than under a parliamentary system.
- The president is elected indirectly by the electoral college. Compared to the chief executive of parliamentary systems, the U.S. president has less power.
- The Supreme Court today has much greater powers than those named in the Constitution. This expansion derives from the adoption of the principle of judicial review, which gives the Court much more power than its counterparts in most other democracies and also acts as a check on the powers of the president, Congress, and the states.
- The scheme of checks and balances prevents any branch from overextending its own power. It grew out of the founders' fears of placing too much trust in any single source. The system provides a great deal of protection from abuses of power, but it also makes it difficult to get things done.
- The Constitution is ambiguous in defining federalism, giving "reserved powers" to the states but providing a "necessary and proper clause" that has allowed tremendous growth of national powers.
- Our understanding of federalism in the United States has evolved from a belief in dual federalism, with distinct policy responsibilities for the national and state governments, to the more realistic cooperative federalism, in which the different levels share responsibility in most domestic policy areas.
- Alternatives to our federal arrangement are unitary systems, which give all effective power to the central government, and confederal systems, in which the individual states (or other subunits) have primary power. The balance of power adopted between central and subnational governments directly affects the national government's ability to act on large policy problems and the subnational units' flexibility in responding to local preferences.
- The growth of national power can be traced to the early decisions of Chief Justice John Marshall, the constitutional consequences of the Civil War, the establishment of national supremacy in economics with the New Deal, and new

national responsibilities in protecting citizens' rights that are associated with the civil rights movement.

- Devolution has required new, and sometimes difficult, agreements between state governments and their citizens. For the most part, state institutions (legislature, courts, governor) have become stronger and more efficient in the process.
- Amending the Constitution—that is, changing the basic rules of politics—is a two-step process of proposal by either Congress or a constitutional convention followed by ratification by the states. Of the thousands of amendments that have been suggested, only twenty-seven have been adopted. The Constitution can also be unofficially changed through the less formal and more controversial process of judicial interpretation.

PRACTICE QUIZ

republic.cqpress.com

1. According to this chapter, all governments must have the power to do what three things?

a. Legislate, administer laws, and adjudicate laws.
b. Make laws, rewrite laws, and declare laws to be unconstitutional.
c. Check other branches of government, divide powers among the branches equally, and oversee state governments.
d. Engage in war, defend against foreign attack, and make peace.
e. Control the people, control political parties, and control interest groups.

2. The necessary and proper clause is the provision in the Constitution that

a. allows each branch of government to exercise some form of control over the others.
b. empowers the Supreme Court to rule on the constitutionality of laws.
c. authorizes Congress to make any law required to carry out its powers.
d. declares that the Constitution is the supreme law of the land.
e. limits judicial, executive, and legislative powers by assigning them to different persons or groups.

3. Why did Alexander Hamilton, in *Federalist* No. 78, claim that the judicial branch would be the "least dangerous branch"?

a. The Constitution ensures that judicial elections occur only in off-year elections.
b. The judiciary would hold the power neither of the "sword" nor the "purse."
c. The judiciary would agree with the president because he appoints its members, which makes it a portion of the executive branch.
d. The founders made sure that the Constitution would clearly provide the legislative branch with the permanent power of judicial review.
e. The judiciary holds the power of the "purse" but not the greater power of the "sword."

4. Which of the following parts of the Constitution is not relevant to understanding federalism?

a. The supremacy clause
b. The elastic clause
c. The necessary and proper clause
d. The Tenth Amendment
e. The Preamble

5. One reason the federal government's power has increased over state governments is that

a. the federal government has increasingly used block grants instead of categorical grants.
b. more people have begun to support the idea of devolution.
c. the civil rights movement brought about new federal responsibilities that protect citizens' rights.
d. states have voluntarily given up power to the federal government.
e. the supremacy clause doesn't make it clear whether to follow state or federal law when state and federal laws conflict.

SUGGESTED RESOURCES

republic.cqpress.com

Books

Beer, Samuel H. 1993. *To Make a Nation: The Rediscovery of American Federalism.* Cambridge, Mass.: Harvard University Press. An exceptional historical examination of American federalism with an emphasis on contrasting nation-centered and state-centered federalism.

Madison, James. 1969. *Notes of Debates in the Federal Convention of 1787.* New York: Norton. A fascinating account of what really happened at the Constitutional Convention from the perspective of James Madison, the father of our Constitution.

Madison, James, Alexander Hamilton, and John Jay. 1961. *The Federalist Papers.* New York: New American Library. Madison, Hamilton, and Jay presented compelling arguments for ratification of the proposed Constitution under the pseudonym Publius. *The Federalist Papers* may be a bit difficult to understand, but they are some of the most important works ever written in the history of the United States.

Rossiter, Clinton. 1966. *1787: The Grand Convention.* New York: Macmillan. In a marvelous account of the Constitutional Convention, Rossiter goes into great detail describing the convention's participants, the debate over ratification, and the early years of the new republic.

Storing, Herbert J. 1981. *What the Anti-Federalists Were For.* Chicago: University of Chicago Press. We hear a great deal about those who supported the new Constitution, but what about those who opposed it? This book is a collection of papers written by Anti-Federalists during the constitutional ratification period.

Web Sites

The Constitution. www.usconstitution.net. A rewarding site for anyone interested in learning more about the Constitution. This page contains general information about the Constitution, the founders, and other landmark documents in U.S. history. It also contains a section on how current events are influenced by the Constitution, and vice versa.

National Conference of State Legislatures. www.ncsl.org. This Web site, dedicated to state-federal issues, includes loads of information on national policies implemented at the state level.

State Constitutions. www.law.cornell.edu/statutes.html. In addition to the U.S. Constitution, this site also has links to each state's constitution. These documents provide useful points of comparison to our national "rule book."

United States Constitution Search. www.law.emory.edu/FEDERAL/usconser.html. An excellent source when you need quick answers about the Constitution.

Murals in one of Indiana University's largest lecture halls (right) depict key moments in the state's history—including its one-time ties to the Ku Klux Klan. For most white students, the image is little more than a surprising and perhaps embarrassing curiosity, but for many black students, it is more reason to feel isolated and powerless at a predominantly white school. School officials and student leaders have struggled to find a solution that protects every student's right to get an education in a safe and secure environment while preserving artistic expression.

FUNDAMENTAL AMERICAN LIBERTIES

5

WHAT'S AT STAKE?

Imagine that you are a freshman, an African American student at a predominantly white university in the Midwest. Sitting in your American Politics classroom with four hundred other students on the first day of class, you realize that you see only four other black faces in the room. This experience alone is not that unusual for you; you have gotten used to finding yourself a racial minority. But up on the wall, two huge murals dominate the lecture hall. Painted by Thomas Hart Benton, a noted artist of the 1930s, the murals show key moments (both good and bad) of your state's history, including a scene of hooded Ku Klux Klan members burning a cross in front of a church steeple. It gives you the creeps, intimidates you, and haunts your thoughts. Your professor is talking about American ideals like equal opportunity and equal protection of the laws. How is this equal protection, you wonder, if your education in a public university has to take place in the shadow of a portrait of the Ku Klux Klan?

This situation is not merely hypothetical. At Indiana University, students have faced this seeming contradiction since the Benton murals were put up in the 1940s in the campus's largest lecture hall in Woodburn Hall. They are part of a series of twenty-one murals that depict Indiana history. Although a plaque on the wall explains that the murals do not celebrate the Klan, but rather show how journalists (in the forefront of the picture) worked to expose the Klan's role in Indiana politics, the plaque is small and the mural is very, very big.

Periodically, the murals had been the target of vandalism and of more legitimate efforts by students to have them removed. Previous student action had resulted in the production of a video, which professors teaching in the lecture hall were asked to show, explaining the history of the murals and acknowledging the bad feelings that they sometimes invoke. In the flurry of activity at the start of the semester, however, the videos often went unshown. In the spring of 2002, the Indiana University Black Student Union tried one more time to have the murals removed.

Claiming that a classroom at a public university is a public space and that students who wanted to take a class that was offered in that room had no choice but to attend, they argued that if the university could not come up with some solution that would relieve students of having to get their education in

(continued)

what felt like a hostile atmosphere, then the murals should be removed, a costly procedure hazardous to preserving the murals. Controversy flared as students and professors found themselves torn between keeping the murals as the historical monument that they were and finding a way to accommodate diverse views and feelings. Why was this situation so difficult? Why not just take down the murals, or tell the students that they would just have to deal with it? What was really at stake in the case of the Thomas Hart Benton murals? We return to this question after we explore some of the issues involved in the protection of our civil liberties. *

"Give me liberty," declared patriot Patrick Henry at the start of the Revolutionary War, "or give me death." "Live Free or Die," proudly proclaims the New Hampshire license plate. Americans have always put a lot of stock in their freedom. Certain that they live in the least restrictive country in the world, Americans celebrate their freedoms and are proud of the Constitution, the laws, and the traditions that preserve them.

And yet, living collectively under a government means that we aren't free to do whatever we want. There are limits on our freedoms that allow us to live peacefully with our fellows, minimizing the conflict that would result if we all did exactly what we pleased. John Locke said that liberty does not equal license; that is, the freedom to do some things doesn't mean the freedom to do everything. Deciding what rights we give up to join civilized society, and what rights we retain, is one of the great challenges of democratic government.

What are these things called "rights" or "liberties," so precious that some Americans are willing to lay down their lives to preserve them? On the one hand, the answer is very simple. *Rights* and *liberties* are synonyms; they mean freedoms or privileges to which one has a claim. In that respect, we use the words more or less interchangeably. But when prefaced by the word *civil,* both rights and liberties take on a more specific meaning, and they no longer mean quite the same thing.

civil liberties individual freedoms guaranteed to the people primarily by the Bill of Rights

Our **civil liberties** are individual freedoms that place limitations on the power of government. In general, civil liberties protect our right to think and act without governmental interference. Some of these rights are spelled out in the Constitution, particularly in the Bill of Rights. These include the rights to express ourselves and to choose our own religious beliefs. Others, like the right to privacy, rest on the shakier ground of judicial decision making. Although government is prevented from limiting these freedoms per se, we will see that sometimes one person's freedom—to speak or act in a certain way—may be limited by another person's rights. Government does play a role in resolving the conflicts between individuals' rights.

civil rights citizenship rights guaranteed to the people (primarily in the Thirteenth, Fourteenth, Fifteenth, Nineteenth, and Twenty-sixth Amendments) and protected by the government

While civil liberties refer to restrictions on government action, **civil rights** refer to the extension of government action to secure citizenship rights to all members of society. When we speak of civil rights, we most often mean that the government must treat all citizens equally, apply laws fairly, and not discriminate unjustly against certain groups of people. Most of the rights we consider civil rights are guaranteed by the Thirteenth, Fourteenth, Fifteenth, Nineteenth, and Twenty-sixth Amendments. These amendments lay out fundamental rights of citizenship, most notably the right to vote but also the right to equal treatment before the law and the right to due process of law.

They forbid government from making laws that treat people differently on the basis of race, and they ensure that the right to vote cannot be denied on the basis of race or gender.

Not all people live under governments whose rules guarantee them fundamental liberties. In fact, we argued earlier that one way of distinguishing between authoritarian and nonauthoritarian governments is that nonauthoritarian governments, including democracies, give citizens the power to challenge government if they believe it has denied their basic rights. When we consider our definition of politics as "who gets what, and how," we see that rights are crucial in democratic politics, where a central tension is the power of the individual pitted against the power of the government. What's at stake in democracy is the resolution of that tension. In fact, democracies depend on the existence of rights in at least two ways. First, civil liberties provide rules that keep government limited, so that it cannot become too powerful. Second, civil rights help define who "we, the people" are in a democracy, and they give those people the power necessary to put some controls on their governments.

We will take two chapters to explore the issues of civil liberties and civil rights in depth. In this chapter we begin with a general discussion of the meaning of rights or liberties in a democracy, and then focus on the traditional civil liberties that provide a check on the power of government. In Chapter 6 we focus on civil rights and the continuing struggle of some groups of Americans—like women, African Americans, and other minorities—to be fully counted and empowered in American politics.

As an introduction to the basic civil liberties guaranteed to Americans, in this chapter you will learn about

- the meaning of rights in a democratic society
- the Bill of Rights as part of the federal Constitution, and its relationship to the states
- freedom of religion in the United States
- freedom of speech and of the press
- the right to bear arms
- the rights of people accused of crimes in the United States
- the right to privacy

RIGHTS IN A DEMOCRACY

The freedoms we consider indispensable to the working of a democracy are part of the everyday language of politics in America. We take many of them for granted: we speak confidently of our freedoms of speech, of the press, of religion, and of our rights to bear arms, to a fair trial, and to privacy. There is nothing inevitable about these freedoms, however.

In fact, there is nothing inevitable about the idea of rights at all. Until the writing of such Enlightenment figures as John Locke, it was rare for individuals to talk about claiming rights against government. Governments were assumed to have all the power, their subjects only such privileges as government was willing to bestow. Locke argued that the rights to life, liberty, and the pursuit of property were conferred on individuals by nature, and that one of the primary purposes of government was to preserve the natural rights of its citizens.

This notion of natural rights and limited government was central to the founders of the American system. In the Declaration of Independence, Thomas Jefferson wrote that men are "endowed by their Creator with certain inalienable rights; that among these are life, liberty, and the pursuit of happiness; that, to secure these rights, governments are instituted among men." John Locke could not have said it better himself.

Practically speaking, of course, any government can make its citizens do anything it wishes, regardless of their rights, as long as it is in charge of the military and the police. But in nonauthoritarian governments, public opinion is usually outraged at the invasion of individual rights. Unless the government is willing to dispense with its reputation as a democracy, it must respond in some way to pacify public opinion. Public opinion can be a powerful guardian of citizens' rights in a democracy.

RIGHTS AND THE POWER OF THE PEOPLE

Just as rights limit government, they also empower its citizens. To claim a right is to claim a power—power over a government that wants to stop publication of an article detailing its plans for war; power over a school board that wants children to say a Christian prayer in school, regardless of their religious affiliation; power over a state legal system that wants to charge suspects with a crime without guaranteeing that a lawyer can be present; power over a state legislature that says residents can't vote because of the color of their skin or the fact that they were born female.

A person who can successfully claim that he or she has rights that must be respected by government is a citizen of that government; a person who is under the authority of a government but cannot claim rights is merely a subject, bound by the laws but without any power to challenge or change them. This does not mean, as we will see, that a citizen can always have things his or her own way. Nor does it mean that noncitizens have no rights in a democracy. It *does* mean that citizens have special protections and powers that allow them to stand up to government and plead their cases when they believe an injustice is being done.

The power of citizenship is nowhere so clearly illustrated as in the Supreme Court case of *Dred Scott v. Sanford.* Dred Scott was an African American slave who, through a transfer of ownership in 1834, was taken from Missouri, a slave state, into Illinois and the Wisconsin Territory, which Congress had declared to be free areas. Scott argued that living in a free territory made him a free man. The Court's decision, handed down in 1857, denied Scott the legal standing to bring a case before the Supreme Court because, according to the Court, Dred Scott, as an African American and as a slave, could not be considered a citizen of the United States. Although several northern states had extended political rights to African Americans by this time, the ruling declaring Scott a noncitizen denied him access to the courts, one of the primary arenas in which the battle for rights is fought.

WHEN RIGHTS CONFLICT

Because rights represent power, they are, like all other forms of power, subject to conflict and controversy. Often for one person to get his or her own way, someone else must lose out.

People clash over rights in two ways. The first type of rights conflict occurs between individuals. One person's right to share a prayer with classmates at the start of the school day conflicts with another student's right not to be subjected to a religious practice against his or her will. Our right as citizens to know about the individuals we elect to office might conflict with a given candidate's right to privacy. What is at stake in these disputes might be an inevitable conflict of interest (for instance, candidate versus voter) or it might be a more fundamental issue like the role of religion in society, gay rights, or the death penalty that reflects not just differences in preferences or interests, but deeply held visions of the "right" kind of society. These visions are often so firmly embedded in people's minds that any challenge is intolerable.

The second way rights conflict is when the rights of individuals are pitted against the needs of society and the demands of collective living. The decision to wear a motorcycle helmet or a seat belt, for instance, might seem like one that should be left up to individuals. But society also has an interest in regulating these behaviors because the failure to wear helmets or seat belts is costly to society in more ways than one. The death or serious injury of its citizens deprives society of productive members who might have lived to make important contributions. Through public education and other social programs, society makes a considerable investment in its citizens, which is lost if those citizens die prematurely. In addition, accident victims might require expensive, long-term medical treatment, usually taking place eventually at public expense. The decision about whether to wear a motorcycle helmet might seem to be a private one, but it has many public repercussions. Similarly, individual acts such as carrying a gun or publishing pornography can have consequences for society.

WHEN RIGHTS CONFLICT—THE CASE OF NATIONAL SECURITY

One very clear example of how individual rights can conflict with the needs of society is the case of national security. After the terrorist attacks of September 11, 2001, Americans were deeply afraid. Determined to prevent a repeat of the horrific attacks, the government federalized airport security and began screening passengers, searching luggage, and allowing armed agents on airplanes. Officials scrutinized the backgrounds of tourists and students from the Middle East and kept a close eye on Arab Americans they suspected of having ties to terrorist organizations. Congress passed and President George W. Bush signed the USA Patriot Act of 2001, which, among other things, made it easier for law enforcement to intercept e-mail and conduct roving wiretaps, gave it access to library records and bookstore purchases, and allowed immigrants suspected of terrorist activity to be held for up to seven days (and sometimes indefinitely) without being charged. The Bush administration, fearful that the evidence required in a U.S. court of law might not be forthcoming to convict a suspected terrorist, issued an executive order that those non–U.S. citizens arrested on grounds of terrorism could be subject to trial in a military tribunal, where usual rules of due process need not apply.

All of these measures may have increased the security of U.S. citizens, but they also reduced their civil liberties. In the immediate aftermath of September 11, such a trade-off struck most Americans as worthwhile. In times of national danger, we are susceptible to calls for locking down our liberties if we believe that it can help lock out threats. Somehow a reduction in freedom does not seem like an unreasonable price to pay for a reduction in fear.

But not all Americans were quick to endorse the sacrifice of their rights in favor of a potentially safer society. Immediately after the Patriot Act was passed, organizations including the American Civil Liberties Union (ACLU) criticized the legislation for infringing on Americans' privacy, violating due process, and being discriminatory.

How Far Do We Go?
The Constitution gives us a number of procedural rights that protect us if we are arrested and guarantee us access to a lawyer. Should these protections be extended to those accused of waging war against the United States? In the spring of 2004, photos surfaced of the U.S. military's use of torture against prisoners captured in the Iraq war and held at the Abu Ghraib prison. While the government disowned the worst of these abuses, we continue to hold people captured in Afghanistan and Iraq at a U.S. base in Guantanamo Bay, Cuba, who have no access to legal counsel to ensure the protection of their rights. How do we ensure our national security while maintaining the long American tradition of protecting civil liberties?

Although their efforts failed, some members of Congress tried to repeal sections of the Act. Even support among the public began to wane as the events of September 11 became more distant. In January 2002 the country was evenly split when asked whether government should take steps to prevent terrorism even if civil liberties were violated. By November 2003, 64 percent of the public responded that government should take steps to prevent additional terrorist attacks but not violate civil liberties; only 31 percent said that steps should be taken even if civil liberties were violated.[1]

The balancing of public safety with individuals' rights is complex. We could ensure our safety from most threats, perhaps, if we were willing to give up all of our freedom; with complete control over our movements, with the ability to monitor all our communications, with information on all our spending decisions, government could keep itself informed about which of us was likely to endanger others. The ultimate problem, of course, is that without our civil liberties, we have no protection from government itself.

HOW DO WE RESOLVE CONFLICTS ABOUT RIGHTS?

Because we are fortunate enough to be political and, we hope, rational beings, we can resolve disputes over rights without necessarily resorting to violence. But that doesn't make their resolution easy or necessarily "fair." Much of the conflict over rights in this country is between competing visions of what is fair. Because so much is at stake, the resulting battles are often politics at its messiest. Adding to the general political untidiness is the fact that so many actors get involved in the process: the courts, Congress, the president, and the people themselves. Although we focus on these actors in depth later in this book, we now look briefly at the role each one plays in resolving conflicts over rights.

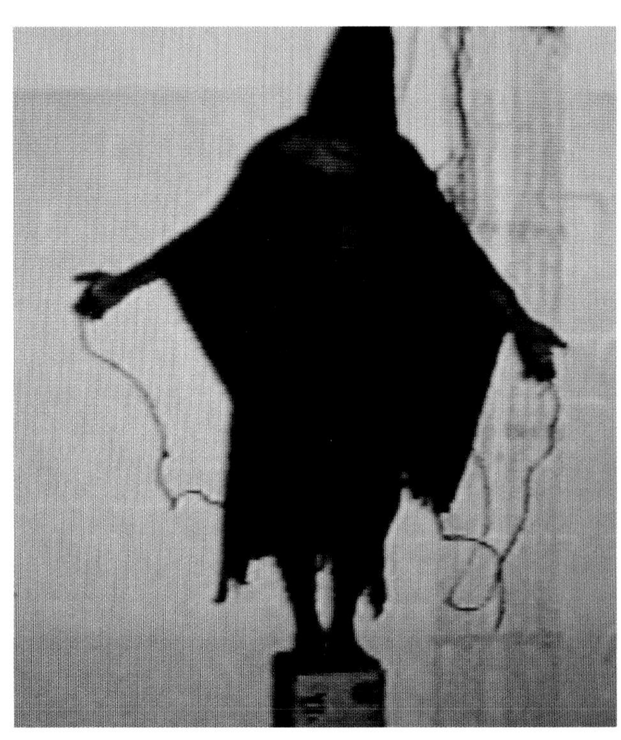

The Courts One of the jobs of the judiciary system is to arbitrate disputes among individuals about such things as rights. In this country, the highest you can go in seeking justice through the courts—that is, the highest court of appeal—is the U.S. Supreme Court. For legal and practical reasons, the Supreme Court can hear only a fraction of the cases that are appealed to it, so the Court agrees to hear cases when it wants to send a message to lower courts about how the Constitution should be interpreted. As we discussed in Chapter 4 the Supreme Court may exercise a power called judicial review, which enables it to decide if laws of Congress or the states are consistent with the Constitution and, if they are not, to invalidate them. Judicial review is generally used sparingly by the Court, but it can offer a remedy when rights conflict.

Even though we typically think of the Supreme Court as the ultimate judge of what is fair in the United States, the truth is that its rulings have varied as the membership of the Court has changed. There is no guarantee that the Court will reach some unarguably "correct" answer to a legal dilemma; the justices are human beings influenced by their own values, ideals, and biases in interpreting and applying the laws. In addition, although the founders had hoped that the Supreme Court justices would be above the political fray, they are in fact subject to all sorts of political pressures, from the ideology of the presidents who appoint them to the steady influence of public opinion and the media. How else can we account for the fact that the same institution that denied Dred Scott his right to use the court system was responsible a century later for breaking down the barriers between blacks and whites in the South? At times in our history the Court has championed what seem like underdog interests that fight the mainstream of American public opinion, for example, ruling in favor of those who refuse to salute the American flag on religious grounds.[2] It has also tempered some of the post–September 11 legislation by ruling, for instance, that enemy combatants do have some due process rights, although it has not yet spelled them out.[3] At other times the Supreme Court has been less expansionary in its interpretation of civil liberties, and its rulings have favored the interests of big business over the rights of ordinary Americans, have blocked the rights of racial minorities, and have even put the stamp of constitutional approval on the World War II incarceration of Japanese Americans in internment camps,[4] an action we, as a nation, have since apologized for.

Congress Another actor involved in the resolution of conflicts over rights in this country is Congress. Sometimes Congress has chosen to stay out of disputes about rights. At other times it has taken decisive action either to limit or to expand the rights of many Americans. For example, the Smith Act, passed by Congress in 1940, made it illegal to advocate the overthrow of the U.S. government by force or to join any organization that advocated government subversion. A decade later, in the name of national security, the House Un-American Activities Committee investigated and ruined the reputations of many Americans suspected of having sympathy for the Communist Party, sometimes on the flimsiest of evidence.[5] But Congress has also acted on the side of protecting rights. When the courts became more conservative in the 1980s and 1990s, with appointments made by Republican presidents Ronald Reagan and George H. W. Bush, the judiciary narrowed its protections of civil rights issues. The Democratic-led Congress of the time countered with the Civil Rights Act of 1991, which broadened civil rights protection in the workplace. Congress has also worked to balance the rights of gun owners with the rights of crime victims by passing the Brady Bill, which imposes a waiting period and background check on handgun purchases, and the 1994 Crime Bill, which outlaws some kinds of assault weapons.

The President Presidents as well can be involved in resolving disputes over rights. They can get involved by having administration officials lobby the Supreme Court to encourage outcomes they favor. Popular presidents can also try to persuade Congress to go along with their policy initiatives by bringing public pressure to bear. Their influence can be used to expand or contract the protection of individual rights. In the 1950s President Dwight Eisenhower was reluctant to enforce desegregation in the South, believing that it was the job of the states, not the federal government.[6] President John Kennedy chose more active involvement when he sent Congress a civil rights bill in 1963 (it was signed by Lyndon Johnson in 1964). More recently, President Bush used his post–September 11 popularity to urge Congress to pass the Patriot Act, and, as we have seen, it was his executive order that declared that noncitizens could be subject to trial by military tribunal.

The Czar of Un-American Activity
Playing on American anxieties about communism in the 1950s, Senator Joseph R. McCarthy led an aggressive investigation of suspected communists in the U.S. government. Although his sensational and clever tactics ruined many careers—and kept his name in the headlines—he failed to find evidence of a single "card-carrying communist" in any government department. McCarthy, censured by the Senate in 1954, died in disgrace three years later.

The People Finally, the American people themselves are actors in the struggle over rights. Individual Americans may use the courts to sue for what they perceive as their rights, but more often individuals act in groups. One of the best known of these groups is the ACLU. The ACLU's goal is to defend the liberties of Americans, whatever their ideological position. Thus the ACLU would be just as likely to fight for the right of an American Nazi Party to stage a march as it would be to support a group of parents and students challenging the removal of books with gay themes from a high school library. Other interest groups that get involved in the effort to resolve rights conflicts include the National Association for the Advancement of Colored People (NAACP), the National Organization for Women (NOW), the Christian Coalition, Common Cause, environmental groups like the Sierra Club, AARP (formerly the American Association of Retired Persons), and the National Rifle Association (NRA). These groups and many others like them engage in fundraising and public relations activities to publicize their views and work to influence government directly, by meeting with lawmakers and testifying at congressional hearings. Even though individuals may not feel very effective in trying to change what government does, in groups their efforts are magnified, and the effects can be considerable.

WHO, WHAT, HOW Citizens of democracies have a vital stake in the issue of fundamental rights. What they stand to gain is more power for themselves and less for government. But citizens also have at stake the resolution of the very real conflicts that arise as all citizens try to exercise their rights simultaneously. And as citizens try to maximize their personal freedoms, they are likely to clash with governmental rules that suppress some individual freedom in exchange for public order.

The means for resolving these conflicts are to be found in the Constitution, in the exercise of judicial review by the Supreme Court, in congressional legislation and pres-

Mercury Rising
This Sierra Club protester is acting to secure what he and others see as their right to clean air and water. The object of their wrath is lax government regulation of mercury cleanup from coal-fired power plants. The freedom from government regulation that power companies seek clashes with their critics' freedom to live in a clean environment. Alone, individuals cannot do much to persuade agencies sympathetic to strong financial interests like power companies, but united in group action, citizens have been and can be quite effective at changing government policies to protect their rights.

idential persuasion, and in the actions of citizens themselves, engaging in interest group activities and litigation.

THE BILL OF RIGHTS AND THE STATES

The Bill of Rights looms large in any discussion of American civil liberties, but the document that today seems so inseparable from American citizenship had a stormy birth. Controversy raged over whether a bill of rights was necessary in the first place, deepening the split between Federalists and Anti-Federalists during the founding. And the controversy did not end once it was firmly established as the first ten amendments to the Constitution. Over a century passed before the Supreme Court agreed that at least some of the restrictions imposed on the national government by the Bill of Rights should be applied to the states as well.

WHY IS A BILL OF RIGHTS VALUABLE?

Recall from Chapter 3 that we came very close to not having any Bill of Rights in the Constitution at all. The Federalists had argued that the Constitution itself was a bill of rights, that individual rights were already protected by many of the state constitutions, and that to list the powers that the national government did *not* have was dangerous, as it implied that it *did* have every other power. Hamilton had spelled out this argument in *Federalist* No. 84, and James Madison agreed, at least initially, calling the effort to pass such "parchment barriers," as he called the first ten amendments, a "nauseous project." [7]

But Madison, in company with some of the other Federalists, came to agree with such Anti-Federalists as Thomas Jefferson, who wrote, "A bill of rights is what the people are entitled to against every government on earth." [8] Even though, as the Federalists argued, the national government was limited in principle by popular sovereignty (the concept that ultimate authority rests with the people), it could not hurt to limit it in practice as well. A specific list of the rights held by the people would give the judiciary a more effective check on the other branches.

habeas corpus the right of an accused person to be brought before a judge and informed of the charges and evidence against him or her

bills of attainder laws under which specific persons or groups are detained and sentenced without trial

ex post facto laws laws that criminalize an action *after* it occurs

To some extent Hamilton was correct in calling the Constitution a bill of rights in itself. Protection of some very specific rights is contained in the text of the document. The national government may not suspend writs of **habeas corpus**, which means that it cannot fail to bring prisoners, at their request, before a judge and inform the court why they are being held and what evidence is against them. This provision protects people from being imprisoned solely for political reasons. Both the national and the state governments are forbidden to pass **bills of attainder**, which are laws that single out a person or group as guilty and impose punishment without trial. Neither can they pass **ex post facto laws**, which are laws that make an action a crime after the fact, even though it was legal when carried out. States may not impair or negate the obligation of contracts; here the founders obviously had in mind the failings of the Articles of Confederation. And the citizens of each state are entitled to "the privileges and immunities of the several states," which prevents any state from discriminating against citizens of other states. This provision protects a nonresident's right to travel freely, conduct business, and have access to state courts while visiting another state.[9] Of course, nonresidents are discriminated against when they have to pay a higher nonresident tuition to attend a state college or university, but the Supreme Court has ruled that this type of "discrimination" is not a violation of the privileges and immunities clause.

For the Anti-Federalists, these rights, almost all of them restrictions on the national and state governments with respect to criminal laws, did not provide enough security against potential abuse of government power. The first ten amendments add several more categories of restrictions on government. Although twelve amendments had been proposed, two were not ratified: one concerned the apportionment of members of Congress, and the other barred midterm pay raises for congressmen. (The congressional pay raise amendment, which prevents members of Congress from voting themselves a salary increase effective during that term of office, was passed as the Twenty-seventh Amendment in 1992.) Amendments One through Ten were ratified on December 15, 1791. See Table 5.1 for details on the provisions of the Bill of Rights.

APPLYING THE BILL OF RIGHTS TO THE STATES

If you look closely at the Bill of Rights, you'll see that most of the limitations on government action are directed toward Congress. "Congress shall make no law . . . ," begins the First Amendment. Nothing in the text of the first ten amendments would prevent the Oregon legislature, for instance, from passing a law restricting the freedoms of Oregon newspaper editors to criticize the government. Until about the turn of the twentieth century, the Supreme Court clearly stipulated that the Bill of Rights applied only to the national government and not to the states.[10]

Not until the passage of the Fourteenth Amendment in 1868 did the Constitution make it possible for the Court to require that states protect their citizens' basic liberties. That post–Civil War amendment was specifically designed to force southern

TABLE 5.1 Protections of the Bill of Rights

The first ten amendments to the Constitution, known as the Bill of Rights, were passed by Congress on September 25, 1789, and ratified two years later, on December 15, 1791. See the Appendix for the actual wording of each amendment.

First Amendment	Prohibits government establishment of religion Protects the free exercise of religion Protects freedom of speech and the press Protects freedom of assembly Protects the right to petition government "for a redress of grievances"
Second Amendment	Protects the right to bear arms in order to maintain a well-regulated militia
Third Amendment	Prohibits the quartering of soldiers in homes during peacetime Requires legal authorization for quartering of soldiers during war
Fourth Amendment	Protects against "unreasonable searches and seizures" Allows judges to issue search warrants only with "probable cause"
Fifth Amendment	Requires a grand jury indictment before a person can be tried for a serious crime Prohibits "double jeopardy" (repeated prosecution for the same offense after being found innocent) Prohibits the government from forcing any person in a criminal case to be a witness against himself Prohibits the government from depriving a person of "life, liberty, or property" without due process Requires that just compensation be paid for property taken for public use
Sixth Amendment	Requires that the accused in a criminal case receive a speedy and public trial, heard by a jury in the district where the crime took place Requires that the accused be informed of the nature and cause of the accusation, be confronted with the witnesses against him, have the right to call witnesses who could be favorable to his case, and receive the assistance of counsel
Seventh Amendment	Requires a jury trial in civil cases involving more than $20 and requires that juries be the final finders of fact except as provided for by common law
Eighth Amendment	Prohibits excessive bail and excessive fines Prohibits cruel and unusual punishment
Ninth Amendment	States that the rights of the people are not limited to those spelled out in the Constitution
Tenth Amendment	Guarantees that the states or the people retain any powers not expressly given to the national government or prohibited to the states

states to extend the rights of citizenship to African Americans, but its wording left it open to other interpretations. The amendment says, in part,

> No state shall make or enforce any law which shall abridge the privileges and immunities of citizens of the United States; nor shall any state deprive any person of life, liberty, or property, without due process of law; nor deny to any person within its jurisdiction the equal protection of the laws.

In 1897 the Supreme Court tentatively began the process of nationalization, or **incorporation**, of most (but not all) of the protections of the Bill of Rights into the states' Fourteenth Amendment obligations to guarantee their citizens due process of law.[11]

incorporation Supreme Court action making the protections of the Bill of Rights applicable to the states

Not until the case of *Gitlow v. New York* (1925), however, did the Court begin to articulate a clear theory of incorporation. In *Gitlow,* Justice Edward Sanford wrote, "We may and do assume that freedom of speech and of the press . . . are among the fundamental rights and liberties protected . . . from impairment by the states."[12] Without any great fanfare, the Court reversed almost a century of ruling by assuming that some rights are so fundamental that they deserve protection by the states as well as the federal government. This approach meant that all rights did not necessarily qualify for incorporation; the Court had to consider each right on a case-by-case basis to see how fundamental it was. This was a tactic that Justice Benjamin N. Cardozo called **selective incorporation**. Over the years the Court has switched between a theory of selective incorporation and total incorporation. As a result, almost all of the rights in the first ten amendments have been incorporated, with some notable exceptions, such as the Second Amendment (see Figure 5.1).

selective incorporation incorporation of rights on a case-by-case basis

Keep in mind that since incorporation is a matter of interpretation rather than an absolute constitutional principle, it is a judicial creation. What justices create they can also uncreate if they change their minds or if the composition of the Court changes. Like all other judicial creations, the process of incorporation is subject to reversal, and it is possible that such a reversal may currently be under way as today's more conservative Court narrows its understanding of the rights that states must protect.

WHO, WHAT, HOW Because rights are so central to a democracy, citizens clearly have a stake in seeing that they are guaranteed these rights at every level of government. The Bill of Rights guarantees them at the federal level, but it is through the process of incorporation into the Fourteenth Amendment

FIGURE 5.1

Applying the Bill of Rights to the States

AMENDMENT	ADDRESSES	CASE	YEAR
Fifth	Just compensation	*Chicago, Burlington & Quincy v. Chicago*	1897
First	Freedom of speech	*Gilbert v. Minnesota* *Gitlow v. New York* *Fiske v. Kansas*	1920 1925 1927
	Freedom of the press	*Near v. Minnesota*	1931
Sixth	Counsel in capital cases	*Powell v. Alabama*	1932
First	Religious freedom (generally)	*Hamilton v. Regents of California*	1934
	Freedom of assembly	*DeJonge v. Oregon*	1937
	Free exercise	*Cantwell v. Connecticut*	1940
	Religious establishment	*Everson v. Board of Education*	1947
Sixth	Public trial	In re *Oliver*	1948
Fourth	Unreasonable search and seizure	*Wolf v. Colorado*	1949
	Exclusionary rule	*Mapp v. Ohio*	1961
Eighth	Cruel and unusual punishment	*Robinson v. California*	1962
Sixth	Counsel in felony cases	*Gideon v. Wainwright*	1963
Fifth	Self-incrimination	*Malloy v. Hogan*	1964
Sixth	Impartial jury Speedy trial Jury trial in serious crimes	*Parker v. Gladden* *Klopfer v. North Carolina* *Duncan v. Louisiana*	1966 1967 1968
Fifth	Double jeopardy	*Benton v. Maryland*	1969

that they are guaranteed at the state level unless the state constitution also provides guarantees. Incorporation, as a judicial creation, is not on as firm a ground as the Bill of Rights because it can be reversed if the Supreme Court changes its mind.

The Supreme Court also has a stake here. It has considerably expanded its power over the states and within the federal government by virtue of its interpretation of the Fourteenth Amendment and its creation of the process of incorporation.

THE FIRST AMENDMENT: FREEDOM OF RELIGION

The First Amendment reads, "Congress shall make no law respecting an establishment of religion, or prohibiting the free exercise thereof; or abridging the freedom of speech, or of the press; or the right of the people peaceably to assemble, and to petition the government for a redress of grievances." These are the "democratic freedoms," the liberties that the founders believed to be necessary to maintain a representative democracy by ensuring a free and unfettered people. For all that, none of these liberties has escaped controversy, and none has been interpreted by the Supreme Court to be absolute or unlimited. Beginning with freedom of religion, we will look at each clause of the First Amendment, the controversy and power struggles surrounding it, and the way the courts have interpreted and applied it.

The briefest look around the world tells us what happens when politics and religion are allowed to mix. When it comes to conflicts over religion, over our fundamental beliefs about the world and the way life should be lived, the stakes are enormous. Passions run deep, and compromise is difficult.

So far the United States has been spared the sort of violent conflict that arises when one group declares its religion to be the one true faith for the whole polity. One reason for this is that Americans are largely Christian, although they belong to many different sects (see "*Who Are We?* Americans and Religion"), so there hasn't been too much disagreement over basic beliefs. But another reason that violent conflict over religion is limited in the United States is the First Amendment, whose first line guarantees that "Congress shall make no law respecting an establishment of religion or prohibiting the free exercise thereof." Although this amendment has generated a tremendous amount of controversy, it has at the same time established general guidelines with which most people can agree and a venue (the courts) where conflicts can be aired and addressed. The establishment clause and the free exercise clause, as the two parts of that guarantee are known, have become something of a constitutional battleground in American politics, but they have kept the United States from becoming a battleground of a more literal sort by deflecting religious conflict to the courts.

WHY IS RELIGIOUS FREEDOM VALUABLE?

While not all the founders endorsed religious freedom for everyone, some of them, notably Jefferson and Madison, cherished the notion of a universal freedom of conscience, the right of all individuals to believe as they pleased. Jefferson wrote that the First Amendment built "a wall of separation between church and state." [13] They based their view of religious freedom on three main arguments. First, history has shown, from the Holy Roman Empire to the Church of England, that when church and state

Who Are We?

Americans and Religion

America is a religious nation. More of us say we are religious than do citizens in other Western nations (even those with official state churches), and many of us see our religion as a source of our national strength. Yet we are also tolerant of religious views other than our own, and half of us feel that it is possible to live a moral life without believing in God. This combination of faith and tolerance echoes the conflicts inherent in the First Amendment. What is the relationship between religious values and a nation's civic life?

Our Religious Identities: Very religious, but many religions

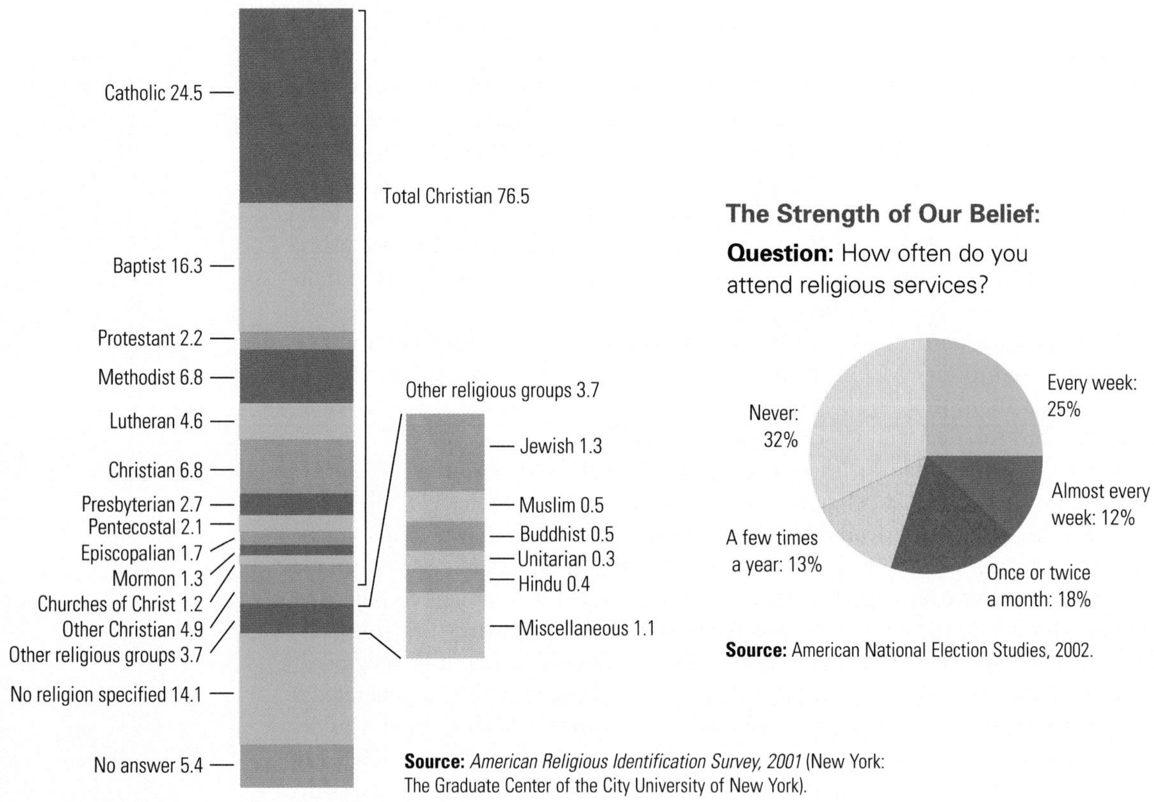

Source: *American Religious Identification Survey, 2001* (New York: The Graduate Center of the City University of New York).

Source: American National Election Studies, 2002.

are linked, all individual freedoms are in jeopardy. After all, if government is merely the arm of God, what power of government cannot be justified?

A second argument for practicing religious freedom is based on the effect that politics can have on religious concerns. Early champions of a separation between politics and religion worried that the spiritual purity and sanctity of religion would be ruined if it mixed with the worldly realm of politics, with its emphasis on power and influence.[14] Further, if religion became dependent on government, in Madison's words, it would result in "pride and indolence in the clergy; ignorance and servility in the laity; in both, superstition, bigotry and persecution."[15]

Religious Tolerance and the Role of Religion in American Life: Which is closer to your own views?

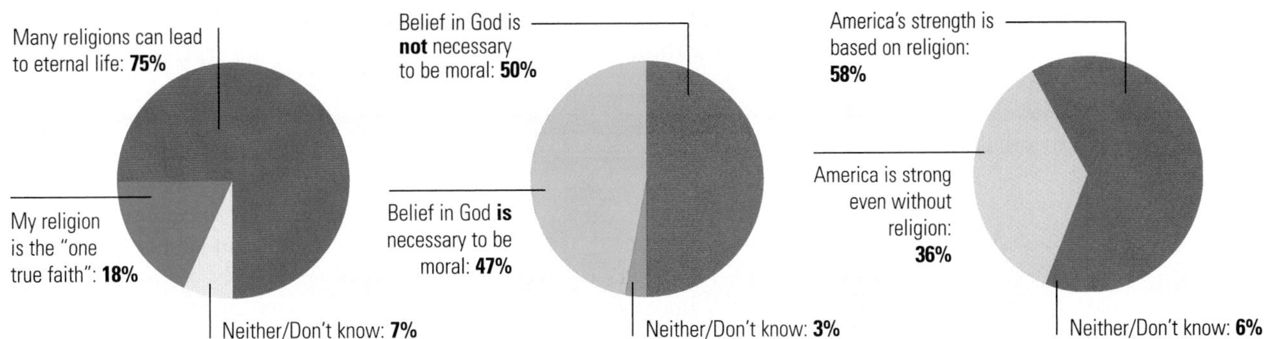

Source: "Americans Struggle with Religion at Home and Abroad." Pew Research Center for the People and the Press. The Pew Forum on Religious and Public Life. Press release, March 20, 2002.

Our Religious Beliefs Compared to Other Nations: Americans take religion very seriously.

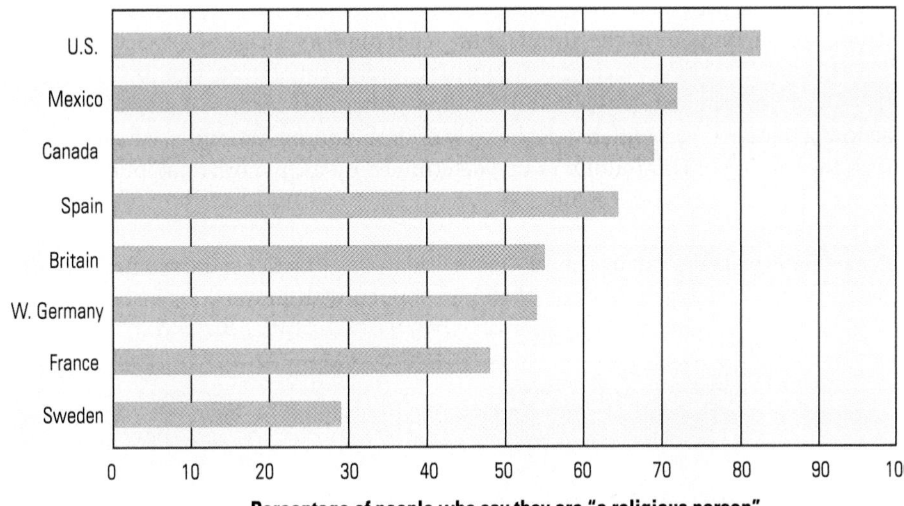

Source: *The Public Perspective,* October/November 1997. Survey by the World Values Study Group, 1990–1993.

Finally, as politics can have negative effects on religion, so too can religion have negative effects on politics, dividing society into the factions that Madison saw as the primary threat to republican government. Religion, Madison feared, could have a divisive effect on the polity only if it became linked to government.

THE ESTABLISHMENT CLAUSE: SEPARATIONISTS VERSUS ACCOMMODATIONISTS

establishment clause the First Amendment guarantee that the government will not create and support an official state church

The beginning of the First Amendment, forbidding Congress to make laws that would establish an official religion, is known as the **establishment clause.** Americans have fought over the meaning of the establishment clause almost since its inception. While founders like Jefferson and Madison were clear on their position that church and state should be separate realms, other early Americans were not. After independence, for instance, all but two of the former colonies had declared themselves to be "Christian states." [16] Non-Christian minorities were rarely tolerated or allowed to participate in politics. Jews could not hold office in Massachusetts until 1848.[17] It may be that the founders were sometimes less concerned with preserving the religious freedom of others than with guaranteeing their own.

separationists supporters of a "wall of separation" between church and state

accomodationists supporters of government nonpreferential accommodation of religion

A similar division continues today between the **separationists**, who believe that a "wall" should exist between church and state, and the nonpreferentialists, or **accommodationists**, who contend that the state should not be separate from religion but rather should accommodate it, without showing a preference for one religion over another. These accommodationists argue that the First Amendment should not prevent governmental aid to religious groups, prayer in school or in public ceremonies, public aid to parochial schools, the posting of religious documents such as the Ten Commandments in public places, or the teaching of the Bible's story of creation along with evolution in public schools. Adherents of this position claim that a rigid interpretation of separation of church and state amounts to intolerance of their religious rights or, in the words of Supreme Court Justice Anthony Kennedy, to "unjustified hostility to religion." [18] President Reagan, both Presidents Bush, and many Republicans have shared this view, as have many powerful interest groups such as the Christian Coalition.

A lot is clearly at stake in the battle between the separationists and the accommodationists. On one side of the dispute is the separationists' image of a society in which the rights of all citizens, including minorities, receive equal protection by the law. In this society, private religions abound, but they remain private, not matters for public action or support. Very different is the view of the accommodationists, which emphasizes the sharing of community values, determined by the majority and built into the fabric of society and political life.

Recent Rulings on the Establishment Clause Today U.S. practice stands somewhere between these two images. Sessions of Congress open with prayers, for instance, but a

The Devil Is in the Details
Supporters of intelligent design theory seek to replace accounts of evolution in schoolbooks with the notion that the universe is created by a higher power according to a divine plan. Critics of this movement, such as this cartoonist, claim that this asks public schools to take a role in teaching religion, which they believe is forbidden by the First Amendment.

schoolchild's day does not. Religion is not kept completely out of our public lives, but the Court has generally leaned toward a separationist stance. In the 1960s the Court tried to cement this stance, refining a test that made it unconstitutional for the government to pass laws that affect religion unless the laws have a "secular intent" (that is, a nonreligious intent) and "a primary effect that neither advances nor inhibits religion." [19] In two separate cases the Court decided that laws requiring prayer or the reading of biblical verses in public schools violated the Constitution, and that permitting children to be excused did not reduce the unconstitutionality of the original laws.[20] In an earlier case the Court had ruled that even nondenominational prayer could not be required of children in public schools,[21] and in 1968 the Court struck down an Arkansas law prohibiting the teaching of evolution in public schools.[22] With these rulings the Court was aligning itself firmly with the separationist interpretation of the establishment clause.

The *Lemon* Test But the Court in the 1960s, under the leadership of Chief Justice Earl Warren, was known for its liberal views, even though Warren, himself a Republican, had been appointed to the Court by President Eisenhower. As the more conservative appointments of Republican presidents Richard Nixon and Reagan began to shape the Court, the Court's rulings moved in a more accommodationist direction. In *Lemon v. Kurtzman* (1971), the Court added to the old test a third provision that a law not foster "an excessive government entanglement with religion." [23] Under the new ***Lemon* test** the justices had to decide how much entanglement there was between politics and religion, leaving much to their own discretion.

***Lemon* test** three-pronged rule used by the courts to determine whether the establishment clause is violated

As the current rule in deciding establishment cases, the *Lemon* test is not used consistently, primarily because the justices have not settled among themselves the underlying issue of whether religion and politics should be separate, or whether state support of religion is permissible.[24] While the justices still lean in a separationist direction, their rulings occasionally nod at accommodationism. In 1984 they allowed a Rhode Island display of a crèche at Christmas (accommodationist);[25] in 1985 they struck down an Alabama law requiring a moment of silence before the public school day began (separationist);[26] in 1987 they rejected a Louisiana law requiring schools to teach creationism (separationist);[27] in 1990 they upheld a federal law (the Equal Access Act of 1984) requiring public high schools to permit religious and political clubs to meet as extracurricular activities (accommodationist);[28] in 1992 they disallowed prayer at graduation ceremonies (separationist);[29] in 2000 the Court ruled that prayers led by students at high school football games were unconstitutional (separationist);[30] and in 2004 they ruled that a state could keep a state scholarship from a student who wanted to major in pastoral ministries (separationist).[31] Also in 2004, the Supreme Court heard a case on the inclusion of the phrase "one nation under God" in the Pledge of Allegiance. The Court failed to rule on the merits of the case this time, making its decision on other grounds, but the Court will likely have to rule on the constitutionality of the Pledge at some point in the future.

THE FREE EXERCISE CLAUSE: WHEN CAN STATES REGULATE RELIGIOUS BEHAVIOR?

Religious freedom is controversial in the United States not just because of the debate between the separationists and the accommodationists. Another question that divides the public and justices alike is what to do when religious beliefs and practices conflict with state goals. The second part of the First Amendment grant of religious freedom guarantees that Congress shall make no law prohibiting the free exercise of religion. Seemingly straightforward, the **free exercise clause**, as it is called, has generated as much controversy as the establishment clause. For example, what is the solution when a religious belief against killing clashes with compulsory military service during a war, or when religious holy days are ignored by state legislation about the days individuals should be expected to work? When is the state justified in regulating religions? The Court decided in 1940 that there is a difference between the freedom to believe and the freedom to act on those beliefs.[32] While Americans have an absolute right to believe whatever they want, their freedom to act is subject to government regulation. The state's **police power** allows it to protect its citizens, providing social order and security. If it needs to regulate behavior, it may. These two valued goods of religious freedom and social order are bound to conflict, and the Court has had an uneasy time trying to draw the line between them.

free exercise clause the First Amendment guarantee that citizens may freely engage in the religious activities of their choice

police power the ability of the government to protect its citizens and maintain social order

The Court's ambivalence can be seen in two cases, three years apart, concerning the obligation to salute the flag. In *Minersville School District v. Gobitis* (1940), two children of a Jehovah's Witness family were expelled from school for violating a rule that required them to salute the flag each day.[33] For a Jehovah's Witness, saluting the flag would amount to worshiping a graven image (idol), which their religion forbids. Their father brought suit, claiming that the rule violated his children's freedom of religion. The Court rejected his claim, arguing that children are required to salute the flag to promote national unity, which in turn fosters national security. Within three years, however, the composition of the Court had changed, and several members had changed their minds. In *West Virginia State Board of Education v. Barnette* (1943), children of Jehovah's Witnesses were again expelled for refusing to salute the flag, but this time the Court overturned the school board's rule requiring the salute.[34]

While *Barnette* still holds, the Court has gone back and forth on other religious freedom issues as it has struggled to define what actions the state might legitimately seek to regulate. Under their police power, states have been allowed to require that businesses close on Sundays, or that certain merchandise not be sold then. In *The Blue Law Cases*, the Court argued that the states are within their rights to require Sunday closings as a provision for a day of rest, and that the Sunday closing laws, while religious in origin, no longer contain religious intent.[35] In *Sherbert v. Verner* (1963), however, the Court seemed to contradict itself. A Seventh Day Adventist, for whom Saturday is the Sabbath, was fired from a company for refusing to work on Saturday and was denied unemployment compensation when she refused to take other jobs with compulsory Saturday hours. A lower court ruled in favor of the woman, and the case was appealed to the Supreme Court. The Court upheld *Sherbert*, finding the denial of benefits to be a clear violation of her constitutional rights. The Court wrote that any incidental burden placed on religious freedom must be justified by a **compelling state interest**; that is, the state must show that it is absolutely necessary for some fundamental state purpose that the religious freedom be limited.[36] How the Court determines what is and what is not a compelling state interest is examined in Chapter 6.

compelling state interest a fundamental state purpose, which must be shown before the law can limit some freedoms or treat some groups of people differently

The Court rejected this compelling state interest test, however, in *Employment Division, Department of Human Resources v. Smith*, when it upheld a law denying state unemployment benefits to employees of a drug rehabilitation organization who were fired for using peyote, a hallucinogenic drug, for sacramental purposes in religious ceremonies.[37] Here the Court abandoned its ruling in *Sherbert* and held that if the infringement on religion is not intentional but is rather the byproduct of a general law prohibiting socially harmful conduct, applied equally to all religions, then it is not unconstitutional. It found that the compelling state interest test, while necessary for cases dealing with matters of race and free speech, was inappropriate for religious freedom issues. Under the *Smith* ruling, a number of religious practices have been declared illegal by state laws on the grounds that the laws do not unfairly burden any particular religion.

Religious groups consider the *Smith* ruling a major blow to religious freedom because it places the burden of proof on the individual or church to show that its religious practices should not be punished, rather than on the state to show that the interference with religious practice is absolutely necessary. In response to the *Smith* decision, Congress in 1993 passed the Religious Freedom Restoration Act (RFRA). This act, supported by a coalition of ninety religious groups, restored the compelling state interest test for state action limiting religious practice and required that when the state did restrict religious practice, it be carried out in the least burdensome way. The Supreme Court, however, did not allow the law to stand. In the 1997 case of *City of Boerne v. Flores,* the Court held that the RFRA was an unconstitutional exercise of congressional power and that it constituted too great an intrusion on government power.[38] Religious groups have declared the *Boerne* ruling an assault on religious freedom and have called for the passage of RFRA legislation at the state level. Some groups even support an amendment to the federal Constitution to restore the protection of the former interpretation of the First Amendment.

WHEN IS A RELIGION A RELIGION?

Finally, religious freedom is controversial because it raises a thorny question: What *is* religion? Can any group call itself a religion? If it does so, is it entitled to constitutional protection? Are all its practices protected? Should nonreligion (like atheism or agnosticism) be similarly protected?

In *Reynolds v. U.S.* (1878), and subsequent cases, the Court has upheld a congressional statute prohibiting polygamy against a Mormon who claimed that his religion required him to marry many wives.[39] In *Reynolds,* the Court said that because religion is not defined in the Constitution, the justices must look elsewhere to determine the founders' intentions. A historical analysis led them to the conclusion that, as the Mormon Church did not exist at the time of the founding, and polygamy was not associated with any religion practiced then, it was not a behavior the founders would have meant to protect. The law was constitutional, given government's right to enforce standards of "civilized society."

The Court also confronted the question of what constitutes religion in a number of cases dealing with conscientious objections to serving in war. Here the question was not whether Congress could force someone to go to war against his religious beliefs. Congress had already passed several laws exempting the conscientious objector from military service—first members of well-recognized religious sects like the Quakers and then, in 1940, anyone whose objection was based on "religious training and belief." The Court has had to decide what claims to exemptions under this law were legitimate, and what Congress could and could not exempt without violating anyone's rights. The Court eventually came to argue that "religious training and belief" could be broadly understood, and that even nonreligious objectors could be exempt if they held ethical and moral beliefs parallel to and just as strong as religious convictions.[40] Thus, in some cases, the Court protected the rights of atheists and agnostics as well as members of organized religious groups.

WHO, WHAT, HOW All citizens have a stake in a society where they are not coerced to practice a religion in which they do not believe, and where they cannot be prevented from practicing the religion in which they do believe. The rules that help them get what they want here are the establishment clause and the free exercise clause of the First Amendment.

There is, however, an inherent conflict between those two clauses. If there truly is a wall of separation between church and state, as the separationists want, then restrictions on religious practice are permissible, which is the opposite of what the accommodationists seek. The only solution is to find a level of separation that the separationists can tolerate that is compatible with a level of protection that accommodationists can agree to.

THE FIRST AMENDMENT: FREEDOM OF EXPRESSION

Among the most cherished of American values is the right to free speech. The First Amendment reads that "Congress shall make no law . . . abridging the freedoms of speech, or of the press" and, at least theoretically, most Americans agree.[41] When it comes to actually practicing free speech, however, our national record is less impressive. In fact, time and again, Congress *has* made laws abridging freedom of expression, often with the enthusiastic support of much of the American public. As a nation we have never had a great deal of difficulty restricting speech we don't like, admire, or respect. The challenge of the First Amendment is to protect the speech we despise.

The ongoing controversy surrounding free speech has kept the Supreme Court busy. On the one hand are claims that the right to speak freely should be absolute, that we should permit no exceptions whatsoever. On the other hand are demands that speech should be limited—perhaps because it threatens national security or unity or certain economic interests; because it is offensive, immoral, or hurtful; because it hinders the judicial process; or because it injures reputations. The Supreme Court has had to navigate a maze of conflicting arguments as it has assessed the constitutionality of a variety of congressional and state laws that do, indeed, abridge the freedom of speech and of the press.

WHY IS FREEDOM OF EXPRESSION VALUABLE?

It is easier to appreciate what is at stake in the battles over when and what kind of speech should be protected if we think about just why we value free speech so much in the first place. Four arguments for keeping speech free of restrictions deserve our particular attention:

- *An informed citizenry.* In a democracy, citizens are responsible for participating in their government's decisions. Democratic theory holds that, to participate wisely, citizens must have information about what their government is doing. This requires, at the least, a free press, able to report fully on government's activities. Otherwise, citizens are easily manipulated by those people in government who control the flow of information.
- *A watchdog for government.* By being free to voice criticism of government, to investigate its actions, and to debate its decisions, both citizens and journalists are

able to exercise an additional check on government that supplements our valued principle of checks and balances. This watchdog function of freedom of expression helps keep government accountable and less likely to step on our other rights. A perfect example of this was the investigation into the Watergate activities by reporters from the *Washington Post* and other newspapers. Had we not had a free press that allowed the investigation of Watergate, the unscrupulous politics or so-called dirty tricks of the Nixon administration would have continued unchecked.

- *A voice for the minority.* Another reason for allowing free speech in society—even (or especially) speech of which we do not approve—is the danger of setting a precedent of censorship. Censorship in a democracy usually allows the voice of the majority to prevail. One of the reasons to support minority rights as well as majority rule, however, is that we never know when we may fall into the minority on an issue. If we make censorship a legitimate activity of government, we too will be potentially vulnerable to it.
- *Preservation of the truth.* Political theorist John Stuart Mill argued that the free traffic of all ideas, those known to be true as well as those suspected to be false, is essential in a society that values truth. By allowing the expression of all ideas, we discover truths that we had previously believed to be false (the world is not flat, after all), and we develop strong defenses against known falsehoods like racist and sexist ideas.

If free speech is so valuable, why is it so controversial? Like freedom of religion, free speech requires tolerance of ideas and beliefs other than our own, even ideas and be-

Media Watchdogs
The work of two relatively inexperienced *Washington Post* reporters, Bob Woodward (center) and Carl Bernstein (second from left), demonstrated the fundamental importance of a free press. Their reporting of the Watergate break-in and cover-up led to congressional investigations, which resulted in President Richard Nixon's resignation in 1974, shortly before he would have been impeached. Here they discuss developments in the story with the *Post*'s publisher Katharine Graham, managing editor Howard Simons, and executive editor Benjamin Bradlee.

liefs that we find personally repugnant. Those who are convinced that their ideas are eternally true see no real reason to practice toleration, especially if they are in the majority. It is clear to them that language they view as offensive should be silenced, to create the sort of society they believe should exist.

It is the Supreme Court that has had to balance the claims of those who defend the rights of all speakers and those who think they should be limited. The Court has had to make difficult decisions about how to apply the First Amendment to speech that criticizes government, symbolic speech, obscenity, and other offensive speech, as well as about freedom of the press. How the Court arrived at the very complex and rich interpretation that it generally uses today is a political tale.

SPEECH THAT CRITICIZES THE GOVERNMENT

sedition speech that criticizes the government

Speech that criticizes the government, called **sedition**, has long been a target of restrictive legislation, and most of the founders were quite content that it should be so. Of course, all of the founders had engaged daily in the practice of criticizing their government when *they* were in the process of inciting their countrymen to revolution against England, so they were well aware of the potential consequences of seditious activity. Now that the shoe was on the other foot, and they were the government, many were far less willing to encourage dissent. It was felt that criticism of government undermined authority and destroyed patriotism, especially during wartime.

Early Restrictions on Speech It didn't take long for American "revolutionaries" to pass the Alien and Sedition Act of 1798, which outlawed "any false, scandalous writing against the government of the United States." In the early 1800s, state governments in the South punished speech advocating the end of slavery and even censored the mail to prevent the distribution of abolitionist literature. Throughout that century and into the next, all levels of government, with the support and encouragement of public opinion, squashed the views of radical political groups, labor activists, religious sects, and other minorities.[42]

By World War I (1914–1918), freedom of speech and of the press were a sham for many Americans, particularly those holding unorthodox views or views that challenged the status quo. War in Europe was seen as partly due to the influence of evil ideas, and leaders in America were determined to keep those ideas out of the United States. Government clamped down hard on people promoting socialism, anarchism, revolution, and even labor unions. By the end of World War I, thirty-two of forty-eight states had laws against sedition, particularly prohibiting speech that advocated the use of violence or force to bring about industrial or political change. In 1917 the U.S. Congress had passed the Espionage Act, which made it a crime to "willfully obstruct the recruiting or enlistment service of the United States," and a 1918 amendment to the act spelled out what that meant. It became a crime to engage in "any disloyal . . . scurrilous, or abusive language about the form of government of the United States, . . . or any language intended to bring the form of government of the United States . . . into contempt, scorn, contumely, or disrepute."[43] Such sweeping prohibitions made it possible to arrest people on the flimsiest of pretexts.

The Role of the Supreme Court Those arrested and imprisoned under the new sedition laws looked to the Supreme Court to protect their freedom to criticize their government, but they were doomed to disappointment. The Court did not dispute the idea

Bill Maher

Bill Maher is a big fan of the First Amendment.

That's because he says what few of us dare to say, what most of us dare not even think. The gasp of laughter that follows the comedian's one-liners is not just shocked amusement, it's shocked recognition that, uncomfortable, unflattering, unpalatable as his observations are, they're often right on target. Maher has made a career out of mocking the emperor's anatomy, while most of us are still oohing and awing over the splendor of his new clothes. Usually the First Amendment saves his bacon.

". . . if you want to teach somebody something, it's got to be like a pill in the dog's food."

And sometimes it doesn't. On September 17, 2001, he went on his ABC comedy show, *Politically Incorrect,* and said, about the suicide bombing of the World Trade Center: "We have been the cowards, lobbing cruise missiles from 2,000 miles away. That's cowardly. Staying in the airplane when it hits the building—say what you want about it, it's not cowardly."

Predictably, in those shaky days of national trouble, all hell broke loose. Asked about Maher's comment at a White House press briefing, then–Press Secretary Ari Fleischer replied: "All Americans . . . need to watch what they say, watch what they do." Advertisers balked, and Maher's show was canceled.

He's back now, with a cable show called *Real Time with Bill Maher,* where he continues to speak his mind. Still, there are limits. He says: "I can't get up there every week and just rail about the environment and global warming and whatever is going on that I think is most important. But I push it as far as I can. You've got to try to find entertaining ways to get the message through. I always say, in America if you want to teach somebody something, it's got to be like a pill in the dog's food. You've got to wrap it in the bologna . . . stick it right at the back of his throat so he doesn't even know it's there."

The trouble, as he sees it, is that Americans want to fit their beliefs into tidy categories of "liberal" and "conservative" as if that sums up the whole debate. Maher wants us to dig our way out of our comfortable platitudes to reach new truths, even if they're unpopular. He recalls getting booed once on the *Tonight Show* after he berated an animal trainer who had appeared with his tiger. "They're like, please, Mr. Comedown. We just enjoyed a delightful animal show, and I pointed out that animals really don't want to be in show business." New rule, as Maher would say today.

Maher is a libertarian, but, true to his own creed, he is also a bit of everything else, believing fiercely in causes like animal rights, the environment, personal responsibility, and civic education. Today, he says, we've lost the thread to the things that matter. Raised by parents who served in World War II, Maher grew up thinking that there was a common good worth sacrificing for, "that the world had been to the brink and good citizenship was responsible for saving it. And we have nothing like that today. Nothing." Here's more Maher:

On patriotism:

Well, it means being loyal to your country above other countries. And I am. . . . [But] it has to be put in context and also it has to be put side by side with a greater humanity. . . . Americans who say, "This is the greatest country in the world," without having any clue what goes on in any other countries are just pulling it out of nowhere. There are many things that I'm proud of in this country. I'm proud of how my parents and other people stopped fascism and communism. I'm certainly proud of what we started in 1776. It was a new dawn of freedom and liberty in the world. But I'm not proud of slavery. I'm not proud of the genocide of the Indians. I'm not proud of much of what goes on today. So I still believe in the promise of America, but most of America looks at itself through rose-colored glasses. And that's not healthy.

On keeping the republic:

Take it upon [yourself] to learn the basics. . . . [K]ids need . . . to learn history. Because kids say to me all the time when I say something from history: "How should I know about that, I wasn't born." Oh, really? So nothing happened before you were born? . . . Kids need to learn history so they can put themselves in the proper place, which is of great insignificance. . . . The problem with kids today is not too little self-esteem, it's too much. And history, I think, learning a big picture, is very important in that.

Source: Bill Maher spoke with Christine Barbour and Gerald Wright on May 9, 2005.

that speech criticizing the government could be punished. The question it dealt with was just how bad the speech had to be before it could be prohibited. The history of freedom of speech cases is a history of the Court devising tests for itself to determine if certain speech should be protected or could be legitimately outlawed. In four cases upholding the Espionage Act, the Court used a measure it called the **bad tendency test**, which simply required that for the language to be regulated, it must have "a natural tendency to produce the forbidden consequences." That is, if Congress has the right to outlaw certain actions, it also has the right to outlaw speech that is likely to lead to those actions. This test is pretty easy for prosecutors to meet, so most convictions under the act were upheld.[44]

bad tendency test rule used by the courts that allows speech to be punished if it leads to punishable actions

But in two of those cases, *Schenck v. United States* (1919) and *Abrams v. United States* (1919), Justice Oliver Wendell Holmes began to articulate a new test, which he called the **clear and present danger test**. This test, as Holmes conceived it, focused on the circumstances in which language was used.[45] If no immediately threatening circumstances existed, then the language in question would be protected and Congress could not regulate it. But Holmes's views did not represent the majority opinion of the Court, and the clear and present danger test was slow to catch on.

clear and present danger test rule used by the courts that allows language to be regulated only if it presents an immediate and urgent danger

With the tensions that led to World War II, Congress again began to fear the power of foreign ideas, especially communism, which was seen as a threat to the American way of life. The Smith Act of 1940 made it illegal to advocate the violent overthrow of the government or to belong to an organization that did so. Similarly, as the communist scare picked up speed after the war, the McCarran Act of 1950 required members of the Communist Party to register with the U.S. attorney general. At the same time, Senator Joseph McCarthy was conducting investigations of American citizens to search out communists, and the House Un-American Activities Committee was doing the same thing. The suspicion or accusation of being involved in communism was enough to stain a person's reputation irreparably, even if there were no evidence to back up the claim. Many careers and lives were ruined in the process.

Again the Supreme Court did not weigh in on the side of civil liberties. Convictions under both the Smith and McCarran Acts were upheld. The Court had used the clear and present danger test intermittently in the years since 1919, but usually not as originally intended, to limit speech only in the rarest and most dire of occasions. Instead the clear and present danger test came to be seen as a kind of balancing test where the interests of society in prohibiting the speech were weighed against the value of free speech; consequently, the emphasis on an obvious and immediate danger was lost.

The Court's record as a supporter of sedition laws finally ended with the personnel changes that brought Earl Warren to the position of chief justice. In 1969 the Court overturned the conviction of Charles Brandenburg, a Ku Klux Klan leader who had been arrested under Ohio's criminal syndicalism law. In this case the Court ruled that abstract teaching of violence is not the same as incitement to violence. In other words, political speech could be restricted only if it was aimed at producing or was likely to produce "imminent lawless action." Mere advocacy of specific illegal acts was protected unless it led to immediate illegal activity. In a concurring opinion, Justice William O. Douglas pointed out that it was time to get rid of the clear and present danger test because it was so subject to misuse and manipulation. Speech, except when linked with action, he said, should be immune from prosecution.[46] The **imminent lawless action test** continues to be the standard for regulating political speech today.

imminent lawless action test rule used by the courts that restricts speech only if it is aimed at producing or is likely to produce imminent lawless action

SYMBOLIC SPEECH

The question of what to do when speech *is* linked to action, of course, remained. Many forms of expression go beyond mere speech or writing. Should they also be protected? No one disputes that government has the right to regulate actions and behavior if it believes it has sufficient cause, but what happens when that behavior is also expression? When is an action a form of expression? Is burning a draft card, or wearing an armband to protest a war, or torching the American flag an action or an expression? All of these questions, and more, have come before the Court, which generally has been more willing to allow regulation of symbolic speech than of speech alone, especially if the regulation is not a direct attempt to curtail the speech.

We already saw, under freedom of religion, that the Court has decided that some symbolic expression, such as saluting or not saluting the American flag, is a protected form of speech. But drawing the line between what is and is not protected has been extremely difficult for the Court. In *United States v. O'Brien* (1968), the Court held that burning a draft card at a rally protesting the Vietnam War was *not* protected speech because the law against burning draft cards was legitimate and not aimed at restricting expression. In that case, Chief Justice Earl Warren wrote, "We think it clear that a government regulation is sufficiently justified if it is within the constitutional power of the Government; if it furthers an important or substantial governmental interest; if the governmental interest is unrelated to the suppression of free expression; and if the incidental restriction on alleged First Amendment freedoms is no greater than is essential to the furtherance of that interest." [47] Following that reasoning, in 1969 the Court struck down a school rule forbidding students to wear black armbands as an expression of their opposition to the Vietnam War, arguing that the fear of a disturbance was not a sufficient state interest to warrant the suppression.[48]

One of the most divisive issues of symbolic speech that has confronted the Supreme Court, and indeed the American public, concerns that ultimate symbol of our country, the American flag. There is probably no more effective way of showing one's dissatisfaction with the United States or its policies than burning the Stars and Stripes. In 1969 the Court split five to four when it overturned the conviction of a person who had broken a New York law making it illegal to deface or show disrespect for the flag (he had burned it).[49] Twenty years later, with a more conservative Court in place, the issue was raised again by a similar Texas law. Again the Court divided five to four, voting to protect the burning of the flag as symbolic expression.[50] Because the patriotic feelings of so many Americans were fired up by this ruling, Congress passed the federal Flag Protection Act in 1989, making it a crime to desecrate the flag. In *United States v. Eichman*, the Court declared the federal law unconstitutional for the same reasons it had overturned the New York and Texas laws: all were aimed specifically at "suppressing expression." [51] The only way to get around a Supreme Court ruling of unconstitutionality is to amend the Constitution. Efforts to pass an amendment failed by a fairly small margin in the House and the Senate, meaning that despite the strong feeling of many, flag burning is still considered protected speech in the United States.

The Court has recently proved willing to restrict symbolic speech, however, if it finds that the speech goes beyond expression of a view. In a 2003 ruling, the Court held that cross burning, a favored practice of the Ku Klux Klan and other segregationists that it had previously held to be protected speech, was not protected under the First Amendment if it was intended as a threat of violence. "When a cross burning is used to intimidate, few if any messages are more powerful," wrote Justice Sandra Day O'Connor, speaking for a six-to-three majority. "A state may choose to prohibit only those forms of intimidation that are most likely to inspire fear of bodily harm," if the intent to stir up such fear is clear.[52] The Court noted that cross burning would still be protected as symbolic speech in certain cases, such as at a political rally.

freedom of assembly the right of the people to gather peacefully and to petition government

Closely related to symbolic speech is an additional First Amendment guarantee, **freedom of assembly**, or "the right of the people peaceably to assemble, and to petition the government for a redress of grievances." The courts have interpreted this provision to mean not only that people can meet and express their views collectively, but also that their very association is protected as a form of political expression. So, for instance, they have ruled that associations like the NAACP cannot be required to make their membership lists public[53] (although groups deemed to have unlawful purposes do not have such protection) and that teachers do not have to reveal the associations to which they belong.[54] In addition, the Court has basically upheld people's rights to associate with whom they please, although it held that public[55] and, in some circumstances, private groups cannot discriminate on the basis of race or sex.[56]

OBSCENITY AND PORNOGRAPHY

Of all the forms of expression, obscenity has probably presented the Court with its biggest headaches. In attempting to define it in 1964, Justice Potter Stewart could only conclude, "I know it when I see it." [57] The Court has used a variety of tests for determining whether material is obscene, but until the early 1970s, only the most hard-core pornography was regulated.

Coming into office in 1969, however, President Nixon made it one of his administration's goals to control pornography in America. Once the Court began to reflect the ideological change that came with Nixon's appointees, rulings became more restric-

Freedom Isn't Always Pretty
A Ku Klux Klan rally in Gainesville, Georgia, sparked a counterdemonstration by residents who did not want their community associated with KKK views. Extending First Amendment rights to all groups regardless of belief is a necessary cost of living in a democracy.

tive. In 1973 the Court developed the ***Miller* test**, which returned more control over the definition of obscenity to state legislatures and local standards. Under the *Miller* test, the Court asks "whether the work depicts or describes, in a patently offensive way, sexual conduct specifically defined by state law" and "whether the work, taken as a whole, lacks serious literary, artistic, political or scientific value" (called the SLAPS test).[58] These provisions have also been open to interpretation, and the Court has tried to refine them over time. The emphasis on local standards has meant that pornographers can look for those places with the most lenient definitions of obscenity in which to produce and market their work, and the Court has let this practice go on.

***Miller* test** rule used by the courts in which the definition of *obscenity* must be based on local standards

The question of whether obscenity should be protected speech raises some fundamental issues, and has created some unlikely alliances. Justice John Marshall Harlan was quite right when he wrote that "one man's vulgarity is another man's lyric."[59] People offended by what they consider to be obscenity believe that their values should be represented in their communities. If that means banning adult bookstores, nude dancing at bars, and naked women on magazine covers at the supermarket, then so be it. But opponents argue that what is obscene to one person may be art or enjoyment to another. The problem of majorities enforcing decisions on minorities is inescapable here. A second issue that has generated debate over these cases is the feminist critique of pornography: that it represents aggression toward women and should be banned primarily because it perpetuates stereotypes and breeds violence. Thus radical feminists, usually on the left end of the political spectrum, have found themselves in alliance with conservatives on the right. There is a real contradiction here for feminists, who are more often likely to argue for the expansion of rights, particularly as they apply to women. Feminists advocating restrictions on pornography reconcile the contradiction by arguing that the proliferation of pornography ultimately limits women's rights by making life more threatening and fundamentally unequal.

FIGHTING WORDS AND OFFENSIVE SPEECH

Among the categories of speech that the Court has ruled may be regulated is one called "**fighting words**," words whose express purpose is to create a disturbance and incite violence in the person who hears the speech.[60] However, the Court rarely upholds legislation designed to limit fighting words unless the law is written very carefully and specifically. Consequently it has held that threatening and provocative language is protected unless it is likely to "produce a clear and present danger of serious substantive evil that rises far above public inconvenience, annoyance, or unrest."[61]

fighting words speech intended to incite violence

The Court has also ruled that offensive language, while not protected by the First Amendment, may occasionally contain a political message, in which case constitutional protection applies. For instance, the Court overturned the conviction of a young California man named Paul Cohen who was arrested for violating California's law against "maliciously and willfully disturb[ing] the peace or quiet of any neighborhood or person . . . by . . . offensive conduct." Cohen had worn a jacket in a Los Angeles courthouse that had "Fuck the Draft" written across the back, in protest of the Vietnam War. The Court held that this message was not directed to any specific person who was likely to see the jacket and, further, there was no evidence that Cohen was in fact inciting anyone to a disturbance. Those who were offended by the message on Cohen's jacket did not have to look at it.[62]

These cases have taken on modern-day significance in the wake of the **political correctness** movement that swept the country in the late 1980s and 1990s, especially

political correctness the idea that language shapes behavior and therefore should be regulated to control its social effects

Free Speech on Campus

What's the purpose of a college education: to reinforce our currently held ideas, or to expose us to new ones? That's what students and faculty debated on the University of North Carolina, Chapel Hill, campus in 2002 when freshmen were assigned *Approaching the Qur'an,* a book that includes excerpts from the Koran. Why should the Koran be taught instead of the Bible, some angry parents and students demanded to know, claiming that the reading assignment amounted to "forced Islamic indoctrination." Understanding other cultures is what makes peace and tolerance possible, argued others. Hey, said the faculty, this is about academic freedom—aren't *we* the ones who get to decide what we teach in our classes? [1]

But the issue of academic freedom—traditionally understood as the right of faculty to teach, research, and write about what they think is important without fear of reprisal [2]—is gradually being redefined by both conservative and liberal students as the right not to have to be taught ideas they disagree with or find offensive. Both sides say the issue is about basic civil liberties and each accuses the other of wanting to indoctrinate students rather than to teach them. The two sets of beliefs are on a collision course, and they may be crashing into each other on a college campus, and maybe even in a state legislature, near you.

As we noted in the Consider the Source feature in Chapter 3, liberal critics of campus culture in the late twentieth century argued that academia was dominated by white middle-class males who perpetuated a Eurocentric view of the world. These critics demanded that college curricula, hiring practices, admissions standards, and campus life generally should acknowledge the growing diversity of the United States. Multiculturalism and the political correctness movement (see p. 179 in this chapter) are two of the consequences of that effort to make colleges and universities more representative of American diversity.

But increasingly conservatives argue that the pendulum has swung way too far in that direction. They say that many college professors are too liberal, that students are captive audiences in classes where they are told only one side of the story, and that they are then graded on whether they support the professor's position. They also argue that because students are still developing their opinions about politics and the world, their exposure to liberal professors makes them more likely to leave college with liberal ideas. One Georgia Tech student was particularly mad. "I feel like professors abuse their power by using the classroom to indoctrinate students," she fumed. "I'm not in class to learn their political agenda." [3]

Conservative activist David Horowitz feels so strongly about the issue that he created Students for Academic Freedom, an organization that is chartered on more than 130 college campuses and that aims to expose professors who promote their personal beliefs in the classroom. One of the group's goals is to get state legislatures and the U.S. Congress to pass an "Academic Bill of Rights" that urges universities to recognize and promote intellectual diversity on college campuses by promoting ideological diversity in the classroom and encouraging schools to hire more conservative professors.[4] The group has had some success.

on college campuses. Political correctness refers to an ideology, held primarily by some liberals, including some civil rights activists and feminists, that language shapes society in critical ways, and therefore racist, sexist, homophobic, or any other language that demeans any group of individuals should be silenced to minimize its social effects. An outgrowth of the political correctness movement was the passing of speech codes on college campuses that ban speech that might be offensive to women and ethnic and other minorities. Critics of speech codes, and of political correctness in general, argue that such practices unfairly repress free speech, which should flourish, of all places, on

The Georgia Senate passed a resolution "encouraging public colleges and universities to refrain from discriminating against students because of their political or religious beliefs,"[5] and similar bills are pending in Colorado, Missouri, Ohio, and Indiana.

Nor is Students for Academic Freedom the only conservative group that considers itself a watchdog for liberal bias on college campuses. NoIndoctrination.org, for instance, provides students with the opportunity to post complaints about biased professors on a web site and, in the days following September 11, groups such as the American Council of Trustees and Alumni—founded by Vice President Dick Cheney's wife, Lynne—tried to limit speech in the classroom that criticized the country or President Bush.[6]

Not surprisingly, these groups have met with criticism in their own turn. Many students disagree that professors are pushing their views in the classroom. "I don't think that bias on campus is really an issue, whether liberal or conservative, said one University of Colorado student. "From my experience [at CU], once you enter the classroom, it's a joining of different perspectives and ideas."[7] Furthermore, university faculty and administrators claim that the conservative organizations are engaging in a witch-hunt to stifle thought and limit speech. The American Association of University Professors opposes the bills pushed by Students for Academic Freedom on the grounds that these bills infringe on what they call academic freedom—that it imposes political standards for hiring, for instance, instead of the standards of academic rigor they believe are important, and places external controls over what can be taught in the classroom.

What are liberals and conservatives really battling over? In a sense, each side has grown in response to the other. Each wants to restrict speech in the classroom that they find offensive. Liberals want open, honest debate on American foreign policy, for instance, but want to limit speech that some minorities might find offensive. Conservatives want open, honest debate on issues such as the influence of the American founders or affirmative action but want to limit speech that criticizes the current government. Each side wants to censor the other in the name of academic freedom, but neither of these two sides is really so much about academic freedom as it is about freedom to tell one's story as the dominant story. It's not surprising that college campuses, filled with bright young minds and youthful energy, should have become battlegrounds in this fight, but the stakes there are unusually high. If either side manages to "win" the war, the losers, if John Stuart Mill is to be believed, will be critical thinking, the ability to find and defend the truth, and ultimately, the fate of democracy itself.

1. Kate Zernike, "Talk, and Debate, on Koran as Chapel Hill Classes Open," *New York Times,* August 20, 2002, A1.
2. See the American Association of University Professors' Statement on Academic Tenure, http://aaup.org/statements/Redbook/1940stat.htm.
3. Kelly Simmons, "Students Fight Alleged Political Prejudice," *Atlanta Journal-Constitution,* March 24, 2004, 1B.
4. Ibid.
5. Ibid.
6. David Glenn, "The War on Campus: Will Academic Freedom Survive?" *The Nation,* December 3, 2001, 11–13.
7. Dave Curtin, "Students' Site Solicits Allegations of CU Bias," *Denver Post,* January 20, 2004, A1.

college campuses. In 1989 and 1991, federal district court judges agreed, finding speech codes on two campuses, the University of Michigan and the University of Wisconsin, in violation of students' First Amendment rights.[63] Neither school appealed. The Supreme Court spoke on a related issue in 1992 when it struck down a Minnesota "hate crime law." The Court held that it is unconstitutional to outlaw broad categories of speech based on its content. The prohibition against activities that "arouse anger, alarm or resentment in others on the basis of race, color, creed, religion or gender" was too sweeping and thus unconstitutional.[64]

FREEDOM OF THE PRESS

The First Amendment covers not only freedom of speech but also freedom of the press. Many of the controversial issues we have already covered apply to both of these areas, but some problems are confronted exclusively, or primarily, by the press: the issue of prior restraint, libel restrictions, and the conflict between a free press and a fair trial.

prior restraint censorship of or punishment for the expression of ideas before the ideas are printed or spoken

Prior Restraint The founders modeled their ideas about freedom of expression on British common law, which held that it is acceptable to censor writing and speech about the government as long as the censorship occurs *after* publication. **Prior restraint**, a restriction on the press before its message is actually published, was seen as a more dangerous form of censorship since the repressed ideas never entered the public domain and their worth could not be debated. The Supreme Court has shared the founders' concern that prior restraint is a particularly dangerous form of censorship and almost never permits it. Two classic judgments illustrate their view. In *Near v. Minnesota,* Jay Near's newspaper *The Saturday Press* was critical of African Americans, Jews, Catholics, and organized labor. His paper was shut down in 1927 under a Minnesota law that prohibited any publication of "malicious, scandalous and defamatory" materials. If he continued to publish the paper, he would have been subject to a $1,000 fine or a year in jail. The Court held that the Minnesota law infringed on Near's freedom of the press. While extreme emergency, such as war, might justify previous restraint on the press, wrote Justice Charles Evans Hughes, the purpose of the First Amendment was to limit it to those rare circumstances.[65] Similarly, and more recently, in *New York Times Company v. United States,* the Court prevented the Nixon administration from stopping the publication by the *New York Times* and the *Washington Post* of a "top secret" document about U.S. involvement in Vietnam. These so-called Pentagon Papers were claimed by the government to be too sensitive to national security to be published. The Court held that "security" is too vague to be allowed to excuse the violation of the First Amendment; to grant such power to the president, it ruled, would be to run the risk of destroying the liberty that the government is trying to secure.[66]

libel written defamation of character

Libel Freedom of the press also collides with the issue of **libel**, the written defamation of character (verbal defamation is called *slander*). Obviously it is crucial to the watchdog and information-providing roles of the press that journalists be able to speak freely about the character and actions of those in public service. But at the same time, because careers and reputations are easily ruined by rumors and innuendo, journalists ought to be required to "speak" responsibly. The Supreme Court addressed this issue in *New York Times v. Sullivan.* In 1960 a Montgomery, Alabama, police commissioner named Sullivan claimed he had been defamed by an advertisement that had run in the *Times.* The ad, paid for by the Committee to Defend Martin Luther King, had alleged that various acts of racism had taken place in the South, one in particular supported by police action on a Montgomery college campus. Sullivan, claiming that as police commissioner he was associated with the police action and was thus defamed, and arguing that there were factual errors in the story (although only minor ones), sued the *Times* for libel and won.

The *Times* was convinced that officials illegally resisting desegregation in the South would use libel cases to deflect attention from the northern press if this judgment were not challenged. The paper brought a unique defense to the case when it appealed to the Supreme Court. It argued that if government officials could claim personal damages when institutions they controlled were portrayed negatively in the press, and if any inaccuracy at all in the story were sufficient to classify the story as false and thus libelous, then libel law would have the same effect that antisedition laws had once had: neither citizens nor the press could criticize the government—dramatically weakening the protection of the First Amendment.[67]

The Supreme Court accepted the *New York Times* argument, and libel law in the United States was revolutionized. No longer simply a state matter, libel became a constitutional issue under the First Amendment. The Court held that public officials, as opposed to private individuals, when suing for libel, must show that a publication acted with "actual malice," which means not that the paper had an evil intent but only that it acted with "knowledge that [what it printed] was false or with reckless disregard for whether it was false or not." [68] Shortly afterward, the Court extended the ruling to include public figures such as celebrities and political candidates—anyone whose actions put them in a public position.

The Court's rulings attempt to give the press some leeway in its actions. Without *Sullivan,* investigative journalism would never have been able to uncover the U.S. role in Vietnam, for instance, or the Watergate cover-up. Freedom of the press, and thus the public's interest in keeping a critical eye on government, is clearly the winner here. The Court's view is that when individuals put themselves into the public domain, the public's interest in the truth outweighs the protection of those individuals' privacy.

The Right to a Fair Trial Freedom of the press also confronts head-on another Bill of Rights guarantee, the right to a fair trial. Media coverage of a crime can make it very difficult to find an "impartial jury," as required by the Sixth Amendment. On the other side of this conflict, however, is the "public's right to know." The Sixth Amendment promises a "speedy and public trial," and many journalists interpret this provision to mean that the proceedings ought to be open. The courts, on the other hand, have usually held that this amendment protects the rights of the accused, not of the public. But while the Court has overturned a murder verdict because a judge failed to control the media circus in his courtroom,[69] on the whole it has ruled in favor of media access to most stages of legal proceedings. Likewise, courts have been extremely reluctant to uphold gag orders, which would impose prior restraint on the press during those proceedings.[70]

CENSORSHIP ON THE INTERNET

Lawmakers do not always know how to deal with new outlets for expression as they become available. Modern technology has presented the judiciary with a host of free speech issues the founders never anticipated. The latest to make it to the courts is the question of censorship on the Internet. Some web sites contain explicit sexual material, obscene language, and other content that many people find objectionable. Since children often find their way onto the Internet on their own, parents and groups of other concerned citizens have clamored for regulation of this medium. Congress obliged in 1996 with the Communications Decency Act (CDA), which made it illegal to knowingly send or display indecent material over the Internet. In 1997 the Supreme

How to Be a Savvy Web Surfer

P. T. Barnum said there's a sucker born every minute–and that was decades *before* the advent of the Internet. He would have rubbed his hands in glee over the gullibility of people in the electronic age. While freedom of speech is a powerful liberty, as we have seen in this chapter, one consequence is that it makes it very difficult to silence those making fraudulent or misleading claims. We regulate radio and television, of course, but that is because these media were originally (before the days of cable and satellites) held to be scarce resources that belonged to the public. Private publishers can enforce standards of excellence, or accuracy, or style, on what they publish, but when a medium is quasipublic, like the Internet, and access to it is easy and cheap, it is impossible to restrict the views and ideas that are published without also doing some serious damage to freedom of speech. Consequently anything goes, and it is up to us as consumers to sort the grain from the chaff.

Today we have access to more information than we could ever have imagined, but we are not trained to use it critically and competently. Case in point: A father and son traveled six hours from Canada to Mankato, Minnesota, lured by a Web site singing the praises of Mankato's sunny beaches and whale watching opportunities.[1] The site turned out to be a spoof perpetrated by winter-weary Mankato residents. Confronted with the reality of more of the frozen north they had just left, the disillusioned dad was angry, but a reasonable target of his anger might have been his own eagerness and willingness to believe unquestioningly what he read on the web.

All of us, of course—professors, students, politicians, journalists, doctors, lawyers, CEOs, and anyone else with access to the Web—are potential suckers. The Internet is merely an electronic link between those who have information to give and those who want information—much like the telephone. Anyone who has the small amount of money needed to set up a Web page can get on the Internet and disseminate information. Discussing the curious willingness of Pierre Salinger, former press secretary to President Kennedy, to believe an Internet report that the 1996 crash of TWA flight 800 was due to "friendly fire" from American military aircraft, one author likens it to the conviction that something is true just because we heard it on the phone, or found it on a document "blowing across a busy city street." [2]

The fact that some piece of information appears on a computer screen does not confer any special distinction on it, or make it more reliable than any other rumor we may happen to hear. This is not to disparage everything that you find on the Internet. Some of it is terrific, and our ability to surf the web in search of new information expands our intellectual horizons like nothing has since the invention of the printing press. What allows us to rely on what we find on the Internet is our own hard work and careful scrutiny. Here are some tips to help you become a savvy surfer of the World Wide Web:

1. **Find out the source of the Web site.** Examine the Web address, or URL, for clues. Web addresses end with .com, .org, .gov, .net, or .edu to indicate, respectively, commercial, nonprofit, government, network, or educational sites. Sites from other countries end with abbreviations of the nation. For example, .kr indicates the site is from Korea and .fr indicates France. If a tilde (~) appears in the address, it is likely to be a personal home page rather than an official site.[3] Remember, however, that anyone can purchase rights to a Web address; an official-looking address does not necessarily confer legitimacy on a site.
2. **Check out the author of the site.** Sometimes the author is not who it seems to be—many authors try to disguise the source of their sites to gain respectability for their ideas or to lure users further into a site, or they may seem to support groups or individuals who turn out to be their targets. For example, people looking for information on George W. Bush who visited georgewbush.org or bush2004.com would be surprised to learn that the sites are actually maintained by critics of the president. Bush's official Web site is www.georgewbush.com. Similarly, a site that at first appears to be a tribute to Martin Luther King accuses him several links later of being "just a degenerate, an America-hating Communist." [4]
3. **If something about a site does not look right (what one author calls the "J.D.L.R.," or the Just Doesn't Look Right, test), investigate more closely.**[5] Be sus-

picious if, for example, you notice lots of misspellings or grammatical errors, or if the site has an odd design. Analyze the site's tone and approach. A very shrill or combative tone could signal a lack of objectivity. When a familiar site doesn't look the way you expect it to, consider the possibility that hackers have broken into it and changed its content. People looking to get their news from Al-Jazeera's Web page in March 2003 were surprised to find a U.S. flag and the message "Let Freedom Ring" on the site. A group based in Salt Lake City, Utah, called Freedom Cyber Force Militia hacked into Al-Jazeera's Web page.[6] Sometimes hackers go for more subtle alterations that are not immediately obvious. Ultimately, remember this: anyone can put up a Web site—even you. Are you a reliable enough source to be quoted in a college student's research paper?

4. **Find out who is footing the bill.** Whoever said there is no such thing as a free lunch might have been speaking of the Internet. Ultimately our access to the glorious world of cyberspace must be paid for, and since we as consumers seem to be singularly unwilling to pay for the information we find, providers of that information are increasingly looking to advertisers to pick up the bill.[7] Commercial interests can shape the content of what we find on the web in any number of ways: links to sponsors' pages may appear prominently on a web page, web sites may promote the products of their advertisers as if they were objectively recommending them without making the financial relationship clear, or the commercial bias may be even more subtle. Amazon.com, an on-line bookseller that provides reviews of the books it sells, admitted in early 1999 that it showcased the reviews of books whose publishers paid for this special treatment. Such behavior, while perfectly legal, is misleading to the consumer, who has no way of knowing whether he or she is getting straight advice or a paid advertisement. Even the search engines you use to find the sites, such as Yahoo! or Lycos, are supported by advertisers and may give preference to their sponsors' sites when you think you are conducting an impartial search. One author says that "trusting an Internet site to navigate the World Wide Web . . . is like following a helpful stranger in Morocco who offers to take you to the best rug store. You may very well find what you are looking for, but your guide will get a piece of whatever you spend." [8]

5. **Use the Internet to evaluate the Internet.** You can find out who runs a site by going to www.internic.net and using the "whois" search function. This will give you names and contact information but is not, warns Tina Kelly of the *New York Times,* conclusive. Similarly, she suggests running authors' names through a search engine or groups-beta.google.com, which searches newsgroups, to see what you can find out about them. Some browsers will tell you when a site was last updated. On Netscape, for instance, you can get this information by clicking on the View option and going to Page Info or Document Info. And remember that you can always e-mail authors of a site and ask for their credentials.[9] If no contact information for the author is available on the site itself, that alone can tell you something about its reliability. For more information on how to evaluate various types of Web sites, check out the Widener University Wolfgram Memorial Library's "Evaluate Web Pages" at www.widener.edu/?pageId=480 and click on "Evaluate Web Pages."

6. **Note the other kinds of information the site directs you to.** If you are in doubt about a site's legitimacy, check some of its links to external sites. Are they up-to-date and well maintained? Do they help you identify the ideological, commercial, or other bias the site may contain? If there are no links to other sites, ask yourself what this might mean.

1. Tina Kelly, "Whales in the Minnesota River? Only on the Web, Where Skepticism Is a Required Navigational Aid," *New York Times,* March 4, 1999, D1.
2. David Sieg, "The Internet as an Information Source," December 17, 1996, www.tricon.net/Features/infosources.html.
3. Kelly, D9.
4. Michel Marriot, "Rising Tide: Sites Born of Hate," *New York Times,* March 18, 1999, G1.
5. Kelly, D1.
6. "Al-Jazeera Web Traffic Hijacked," *Boston Globe,* March 28, 2003, A20.
7. Saul Hansell and Army Harmon, "Caveat Emptor on the Web: Ad and Editorial Lines Blur," *New York Times,* February 26, 1999, A1.
8. Ibid.
9. Kelly, D9.

Court ruled that such provisions constituted a violation of free speech, and that communication over the Internet, which it called a modern "town crier," is subject to the same protections as nonelectronic expression.[71] When Congress tried again with a more narrowly tailored bill, the Child Online Protection Act, the Court struck it down, too.[72]

The Court has not always ruled on the side of a completely unregulated Internet. While not restricting the creation of content, in 2003 the Supreme Court did uphold the Children's Internet Protection Act, which required public libraries that received federal funds to use filtering software to block material that is deemed harmful to minors, such as pornography.[73] However, these filters can create some problems. Many companies and institutions use them to screen offensive incoming e-mail, but such filters often have unwanted consequences. Since the filters cannot evaluate the material passing through, they can end up blocking even legitimate messages and publications. One editor of a newsletter on technology has resorted to intentionally misspelling words (for example, writing "sez" instead of "sex") to avoid the automatic sensors that screen many of his readers' mail.[74]

The Internet can also have the effect of freeing people from censorship, however. As many people who have worked on their high school newspapers know, the Court has ruled that student publications are subject to censorship by school officials if the restrictions serve an educational purpose. The Internet, however, offers students an alternate medium of publication that the courts say is not subject to censorship. As a result, students have been able to publish such matters as the results of investigations into school elections and campus violence that have been excluded from the hard-copy newspaper.[75] We can probably expect some flux in the laws on Internet censorship as the courts become more familiar with the medium itself and the issues surrounding it. (See "*Consider the Source:* How to Be a Savvy Web Surfer" for some tips on how to evaluate what you find on the Internet.)

WHO, WHAT, HOW No less than the success of free democratic government is at stake in the issue of freedom of expression. This First Amendment liberty, we have argued, produces information about government, limits corruption, protects minorities, and helps maintain a vigorous defense of the truth. But something else is at stake as well—preservation of social order; stable government; and protection of civility, decency, and reputation.

It has been left to the courts, using the Constitution, to balance these two desired goods: freedom of expression on the one hand, and social and moral order on the other. The courts have devised several rules, or tests, to try to reconcile the competing claims. Thus we have had the bad tendency test, the clear and present danger test, the *Miller* test, and revised libel laws. The tension between freedom and order lends itself not to a permanent solution, since the circumstances of American life are constantly in flux, but rather to a series of uneasy truces and revised tests.

THE RIGHT TO BEAR ARMS

The Second Amendment to the Constitution reads, "A well regulated militia, being necessary to the security of a free state, the right of the people to keep and bear arms, shall not be infringed." This amendment has been the subject of some of the fiercest debates in American politics. Originally it was a seemingly straightforward effort by opponents of the Constitution to keep the federal government in check by limiting the power of standing, or permanent, armies. Over time it has become a rallying point for those who want to engage in sporting activities involving guns, those who believe that firearms are necessary for self-defense, those who oppose contemporary American policy and want to use revolution to return to what they think were the goals of the founders, and those who simply don't believe that it is government's business to make decisions about who can own guns. (See "*Who Are We?* Gun Ownership in America.")

Although various kinds of gun control legislation have been passed at the state and local levels, powerful interest groups like the NRA have kept it to a minimum at the federal level. The 1990s, however, saw the passage of three federal bills that affect the right to bear arms: the 1993 Brady Bill, requiring background checks on potential handgun purchasers (see Figure 5.2); the 1994 Crime Bill barring semiautomatic assault weapons; and a 1995 bill making it illegal to carry a gun near a school. The 1995 law and the interim provisions of the Brady Bill, which imposed a five-day waiting period for all gun sales, with local background checks until a national background check system could be established, were struck down by the Supreme Court on the grounds that they were unconstitutional infringements of the national government into the realm of state power.[76] In September 2004, Congress let the ban on semiautomatic weapons expire, largely at the urging of House Majority Leader Tom DeLay. While some Democrats in Congress promised to reintroduce the ban, many members have been reluctant to act, possibly because the NRA continues to target gun control candidates for defeat in reelections.

WHY IS THE RIGHT TO BEAR ARMS VALUABLE?

During the earliest days of American independence, the chief source of national stability was the state militia system—armies of able-bodied men who could be counted on to assemble, with their own guns, to defend their country from external and internal threats, whether from the British, the Native Americans, or local insurrection. Local militias were seen as far less dangerous to the fledgling republic than a standing army under national leadership. Such an army could seize control and create a military dictatorship, depriving citizens of their hard-won rights. Madison, Hamilton, and Jay devoted five *Federalist Papers* to the defense of standing armies and the unreliability of the militia, but they did not persuade the fearful Anti-Federalists. The Second Amendment was designed to guard against just that tyranny of the federal government.

Arguments in Defense of the Second Amendment Today The restructuring of the U.S. military, and the growing evidence that under civilian control it did not pose a threat to the liberties of American citizens, caused many people to view the Second Amendment as obsolete. But although the militia system that gave rise to the amendment is now defunct, supporters of rights for gun owners, like the NRA, argue that the amendment is as relevant as ever. They offer at least four reasons the right to bear arms should be unregulated. First, they argue that hunting and other leisure activities involving guns do not hurt anybody (except, of course, the hunted) and are an important part of American culture. They are concerned that even the restriction of weapons not used for hunting, such as assault weapons, will harm their sport by making the idea of regulation more acceptable to Americans and starting society down the

Gun Ownership in America

When asked, "In general, do you feel that laws covering the sale of firearms should be made more strict, less strict, or kept as they are now?" 54 percent of the public preferred stricter gun control laws. When asked, "Do you have a gun in your home?" 43 percent of Americans polled said yes. While a majority of people want stricter gun control and do not own guns, this majority is often less vocal than those on the other side of the issue. How might this affect the stance that politicians are likely to take on gun control?

Source: Darren K. Carlson, "Americans Softening on Tougher Gun Laws?" *Gallup Poll*, November 30, 2004.

Gun Ownership in the U.S.

Question: Should laws covering the sale of firearms be made more strict, less strict, or kept as they are now?

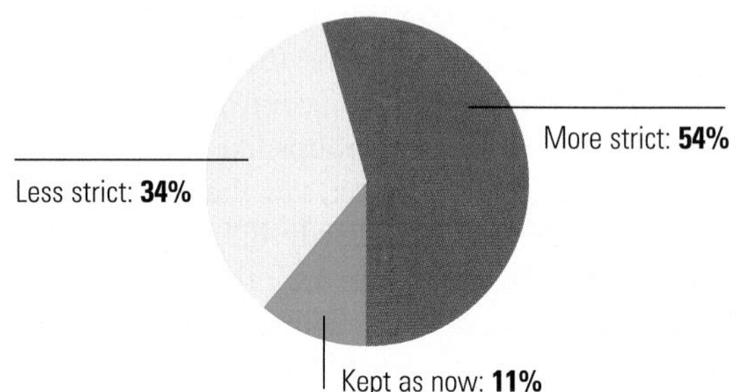

FIGURE 5.2
Firearms Crimes Before and After Passage of the Brady Bill (1993)

Crimes committed with firearms, 1973–2003

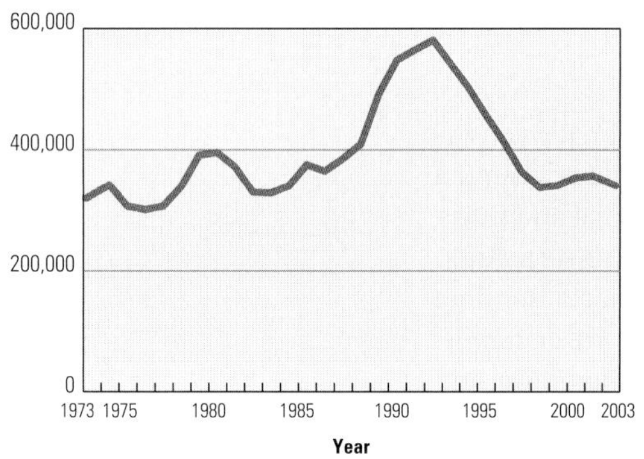

Source: U.S. Department of Justice Bureau of Justice Statistics "Crimes committed with firearms 1973–2003." Retrieved from www.ojp.usdoj.gov/bjs/glance/tables/guncrimetab.htm.

slippery slope of gun control. Second, gun rights advocates claim that possession of guns is necessary for self-defense. They believe that gun control means that only criminals, who get their guns on the black market, will be armed, making life even more dangerous. Their third argument is that citizens should have the right to arm themselves to protect their families and property from a potentially tyrannical government, just as the American revolutionaries did. Finally, advocates of unregulated gun ownership say that it is not government's business to regulate gun use. The limited government they insist the founders intended does not have the power to get involved in such questions, and any federal action is thus illegitimate.

Arguments Against the Right to Bear Arms Opponents of these views—such as Handgun Control, Inc., and the Coalition to Stop Gun Violence—counter that none of these claims has anything to do with the Second Amendment, which refers only to the use and ownership of guns by state militia members. They say that gun owners want to make this an issue about rights because that gives their claims a higher status in American discourse, but in fact the issue is merely about their wants and preferences. Americans have long held that wants and preferences can be limited and regulated if they have harmful effects on society. Focusing the debate on rights rather than policy increases the conflict and decreases the chance for resolution.[77] Opponents also assemble facts and comparative data to support their claims that countries with stricter gun control laws have less violence and fewer gun deaths. They remind us that none of the rights of Americans, even such fundamental ones as freedom of speech and of the press, is absolute, so why should the right to bear arms not also carry limitations and exceptions? And, finally, they point out the irony of claiming the protection of the Constitution to own weapons that could be used to overturn the government that Constitution supports.[78]

JUDICIAL DECISIONS

The Supreme Court has ruled on only a handful of cases that have an impact on gun rights and the Second Amendment. Because federal gun control legislation has been scarce until recently, most of the cases deal with gun control efforts at the state and local levels. In these cases the Court has kept a narrow definition of the Second Amendment as intending to arm state militias, and it has let state gun-related legislation stand.[79] There was no further action at the Supreme Court level until it struck down the legislation concerning possession of guns near schools and reversed one provision of the Brady Bill on federalism, not Second Amendment, grounds. In the close Brady case, four dissenters argued that the burden put on the localities was not disproportionate to the good done by addressing what they called an "epidemic of gun violence." [80] More recently the Supreme Court has—indirectly at least—taken the side of gun control advocates. In 2004 the Court let stand a lower court's ruling that supported a California ban on assault rifles on the grounds that the Second Amendment did not protect individual gun owners. The ruling applies only to those states in the Ninth Circuit, however, and does not require a state to ban assault rifles.

WHO, WHAT, HOW Some citizens want a protected right to own whatever guns they choose, and others want some regulation on what guns can be owned by private citizens. The rule that should determine who wins and who loses here is the Second Amendment, but though the Supreme Court has been fairly clear that the amendment does not confer an unqualified right to gun ownership on Americans, it also has been reluctant to allow the federal government to impose its will on the states. Consequently the battle is played out in state legislatures and in Congress.

THE RIGHTS OF CRIMINAL DEFENDANTS

A full half of the amendments in the Bill of Rights, and several clauses in the Constitution itself, are devoted to protecting the rights of people who are suspected or accused of committing a crime. These precautions were a particular concern for the founders, who feared an arbitrary government that could accuse and imprison people without evidence or just cause. Governments tend to do such things to shore up their power and to silence their critics. The authors of these amendments believed that, to limit government power, people needed to retain rights against government throughout the process of being accused, tried, and punished for criminal activities. Amendments Four through Eight protect people against unreasonable searches and seizures, self-incrimination, and cruel and unusual punishment, and guarantee them a right to legal advice, a speedy and public trial, and various other procedural protections.

WHY ARE THE RIGHTS OF CRIMINAL DEFENDANTS VALUABLE?

As we indicated, a primary reason for protecting the rights of the accused is to limit government power. One way governments can stop criticism of their actions is by eliminating the opposition, imprisoning them or worse. The guarantees in the Bill of Rights provide checks on government's ability to prosecute its enemies.

Another reason for guaranteeing rights to those accused of crimes is the strong tradition in American culture, coming from our English roots, that a person is innocent until proven guilty. An innocent person, naturally, still has the full protection of the Constitution, and even a guilty person is protected to some degree, for instance, against cruel and unusual punishment. All Americans are entitled to what the Fifth and Fourteenth Amendments call due process of law. **Due process of law** means that laws must be reasonable and fair, and that those accused of breaking the law, and who stand to lose life, liberty, or property as a consequence, have the right to appear before their judges to hear the charges and evidence against them, to have legal counsel, and to present any contradictory evidence in their defense. Due process means essentially that those accused of a crime have a right to a fair trial.

due process of law guarantee that laws will be fair and reasonable and that citizens suspected of breaking the law will be fairly treated

During the 1960s and 1970s the Supreme Court expanded the protection of the rights of the accused and incorporated them so that the states had to protect them as well. And yet the more conservative 1980s and 1990s witnessed a considerable backlash against a legal system perceived as having gone soft on crime—overly concerned with the rights of criminals at the expense of safe streets, neighborhoods, and cities, and deaf to the claims of victims of violent crimes. We want to protect the innocent, but when the seemingly guilty go free because of a "technicality," the public is often incensed. The Supreme Court has had the heavy responsibility of drawing the line between the rights of defendants and the rights of society. We can look at the Court's deliberations on these matters in four main areas: the protection against unreasonable searches and seizures, the protection against self-incrimination, the right to counsel, and the protection against cruel and unusual punishment.

PROTECTION AGAINST UNREASONABLE SEARCHES AND SEIZURES

The Fourth Amendment says,

> The right of the people to be secure in their persons, houses, papers, and effects, against unreasonable searches and seizures, shall not be violated, and no warrants shall issue but upon probable cause, supported by oath or affirmation, and particularly describing the place to be searched, and the persons or things to be seized.

The founders were particularly sensitive on this question because the king of England had had the right to order the homes of his subjects searched without cause, looking for any evidence of criminal activity. For the most part this amendment has been interpreted by the Court to mean that a person's home is private and cannot be invaded by police without a warrant, obtainable only if they have very good reason to think that criminal evidence lies within.

What's Reasonable? Under the Fourth Amendment, there are a few exceptions to the rule that searches require warrants. Automobiles present a special case, for example, since by their nature they are likely to be gone by the time an officer appears with a warrant. Cars can be searched without warrants if the officer has probable cause to think a law has been broken, and the Court has gradually widened the scope of the search so that it can include luggage or closed containers in the car.

Modern innovations like wiretapping and electronic surveillance presented more difficult problems for the Court because previous law had not allowed for them. A "search" was understood legally to require some physical trespass, and a "seizure" involved taking some tangible object. Listening in on a conversation—electronically from afar—was simply not covered by the law. In fact, in the first case in which it was addressed, the Court held that bugging did not constitute a search.[81] That ruling held for forty years, until the case of *Katz v. United States* (1967), when it was overturned by a Court that required, for the first time, that a warrant be obtained before phones could be tapped.[82] In the same year, the Court ruled that conversations were included under Fourth Amendment protection.[83] A search warrant is thus needed in order to tap a phone, although, as we noted earlier, the 2001 Patriot Act makes it a good deal easier to get a warrant.

Yet another modern area in which the Court has had to determine the legality of searches is mandatory random testing for drug or alcohol use, usually by urine or blood tests. These are arguably a very unreasonable kind of search, but the Court has tended to allow them where the violation of privacy is outweighed by a good purpose, for instance, discovering the cause of a train accident,[84] preventing drug use in schools,[85] or preserving the public safety by requiring drug tests of train conductors and airline pilots.

Good Doggie
Officer Taylor Finder of the Ogden, Utah, police department is aided by his dog in their search for illegal drugs in lockers at Mound Fort Middle School. Some who advocate such searches, along with other techniques like random drug testing, argue that these actions are a legitimate means to prevent drug use in schools; others say they are a violation of privacy and students' rights. The courts tend to side with the former, allowing searches like this one.

The Exclusionary Rule By far the most controversial part of the Fourth Amendment rulings has been the exclusionary rule. In a 1914 case, *Weeks v. United States,* the Court confronted the question of what to do with evidence that had, in fact, been obtained illegally. It decided that such evidence should be excluded from use in the defendant's trial.[86] This **exclusionary rule**, as it came to be known, meant that even though the police might have concrete evidence of criminal activity, if obtained unlawfully, it could not be used to gain a conviction of the culprit.

exclusionary rule rule created by the Supreme Court that evidence illegally seized may not be used to obtain a conviction

The exclusionary rule has been controversial from the start. In some other countries, including England, illegally obtained evidence can be used at trial, but the defendant is allowed to sue the police in a civil suit or bring criminal charges against them. The object is clearly to deter misbehavior on the part of the police, while not allowing guilty people to go free. But the exclusionary rule, while it does serve as a deterrent to police, helps criminals avoid punishment. The Court itself has occasionally seemed uneasy about the rule. When the Fourth Amendment was incorporated, in *Wolf v. Colorado,* the exclusionary rule was not extended to the states. The Court ruled that it was a judicial creation, not a constitutionally protected right.[87] Not until the 1961 case of *Mapp v. Ohio* was the exclusionary rule finally incorporated into state as well as federal practice.[88]

But extending the reach of the exclusionary rule did not end the controversy. While the Warren Court (1953–1969) continued to uphold it, the Burger and Rehnquist Courts (1969–present) have cut back on the protections it offers. In 1974 they ruled that the exclusionary rule was to be a deterrent to abuse by the police, not a constitutional right of the accused.[89] The Court subsequently ruled that illegally seized evidence could be used in civil trials[90] and came to carve out what it called a *good faith exception,* whereby evidence is admitted to a criminal trial, even if obtained illegally, if the police are relying on a warrant that appears to be valid at the time or on a law that appears to be constitutional (though either may turn out to be defective).[91] The Court's more conservative turn on this issue has not silenced the debate, however. Some observers are appalled at the reduction in the protection of individual rights, whereas others do not believe that the Court has gone far enough in protecting society against criminals.

PROTECTION AGAINST SELF-INCRIMINATION

No less controversial than the rulings on illegally seized evidence are the Court's decisions on unconstitutionally obtained confessions. The Fifth Amendment provides for a number of protections for individuals, among them that no person "shall be compelled in any criminal case to be a witness against himself." The Supreme Court has expanded the scope of the protection against self-incrimination from criminal trials, as the amendment dictates, to grand jury proceedings, legislative investigations, and even police interrogations. It is this last extension that has proved most controversial.

Court rulings in the early 1900s ordered that police could not coerce confessions, but they did not provide any clear rule for police about what confessions would be admissible. Instead the Court used a case-by-case scrutiny that depended on "the totality of the circumstances" to determine whether confessions had been made voluntarily. This approach was not very helpful to police in the streets trying to make arrests and conduct investigations that would later hold up in court. In 1966 the Warren Court ruled, in *Miranda v. Arizona,* that police had to inform suspects of their rights to remain silent and to have a lawyer present during questioning to prevent them from incriminating themselves. The *Miranda* rights are familiar to viewers of police dramas: "You have the right to remain silent. Anything you say can and will be used against you . . . " If a lawyer could show that a defendant had not been "read" his or her rights, information gained in the police interrogation would not be admissible in court. Like the exclusionary rule, the *Miranda* ruling could and did result in criminals going free even though the evidence existed to convict them.

Reacting to public and political accusations that the Warren Court was soft on crime, Congress passed the Crime Control and Safe Streets Act of 1968, which allowed confessions to be used in federal courts not according to the *Miranda* ruling but according to the old "totality of the circumstances" rule. *Miranda* was still effective in the states, however. Vowing to change the liberal tenor of the Warren Court, 1968 presidential candidate Richard Nixon pledged to appoint more conservative justices. True to his campaign promise, once elected he appointed Warren Burger as chief justice. Under the Burger Court, and later the Rehnquist Court, the justices have backed off the *Miranda* decision to some degree. In 2000, despite the fact that some justices had been highly critical of the *Miranda* ruling over the years, the Court upheld the 1966 decision, stating that it had become an established part of the culture, and held the 1968 Crime Control Act to be unconstitutional.[92]

RIGHT TO COUNSEL

Closely related to the *Miranda* decision, which upholds the right to have a lawyer present during police questioning, is the Sixth Amendment declaration that the accused shall "have the assistance of counsel for his defense." The founders' intentions on this amendment are fairly clear from the 1790 Federal Crimes Act, which required courts to provide counsel for poor defendants only in capital cases, that is, in those punishable by death. Defendants in other trials had a right to counsel, but the government had no obligation to provide it. The Court's decisions were in line with that act until 1938, when in *Johnson v. Zerbst* it extended the government's obligation to provide counsel to impoverished defendants in all criminal proceedings in federal courts.[93] Only federal crimes, however, carried that obligation, until 1963. In one of the most dramatic tales of courtroom appeals, a poor man named Clarence Earl Gideon was convicted of breaking and entering a pool hall and stealing money from the vending machine. Gideon asked the judge for a lawyer, but the judge told him that the state of Florida was not obligated to give him one. He tried to defend the case himself but lost to the far more skilled and knowledgeable prosecutor. Serving five years in prison for a crime he swore he did not commit, he filed a handwritten appeal with the Supreme Court. In a landmark decision, *Gideon v. Wainwright,* the Court incorporated the Sixth Amendment right to counsel.[94]

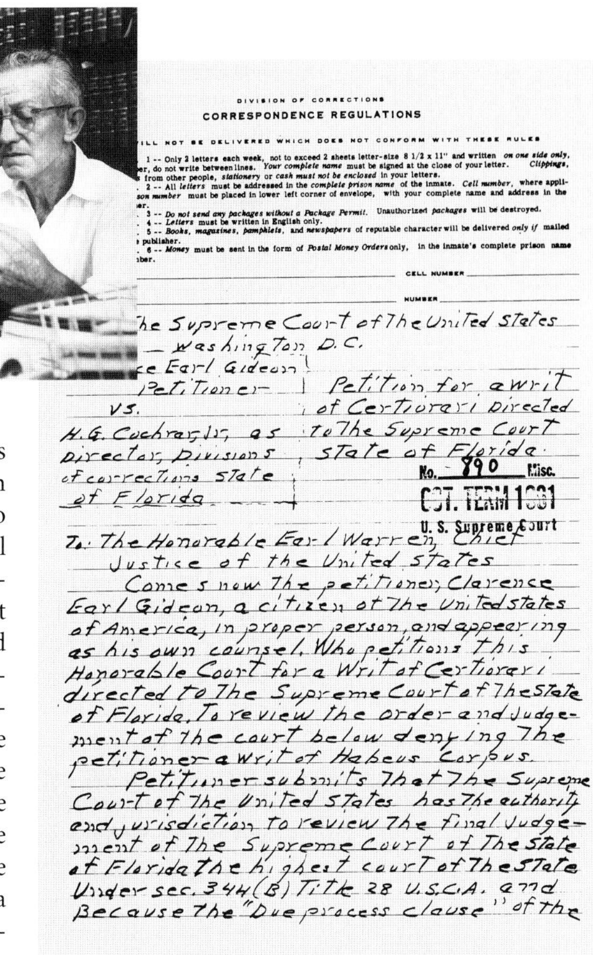
DIVISION OF CORRECTIONS
CORRESPONDENCE REGULATIONS
…ILL NOT BE DELIVERED WHICH DOES NOT CONFORM WITH THESE RULES
1 -- Only 2 letters each week, not to exceed 2 sheets letter-size 8 1/2 x 11" and written *on one side only,* …er, do not write between lines. *Your complete name* must be signed at the close of your letter. *Clippings,* …s from other people, *stationery* or *cash must not be enclosed* in your letters.
2 -- All *letters* must be addressed in the *complete prison name* of the inmate. *Cell number,* where appli… …son number must be placed in lower left corner of envelope, with your complete name and address in the …er.
3 -- *Do not send any packages without a Package Permit.* Unauthorized *packages* will be destroyed.
4 -- *Letters* must be written in English only.
5 -- *Books, magazines, pamphlets,* and *newspapers* of reputable character will be delivered *only if* mailed … publisher.
6 -- *Money* must be sent in the form of *Postal Money Orders* only, in the inmate's complete prison name …ber.

CELL NUMBER

NUMBER

…he Supreme Court of The United States
washington D.C.
…ce Earl Gideon
Petitioner | Petition for a writ
vs. | of Certiorari Directed
H. G. Cochran, Jr, as | to The Supreme Court
director, Divisions | state of Florida.
of corrections state | No. 890 Misc.
of Florida | OCT. TERM 1961
U. S. Supreme Court

To: The Honorable Earl Warren, Chief Justice of the United states

Comes now the petitioner, Clarence Earl Gideon, a citizen of The United states of America, in proper person, and appearing as his own counsel. Who petitions this Honorable Court for a Writ of Certiorari directed to The Supreme Court of The State of Florida. To review the order and Judgement of the court below denying The petitioner a writ of Habeus Corpus.

Petitioner submits That The Supreme Court of The United States has The authority and jurisdiction to review The final Judgement of The Supreme Court of The State of Florida the highest court of The State Under sec. 344(B) Title 28 U.S.C.A. and Because the "Due process clause" of the

© Flip Schulke

Rights of the Accused
Clarence Earl Gideon spent much of his five years in prison studying the law. His handwritten appeal to the Supreme Court resulted in the landmark decision *Gideon v. Wainwright,* which granted those accused of crimes the right to counsel.

Not just in Florida, but all over the country, poor people in prison who had not had legal counsel had to be tried again or released. Gideon himself was tried again with a court-appointed lawyer, who proved to the jury not only that Gideon was innocent but that the crime had been committed by the chief witness against him. Conservatives believed that *Gideon* went far beyond the founders' intentions. Again, both the Burger and Rehnquist Courts have succeeded in rolling back some of the protections won by *Gideon,* ruling, for instance, that the right to a court-appointed attorney does not extend beyond the filing of one round of appeals, even if the convicted indigent person is on death row.[95]

Though the right to counsel is now seen by most people as an essential right, many argue that this right is in reality often violated because of overworked public defenders or state laws that limit who can receive court-appointed counsel. According to a study by the National Association of Criminal Defense Lawyers, the Bucks County, Pennsylvania, public defenders office handled 4,173 cases in 1980. "Twenty years later, with the same number of attorneys, the office handled an estimated 8,000 cases." In Wisconsin, "more than 11,000 people go unrepresented annually because anyone with an annual income of more than $3,000 is deemed able to pay a lawyer." [96]

PROTECTION AGAINST CRUEL AND UNUSUAL PUNISHMENT

The final guarantee we look at in this section has also generated some major political controversies. The Eighth Amendment says, in part, that "cruel and unusual punishments" shall not be inflicted. Like some of the earlier amendments, this one reflects a concern of English law, which sought to protect British subjects from torture and inhumane treatment by the king. The Americans inherited the concern and wrote it into their Constitution. It is easy to see why it would be controversial, however. What is "cruel"? And what is "unusual"? Can we protect American citizens from cruel and unusual punishment delivered in other countries?

The Court has ruled that not all unusual punishments are unconstitutional, because all new punishments—electrocution or lethal injection, for instance—are unusual when they first appear, but they may be more humane than old punishments like hanging or shooting.[97] Despite intense lobbying on the part of impassioned interest groups, however, the Court has not ruled that the death penalty itself is cruel or unusual (except in the case of mentally retarded individuals[98]), and the majority of states have death penalty laws (see Figure 5.3).

The strongest attack on the death penalty began in the 1970s, when the NAACP Legal Defense Fund joined with the ACLU and the American Bar Association to argue that the death penalty was disproportionately given to African Americans, especially those convicted of rape. They argued that this was a violation of the Eighth Amendment, and also the Fourteenth Amendment guarantee of equal protection of the laws. Part of the problem was that state laws differed about what constituted grounds for imposing the death penalty, and juries had no uniform standards on which to rely. Consequently, unequal patterns of application of the penalty developed.

In *Furman v. Georgia* (1972) and two related cases, the Court ruled that Georgia's and Texas's capital punishment laws were unconstitutional, but the justices were so far from agreement that they all filed separate opinions, totaling 231 pages.[99] Thirty-five states passed new laws trying to meet the Court's objections and to clarify the standards for capital punishment. By 1976, six hundred inmates waited on death row for the Court to approve the new laws. That year the Court ruled in several cases that the death penalty was not unconstitutional, although it struck down laws requiring the

FIGURE 5.3
Capital Punishment by State

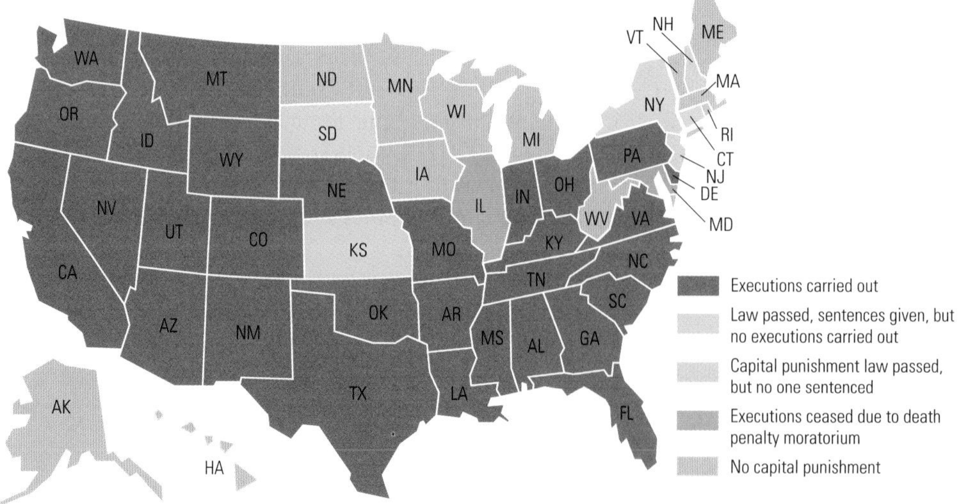

death penalty for certain crimes.[100] The Court remained divided over the issue. In 1977, Gary Gilmore became the first person executed after a ten-year break. Executions by state since 1976 are listed in Figure 5.4.

In 1987, *McClesky v. Kemp* raised the race issue again, but by then the Court was growing more conservative.[101] It held, five to four, that statistics showing that blacks who murder whites received the death penalty more frequently than whites who murder blacks did not prove a racial bias in the law or in how it was being applied.[102] The Rehnquist Court has continued to knock down procedural barriers to imposing the death penalty.

In recent years, however, public support for capital punishment appears to be softening, not because of opposition in principle but because of fears that the system might be putting innocent people on death row. This feeling has grown as DNA testing has cleared some death row residents, and careful investigation has shown that others, too, are innocent. Gallup polls indicate that the percentage of people who believe that an innocent person has been sentenced to death rose from 82 percent in 1995 to 91 percent in 2000.[103]

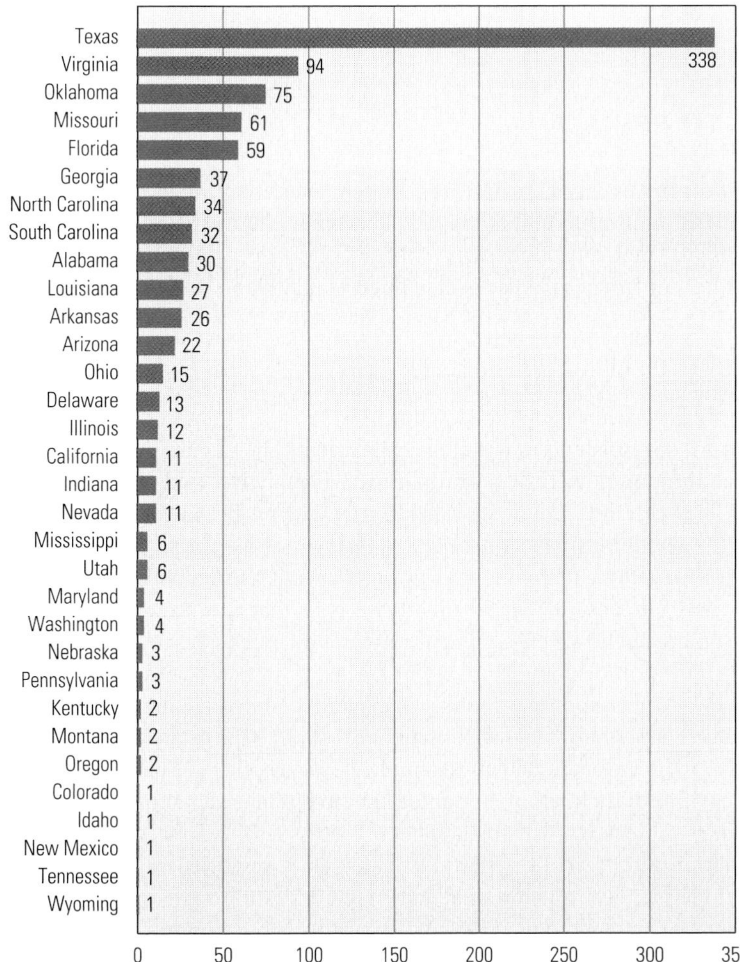

FIGURE 5.4
Executions Since 1976

Source: Death Penalty Information Center Through January 26, 2005.

After thirteen death row convicts in his state were exonerated between 1977 and 2000, Illinois governor George Ryan, a moderate Republican who supports the death penalty in principle, called for a statewide halt to executions. "I cannot support a system, which, in its administration, has proven so fraught with error," Ryan explained, "and has come so close to the ultimate nightmare, the state's taking of an innocent life." [104] Ryan's action has not changed the tide of public opinion about the death penalty in America, however. Following his lead, then–Maryland governor Parris Glendening issued a moratorium in 2002, but that action was quickly reversed by the new governor, Robert Ehrlich, in January 2003. And despite doubts, support for the death penalty still remains strong among Americans. According to a May 2004 Gallup Poll, roughly 70 percent of the public supports the death penalty.

WHO, WHAT, HOW Every citizen has a huge stake in the protection of the rights of criminal defendants. If the government were allowed to arrest, imprison, and punish citizens at will, without legal protections, in secrecy, and without record, then all of us, criminal or not, would be vulnerable to persecution, perhaps for who we are, how we vote, what we say, or what we believe. It is the rules of due process that protect us from an unpredictable and unaccountable legal system.

THE RIGHT TO PRIVACY

One of the most controversial rights in America is not even mentioned in the Constitution or the Bill of Rights: the right to privacy. This right is at the heart of one of the deepest divisions in American politics, the split over abortion rights, and is fundamental to two other controversial areas of civil liberties: gay rights and the right to die.

WHY IS THE RIGHT TO PRIVACY VALUABLE?

Although the right to privacy is not spelled out in the Bill of Rights, it goes hand in hand with the founders' insistence on limited government. Their goal was to keep government from getting too powerful and interfering with the lives and affairs of individual citizens. They certainly implied a right to privacy, and perhaps even assumed such a right, but they did not make it explicit.

The right to privacy, to be left alone to do what we want, is so obviously desirable that it scarcely needs a defense. The problem, of course, is that a right to privacy without any limits is anarchy, the absence of government altogether. Clearly governments have an interest in preventing some kinds of individual behavior—murder, theft, and rape, for example. But what about more subtle behaviors that do not directly affect the public safety but arguably have serious consequences for the public good—prostitution; drug use; gambling; even, to take the example we used earlier in this chapter, riding a motorcycle without a helmet? Should these behaviors fall under a right to privacy, or should the state be able to regulate them? The specific issues the Court has dealt with related to this topic are contraception use and abortion, laws restricting the behavior of homosexuals, and laws preventing terminally patients from ending their lives.

A right to privacy per se did not enter the American legal system until 1890, when an article called "The Right to Privacy" appeared in the *Harvard Law Review*.[105] In the years after the article appeared, states began to add a privacy right to their own bodies of statutory or constitutional law. The Supreme Court had dealt with privacy in some respects when it ruled on cases under the Fourth and Fifth Amendments, but it did not "discover" a right to privacy until 1965, and whether such a right exists remains controversial. None of the rights guaranteed by the first ten amendments to the Constitution is absolute; all, as we have seen, include limitations and contradictions. The right to privacy, without firm constitutional authority, is the least certain of all.

REPRODUCTIVE RIGHTS

Throughout the 1940s, people had tried to challenge state laws that made it a crime to use birth control, or even to give out information about how to prevent pregnancies. The Supreme Court routinely refused to hear these challenges until the 1965 case of *Griswold v. Connecticut.* Connecticut had a law on its books making it illegal to use contraceptive devices or to distribute information about them. Under that law, Griswold, the Connecticut director of Planned Parenthood, was convicted and fined $100 for counseling married couples about birth control.

The Court held that while the right to privacy is not explicit in the Constitution, a number of other rights, notably those in Amendments One, Three, Four, Five, and Nine, create a "zone of privacy" in which lie marriage and the decision to use contraception. It said that the specific guarantees in the Bill of Rights have "penumbras," or outlying shadowy areas, in which can be found a right to privacy. The Fourteenth Amendment applies that right to the states, and so Connecticut's law was unconstitutional.[106] In 1972 the Court extended the ruling to cover the rights of unmarried people to use contraception as well.[107]

Because of the Court's insistence that reproductive matters are not the concern of the government, abortion rights advocates saw an opportunity to use the *Griswold* ruling to strike down state laws prohibiting or limiting abortion. Until the Civil War, such laws were uncommon; most states allowed abortions in the early stages of pregnancy. After the war, however, opinion turned, and by 1910 every state except Kentucky had made abortions illegal. In the 1960s, legislation was again becoming more liberal, but abortions were still unobtainable in many places.

The Court had tried to avoid ruling on the abortion issue, but by 1973 it had become hard to escape. In *Roe v. Wade,* the justices held that the right to privacy did indeed encompass the right to abortion. It tried to balance a woman's right to privacy in reproductive matters with the state's interest in protecting human life, however, by treating the three trimesters of pregnancy differently. In the first three months of pregnancy, it held, there can be no compelling state interest that offsets a woman's privacy rights. In the second three months, the state can regulate access to abortions if it does so reasonably. In the last trimester, the state's interest becomes far more compelling, and a state can limit or even prohibit abortions as long as the mother's life is not in danger.[108]

The *Roe* decision launched the United States into an intense and divisive battle over abortion. States continued to try to limit abortions by requiring the consent of husbands or parents, by outlawing clinic advertising, by imposing waiting periods, and by erecting other roadblocks. The Court struck down most of these efforts, at least until 1977 when it allowed some state limitations. But the battle was not confined to statehouses. Congress, having failed to pass a constitutional amendment banning abortions, passed over thirty laws restricting access to abortions in various ways. For instance, it limited federal funding for abortions through Medicaid, a move the Supreme

Court upheld in 1980.[109] Presidents got into the fray as well. President Reagan and the first President Bush were staunch opponents of *Roe* and worked hard to get it overturned. Reagan appointed only antiabortion judges to federal courts, and his administration was active in pushing litigation that would challenge *Roe.*

The balance on the Supreme Court was crucial. *Roe* had been decided by a seven-to-two vote, but many in the majority were facing retirement. When Burger retired, Reagan elevated Rehnquist, one of the two dissenters, to chief justice, and appointed conservative Antonin Scalia in his place. Reagan's appointees did finally turn the Court in a more conservative direction, but even they have not been willing to overturn *Roe.* The 1973 ruling has been limited in some ways, but Rehnquist has not succeeded in gathering a majority to strike it down.[110] The debate over abortion in this country is certainly not over. It has become a rallying point for the Christian Right, organized since 1989 as the Christian Coalition, which has become a powerful part of the Republican Party. Since 1980 the Republicans have included a commitment to a constitutional amendment banning abortion in their presidential party platform. President George W. Bush is a strong opponent of abortion rights; one of his first acts as president was to ban federal funds to groups that provide or promote abortions overseas, and he later signed the controversial "partial-birth abortion" bill. But since a majority of Americans support at least some rights to abortion and the issue has proved damaging for the electoral fortunes of some Republicans, Bush has downplayed the issue in his presidential campaigns, preferring to say that he supports a "culture of life."

GAY RIGHTS

The *Griswold* and *Roe* rulings have opened up a variety of difficult issues for the Supreme Court. If there is a right to privacy, what might be included under it? On the whole, the Court has been very restrictive in expanding it beyond the reproductive rights of the original cases. Most controversial was its ruling in *Bowers v. Hardwick* (1986).[111]

Michael Hardwick was arrested under a Georgia law outlawing heterosexual and homosexual sodomy. A police officer, seeking to arrest him for failing to show up in court on a minor matter, was let into Hardwick's house by a friend and directed to his room. When the officer entered, he found Hardwick in bed with another man, and arrested him. Hardwick challenged the law (although he wasn't prosecuted under it), claiming that it violated his right to privacy. The Court disagreed. Looking at the case from the perspective of whether there was a constitutional right to engage in sodomy, rather than from the dissenting view that what took place between consenting adults was a private matter, the Court held five to four that the state of Georgia had a legitimate interest in regulating such behavior.

Justice Lewis Powell, who provided the fifth vote for the majority, said after his retirement that he regretted his vote in the *Bowers* decision, but by then, of course, it was too late. Several states were critical of the Court's ruling, Kentucky's Supreme Court going so far in 1992 as to strike down Kentucky's sodomy law as unconstitutional on the grounds the U.S. Supreme Court refused to use.[112] The Georgia Supreme Court itself struck down Georgia's sodomy law in 1998 on privacy grounds, but in a case involving heterosexual rather than homosexual activity. Not until 2003, in *Lawrence v. Texas,* did the Court, in a six-to-three decision, finally overturn *Bowers* on privacy grounds.[113] Interestingly, despite its longtime reluctance to overturn *Bowers,* the Court in 1996 used the equal protection clause of the Fourteenth Amendment to strike down a Colorado law that would have made it difficult for gays to use the Colorado courts to fight discrimination.[114] Thus the Court can pursue several constitutional avenues to expand the rights of gay Americans, should it want to do so.

THE RIGHT TO DIE

A final right-to-privacy issue that has stirred up controversy for the Court is the so-called right to die. In 1990 the Court ruled on the case of Nancy Cruzan, a woman who had been in a vegetative state and on life-support systems since she was in a car accident in 1983. Her parents asked the doctors to withdraw the life support and allow her to die, but the state of Missouri, claiming an interest in protecting the "sanctity of human life," blocked their request. The Cruzans argued that the right to privacy included the right to die without state interference, but the Court upheld Missouri's position, saying it was unclear that Nancy's wishes in the matter could be known for sure but that when such wishes were made clear, either in person or via a living will, a person's right to terminate medical treatment was protected under the Fourteenth Amendment's due process clause.[115]

The right-to-die issue surged back into national prominence in 2005 by a case involving Terri Schiavo, a young woman who had been in a persistent vegetative state for over fifteen years. Claiming that Schiavo had not wished to be kept alive by artificial measures, her husband asked a state court to have her feeding tube removed. Her parents challenged the decision, but after numerous appeals the court ordered the tube removed in accordance with the precedent set in the Cruzan case. Social conservatives in Congress passed a law that allowed the federal courts to review the case, but there were no legal grounds for federal court action and they all refused, including the Supreme Court. Schiavo died soon after. Angered by their inability to overturn the state court ruling, conservative groups vowed to fight for judicial appointments to the federal courts who would be more likely to intervene in such cases.

The Schiavo case did not change the prevailing legal principles—that this is a matter for individuals to decide and that when their wishes are known they should be respected by the doctors and the courts. In this matter, at least, public opinion seems to be consistent with the law. Polls showed the public strongly opposed to Congress's

'Don't tell me... You're here about a living will.'

You Can't Take It With You
The fate of Terri Schiavo, a terminally ill woman who had not left a living will but whose husband claimed she would not want to be kept alive by extraordinary measures, was finally settled in the courts in 2005. The spectacle of relatives fighting over her treatment when she could not speak for herself sent thousands of Americans to their lawyers to get living wills to make their own wishes clear.

intervention to prevent Schiavo's death, and large majorities supported the removal of her feeding tube. In the wake of the case, 70 percent of Americans said they were thinking about getting their own living wills.[116]

The question of a person's right to suspend treatment is different from another legal issue—whether individuals have the right to have assistance ending their lives when they are terminally ill and in severe pain. Proponents of this right argue that patients should be able to decide whether to continue living with their conditions, and since such patients are frequently incapacitated or lack the means to end their lives painlessly, they are entitled to help if they want to die. Opponents, on the other hand, say a patient's right to die may require doctors to violate their Hippocratic Oath, and that it is open to abuse. Patients, especially those whose illnesses are chronic and costly, might feel obligated to end their lives out of concern for family or financial matters. In 1997 the Supreme Court ruled that the issue be left to the states and left open the possibility that dying patients might be able to make a claim to a constitutional right to die in the future.[117]

Oregon provided the first test of this policy. In 1997 it passed a referendum allowing doctors under certain circumstances to provide lethal doses of medication to enable terminally ill patients to end their lives. In late 2001, U.S. Attorney General John Ashcroft effectively blocked the law by announcing that doctors who participated in assisted suicides would lose their licenses to prescribe federally regulated medications, an essential part of medical practice. In 2004 a federal appellate court ruled that Ashcroft overstepped his authority under federal law and in early 2005 the Supreme Court agreed to hear an appeal of that case.

WHO, WHAT, HOW What's at stake in the right to privacy seems amazingly simple given the intensity of the debate about it. In short, the issue is whether citizens have the right to control their own bodies in fundamentally intimate matters like birth, sex, and death. The controversy arises when opponents argue that citizens do not have that right, but rather should be subject to religious rules, natural laws, or moral beliefs that dictate certain behaviors with respect to these matters. They promote legislation and constitutional amendment that seek to bring behavior into conformity with their beliefs. The founders did not act to protect this right, possibly because they did not anticipate that they had created a government strong enough to tell people what to do in such personal matters, or possibly because technology has put choices on the table today that did not exist more than two hundred years ago. In the absence of constitutional protection or prohibition of the right to privacy, the rule that provides for it today derives from a series of Court cases that could just as easily be overturned should the Court change its mind.

THE CITIZENS AND CIVIL LIBERTIES

In the United States we are accustomed to thinking about citizenship as a status that confers on us certain rights. We have explored many of those rights in detail in this chapter. But as we stand back and ask ourselves why each of these rights is valuable, an interesting irony appears. Even though these are *individual* rights, valued for granting freedoms to individuals and allowing them to make claims on their government, we value them also because they lead to *collective* benefits—we are better off as a society if individuals possess these rights. Democratic government is preserved if criticism is allowed; religion can prosper if it is not entangled in politics; militias may defend the security of a free state if individual citizens are armed; justice will be available to all if it is guaranteed to each.

The collective as well as the individual nature of American civil liberties recalls the argument we made in Chapter 1 that there are two strands of thinking about citizenship in the United States—one focused on individual rights and the self-interest of citizens and the other emphasizing obligations or duties seen as necessary to protect the public interest. We said these traditions have existed side by side throughout our history. They have done so because neither can exist solely by itself in a democracy: obligation without rights is an authoritarian dictatorship, rights without obligation lead to a state of nature, or anarchy, with no government at all. Citizenship in a democracy plainly carries both rights and duties.

The final section of a chapter on civil liberties is an interesting place to speculate about the duties attached to American citizenship. We have explored the Bill of Rights. What might a Bill of Obligations look like? The Constitution itself suggests the basics. Obligations are very much the flip side of rights; for every right guaranteed, there is a corresponding duty to use it. For instance, the provisions for elected office and the right to vote imply a duty to vote. Congress is authorized to collect taxes, duties, and excises, including an income tax; citizens are obligated to pay those taxes. Congress can raise and support armies, provide and maintain a navy, provide for and govern militias; correspondingly, Americans have a duty to serve in the military. The Constitution defines treason as waging war against the states or aiding or abetting their enemies; citizens have an obligation not to betray their country or state. Amendments Five and Six guarantee grand juries and jury trials to those accused of crimes; it is citizens who must serve on those juries.

As citizenship obligations around the world go, these are not terribly onerous. In Europe such obligations are explicitly extended to include providing for the welfare of those who cannot take care of themselves, for instance. Tax burdens are much higher in most other industrialized nations than they are in the United States. In some countries the obligation to vote is legally enforced, and others have mandatory military service for all citizens, or at least all male citizens.

Still, many people find the obligations associated with American citizenship to be too harsh. For instance, two *Wall Street Journal* reporters wrote, "We [Americans] are a nation of law breakers. We exaggerate tax-deductible expenses, lie to customs officials, bet on card games and sports events, disregard jury notices, drive while intoxicated . . . and hire illegal child care workers. . . . Nearly all people violate some laws, and many run afoul of dozens without ever being considered or considering themselves criminals."[118] While 90 percent of Americans value their right to a trial by jury, only 12 percent are willing to accept the jury duty that makes that right possible.[119] We have already seen that voter turnout in the United States falls far behind that in most other nations.

How much fulfillment of political obligation is enough? Most Americans clearly obey most of the laws, most of the time. When there is a war and a military draft, most draft-aged males have agreed to serve. If we do not pay all the taxes we owe, we pay much of them. If we do not vote, we get involved in our communities in countless other ways. As a nation, we are certainly getting by, at least for now. But perhaps we should consider the long-term political consequences to a democratic republic if the emphasis on preserving civil liberties is not balanced by a corresponding commitment to fulfilling political obligations.

WHAT'S AT STAKE REVISITED

When the Black Student Union at Indiana University asked the administrators to do something about the presence of Ku Klux Klan figures in the murals in Woodburn Hall, many students, both white and black, supported them. The murals, without any prominent explanation to put them into context, seemed peculiar at best, and racist at worst. And many students felt that the fact that some students felt intimidated was enough to warrant removing the paintings.

But the request also drew fire from those who argued that taking down the murals would be political correctness run amok. They said that free speech required that a historically accurate painting that wasn't racist in intent not be taken down because some people felt uncomfortable in its presence. Other people said that serious Klan action was a regrettable but undeniable part of Indiana history, and to take down the murals was to sweep it under the rug and pretend that it had not happened. And still others argued that the murals presented a perfect opportunity to teach students about the place of racism in U.S. history and that professors should work harder to do their jobs and use the murals in a pedagogically responsible way.

Thinking Outside the Box

- Should the founders have provided a Bill of Obligations as well as a Bill of Rights?
- In the delicate balance between security and freedom, on which side should we err?
- How much free speech do we need on our college campuses?

It is clear from what we learned in this chapter that a great deal is at stake in the question of what should happen to the murals. Indeed, universities are obligated to provide to their students an environment in which they can comfortably learn. But universities have other obligations as well, and one of those is to preserve freedom of speech and promote the free expression of ideas. If all groups asked to have a veto over what could be displayed publicly, there might be no art displayed at all. And, some people argue, real education is never a comfortable experience. The process of having one's old ideas shaken up and new ideas tried out is sometimes a painful process, but one necessary for intellectual growth and maturity.

Indiana University's chancellor echoed some of this reasoning in her decision to keep the murals where they are. To remove them, she said, would be to do what the artist, Benton, had refused to do: "It would hide the shameful aspects of Indiana's past." To provide context for the murals, the chancellor announced a plan to strengthen campus education about the murals, to create a fund to bring more diverse art to the campus, and to enhance the campus's commitment to diversity. The controversy subsided as most students agreed that the solution addressed their concerns.

Philosophers like John Stuart Mill would argue that free expression should always prevail, lest we lose our ability to defend the truth, that only in the free flow of ideas, no matter how heinous some of them might be, do we learn to formulate and support what we know to be true. And there is a good deal of value in this argument. It is undeniable as well, however, that it has always been the people with power who get to decide what goes up on the walls, and that it can be very important to be willing to transfer some of that power to groups that have traditionally had none. One student, commenting on the mural controversy, said that it didn't really matter so much whether the murals were indeed art, or part of history. What mattered to her, she said, was whether she and her fellow students were really being heard, whether they had the power to make themselves heard. And in the end, conflicts about rights often come down to conflicts about power. As we will see again in Chapter 6, on civil rights, that is almost always what is at stake when rights conflict.

To Sum Up

KEY TERMS

republic.cqpress.com

accommodationists (p. 168)
bad tendency test (p. 176)
bills of attainder (p. 162)
civil liberties (p. 154)
civil rights (p. 154)
clear and present danger test (p. 176)
compelling state interest (p. 170)
due process of law (p. 190)
establishment clause (p. 167)
exclusionary rule (p. 191)
ex post facto laws (p. 162)
fighting words (p. 179)
freedom of assembly (p. 178)
free exercise clause (p. 170)
habeas corpus (p. 162)
imminent lawless action test (p. 176)
incorporation (p. 163)
Lemon test (p. 169)
libel (p. 182)
Miller test (p. 179)
police power (p. 170)
political correctness (p. 179)
prior restraint (p. 182)
sedition (p. 174)
selective incorporation (p. 164)
separationists (p. 168)

Key terms, chapter summaries, practice quizzes, Internet links, and other study aids are available on the companion Web site at: republic.cqpress.com.

SUMMARY

republic.cqpress.com

- Our civil liberties are individual freedoms that place limitations on the power of government. Most of these rights are spelled out in the text of the Constitution or in its first ten amendments, the Bill of Rights, but some have developed over the years through judicial decision making.
- Sometimes rights conflict, and when they do, government, guided by the Constitution and through the institutions of Congress, the executive, and the actions of citizens themselves, is called upon to resolve these conflicts.
- According to the establishment and free exercise clauses of the First Amendment, citizens of the United States have the right not to be coerced to practice a religion in which they do not believe, as well as the right not to be prevented from practicing the religion they espouse. Because these rights can conflict, religious freedom has been a battleground ever since the founding of the country. The courts have played a significant role in navigating the stormy waters of religious expression since the founding.
- Freedom of expression, also provided for in the First Amendment, is often considered the hallmark of our democratic government. Freedom of expression produces information about government, limits corruption, protects minorities, and helps maintain a vigorous defense of the truth. But this right may at times conflict with the preservation of social order and protection of civility, decency, and reputation. Again, it has been left to the courts to balance freedom of expression with social and moral order.
- The right to bear arms, supported by the Second Amendment, has also been hotly debated—more so in recent years than in the past, as federal gun control legislation has been enacted only recently. Most often the debate over gun laws is carried out in state legislatures.
- The founders believed that to limit government power, people needed to retain rights against government throughout the process of being accused, tried, and punished for criminal activities. Thus they devoted some of the text of the Constitution as well as the Bill of Rights to a variety of procedural protections, including the right to a speedy and public trial, protection from unreasonable search and seizure, and the right to legal advice.
- Though the right to privacy is not mentioned in either the Constitution or the Bill of Rights—and did not even enter the American legal system until the late 1800s—it has become a fiercely debated right on a number of different levels, including reproductive rights, gay rights, and the right to die. In the absence of constitutional protection, the series of court cases on these matters determines how they are to be resolved. Many of these issues are still on shaky ground, as the states create their own legislation and the courts hand down new rulings.

PRACTICE QUIZ

republic.cqpress.com

1. Because rights represent power in a democratic society,

a. rights are subject to the whims of the majority.
b. a rigid hierarchy of rights exists.
c. the exercise of rights is inevitably subject to conflict and controversy.
d. the powerful have a monopoly on rights.
e. many rights are often limited.

2. Both freedom of speech and freedom of religion require

a. strong acceptance of majority views.
b. free and periodic elections.
c. strict regulation by government.
d. tolerance of ideas that we reject or find repugnant.
e. limited protection from Congress.

3. The right to bear arms was initially established

a. to keep the federal government in check by limiting the power of permanent armies.
b. because the right to bear arms has historically been an important element of a free society.
c. because the right to bear arms was critical to a society that got most of its food from hunting.
d. to protect the United States from foreign invasion.
e. because most of the founders were gun owners.

4. Amendments Four through Eight deal largely with

a. rights of expression.
b. limits on the power of the government to accuse, try, and punish criminal activities.
c. powers of state government.
d. limits on the power of government to take or restrict property rights.
e. voting rights.

5. This chapter states that citizenship obligations

a. are almost never met.
b. are quite oppressive.
c. affect the poor and not the wealthy.
d. are brought to bear more heavily on women and minorities.
e. are not terribly onerous.

SUGGESTED RESOURCES

republic.cqpress.com

Books

Bailyn, Bernard. 1967. *The Ideological Origins of the American Revolution.* Cambridge, Mass.: Belknap Press. An exceptionally detailed account of the pamphlets and other writings that convinced the thirteen colonies to revolt from Mother England.

Carter, Stephen L. 1993. *The Culture of Disbelief: How American Law and Politics Trivialize Religious Devotion.* New York: Basic Books. In an intriguing argument, Carter asserts that Americans can preserve the separation of church and state while at the same time embracing spirituality.

Cottrell, Robert C. 2001. *Roger Nash Baldwin and the American Civil Liberties Union.* New York: Columbia University Press. This straightforward biography of the founder of the ACLU documents the story of the man behind this important organization.

Downs, Donald A. 2005. *Restoring Free Speech and Liberty on Campus.* Cambridge, U.K.: Cambridge University Press. In a book written from his personal experience, Downs argues that academic freedom on college campuses has declined since the 1990s. Downs maintains that constitutional rights and free inquiry will prevail only if individuals or groups stand up to protect them in the face of pressure.

Epstein, Lee, and Thomas G. Walker. 2004. *Constitutional Law for a Changing America,* 5th ed. Washington, D.C.: CQ Press. This book presents two detailed yet accessible volumes for beginning constitutional law students.

Fish, Stanley. 1994. *There's No Such Thing as Free Speech and It's a Good Thing, Too.* New York: Oxford University Press. Fish, a noted law professor, believes that free speech can be dangerous, making limits necessary for certain kinds of speech.

Garrow, David. 1994. *Liberty and Sexuality: The Right to Privacy and the Making of* Roe v. Wade. New York: Macmillan. This book offers a comprehensive historical analysis of the debate surrounding *Roe v. Wade,* both before and after the decision.

Hentoff, Nat. 1992. *Free Speech for Me—But Not for Thee: How the American Left and Right Relentlessly Censor Each Other.* New York: HarperCollins. This book offers an excellent and somewhat frightening account of how both the left and right attempt to censor speech and publications they oppose.

Prejean, Helen. 1993. *Dead Man Walking: An Eyewitness Account of the Death Penalty in the United States.* New York: Random House. Written by a Catholic nun who befriended two inmates on Louisiana's death row, this thought-provoking memoir offers a first-hand glimpse at the harsh realities of the criminal justice system and an impassioned plea to end capital punishment. Adapted for the screen in a 1996 film by Tim Robbins, starring Susan Sarandon and Sean Penn.

Web Sites

FindLaw. www.findlaw.com/casecode/supreme.html. This database allows you to search and read the full text of every Supreme Court decision handed down since 1893 and selected earlier cases.

Note: The following are just two of the many Web sites that address civil liberties issues. For links to other sites, see our web page at republic.cqpress.com.

American Civil Liberties Union. www.aclu.org. A fact-filled resource with information on ACLU issues, current events in Congress and the courts, and the history of the organization.

National Rifle Association. www.nra.org. Everything you need to know about the history of the NRA and current gun control legislation; includes links to news commentary on firearms-related stories.

Movies

***Bowling for Columbine.* 2002.** A controversial and, at times, humorous filmmaker, Michael Moore attempts to uncover why the United States has so many firearms-related deaths.

***Gideon's Trumpet.* 1979.** An inspiring movie about the 1963 Supreme Court case *Gideon v. Wainwright.* Based on Anthony Lewis's book published in 1964.

***Minority Report.* 2002.** Adapted from a short story by science fiction writer Philip K. Dick, this film portrays civil liberties gone awry in a grim future where criminals are arrested "precrime."

***The People vs. Larry Flynt.* 1996.** Director Milos Forman chronicles the notorious publisher's journey from "smut peddler" to champion of free speech, culminating in the Supreme Court's 1988 landmark decision in his favor. Starring Woody Harrelson, Courtney Love, and Edward Norton.

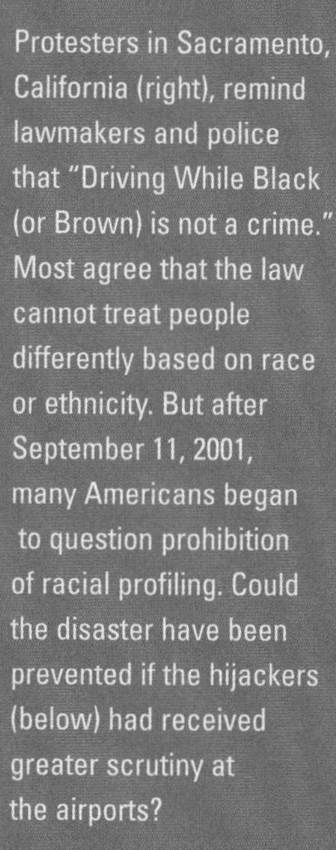

Protesters in Sacramento, California (right), remind lawmakers and police that "Driving While Black (or Brown) is not a crime." Most agree that the law cannot treat people differently based on race or ethnicity. But after September 11, 2001, many Americans began to question prohibition of racial profiling. Could the disaster have been prevented if the hijackers (below) had received greater scrutiny at the airports?

THE STRUGGLE FOR EQUAL RIGHTS

6

(continued)

WHAT'S AT STAKE?

On Wednesday, April 19, 1995, a thirty-one-year-old computer technician named Abrahim Ahmed left Oklahoma City, where he had lived for thirteen years, on a visit to his family in his native Jordan. At a stopover in Chicago, he heard the news on television: terrorists had blown apart the Alfred P. Murrah Federal Building in Oklahoma City, killing nearly two hundred people, many of them children at an on-site day-care facility. Ahmed's Middle Eastern name and his Oklahoma City–to–Jordan itinerary caught the attention of airport officials who, along with many other Americans, immediately suspected that the bombing was the work of Islamic extremists like those accused of setting off a bomb at New York's World Trade Center two years earlier.

Authorities stopped Ahmed in Chicago, searching his baggage and questioning him so thoroughly that he missed his connecting flight to Rome and had to fly to London instead. Once in London, he was handcuffed and interrogated again for several hours. Tools he was bringing to Jordan to give as gifts looked to authorities as if they could be used to make bombs. He was put on a flight back to the United States and held in an office near Dulles Airport for several more hours, before he was finally told he was free to go. Several days later, agents arrested two white American males and charged them with blowing up the Murrah building. Despite the nation's fears of Arab extremism, Timothy McVeigh's and Terry Nichols's terrorism was homegrown.

The practice of singling out people for suspicion because they are the same race as other suspects or because you believe people of one racial or ethnic group are more likely than others to commit crimes is called *racial profiling.* The Oklahoma City bombing was neither the first nor the last time Americans engaged in it. At the start of World War II, as we mentioned in Chapter 5, President Franklin Roosevelt ordered Japanese Americans rounded up and put into internment camps in case any of them were spies or saboteurs. In 2000, police departments in New Jersey, New York, and Maryland, among other places, were accused of racial profiling when evidence showed that they were more likely to stop blacks and Hispanics on the highways for traffic violations or to look for illegal drugs. The police argued that they did so because these groups were statistically more likely to commit crimes.

And after the September 11, 2001, terrorist attacks, which did turn out to be the work of Islamic extremists, many Americans again made Middle Easterners the target of their fear and suspicion. Some, for instance, were afraid to fly on planes with Middle Eastern–looking passengers. In one of several similar incidents, a man en route to his brother's wedding in Pakistan was told to get off the plane because the flight crew did not "feel safe flying with" him. Feeling shamed, he left the plane and missed the wedding.[1] In an indication of just how torn Americans were between their fears and their consciences, even several African Americans who have long abhorred the whole idea of racial profiling found themselves carefully watching their fellow airplane passengers who appeared to be Arabs or Muslims in the weeks immediately following September 11.[2] Airplanes were not the only places where Arabs were singled out. Arab Americans or visitors were harassed on the streets, in their cars, and at home (by phone). They were pulled over by police, interrogated on trains, and arrested in significant numbers. Many were let go quickly. Others sat in jail, usually on immigration-related charges, until they were finally released. Still others really did turn out to be involved with organizations that planned to terrorize Americans, making it difficult to see the practice of racial profiling as a clear-cut problem of right versus wrong.

What lessons do we learn from these experiences? Is racial profiling necessary when the nation is under threat? Does it help reduce crime rates when it is not? And what degree of increased security or order justifies infringement on innocent people's rights, just because they happen to fit the profile of a criminal? Just what is at stake for our nation in the practice of racial profiling? We return to this question after we study just how difficult the battle for equal rights has been in this country for many of the groups concerned. *

When you consider where we started, the progress toward racial equality in the United States can look pretty impressive. Just fifty years ago, it was illegal for most blacks and whites to go to the same schools in the American South or to use the same public facilities, like swimming pools and drinking fountains. Today, for most of us, the segregated South seems like a distant memory. At a 2002 White House ceremony commemorating Martin Luther King Day, Condoleezza Rice watched from the audience as a portrait of the fallen civil rights leader was unveiled. Once a young girl living through the violent days of the civil rights movement in Birmingham, Alabama, Rice is now the nation's second African American secretary of state and one of two black cabinet-level appointees in the second George W. Bush administration. Such moments, caught in the media spotlight, illuminate a stark contrast between now and then.

But in some ways, the changes highlighted at such moments are only superficial. Though there are indeed two black members of Bush's cabinet—the other is Alphonso Jackson at Housing and Urban Development—there are remarkably few blacks in national elected office. *USA Today* pointed out in 2002 that "if the US Senate and the National Governors Association were private clubs, their membership rosters would be a scandal. They're virtually lily white." [3] Throughout our history, only one elected governor and five U.S. senators have been black, and none of them was in office in 2002, as Rice watched the Martin Luther King ceremony at the White House (although Barack Obama was elected senator from Illinois in 2004).

Even though legal discrimination ended nearly fifty years ago, inequality still pervades the American system and continues to be reflected in economic and social statistics. On average, blacks are less educated and much poorer than whites, they experience higher crime rates, they live disproportionately in poverty-stricken areas, they score lower on standardized tests, and they rank at the bottom of most social measurements. Life expectancy is lower for African American men and women than for their white counterparts, and a greater percentage of African American children live in single-parent homes than do white or Hispanic children. The statistics illustrate what we suggested in Chapter 5—that rights equal power, and long-term deprivation of rights results in powerlessness. Unfortunately, the granting of formal **civil rights**, which we defined in Chapter 5 as the citizenship rights guaranteed by the Thirteenth, Fourteenth, Fifteenth, Nineteenth, and Twenty-sixth Amendments, does not immediately bring about change in social and economic status.

civil rights citizenship rights guaranteed to the people (primarily in the Thirteenth, Fourteenth, Fifteenth, Nineteenth, and Twenty-sixth Amendments) and protected by the government

African Americans are not the only group that shows the effects of having been deprived of its civil rights. Native Americans, Hispanics, and Asian Americans have all faced or face unequal treatment in the legal system, the job market, and the schools. Women, making up over half the population of the United States, have long struggled to gain economic parity with men. People in America are denied rights, and consequently power, on the basis of their sexual orientation, their age, their physical abilities, and their citizenship status. A country once praised by French observer Alexis de Tocqueville as a place of extraordinary equality, the United States today is haunted by traditions of unequal treatment and intolerance that it cannot entirely shake.

In this chapter we look at the struggles of these groups to gain equal rights and the power to enforce those rights. The struggles are different because the groups themselves, and the political avenues open to them, vary in important ways. In order to understand how groups can use different political strategies to change the rules and win power, in this chapter you will learn about

- the meaning of political inequality
- the struggle of African Americans to claim rights denied to them because of race
- the struggle of Native Americans, Hispanics, and Asian Americans to claim rights denied to them because of race or ethnicity
- women's battle for rights denied to them on the basis of gender
- the fight by other groups in society to claim rights denied to them on a variety of bases
- the relationship of citizens to civil rights

THE MEANING OF POLITICAL INEQUALITY

Despite the deeply held American expectation that the law should treat all people equally, laws by nature must treat some people differently from others. Not only are laws designed in the first place to discriminate *between* those who abide by society's rules and those who don't,[4] but the laws can also legally treat criminals differently once they are convicted. For instance, in forty-six states and the District of Columbia, convicted felons are denied the right to vote while in prison, and in fourteen of those states convicts lose the right to vote for life.[5] But when particular groups are treated differently because of some characteristic like race, religion, gender, sexual orientation, age, or wealth, we say that the law discriminates *against* them, that they are denied equal protection of the laws. Throughout our history, legislatures, both state and national, have passed laws treating groups differently based on characteristics such as these. Sometimes those laws have seemed just and reasonable, but often they have not. Deciding which characteristics may fairly be the basis of unequal treatment, and which may not, is the job of all three branches of our government, but especially of our court system.

WHEN CAN THE LAW TREAT PEOPLE DIFFERENTLY?

The Supreme Court has expended considerable energy and ink on this problem, and its answers have changed over time as various groups have waged the battle for equal rights, against a backdrop of ever-changing American values, public opinion, and politics. Before we look at the struggles those groups have endured in their pursuit of equal treatment by the law, we look briefly at the Court's formula for determining what sorts of discrimination need what sorts of legal remedy.

Legal Classifications The Court has divided the laws that treat people differently into three tiers (see Table 6.1).

- The top tier refers to those ways of classifying people that are so rarely constitutional that they are immediately "suspect." **Suspect classifications** require that the government have a *compelling state interest* for treating people differently. Race is a suspect classification. To determine whether laws making suspect classifications are constitutional, the Court subjects them to a heightened standard of review called **strict scrutiny**. Strict scrutiny means that the Court looks very carefully at the law and the government interest involved. As we saw in Chapter 5, laws that deprived people of some fundamental religious rights were once required to pass the compelling state interest test; at that time, religion was viewed by the Court as a suspect category.
- Classifications that the Court views as less potentially dangerous to fundamental rights fall into the middle tier. These "quasisuspect" classifications may or may not be legitimate grounds for treating people differently. Such classifications are subject not to strict scrutiny but to an **intermediate standard of review**. That is, the Court looks to see if the law requiring different treatment of people bears a substantial relationship to an important state interest. An "important interest test" is not as hard to meet as a "compelling interest test." Laws that treat women differently than men fall into this category.
- Finally, the least scrutinized tier of classifications is that of "nonsuspect" classifications; these are subject to the **minimum rationality test**. The Court asks whether the government had a *rational basis* for making a law that treats a given class of people differently. Laws that discriminate on the basis of age, such as a curfew for young people, or on the basis of economic level, such as a higher tax rate for those in a certain income bracket, need not stem from compelling or important government interests. The government must merely have had a rational basis for making the law, which is fairly easy for a legislature to show.

suspect classifications classifications, such as race, for which any discriminatory law must be justified by a compelling state interest

strict scrutiny a heightened standard of review used by the Supreme Court to assess the constitutionality of laws that limit some freedoms or that make a suspect classification

intermediate standard of review standard of review used by the Court to evaluate laws that make a quasisuspect classification

minimum rationality test standard of review used by the Court to evaluate laws that make a nonsuspect classification

TABLE 6.1 **When Can the Law Treat People Differently**

LEGAL CLASSIFICATION	WHEN LAWS TREAT PEOPLE DIFFERENTLY BECAUSE OF . . .	THE COURT APPLIES . . .	THE COURT ASKS . . .	EXAMPLE: TEST USED TO UPHOLD A CLASSIFICATION	EXAMPLE: TEST USED TO STRIKE DOWN A CLASSIFICATION
Suspect	Race (or legislation that infringes on some fundamental rights)	Strict scrutiny standard of review	Is there a *compelling state interest* in this classification?	Government had a compelling state interest (national security) in relocating Japanese Americans from the West Coast during World War II. *Korematsu v. United States* (1944)	State government had no compelling reason to segregate schools to achieve state purpose of educating children. *Brown v. Board of Education* (1954)
Quasisuspect	Gender	Intermediate standard of review	Is there an *important state purpose* for this classification, and are the means used by the law substantially related to the ends?	Court upheld federal law requiring males but not females to register for military service (the draft). *Rostker v. Goldberg* (1981)	Court struck down an Alabama law requiring husbands but not wives to pay alimony after divorce. *Orr v. Orr* (1979)
Nonsuspect	Age, wealth, sexual orientation	Minimum rationality standard of review	Is there a *rational basis* for this classification?	Court found a Missouri law requiring public officials to retire at age 70 to have a rational basis. *Gregory v. Ashcroft* (1991)	Court struck down an amendment to the Colorado constitution that banned legislation to protect people's rights on the basis of their sexual orientation because it had no rational relation to a legitimate state goal. *Romer v. Evans* (1996)

The Fight for Suspect Status The significance of the three tiers of classifications and the three review standards is that all groups that feel discriminated against want the Court to view them as a suspect class so that they will be treated as a protected group. Civil rights laws might cover them anyway, and the Fourteenth Amendment, which guarantees equal protection of the laws, may also formally protect them. However, once a group is designated as a suspect class, the Supreme Court is very unlikely to permit *any* laws to treat them differently. Thus gaining suspect status is crucial in the struggle for equal rights.

After over one hundred years of decisions that effectively allowed people to be treated differently because of their race, the Court finally agreed in the 1950s that race is a suspect class. Women's groups, however, have failed to convince the Court, or to amend the Constitution, to make gender a suspect classification. The intermediate standard of review was devised by the Court to express its view that it is a little more dangerous to classify people by gender than by age or wealth, but not as dangerous as classifying them by race or religion. Some groups in America—homosexuals, for instance—have not even managed to get the Court to consider them in the quasisuspect category. Although some states and localities have passed legislation to prevent discrimination on the basis of sexual orientation, gays can be treated differently by law as long as the state can demonstrate a rational basis for the law.

These standards of review make a real difference in American politics—they are part of the rules of politics that determine society's winners and losers. Americans who are treated unequally by the laws consequently have less power to use the democratic system to get what they need and want (like legislation to protect and further their interests), to secure the resources available through the system (like education and other government benefits), and to gain new resources (like jobs and material goods). People who cannot claim their political rights have little if any standing in a democratic society.

WHY DO WE DENY RIGHTS?

People deny rights to others for many reasons, although they are not always candid about what those reasons are. People usually explain their denial of others' rights by focusing on some group characteristic. They may say that the other group is not "civilized" or does not recognize the "true God," or that its members are in some other way unworthy or incapable of exercising their rights. People feel compelled to justify poor treatment by blaming the group they are treating poorly.

But usually there is something other than simple fault-finding behind the denial of rights. People deny the rights of others because rights are power. To deny people rights is to have power over them and to force them to conform to our will. Thus we have compelled slaves to work for our profit, we have deprived wives of the right to divorce their husbands, and we have driven Native Americans from their homes so that we could develop their land. Denying people rights keeps them dependent and submissive. Grant them rights, and they soon leave their subservience behind.

People also deny rights to others for another reason. Isolating categories of people, be they recent immigrants who speak English poorly, homosexuals whose lifestyle seems threatening, or people whose religious beliefs are unfamiliar, helps groups to define who they are, who their relevant community is, and who they are *not*. Communities can believe that they, with their culture, values, and beliefs, are superior to people who are different. This belief promotes cohesion and builds loyalty to "people who are like us"; it also intensifies dislike of and hostility to those who are "not our kind." It is only a small step from there to believing that people outside the community do not really deserve the same rights as those "superior" people within.

DIFFERENT KINDS OF EQUALITY

The notion of equality is very controversial in America. The disputes arise in part because we often think that "equal" must mean "identical" or "the same." Thus equality can seem threatening to the American value system, which prizes people's freedom to be different, to be unique individuals. We can better understand the controversies over the attempts to create political equality in this country if we return briefly to a distinction we made in Chapter 2 between substantive and procedural equality.

In American political culture, we prefer to rely on government to guarantee fair treatment and equal opportunity (a *procedural* view), rather than to manipulate fair and equal outcomes (a *substantive* view). We want government to treat everyone the same, and we want people to be free to be different, but we do not want government to treat people differently in order to make them equal at the end. This distinction poses a problem for the civil rights movement in America, the effort to achieve equal treatment by the laws for all Americans. When the laws are changed, which is a procedural solution, substantive action may still be necessary to ensure equal treatment in the future.

WHO, WHAT, HOW In the struggle for political equality, the people with the most at stake are members of groups that, because of some characteristic beyond their control, have been denied their civil rights. What they seek is equal treatment by the laws. The rules the Supreme Court uses to determine if they should have it are the three standards of strict scrutiny, the intermediate standard of review, and the minimum rationality test.

But minority groups are not the only ones with a stake in the battle for equal rights. Those who support discrimination want to maintain the status quo, which bolsters their own power and the power of those like them. The means open to them are maintaining discriminatory laws and intimidating those they discriminate against.

RIGHTS DENIED ON THE BASIS OF RACE: AFRICAN AMERICANS

We cannot separate the history of our race relations from the history of the United States. Americans have struggled for centuries to come to terms with the fact that citizens of African nations were kidnapped, packed into sailing vessels, exported to America, and sold, often at great profit, into a life that destroyed their families, their spirit, and their human dignity. The stories of white supremacy and black inferiority, told to numb the sensibilities of European Americans to the horror of their own behavior, have been almost as damaging as slavery itself and have lived on in the American psyche—and in political institutions—much longer than the practice they justified. **Racism**, institutionalized power inequalities in society based on the perception of racial differences, is not a "southern problem" or a "black problem"; it is an American problem, and one that we have not yet managed to eradicate from national culture.

racism institutionalized power inequalities in society based on the perception of racial differences

Not only has racism had a decisive influence on American culture, it has also been central to American politics. From the start, those with power in America have been torn by the issue of race. The framers of the Constitution were so ambivalent that they would not use the word *slavery*, even while that document legalized its existence. Although some early politicians were morally opposed to the institution of slavery, they were, in the end, more reluctant to offend their southern colleagues by taking an antislavery stand. Even the Northwest Ordinance of 1787, which prohibited slavery in the northwestern territories, contained the concession to the South that fugitive slaves could legally be seized and returned to their owners. Sometimes in politics the need to compromise and bargain can cause people to excuse the inexcusable for political gain.

BLACKS IN AMERICA BEFORE THE CIVIL WAR

At the time of the Civil War there were almost four million slaves in the American South and nearly half a million free blacks living in the rest of the country. Even where slavery was illegal, blacks as a rule did not enjoy full rights of citizenship. In fact, in *Dred Scott v. Sanford* (1857), the Supreme Court had ruled that blacks could not be citizens because the founders had not intended them to be citizens. "On the contrary," wrote Justice Roger Taney, "they were at that time considered as a subordinate and inferior class of beings, who had been subjugated by the dominant race, and whether emancipated or not, yet remained subject to their authority." [6]

Congress was no more protective of blacks than the Court was. Laws such as the Fugitive Slave Act of 1850 made life precarious even for free northern blacks. When national institutions seemed impervious to their demands for black rights, the abolitionists, a coalition of free blacks and northern whites working to end slavery altogether, tried other strategies. The movement put pressure on the Republican Party to take a stand on political equality and persuaded three state legislatures (Iowa, Wisconsin, and New York) to hold referenda (statewide votes) on black suffrage between 1857 and 1860. The abolitionists lost all three votes by large margins. Even in the North, on the eve of the Civil War, public opinion did not favor rights for blacks.

THE CIVIL WAR AND ITS AFTERMATH: WINNERS AND LOSERS

We can't begin to speculate here on all the causes of the Civil War. Suffice it to say that the war was not fought simply over the moral evil of slavery. Slavery was an economic and political issue as well as an ethical one. The southern economy depended on slavery, and when, in an effort to hold the Union together in 1863, President Abraham Lincoln issued the Emancipation Proclamation, he was not simply taking a moral stand; he was trying to use economic pressure to keep the country intact. The proclamation, in fact, did not free all slaves, only those in states rebelling against the Union.[7]

It is hard to find any real "winners" in the American Civil War. Indeed the war took such a toll on North and South that neither world war in the twentieth century would claim as many American casualties. The North "won" the war, in that the Union was restored, but the costs would be paid for decades afterward. Politically, the northern Republicans, the party of Lincoln, were in the ascendance, controlling both the House and the Senate, but their will was often thwarted by President Andrew Johnson, a Democrat from Tennessee who was sympathetic toward the South.

black codes a series of laws in the post–Civil War South designed to restrict the rights of former slaves before the passage of the Fourteenth and Fifteenth Amendments

The Thirteenth Amendment, banning slavery, was passed and ratified in 1865. In retaliation, and to ensure that their political and social dominance of southern society would continue, the southern white state governments legislated **black codes**. Black codes were laws that essentially sought to keep blacks in a subservient economic and political position by restoring as many of the conditions of slavery as possible. As one scholar describes it, "Twenty years after freedom, a former slave was apt to be a black peasant, apathetically scratching a crop out of exhausted soil not his own, with scrawny mules and rusted plows and hoes that he had neither the incentive nor the means to improve." [8] In all likelihood, he was still working for, or at least on the land of, his former master. "Freedom" did not make a great deal of difference in the lives of most former slaves after the war.

Reconstruction and Its Reversal Congress, led by northern Republicans, tried to check southern obstruction of its will by instituting a period of federal control of southern politics called **Reconstruction**, which began in 1865. In an attempt to make the black codes unconstitutional, the Fourteenth Amendment was passed, guaranteeing all people born or naturalized in the United States the rights of citizenship. Further, no state could deprive any person of life, liberty, or property without due process of the law, or deny any person equal protection of the law. As we saw in Chapter 5, the Supreme Court has made varied use of this amendment, but its original intent was to bring some semblance of civil rights to southern blacks. The Fifteenth Amendment followed in 1870, effectively extending the right to vote to all adult males.

Reconstruction the period following the Civil War during which the federal government took action to rebuild the South

At first Reconstruction worked as the North had hoped. Under northern supervision, southern life began to change. Blacks voted, were elected to some local posts, and cemented Republican dominance with their support. But soon southern whites responded with violence. Groups like the Ku Klux Klan terrorized blacks in the South and made them reluctant to claim the rights to which they were legally entitled for fear of reprisals. Lynchings, arson, assaults, and beatings made claiming one's rights or associating with Republicans a risky business. Congress fought back vigorously and suppressed the reign of terror for a while, but its efforts earned accusations of military tyranny, and the Reconstruction project began to run out of steam. Plagued by political problems of their own, the Republicans were losing electoral strength and seats in Congress. Meanwhile, the Democrats were gradually reasserting their power in the southern states. By 1876, Reconstruction was effectively over, and shortly after that, southern whites set about the business of disenfranchising blacks, or taking away their newfound political power.

Segregation and the Era of Jim Crow Without the protection of the northern Republicans, disenfranchisement turned out to be easy to accomplish. The strategy chosen by

Control, At Any Cost
After Reconstruction, the fever to reestablish and maintain white supremacy in southern and border states led to acts of terror. Between 1882 and 1951, 3,437 African Americans were lynched by mobs. Local authorities usually claimed the killers could not be identified, although the mobs often posed for photographs, like this one, that were then turned into postcards and saved as macabre souvenirs.

the Democrats, who now controlled the southern state governments, was a sly one. Under the Fifteenth Amendment the vote could not be denied on the basis of race, color, or previous condition of servitude, so they set out to deny it on other, legal, bases that would have the primary effect of targeting blacks. **Poll taxes**, which required the payment of a small tax before voters could cast their votes, effectively took the right to vote away from the many blacks who were too poor to pay, and **literacy tests**, which required potential voters to demonstrate some reading skills, excluded most blacks who, denied an education, could not read. Even African Americans who were literate were often kept from voting because a white registrar administered the test unfairly. To permit illiterate whites to vote, literacy tests were combined with **grandfather clauses**, which required passage of such tests only by those prospective voters whose grandfathers had not been allowed to vote before 1867. Thus, unlike the black codes, these new laws, called **Jim Crow laws**, obeyed the letter of the Fifteenth Amendment, never explicitly saying that they were denying blacks the right to vote because of their race, color, or previous condition of servitude. This strategy proved devastatingly effective, and by 1910, registration of black voters had dropped dramatically, and registration of poor, illiterate whites had fallen as well.[9] Southern Democrats were back in power and had eliminated the possibility of competition.

poll taxes taxes levied as a qualification for voting

literacy tests tests requiring reading or comprehension skills as a qualification for voting

grandfather clauses provisions exempting from voting restrictions the descendants of those able to vote in 1867

Jim Crow laws Southern laws designed to circumvent the Thirteenth, Fourteenth, and Fifteenth Amendments and to deny blacks rights on bases other than race

segregation the practice and policy of separating races

Jim Crow laws were not just about voting but also concerned many other dimensions of southern life. The 1900s launched a half-century of **segregation** in the South, that is, of separate facilities for blacks and whites for leisure, business, travel, education, and other activities. The Civil Rights Act of 1875 had guaranteed that all people, regardless of race, color, or previous condition of servitude, were to have full and equal accommodation in "inns, public conveyances on land or water, theaters, and other places of public amusement," but the Supreme Court struck down the law, arguing that the Fourteenth Amendment only restricted the behavior of states, not of private individuals.[10] Having survived the legal test of the Constitution, Jim Crow laws continued to divide the southern world in two. But it was not a world of equal halves. The whites-only facilities were invariably superior to those intended for blacks; they were newer, cleaner, more comfortable. Before long, the laws were challenged by blacks who asked why equal protection of the law shouldn't translate into some real equality in their lives.

One Jim Crow law, a Louisiana statute passed in 1890, required separate accommodations in all trains passing through the state. Homer Plessy, traveling through Louisiana, chose to sit in the white section. Although Plessy often passed as a white person, he was in fact one-eighth black, which made him a black man according to Louisiana law. When he refused to sit in the "Colored Only" section, Plessy was arrested. He appealed his conviction all the way to the Supreme Court, which ruled against him in 1896. In ***Plessy v. Ferguson***, the Court held that enforced separation of the races did not mean that one race was inferior to the other. As long as the facilities provided were equal, states were within their rights to require them to be separate. Rejecting the majority view, Justice John Marshall Harlan wrote in a famous dissent, "Our Constitution is color-blind, and neither knows nor tolerates classes among citizens." [11] It would be over fifty years before a majority on the Court shared his view. In the meantime, everyone immediately embraced the "separate," and forgot the "equal," part of the ruling. Segregated facilities for whites and blacks had received the Supreme Court's seal of approval.

Plessy v. Ferguson Supreme Court case that established the constitutionality of the principle "separate but equal"

THE LONG BATTLE TO OVERTURN *PLESSY*: THE NAACP AND ITS LEGAL STRATEGY

The years following the *Plessy* decision were bleak ones for African American civil rights. The formal rules of politics giving blacks their rights had been enacted at the national level, but no branch of government at any level was willing to enforce them. The Supreme Court had firmly rejected attempts to give the Fourteenth Amendment more teeth. Congress was not inclined to help since the Republican fervor for reform had worn off. Nor were the southern state governments likely to support black rights.

In the early days of the twentieth century, African Americans themselves did not agree on the best political strategy to follow. Booker T. Washington, president of the Tuskegee Institute, a black college, advocated an accommodationist approach. Blacks should give up demanding political and social equality, he said, and settle for economic opportunity. Through hard work and education they would gradually be recognized on their merits and accorded their rights. This philosophy, popular with whites because it asked so little and seemed so unthreatening, angered many other blacks who felt that they had accommodated whites long enough. People like W. E. B. Du Bois took a far more assertive approach. Only by demanding their rights and refusing to settle for second-class treatment, he argued, would blacks ever enjoy full citizenship in the United States.[12]

Du Bois was influential in starting one of a handful of African American groups born in the early 1900s to fight for civil rights. The **National Association for the Advancement of Colored People** (**NAACP**), founded in 1910, aimed to help individual blacks, to raise white society's awareness of the atrocities of contemporary race relations, and most important, to change laws and court rulings that kept blacks from true equality. The NAACP, over time, was able to develop a legal strategy that was finally the undoing of Jim Crow and the segregated South.

National Association for the Advancement of Colored People (NAACP) an interest group founded in 1910 to promote civil rights for African Americans

By the 1930s, political changes suggested to the legal minds of the NAACP that the time might be right to challenge the Court's "separate but equal" decision. Blacks had made some major political advances in the North, not so much by convincing Republicans to support them again, but by joining the coalition that supported Democratic President Franklin Roosevelt's New Deal. Wanting to woo black voters from the Republican Party, the Democrats gave as much influence to blacks as they dared without alienating powerful southern Democratic congressmen. The Supreme Court had even taken some tentative steps in the direction of civil rights, such as striking down grandfather clauses in 1915.[13] But after four decades the *Plessy* judgment was still intact.

The Early Education Cases The NAACP, with the able assistance of a young lawyer named Thurgood Marshall, decided to launch its attack in the area of education. Segregation in education was particularly disastrous for blacks because the poor quality of their schools limited their potential, which in turn reinforced southern beliefs about their inferiority. Knowing that a loss reinforcing *Plessy* would be a major setback, the lawyers at the NAACP chose their case very carefully. Rather than trying to force the immediate integration of elementary schools, a goal that would have terrified and enraged whites, they began with law schools. Not only would this approach be less threatening, but law schools were clearly discriminatory (most states didn't even have black law schools) and were an educational institution the justices on the Court knew well. The NAACP decision to lead with law school cases was a masterful legal strategy.

The first education case the NAACP took to the Court was *Missouri ex rel Gaines v. Canada*. Lloyd Gaines, a black man, wanted to go to law school in Missouri.

Missouri had no law school for blacks but promised to build one. In the meantime, they told him, they would pay his tuition at an out-of-state law school. Gaines sued the state of Missouri, claiming that the facilities open to him under Missouri law were not equal to those available to white students. The Court, in 1938, agreed. It argued that Missouri had failed in its obligation to provide equal facilities and that black students in Missouri had an equal right to go to law school in-state.[14] The *Gaines* case was significant because the Court was looking at something it had ignored in *Plessy:* whether the separate facilities in question were truly equal.

Twelve years later, the *Gaines* decision was expanded in *Sweatt v. Painter.* Again a black law school candidate, Herman Sweatt, applied to a white law school, this time in Texas. The law school denied him admission, but mindful of the Missouri ruling, Texas offered to provide Sweatt with a school of his own in three downtown basement rooms, with a part-time faculty and access to the state law library. Again the NAACP argued before the Court that this alternative would not be an equal facility. But this time it went further and claimed that even if the schools *were* comparable, Sweatt's education would still be unequal because of the intangible benefits he would lose: the reputation of the school, talking with classmates, and making contacts for the future, for example. The justices agreed. Perhaps they were aware of how different their own legal educations would have been, isolated in three basement rooms by themselves. If the separate education was not equal, they said, it was unconstitutional under the Fourteenth Amendment.[15]

The ruling striking down "separate but equal" laws were aided by an unrelated case that, ironically, had the effect of depriving Japanese American citizens of many of their civil rights during World War II. In *Korematsu v. United States* (1944), Justice Hugo Black articulated the strict scrutiny test described earlier in this chapter: "All legal restrictions which curtail the civil rights of a single racial group are immediately suspect. That is not to say that all such restrictions are unconstitutional. It is to say that courts must subject them to the most rigid scrutiny." [16] After applying strict scrutiny, the Court allowed the laws that limited the civil rights of Japanese Americans to stand because it felt that the racial classification was justified by considerations of national security. The ruling was disastrous for Japanese Americans, but it would give blacks more ammunition in their fight for equal rights. From that point on, a law that treated people differently on the basis of race had to be based on a compelling governmental interest, or it could not stand.

Brown v. Board of Education By the early 1950s the stage was set for tackling the issue of education more broadly. The NAACP had four cases pending that concerned the segregation of educational facilities in the South and the Midwest. The Court ruled on all of them under the case name ***Brown v. Board of Education of Topeka.*** In its now-familiar arguments, the NAACP emphasized the intangible aspects of education, including how it made black students feel to be made to go to a separate school. They cited sociological evidence of the low self-esteem of black schoolchildren, and they argued that it resulted from a system that made black children feel inferior by treating them differently.

Brown v. Board of Education of Topeka Supreme Court case that rejected the idea that separate could be equal in education; catalyst for civil rights movement

Under the new leadership of Chief Justice Earl Warren, the Court ruled unanimously in favor of Linda Brown and the other black students. Without explicitly denouncing segregation or overturning *Plessy,* lest the South erupt in violent outrage again, the Warren Court held that separate schools, by their very definition, could never be equal because it was the fact of separation itself that made black children feel unequal. Segregation in education was inherently unconstitutional.[17] The principle of "separate but equal" was not yet dead, but it had suffered serious injury.

The *Brown* decision did not bring instant relief to the southern school system. The Court, in a 1955 follow-up to *Brown,* ruled that school desegregation had to take place "with all deliberate speed." [18] Such an ambiguous direction was asking for school districts to drag their feet. The most public and blatant attempt to avoid compliance took place in Little Rock, Arkansas, in September 1957, when Governor Orval Faubus posted the National Guard at the local high school to prevent the attendance of nine African American children. Rioting white parents, filmed for the nightly news, showed the rest of the country the faces of southern bigotry. Finally President Dwight Eisenhower sent one thousand federal troops to guarantee the safe passage of the nine black children through the angry mob of white parents who threatened to lynch them rather than let them enter the school. The *Brown* case, and the attempts to enforce it, proved to be a catalyst for a civil rights movement that would change the whole country. See "*Who Are We?* Education in America" for data on educational disparities that still exist.

THE CIVIL RIGHTS MOVEMENT

In the same year that the Court ordered school desegregation to proceed "with all deliberate speed," a woman named Rosa Parks sat down on a bus in Montgomery, Alabama, and started a chain of events that would end with a Court order to stop segregation in all aspects of southern life.

As law required, Parks sat in the black section at the back of the bus. As the bus filled, all the white seats were taken, and the driver ordered Parks and the other blacks

Looking Back at the Pain
The scene was chaotic and ugly in 1957 when Elizabeth Eckford and eight other black students integrated Central High School in Little Rock, Arkansas. Forty years later, Eckford and a member of the mob that had taunted her, Hazel Bryan Massery, met again in front of the school, this time on friendly terms (Massery had telephoned Eckford in 1962 to apologize for her part in the disturbance).

Education in America

In the years since the NAACP's historic fight to overturn *Plessy*, education has indeed been on the rise for all groups. But despite these historic inroads, America's minority groups are still lagging behind whites in education. Higher education is clearly linked to economic success, but even where education levels are similar, minorities and women continue to earn much less than their white male counterparts. Why do these disparities continue to exist? Whose responsibility is it to eliminate them?

Earnings by Race and Education: Income by highest degree earned

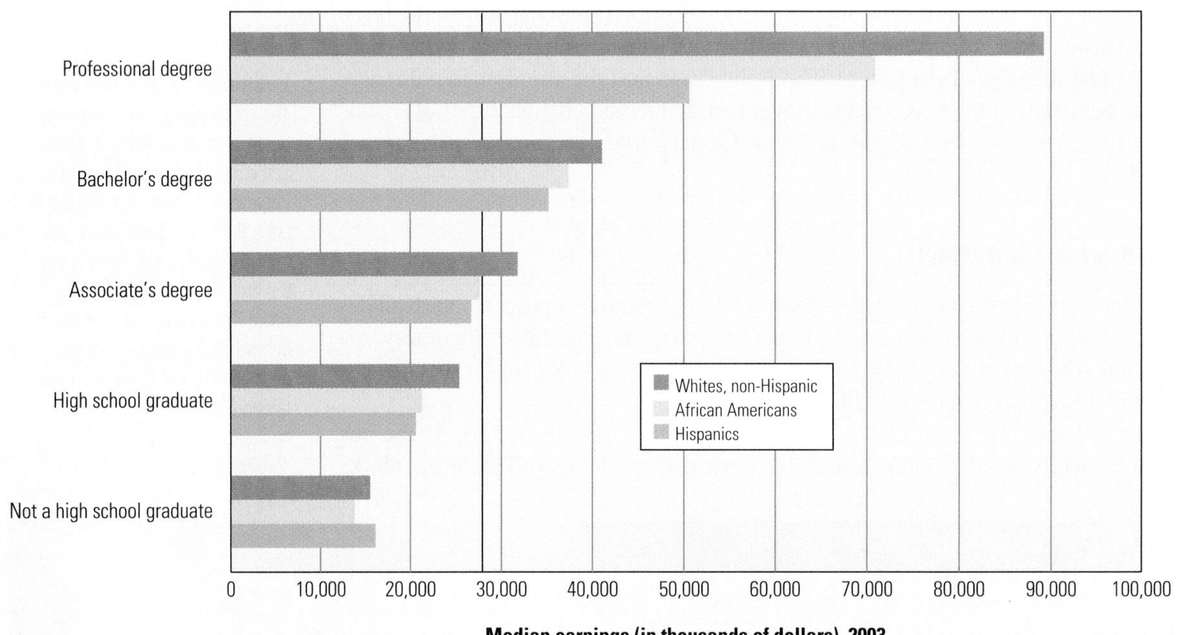

Source: U.S. Census Bureau, *Current Population Survey, 2004,* Educational Attainment in the United States, Table 9.

in her row to stand. Tired from a fatiguing day as a seamstress, Parks refused. She was arrested and sent to jail.

boycott refusal to buy certain goods or services as a way to protest policy or force political reform

Overnight, local groups in the black community organized a boycott of the Montgomery bus system. A **boycott** seeks to put economic pressure on a business to do something by encouraging people to stop purchasing its goods or services. Montgomery blacks, who formed the base of the bus company's clientele, wanted the bus company to lose so much money that it would force the local government to change the bus laws. Against all expectations, the bus boycott continued for over a year. Despite their dependence on public transportation (fewer blacks owned cars than whites), boycotters found the stamina to walk, carpool, and otherwise avoid the buses to make a political statement that was heard around the country. In the meantime the case wound its way through the legal system, and a little over a year after the boycott began, the Supreme Court affirmed a lower court's judgment that Montgomery's law

Education Among Selected Groups, 2003:
Highest degree earned, by race and gender.

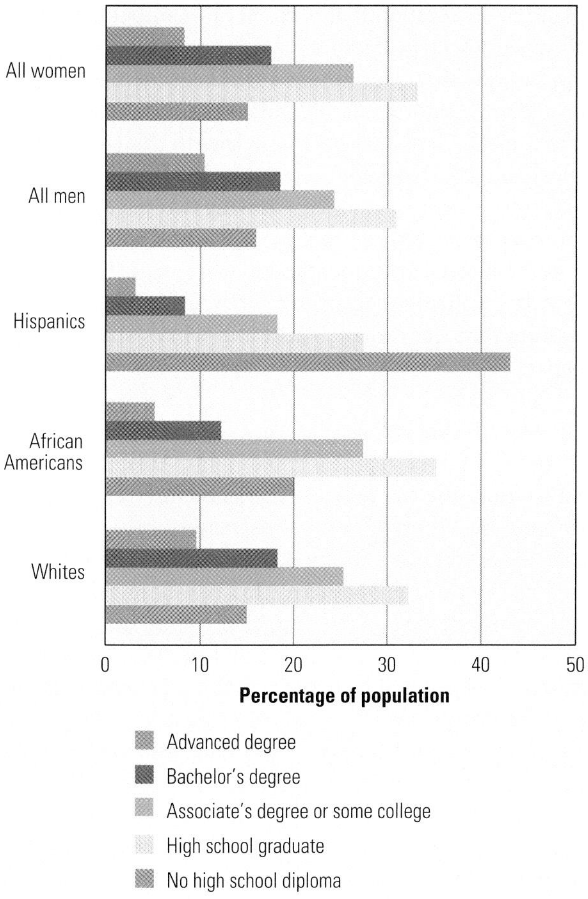

Source: U.S. Census Bureau, *Statistical Abstract of the United States,* 2005, Table 214.

Educational Attainment, 1960–2003:
Education is on the rise for all groups.

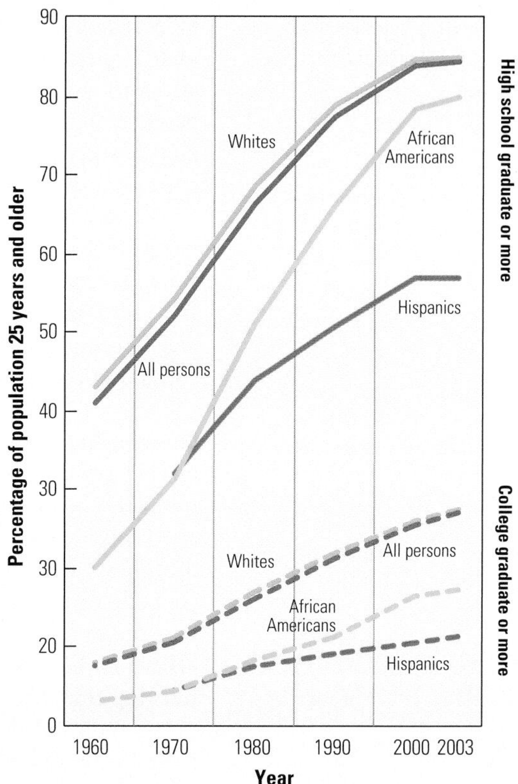

Source: U.S. Census Bureau, *Statistical Abstract of the United States,* 2005, Table 212.

was unconstitutional.[19] Separate bus accommodations were not equal. (The Montgomery bus boycott was portrayed in the movie *The Long Walk Home.* Watching a historical film—especially one based on a real person or event—requires critical thinking skills similar to those needed to read a newspaper or surf the web. See "*Consider the Source:* How to Be a Critical Movie Reviewer" for some suggestions on how to get the most out of the movies you view.)

Two Kinds of Discrimination The civil rights movement launched by the Montgomery bus boycott confronted two different types of discrimination. **De jure discrimination** (discrimination by law) is created by laws that treat people differently based on some characteristic like race. This is the sort of discrimination most blacks in the South faced. Especially in rural areas, blacks and whites lived and worked side by side, but by law they used separate facilities. Although the process of changing the laws was

de jure discrimination discrimination arising from or supported by the law excruciatingly painful, once the laws were changed and the new laws were enforced, the result was integration.

de facto discrimination discrimination that is the result not of law but rather of tradition and habit

The second sort of discrimination, called **de facto discrimination** (discrimination in fact), however, produces a kind of segregation that is much more difficult to eliminate. Segregation in the North was of this type because blacks and whites did not live and work in the same places to begin with. It was not laws that kept them apart, but past discrimination, tradition, custom, economic status, and residential patterns. This kind of segregation is so hard to remedy because there are no laws to change; the segregation is woven more complexly into the fabric of society.

We can look at the civil rights movement in America as having two stages. The initial stage involved the battle to change the laws so that blacks and whites would be equally protected by the laws, as the Fourteenth Amendment guarantees. The second stage, and one that is ongoing today, is the fight against the aftereffects of those laws, and of centuries of discrimination, that leave many blacks and whites still living in communities that are worlds apart.

Changing the Rules: Fighting De Jure Discrimination Rosa Parks and the Montgomery bus boycott launched a new strategy in blacks' fight for equal rights. Although it took the power of a court judgment to move the city officials, blacks themselves had exercised considerable power through peaceful protest and massive resistance to the will of whites. One of the leaders of the boycott was a young Baptist minister named Martin Luther King, Jr. A founding member of the Southern Christian Leadership Conference, a group of black clergy committed to expanding civil rights, King became known for his nonviolent approach to political protest. This philosophy of peacefully resisting enforcement of laws perceived to be unjust, and marching or "sitting in" to express political views, captured the imagination of supporters of black civil rights in both the South and the North. Black college students, occasionally joined by whites, staged peaceful demonstrations, called sit-ins, to desegregate lunch counters in southern department stores and other facilities. The protest movement was important for the practices it challenged directly—such as segregation in motels and restaurants, on beaches, and in other recreational facilities—but also for the pressure it brought to bear on elected officials and the effect it had on public opinion, particularly in the North, which had been largely unaware of southern problems.

The nonviolent resistance movement, in conjunction with the growing political power of northern blacks, brought about remarkable social and political change in the 1960s. The administration of Democratic president John F. Kennedy, not wanting to alienate the support of southern Democrats, tried at first to limit its active involvement in civil rights work. But the political pressure of black interest groups forced Kennedy to take a more visible stand. The Reverend King was using his tactics of nonviolent protest to great advantage in the spring of 1963. The demonstrations he led to protest segregation in Birmingham, Alabama, were met with extreme police violence. With an eye to the national media, King included children in the march. When the police turned on the demonstrators with swinging clubs, vicious dogs, and high-pressure hoses, the horror was brought to all Americans with their morning newspapers. Kennedy responded to the political pressure, so deftly orchestrated by King, by sending to Birmingham federal mediators to negotiate an end to segregation, and then by sending to Congress a massive package of civil rights legislation.

Kennedy did not live to see his proposals become law, but they became the top priority of his successor, Lyndon Johnson. During the Johnson years, the president, majorities in Congress, and the Supreme Court were in agreement on civil rights issues, and their joint legacy is impressive. The Kennedy-initiated Civil Rights Bill of 1964 reinforced the voting laws, allowed the attorney general to file school desegregation lawsuits, permitted the president to deny federal money to state and local programs that practiced discrimination, prohibited discrimination in public accommodations and in employment, and set up the Equal Employment Opportunity Commission (EEOC) to investigate complaints about job discrimination. Johnson also sent to Congress the Voting Rights Act of 1965, which, when passed, disallowed discriminatory tests like literacy tests and provided for federal examiners to register voters throughout much of the South. The Supreme Court, still the liberal Warren Court that had ruled in *Brown,* backed up this new legislation.[20] In addition, the Twenty-fourth Amendment, outlawing poll taxes in federal elections, was ratified in 1964.

Because of the unusual cooperation among the three branches of government, by the end of the 1960s life in the South, though far from perfect, was radically different for blacks. In 1968, 18 percent of southern black students went to schools with a majority of white students; in 1970 the percentage rose to 39 and in 1972 to 46. The comparable figure for black students in the North was only 28 percent in 1972.[21] Voter registration had also improved dramatically: from 1964 to 1969, black voter registration in the South nearly doubled, from 36 to 65 percent of adult blacks.[22]

Changing the Outcomes: Fighting De Facto Discrimination Political and educational advances did not translate into substantial economic gains for blacks. As a group, they remained at the very bottom of the economic hierarchy, and ironically, the problem was most severe not in the rural South but in the industrialized North. Many southern blacks who had migrated to the North in search of jobs and a better quality of life found conditions not much different from those they had left behind. Abject poverty, discrimination in employment, and segregated schools and housing led to frustration and inflamed tempers. In the summers of 1966 and 1967, race riots flashed across the northern urban landscape, leaving death, destruction, and ashes in their wake. Impatient with the passive resistance of the nonviolent protest movement in the South, many blacks became more militant in their insistence on social and economic change. The Black Muslims, led by Malcolm X until his assassination in 1965; the Black Panthers; and the Student Nonviolent Coordinating Committee all demanded "black power" and radical change. These activists rejected the King philosophy of working peacefully through existing political institutions to bring about gradual change.

Northern whites who had applauded the desegregation of the South grew increasingly nervous as angry African Americans began to target segregation in the North. As we explained earlier, the de facto segregation in the North was not the product of laws that treated blacks and whites differently, but instead resulted from different residential patterns, socioeconomic trends, and years of traditions and customs that subtly discriminated against blacks. Black inner-city schools and white suburban schools were often as segregated as if the hand of Jim Crow had been at work.

In the 1970s the courts and some politicians, believing that they had a duty not only to end segregation laws in education but also to integrate the schools, instituted a policy of **busing** in some northern cities. Students from majority-white schools would be bused to mostly black schools, and vice versa. The policy was immediately controversial; riots in South Boston in 1974 resembled those in Little Rock seventeen years earlier.

busing achieving racial balance by transporting students to schools across neighborhood boundaries

Consider the Source

How to Be a Critical Movie Reviewer

Throughout this book, we've made suggestions for films—both dramas and documentaries—that offer some insights into the political events that have shaped our history. Movies like *The Long Walk Home* (1990), which portrays events surrounding the historic Montgomery bus boycott, and *Mississippi Burning* (1988), which dramatizes the murder of three young civil rights workers in the rural South, do indeed stir emotional responses and invite viewers to consider the more human aspects of the civil rights movement in America. But are they good history? Do they enhance the audience's understanding of events? Do they tell the whole truth?

Of course not. Movies are created to make money, to tell stories in a dramatic and compelling manner, and often to promote a particular cause or idea. Stories inspired by real events are retold through the eyes of producers, writers, directors, and actors who bend the truth to create a particular artistic and commercial vision. Even films with no commercial ambitions whatsoever—independent documentaries, for example—are shot (and, perhaps more important, edited) by filmmakers who inevitably have their own agenda. Thus even the most even-handed and objective treatment of an issue is bound to be informed somewhat by the filmmaker's basic feelings. Ken Burns's *Civil War* (1990), for example, is a critically acclaimed, thorough, and fact-based documentation of the war between the states. But it is colored by Burns's own feelings and by the culture in which it was produced. A different filmmaker, living at a different time or in a different place, might have used the same facts and materials to create a very different film.

How then can you distinguish the well-established historical fact from the artist's fancy? Is it possible for a film to enhance our understanding of political events without manipulating us? It is—*if* you keep a critical eye. The next time you settle in for a movie about politics, history, or social movements, ask yourself the following questions:

1. **What kind of film are you watching?** A big Hollywood release such as *Pearl Harbor* (2001) is meant to draw in a huge audience and make lots of money. That often means that factual accuracy is less important than action, romance, or drama. Even films that purport to be inspired by true stories often bend, gloss over, or ignore crucial facts, or even create new ones.
2. **Who made the movie?** Do the producers have a stake in a particular interpretation of events? Does the director have an ax to grind or some personal experience that might inspire or influence his vision? How might a film like *Malcolm X* (1992) have been different

Not all opponents of busing were reacting from racist motives. Busing students from their homes to a distant school strikes many Americans as fundamentally unjust. Parents seek to move to better neighborhoods so that they can send their children to better schools, only to see those children bused back to the old schools. Parents want their children to be part of a local community and its activities, which is hard when the children must leave the community for the better part of each day. And they fear for the safety of their children when they are bused into poverty-stricken areas with high crime rates. Even many African American families were opposed to busing because of fears for their children's safety and because of the often long bus rides into predominantly white neighborhoods.

The Supreme Court has shared America's ambivalence about busing. Although it endorsed busing as a remedy for segregated schools in 1971,[23] three years later it ruled that busing plans could not merge inner-city and suburban districts unless officials could prove that the district lines had been drawn in a racially discriminatory manner.[24] Since many whites were moving out of the cities, there were fewer white students to bus, and busing did not really succeed in integrating schools in many urban areas. Fifty years after the *Brown* decision, many schools, especially those in urban areas, remain largely segregated.[25]

had it been made by a white director rather than Spike Lee? Would the story of female baseball players told by Penny Marshall in *A League of Their Own* (1993) have been told differently by a man?

3. **What is the filmmaker's reputation?** Some filmmakers are known for striving to be historically accurate, others for taking artistic license, and still others are known for using the medium to promote their own beliefs or philosophies. For example, Michael Moore is well known for using his movies, such as *Bowling for Columbine* (2002) and *Fahrenheit 9/11* (2004) to promote his political views; and Mel Gibson used his film *The Passion of the Christ* (2004) to express his interpretation of particular religious events. Many of Oliver Stone's movies have dramatized his theories of the nefarious forces behind various political and social events. *JFK* (1991) in particular was condemned by many both in and out of government as stoking irresponsible conspiracy theories about the Kennedy assassination.
4. **Where and when was it made?** Films are informed by the times in which they were produced and must be viewed with that in mind. Movies that were considered progressive at the time they were released might seem racist or sexist now.
5. **What is the primary source for historical material?** Filmmakers often consult historians and other experts to add factual and dramatic accuracy to their movies. For example, Steven Spielberg accomplished his spectacular dramatization of the Allied invasion of Europe during World War II for *Saving Private Ryan* (1998) with the help of noted experts on the subject, including Stephen Ambrose, one of today's foremost World War II historians.
6. **Who's telling the story?** Consider the movie's perspective. Films about the civil rights movement as seen by the U.S. attorney general, a nonviolent protester, or a southern sheriff would prove very different from beginning to end.
7. **What have the critics said about it?** Thorough reviews of films from reputable critics and historians can offer insights into any hidden agendas. *Mississippi Burning,* for example, is a powerful film, but it has been widely criticized by historians for its grossly misleading account of the investigation into the murder of three civil rights workers in the rural South.

Early Efforts at Affirmative Action The example of busing highlights a problem faced by civil rights workers and policymakers: deciding whether the Fourteenth Amendment guarantee of equal protection simply requires that the states not sanction discrimination or imposes an active obligation on them to integrate blacks and whites. As the northern experience shows, the absence of legal discrimination does not mean equality. In 1965 President Johnson issued Executive Order 11246, which not only prohibited discrimination in firms doing business with the government but also ordered them to take **affirmative action** to compensate for past discrimination. In other words, if a firm had no black employees, it wasn't enough not to have a policy against hiring them; the firm now had to actively recruit and hire blacks. The test would not be federal law or company policy, but the actual racial mix of employees.

affirmative action a policy of creating opportunities for members of certain groups as a substantive remedy for past discrimination

Johnson's call for affirmative action was taken seriously not only in employment situations but also in university decisions. Patterns of discrimination in employment and higher education showed the results of decades of decisions by white males to hire or admit other white males. Blacks, as well as other minorities and women, were relegated to low-paying, low-status jobs. After Johnson's executive order, the EEOC decided that the percentage of blacks working in firms should reflect the percentage of blacks in the labor force. Many colleges and universities reserved space on their admissions lists for minorities, sometimes accepting minority applicants with grades and test scores lower than those of whites.

Like busing, affirmative action has proved controversial among the American public. We have talked about the tension in American politics between procedural and substantive equality, between equality of treatment and equality of results. That is precisely the tension that arises when Americans are faced with policies of busing and affirmative action, both of which are instances of American policy attempting to bring about substantive equality. The end results seem attractive, but the means to get there—treating people differently—seem inherently unfair in the American value system.

The Court reflected the public's unease with these affirmative action policies when it ruled in *Regents of the University of California v. Bakke* in 1978. A white applicant for admission, Alan Bakke, had been rejected from the medical school at the University of California, Davis, even though minorities with lower grades and scores had been accepted. He challenged Davis's policy, claiming that it denied him admission to medical school on account of his race—effectively resulting in "reverse discrimination." The Court agreed with him, in part. It ruled that a quota system like Davis's, holding sixteen of one hundred spots for minorities, was a violation of the equal protection clause. But it did not reject the idea of affirmative action, holding that schools can have a legitimate interest in having a diversified student body, and that they can take race into account in admissions decisions just as they can take geographical location, for instance.[26] In this and several later cases, the Court signaled its approval of the intent of affirmative action, even though it occasionally took issue with specific implementations.[27]

Few of the presidents who immediately followed Kennedy and Johnson took strong pro–civil rights positions, but none effected a real reversal in policy until Ronald Reagan. The Reagan administration lobbied the Court strenuously to change its rulings on the constitutionality of affirmative action. In 1989 the Court fulfilled civil rights advocates' most pessimistic expectations. In a series of rulings, it struck down a variety of civil rights laws, holding that the Fourteenth Amendment did not protect workers from racial harassment on the job,[28] that the burden of proof in claims of employment discrimination was on the worker,[29] and that affirmative action was on shaky constitutional ground.[30] The Democratic-led Congress sought to undo some of the Court's late-1980s rulings by passing the Civil Rights Bill of 1991, which made it easier for workers to seek redress against employers who discriminate.

BLACKS IN CONTEMPORARY AMERICAN POLITICS

The Supreme Court's use of strict scrutiny on laws that discriminate on the basis of race has put an end to most de jure discrimination. However, de facto discrimination remains, with all the consequences that stem from the fact that tradition and practice in the United States endorse a fundamental inequality of power. In addition, African Americans continue to grapple with issues such as racial profiling, which, like the inequities in the criminal justice system that we discuss in Chapter 10, mean they often feel that the American political system treats them differently.

Race relations in this country are complicated by the growing diversity within the black community itself. Many blacks in America are in fact not native-born African Americans. They may come from Haiti, or the West Indies, or they may be African immigrants, and not Americans at all. In Miami, 48 percent of the black population is

West Indian, and a third of New York City blacks are foreign-born immigrants, as are a third of the blacks in Massachusetts and 8 percent of the blacks in Washington, D.C. One researcher points out that "the foreign-born African Americans and native-born African Americans are becoming as different from each other as foreign-born and native-born whites, in terms of culture, social status, aspirations, and how they think of themselves." [31]

This growing diversity signals problems for intraracial relations. Blacks born in other countries, where they were very likely not a minority, often have difficulty identifying with the experience of American blacks and seeing themselves as part of the same group with the same concerns and interests. Their primary identity might be nationality (they might see themselves as primarily Somali, or Ethiopian, or Jamaican, or Haitian) rather than race. Native-born black Americans, for their part, often view black immigrants with the same general suspicion and stereotypes that Americans have traditionally directed toward immigrants. As this trend toward diversity grows, it will become even harder than it is now to characterize the "black experience" in America. In this section, we examine some of the other critical issues facing blacks in contemporary American politics.

The Economic Outlook for Blacks We began this chapter noting that blacks fall behind whites on most socioeconomic indicators, although we should not disregard the existence of a growing black middle class. The median household income for African Americans in 2003 was $29,689; for whites, it was $45,631. Though blacks constituted about 12 percent of the U.S. population in 1997, they owned only 4 percent of U.S. businesses. The racial income gap is blamed, in part, on lack of enforcement of antidiscrimination laws, showing that even when laws change, the results may not.[32] (See "*Who Are We?* Poverty and Prosperity Among Ethnic and Racial Groups" for more comparisons.)

Diversity Redefined
In the United States, diversity abounds even within groups. At this New York cultural festival paying homage to the "Haitian experience," Haitian Americans celebrate their distinct heritage with performances, art, film, and food. The black population in America comprises a wide spectrum of people who trace their heritage to the West Indies, Haiti, and Africa, whether from slave times or as more recent, voluntary immigrants.

Poverty and Prosperity Among Ethnic and Racial Groups

A glance at family income and poverty rates shows that, in America, all groups do not fare the same. Asian Americans earn well above the national average, while most other minority groups earn far less. About a quarter of African Americans, Hispanics, and Native Americans live in poverty as defined by the U.S. Census Bureau. This rate is over twice that for whites and Asians. What explanations might account for these differences? Should government play a role in bringing about more equality?

Poverty in America: Poverty rate by race and Hispanic origin, 2003

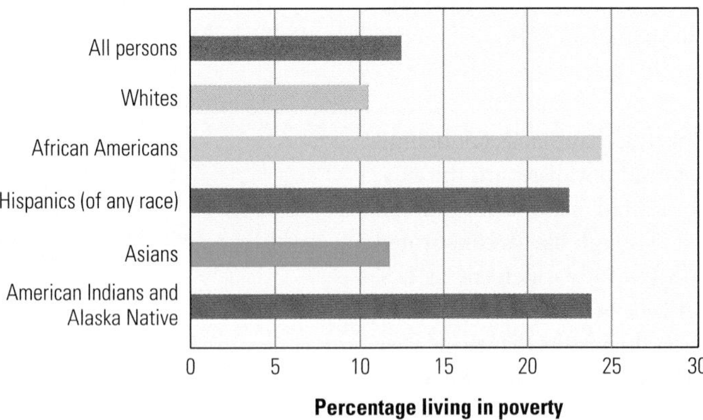

Source: U.S. Census Bureau, *Historical Poverty Tables,* Table 24.

Poverty in America: Median Family Income by Race and Hispanic Origin, 1985–2002

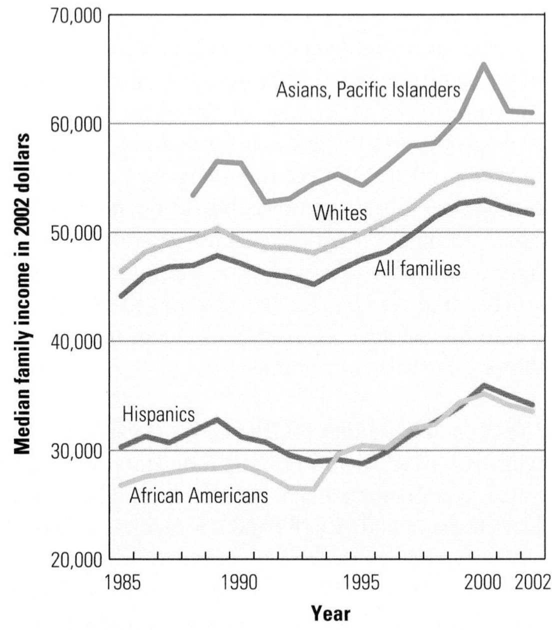

Source: U.S. Census Bureau, *Statistical Abstract of the United States,* 2005, Table 671.

But even when overt discrimination is not present, the differences persist. One study by two sociologists uncovered the dispiriting fact that, all other things being equal, African American doctors, lawyers, and real estate managers make less than their white counterparts. Those in securities and financial services fields make seventy-two cents for every dollar earned by a white man in the same job. They speculate that perhaps the gap is due to blacks tending to be assigned by employers to black clients, who are often less financially well off than whites.[33] Such studies show how subtle and yet how pervasive economic inequities can be.

Political Gains and Losses Because people of lower income and education levels are less likely to vote, African Americans' economic disadvantage translates into a political limitation as well. And although voting discrimination is clearly illegal, some racial patterns in disenfranchisement still need further examination. The most notorious case in point is the 2000 presidential election vote in Florida. Numerous studies show that many people's votes ultimately went uncounted in Florida, most likely costing Vice President Al Gore the election, but African American, Hispanic, and elderly voters were especially hard hit. In a *New York Times* analysis of the vote, ballots went uncounted in black precincts three times more often than in white precincts, even after income, education levels, and confusing ballot designs were taken into account.[34] While it is unclear whether intentional discrimination took place (although some people allege that it did),[35] the U.S. Civil Rights Commission, noting that Florida blacks were at least ten times more likely than whites to have had their ballots thrown out in 2000, asked the Justice Department to investigate.[36] Nor was the problem confined to Florida. A *Washington Post* analysis found that in some black precincts in Chicago, one in six ballots was disqualified, while in some of the suburbs, almost none were. Less extreme examples were found in other states as well.[37]

African Americans have had difficulty overcoming barriers not just on the voting side of the democratic equation. In terms of elected officials, progress has been mixed. By 2001, there were slightly more than nine thousand black elected officials in the United States, in posts ranging from local education and law enforcement jobs to the U.S. Congress. But the number of African Americans is much higher at local levels of government, where the constituents who elect them are more likely to be African American themselves. As the constituencies grow larger and more diverse, the task of black candidates gets tougher. In the 109th Congress, elected in 2004, 40 of 435 members of the House of Representatives were black, and Barack Obama became only the fifth black senator in U.S. history. In 2004, there were 526 black mayors. There are currently no African American governors (the only African American governor ever elected, Douglas Wilder of Virginia, is no longer in office). And even though, as we mentioned, there are two black cabinet members, those are appointed, not elected, positions.

Public opinion polls have indicated that more than 140 years after the end of the Civil War, Americans may very well be ready to elect a black president.[38] But the reality that black candidates face is more daunting. They attribute their difficulties achieving statewide and national office to four factors: the scarcity of blacks in lesser state offices, from which statewide candidates are often recruited; the fact that many good black politicians are mayors, who traditionally have trouble translating urban political success to statewide success; the fact that black politicians have fewer deep pockets from which to raise funds since they often represent lower-income areas; and "old fashioned prejudice"—their belief that nonblacks are less likely to vote for them and that party officials are less likely to encourage them to run for higher office because of that.[39]

Affirmative Action Today Affirmative action continues to be a controversial policy in America. In 1996, voters in California declared affirmative action illegal in their state, and voters in Washington did the same in 1998. The American public remains divided: opinion polls show support for the ideals behind affirmative action but not for the way it is practiced, and support is divided along racial and gender lines, with white males more opposed.[40]

The federal courts have taken the notion that race is a suspect classification to mean that any laws treating people differently according to race must be given strict scrutiny. Even though strict scrutiny has traditionally been used to support the rights of racial minorities, when applied consistently across the board, it can also preclude laws that give them special treatment or preferences, even if those preferences are meant to create more equality. That doesn't necessarily mean that the courts throw out the laws, but they do hold them to a higher standard. In a 2001 case rejecting a University of Michigan Law School affirmative action policy, a federal district court judge stated the principle bluntly: "All racial distinctions are inherently suspect and presumptively invalid. . . . Whatever solution the law school elects to pursue, it must be race-neutral." [41] A few months later, a federal appeals court held that the University of Georgia's affirmative action policy was unconstitutional. It said that while a university can strive to achieve a diverse student body, race could not be the only factor used to define diversity.[42]

The University of Michigan law school case eventually found its way to the Supreme Court along with another that dealt with Michigan's undergraduate admissions policy. As in *Bakke,* students who had been rejected with higher grade point averages and test scores than some admitted students challenged the constitutionality of Michigan's policies, again on Fourteenth Amendment grounds. The Supreme Court handed down two decisions, the results of which were essentially in line with the *Bakke* decision. The Court threw out the university's undergraduate admissions policy because it was tantamount to racial quotas.[43] In a five-to-four decision, however, the Court held that the law school's holistic approach of taking into account the race of the applicant was constitutional because of the importance of creating a diverse student body.[44]

Despite the controversy, there remains considerable support for affirmative action in the United States. Efforts to end affirmative action in state legislatures failed in New Jersey, Michigan, Arizona, and almost a dozen other states, most recently Colorado in 2004. Also in 2004, a Michigan judge ruled that a state ballot initiative banning affirmative action was unconstitutional.

The issues raised by the affirmative action debate in America deserve to be taken seriously by students of American politics. Unlike many earlier debates in American civil rights politics, this one cannot be reduced to questions of racism and bigotry. What is at stake are two competing images of what America ought to be about. On the one side is a vision of an America whose discriminatory past is past and whose job today is to treat all citizens the same. This view, shared by many minorities as well as many white Americans, argues that providing a set of lower standards for some groups is not fair to anybody. Ward Connerly, an African American businessman and a former member of the University of California Board of Regents, whose American Civil Rights Institute is a strong opponent of affirmative action, says that "people tend to perform at the level of competition. When the bar is raised, we rise to the occasion. That is exactly what black students will do in a society that has equal standards for all." [45] (See "*Profiles in Citizenship* Ward Connerly.")

On the other side of the debate are those who argue that affirmative action programs have made a real difference in equalizing chances in society, and although they are meant to be temporary, their work is not yet done. These advocates claim that the old patterns of behavior are so ingrained that they can be changed only by conscious effort. *New York Times* writer David Shipler says, "White males have long benefited from unstated preferences as fraternity brothers, golfing buddies, children of alumni and the like—unconscious biases that go largely unrecognized until affirmative action forces recruiters to think about how they gravitate toward people like themselves." [46]

WHO, WHAT, HOW All Americans have had a great deal at stake in the civil rights movement. Blacks have struggled, first, to be recognized as American citizens and, then, to exercise the rights that go along with citizenship. Lacking fundamental rights, they also lacked economic and social power. Those who fought to withhold their rights knew that recognizing them would inevitably upset the traditional power structure in both the South and the North.

Ward Connerly

Ward Connerly is a reluctant warrior. He didn't set out to become the go-to guy in the battle against affirmative action; he didn't even want a political life. While he wanted to leave the world a better place than he found it, he was content to contribute to the political campaigns of others while building his successful California business and enjoying his family. For Connerly, a Republican, the agent of change should be the individual, not government—he was committed to private enterprise and hard work.

". . . if I believe in freedom then it's got to be for everybody.

That's what he told his friend, Republican governor Pete Wilson, when Wilson asked Connerly to join his administration. Still, Wilson was persuasive and, in 1993, Connerly found himself beginning a twelve-year term as one of the eighteen people on the hugely powerful University of California Board of Regents.

To Connerly, service on the board was "an awesome responsibility." So when the issue of affirmative action came up, he took it seriously. Connerly had had reservations about the policy from the start. Although he grew up poor, his Uncle James and his grandmother had taught him to value the dignity that comes from self-reliance and the pride that comes from hard work.

Still, he wasn't looking to launch a major controversy when he was approached by the parents of a highly qualified white student who could not gain admission to the UC system. Investigating, he found what he called a system-wide pattern of discrimination against whites and Asians. Affirmative action did not seem to him to be a program of outreach but rather a program of racial preferences, which he found as distasteful when offered to blacks as when offered to whites, and which he believed would weaken black students in the bargain.

The story of how he overturned the UC affirmative action policy is recounted in his book, *Creating Equal.* Although the battle left him feeling bruised, it also strengthened his belief that affirmative action was unfair to whites and debilitating to blacks, and he ended up leading the successful effort to pass Proposition 209, an initiative that ended affirmative action statewide in California.

Undaunted, he took on another fight in 1997 over the issue of domestic partner benefits for gays. Originally "close to homophobic," he realized, meeting with long-term gay faculty couples, that "[it was] the real deal, you know. There was no difference except it was two women or two men rather than a man and woman but it was clear to me that they loved each other, that families can come in different forms and . . . that I needed to rethink my position." Concluding that "if I believe in freedom, then it's got to be for everybody," he led the effort that secured the benefits.

Having infuriated liberals with his stance on affirmative action, Connerly was now annoying his fellow conservatives, including the governor who appointed him. "I was an equal opportunity offender," he says wryly. But the values that informed the one battle underlay the other as well—an abiding commitment to fair play and hard work, to procedural guarantees, not substantive results.

So today, his long term on the board finally ended, Connerly is back to running his own business full-time, but also running the American Civil Rights Institute—a national, not-for-profit organization aimed at educating the public about the need to move beyond racial and gender preferences. Although he tried to leave the issue behind, he could not. "Once you get involved in race you can't extricate yourself from it. It's just something that begins to eat at you, and you can't finish until the job is done. And the job is never done." Here's what else he says:

On having the courage of your convictions:

It requires an awful lot of guts. An awful lot of courage . . . . There will be those who will question whether you're comfortable in your own skin and are you betraying your race and your gender and all of that stuff, which will require that you be very, very secure. . . . [I]t requires you to think hard about who you are, what you want to accomplish. . . . As my grandmother used to often say, "like a tree standing by the water, I shall not be moved." And that was the creed that I adapted and that served me well for those twelve years.

On keeping the republic:

Realize that you live in a great place. And it has been made great by a lot of people over the years who have worked hard to make it great. Every one of your ancestors has made some contribution along the way . . . . [I]t's not the elected official who's made it great, it's the people themselves. . . . That falls on the back of the ordinary citizen. Take it seriously because it's an awesome responsibility.

Source: Ward Connerly spoke with Christine Barbour and Gerald Wright on April 1, 2005.

The formal citizenship rights granted African Americans by way of the Thirteenth, Fourteenth, and Fifteenth Amendments should have changed the rules of American politics sufficiently to allow blacks to enter the political world on an equal footing with whites. Yet when Congress and the courts failed to enforce the Reconstruction amendments, southern blacks were at the mercy of discriminatory state and local laws for nearly a century. Those laws were finally changed by a combination of tactics that succeeded in eliminating much of the de jure discrimination that had followed the Civil War. However, they were not very effective in remedying the de facto discrimination that persisted, particularly in the North. Efforts to get rid of de facto discrimination generally involve substantive remedies like affirmative action, which remain controversial with procedure-loving Americans. The remnants of past discrimination, in the form of greater poverty and lower education levels for blacks, mean that increased political rights are not easily translated into equal economic and social power.

RIGHTS DENIED ON THE BASIS OF RACE AND ETHNICITY: NATIVE AMERICANS, HISPANICS, AND ASIAN AMERICANS

African Americans are by no means the only Americans whose civil rights have been denied on racial or ethnic grounds. Native Americans, Hispanics, and Asian Americans have all faced their own particular kind of discrimination. For historical and cultural reasons, these groups have had different political resources available to them, and thus their struggles have taken shape in different ways.

NATIVE AMERICANS

Native Americans of various tribes shared the so-called New World for centuries before it was discovered by Europeans. The relationship between the original inhabitants of this continent and the European colonists and their governments has been difficult, marked by the new arrivals' clear intent to settle and develop the Native Americans' ancestral lands, and complicated by the Europeans' failure to understand the Indians' cultural, spiritual, and political heritage. The lingering effects of these centuries-old conflicts continue to color the political, social, and economic experience of Native Americans today.

Native Americans and the U.S. Government The precise status of Native American tribes in American politics and in constitutional law is somewhat hazy. The Indians always saw themselves as sovereign independent nations, making treaties, waging war, and otherwise dealing with the early Americans from a position of strength and equality. But that sovereignty has not consistently been recognized by the United States. The commerce clause of the Constitution (Article I, Section 8) gives Congress the power to regulate trade "with foreign nations, among the several states, and with the Indian tribes." The U.S. perception of Indian tribes as neither foreign countries nor states was underscored by Chief Justice John Marshall in 1831. Denying the Cherokees the right to challenge a Georgia law in the Supreme Court, as a foreign nation would be able to do, Marshall declared that the Indian tribes were "domestic dependent nations."[47]

Until 1871, however, Congress continued to treat the tribes outwardly as if they were sovereign nations, making treaties with them to buy their land and relocate them. The truth is that regardless of the treaties, the tribes were often forcibly moved from their traditional lands; by the mid-1800s, most were living in western territories on land that had no spiritual meaning for them, where their hunting and farming traditions were ineffective, leaving them dependent on federal aid. Their actual relationship with the government was more one of conquered and conqueror, and the commerce clause was interpreted as giving Congress guardianship over Indian affairs. The creation of the Bureau of Indian Affairs in 1824 as part of the Department of War (moved, in 1849, to the Department of the Interior) institutionalized that guardian role. When Congress ended the pretense of treating tribes as sovereign nations, the central issues became what the role of the federal government would be and how much self-government the Indians should have.[48]

Congressional policy toward the Native Americans has varied between trying to assimilate them into the broader, European-based culture and encouraging them to develop economic independence and self-government. The combination of these two strategies—stripping them of their native lands and cultural identity, and reducing their federal funding to encourage more independence—has resulted in tremendous social and economic dislocation in the Indian communities. Poverty, joblessness, and alcoholism have built communities of despair and frustration for many Native Americans. Their situation has been aggravated as Congress has denied them many of the rights promised in their treaties in order to exploit the natural resources so abundant in the western lands they have been forced onto, or as they have been forced to sell rights to those resources in order to survive.

Political Strategies The political environment in which Native Americans found themselves in the mid–twentieth century was very different from the one faced by African Americans. What was at stake were Indians' civil rights and their enforcement, and the fulfillment of old promises and the preservation of a culture that did not easily coexist with modern American economic and political beliefs and practice. For cultures that emphasized the spirituality of living in harmony with lands that cannot really "belong" to anyone, haggling over mining and fishing rights seems the ultimate desecration. But the government they rejected in their quest for self-determination and tribal traditions was the same government they depended on to keep poverty at bay.

It was not clear what strategy the Native Americans should follow in trying to get their rights recognized. State politics did not provide any remedies, not merely because of local prejudice but also because the Indian reservations were separate legal entities under the federal government. Because Congress itself has been largely responsible for the plight of Native Americans, it was not a likely source of support for the expansion of Native American rights. Too many important economic interests with influence in Congress have had a lot at stake in getting their hands on Indian-held resources. In 1977 a federal review commission found the Bureau of Indian Affairs guilty of failing to safeguard Indian legal, financial, and safety interests. Nor were the courts anxious to extend rights to Native Americans. Most noticeably in cases concerning religious freedom, the Supreme Court has found compelling state interests to outweigh most Indian claims to religious freedom. In 1988, for instance, the Court ruled that the forest service could allow roads and timber cutting in national forests that had been used by Indian tribes for religious purposes.[49] And in 1990 the Court held that two Native American drug counselors who had been dismissed for using peyote, a hallucinogenic drug traditionally used in Native American religious ceremonies, were not entitled to unemployment benefits from the state of Oregon.[50]

Are We There Yet?
Following strict tribal protocol, these members of a visiting tribe have just received permission from Tulalip officials to come ashore on their land at the shore of Tulalip Indian Reservation near Marysville, Washington. This was the last of 50 ocean-going canoes carrying more then 3,000 tribal members from Canada and the Northwest to the Tulalip reservation as part of an annual celebration of Native cultures, which have their own customs and laws, nested inside the framework of the American legal system.

Like many other groups shut out from access to political institutions, Native Americans took their political fate into their own hands. In the 1960s and after, they focused on working outside the system to change public opinion and to persuade Congress to alter public policy. Not unlike the black protest movement of the sixties, but without their foundation of judicial victories, the Indians formed interest groups to fight for their cause. The most well known of these activist groups was the American Indian Movement, founded in 1968. This group staged dramatic demonstrations, such as the 1969 takeover of Alcatraz Island in San Francisco Bay and the 1973 occupation of a reservation at Wounded Knee (the location of an 1890 massacre of Sioux Indians). The American Indian Movement drew public attention to the plight of many Native Americans and, at the same time, to the divisions within the Indian community on such central issues as self-rule, treaty enforcement, and the role of the federal government.

Contemporary Challenges But for all the militant activism of the sixties and seventies, Native Americans have made no giant strides in redressing the centuries of dominance by white people. They remain at the bottom of the income scale in America, earning less than African Americans on average, and their living conditions are often poor. In 2003, 23.8 percent of American Indians lived in poverty, compared to only 12.5 percent of the total U.S. population.[51] And in 2002 the graduation rate of Native Americans was only 51.1 percent, compared to 68 percent of the overall population.[52] Consider, for example, the Navajos living on and off the reservation in Montezuma Creek, Utah. Sixty percent have no electricity or running water, half don't have jobs, fewer than half have graduated from high school, and 90 percent receive some kind of governmental support.[53]

Since the 1980s, however, an ironic twist of legal interpretation has enabled some Native Americans to parlay their status as semisovereign nations into a foundation for economic prosperity. As a result of two court cases,[54] and Congress's 1988 Indian

Gaming Regulatory Act, if a state allows any form of legalized gambling at all, even a state lottery, then Indian reservations in that state may allow all sorts of gambling, subject only to the regulation of the Bureau of Indian Affairs. Many reservations now have casinos to rival Las Vegas in gaudy splendor, and the money is pouring into their coffers. Close to thirty states now allow Indian gambling casinos, and in 2003 they brought in close to $17 billion, more than Native Americans received in federal aid.[55]

Casino gambling is controversial on several counts. Native Americans themselves are of two minds about it—some see gambling as their economic salvation and others as spiritually ruinous. The revenue created by the casinos has allowed Indian tribes to become major donors to political campaigns in states such as California, which has increased their political clout though leaving them open to criticism for making big money donations while many reservations remain poverty stricken. Many other Americans object for economic reasons. Opponents like casino owner Donald Trump claim that Congress is giving special privileges to Native Americans that may threaten their own business interests. Regardless of the moral and economic questions unleashed by the casino boom, for many Native Americans it is a way to recoup at least some of the resources that were lost in the past.

Politically, there is the potential for improvement as well. While recent Supreme Court cases failed to support religious freedom for Native Americans, some lower court orders have supported their rights. In 1996 President Bill Clinton issued an executive order that requires federal agencies to protect and provide access to sacred religious sites of American Indians, which has been a major point of contention in Indian-federal relations. Until the Supreme Court ruled in 1996 that electoral districts could not be drawn to enhance the power of particular racial groups, Native Americans had been gaining strength at the polls, to better defend their local interests. Still, the number of American Indian state representatives has increased slightly in the past few years, although there is currently only one American Indian, Tom Cole of Oklahoma, serving in the House of Representatives. There are no American Indians in the Senate now that Senator Ben Nighthorse Campbell of Colorado retired after his term expired in 2005.

HISPANIC AMERICANS

Hispanic Americans, sometimes also called Latinos, are a diverse group with yet another story of discrimination in the United States. They did not have to contend with the tradition of slavery that burdened blacks, and they don't have the unique legal problems of Native Americans, but they face peculiar challenges of their own in trying to fight discrimination and raise their standing in American society. Among the reasons that the Hispanic experience is different are the diversity within the Hispanic population, the language barrier that many face, and the political reaction to immigration, particularly illegal immigration, from Mexico into the United States.

Hispanics are the largest minority group in the United States today, making up 13 percent of the population. Their numbers have more than doubled in the past twenty-plus years, from 14.6 million in 1980 to nearly 40 million in 2003. Since 1990 the Hispanic population has grown by nearly 60 percent, compared with an increase of less than 10 percent among non-Hispanics. This population explosion means that the problems facing Hispanics will become much more central to the country as a whole as the twenty-first century unfolds.

Diversity A striking feature of the Hispanic population is its diversity. While Hispanics have in common their Spanish heritage, they have arrived in the United States traveling different routes, at different times. As illustrated in "*Who Are We?* America's Fastest-Growing Minority Groups," the current Hispanic population is quite diverse, even though the vast majority is Mexican. Americans with Mexican backgrounds, called Chicanos or Chicanas, do not necessarily share the concerns and issues of more recent Mexican-born immigrants, so there is diversity even within this group. Immigrants from different countries have settled across the United States. Mexican Americans are concentrated largely in California, Texas, Arizona, and New Mexico; Puerto Ricans are in New York, New Jersey, and other northern states; and Cubans tend to be clustered in South Florida.

These groups differ in more than place of origin and settlement. Cubans are much more likely to have been political refugees, escaping the communist government of Fidel Castro, whereas those from other countries tend to be economic refugees looking for a better life. Because educated, professional Cubans are the ones who fled, they have largely regained their higher socioeconomic status in this country. For instance, almost 20 percent of Cuban Americans are college educated, a percentage matching that found in the U.S. population as a whole, but only 7.6 percent of Mexican Americans and 14 percent of Puerto Ricans are college graduates. Consequently, Cuban Americans also hold more professional and managerial jobs, and their standard of living, on average, is much higher. What this diversity means is that there is little reason for Hispanics to view themselves as a single ethnic group with common interests and thus to act in political concert. While their numbers suggest that if they acted together they would wield considerable clout, their diversity has led to fragmentation and powerlessness.

The English-Only Movement Language has also presented a special challenge to Hispanics. The United States today ranks sixth in the world in the number of people who consider Spanish a first language, with an active and important Spanish-language media of radio, television, and press. This preponderance of Spanish speakers is probably due less to a refusal on the part of Hispanics to learn English than to the fact that new immigrants are continually streaming into this country.[56] Nonetheless, especially in areas with large Hispanic populations, white Anglos feel threatened by what they see as the encroachment of Spanish, and as we saw in "What's at Stake?" in Chapter 2, many communities have launched **English-only movements** to make English the official language, precluding foreign languages from appearing on ballots and official documents. The English-only controversy is clearly about more than language—it is about national and cultural identity, a struggle to lay claim to the voice of America.

English-only movements efforts to make English the official language of the United States

The Controversy over Immigration A final concern that makes the Hispanic struggle for civil rights unique in America is the reaction against immigration, particularly illegal immigration from Mexico. As we saw in Chapter 2, illegal immigration is a critical problem in some areas of the country. A backlash against illegal immigration has some serious consequences for Hispanic American citizens, who may be indistinguishable in appearance, name, and language from recent immigrants. They have found themselves suspected, followed, and challenged by the police; forced to show proof of legal residence on demand; and subjected to unpleasant reactions from non-Hispanic citizens who blame an entire ethnic group for the perceived behavior of a few of its members. All of this makes acceptance into American society more difficult for Hispanics; encourages segregation; and makes the subtle denial of equal rights in employment, housing, and education, for instance, easier to carry out.

Political Strategies Though Hispanics face formidable barriers to assimilation, their political position is improving. Like African Americans, they have had some success in organizing and calling public attention to their circumstances. Cesar Chavez, as leader of the United Farm Workers in the 1960s, drew national attention to the conditions under which farm workers labored. Following the principles of the civil rights movement, he highlighted concerns of social justice in his call for a nationwide boycott of grapes and lettuce picked by nonunion labor, and in the process he became a symbol of the Hispanic struggle for equal rights. Groups like the Mexican American Legal Defense and Education Fund (MALDEF) and the League of United Latin American Citizens (LULAC) continue to lobby to end discrimination against Hispanic Americans.

There are twenty-three Hispanic representatives in the 109th Congress and two Hispanic Senators. There is one Hispanic governor (Bill Richardson of New Mexico). In 2004 President Bush appointed Alberto Gonzales to be the first Hispanic attorney general, and Carlos Gutierrez as secretary of commerce. Many Hispanics have been appointed to high-level state offices as well. The voter turnout rate for Hispanics has traditionally been low because they are disproportionately poor and poor people are less likely to vote, but this situation is changing. Where the socioeconomic status of Hispanics is high and where their numbers are concentrated, as in South Florida, their political clout is considerable, as the intense controversy over the custody of young Cuban refugee Elian Gonzalez in 1999–2000 made clear. Presidential candidates, mindful of Florida's twenty-five electoral votes, regularly make pilgrimages to South Florida to denounce Cuba's communist policies, a position popular among the Cuban American voters there. Grassroots political organization has also paid off for Hispanic communities. In Texas, for instance, local groups called Communities Organized for Public Service (COPS) have brought politicians to Hispanic neighborhoods so that poor citizens can meet their representatives and voice their concerns. Citizens who feel that they are being listened to are more likely to vote, and COPS was able to organize voter registration drives that boosted Hispanic participation. Similarly, the Southwest Voter Registration Education Project has led over one thousand voter registration drives in several states, including California, Texas, and New Mexico. In 1996, Latino Vote USA targeted Hispanics in thirty-one states and Washington, D.C., to register them to vote and encourage them to turn out at the polls. Such movements have increased registration of Hispanic voters by more than 50 percent. In 2000, Hispanics made up 14 percent of California's 11 million registered voters. Since 1990, more than 40 percent of California's new voters have been Hispanic, and they have been voting at rates higher than the rest of the population.[57]

Because of the increase in the number of potential Hispanic voters, and because

Waking the Sleeping Giant
Although Hispanics are one of the fastest-growing ethnic groups in the United States, they remain one of the least mobilized groups in American politics. In 2004, 47 percent of voting-age Hispanics went to the polls. During that year's election campaign, many groups targeted Hispanics in voter registration drives. Here, a volunteer with the group Election Protection, sits outside a polling station in a largely Hispanic precinct of Orlando, Florida, to answer voting questions.

America's Fastest-Growing Minority Groups

America is becoming increasingly diverse. Latinos and Asians are the fastest-growing racial and ethnic groups in the United States. By midcentury, Hispanics will make up a quarter of the population, and Asians and Pacific Islanders will have doubled their numbers.

The different groups that make up the U.S. population are themselves becoming more diverse. Whereas in the past most Hispanics in the United States had origins in Mexico, Puerto Rico, and Cuba, today many can be called the "New Latinos"—immigrants from Central and South America and the Dominican Republic. Meanwhile Asians continue to come from an array of countries, each with quite distinct cultural traditions. Do you think this growing diversity will lead to greater understanding and appreciation for America's rich and diverse heritage, or is it likely to lead to increased intergroup hostility, competition, and racism? Can government do anything to smooth relations among and within groups?

Diversity Among Hispanics

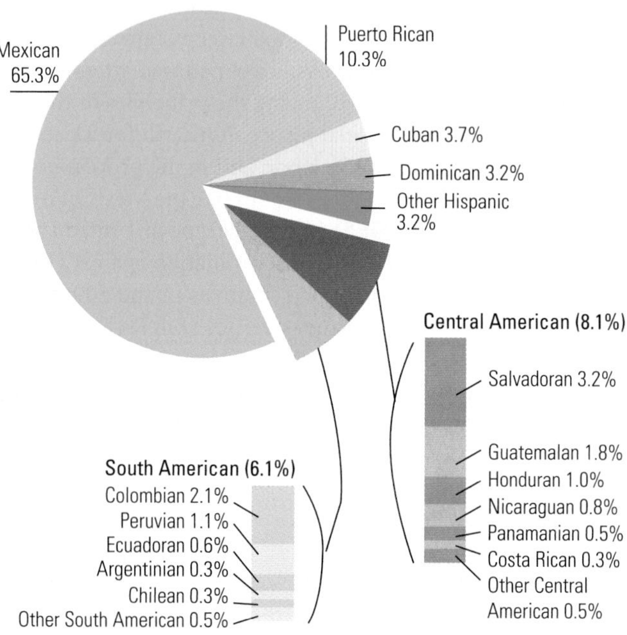

Source: Report by the Lewis Mumford Center for Comparative Urban and Regional Research, University at Albany.

of the prominence of the Hispanic population in battleground states such as Florida, New Mexico, Colorado, Nevada, and even in places such as Iowa, where one might not expect a significant Hispanic population, both George W. Bush and John Kerry actively courted Hispanic voters in the 2004 presidential election. Each candidate ran several advertisements entirely in Spanish and Kerry considered choosing New Mexico governor Bill Richardson, who is Hispanic, as his running mate. According to exit polls, Bush's efforts to win Hispanic votes paid off; he carried 44 percent of the Hispanic vote, a 9-percent increase from 2000.[58]

America's Hispanic Population Growth

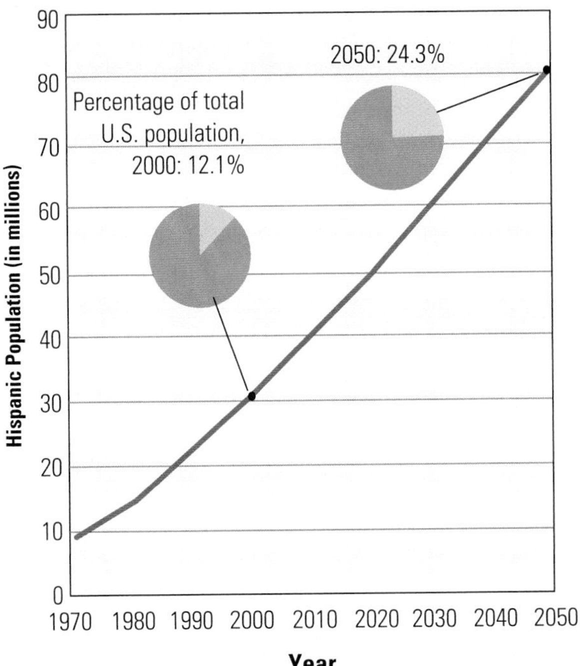

Note: 2010–2050

Source: U.S. Bureau of the Census.

America's Asian Population Growth, Foreign born

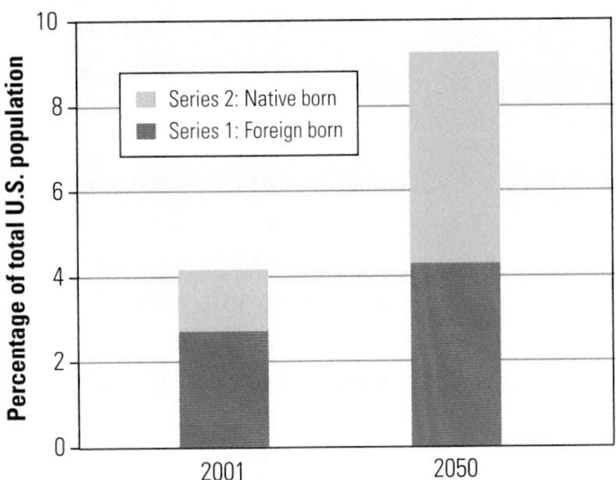

Source: U.S. Bureau of the Census, (NP-T5) Projections of the Resident Population by Race, Hispanic Origin, and Nativity, Middle Series, 1999–2100.

Diversity Among Asians, Native born

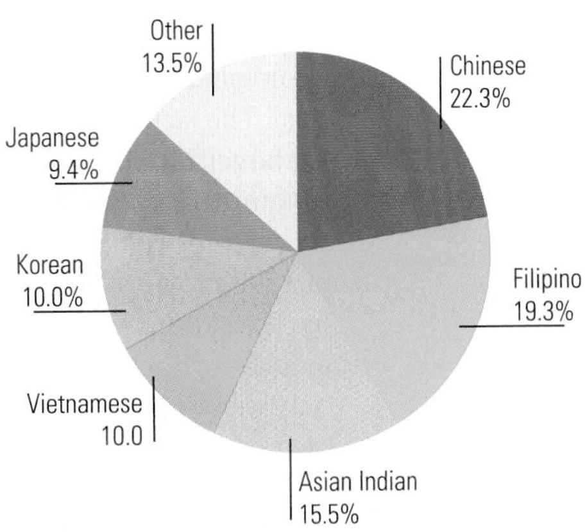

Source: Report by the Lewis Mumford Center for Comparative Urban and Regional Rsearch, University at Albany.

ASIAN AMERICANS

Asian Americans share some of the experiences of Hispanics, facing cultural prejudice as well as racism and absorbing some of the public backlash against immigration. Yet the history of Asian American immigration, the explosive events of World War II, and the impressive educational and economic success of many Asian Americans mean that the Asian experience is also in many ways unique.

Diversity Like Hispanics, the Asian American population is diverse. (See the "Diversity Among Asians" figure in "*Who Are We?* America's Fastest-Growing Minority Groups.") There are Americans with roots in China, Japan, Korea, the Philippines,

India, Vietnam, Laos, and Cambodia, to name just a few. Asian Americans vary not only by their country of origin but also by the time of their arrival in the United States. There are Chinese and Japanese Americans whose families have lived here for well over a century and a half, arriving with the waves of immigrants in the early 1800s who came to work in the frontier West. In part because of the resentment of white workers, whose wages were being squeezed by the low pay the immigrants would accept, Congress passed the Chinese Exclusion Act in 1882, halting immigration from China, and the National Origin Act of 1925, barring the entry of the Japanese. It was 1943 before Congress repealed the Chinese Exclusion Act, and 1965 before Asian immigrants were treated the same as those of other nationalities. Asians and Pacific Islanders are currently the fastest-growing immigrant group in America, arriving from all over Asia but in particular from the war-torn countries of Vietnam, Laos, and Cambodia.

Today Asian Americans live in every region of the United States. In 2003, Asians and Pacific Islanders comprised 51.3 percent of the population in Hawaii and 12.1 percent of that in California. New York City has the largest Chinese community outside China. The more recent immigrants are spread throughout the country. The Asian population in the South is especially fast growing; there, from 1980 to 1990, the Asian and Pacific Islander population increased 146 percent, compared to 103 percent in the rest of the country.[59]

Discrimination Asians have faced discrimination in the United States since their arrival. The fact that they are identifiable by their appearance has made assimilation into the larger European American population difficult. While most immigrants dream of becoming citizens in their new country, and eventually gaining political influence through the right to vote, that option was not open to Asians. The Naturalization Act of 1790 provided only for white immigrants to become naturalized citizens, and with few exceptions—for Filipino soldiers in the U.S. Army during World War II, for example—the act was in force until 1952. Branded "aliens ineligible for citizenship," not only were Asians permanently disenfranchised, but in many states they could not even own or rent property. Female citizens wishing to marry Asian "aliens" lost their own citizenship. The exclusionary immigration laws of 1882 and 1925 reflect this country's hostility to Asians, but at no other time was anti-Asian sentiment so painfully evident than in the white American reaction to Japanese Americans during World War II.

When the United States found itself at war with Japan, there was a strong backlash against Asian Americans. Because most Americans could not tell the difference between people from different Asian heritages, non-Japanese citizens found it necessary to wear buttons proclaiming "I am Korean" or "I am Filipino" to avoid having rocks and racial insults hurled at them.[60] In 1942, however, the U.S. government began to round up Japanese Americans, forcing them to abandon or sell their property, and putting them in detention camps for purposes of "national security." While the government was worried about security threats posed by those with Japanese sympathies, two-thirds of the 120,000 incarcerated were American citizens. Neither German Americans nor Italian Americans, both of whose homelands were also at war with the United States, were stripped of their rights. Remarkably, after they were incarcerated, young Japanese men were asked to sign oaths of loyalty to the American government so that they could be drafted into military service. Those who refused in outrage over their treatment were imprisoned. The crowning insult was the Supreme Court approval of curfews and detention camps for Japanese Americans.[61] Though the government later backed down and, in fact, in 1988 paid $1.25 billion as reparation to survivors of the ordeal, the Japanese internment camps remain a major scar on America's civil rights record.

The Price of Prosperity One unusual feature of the Asian American experience is their overall academic success and corresponding economic prosperity. Although all Asian groups have not been equally successful (groups that have immigrated primarily as refugees—like the Vietnamese—have higher rates of poverty than do others), median household income in 2003 was $55,262 for Asian and Pacific Islanders, compared with $45,631 for whites, $32,997 for Hispanics, and $29,689 for blacks. A number of factors probably account for this success. Forced out of wage labor in the West in the 1880s by resentful white workers, Asian immigrants developed entrepreneurial skills and many came to own their own businesses and restaurants. A cultural emphasis on hard work and high achievement lent itself particularly well to success in the American education system and culture of equality of opportunity. Furthermore, many Asian immigrants were highly skilled and professional workers in their own countries and passed on the values of their achievements to their children.

High school and college graduation rates are higher among Asian Americans than among other ethnic groups, and are at least as high as, and in some places higher than, those of whites. In 2003, 19 percent of the students at Harvard were Asian, as were 26 percent at Stanford, 30 percent at MIT, and 42 percent at the University of California, Berkeley.[62] What their high levels of academic success often mean for Asian Americans is that they become the targets of racist attacks by resentful whites.[63] Asian Americans have accused schools like Stanford, Brown, Harvard, and Berkeley of "capping" the number of Asians they admit, and white alumni who feel that slots at these elite schools should be reserved for their children have complained about the numbers of Asians in attendance. Although the schools deny the capping charges, Asian American students won favorable judgments in sixteen out of forty complaints they filed with the Department of Education between 1988 and 1995, a much higher rate than that achieved by any other racial group.[64] Their success also means that Asian Americans stand in an odd relationship to affirmative action, a set of policies that usually helps minorities blocked from traditional paths to economic prosperity. While affirmative action policies might benefit them in hiring situations, they actually harm Asian Americans seeking to go to universities or professional schools. Because these students are generally so well qualified, more of them would be admitted if race were not taken into account to permit the admission of Hispanic and African American students. Policies that pit minority groups against each other in this way do not promote solidarity and community among them and make racist attitudes even harder to overcome.

Political Strategies According to all our conventional understanding of what makes people vote in the United States, participation among Asian Americans ought to be quite high. Voter turnout usually rises along with education and income levels, yet Asian American voter registration and turnout rates have been among the lowest in the nation. Particularly in states with a sizable number of Asian Americans such as California, where they constitute 12 percent of the population, their political representation and influence do not reflect their numbers.

Political observers account for this lack of participation in several ways. Until after World War II, as we saw, immigration laws restricted the citizenship rights of Asian Americans. In addition, the political systems that many Asian immigrants left behind did not have traditions of democratic political participation. Finally, many Asian Americans came to the United States for economic reasons and have focused their attentions on building economic security rather than learning to navigate an unfamiliar political system.[65]

Some evidence indicates, however, that this trend of nonparticipation is changing. Researchers have found that where Asian Americans do register, they tend to vote at rates higher than those of other groups.[66] In the 1996 election, concerted efforts were made to register and turn out Asian Americans by a national coalition of Asian American interest groups seeking to maximize their impact at the polls. The results included the election of Gary Locke as the first Asian American governor of a mainland state (Washington), and in 1998 there were two thousand elected officials of Asian and Pacific Islander descent—up 10 percent from 1996.[67] About 33 percent of the Asian American voters in California in 1996 were first-time voters.[68] Still, even with the added emphasis on Asian American turnout, they comprised only 4 percent of the electorate in California, New York, and New Jersey in 2004. Only in Hawaii did Asian Americans constitute a larger percentage (26 percent) of the electorate.[69]

One reason for the increased participation of Asian Americans in 1996, in addition to the voter registration drives, is that many Asian Americans are finding themselves more and more affected by public policies. Welfare reform that strips many elderly legal immigrants of their benefits, changes in immigration laws, and affirmative action are among the issues driving Asian Americans to the polls. However, even continued efforts to register this group are unlikely to bring about electoral results as dramatic as those that we are starting to see for Hispanics, because Asian Americans tend to split their votes more or less equally between Democrats and Republicans.[70] Whereas African Americans vote for Democratic candidates over Republicans at a ratio of eight to one, and Hispanics, two to one, Asian Americans favor the Democrats only slightly.[71] In 2004, John Kerry carried 56 percent of the Asian American vote.[72] Interestingly, a recent survey of Asian Americans found that an astonishing 50 percent of Asians claim no partisan affiliation.[73]

WHO, WHAT, HOW Native Americans' rights have been denied through the Supreme Court's interpretation of the commerce clause, giving Congress power over them and their lands. Because neither Congress nor the courts have been receptive to the claims of Native Americans, they have sought to force the American government to fulfill its promises to them and to gain political rights and economic well-being by working outside the system and using the resources generated from running casinos.

Hispanics too have been denied their rights, partly through general discrimination but partly through organized movements such as the English-only movement and anti-immigration efforts. Because of their diversity and low levels of socioeconomic achievement, they have not been very successful in organizing to fight for their rights politically. Tactics that Hispanic leaders use include boycotts and voter education and registration drives.

Finally, Asian Americans, long prevented by law from becoming citizens and under suspicion during World War II, have also had to bear the collective brunt of Americans' discriminatory actions. As diverse as Hispanics, Asian Americans have also failed to organize politically. Their socioeconomic fate, however, has been different from that of many Hispanic groups, and as a group, Asian Americans have managed to thrive economically in their own communities despite political discrimination.

RIGHTS DENIED ON THE BASIS OF GENDER: WOMEN

Of all the battles fought for equal rights in the American political system, the women's struggle has been perhaps the most peculiar, because women, while certainly denied most imaginable civil and economic rights, were not outside the system in the same way that racial and ethnic groups have been. Most women lived with their husbands or fathers, and many shared their view that men, not women, should have power in the political world. Women's realm, after all, was the home, and the prevailing belief was that women were too good, too pure, too chaste, to deal with the sordid world outside. As a New Jersey senator argued in the late 1800s, women should not be allowed to vote because they have "a higher and holier mission. . . . Their mission is at home."[74] Today there are still some women as well as men who agree with the gist of this sentiment. That means that the struggle for women's rights not only has failed to win the support of all women but also has been actively opposed by some, as well as by many men whose power, standing, and worldview it has threatened.

WOMEN'S PLACE IN THE EARLY NINETEENTH CENTURY

The legal and economic position of women in the early nineteenth century, though not exactly "slavery," in some ways was not much different. According to English common law, on which our system was based, when a woman married, she merged her legal identity with her husband's, which is to say in practical terms, she no longer had one. Once married, she could not be a party to a contract, bring a lawsuit, own or inherit property, earn wages for any service, gain custody of her children in case of divorce, or initiate divorce from an abusive husband. If her husband were not a U.S. citizen, she lost her own citizenship. Neither married nor unmarried women could vote. In exchange for the legal identity his wife gave up, a husband was expected to provide security for her, and if he died without a will, she was entitled to one-third of his estate. If he made a will and left her out of it, however, she had no legal recourse to protect herself and her children.[75]

Opportunities were not plentiful for women who preferred to remain unmarried. Poor women worked in domestic service and, later, in the textile industry. But most married women did not work outside the home. For unmarried women, the professions available were those that fit their supposed womanly nature and that paid too little to be attractive to men, primarily nursing and teaching. Women who tried to break the occupational barriers were usually rebuffed, and for those who prevailed, success was often a mixed blessing. When in 1847, after many rejections and a miserable time in medical school, Elizabeth Blackwell graduated at the top of her class to become the first woman doctor in the United States, the only way she could get patients was to open her own hospital for women and children. The legal profession did not welcome women either, because once women were married, they could no longer be recognized in court. In 1860 Belle Mansfield was admitted to the Iowa bar by a judge sympathetic to the cause of women's rights. But when Myra Bradwell became the first woman law school graduate ten years later, the Illinois bar refused to admit her. Rather than support her, the U.S. Supreme Court ruled that admission to the bar was the states' prerogative.[76]

THE BIRTH OF THE WOMEN'S RIGHTS MOVEMENT

The women's movement is commonly dated from an 1848 convention on women's rights held in Seneca Falls, New York. There, men and women who supported the extension of rights to women issued a Declaration of Principles that deliberately sought to evoke the sentiments of those calling for freedom from political oppression. Echoing the Declaration of Independence, it stated:

> We hold these truths to be self-evident: that all men and women are created equal; that they are endowed by their Creator with certain inalienable rights; that among these are life, liberty and the pursuit of happiness.

Against the advice of many of those present, a resolution was proposed to demand the vote for women. It was the only resolution not to receive the convention's unanimous support—even among supporters of women's rights, the right to vote was controversial. Other propositions were enthusiastically and unanimously approved, among them calls for the right to own property, to have access to higher education, and to receive custody of children after divorce. Some of these demands were realized in New York by the 1848 Married Women's Property Act, and still others in an 1860 New York law, but these rights were not extended to all American women, and progress was slow.

The women's movement picked up steam after Seneca Falls and the victories in New York, but it had yet to settle on a political strategy. The courts were closed to women, of course, much as they had been for Dred Scott; women simply weren't allowed access to the legal arena. For a long time, women's rights advocates worked closely with the antislavery movement, assuming that when blacks received their rights, as they did with the passage of the Fourteenth Amendment, they and the Republican Party would rally to the women's cause. Not only did that fail to happen, but the passage of the Fourteenth Amendment marked the first time the word *male* appeared in the Constitution. There was a bitter split between the two movements, and afterward it was not unheard of for women's rights advocates to promote their cause, especially in the South, with racist appeals, arguing that giving women the right to vote would dilute the impact of black voters.

In 1869 the women's movement itself split into two groups, divided by philosophy and strategy. The National Woman Suffrage Association took a broad view of the suffrage issue and included among its goals the reform of job discrimination, labor conditions, and divorce law. It favored a federal suffrage amendment, which required work at the national level. Regularly, from 1878 to 1896 and again after 1913, the Susan B. Anthony Amendment, named after an early advocate of women's rights, was introduced into Congress but failed to pass. The American Woman Suffrage Association, on the other hand, took a different tack, focusing its efforts on the less dramatic but more practical task of changing state electoral laws. It was this state strategy that would prove effective and finally create the conditions under which the Susan B. Anthony Nineteenth Amendment would be passed and ratified in 1920.

THE STRUGGLE IN THE STATES

The state strategy was a smart one for women. Unlike the situation that blacks faced after the war, the national government did not support the women's cause. It was possible for women to have an impact on state governments, however. Different states have different cultures and traditions, and the Constitution allows them to decide who may legally vote. Women were able to target states that were sympathetic to them and gradually gain enough political clout that their demands were listened to on the national level.

Women had been able to vote since 1869 in the Territory of Wyoming. In frontier country, it wasn't possible for women to be as protected as they might be back East, and when they proved capable of taking on a variety of other roles, it was hard to justify denying them the same rights as men. When Wyoming applied for statehood in 1889, Congress tried to impose the disenfranchisement of women as the price of admission to the Union. The Wyoming legislature responded, "We will remain out of the Union a hundred years rather than come in without the women." [77] When Wyoming was finally admitted to the United States, it was the first state to allow women to vote.

That success was not to prove contagious, however. From 1870 to 1910, women waged 480 campaigns in thirty-three states, caused seventeen referenda to be held in eleven states, and won in only two of them: Colorado (1893) and Idaho (1896). In 1890 the National and American Woman Suffrage Associations merged, becoming the National American Woman Suffrage Association (NAWSA), and began to refine their state-level strategy. By 1912, women could vote in states, primarily in the West, that controlled 74 of the total 483 electoral college votes that decided the presidency, but the movement was facing strong external opposition and was being torn apart internally by political differences.

In 1914 an impatient, militant offshoot of NAWSA began to work at the national level again, picketing the White House and targeting the president's party, contributing to the defeat of twenty-three of forty-three Democratic candidates in the western states where women could vote. The appearance of political power lent momentum to the state-level efforts. In 1917 North Dakota gave women presidential suffrage; then Ohio, Indiana, Rhode Island, Nebraska, and Michigan followed suit. Arkansas and New York joined the list later that year. NAWSA issued a statement to members of Congress that if they would not pass the Susan B. Anthony Amendment, it would work to defeat every legislator who opposed it. The amendment passed in the House, but not the Senate, and NAWSA targeted four senators. Two were defeated, and two held onto their seats by only narrow margins. Nine more states gave women the right to vote in presidential elections (see Figure 6.1).

In 1919 the Susan B. Anthony Amendment was reintroduced into Congress with the support of President Woodrow Wilson and passed by the necessary two-thirds majority in both houses. When, in August 1920, Tennessee became the thirty-sixth state to ratify the Nineteenth Amendment, for the required total of three-fourths of the state legislatures, women finally had the vote nationwide. Unlike the situation faced by African Americans, the legal victory ended the battle. Enforcement was not as difficult as enforcement of the Fifteenth Amendment, although many women were not inclined to use their newly won right. But until the end, the opposition had been petty and virulent, and the victory was only narrowly won. (See the box, "Comparing Women's Rights in the United States and Around the World.")

WINNERS AND LOSERS IN THE SUFFRAGE MOVEMENT

The debate over women's suffrage, like the fight over black civil rights, hit bitter depths because so much was at stake. If women were to acquire political rights, opponents feared, an entire way of life would be over. And, of course, in many ways they were right.

Comparing Women's Rights in the United States and around the World

Women's rights as citizens have varied dramatically throughout history and around the world. Beginning with the right to vote, women in the United States saw great improvement in their civil rights during the twentieth century. In many respects, what seem like basic rights afforded to women in the United States—the right to a divorce or the right to own property—are lofty goals to women in more oppressive countries. Nevertheless, women in the United States still do not share some of the more expansive rights granted to women in other countries today, for instance, adequate paid maternity leave. Here, we compare the rights of women in the United States to those around the world to see where the United States fits into the fight for women's rights.

ISSUE AREA/RIGHT	UNITED STATES	AROUND THE WORLD
Voting rights	Women were granted the right to vote in the 19th Amendment in 1920; black women and other minorities were aided by the 1965 Voting Rights Act.	Women in Finland gained the right to vote in 1906, in Switzerland in 1971; Kuwait is the only country that still specifically denies women the right to vote, and a bill to extend suffrage is before the Kuwaiti Parliament.
Marriage	Polygamy was outlawed in the United States in 1862 and officially forbidden by the Mormon Church in 1890, although cases of the practice have been reported as recently as 2004 in the United States.	Polygamy is legal in Kenya, Senegal, Somalia, Tanzania, and Sudan; moreover, the president of Sudan urged polygamy in his country in 2001 to boost the population.
Divorce	Although state laws vary, women hold the right to divorce their husbands; the first "no-fault" divorce laws in the United States, allowing couples to divorce by mutual consent, were enacted in California in 1969; all states had no-fault laws by 1985.	In 1999, France granted legal rights to people cohabiting to collect insurance and retain property in the event of a separation even without a legal marriage; women in Morocco gained the right to divorce an adulterous husband in 2000; women in Turkey gained the same right in 2002.
Maternity leave	Women in the United States are allowed up to 12 weeks' unpaid medical or maternity leave in a year under the Family and Medical Leave Act of 1993.	Women in France receive 26 weeks' paid maternity leave; women in the Netherlands and Vietnam get 16 weeks' paid leave; women in Germany and Algeria receive 14 weeks' paid leave; women *maquila* (textile) workers in Guatemala are denied health benefits guaranteed by Guatemalan law and can be fired for becoming pregnant.

The opposition to women's suffrage came from a number of different directions. In the South, white men rejected women's suffrage for fear that women would encourage enforcement of the Civil War amendments, giving political power to blacks. And if women could vote, then of course black women could vote, further weakening the white male position. Believing that women would force temperance on the nation,

ISSUE AREA/RIGHT	UNITED STATES	AROUND THE WORLD
Domestic violence	The Violence Against Women Act, authorized by Congress in 1998, provides funds for training authorities about domestic violence against women, shelters for battered women, and counseling.	In Jordan, men who kill their wives in so-called honor crimes, or because they believe their wives have committed acts that violate social mores (such as adultery), receive reduced penalties from the state; Ecuador outlawed physical and mental assaults against women in 1995.
Workplace rights	Paying women lesser wages than men for the same job was outlawed by the 1963 Equal Pay Act, yet women in the United States earn 76 percent of what men make (and even less for minority women), because women often hold lower-paying jobs.	Women in Turkey were granted the right to get a job without their husband's consent only in 2002; in Sweden, both men and women are eligible for paid leave from their jobs when they have new children.
Violence against women	The first marital rape law, making it illegal for a husband to rape his wife, was put into law in Nebraska in 1976; marital rape is now illegal in all 50 states.	Female genital mutilation, or the practice of removing a women's clitoris and/or stitching the vulva together to discourage sexual contact or promiscuity, is officially forbidden in Somalia, Kenya, Senegal, and Togo, but UNICEF estimates 130 million women worldwide are still subjected to the practice each year, and few measures are taken to prevent the practice effectively.
Dress codes for women	Traditional dress codes for women (prohibiting wearing pants to work, etc.) have effectively fallen out of fashion, but women were not officially given the right to wear pants to work in California until 1995; a 2001 Supreme Court decision upheld a similar 1989 decision making sex-specific dress codes legal in the workplace.	Women under the Taliban regime in Afghanistan were required to wear a *burqa*, or garment that covers them from head to toe with only a mesh opening at the mouth and eyes to see and breathe through, as well as shoes that do not make any noise.

Sources: Human Rights Watch, Women's Human Rights, www.hrw.org/women; National Organization for Women, www.now.org; U.S. Equal Employment Opportunity Commission, www.eeoc.gov; "How We Compare," *The Advertiser* (Australia), December 21, 2001; The Learning Partnership, http://learningpartnership.org; Web Journal of Current Legal Issues, http://webjcli.nclac.uk; Ewan Winning, "Dress Codes: Women Get the Right to Wear Pants," 1997, www.ewin.com/articles/dressed.htm; Find Law's Legal Commentary, http://writ.news.findlaw.com/grossman/20010717.html; UNICEF, www.unicef.org; www.infoplease.com/spot/womenstimeline1.html.

brewing and liquor interests fought the women's campaign vigorously, stuffing ballot boxes and pouring huge sums of money into antisuffrage efforts. In the East, industrial and business interests, concerned that voting women would pass enlightened labor legislation, also opposed suffrage. Antisuffrage women's groups, usually composed of upper-class women, claimed that their duties at home were more than enough for

FIGURE 6.1
Women's Right to Vote Before the Nineteenth Amendment

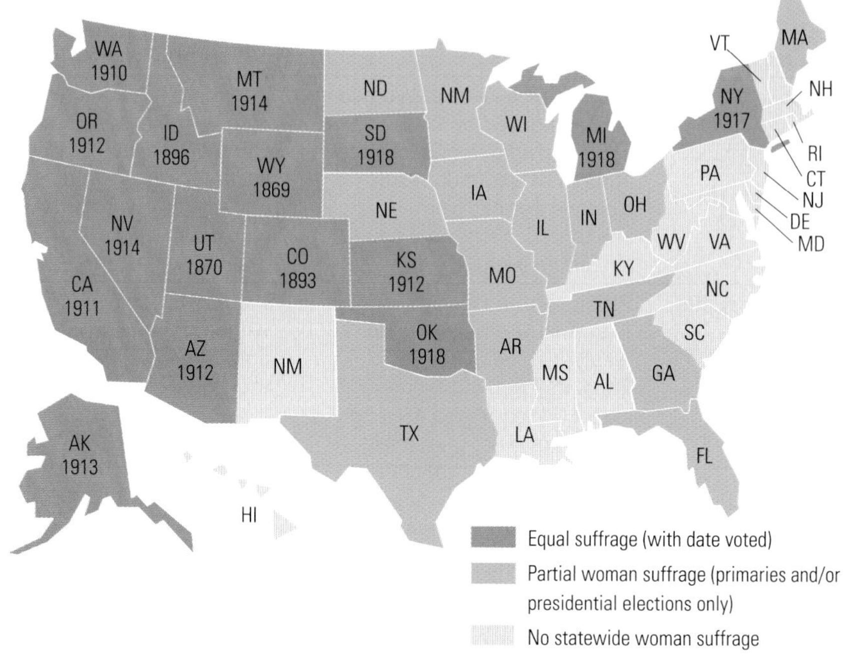

women, and that suffrage was unnecessary since men represented and watched out for the interests of women.[78] For some well-to-do women, the status quo was comfortable, and changing expectations about women's roles could only threaten that security.

Eventually, everything these opponents feared came to pass, although not necessarily as the result of women voting. In fact, in the immediate aftermath of the Nineteenth Amendment, the results of women's suffrage were disappointing to supporters. Blacks and immigrants were still being discriminated against in many parts of the country, effectively preventing both males and females from voting. Political parties excluded women, and most women lacked the money, political contacts, and experience to get involved in politics. Perhaps most important, general cultural attitudes worked against women's political participation. Politically active women were ostracized and accused of being unfeminine, making political involvement costly to many women.[79] While the women's rights advocates were clear winners in the suffrage fight, it took a long time for all the benefits of victory to materialize. As the battle over the Equal Rights Amendment (ERA) was to show, attitudes toward women were changing at a glacial pace.

Going to the Dance
In 1919, with the Nineteenth Amendment headed toward final ratification, women began to sense the first signs of real political power.

The Suffragist

Democrat: May I have the Honor?
Republican: May I have the Honor?

THE EQUAL RIGHTS AMENDMENT

The Nineteenth Amendment gave women the right to vote, but it did not ensure the constitutional protection against discrimination that the Fourteenth Amendment had provided for African Americans. Even though the Fourteenth Amendment technically applied to women as well as men, the courts did not interpret it that way. It was not unconstitutional to treat people differently on account of gender. Since the ratification of the Nineteenth Amendment in 1920, some women's groups had been working for the passage of an additional **Equal Rights Amendment** that would ban discrimination on the basis of sex and guarantee women the equal protection of the laws. Objections to the proposed amendment again came from many different directions. Traditionalists, both men and women, opposed changing the status quo and giving more power to the federal government. But there were also women, and supporters of women's rights, who feared that requiring laws to treat men and women the same would actually make women worse off by nullifying the variety of legislation that sought to protect women. Many social reformers, for instance, had worked for laws that would limit working hours or establish minimum wages for women, which now would be in jeopardy. Opponents also feared that an ERA would strike down laws preventing women from being drafted and sent into combat. Many laws in American society treat men and women differently, and few, if any, would survive under such an amendment. Nonetheless, an ERA was proposed to Congress on a fairly regular basis.

Equal Rights Amendment constitutional amendment passed by Congress but *never ratified* that would have banned discrimination on the basis of gender

In the 1960s the political omens started to look more hopeful for expanding women's rights. Support for women's rights more generally came from an unlikely quarter, however. Title VII of the Civil Rights Act of 1964, intended to prohibit job discrimination on the basis of race, was amended to include discrimination on the basis of gender as well, in the hopes that the addition would doom the bill's passage. Unexpectedly, the amended bill passed.

In 1967 the National Organization for Women (NOW) was organized to promote women's rights and lent its support to the ERA. Several pieces of legislation that passed in the early seventies signaled that public opinion was favorable to the idea of expanding women's rights. Title IX of the Education Amendments of 1972 banned sex discrimination in schools receiving federal funds, which meant, among other things, that schools had to provide girls with the equal opportunity and support to play sports in school. The Revenue Act of 1972 provided for tax credits for child care.

World Class Women
The U.S. women's soccer team celebrates victory against Brazil after the final game of the Athens 2004 Summer Olympics. Many people credit Title IX of the Higher Education Act (aimed at ending discrimination in athletic programs at federally funded institutions) with giving female athletes in the United States the opportunities they needed to make this victory possible.

In 1970 the ERA was again introduced in the House, and this time it passed. But the Senate spent the next two years refining the language of the amendment, adding and removing provisions that would have kept women from being drafted. Arguing that such changes would not amount to true equality, advocates of equal rights for women managed to defeat them. Finally, on March 22, 1972, the ERA passed in the Senate. The exact language of the proposed amendment read:

1. Equality of rights under the law shall not be denied or abridged by the United States or by any State on account of sex.
2. The Congress shall have the power to enforce, by appropriate legislation, the provisions of this article.
3. This amendment shall take effect two years after the date of ratification.

When both Houses of Congress passed the final version of the amendment, the process of getting approval of three-quarters of the state legislatures began. Thirty states had ratified the amendment by early 1973. But while public opinion polls showed support for the idea of giving constitutional protection to women's rights, the votes at the state level began to go the other way. By 1977 only thirty-five states had voted to ratify, three short of the necessary thirty-eight. Despite the extension of the ratification deadline from 1979 to 1982, the amendment died unratified.

Why did a ratification process that started out with such promise fizzle so abruptly? The ERA failed to pass for several reasons. First, while most people supported the idea of women's rights in the abstract, they weren't sure what the consequences of such an amendment would be, and people feared the possibility of radical social change. Second, the ERA came to be identified in the public's mind with the 1973 Supreme Court ruling in *Roe v. Wade* that women have abortion rights in the first trimester of their pregnancies. Professor Jane Mansbridge argued that conservative opponents of the ERA managed to link the two issues, claiming that the ERA was a rejection of motherhood and traditional values, turning ERA votes into referenda on abortion.[80]

Finally, the Supreme Court had been striking down some (though not all) laws that treated women differently from men, using the equal protection clause of the Fourteenth Amendment.[81] This caused some people to argue that the ERA was unnecessary, which probably reassured those who approved the principle of equality but had no desire to turn society upside-down.

GENDER DISCRIMINATION TODAY

Despite the failure of the ERA, today most of the legal barriers to women's equality in this country have been eliminated. But because the ERA did not pass, and there is no constitutional amendment specifically guaranteeing equal protection of the laws regardless of gender, the Supreme Court has not been willing to treat gender as a suspect classification, although it has come close at times. Laws that treat men and women differently are subject only to the intermediate standard of review, not the strict scrutiny test. There must be only an important government purpose for laws that discriminate against women, not a compelling interest. Examples of laws that have failed that test, and thus have been struck down by the Court, include portions of the Social Security Act that give benefits to widows but not to widowers, and laws that require husbands but not wives to be liable for alimony payments.[82] Some laws that do treat men and women differently—for instance, statutory rape laws and laws requiring that only males be drafted—have been upheld by the Court.

Gender and Equality

The traditional notion of the male as the sole breadwinner of a household has long been in decline. Today, levels of education among men and women are almost equal. The wage gap between men and women has shrunk, although even for those with similar levels of education, the incomes of men exceed those of women. As women have become more equal in terms of work and income, they have also become a distinctive political group—one that tends to be more Democratic and more liberal than men on many issues. How might the gender gap in wages relate to this ideological gender gap? What social and political changes are likely to follow from the changing economic positions of men and women?

Earning by Gender and Education: At every level of education, women earn less than men.

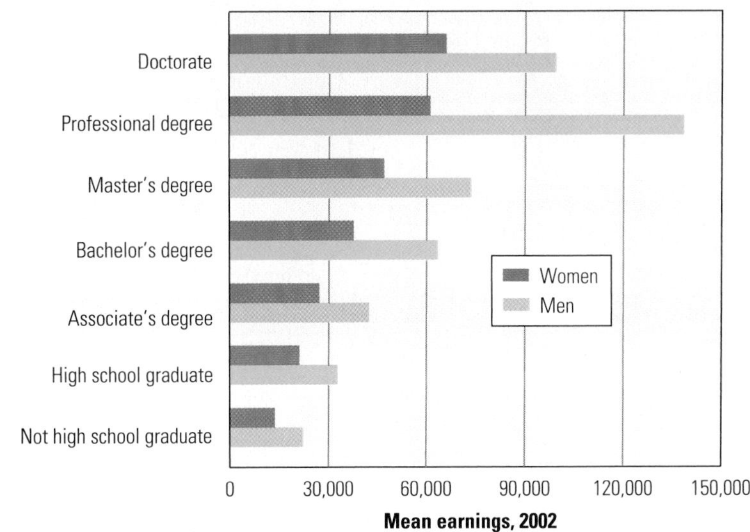

Source: U.S. Bureau of the Census, *Statistical Abstract of the United States,* 2005, Common Table 215.

Percentage of Men and Women in the Work Force: A greater percentage of women are entering the work force.

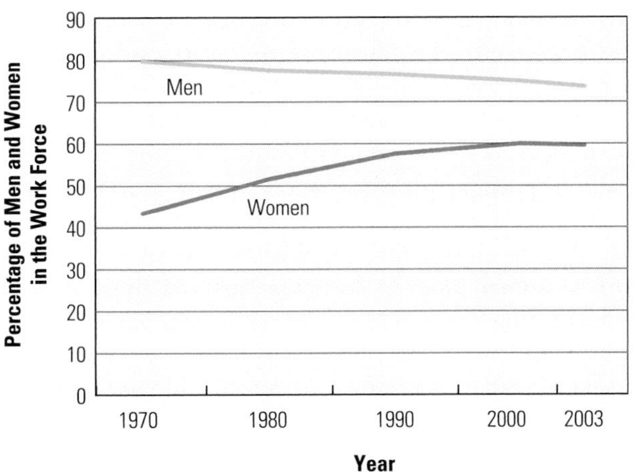

Source: U.S. Bureau of the Census, *Statistical Abstract of the United States,* 2005, Common Table 571.

Changes in Median Income, by Sex: The wage gap is shrinking.

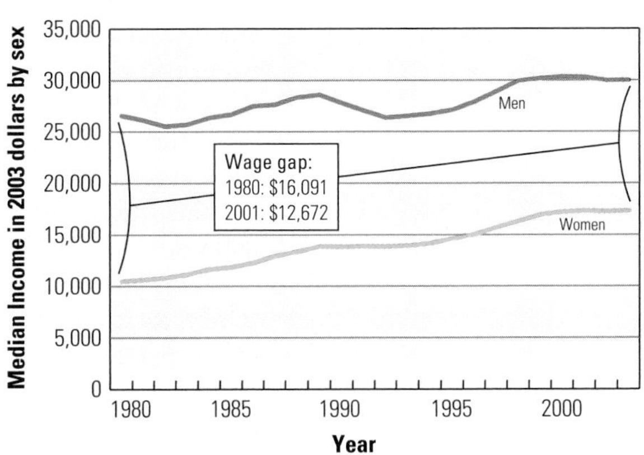

Source: U.S. Bureau of the Census, *Historical Income Tables,* Table P-8.

Having achieved formal equality, women still face some striking discrimination in the workplace. (See "*Who Are We?* Gender and Equality.") Women today earn seventy-six cents for every dollar earned by men, and the National Committee on Pay Equity, a nonprofit group in Washington, calculates that that pay gap may cost women almost a half a million dollars over the course of their work lives.[83]

'Three-fourths of a penny for your thoughts...'

In addition, women are tremendously underrepresented at the upper levels of corporate management, academic administration, and other top echelons of power. Some people argue that women fail to achieve levels of power and salary on a par with men because many women may leave and enter the job market several times or put their careers on hold to have children. Such interruptions prevent them from accruing the kind of seniority that pays dividends for men. The so-called Mommy track has been blamed for much of the disparity between men's and women's positions in the world. Others argue, however, that there is an enduring difference in the hiring and salary patterns of women that has nothing to do with childbearing, or else reflects male inflexibility when it comes to incorporating motherhood and corporate responsibility. These critics claim that there is a "glass ceiling" in the corporate world, invisible to the eye but impenetrable, that prevents women from rising to their full potential. The Civil Rights Act of 1991 created the Glass Ceiling Commission to study this phenomenon, and among the commission's conclusions was the observation that business is depriving itself of a large pool of talent by denying leadership positions to women.

Ever since President Johnson's executive order of 1965 was amended in 1968 to include gender, the federal government has had not only to stop discriminating against women in its hiring practices but also to take affirmative action to make sure that women are hired. Many other levels of government take gender into consideration when they hire, and the Supreme Court has upheld the practice.[84] But it is hard to mandate change in leadership positions when the number of jobs is few to begin with and the patterns of discrimination appear across corporations, universities, and foundations.

Some analysts have argued that the glass ceiling is a phenomenon that affects relatively few women, and that most women today are less preoccupied with moving up the corporate ladder than with making a decent living, or getting off what one observer has called the "sticky floor" of low-paying jobs.[85] While the wage gap between men and women with advanced education is narrowing, women still tend to be excluded from the more lucrative blue-collar positions in manufacturing, construction, communication, and transportation.[86]

Getting hired, maintaining equal pay, and earning promotions are not the only challenges women face on the job. They are often subject to unwelcome sexual advances, comments, or jokes that make their jobs unpleasant, offensive, and unusually stressful. **Sexual harassment**, brought to national attention during the Senate confirmation hearings for Clarence Thomas's appointment to the Supreme Court in 1991, often makes the workplace a hostile environment for women. Now technically illegal, it is often difficult to define and document, and women have traditionally faced retribution from employers and fellow workers for calling attention to such practices. In the late 1990s it became clear that even when the U.S. government is the employer, sexual

sexual harassment unwelcome sexual speech or behavior that creates a hostile work environment harassment can run rampant. The much-publicized cases of sexual harassment in the military show that progress toward gender equality in the armed forces still has a long way to go, and cases as recent as 2004 against such prominent private employers as Merrill Lynch, Morgan Stanley, and Boeing indicate that the problem continues to plague the private sector too. Another form of employment discrimination is highlighted in the recent dramatic rise in the number of cases of discrimination reported by pregnant women. Between fiscal years 1992 and 2003, pregnancy discrimination complaints filed with the EEOC jumped 39 percent, outpacing sexual harassment claims.[87] Allegations of pregnant women being unfairly fired or denied promotion have been made against several companies including Wal-Mart and Hooters. In one study, roughly half of the sample of pregnant women stated that their bosses had had negative reactions to the pregnancies.

Nor is employment the only place where women continue to face unequal treatment. A 1995 California law, the Gender Tax Repeal Act, for instance, bans businesses from charging women more than men for the same services, such as haircuts, dry cleaning, and car repairs, and a number of other states are following suit. That such laws are called for is indicated by a 1996 Washington state study: it found that while women generally earn less than men, 36 percent of hair stylists charge women an average of $5.58 more than men for the same basic short cut, and 86 percent of dry cleaners charge women about two dollars more to clean a shirt.[88] Other recent legal action tries to correct price differences in catalogs sent to men and women, and the practice of golf courses reserving their best tee times for men.[89] As these examples indicate, the struggle for gender equity in America is far from over.

WOMEN IN CONTEMPORARY POLITICS

Women have faced discrimination not only in the boardroom and the barbershop but in politics as well. While more women today hold elected office than at any other time in history, women still remain the most underrepresented group in Congress and the state legislatures. In the 109th Congress, only 65 of 435 members of the House of Representatives are female. There are currently fifteen female senators and eight female governors. As of 2005, 38 cities with populations of more than 100,000 had female mayors (15.6 percent).[90]

Women have been underrepresented in government for many reasons. Some observers argue that women may be less likely to have access to the large amounts of money needed to run a successful campaign. A study of U.S. House candidates from the 1970s to the 1990s shows that women candidates raised and spent about three-fourths of what a male candidate did between 1974 and 1980. However, by 1990, women candidates for the House raised and spent *more* money than did male candidates; women candidates raised 111 percent of what male candidates did for the 1992 race.[91] Others argue that women are not as likely as men to want to go into politics. For instance, more women candidates for state legislative office report waiting to wage a campaign until after they were asked to run by a party or legislative official.[92] And, while sexism has abated to some extent, many men (and even some women) are unwilling to vote for a female candidate. In a February 2005 poll, only 62 percent of those surveyed agreed that the United States was ready for a woman president in 2008.[93]

However, the representation of women in government is clearly better than it was. In 1971, women comprised only 2 percent of Congress members and less than 5 percent of state legislators. Today 14.8 percent of Congress members and 22.5 percent of state legislators are female, both all-time highs. In 2005, women held 25 percent of all statewide elective offices, including sixteen lieutenant governorships. While this percentage is below the high of 27.6 in 2001, it is a substantial increase from the 11 percent in 1979.[94] In 2002, women entered more than half of the thirty-six gubernatorial races.[95] Many observers argue that the increase in the number of female candidates running for and winning office expands future electoral opportunities for women. We discuss this issue further in Chapter 8.

WHO, WHAT, HOW Supporters and opponents of the women's movement struggled mightily over the extension of rights to women. As in the battles we discussed earlier, at stake was not just civil rights but social and economic power as well.

Because the courts and Congress were at first off-limits to the women's movement, women took their fight to the states, with their more accepting cultures and less restrictive rules. Having finally gained the vote in enough states to allow them to put electoral pressure on national officials, women got the national vote in 1920. The Nineteenth Amendment, however, did not give them the same equal protection of the laws that the Fourteenth Amendment had given blacks. Today the courts give women greater protection of the law, but the failure of the ERA to be ratified means that laws that discriminate against them are still subject to only an intermediate standard of review.

RIGHTS DENIED ON OTHER BASES

Race, gender, and ethnicity, of course, are not the only grounds on which the laws treat people differently in the United States. Four other classifications that provide interesting insights into the politics of rights in America are sexual orientation, age, disability, and lack of citizenship.

SEXUAL ORIENTATION

Gays and lesbians have faced two kinds of legal discrimination in this country. On the one hand, overt discrimination simply prohibits some behaviors: gays cannot serve openly in the military, for instance, and in some states they cannot adopt children or teach in public schools. But a more subtle kind of discrimination doesn't forbid their actions or behavior; it simply fails to recognize them legally. Thus in most states gays cannot marry or claim the rights that married people share, such as collecting their partner's social security, being covered by a partner's insurance plan, being each other's next of kin, or having a family. Some of these rights can be mimicked with complicated and expensive legal arrangements, some are possible because of the good will of particular companies toward their employees, but others, under the current laws, are out of reach. Being gay, unlike being black or female or Asian, is something that can be hidden from public view, and until the 1970s many gays escaped overt discrimination by denying or concealing who they were, but that too, many people argue, is a serious deprivation of civil rights.[96]

Political Strategies: The Courts As we discussed in Chapter 5, the case of *Bowers v. Hardwick* failed to advance the rights of gays and lesbians. The Court ruled that a Georgia statute against sodomy was a legitimate exercise of the state's power and that it met the minimum rationality test described earlier in this chapter.[97] The Court did not require that a law that treated people differently on the basis of sexual orientation had to fulfill either a compelling or an important state purpose; it merely had to be a reasonable use of state power. The four justices who dissented from that opinion did not want to tackle the issue of whether homosexuality was right or wrong. Rather they claimed that, as a privacy issue, what consenting adults do is none of government's business.

Gay rights again took a hit in 1995, when the Court ruled that the South Boston Allied War Veterans Council did not have to let the Irish-American Gay, Lesbian and Bisexual Group of Boston march in its annual St. Patrick's Day parade under a banner proclaiming their sexual orientation. But the decision did not touch on the rights of homosexuals; it was based solely on the question of the veterans' group's right to freedom of expression.[98]

More recently, however, gays and lesbians have had some major victories in the courts. In 1996 a bitterly divided Court struck down an amendment to the Colorado constitution that would have prevented gays from suing for discrimination in housing and employment. The amendment had been a reaction on the part of conservative groups to legislation in several cities that would have made it illegal to discriminate against gays in housing, employment, and related matters. The Court ruled that gays could not be singled out and denied the fundamental protection of the laws, that "a state cannot deem a class of persons a stranger to its laws." While the majority on the Court did not rule in this case that sexual orientation was a suspect classification, it did hint at greater protection than the minimum rationality test would warrant.[99] For the first time, it treated gay rights as a civil rights issue.

In 2000 a bare majority on the Court relied on their precedent in the parade case to rule on First Amendment grounds that the Boy Scouts of America had the right to exclude gay leaders because doing so was part of their "expressive message."[100] This ruling did not do anything to limit the more general civil rights issues that the Colorado case advanced.

The two biggest victories for gays and lesbians in a court of law, however, came in 2003. First, in *Lawrence v. Texas,* the Supreme Court overturned the *Bowers* decision, ruling that state sodomy laws were a violation of the right to privacy.[101] Even though many states had already repealed their sodomy laws, or failed to enforce them, the *Lawrence* decision was substantively and symbolically a break with previous judicial opinion that allowed the states to regulate the sexual behavior of gays and lesbians.

The gay and lesbian movement received another unexpected legal victory in 2003, when the Massachusetts Supreme Judicial Court ruled, in an extremely controversial four-to-three decision, that marriage was a civil right and that the state's law banning homosexual marriage violated the equal protection and due process clauses in the Massachusetts constitution.[102] The Massachusetts court ruling sent shockwaves throughout the country as the nation's first legal gay marriages were performed in Massachusetts. (Some local officials in California and New York began to conduct gay marriages as well, though these were later determined to be illegal.)

Critics on the right (and even some on the left) argued that the ruling was an example of judicial activism—of judges trying to legislate from the bench. They claimed that the court had overstepped its bounds and that decisions regarding marriage

Mrs. and Mrs. Goodridge
The struggle of gays and lesbians for equal rights includes the right to marry. The issue got new life when the Massachusetts Supreme Court found for two of the plaintiffs, Hillary and Julie Goodridge, shown at their wedding ceremony with their daughter, Annie. The court ruled that the state constitution provides no basis for a state law against same-sex marriages. While this was a victory for the movement, it was a catalyst for an explosion of political activity as states scrambled to amend their constitutions and activists started pushing to amend the U.S. Constitution to restrict Americans' choice of a marriage partner to those of the opposite sex.

should be left to the state legislatures. Opponents of the decision also noted that the majority of the public opposed same-sex marriage. Almost immediately after the ruling, President George W. Bush announced his support for an amendment to the Constitution defining marriage as a union between a man and a woman. However, because Congress had already passed a Defense of Marriage Act in 1996 (DOMA) stating that states need not recognize gay marriages performed in other states, the amendment failed to garner much immediate congressional support although conservative groups still strongly support it. Should the Supreme Court strike down DOMA in the future, that may change. In reaction to the Massachusetts Supreme Court ruling, eleven states overwhelmingly passed propositions in 2004 that banned same-sex marriage.

Political Strategies: Elections The courts are not the only political avenue open to gays in their struggle for equal rights. Gays have also been effective in parlaying their relatively small numbers into a force to be reckoned with electorally. Although it is difficult to gain an accurate idea of the size of the gay population in the United States,[103] between 4 and 5 percent of the electorate self-identifies as gay, lesbian, or bisexual—a larger portion of the electorate than Hispanics or Jews or other groups that are courted by the political parties.[104] It is not only as individuals that gays wield political power, however. Gays began to organize politically in 1969 after riots following police harassment at a gay bar in New York City, the Stonewall Inn. Today many interest groups are organized around issues of concern to the gay community. The largest, the Human Rights Campaign, gave $1.3 million to federal candidates in 2004.[105] While in the past gays have primarily supported the Democratic Party, a growing number identify themselves as independent, and a group of conservative gays calling themselves the Log Cabin Republicans have become active on the political right. Openly gay congressmen have been elected from both sides of the partisan divide.

In 1992, acting on a campaign promise made to gays, President Clinton decided to end the ban on gays in the military with an executive order, much as President Truman had ordered the racial integration of the armed forces in 1948. Clinton, however, badly misestimated the public reaction to his move. The Christian Right and other conservative and military groups were outraged. In the ensuing storm, Clinton backed off his support for ending the ban and settled instead for a "don't ask, don't tell" policy: members of the armed forces need not disclose their sexual orientation, but if they reveal it, or the military otherwise finds out, they can still be disciplined or discharged. For example, shortly after the September 11 attacks, at a time when the military was already facing a shortage of translators who could speak Arabic, six army linguists who spoke Arabic were dismissed when it was discovered that they were gay.[106] Some lingering evidence indicates as well that the military continues to ask about its members' sexual orientations.[107]

Gays have also tried to use their political power to fend off the earlier-mentioned legislation banning gay marriage. The legislation was prompted in the mid-1990s, by a case in the Hawaiian courts that could have allowed gays to marry in that state. Under the Constitution's "full faith and credit" clause, the other states would have to recognize those marriages as legal. State legislators rushed to create laws rejecting gay marriage, and in 1996 Congress passed DOMA to prevent federal recognition of gay marriage and allow states to pass laws denying its legality. President Clinton, who opposed the idea of gay marriage, signed the bill under protest, claiming that the bill was politically motivated and mean-spirited. In 2000, Vermont passed a law creating civil unions that stop short of achieving the status of marriage but that allow same-sex couples to have all the rights and responsibilities of married couples. Although this law has been deeply divisive in the state, efforts to roll it back have so far proved unavailing and other states, including New Jersey, California, and Connecticut, have begun to follow Vermont's lead.

Another issue of active concern to gays is workplace discrimination. The Employment Non-Discrimination Act (ENDA) would make it illegal to discriminate on the basis of sexual orientation in hiring, firing, pay, and promotion decisions. Introduced to Congress for the fifth time in the summer of 2001, it has yet to come up for a vote in the House, and the Senate, while coming within one vote in 1996, has not yet passed it.

The issue of gay rights has come to the forefront of the American political agenda not only because of gays' increasing political power but also because of the fierce opposition of the Christian Right. Their determination to banish what they see as an unnatural and sinful lifestyle—and their conviction that protection of the basic rights of homosexuals means that they will be given "special privileges"—has focused tremendous public attention on issues that most of the public would rather remained private. The spread of AIDS and the political efforts of gay groups to fight for increased resources to battle the disease have also heightened public awareness of gay issues. Public opinion remains mixed on the subject, but tolerance is increasing. In 2004, 70 percent or more of Americans favored lifting the ban on gays in the military and supported laws that protect gays and lesbians against job discrimination and housing discrimination. Still, more than half opposed same-sex adoption and 72 percent opposed gay marriage, though only a bare majority supported a constitutional amendment banning it. Interestingly, young people consistently support issues of gay and lesbian rights in far greater numbers than their elders, an indication that change may be on the horizon. For example, whereas 70 percent of those aged 65 years or older opposed gay adoption, only 43 percent of those aged 18–29 years did so.[108]

AGE

In 1976 the Supreme Court ruled that age is not a suspect classification.[109] That means that if governments have rational reasons for doing so, they may pass laws that treat younger or older people differently from the rest of the population, and courts do not have to use strict scrutiny when reviewing those laws. Young people are often not granted the full array of rights of adult citizens, being subject to curfews or locker searches at school, nor are they subject to the laws of adult justice if they commit a crime. Some observers have argued that children should have expanded rights to protect them in dealings with their parents.

Older people face discrimination most often in the area of employment. Compulsory retirement at a certain age regardless of an individual's capabilities or health may be said to violate basic civil rights. The Court has generally upheld mandatory retirement requirements.[110] Congress, however, has sought to prevent age discrimination with the Age Discrimination Act of 1967, outlawing discrimination against people up to seventy years of age in employment or in the provision of benefits, unless age can be shown to be relevant to the job in question. In 1978 the act was amended to prohibit mandatory retirement before age seventy, and in 1986 all mandatory retirement policies were banned except in special occupations.

Unlike younger people, who can't vote until they are eighteen and don't vote in great numbers after that, older people defend their interests very effectively. Voter participation rates rise with age, and older Americans are also extremely well organized politically. AARP (formerly the American Association of Retired Persons), a powerful interest group with over 30 million members, has been active in pressuring government to preserve policies that benefit elderly people. In the debates in the mid-1990s about cutting government services, AARP was very much present, and in the face of the organization's advice and voting power, programs like social security and Medicare (providing health care for older Americans) remained virtually untouched.

DISABILITY

People with physical and mental disabilities have also organized politically to fight for their civil rights. Advocates for the disabled include people with disabilities themselves, people who work in the social services catering to the disabled, and veterans' groups. Even though laws do not prevent disabled people from voting, staying in hotels, or using public phones, circumstances often do. Inaccessible buildings, public transportation, and other facilities can pose barriers as insurmountable as the law, as can public attitudes toward and discomfort around disabled people.

The 1990 Americans with Disabilities Act (ADA), modeled on the civil rights legislation that empowers racial and gender groups, protects the rights of the more than 44 million mentally and physically disabled people in this country. Disabilities covered under the act need not be as dramatic or obvious as confinement to a wheelchair or blindness. People with AIDS, recovering drug and alcohol addicts, and heart disease and diabetes patients are among those covered. The act provides detailed guidelines for access to buildings, mass transit, public facilities, and communication systems. It also guarantees protection from bias in employment; the EEOC is authorized to handle cases of job discrimination because of disabilities, as well as race and gender. The act was controversial because many of the required changes in physical accommodations, such as ramps and elevators, are extremely expensive to install. Advocates for the disabled respond that these expenses will be offset by increased business from disabled people and by the added productivity and skills that the disabled bring to the workplace. The reach of the act was limited in 2001, when the Supreme Court ruled that state employees could not sue their states for damages under the ADA because of the seldom discussed, but extremely important, Eleventh Amendment, which limits lawsuits that can be filed against the states.[111] The Court's five-to-four decision was criticized by disability rights advocates as severely limiting the ADA.

CITIZENSHIP

The final category of discrimination we discuss is discrimination against people who are not citizens. Should noncitizens have the same rights as U.S. citizens? Should all noncitizens have those rights? Illegal visitors as well as legal? Constitutional law has been fairly clear on these questions, granting citizens and aliens most of the same constitutional rights except the right to vote. (Even legal aliens who serve in the military are unable to vote.) Politics and the Constitution have not always been in sync on these points, however. Oddly for a nation of immigrants, the United States has periodically witnessed backlashes against the flow of people arriving from other countries, often triggered by fear that the newcomers' needs will mean fewer resources, jobs, and benefits for those who arrived earlier. During these backlashes, politicians have vied for public favor by cutting back on immigrants' rights. The Supreme Court responded in 1971 by declaring that alienage like a race and religion, is a suspect classification, and that laws that discriminate against aliens must be backed by a compelling government purpose.[112] To be sure, the Court has upheld some laws restricting the rights of immigrants, but it has done so only after a strict scrutiny of the facts. In light of the ruling, it has even supported the rights of illegal aliens to a public education.[113]

Among the groups who fight for the rights of immigrants are the Coalition for Humane Immigrant Rights and many politically active Hispanic groups. The people they represent, however, are often among the poorest, and the most politically silent, in society. Illegal immigrants, especially, do not have much money or power, and they are thus an easy target for disgruntled citizens and hard-pressed politicians. However, considerable evidence suggests that while immigrants, particularly the larger groups like Mexicans, tend to be poor, they do become assimilated into American society. The average wages of second- and third-generation Mexican Americans, for instance, rise to about 80 percent of the wages of whites.[114] And their wage levels do not necessarily depress the overall wage levels. In the 1980s wages rose faster in parts of the country with higher immigrant populations.[115] Although many immigrant groups are certainly poor, and a gap remains between their average standards of living and those of longer-term residents, the reaction against immigration in this country may be out of proportion to the problem.

WHO, WHAT, HOW Even groups who already enjoy basic civil rights can face considerable discrimination. Opposition to the extension of more comprehensive rights to these groups comes from a variety of directions.

In the case of gays and lesbians, opponents claim that providing a heightened standard of review for laws that discriminate on the basis of sexual orientation would be giving special rights to gays. Gays and lesbians are politically sophisticated and powerful, however, and the techniques they use are often strategies that had originally been closed off to minorities and women. Both they and their opponents use the courts, form interest groups, lobby Congress, and support presidential candidates to further their agendas. In the case of age discrimination, opponents are motivated not by moral concerns but by issues of social order and cost-efficiency. Older people are able to protect their rights more effectively than younger people because of their higher voter turnout.

People resist giving rights to the disabled generally out of concern for the expense of making buildings accessible and the cost-efficiency of hiring disabled workers. Organization into interest groups and effective lobbying of Congress have resulted in considerable protection of the rights of the disabled.

Finally, noncitizens seeking rights face opposition from a variety of sources. Although immigrants themselves are not usually well organized, the biggest protection of their rights comes from the Supreme Court, which has ruled that alienage is a suspect classification and therefore laws that discriminate on the basis of citizenship are subject to strict scrutiny.

THE CITIZENS AND CIVIL RIGHTS TODAY

The stories of America's civil rights struggles are the stories of citizen action. But clearly, citizens acting individually have not been able to bring about all the changes that civil rights groups have achieved. Although great leaders and effective organizers have played an important role in the battles for rights, the battles themselves have been part of a group movement.

In Chapter 1 we discussed three models of democracy that define options for citizen participation: elite, pluralist, and participatory. Of the three, the pluralist model best describes the actions that citizens have taken to gain the government's protection of their civil rights. Pluralism emphasizes the ways that citizens can increase their individual power by organizing into groups. The civil rights movements in the United States have been group movements, and to the extent that groups have been unable to organize effectively to advance their interests, their civil rights progress has been correspondingly slowed.

As we will see in Chapter 13, what have come to be known as *interest groups* play an increasingly important role in American politics. In fact, from the 1960s through the end of the century, the number of national associations in the United States grew by over 250 percent, to about 23,000, and the number of groups organized specifically to advocate the rights of African Americans, Hispanics, Asian Americans, and women have multiplied by six times during that period.[116] Scholars do not agree on whether this proliferation of groups increases the quality of democracy or skews its results. Groups that are well organized, well financed, and well informed and that have particularly passionate members (who put their votes where their hearts are) are likely to carry greater weight with lawmakers than are groups that are less focused and less well to do. On the one hand, money, information, and intensity of opinion all can make interest groups more powerful than their numbers, a fact that seems at odds with notions of political equality and democracy. On the other hand, as we have seen, individuals can accomplish things together in groups that they can only dream of doing alone. In the case of the civil rights movement, democracy would have clearly been impoverished without the power of groups to work on distributing citizenship rights more broadly. We return to the question of how democratic a pluralist society can be in Chapter 13, when we investigate in more depth the role of interest groups in American politics.

WHAT'S AT STAKE REVISITED

Racial profiling can sometimes seem reasonable, especially to those who are not targeted by it. After all, we profile in other, nonracial ways all the time. For instance, all young people pay more for car insurance, because we know that statistically they are more likely to get into costly accidents than are older people. Similarly, all older people pay more for health insurance because they are more likely to get sick. If statistics tell us that Middle Easterners are more likely to be terrorists than are other members of the population, or that a higher percentage of blacks than whites commit street crimes, what is really at stake in looking for those people when we are investigating a crime or questioning them to see if they are involved?

As our experience in the period ushered in by the September, 11, 2001, attacks makes clear, this question can be very difficult to answer. Those opposed to racial profiling argue that it violates the Constitution's guarantee of equal protection of the laws and that it should not be permitted under any circumstances. One defender of the practice says, on the other hand, that when we prohibit racial profiling, we tie the hands of law enforcement. "Investigating means following hunches," he says, and hunches cannot be neatly legislated.[117]

The American courts have not found the issue easy to deal with either. Even though they have said that race is a suspect category and laws that treat people differently need to be scrutinized strictly, that doesn't mean that if they see a compelling reason to categorize people by race, they do not allow it. A federal appeals court in 1992 allowed a conviction to stand, even though the arrest of the suspect had been based, in part, on his race. The court held that "facts are not to be ignored simply because they are unpleasant."[118]

Michael Kinsley, a political journalist, points out that the complexities of racial profiling are mirrored in another controversial practice: affirmative action. He says, "When the cops stop black drivers or companies make special efforts to hire black employees, they are both giving certain individuals special treatment based on racial generalizations. The only difference is that in one case the special treatment is something bad and in the other it's something good. Yet defenders of affirmative action tend to deplore racial profiling and vice versa."[119]

Kinsley concludes that support for these practices needs to be based on an estimation of what is at stake in allowing or forbidding a particular act of racial discrimination, and he uses something much like a "clear and present danger test" to decide. If it is known that someone on a plane has planted a bomb and time is of the essence, it may make sense to target for questioning the Arab-looking person, who is statistically more likely to be involved. But if people have been cleared by airport security and are asked to leave a plane because the pilot or passengers are just uncomfortable, he says, that is simply racism.

As this chapter has shown us, racism in this country has left a painful scar. Perhaps in a nation without our history of racism, stopping Middle Easterners when a crime is thought to have been committed by an Arab would be fraught with no more controversy than stopping blond people to search for a suspect who is reputed to have blond

continued

Thinking Outside the Box

- What would a legal system that treated all people exactly the same look like?
- Is it possible to have too much equality?
- Can we end de facto discrimination without imposing substantive solutions?

WHAT'S AT STAKE REVISITED *(continued)*

hair, or charging a young person more for automobile insurance. Our history, however, means that we cannot be casual about the sorts of behavior that followed the September 11 attacks or the kinds of behavior engaged in by certain police departments. Even before September 11, the U.S. Justice Department had declared that racial profiling by police was a practice that should not stand. What was at stake was clearly equality and freedom, valued prizes that had been too hard won by African Americans and other minorities to be taken lightly on the off-chance that a petty criminal might be found.

But in the aftermath of September 11, the stakes of freedom and equality seemed to be countered by immediate threats to our security. In a testimony, perhaps, to a sensitivity born of the long struggle against racism in this country, many Americans reached out to members of the Islamic faith, even as they kept wary eyes on their fellow travelers. In addressing the nation on the evening of the attacks, President Bush called for tolerance and respect. Many Arab Muslims, expecting to be harassed at the workplace, found support there instead.[120] Arab children were walked to school by non-Arab volunteers so that their mothers wearing traditional garb could stay safely off the streets. On college campuses around the country, hundreds of students came forward to escort their fellow students to class to protect them from intimidation. And concerned residents held candlelight vigils and neighborhood watches to guard local mosques. Do these responses take the edge off the painful racial profiling and frankly racist incidents they were designed to protest? Probably not, but they do show a deep and sincere effort on the part of many Americans to keep their troubled past from becoming part of a troubled future.

To Sum Up

KEY TERMS

republic.cqpress.com

affirmative action (p. 225)
black codes (p. 214)
boycott (p. 220)
Brown v. Board of Education of Topeka (p. 218)
busing (p. 223)
civil rights (p. 209)
de facto discrimination (p. 222)
de jure discrimination (p. 221)
English-only movements (p. 236)
Equal Rights Amendment (p. 249)
grandfather clauses (p. 216)
intermediate standard of review (p. 210)
Jim Crow laws (p. 216)
literacy tests (p. 216)
minimum rationality test (p. 210)
National Association for the Advancement of Colored People (NAACP) (p. 217)
Plessy v. Ferguson (p. 216)
poll taxes (p. 216)
racism (p. 213)
Reconstruction (p. 215)
segregation (p. 216)
sexual harassment (p. 252)
strict scrutiny (p. 210)
suspect classifications (p. 210)

Key terms, chapter summaries, practice quizzes, Internet links, and other study aids are available on the companion Web site at: republic.cqpress.com.

SUMMARY

republic.cqpress.com

- Throughout U.S. history, various groups, because of some characteristic beyond their control, have been denied their civil rights and have fought for equal treatment under the law. All three branches of the government have played an important role in providing remedies for the denial of equal rights.
- Groups that are discriminated against may seek procedural remedies, such as changing the law to guarantee *equality of opportunity*, or substantive remedies, such as the institution of affirmative action programs, to guarantee *equality of outcome*.
- African Americans have experienced both *de jure discrimination*, created by laws that treat people differently, and *de facto discrimination*, which occurs when societal tradition and habit lead to social segregation.
- African Americans led the first civil rights movement in the United States. By forming interest groups such as the NAACP and developing strategies such as nonviolent resistance, African Americans eventually defeated de jure discrimination.
- De facto discrimination persists in America, signified by the education and wage gap between African Americans and whites. Programs like affirmative action, which could remedy such discrimination, remain controversial. Although African Americans have made great strides in the last fifty years, much inequality remains.
- Native Americans, Hispanics, and Asian Americans have also fought to gain economic and social equality. Congressional control over their lands has led Native Americans to assert economic power through the development of casinos. Using boycotts and voter education drives, Hispanics have worked to stem the success of English-only movements and anti-immigration efforts. Despite their smaller numbers, Asian Americans also aim for equal political clout, but it is through a cultural emphasis on scholarly achievement that they have gained considerable economic power.
- Women's rights movements represented challenges to power, to a traditional way of life, and to economic profit. Early activists found success through state politics because they were restricted from using the courts and Congress; efforts now focus on the courts to give women greater protection of the law.
- Gays, youth, the elderly, and the disabled enjoy the most fundamental civil rights, but they still face de jure and de facto discrimination. While moral concerns motivate laws against gays, social order and cost-efficiency concerns mark the restrictions against youth, the elderly, and disabled Americans.

PRACTICE QUIZ

republic.cqpress.com

1. Suspect classifications are defined as

a. ways of ranking criminal behavior as felonies or misdemeanors.

b. a standard of review in which the Court defines certain laws as most likely unconstitutional and in need of review.

c. classifications that need review before going into effect.

d. classifications, such as race or religion, for which a discriminatory law must be justified by a compelling state interest.

e. classifications for which strict scrutiny is not applied.

2. In the North, the civil rights movement fought to combat ______ discrimination.

a. ex post facto

b. de facto

c. de jure

d. de solis

e. ad hoc

3. While significant in numbers, the diversity of Hispanic Americans has

a. allowed them to avoid the stereotyping affecting other minority groups.

b. led to fragmentation and powerlessness.

c. allowed them to form alliances with other minorities.

d. limited their ability to assimilate into traditional American society.

e. made them more likely to compromise.

4. The Seneca Falls Convention showed that

a. support for women's rights existed but not when it came to voting rights.

b. African Americans did not support the women's movement.

c. southerners were supportive of women's rights.

d. women were not well organized politically.

e. women actually had more rights than was previously believed.

5. The model of democracy that best describes the actions American citizens have taken to gain the government's protection of their civil rights is ________ democracy.

a. participatory

b. elite

c. pluralist

d. direct

e. representative

SUGGESTED RESOURCES

republic.cqpress.com

Books

Correspondents of the *New York Times*. 2001. *How Race Is Lived in America: Pulling Together, Pulling Apart*. New York: Times Books. Originally published as a year-long series in the *New York Times*, this extraordinary compilation offers fifteen provocative and often touching stories that document the way that race is experienced in modern America.

Cushman, Clare, ed. 2002. *Supreme Court Decisions and Women's Rights: Milestones to Equality*. Washington, D.C.: Congressional Quarterly Press/ Supreme Court Historical Society. An authoritative, illustrated examination of precedent-setting cases involving women's rights and gender issues.

Deloria, Vine, Jr., and Clifford M. Lytle. 1984. *The Nations Within: The Past and Future of Indian Sovereignty*. New York: Pantheon. A thorough history of federal Indian law, this book effectively lays out the struggles that Native Americans encountered as the United States expanded westward.

Ferriss, Susan, and Ricardo Sandoval. 1997. *The Fight in the Fields: Cesar Chavez and the Farmworkers Movements*. New York: Harcourt Brace. An examination of the life and work of the founder of the United Farm Workers union. Also a PBS documentary.

Gerstmann, Evan. 2004. *Same-Sex Marriage and the Constitution*. New York: Cambridge University Press. An engaging, clearly written review of the arguments for and against same-sex marriage.

Hacker, Andrew. 1992. *Two Nations: Black and White, Separate, Hostile, Unequal.* New York: Scribner's. A bleak, but unfortunately realistic, account of the differences that exist between black and white Americans. Hacker's book is a must for students interested in race relations.

Ogletree, Charles J., Jr. 2004. *All Deliberate Speed: Reflections on the First Half Century of* Brown v. Board of Education. New York: Norton. An interesting examination of the *Brown* decision fifty years later. Ogeltree argues that the reforms promised in *Brown* have been systematically undermined.

Switzer, Jacqueline Vaughn. 2003. *Disabled Rights: American Disability Power and the Fight for Equality.* Washington, D.C.: Georgetown University Press. A thorough account of the history and politics of the disabilities movement in the United States.

Wu, Frank H. 2002. *Yellow: Race in America Beyond Black and White.* New York: Basic Books. In this personal account of growing up as an Asian American in the United States, Wu, a law professor at Howard University, adds another dimension to the debate over race in America.

Web Sites

Human Rights Campaign. www.hrc.org. The HRC's Web site contains information on every major current issue faced by the gay, lesbian, and transgender communities. It also includes a scorecard of how well members of Congress rate on these issues.

League of United Latin American Citizens. www.lulac.org. The LULAC works toward advancing the civil rights of the U.S. Hispanic population. Its Web site contains a wealth of information on the organization's activities and how others can participate in their efforts.

National Association for the Advancement of Colored People. www.naacp.org. The NAACP is the country's oldest civil rights organization. Its Web site includes information about the organization's history, the various ways in which it is active, and how you can get involved.

National Organization for Women. www.now.org. The preeminent women's rights organization, NOW publishes policy briefs on a wealth of issues relevant to bringing about equality for women.

U.S. Department of Justice Civil Rights Division. www.usdoj.gov/crt/. This site, representing the Justice Department agency responsible for enforcing the nation's civil rights statutes, includes guides to civil rights laws, cases in which the agency is currently involved, and reports on various topics.

You can connect with many of the other civil rights organizations mentioned in this chapter, as well as additional resources, from the *Keeping the Republic* Web site. Just go to *republic.cqpress.com* and select the Chapter 6 Explore section.

Movies

Many fine films have documented the struggle for equal rights in America, among them *Iron Jawed Angels* (2004), *The Long Walk Home* (1990), *Glory* (1989), and *Malcolm X* (1992). Be sure to read the *Consider the Source* feature in this chapter for tips on becoming a critical movie reviewer.

Actions speak louder than words. In 2003, Democrats from both houses of the Texas legislature left the state to prevent Republican-proposed redistricting plans from coming to a vote. On May 15 of that year, the fifty-three representatives who had fled to Oklahoma held a press conference to explain their actions (right). A year later, Republican House Majority Leader Tom DeLay (below), a major force in the redistricting strategy, showed his victory spirit after seeing the plan succeed in increasing the Republican majority in the House and after winning his own eleventh term of office.

CONGRESS

7

WHAT'S AT STAKE?

It could have been a scene from an old-time Western—only the date was May 13, 2003. Fifty-one Democratic Texas legislators were on the lam, holed up across the Oklahoma border. Some called them cowards for not standing and fighting, but these Democrats claimed they had no choice but to flee the Lone Star state. Determined to bring them home, their Republican colleagues in the Texas House sent for the Texas Rangers. When the Rangers failed to retrieve them, Tom DeLay, the Republican majority leader of the U.S. House of Representatives (and a native Texan), asked Federal Aviation Administration (FAA) officials to help out. The president of the United States chimed in, telling DeLay that he supported his efforts. At one point, inquiries were even made of the Department of Homeland Security and the FBI, to see if they had jurisdiction to bring the errant representatives home. As federal agents, of course, they did not (nor did the FAA, as DeLay was told when he was admonished for an ethics violation months later), but tempers were getting hot in Texas and the Republicans were pulling out all the stops. And though the representatives eventually came home of their own volition, eleven Democratic members of the Texas Senate took off for New Mexico three months later, leaving home so quickly that one forgot his belt and another his wallet.

Now, what was *that* all about?

The Democrats were trying to prevent a vote in the Texas legislature that they knew they would lose. Texas law requires a quorum of two-thirds of the members (or 100 of 150 members in the House and 21 of 31 in the Senate) be present for a vote, and by staying out of reach of state police, the runaway Democrats could keep that vote from happening.

And what was this vote? What issue was so important that it could send these legislators into exile, living without their families and the comforts of home in the Ardmore, Oklahoma, Holiday Inn and the Albuquerque Marriott? For the Democrats, it was very serious business indeed.

The vote was all about redrawing the Texas congressional districts, an issue we talk more about later in this chapter, in the section on congressional elections. At the start of every new decade, after the nation's population is tallied in the constitutionally mandated census, many states must redraw their districts for the U.S. House of Representatives to match the population shifts that have occurred within the country. This is a way of making sure that districts stay of roughly equal size, but political parties in the state legislatures have long taken the opportunity to enhance their own political clout at the same time, by drawing the districts to maximize the number of representatives their parties will get. Parties in the majority when the census is taken have lucked out until the next census, ten years later.

The Texas map was redrawn after 2000, when final district lines were determined by a three-judge federal court because the Democrats (then in the majority in the state legislature) failed to bring it to a vote. The redistricting kept the map mostly as it was, which benefited the Democrats who were likely to win seventeen of the thirty-two districts. Then, in 2002 the Republicans won a controlling majority of the Texas legislature and decided, largely at the urging of Tom DeLay, to redraw the map again, an unprecedented mid-decade redistricting. DeLay believed that, under his plan, Republicans would be much more likely to win four to seven additional U.S. House seats in Texas, helping to solidify the Republican majority there and giving DeLay himself considerably more influence. When Republicans sought to bring the new redistricting to a vote, Democrats left the state in an attempt to prevent it. Eventually they came home and the vote took place, with exactly the consequences they feared. Districts were redrawn to hurt the Democrats' chances in November 2004, and sure enough, when the election rolled around, five Texas Democrats lost their seats, helping to boost the overall Republican majority in the House by three.

Why were Texas Republicans willing to go to such lengths to shore up their majority in Congress? Why were the Democrats willing to leave their families and homes to live in hotels at their own expense to prevent them? Why was the majority leader of the U.S. House of Representatives willing to get involved in state politics, something that on its face was none of his business? And why did one Texas Democrat say that this was really all about the future of democracy?[1] What was really at stake in which party controlled the U.S. Congress? We return to this question after we learn more about how Congress works and what it can do. *

The U.S. Congress is the world's longest-running and most powerful democratic legislature. If politics is all about who gets what, and how, then Congress is arguably also the center of American national politics. Not only does it often decide exactly who gets what, but Congress also has the power to alter many of the rules (or the how) that determine who wins and who loses in American political life.

The Capitol building in Washington, D.C., home to both the House of Representatives and the Senate, has become as much a symbol of America's democracy as are the Stars and Stripes or the White House. We might expect Americans to express considerable pride in their national legislature, with its long tradition of serving democratic government. But if we did, we would be wrong.

Congress is generally distrusted, seen by the American public as incompetent, corrupt, torn by partisanship, and at the beck and call of special interests.[2] And yet, despite their contempt for the institution of Congress as a whole, Americans typically revere their representatives and senators and reelect them so often that critics have long been calling for term limits to get new people into office (see the box, "Citizens' Love-Hate Relationship With Congress"). How can we understand this bizarre paradox?[3]

There are two main reasons for America's love-hate relationship with Congress. The first is that citizens have conflicting expectations when it comes to the operation of their national legislature. On the one hand, they want their representatives in Washington to take care of their local or state interests and to ensure that their home district gets a fair share of national resources. On the other hand, citizens also want Congress to take care of the nation's business. This can pose a quandary for the legislator because what is good for the home district might not be good for the nation as a whole. Legislators trying to meet both sets of citizens' expectations often end up disappointing someone.

The second reason for citizens' love-hate relationship with Congress is that the rules that determine how Congress works were designed by the founders to produce slow, careful lawmaking that can seem motionless to an impatient public. When citizens are looking to Congress to produce policies that they favor or to distribute national resources, the built-in slowness can look like intentional foot dragging and partisan bickering. That it is instead a constitutional safeguard is part of a civics lesson most Americans have long forgotten.

Keeping in mind these two dynamics, our legislators' struggle to meet our conflicting expectations, and our own frustration with Congress's institutionalized slowness, will take us a long way toward understanding our mixed feelings about our national legislature. In this chapter we explore those dynamics as we look at who—including citizens, other politicians, and members of Congress themselves—gets the results they want from Congress, and how the rules of legislative politics help or hinder them. You will learn about

- the clash between representation and lawmaking
- the powers and responsibilities of Congress
- congressional membership and elections
- the organization of Congress and the rules of congressional operation
- the relationship of citizens to Congress

CONGRESS: REPRESENTATION AND LAWMAKING

We count on our elected representatives in both the House and the Senate to perform two major functions: representation and lawmaking. By **representation**, we mean that those we elect should represent, or look out for, our local interests and carry out our will. At the same time, we expect our legislators to address the country's social and economic problems by **national lawmaking**—passing laws that serve the interest of the entire nation.

representation the efforts of elected officials to look out for the interests of those who elect them

national lawmaking the creation of policy to address the problems and needs of the entire nation

The functions of representation and lawmaking often conflict. What is good for us and our local community may not serve the national good. One of the chief lessons of this chapter is that the rules under which Congress operates make it likely that when these primary functions do conflict, members of Congress will usually favor their jobs as representatives. That is, a member of Congress will usually do what the local district wants. Thus national problems go unaddressed while local problems get atten-

Citizens' Love-Hate Relationship With Congress

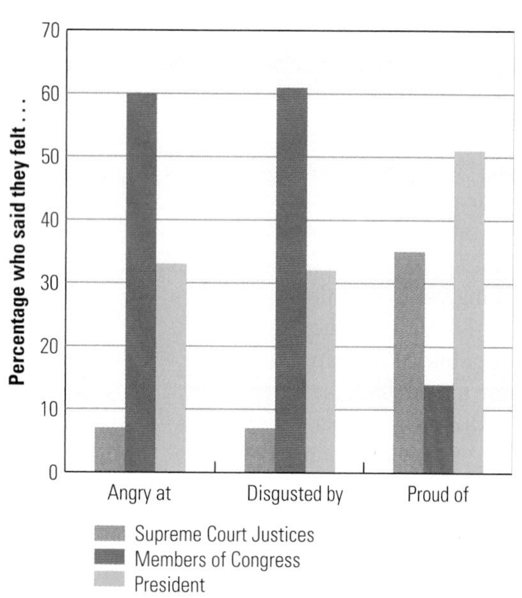

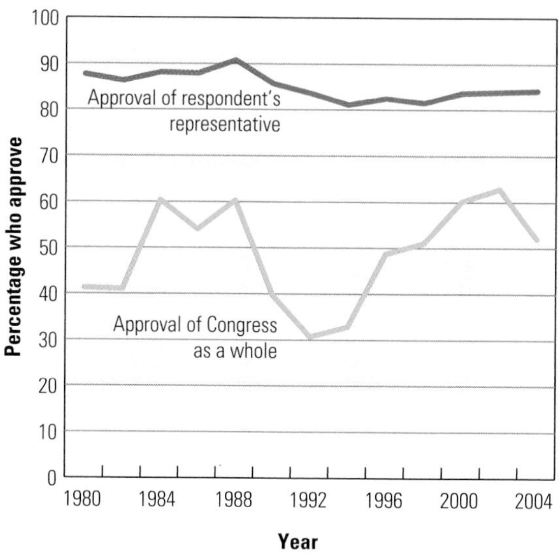

Question: Please tell me how you would rate the honesty and ethical standards of people in these different fields (very high, high, average, low, or very low)?

Nurses	(79%)	Judges	(53%)	Newspaper reporters	(21%)
Pharmacists	(72%)	Day care providers	(49%)	Senators	(20%)
Military officers	(72%)	Bankers	(36%)	Business executives	(20%)
Medical doctors	(67%)	Auto mechanics	(26%)	Lawyers	(18%)
Police officers	(60%)	Local officeholders	(26%)	Congressmen	(10%)
College teachers	(59%)	Nursing home operators	(24%)	Advertising Practitioners	(10%)
Clergy	(56%)	TV reporters	(23%)	Car salesmen	(9%)

Note: Rank is by very high/high combined.

Source: Data are from John R. Hibbing and Elizabeth Theiss-Morse, *Congress as Public Enemy* (New York: Cambridge University Press, 1995), 58; American National Election Studies Cumulative File, 1948–2002; National Election Study 2004 Pre-Post Study (advanced release), January 31, 2005; Joseph Carroll, "Public Rates Nursing as Most Honest and Ethical Profession," Gallup Organization Poll Analysis, Gallup News Service (December 1, 2003); "Nurses Top List for Honesty," CBSNews.com (December 8, 2004).

Public Feelings Toward Congress

Measured several different ways, the public's attitudes toward Congress are unfavorable: compared to the other branches of government, Congress is more frequently the target of American anger and disgust. Compared to other occupations, members of Congress in general are held in low esteem. However, individual representatives achieve much higher approval ratings by their own constituents than does Congress as a whole. Members' intense efforts at representation result in a situation in which many Americans love their congresspeople but hate their Congress.

tion, resources, and solutions. No wonder we love our individual representatives but think poorly of the job done by Congress as a national policymaking institution.

FOUR KINDS OF REPRESENTATION

Representation means working on behalf of one's **constituency**, the folks back home in the district who voted for the member as well as those who did not. To help us understand this complex job, political scientists often speak about four types of representation.[4] Most members of Congress try to excel at all four functions so that constituents will rate them highly and reelect them.

constituency the voters in a state or district

Policy Representation **Policy representation** refers to congressional work for laws that advance the economic and social interests of the constituency. For example, House members and senators from petroleum-producing states can be safely predicted to vote in ways favorable to the profitability of the oil companies, members from the Plains states try to protect subsidies for wheat farmers, and so on. It is rarer for a member to champion a national interest, since it is in the local constituency that he or she will face reelection, but some members do focus on such issues as foreign policy, campaign finance reform, or the environment.

policy representation congressional work to advance the issues and ideological preferences of constituents

Allocative Representation Voters have also come to expect a certain amount of **allocative representation**, in which the congressperson gets projects and grants for the district. Such perks are called **pork barrel** benefits, paid for by all the taxpayers but enjoyed by just a few. Congresspeople who are good at getting pork barrel projects for their districts (e.g., highway construction or the establishment of a research institution) are said to "bring home the bacon."

allocative representation congressional work to secure projects, services, and funds for the represented district

pork barrel public works projects and grants for specific districts paid for by general revenues

Casework Senators and representatives also represent their states or districts by taking care of the individual problems of constituents, especially problems that involve the

Bringing Home the Bacon
Pork barrel projects are quite popular, because they have the appearance of being free to constituents. Democratic senator Robert Byrd of West Virginia (second from left) is so good at bringing home the bacon—including an FBI identification center, an IRS processing center, and a NASA research center—that he has earned a reputation as the "King of Pork." Here, he takes part in a groundbreaking ceremony for the Blanchette Rockefeller Neurosciences Institute, billed as the largest basic science research venture in West Virginia history. The project is affiliated with the National Institutes of Health and West Virginia University, for which Byrd has appropriated millions of dollars over the years.

casework legislative work on behalf of individual constituents to solve their problems with government agencies and programs

franking the privilege of free mail service provided to members of Congress

symbolic representation efforts of members of Congress to stand for American ideals or identify with common constituency values

federal bureaucracy. This kind of representation is called **casework**, or constituency service, and it covers things such as finding out why a constituent's Social Security check has not shown up, sending a flag that has flown over the nation's capitol to a high school in the district, or helping with immigration and naturalization problems. To promote their work for constituents, members maintain web pages and send information to the homes of voters through more traditional channels. (See "*Consider the Source:* How to Be a Critical Constituent," for some tips on how to be a savvy consumer of congressional information.) The congressional privilege of **franking** allows members to use the U.S. mail at no charge. This free postal service fulfills the democratic purpose of keeping citizens informed about their lawmakers' activities, but because only positive information about and images of the congressperson are sent out, it is also self-serving.

Symbolic Representation A fourth kind of representation is called **symbolic representation**. In this elusive but important function, the member of Congress represents many of the positive values Americans associate with public life and government. Thus members are glad to serve as commencement speakers at high school graduations or attend town meetings to explain what is happening in Washington. Equally important are the ways members present themselves to their districts—using colloquialisms such as "y'all" even if they are not from the South and wearing a denim work shirt to county fairs. These appearances are part of a member's "home style" and help to symbolize the message "I am one of you" and "I am a person you can trust; I share your values and interests."[5]

NATIONAL LAWMAKING

As we explained earlier, representation is not the only business of our senators and representatives. A considerable part of their job involves working with one another in Washington to define and solve the nation's problems. We expect Congress to create laws that serve the common good. One scholar calls this view of effective lawmaking "collective responsibility."[6] By this he means that Congress should be responsible for the effectiveness of its laws in solving national problems. A variety of factors go into a representative's calculation of how to vote on matters of national interest. He or she might be guided by conscience or ideology, by what opinion polls say the local constituents want, or by party position. And these considerations may very well be at odds with the four kinds of representation just described, which frequently make it difficult, if not impossible, for members to fulfill their collective responsibility.

Imagine, for instance, the dilemma of a Democratic congresswoman representing an industrial midwestern district with an automotive plant that builds large, fuel-inefficient sport-utility vehicles. What is good for her constituency—fewer fuel-efficiency requirements on automobiles and more tax breaks for companies purchasing heavy-duty vehicles—might conflict sharply with the national public good. For instance, stricter fuel-efficiency standards could lower America's dependence on foreign sources of oil and reduce harmful automotive emissions that lower air quality. Our congresswoman would have to consider tough questions that affect the public good, her policy goals, and her reelection.

In this case, what's best for the local district clearly clashes with the national interest. And the scenario holds true again and again for every representative and senator. Thus the potential for conflict is great when one works for one's constituents as well as for the entire nation. We all want a Congress that focuses on the nation's problems, but as voters we tend to reward members for putting constituency concerns first.

WHO, WHAT, HOW Both citizens and their representatives have something serious at stake in the tension between representation and lawmaking. Citizens want their local interests protected. But citizens also want sound national policy, and here they are often disappointed. The need to secure reelection by catering to local interests often means that their representatives have fewer incentives to concentrate on national lawmaking.

In fact, members of the House and the Senate face a true dilemma. On the one hand, they want to serve their constituents' local interests and needs, and they want to be reelected to office by those constituents. But they also must face personal, party, and special interest demands to take stands that might not suit the voters back home.

CONGRESSIONAL POWERS AND RESPONSIBILITIES

The Constitution gives the U.S. Congress enormous powers, although it is safe to say that the founders could not have imagined the scope of contemporary congressional power since they never anticipated the growth of the federal government to today's size. As we will see, they were less concerned with the conflict between local and national interests we have been discussing than they were with the representation of short-term popular opinion versus long-term national interests. The basic powers of Congress are laid out in Article I, Section 8, of the Constitution (see Chapter 4). They include the powers to tax, to pay debts, and to provide for the common defense and welfare of the United States, among many other things.

DIFFERENCES BETWEEN THE HOUSE AND THE SENATE

The term *Congress* refers to the institution that is formally made up of the U.S. House of Representatives and the U.S. Senate. Congresses are numbered so that we can talk about them over time in a coherent way. Each congress covers a two-year election cycle. The 109th Congress was elected in November 2004, and its term runs from January 2005 through the end of 2006. The **bicameral** (two-house) **legislature** is laid out in the Constitution. As we discussed in earlier chapters, the founders wanted two chambers so that they could serve as a restraint on each other, strengthening the

bicameral legislature
legislature with two chambers

Consider the Source

How to Be a Critical Constituent

Being a critical constituent means more than sitting around the dinner table griping about Congress. It means knowing what your representatives are doing so that you can evaluate how well they are representing your interests. How can you learn about your representative's or senators' performance in Congress? There is an abundance of information, but it is not all equally reliable or equally easy to find. Here is a guide to sources that can help you discover and evaluate what your elected representatives are up to.

1. For the average citizen, one of the best sources of information about members of Congress comes from a nonpartisan organization, Project Vote Smart (PVS). PVS collects information on the background, issue positions, campaign finances, and voting records of over 13,000 officeholders and candidates for president, governor, Congress, and the state legislatures. It also tracks performance evaluations for members of Congress from special interest groups that provide them. These evaluations represent the frequency with which the member of Congress voted with that organization's preferred position on a number of votes identified as key in their issue area. One big advantage of PVS is that it attempts to provide data on all candidates, not just incumbents, and it makes its information available during the campaign. All information is free and available on-line at **www.vote-smart.org**.
2. For an overview of the debates going on in Congress, you can find the detailed proceedings of past sessions in the *Congressional Record,* which is available in print at many university libraries and on-line (**www.thomas.loc.gov**) for the past few congressional sessions. The *Congressional Record* is informative, but it can be tedious to read. Moreover, it is not an exact transcript of congressional proceedings. Members are regularly given permission, by unanimous consent, to "extend and revise" their remarks even to the extent of adding entirely new speeches they never gave. Read this source with some skepticism.

principle of checks and balances. The framers' hope was that the smaller, more elite Senate would "cool the passions" of the people represented in the House. Accordingly, while the two houses are equal in their overall power—both can initiate legislation (although tax bills must originate in the House), and both must pass every bill in identical form before it can be signed by the president to become law—there are also some key differences, particularly in the extra responsibilities assigned to the Senate. In addition, the two chambers operate differently, and they have distinct histories and norms of conduct (that is, informal rules and expectations of behavior).[7] Some of the major differences are outlined in Table 7.1.

The single biggest factor determining differences between the House and the Senate is size. With 100 members, the Senate is less formal; the 435-person House needs more rules and hierarchy in order to function efficiently. The Constitution also provides for differences in terms: two years for the House, six for the Senate (on a staggered basis—all senators do not come up for reelection at the same time). In the modern context, this means that House members (also referred to as congresspersons or members of Congress, a term that sometimes applies to senators as well) never stop campaigning. Senators, in contrast, can suspend their preoccupation with the next campaign for the first four or five years of their terms and thus, at least in theory, have more time to spend on the affairs of the nation. The minimum age of the candidates is different as well: members of the House must be at least twenty-five years old, senators thirty. This again reflects the founders' expectation that the Senate would be older, wiser, and better able to deal with national lawmaking. This distinction was reinforced in the constitutional provision that senators be elected not directly by the

3. A number of media sources, both local and national, track congressional action. Your local paper should cover the activities of your state's senators and representatives through articles and editorials and may report on how each representative votes on proposed legislation. The national media may cover your representatives as well, as do *CQ Weekly* and *National Journal* (most college libraries have these publications). You can also go to the highly readable biennial almanacs that provide detailed portraits of members of Congress and their districts and states: *The Almanac of American Politics,* published by National Journal, and *Politics in America,* published by CQ (Congressional Quarterly) Press.

4. Follow the money. A good clue to what your congressperson is up to can be found in the records of who has given money to him or her. Check out **www.crp.org**, the web site for the Center for Responsive Politics. This center tracks campaign contributions and can even tell you who in your ZIP code area has given how much money to which political causes or candidates.

5. Get to know your elected representatives. Members regularly come home for long weekends in part to maintain contact with constituents. Send an e-mail or letter to your congressperson asking when he or she will be nearby. Staff will be happy to tell you of any upcoming town meetings or visits to district offices to meet with constituents. This is harder to arrange for a U.S. senator from a large state, but most citizens can meet with their U.S. representative with just a bit of effort.

Getting the facts is only part of the job of being a critical constituent. Evaluating them is no less important. Any time you engage in evaluation, you need a clear yardstick against which to hold up the thing you are evaluating. Here it may be helpful to remember the twin pressures on a member of Congress to be both a representative and a national lawmaker. Which do you think is more important? What kind of balance should be struck between them? How does your congressperson measure up?

people, as were members of the House, but by state legislatures. Although this provision was changed by constitutional amendment in 1913, its presence in the original Constitution reflects the convictions of its authors that the Senate was a special chamber, one step removed from the people.

Budget bills are initiated in the House of Representatives. In practice this is not particularly significant since the Senate has to pass budget bills as well, and most of the time differences are negotiated between the two houses. The budget process has gotten quite complicated, as demonstrated by congressional struggles in the 1980s and 1990s to deal with the deficit, which called for reductions in spending at the same time that constituencies and interest groups were pleading for expensive new programs. The budget process illustrates once again the constant tension for members of Congress between being responsive to local or particular interests and at the same time trying to make laws in the interest of the nation as a whole.

Other differences between the House and the Senate include the division of power on impeachment of public figures such as presidents and Supreme Court justices. The House impeaches, or charges the official with "treason, bribery, or other high crimes and misdemeanors," and the Senate tries the official. Both Andrew Johnson and Bill Clinton were impeached by the House, but in both cases the Senate failed to find the president guilty of the charges brought by the House. In addition, only the Senate is given the responsibility of confirming appointments to the executive and judicial branches, and of sharing the treaty-making power with the president, responsibilities we explore in more detail in the next section.

TABLE 7.1 Differences Between the House and the Senate

	HOUSE	SENATE
Constitutional Differences		
Term length	2 years	6 years
Minimum age	25	30
Citizenship required	7 years	9 years
Residency	In state	In state
Apportionment	Changes with population	Fixed; entire state
Impeachment	Impeaches official	Tries the impeached official
Treaty-making power	No authority	2/3 approval
Presidential appointments	No authority	Majority approval
Organizational Differences		
Size	435 members	100 members
Number of standing committees	20	16
Total committee assignments per member	Approx. 6	Approx. 11
Rules Committee	Yes	No
Limits on floor debate	Yes	No (filibuster possible)
Electoral Differences		
Costs of elections		
Incumbents	$1.1 million	$8.5 million
Challengers	$190,024	$971,379
Open seat	$550,839	$3.0 million
Incumbency advantage	98% reelected (93.4% 50-year average)	96% reelected (80.4% 50-year average)

Source: Roger Davidson and Walter Oleszek, *Congress and Its Members,* 9th ed. (Washington, D.C.: CQ Press, 2004), 60, 205; Federal Election Commission data compiled by Center for Responsive Politics; calculations by authors.

CONGRESSIONAL CHECKS AND BALANCES

The founders were concerned about the abuse of power by the executive and legislative branches, and even by the people. But, as we saw in Chapter 3, they were most anxious to avoid executive tyranny, and so they granted Congress an impressive array of powers. Keeping Congress at the center of national policymaking is the power to regulate commerce; the exclusive power to raise and to spend money for the national government; the power to provide for economic infrastructure (roads, postal service, money, patents); and significant powers in foreign policy, including the power to declare war, to ratify treaties, and to raise and support the armed forces.

As we discussed in Chapter 4, the Supreme Court has generally interpreted the necessary and proper clause of the Constitution quite favorably for the expansion of congressional power. But the Constitution also limits congressional powers through the protection of individual rights and by the watchful eye of the other two branches of government, with which Congress shares power. We look briefly at those relationships here.

Congress and the President Our system of checks and balances means that to exercise its powers, each branch has to have the cooperation of the others. Thus Congress has the responsibility for passing bills, but the bills do not become law unless (1) the president signs them or, more passively, refrains from vetoing them, or (2) both houses of Congress are able to muster a full two-thirds majority to override a presidential veto. While the president cannot vote on legislation or even introduce bills, the Constitution gives the chief executive a powerful policy formulation role in calling for the president's annual State of the Union address and in inviting the president to recommend to Congress "such measures as he shall judge necessary and expedient."

Cooperation between Congress and the president is also necessitated by the requirement that major presidential appointments, for instance to cabinet posts, ambassadorships, and the federal courts, must be confirmed by the Senate. Historically, most presidential appointments have proceeded without incident, but in recent administrations, appointments have become increasingly political. Senators sometimes use their confirmation powers to do more than "advise and consent" on the appointment at hand. They can, and do, tie up appointments, either because they oppose the nominee on account of his or her ideology or because they wish to extract promises and commitments from the president. Traditionally, just a single senator could put a hold on a judicial nominee from his or her state, though that practice has been challenged during the Bush administration.[8] During the Clinton administration, the Republican majority in the Senate opposed so many of the president's nominees that one-tenth of the seats on the federal bench were left empty, causing a large backlog of cases that the courts were unable to process.[9] In his turn, President George W. Bush has faced intense nomination battles with Senate Democrats. At least some of these Democrats have suggested that they were motivated in part by resentment over the way Clinton's nominees were treated, with one senator declaring that he would not "reward the president's party for the vacancies created by their obstructionism during the last six years."[10] The battle of wills between the Senate Democrats and the Repub-

Laughter, the Best Medicine
After weeks of political stalemate, during which Republicans in the U.S. Senate threatened to use a "nuclear option" to prevent the Democratic minority from using the filibuster to block the president's nominees to federal benches, cooler heads managed to prevail. A "gang of fourteen" moderates—seven Democrats and seven Republicans—pulled together a last-minute compromise that saved the constitutional right to filibuster and got several of President George W. Bush's nominees approved. Joe Lieberman, D-Conn., at the podium, and his jovial colleagues announced the deal at a press conference on May 23, 2005.

lican administration was at least temporarily resolved in the spring of 2005, when a group of moderate senators of both parties negotiated a compromise to gain approval for most of Bush's nominees.

A continuing source of institutional conflict between Congress and the president is the difference in constituencies. The president looks at each policy in terms of a national constituency and his own policy program, whereas members of Congress necessarily take a narrower view. For example, the president may decide that clean air should be a national priority. For some members of Congress, however, a clean air bill might mean closing factories in their districts because it would not be profitable to bring them up to emissions standards, or shutting down soft coal mines because the bill would kill the market for high-sulfur coal. Often, public policy looks very different from the perspective of congressional offices than it does from the presidential Oval Office at the other end of Pennsylvania Avenue.

Congress and the Courts The constitutional relationship between the federal courts and Congress is simple in principle: Congress makes the laws, and the courts interpret them. The Supreme Court also has the lofty job of deciding whether laws and procedures are consistent with the Constitution, although this power of judicial review is not actually mentioned in the Constitution.

We think of the judiciary as independent of the other branches, but this self-sufficiency is only a matter of degree. Congress, for example, is charged with setting up the lower federal courts and determining the salaries for judges, with the interesting constitutional provision that a judge's salary cannot be cut. Congress also has considerable powers in establishing some issues of jurisdiction—that is, deciding which courts hear which cases (Article III, Section 2). And, as we just indicated, in accepting and rejecting presidential Supreme Court and federal court nominees the Senate influences the long-term operation of the courts.[11]

A final way Congress exerts power over the courts is by passing laws that limit the courts' discretion to rule or impose sentences as judges think best. For example, in the 1980s, Congress passed strict drug laws that required mandatory sentences for offenders; judges could not sentence someone for less than the minimum time that Congress defined in legislation. Similarly, Congress, with the support of President Bush, would like to pass tort reform that would place limits on the compensation an individual can receive in a civil lawsuit. Finally, though it is hard to do, Congress can remove the ability of federal courts and the Supreme Court to interpret constitutional issues by trying to amend the Constitution itself.

WHO, WHAT, HOW The Constitution gives great power to both the House and the Senate, but it does so in the curiously backhanded way known as checks and balances. The House and the Senate share most lawmaking functions, but the fact that they *both* must approve legislation gives them a check over each other. They in turn are checked by the power of the president and the courts. The legislature is unable to operate without the cooperation of the other two branches unless it can demonstrate unusual internal strength and consensus, allowing it to override presidential vetoes and, in more extreme circumstances, amend the Constitution and impeach presidents.

CONGRESSIONAL ELECTIONS: CHOOSING THE MEMBERS

The first set of rules a future congressperson or senator has to contend with are those that govern congressional elections. These, more than any others, are the rules that determine the winners and losers in congressional politics. No matter what a legislator might hope to accomplish, he or she cannot achieve it as a legislator without winning and keeping the support of voters. With House elections every two years and Senate elections every six years, much of the legislator's life is spent running for reelection. In fact, one professor argues that most aspects of Congress are designed to aid the reelection goals of its members.[12] With elections so central, let us take a look at how the rules work, who runs for office, and how the electoral process shapes what members do in Washington.

THE POLITICS OF DEFINING CONGRESSIONAL DISTRICTS

As a result of the Great Compromise in 1787, the Constitution provides that each state will have two senators and that seats in the House of Representatives will be allocated on the basis of population. Two important political processes regulate the way House seats are awarded on this basis. One is **reapportionment**, in which the 435 House seats are reallocated among the states after each ten-year census. States whose populations grow gain seats, which are taken from those whose populations decline or remain steady. Figure 7.1 shows the current apportionment for each state in the 2000s and the projected changes for the 2010s. The winners are mostly in the rapidly growing Sun Belt states of the South and Southwest; the losers are largely in the Northeast and Midwest.

reapportionment a reallocation of congressional seats among the states every ten years, following the census

Since areas that lose population will also lose representatives, just how you count the population becomes critical. Democrats in 2000 proposed using what they claimed was a more precise statistical sampling technique that would allow census workers to get a better estimate of hard-to-count portions of the population such as

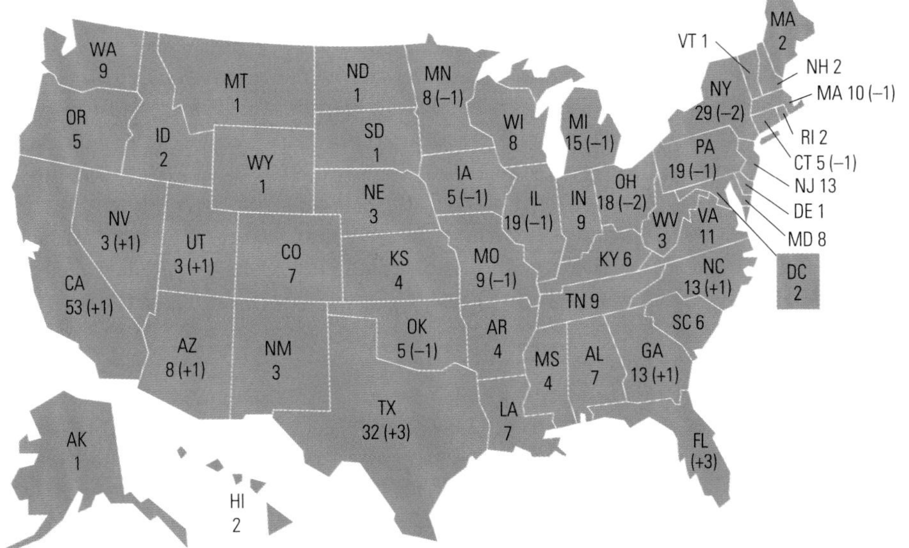

FIGURE 7.1
House Apportionment in the 2000s and Estimates for the 2010s

Note: Numbers in parentheses show estimated gains and losses following the 2010 census, based on U.S. Census Bureau population projections. These projections mirror states' gain-and-loss trends over recent decades, although the numbers may not all be borne out by the 2010 count.

Source: Roger H. Davidson and Walter J. Oleszek, *Congress and Its Members*, 10th ed. (Washington, D.C.: CQ Press, 2006), Figure 3.1.

poor people and immigrants. Fearing that this would add to the population of Democratic districts, and thus increase Democratic representation, Republicans balked. The Supreme Court sided with the Republicans, ruling that the Constitution and the legislation on the books required that, for purposes of reapportionment, the census had to reflect an actual count of the population.

Even more political, however, is the second process that regulates the way districts are drawn. Until the 1960s the states often suffered from malapportionment, the unequal distribution of population among the districts so that some had many fewer residents than others. This, in effect, gave greater representation to those living in lower population districts. This difference is built into the Constitution in the case of the U.S. Senate, but the Supreme Court decided in 1964 that for the U.S. House of Representatives as well as for both houses of the state legislatures, Americans should be represented under the principle of "one person, one vote" and that the districts therefore must have equal populations.[13] The average size of a house district in the year 2000 was 646,952.[14] Districts are equalized following the census through a political process called **redistricting**, or the redrawing of district lines in states with more than one representative. This procedure, which is carried out by the state legislators (or by commissions they empower), can turn into a bitter political battle because how the district lines are drawn will have a lot to do with who has, gets, and keeps power in the states. In the What's at Stake? that opened this chapter we saw how divisive redistricting became in Texas when Republicans decided to carry it out in a noncensus year.

redistricting process of dividing states into legislative districts

gerrymandering redistricting to benefit a particular group

Gerrymandering is the process of drawing district lines to benefit one group or another, and it can result in some extremely strange shapes by the time the state politicians are through. Gerrymandering usually is one of three kinds. Pro-incumbent gerrymandering takes place when a state legislature is so closely divided that members can't agree to give an advantage to one party or the other, so they agree to create districts that reinforce the current power structure by favoring the people who already hold the seats.[15]

A second kind of gerrymandering is partisan gerrymandering. Generally, the goal of the party controlling the redistricting process in a particular state legislature is to draw districts to maximize the number of House seats their party can win. Consequently, Democrats might draw districts that would split a historically Republican district and force an incumbent Republican to run in a new, more liberal district, or even draw districts in a way that would pit two incumbent Republicans in the same district, forcing them to run against each other in a primary. Partisan gerrymandering was the goal of the Texas Republicans who redistricted in 2003.

The First Gerrymander

In 1812, during the administration of Governor Elbridge Gerry, district lines for the Massachusetts senate were drawn to concentrate Federalist Party support in a few districts, thereby helping to elect more Democratic-Republicans. This contemporary cartoon likened one particularly convoluted district to a long-necked monster.

Finally, **racial gerrymandering** occurs when district lines are drawn to favor or disadvantage an ethnic or racial group. For many years, states in the Deep South drew district lines to ensure that black voters would not constitute a majority that could elect an African American to Congress. Since the 1982 Voting Rights Act, the drawing of such lines has been used to maximize the likelihood that African Americans will be elected to Congress. Both Republicans and African American political activists have backed the formation of *majority-minority districts*, in which African Americans or Hispanics constitute majorities. This has the effect of concentrating enough minority citizens to elect one of their own, and at the same time, it takes these (usually Democratic) voters out of the pool of voters in other districts, thus making it easier for nonminority districts to be won by Republicans.[16] The boundaries for the First and Twelfth Districts of North Carolina, for instance, were redrawn after the 1990 census to consolidate the state's African American population. The Twelfth District was particularly oddly shaped, snaking for over 160 miles along a narrow stretch of Interstate 85 (see Figure 7.2). The gerrymandering accomplished its purpose: two African Americans—the first since 1889—were elected to represent North Carolina in Congress in 1992.[17]

racial gerrymandering redistricting to enhance or reduce the chances that a racial or ethnic group will elect members to the legislature

Racial gerrymandering, however, remains highly controversial. While politicians and racial and ethnic group leaders continue to jockey for the best district boundaries for their own interests, the courts struggle to find a "fair" set of rules for drawing district lines. In recent cases the Supreme Court declared that race cannot be the predominant factor in drawing congressional districts. It can be taken into account, but so must other factors, such as neighborhood and community preservation. Since, as we discussed in Chapter 6, race is a suspect classification, it is subject to *strict scrutiny* whenever the law uses it to treat citizens differently, and the law must fulfill a compelling state purpose whether it penalizes them or benefits them.[18] After holding an earlier effort unconstitutional, the Court allowed a later redrawing of the North Carolina district to stand, arguing that where black voters are mostly Democrats, disentangling race from politics can be difficult, and that race can be a legitimate concern in redistricting as long as it is not the "dominant and controlling" consideration.[19]

DECIDING TO RUN

Imagine that your interest in politics is piqued as a result of your American politics class. You decide the representative from your district is out of touch with the people, too wrapped up in Washington-centered politics, and you start thinking about run-

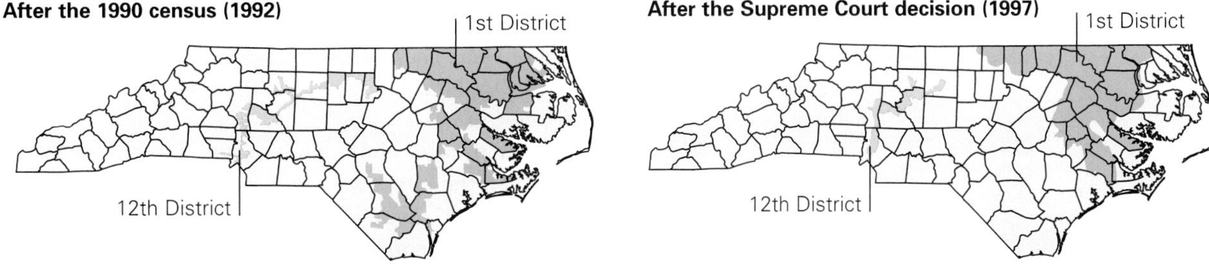

FIGURE 7.2 **Gerrymandering in the 1990s**

The First and Twelfth Districts of North Carolina were redrawn in 1992 (based on the 1990 census) to consolidate African American communities. The Supreme Court invalidated the gerrymandered districts, and they were redrawn in 1997.

ning for office. What sorts of things should you consider? What would you have to do to win? Even if you never contemplate a life in Washington politics, you will understand much more about how Congress works if you put yourself, temporarily, in the shoes of those who do.

Who Can Run? The formal qualifications for Congress are not difficult to meet. In addition to the age and citizenship requirements listed in Table 7.1, the Constitution requires that you live in the state you want to represent, although state laws vary on how long or when you have to have lived there. In three recent high-profile races, candidates who had been living somewhere else decided to move to a state in order to run for the Senate. Hillary Clinton won the New York seat in 2000, and Elizabeth Dole won in North Carolina in 2002. Two years later, Alan Keyes staged an unsuccessful run in Illinois. Custom also dictates that if you are running for the House, you live in the district you want to represent. There are no educational requirements for Congress. Although, as we will see, many members of Congress are lawyers, you certainly do not need to be one. In fact, you don't even need to have graduated from college or high school. In many ways, the qualifications for Congress are lighter than for most jobs you might apply for when you graduate, but you do have to be prepared to expose yourself to the critical scrutiny of your prospective constituents—not a pleasant prospect if you value your privacy!

Why Would Anyone Want This Job? Perhaps you want to run for Congress because you want to serve your country. Many people run from a sense of duty to country or to party, or from a wish to realize certain ideals. Although the institution of Congress sometimes makes it difficult by throwing conflicting incentives and temptations in their way, many, if not most, members of Congress are there because they have the best interests of their constituents and the nation at heart, and because they are fighting hard to make policy that reflects what they think is best. If you are contemplating a run for Congress these days, you are increasingly likely to be a strong ideologue—a conservative Republican or a liberal Democrat who wants to run from a sense of personal conviction and commitment to enact policy that represents your values. As an ideologically motivated candidate, you would enjoy all the benefits of strong support from your party and from concerned interest groups that can give you an advantage as you run against a more moderate opponent.

But your wish to run for Congress may also be enhanced by the fact that it is a very attractive job in its own right. First, there is all the fun of being in Washington, living a life that is undeniably exciting and powerful. The salary, $162,100 in 2005, puts representatives and senators among the top wage earners in the nation, and the "perks" of office are rather nice as well. These include generous travel allowances, ample staff, franking privileges, free parking at Reagan National Airport, health and life insurance, and a substantial pension.[20]

Not only is this a nice benefits package, but many of the benefits have the added advantage of helping you keep the job you worked so hard to get. Franking privileges, videotaping services, and trips home were all designed by members of Congress to help themselves continue to be members of Congress—all at taxpayer expense.

Along with the benefits and salary comes a certain amount of power and recognition. As a member of Congress you will be among the very important people (VIPs) of your community. You will get a title ("The Honorable So-and-So") and will be asked to speak at all sorts of gatherings, from high school graduations to ribbon-cutting ceremonies and Rotary Club meetings. You could build a power base through service to your district or state and try to hold on to your seat as long as possible, or you could use your position and its resources as a jumping-off point for even higher office.

Offsetting these enviable aspects of serving in Congress are the facts that the work is awfully hard and the job security nonexistent. To do the job successfully, you will put in long hours, practice diplomacy, and spend a lot of time away from home and family. Then, no matter how hard you work, you are sure to face an opponent in the next election who claims you did not do enough and declares that it's "time for a change." So you have to work all the harder, raise more money, and be even more popular than you were to begin with, just to keep your job.

Also, despite the seemingly high salary, the job of being a member of Congress is expensive. Most members have to maintain two households, one in Washington and one at home. Many find it hard to manage on their congressional salaries.[21] It is also hard on families, who must either divide their time between two homes or live without one parent for part of the year. Finally, more and more members claim that the level of conflict in Congress is so high, and the interest group pressure and fundraising needs so intense, that "the job just isn't any fun any more."[22]

How Can I Win? To have an outside chance of winning, nonincumbent candidates for Congress must have more than just a strong commitment to public service or a cause they dearly believe in: they also need political and financial assets. The key political asset for a potential candidate is experience, including working for other candidates, serving as a precinct chair, or holding an office in the county party organization. Even more helpful is experience in elective office. Those without such experience are called political amateurs and are considered "low-quality" candidates for Congress because they almost never win—unless they happen to be famous sports stars, television personalities, or wealthy businesspeople who have personal resources that can help them beat the odds.[23] Candidates with political experience—especially those who have held elective office—are considered "high-quality" candidates, not because they are superior people but because their political connections, visibility among voters, and knowledge of campaigns give them a much better chance of winning when they run for Congress.

Candidates with such political assets need to be careful not to squander them. They do not want to use up favors and political credibility in a losing effort, especially if they have to give up something valuable, like money or an office they currently hold, in order to run. **Strategic politicians** act rationally and carefully in deciding when to run and what office to run for. Any potential candidate approaching an election strategically will answer at least four questions. As a strategic candidate yourself, consider these questions:

strategic politicians office-seekers who base the decision to run on a rational calculation that they will be successful

1. *Is this the right district or state for me?* People want to vote for and be represented by people like themselves, so determine whether you and the district are compatible. Liberals do not do well in conservative parts of the South, African Americans have great difficulty getting elected in predominantly white districts, Republicans have a hard time in areas that are mostly Democratic, and so forth.

2. *What is the strategic situation in the district?* The strategic situation is largely governed by the **incumbency advantage**, which refers to the edge in visibility, experience, organization, and fundraising ability possessed by the incumbents, the

incumbency advantage the electoral edge afforded to those already in office

Profiles in Citizenship

Russ Feingold

The conference room in Senator Russ Feingold's Middleton, Wisconsin, office is papered with posters showing his listening sessions—one for every year he's been in office. Seventy-two town meetings a year, that's one per county, times thirteen years in office, that's more than 900 so far. And boy, is he proud of that. He made a campaign promise when he first ran for the Senate that he would make the visits to keep in touch with his constituents, about which one journalist said, "What a stupid pledge. He'll never be able to do it." That reporter has since had to eat his words because if there is one thing you can say about Russ Feingold, he believes in keeping his promises.

"I'm not afraid of people being mad at me in Washington, or any of that, because what matters to me is that people think I'm doing a good job."

Leaning back in his chair, relaxed and casual in a green golf shirt, Feingold explains how it came about. "[T]he reason I'm doing all these [sessions] is that people kept saying to me, when I was running and nobody really knew who I was, 'hey you seem like a nice guy but we know how this works. You're going to get elected, you go out there and we never see you again.' And I thought, 'OK, how can I break that image? How can I change peoples' feeling about their representative by doing something that will guarantee them access?' So I made this pledge. Kind of a crazy pledge but everybody in this state knows that in their county every year, they can come talk to me, they can say whatever they want to me, in their own home county without an appointment, without making a campaign contribution."

Compared to most of us, whose senators are protected by barricades of staff and protocol, Feingold's constituents have amazing access. He has clearly given a lot of thought to what it means to be a representative, and says it this way: "I work for the people of Wisconsin. And they're my boss. They've elected me to listen to them and to try to agree with them and help them with their views if I can justify them as being a good thing for Wisconsin and America. And they expect me to lead."

That clarity about what his job is and who he answers to has given Feingold the courage to take some strong, unconventional but principled stands. One of course, is the pledge on the listening tours. Another was the cosponsorship, with the Republican senator from Arizona, John McCain, of the campaign finance legislation that was enacted in 2002. Another was the refusal to accept any soft money from his party in his reelection campaign in 1998—an election he almost lost and in which the money he turned down would have come in mighty handy. Then there was the PATRIOT ACT—in the frightening days after September 11, Feingold was the only senator to vote against it. And in the summer of 2005, he was the first senator to demand a timetable for finishing the war in Iraq.

Feingold has the courage to stand on his convictions because he believes his constituents trust him, counting on him to do his homework, to tell the truth, and to keep his promises, even where they might disagree

people who already hold the job. It can make them hard to defeat (see the box, "The 109th Congress"). Three possibilities exist:

a. An incumbent of your party already holds the seat. In this case, winning the nomination is a real long shot. From 1984 through 2004, only forty-seven incumbents lost in primary battles to determine a party's nominee, or about 1 percent of all those seeking reelection.[24]
b. An incumbent of the opposite party holds the seat. In this case, winning the primary to get your party's nomination will probably be easier, but the odds are against winning in the general election unless the incumbent has been weak-

with some of his views. "I'm not afraid of people being mad at me in Washington, or any of that, because what matters to me is that people think I'm doing a good job."

Feingold clearly relishes the job he is doing—not surprising since being in politics is what he's wanted to do since he was a kid. His lawyer dad was one of a handful of progressive Democrats in a county of Wisconsin Republicans, and fascinating people, stalwarts in the Progressive tradition, came through the family home, firing young Russ with a desire to share the excitement of politics. He can remember clearly being seven when John F. Kennedy became president, and determining that he, too, would like to be president one day (an ambition his family and childhood friends don't let him forget). Growing up in a turbulent, stimulating time—civil rights, the environment, the women's movement, Vietnam—helped shape his consciousness and propelled him into a life of public service. He's there because he believes deeply in the issues he works for and feels the weight of having to make the right calls in the troubled times we live in. But, push him a little, and he admits that it's a lot of fun as well. He says with a grin, "And of course, I like the excitement. I don't like to be bored and I'm not bored in this shop." Here's what else he has to say:

On living in interesting times:

But to me, to love history, to be involved as it's occurring is a very exciting thing. [A]s I studied great, frightening events in human history and what it means to be involved in foreign policy, what I didn't anticipate is that the most interesting times are also the most upsetting. And that those are really truly tragic times. And what 9/11 really made me realize [is] that the most exquisitely interesting questions are raised at a time when you're almost devastated by the difficulties that this country is going through. So, you know, some say it's Confucius, some say it's Scottish, but the sentiment "may you live in interesting times" is a curse.

On keeping the republic:

Obviously John F. Kennedy said it best in his inaugural address. And that greatly inspired all of us because he gave all of us a clean phrase. "Ask not what your country can do for you, ask what you can do for your country". . . . It's an invitation to pick something that you can do, that you'll enjoy, but that'll help this nation get through this difficult period and continue to be the great nation that it is. It's a wonderful feeling. It's part of feeling good about yourself. And I want young people to think of it that way. It's not just about doing your duty. It feels good to help this country move forward. It's good for your family, it's good for everybody around you, it's good for you. . . . I love that expression. In fact, when we were trying to stop this ridiculous attempt to take away the filibuster about the judges, that was the quote that was used. Because Thomas Jefferson said that the Senate was supposed to be the cooling saucer and that's what Franklin was talking about. It's a republic. It's not a direct democracy. It is a republic if you can keep it.

Source: Senator Feingold spoke with Christine Barbour and Gerald Wright on August 19, 2005.

ened by scandal, redistricting, or a challenge from within his party. Over 94 percent of incumbents running won in their general election contests from 1984 to 2004.

c. The incumbent is not running. This is an "open seat," your best chance for success. However, because others know this as well, both the primary and the general elections are likely to be hard fought by high-quality candidates.

3. *Do I have access to the funds necessary to run a vigorous campaign?* Modern political campaigns are expensive, and campaigns run on a budget and a prayer are hardly

ever successful. Winning nonincumbents in 2004, for example, spent almost four-and-a-half times as much as nonincumbents who did not win, and even then nonincumbents could not keep up with the spending of incumbents.[25] Incumbents have access to a lot more political action committee (PAC) money and other contributions than do nonincumbents. (PACs are money-raising organizations devoted to a particular interest group, such as a labor union or trade association; they make donations to candidates that best represent their interests. We'll hear more about PACs in Chapter 13, on interest groups.) As a nonincumbent, you must raise on average about $685,000 to have even a chance of winning in the House.[26] Senate contests, with their much larger constituencies, cost much more.

4. *How are the national tides running?* Some years are good for Democrats, some for Republicans. These tides are a result of such things as presidential popularity, the state of the economy, and military engagements abroad. If it is a presidential election year, a popular presidential candidate of your party might sweep you to victory on his or her coattails. The **coattail effect**, less significant in recent days as people have begun to identify less closely with parties, refers to the added votes congressional candidates of the winning presidential party receive in a presidential election year as voters generalize their enthusiasm for the national candidate to the whole party.

coattail effect the added votes received by congressional candidates of a winning presidential party

While the strength of coattails might be declining, until 1998 there was no arguing with the phenomenon of the **midterm loss**. This is the striking regularity with which the presidential party loses seats in Congress in the midterm elections, also called "off-year" elections—those congressional elections that fall in between presidential election years. Before 1998 the presidential party lost seats in the House of Representatives in every midterm election of the twentieth century except in 1934. The 1994 election that brought Republicans to power in Congress for the first time in forty years (see Figure 7.3) was a striking example of the midterm loss: fifty-three seats changed from Democratic to Republican control, making it the largest change of this sort in fifty years.[27] In general, the presidential party losses depend on the president's standing with the public and the state of the economy; an unpopular president and a sour economy spell bad news for congressional candidates of the presidential party in an off-year election.[28]

midterm loss the tendency for the presidential party to lose congressional seats in off-year elections

In 1998 and again in 2002, however, unusual circumstances not only eliminated the midterm loss but also led the president's party to pick up seats. In 1998 the economy was sound and President Clinton's popularity was relatively high. House Republican leaders were pursuing impeachment charges against Clinton despite opinion polls demonstrating that most Americans did not want Clinton removed. This sentiment came home to roost when Republicans lost five House seats in the midterm election and held even in the Senate. In 2002, President Bush's high popularity rating following the September 11, 2001, attacks remained strong, and he was able to keep the public focused on national security—an issue that Republicans have historically been seen as better able to handle than Democrats. The combination of beneficial redistricting after the 2000 election, a popular president's rigorous campaigning, and a favorable issue agenda allowed Republicans to pick up seats in both the House and the Senate.

The 109th Congress

Incumbents of both parties triumphed in the 2004 congressional election with 25 of 26 (96 percent) of the Senate incumbents who ran keeping their seats and 394 of 403 (98 percent) of the House incumbents who ran keeping theirs. Nevertheless, Republicans solidified their majorities in both houses of Congress, picking up three seats in the House and four in the Senate. Although slight, these gains were dramatic because Republicans defeated the Democratic Senate leader Tom Daschle, D-S.D., and picked up five open Senate seats previously held by Democrats. Republicans ended up with a 55–44 advantage over Democrats in the Senate (there is one independent). In the House, the Texas redistricting meant that Republicans added seats and headed into the 109th Congress with a 232–202 advantage (again with one independent), despite having lost ground to Democrats in House elections outside of Texas.

Among the new faces in Congress were more minorities. Three new African American members were elected to the House, and Democrat Barack Obama won the Senate race in Illinois (against another African American, Alan Keyes) to become the only black member of that house. The Senate also added two Hispanics (one from each party), and the House added one Hispanic member. Bobby Jindal, R-La., became only the second Asian Indian American in history to serve in Congress.

Following the defeat of their Senate leader, Democrats chose Harry Reid, D-Nev., as the minority leader. Senator Bill Frist, R-Tenn., remained the Republican's choice as the majority leader. On the House side of Capitol Hill, party leadership remained as it was under the 108th Congress. Speaker of the House Dennis Hastert, R-Ill., and House majority leader Tom DeLay, R-Texas, led the Republicans in the 109th, and Nancy Pelosi, D-Calif., remained the Democratic House minority leader. After crafting the Texas strategy that benefited Republicans, DeLay remained popular with most Republicans and was widely considered to be the most powerful person on the Hill, despite the scandals that plagued him.

Because conservative Republicans replaced defeated or retiring moderate Democrats in the 2004 elections, both parties have become more ideologically polarized and internally loyal. Along with President Bush's reelection, the greater Republican congressional majorities should allow for sturdier footing for the Republicans' agenda in the 109th Congress. Thus far, Republicans have taken dramatic action on ideological issues such as toughening up bankruptcy laws, forcing the federal courts to consider whether a feeding tube could be removed from the brain-damaged Terri Schiavo (see Chapter 5), and, in the Senate, weighing the so-called "nuclear option," which would eliminate the filibuster for voting on judicial nominees. Democrats, in turn, have unified against President Bush's Social Security reform and have remained uniformly opposed to many Bush court nominees. Some Republican moderates have balked at elements of their party's more conservative agenda, making them heavily courted by both sides.

WHO GETS ELECTED?

The founders intended that the House of Representatives, which was elected directly by the people, would be the "people's house," reflecting the opinions and interests of the mass of American citizenry. The Senate was to be a more elite institution, composed of older men of virtue, education, and property like the founders themselves, whom they believed would have the wisdom to balance the impulses of the popularly elected House. In a way, the division of representational duties between the House and the Senate reflects the distinction between the dual tasks of constituent representation on the one hand and national lawmaking on the other that we have said forms the central dilemma for legislators today.

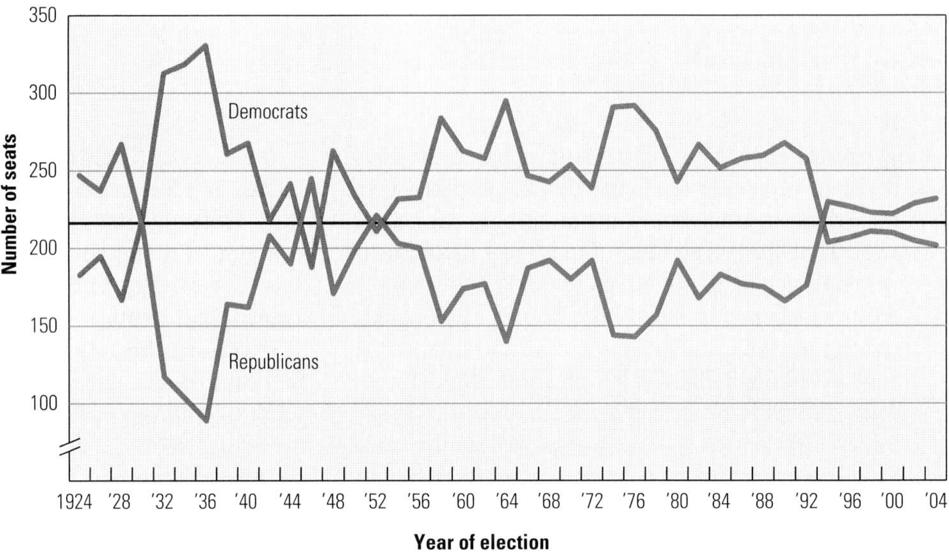

FIGURE 7.3
Party Control in Congress, 1925–2005

After a long period of uninterrupted dominance by the Democratic Party, Republicans have controlled the House of Representatives for over a decade since the "Republican Revolution" of 1994. The small Republican edge in seats increased in both the 2002 and 2004 elections, but the historically small margin ensures intense partisan struggle for the 2006 election and beyond.

But today we no longer see the responsibility of making national policy as the sole province of the Senate, nor do we believe that responding to public opinion, interests, and demands is a lower order of representation belonging just to the House. In fact, our expectations about the House and the Senate have changed dramatically since the days of the founding. Most of us have more trust in the people and—as we saw at the outset of this chapter—considerably less regard for politicians, even those with education and property. In this section we look at what kind of legislature the people choose.

descriptive representation the idea that an elected body should mirror demographically the population it represents

The first question we can ask is whether Congress measures up to the definition of what we call **descriptive representation**, in which the legislature is expected to mirror the demographics of those it represents. Founder and president John Adams said a representative assembly "should be in miniature an exact portrait of the people at large. It should think, feel, reason, and act like them."[29] In this regard, Congress fails quite miserably. Congress today, almost as much as the 1787 Constitutional Convention in Philadelphia, is dominated by relatively well-educated, well-to-do white males. The poor, the less educated, women, and minorities are not represented proportionately to their numbers in the population, although there are several trends in the direction of a more demographically representative Congress. (See "*Who Are We?* Our Representatives in Congress.")

Occupations Americans work in many kinds of jobs. Only a relatively few have professional careers; far more are skilled and semiskilled workers, service economy workers, sales representatives, managers, and clerical workers. Yet this large bulk of the population does not send many of its own to Congress. Rather, Congress is dominated by lawyers and businesspeople (see Table 7.2). Forty-five percent of members of the 109th Congress are lawyers, although this proportion is down considerably from the turn of the last century and earlier, when over 60 percent of the members were lawyers. Recent years have seen substantial increases in members with occupations in business, banking, and education.[30] While the occupations tend to split more or less evenly between the parties, the Republicans draw much more heavily from business and banking, and the Democrats are more likely to have come from public service careers.

Patience Rewarded
If at first you don't succeed . . . try, and try again. Rep. Shelia Jackson Lee, D-Texas, Sen. Barack Obama, D-Ill., Del. Eleanor Holmes Norton, D-D.C., and Rep. William Clay Jr., D-Mo., were among the members of the Congressional Black Caucus to meet with President George W. Bush in January 2005, after four years of chilly relations between the White House and the all-Democratic group. Members of the caucus had been trying for some time to present the needs of their constituents to the president.

Despite the prevalence of these conventional professions, recent elections have seen a growth in the number of members with more unusual backgrounds. In the 109th Congress, these included people with experience as a professional magician, a librarian, a vintner, a "jackeroo" (a cowboy on a sheep-cattle ranch), a race track blacksmith, a riverboat captain, a toll collector, a hotel bellhop, and a taxicab driver.[31]

Education and Income Given what we have said so far, you can guess that Congress is also highly unrepresentative in terms of education and income. In the adult population at large, 26.7 percent graduated from college and only 8.9 percent have advanced degrees. In contrast, all but a handful of Congress's 535 members have a college degree, and three-quarters have graduate degrees. Their income is well above the average American's income as well. Many House members—and an even greater percentage of senators—are millionaires.[32]

By these standards, Congress is an educational, occupational, and income elite. Those lower in the socioeconomic ranks do not have people like themselves in Washington working for them. A hard question to answer is whether it matters. Who can do a better job of representing, say, a working-class man who did not finish high school: people like himself, or those with the education and position to work in the halls of Congress on his behalf? We get hints of an answer to this tricky question when we look at the representation of women and minorities in Congress.

Race and Gender Over the long haul, women and minorities have not been well represented in Congress (as indicated in "*Who Are We?* Our Representatives in Congress"). Congress, however, is more representative today than it has been through most of our history. Until the civil rights movement in the 1960s, there were hardly any blacks or Hispanics in the House. Women seemed to have fared somewhat better, partly because of the once-common practice of appointing (and sometimes then electing) a congressman's widow to office when the member died. This tactic was

Who Are We?

Our Representatives in Congress

The 109th Congress is the most diverse yet. A record number of women serve in both houses from both parties, and there are more Hispanics and African Americans in both chambers than ever before. Despite these advances, both chambers remain predominantly male and almost entirely white. The Senate has fourteen women, one African American, and two Hispanics, but this still means that 83 percent of the institution's members remain white males. Is the underrepresentation of women and minorities in Congress something that Americans should be concerned about? Should a legislature look like the people it represents?

Race and Gender in Congress Over Time

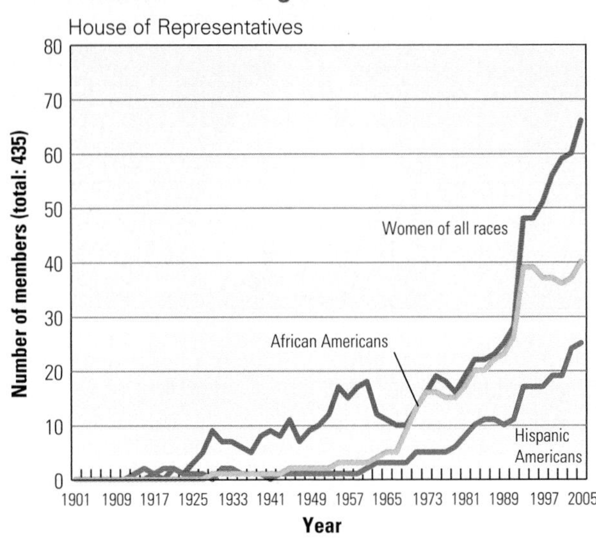

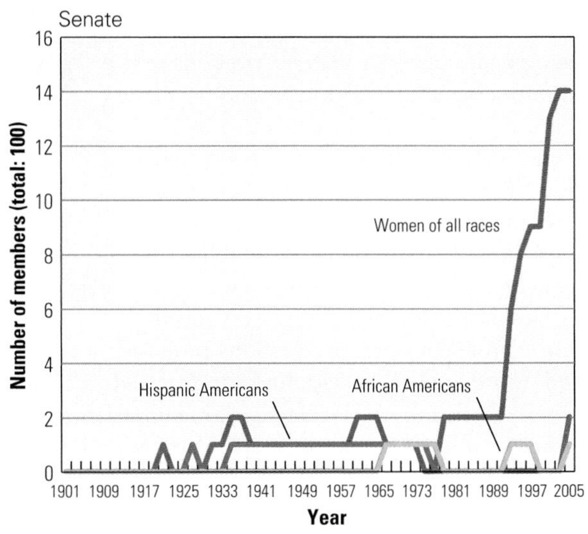

Source: Norman J. Ornstein, Thomas E. Mann, and Michael J. Malbin, *Vital Statistics on Congress, 2001–2002* (Washington, D.C.: AEI Press, 2002), 53–55; Mildred L. Amer, "Membership of the 108th Congress: A Profile," *Congressional Research Service*, October 25, 2004; Mildred L. Amer, "Membership of the 109th Congress: A Profile," *Congressional Research Service*, December 20, 2004.

thought to minimize intraparty battles for the appointment. Not until the 1970s did female candidates begin to be elected and reelected on their own in significant numbers.

In the 1990s, representation of all three groups, especially blacks and women, began to improve. The reasons, however, are quite different. Women have been coming into their own as candidates, a natural extension of their progress in education and the workplace. Women's political status has also been reinforced by the growing salience of issues that are of particular concern to them, from abortion to family leave policy to sexual harassment. For example, in 1991, when Anita Hill came forward to charge Supreme Court nominee Clarence Thomas with sexual harassment and was asked to testify at the televised hearings, women across the country were appalled at the seeming insensitivity of the all-male Senate Judiciary Committee. In the following 1992 congressional election, women were phenomenally successful. In what has been dubbed the "Year of the Woman," women increased their representation in the House by two-thirds (from twenty-eight to forty-seven seats) and tripled their representation in the Senate (from two to six). Each election since has seen the addition of at least one new female senator, and they have come from both

Race and Gender in the 109th Congress and in the U.S. Public

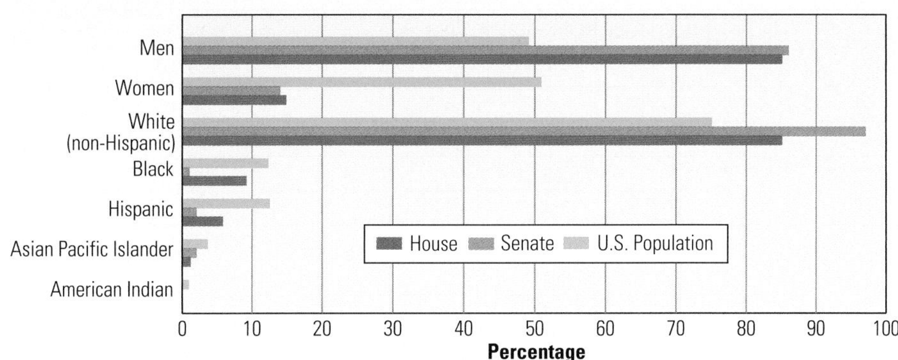

Note: Percentages may not add up to 100 because some racial/ethnic categories do not have representation in Congress, and both the public and members of Congress were allowed to identify with more than one racial/ethnic group.

Source: Mildred L. Amer, "Membership of the 109th Congress: A Profile," *Congressional Research Service*, December 20, 2004; U.S. Census Bureau, "Overview of Race and Hispanic Origin, 2000," Census Brief (Washington, D.C.: U.S. Census Bureau, 2001), 3, Web version; "Portrait of the U.S. Population," in *2005 New York Times Almanac* (New York: Penguin Group, 2005), 264.

Education: Congress and the Public: Degrees held by members of the 109th Congress compared to the U.S. public

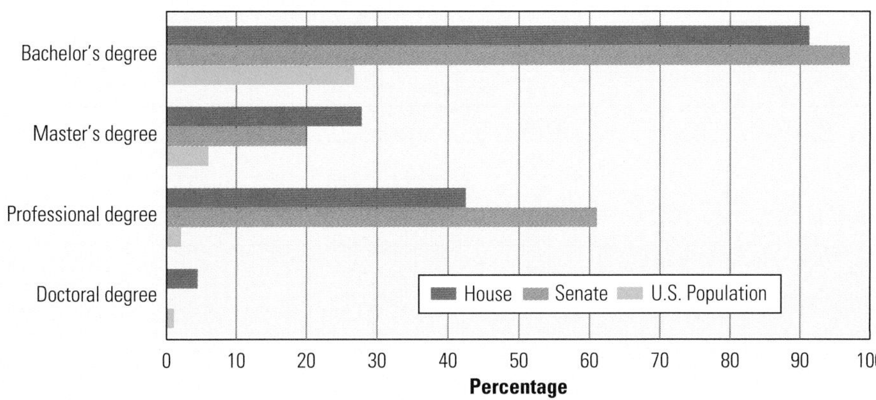

Source: Mildred L. Amer, "Membership of the 109th Congress: A Profile," *Congressional Research Service*, December 20, 2004; Kurt Bauman and Nikki Graf, *Educational Attainment: Census 2000 Brief* (Washington, D.C.: U.S. Census Bureau, August 2003), Figure 2, Web version.

parties (nine Democrats and five Republicans). The House has had a similar increase.

The pattern of black representation showed steady increases during the 1970s and 1980s, followed by a comparatively large jump in the 1990s with the advent of racial gerrymandering. The constitutionality of racially based districting will depend on future Supreme Court rulings.[33] However, evidence that whites are increasingly likely to vote for African American candidates (indicated by the broad-based support that Illinois senator Barack Obama received in his 2004 election) may make the constitutionality of majority-minority districts less crucial to their electoral fortunes.

Hispanics have been even more underrepresented in Congress than have blacks because Hispanic populations do not tend to be as solidly concentrated as African Americans, they do not vote as consistently for a single party, and many do not vote at all. Underrepresentation of this group may be poised to change, however. Because the Hispanic population is growing so rapidly in America, both parties have pushed for Hispanics to run for office and have also worked hard to mobilize Hispanics to vote.

Does representation of these traditionally underrepresented groups matter? In the case of women, the answer is yes. Congress has begun to deal with issues that previously

TABLE 7.2 **Prior Occupations of Members of the 109th Congress (2005–2006)**

	HOUSE OF REPRESENTATIVES	SENATE
Acting/entertainment or artistic/creative	5	0
Aeronautics	2	0
Agriculture	29	5
Business	205	40
Clergy	3	0
Education	91	13
Engineering	4	1
Healthcare	6	0
Homemaker/domestic	4	0
Journalism	11	7
Labor (blue collar or skilled)	12	3
Law	178	64
Law enforcement	9	1
Medicine	16	4
Military	3	1
Professional sports	2	1
Public service/politics	209	45
Real estate	39	3
Science	6	0
Secretarial/clerical	4	0
Miscellaneous	3	0

Source: Gregory L. Giroux, "A Touch of Gray on Capitol Hill," *CQ Weekly,* January 31, 2005, 241.

never made it onto the congressional agenda. The picture is less clear for Hispanics, since their interests are diverse, or for African Americans in Congress. Although African Americans, organized as the Congressional Black Caucus, had been quite influential on some issues when the Democrats had majority control of Congress, they've lost a good deal of their political muscle since the Republicans took control.[34]

WHO, WHAT, HOW Congressional elections are the meeting ground for citizens and their representatives, where each brings their own goals and their own stakes in the process. Citizens want a congressperson who will take care of local affairs, mind the nation's business, and represent them generally on political and social issues. The rules of local representation and electoral politics, however, mean that citizens are more likely to get someone who takes care of local interests and affairs at the expense of national interests and general representation.

Members of Congress want election, and then reelection. Because they make many of the rules that control electoral politics, the rules often favor those already in office. While many members may wish to turn to national affairs, to do what is best for the nation regardless of their local district or state, they have to return continually to the local issues that get them elected.

HOW CONGRESS WORKS: ORGANIZATION

Despite of the imperatives of reelection and the demands of constituency service, the primary business of Congress is making laws. Lawmaking is influenced a great deal by the organization of Congress—that is, the rules of the institution that determine where the power is and who can exercise it. In this section we describe how Congress organizes itself and how this structure is influenced by members' goals.

THE CENTRAL ROLE OF PARTY

Political parties are central to how Congress functions for several reasons. First, Congress is organized along party lines. In each chamber, the party with the most members—the **majority party**—decides the rules for each chamber and it gets the top leadership posts, such as the Speaker of the House, the majority leader in the Senate, and the chairmanships of all the committees and subcommittees.

majority party the party with the most seats in a house of Congress

Party is also important in Congress because it is the mechanism for members' advancement. Because all positions are determined by the parties, members have to advance within their party to achieve positions of power in the House or the Senate, whether as a committee chair or in the party leadership.

Finally, party control of Congress matters because the parties stand for very different things. Across a wide range of issues, Democrats embrace more liberal policies, whereas Republicans advocate more conservative ones. Figure 7.4 shows that on issues from abortion to raising the minimum wage to affirmative action programs, Democratic House candidates are more liberal and Republican House candidates are much

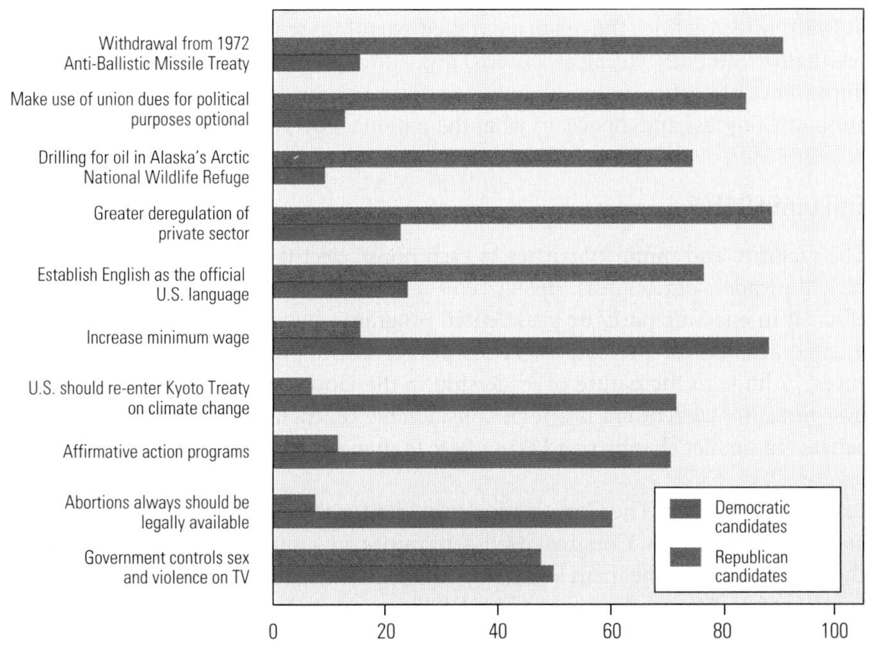

FIGURE 7.4
Party Differences Among House Candidates on Policy Stances, 2002

Source: Robert S. Erikson and Gerald C. Wright, "Voters, Candidates, and Issues in Congressional Elections," in *Congress Reconsidered,* 8th ed., ed. Lawrence C. Dodd and Bruce I. Oppenheimer (Washington, D.C.: CQ Press, 2005), 85.

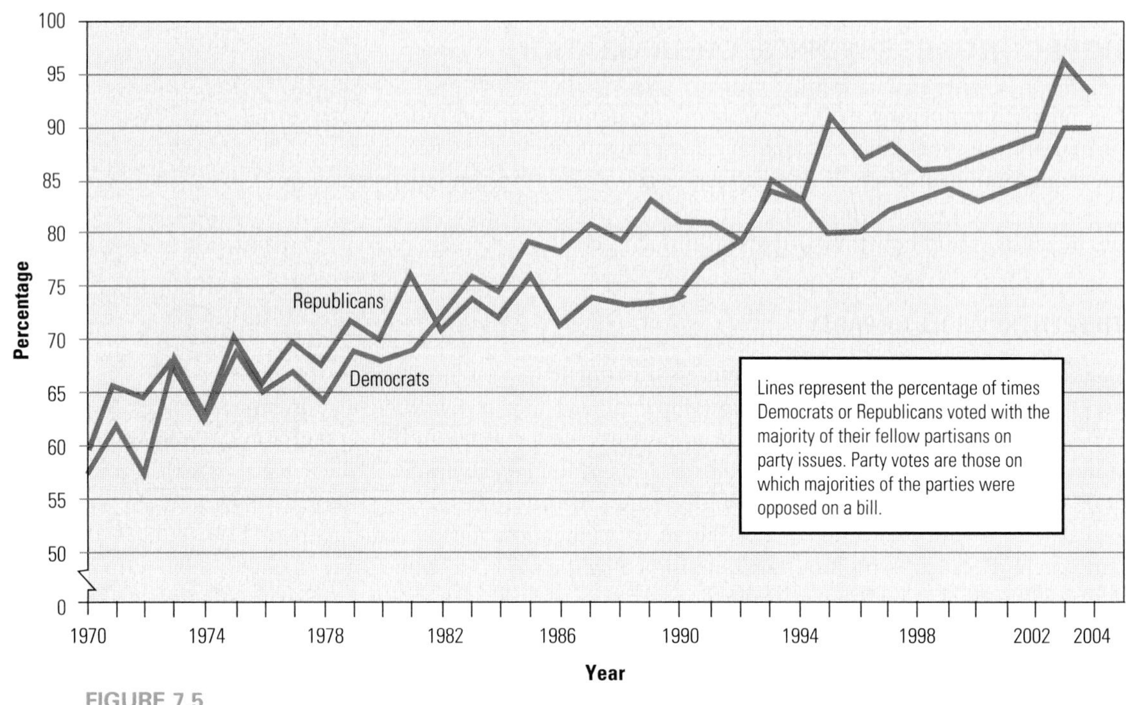

FIGURE 7.5
Party Voting in Congress, 1970–2004

Source: Roger H. Davison and Walter J. Oleszek, *Congress and Its Members,* 10th ed. (Washington, D.C.: CQ Press, 2006), Figure 9-2.

more conservative. Upon winning office, these candidates vote very differently from each other. As Figure 7.5 illustrates, Democratic members of the House are increasingly likely to vote with the majority of their party and are opposed by Republican representatives similarly voting as a bloc. Thus, although Americans like to downplay the importance of parties in their own lives, political parties are fundamental to the operation of Congress and, hence, to what the national government does.

THE LEADERSHIP

The majority and minority parties in each house elect their own leaders, who are, in turn, the leaders of Congress. Strong, centralized leadership allows Congress to be more efficient in enacting party or presidential programs, but it gives less independence to members to take care of their own constituencies or to pursue their own policy preferences.[35] Although the nature of leadership in the House of Representatives has varied over time, the current era is one of considerable centralization of power. Because the Senate is a smaller chamber and thus easier to manage, its power is more decentralized.

Leadership Structure The Constitution provides for the election of some specific congressional officers, but Congress itself determines how much power the leaders of each chamber will have. The main leadership offices in the House of Representatives are the Speaker of the House, the majority leader, the minority leader, and the whips (see Figure 7.6). The real political choice about who the party leader should be occurs within the party groupings in each chamber. The **Speaker of the House** is elected by the ma-

Speaker of the House the leader of the majority party who serves as the presiding officer of the House of Representatives

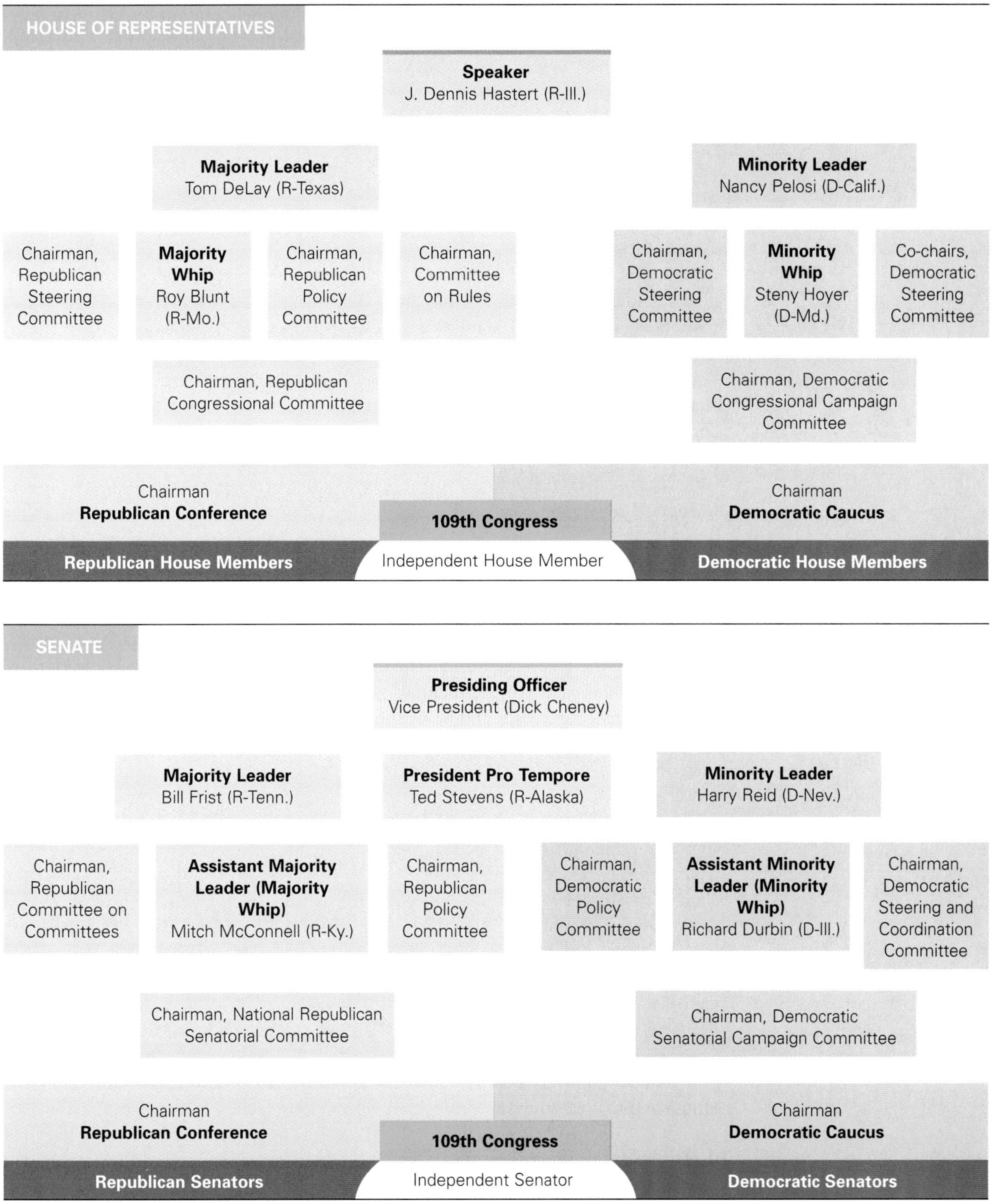

HOUSE OF REPRESENTATIVES

Speaker
J. Dennis Hastert (R-Ill.)

Majority Leader
Tom DeLay (R-Texas)

Chairman, Republican Steering Committee

Majority Whip
Roy Blunt (R-Mo.)

Chairman, Republican Policy Committee

Chairman, Committee on Rules

Chairman, Republican Congressional Committee

Minority Leader
Nancy Pelosi (D-Calif.)

Chairman, Democratic Steering Committee

Minority Whip
Steny Hoyer (D-Md.)

Co-chairs, Democratic Steering Committee

Chairman, Democratic Congressional Campaign Committee

Chairman
Republican Conference

109th Congress

Chairman
Democratic Caucus

Republican House Members

Independent House Member

Democratic House Members

SENATE

Presiding Officer
Vice President (Dick Cheney)

Majority Leader
Bill Frist (R-Tenn.)

President Pro Tempore
Ted Stevens (R-Alaska)

Minority Leader
Harry Reid (D-Nev.)

Chairman, Republican Committee on Committees

Assistant Majority Leader (Majority Whip)
Mitch McConnell (R-Ky.)

Chairman, Republican Policy Committee

Chairman, Democratic Policy Committee

Assistant Minority Leader (Minority Whip)
Richard Durbin (D-Ill.)

Chairman, Democratic Steering and Coordination Committee

Chairman, National Republican Senatorial Committee

Chairman, Democratic Senatorial Campaign Committee

Chairman
Republican Conference

109th Congress

Chairman
Democratic Caucus

Republican Senators

Independent Senator

Democratic Senators

FIGURE 7.6
Structure of the House and Senate Leadership in the 109th Congress

jority party and, as the person who presides over floor deliberations, is the most powerful House member. The House majority leader, second in command, is given wide-ranging responsibilities to assist the Speaker.

The leadership organization in the Senate is similar but not as elaborate. The presiding officer of the Senate is the vice president of the United States, who can cast a tie-breaking vote when necessary but otherwise does not vote. When the vice president is not present, which is almost always the case, the president pro tempore of the Senate officially presides, although the role is almost always performed by a junior senator. Because of the Senate's much freer rules for deliberation on the floor, the presiding officer has less power than in the House, where debate is generally tightly controlled. The locus of real leadership in the Senate is the majority leader and the minority leader. Each is advised by party committees on both policy and personnel matters, such as committee appointments.

In both chambers, Democratic and Republican leaders are assisted by party whips. (The term *whip* comes from an old English hunting expression; the "whipper in" was charged with keeping the dogs together in pursuit of the fox.) Elected by party members, whips find out how people intend to vote so that on important party bills, the leaders can adjust the legislation, negotiate acceptable amendments, or employ favors (or, occasionally, threats) to line up support. Whips work to persuade party members to support the party on key bills, and they are active in making sure favorable members are available to vote when needed.

Leadership Powers Leaders can exercise only the powers that their party members give them. From the members' standpoint, the advantage of a strong leader is that he or she can move legislation along, get the party program passed, do favors for members, and improve the party's standing. The disadvantage is that a strong party leader can pursue national party (or presidential) goals at the expense of members' pet projects and constituency interests, and he or she can withhold favors.

seniority system the accumulation of power and authority in conjunction with the length of time spent in office

The power of the Speaker of the House has changed dramatically over time. At the turn of the century, the strong "boss rule" of Speaker Joe Cannon greatly centralized power in the House. Members rebelled at this and moved to the **seniority system**, which vested great power in committee chairs instead of the Speaker. Power followed seniority, or length of service on a committee, so that once a person assumed the chairmanship of a committee, business was run very much at the pleasure of the chair.[36] The seniority system itself was reformed in the 1970s by a movement that weakened the grip of chairs and gave some power back to the Speaker and the party caucuses, as well as to members of the committees, and especially subcommittees.[37]

The Speaker's powers were further enhanced with the Republican congressional victories in the 1994 election, when Rep. Newt Gingrich, R-Ga., became Speaker (see the *Profiles in Citizenship* in Chapter 3). Gingrich quickly became the most powerful Speaker since the era of boss rule. His House Republican colleagues were willing to give him new powers because his leadership enabled them to take control of the House and to enact the well-publicized conservative agenda that they called the *Contract With America.*[38] Gingrich continued as the powerful Republican congressional spokesperson and leader until he resigned in the wake of the almost unprecedented reversal of the 1998 midterm loss.

Gingrich's replacement as Speaker, Dennis Hastert, R-Ill., does not have the power-grabbing, headline-making style of a Newt Gingrich, and often leaves the party spokesperson role to the very powerful House majority leader, Tom DeLay, R-Texas.

Nevertheless, Hastert has become adept at wielding power effectively, skillfully keeping the Republican majority cohesive and using rules to advance his party's agenda.[39] If recent history is a guide and parties remain numerically close and as ideologically divided in the House, speakers will likely continue to utilize every rule they can to assure their party's agenda is fulfilled in the House.

The leaders of the Senate have never had as much formal authority as those in the House, and that remains true today. The traditions of the Senate, with its much smaller size, allow each senator to speak or to offer amendments when he or she wants. The highly individualistic Senate would not accept the kind of control that Speaker Gingrich achieved in the House. But though the Senate majority leader cannot control senators, he or she can influence the scheduling of legislation, a factor that can be crucial to a bill's success. The majority leader may even pull a bill from consideration, a convenient exercise of authority when defeat would embarrass the leadership.

The Treatment
As Senate majority leader in the 1950s, Lyndon B. Johnson was legendary for his ability to cajole, charm, bully, and—by all means necessary—persuade others to see things his way. Here, with Senator Theodore Francis Green, D-R.I., he leans in for the kill.

THE COMMITTEE SYSTEM

Meeting as full bodies, it would be impossible for the House and the Senate to consider and deliberate on all of the 10,000 bills and 100,000 nominations they receive every two years.[40] Hence, the work is broken up and handled by smaller groups called committees.

The Constitution says nothing about congressional committees; they are completely creatures of the chambers of Congress they serve. The committee system has developed to meet the needs of a growing nation as well as the evolving goals of members of Congress. Initially, congressional committees formed to consider specific issues and pieces of legislation; after they made their recommendations to the full body, they dispersed. As the nation grew, and with it the number of bills to be considered, this ad hoc system became unwieldy and Congress formed a system of more permanent committees. Longer service on a committee permitted members to develop expertise and specialization in a particular policy area, and thus bills could be considered more efficiently. Committees also provide members with a principal source of institutional power and the primary position from which they can influence national policy.

What Committees Do It is at the committee and, even more, the subcommittee stage that the nitty-gritty details of legislation are worked out. Committees and subcommittees do the hard work of considering alternatives and drafting legislation. Committees are the primary information gatherers for Congress. Through hearings, staff reports, and investigations, members gather information on policy alternatives and discover who will support different policy options. Thus committees act as the eyes, ears, and workhorses of Congress in considering, drafting, and redrafting proposed legislation.

Committees do more, however, than write laws. Committees also undertake **legislative oversight**; that is, they check to see that executive agencies are carrying out the laws as Congress intended them to. Committee members gather information about

legislative oversight a committee's investigation of government agencies to ensure they are acting as Congress intends agencies from the media, constituents, interest groups, staff, and special investigations (see the discussion of the Government Accountability Office, later in this chapter). A lot of what is learned in oversight is reflected in changes to the laws giving agencies their power and operating funds.

Members and the general public all strongly agree on the importance of congressional oversight; it is part of the "continuous watchfulness" that Congress mandated for itself in the Legislative Reorganization Act of 1946 and reiterated in its Legislative Reorganization Act of 1970. Nevertheless, oversight tends to be slighted in the congressional process. The reasons are not hard to find. Oversight takes a lot of time, and the rewards to individual members are less certain than from other activities like fundraising or grabbing a headline in the district with a new pork project. Consequently, oversight most often takes the form of "fire-alarm" oversight, in which some scandal or upsurge of public interest directs congressional attention to a problem in the bureaucracy rather than careful and systematic reviews of agencies' implementation of congressional policies.[41]

standing committees permanent committees responsible for legislation in particular policy areas

Types of Committees Congress has four types of committees: standing, select, joint, and conference. The vast majority of work is done by the **standing committees**. These are permanent committees, created by statute, that carry over from one session of Congress to the next. They review most pieces of legislation that are introduced to Congress. So powerful are the standing committees that they scrutinize, hold hearings on, amend, and, frequently, kill legislation before the full Congress ever gets the chance to discuss it.

The standing committees of the 109th Congress are listed in Table 7.3, and as their names indicate, most deal with issues in specific policy areas, such as agriculture, foreign relations, or justice. Each committee is typically divided into many subcommittees that focus on detailed areas of policy. There are twenty standing committees and ninety-seven subcommittees in the House. The Senate has sixteen committees and seventy subcommittees. Not surprisingly, committees are larger in the House, with membership rising to more than seventy on some committees, compared to fewer than thirty on the Senate committees. The size of the committees and the ratio of majority to minority party members on each are determined at the start of each Congress by the majority leadership in the House and by negotiations between the majority and minority leaders in the Senate. Standing committee membership is relatively stable as seniority on the committee is a major factor in gaining subcommittee or committee chairs; the chairs wield considerable power and are coveted positions.

House Rules Committee the committee that determines how and when debate on a bill will take place

The policy areas represented by the standing committees of the two houses roughly parallel each other, but the **House Rules Committee** exists only in the House of Representatives. (There is a Senate Rules and Administration Committee, but it does not have equivalent powers.) The House Rules Committee provides a "rule" for each bill that specifies when it will be debated, how long debate can last, how it can be amended, and so on. Because the House is so large, debate would quickly become chaotic without the organization and structure provided by the Rules Committee. Such structure is not neutral in its effects on legislation, however. Since the committees are controlled by the majority party in the House, and especially by the Speaker, the rule that structures a given debate will reflect the priorities of the majority party.

select committee a committee appointed to deal with an issue or problem not suited to a standing committee

When a problem before Congress does not fall into the jurisdiction of a standing committee, a **select committee** may be appointed. These committees are usually temporary and do not recommend legislation per se. They are used to gather information

TABLE 7.3 **Standing Committees in the 109th Congress**

House of Representatives	Senate
20 Standing Committees	*16 Standing Committees*
Agriculture	Agriculture, Nutrition, and Forestry
Appropriations	Appropriations
Armed Services	Armed Services
Budget	Banking, Housing, and Urban Affairs
Education and the Workforce	Budget
Energy and Commerce	Commerce, Science, and Transportation
Financial Services	Energy and Natural Resources
Government Reform	Environment and Public Works
Homeland Security	Finance
House Administration	Foreign Relations
International Relations	Health, Education, Labor, and Pensions
Judiciary	Homeland Security and Governmental Affairs
Resources	Judiciary
Rules	Rules and Administration
Science	Small Business and Entrepreneurship
Small Business	Veterans Affairs
Standards of Official Conduct	(*70 Subcommittees*)
Transportation and Infrastructure	
Veterans Affairs	
Ways and Means	
(*97 Subcommittees*)	

on specific issues, like the Select Committee on Homeland Security did after the September 11 terror attacks, or to conduct an investigation, as did the Senate Select Committee on Whitewater, which in 1995 investigated the allegations concerning President Clinton's financial dealings in Arkansas.

Joint committees are made up of members of both houses of Congress. While each house generally considers bills independently (making for a lot of duplication of effort and staff), in some areas they have coordinated activities to expedite consideration of legislation. The joint committees in the 109th Congress were on economics, taxation, and printing.

joint committees combined House-Senate committees formed to coordinate activities and expedite legislation in a certain area

Before a bill can become law, it must be passed by both houses of Congress in exactly the same form. But because the legislative process in each house often subjects bills to different pressures, they may be very different by the time they are debated and passed. **Conference committees** are temporary committees made up of members of both houses of Congress commissioned to resolve these differences, after which the bills go back to each house for a final vote. Members of the conference committees are appointed by the presiding officer of each chamber, who usually taps the senior members, especially the chair, of the committees that considered the bill. Most often the conferees are members of those committees.

conference committees temporary committees formed to reconcile differences in House and Senate versions of a bill

In the past, conference committees have tended to be small (five to ten members). In recent years, however, as Congress has tried to work within severe budget restrictions, it has taken to passing huge "megabills" that collect many proposals into one. Conference committees have expanded in turn, sometimes ballooning into gigantic affairs with many "subconferences."[42]

Getting on the Right Committees Getting on the right standing committee is vital for all members of Congress because so much of what members want to accomplish is realized through their work on these committees. Political scientist Richard Fenno identified three goals for members—reelection, lawmaking (also called policymaking), and influence in Congress—and argued that committee memberships are the principal means for achieving these goals.[43] Because members are concerned with reelection, they try to get on committees that deal with issues of concern to constituents. Examples of good matches include the Agriculture Committee for farm states' legislators and the Defense Committee for members with military bases or contractors in their districts.

Members who like to focus on national lawmaking might try to get assigned to committees like Commerce or Foreign Affairs, which have broad jurisdictions and often deal with weighty, high-profile concerns. The House Ways and Means Committee and the Senate Finance Committee, because they deal with taxation—a topic of interest to nearly everyone—are highly prized committee assignments.

When it comes to committee assignments that serve the third goal, achieving power within Congress, an excellent choice is the House Rules Committee. Because it plays the central "traffic cop" role we discussed earlier, its members are in a position to do a lot of favors for members whose bills have to go through Rules. Almost all senators have the opportunity to sit on one of the four most powerful Senate committees: Appropriations, Armed Services, Finance, and Foreign Relations.[44]

Decisions on who gets on what committee vary by party and chamber. Although occasionally the awarding of committee assignments has been used by the parties to reward those who support party positions, in general both the Democrats and the Republicans accommodate their members when they can, since the goal of both parties is to support their ranks and help them be successful.

Committee Chairs For much of the twentieth century, congressional power rested with the chairmen and chairwomen of the committees of Congress; their power was unquestioned under the seniority system. Today, seniority remains important, but chairs serve at the pleasure of their party caucuses and the party leadership. The committees, under this system, are expected to reflect more faithfully the preferences of the average party member rather than just those of the committee chair or current members.[45]

CONGRESSIONAL RESOURCES

For Congress to knowledgeably guide government lawmaking, it needs expertise and information. Members find, however, that alone they are no match for the enormous amount of information generated by the executive branch, on the one hand, or the sheer informational demands of the policy process—economic, social, military, and foreign affairs—on the other. The need for independent, expert information, along with the ever-present reelection imperative, has led to a big growth in what we call the congressional bureaucracy. Congress has over 26,000 employees, paid for by the federal government. This makes it by far the largest staffed legislature in the world. Figure 7.7 shows the tremendous growth over time in the number of people working for Congress.

Congressional Staff The vast majority of congressional staff—secretaries, computer personnel, clericals, and professionals—work for individual members or committees. Notice in Figure 7.7 that a disproportionate amount of the growth has been in per-

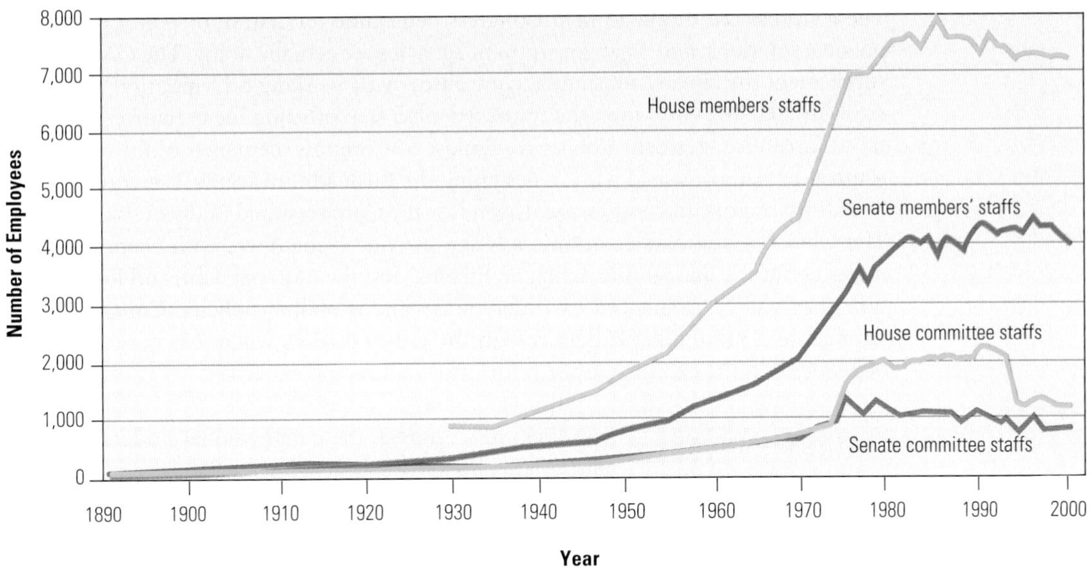

FIGURE 7.7
Growth in Congressional Staff, 1891–2001

Source: Norman J. Ornstein, Thomas E. Mann, and Michael J. Malbin, *Vital Statistics on Congress, 2001–2002* (Washington, D.C.: AEI Press), 126–128.

sonal staff. House members have an average staff of eighteen per member, while the Senate averages twice that, with the sizes of Senate staff varying with state population. Staff members can be assigned to either legislative work or constituency service, at the member's discretion; those doing primarily constituency work are usually located in the district or state, close to constituents, rather than in Washington.

The committees' staffs (about 2,200 in the House and 1,200 in the Senate) do much of the committee work, from honing ideas, suggesting policy options to members, scheduling hearings, and recruiting witnesses, to actually drafting legislation.[46] In most committees each party also has its own staff. Following the 1994 election, committee staffs were cut by one-third; however, members did not force any cuts in sizes of their personal staffs.

Congressional Bureaucracy Reflecting a reluctance dating from Vietnam and Watergate to be dependent on the executive branch for information, Congress has built its own research organizations and agencies to facilitate its work. Unlike personal or committee staffs, these are strictly nonpartisan, providing different kinds of expert advice and technical assistance. The Congressional Research Service (CRS), a unit of the Library of Congress, employs over eight hundred people to do research for members of Congress. For example, if Congress is considering a bill to relax air quality standards in factories, it can have the CRS determine what is known about the effects of air quality on worker health.

The Government Accountability Office (formerly the General Accounting Office but still known as the GAO), with its five thousand employees, audits the books of executive departments and conducts policy evaluation and analysis. It issues reports such as *Illegal Aliens: Extent of Welfare Benefits Received on Behalf of U.S. Citizen Children* and *Combating Terrorism: Efforts to Protect U.S. Forces in Turkey and the Middle East.*[47]

These studies are meant to help Congress determine the nature of policy problems, possible solutions, and what government agencies are actually doing. The GAO studies supplement the already substantial committee staffs working on legislation and oversight. In 2002 the GAO took the unprecedented step of suing the executive branch to try to force Vice President Cheney to disclose to Congress the names of the energy executives he had consulted with in designing the Bush administration's energy bill.

A third important congressional agency is the Congressional Budget Office (CBO). The CBO is Congress's economic adviser, providing members with economic estimates about the budget, the deficit or surplus, and the national debt, and forecasts of how they will be influenced by different tax and spending policies. Congress has a stronger and more independent role in the policy process when it is not completely dependent on the executive branch for information and expertise.

WHO, WHAT, HOW Members of Congress, the congressional leaders, and the parties are all vitally concerned with the rules of congressional organization. The members want autonomy to do their jobs and to respond to their constituents. But they are dependent on their leaders and thus on their parties for the committee assignments that enhance their job performance and help them gain expertise in areas that their constituents care about. Without party and leadership cooperation, the individual member of Congress, especially in the House where party control is stronger, is isolated and relatively powerless.

Congressional leaders want tight rules of organization so that they can control what their members do and say. Members of the House and Senate make their own organizational rules, which give the dominant party in each house power over the internal rules and, consequently, over the policies produced.

HOW CONGRESS WORKS: PROCESS AND POLITICS

The policies passed by Congress are a result of both external and internal forces. The external environment includes the problems that are important to citizens at any given time—sometimes the economy, sometimes foreign affairs, at other times national security or the federal deficit or the plight of the homeless and so forth. The policy preferences of the president loom large in this external environment as well. It is often said, with some exaggeration but a bit of truth, that "the president proposes, the Congress disposes" of important legislation. Parties, always important, have been increasing their influence in the policymaking arena, and organized interests play a significant role as well.

THE CONTEXT OF CONGRESSIONAL POLICYMAKING

Congress also has a distinct internal institutional environment that shapes the way it carries out its business. Three characteristics of this environment are especially important.

Separate Houses, Identical Bills First, the Constitution requires that almost all congressional policy has to be passed in identical form by both houses. This requirement, laid out by the founders in the Constitution, makes the policy process difficult because the two houses serve different constituencies and operate under different decision-making procedures. Interests that oppose a bill and lose in one chamber can often be successful at defeating a bill in the other chamber. The opposition only has to stop a bill in one place to win, but the proponents have to win in both. In Congress, it is much easier to play defense than offense.

Fragmentation The second overriding feature of the institutional environment of Congress as a policymaking institution is its fragmentation. As you read the next section on how a bill becomes a law, notice how legislation is broken into bits, each considered individually in committees. It is very difficult to coordinate what one bill does with those laws that are already on the books or with what another committee might be doing in a closely related area. Thus we do such seemingly nonsensical things as simultaneously subsidizing tobacco growers and antismoking campaigns. This fragmentation increases opportunities for constituencies, individual members, and well-organized groups to influence policy in those niches about which they really care. The process also makes it very hard for national policymakers—the president or the congressional leaders—who would like to take a large-scale, coordinated approach to our major policy problems.

Norms of Conduct The third critical feature of the institutional environment of Congress is the importance of **norms**, or informal rules that establish accepted ways of doing things. These are sometimes called "folkways" and are quickly learned by newcomers when they enter Congress. Norms include the idea that members should work hard, develop a specialization, treat other members with the utmost courtesy, reciprocate favors generally, and take pride in their chambers and in Congress. The purpose of congressional norms is to constrain conflict and personal animosity in an arena where disagreements are inevitable, but they also aid in getting business done. Although congressional norms continue to be important, they are less constraining on members today than they were in the 1950s and 1960s.[48] The current norms allow for more individualistic, media-oriented, and adversarial behavior than in the past.

norms informal rules that govern behavior in Congress

HOW A BILL BECOMES A LAW—SOME OF THE TIME

When we see something that seems unfair in business or in the workplace, when disaster strikes and causes much suffering, when workers go on strike and disrupt our lives—whenever a crisis occurs, we demand that government do something to solve the problem that we cannot solve on our own. This means government must have a policy, a set of laws, to deal with the problem. Because so many problems seem beyond the ability of individual citizens to solve, there is an almost infinite demand for new laws and policies, often with different groups demanding quite contradictory responses from the government.

This section briefly considers how demands for solutions become laws. We will consider two aspects of congressional policy here: (1) the agenda, or the source of ideas for new policies; and (2) the legislative process, or the steps a bill goes through to become law. Very few proposed policies, as it turns out, actually make it into law, and those that do have a difficult path to follow.

Setting the Agenda Before a law can be passed, it must be among the things that Congress thinks it ought to do. There is no official list of actions that Congress needs to

legislative agenda the slate of proposals and issues that representatives think it worthwhile to consider and act on

take, but when a bill is proposed, it must seem like a reasonable thing for members to turn their attention to—a problem that is possible, appropriate, and timely for them to try to solve with a new policy. That is, it must be on the **legislative agenda**. Potential new laws can get on Congress's agenda in several ways. First, because public attention is focused most closely on presidential elections and campaigns, new presidents are especially effective at setting the congressional agenda. Later in their terms, presidents also use their yearly State of the Union addresses to outline the legislative agenda they would like Congress to pursue. Because the media and the public pay attention to the president, Congress does too. This does not guarantee presidential success, but it means the president can usually get Congress to give serious attention to his major policy proposals. His proposals may be efforts to fulfill campaign promises, to pay political debts, or to realize ideological commitments. Partly because of all three, George W. Bush came into office determined to get Congress to pass a tax cut, which it did soon after his inauguration.

A second way an issue gets on the legislative agenda is when it is triggered by a well-publicized event, even if the problem it highlights is not a new one at all. For example, airport security, long a concern of politicians, leaped to the forefront of the agenda after September 11, and Congress quickly federalized the system. Although, arguably, such reforms would have done little to prevent the terrorist attacks, those attacks put the issue on the legislative agenda. The media are often key players in getting issues and problems onto the congressional agenda.

policy entrepreneurship practice of legislators becoming experts and taking leadership roles in specific policy areas

A third way an idea gets on the agenda is for some member or members to find it in their own interests, either political or ideological, to invest time and political resources in pushing the policy. Many members of Congress want to prove their legislative skills to their constituents, key supporters, the media, and fellow lawmakers. The search for the right issue to push at the right time is called **policy entrepreneurship**. Most members of Congress to greater or lesser degrees are policy entrepreneurs. Those with ambition, vision, and luck choose the issues that matter in our lives and that can bring them fame and respect. Arizona senator John McCain, in the aftermath of his own involvement in a campaign finance scandal, became a leading advocate of campaign finance reform, making it the centerpiece of his 2000 run for the Republican presidential nomination and finally shepherding the bill to victory in spring 2002. Policy entrepreneurship by members is important in setting the congressional policy agenda, and it can reap considerable political benefits for those associated with important initiatives.

Legislative Process: Beginning the Long Journey Bills, even those widely recognized as representing the president's legislative program, must be introduced by members of Congress. The formal introduction is done by putting a bill in the "hopper" (a wooden box) in the House, where it goes to the clerk of the House, or by giving it to the presiding officer in the Senate. The bill is then given a number (for example, HR932 in the House or S953 in the Senate) and begins the long journey that *might* result in its becoming law. Figure 7.8 shows the general route for a bill once it is introduced in either the House or the Senate, but the actual details can get messy, and there are exceptions (as Figure 7.9 shows). A bill introduced in the House goes first through the House and then on to the Senate, and vice versa. However, bills may be considered simultaneously in both houses.

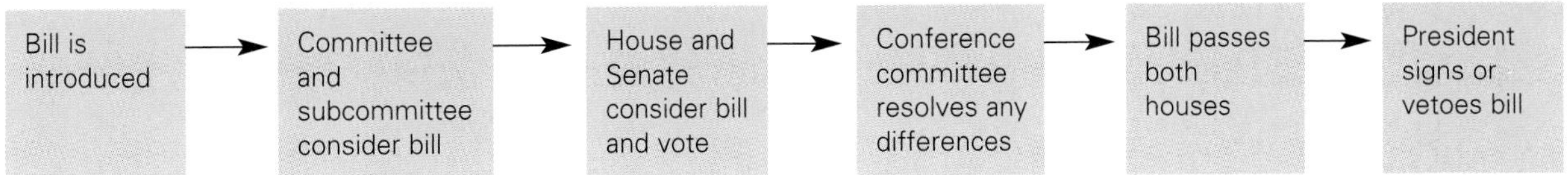

FIGURE 7.8
How a Bill Becomes Law: Short Version

Legislative Process: Moving Through Committee The initial stages of committee consideration are similar for the House and the Senate. The bill first has to be referred to committee. This is largely automatic for most bills; they go to the standing committee with jurisdiction over the content of the bill. A bill to change the way agricultural subsidies on cotton are considered would start, for example, with the House Committee on Agriculture. In some cases, a bill might logically fall into more than one committee's jurisdiction, and here the Speaker exercises a good deal of power. He can choose the committee that will consider the bill or even refer the same bill to more than one committee. This gives him important leverage in the House because he often knows which committees are likely to be more or less favorable to different bills. Senators do not worry quite as much about where bills are referred because they have much greater opportunity to make changes later in the process than representatives do. We'll see why when we discuss floor consideration.

Bills then move on to subcommittees, where they may, or may not, get serious consideration. Most bills die in committee because the committee members either don't care about the issue (it isn't on their agenda) or actively want to block it. Even if the bill's life is brief, the member who introduced it can still campaign as its champion. In fact, a motivation for the introduction of many bills is not that the member seriously believes they have a chance of passing but that the member wants to be seen back home as taking some action on the issue.

Bills that subcommittees decide to consider will have hearings—testimony from experts, interest groups, executive department secretaries and undersecretaries, and even other members of Congress. The subcommittee deliberates and votes the bill back to the full committee. There the committee further considers the bill and makes changes and revisions in a process called *markup*. If the committee votes in favor of the final version of the bill, it goes forward to the floor. Here, however, a crucial difference exists between the House and the Senate.

Getting to the Floor: House Rules In the House, bills go from the standing committee to the Rules Committee. This committee, highly responsive to the Speaker of the House, gives each bill a "rule," which includes when and how the bill will be considered. Some bills go out under an "open rule," which means that any amendments can be proposed and added as long as they are germane, or relevant, to the legislation under consideration. More typically, especially for important bills, the House leadership gains more control by imposing restrictive rules that limit the time for debate and restrict the amendments that can be offered. For example, if the leadership knows that there is a lot of sentiment in favor of action on a tax cut, it can control the form of the tax cut by having a restrictive rule that prohibits any amendments to the committee's bill. In this way, even members who would like to vote for a different kind of tax cut face pressure to go along with the bill because they can't amend it; it is either this tax cut or none at all, and

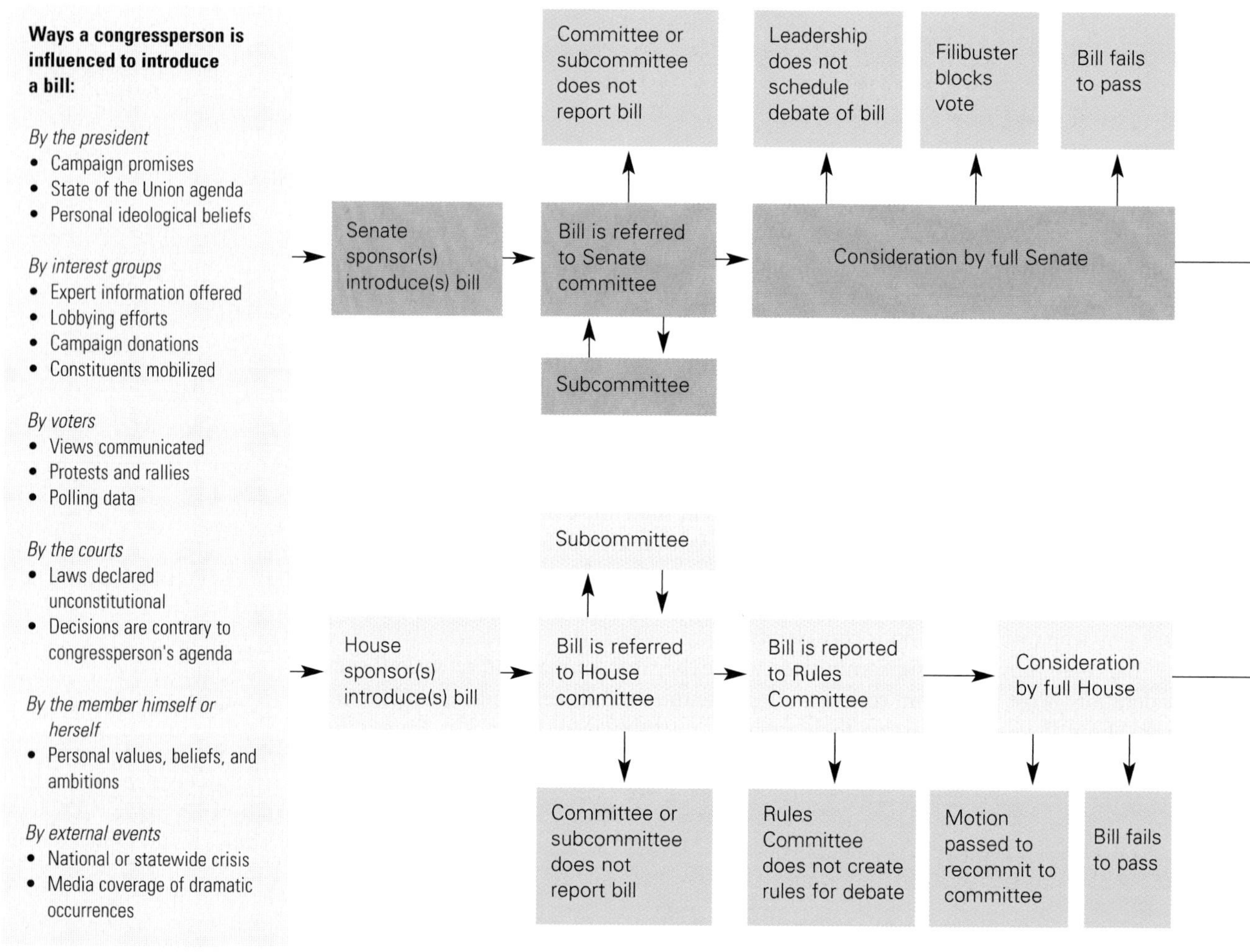

FIGURE 7.9
How a Bill Becomes Law: Long Version

they don't want to vote against a tax cut. Thus, for some bills, not only can the House Rules Committee make or break the bill, but it can also influence the bill's final content.

Getting to the Floor: Senate Rules The Senate generally guarantees all bills an "open rule" by default and, unlike in the House, there is no germane rule that says that an amendment must logically relate to the policy being considered. The majority leader, usually in consultation with the minority leader, schedules legislation for consideration. Their control, however, is fairly weak because any senator can introduce any proposal as an amendment to any bill, sometimes called a rider, and get a vote on it. Thus senators have access to the floor for whatever they want in a way that is denied to representatives. Furthermore, whereas in the House the rule for each bill stipulates how long a member can debate, under the Senate's tradition of "unlimited debate," a member can talk indefinitely. Senators opposed to a bill can engage in a **filibuster**, which is

filibuster a practice of unlimited debate in the Senate in order to prevent or delay a vote on a bill

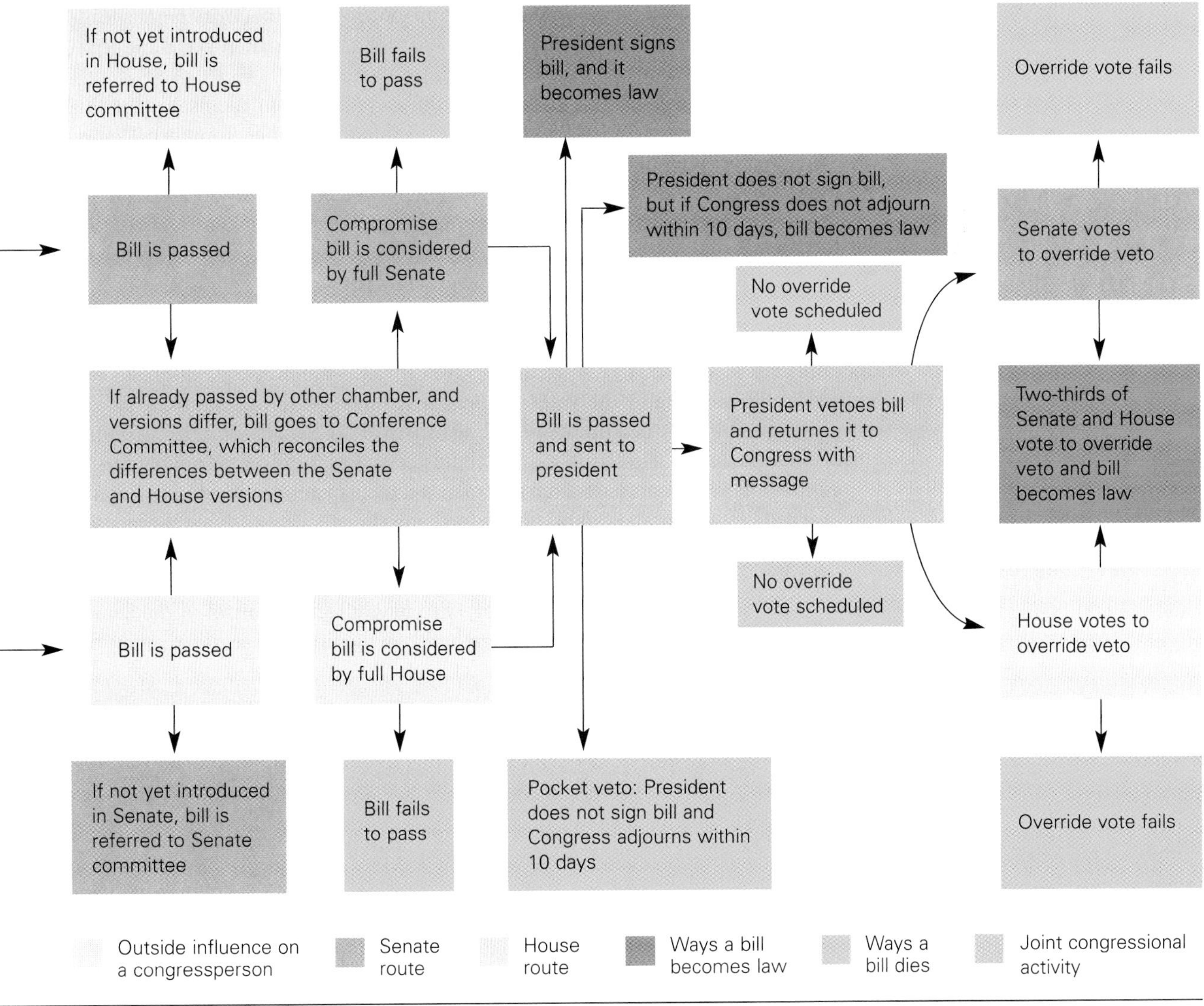

an effort to tie up the floor of the Senate in nonstop debate to stop the Senate from voting on a bill. A filibuster can be stopped only by **cloture**. Cloture, a vote to cut off debate and end a filibuster, requires an extraordinary three-fifths majority, or sixty votes. A dramatic example of a filibuster occurred when southern senators attempted to derail Minnesota senator Hubert Humphrey's efforts to pass the Civil Rights Act of 1964. First, they filibustered Humphrey's attempt to bypass the Judiciary Committee, whose chair, a southern Democrat, opposed the bill. This was known as the "mini-buster" and it stopped Senate business for sixteen days.[49] It was considered "mini" because from March 30 to June 30, 1964, these same southern Democrats filibustered the Civil Rights Act and created a twenty-week backlog of legislation.[50] Often these senators resorted to reading the telephone book in order to adhere to the rules of constant debate. The consequence of a filibuster, as this example suggests, is that a minority in the Senate is able to thwart the will of the majority. Even one single senator can halt

cloture a vote to end a Senate filibuster; requires a three-fifths majority, or sixty votes action on a bill by placing a hold on the legislation, notifying the majority party's leadership that he or she plans to filibuster a bill. That threat alone often keeps the leadership from going forward with the legislation.[51]

Recent congressional sessions have seen a striking increase in the use of the filibuster, as shown in Figure 7.10. Rarely used until the 1960s, when southern Democrats unpacked it to derail civil rights legislation, it has become increasingly popular, with congresses now averaging around forty attempts at cloture. Only about a third of these have been successful in mustering the necessary sixty votes, so a minority has prevailed over the majority most of the time. The use of the filibuster is considered "hardball politics"; its greater use reflects the growing partisan ideological conflicts of the past fifteen to twenty years.

Partisan battles over the filibuster came to a head in 2005, when Senate majority leader Bill Frist threatened to use what Republicans called the "nuclear option" to end Democratic filibustering of the votes on President Bush's judicial nominees. Essentially, Frist would have called on the presiding officer of the Senate for a ruling on the constitutionality of the use of the judicial filibuster and that officer (probably Bush's vice president, Dick Cheney) would have ruled it unconstitutional. Moderate Republicans warned that their party would not always be in the majority and that they would someday regret it if they eliminated the traditional protection for a Senate minority. Along with moderate Democrats, they crafted a compromise that averted the nuclear option, at least for a time. For a political party to have effective control of the Senate these days, it still needs to have sixty seats rather than the fifty-one seats necessary for a simple majority.

Final Challenges: A Bill Becomes a Law Clearly, a bill must survive a number of challenges to get out of Congress alive. A bill can be killed, or just left to die, in a sub-

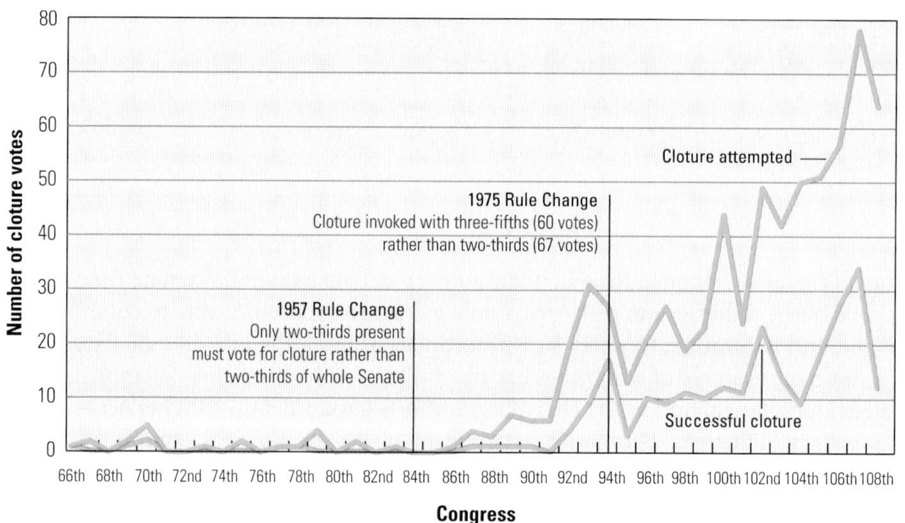

FIGURE 7.10
Cloture Votes to End Filibusters in the 66th to 109th Congresses (1919–2005)

Source: Norman J. Ornstein, Thomas E. Mann, and Michael J. Malbin, *Vital Statistics on Congress, 2001–2002* (Washington, D.C.: AEI Press, 2002), Table 6-7, p. 152; "Cloture Motions—108th Congress," "Cloture Motion—107th Congress—2nd Session," "Cloture Motions—107th Congress—1st Session," U.S. Senate Virtual Reference Desk, 2005, www.senate.gov.

committee, the full committee, the House Rules Committee, or any of the corresponding committees in the Senate, and, of course, it has to pass votes on the floors of both houses.

The congressional decision-making process really begins with the individual member's decision on how to vote. Congressional voting is called **roll call voting**, and all votes are a matter of public record.

roll call voting publicly recorded votes on bills and amendments on the floor of the House or Senate

A variety of influences come to bear on the senator or member of Congress as he or she decides how to vote. Studies have long shown that party affiliation is the most important factor in determining roll call voting, but constituency also plays a big role, as does presidential politics. Busy representatives often take cues from other members whom they respect and generally agree with.[52] They also consult with their staff, some of whom may be very knowledgeable about certain legislation. Finally, interest groups have an effect on how a member of Congress votes, but studies suggest that their impact is much less than we usually imagine. Lobbying and campaign contributions buy access to members so that the lobbyists can try to make their case, but they do not actually buy votes.[53]

The congressperson or senator who is committed to passing or defeating a particular bill cannot do so alone, however, and he or she looks to find like-minded members for political support. Once a representative or senator knows where he or she stands on a bill, there are a variety of methods for influencing the fate of that bill, many of them effective long before the floor vote takes place. Congressional politics—using the rules to get what one wants—can entail many complex strategies, including controlling the agenda (whether a bill ever reaches the floor), proposing amendments to a bill, influencing its timing, and forming coalitions with other members to pass or block a bill. Knowing how to use the rules makes a huge difference in congressional politics.

If a bill emerges from the roll call process in both houses relatively intact, it goes to the president, unless the chambers passed different versions. If the bills differ, then the two versions go to a conference committee made up of members of both houses, usually the senior members of the standing committees that reported the bills. If the conferees can reach an agreement on a revision, then the revised bill goes back to each

A Rare Moment of Unanimous Acclaim
Making laws usually means making someone unhappy, but occasionally a significant piece of legislation is universally applauded. Such was the case when President Franklin D. Roosevelt signed the Social Security Bill on August 15, 1935. The bill was designed to provide old-age pensions and unemployment insurance, and the Social Security program is still in existence today.

house to be voted up or down; no amendments are permitted at this point. If the bill is rejected, that chamber sends it back to the conference committee for a second try.

Finally, any bill still alive at this point moves to the president's desk. He has several choices of action. The simplest choice is that he signs the bill and it becomes law. If he doesn't like it, however, he can veto it. In that case, the president sends it back to the originating house of Congress with a short explanation of what he does not like about the bill. Congress can then attempt a **veto override**, which requires a two-thirds vote of both houses. Because the president can usually count on the support of *at least* one-third of *one* of the houses, the veto is a powerful negative tool; it is hard for Congress to accomplish legislative goals that are opposed by the president. They can, however, bundle policies together, so that the bill that arrives on the president's desk contains elements that he would normally want to veto along with legislation that is very hard for him to turn down. To get around this practice, Congress introduced and passed in 1996 a controversial line-item veto bill, which would have allowed presidents to strike out spending provisions they didn't like, but the Supreme Court ruled in June 1998 that the line-item veto was unconstitutional.[54]

veto override reversal of a presidential veto by a two-thirds vote in both houses of Congress

The president can also kill a bill with the **pocket veto**, which occurs when Congress sends a bill to the president within ten days of the end of a session and the president does not sign it. The bill fails simply because Congress is not in session to consider a veto override. The president might choose this option when he wants to veto a bill without drawing much public attention to it. Similarly, the president can do nothing, and if Congress remains in session, a bill will automatically become law in ten days, excluding Sundays. This seldom-used option signals presidential dislike for a bill but not enough dislike for him to use his veto power.

pocket veto presidential authority to kill a bill submitted within ten days of the end of a legislative session by not signing it

The striking aspect of our legislative process is how many factors have to fall into place for a bill to become law. At every step there are ways to kill bills, and a well-organized group of members in the relatively decentralized Congress has a good chance, in most cases, of blocking a bill to which these members strongly object. In terms of procedures, Congress is better set up to ensure that bills do not impinge on organized interests than it is to facilitate coherent, well-coordinated attacks on the nation's problems. Once again, we see a balance between representation and effective lawmaking, with the procedures of passage tilted toward the forces for representation.

WHO, WHAT, HOW All American political actors, those in Washington and those outside, have something important at stake in the legislative process. The president has a huge stake in what Congress does in terms of fulfilling his own campaign promises, supporting his party's policy goals, and building his political legacy. He can influence the legislative agenda, try to persuade his fellow party members in Congress to support his policies, take his case to the people, or, once the process is under way, threaten to veto or, in fact, use several different veto techniques. But it is Congress that has the most range and flexibility when it comes to passing or stopping legislation. Members want to satisfy constituents, build national reputations or platforms on which to run for future office, and accomplish ideological goals. They have a wealth of legislative tools and strategies at their disposal. But success is not just a matter of knowing the rules. It is personality, luck, timing, and context, as well as political skill in using the rules that make a successful legislator. Repeated filibusters may accomplish a political goal, but if they earn a party a reputation as partisan and uncooperative, they could also cause voter backlash. Legislative politics is a complex balance of rules and processes that favors the skilled politician.

THE CITIZENS AND CONGRESS

Academics and journalists spend a great deal of time speculating about what the decline in public support for our political institutions means for American democracy.[55] In this final section we look at the implications for citizens of their increasingly negative views of the U.S. Congress. While public approval of Congress spiked in the wake of September 11, from 1974 through the 1990s, periodic Gallup polls showed that less than a third of the public "approves of the way Congress is handling its job." In 1992 this proportion dropped to just 18 percent! Part of the blame may be attributed to a general decline in respect for societal institutions ranging from government to organized religion to the media.[56] But the behavior of Congress itself must also be examined.

WHY THE PUBLIC DISLIKES CONGRESS

Four factors help to explain why citizens are so angry at Congress:

- *The changing nature of campaigns.* Recent years have seen a marked increase in voter cynicism about government as well as a decrease in voter reliance on parties to help in the voting decision. Smart candidates have positioned themselves as champions of the districts and states, fighting the good fight against special interests, bureaucrats, and the general incompetence of Washington. In short, members of Congress have increasingly "run for Congress by running against it."[57] A successful campaign may put a candidate into office, but it may also diminish that office in the public's eyes.
- *Negative media coverage of Congress.* Prior to the Watergate scandal in the 1970s, the press did not play up what were considered inconsequential improprieties. After Watergate, however, all aspects of political life became fair game for "investigative reporters" anxious to get a byline with the latest exposé. Impartial observers say that Congress is probably less corrupt than ever before, but the reports of scandals have increased dramatically.
- *The role of money in congressional elections.* Before the 1970s, citizens really had no way of knowing how much campaigns cost or who was contributing. Federal reforms in the 1970s instituted strict reporting requirements about where the money comes from and where it goes. During this same period, campaign costs have soared. More expenses mean that members and challengers have to spend more time and effort at fundraising; it means more PAC involvement, and it probably means more access for the interests that provide the funds candidates need to run. The heavy involvement of special interests casts a shadow of suspicion on the entire process, raising the concern that congressional influence can be bought.
- *Dissatisfaction with the practice of democracy as it is played out in congressional politics.*[58] Americans want to see their representatives agree and get along, not bicker and quarrel. They want efficiency in policymaking, not endless committee hearings and delays. They want their politicians to stand firm on principle and not give way to compromise and deal making. And they want their government to be responsive to their interests, all the time.

  The truth is, however, that democracy is messy. Bickering arises in Congress because the members represent all different kinds of Americans with varied in-

> terests and goals. Dissent is natural given the diversity of America. The inefficiency we see in Congress comes from the variety of interests that must be heard and the conflicting roles we ask our members of Congress to play. They make deals because politics is about deal making. Compromise allows several sides to win and collective life to go on. Standing on principle means all sides but one must lose, and keeping the losers happy and committed to the system is a difficult task. Finally, Congress is responsive, but it cannot possibly give citizens all they want, all the time. If it were possible for everyone to have that, we wouldn't need Congress to make the tough choices for us in the first place. The harmonious view of politics by which some Americans measure Congress is not very realistic. It is precisely our bickering, our inefficiency, our willingness to compromise, to give and take, that preserve the freedoms Americans hold dear. It is the nature of representative government.[59]

PROSPECTS FOR THE FUTURE

Given the reasons that many Americans are unhappy with Congress, the reforms currently on the agenda are not likely to change their minds. One of the most popular reforms being advocated is term limits. The specific proposals vary, but the intent is to limit the number of terms a member of Congress can serve, usually to somewhere between eight and twelve years. The idea is that this will open up the process, drawing in more amateur representatives and ousting "professional politicians." Would citizens be happier with a Congress of amateurs? Will less experience change what candidates say about each other and about Washington? Probably not. Nor is it likely to change the career incentives of journalists, who focus on isolated instances of wrongdoing. Term limits might work if there were evidence that serving in Congress corrupts good people, but there is no evidence of this at all. It just puts them in the public eye.

Term limits will not cut the cost of campaigns or the role of interest groups either. Candidates will be competing with one another for available funds, just as they do now, with more open seats. Nor will term limits make Congress act faster. There will still be the electoral incentives for members to represent their districts and states, and thus to make sure many voices are heard. That means there will still be delay and members will still have to make deals.

Other reforms might, however, make a difference in public support for Congress. Campaign finance reforms, enacted in 2002 with the passage of the McCain-Feingold bill, could have a significant impact. The primary intent of this law is to limit the power of special interest groups by restricting the amount of previously unregulated "soft money" donations they can make to political parties. In theory, this would allow candidates to be freer of special interests and PAC contributions, making more contests competitive. In reality, however, the advantages of incumbency are hard to overcome,[60] and as soon as the reforms were passed, political parties started scrambling to find alternative forms of funding. In the 2004 election, new groups, called 527 groups (named after the section of the law that regulates them), used loopholes in the McCain-Feingold regulations to spend huge unregulated amounts of money in the campaign, disappointing many of the supporters of campaign finance reform, and casting into doubt the long-range success of the bill.

Institutional reforms can also make a big difference. Strengthening the power of the party leadership, particularly the majority party, for example, can cut down on de-

lays and the necessity to compromise over every little complaint some member might have. The Senate, for example, is much more hostage to individual members' objections to almost any piece of legislation than is the House, where the leadership has more tools for controlling the flow of legislation.

Such reforms, however, will probably not fundamentally change how the public feels about Congress. Congress does have the power to act, and when it is unified and sufficiently motivated, it usually does. When Congress reflects our sharply divided society, however, it has a harder time acting. Its inability to act is *because it is a representative institution,* not because members are inattentive to their districts or in the grip of special interests. Furthermore, Congress has more incentives on a daily basis to be a representative institution than a national lawmaking body. It is important to remember, too, that this is not entirely an accident. It was the founders' intention to create a legislature that would not move hastily or without deliberation. The irony is that the founders' mixed bag of incentives works so well that Congress today often does not move very much at all.

We conclude where we began. Congress has the dual goals of lawmaking and representation. These goals often and necessarily conflict. The practice of congressional politics is fascinating to many close-up observers but looks rather ugly as we average citizens understand it, based on the nightly news and what we hear during campaigns. It is important to understand, however, that this view of Congress stems from the contradictions in the expectations we place on the body more than the failings of the people we send to Washington.

WHAT'S AT STAKE REVISITED

We began this chapter by asking why Democrats and Republicans in the Texas legislature, and indeed, the majority leader of the House of Representatives and even the president of the United States, were willing to get involved in an extended squabble over the Texas redistricting plan. What was at stake, we asked, in the Republicans' ability to increase their majority in the U.S. House?

As we have seen, the U.S. Congress has a huge amount of power, even given the constraints of checks and balances and the sometimes tortured legislative process the founders bequeathed to us. The people who call the shots in Congress can control the

continued

WHAT'S AT STAKE REVISITED *(continued)*

agenda of national policymaking and even national debate. For much of the twentieth century, these people were Democrats, but from the 1990s through the early years of the twenty-first century, the U.S. population has been closely divided between Republicans and Democrats and the balance of power in Congress has been tightly contested.

In addition, the process of partisan gerrymandering has yielded congressional districts that are no longer very competitive. Drawn to enhance the power of one party or another, districts are more and more likely to stay in that party's control. Despite the fact that the Texas districts had already been redrawn after the 2000 census, once the Republican Party had control in the Texas legislature, four to seven seats were at stake if the party could manage to stage a mid-decade redrawing of the lines.

Such redistricting, and the consequent gain in seats for the Republicans in 2004, means that the Republican leaders in the House have a bigger comfort margin in passing legislation—they can afford to lose more votes to dissenting members and still win key votes. President Bush was happy with the results because, with an ambitious legislative agenda for his second term, including making tax cuts permanent and reshaping Social Security, a larger Republican majority increases his chances for victory.

The Democrats have a large stake here as well. Not only did they lose five seats they otherwise would have held on to (which, combined with their wins elsewhere in the country, would have narrowed the Republican majority in the House to about twenty seats), but they claim that the Republican efforts have endangered democracy itself. Their argument is that the Republicans are trying to increase their narrow power base in a closely divided America by changing the rules to solidify their power and make it harder for the Democrats to participate. They count the Texas redistricting in that effort, as well as the successful Republican effort to recall California governor Gray Davis in 2003, replacing him with Republican Arnold Schwarzenegger, and the attempt in 2005 by the Republican Senate majority to disallow the filibuster in votes for judicial nominees, to enable President Bush's picks for the courts to go through with a simple majority vote. "These folks don't want to govern," said one Texas Democrat. "They want to rule."[61] Democrats fear that if the courts allow this mid-decade redistricting in Texas, they will go about redrawing districts in all states that allow it, stacking the decks against a Democratic return to power. The practice was upheld by a federal court in June 2005, but an appeal to the Supreme Court is likely.[62]

Finally, the American citizens have a real and important stake in the control of Congress. The founders put checks and balances into place to ensure slow, deliberate policymaking and the protection of civil liberties. To the extent that a single party controls both houses of the legislature and the presidency by a large margin, checks and balances are reduced and our system comes to look more like the parliamentary systems we discussed in Chapter 4. This can have the advantage of increased legislative efficiency and party accountability (it is easier to pass legislation and clearer whom to blame if it doesn't work out). However, it also can mean that less heed is given to minority voices and that individual rights have fewer protections. Secure single-party control of Congress and the presidency can be a heady experience for the party that wins it, but it carries political risks for many concerned.

Thinking Outside the Box

- Does the local interest have to clash with the national interest?
- Why is geography a better base for congressional representation than, say, race, religion, gender, occupation, or socio-economic group?
- What difference does it make that Americans dislike Congress so much?

To Sum Up

KEY TERMS
republic.cqpress.com

allocative representation (p. 271)
bicameral legislature (p. 273)
casework (p. 272)
cloture (p. 307)
coattail effect (p. 286)
conference committees (p. 299)
constituency (p. 271)
descriptive representation (p. 288)
filibuster (p. 306)
franking (p. 272)
gerrymandering (p. 280)
House Rules Committee (p. 298)
incumbency advantage (p. 283)
joint committees (p. 299)
legislative agenda (p. 304)
legislative oversight (p. 297)
majority party (p. 293)
midterm loss (p. 286)
national lawmaking (p. 269)
norms (p. 303)
pocket veto (p. 310)
policy entrepreneurship (p. 304)
policy representation (p. 271)
pork barrel (p. 271)
racial gerrymandering (p. 281)
reapportionment (p. 279)
redistricting (p. 280)
representation (p. 269)
roll call voting (p. 309)
select committee (p. 298)
seniority system (p. 296)
Speaker of the House (p. 294)
standing committees (p. 298)
strategic politician (p. 283)
symbolic representations (p. 272)
veto override (p. 310)

Key terms, chapter summaries, practice quizzes, Internet links, and other study aids are available on the companion Web site at: republic.cqpress.com.

SUMMARY
republic.cqpress.com

- Members of Congress are responsible for both representation and lawmaking. These two duties are often at odds because what is good for a local district may not be beneficial for the country as a whole.
- Representation style takes four different forms—policy, allocative, casework, and symbolic—and congresspersons attempt to excel at all four. However, since the legislative process designed by the founders is meant to be very slow, representatives have fewer incentives to concentrate on national lawmaking when reelection interests, and therefore local interests, are more pressing.
- The founders created our government with a structure of checks and balances. In addition to checking each other, the House and the Senate may be checked by either the president or the courts. Congress is very powerful but must demonstrate unusual strength and consensus to override presidential vetoes and to amend the Constitution.
- Citizens and representatives interact in congressional elections. The incumbency effect is powerful in American politics because those in office often create legislation that makes it difficult for challengers to succeed.
- Representatives want autonomy and choice committee assignments to satisfy constituent concerns. They achieve these goals by joining together into political parties and obeying their leadership and party rules. House and Senate members make their own organizational rules, which means that the dominant party in each house has great power over the internal rules of Congress and what laws are made.
- Citizens, interest groups, the president, and members of Congress all have a stake in the legislative process. Voters organized into interest groups may have a greater impact on legislative outcomes than may the individual. Yet Congress, with various legislative tools and strategies, holds the most sway over the fate of legislation.

PRACTICE QUIZ

republic.cqpress.com

1. What does it mean that the U.S. Congress is a bicameral legislature?

a. It has only one legislative chamber.
b. It has two legislative chambers, but one (the Senate) has more powers.
c. It has two legislative chambers, with each having equal power overall.
d. It has one chamber with legislative power and one chamber with executive power.
e. It has two legislative chambers with equal power, but they have no checks upon one another.

2. The reallocation of U.S. House seats among the states every ten years is called

a. the census.
b. reapportionment.
c. redistricting.
d. gerrymandering.
e. partisan gerrymandering.

3. Which of the following is NOT a factor that explains why citizens today are generally angry at Congress?

a. Successful campaigning for Congress often takes the form of running against the institution of Congress.
b. The media have increased negative coverage of Congress.
c. The importance of money in campaigns makes the public suspicious of the involvement of special interests in lawmaking.
d. The public has a poor view of how democracy fares in congressional politics, because of such things as long debates, compromise, and deal making.
e. The public is frustrated with their representatives and senators for putting the national interest in front of their district's or state's interests.

4. The majority of work done in Congress is done in what type of committee?

a. Conference committees
b. Rules committees
c. Ethics committees
d. Standing committees
e. Select committees

5. Which of the following statements does NOT describe part of the process of how a bill becomes a law?

a. It is difficult for a bill to get on the congressional agenda.
b. Most bills die in standing committees.
c. The rules and steps for passage are identical in the House and the Senate.
d. The process has numerous complex steps with drawbacks at many stages.
e. A bill might not pass even if a strong majority supports the legislation.

SUGGESTED RESOURCES

republic.cqpress.com

Books

Bell, Lauren Cohen. *Master the U.S. Congress: A Simulation for Students.* Belmont, Calif.: Wadsworth. Provides a hands-on simulation of how Congress functions and how representatives and senators behave given the structure of Congress and the challenges of both representing constituents and making law.

Caro, Robert A. 2002. *Master of the Senate: The Years of Lyndon Johnson.* New York: Knopf. The third in a planned series of four books about Johnson. This lengthy book details Johnson's expert use of power to rise to the top leadership position in the Senate.

***CQ's Politics in America.* 2006. Washington, D.C.: CQ Press.** Make this your first stop when researching individual members of Congress, their districts, or their states. Contains voting records, campaign expenditures, state and district demographics, and more.

CQ Weekly. The best source for the most recent happenings in Congress. Congressional Quarterly has especially great election coverage.

Davidson, Roger, and Walter Oleszek. 2006. *Congress and Its Members,* 10th ed. Washington, D.C.: CQ Press. Clarifies even the most complex aspects of Congress.

Dodd, Larry, and Bruce Oppenheimer, eds. 2005. *Congress Reconsidered,* 8th ed. Washington, D.C.: CQ Press. A rich collection on some of the most pressing issues regarding Congress.

Fenno, Richard F., Jr. 1978. *Home Style: House Members in Their Districts.* Boston: Little, Brown. The author hits the campaign trail with several members of Congress to get a better understanding of the congressperson-constituent relationship.

Herrnson, Paul S. 2004. *Congressional Elections: Campaigning at Home and in Washington,* 4th ed. Washington, D.C.: CQ Press. An informative book on congressional elections and how their campaigns are waged.

Jacobson, Gary C. 2001. *The Politics of Congressional Elections,* 5th ed. New York: Longman. An in-depth examination of congressional elections emphasizing challengers' decisions to run for office.

Parker, Glenn R. 1986. *Homeward Bound: Explaining Changes in Congressional Behavior.* Pittsburgh: University of Pittsburgh Press. An insightful and well-documented account of why and when members of Congress visit their home states and districts.

Sinclair, Barbara. 2000. *Unorthodox Lawmaking: New Legislative Processes in the U.S. Congress,* 2d ed. Washington, D.C.: CQ Press. An inside view of the modern Congress that, as this chapter suggests, illustrates how different lawmaking and politics are in Congress than most "textbook" descriptions suggest.

Web Sites

See "*Consider the Source*: How to Be a Critical Constituent" for many useful congressional Internet sources.

Thomas. thomas.loc.gov. This Library of Congress Web site is designed to provide legislative information to the public. It provides voting records, committee reports, and current legislation and even allows an interested web surfer to search the *Congressional Record* to see what anyone in Congress has said about any particular subject.

U.S. House of Representatives. www.house.gov. The official Web site of the U.S. House of Representatives provides an entry into individual representatives' web sites and those of different House committees, as well as information on the processes, calendar, and votes of Congress.

U.S. Senate. www.senate.gov. The official Senate Web site provides contact information for senators and Senate committees; information on bill traffic and calendars; and quizzes, art history, and facts about this chamber.

The Center on Congress at Indiana University. congress.indiana.edu. This useful Web site provides historical and institutional information about the work and role of Congress, especially highlighting the positive role Congress has played in the lives of Americans.

Movies

The Candidate. 1972. Robert Redford plays a charismatic Senate candidate.

Mr. Smith Goes to Washington. 1939. Frank Capra's classic story about a young politician who is appointed to the Senate and, defying his party's bosses, fights the leaders' corruption.

President Bush and his father, former president George H. W. Bush, arrive at Fort Hood Army Base in Texas in April 2004 (right). Like most recent presidents, both Bushes made use of executive privilege—the right to withhold certain communications between the president and his staff from Congress and the courts—during their terms of office. Although the Supreme Court has ruled against presidents Richard Nixon (below) and Bill Clinton as they sought to withhold information during their impeachment inquiries, presidents continue to claim executive privilege—usually successfully—as power necessary to get their job done.

THE PRESIDENCY

8

WHAT'S AT STAKE?

When President Bush nominated Judge John G. Roberts Jr. to fill the Supreme Court vacancy created by Sandra Day O'Connor's retirement, voices of opposition were muted. Even liberals who wanted to oppose the conservative Roberts's nomination had a hard time finding grounds on which to oppose him. As part of the confirmation process, Democratic senators asked the White House to release documents from Roberts's tenure in the Reagan and first Bush administrations. The White House released some of them but refused to release those pertaining to Roberts's service as deputy solicitor general. Even when the debate over Roberts heated up, after September 5, 2005, when Bush renominated him for the position of chief justice, following William Rehnquist's death, the president was adamant; he would not release the papers.

The arguments made by the Bush White House were the same that had been made just months earlier over the release of papers pertaining to the executive service of John R. Bolton, Bush's nominee for UN ambassador. When Democrats balked at confirming Bolton without seeing the papers, Bush got around their demands by making a seventeen-month recess appointment that would put Bolton at the UN until the next Congress reconvened. As then, President Bush claimed that to release the papers would violate *executive privilege,* the right of the president to keep confidential certain sensitive information or his conversations with close advisers, so that he can trust them to give him "truthful" advice—advice untainted by considerations of how it might look if revealed to the general public.[1]

Vice President Dick Cheney had made similar arguments earlier in 2001, when he declared that he should not have to release the names of energy industry executives he met with in formulating the Bush administration's energy policy. Cheney's decision became more controversial with the bankruptcy of energy giant Enron, but when Congress wanted to investigate whether Enron had sought or received help from the administration to which it had made hefty financial contributions, Cheney insisted that his task force was not a federal agency and that to give in to Congress would be to weaken the presidency. When the Government Accountability Office, known at the time as the General Accounting Office (GAO), disagreed and sued Cheney for the information in early 2002, the courts ruled against the agency.

Although presidents have been claiming that they are entitled to the protections of executive privilege since the days of George Washington, this protection is not in the Constitution. In fact, the Supreme Court did not recognize it until 1974, when it confronted President Richard Nixon's claim that he should not have to release tapes made in the Oval Office because they would violate executive privilege. The Court ruled that courts should indeed be sensitive to presidents' need for "complete candor and objectivity" from advisers, but that the information was not protected in a criminal investigation.[2]

Debates between Congress and the president (and sometimes the courts) over executive privilege are usually heated, although often both sides back down and reach a compromise about how much information should be turned over. President Bill Clinton gave up his claims of executive privilege to protect conversations with aides during the investigation of his affair with White House intern Monica Lewinsky and settled his four claims of executive privilege with Congress outside the courts as well. One writer says that "this is the usual outcome; after making a political show, both sides make accommodations."[3]

The Bush administration insisted, however, that there would be no backing down—that there were principles involved that could not be sacrificed. Was this true? What is really at stake in this controversial issue of executive privilege? We return to this question after we examine the powers and limitations of the U.S. president. *

Ask just about anyone who the most powerful person in the world is and the answer will probably be "the president of the United States." He, or perhaps someday soon, she, is the elected leader of the nation that has one of the most powerful economies, one of the greatest military forces, and the longest-running representative government that the world has ever seen. Media coverage enforces this belief in the importance of the U.S. president. The networks and news services all have full-time reporters assigned to the White House. The evening news tells us what the president has been doing that day; even if he only went to church or played a round of golf, his activities are news. This attention is what one scholar calls the presidency's "monopolization of the public space."[4] It means that the president is the first person the citizens and the media think of when anything of significance happens, whether it is a terrorist attack, a natural disaster, or a big drop in the stock market. We look to the president to solve our problems and to represent the nation in our times of struggle, tragedy, and triumph. The irony is that the U.S. Constitution provides for a relatively weak chief executive, and the American public's and, indeed, the world's expectations of the president constitute a major challenge for modern presidents.

The challenge of meeting the public's expectations is made all the more difficult because so many political actors have something at stake in the office of the presidency. Most obviously, the president himself wants to widen his authority to act so that he can deliver on campaign promises and extend the base of support for himself and his party. Although the formal rules of American politics create only limited presidential powers, informal rules help him expand them. Citizens, both individually and in groups, often have high expectations of what the president will do for them and for the country, and they may be willing to allow him more expanded powers to act. An unpopular president, however, will face a public eager to limit his options and ready to complain about any perceived step beyond the restrictive constitutional bounds. Congress, too, stands to gain or lose based on the president's success. Members of the president's party will share some of his popularity, but in general the more power the president has, the less Congress has. This is especially true if the majority party in Congress is different from the president's. So Congress has a stake in limiting what the president may do.

This chapter tells the story of who gets what from the American presidency and how they get it. You will learn about

- the double expectations gap between what Americans want the president to do and what he can deliver
- the evolution of the American presidency from its constitutional origins to the modern presidency
- the president's struggle for power
- the organization and functioning of the executive office
- the role of presidential character
- the relationship of citizens to the presidency

THE DOUBLE EXPECTATIONS GAP

Presidential scholars note that one of the most remarkable things about the modern presidency is how much the office has become intertwined with public expectations and perceptions. The implication, of course, is that we expect one thing and get something less—that there is a gap between our expectations and reality. In fact, we can identify two different expectations gaps when it comes to popular perceptions of the presidency. One is between the very great promises that presidents make, and that we want them to keep, on the one hand, and the president's limited constitutional power to fulfill those promises on the other. The second gap is between two conflicting roles that the president is expected to play, between the formal and largely symbolic role of head of state and the far more political role of head of government. These two expectations gaps form a framework for much of our discussion of the American presidency.

THE GAP BETWEEN PRESIDENTIAL PROMISES AND THE POWERS OF THE OFFICE

The first gap between what the public expects the president to do and what he can actually accomplish is of relatively recent vintage. Through the 1930s the presidency in the United States was pretty much the office the founders had planned, an administrative position dwarfed by the extensive legislative power of Congress. During Franklin Roosevelt's New Deal, however, public expectations of the president changed. Roosevelt did not act like an administrator with limited powers; he acted like a leader whose strength and imagination could be relied on by an entire nation of citizens to rescue them from the crisis of the Great Depression. Over the course of Roosevelt's four terms in office, the public became used to seeing the president in just this light, and future presidential candidates promised similarly grand visions of policy in

TOLES © 1993 *The Washington Post.* Reprinted with permission of UNIVERSAL PRESS SYNDICATE.

their efforts to win supporters. Rather than strengthening the office to allow presidents to deliver on such promises, however, the only constitutional change in the presidency weakened it. In reaction to Roosevelt's four elections, the Twenty-second Amendment was passed, limiting the number of terms a president can serve to two.

Today's presidents suffer the consequences of this history. On the one hand, we voters demand that they woo us with promises to change the course of the country, to solve our problems, and to enact visionary policy. On the other hand, we have not increased the powers of the office to meet this greatly expanded job description. Thus, to meet our expectations, the president must wheel, deal, bargain, and otherwise gather the support needed to overcome his constitutional limitations. And if the president doesn't meet our expectations, or if the country doesn't thrive the way we think it should, even if it isn't his fault and there's nothing he could have done to change things, we hold him accountable and vote him out of office. Some evidence of this can be seen in the fates of the past nine presidents; only four have been reelected to a second term, and of those, Nixon resigned after Watergate, Ronald Reagan faced the Iran-contra scandal and his party lost its majority in the Senate, Bill Clinton was impeached, and George W. Bush won reelection by the smallest margin of any reelected president. The inability of some of our most skilled politicians to survive for even two full terms of office (see Table 8.1) suggests that our expectations of what can be done potentially outstrip the resources and powers of the position.

THE GAP BETWEEN CONFLICTING ROLES

The second expectations gap that presidents face is in part a product of the first. Since we now expect our presidents to perform as high-level legislators as well as administrators, holders of this office need to be adept politicians. That is, today's presidents need to be able to get their hands dirty in the day-to-day political activities of the nation or, as we just said, to wheel, deal, and bargain. But the image of their president as a politician, an occupational class not held in high esteem by most Americans, often doesn't sit well with citizens who want to hold their president above politics as a symbol of all that is good and noble about America. Thus, not only must presidents contend with a job in which they are required to do far more than they are given the power to do, but they must also cultivate the talents to perform two very contradictory roles: the essentially political head of government, who makes decisions about who will get scarce resources, and the elevated and apolitical head of state, who should unify rather than divide the public. Few presidents are skilled enough to carry off both roles with aplomb; the very talents that make a president good at one side of this equation often disqualify him from being good at the other.

TABLE 8.1 **Length of Time in Office for the Last Nine Presidents**

PRESIDENT	TERMS SERVED
John Kennedy	Assassinated in the third year of his first term.
Lyndon Johnson	Served out Kennedy's term, elected to one term of his own. Chose not to run for reelection, knowing he would lose.
Richard Nixon	Served one full term, reelected, resigned halfway through second term.
Gerald Ford	Served out Nixon's term. Ran for reelection and lost.
Jimmy Carter	Served one full term. Ran for reelection and lost.
Ronald Reagan	Served two full terms.
George H. W. Bush	Served one full term. Ran for reelection and lost.
Bill Clinton	Served two full terms. Impeached but acquitted halfway through second term.
George W. Bush	Served one full term, reelected, and serving second term.

Head of State The **head of state** serves as the symbol of the hopes and dreams of a people and is responsible for enhancing national unity by representing that which is common and good in the nation. Most other nations separate the head-of-state role from the head-of-government role so that clearly acknowledged symbolic duties can be carried out without contamination by political considerations. One of the clearest examples is the monarchy in Britain. As head of state, Queen Elizabeth remains a valued symbol of British nationhood. Her Christmas speech is listened to with great interest and pride by the nation, and, even with her family troubles, she continues to be an important symbol of what it means to be British. Meanwhile, the prime minister of England can get on with the political business of governing.

head of state the apolitical, unifying role of the president as symbolic representative of the whole country

That the founders wanted the presidency to carry the dignity, if not the power, of a monarch is evident in George Washington's wish that the president might bear the title "His High Mightiness, the President of the United States and the Protector of their Liberties."[5] While Americans were not ready for such a pompous title, we nevertheless do put presidents, as the embodiment of the nation, on a higher plane than other politicians. Consequently the American president's job includes a ceremonial role for activities like greeting other heads of state, attending state funerals, tossing out the first baseball of the season, hosting the annual Easter egg hunt on the White House lawn, and consoling survivors of national tragedies. The vice president can relieve the president of some of these responsibilities, but there are times when only the president's presence will do.

Head of Government The president is elected to do more than greet foreign dignitaries, wage war, and give electrifying speeches, however. As **head of government**, he is also supposed to run the government and function as the head of a political party. These are the functions that have expanded so greatly since Roosevelt's presidency.

head of government the political role of the president as leader of a political party and chief arbiter of who gets what resources

Running the country, as we shall see throughout this chapter, involves a variety of political activities. First, the president is uniquely situated to define the nation's policy agenda—that is, to get issues on the unofficial list of business that Congress and the

Head of State, Head of Government
All presidents fill two roles. Sometimes a president acts as head of state, appearing as a symbol of the entire nation. On April 6, 2005, President George W. Bush led a U.S. delegation that included First Lady Laura Bush, Secretary of State Condoleeza Rice, and former presidents George H. W. Bush and Bill Clinton to Rome for the funeral of Pope John Paul II. Bush was the first president to attend a pope's funeral. At other times, a president acts as head of government, working for the party, its supporters, or programs. Late in his first term of office, Bush signed the Intelligence Reform and Terrorism Prevention Act of 2004 into law. The law set into motion the largest overhaul of U.S. intelligence gathering in fifty years, with the hope of improving the spy network that failed to prevent the September 11, 2001, attacks.

public think should be taken care of. The media's constant coverage of the president, combined with the public's belief in the centrality of the office, means that modern presidents have great influence in deciding what policy issues will be addressed.

An effective head of government must do more than simply bring issues to national attention, however. We also expect him to broker the deals, line up the votes, and work to pass actual legislation. This may seem peculiar since Congress makes the laws, but the president is often a critical player in developing political support from the public and Congress to get these laws passed. Thus the president is also seen as the nation's chief lawmaker and coalition builder. An excellent example of the president's role in making law and building coalitions can be seen in President Clinton's efforts to build bipartisan support to get the North American Free Trade Agreement (NAFTA) passed. Political cartoonists lampooned his willingness to carve out exceptions and make deals for individual legislators, but in the end he, a Democrat, was able to garner support in a Democratic-led Congress for a policy mostly favored by Republicans. (For more on the tools cartoonists use to make their points, see "*Consider the Source*: How to Be a Savvy Student of Political Cartoons.")

In addition to helping to make the laws, the president is supposed to make government work. When things go okay, no one thinks much about it. But when things go wrong, the president is the one who has to have an explanation—he is accountable. President Harry Truman kept a sign on his desk that read "The Buck Stops Here," nicely summarizing this presidential responsibility.

The president does not just lead the nation; he leads his political party as well. As its head, he appoints the chair of his party's national committee and can use his powers as president—perhaps vetoing a bill, directing discretionary funds, or making appointments—to reward loyalty or punish a lack of cooperation. He also has considerable patronage at his disposal to reward the party faithful, although this practice is fading (see Chapter 9). The president can, if he wants, have a major influence on his party's platform. And finally, the president is an important fundraiser for his party. By assisting in the election of party members, he helps to ensure support for the party's program in Congress.

We explore the president's powers in greater detail later in this chapter. What is important for our purposes here is that all these roles are *political* aspects of the president's job. Remember that "political" means allocating resources and benefits to some people over others, deciding who wins and who loses. Thus the responsibilities of the office place the president in an inherently and unavoidably contradictory position. On the one hand he is the symbol of the nation, representing all the people (head of state); and on the other he has to take the lead in politics that are inherently divisive (head of government). Almost all changes in public policy—for example, tax, environmental, welfare, or economic policy—will result in some citizens winning more than others, some losing, and some becoming angry. Thus the political requirements of the president as head of government necessarily undermine his unifying role as head of state. In addition, the image of the president wheeling and dealing can tarnish the stature considered crucial to the leader of the United States.

WHO, WHAT, HOW Presidents want to leave a legacy, a reputation for having led the country in a meaningful way. To do this they make grand promises that they may not necessarily have the power to fulfill. Their job is complicated by the requirement that they serve as head of state, even as they are forced to act as head of government to accomplish their political goals. The people who hold the conflicting expectations of the president are, of course, the American voters. Citizens have a stake in having a successful president, but their expectations make it unlikely that he will succeed. Since voters choose among presidential candidates on the basis of their campaign promises, candidates are only encouraged to make grander promises, in the hopes of getting elected—ultimately increasing the expectations gaps as they are unable to deliver on their extravagant pledges.

THE EVOLUTION OF THE AMERICAN PRESIDENCY

The framers designed a much more limited presidency than the one we have today. The constitutional provisions give most of the policymaking powers to Congress, or at least require power sharing and cooperation. For most of our history, this arrangement was not a problem. As leaders of a rural nation with a relatively restrained governmental apparatus, presidents through the nineteenth century were largely content

Consider the Source

How to Be a Savvy Student of Political Cartoons

Political cartoons are not just for laughs. While they may often use humor as a way of making a political point, that point is likely to be sharp and aimed with uncanny accuracy at political targets. In fact, noted cartoonist Jeff MacNelly, who won a Pulitzer Prize for his work, once said that if cartoonists couldn't draw, most of them would probably have become hired assassins.[1]

Since the first days of our republic, Americans have been using drawings and sketches to say what mere words cannot. Benjamin Franklin and Paul Revere, among others, used pen, ink, and engraving tools to express pointed political views.[2] Moreover, their hapless targets have been acutely aware of the presence of these "annoying little pups, nipping at the heels. . . ."[3] Politicians crave the attention, knowing they have arrived when a cartoonist can draw them without having to indicate their names, but at the same time they dread the sharp sting of the cartoonist's pen.

In the 1870s, Boss Tweed of Tammany Hall (a powerful New York City politician who dominated local party politics) reportedly offered cartoonist Thomas Nast $100,000 to stop drawing cartoons about him (such as the one on page 515 in Chapter 12),[4] saying: "Stop them damn pictures. I don't care so much what the papers write about me. My constituents can't read. . . . But, damn it, they can see pictures."[5] By the early 1900s, legislatures in four states—Pennsylvania, California, Indiana, and Alabama—had introduced anti–cartoon censorship bills to protect the First Amendment freedoms of the political cartoonist.[6]

Political cartoons do more than elicit a laugh or a chuckle. Frequently they avoid humor altogether, going for outrage, indignation, ridicule, or scathing contempt. Their goal is to provoke a reaction from their audience, and they use the tools of irony, sarcasm, symbolism, and shock as well as humor. With this barrage of weapons aimed at you, your critical skills are crucial. The next time you are confronted with a political cartoon, ask yourself these questions:[7]

1. **What is the event or issue that inspired the cartoon?** Political cartoonists do not attempt to inform you about current events; they assume that you already know what has happened. Their job is to comment on the news, and so your first step in savvy cartoon readership is to be up on what's happening in the world. The cartoon shown here assumes that you are familiar with President George W. Bush (the driver in the cartoon) and the fact that, although he was continually supportive verbally of the troops serving in Iraq (and sometimes deflected criticism of the war effort by claiming that such criticism subverted the troops' efforts), his 2005 budget also proposed reductions in some veterans' benefits. The cartoon also plays on the American fad of putting magnetic ribbons on the back of one's car, by providing two magnets: one the familiar yellow ribbon proclaiming support of the troops and the other in the shape of scissors.
2. **Are there any real people in the cartoon? Who are they?** Cartoonists develop caricatures of prominent politicians that exaggerate some gesture or facial feature (often the nose, the ears, or the eyebrows, although cartoonists had a field day with Ronald Reagan's hair) that makes them immediately identifiable.[8] Richard Nixon's ski jump nose and swarthy complexion were frequently lampooned, as was his habit of raising his hands over his head in a victory salute. Clinton often appeared as a bulbous-nosed, chubby-cheeked childlike figure. Bush is often drawn as a small figure with a monkey-like face, often with huge ears. Here, although the face is not visible, the ears clue you in that the driver is meant to be Bush.

with a limited authority that rested on the grants of powers provided in the Constitution. But the presidency of Franklin Roosevelt, beginning in 1932, ushered in a new era in presidential politics.

THE FRAMERS' DESIGN FOR A LIMITED EXECUTIVE

The presidency was not a preoccupation of the framers when they met in Philadelphia in 1787. Most of their debates and compromises concerned the powers and arrange-

STAR TRIBUNE SACK

Many cartoonists do not confine their art to real people. Some will use a generic person sometimes labeled to represent a group (big business, U.S. Senate, environmentalists). In the cartoon on page 272, an anonymous, overweight politician is meant to reflect the tendency of representatives to fight harmful effects on their districts. Other cartoonists draw stereotypically middle-class citizens, talking television sets, or multipaneled "talking head" cartoons to get their views across.[9]

3. **Are there symbols in the cartoon? What do they represent?** Without a key to the symbols cartoonists use, their art can be incomprehensible. Uncle Sam stands in for the United States, donkeys are Democrats, and elephants are Republicans. Tammany Hall frequently appeared as a tiger in political cartoons of the time. Often these symbols are combined in unique ways. (See the cartoon on page 534, which shows a confused Uncle Sam standing outside an Oval Office door made to look like th entrance to a church to show the Bush administration's close relationship with the religious right). The cartoon on page 322 depicts presidential power as a giant, complicated, and frightening-looking machine, in front of which the president stands, awestruck. However, as politics has focused more on image and personality, symbols, although still important, have taken a back seat to personal caricature.[10]

4. **What is the cartoonist's opinion about the topic of the cartoon? Do you agree with it or not? Why?** A cartoon is an editorial as surely as are the printed opinion pieces we focused on in Chapter 4. The cartoon has no more claim to objective status than does someone else's opinion, and you need to evaluate it critically before you take what it says to be accurate. Often this evaluation is harder with a cartoon than with text, because the medium can be so effective in provoking a reaction from us, whether it is shock, laughter, or scorn. Furthermore, a single cartoon can be interpreted in multiple ways.

   In the drawing here, the cartoonist is likely trying to highlight an apparent inconsistency in Bush's support for the military. During the 2004 campaign, Bush attacked his opponent's criticism of his handling of the war in Iraq by claiming that such criticism undermined the American troops in the field. But the scissors-ribbon illustrates that the cartoonist views cutting veterans' benefits to be unsupportive of the troops—that Bush's use of patriotic symbols is not backed by political action.

1. Kirkus Reviews, review of *Them Damned Pictures: Explorations in American Political Cartoon Art,* by Roger A. Fischer, January 15, 1996.
2. Richard E. Marschall, "The Century in Political Cartoons," *Columbia Journalism Review,* May–June 1999, 54.
3. Richard Ruelas, "Editorial Cartoonists Nip at the Heels of Society," *Arizona Republic,* June 9, 1996, A1.
4. Marschall.
5. Ira F. Grant, "Cartoonists Put the Salt in the Stew," *Southland (New Zealand) Times,* February 20, 1999, 7.
6. Marschall.
7. Questions are from the PoliticalCartoons.com teachers' guide, http://cagle.slate.msn.com/teacher.
8. Robert W. Duffy, "Art of Politics: Media With a Message," *St. Louis Post-Dispatch Magazine,* September 2, 1992, 3D.
9. Marschall.
10. Ibid.

ments for the new Congress. The legislature was presumed by all to be the first branch of government, the real engine of the national political system, but the breakdown of the national government under the Articles of Confederation demonstrated the need for a central executive. But the founders were divided over how powerful the executive should be and how it should be constituted and chosen.

The most common form of the executive among advanced democracies today is the parliamentary system in which the chief executive—the prime minister—is one of the elected legislators. As we saw in Chapter 4, this system eliminates separation of powers by merging the executive and the legislature and by greatly concentrating power in the legislative branch of government and strengthening the prime minister's hand.

The American founders, in contrast, were committed to separation of powers, but they were also nervous about trusting the general public to choose the executive. (Remember that not even senators were directly elected by the people in the original Constitution.) The founders compromised by providing for an electoral college, a group of people who would be chosen by the state for the sole purpose of electing the president. The assumption was that this body would be made up of leading citizens who would exercise care and good judgment in casting ballots for president and who would not make postelection claims on him. Clearly the founding fathers did not envision a presidency based on massive popular support. The electoral college was intended to insulate him from the winds of public opinion. Even today the president is officially chosen by the electoral college rather than by popular vote. We look a good deal more closely at this electoral mechanism in Chapter 14, on elections.

Because of their experience with King George III, the founders also wished to avoid the concentration of power that could be abused by a strong executive. Their compromise was a relatively limited scope for presidential authority as laid out in the Constitution. Even on this point they were divided, however, with Alexander Hamilton far more willing than most of the others to entertain the notion of a strong executive. Although the majority's concept of a limited executive is enshrined in the Constitution, Hamilton's case for a more "energetic" president, found in *Federalist* No. 70, foreshadows many of the arguments for the stronger executive we have today.

QUALIFICATIONS AND CONDITIONS OF OFFICE

The framers' conception of a limited presidency can be seen in the brief attention the office receives in the Constitution. Article II is short and not very precise. It provides some basic details on the office of the presidency:

- The president is chosen by the electoral college to serve four-year terms. The number of terms was unlimited until 1951 when, in reaction to Roosevelt's unprecedented four terms in office, the Constitution was amended to limit the president to two terms.
- The president must be a natural-born citizen of the United States, at least thirty-five years old, and a resident for at least fourteen years. As we saw in Chapter 4, however, a movement is under way to amend the Constitution by removing the requirement that the president be natural born.
- The president is succeeded by the vice president if he dies or is removed from office. The Constitution does not specify who becomes president in the event that the vice president, too, is unable to serve, but in 1947 Congress passed the Presidential Succession Act, which establishes the order of succession after the vice president (see Table 8.2). While the rules for succession following vacancies are clear, the rules for replacing a president because of *disability* are not. President Woodrow Wilson, for example, suffered an incapacitating stroke, but his vice president, Thomas Riley Marshall, never came forward because no one wanted to remove a living president. Consequently the executive department could not

function; no cabinet meetings were held, and no one could argue to save Wilson's Versailles Treaty (and the League of Nations) from failure in the Senate. Ronald Reagan's failing memory in the last years of his presidency may have been an early indication of the Alzheimer's disease that later killed him. At what point is a president too disabled to handle the demands of office? The Twenty-fifth Amendment states that a vice president can take over when either a president himself or the vice president and a majority of the cabinet report to Congress that the president is unable to serve. Two-thirds of Congress must agree that the president is incapacitated if reports are contradictory.[6]

- The president can be removed from office by impeachment and conviction by the House of Representatives and the Senate for "treason, bribery, or other high crimes and misdemeanors." The process of removal involves two steps: First, after an in-depth investigation, the House votes to impeach by a simple majority vote, which charges the president with a crime. Second, the Senate tries the president on the articles of impeachment and can convict by a two-thirds majority vote. Only two American presidents, Andrew Johnson and Bill Clinton, have been impeached (in 1868 and 1998), but neither was convicted. The Senate failed, by one vote, to convict Johnson and could not assemble a majority against Clinton. The power of impeachment is meant to be a check on the president, but it is often used for partisan purposes. Impeachment resolutions were filed against both Reagan (over the invasion of Grenada and the Iran-contra affair) and George H. W. Bush (over Iran-contra), without a vote ever getting to the floor of the House.[7] For more details on the politics of impeachment, see the box "Grounds for Impeachment?"

TABLE 8.2 **Who Does the President's Job When the President Cannot?**

PRESIDENTIAL ORDER OF SUCCESSION
Vice president
Speaker of the House
President pro tempore of the Senate
Secretary of state
Secretary of the Treasury
Secretary of defense
Attorney general
Secretary of the interior
Secretary of agriculture
Secretary of commerce
Secretary of labor
Secretary of health and human services
Secretary of housing and urban development
Secretary of transportation
Secretary of energy
Secretary of education
Secretary of veterans affairs
Secretary of homeland security

Note: It seems impossible that all in the line of succession could die simultaneously. Nevertheless, during the State of the Union address, when Congress and the cabinet are present with the president and vice president, one cabinet member does not attend in order to ensure that a catastrophe could not render our government leaderless. Some in Congress have pushed legislation that would leapfrog the Secretary of Homeland Security to eighth in line (one behind the attorney general), arguing that because of that secretary's particular familiarity with crises that would obviously have occurred if the succession had reached the eighth official—he or she would be best able to lead the country.

THE CONSTITUTIONAL POWER OF THE PRESIDENT

The Constitution uses vague language to discuss some presidential powers and is silent on the range and limits of others. It is precisely this ambiguity that allowed the Constitution to be ratified by both those who wanted a strong executive power and those who did not. In addition, this vagueness has allowed the powers of the president to expand over time without constitutional amendment. We can think of the president's constitutional powers as falling into three areas: executive authority to administer government, and legislative and judicial power to check the other two branches.

Executive Powers Article II, Section 1, of the Constitution begins, "The executive power shall be vested in a president of the United States of America." However, the document does not explain exactly what "executive power" entails, and scholars and presidents through much of our history have debated the extent of these powers.[8] Section 3 states the president "shall take care that the laws be faithfully executed." Herein lies much of the executive authority; the president is the **chief administrator** of the nation's laws. This means that he is the chief executive officer of the country, the per-

chief administrator the president's executive role as the head of federal agencies and the person responsible for the implementation of national policy

Grounds for Impeachment?

The framers' worries about an overly powerful executive led them to create a means of presidential removal. Article II, Section 4, of the Constitution provides: "The president, vice-president and all civil officers of the United States shall be removed from office on impeachment for, and on conviction of, treason, bribery, or other high crimes and misdemeanors." Although the definitions of treason and bribery are not controversial, the meaning of "other high crimes and misdemeanors" has never been clear. Why was Vice President Aaron Burr not impeached after he killed Alexander Hamilton in a duel, but President Andrew Johnson was impeached and nearly convicted for, among other things, calling Congress "fractious and domineering"?[1] More recently, why did the Judiciary Committee decide obstruction of justice, abuse of power, and contempt of Congress were impeachable offenses against Richard Nixon but that two counts of tax fraud were not?

When former president Gerald Ford was House minority leader, he suggested that "an impeachable offense is whatever the majority of the House of Representatives considers it to be at a given moment in history." Similarly, then–solicitor general Kenneth Starr claimed that impeachment could result from something as trivial as poisoning a neighbor's cat.[2]

Many observers have argued that the impeachment process is too crippling to be an effective check, that with the House Judiciary Committee investigating the president, the Senate listening to enormous amounts of testimony, the president struggling to defend himself, and the Chief Justice leaving his duties at the Supreme Court, impeachment paralyzes all branches of the government.[3] The independent counsel statute of 1978 attempted to avoid such an overload by providing for the appointment of a prosecutor from outside the Justice Department. The independent counsel's job was to notify the House of any "substantial and credible information" that could lead to an impeachment, but the office came under increasing criticism because it was not subject to any limits. In the wake of President Clinton's impeachment in 1998, Congress allowed the independent counsel statute to lapse on June 30, 1999. The three presidential impeachment investigations summarized here show how the rules of impeachment have shaped the American presidency in the latter half of the twentieth century.

WATERGATE

Overview The Watergate scandal, uncovered largely by *Washington Post* reporters Bob Woodward and Carl Bernstein, led to the resignation of President Nixon in 1974. Investigations by the media, Congress, and a special prosecutor appointed by the Justice Department tied top administration officials to the planning and cover-up of a burglary at the Democratic National Committee (DNC) headquarters in the Watergate Hotel in Washington, D.C. The White House used the CIA, FBI, and Internal Revenue Service to eavesdrop on and bully investigators and potential witnesses. On the discovery that Nixon was in the habit of taping discussions that took place in the Oval Office, the Supreme Court ordered him to turn over tapes of conversations he had had with his staff. When, after refusing initially, Nixon finally handed over the tapes, eighteen minutes were missing. Even so, the tapes provided overwhelming evidence that the president either knew about or directed the crimes.

Actions Taken The House Judiciary Committee passed three articles of impeachment in July 1974 charging the president with obstruction of justice, abuse of power, and contempt of Congress. On August 9, 1974, on receiving the news that there were enough votes in the Senate to convict him, Richard Nixon became the first president to resign from office.

Outcome for the Presidency Watergate demonstrated that our system of government works: two branches checked abuses of power by the third. In the aftermath, Watergate is often blamed for the widespread cynicism that pervades today's politics. News reports on subsequent political scandals usually have "-gate" attached somewhere in the headline, and many historians trace the roots of today's aggressive investigative media to this era. Watergate was also responsible for the Independent Counsel Act, passed by Congress in 1978 to remove the investigation and prosecution of wrongdoing by the executive branch from the executive branch and thus to get around the possibility that a president could fire his own special prosecutor, as Nixon had done.

IRAN-CONTRA

Overview In the fall of 1986 a Beirut, Lebanon, magazine revealed that foreign policy makers in the Reagan administration had sold arms to Iran in exchange for the release of American hostages. It later transpired that they had used the proceeds from the arms sales to assist "contra" rebels fighting against the Marxist Sandinista government in Nicaragua, in direct contradiction to Congress's wishes. Reagan insisted that his administration had not dealt with terrorists, because Iran did not actually hold the hostages, and that he did not know about the diversion of funds to the contras. Critics claimed that the Iran-contra dealings amounted to the White House's taking foreign policy into its own hands, ignoring the Constitution and bypassing checks and balances.

Actions Taken Independent counsel Lawrence Walsh's investigation lasted seven years and resulted in the indictments of fourteen people. President George H. W. Bush pardoned six of them, while Walsh released two others in exchange for testimony. The investigation implicated many of President Reagan's national security staff who either directed or had knowledge of the operations. However, Walsh failed to find solid proof that Reagan himself knowingly approved the illegal sales and directed the profits to another illegal operation. Had such evidence been found, it may well have precipitated impeachment hearings.

Outcome for the Presidency The Iran-contra scandal deeply scarred President Reagan's legacy. Even his supporters perceived him as "out of the loop" in his own presidency, and his severest critics called him a liar. The scandal had an impact on Bush's presidency as well; only days before Bush's 1992 reelection defeat, Walsh indicted former defense secretary Caspar Weinberger, whose notes apparently indicated that then–Vice President Bush knew more than he claimed. After he lost the election, Bush pardoned Weinberger and five others, declaring that the investigation was politically motivated. Apart from having a damaging effect on two presidencies, the scandal further weakened the office of the presidency itself, making it vulnerable to media scrutiny and the unrestricted investigations of a powerful independent counsel.

WHITEWATER

Overview "Whitewater" refers to a private real estate investment by then-governor of Arkansas Bill Clinton. The question was whether Clinton improperly used his office to finance the deal, and whether Hillary Clinton had improperly represented a state-regulated savings and loan while her husband was governor. The investigation of Whitewater expanded to cover other questionable White House activity, such as the firing of White House Travel Office employees, the suicide of White House deputy counsel Vince Foster, and the use of FBI files to investigate prominent Republicans.

Actions Taken Independent counsel Kenneth Starr was unable to tie Clinton to the Whitewater deal or to the other targets of his investigation. In the course of his inquiries, however, it was brought to his attention that Clinton was allegedly having an affair with a White House intern, which Clinton had not admitted in his testimony in a sexual harassment lawsuit brought against him by former Arkansas state employee Paula Jones. When damaging evidence came to light, Clinton confessed to the relationship despite his previous testimony and repeated public denials. Starr sent a report to Congress outlining eleven offenses that he believed were impeachable; all focused on Clinton's efforts to dissemble about the affair.

The House Judiciary Committee passed four articles of impeachment in December 1998: two counts of perjury and one count each for obstructing justice and abusing power. On December 19, 1998, Clinton became the second president to be impeached when the full House approved, largely along party lines, two of

Grounds for Impeachment? (continued)

the four articles. The Senate failed to achieve the necessary sixty-seven votes for either article (obstruction of justice and perjury) and acquitted President Clinton on February 12, 1999.

Outcome for the Presidency Clinton became the only modern president to be impeached. Although he enjoyed high approval ratings throughout the impeachment process, the whole affair led many to view Clinton as a highly polarizing figure. Supporters of the president believed the process to be a vindictive, personal attack by Republicans and argued that attention was distracted from more pressing issues like the Kosovo crisis. Rulings by the Supreme Court that allowed the sexual harassment lawsuit to proceed against the president and that permitted the subpoena of Secret Service personnel will greatly affect the executive privilege and privacy of future presidents. Finally, the ability of Congress to tie up the nation's business in an attempt to remove a president for reasons that most Americans did not feel rose to the level of high crimes and misdemeanors damaged the principle of separation of powers and weakened the presidency.

1. Stephen Gettinger, "When Congress Decides a President's 'High Crimes and Misdemeanors,'" *Congressional Quarterly Weekly Report,* March 7, 1998, 565.
2. Aaron Epstein, "What Is an Impeachable Act? Constitution Called Confusing," *Detroit Free Press,* September 10, 1998, A1.
3. Robert DiClerico, *The American President,* 4th ed. (Englewood Cliffs, N.J.: Prentice Hall, 1995), 99.

son who, more than anyone else, is held responsible for agencies of the national government and the implementation of national policy.

The Constitution also specifies that the president, with the approval of the majority of the Senate, will appoint the heads of departments, who will oversee the work of implementation. These heads, who have come to be known collectively as the **cabinet**, report to the president. Today the president is responsible for the appointments of more than four thousand federal employees: cabinet and lower administrative officers, federal judges, military officers, and members of the diplomatic corp. His responsibilities place him at the top of a vast federal bureaucracy. But his control of the federal bureaucracy is limited, as we will see in Chapter 9, by the fact that though he can make a large number of appointments, he is not able to fire many of the people he hires.

cabinet a presidential advisory group selected by the president, made up of the vice president, the heads of the federal executive departments, and other high officials to whom the president elects to give cabinet status

Other constitutional powers place the president, as **commander-in-chief**, at the head of the command structure for the entire military establishment. The Constitution gives Congress the power to declare war, but as the commander-in-chief, the president has the practical ability to wage war. These two powers, meant to check each other, instead provide for a battleground on which Congress and the president struggle for the power to control military operations. After the controversial Vietnam War, which was waged by Presidents Lyndon Johnson and Richard Nixon but never officially declared by Congress, Congress passed the War Powers Act of 1973, which was intended to limit the president's power to send troops abroad without congressional approval. Most presidents have ignored the act, however, when they wished to engage in military action abroad, and since public opinion tends to rally around the president at such times, Congress has declined to challenge popular presidential actions. The War Powers Act remains more powerful on paper than in reality.

commander-in-chief the president's role as the top officer of the country's military establishment

Finally, under his executive powers, the president is the **chief foreign policy maker**. This role is not spelled out in the Constitution, but the foundation for it is laid in the

chief foreign policy maker the president's executive role as the primary shaper of relations with other nations

Commander-in-Chief or Commander-in-Chef?
The Constitution puts the president in charge of the U.S. armed forces, with the power to send troops to resolve conflicts. Since most "wars" are fought without a congressional declaration of war, presidents wield substantial military power. On Thanksgiving Day 2003, President Bush paid a surprise visit to Iraq, where he served turkey to troops at Baghdad International Airport. The mission's intent was to rally troops and boost morale during the war on terrorism.

provision that the president negotiates **treaties**—formal international agreements with other nations—with the approval of two-thirds of the Senate. The president also appoints ambassadors and receives ambassadors of other nations, a power that essentially amounts to determining what nations the United States will recognize.

treaties formal agreements with other countries; negotiated by the president and requiring approval by two-thirds of the Senate

While the requirement of Senate approval for treaties is meant to check the president's foreign policy power, the president can get around the senatorial check by issuing an **executive agreement** directly with the heads of state of other nations. The executive agreement allows the president the flexibility of negotiating, often in secret, to set important international policy without creating controversy or stirring up opposition. For example, U.S. military bases set up in Egypt, Saudi Arabia, Kuwait, and other Gulf states are the result of executive agreements made between the president and the leaders of those countries. Executive agreement is used frequently; 9,472 executive agreements were issued between 1969 and 2002, compared to just 850 treaties.[9] This capability gives the president considerable power and flexibility in the realm of foreign policy—more than 90 percent of the agreements the United States reaches with foreign nations are made by executive agreement.[10] However, even though the executive agreement is a useful and much-used tool, Congress may still thwart the president's intentions by refusing to approve the funds needed to put an agreement into action. Executive agreements are not only used to get around the need for Senate approval. Often they concern routine matters and are issued for the sake of efficiency. If the Senate had to approve each agreement, it would have to act at the rate of one per day, tying up its schedule and keeping it from many more important issues.[11]

executive agreement a presidential arrangement with another country that creates foreign policy without the need for Senate approval

The framers clearly intended that the Senate would be the principal voice and decision maker in foreign policy, but that objective was not realized even in George Washington's presidency. At subsequent points in our history, Congress has exerted more authority in foreign policy, but for the most part, particularly in the twentieth century, presidents have taken a strong leadership role in dealing with other nations.

Part of the reason for this is that Congress has more jealously guarded its prerogatives in domestic policy because those are so much more crucial in its members' reelection efforts. This has changed somewhat in recent years as the worldwide economy has greatly blurred the line between domestic and foreign affairs.

Legislative Powers Even though the president is the head of the executive branch of government, the Constitution also gives him some legislative power to check Congress. He "shall from time to time give to the Congress information of the state of the union, and recommend to their consideration such measures as he shall judge necessary and expedient." Although the framers' vision of this activity was quite limited, today the president's **State of the Union address**, delivered before the full Congress every January, is a major statement of the president's policy agenda.

State of the Union address a speech given annually by the president to a joint session of Congress and to the nation announcing the president's agenda

The Constitution gives the president the nominal power to convene Congress and, when there is a dispute about when to disband, to adjourn it as well. Before Congress met regularly, this power, though limited, actually meant something. Today we rarely see it invoked. Some executives, such as the British prime minister who can dissolve Parliament and call new elections, have a much more formidable convening power than that available to the U.S. president.

The principal legislative power given the president by the Constitution is the **presidential veto**. If the president objects to a bill passed by the House and the Senate, he can veto it, sending it back to Congress with a message indicating his reasons. Congress can override a veto with a two-thirds vote in each house, but because mustering the two-thirds support is quite difficult, the presidential veto is a substantial power. Even the threat of a presidential veto can have a major impact in getting congressional legislation to fall in line with the administration's preferences.[12] Table 8.3 shows the number of bills vetoed since 1933 and the number of successful veto overrides by Congress. The elder President Bush was particularly successful in using the veto—he used it often against the Democratic Congress and was overridden only once. President Clinton never used the veto in 1993 and 1994, when he had Democratic majorities in Congress.

presidential veto a president's authority to reject a bill passed by Congress; may only be overridden by a two-thirds majority in each house

Measured Responses
A president's State of the Union address usually receives polite support from the opposition. Yet the ambivalent feelings of many Democratic members of Congress were clearly evident as they remained seated during President George W. Bush's February 2005 speech. On the other side of the aisle, much happier with his words, Republicans stood and applauded in praise. The Democrats' discontent with the president's speech foreshadowed a year of opposition politics, in which they attempted to block several of Bush's appointees and tried to undercut his plans to privatize Social Security.

However, over the next four years, when he faced a mostly Republican Congress, he attempted to stop twenty-five bills; Congress was able to override him only twice. With Republican majorities in the House and the Senate for most of his first term, as well as the unusual atmosphere of bipartisanship that appeared in Washington after September 11, 2001, George W. Bush joined John Quincy Adams and Thomas Jefferson as the only presidents who did not veto a bill during their first term.[13]

Congress has regularly sought to get around the obstacle of presidential vetoes by packaging a number of items together in a bill. Traditionally, presidents have had to sign a complete bill or reject the whole thing. Thus, for example, Congress regularly adds such things as a building project or a tax break for a state industry onto, say, a military appropriations bill that the president wants. Often presidents calculate that it is best to accept such add-ons, even if they think them unjustified or wasteful, in order to get passed what they judge to be important legislation.

Before it was ruled unconstitutional by the Supreme Court in 1998, the short-lived *line-item veto* promised to provide an important new tool for presidents. Favored by conservatives and by President Clinton, the 1996 line-item veto was supposed to save money by allowing presidents to cut some items, like pork barrel projects, from spending bills without vetoing the entire package. The Supreme Court declared the law unconstitutional because the Constitution says that all legislation is to be passed by both houses and then presented as a whole to the president for his approval.

Another of the president's key legislative powers comes from the vice president's role as presiding officer of the Senate. Although the vice president rarely presides over the Senate, Article I, Section 3 says that he may cast a tie-breaking vote when the 100-member Senate is evenly divided. Some recent examples illustrate just how important this has been to presidential prerogatives. In 1993, Vice President Al Gore voted to break a tie that enabled President Clinton's first budget to pass. The bill included con-

TABLE 8.3 **Presidential Vetoes, Roosevelt to Bush**

YEARS	PRESIDENT	TOTAL VETOES	REGULAR VETOES	POCKET VETOES	VETOES OVERRIDDEN	VETO SUCCESS RATE
1933–1945	Franklin Roosevelt	635	372	263	9	97.6%
1945–1953	Harry Truman	250	180	70	12	93.3
1953–1961	Dwight Eisenhower	181	73	108	2	97.3
1961–1963	John Kennedy	21	12	9	0	100.0
1963–1969	Lyndon Johnson	30	16	14	0	100.0
1969–1974	Richard Nixon	43	26	17	7	73.1
1974–1977	Gerald Ford	66	48	18	12	75.0
1977–1981	Jimmy Carter	31	13	18	2	84.6
1981–1989	Ronald Reagan	78	39	39	9	76.9
1989–1993	George H. W. Bush	46	29	17*	1	96.6
1993–2001	Bill Clinton	36	36	0	2	94.4
2001–2005	George W. Bush	0	0	0	0	n/a

*Although they are counted here, Congress did not recognize two of Bush's pocket vetoes and considered the legislation enacted. n/a = not applicable.

Source: Mitchel A. Sollenberger, "The Presidential Veto and Congressional Procedure" in CRS Report for Congress, updated February 27, 2004, 4. Retrieved from www.senate.gov/reference/resources/pdf/RS21750.pdf; Joseph J. Schatz, "With a Deft and Light Touch, Bush Finds Ways to Win," *CQ Weekly,* December 11, 2004, 2900–2904; veto success rate calculated by authors.

troversial tax increases and spending cuts but ultimately helped create a budget surplus. Eight years later, Vice President Dick Cheney broke a tie vote on Bush's first budget, which ironically undid some of the Clinton tax increases but also included numerous other tax reductions. Both of these pieces of legislation were hallmarks of their respective presidents' agendas. The fact that a president can count on his vice president to break a tie when the Senate is split over controversial legislation is an often underappreciated legislative power.

Although the Constitution does not grant the president the power to make law, his power to do so has grown over time and now is generally accepted. Presidents can issue **executive orders** (not to be confused with the executive agreements he can make with other nations), which are supposed to be clarifications of how laws passed by Congress are to be implemented by specific agencies. Some of the most significant presidential actions have come from executive orders, including President Franklin Roosevelt's order to hold Japanese Americans in internment camps in World War II, President Truman's order that black and white military troops be integrated, President Kennedy's and President Johnson's affirmative action programs, and many of the post–September 11 security measures such as the establishment of military tribunals for cases against terrorists. Perhaps the most contentious arguments in George W. Bush's presidency have concerned the administration's executive orders easing environmental regulations on businesses, limiting federal funding for stem cell research, or instructing agencies to provide grants for faith-based groups to carry out social services.

executive order a clarification of congressional policy issued by the president and having the full force of law

Historically, executive orders spike when there are national crises. Patterns also suggest that executive orders are released at a higher rate at the beginning of a president's term as he immediately implements key policies and at the end of his term as he tries to leave his legacy.[14] Indeed, presidents often release particularly symbolic executive orders on their first days in office, as President Clinton did within days of his inauguration when he reversed the Reagan and Bush ban on funding for international family planning, or as President George W. Bush did after his inauguration when he undid Clinton's order.

Judicial Powers Presidents can have tremendous long-term impact on the judiciary, but in the short run their powers over the courts are meager. Their continuing impact comes from nominating judges to the federal courts, including the Supreme Court. The political philosophies of individual judges influence significantly how they interpret the law, and this is especially important for Supreme Court justices, who are the final arbitrators of constitutional meaning. Since judges serve for life, presidential appointments have a long-lasting effect. For instance, today's Supreme Court is considered to be distinctly more conservative than its immediate predecessors due to the appointments made by Presidents Reagan and Bush in the 1980s and early 1990s. Moreover, President Reagan is credited by many with having ushered in a "judicial revolution." He, together with his successor, George H. W. Bush, appointed 550 of the 837 federal judges, most of them conservatives. Clinton appointed moderates to the courts, angering many Democrats, who felt that his appointees should have been more liberal. President George W. Bush has revived the conservative trend that was halted under Clinton.[15]

Presidents cannot always gauge the judicial philosophy of their appointees, however, and they can be sadly disappointed in their choices. Republican president Dwight Eisenhower appointed Chief Justice Earl Warren and Justice William Brennan, both of whom turned out to be more liberal than the president had anticipated. When asked if he had any regrets as president, Eisenhower answered, "Yes, two, and they are both sitting on the Supreme Court."[16]

The presidential power to appoint is limited to an extent by the constitutional requirement for Senate approval of federal judges. Traditionally, most nominees have been approved, with occasional exceptions. Sometimes rejection stems from questions about the candidate's competence, but in other instances rejection is based more on style and judicial philosophy. The Democratic-led Senate's rejection of President Reagan's very conservative Supreme Court nominee Robert Bork in 1987 is one of the more controversial cases.[17] Some observers believe that the battle over the Bork nomination signaled the end of deference to presidents and opened up the approval process to endless challenges and partisan bickering.[18] As we saw in Chapter 7, some of the harshest battles between the president and Congress in recent years have come from partisan Senate challenges to judicial nominations by both the Clinton and Bush administrations. Senate Republicans blocked many of Clinton's nominations, and even though they were typically in the minority during Bush's first term, Democrats filibustered a handful of Bush judicial nominations, prompting some Republicans to call for parliamentary maneuvers that would eliminate the use of the filibuster for judicial nominations in his second term. A deal cut by Senate moderates allowed most of Bush's nominees to be confirmed while preserving the filibuster for extraordinary cases.[19]

A president's choice of judges for the federal district courts is also limited by the tradition of **senatorial courtesy**, whereby senior senators of the president's party from the states in which the appointees reside have what amounts to a veto power over the president's choice. If presidents should ignore the custom of senatorial courtesy and push a nomination unpopular with one of the home state senators, fellow senators will generally honor one another's requests and refuse to confirm the appointee.

senatorial courtesy tradition of granting senior senators of the president's party considerable power over federal judicial appointments in their home states

Though presidents can leave a lasting imprint on the judiciary, in the short run they do little to affect court decisions. They do not contact judges to plead for decisions; they do not offer them inducements as they might a fence-sitting member of Congress. When, as happens rarely, a president criticizes a federal judge for a decision, the criticism is usually poorly received. For example, when spokespeople for President Clinton went so far as to threaten to ask for the resignation of a federal judge after he made a widely publicized and unpopular decision, a flood of editorials cried foul.[20]

The least controversial way a president can try to influence a court decision is to have the Justice Department invest resources in arguing a case. The third-ranking member of the Justice Department, the **solicitor general**, is a presidential appointee whose job it is to argue cases for the government before the Supreme Court. The solicitor general is thus a bridge between the executive and the judiciary, not only deciding which cases the government will appeal to the Court, but also filing petitions stating the government's (usually the president's) position on cases to which the government is not even a party. These petitions, called *amicus curiae* ("friend of the court") briefs, are taken very seriously by the Court. The government is successful in its litigation more often than any other litigant, winning over two-thirds of its cases in the past half-century, and often having its arguments cited by the justices themselves in their opinions.[21]

solicitor general the Justice Department officer who argues the government's cases before the Supreme Court

One additional judicial power granted to the president by the Constitution is the **pardoning power**, which allows a president to exempt a person, convicted or not, from punishment for a crime. This power descends from a traditional power of kings as the court of last resort and thus a check on the courts. Pardons are usually not controver-

pardoning power a president's authority to release or excuse a person from the legal penalties of a crime sial, although they have occasionally backfired in dramatic ways. After President Gerald Ford pardoned Richard Nixon, in the hopes that the nation would heal from its Watergate wounds more quickly if it didn't have to endure the spectacle of its former president on trial, Ford experienced a tremendous backlash that may have contributed to his 1976 loss to Jimmy Carter. Similarly, President George Bush's pardon—after he had already lost to Bill Clinton in 1992—of the people who could have conceivably been charged with wrongdoing in the Iran-contra affair, was received extremely negatively. Clinton's turn came in 2001 when, shortly after he left office, he was investigated for trading political favors and contributions for pardons. Perhaps the lesson for future presidents is that pardons that are perceived to be partisan in nature rather than a disinterested check on the power of the courts are likely to be taken amiss by a public and media on the lookout for abuses of the public trust.[22]

THE TRADITIONAL PRESIDENCY

The presidency that the founders created and outlined in the Constitution is not the presidency of today. In fact, so clearly have the effective rules governing the presidency changed that scholars speak of the era of the *traditional presidency,* from the founding to the 1930s, and the era of the *modern presidency,* from the 1930s to the present. Although the constitutional powers of the president have been identical in both eras, the interpretation of how far the president can go beyond his constitutional powers has changed dramatically.

The founders' limited vision of the office survived more or less intact for a little over one hundred years. There were exceptions, however, to their expectations that echoed Hamilton's call for a stronger executive. Several early presidents exceeded the powers granted in the Constitution. Washington expanded the president's foreign policy powers, Jefferson entered into the Louisiana Purchase, and Andrew Jackson developed the role of president as popular leader. In one of the most dramatic examples, Abraham Lincoln, during the emergency conditions of the Civil War, stepped outside his constitutional role to call up state militias, to enlarge the army and use tax money to pay for it, and to blockade the southern ports. He claimed that his actions, though counter to the Constitution, were necessary to save the nation.[23]

inherent powers presidential powers implied but not explicitly stated in the Constitution

These presidents believed that they had what modern scholars call **inherent powers** to fulfill their constitutional duty to "take care that the laws be faithfully executed." Some presidents, like Lincoln, claimed that national security required a broader presidential role. Others held that the president, as our sole representative in foreign affairs, needed a stronger hand abroad than at home. Inherent powers are not explicitly listed in the Constitution but are implied by the powers that are granted, and they have been supported, to some extent, by the Supreme Court.[24] But most nineteenth- and early-twentieth-century presidents, conforming to the founders' expectations, took a more retiring role, causing one observer to claim that "twenty of the twenty-five presidents of the nineteenth century were lords of passivity."[25] The job of the presidency was seen as a primarily administrative office, in which presidential will was clearly subordinate to the will of Congress.

THE MODERN PRESIDENCY

The simple rural nature of life in the United States changed rapidly in the century and a half after the founding. The country grew westward, and the nation became more industrialized. More people worked in factories, fewer on the land. The postal system expanded greatly, and the federal government became involved in American Indian affairs, developed national parks, and enacted policies dealing with transportation, especially the railroads. Government in the nineteenth century sought bit by bit to respond to the new challenges of its changing people and economy, and as it responded, it grew beyond the bounds of the rudimentary administrative structure supervised by George Washington. With the crisis of the Great Depression and Franklin Roosevelt's New Deal solution, the size of government exploded and popular ideas about government changed radically. From being an exception, as it was in our early history, the use of strong presidential power became an expectation of the modern president.

Nothing in their prior experience had prepared Americans for the calamity of the Great Depression. Following the stock market crash of October 1929, the economy went into a tailspin. Unemployment soared to 25 percent while the gross national product plunged from around $100 billion in 1928 to under $60 billion in 1932.[26] President Herbert Hoover held that government had only limited powers and responsibility to deal with what was, he believed, a private economic crisis. There was no widespread presumption, as there is today, that government was responsible for the state of the economy or for alleviating the suffering of its citizens.

Roosevelt's election in 1932, and his subsequent three reelections, initiated an entirely new level of governmental activism. For the first time, the national government assumed responsibility for the economic well-being of its citizens on a substantial scale. Relying on the theory mentioned earlier, that foreign affairs are thought to justify greater presidential power than domestic, Roosevelt portrayed himself as waging a war against the Depression and sought from Congress the powers "that would be given to me if we were in fact invaded by a foreign foe."[27] The New Deal programs he put in place tremendously increased the size of the federal establishment and its budget. The number of civilians (nonmilitary personnel) working for the federal government increased by over 50 percent during Roosevelt's first two terms (1933–1939). The crisis of the Great Depression created the conditions for extraordinary action, and

Birth of the Modern Presidency
New Deal policies and programs expanded the national government and created the powerful modern presidency. Seated in the rear of the car at the left of this image, President Franklin D. Roosevelt inspects the progress of construction of the Grand Coulee Dam in Washington State in October 1937. The dam was constructed at a cost of $200,000,000 and still provides irrigation and power to more than a million acres of the Columbia River basin.

the leadership of Roosevelt created new responsibilities and opportunities for the federal government. Congress delegated a vast amount of discretionary power to Roosevelt so that he could implement his New Deal programs.

The legacy of the New Deal is that Americans now look to their president and their government to regulate their economy, solve their social problems, and provide political inspiration. Roosevelt's New Deal was followed by Truman's Fair Deal. Eisenhower's presidency was less activist, but it was followed by Kennedy's New Frontier and Johnson's Great Society. All of these comprehensive policy programs did less than they promised, but they reinforced the belief of Americans that it is government's and, in particular, the president's job to make ambitious promises. While presidents from Carter to Reagan to Clinton enthusiastically promoted plans for cutting back the size of government, few efforts were successful. Not even President Reagan, more conservative and therefore more hostile to "big government," was able to significantly reduce government size and popular expectations of government action.

The growth of domestic government is not the only source of the increased power of the modern president, however. As early as 1936, the Supreme Court confirmed in *United States v. Curtiss-Wright Corporation* the idea that the president has more inherent power in the realm of foreign affairs than in domestic politics.[28] This decision became more significant as the U.S. role in world politics expanded greatly in the post–World War II years. The ascendance of the United States as a world power; its engagement in the Cold War; its participation in such undeclared wars as Korea, Vietnam, the Persian Gulf, Kosovo, and the war against terrorism; and its current status as the sole global superpower make the person at the head of that government very powerful indeed.

Thus the modern presidency is characterized by a tremendous growth in the policy and leadership responsibilities of the president, based not on his constitutional role but on his inherent powers. In the so-called steel seizure case (1952), the Supreme Court struck down a particular exercise of inherent powers on the part of President Truman, but only two of the justices rejected the idea of inherent powers.[29] In this era the dominance of the legislature recedes and observers write about an "imperial presidency."

THE MODERN PRESIDENCY TODAY

Whether or not the power of the modern presidency ever approached "imperial" status at one time, there is no doubt that the 1970s brought a reaction to the Vietnam War and the Watergate scandal that made it harder for the modern president to act. Congress, the media, and the courts began to check the president in ways they had not done earlier in the era of the modern presidency.

Many in Congress felt that neither the Johnson nor the Nixon administrations had been sufficiently forthcoming over the Vietnam War. Frustration with that, as well as with Nixon's abuse of his powers during Watergate and his unwillingness to spend budgeted money as Congress had appropriated it, led Congress to develop its own mechanisms for getting information about public policy to use as a check on presidential power.[30] Congress also weakened the office of the presidency by the passage of the Independent Counsel Act of 1978 (see the box "Grounds for Impeachment?"), which was intended to provide an impartial check on a president's activities but which was ultimately left open to abuse by his opponents.

At the same time, fresh from the heady success of the *Washington Post*'s discovery of the Watergate scandal, the Washington press corps abandoned the discretion that had kept them from reporting Franklin Roosevelt's inability to walk or John Kennedy's extramarital affairs, and began to subject the president to closer scrutiny. Reporters, eager to make a name as investigative journalists, became far more aggressive in their coverage of the White House.

Even the Supreme Court served to limit the power and stature of the presidency, as when it ruled unanimously in 1997 that a sitting president does not have immunity from civil lawsuits while he is in office, adding that the process of such a case was unlikely to prove a disruption of his duties.[31] Paula Jones's lawsuit against Bill Clinton, of course, proved to be disruptive of his presidency in the extreme, and ended up leading to his impeachment, although on grounds that had nothing to do with the case. Had the Court not made that decision, Clinton's affair with Monica Lewinsky would not have come to light, and he would most likely not have been impeached.

The modern presidency had been so diminished by post-Watergate developments and the Clinton impeachment that the George W. Bush administration came to power determined to restore the luster and power of the office. In January 2002, Vice President Cheney remarked that the presidency is "weaker today as an institution because of the unwise compromises that have been made over the last 30 to 35 years," and he highlighted the "erosion of the powers and the ability of the president" of the United States to do his job.[32] Indeed, many of Bush's executive orders were designed to reinstate those powers, as were the claims of executive privilege made by his administration (see, for example, the What's at Stake? discussion that opens this chapter).

WHO, WHAT, HOW The politicians who initially had something important at stake in the rules governing the executive were the founders themselves. Arranged by those, like Alexander Hamilton, who wanted a strong leader and by others who preferred a multiple executive to ensure checks on the power of the office, the constitutional compromise provides for a stronger position than many wanted, but one still limited in significant ways from becoming overly powerful and independent.

Until the 1930s, presidents were mostly content to live within the confines of their constitutional restrictions, with only occasional excursions into the realm of inherent powers. But since the 1930s, presidents and citizens have entered into a complex relationship. Seeking effective leadership in an increasingly sophisticated world, citizens have been willing to expand the informal rules of presidential power provided they approve of the ways in which the president uses it. When the powers of the presidency have seemed to have gotten out of hand, however, Congress, the courts and the media have been quick to limit it, showing how well the founders' system of checks and balances functions.

PRESIDENTIAL POLITICS: THE STRUGGLE FOR POWER

Presidential responsibilities and the public's expectations of what the president can accomplish have increased greatly since the start of the twentieth century, but as we have discussed, the Constitution has not been altered to give the president more power. To avoid failure, presidents have to seek power beyond that which is explicitly granted by the Constitution, and even beyond what they can claim as part of their inherent powers.

THE EXPECTATIONS GAP AND THE NEED FOR PERSUASIVE POWER

Even presidents who have drawn enthusiastically on their inherent powers to protect national security or conduct foreign policy still cannot summon the official clout to ensure that their legislation gets through Congress, that the Senate approves their appointments, and that other aspects of their campaign promises are fulfilled. Some scholars believe that presidents should be given the power necessary to do the job correctly. Others argue that no one can do the job; it is not a lack of power that is the problem, but rather, no human being is up to the task of solving everyone's problems on all fronts. The solution according to this view is to lower expectations and return the presidency to a position of less prominence.[33]

New presidents quickly face the dilemma of high visibility and status, and limited constitutional authority. Of course, they do not want to fail. It would be political suicide for them to be candid and say, "Gee, America, this job is a lot tougher than I thought it would be. The truth is, I don't have the power to do all the stuff I promised." Presidential frustration with the limits of the office is nicely captured by President Truman's remarks about his successor, President Eisenhower, a former general. "He'll sit here," Truman would remark (tapping his desk for emphasis) "and he'll say, 'Do this! Do that!' *And nothing will happen.* Poor Ike—it won't be a bit like the Army. He'll find it very frustrating."[34]

Yet people continue to run for and serve as president. How do they deal with the expectations gap? The answer is that they attempt to augment their power. In addition to the inherent powers we have already discussed, the primary extraconstitutional power the president tries to use is, in one scholar's phrase, the **power to persuade.**[35] To achieve what is expected of them, presidents must persuade others to cooperate with their agendas—most often members of Congress, but also the courts, the media, state and local officials, bureaucrats, foreign leaders, and even the American public itself.

power to persuade a president's ability to convince Congress, other political actors, and the public to cooperate with the administration's agenda

GOING PUBLIC

One central strategy that presidents follow in their efforts to persuade people "inside the Beltway" (that is, the Washington insiders) to go along with their agenda is to reach out and appeal to the public directly for support. This strategy of **going public** is based on the expectation that public support will put pressure on other politicians to give the president what he wants.[36] Presidents use their powers as both head of government and head of state to appeal to the public.[37] A president's effort to go public can include a trip to an international summit, a town-meeting-style debate on a controversial issue, or even the president's annual State of the Union address or other nationally televised speeches. President Clinton used this strategy to garner and maintain public support in 1998, when he faced allegations that he had had an affair with a White House intern and lied about it to a grand jury. Soon after the scandal became widely publicized, Clinton gave his State of the Union address to such public acclaim that his approval ratings rose as the scandal unfolded. Congress's approval ratings declined as it was seen to attack and then impeach such a popular president.

going public a president's strategy of appealing to the public on an issue, expecting that public pressure will be brought to bear on other political actors

Somewhat less successfully, President George W. Bush used his 2005 State of the Union address and subsequent sixty-day "coast-to-coast blitz" of town hall meetings to publicly promote his Social Security reforms.[38] The administration's sales pitch was meant to pressure congressional Democrats, whom Bush openly warned would pay a political price if they did not work with him on the issue.[39] While the public did not

Going Public by Going to the People
Presidents' access to the media allows them to present their policy proposals to the public, in the hope that the policies will win popular support that will, in turn, persuade Congress to pass their favored legislation. In 2005, President Bush took to the road with a series of carefully orchestrated town meetings like this one in Raleigh, North Carolina, where the participants were carefully screened to provide a supportive backdrop for him to present his ideas.

fully back Bush's plan, allowing Democrats to resist his reforms, going public did help Bush to convince a majority of Americans that Social Security needed reform.

The Presidency and the Media At the simplest level of the strategy of going public, the president just takes his case to the people. Consequently, presidential public appearances have greatly increased in the era of the modern presidency. Recent presidents have had some sort of public appearance almost every day of the week, year round. Knowing that the White House press corps will almost always get some airtime on network news, presidents want that coverage to be favorable. Shaping news coverage so that it generates favorable public opinion for the president is now standard operating procedure.[40]

The Ratings Game Naturally, only a popular president can use the strategy of going public effectively, so popularity ratings become crucial to how successful a president can be. Since the 1930s the Gallup organization has been asking people, "Do you approve or disapprove of the way [the current president] is handling his job as president?" The public's rating of the president—that is, the percentage saying they approve of how the president is handling his job—varies from one president to the next and also typically rises and falls within any single presidential term. The president's ratings are a kind of political barometer: the higher they are, the more effective the president is with other political and economic actors; the lower they are, the harder he finds it to get people to go along. For the modern presidency, the all-important power to persuade is intimately tied to presidential popularity.

Three factors in particular can affect a president's popularity: a cycle effect, the economy, and unifying or divisive current events.[41]

cycle effect the predictable rise and fall of a president's popularity at different stages of a term in office

- The **cycle effect** refers to the tendency for most presidents to begin their terms of office with relatively high popularity ratings, which decline as they move through

honeymoon period the time following an election when a president's popularity is high and congressional relations are likely to be productive

their four-year terms (see Figure 8.1). During the very early months of this cycle, often called the **honeymoon period**, presidents are frequently most effective with Congress. Often, but not always, presidential ratings rise going into reelection, but this seldom approaches the popularity the president had immediately after being elected the first time.

The post-honeymoon drop in approval demonstrated in Figure 8.1 may occur because, by then, presidents have begun to try to fulfill the handsome promises on which they campaigned. Fulfilling promises requires political action, and as presidents exercise their head-of-government responsibilities, they lose the head-of-state glow they bring with them from the election. Political change seldom favors everyone equally, and when someone wins, someone else usually loses. Some citizens become disillusioned as the president makes divisive choices, acts as a partisan, or is attacked by Congress and interests that do not favor his policies. For some citizens, the president then becomes "just another politician," not the dignified head of state they thought they were electing. The cycle effect means that presidents need to present their programs early while they enjoy popular support. Unfortunately, much opportunity available during the honeymoon period can be squandered because of inexperience, as it was at the start of the Clinton administration. In contrast, the Bush team came into office experienced (in part because it benefited from veterans of the previous Bush presidency) and ready to act. Despite the lingering controversy over the contested 2000 election, Republican majorities in both houses of Congress handed Bush several significant legislative victories, including his signature tax cut. By summer 2001, however, there were definite signs that Bush's honeymoon was over.

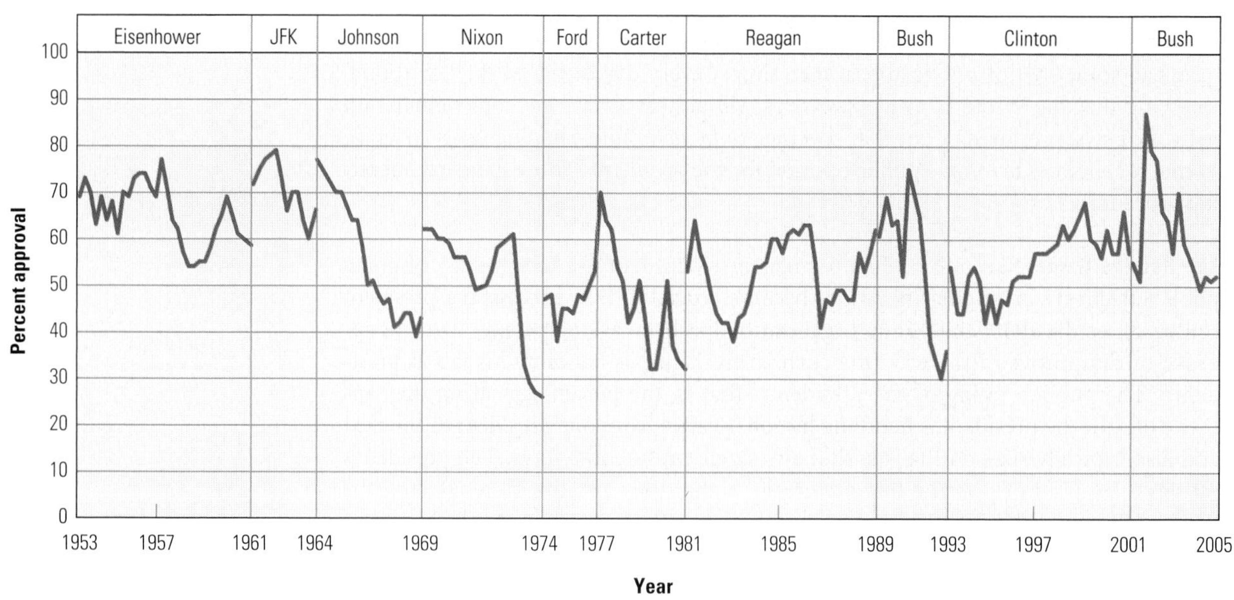

FIGURE 8.1

Average Quarterly Presidential Approval Ratings, From Eisenhower to Bush

Note: Respondents were asked, "Do you approve or disapprove of the way [the current president] is handling his job as president?"

Source: Quarterly data from 1953–2000 provided by Robert S. Erickson; developed for Robert S. Erikson, James A. Stimson, and Michael B. MacKuen, *The Macro Polity* (Cambridge: Cambridge University Press, 2002); data for 2000–2005 calculated by authors from the Gallup Organization.

- The second important factor that consistently influences presidential approval is the state of the economy. At least since Roosevelt, the government has taken an active role in regulating the national economy, and every president promises economic prosperity. In practice, presidential power over the economy is quite limited, but we nevertheless hold our presidents accountable for economic performance. President George H. W. Bush lost the presidency in large measure because of the prolonged recession in the latter part of his administration. Clinton won it with a campaign focused on his plan for economic recovery. From 1992, Clinton presided over the nation's longest postwar period of economic growth, and this was a big factor in his relatively easy victory in 1996 and his healthy approval ratings even in the face of the string of embarrassing and headline-grabbing allegations of wrongdoing that led to his impeachment.[42] The economy was troubled for most of President George W. Bush's first term. Growth was slow, especially after the 2001 terror attacks, and because of his tax cuts and the cost of the wars that followed the attacks, the Clinton surplus had turned into the Bush deficit. Bush's extraordinarily high post–September 11 approval ratings dropped throughout 2004 as news about the economy and the war in Iraq became increasingly negative. By the time of the 2004 election, Bush's ratings were similar to his father's and Jimmy Carter's, both of whom failed to be reelected. Bush did manage to win election but with a smaller margin than any other reelected president.

- Newsworthy events can influence presidential approval. Divisive events hurt the president, and unifying events help him. Divisive events usually sink approval ratings. Presidential vetoes and political controversy in general erode presidential stature,[43] because people prefer not to see their executive as a politicking head of government. This element of the expectations gap means that many events and presidential actions can generate public criticism: taking any kind of a stand on abortion; quelling a strike; vetoing many bills; raising taxes; opposing tax breaks, subsidies, or payment levels to groups; calling for more regulation or calling for less regulation. Scandals can hurt presidential approval as well.[44]

  Unifying events tend to be those that focus attention on the president's head-of-state role. Television footage of the president signing agreements with other heads of state is guaranteed to make the incumbent "look presidential." The same effect usually occurs when the United States confronts or makes war on other nations. President George H. W. Bush's ratings soared during the Gulf War, but his high profile was topped by his son's ratings following the terrorist attacks of 2001. George W. Bush's ratings stayed at unprecedented levels well into 2002. Seeking to capitalize on his high approval ratings, Bush took care to frame political issues as if they were about the war even though many of them (for instance, his tax cut, energy policy, and military spending) were on his agenda prior to September 11.

Thus presidents necessarily play the ratings game.[45] Those who choose not to play suffer the consequences: Truman, Johnson, and Ford tended not to heed the polls so closely, and they either had a hard time in office or were not reelected.[46]

WORKING WITH CONGRESS

Presidents do not always try to influence Congress by going public. Sometimes they deal directly with Congress itself, and sometimes they combine strategies and deal with the public and Congress at the same time. The Constitution gives the primary lawmaking powers to Congress. Thus, to be successful with his policy agenda, the president has to have congressional cooperation. This depends in part on the reputation he has with members of that institution and other Washington elites for being an effective leader.[47] Such success varies with several factors, including the compatibility of the president's and Congress's goals and the party composition of Congress.

Shared Powers and Conflicting Policy Goals Presidents usually conflict with Congress in defining the nation's problems and their solutions. In addition to the philosophical and partisan differences that may exist between the president and members of Congress, each has different constituencies to please. The president, as the one leader elected by the whole nation, needs to take a wider, more encompassing view of the national interest. Members of Congress have relatively narrow constituencies and tend to represent their particular interests. Thus, in many cases, members of Congress do not want the same things the president does.

What can the president do to get his legislation through a Congress made up of members whose primary concern is with their individual constituencies? For one thing, presidents have a staff of assistants to work with Congress. The **legislative liaison** office specializes in determining what members of Congress are most concerned about, what they need, and how legislation can be tailored to get their support. In some cases, members just want their views to be heard; they do not want to be taken for granted. In other cases, the details of the president's program have to be adequately explained. It is electorally useful for members to have this done in person, by the president, complete with photo opportunities for release to the papers back home.

legislative liaison executive personnel who work with members of Congress to secure their support in getting a president's legislation passed

In recent presidential races, some candidates have claimed to be running for office as "outsiders," politicians beyond or above the politics-as-usual world of Washington and therefore untainted by its self-interest and contentiousness. This can just be a campaign ploy, but when presidents such as Carter and Clinton are elected who truly *do* lack experience in Washington politics, they may fail to understand the sensitivities of members of Congress and the dynamics of sharing powers. President Carter, even though he had a healthy Democratic majority, had a very difficult time with Congress because he did not realize that, from the perspective of Capitol Hill, what was good for the nation and for Jimmy Carter might not be considered best for each member.[48] Bill Clinton may have learned from Carter's experience. In seeking to pass NAFTA, President Clinton painstakingly spent hours with individual members of Congress in an effort to convince them that he would protect the particular interests of their constituencies. His efforts paid off as Congress approved the free trade agreement in November 1993. The president and his staff inevitably have to do a lot of coalition building with members of Congress if they hope to get the cooperation they require to get their bills through.

Partisanship and Divided Government When the president and the majority of Congress are of the same party, the president is more successful at getting his programs passed. When the president faces **divided government**—that is, when he is of a different party than the majority in one or both houses—he does not do as well.[49] The problem is not just that members of one party act to spite a president of the other party, although that does occur at times. Rather, members of different parties stand for different approaches and solutions to the nation's problems. Democratic presidents and members of Congress tend to be more liberal than the average citizen, and Republican presidents and members of Congress tend to be more conservative.

divided government political rule split between two parties: one controlling the White House and the other controlling one or both houses of Congress

Figure 8.2 shows a hypothetical example of the positions that President George W. Bush might take in dealing with a Republican-led Congress as opposed to a Democratic-led one. When the same party controls the presidency and Congress, the two institutions can cooperate relatively easily on ideological issues, because the majority party wants to go in the same direction as the president. The president prefers his own position, but he would be happy to cooperate with the Republican majority on proposal A because this is much closer to what he wants than is the status quo or the opposition party's proposal. This has been the situation since 2003, when the Republi-

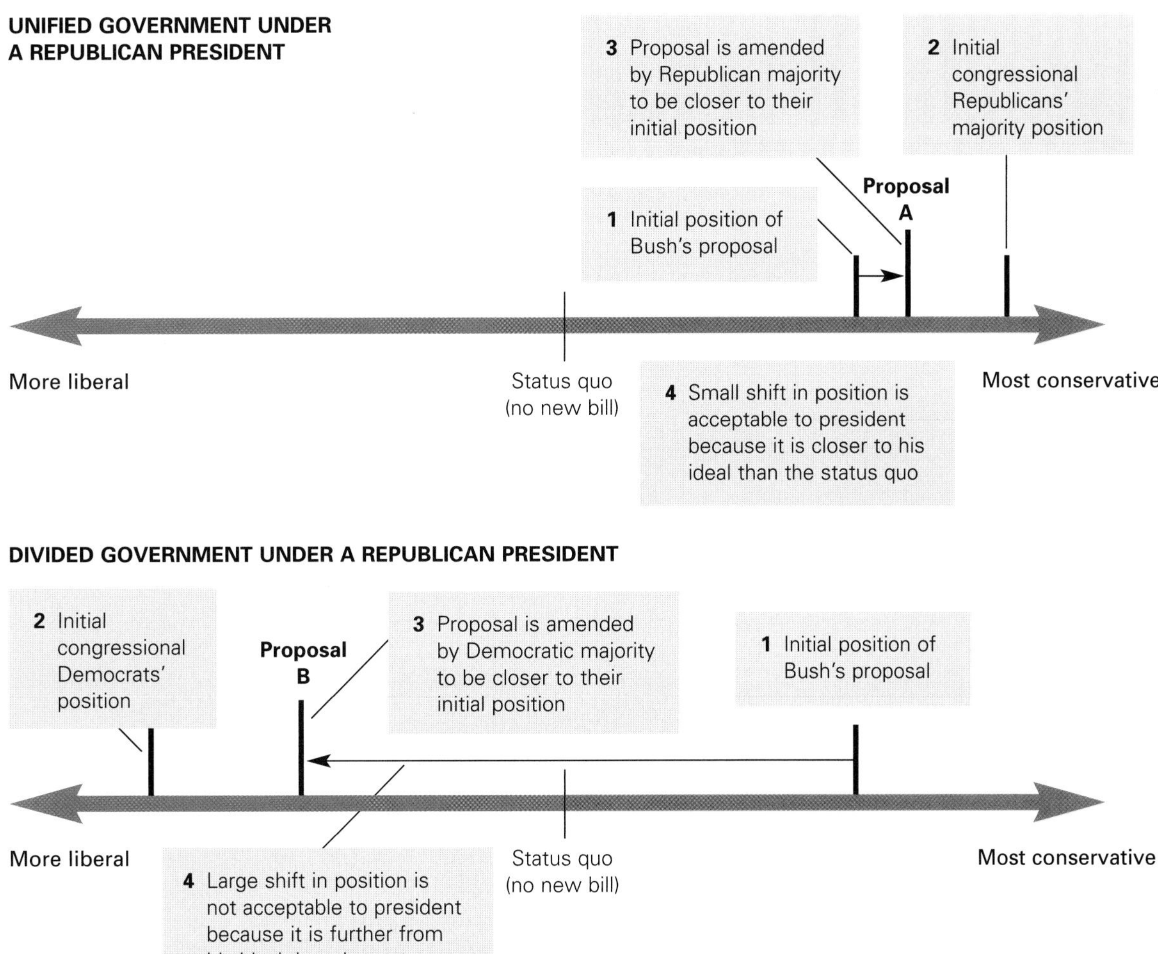

Figure 8.2
Hypothetical Policy Alternatives Under Unified and Divided Government
It is much easier to pass legislation under unified government, where the president's position and that of Congress start out relatively close together, than under divided government, where there is a large gap between the initial positions of the president and Congress. Presidential success in getting bills passed is much higher under unified government than it is when the opposition party has a majority in Congress.

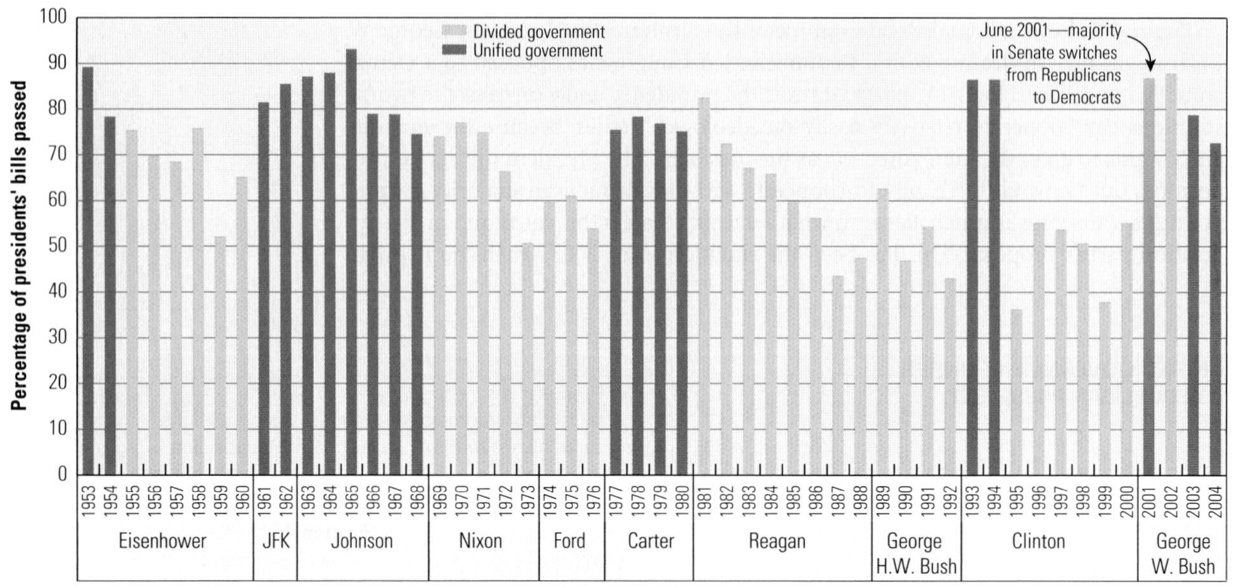

FIGURE 8.3 **Presidential Success Under Unified and Divided Government, Eisenhower to George W. Bush**
When the president faces a divided government—that is, when the opposing party controls one or both houses of Congress—he usually finds it harder to get his bills passed.

Source: Data from "Presidential Support Background," *CQ Weekly*, December 11, 2004, 2946.

cans, already in control of the presidency and the House, gained control of the Senate as well. Consider how different the situation was when the Democrats had the majority in the Senate from May 2001 to January 2003 and there was divided government. Whenever the president pushed for a bill like proposal A, the Senate could ignore it or amend it to something more palatable, such as proposal B. Notice, however, that if the Democratic Senate then sent a bill like proposal B to the president, he would want to veto it because he prefers the alternative of no bill, the status quo, to what Congress might pass. Thus, under divided government, Congress tends to ignore what the president wants, and the president tends to veto what the majority party in Congress offers.

Under a divided government, presidential success is likely to falter, as history has shown. Figure 8.3 shows the percentage of bills passed that were supported by each president from Eisenhower to George W. Bush. Notice that the success rate is consistently higher under unified government. A dramatic example of the impact of divided government can be seen in the Clinton administrations. For his first two years in office, Clinton worked with a Democratic majority in both houses, and Congress passed 86 percent of the bills he supported. The next two years (1995–1996) the Republicans had a majority in both houses, and Clinton's success rate dropped to 46 percent.[50]

Divided government, however, does not doom Washington to inaction. When national needs are pressing or the public mood seems to demand action, the president and opposition majorities have managed to pass important legislation.[51] For example, the government was divided with a Democrat in the White House and Republicans in control of both houses of Congress when major welfare reform was passed with the Personal Responsibility and Work Opportunity Act of 1996.

WHO, WHAT, HOW The president wants to get his policy agenda enacted with congressional cooperation and to get and maintain the public approval necessary to keep the expanded powers he needs to do his job. He tries to accomplish these goals with his constitutional powers, by maintaining his reputation among Washington elites as an effective leader, by building coalitions among members of Congress, by going public, by skillfully using the media, and by trying to keep the economy healthy.

Citizens have an enormous amount of power in this regard because, distant though Washington may seem to most citizens, presidents are driven by the need for public approval to get most of the things that they want. Congress too has goals; members want to get policy passed so that they may go home to the voters and claim to have supported their interests and to have brought home the bacon. Legislators need to meet the expectations of a different constituency than does the president, but few members of Congress want to be seen by the voters as an obstacle to a popular president. A president who has a strong reputation inside Washington and who has broad popularity outside comes to Congress with a distinct advantage, and members of Congress will go out of their way to cooperate and compromise with him.

MANAGING THE PRESIDENTIAL ESTABLISHMENT

We tend to think of the president as one person—what one presidential scholar calls the "single executive image."[52] However, despite all the formal and informal powers of the presidency, the president is limited in what he can accomplish on his own. In fact, the modern president is one individual at the top of a large and complex organization called the presidency, which itself heads the even larger executive branch of government. George Washington got by with no staff to speak of and consulted with his small cabinet of just three department heads, but citizens' expectations of government, and consequently the sheer size of the government, have grown considerably since then, and so has the machinery designed to manage that government.

Today the executive branch is composed of the cabinet with its fifteen departments, the Executive Office of the President, and the White House staff, amounting altogether to hundreds of agencies and 2.71 million civilian employees and almost a million and a half active-duty military employees. The modern president requires a vast bureaucracy to help him make the complex decisions he faces daily, but at the same time the bureaucracy itself presents a major management challenge for the president. The reality of the modern presidency is that the president is limited in his ability to accomplish what he wants by the necessity of dealing with this complex bureaucracy. The executive bureaucracy becomes part of the "how" through which the president tries to get what he wants—for the country, his party, or himself as a politician. But at the same time it becomes another "who," a player in government that goes after its own goals and whose goals can conflict with those of the president.

THE CABINET

Each department in the executive branch is headed by a presidential appointee; collectively, these appointees form the president's cabinet. Today the cabinet comprises fifteen posts heading up fifteen departments. (See Table 9.1 on page 384 for a complete list.) The newest cabinet-level department is the Department of Homeland Security, which was created in 2003. The cabinet is not explicitly set up in the Constitution, though that document does make various references to the executive departments, indicating that the founders were well aware that the president would need specialty advisers in certain areas. President Washington's cabinet included just secretaries of state, Treasury, and war (now called the secretary of defense). The original idea was for the cabinet members to be the president's men overseeing areas for which the president was responsible but that he was unable to supervise personally.

All of that has changed. Today the president considers the demands of organized interests and the political groups and the stature of his administration in putting his cabinet together. The number of departments has grown as various interests (for example, farmers, veterans, workers) have pressed for cabinet-level representation. Appointments to the cabinet have come to serve presidential political goals after the election rather than the goal of helping run the government. Thus the cabinet secretaries typically are chosen to please—or at least not alienate—the organized interests of the constituencies most affected by the departments. Democrats and Republicans will not always choose the same sort of person to fill a cabinet post, however. For example, a Democratic president would be likely to choose a labor leader for secretary of labor, whereas a Republican president would be more likely to fill the post with a representative of the business community.

Presidents may also seek ethnic and gender balance in their cabinet choices. Bill Clinton followed through on his promise to appoint a cabinet of exceptional diversity, and George W. Bush's first- and second-term cabinets have followed suit. Bush has four women, two Hispanics, two African Americans, and two Asian Americans serving in his second-term cabinet. In addition, the president chooses cabinet members who have independent stature and reputation before their appointments. The president's sense of legitimacy is underscored by having top-quality people working in his administration. Last, but certainly not least, a president wants people who are ideologically similar to him in the policy areas they will be handling.[53] This is not easily achieved (and may not be possible) given the other considerations presidents must weigh.

The combination of these factors in making cabinet choices—political payoffs to organized interests, and the legitimacy provided by top people in the area—often results in a "team" that may not necessarily be focused on carrying out the president's agenda. There are exceptions to the typically antagonistic relationship between cabinet members and the president, but they prove the rule. President Kennedy appointed his brother Robert as attorney general. George H. W. Bush appointed his very close friend and personal adviser James Baker as treasury secretary. In these cases, however, the close relationship with the president preceded appointment to the cabinet.

A Diverse Cabinet
Sue Ellen Woodridge, solicitor for the Department of the Interior, Michael Leavitt, secretary of health and human services, and Condoleeza Rice, secretary of state, attend George W. Bush's second cabinet meeting of his second term on April 5, 2005. Part of the balancing act in putting together a cabinet is concern for the many different constituencies represented.

In his second term, George W. Bush's cabinet appointments have come closer to his own ideological views, as those like Secretary of State Colin Powell, who did not always see eye to eye with him, were replaced by more trusted policy advisers such as Condoleezza Rice (see "*Profiles in Citizenship:* Condoleezza Rice"). However Bush's current cabinet is unusual in its ideological cohesion and loyalty to the president. In general, the political considerations of their appointment, coupled with their independent outlook, mean that cabinet members will provide the president with a wide variety of views and perspectives. They do not usually, as a group, place loyalty to the president's agenda above other considerations in their advice to the president. Consequently, presidents tend to centralize their decision making by relying more on their advisers in the Executive Office of the President for advice they can trust.[54]

EXECUTIVE OFFICE OF THE PRESIDENT

The **Executive Office of the President** (EOP) is a collection of organizations that form the president's own bureaucracy. Instituted by Franklin Roosevelt in 1939, the EOP was designed specifically to serve the president's interests, supply information, and provide expert advice.[55] Among the organizations established in the EOP is the **Office of Management and Budget** (OMB), which helps the president exert control over the departments and agencies of the federal bureaucracy by overseeing all their budgets. The director of OMB works to ensure that the president's budget reflects his own policy agenda. Potential regulations created by the agencies of the national government must be approved by OMB before going into effect. This provides the president an additional measure of control over what the bureaucracy does.

Executive Office of the President, or EOP collection of nine organizations that help the president with policy and political objectives

Office of Management and Budget organization within the EOP that oversees the budgets of departments and agencies

Because modern presidents are held responsible for the performance of the economy, all presidents attempt to bring about healthy economic conditions. The job of the **Council of Economic Advisers** is to predict for presidents where the economy is going and to suggest ways to achieve economic growth without much inflation.

Council of Economic Advisers organization within the EOP that advises the president on economic matters

Other departments in the EOP include the **National Security Council** (NSC), which gives the president daily updates about events around the world. The NSC's job is to provide the president with information and advice about foreign affairs; however, the council's role has expanded at times into actually carrying out policy—sometimes illegally, as in the Iran-contra affair.[56] When the existing federal bureaucracy is less than fully cooperative with the president's wishes, some presidents have simply bypassed the agencies by running policy from the White House.

National Security Council organization within the EOP that provides foreign policy advice to the president

WHITE HOUSE OFFICE

Closest to the president, both personally and politically, are the members of the **White House Office**, which is included as a separate unit of the EOP. White House staffers have offices in the White House (see Figure 8.4), and their appointments do not have to be confirmed by the Senate. Just as the public focus on the presidency has grown, so has the size of the president's staff. The White House staff, around 60 members under Roosevelt, grew to the 300–400 range under Eisenhower and now rests at about 400.[57] The organization of the White House Office has also varied greatly from administration to administration. Presidential scholar James Pfiffner has described this organization generally in terms of the following three functional categories: policymaking, outreach and communications, and internal coordination (see Figure 8.5).

White House Office the approximately four hundred employees within the EOP who work most closely and directly with the president

Central to the White House Office is the president's **chief of staff**, who is responsible for the operation of all White House personnel. Depending on how much power the president delegates, the chief of staff may decide who gets appointments with the president and whose memoranda he reads. The chief of staff also has a big hand in

chief of staff the person who oversees the operations of all White House staff and controls access to the president

Profiles in Citizenship

Condoleezza Rice

The high-stakes world of international diplomacy is fraught with stress and tension, but watching Secretary of State Condoleezza Rice stride through it, confident and smiling, only one conclusion is possible: she's having a blast. Ask her if she's enjoying herself, and she laughs. "I am," she confirms with a grin in her voice.

What's so much fun? She says it's the sense that she is very fortunate to be part of an age when big things are happening in the world. "You just don't get a chance unless you're very, very blessed to both have an opportunity to work at this level and to work at this level at a time when so much is at stake," she explains. "This president is really ambitious and bold in what he thinks is possible. . . . [P]eople who've studied international politics or studied international history know of the big cataclysmic changes that have taken place over the centuries, and we're in one of those periods of time. And it's hard and it's complicated and it's messy, but I have enormous optimism about the outcomes here. And so I just feel really very lucky to get up every day and be able to do that. And I don't experience it as a burden. I experience it as . . . how did I get so lucky to get afforded this opportunity?"

> **"It's hard and it's complicated and it's messy, but I have enormous optimism about the outcomes. . . ."**

How did she get so lucky? Listen to Secretary Rice talk about her background and it's apparent that she thinks the biggest piece of luck in her life was being born to John and Angelena Rice. They were "extraordinary people," she says, "and I knew that from very young." Her grandparents too were central in shaping who she is, particularly her paternal grandfather, who died two months before she was born. Although she never knew him, "he was a towering figure in the family because he had managed to get a college education even though he was a sharecropper's son in the early teens of the century. And then he was a kind of educational evangelist. He went around the South starting schools and churches everywhere."

In fact, if there is a single theme in Rice's upbringing, it is, as she puts it, "education, education, education."

Although she grew up as a black child in Birmingham, Alabama, during the height of the civil rights movement, she lived in a protected cocoon. In the seven-square block community where she was raised, parents worked hard to be sure their kids weren't scarred by the violence around them. Education was one way to ensure that these children would be equipped to compete and succeed in the complicated world that was emerging from the embers of the segregated South.

It was a strategy that clearly worked: that seven-block neighborhood produced the first black governor of the International Monetary Fund, a president of the University of Maryland at Baltimore, the head of the largest trauma unit in Los Angeles, the first black National Merit Scholar in Alabama, and, don't forget, of course, a secretary of state.

As Rice was growing up in Alabama and later in Colorado, her parents made sure she was aware of the politics that surrounded her. She remembers, for instance, staying up all night with them, watching the Republican conventions on television. But while her family shared an interest in politics, it never occurred to Rice that she would choose it as a career, because she had her heart set on becoming a great concert pianist. It was only when she decided that she didn't have the talent to take it to the top that she gave up music and changed her major.

Ironically, it was a class at the University of Denver with Josef Korbel (the father of one of Rice's predecessors at the State Department, Madeline Albright) that turned her on to international politics. Even though she hadn't even been out of the country at that point (except to ice skate competitively in Canada), she says, "I was always more interested in world history than anything else." Ask her why, and she laughs. "Well, I was just fascinated by it. . . . I said once that it's a little bit like love. You can't describe why it happens; it just does."

So Rice became an academic, teaching political science at Stanford University before becoming provost there—the first female, the first black, and the youngest person ever to hold the job. From there she became an adviser to the first President Bush and then to his son, holding the post of national security adviser in his first term before being appointed as Colin Powell's successor at State in his second.

Now that she is up to her ears in the political world, she has a view of it that is both practical and almost affectionate. Asked about what seems like the extreme partisanship in politics today, which so many students say turns them off, she takes a long view. "I sometimes think we have very short historical memory in the United States," she says, "which sometimes is not a bad thing because it helps us get over our history. I have a lot of contact with countries where they're still fighting what happened a thousand years ago. But our short historical perspective sometimes makes us overstate the degree to which things are so partisan now or so red and blue. I've been reading lately the biographies of the founding fathers, and it's been really fun for me. I read Alexander Hamilton and I read Ben Franklin. I just finished a great biography of George Washington. Politics was literally a blood sport." She chuckles at this. "You know, I mean it was rough. And the press was rough, and the rumors were rough, and Thomas Jefferson spread rumors about George Washington being senile. It was pretty awful. So I don't mean to excuse the roughness of politics, but I also don't think that the republic necessarily is going to be weakened because the politics gets rough." Here are some more of her views:

On patriotism:

I think it means, first and foremost, not just loving your country but appreciating and respecting what your country stands for. And sometimes patriotism, I think, is confused with what I'll call "jingoism" or just my country, right or wrong. Well, in fact, our country, the United States of America, is a very human institution. And so sometimes it's been right, and sometimes it's been wrong. But it's always stood for principles that I think are very right. And it's always struggled toward those principles.

And for someone like me who comes from the segregated South and who recognizes that it was not that long ago that many of my ancestors were slaves, it's not seeing the United States through rose-colored glasses, but it's seeing that when the United States is at its best, when the United States is really acting on its principles, it's mostly done good in the world.

On keeping the republic:

Recognize that democracy works not just on the rights that you personally are afforded. We're actually very good at defending our individual rights—it's my right to do this, it's my right to do that—but [there are] obligations that go with that. And you can fulfill those obligations, I think, by acting on the other side of democracy. There is also a communitarian part of it. If it's just a group of individuals, it's not going to hold together.

If you look at what really makes America work, it is rotary clubs and Boys and Girls Clubs and the kind of institutions that bring communities together to make life better for people who aren't so lucky as you are. Whenever I spoke to students at Stanford, I would say that, to me, the obligation is to recognize that you are where you are, not necessarily because you were the smartest or the best. There were probably a lot of people who were smarter and better who, by reason of circumstance, didn't make it there. And then that bestows on you an obligation to reach back and to help those who didn't have the circumstances. Maybe they didn't have the parents [who] pushed them, or maybe they didn't get the one teacher who stimulated them in school.

And if you can reach back and make sure that you are that person for a child who needs tutoring or be a Big Sister or whatever, that's all a part of democracy, too. We often think of keeping the republic as just the politics of it: voting, defending individual rights, having a voice. But it's also this communitarian side of democracy because that's what holds us together.

Source: Condoleezza Rice talked with Christine Barbour on August 16, 2005.

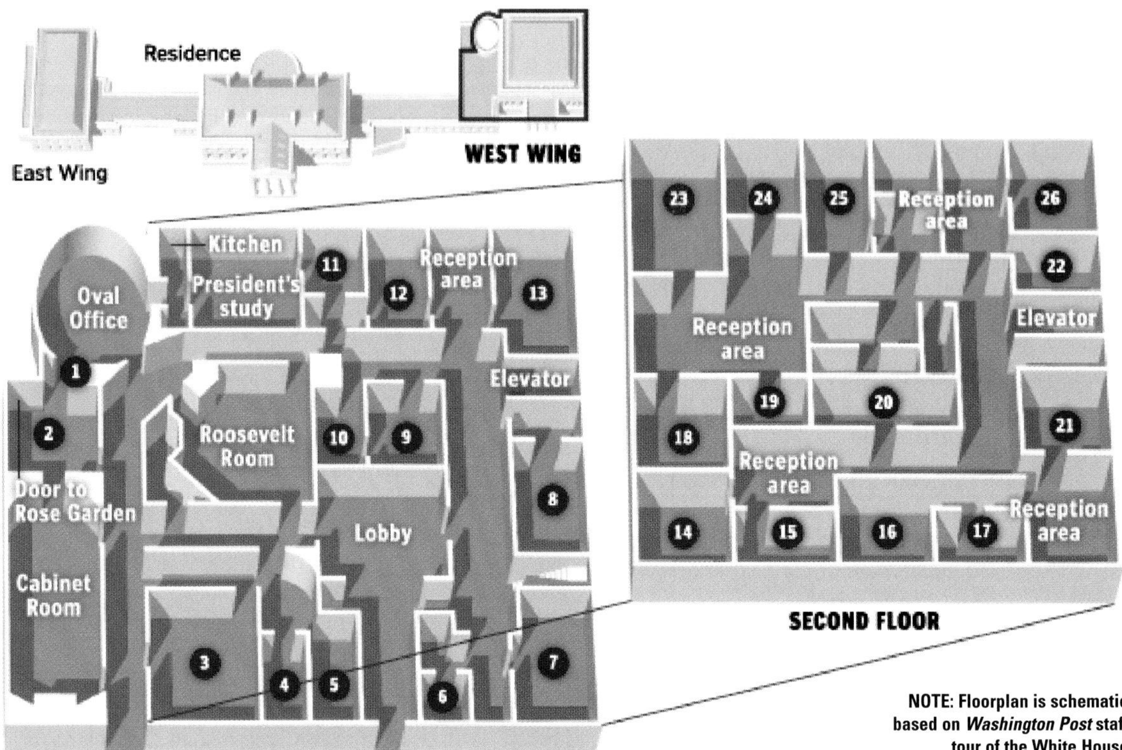

First Floor

1. **Blake Gottesman,** Special Assistant to the President and Personal Aide
2. **Karen Keller,** Special Assistant to the President and Personal Secretary
3. **Scott McClellan,** Assistant to the President and Press Secretary
4. Unoccupied
5. **Erin Healy,** Assistant Press Secretary
6. **J.D. Crouch,** Assistant to the President and Deputy National Security Advisor
7. **Steve Hadley,** Assistant to the President for National Security Affairs
8. **Richard B. Cheney,** Vice President
9. **Susan Ralston,** Special Assistant to the President and Assistant to the Senior Advisor
   Steve Atkiss, Special Assistant to the President for Operations
10. **Mike Gerson,** Assistant to the President for Policy and Strategic Planning
11. **Joseph Hagin,** Assistant to the President and Deputy Chief of Staff
12. **Karl Rove,** Assistant to the President, Deputy Chief of Staff and Senior Advisor
13. **Andrew H. Card Jr.,** Assistant to the President and Chief of Staff

Second Floor

14. **Dan Bartlett,** Counselor to the President
15. **Nicolle Devenish,** Assistant to the President for Communications
16. **Candi Wolff,** Assistant to the President for Legislative Affairs
17. **Doug Badger,** Deputy Assistant to the President for Legislative Affairs
18. **Allan Hubbard,** Assistant to the President for Economic Policy and Director, National Economic Council
19. **Keith Hennessey,** Deputy Assistant to the President for Economic Policy and Deputy Director, National Economic Council
20. **Bill McGurn,** Assistant to the President for Speechwriting
21. **Dina Powell,** Assistant to the President for Presidential Personnel
22. **Bill Kelley,** Deputy Counsel to the President
23. **Claude Allen,** Assistant to the President for Domestic Policy
24. **Tevi Troy,** Deputy Assistant to the President for Domestic Policy
25. **Kristen Silverberg,** Deputy Assistant to the President and Advisor to the Chief of Staff
26. **Harriet Miers,** Counsel to the President

FIGURE 8.4
Floor Plan of the West Wing

Source: © 2005, the *Washington Post.* "Inside the Real West Wing." www.washingtonpost.com/wp-dyn/content/custom/2005/06/06/CU2005060601310.html.

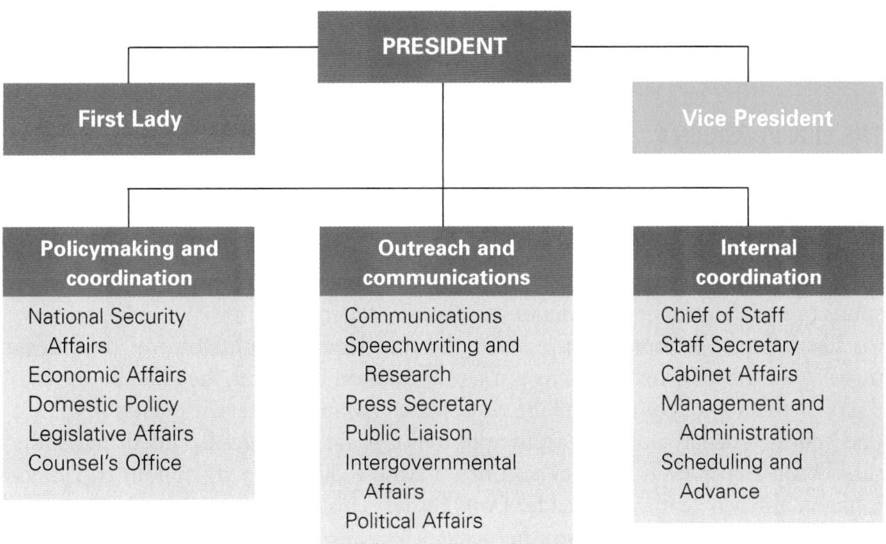

FIGURE 8.5
Organization of the White House Office

Source: James P. Pfiffner, *The Modern Presidency,* 2d ed. (New York: St. Martin's, 1998), 87.

hiring and firing decisions at the White House. Critics claim that the chief of staff isolates the president by removing him from the day-to-day control of his administration, but demands on the president have grown to the point that now a chief of staff is considered a necessity. Presidents Carter and Ford tried to get by without a chief of staff, but each gave up and appointed one in the middle of his term to make his political life more manageable.[58]

The chief of staff and the other top assistants to the president have to be his eyes and ears, and they act on his behalf every day. The criteria for a good staffer are very different from those for a cabinet selection. First and foremost, the president demands loyalty. This loyalty is developed from men and women who have hitched their careers to the president's. That is why presidents typically bring along old friends and close campaign staff as personal assistants. For instance, George W. Bush brought with him people who had served in previous Republican administrations, friends of his father, and members of his staff in Texas. The Bush administration is known for its solid loyalty to the president, with none of the leaks and backstabbing that had plagued Clinton, especially during the early years of his presidency.

A general principle presidents employ is that their staffs exist only to serve them. When things go well, the president gets the credit; when they do not, the staff takes the blame, sometimes even being fired or asked to resign. Such replacements are not unusual at all as presidents change personnel and management strategies to maximize their policy effectiveness and political survival.

The different backgrounds and perspectives of the White House staff and the cabinet mean that the two groups are often at odds. The cabinet secretaries, dedicated to large departmental missions, want presidential attention for those efforts; the staff want the departments to put the president's immediate political goals ahead of their departmental interests. As a result, the past several decades have seen more and more centralization of important policymaking in the White House, and more decisions being taken away from the traditional turf of the departments.[59]

THE VICE PRESIDENT

For most of our history, vice presidents have not been important actors in presidential administrations. Because the original Constitution awarded the vice presidency to the second-place presidential candidate, these officials were seen as potential rivals to the president and were excluded from most decisions and any meaningful policy responsibility. That was corrected with the Twelfth Amendment (1804), which provided for electors to select both the president and the vice president. However, custom for most of the period since then has put a premium on balancing the ticket in terms of regional, ideological, or political interests, which has meant that the person in the second spot is typically not close to the president. In fact, the vice president has sometimes been a rival even in modern times, as when John Kennedy appointed Lyndon Johnson, the Senate majority leader from Texas, as his vice president in 1960 in an effort to gain support from the southern states.

Since the Constitution provides only that the vice president act as president of the Senate, which carries no power unless there is a tie vote, most vice presidents have tried to make small, largely insignificant jobs seem important, often admitting that theirs was not an enviable post. Thomas Marshall, Woodrow Wilson's vice president, observed in his inaugural address that "I believe I'm entitled to make a few remarks because I'm about to enter a four-year period of silence."[60] Roosevelt's first vice president, John Nance Garner, expressed his disdain for the office even more forcefully, saying that the job "is not worth a pitcher of warm piss."[61]

Ultimately, however, the job of vice president is what the president wants it to be. President Reagan largely ignored George H. W. Bush, for instance, whereas President

More than a Master of Ceremonies
Vice presidents have traditionally been relegated to ceremonial duties, but that trend has changed significantly in recent administrations. Former vice president Al Gore was a key adviser in the Clinton administration, and Vice President Dick Cheney, shown here in deep discussion with George W. Bush on the White House Colonnade, brought a record of service, experience, and connections that has made him one of the principal forces in the Bush administration.

Carter created a significant policy advisory role for Walter Mondale, who brought to the job a considerable Washington expertise that Carter lacked. Former Tennessee senator Al Gore, serving under President Clinton, had an even more central advisory role, in addition to heading up the National Performance Review, which streamlined the bureaucracy and cut government personnel and costs.[62]

Dick Cheney also brings a good deal of Washington experience upon which President George W. Bush can rely, leading many observers to speculate that the Texas governor selected him for that very reason. Previously serving as a congressman from Wyoming, former chief of staff in the Ford White House, and secretary of defense under Bush's father, Cheney has a stronger résumé than many presidents bring to office and has wielded much more power than previous vice presidents.

Thus, even though the office of the vice presidency is not a powerful one, vice presidents who establish a relationship of trust with the president can have a significant impact on public policy. The office is important as well, of course, because it is the vice president who assumes the presidency if the president dies, is incapacitated, resigns, or is impeached. Many vice presidents also find the office a good launching pad for a presidential bid. Four of the last ten vice presidents—Lyndon Johnson, Richard Nixon, Gerald Ford, and George H. W. Bush—ended up in the Oval Office, although Al Gore did not enjoy similar success in 2000.

THE FIRST LADY

The office of the first lady (even the term seems strangely antiquated) is undergoing immense changes that reflect the tremendous flux in Americans' perceptions of the appropriate roles for men and women. But the office of first lady has always contained controversial elements, partly the result of conflict over the role of women in politics, but also because the intimate relationship between husband and wife gives the presidential spouse, an unelected position, unique insight into and access to the president's mind and decision-making processes. For all the checks and balances in the American system, there is no way to check the influence of the first spouse. Even though the president is free to appoint other trusted friends and even relations as advisers, the presence of the first lady as an unelected political consultant in the White House has been viewed with suspicion by some. It will be interesting to see whether first "gentlemen" become as controversial as their female counterparts (see the box "Madam President?" for the prospects of a woman president).

First ladies' attempts to play a political role are almost as old as the Republic. In fact, as her husband, John, was preparing to help with the writing of the Constitution, future first lady Abigail Adams admonished him to "remember the ladies," although there is no evidence that he actually did. Much later, in 1919, first lady Edith Bolling Galt Wilson virtually took over the White House following the illness of her husband, Woodrow, controlling who had access to him and perhaps even issuing presidential decisions in his name. And Eleanor Roosevelt, like her husband, Franklin, took vigorously to political life and kept up an active public role even after his death.

But since the 1960s and the advent of the women's movement, the role of the first lady is seen by the public as less an issue of individual personality and quirks, and more a national commentary on how women in general should behave. As a surrogate for our cultural confusion on what role women should play, the office of the first lady has come under uncommon scrutiny. Jacqueline Kennedy brought grace and sophistication and a good deal of public attention to the office; she created an almost

Madam President?

In the United States, the idea of Madam President is just that—still an idea. In many other countries, however, the idea of a woman executive has become a reality. Women have served as elected national leaders in twenty-one countries, beginning in 1960 with Sirimavo Bandaranaike of Sri Lanka, the first elected woman prime minister; in 1980, Vigdis Finnbogadottir of Iceland became the first elected woman head of state.[1] The list below gives only a sample of the women who have served as national leaders, including several who remain in power today.

Why has the United States lagged behind other nations in electing a woman to its highest political office? American women were among the first women in the world to gain the right to vote, in 1920, well before women living in several of the countries listed in the table. Women leaders have served or are serving in countries such as Pakistan and Senegal, where women currently have fewer civil rights than do women in the United States. Culture does not seem to offer an explanation, because women have been chief executives in Islamic, South American, southern European, Asian, and African countries, where the social and cultural separation between male and female roles has been most pronounced. Furthermore, countries with social and cultural traditions more similar to the United States, such as Britain and Canada, have also had women as national leaders.

So why has the United States not had a female president? In public opinion polls, Americans seem to indicate that they are willing to give it a try. In 2003 a Gallup poll indicated that 87 percent of the public say they would vote for a woman presidential candidate,[2] up from 78 percent in 1984 and only 53 percent in 1969—though down from 92 percent in 2001.[3] (See figure.) In addition, 60 percent of all U.S. voters recently reported that they think the country is ready for a female president.[4]

The most likely explanation for the lack of a woman leader in the United States is that there aren't many women in the pipeline, in jobs like vice president, senator, or state governor, which generate presidential candidates. While these jobs contain many potential male candidates for president, there are relatively few women in line to become candidates for president or even vice president. This is partly because women enter politics on average a decade later than do men, meaning they begin climbing the political ladder later than do most men.[5] The number of female senators from both par-

LEADER	COUNTRY	POSITION	YEARS
Indira Gandhi	India	PM	1966–1977; 1980–1984
Golda Meir	Israel	PM	1969–1974
Margaret Thatcher	UK	PM	1979–1990
Corazon Aquino	Philippines	President	1986–1992
Benazir Bhutto	Pakistan	PM	1988–1990; 1993–1996
Violetta Chamorro	Nicaragua	President	1990–1996
Mary Robinson	Ireland	President	1990–1997
Hanna Suchocka	Poland	PM	1992–1993
Kim Campbell	Canada	PM	1993
Tansu Ciller	Turkey	PM	1993–1996
Chandrika Kumaratunga	Sri Lanka	President	1994–present
Sheikh Hasina Wazed	Bangladesh	PM	1996–2001
Janet Jagan	Guyana	President	1997–1999
Mary McAleese	Ireland	President	1997–present
Jennifer Smith	Bermuda	PM	1998–2003
Helen Clark	New Zealand	PM	1999–present
Mireya Moscoso	Panama	President	1999–2004
Vaira Vike-Freiberga	Latvia	President	1999–present
Tarja Halonen	Finland	President	2000–present
Gloria Arroyo	Philippines	President	2001–present
Madior Boye	Senegal	PM	2001–2002
Megawati Sukarnoputri	Indonesia	President	2001–2004
Anneli Jaatteenmaki	Finland	PM	2003
Yulia Tymoshenko	Ukraine	PM	2005

Note: PM = Prime Minister

Source: Women World Leaders, www.geocities.com/CapitolHill/Lobby/4642/#section1.

Question: "If your party nominated a generally well-qualified person for president who happened to be a woman, would you vote for that person?"

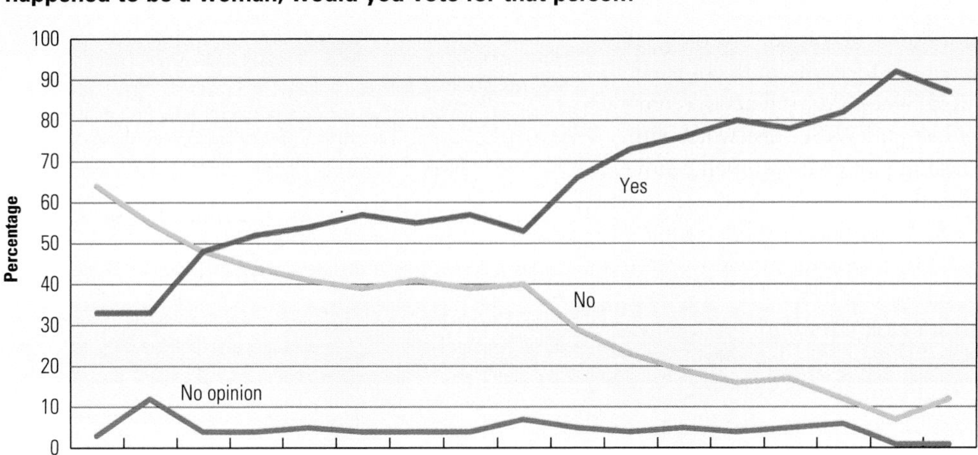

Source: Authors' update of data from the California State University Social Sciences Research and Instructional Council, http://www.csubak.edu/ssric/Modules/Others/disk1/gallup.htm; and Gallup/CNN/*USA Today* poll, June 10, 2003, Roper Center at the University of Connecticut, Public Opinion Online.

ties continues to rise, but it remains well below the average percentage of women in American society. Perhaps more important, the number of female governors (four of our past five presidents were governors) has remained limited. Only eight women (six Democrats and two Republicans) currently serve as governors, one of whom was not elected and another who cannot run for president because she is not a native-born American. In 2004, only one woman (Carol Moseley Braun) ran in the Democratic presidential primary, and she was the first candidate to drop out of contention. Further, the eventual Democratic nominee, John Kerry, never really considered any women for the vice presidential slot. In fact, the only woman candidate for vice president for either party was Geraldine Ferraro, who ran with Walter Mondale in 1984.

In general, the overall pool of elected women in the United States is small. Women legislators hold only 22.5 percent of state legislative seats across the country and even fewer of the national legislative seats in Congress (14.8 percent of seats in the House of Representatives and Senate).[6] In this respect, the United States lags far behind other countries. In 2003, 38 percent of the seats in the Danish legislature were held by women, 49 percent in Rwanda, 31 percent in Argentina, 23 percent in Mexico, 22 percent in Pakistan, and 25 percent in Australia.[7] In addition, only thirty-three women have ever served in the U.S. Senate, only twenty-eight women have served as governors (only twenty-one of whom were elected rather than succeeding another governor),[8] and no woman has ever served as U.S. vice president.[9]

Nevertheless, several researchers point to important advances for women in prominent political positions that may lead to a deeper pool of women candidates for president in the future. Nancy Pelosi, D-Calif., is the minority leader of the House of Representatives, the highest Democratic post in the House. The continued appointment of women to key executive posts dealing with international affairs, especially including two secretaries of state, also encourages the idea that women can handle crisis-filled political situations.[10] Further, when asked the person they would most likely support in the 2008 Democratic presidential primary, most Democrats have listed Hillary Rodham Clinton, the junior senator from New York.[11]

(continued)

Madam President? (continued)

Several organizations are working toward the goal of electing more women to office, and to the office of president, in the United States. Political action committees like EMILY's List and WISH List work with the primary aim of raising money for women candidates for major political offices. The White House Project (www.thewhitehouseproject.org) is a nonpartisan initiative dedicated to raising the public's awareness of women political leaders in the United States and to putting a woman in the White House. Another group, American Women Presidents (and its Ms. President political action committee), also promotes women of both parties in elections that will deepen the pool of women candidates.

An important question remains in the issue of a future woman president. Are Americans ready for a "first husband"? Apparently they are. Ninety-one percent of Americans said that if the president of the United States were a woman, they would find it appropriate for the husband to serve as official host at the White House.[12]

1. The History Net, "Women Prime Ministers and Presidents—20th Century Heads of State," http://womenshistory.about.com/cs/rulers20th/?once=true&.
2. CNN/*USA Today*/Gallup poll, May 30–June 1, 2003, iPOLL databank, the Roper Center for Public Opinion Research, University of Connecticut, www.ropercenter.uconn.edu/ipoll.html.
3. California State University Social Sciences Research and Instructional Council, "65 Years of Gallup Polling. Mystery Table Three: Willingness to Support a Woman for President," www.csubak.edu/ssric/modules/other/disk1/gallup.htm.
4. Associated Press, "60% of Voters Support Idea of Female President." Fort Wayne *Journal Gazette*, February 23, 2005, 2A.
5. Eleanor Clift and Tom Brazaitis, *Madam President* (New York: Routledge, 2003), 227.
6. Center for American Women and Politics, Eagleton Institute of Politics, Rutgers University, "Facts on Women Candidates and Elected Officials," www.rci.rutgers.edu/~cawp/facts.html.
7. United Nations Statistics Division, "Statistics and Indicators on Women and Men. Table 6.A: Women in Public Life," http://unstats.un.org/unsd/demographic/products/indwm/table6a.htm.
8. Clift and Brazaitis, *Madam President*, 181; updated with authors' calculation from "Female Governors" table from National Governors Association Web site, www.nga.org/governors/1%2C1169%2CC_TRIVIA^D_2117%2C00.html.
9. Center for American Women and Politics, Eagleton Institute of Politics, Rutgers University, "Women in Elective Office 2005," "Women in the U.S. Senate, 1922–2005," and "Statewide Elective Executive Women," www.cawp.rutgers.edu/facts.html.
10. American Women Presidents, "More Women. . . ," www.americanwomenpresidents.org/why_we_haven't_had_women_presidents.htm#_ftnref4.
11. CNN/*USA Today*/Gallup poll, February 4–6, 2005, www.pollingreport.com/2008.htm.
12. *USA Today*/Gallup poll, September 13–15, 2004, iPOLL databank, the Roper Center for Public Opinion Research, University of Connecticut, www.ropercenter.uconn.edu/ipoll.html.

fantasy "first family," sometimes referred to as Camelot, after the legendary medieval court of King Arthur. This public image certainly contributed to Kennedy's effectiveness as head of state, as, for instance, following Jacqueline's enthusiastic reception in Paris, he introduced himself to the French as "Jacqueline Kennedy's husband." Barbara Bush's autobiography portrays the traditional role of first lady perfectly, a totally supportive wife of a president and self-sacrificing mother of a future president whose ambitions were centered on her family.[63]

Offsetting this traditional vision was the more directly involved and equally supportive Rosalyn Carter, who even attended cabinet meetings at her husband's request. Public objections to her activities and her position as informal presidential adviser showed that the role of the first lady was controversial even in the late 1970s. Far more in the Carter than the Bush mode, Hillary Rodham Clinton did the most to shake up public expectations of the first lady's role. A successful lawyer who essentially earned the family income while her husband, Bill, served four low-paid terms as governor of Arkansas, Hillary was the target of both public acclaim and public hatred. Her nontraditional tenure as first lady was capped in 2000, at the end of Clinton's second term,

Laura the Explorer
As part of her goodwill trip to Israel and the Middle East in May 2005, First Lady Laura Bush visited the set of Egypt's version of *Sesame Street, Alam Simsim.* As a former librarian, literacy and education are two of Mrs. Bush's primary causes.

by her successful campaign to become the junior senator from New York. Speculation has been rife ever since that she might someday launch her own campaign for the presidency.

The politically safest strategy for a first lady appears to be to stick with a noncontroversial moral issue and ask people to do what we all agree they ought to do. Lady Bird Johnson beseeched us, rather successfully, to support highway beautification, Rosalyn Carter called for more attention to mental health, and Nancy Reagan suggested, less successfully, that we "just say no" to drugs.

Laura Bush is far closer to the tradition of her mother-in-law than to Senator Clinton. During her husband's first campaign she went out of her way to say that she would not sit in on cabinet meetings and that she considered herself a wife, not an adviser. A former teacher and school librarian, she focuses on the issues of education, youth, and literacy. In his second term, President Bush appointed her to head an expanded White House program aiming to steer at-risk youth, particularly boys, away from gangs and violence.

WHO, WHAT, HOW The purpose of the executive bureaucracy is to help the president do his job by providing information, expertise, and advice. But while the president's closest advisers are usually focused on his interests, various cabinet officers, staff members, and agency heads may develop agendas of their own that may be at odds with those of the president. He has an easier time controlling members of the EOP, whose job is more clearly to serve him. The vice president and first lady are also more likely to find an agenda that is consistent with the president's. The president employs different management styles in an effort to keep a tight rein on the bureaucracy, but the talents and skills that help one get elected president are not necessarily those of a skillful manager.

PRESIDENTIAL CHARACTER

Effective management of the executive branch is one feature of a successful presidency, but there are many others. Historians and presidential observers regularly distinguish presidential success and failure, even to the extent of actually rating presidential greatness.[64] Political scientists also assess presidential success, usually in terms of how frequently presidents can get their legislative programs passed by Congress.[65] We have already discussed the powers of the president, the challenges to success provided by the need for popularity, the difficulties of dealing with Congress, and the enormous management task faced by the president. In this section we look at the personal resources of a president that lead to success or contribute to failure. We begin by exploring what kinds of people are driven to become president in the first place.

CLASSIFYING PRESIDENTIAL CHARACTER

Most presidents share some personality characteristics—giant ambition and large egos, for instance—but this does not mean that they are carbon copies of one another. They clearly differ in fundamental ways. A number of scholars have developed classification schemes of presidential personalities. Each of these schemes is based on the expectation that knowing key dimensions of individual presidential personalities will help explain, or even predict, how presidents will behave in certain circumstances. The most famous of these schemes was developed by James David Barber, who classifies presidents on two dimensions: their energy level (passive or active) and their orientation toward life (positive or negative).[66] This scheme yields four types of presidents: active-positive, active-negative, passive-positive, and passive-negative (see Figure 8.6).

Some of our best and most popular presidents have been active-positives. They have had great energy and a very positive orientation toward the job of being president. Franklin Roosevelt, John Kennedy, and Bill Clinton represent this type. Others have had less energy (passives) or have been burdened by the job of being president (negatives). They have acted out their roles, according to Barber, as they thought they should, out of duty or obligation. George W. Bush fits the model of the passive-positive president. He likes being a leader but believes that his job is one of delegating and setting the tone rather than of taking an active policymaking role. Some scholars use Barber's classification scheme to explain political success and failure. Richard Nixon is usually offered as one of the clearest examples of an active-negative president; he had lots of energy but could not enjoy the job of being president. According to this theory, Nixon's personality caused him to make unwise decisions that led to the Watergate scandal and, eventually, to his political ruin.

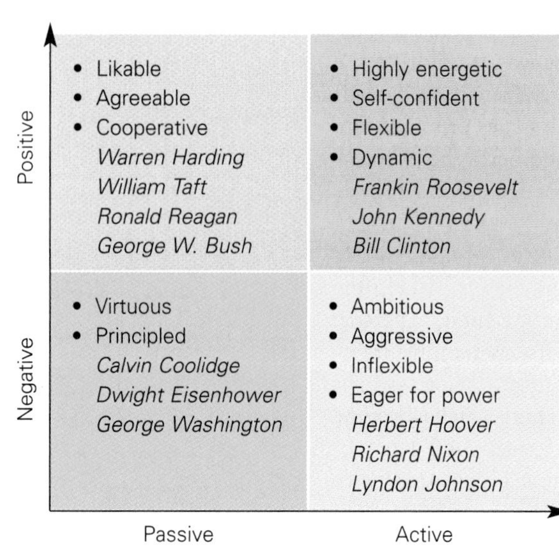

FIGURE 8.6
Classification of Presidents

Assessing individual personalities is a fascinating enterprise, but it is fraught with danger. Few politicians fit neatly into Barber's boxes (or the categories of other personality theorists) in an unambiguous way. Although some scholars find that personality analysis adds greatly to their understanding of the differences between presidencies, others discount it altogether, claiming that it leads one to overlook the ways in which rules and external forces have shaped the modern presidency.[67]

PRESIDENTIAL STYLE

In addition to their personality differences, each president strives to create a **presidential style**, or an image that symbolically captures who he is for the American people and for leaders of other nations. These personal differences in how presidents present themselves are real, but they are also carefully cultivated. Each also strives to distinguish himself from his predecessors, to set himself apart, and to give hope for new, and presumably better, presidential leadership.[68]

presidential style image projected by the president that represents how he would like to be perceived at home and abroad

For example, Harry Truman was known for his straight, sometimes profane, talk and no-nonsense decision making. In contrast, Dwight Eisenhower developed his "Victorious General" image as a statesman above the fray of petty day-to-day politics. John Kennedy, whose term followed Eisenhower's, evoked a theme of "getting the country moving again" and embodied this with a personal image of youth and energy. Photos of the Kennedys playing touch football at their family compound in Hyannisport, or of Kennedy on his sailboat, with windswept hair and full of confidence and fun, was a refreshing image that promised a different style of leadership.

More recently, in the wake of Watergate and the disgrace of Richard Nixon, Jimmy Carter hit a winning note with a style promising honesty and competent government. Carter was honest, but his self-doubts and admissions that the United States faced problems that government might not be able to solve disappointed many Americans. In contrast, Ronald Reagan's "it's-morning-in-America" optimism and his calming, grandfatherly presence were soaked up by an eager public.

The Great Communicator This was the label many people applied to President Ronald Reagan because of his ability to connect with the American public. His effectiveness as a communicator had little to do with explaining complex policy decisions. Rather, he conveyed a sense of confidence, trustworthiness, and warmth. He made people feel good.

Bill Clinton's style combined the image of the highly intellectual Rhodes scholar with that of a compassionate leader, famous for "feeling America's pain." Sometimes the president's style cannot override other image problems, however. While people approved of Clinton's leadership through the end of his presidency, the charges of extramarital affairs and his association with the Whitewater scandal gave a majority of citizens concern about his honesty and moral character.

George W. Bush came into office with an opposite set of characteristics. Widely perceived as a nonintellectual who joked that C students could grow up to be president, he cultivated the image of the chief executive officer he was: a president primarily interested in results, not academic debates, who was willing to set a course and leave others to get the job done. Despite a reputation for hard drinking and high living in his youth, including a drunk driving arrest, his pledge of abstinence, traditional marriage, and frequent references to Jesus Christ helped to put a moral tone on his presidency that Clinton's had lacked. Figure 8.7 compares public opinion about Clinton's character as he left office in 2000 with public opinion about Bush's during his 2004 reelection campaign.

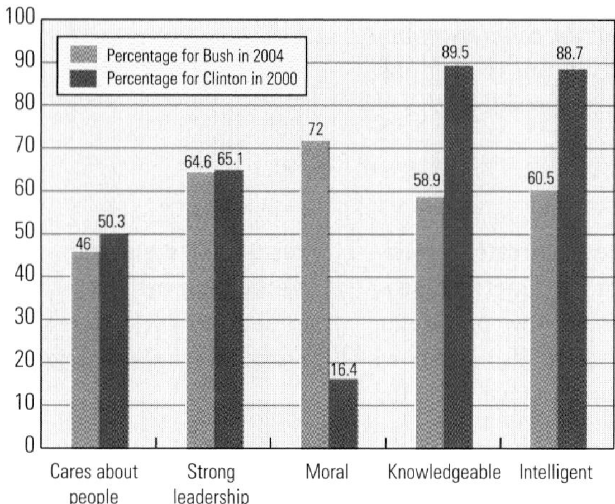

FIGURE 8.7
Presidential Style: A Comparison of the Public's Image of Clinton and Bush

Source: American National Election Study, 2000; American National Election Study, 2004 Pre-Post Study, Version 20050131 (Advanced Release, January 31, 2005).

Presidential style is an important but subtle means by which presidents communicate. It can be an opportunity for enhancing public support and thereby the president's ability to deal effectively with Congress and the media. But any style has its limitations, and the same behavioral and attitudinal characteristics of a style that help a president at one juncture can prove a liability later. Furthermore, as Clinton's experience shows, the president does not always have total control over the image of him that the public sees. Political enemies and an investigative press can combine to counter the image the president wants to project. A significant portion of the president's staffers concern themselves with "image management." In the wake of September 11, Bush's staffers, worried that he would not be perceived as up to the job of dealing with the terrorists, regularly told the press that the president was resolved and focused but calm and determined. Information about how Bush was handling the situation was tightly controlled. When asked if the president used running to help manage his angry or bad moods, then–press secretary Ari Fleischer replied, "I have never seen him be in either."[69]

WHO, WHAT, HOW In the matter of presidential style and personality, the person with the most at stake is undoubtedly the president. His goals are popularity, legislative success, support for his party, and a favorable judgment in the history books. He functions in a number of policy roles as the head of government, but he also serves as our head of state, a role that is merely symbolic at times but can be of tremendous importance for presidential power in times of national crisis or in conflicts with other nations. Because presidents' formal powers to fulfill these functions are limited, and their informal powers depend on their popularity with citizens and with the Washington elite, the personality and style that allow them to win popularity are crucial.

THE CITIZENS AND THE PRESIDENCY

There are approximately 295 million American citizens and only one president. While we all have a reasonable chance of meeting our members of Congress, only the luckiest few will actually shake hands with the president of the United States. With connections this remote, how can we talk about the relationship between the citizens and the president?

Perhaps in the days before technology made mass communication so easy and routine, we could not. But today, while we may never dance at an inaugural ball or even wave at the president from afar, we can know our presidents intimately (and often far more intimately than we want to!). Through the medium of television, we can watch them board airplanes, speak to foreign leaders, swing golf clubs, dance with their wives, and speak directly to us. Skilled communicators, especially like Ronald Reagan and Bill Clinton, can touch us personally—inspire us and infuriate us as if we were family and friends.

So it is fitting, in a way, that the citizens of the United States have the ultimate power over the president. We elect him (and someday her), it is true, but our power goes beyond a once-every-four-years vote of approval or disapproval. Modern polling techniques, as we have seen, allow us to conduct a "rolling election," as the media and the politicians themselves track popular approval of the president throughout his term. The presidential strategy of going public is made possible because all Americans—citizens, president, and members of Congress—know just where the president stands with the public and how much political capital he has to spend.

In 1998 and 1999 we saw perhaps the clearest example of the power that citizens' support can give to a president in the fate of Bill Clinton's imperiled presidency. After a lengthy investigation, independent prosecutor Kenneth Starr sent a report to Congress on September 9, 1998, that he claimed provided grounds for Clinton's impeachment on perjury and obstruction-of-justice charges. As graphic details of Clinton's behavior were made public, Clinton's personal approval ratings sank, yet his job approval ratings stayed high. Questioned on specifics, people said they disapproved of Clinton's moral character and found his behavior repellent, but they thought the impeachment movement was politically motivated and that Clinton's private behavior had no impact on his ability to do his job. They seemed to find him wanting in the symbolic head-of-state role we discussed earlier in this chapter but continued to approve of him as the head of government. In clear rejection of the investigation of the president, Americans went against tradition on Election Day 1998: instead of handing the president's party its usual midterm loss, they supported the Democrats so strongly that they gained five seats in Congress. The day after Clinton was impeached, on December 11, his approval ratings with the American public hit a high of 73 percent.[70]

Of course, we know the end of the story. Clinton went on to be acquitted in the Senate. Once he was no longer under threat, Clinton's ratings dropped too, to the more normal levels of a popular president near the end of his second term. It is arguable that these polls saved Clinton's political life. Had they fallen it would have been much harder for Democrats and moderates in the House and the Senate to support him and the president may well have lost his job.

In a similar vein, although the details are strikingly different, the presidency of George W. Bush also came to depend on unusually high opinion ratings where one might not have expected to find them. Bush claimed the presidency after a contested election in which he received fewer popular votes than his opponent and in which his electoral college victory hinged on an electoral dispute, in a state governed by his brother, that was resolved by the Supreme Court in a five-to-four vote that many believed was politically motivated. Many pundits predicted that his presidency would be a one-term failure. While his early approval ratings showed he was enjoying something of a traditional honeymoon, by the summer of 2001, his ratings were starting to sag.

In September, however, the unthinkable happened. When terrorists flew hijacked planes into the World Trade Center and the Pentagon and launched America into the war on terrorism, Bush was given a clean slate on which to write his presidential legacy. With an experienced foreign policy team behind him, Bush undertook to lead the nation in a time of uncommon turmoil. Making the war against terrorism the keystone of his presidency, his portrayal of the conflict in simple terms reassured Americans, and his early military successes solidified their support for him. Figure 8.8 shows

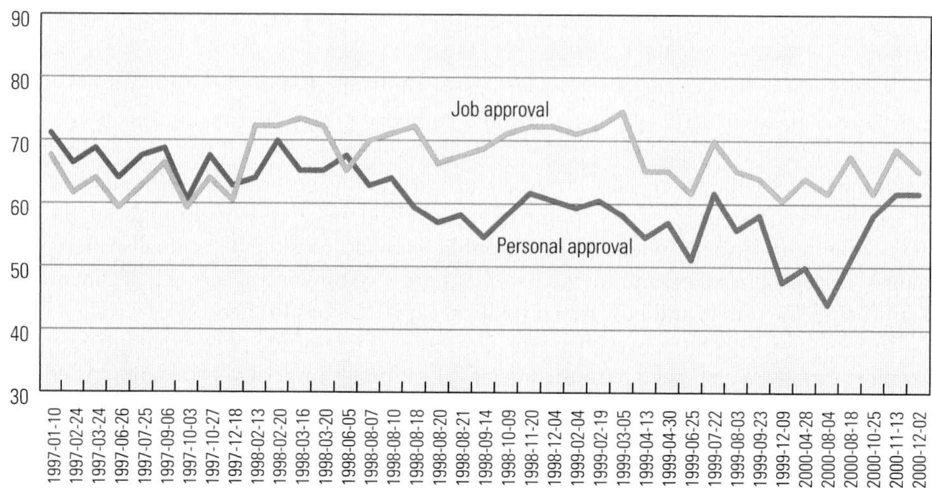

Bush Approval, First Term

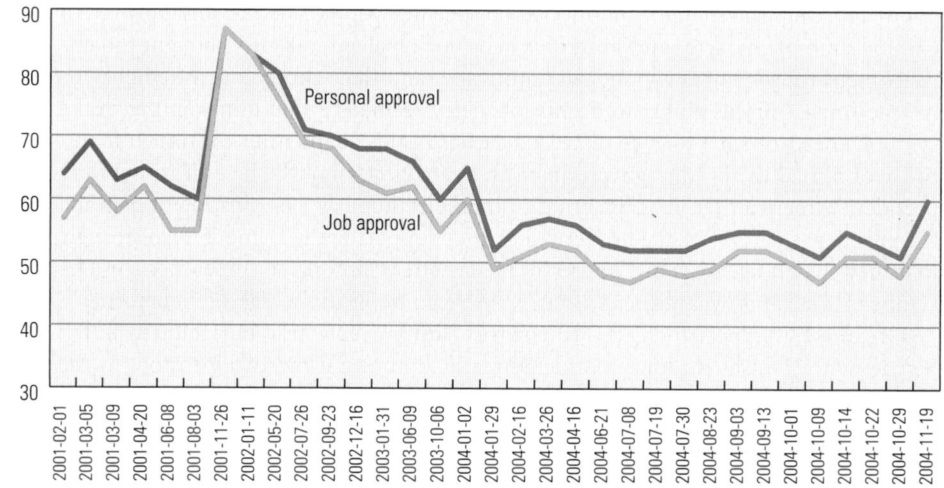

FIGURE 8.8

Personal and Job Approval Ratings for President Bill Clinton and President George W. Bush

Source: Compiled by the authors from Gallup poll data.

the striking change in Bush's image after September 11. His approval rating hit 90 percent—higher than any other president since records have been kept. With high ratings, Bush was as powerful as, if not more powerful than, if he had won the election in a landslide, and the 2002 election again failed to show the traditional midterm loss as Bush's efforts swept Republicans into Congress—building slightly the majority in the House of Representatives and creating a Republican majority in the Senate.

Bush's approval dropped off steadily afterward, except for a slight turn upward following his initial success with the invasion of Iraq. It has since stabilized at around 50 percent, give or take a few percentage points. Nevertheless, unlike the situation for Clinton, the American people have tended to approve of Bush more personally than they have approved of how he has performed his job. Moreover, Bush's personal ap-

proval and job approval go up and down together, whereas the American public largely separated those judgments for Clinton. Thus the public has linked the head-of-state and head-of-government roles for President Bush much more so than they did for President Clinton. Not surprisingly, when Bush ran for reelection in a tight race, many of the images his campaign focused on were those that tried to remind Americans of the post–September 11 era, when he had high job and approval ratings. They also highlighted Bush's personal attributes that the public seemed to prefer over his performance on the job. Even amid a soft economy and a shaky situation in Iraq, the American people returned Bush to office, although with a very narrow margin.

How can we understand the very unusual reaction of Americans who showed overwhelming support for a president whom they had only moderately approved of before his involvement in a tawdry sex scandal, and who rejected one president at the election booth only a year before they gave him the highest approval ratings a president has ever received? For one thing, the public judges presidents on different criteria in part because the office has different roles to fill. Which president are they being asked their opinion of? Americans may have disapproved of President Clinton as head of state, but they certainly supported him as head of government. The opposite might be more the case for President Bush. Second, under everyday circumstances, questions concerning presidential job and personal approval seem straightforward, but the strength of the economy, current political conflicts, external events, and the personal foibles of the president can alter the public's assessment of the president in complex ways that either enhance or limit the president's power. Finally, the institution of the American presidency, like most of the rest of the government designed by the framers, was meant to be insulated from the whims of the public. It is an irony that in contemporary politics the president is often more indebted to the citizens for his power than he is to the electoral college, Congress, the courts, or any of the political elites the founders trusted to stabilize American government.

WHAT'S AT STAKE REVISITED

President Bush and Vice President Cheney insisted that they could not give in to the demands from Congress for information about the president's nominees or about the energy task force because a huge principle was at stake: they argued that the president has the right to get advice without having that advice become public and that to give in to Congress was to weaken the office of the presidency. Were they right?

The question of executive privilege goes to the heart of the principle of checks and balances. The two branches of government, executive and legislative, have opposing interests that cannot easily be resolved. Sometimes the stakes are constitutional—the Constitution assigns the two branches very different roles. The executive deals with issues like national security and military policy that can require secrecy; Congress is the "people's house," where open democracy is supposed to reign. The president needs to be able to get straight and candid advice from those who work for him; Congress's obligation to see that its laws are faithfully carried out requires insight into what the federal bureaucracy, charged with executing the laws, actually does. Another constitutional issue is how strong the executive ought to be. Since the days of executive abuse of power under Nixon, Congress has been vigilant about not allowing the idea of the imperial presidency to rise again. George W. Bush's administration, however, seems to be determined to restore the presidency's lost power. A constitutional power struggle is inevitable.

Sometimes the issues at stake are not about the constitutional division of power at all but rather are about political or partisan advantage. The two branches of government have different constituencies and different imperatives for reelection. Also, they are often led by different parties and may be political rivals. The president wants to keep information out of the hands of his political opponents, while frequently those opponents are sitting in Congress and trying to use their powers to investigate him. Sometimes, as the example of Nixon makes clear, there really is something that requires investigation, and at other times the investigation can be a costly effort to discredit a president that members of the majority party in Congress simply don't like or trust.

Clearly, what's at stake in the issue of executive privilege is the balance of power in Washington. Neither the privilege nor the oversight can be eliminated without seriously offsetting that balance and removing important checks. But if either side insists on having its way and refuses to compromise, the system is gridlocked as courts try to disentangle the mess. As always with areas of constitutional ambiguity, it will be the courts that make the final determination about where the power lies.

Thinking Outside the Box

- Should the president represent the interests of the people who voted for him, or of all Americans?
- How might presidential behavior change if we once again allowed presidents to serve more than two terms?
- What political impact might it have if, following Washington's wishes, the president were known as "His High Mightiness"?

To Sum Up

KEY TERMS
republic.cqpress.com

cabinet (p. 332)
chief administrator (p. 329)
chief foreign policy maker (p. 332)
chief of staff (p. 351)
commander-in-chief (p. 332)
Council of Economic Advisers (p. 351)
cycle effect (p. 343)
divided government (p. 346)
executive agreement (p. 333)
Executive Office of the President (p. 351)
executive order (p. 336)
going public (p. 342)
head of government (p. 323)
head of state (p. 323)
honeymoon period (p. 344)
inherent powers (p. 338)
legislative liaison (p. 346)
National Security Council (p. 351)
Office of Management and Budget (p. 351)
pardoning power (p. 337)
power to persuade (p. 342)
presidential style (p. 363)
presidential veto (p. 334)
senatorial courtesy (p. 337)
solicitor general (p. 337)
State of the Union address (p. 334)
treaties (p. 333)
White House Office (p. 351)

Key terms, chapter summaries, practice quizzes, Internet links, and other study aids are available on the companion Web site at: republic.cqpress.com.

SUMMARY
republic.cqpress.com

- Presidents face a double expectations gap when it comes to their relationship with the American public. The first gap is between what the president must promise in order to gain office and the limitations put on the president by the powers granted by the Constitution. The second gap occurs between conflicting roles. An American president must function as both a political head of government and an apolitical head of state, and often these two roles conflict.
- When it came to defining the functions and powers of the president, the founders devised rules that both empowered and limited the president. While some of the founders argued for a strong leader with far-reaching powers, others argued for several executives who would check each other's power. The constitutional compromise gives us an executive with certain powers and independence, yet checked by congressional and judicial power.
- We have seen two periods of presidential leadership so far. The first period, called the traditional presidency, which lasted until the 1930s, describes chief executives who mainly lived within the limits of their constitutional powers. Since then, in the modern presidency, a more complex relationship exists between the president and the American citizens, in which presidents branch out to use more informal powers yet remain indebted to public approval for this expansion.
- The president is in a constant struggle with Congress and the public for the furthering of his legislative agenda. The president needs both congressional cooperation and public approval in order to fulfill campaign promises. The chief executive uses several strategies to achieve these goals, including going public and building coalitions in Congress.
- The presidential establishment includes the cabinet, the Executive Office of the President, and the White House Office—a huge bureaucracy that has grown considerably since the days of George Washington's presidency. Although the resources are vast, managing such a large and complex organization presents its own problems for the president. The president's closest advisers are generally focused on his interests, but the variety of other staff and agency heads—often with their own agendas and often difficult to control—can make life difficult for the chief executive.

PRACTICE QUIZ
republic.cqpress.com

1. What best describes the era of the modern presidency?

a. Its legacy is that Americans often look to their presidents and government to solve social and economic issues and to inspire the public.

b. It preceded the Great Depression, which exhausted much of the power of the president to deal with social and economic issues.

c. It proved that presidents would continue to fulfill the limited role envisioned by the framers.

d. It occurred during the late eighteenth and throughout the nineteenth centuries, when presidents were overshadowed by congressional power.

e. All of the above

2. Which of the following best explains why there has been an increased centralization of important policymaking in the White House in the past several decades?

a. The scope of government has decreased, which has lessened the president's need to seek outside advice.

b. The Twenty-fifth Amendment has given vice presidents much more control than they had prior to its enactment.

c. The Bipartisan Selection Act of 1960 has centralized the president's policymaking within the Executive Office of the President.

d. The White House staff has successfully put the president's immediate political goals ahead of the multiple demands placed on him by cabinet secretaries.

e. The size of government continues to decrease, making it more efficient to concentrate efforts within the White House.

3. The strategy presidents use to appeal to the public on an issue, in expectation that public pressure will be brought to bear on other political actors, is referred to as

a. converting on the expectations gap.

b. going public.

c. senatorial courtesy.

d. the legislative liaison.

e. presidential approval.

4. How does the presidential character classification scheme supposedly help presidential scholars and citizens in judging presidents?

a. It illustrates how active-positive presidents are always the poorest type of person for the job.

b. It illustrates how active-negative presidents are always the best type of person for the job.

c. It proves that the personality of a president has no impact on how a president will perform in office, given the enormous institutional constraints on the presidency.

d. It alone explains how well a president will perform in office.

e. It may provide a helpful tool in explaining and predicting how a president may perform in certain circumstances.

5. Which of the following is NOT true of the double expectations gap?

a. The public demands that presidential candidates make numerous promises when running for office.

b. Presidents do not often have the constitutional powers to fulfill their campaign promises.

c. Unlike other heads of governments around the world, the president is freed from ceremonial roles carried out by heads of state.

d. The president must fulfill conflicting roles, which saps his ability to carry out one or more of those roles particularly well.

e. Presidents struggle to live up to promises and juggle the different roles of the office.

SUGGESTED RESOURCES

republic.cqpress.com

Books

Abshire, David M., ed. 2001. *Triumphs and Tragedies of the Modern Presidency: Seventy-six Case Studies in Presidential Leadership.* Westport, Conn.: Praeger. Written by top political historians, journalists, and scholars and compiled by the Center for the Study of the Presidency, this intriguing volume documents seventy-six events that have defined the American presidency since Woodrow Wilson's administration.

Barber, James David. 1992. *The Presidential Character,* 4th ed. Englewood Cliffs, N.J.: Prentice Hall. This fun-to-read but somewhat controversial book discusses the impact that presidential personalities have on the president's success in office.

Bond, Jon R., and Richard Fleischer. 1990. *The President in the Legislative Arena.* Chicago: University of Chicago Press. A great source for those interested in the relationship between the president and Congress.

The authors provide a Congress-centered explanation of why some presidents fail and others succeed in the legislative arena.

DeGregorio, William A. 2000. *The Complete Book of U.S. Presidents: From George Washington to George W. Bush,* 6th ed. New York: Wings Books. This comprehensive book contains an extraordinary amount of
information about each of our forty-three presidents, including their biographical backgrounds, highlights of their administrations, and memorable quotations.

Drew, Elizabeth. 1996. *Showdown: The Struggle Between the Gingrich Congress and the Clinton White House.* New York: Simon & Schuster. By drawing on a dramatic conflict between Congress and the president, Drew effectively illustrates how the different agendas of these two branches often collide.

Gergen, David. 2000. *Eyewitness to Power: The Essence of Leadership: From Nixon to Clinton.* New York: Simon & Schuster. The journalistic style used in this insider analysis of the four recent presidents for whom Gergen worked makes it very readable.

Jones, Charles O. 1994. *The Presidency in a Separated System.* Washington, D.C.: Brookings Institution. This presidential scholar successfully integrates previous studies of the presidency to form a new way of understanding the tensions between the president and Congress.

Kernell, Samuel. 1997. *Going Public: New Strategies of Presidential Leadership,* 3d ed. Washington, D.C.: Congressional Quarterly Press. An interesting book on how recent presidents have bypassed Congress and gone straight to the public for support of presidential initiatives in an attempt to put constituent pressure on Congress.

Mayer, Kenneth R. 2002. *With the Stroke of a Pen: Executive Orders and Presidential Power.* Princeton: Princeton University Press. Mayer illustrates how constitutional and institutional powers of the presidency, such as the executive order, allow presidents to follow through on much of their agenda with few checks from Congress.

Neustadt, Richard E. 1990. *Presidential Power and the Modern Presidents: The Politics of Leadership From Roosevelt to Reagan.* New York: Free Press. In perhaps the most widely cited book on the presidency, Neustadt argues that the persuasive powers of presidents are imperative for accomplishing their goals while in office.

Skowronek, Stephen. 1997. *The Politics Presidents Make: Leadership From John Adams to Bill Clinton.* Cambridge, Mass.: Harvard University Press. An important book that all students interested in the presidency should read. Skowronek analyzes how political contexts throughout history have contributed to the success or failure of our presidents.

Tulis, Jeffrey K. 1987. *The Rhetorical Presidency.* Princeton: Princeton University Press. Tulis gives a fascinating account of how the public's demands for a less distant president influenced the behavior of our twentieth-century chief executives.

Web Sites

C-SPAN American Presidents, Life Portraits www.americanpresidents.org/classroom. This Web site presents educational information about presidents and the presidency from C-SPAN, including curricula and teachers' guides on each president and educational activities.

U.S. National Archives and Records Administration Presidential Libraries www.archives.gov/presidential_libraries/addresses/addresses.html. This excellent starting point for research contains links to eleven different presidential libraries and museums, as well as on-line libraries for twelve presidents.

White House www.whitehouse.gov. The White House home page provides recent presidential addresses, pictures, information on key administration officials and presidential and vice presidential family members, as well as facts about the White House and the executive branch.

Movies

***The American President.* 1995.** A young, widowed president's relationship with an environmental lobbyist threatens his reelection chances. While this movie is fun, it also has much to say about the relationship between the president, interest groups, and Congress.

***The American President.* 1999.** This acclaimed PBS documentary explores the lives and careers of the presidents of the United States, offering valuable insights and many little-known facts.

Frontline. Not a movie, but this weekly documentary series on PBS often concentrates on issues of the president, the executive branch, and other key aspects of American democracy.

Many of the growing number of consumers who want organic food turn to local farmers markets (right) for produce that is not genetically altered or sprayed with pesticides. Despite the growing market segment that looks for such products, large agribusiness farms like the one below still dominate the landscape and bring their political influence to the table over regulatory processes like defining what constitutes "organic" food.

THE BUREAUCRACY

9

WHAT'S AT STAKE?

What did the chicken who laid your breakfast egg have for *its* breakfast? Was your hamburger once on drugs? And just what is the pedigree of the french fries you ate at lunch? Do you care? Some people do. Those who worry about eating vegetables that have been grown with the aid of pesticides or chemical fertilizers, or animals that were treated with hormones or antibiotics, or who are concerned with the environmental effects of such practices, form part of a growing number of consumers who look for the label "organic" before they buy food. One estimate says that Americans spend about $5 billion a year on organic foods.[1]

What does it mean to be organic? Without a standardized definition, states, localities, and private agencies were free to define *organic* as they wished. Usually the standards were stringent; for example, many groups required organic farmers to use land on which no artificial or synthetic fertilizers, pesticides, or herbicides had been used for five years. Such farming techniques favor the small, committed organic farmer and are difficult for large agribusinesses to apply.[2]

In an effort to eliminate the patchwork of local regulations and to assure consumers that organic food purchased anywhere in the country was equally safe, the organic food industry repeatedly asked the U.S. Department of Agriculture (USDA) to nationalize standards. When the USDA revealed its standardized definition of *organic*, however, it was a definition traditional organic farmers and consumers didn't recognize. USDA standards proposed in December 1997 would allow the use of genetic engineering, irradiation, antibiotics and hormones, and sewer sludge—techniques that run directly counter to the values of organic farming—in the production of foods to be labeled "organic." Though strongly supported by the conventional food manufacturers and the developers of biotechnology, these standards were bitterly opposed by the organic food industry and its consumers.

Before they issue new regulations, however, all federal agencies must give interested parties and the public the opportunity to be heard. In the battle to win USDA support, the conventional food industry and the food preparers associations had—and used—all the resources of big business; the organic food industry had none. Searching for another strategy for influencing the enormous bureaucracy of the USDA, they began a grassroots campaign, encouraging consumers to write to the USDA objecting to the new standards. Natural food stores posted information and distributed fliers on the proposed regulation, and Horizon Organic Dairy used the back panels of its milk cartons to pass on the information and urge consumer action.[3]

The campaign was successful. Nearly 300,000 letters and e-mails opposing the proposal were received by the USDA. Even Congress went on record against it.[4] The result was that Secretary of Agriculture Dan Glickman eliminated the provision allowing genetic engineering, crop irradiation, and the use of sewage sludge as fertilizer. Said Glickman, "Democracy will work. We will listen to the comments and will, I am sure, make modifications to the rule."[5]

Depending on where you stand, the moral of this story varies. It might be a David-and-Goliath success, or just a quirky tale about a handful of food fanatics. What is really at stake in the issue of whether the organic food industry should be regulated by the USDA? *

Kids have dramatic aspirations for their futures: they want to be adventurers or sports stars, doctors or lawyers, even president of the United States. Almost no one aspires to be what so many of us become: bureaucrats. But bureaucrats are the people who make national, state, and local government work for us. They are the people who give us our driving tests and renew our licenses, who deliver our mail, who maintain our parks, who order books for our libraries. Bureaucrats send us our social security checks, find us jobs through the unemployment office, process our student loans, and ensure we get our military benefits. In fact, bureaucrats defend our country from foreign enemies, chase our crooks at home, and get us aid in times of natural disasters. We know them as individuals. We greet them, make small talk, laugh with them. They may be our neighbors or friends. But as a profession, civil servants are seldom much admired or esteemed in this country. Indeed, they are often the target of scorn or jokes, and the people who work in the organizations we call bureaucracies are derided as lazy, incompetent, power hungry, and uncaring.

Such a jaded view, like most other negative stereotypes, is based on a few well-publicized bureaucratic snafus and the frustrating experiences we all have at times with the bureaucracy. Waiting in endless lines at the post office or driver's license bureau, expecting in the mail a government check that never arrives, reading about USDA definitions of "organic" that seem preposterous—all of these things can drive us crazy. In addition, as demonstrated by the organic food example, the bureaucracy is the source of many of the rules that can help us get what we want from government but that often irritate us with their seeming arbitrariness and rigidity. Though they aren't elected, bureaucrats can have a great deal of power over our lives.

Bureaucracies are essential to running a government. Bureaucracy, in fact, is often the only ground on which citizens and politics meet, the only contact many Americans have with government except for their periodic trips to the voting booth. Bureaucrats are often called "civil servants" because, ultimately, their job is to serve the civil society in which we all live. In this chapter, as we give bureaucracy a closer look, you will learn about

- the definition of *bureaucracy*

- the evolution, organization, and roles of the federal bureaucracy
- politics inside the bureaucracy
- the relationship between the federal bureaucracy and the branches of the federal government
- the relationship of citizens to the bureaucracy

WHAT IS BUREAUCRACY?

In simplest terms, a **bureaucracy** is any organization that is hierarchically structured—that is, in which orders are given at the top by those with responsibility for the success of the organization and followed by those on the bottom. The classic definition comes to us from German sociologist Max Weber. Weber's model of bureaucracy features the following four characteristics:[6]

bureaucracy an organization characterized by hierarchical structure, worker specialization, explicit rules, and advancement by merit

- *Hierarchy.* A clear chain of command exists in which all employees know who their bosses or supervisors are, as well as whom they in turn are responsible for.
- *Specialization.* The effectiveness of the bureaucracy is accomplished by having tasks divided and handled by expert and experienced full-time professional staffs.
- *Explicit rules.* Bureaucratic jobs are governed by rules rather than by bureaucrats' own feelings or judgments about how the job should be done. Thus bureaucrats are limited in the discretion they have, and one person in a given job is expected to make pretty much the same decisions as another. This leads to standardization and predictability.
- *Merit.* Hiring and promotions are often based on examinations but also on experience or other objective criteria. Politics, in the form of political loyalty, party affiliation, or dating the boss's son or daughter, is not supposed to play a part.

Political scientist Herbert Kaufman says that the closer governments come to making their bureaucracies look more like Weber's model, the closer they are to achieving "neutral competence."[7] **Neutral competence** represents the effort to depoliticize the bureaucracy, or to take politics out of administration, by having the work of government done expertly, according to explicit standards rather than personal preferences or party loyalties. The bureaucracy in this view should not be a political arm of the president or of Congress, but rather it should be neutral, administering the laws of the land in a fair, evenhanded, efficient, and professional way.

neutral competence the principle that bureaucracy should be depoliticized by making it more professional

THE SPOILS SYSTEM

Americans have not always been so concerned with the norm of neutral competence in the bureaucracy. Under a form of bureaucratic organization called the **spoils system**, practiced through most of the nineteenth century in the United States, the elected executives—the president, governors, and mayors—were given wide latitude to hire their own friends, family, and political supporters to work in their administrations. The spoils system is often said to have begun with the administration of President Andrew Jackson and gets its name from the adage "To the victor belong the spoils of the enemy," but Jackson was neither the first nor the last politician to see the ac-

spoils system the nineteenth-century practice of rewarding political supporters with public office

patronage system in which successful party candidates reward supporters with jobs or favors

quisition of public office as a means of feathering his cronies' nests. Such activity, referred to as **patronage**, allowed the elected executive to use jobs to pay off political debts as well as to gain cooperation from the officials who were hired this way, thereby strengthening his base of power.

Filling the bureaucracy with political appointees almost guarantees incompetence because those who get jobs for political reasons are more likely to be politically motivated than genuinely skilled in a specific area. Experts who are devoted to the task of the agency soon become discouraged because advancement is based on political favoritism rather than on how well the job is done. America's disgust with the corruption and inefficiency of the spoils system, as well as our collective distrust of placing too much power in the hands of any one person, led Congress to institute various reforms of the American **civil service**, as it is sometimes called, aimed at achieving a very different sort of organization.

civil service nonmilitary employees of the government who are appointed through the merit system

Pendleton Act 1883 civil service reform that required the hiring and promoting of civil servants to be based on merit, not patronage

One of the first reforms, and certainly one of the most significant, was the Civil Service Reform Act of 1883. This act, usually referred to as the **Pendleton Act**, created the initial Civil Service Commission, under which federal employees would be hired and promoted on the basis of merit rather than patronage. It prohibited firing employees for failure to contribute to political parties or candidates. Civil service coverage increased until President Harry Truman in 1948 was successful in getting 93 percent of the federal workforce covered under the merit system.

Hatch Act 1939 law limiting the political involvement of civil servants in order to protect them from political pressure and keep politics out of the bureaucracy

Protection of the civil service from partisan politicians got another boost in 1939 with the passage of the **Hatch Act**. This act was designed to take the pressure off civil servants to work for the election of parties and candidates. It forbids pressuring federal employees for contributions to political campaigns, and it prohibits civil servants from taking leadership roles in campaigns. They cannot run for federal political office, head up an election campaign, or make public speeches on behalf of candidates. However, they are permitted to make contributions, to attend rallies, and to work on registration or get-out-the-vote drives that do not focus on just one candidate or party. The Hatch Act thus seeks to neutralize the political effects of the bureaucracy. However, in doing so, it denies federal employees a number of activities that are open to other citizens.

WHY IS BUREAUCRACY NECESSARY?

Much of the world is organized bureaucratically. Large tasks require organization and specialization. The Wright brothers may have been able to construct a rudimentary airplane, but no two people or even small group could put together a Boeing 747. Similarly, though we idolize individual American heroes, we know that efforts like the D-Day invasion of Europe, the war on terrorism, or the post-hurricane clean-up in New Orleans take enormous coordination and planning. Smaller in scale, but still necessary, are routine tasks like delivering the mail, evaluating welfare applications, ensuring that social security recipients get their checks, and processing student loans.

Obviously many bureaucracies are public, like those that form part of our government. But the private sector has the same demand for efficient expertise to manage large organizations. Corporations and businesses are bureaucracies, as are universities and hospitals. It is not being public or private that distinguishes a bureaucracy; rather, it is the need for a structure of hierarchical, expert decision making. In this chapter we focus on public bureaucracies, the federal bureaucracy in particular.

BUREAUCRACY AND DEMOCRACY

Decision making by experts may seem odd to Americans who cherish the idea of democracy, and it may be why so many Americans dislike so much of our public bureaucracy. If we value democracy and the corresponding idea that public officials should be accountable, or responsible, to the people, how can we also value bureaucracy, in which decisions are often made behind closed doors where accountability cannot be monitored?

Bureaucratic decision making in a democratic government presents a real puzzle unless we consider that democracy may not be the best way to make every kind of decision. If we want to ensure that many voices are heard from, then democracy is an appropriate way to make decisions. But those decisions will be made slowly (it takes a long time to poll many people on what they want to do), and though the decisions are likely to be popular, they are not necessarily made by people who know what they are doing. When we're deciding whether to have open heart surgery, we don't want to poll the American people, or even the hospital employees. Instead we want an expert, a heart surgeon, who can make the "right" decision, not the popular decision, and make it quickly.

Democracy could not have designed the rocket ships that formed the basis of America's space program, or decided the level of toxic emissions allowable from a factory smokestack, or determined the temperature at which beef must be cooked in restaurants to prevent food poisoning. Bureaucratic decision making, by which decisions are made at upper levels of an organization and carried out at lower levels, is essential when we require expertise and dispatch.

ACCOUNTABILITY AND RULES

Bureaucratic decision making does leave open the problem of **accountability**: who is in charge and to whom does that person answer? Where does the buck stop? In a growing and complex society, bureaucracy is necessary but it is not without costs. Because bureaucracies can wield enormous amounts of power in the public realm, we want some assurance that it is not being abused. It is sometimes less difficult to solve the abuse of power problem in private bureaucracies. The chief executive officer (CEO) of General Motors, for instance, may have several professional goals—making a more fuel-efficient automobile, for instance, or gaining market share. That CEO also works for the stockholders, however, and their single goal is profits. The stockholders decide how well this goal is being met; they hold the CEO accountable.

accountability the principle that bureaucratic employees should be answerable for their performance to supervisors, all the way up the chain of command

The lines of accountability are less clear in public bureaucracies, where there are often multiple goals to be served. Because the Constitution does not provide specific rules for the operation of the bureaucracy, Congress has filled in a piecemeal framework for the bureaucracy that, generally speaking, ends up promoting the goals of members of Congress and the interests they represent.[8] The president of the United States, nominally the head of the executive branch of government, also has goals and objectives he would like the bureaucracy to serve. However, our system of checks and balances and our general distrust of high concentrations of power make the president much less powerful over his bureaucracy than any corporate CEO, and he shares his authority with the legislators in Congress, not all of whom agree with his goals and plans for the agencies. Thus, at the very highest level, the public bureaucracy must answer to several bosses who often have conflicting goals.

The problem of accountability exists at a lower level as well. Even if the lines of authority from the bureaucracy to the executive and legislative branches were crystal clear, no president or congressional committee has the interest or time to supervise the day-to-day details of bureaucratic workings. To solve the problem of accountability within the bureaucracy and to prevent the abuse of public power at all levels, we again resort to rules. If the rules of bureaucratic policy are clearly defined and well publicized, it is easier to tell if a given bureaucrat is doing his or her job, and doing it fairly.

What does fairness mean in the context of a bureaucracy? It means, certainly, that the bureaucrat should not play favorites. The personnel officer for a city is not supposed to give special consideration to her neighbors or to her boyfriend's brother. We do not want employees to give preferential treatment to people like themselves, whether that likeness is based on race, ethnicity, religion, or even sexual orientation, or to discriminate against people who are different from them. And we do not want people to run their organizations for their own benefit rather than for the public good. In these and many additional ways, we do not want the people carrying out jobs in any bureaucracy to take advantage of the power they have.

CONSEQUENCES OF A RULE-BASED SYSTEM

The centrality of rules in bureaucracies has important trade-offs. According to the goals of neutral competence, we try to achieve fairness and predictability by insisting that the bureaucrats do their work according to certain rules. If everyone follows his or her job description, the supervisor, boss, or policymaker can know what, within some limits, is likely to happen. Similarly, if an important task is left undone, it should be possible to determine who did not do his or her job.

On the negative side, the bureaucrats' jobs can quickly become rule-bound; that is, deviations from the rules become unacceptable, and individuality and creativity are stifled. Sometimes the rules that bind bureaucrats do not seem relevant to the immediate task at hand, and the workers are rewarded for following the rules, not for fulfilling the goals of the organization. Rigid adherence to rules designed to protect the bureaucracy often results in outcomes that have the opposite effect. Furthermore, compliance with rules has to be monitored, and the best way we have developed to guarantee compliance is to generate a paper record of what has been done. To be sure that all the necessary information will be available if needed, it has to be standardized—hence the endless forms for which the bureaucracy is so famous.

For the individual citizen applying for a driver's license, a student loan, or food stamps, the process can become a morass of seemingly unnecessary rules, regulations, constraints, forms, and hearings. We call these bureaucratic hurdles "**red tape**," after the red tape that seventeenth-century English officials used to bind legal documents.

red tape the complex procedures and regulations surrounding bureaucratic activity

Rules thus generate one of the great trade-offs of bureaucratic life. If we want strict fairness and accountability, we must tie the bureaucrat to a tight set of rules. If we allow the bureaucrat discretion to try to reach goals with a looser set of rules, or to waive a rule when it seems appropriate, we may gain some efficiency, but we lose accountability. Given the vast number of people who work for the federal government, we have opted for the accountability, even while we howl with frustration at the inconvenience of the rules.

WHO, WHAT, HOW The American public is strongly committed to democratic governance, but sometimes decisions need to be made that do not lend themselves to democracy. When what is needed is complex, technical decision making, then some form of specialization and expertise is required. Because we also want accountability and fairness among our decision makers, we want them to stick to a prescribed set of rules. Bureaucratic decision making and administration offer possibilities in governance that democracy cannot, but it also brings its own difficulties and challenges.

THE AMERICAN FEDERAL BUREAUCRACY

Almost three million civilians work for the federal government, with another million and a half or so in the armed forces. Only a relative handful, 2 percent of federal workers, work in the legislative branch (30,190) or the judiciary (34,303). The rest—98 percent of federal workers[9]—are in the executive branch, home of the federal bureaucracy. In this section we look at the evolution of the federal bureaucracy, its present-day organization, and its basic functions.

EVOLUTION OF THE FEDERAL BUREAUCRACY

The central characteristic of the federal bureaucracy is that most of its parts developed independently of the others in a piecemeal and political fashion, rather than emerging from a coherent plan. Some government activities are fundamental; from the earliest days of the republic, the government had departments to handle foreign relations, money, and defense. But other government tasks have developed over time as the result of historical forces, as solutions to particular problems, and as a response to different groups who want government to do something for them. The emerging picture is more like a patchwork quilt than the streamlined efficient government structure we would like to have. Thus the nature and duties of the agencies reflect the politics of their creation and the subsequent politics of their survival and growth.[10] We can understand federal agencies as falling into three categories: those designed to serve essential government functions, those crafted to meet the changing needs and problems of the country, and those intended to serve particular clientele groups.[11]

Serving Essential Government Functions Some departments are created to serve essential government functions, the core operations that any viable government performs. For example, the Departments of State, War, and the Treasury were the first cabinet offices because the activities they handle are fundamental to the smooth functioning of government. The Department of State exists to handle diplomatic relations with other nations. When diplomacy fails, national interests must be protected by force; the Department of Defense (formerly War) supervises the air force, army, navy, and marines, and, in time of war, the coast guard. All nations have expenses and must extract resources in the form of taxes from their citizens to pay for them. The Department of the Treasury, which oversees the Internal Revenue Service (IRS), performs this key tax collection function. Treasury also prints the money we use and oversees the horrendous job of managing the national debt. Imagine the effort required to borrow almost $2 billion a day![12]

Responding to Changing National Needs Other departments and agencies were created to meet the changing needs of the country as we industrialized and evolved into a highly urbanized society. For example, with westward expansion, the growth of manufacturing, and increased commerce came demands for new roles for government. The Department of the Interior was created in 1848 to deal with some of the unforeseen effects of the move westward, including the displacement of Native Americans and the management of western public lands and resources.

Similarly, a number of the negative aspects of industrialization, including child labor abuses, filthy and dangerous working conditions, unsanitary food production, and price gouging by the railroads, led to calls for government intervention to manage the burgeoning marketplace of an industrialized society. Thus began the development of the independent regulatory commissions starting in the late nineteenth century with the Interstate Commerce Commission and continuing into the twentieth century with the Federal Trade Commission, the Federal Reserve System, and others.

Under the New Deal, several new agencies were created and new programs put into place. The federal government's largest single program today, social security, was organized under the Social Security Administration as a supplement for inadequate and failed old-age pensions. For the first time, the national government became directly involved in the economic well-being of individual citizens. Related programs like the Work Progress Administration and the Civilian Conservation Corps were sometimes called government "make-work" programs because their primary purpose was to create jobs and get people back to work. The new obligations of the national government did not vanish with postwar prosperity. Americans came to expect that government would play a large role in managing the economy and in ensuring that people could work, eat, and live in decent housing. President Lyndon Johnson's War on Poverty resulted in the creation of the Office of Economic Opportunity in 1964 and the Department of Housing and Urban Development (HUD) in 1965.

A changing international environment also created needs that required government to grow. The Cold War between the United States and the Soviet Union launched a multipronged policy effort that included investment in military research, science (the National Science Foundation), education (the National Defense Education Act), and space exploration (the National Aeronautics and Space Administration). Much more recently, the September 11, 2001, terror attacks on the United States led to the establishment of

Uncle Sam Lends a Hand

The federal government's response to the Great Depression was Roosevelt's New Deal, which provided assistance to anxious Americans in need of stable work. The Civilian Conservation Corps, featured in this 1941 poster, not only helped preserve the country's forests but also mobilized more than a half million men and women into the labor force.

a new cabinet-level Department of Homeland Security to coordinate efforts to protect the country.

Responding to the Demands of Clientele Groups A number of departments and agencies either were created or have evolved to serve distinct **clientele groups**. These may include interest groups—groups of citizens, businesses, or industry members who are affected by government regulatory actions and who organize to try to influence policy. Or they may include unorganized groups, such as poor people, to which the government has decided to respond. Such departments are sensitive to the concerns of those specific groups rather than being focused on what is good for the nation as a whole. The Department of Agriculture, among the first of these, was set up in 1862 to assist U.S. agricultural interests. It began by providing research information to farmers and later arranged subsidies and developed markets for agricultural products. Politicians in today's budget-cutting climate talk about cutting back on agricultural subsidies, but no one expects the USDA to change its focus of looking out, first and foremost, for the farmer. Similar stories can be told of the Departments of Labor, Commerce, Education, and Veterans Affairs.

clientele groups groups of citizens whose interests are affected by an agency or department and who work to influence its policies

ORGANIZATION OF THE FEDERAL BUREAUCRACY

The federal bureaucracy consists of four types of organizations: (1) cabinet-level departments, (2) independent agencies, (3) regulatory boards and commissions, and (4) government corporations. As you might suspect, some agencies can fit in more than one of those classifications. The difficulty in classifying an agency as one type or another stems partly from Congress's habit of creating hybrids: agencies that act like government corporations, for instance, or cabinet-level departments that regulate. The overall organizational chart of the U.S. government (see Figure 9.1) makes this complex bureaucracy look reasonably orderly. To a large extent the impression of order is an illusion.

Departments The federal government currently has fifteen **departments**. Table 9.1 lists these departments along with their dates of creation, budgets, and functions. The heads of departments are known as secretaries—for example, the secretary of state or the secretary of defense—except for the head of the Department of Justice, who is called the attorney general. These department heads collectively make up the president's cabinet, appointed by the president, with the consent of the Senate, to provide advice on critical areas of government affairs such as foreign relations, agriculture, education, and so on. These areas are not fixed, and presidents may propose different cabinet offices. Although the secretaries are political appointees who usually change when the administration changes (or even more frequently), they sit at the heads of the large, more or less permanent, bureaucracies we call departments. Cabinet heads may not have any more actual power than other agency leaders, but their posts do carry more status and prestige.

department one of the major subdivisions of the federal government, represented in the president's cabinet

When a cabinet department is established, it is a sign that the government recognizes its policy area as a legitimate and important political responsibility. Therefore, groups fight hard to get their causes represented at the cabinet level. During the Clinton administration, environmental groups tried to get the Environmental Protection Agency (EPA) raised to the cabinet level. The fact that it was not elevated, despite President Clinton's campaign promises on the matter, was a sign that the business and development interests that opposed environmental regulation were stronger politically.

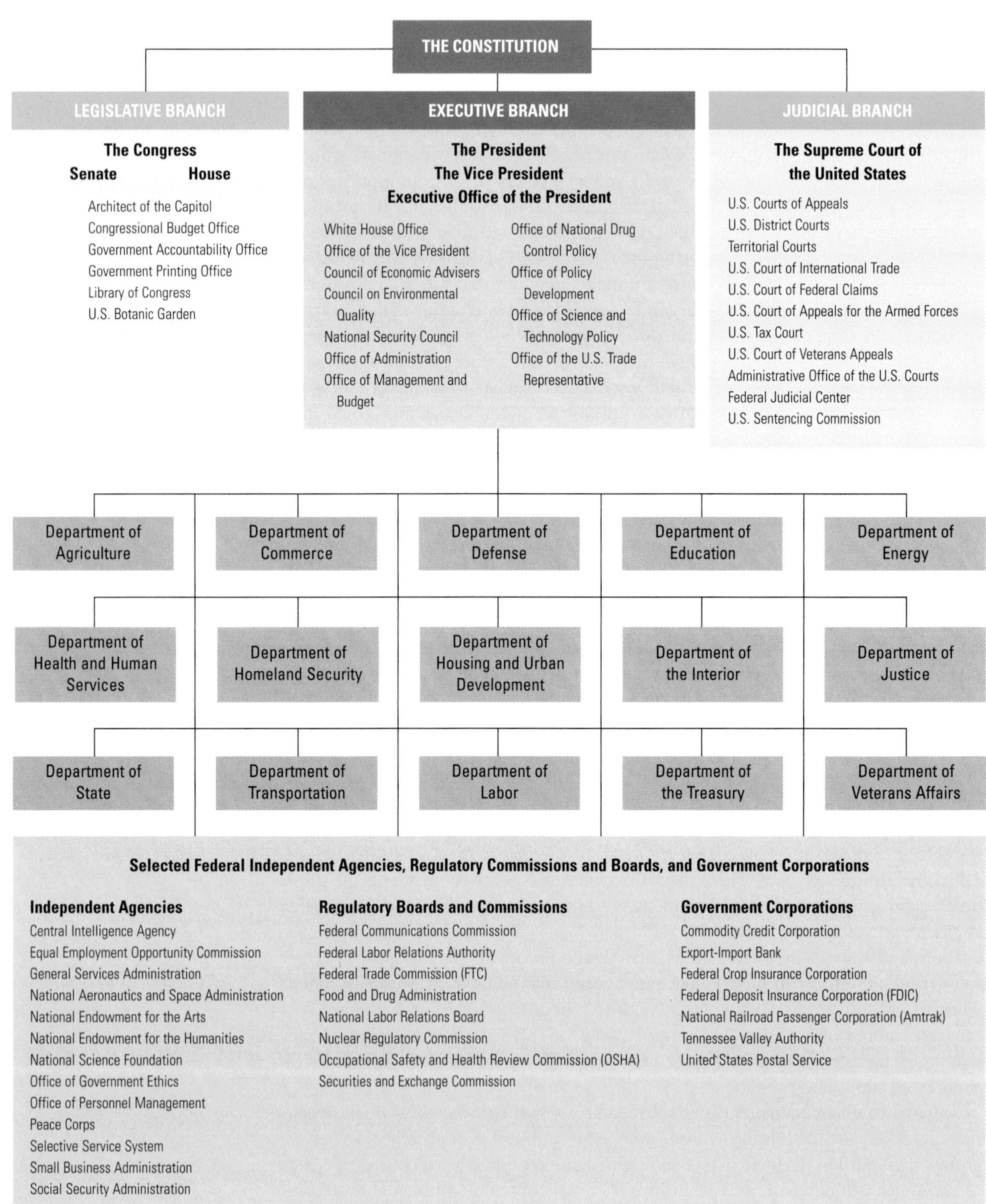

FIGURE 9.1

Organizational Chart of the United States Government

Even though the EPA is not a cabinet-level agency, its director has been asked by various presidents, including Clinton and Bush, to meet with the cabinet, giving him or her cabinet rank and thus more status, even if the agency is not so elevated.

Independent Agencies Congress has established a host of agencies outside the cabinet departments (some are listed in Figure 9.1). The **independent agencies** are structured like the cabinet departments, with a single head appointed by the president. Their areas of jurisdiction, however, tend to be narrower than those of the cabinet departments. Congress does not follow a blueprint about how to make an independent agency or a department. Instead, it expands the bureaucracy to fit the case at hand, given the mix of political forces of the moment—that is, given what groups are demanding what action, and with what resources. As a result, the independent agencies vary tremendously in size, from 300 employees in the Federal Election Commission (FEC) to over 18,000 for the EPA. While agencies are called independent because of their independence from cabinet departments, they vary in their independence from the president. Some agency heads serve at the president's discretion and can be fired at any time; others serve fixed terms, and the president can appoint a new head or commissioner only when a vacancy occurs. Independent agencies also vary in their freedom from judicial review. Congress has established that some agencies' rulings cannot be challenged in the courts, whereas others' can be.[13]

independent agency a government organization independent of the departments but with a narrower policy focus

The establishment and reorganization of independent agencies and cabinet-level departments are the subject of intense political maneuvering. Interests that have become accustomed to dealing with particular agencies and have built relationships with key congressional committees are frequently threatened by the prospect of changes in the location of the agency responsible for their programs or the committee overseeing relevant funding.

Independent Regulatory Boards and Commissions **Independent regulatory boards and commissions** make regulations for various industries, businesses, and sectors of the economy (see Figure 9.1). **Regulations** are simply limitations or restrictions on the behavior of an individual or a business; they are bureaucratically determined prescriptions for how business is to take place. This chapter opened with the battle over a regulation: the guidelines that must be followed for a product to be labeled "organic." Regulations usually seek to protect the public from some industrial or economic danger or uncertainty. The Securities and Exchange Commission, for example, regulates the trading of stocks and bonds on the nation's stock markets, while the Food and Drug Administration regulates such things as how drugs must be tested before they can be safely marketed and what information must appear on the labels of processed foods and beverages sold throughout the country. Regulation usually pits the individual's freedom to do what he or she wants, or a business's drive to make a profit, against some vision of what is good for the public. As long as there are governments, there will be trade-offs between the two because it is for the purpose of managing citizens' collective lives that governments are formed. How each trade-off is made between individual freedom and public safety is a question of public policy.

independent regulatory boards and commissions government organizations that regulate various businesses, industries, or economic sectors

regulations limitations or restrictions on the activities of a business or individual

There are thirty-eight agencies of the federal government whose principal job is to issue and enforce regulations about what citizens and businesses can do, and how they have to do it. This effort employs nearly 185,000 people and takes up about 5 percent of the federal budget.[14] Given the size of the enterprise, it is not surprising that regulation occasionally gets out of hand. If an agency exists to regulate, regulate it proba-

TABLE 9.1 **Departments of the United States Government**

DEPARTMENT	YEAR FORMED	SPENDING 2002 (BILLIONS)	NUMBER OF EMPLOYEES	FUNCTION AND HISTORY
Agriculture	1862	$76.6	131,385	Administers federal programs related to food production and rural life, including price support programs and soil conservation
Commerce	1903	$5.5	37,000	Responsible for economic and technological development; includes Census Bureau; was Commerce and Labor until 1913, when Labor split off
Defense	1789	$330.6	667,750 civilian, 2.3 million military	Manages U.S. Army, Air Force, Navy; created as War Department in 1789; changed to Defense in 1949
Education	1979	$47.6	4,710	Provides federal aid to local school districts and colleges and student college loans; until 1979 was part of Health, Education and Welfare
Energy	1977	$19.1	15,000 federal, 100,000 contractors	Oversees national activities relating to the production, regulation, marketing, and conservation of energy
Health and Human Services	1953	$459.4	65,000	Administers government health and security programs; includes Centers for Disease Control and Food and Drug Administration; formerly Health, Education and Welfare
Homeland Security	2003			Created to prevent terrorist attacks within the United States, make the country less vulnerable to terrorism, and help the nation survive attacks that do occur.
Housing and Urban Development	1965	$30.9	10,300	Administers housing and community development programs
Interior	1849	$10.3	69,718	Manages the nation's natural resources through its eight bureaus, including the Bureau of Land Management and the National Park Service
Justice	1870	$23.1	129,676	Legal arm of executive branch responsible for enforcement of federal laws, including civil rights and antitrust laws
Labor	1903	$58.6	17,432	Responsible for work force safety and employment standards; originated in Interior in 1884, moved to Commerce and Labor in 1903, split from Commerce in 1913
State	1789	$15.9	28,967	Responsible for foreign policy and diplomatic relations
Transportation	1966	$60.8	118,447	Coordinates and administers overall transportation policy, including highways, urban mass transit, railroads, aviation, and waterways
Treasury	1789	$16.8*	150,532	Government's financial agent, responsible for money coming in and going out (including tax collection); advises president on fiscal policy
Veterans' Affairs	1989	$51.5	207,028	Administers programs to help veterans and their families, including pensions, medical care, disability, and death benefits

*Debt financing and tax credits add $365.8 million to Treasury spending.

Sources: *U.S. Government Manual 1997/1998.* Washington, D.C.: Office of the Federal Register, National Archives and Records Administration, 1997–1998. "Summaries by Agency: Table S-10 Discretionary Budget Authority by Agency." *Budget of the United States* (OMB homepage: http://www.access.gpo.gov/usbudget/fy2003/maindown.html). White House homepage (www.whitehouse.gov) has links to each department's homepage.

bly will, whether or not a clear case can be made for restricting action. The average cheeseburger in America, for instance, is the subject of over 40,000 federal and state regulations, specifying everything from the vitamin content of the flour in the bun, to the age and fat content of the cheese, to the temperature at which it must be cooked, to the speed at which the ketchup must flow to be certified Grade A Fancy.[15] Some of these rules are undoubtedly crucial; we all want to be able to buy a cheeseburger without risking food poisoning and possible death. Others are informative; those of us on restrictive diets need to know what we are eating, and none of us likes to be ripped off by getting something other than what we think we are paying for. Others seem merely silly; when we consider that adult federal employees are paid to measure the speed of ketchup, we readily sympathize with those who claim that the regulatory function is getting out of hand in American government.

Nasty Business
The Federal Emergency Management Agency (FEMA) was an independent agency charged with helping Americans cope with disaster until bureaucratic reorganization brought it into the Department of Homeland Security in 2003. That reorganization faced considerable criticism and second guessing in the wake of Hurricane Katrina in 2005, when the placement of the FEMA under the DHS was thought to have slowed that agency's ability to respond to the disaster. Its politically appointed director, Michael Brown (shown here with DHS secretary Michael Chertoff behind him), bore the brunt of the criticism and was eventually reassigned to Washington.

The regulatory agencies are set up to be largely independent of political influence, though some are bureaus within cabinet departments—the federal Food and Drug Administration, for example, is located in the Department of Health and Human Services. Most independent regulatory agencies are run by a commission of three or more people who serve overlapping terms, and the terms of office, usually between three and fourteen years, are set so that they do not coincide with presidential terms. Commission members are nominated by the president and confirmed by Congress, often with a bipartisan vote. Unlike cabinet secretaries and some agency heads, the heads of the regulatory boards and commissions cannot be fired by the president. All of these aspects of their organization are intended to insulate them from political pressures so that they regulate in the public interest and not in the interests of those they hope will reappoint them.

Government Corporations We do not often think of the government as a business, but public enterprises are, in fact, big business. The U.S. Postal Service is one of the larger businesses in the nation in terms of sales and personnel. The Tennessee Valley Authority and the Bonneville Power Administration of the northwestern states are both in the business of generating electricity and selling it to citizens throughout their regions. If you ride the rails as a passenger, you travel by Amtrak, a government-owned corporation (technically called the National Railroad Passenger Corporation). All of these businesses are set up to be largely independent of both congressional and presidential influence. This independence is not insignificant. Consider, for example, how angry citizens are when the postal rates go up. Because the Postal Commission is independent, both the president and Congress avoid the political heat for such unpopular decisions. Figure 9.1 lists some examples of the businesses run by the federal government.

Congress created these publicly owned **government corporations** primarily to provide a good or service that is not profitable for a private business to provide. The Federal Deposit Insurance Corporation (FDIC) is a good example. Following the Great Depression, during which financial institutions failed at an alarming rate, citizens were reluctant to put their money back into banks. A "government guarantee," through FDIC, of the safety of savings gave, and continues to give, citizens much more confidence than if the insurance were provided by a private company, which itself

government corporation
a company created by Congress to provide a good or service to the public that private enterprise cannot or will not profitably provide

could go broke. Similarly, government has acted to bring utilities to rural areas and to ensure that mail is delivered even to the most remote addresses. The government's ownership of Amtrak came about because a national rail service did not prove profitable for private industry but was seen by Congress as a national resource that should not be lost. The rationale is that providing these services entails not just making a profit but also serving the public interest. However, as in so many other aspects of American government, the public is relatively quiet in speaking up for its interests, and so the politics of government corporations become the politics of interested bureaucrats, clientele groups, and congressional subcommittees.

ROLES OF THE FEDERAL BUREAUCRACY

Federal bureaucrats at the broadest level are responsible for helping the president to administer the laws, policies, and regulations of government. The actual work the bureaucrat does depends on the policy area in which he or she is employed. Take another look at the titles of the cabinet departments and independent agencies listed in Table 9.1 and Figure 9.1. Some part of the bureaucracy is responsible for administering rules and policies on just about every imaginable aspect of social and economic life.

Bureaucrats are not confined to administering the laws, however. Although the principle of separation of powers—by which the functions of making, administering, and interpreting the laws are carried out by the executive, legislative, and judicial branches—applies at the highest level of government, it tends to dissolve at the level of the bureaucracy. In practice, the bureaucracy is an all-in-one policymaker. It administers the laws, but it also effectively makes and judges compliance with laws. It is this wide scope of bureaucratic power that creates the problems of control and accountability that we discuss throughout this chapter.

Bureaucracy as Administrator We expect the agencies of the federal government to implement the laws passed by Congress and signed by the president. Operating under the ideal of neutral competence, a public bureaucracy serves the political branches of government in a professional, unbiased, and efficient manner. In many cases this is exactly what happens, and with admirable ability and dedication. The rangers in the national parks help citizens enjoy our natural resources, police officers enforce the statutes of criminal law, social workers check for compliance with welfare regulations, and postal workers deliver letters and packages in a timely way. All these bureaucrats are simply carrying out the law that has been made elsewhere in government.

Bureaucracy as Rule Maker The picture of the bureaucrat as an impartial administrator removed from political decision making is a partial and unrealistic one. The bureaucracy has a great deal of latitude in administering national policy. Because it often lacks the time, the technical expertise, and the political coherence and leverage to write clear and detailed legislation, Congress frequently passes laws that are vague, contradictory, and overly general. In order to carry out or administer the laws, the bureaucracy must first fill in the gaps. Congress has essentially delegated some of its legislative power to the bureaucracy. Its role here is called **bureaucratic discretion**. Top bureaucrats must use their own judgment, which under the ideal of neutral competence should remain minimal, in order to carry out the laws of Congress. Congress does not say how many park rangers should be assigned to Yosemite versus Yellowstone, for instance; the Park Service has to interpret the broad intent of the law and

bureaucratic discretion
top bureaucrats' authority to use their own judgment in interpreting and carrying out the laws of Congress

make decisions on this and thousands of other specifics. Bureaucratic discretion is not limited to allocating personnel and other "minor" administrative details. Congress cannot make decisions on specifications for military aircraft, dictate the advice the agricultural extension agents should give to farmers, or determine whether the latest sugar substitute is safe for our soft drinks. The appropriate bureaucracy must fill in all those details. Similarly, when Congress created the EPA, it chose the broadest language telling the new agency to protect the environment. It has been up to the EPA to translate that lofty goal into specific policies, which means that unelected bureaucrats have made more environmental laws than has Congress.

The procedures of administrative rule making are not completely insulated from the outside world, however. Before they become effective, all new regulations must first be publicized in the ***Federal Register***, which is a primary source of information for thousands of interests affected by decisions in Washington. Before adopting the rules, agencies must give outsiders—the public and interest groups—a chance to be heard, as we saw in the examination of organic farming regulation that began this chapter.

Federal Register publication containing all federal regulations and notifications of regulatory agency hearings

Bureaucracy as Judge The third major function of governments is adjudication, or the process of interpreting the law in specific cases for potential violations and deciding the appropriate penalties when violations are found. This is what the courts do. However, a great deal of adjudication in America is carried out by the bureaucracy. For example, regulatory agencies not only make many of the rules that govern the conduct of business but also are responsible for seeing that individuals, but more often businesses, comply with their regulations. Tax courts, under the IRS, for instance, handle violations of the tax codes.

The adjudication functions of the agencies, while generally less formal than the proceedings of the courts, do have formal procedures, and their decisions have the full force of law. In most cases if Congress does not like an agency ruling, it can work to change it, either by passing new legislation or by more subtle pressures. Nevertheless, agencies often issue rulings that could never have overcome the many hurdles of the legislative process in Congress.

WHO ARE THE FEDERAL BUREAUCRATS?

The full civilian work force of the federal bureaucracy fairly accurately reflects the general population. For example, 50.8 percent of the U.S. population is female and 44.6 percent of the civil service is female. African Americans make up 13.3 percent of the population and 16.9 percent of the civil service. The distributions are similar for other demographic characteristics such as ethnic origin or level of education. This representative picture is disturbed, however, by the fact that not all bureaucratic positions are equal. Policymaking is done primarily at the highest levels, and the upper grades are staffed predominantly by well-educated white males. As illustrated in "*Who Are We*? The Federal Bureaucrats," women and minorities are distinctly underrepresented in the policymaking (and higher-paying) levels of the bureaucracy.[16]

WHO, WHAT, HOW Government exists, among other reasons, to solve citizens' common problems and to provide goods and services that the market does not or cannot provide. The apparatus for problem solving and service providing is primarily the bureaucracy. Congress and the president define the problems, make the initial decisions, and assign responsibility for solving them to a department, an agency, or a regulatory board.

Citizens or groups of citizens who want something from the government must deal with the bureaucracy as well. Finally, the bureaucrats themselves have a stake in performing their mandated jobs in a political context where Congress and the president may hedge on the details of what that job actually is. Consequently, bureaucrats need to go beyond administering the laws to making them and judging compliance with them as well. Though we cautiously separate power, and check and balance it among all our elected officials, it is curious that where the officials are unelected and thus not accountable to the people, powers are fused and to a large extent unchecked. The bureaucracy is therefore a very powerful part of the federal government.

POLITICS INSIDE THE BUREAUCRACY

Politicians and bureaucrats alike are wary about the effects of politics on decision making. They act as if fairness and efficiency could always be achieved if only the struggle over competing interests could be set aside through an emphasis on strict rules and hierarchical organization. We know, of course, that the struggle can't be set aside. As a fundamental human activity, politics is always with us, and it is always shaped by the particular rules and institutions in which it is played out. Politics within bureaucracies is a subset of politics generally, but it takes on its own cast according to the context in which it takes place.

BUREAUCRATIC CULTURE

bureaucratic culture the accepted values and procedures of an organization

The particular context in which internal bureaucratic politics is shaped is called **bureaucratic culture**—the accepted values and procedures of an organization. Consider any place you may have been employed. When you began your job, the accepted standards of behavior may not have been clear, but over time you figured out who had power, what your role was, which rules could be bent and which had to be followed strictly, and what the goals of the enterprise were. Chances are you came to share some of the values of your colleagues, at least with respect to your work. Those things add up to the culture of the workplace. Bureaucratic culture is just a specific instance of workplace culture.

Knowing the four main elements of bureaucratic culture will take us a long way toward understanding why bureaucrats and bureaucracies behave the way they do. Essentially these elements define what is at stake within a bureaucracy, and what bureaucrats need to do to ensure that they are winners and not losers in the bureaucratic

The Federal Bureaucrats

The federal bureaucrats who work for the U.S. government represent a fair cross-section of the American population. But very few women, African Americans, or Hispanics reach the highest grade levels of the civil service ladder. Does this "glass ceiling" make a difference in the way the bureaucracy does its job?

Minorities in the Civil Service

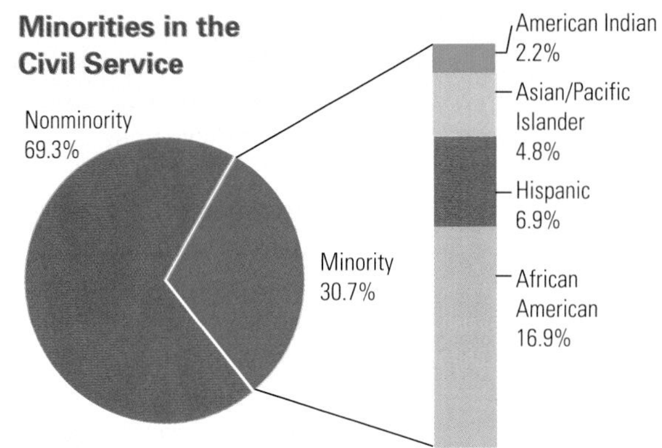

Source: U.S. Office of Personnel Management, Federal Civilian Workforce Statistics, May 2002.

Government Employees by Gender and Race, 2002: Who makes it to the top of the civil service?

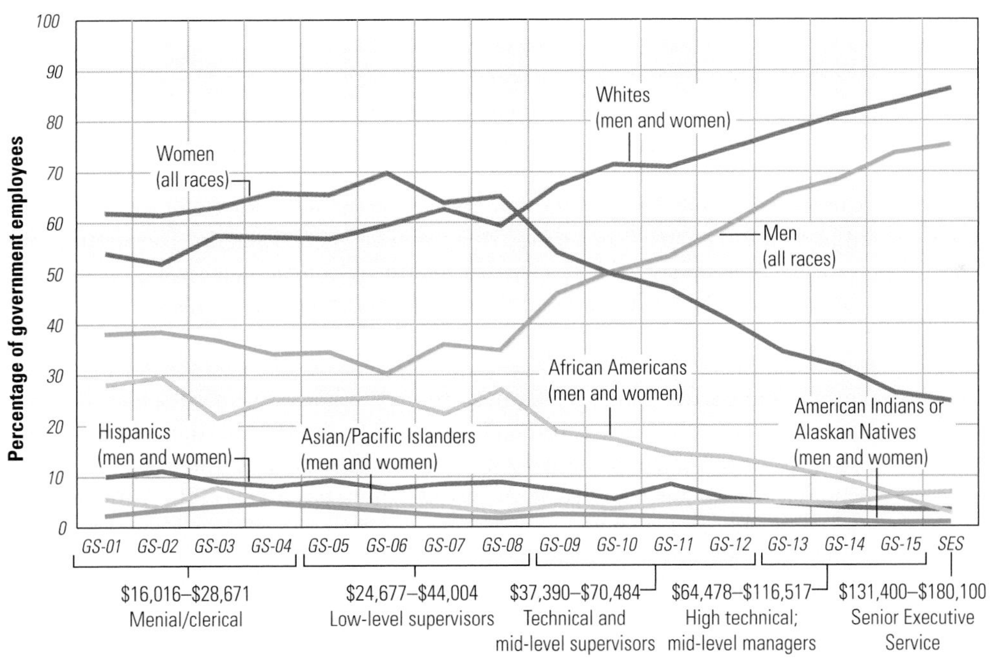

Source: U.S. Office of Personnel Management, *Civilian Workforce Statistics,* May 2004.

world. To explore bureaucratic culture, let's imagine that you have landed a job working in the USDA. Over time, if you are successful in your job, you will come to share the values and beliefs of others working in your department; that is, you will come to share their bureaucratic culture.

Policy Commitment As a good bureaucrat in training, the first thing you will do is develop a commitment to the policy issues of agriculture. No matter if you've never thought much about farming before. As an employee of the USDA, you will eventually come to believe that agricultural issues are among the most important facing the country, just as those working at the National Aeronautics and Space Administration place a priority on investigating outer space, and bureaucrats at the National Institutes of Health believe fervently in health research. You share a commitment to your policy area not only because your job depends on it but also because all the people around you believe in it.

bureaucratese the often unintelligible language used by bureaucrats to avoid controversy and lend weight to their words

Adoption of Bureaucratic Behavior Not long after you join your department, you will start to see the logic of doing things bureaucratically; you may even start to sound like a bureaucrat. **Bureaucratese**, the formal and often (to outsiders) amusing way that bureaucrats sometimes speak in their effort to convey information without controversy, may become your second tongue (see "*Consider the Source:* How to Decipher Bureaucratese"). The elaborate rule structure that defines the bureaucracy will come to seem quite normal to you; you will even depend on it because relying on the rules relieves you of the responsibility of relying on your own judgment.

The hierarchical organization of authority will also make a good deal of sense, and you will, in fact, find yourself spending a lot of your time helping to make your superiors look good to their superiors, even as the people working under you will be helping you to look good to your bosses. Remember that in a hierarchy most of your rewards will come from those over you in the power structure; you will be dependent on your superiors for work assignments, promotions, budget allotments, and vacation authorizations. Your superiors will have the same relationships with their bosses.

As you become committed to the bureaucratic structure, you learn that conformity to the rules and norms of the enterprise is the name of the game. Free spirits are not likely to thrive in a bureaucratic environment where deference, cooperation, and obedience are emphasized and rewarded, and the relentless rule orientation and hierarchy can wear down all but the most committed independent souls.

Specialization and Expertise Early on in your career, you will realize that departments, agencies, and bureaus have specific areas of responsibility. There is not a great deal of interagency hopping; most bureaucrats spend their whole professional lives working in the same area, often in the same department. The lawyers in the Justice Department, scientists at the National Science Foundation, physicians at the National Institutes of Health, and even you as a soybean expert at the USDA all have specialized knowledge as the base of your power.

Because of specialization and expertise, bureaucrats come to know a lot more about their policy areas than do the public or even politicians who must make decisions relevant to those areas. Their possession of critical information gives bureaucrats considerable power in policymaking situations.

Identification With the Agency All three of the characteristics of bureaucratic culture discussed so far lead to the fourth: identification with and protection of the agency. As you become attached to the interests of agriculture, committed to the rules and structures of the bureaucracy, concerned with the fortunes of your superiors, and appreciative of your own and your colleagues' specialized knowledge, your estimation of the USDA rises also. You begin to think that what is good for Agriculture is good for you, and that threats to the department's well-being become threats to you. You identify with the department, not just because your job depends on it but because you believe in what it does.

Consequences of the Bureaucratic Culture This pervasive bureaucratic culture breeds a number of political consequences. On the plus side, it holds the bureaucracy together, fostering values of commitment and loyalty to what could otherwise be seen as an impersonal and alienating work environment. It means that the people who work in the federal government, for the most part, really believe in what they do. Members of the Federal Bureau of Investigation (FBI), for example, are strongly attached to the agency's law enforcement mission and are steeped in one of the most distinctive bureaucratic cultures in the nation. This strong commitment to its law enforcement mission has led to major successes, such as the exposure and arrest of major organized crime figures across the country.

But bureaucratic culture can lead to negative consequences as well. As former FBI agent Coleen Rowley pointed out in testimony before the Senate Judiciary Committee in June 2002, this culture very likely had a role in the failure of our law enforcement and intelligence agencies to foresee and prevent the attacks of September 11, 2001. Rowley's office, in Minneapolis, had known that a possible terrorist, Zacarias Moussaoui, was seeking to take flying lessons. Finding his activities suspicious and worrisome, Minneapolis agents tried to get a warrant to search his computer but were unable to do so. In her testimony, Rowley targeted the FBI's hierarchical culture, with its implicit norm that said field agents did not go over the heads of their superiors, who frequently second-guessed their judgment. "There's a certain pecking order, and it's real strong," she told the committee. "Seven to nine levels is really ridiculous."[17]

Not only did bureaucratic culture keep the FBI from knowing what information it had prior to September 11, but it also kept the FBI and the Central Intelligence Agency (CIA) from communicating with each other about the various pieces of the puzzle they had found. Between them they had much of the information needed to have discovered the plot, but no one "connected the dots." Why? The cultures are different. The FBI is primarily a law enforcement agency; agents are rewarded for making arrests. Its antiterrorist activities prior to September 11 were focused on after-the-fact investigations of terrorist attacks (leading to convictions) but not on preventing such attacks against domestic targets.[18]

The CIA, on the other hand, is focused on clandestine activity to develop information about non-American groups and nations. It is more secretive and less rule-bound, more focused on plans and intentions than on after-the-fact evidence and convictions. Agents focus on relationships, not individual achievement. One reporter covering the two agencies wrote that though the two agencies need to work with each other, "they have such different approaches to life that they remain worlds apart. In fact, they speak such different languages that they can barely even communicate."[19]

When an agency is charged with making the rules, enforcing them, and even adjudicating them, it is relatively easy to cover up less catastrophic agency blunders.

A Tragedy Once Again
An entrenched bureaucratic culture and political pressure to meet a deadline were seen as responsible for the 1986 explosion of the space shuttle *Challenger.* The same factors were at play when the damaged space shuttle *Columbia* (seen here on its final lift-off) broke apart upon reentry into the earth's atmosphere in 2003. Foam insulation was the physical cause of damage to the craft, but NASA managers fostered a culture that stifled discussion and led to practices detrimental to safety—the true culprit of the disaster.

Consider the Source

How to Decipher Bureaucratese

The tortured and twisted language our government bureaucrats seem to love can be so awful that it's actually amusing—*if* you have nothing at stake in figuring out what it means. Try this on for size: "The metropolitan Washington region's transportation system will promote economic sustainability and quality of life through a facilitation of inter- and intra-jurisdictional connectivity of employment and population centers, with a comprehensive multi-modal approach to mobility and utilize available tools to reduce congestion."[1] What a windy way to say that the Washington transportation system will relieve traffic jams by using a variety of methods of transit!

It's no wonder that people have trouble taking what their government says seriously. But what might be merely irritating, or laughable, or just plain stupid when it comes to transportation, can assume a lot more importance when it's something we need to know about. Take taxes: failing to accurately calculate and pay one's taxes can lead to a financial penalty, or worse. But what's a taxpayer to do when confronted with something like this? "If the taxpayer's passive activity gross income from significant participation passive activities (within the meaning of section 1.469-2T-(f)(2)(ii)) for the taxable year (determined without regard to section 1.469-2T-(f)(2) through (4)) exceeds the taxpayer's passive activity deductions from such activities for the taxable year, such activities shall be treated, solely for purposes of applying this paragraph (f)(2)(i) for the taxable year, as a single activity that does not have a loss for such taxable year." Even a nationwide poll of accountants gave this Internal Revenue Service rule the "Most Incomprehensible Government Regulation" award.[2]

The truth is, translating bureaucratese, the bewildering way that government officials often speak, can be quite a project. It would be nice if we could just avoid dealing with government language altogether, but most of us can't. At some time in our lives we register a car, apply for a student loan, get a marriage license, or file a building permit. We may need to register for social security benefits or apply for Medicaid or food stamps. We may fill out a passport application or a form to bring purchases back through customs after traveling abroad. We may want to read a report from the local school committee or the public transportation board. And one thing is certain: we all have to pay taxes. Here are a few hints for deciphering government jargon:

1. **Translate overly complicated terms that refer to common objects and events**. In bureaucratese, "means of egress" are exits, a "grade separation structure" can turn out to be a bridge, "rail movements" are train trips, "agricultural specialists" are farmers, and an application for an "unenclosed premise permit" is a request to build a patio.[3] Such language may result from an effort to be more specific, from a wish to be *less* specific, or just from a desire to make something sound more important than it is. Don't be fooled by lofty or euphemistic language.
2. **Watch out for the use of the passive voice**. Bureaucrats often speak passively: "Action is taken," or "Resources are acquisitioned." The passive voice allows the author to avoid saying who is taking the action or acquiring the resources, often key pieces of information you need or want to know.
3. **Don't be intimidated by the insider language bureaucrats may create for themselves**. Be sure you understand what you are reading or being told. When officials at the Department of Housing and Urban Development in Washington talk about having a "pony to ride," they aren't referring to a childhood pet but to a "senior inside official who would walk a controversial project through various obstacles in the department, much like a pony express rider could deliver the mails in the Old West."[4] At the local level, "public-assistance benefits insurance" (itself a mouthful of

If Congress, the media, or the public had sufficient information and the expertise to interpret it, this would not be as big a problem. However, specialization necessarily concentrates the expertise and information in the hands of the agencies. Congress and the media are generalists. They can tell something has gone wrong when terrorists attack the United States seemingly without warning, but they cannot evaluate the hundreds of less obvious problems that may have led to the failure to warn that only an expert would even recognize.

bureaucratese) is called "Benny" or, even more obscurely, "Jack Benny" by county welfare agents in Buffalo, New York. There is no end to the creative shorthand employed by bureaucrats. If you do not understand what you are told, ask.

4. **Eliminate redundancy—it can make a relatively simple concept sound incredibly complicated**. Bureaucrats are not the only ones guilty of this. An article on writing for lawyers (many of whom go on to work in the government, of course) points out that it is unnecessary to say "green in color," "consensus of opinion," "free gift," or "final outcome."[5] Such wordiness is not only wrong, but it clutters up the language, making it hard to understand what is being said.
5. **Look for nouns that have been turned into verbs**. Bureaucrats are famous for this. *Impact, acquisition,* and *dialogue,* for instance, are used as nouns in everyday language but as verbs in bureaucratese. If a word seems out of place, it probably is. Think creatively when translating government documents.
6. **Never speak or write like this yourself!** Bureaucratese is bad enough coming from bureaucrats and lawyers. There is no substitute for good, clear, crisp writing.

Reading and understanding the bloated jargon of government bureaucratese can be quite a challenge. Those of you with a sweet tooth can practice on Official Government Bureaucracy Cookies.[6]

Official Government Bureaucracy Cookie

Output: six dozen cookie units.

Inputs:

1 cup packed brown sugar
1/2 cup butter, softened
2 eggs
2 1/2 cups all purpose flour
1/2 teaspoon salt
1 cup chopped pecans or walnuts
1/2 cup white sugar
1/2 cup shortening
1 1/2 teaspoons vanilla
1 teaspoon baking soda
12 ounces semisweet chocolate chips

Guidance:

After procurement actions, decontainerize inputs. Perform measurement tasks on a case-by-case basis:

1. In a mixing-type bowl, impact heavily on brown sugar, white sugar, butter, and shortening. Coordinate the interface of eggs and vanilla, avoiding an overrun scenario to the best of your skills and abilities.
2. At this point in time, leverage flour, baking soda, and salt into a bowl and aggregate. Equalize with prior mixture and develop intense and continuous liaison among inputs until well coordinated. Associate with chocolate and nut subsystems and execute stirring options.
3. Within this time frame, take action to prepare the heating environment for throughput by manually setting the oven baking unit to a temperature of 375 degrees F.
4. Drop mixture in an ongoing fashion from a teaspoon implement onto an ungreased cookie sheet at intervals sufficiently apart to permit total and permanent throughputs to the maximum extent particular under operating conditions. Position cookie sheet in a bake situation for 8 to 10 minutes or until cooking action terminates.
5. Initiate coordination of outputs with the cooling rack function. Containerize, wrap in red tape and disseminate to authorized staff personnel on a timely and expeditious basis.

1. Walden Siew, "Ready Readers Respond to Our Gibberish Alert," *Washington Times,* December 1, 1997, 1, Web version.
2. "Have You Hugged Your 1040 Today?" *Washington Times,* April 15, 1991, D2.
3. Laurel Walker, "Functionaries Should Better Utilize Lexicon: Why Do Bureaucrats Insist on Using So Much Unintelligible Jargon?" *Milwaukee Journal Sentinel,* July 5, 1997, 1–2.
4. Bill McAllister and Maralee Schwartz, "'A Pony to Ride': Freshly Minted Bureaucratese," *Washington Post,* May 8, 1990, 1.
5. Tom Goldstein and Jethro K. Lieberman, "Double Negative Use Is Not Unavoidable," *Texas Lawyer,* May 28, 1990, 2.
6. Laura Robin, "Fluent in Bureaucratese? Output These Food Units," *The Ottawa Citizen,* February 18, 1998, 2–3. Reprinted by permission.

Congress has tried to check the temptation for bureaucrats to cover up their mistakes by offering protection to whistle blowers. **Whistle blowers** are employees who expose instances or patterns of error, corruption, or waste in their agencies. They are just good citizens whose consciences will not permit them to protect their agencies and superiors at the expense of what they believe to be the public good. Coleen Rowley, for instance, was asked to testify before the Senate Judiciary Committee because someone had leaked to the media a memo she had written to FBI director Robert

whistle blowers individuals who publicize instances of fraud, corruption, or other wrongdoing in the bureaucracy

Mueller detailing her concerns about the failure of upper-level agency officials to heed her office's worries and to give permission for the search of Moussaoui's computer. Writing that memo was difficult for her because it required her to break with her loyalty to an agency she loved in order to hold it to standards she believed it should meet (see "*Profiles in Citizenship:* Coleen Rowley").

Whistle blowers are not popular with their bosses, as you can well imagine. The Whistleblower Protection Act of 1989 established an independent agency to protect employees from being fired, demoted, or otherwise punished for exposing wrongdoing. Examples of the types of activities whistle blowers have exposed are shown in the box "The Whistle Blower Hall of Fame." Protecting whistle blowers is certainly a step in the direction of counteracting a negative tendency of organizational behavior, but it does very little to offset the pervasive pressure to protect the programs and the agencies from harm, embarrassment, and budget cuts.

PRESIDENTIAL APPOINTEES AND THE CAREER CIVIL SERVICE

Another aspect of internal bureaucratic politics worth noting is the giant gulf between those at the very top of the department or agency who are appointed by the president and those in the lower ranks who are long-term civil service employees. Of the 1.8 million civilian employees in the U.S. civil service, the president or his immediate subordinates appoint about three thousand.

Conflicting Agendas The presidential appointees are sometimes considered "birds of passage" by the career service because of the regularity with which they come and go. Though generally quite experienced in the agency's policy area, appointees have their own careers or the president's agenda as their primary objective rather than the long-established mission of the agency. The rank-and-file civil service employees, in contrast, are wholly committed to their agencies. Minor clashes are frequent, but they can intensify into major rifts when the ideology of a newly elected president varies sharply from the central values of the operating agency. When Ronald Reagan was elected president in 1980, he brought in a distinctly conservative ideology. His appointees to agencies such as the Department of Education and the EPA were charged with reversing the growing federal presence in education and countering the EPA's advocacy of environmental protection over business interests. While President Reagan succeeded in making changes, they were not as extensive as conservatives had hoped, partly because the agencies resisted all the way. President George W. Bush is now engaged in much the same effort to make bureaucratic appointments loyal to his conservative agenda, and many observers expect his efforts to be more successful than Reagan's.[20]

Conflicting Time Frames Political appointees have short-term outlooks; they are viewed by career bureaucrats as "birds of passage."[21] The professionals, in contrast, serve long tenures in their positions; the average upper-level civil servant has worked in his or her agency for over seventeen years, and expects to remain there.[22] Chances are the professionals were there before the current president was elected, and they will be there after he leaves office. Thus, while the political appointees have the advantage of higher positions of authority, the career bureaucrats have time working on their side. Not surprisingly, the bureaucrat's best strategy when the political appointee presses for a new but unpopular policy direction is to stall. This is

Coleen Rowley

Coleen Rowley knew what she wanted to do with her life from the time she was in the fifth grade. Watching TV at home in Iowa, she was enthralled by the exotic adventures of the spies on her favorite show *Man from U.N.C.L.E.*, and determined to join their ranks as soon as she could.

Even then, Rowley must have been the most goal-oriented, determined person you could ever meet. Having chosen her future career, she set about making it happen—at the age of eleven. She wrote to a local newspaper for more information and was chagrined to find out that U.N.C.L.E. was just a fictional organization. But, the newspaper told her, the United States had a similar agency called the FBI, so young Coleen immediately wrote to them instead.

"History has proven over and over that mistakes and problems occur when people fall asleep at the helm . . . ."

The FBI responded with a packet of information that she devoured, stoking her interest in joining up. She checked briefly at one question buried in the material: "Why can't women become FBI agents?" The answer was "an elaborate, contrived creative writing exercise," she says, "about the job being so difficult and demanding . . . requiring agents to be capable of bounding into the room and dominating the situation." But it never said why women couldn't do those things (and, adds Coleen, she's never known a man to bound into a room anyway). "I remember thinking, 'Well, this is dumb. This will have to change.'"

She wasn't deterred for a minute. In preparation for her future career she organized seven or eight girlfriends into the World Organization of Secret Spies Club, where they picked the kind of names they imagined covert agents might have—cool, tough-girl names like Tuesday West and Nicky Slate. Although the WOSS club died out the next year about the time of the first "boy-girl" party in sixth grade, Rowley never gave up her dream of being a government agent.

Right out of college she applied to the FBI (which had reluctantly begun to hire women in 1972) but ended up going on to law school instead. But for her, private law practice held no attractions; it was "government service always." In her last year of law school, she applied to the CIA and the Foreign Service before settling on the FBI.

And so it has been ever since. Coleen Rowley has ended up serving her government in ways she could have never imagined—going from fairly traditional law enforcement officer (she worked for a few years in New York City helping bring organized crime figures to justice) to *Time* Magazine Person of the Year in 2002 (for bringing to light internal FBI failures to connect the dots in their intelligence about potential terrorist activity in the days prior to 9-11), to Democratic candidate for Congress in Minnesota's 2nd district.

Rowley is not heroic or noble about any of this—in fact she is so phlegmatic and matter-of-fact that you almost miss how very unusual she is. The fearless, seize-the-initiative stance to the world that she had at eleven years old has only matured and seasoned with time. She no longer has a romantic vision of what government service entails—while there were some exciting moments in her FBI career, she wasn't always living the action-packed dreams inspired by the *Man from U.N.C.L.E.* But when push came to shove in the days after September 11, she called on a kind of personal courage and integrity that goes far beyond the ability to bound into a room.

On the courage to make tough decisions:

Keep your head on straight and don't let other people's reactions affect you. It's really ingrained in us that popularity is key. It's key to a lot of success in life [as is] not rubbing people the wrong way. However, if you can figure out constructive ways of addressing wrongs—and there are ways—you will be surprised to see that sometimes it works out. You may pay some price, but I still think it's worth it.

On keeping the republic:

You can serve your country in all kinds of ways. Obviously people think of military service, but there is civilian service and actually citizens serve their country by being informed and being discerning. . . . History has proven over and over that mistakes and problems occur when people fall asleep at the helm and they blindly follow orders. It didn't work in Nuremberg, My Lai Massacre, all these situations. People are afraid to serve their country by rocking the boat and doing the right thing. First you have to discern right from wrong, and many times that's hard. And then when you have discerned it, you've got to have the courage to follow through. I think that's patriotism.

Source: Coleen Rowley spoke with Christine Barbour on March 28, 2005.

The Whistle Blower Hall of Fame

WHISTLER	TARGET	CIRCUMSTANCES
Sibel Edmonds 2002, Washington, D.C.	FBI Counterintelligence Translation	Fired after complaining that bureau incompetence had left Middle Eastern–language wiretap espionage tapes untranslated and that one coworker was connected to a group under surveillance.
Coleen Rowley (see Profiles in Citizenship, page 395)	FBI	Complained that FBI headquarters hindered Minneapolis FBI agents' investigation of Zacarias Moussaoui, whose bizarre flight training behavior may have signaled the 9/11 hijackers' training to the FBI.
Jennifer Long 1997, Houston, Texas	IRS	Testified to the Senate that the IRS, without legal basis, encouraged their agents to target individuals who because of either financial or legal difficulty could not defend themselves against such IRS audits.
Frederic Whitehurst 1997, Washington, D.C.	FBI Crime Lab	Criticized the FBI lab for poor lab conditions and work that could have contaminated findings in such important cases as the first World Trade Center bombing in 1993 and the 1995 Oklahoma City bombing.
Lieut. Paula Coughlin 1991, Las Vegas, Nev.	U.S. Navy	Went public about the groping and sexual harassment of naval women by pilots at the navy's annual "Tailhook" convention. This led to the resignation of many naval officers and focused attention on sexual harassment in the military.
Richard Cook 1986, Washington, D.C.	NASA	Publicly claimed that the company that produced the O-rings knew about the problems that caused the explosion of the *Challenger* shuttle and that the investigation into the explosion also ignored this evidence.
John McMahon 1985, Washington, D.C.	CIA	Insisted that the Reagan administration report secret arms sales to Iran that it had previously refused to disclose. Having this evidence proved that there had been an attempt to cover up the arms sales in the Iran-contra scandal.
Dr. Tony Morris 1976, Washington, D.C.	Food and Drug Administration	Claimed that the influenza vaccine might be dangerous; injuries and deaths from the vaccine have since led to changes and safeguards in national flu vaccine shots.
Dr. Daniel Ellsberg 1971, Washington, D.C.	Department of Defense	Released the so-called Pentagon Papers to the *New York Times* that proved the government systematically misled the public about the Vietnam War.
A. Ernest Fitzgerald 1969, Washington, D.C.	Department of Defense	Disclosed a $2 billion cost overrun on the C-5A cargo plane by the military contractor; President Nixon was so angry that he ordered staffers to "get rid of that son of a bitch."

easily achieved by consulting the experts on feasibility, writing reports, drawing up implementation plans, commissioning further study, doing cost-benefit analyses, consulting advisory panels of citizens, and on and on.

Presidential Strategies Given the difficulty that presidents and their appointees can have in dealing with the entrenched bureaucracy, presidents who want to institute an innovative program are better off starting a new agency than trying to get an old one to adapt to new tasks. In the 1960s, when President John Kennedy wanted to start the Peace Corps, a largely volunteer organization that provided assistance to Third World countries by working at the grassroots level with the people themselves, he could have added it to any number of existing departments. He might have argued to have it placed in the State Department (which traditionally works through diplomacy at the highest levels of international politics), or in the CIA (which employs people in other countries in its intelligence-gathering operations), or in the Agency for International Development (which consists of experts at administering foreign aid). The problem was that either these existing agencies were unlikely to accept the idea that nonprofessional volunteers could do anything useful, or they were likely to subvert them to their own purposes, such as spying or managing aid. Thus President Kennedy was easily persuaded to have the Peace Corps set up as an independent agency, a frequent occurrence in the change-resistant world of bureaucratic politics.[23]

"Ask What You Can Do for Your Country"
President Bill Clinton created AmeriCorps in 1994, bringing together volunteers like those shown here to meet the country's needs in education, public safety, health, and the environment. Throughout his presidency, Clinton called on Congress to expand the participation level in AmeriCorps and vowed to veto any bill that would eliminate its funding.

WHO, WHAT, HOW Life inside the bureaucracy is clearly as political as life outside. Many actors attempt to use the rules to advance themselves and the interests of their agency or clientele group, but the bureaucracy has its own culture in which the rules are played out.

Individual bureaucrats want to succeed in their jobs and promote their agencies. Here time, bureaucratic culture, and the rigid nature of bureaucratic rules are in their favor. Congress has helped bureaucrats who wish to challenge an agency to correct a perceived wrong or injustice by passing the Whistleblower Protection Act.

The president has an enormous stake in what the bureaucracy does, and so do his political appointees, who have their own agendas for advancement. But the entrenched civil service can often and easily outlast them, and ultimately prevail.

EXTERNAL BUREAUCRATIC POLITICS

Politics affects relationships not only within bureaucratic agencies but also between those agencies and other institutions. While the bureaucracy is not one of the official branches of government, since it falls technically within the executive branch, it is often called the fourth branch of government because it wields so much power. It can be checked by other agencies, by the executive, by Congress, or even by the public, but it is not wholly under the authority of any of those entities. In this section we examine the political relationships that exist between the bureaucracy and the other main actors in American politics.

INTERAGENCY POLITICS

As we have seen, agencies are fiercely committed to their policy areas, their rules and norms, and their own continued existence. The government consists of a host of agencies, all competing intensely for a limited amount of federal resources and political support. They all want to protect themselves and their programs, and they want to grow, or at least to avoid cuts in personnel and budgets.

To appreciate the agencies' political plight, we need to see their situation *as they see it.* Bureaucrats are a favorite target of the media and elected officials. Their budgets are periodically up for review by congressional committees and the president's budget department. Consequently, agencies are compelled to work for their survival and growth. They have to act positively in an uncertain and changing political environment in order to keep their programs and their jobs.

Constituency Building One way agencies compete against other agencies is by building groups of supporters. Members of Congress are sensitive to voters' wishes, and because of this, support among the general public as well as interest groups is important for agencies. Congress will not want to cut an agency's budget, for instance, if doing so will anger a substantial number of voters.

As a result, agencies try to control some services or products that are crucial to important groups. In most cases, the groups are obvious, as with the clientele groups of, say, the USDA. Department of Agriculture employees work hard for farming interests, not just because they believe in the programs but also because they need strong support from agricultural clienteles to survive. Agencies whose work does not earn them a lot of fans, like the IRS whose mission is tax collection, have few groups to support them. When Congress decided to reform the IRS in 1998, there were no defenders to halt the changes.[24] The survival incentives for bureaucratic agencies do not encourage agencies to work for the broader public interest but rather to cultivate special interests that are likely to be more politically active and powerful.

Even independent regulatory commissions run into this problem. Numerous observers have noted how commissions tend to be *captured* by the very interests they are supposed to regulate. In other words, as the regulatory bureaucrats become more and more immersed in a policy area, they come to share the views of the regulated industries. The larger public's preferences tend to be less well formed and certainly less well expressed because the general public does not hire teams of lawyers, consultants, and lobbyists to represent its interests. An excellent case in point is the USDA's proposed definition of *organic*, which seemed designed to benefit big food industries and agribusiness rather than the public and small farmers. The regulated industries have a tremendous amount at stake. Over time, regulatory agencies' actions may become so favorable to regulated industries that in some cases the industries themselves have fought deregulation, as did the airlines when Congress and the Civil Aeronautics Board deregulated air travel in the 1980s.[25]

Guarding the Turf Agencies want to survive, and one way to stay alive is to offer services that no other agency provides. Departments and agencies are set up to deal with the problems of fairly specific areas. They do not want to overlap with other agencies because duplication of services might indicate that one of them is unnecessary, inviting congressional cuts. Thus, in many instances, agencies reach explicit agreements about dividing up the policy turf to avoid competition and duplication. This does not mean that agencies do not get in one another's way or that their rules and regulations are never contradictory. Rather, to ensure supportive constituencies, they do not want anyone else to do what they do.

This turf jealousy can undermine good public policy. Take, for example, the military: for years, the armed services successfully resisted a unified weapons procurement, command, and control system. Each branch wanted to maintain its traditional independence in weapons development, logistics, and communications technologies, costing the taxpayers millions of dollars. Getting the branches to give up control of their turf was politically difficult, although it was eventually accomplished.

THE BUREAUCRACY AND THE PRESIDENT

As we discussed in Chapter 8, one of the president's several jobs is that of chief administrator. In fact, organizational charts of departments and agencies suggest a clear chain of command with the cabinet secretary at the top reporting directly to the president. But in this case, being "the boss" does not mean that the boss always, or even usually, gets his way. The long history of the relationship between the president and the bureaucracy is largely one of presidential frustration. President Kennedy voiced this exasperation when he said that dealing with the bureaucracy "is like trying to nail jelly to the wall." Presidents have more or less clear policy agendas that they believe they have been elected to accomplish, and with amazing consistency presidents complain that "their own" departments and agencies are uncooperative and unresponsive. The reasons for presidential frustration lie in the fact that, although the president has some authority over the bureaucracy, the bureaucracy's different perspectives and goals often thwart the chief administrator's plans.

Appointment Power Presidents have some substantial powers at their disposal for controlling the bureaucracy. The first is the power of appointment. For the departments, and for quite a few of the independent agencies, presidents appoint the heads and the next layer or two of undersecretaries and deputy secretaries. These cabinet secretaries and agency administrators are responsible for running the departments and agencies. The president's formal power, though quite significant, is often watered down by the political realities of the appointment and policymaking processes.

Cabinet secretaries are supposed to be "the president's men and women," setting directions for the departments and agencies that serve the president's overall policy goals. The reality is that although the president does select numerous political appointees, they also have to be approved by the Senate. The process begins at the start of the president's administration when he is working to gain support for his overall program, so he doesn't want his choices to be too controversial. This desire for early widespread support means presidents tend to play it safe and to nominate individuals with extensive experience in the policy areas they will oversee. Their backgrounds mean that the president's men and women are only partially his. They arrive on the job with some sympathy for the special interests and agencies they are to supervise on the president's behalf as well as loyalty to the president.

President George W. Bush has been unusually aggressive in taking steps to counteract this tendency of bureaucrats to have divided loyalties.[26] Especially in his second term, he has been effective at appointing cabinet secretaries who are wholly committed to his policy agenda. Significant examples include Donald Rumsfeld, who as Bush's secretary of defense was a central figure in the president's decision to go to war in Iraq; Condoleezza Rice, his trusted former national security adviser from his first term, appointed as secretary of state in his second; and Alberto Gonzales, one of Bush's closest legal advisers since his days as governor of Texas, as attorney general. Having long-trusted associates heading the departments can help overcome the tendency of cabinet secretaries and other political appointees to become advocates for the agencies of the bureaucracy rather than the president's policy agenda.

Bush has also engaged in more systematic and far-reaching bureaucratic "house cleaning" to get his views represented. For instance, in the wake of criticisms that the CIA had been too lax prior to September 11, he appointed Porter Goss as the agency's new director. Goss immediately declared, "We support the administration and its policy in our work." Shortly after, twenty CIA officials resigned, many of whom were replaced with Republican operatives loyal to the administration.[27]

The Budget Proposal The president's second major power in dealing with the bureaucracy is his key role in the budget process. About fifteen months before a budget request goes to Congress, the agencies all send their preferred budget requests to the Office of Management and Budget (a White House agency serving the preferences of the president), which can lower, or raise, departmental budget requests. Thus the president's budget, which is sent to Congress, is a good statement of the president's overall program for the national government. It reflects his priorities, new initiatives, and intended cutbacks. His political appointees and the civil servants who testify before Congress are expected to defend the president's budget.

And they do defend the president's budget, at least in their prepared statements. However, civil servants have contacts with interest group leaders, congressional staff, the media, and members of Congress themselves. Regardless of what the president wants, the agencies' real preferences are made known to sympathetic members of the key authorizations and appropriations committees. Thus the president's budget is a beginning bargaining point, but Congress can freely add to or cut back presidential requests, and most of the time it does so. The president's budget powers, while not insignificant, are no match for an agency with strong interest group and congressional support. Presidential influence over the bureaucratic budget is generally more effective in terminating an activity that the president opposes than in implementing a program that the agency opposes.[28]

The Presidential Veto The third major power of the president is the veto. As we argued in Chapter 8, the presidential veto can be an effective weapon for derailing legislation, but it is a rather blunt tool for influencing the bureaucracy. First, many spending bills are bundled together. The president may want a different set of funding priorities for, say, mass transit systems, but such funding is buried in a multibillion-dollar multiagency appropriation. He may not like everything in the bill, but he does not want to risk shutting down the government or starting a public battle. Without a line-item veto, the veto can only be used as a threat in political bargaining. By itself, it does not guarantee the president what he wants.

Government Reorganization In addition to his other efforts, the president can try to reorganize the bureaucracy, combining some agencies, eliminating others, and generally restructuring the way government responsibilities are handled. Such reorganization efforts have become a passion with some presidents, but they are limited in their efforts by the need for congressional approval.[29]

One recent effort at reorganization was the creation of the Department of Homeland Security in response to the terrorist attacks of September 11, 2001. The goal of the new department is to refocus the activities of multiple agencies whose jurisdictions touch on security issues, bringing them under the leadership of a single organization. More typical of reorganization efforts in the sense that it was intended to make government leaner and more efficient was President Clinton's National Performance Review (NPR), which later became the National Partnership for Reinventing Government. The goal of this commission, headed by Vice President Al Gore, was to trim the federal payroll by a quarter of a million jobs and to produce savings of $100 billion by decentralizing, deregulating, and freeing government employees to show more initiative in getting their jobs done. In fact, as of 1998, the federal government had 350,000 fewer civilian positions than it had when Clinton took office and had cut thousands of pages of internal bureaucratic regulations.[30] But these efforts, while effective, have some limitations. Greater discretion available to bureaucrats at lower levels, for instance, opens up the opportunity for arbitrary decisions based on racial, gender, family, or personal preferences. This latitude has the potential to make the public just as angry as the atmosphere of suffocating red tape, delay, and seemingly irrelevant rules. We need to be cautious in our expectations of what NPR or any other reform effort can accomplish.

Funding the Bureaucracy
The fight over power and resources in politics often comes down to money. The winners and losers in the process are reflected in the annual budget. In 2005 President George W. Bush proposed a $2.5 trillion budget that slashed domestic programs from farm aid to housing grants for the poor in an attempt to rein in budget deficits.

Powers of Persuasion The president's final major power over the bureaucracy is an informal one, the prestige of the office itself. The Office of the President impresses just about everyone. If the president is intent on change in an agency, his powers of persuasion and the sheer weight of the office can produce results. Few bureaucrats could stand face to face with the president of the United States and ignore a legal order. But the president's time is limited, his political pressures are many, and he needs to choose his priorities very carefully. The media, for example, will not permit him to spend a good part of every day worrying about a little program that they think is trivial. He will be publicly criticized for wasting time on "minor matters." Thus the president and his top White House staff have to move on to other things. The temptation for a bureaucracy that does not want to cooperate with a presidential initiative is to wait it out, to take the matter under study, to be "able" to accomplish only a minor part of the president's agenda. The agency or department can then begin the process of regaining whatever ground it lost. It, after all, will be there long after the current president is gone.

THE BUREAUCRACY AND CONGRESS

Relationships between the bureaucracy and Congress are not any more clear-cut than those between the agencies and the president, but in the long run individual members of Congress, if not the whole institution itself, have more control over what bureaucracies do than does the executive branch. This is not due to any particular grant of power by the Constitution but rather to informal policymaking relationships that have grown up over time and are now all but institutionalized.

iron triangle the phenomenon of a clientele group, congressional committee, and bureaucratic agency cooperating to make mutually beneficial policy

Iron Triangles Much of the effective power in making policy in Washington is lodged in what political scientists call **iron triangles**. An iron triangle is a tight alliance between congressional committees, interest groups or representatives of regulated industries, and bureaucratic agencies, in which policy comes to be made for the benefit of the shared interests of all three, not for the benefit of the greater public. Politicians are themselves quite aware of the pervasive triangular monopoly of power. Former secretary of Health, Education, and Welfare John Gardner once declared before the Senate Government Operations Committee, "As everyone in this room knows but few people outside of Washington understand, questions of public policy nominally lodged with the Secretary are often decided far beyond the Secretary's reach by a trinity—not exactly a holy trinity—consisting of (1) representatives of an outside lobby, (2) middle-level bureaucrats, and (3) selected members of Congress."[31]

A good example of an iron triangle is public land use policy, as shown in Figure 9.2. The Forest Service (part of the USDA) has long worked closely with the nation's timber interests. Not surprisingly, many of the key congressional leaders on the committees with jurisdiction over policies governing the use of federal lands are from states with larger timber, grazing, and mining interests. For example, Rep. Greg Walden, R-Ore., who became chair of the Subcommittee on Forests and Forest Health in 2003 has eleven national forests in his district. The Forest Service wants Congress to continue to authorize its budget and support its activities in administering the federal policies governing the national forests. When important administrators such as Undersecretary of Agriculture Mark Rey come to their jobs after being a timber lobbyist, it is easy to see why the agency is sympathetic to the industry. The third portion of the triangle, the timber industry interests, are also very involved. The large U.S. lumber companies have worked together to promote the interests of their industry through such interest groups as the American Forest & Paper Association and the American Forest Resources Council. The industry's contributions to congressional candidates ensure that their interests are heard on the key committees.[32] They benefit by getting policies favorable to logging in the national forests.

issue network a complex system of relationships between groups that influence policy, including elected leaders, interest groups, specialists, consultants, and research institutes

The metaphor of the iron triangle has been refined by scholars, who speak instead of **issue networks**.[33] The iron triangle suggests a particular relationship among a fixed interest group and fixed agencies and fixed subcommittees. The network idea suggests that the relationships are more complex than a simple triangle. There are really clusters of interest groups, policy specialists, consultants, and research institutes ("think tanks") that are influential in policy areas. To continue with the timber example, en-

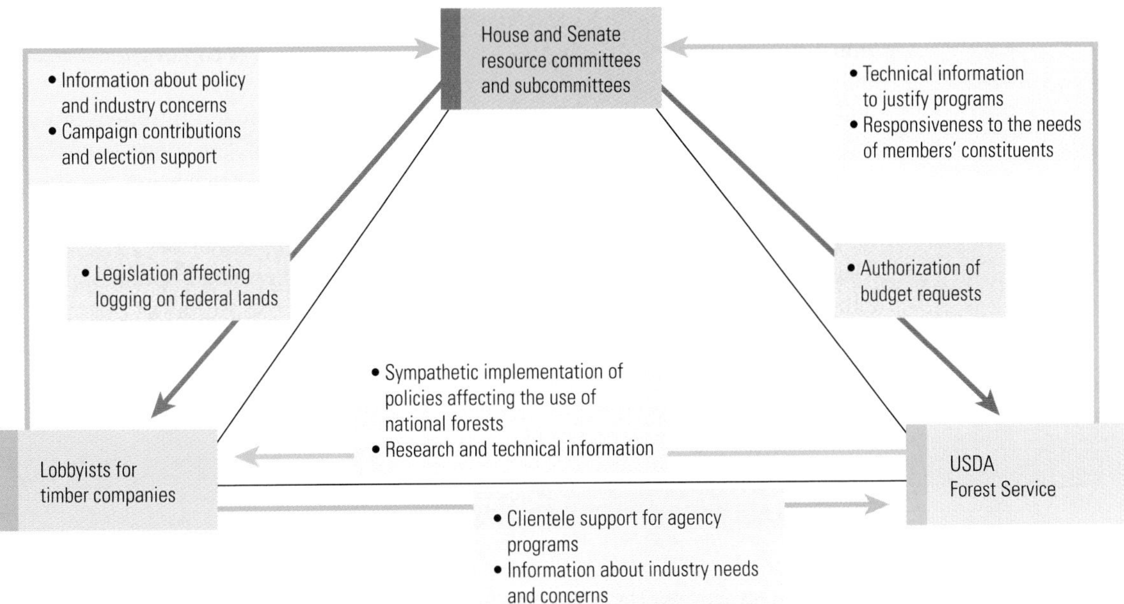

FIGURE 9.2
The Timber–Forest Service Iron Triangle
Iron triangles (involving Congress, the bureaucracy, and special interest groups) exist on nearly every subgovernment level. In this example, you can see how the Forest Service (which depends on the House and Senate for its budget) influences and is influenced by timber company lobbyists, who in turn influence and are influenced by House and Senate committees and subcommittees. This mutual interdependence represents a powerful monopoly of power.

vironmental groups such as the Wilderness Society and Sierra Club work to weaken the dominance of the timber industry iron triangle. They use the courts and sympathetic members of Congress to contest the Bush administration's reinterpretations of existing laws, such as the Endangered Species Act and the National Forest Management Act, that lessen the constraints on logging and other commercial uses of federal lands.[34] Their participation shows that the concept of an iron triangle does not always incorporate all the actors in a particular policy area. That is, while the relationships identified by the iron triangle remain important, the full range of politics is frequently better captured by the concept of issue networks.

Congressional Control of the Bureaucracy Congressional control of the bureaucracy is found more in the impact of congressional committees and subcommittees than in the actions of the institution as a whole. Congress, of course, passes the laws that create the agencies, assigns them their responsibilities, and funds their operations. Furthermore, Congress can, and frequently does, change the laws under which the agencies operate. Thus Congress clearly has the formal power to control the bureaucracy. It also has access to a good deal of information that helps members monitor the bureaucracy. Members learn about agency behavior through required reports, oversight hearings, reports by congressional agencies such as the Office of Technology Assessment and the Government Accountability Office, and from constituents and organized interests. But Congress is itself often divided about what it wants to do and is unable to set clear guidelines for agencies. Only when a congressional consensus exists on what an agency should be doing is congressional control fully effective.

In general, agencies are quite responsive to the congressional committees most directly involved with their authorizations and appropriations. The congressional control that committees and subcommittees exert on the bureaucracy is not the same as the control exercised by Congress as a whole. This is because the subcommittee policy preferences do not always reflect accurately the preferences of the full Congress. Members of Congress gravitate to committees in which they have a special interest—either because of the member's background and expertise or because of the committee's special relevance for the home constituency.[35] Thus, in being responsive to the relevant committees and subcommittees, usually with the support of the organized interests served by the agencies, bureaucrats are clearly less sensitive to preferences of Congress as a whole, the president, and the general public.

THE BUREAUCRACY AND THE COURTS

Agencies can be sued by individuals and businesses for not following the law. If a citizen disagrees with an agency ruling on welfare eligibility, or the adequacy of inspections of poultry processing plants, or even a ruling by the IRS, he or she can take the case to the courts. In some cases the courts have been important. A highly controversial example involves the timber industry we have been discussing. Environmentalists sued the Department of the Interior and the U.S. Forest Service to prevent logging in some of the old-growth forests of the Pacific Northwest. They sought protection for the spotted owl under the terms of the Endangered Species Act. Since 1992, and after a decade-long struggle, logging has been greatly restricted in the area, despite opposition by the economically important timbering interests of the region. However, under the more business-friendly Bush administration, the issue is once again on the agenda and the timber industry has been gaining ground.

More often, though, the courts play only a modest role in controlling the bureaucracy. One of the reasons for this limited role is that, since the Administrative Procedures Act of 1946, the courts have tended to defer to the expertise of the bureaucrats when agency decisions are appealed. That is, unless a clear principle of law is violated, the courts usually support administrative rulings.[36]

Another reason is that Congress explicitly puts the decisions of numerous agencies, such as the Department of Veterans Affairs, beyond the reach of the courts. They do this, of course, when members expect they will agree with the decisions of an agency but are uncertain about what the courts might do. Finally, even without these restrictions, the courts' time is extremely limited. The departments and independent agencies make thousands and thousands of important decisions each year; the courts can act on only those decisions about which someone feels sufficiently aggrieved to take the agency to court. Court proceedings can drag on for years, and meanwhile the agencies go about their business making new decisions. In short, the courts can, in specific instances, decide cases that influence how the bureaucracy operates, but such instances are the exception rather than the rule.

WHO, WHAT, HOW All of Washington and beyond has something at stake in bureaucratic politics. The agencies themselves battle over scarce resources, using the tools of constituency building to keep pressure on Congress

Attorney General Alberto Gonzales and FBI Director Robert Mueller argue their case for Justice Department funding to the Senate Appropriations Subcommittee on Commerce, Justice, and Science. Proceedings such as these allow members of Congress to keep bureaucratic direction in line with their own policy preferences. It is in the agency heads' best interest to be cooperative to the committees' questioning.

to maintain their funding levels, and keeping their functions separate from other agencies even if the result is redundancy and inefficiency.

The president can employ a variety of techniques to control the bureaucracy, but given time constraints and the weight of bureaucratic norms, he is generally unsuccessful at wresting control from the bureaucrats.

Congress has much at stake in its interactions with the bureaucracy. The bottom line in bureaucratic politics is that the bureaucracy is ultimately responsible to Congress. It is difficult to speak of Congress as a whole institution guided by a common interest, but individual members of Congress certainly have identifiable interests. Because policymaking in Congress so often takes place at the committee and subcommittee levels, and because those committees develop iron triangle relationships with interest groups and the bureaucracies that serve them, members of Congress have quite a lot of input into what bureaucracy does.

THE CITIZENS AND THE BUREAUCRACY

The picture that emerges from a look at the politics of the bureaucracy is one of a powerful arm of government, somewhat answerable to the president, more responsible to Congress, but with considerable discretion to do what it wants, often in response to the special interests of clientele groups or regulated industry. If anyone is forgotten in this policymaking arrangement, it is the American public, the average citizens and consumers who are not well organized and who may not even know that they are affected by an issue until the policy is already law. We can look at the relationship between the bureaucracy and the public to determine how the public interest is considered in bureaucratic policymaking.

First, we should figure out what the "public interest" in a democracy really means. Is it the majority preference? If so, then what happens to the minority? Is it some unknown, possibly unpleasant goal that we would favor unanimously if only we could be detached from our particular interests—a sort of national equivalent of eating our spinach because it's good for us? We can imagine some interests that would be disadvantaged by any notion of the public good, no matter how benign. Industries that pollute are disadvantaged by legislation promoting clean air and water; manufacturers of bombs, warplanes, and tanks are disadvantaged by peace. The point here is not to argue that there is no such thing as a "public interest" but to point out that in a democracy it may be difficult to reach consensus on it. To that end, the public interest can probably best be determined by increasing the number of people who have input into deciding what it is. The facts of political life are that the most organized, vocal, and well-financed interests usually get heard by politicians, including bureaucrats. When we speak of the public interest, we usually refer to the interest that would be expressed by the unorganized, less vocal, poorer components of society, if they would only speak. In this final section we look at efforts to bring more people into the bureaucratic policymaking process so as to make policy more responsive to more citizens.

To help increase bureaucratic responsiveness and sensitivity to the public, Congress has made citizen participation a central feature in the policymaking of many agencies. This frequently takes the form of **citizen advisory councils** that, by statute, subject key policy decisions of agencies to outside consideration by members of the public. There are over 1,200 such committees and councils in the executive branch. The people who participate on these councils are not representative of the citizenry; rather, they are typically chosen by the agency and have special credentials or interests relevant to the agencies' work. Thus citizen advisory councils are hardly a reflection of the general population.

citizen advisory council a citizen group that considers the policy decisions of an agency; a way to make the bureaucracy responsive to the general public

Seven different types of citizen advisory councils have been called over the years (1937 through 1996) to make recommendations on the social security system. All have favored the existing programs and recommended expansion. Why? Because members of the councils were carefully selected from among people who already thought highly of social security. What political scientist Martha Derthick concluded about the social security councils is probably true generally: "The outsiders tended to become insiders as they were drawn into the council's deliberations. . . . Typically, advisory council reports paved the way for program executives' own current recommendations."[37]

Given the chance, such groups can generally be counted on to praise existing efforts—unless they are genuinely flawed or the council is investigating some policy disaster—and then to call for a greater commitment and more resources to deal with whatever problems they are considering. This arrangement serves the interests of the bureaucracy, interest groups, Washington consultants, and elected officials. It probably does not achieve the goal of making public policy more responsive to the broader public interest.

Other reform efforts have attempted to make the bureaucracy more accessible to the public. Citizen access is enhanced by the passage of **sunshine laws** that require that meetings of policymakers be open to the public. Thus the Open Meeting Law was passed in 1976 requiring important agency reviews, hearings, and decision-making sessions to be open to the public, along with most congressional committee and subcommittee meetings. However, most national security and personnel meetings and

sunshine laws legislation opening the process of bureaucratic policymaking to the public many criminal investigative meetings are exempted. The right to attend a meeting is of little use unless one can find out that it is being held. The Administrative Procedures Act requires advanced published notices of all hearings, proposed rules, and new regulations so that the public can attend and comment on decisions that might affect them. These announcements appear in the *Federal Register.* In a separate section, the *Federal Register* also contains major presidential documents including executive orders, proclamations, transcripts of speeches and news conferences, and other White House releases.

With all this information about every meeting, every proposed regulation, and more, the *Federal Register* becomes very large—over 70,000 pages a year. Such size makes it quite forbidding to the average citizen; fortunately, a government booklet, "The *Federal Register*: What It Is and How to Use It," is generally available in libraries and on the Internet, and it greatly eases the task of navigating the *Register.* An on-line edition of the *Federal Register* is also available (www.nara.gov/fedreg).

A related point of access is the **Freedom of Information Act** (FOIA), which was passed in 1966 and has been amended several times since. This act provides citizens with the right to copies of most public records held by the agencies. These records include the evidence used in agency decisions, correspondence pertaining to agency business, research data, financial records, and so forth. The agency has to provide the information requested or let the applicant know which provisions of the FOIA allow the agency to withhold the information.

Freedom of Information Act a 1966 law that allows citizens to obtain copies of most public records

Citizens also receive protection under the **Privacy Act of 1974**, which gives them the right to find out what information government agencies have about them. It also sets up procedures so that erroneous information can be corrected and ensures the confidentiality of social security, tax, and related records.

Privacy Act of 1974 a law that gives citizens access to the government's files on them

These reforms may provide little practical access for most citizens. Few of us have the time, the knowledge, or the energy to plow through the *Federal Register* and to attend dull meetings. Similarly, while many citizens no doubt feel they are not getting the full story from government agencies, they also do not have much of an idea of what it is they don't know. Hence, few of us ever use the FOIA.

In fact, few Americans try to gain access to the bureaucracy because of negative images that tell us that it is too big, too remote, too complex, and too devoted to special interests. The public does not think well of the bureaucracy or the government, although it does report favorably on its interaction with individual bureaucrats and agencies.[38] One reason for the public disaffection with the bureaucracy may be that it is so constantly under attack by a frustrated president and by members of Congress who highlight the failings of some aspects of government to divert attention from those that are serving their interests only too well.

Political scientist Kenneth Meier suggests that although countries usually get bureaucracies no worse than they deserve, the United States has managed to get one that is much better than it deserves, given citizen attitudes and attentiveness toward it. He says that in terms of responsiveness and competency, the U.S. federal bureaucracy is "arguably the best in the world."[39] He places the responsibility for maintaining the quality of the system squarely with the citizens and, to some extent, with the media, suggesting that citizens contact bureaucratic agencies about issues of concern, vote with an elected official's bureaucratic appointments in mind, keep realistic expectations of what government can do, and encourage the media in its watchdog role. Keeping the republic may require public participation in bureaucracy as well as in democracy.

WHAT'S AT STAKE REVISITED

Let's go back to the question of what's at stake in the dispute over the USDA's organic food regulation. Remember that regulations are a form of rules, and rules determine who the winners and losers are likely to be. Regulations can serve a variety of interests. They could serve the public interest, simply making it easier for consumers to buy organic food by standardizing what it means to be organic. But regulations can also serve interests besides the public interest. In this case, there were competing business interests as well. Agribusiness and the food preparation industry wanted to use regulations to break into a lucrative market previously closed to them because of the labor-intensive nature of organic farming. For the traditional organic farmers, the proposed regulations spelled disaster.

As far as big business was concerned, this case was like many others. Businesses in the United States are able to freely lobby the government to try to get rules and regulations passed that enhance their positions, and to try to stop those that will hurt them. As we will see in Chapter 13, on interest groups, the larger sums of money that big business can bring to the lobbying effort usually give them an edge in influencing government. If the larger businesses were allowed to compete as organic food producers, the small businesses would lose the only advantage they had, and they would have been forced out of business. In this case, the small businesses were aided by citizen action. This example shows that it is possible to energize a public audience to respond to the bureaucracy. Because those consumers who choose to eat organic foods were a focused, committed, and assertive segment of the population, they were able to follow through with political action.

Thinking Outside the Box

- Are some essential services now provided by the federal bureaucracy better left to the private sector?
- When does bureaucratic decision making become a threat to democracy?
- When is rocking the bureaucratic boat (blowing the whistle) a good thing, and when is it not?

To Sum Up

KEY TERMS
college.cqpress.com/ktr

accountability (p. 377)
bureaucracy (p. 375)
bureaucratese (p. 390)
bureaucratic culture (p. 388)
bureaucratic discretion (p. 386)
citizen advisory council (p. 406)
civil service (p. 376)
clientele groups (p. 381)
department (p. 381)
Federal Register (p. 387)
Freedom of Information Act (p. 407)
government corporation (p. 385)
Hatch Act (p. 376)
independent agency (p. 383)
independent regulatory boards and commissions (p. 383)
iron triangle (p. 402)
issue network (p. 402)
neutral competence (p. 375)
patronage (p. 376)
Pendleton Act (p. 376)
Privacy Act of 1974 (p. 407)
red tape (p. 378)
regulations (p. 383)
spoils system (p. 375)
sunshine laws (p. 406)
whistle blowers (p. 393)

Key terms, chapter summaries, practice quizzes, Internet links, and other study aids are available on the companion Web site at: republic.cqpress.com.

SUMMARY
republic.cqpress.com

- Bureaucracies are everywhere today, in the private as well as the public sphere. They create a special problem for democratic politics because the desire for democratic accountability often conflicts with the desire to take politics out of the bureaucracy. We have moved from the spoils system of the nineteenth century to a civil service merit system with a more professionalized bureaucracy.
- The U.S. bureaucracy has grown from just three cabinet departments at the founding to a gigantic apparatus of fifteen cabinet-level departments and hundreds of independent agencies, regulatory commissions, and government corporations. This growth has been in response to the expansion of the nation, the politics of special economic and social groups, and the emergence of new problems.
- Many observers believe that the bureaucracy should simply administer the laws the political branches have enacted. In reality, the agencies of the bureaucracy make government policy, and they play the roles of judge and jury in enforcing those policies. These activities are in part an unavoidable consequence of the tremendous technical expertise of the agencies because Congress and the president simply cannot perform many technical tasks.
- The culture of bureaucracy refers to how agencies operate—their assumptions, values, and habits. The bureaucratic culture increases employees' belief in the programs they administer, their commitment to the survival and growth of their agencies, and the tendency to rely on rules and procedures rather than goals.
- Agencies work actively for their political survival. They attempt to establish strong support outside the agency, to avoid direct competition with other agencies, and to jealously guard their own policy jurisdictions. Presidential powers are only modestly effective in controlling the bureaucracy. The affected clientele groups working in close cooperation with the agencies and the congressional committees that oversee them form powerful iron triangles.
- Regardless of what the public may think, the U.S. bureaucracy is actually quite responsive and competent when compared with the bureaucracies of other countries. Citizens can increase this responsiveness by taking advantage of opportunities for gaining access to bureaucratic decision making.

PRACTICE QUIZ

republic.cqpress.com

1. A bureaucracy is a(n)

a. hierarchically structured organization with worker specialization, explicit rules, and advancement by merit.

b. hierarchically structured organization in which workers have great discretion.

c. organization of elected officials who work together in a legislative or executive body of government.

d. broad organization in which workers have many specialties.

e. organization in which political supporters are rewarded with public jobs.

2. Which of the following is NOT a reason why the federal bureaucracy has grown over time?

a. To fulfill essential government functions like defense, diplomacy, and currency

b. To respond to the changes in society and the economy with westward expansion, industrialization, and the Great Depression

c. To respond to the increasing power of the state governments

d. To serve particular clientele groups like industries or special interest groups

e. To respond to changing international conditions like the Cold War and the September 11, 2001, terrorist attacks

3. Which of the following is a characteristic of a bureaucratic culture?

a. Departments all have a similar culture but one that is different from independent agencies.

b. Bureaucrats tend to identify with their particular agency and, because of their expertise in the area, they are typically very committed to the particular policies of that agency.

c. Bureaucrats tend to take on the identity of the judicial branch rather than the executive branch.

d. Bureaucrats tend to convey information to the public using very clear and accessible language.

e. Bureaucrats often lack expertise because government workers constantly shift from one agency to another.

4. In what way do bureaucrats challenge the authority of the president, even though he is their "boss"?

a. Bureaucrats tend to have less expertise on most issues than the president.

b. Bureaucrats often campaign against the president.

c. Bureaucrats often successfully appoint political heads of their agencies, like cabinet secretaries, who are only sympathetic to their own policy interests.

d. Bureaucrats control the Office of Management and Budget, so they fund the policies they find important and the president is powerless to influence budgetary politics.

e. Bureaucrats often have better established relationships with interest groups and are committed to particular policies, so they often thwart a president's plans to change policies.

5. What have sunshine laws done for citizens' accessibility to bureaucratic decision making?

a. Reduced accessibility, because citizens have access to such information only after the sun has set on a particular administration

b. Increased accessibility to bureaucratic decisions regarding defense policy but not environmental policy

c. Required public access to most bureaucratic decision-making sessions

d. Helped interest groups, but not individual citizens, hold bureaucratic departments accountable

e. Added an extra level of bureaucracy, making it more difficult for citizens to access records

SUGGESTED RESOURCES

republic.cqpress.com

Books

Brown, Anthony. 1987. *The Politics of Airline Deregulation.* Knoxville: University of Tennessee Press. An insightful look at the events behind the rapid deregulation of one of America's most heavily regulated industries.

Downs, Anthony. 1967. *Inside Bureaucracy.* Boston: Little, Brown. In this ground-breaking work on the bureaucracy, Downs develops a theory of bureaucratic decision making in which bureaucrats are motivated by self-interest.

Goodsell, Charles T. 2003. *The Case for Bureaucracy: A Public Administration Polemic,* 4th ed. Washington, D.C.: CQ Press. The majority of the public believes that the bureaucracy is too complex and entangled in red tape. This former bureaucrat takes the opposite view and discusses the positive aspects of bureaucracies.

Heclo, Hugh. 1977. *A Government of Strangers: Executive Politics in Washington.* Washington, D.C.: Brookings Institution. The best book written to date on the conflict between appointed officials and career bureaucrats.

Kettl, Donald F., and James W. Fesler. 2005. *The Politics of the Administrative Process,* 3d ed. Washington, D.C.: CQ Press. An excellent and easily understandable textbook on public administration that raises several pertinent questions about the bureaucracy.

Khademian, Anne. 2002. *Working With Culture: The Way the Job Gets Done in Public Programs.* Washington, D.C.: CQ Press. A short overview of agency culture in federal, state, and local bureaucracies, as well as a demonstration of how management of an agency's culture can lead to successful reform.

Meier, Kenneth. 2000. *Politics and the Bureaucracy: Policymaking in the Fourth Branch of Government,* 4th ed. Fort Worth, Texas: Harcourt-Brace. An excellent, readable introduction to politics within the bureaucracy and to the struggles of the bureaucracy with the president and Congress.

Pressman, Jeffrey L., and Aaron Wildavsky. 1984. *Implementation,* 3d ed. Berkeley: University of California Press. Once a bill is passed in Washington, it still faces a long and difficult journey to be successfully implemented. Pressman and Wildavsky illustrate just how complex and frustrating this process can be.

Radin, Beryl. 2002. *The Accountable Juggler: The Art of Leadership in a Federal Agency.* Washington, D.C.: CQ Press. This case study of the Department of Health and Human Services illustrates how bureaucratic bosses must balance the disparate demands of their agencies.

Reich, Robert. 1997. *Locked in the Cabinet.* New York: Knopf. Clinton's long-time friend and first secretary of labor gives a firsthand look at the politics behind the Clinton administration.

Riley, Dennis D. 1987. *Controlling the Federal Bureaucracy.* Philadelphia: Temple University Press. In this intriguing analysis of the federal bureaucracy, Riley argues that the bureaucracy is irresponsible because of a complex policymaking process dominated by special interests, congressional committees, and career public employees.

Web Sites

Fed World Information Network. www.fedworld.gov. Sponsored by the Department of Commerce, this site provides a comprehensive central access point for searching, locating, and acquiring government and business information.

FirstGov. www.firstgov.gov. Billed as the U.S. government's official Web portal, this site has links to individual federal agencies, as well as state, local, and tribal governments. There is also a special section "for citizens" to help them navigate services they may need.

National Archives and Records Administration. www.nara.gov. NARA is an independent federal agency charged with the management of federal records and with ensuring citizen access to the documents that record the rights of American citizens, the actions of federal officials, and the national experience. This site provides electronic access to a huge array of historical documents, including speeches and photos, as well as federal agency records.

Movies

***The Insider.* 1999.** Based on a true story about a 1994 *60 Minutes* episode on malpractices in the tobacco industry that was never aired because Westinghouse, the parent company of CBS, objected.

***Silkwood.* 1983.** The true story of a plutonium plant worker who died mysteriously after blowing the whistle on the dangerous conditions in the plant.

The magnificence of the Supreme Court building (right) reflects the deference Americans have had for their high court. However, this does not completely insulate the Court from citizens' protests when the Court is seen as making policy that affects our lives. Demonstrators on both sides of the partisan divide rallied over the U.S. Supreme Court's decision not to allow a recount in Florida following the 2000 presidential election (below)—a decision many Gore supporters felt gave George W. Bush the presidency.

THE AMERICAN LEGAL SYSTEM AND THE COURTS

WHAT'S AT STAKE?

The 2000 presidential election must have set Alexander Hamilton spinning in his grave. In the *Federalist Papers* the American founder confidently wrote that the Supreme Court would be the least dangerous branch of government. Having the power of neither the sword nor the purse, it could do little other than judge, and Hamilton blithely assumed that those judgments would remain legal ones, not matters of raw power politics.

More than two hundred years later, however, without military might or budgetary power, the Supreme Court took into its own hands the very political task of deciding who would be the next president of the United States and, what's more, made that decision right down party lines. On a five-to-four vote (five more conservative justices versus four more liberal ones), the Supreme Court overturned the decision of the Florida Supreme Court to allow a recount of votes in the contested Florida election and awarded electoral victory to Republican George W. Bush.

How did it come to this? The presidential vote in Florida was virtually tied, recounts were required by law in some locations, and voting snafus in several other counties had left untold votes uncounted. Whether those votes should, or even could, be counted or whether voter error and system failure had rendered them invalid was in dispute. Believing that a count of the disputed ballots would give him the few hundred votes he needed for victory, Al Gore wanted the recount; Bush did not. The Florida secretary of state, a Republican appointed by the governor, Bush's brother, ordered the vote counting finished. The Florida Supreme Court, heavily dominated by Democrats, ruled instead that a recount should go forward.

Bush appealed to the Supreme Court, asking it to overturn the Florida Supreme Court's decision and to stay, or suspend, the recount pending its decision. A divided Court issued the stay. Justice John Paul Stevens took the unusual route of writing a dissent from the stay, arguing that it was unwise to "stop the counting of legal votes." Justice Antonin Scalia wrote in response that the recount would pose "irreparable harm" to Bush by "casting a cloud on what he claims to be the legitimacy of his election."

The split between the justices, so apparent in the order for the stay, reappeared in the final decision, where six separate opinions ended up being written. On a five-to-four vote, the majority claimed that if the recount went forward under the Florida Supreme Court's order with different standards for counting the vote in different counties, it would amount to a denial of equal protection of the laws. The amount of work required to bring about a fair recount could not be accomplished before the December 12 deadline. A three-person subset of the majority added that the Florida court's order was illegal in the first place.

The dissenters argued instead that the December 12 deadline was not fixed and that the recount could have taken place up to the meeting of the electoral college on December 18, that there was no equal protection issue, that the Supreme Court should defer to the Florida Supreme Court on issues of state law, and that by involving itself in the political case, the Court risked losing public trust. While the winner of the election was in dispute, wrote Stevens, "the loser is perfectly clear. It is the nation's confidence in the judge as an impartial guardian of the rule of law."

Who was right here? The issue was debated by everyone from angry demonstrators outside the Court to learned commentators in scholarly journals, from families at the dinner table to editorial writers in the nation's press. Was Scalia correct that Bush had really already won and that it was up to the Court to save the legitimacy of his claim to power? Or was Stevens right: that by engaging in politics so blatantly, the Court had done itself irremediable damage in the eyes of the public? What was really at stake for the Court and for America in the five-to-four decision of *Bush v. Gore*? ❋

Imagine a world without laws. You careen down the road in your car, at any speed that takes your fancy. You park where you please and enter a drugstore that sells drugs of all sorts, from Prozac to LSD to vodka and beer. You purchase what you like—no one asks you for proof of your age or for a prescription—and there are no restrictions on what or how much you buy. There are no rules governing the production or usage of currency either, so you hope that the dealer will accept what you have to offer in trade.

Life is looking pretty good as you head back out to the street, only to find that your car is no longer there. Theft is not illegal, and you curse yourself for forgetting to set the car alarm and for not using your wheel lock. There are no police to call, and even if there were, tracking down your car would be virtually impossible since there are no vehicle registration laws to prove you own it in the first place.

Rather than walk—these streets are quite dangerous, after all—you spot a likely car to get you home. You have to wrestle with the occupant, who manages to clout you over the head before you drive away. It isn't much of a prize, covered with dents and nicks from innumerable clashes with other cars jockeying for position at intersections where there are neither stop signs nor lights and the right of the faster prevails. Arriving home to enjoy your beer in peace and to gain a respite from the war zone you call your local community, you find that another family has moved in while you were shopping. Groaning with frustration, you think that surely there must be a better way!

And there is. As often as we might rail against restrictions on our freedom, such as not being able to buy beer if we are under twenty-one, or having to wear a motorcycle helmet, or not being able to speed down an empty highway, laws actually do us much more good than harm. British philosophers Thomas Hobbes and John Locke, whom we discussed in Chapter 1, both imagined a "prepolitical" world without laws. Inhabitants of Hobbes's state of nature found life without laws to be dismal or, as he put it, "solitary, poor, nasty, brutish and short." And although residents of Locke's state of nature merely found the lawless life to be "inconvenient," they had to mount a constant defense of their possessions and their lives. One of the reasons both Hobbes and Locke thought people would be willing to leave the state of nature for civil society, and to give up their freedom to do whatever they wanted, was to gain security, order, and predictability in life. Because we tend to focus on the laws that stop us from doing the things we want to do, or that require us to do things we don't want to do, we often forget the full array of laws that make it possible for us to live together in relative peace and to leave behind the brutishness of Hobbes's state of nature and the inconveniences of Locke's.

Laws occupy a central position in any political society, but especially in a democracy, where the rule is ultimately by law and not the whim of a tyrant. Laws are the "how" in the formulation of politics as "who gets what, and how"—they dictate how our collective lives are to be organized, what rights we can claim, what principles we should live by, and how we can use the system to get what we want. Laws can also be the "what" in the formulation, as citizens and political actors use the existing rules to create new rules that produce even more favorable outcomes.

In this chapter you will learn about the following aspects of law:

- the notion of law and the role that it plays in democratic society in general, and in the American legal system in particular
- the constitutional basis for the American judicial system
- the dual system of state and federal courts in the United States
- the Supreme Court and the politics that surround and support it
- the relationship of citizens to the courts in America

LAW AND THE AMERICAN LEGAL SYSTEM

Thinking about the law can be confusing. On the one hand, laws are the sorts of rules we have been discussing: limits and restrictions that get in our way, or that make life a little easier. But on the other hand, we would like to think that our legal system is founded on rules that represent basic and enduring principles of justice, that create for us a higher level of civilization. Laws are products of the political process, created by political human beings to help them get valuable resources. Those resources may be civil peace and security, or a particular moral order, or power and influence, or even goods or entitlements. Thus, for security, we have laws that eliminate traffic chaos, enforce contracts, and ban violence. For moral order (and for security as well!), we have laws against murder, incest, and rape. And for political advantage, we have laws like those that give large states greater power in the process of electing a president and those that allow electoral districts to be drawn by the majority party. Laws dealing with more concrete resources are those that, for example, give tax breaks to homeowners or subsidize dairy farmers.

Different political systems produce different systems of laws as well. In small communities where everyone shares values and experiences, formal legal structures may be unnecessary since everyone knows what is expected of him or her, and the community can force compliance with those expectations, perhaps by ostracizing nonconformists. In authoritarian systems, like those of the former Soviet Union, or North Korea or China, laws exist primarily to serve the rulers and the state, and they are subject to sudden change at the whim of the rulers. In systems that merge church and state, such as the Holy Roman Empire, pre-Enlightenment Europe, or some Islamic countries today, laws are assumed to be God-given, and violations of the law are analogous to sin against an all-powerful creator. These sorts of legal systems are not much more convenient for the "ruled" than is Locke's state of nature, though they may be more secure.

In nonauthoritarian countries, where citizens are more than mere subjects and can make claims of rights against the government, laws are understood to exist for the purpose of serving the citizens. That is, laws make life more convenient, even if they have to restrict our actions to do so. But laws, and the courts that interpret and apply them, perform a variety of functions in a democratic society, some of which we commonly recognize, and others of which are less obvious.

THE ROLE OF LAW IN DEMOCRATIC SOCIETIES

For the purpose of understanding the role of law in democratic political systems, we can focus on five important functions of laws.[1]

- The first, and most obvious, function follows directly from Hobbes and Locke: laws *provide security* (for people and their property) so that we may go about our daily lives in relative harmony.
- Laws *provide predictability,* allowing us to plan our activities and go about our business without fearing a random judgment that tells us we have broken a law we didn't know existed.
- The fact that laws are known in advance and identify punishable behaviors leads to the third function of laws in a democracy, that of *conflict resolution,* through neutral third parties known as **courts**.
- A fourth function of laws in a democratic society is *to reflect and enforce conformity to society's values*—for instance, that murder is wrong or that parents should not be allowed to abuse their children.
- A fifth function of laws in a democracy is *to distribute the benefits and rewards society has to offer and to allocate the costs of those good things,* whether they are welfare benefits, civil rights protection, or tax breaks.

courts institutions that sit as neutral third parties to resolve conflicts according to the law

THE AMERICAN LEGAL TRADITION

We mentioned earlier that different political systems have different kinds of legal systems—that is, different systems designed to provide order and resolve conflict through the use of laws. Most governments in the industrialized world, including many European countries, South America, Japan, the province of Quebec in Canada, and the state of Louisiana (because of its French heritage), have a legal system founded on a **civil law tradition**, based on a detailed, comprehensive legal code usually generated by the legislature. Some of these codes date back to the days of Napoleon (1804). Such codified systems leave little to the discretion of judges in determining what the law is. Instead, the judge's job is to take an active role in getting at the truth. He or she

civil law tradition a legal system based on a detailed comprehensive legal code, usually created by the legislature investigates the facts, asks questions, and determines what has happened. There are fewer procedural protections for trial participants, like rights of the accused, for instance. The emphasis is more on getting the appropriate outcome than on maintaining the integrity of the procedures, although fair procedures are still important. While this system is well entrenched in much of the world, and has many defenders, the legal system in the United States is different in three crucial ways.

The Common Law Tradition To begin, the U.S. legal system, and that of all fifty states except Louisiana, is based on common law, which developed in Great Britain and the countries that once formed the British Empire. The **common law tradition** relied on royal judges making decisions based on their own judgment and on previous legal decisions, which were applied uniformly, or *commonly,* across the land. The emphasis was on preserving the decisions that had been made before, what is called relying on **precedent**, or *stare decisis* (Latin for "let the decision stand"). Judges in such a system have far more power in determining what the law is than do judges in civil law systems, and their job is to determine and apply the law as an impartial referee, not to take an active role in discovering the truth.

common law tradition a legal system based on the accumulated rulings of judges over time, applied uniformly—judgemade law

precedent a previous decision or ruling that, in common law tradition, is binding on subsequent decisions

The legal system in the United States, however, is not a pure common law system. Legislatures do make laws, and attempts have been made to codify, or organize, them into a coherent body of law. American legislators, however, are less concerned with creating such a coherent body of law than with responding to the various needs and demands of their constituents. As a result, American laws have a somewhat haphazard and hodgepodge character. But the common law nature of the legal system is reinforced by the fact that American judges still use their considerable discretion to decide what the laws mean, and they rely heavily on precedent and the principle of *stare decisis.* Thus, when a judge decides a case, he or she will look at the relevant law but will also consult previous rulings on the issue before making a ruling of his or her own.

The United States as an Adversarial System Related to its origins in the British common law tradition, a second way in which the American legal system differs from many others in the world is that it is an adversarial system. By **adversarial system**, we mean that our trial procedures are "presumed to reveal the truth through the clash of skilled professionals vigorously advocating competing viewpoints."[2] The winner may easily be the side with the most skilled attorneys, not the side that is "right" or "deserving" or that has "justice" on its side. Judges have a primarily passive role; they apply the law, keep the proceedings fair, and make rulings when appropriate, but their role does not include that of active "truth seeker."

adversarial system trial procedures designed to resolve conflict through the clash of opposing sides, moderated by a neutral, passive judge who applies the law

Other legal systems offer an alternative to the adversarial system, and a comparison with these **inquisitorial systems** can help us understand the strengths and weaknesses of our own. The difference can be summed up this way: adversarial systems are designed to determine whether a particular accused person is guilty, whereas inquisitorial systems are intended to discover "who did it."[3] While Britain shares our adversarial tradition, many civil law European countries, like France and Germany, have trial procedures that give a much more active role to the judge as a fact-finder. In these systems, the judge questions witnesses and seeks evidence, and the prosecution (the side bringing the case) and the defense have comparatively minor roles.

inquisitorial systems trial procedures designed to determine the truth through the intervention of an active judge who seeks evidence and questions witnesses

Such a system has obvious advantages. Delegating to a neutral third party the job of establishing what evidence is necessary and obtaining that evidence helps keep the focus of the case away from irrelevant red herrings and on the issues at hand. Such

Pouring Over the Evidence Judges in the U.S. system do not need to spend nearly as much time studying documents and evidence as judges like the French one here. In inquisitorial systems, such as in France, judges are actively involved in determining the facts of a case rather than serving as an impartial referee between the prosecution and defense.

trials are faster, and thus cheaper, than those trials in which both sides engage in lengthy and costly fishing expeditions to find evidence that might support their case, or that might distract the judge and jury from other evidence that damages their case. In an era when American courtrooms have become theatrical stages and trials are often media extravaganzas, the idea of a system that focuses on finding the truth, that reduces the role of lawyers, that limits the expensive process of evidence gathering, and that makes trials cheaper and faster in general sounds very appealing.

There are both cultural and political reasons that we are unlikely to switch to a more inquisitorial system, however. It can be argued, for instance, that the adversarial system makes it easier to maintain that key principle of American law, "innocent until proven guilty." Once a judge in an inquisitorial system has determined that there is enough evidence to try someone, he or she is in fact assuming that the defendant is guilty.[4] In addition, the adversarial system fits with our cultural emphasis on individualism and procedural values, and it gives tremendous power to lawyers, who have a vested interest in maintaining such a system.[5]

The United States as a Litigious System Not only is the U.S. system adversarial, but it is also *litigious*, which is another way of saying that American citizens sue one another, or litigate, a lot. Legal scholars differ on whether Americans are more litigious than citizens of other nations. Certainly there are more lawyers per capita in the United States than elsewhere (three times as many as in England, for instance, and twenty times as many as in Japan), but other countries have legal professionals other than lawyers who handle legal work and the number of actual litigators (lawyers who practice in court) is sometimes limited by professional regulations.

Some evidence, however, suggests that Americans *do* file civil suits—that is, cases seeking compensation from actions that are not defined as crimes, such as medical malpractice or breach of contract—more often than do citizens of many other countries. While the American rate of filing civil suits is roughly the same as the English, Americans file 25 percent more civil cases per capita than do the Germans, and 30 to 40 percent more cases per capita than do the Swedes.[6] Comparisons aside, it remains true that forty-four lawsuits are filed annually for every thousand people in the population.[7]

Why do Americans spend so much time in the courtroom? Scholars argue that the large number of lawsuits in the United States is a measure of our openness and democratic concern for the rights of all citizens,[8] and that litigation is unavoidable in democracies committed to individuals' freedoms and to citizens' rights to defend themselves from harm by others.[9] Americans also sue one another a lot because our society lacks other mechanisms for providing compensation and security from risk. For instance, other kinds of security, like health care or disability, must be privately arranged, often at great cost. Many Americans lack health and disability insurance, basic securities that in many other countries are provided by the government. When disaster strikes, in the form of a car accident or a doctor's error or a faulty product, the only way the individual can cover expenses is to sue. One legal scholar says we use litigation as a method of "compensation and deterrence" for personal injury, medical malpractice, and product liability, that is, as a way of getting paid for the costs we incur when we are injured and as a way of discouraging those who might injure us.[10]

The large number of lawsuits in America, however, has a negative as well as a positive side. Some experts argue that Americans have come to expect "total justice," that everything bad that happens can be blamed on someone, who should compensate them for their harm.[11] In addition, our propensity to litigate means that the courts get tied up with what are often frivolous lawsuits, as when a prisoner filed a million-dollar lawsuit against New York's Mohawk Correctional Facility claiming "'cruel and unusual' punishment for incidents stemming from a guard's refusal to refrigerate the prisoner's ice cream." [12] Such suits are costly not only to the individuals or institutions that must defend themselves, but also to taxpayers, who support the system as a whole, paying the salaries of judges and legal staff. Politicians make occasional attempts to limit lawsuits (for instance the recent Republican effort to cap medical malpractice awards), but these efforts often have political motivations and usually come to nothing.

Flirting with Disaster
The label on this coffee cup, "Caution . . . I'm Hot" is not just a benevolent warning to sip carefully, but also the result of a major lawsuit in which a customer sued a chain for serving dangerously hot coffee. Many criticized the verdict, which favored the plaintiff, saying it represented Americans' propensity to sue, whereas others noted that the plaintiff suffered severe burns that required skin grafts, and the jury award enabled her to pay medical bills. Litigation is one way Americans help to cover the risks of everyday life.

KINDS OF LAW

Laws are not all of the same type, and distinguishing among them can be very difficult. It's not important that we understand all the shades of legal meaning; in fact, it often seems that lawyers speak a language all their own. Nevertheless, most of us will have several encounters with the law in our lifetime, and it's important that we know what laws regulate what sorts of behavior. To get a better understanding of the various players in the court's legal arena, see "*Consider the Source*: A Critical Guide to Going to Court."

Substantive and Procedural Laws We have used the terms *substantive* and *procedural* elsewhere in this book, and though the meanings we use here are related to the earlier ones, these are precise legal terms that describe specific kinds of laws. **Substantive laws** are those whose actual content or "substance" defines what we can and cannot legally do. **Procedural laws**, on the other hand, establish the procedures used to conduct the law—that is, how the law is used, or applied, and enforced. Thus a substantive law spells out what behaviors are restricted, for instance, driving over a certain speed or killing someone. Procedural laws refer to how legal proceedings are to take place: how evidence will be gathered and used, how defendants will be treated, and what juries can be told during a trial. Because our founders were concerned with limiting the power of government to prevent tyranny, our laws are filled with procedural protections for

substantive laws laws whose content, or substance, define what we can or cannot do

procedural laws laws that establish how laws are applied and enforced—how legal proceedings take place

A Critical Guide to Going to Court

A cherished principle of our legal system is that everyone is entitled to his or her day in court. If you get into trouble, you are guaranteed access to the courts to redress your wrongs or to defend yourself against false claims. And the way life is in America these days, you are increasingly likely to end up there. If you don't find yourself in court physically, you will certainly watch legal proceedings on television or read about someone's legal travails in a book, newspaper, or magazine. In a society with a heavy emphasis on due process rights, with a litigious disposition to boot, the legal system plays a prominent role in many of our lives at one time or another.

But the legal system is run by lawyers, and legal jargon, like the bureaucratese we studied in Chapter 9, is not easy to understand. In fact, lawyers have a vested interest in our *not* understanding legalese in the same way that accountants benefit from an incomprehensible tax code. The more we cannot understand the language of the law, the more we need lawyers to tell us what it all means. We cannot condense three years of law school vocabulary here, but we can arm you with some basics to keep in mind if (or when!) you have your day in court.

ENTRY-LEVEL OR APPEALS COURT?

One critical question, when trying to sort out what is happening in a court of law, is whether we are looking at a proceeding in an entry-level or an appeals court. The personnel and the procedures differ, depending on what kind of court it is.

- **Entry-level court.** This is the court in which a person is initially accused of breaking a criminal or a civil law. The questions to be decided in this court are (1) what is the relevant law and (2) is the person accused guilty of a crime or responsible for violating the civil law? The first question is a question of law, the second a question of fact. The entry-level court produces a verdict based on the application of law to a finding of fact.

- **Appeals court.** This is a court that handles cases when one party to an entry-level proceeding feels that a point of law was not properly applied. Cases are appealed only on points of law, not on interpretations of facts. If new facts are shown to be present, a new trial at the entry level can be ordered.

WHO'S WHO?

It's almost impossible to follow the legal action if you aren't familiar with the players. Here we have grouped them under three headings: the people who are themselves involved in the dispute, the people who represent them in court, and the people who make the decisions.

People Involved in the Dispute

The parties to the dispute have different names, depending on whether the case is being heard for the first time or on appeal.

- **Plaintiff.** The person bringing the charges or the grievance if the case is in its original, or entry-level, court. If the case is a criminal case, the plaintiff will always be the government, because crimes are considered to be injuries to the citizens of the state, no matter who is really harmed.
- **Defendant.** The person being accused of a crime or of injuring someone.
- **Petitioner.** The person filing an appeal. The petitioner can be either the plaintiff or the defendant from the lower court trial. It is always the loser of that trial, however.
- **Respondent.** The other party in an appeal. As there may be several layers of appeals, the petitioner in one case may later find himself or herself the respondent in a further appeal.

When you see a case name written out it will look like this: *Name of Plaintiff v. Name of Defendant,* or *Name of Petitioner v. Name of Respondent.* The names of the cases may switch back and forth as the case moves its way through various appeals. The historic case known as *Gideon v. Wainwright,* for example, began as a simple criminal case of Wainwright, the prosecutor for Florida, as the plaintiff, against Clarence Gideon, the defendant. When Gideon decided to file his appeal with the Supreme Court, he became the petitioner against Wainwright, now the respondent.

People Who Represent the Parties in Court

- **Lawyers or attorneys.** Professionals who represent the two sides in a dispute. Unlike in other countries, in the United States the same lawyer who works on the case behind the scenes will also represent the client in court.

- **Prosecuting attorney.** The lawyer for the plaintiff. In criminal cases the prosecutor is always a representative of the government—a district or prosecuting attorney at the state level, and a U.S. attorney at the federal level.
- On appeal the government's case is argued by the **state attorney general** (at the state level), the **U.S. attorney** (at the federal level), and the **solicitor general** (if the case goes all the way to the Supreme Court).
- **Defense attorney (also called a defense counsel).** The representative of the defendant. In a criminal case, the Constitution guarantees that a poor defendant be provided with an attorney free of charge, so it can happen that both the prosecutor and the defense counsel are being paid by the same government to represent the two opposing interests in the case.

People Who Make the Decisions

The final group of players are the decision makers. Two kinds of decisions have to be made in a court of law: decisions about facts (what actually happened) and decisions about law. Generally the facts are decided on by citizens, and the law is applied by legal professionals.

- **Juries.** Groups of citizens who decide on the facts in a case. Juries are intended to be a check by citizens on the power of the courts. The Constitution guarantees us a jury of our peers, or equals, although we can waive our right to a jury trial, in which case the judge will make the findings of fact. Lawyers representing the two sides choose from a pool that is representative of the general population, according to a detailed set of rules. In recent years, lawyers have become expert at picking juries that they believe will give maximum advantage to their clients. Questions of fact arise only in entry-level cases, so there are no juries in appeals courts. Citizens can be asked to sit on **grand juries** (to decide if there is enough factual evidence to warrant bringing a case to trial) or **trial juries** (to decide whether or not someone is guilty as charged).
- **Jurors.** Participants on a jury, either trial or grand, chosen from a pool of citizens on jury duty at the time.
- **Judges.** Deciders of questions of law. In entry-level courts, judges make rulings on points of law and instruct the jury on the law, so that they know how to use the facts they decide on. If there is no jury, the judge finds facts and applies the law as well. In appeals courts, panels of judges rule on legal questions that are alleged to have arisen from an earlier trial (for example, if a defendant was not given the opportunity to speak to a lawyer, was that a violation of due process?).
- **Justices.** Panels of justices in appeals courts in a state court or the federal Supreme Court. There are no witnesses, and no evidence is presented that would raise any factual questions. If new evidence is thought to be present, the justices order a new trial at the entry level.

QUESTIONS TO ASK IF YOU SHOULD FIND YOURSELF HAVING A DAY IN COURT

1. **Does the dispute I am involved in need to be solved in a court of law?** If you have been arrested, you probably have little choice about whether you go to court, but if you are involved in a civil dispute, there are ways to solve conflicts outside the courtroom. Explore options involving mediation and arbitration if you want to avoid a lengthy and possibly acrimonious legal battle.
2. **Do I need a lawyer?** Americans are increasingly getting into the do-it-yourself legal business, but before you take on such a project, carefully evaluate whether hiring a lawyer will serve your interests. Remember that the legal system has been designed by lawyers, and they are trained to know their way around it. Will you be at a disadvantage in resolving your dispute if you don't have a lawyer? It's one thing to draw up your own will but quite another to undertake your own criminal defense. Disputes such as divorce, child custody, and small claims fall somewhere in between, but as a general rule, if the person whose claims you are contesting has a lawyer, you might want one too.
3. **Is the case worth the potential cost in money, time, and emotional energy?** Again, if you are in criminal court, you may not have any choice over whether you go to court, but often people enter into civil disputes without a clear idea of the costs involved, seeing them sometimes as a "get-rich-quick" option. Will your lawyer work on a contingency basis

(taking a percentage, usually 30 percent, of the settlement he or she wins for you), or will you have to pay an hourly rate? Billable hours can add up quite quickly. Is there a higher principle involved, or is it all about money? Will it be worth it to bring or contest a losing case, only to be left with substantial attorney's fees? You might be willing to sacrifice more for an important cause than for a monetary settlement. Cases can drag on for years, through multiple levels of appeals, and can become a major drain on one's energy and resources.

4. **Should I serve on a jury if called?** Serving on a jury is a good opportunity to see how the system works from the inside, as well as to make a contribution to the nation. Finding a reason to be excused from jury duty sometimes seems like an attractive option when we are besieged by the demands of daily life, but there are real costs to avoiding this civic duty. Since all citizens are entitled to a jury trial, having an active pool of willing jurors is important to the civic health of the nation.

procedural due process procedural laws that protect the rights of individuals who must deal with the legal system

those who must deal with the legal system—what we call guarantees of **procedural due process**. Given their different purposes, these two types of laws sometimes clash. For instance, someone guilty of breaking a substantive law might be spared punishment if procedural laws meant to protect him or her were violated because the police failed to read the accused his or her rights or searched the accused's home without a warrant. Such situations are complicated by the fact that not all judges interpret procedural guarantees in the same way.

criminal laws laws prohibiting behavior the government has determined to be harmful to society; violation of a criminal law is called a crime

Criminal and Civil Laws **Criminal laws** prohibit specific behaviors that the government (state, federal, or both) has determined are not conducive to the public peace, behaviors as heinous as murder or as relatively innocuous as stealing an apple. Since these laws refer to crimes against the state, it is the government that prosecutes these cases rather than the family of the murder victim or the owner of the apple. The penalty, if the person is found guilty, will be some form of payment to the public, for example, community service, jail time, or even death, depending on the severity of the crime and the provisions of the law. In fact, we speak of criminals having to pay their "debt to society," because in a real sense, their actions are seen as a harm to society.

civil laws laws regulating interactions between individuals; violation of a civil law is called a tort

Civil laws, on the other hand, regulate interactions between individuals. If one person sues another for damaging his or her property, or causing physical harm, or failing to fulfill the terms of a contract, it is not a crime against the state that is alleged but rather an injury to a specific individual. A violation of civil law is called a *tort* instead of a crime. The government's purpose here is not to prosecute a harm to society but to provide individuals with a forum in which they can peacefully resolve their differences. Apart from peaceful conflict resolution, government has no stake in the outcome.

Sometimes a person will face both criminal charges and a civil lawsuit for the same action. An example might be a person who drives while drunk and causes an accident that seriously injures a person in another car. The drunk driver would face criminal charges for breaking laws against driving while intoxicated and might also be sued by the injured party to receive compensation for medical expenses, missed income, and pain and suffering. Such damages are called *compensatory damages*. The injured person might also sue the bar that served the alcohol to the drunk driver in the first place; this is because people suing for compensation often target the involved party with the deepest pockets, that is, the one with the best ability to pay. A civil suit may also include a fine intended to punish the individual for causing the injury. These damages are called *punitive damages*.

Probably the most famous instance of a person facing both criminal and civil suits for the same action is O. J. Simpson. Found not guilty in a criminal court for the murder of his ex-wife and a friend of hers, he was found responsible for their wrongful deaths in a civil court and ordered to pay damages to the victims' families.

A number of reasons accounted for the different outcomes of these two cases, but the main one was that while the substantive laws in each case were similar (killing someone violates the law), the procedural laws governing the trials were different, providing, among other things, for different "burdens of proof." In the criminal trial the jury was told that it had to find Simpson guilty "beyond a reasonable doubt." In the civil trial his responsibility had to be shown only by a "preponderance of the evidence." In other words, jurors had to be a lot more certain of their verdict in the criminal case than in the civil case. In addition, the jurors in the criminal case would have had to unanimously find Simpson guilty, but in the civil case, only seven of the twelve jurors had to find Simpson responsible for the wrongful deaths. This difference reflects our system's deep-seated belief that citizens need more stringent protections against their government than against each other. Notice how different rules can yield very different results, even when applied to the same situation.

Constitutional Law One kind of law we have discussed often in this book so far is **constitutional law**. This refers, of course, to the laws that are in the Constitution, that establish the basic powers of and limitations on governmental institutions and their interrelationships, and that guarantee the basic rights of citizens. In addition, constitutional law refers to the many decisions that have been made by lower court judges in America, as well as by the justices on the Supreme Court, in their attempts to decide precisely what the Constitution means and how it should be interpreted. Because of our common law tradition, these decisions, once made, become part of the vast foundation of American constitutional law.

constitutional law law stated in the Constitution or in the body of judicial decisions about the meaning of the Constitution handed down in the courts

All of the cases discussed in Chapters 5 and 6 on civil liberties and equal rights are part of the constitutional law of this country. As we have seen, constitutional law evolves over time as circumstances change, justices are replaced, cases are overturned, and precedent is reversed.

Statutory Law, Administrative Law, and Executive Orders Most laws in the country are made by Congress and the state legislatures, by the bureaucracy under the authority of Congress, and even by the president. **Statutory laws** are those laws that legislatures make at either the state or the national level. Statutes reflect the will of the bodies elected to represent the people, and they can address virtually any behavior. Statutes tell us to wear seatbelts, pay taxes, and stay home from work on Memorial Day. According to the principle of judicial review, judges may declare statutes unconstitutional if they conflict with the basic principles of government or the rights of citizens established in the Constitution.

statutory laws laws passed by a state or the federal legislature

Because legislatures cannot be experts on all matters, they frequently delegate some of their lawmaking power to bureaucratic agencies and departments. When these bureaucratic actors exercise their lawmaking power on behalf of Congress, they are making **administrative law**. Administrative laws include the thousands of regulations that agencies make concerning how much coloring and other additives can be in the food we buy, how airports will monitor air traffic, what kind of material can be used to make pajamas for children, and what deductions can be taken legally when figuring your income tax. These laws, although made under the authority of elected representatives,

administrative law law established by the bureaucracy, on behalf of Congress are not, in fact, made by people who are directly accountable to the citizens of America. The implications of the undemocratic nature of bureaucratic decision making were discussed in Chapter 9.

executive orders clarifications of congressional policy issued by the president and having the full force of law

Finally, some laws, called **executive orders**, are made by the president himself. These, as we explained in Chapter 8, are laws made without any participation by Congress, and need be binding only during the issuing president's administration. Famous executive orders include President Harry Truman's desegregation of the armed forces in 1948 and President Lyndon Johnson's initiation of affirmative action programs for companies doing business with the federal government in 1967.

WHO, WHAT, HOW Citizens have a broad stake in a lawful society. They want security, predictability, peaceful conflict resolution, conformity to social norms, and a nondisruptive distribution of social costs and benefits, and they use laws to try to achieve these things. They use the full array of laws and legal traditions available to them in the American legal system to accomplish their goals. The results of the legal process are shaped by the distinctive nature of the American system—its common law roots and its adversarial and litigious nature.

CONSTITUTIONAL PROVISIONS AND THE DEVELOPMENT OF JUDICIAL REVIEW

Americans may owe a lot of our philosophy of law (called *jurisprudence*) to the British, but the court system we set up to administer that law is uniquely our own. Like every other part of the Constitution, the nature of the judiciary was the subject of hot debate during the nation's founding. Large states were comfortable with a strong court system as part of the strong national government they advocated; small states, cringing at the prospect of national dominance, preferred a weak judiciary. Choosing a typically astute way out of their quandary, the authors of the Constitution postponed it, leaving it to Congress to settle later.

Article III, Section 1, of the Constitution says simply this about the establishment of the court system: "The judicial power of the United States, shall be vested in one supreme court, and in such inferior courts as Congress may from time to time ordain and establish." It goes on to say that judges will hold their jobs as long as they demonstrate "good behavior"—that is, they are appointed for life—and that they will be paid regularly and cannot have their pay reduced while they are in office. The Constitution does not spell out the powers of the Supreme Court. It only specifies which cases must come directly to the Supreme Court (cases affecting ambassadors, public ministers and consuls, and states); all other cases come to it only on appeal. It was left to Congress to say how. By dropping the issue of court structure and power into the lap of a future Congress, the writers of the Constitution neatly sidestepped the brewing controversy. It would require an act of Congress, the Federal Judiciary Act of 1789, to begin to fill in the gaps on how the court system would be organized. We turn to that act and its provisions shortly. First, we look at the controversy surrounding the birth of the one court that Article III does establish, the U.S. Supreme Court.

THE LEAST DANGEROUS BRANCH

The idea of an independent judiciary headed by a supreme court was a new one to the founders. No other country had one, not even England. Britain's highest court was also its Parliament, or legislature. To those who put their faith in the ideas of separation of powers and checks and balances, an independent judiciary was an ideal way to check the power of the president and the Congress. But to others it represented an unknown threat. To put those fears to rest, Alexander Hamilton penned *Federalist* No. 78, arguing that the judiciary was the least dangerous branch of government. It lacked the teeth of the other branches; it had neither the power of the sword (the executive power) nor the power of the purse (the legislative budget power), and consequently it could exercise "neither force nor will, but merely judgment."[13]

For a while, Hamilton was right. The Court was thought to be such a minor player in the new government that several of George Washington's original appointees to that institution turned him down.[14] Many of those who served on the Court for a time resigned prematurely to take other positions thought to be more prestigious. Further indicating the Court's lack of esteem was the fact that when the capital was moved to Washington, D.C., city planners forgot to design a location for it. As a result, the highest court in the land had to meet in the basement office of the clerk of the U.S. Senate.[15]

JOHN MARSHALL AND JUDICIAL REVIEW

The low prestige of the Supreme Court was not to last for long, however, and its elevation was due almost single-handedly to the work of one man. John Marshall was the third chief justice of the United States and an enthusiastic Federalist. During his tenure in office, he found several ways to strengthen the Court's power, the most important of which was having the Court create the power of **judicial review**. This is the power that allows the Court to review acts of the other branches of government and to invalidate them if they are found to run counter to the principles in the Constitution. For a man who attended law school for only six months (as was the custom in his day, he learned the law by serving as an apprentice), his legacy to American law is truly phenomenal.

judicial review the power of the courts to determine the constitutionality of laws

***Federalist* No. 78** Marshall was not the first American to raise the prospect of judicial review. While the Constitution was silent on the issue of the Court's power and Hamilton had been quick to reassure the public that he envisioned only a weak judiciary, he dropped a hint in *Federalist* No. 78 that he would approve of a much stronger role for the Court. Answering critics who declared that judicial review would give too much power to a group of unelected men to overrule the will of the majority as expressed through the legislature, Hamilton said that in fact the reverse was true. Since the Constitution was the clearest expression of the public will in America, by allowing that document to check the legislature, judicial review would actually place the true will of the people over momentary passions and interests that were reflected in Congress.

Marbury v. Madison The Constitution does not give the power of judicial review to the Court, but it doesn't forbid the Court to have that power either. Chief Justice John Marshall shrewdly engineered the adoption of the power of judicial review in ***Marbury v. Madison*** in 1803. This case involved a series of judicial appointments to federal courts made by President John Adams in the final hours of his administra-

Marbury v. Madison the landmark case that established the U.S. Supreme Court's power of judicial review

Freedom Fighter
Thurgood Marshall (center) secured his place in legal history when, as special counsel for the National Association for the Advancement of Colored People (NAACP), he convinced the Supreme Court to overturn segregation with the landmark 1954 ruling *Brown v. Board of Education*. In 1967, Marshall himself became a Supreme Court justice, appointed by President Lyndon B. Johnson.

tion. Most of those appointments were executed by Adams's secretary of state, but the letter appointing William Marbury to be justice of the peace for the District of Columbia was overlooked and not delivered. (In an interesting twist, John Marshall, who was finishing up his job as Adams's secretary of state, had just been sworn in as chief justice of the United States; he would later hear the case that developed over his own incomplete appointment of Marbury.) These "midnight" (last-minute) appointments irritated the new president, Thomas Jefferson, who wanted to appoint his own candidates, so he had his secretary of state, James Madison, throw out the letter, along with several other appointment letters. According to the Judiciary Act of 1789, it was up to the Court to decide whether Marbury got his appointment, which put Marshall in a fix. If he exercised his power under the act and Jefferson ignored him, the Court's already low prestige would be severely damaged. If he failed to order the appointment, the Court would still look weak.

From a legal point of view, Marshall's solution was breathtaking. Instead of ruling on the question of Marbury's appointment, which was a no-win situation for him, he instead focused on the part of the act that gave the Court authority to make the decision. This he found to go beyond what the Constitution had intended; that is, according to the Constitution, Congress didn't have the power to give the Court that authority. So Marshall ruled that although he thought Marbury should get the appointment (he had originally made it, after all), he could not enforce it because the relevant part of the Judiciary Act of 1789 was unconstitutional and therefore void. He justified the Court's power to decide what the Constitution meant by saying "it is emphatically the province of the judicial department to say what the law is."[16]

The Impact of Judicial Review With the *Marbury* ruling, Marshall chose to lose a small battle in order to win a very large war. By creating the power of judicial review, he vastly expanded the potential influence of the Court and set it on the road to being the powerful institution it is today. While Congress and the president still have some checks on the judiciary through the powers to appoint, to change the number of members and jurisdiction of the Court, to impeach justices, and to amend the Constitution, the Court now has the ultimate check over the other two branches: the power to declare what they do to be null and void. What is especially striking about the gain of this enormous power is that the Court gave it to itself. What would have been the public reaction if Congress had voted to make itself the final judge of what is constitutional?

Aware of just how substantially their power was increased by the addition of judicial review, justices have tended to use it sparingly. The power was not used from its inception in 1803 until 1857, when the Court struck down the Missouri Compromise.[17] Since then it has been used only 158 times to strike down acts of Congress, although much more frequently (1,261 times) to invalidate acts of the state legislatures.[18]

WHO, WHAT, HOW The Constitution is largely silent about the courts, leaving the task of designing the details of the judicial system to Congress. It was not the Constitution or Congress but John Marshall, the third chief justice, who used the common law tradition of American law to give the Court the extraconstitutional power of judicial review. Once Marshall had claimed the power and used it in a ruling (*Marbury v. Madison*), it became part of the fundamental judge-made constitutional law of this country.

THE STRUCTURE AND ORGANIZATION OF THE DUAL COURT SYSTEM

In response to the Constitution's open invitation to design a federal court system, Congress immediately got busy putting together the Federal Judiciary Act of 1789. The system created by this act was too simple to handle the complex legal needs and the growing number of cases in the new nation, however, and it was gradually crafted by Congress into the very complex network of federal courts we have today. But, understanding just the federal court system is not enough. Our federal system of government requires that we have two separate court systems, state and national, and, in fact, most of the legal actions in this country take place at the state level. Because of the diversity that exists among the state courts, some people argue that in truth we have fifty-one court systems. Since we cannot look into each of the fifty state court systems, we will take the "two-system" perspective and consider the state court system as a whole (see Figure 10.1).

UNDERSTANDING JURISDICTION

A key concept in understanding our dual court system is the issue of **jurisdiction**, the courts' authority to hear particular cases. Not all courts can hear all cases. In fact, the rules regulating which courts have jurisdiction over which cases are very specific. Most cases in the United States fall under the jurisdiction of state courts. As we will see, cases go to federal courts only if they qualify by virtue of the kind of question raised or the parties involved.

jurisdiction a court's authority to hear certain cases

The choice of a court, though dictated in large part by constitutional rule and statutory law (both state and federal), still leaves room for political maneuvering. Four basic characteristics of a case help determine which court has jurisdiction over it: the involvement of the federal government (through treaties or federal statutes) or the Constitution, the parties to the case (if, for instance, states are involved), where the case arose, and how serious an offense it involves.[19]

Once a case is in either the state court system or the federal court system, it almost always remains within that system. It is extremely rare for a case to start out in one system and end up in the other. Just about the only time this occurs is when a case in the highest state court is appealed to the U.S. Supreme Court, and this can happen only for cases involving a question of federal law.

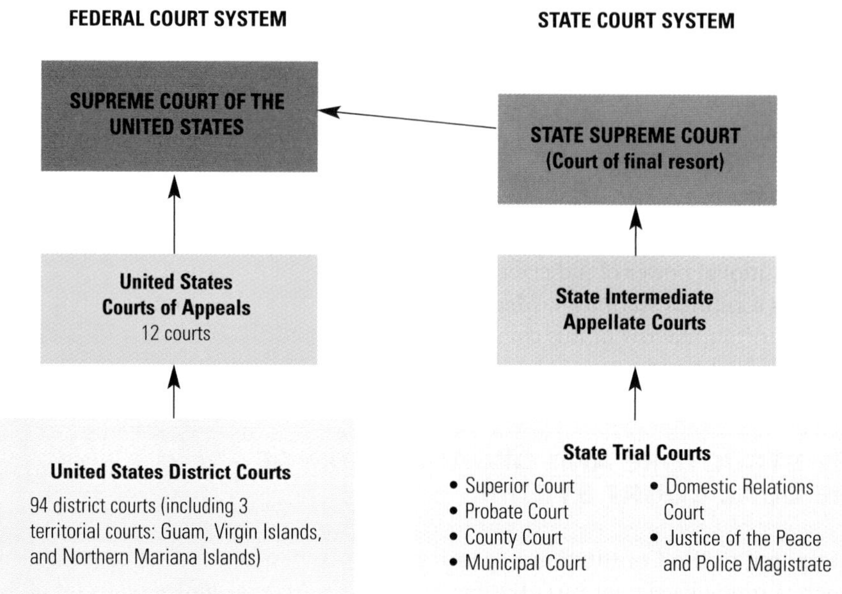

FIGURE 10.1
The Dual Court System

original jurisdiction the authority of a court to hear a case first

appellate jurisdiction the authority of a court to review decisions made by lower courts

appeal a rehearing of a case because the losing party in the original trial argues that a point of law was not applied properly

Cases come to state and federal courts under either their original jurisdiction or their appellate jurisdiction. A court's **original jurisdiction** refers to those cases that can come straight to it without being heard by any other court first. The rules and factors just discussed refer to original jurisdiction. **Appellate jurisdiction** refers to those cases that a court can hear on **appeal**—that is, when one of the parties to a case believes that some point of law was not applied properly at a lower court and asks a higher court to review it. Almost all the cases heard by the U.S. Supreme Court come to it on appeal. The Court's original jurisdiction is limited to cases that concern ambassadors and public ministers and to cases in which a state is a party—usually amounting to no more than two or three cases a year.

All parties in U.S. lawsuits are entitled to an appeal, although more than 90 percent of losers in federal cases accept their verdicts without appeal. After the first appeal, further appeals are at the discretion of the higher court; that is, the court can choose to hear them or not. The highest court of appeals in the United States is the U.S. Supreme Court, but its appellate jurisdiction is also discretionary. When the Court refuses to hear a case, it may mean, among other things, that the Court regards the case as frivolous or that it agrees with the lower court's judgment. Just because the Court agrees to hear a case, though, does not mean that it is going to overturn the lower court's ruling, although it does so about 70 percent of the time. Sometimes the Court hears a case in order to rule that it agrees with the lower court and to set a precedent that other courts will have to follow.

STATE COURTS

Although each state has its own constitution, and therefore its own set of rules and procedures for structuring and organizing its court system, the state court systems are remarkably similar in appearance and function (see Figure 10.1). State courts generally fall into three tiers, or layers. The lowest, or first, layer is the trial court, including major trial courts and courts where less serious offenses are heard. The names of these courts vary—for example, they may be called county and municipal courts at the minor level and superior or district courts at the major level. Here cases are heard for the first time, under original jurisdiction, and most of them end here as well.

Occasionally, however, a case is appealed to a higher decision-making body. In about three-fourths of the states, intermediate courts of appeals hear cases appealed from the lower trial courts. In terms of geographic organization, subject matter jurisdiction, and number of judges, courts of appeals vary greatly from state to state. The one constant is that these courts all hear appeals directly from the major trial courts and, on very rare occasions, directly from the minor courts as well.

Each of the fifty states has a state supreme court, although again the names vary. Since they are appeals courts, no questions of fact can arise, and there are no juries. Rather, a panel of five to nine *justices*, as supreme court judges are called, meet to discuss the case, make a decision, and issue an opinion. As the name suggests, a state's supreme court is the court of last resort, or the final court of appeals, in the state. All decisions rendered by these courts are final unless a case involves a federal question and can be heard on further appeal in the federal court system.

Judges in state courts are chosen through a variety of procedures specified in the individual state constitutions. The procedures range from appointment by the governor or election by the state legislature to the more democratic method of election by the state population as a whole. Thirty-nine states hold elections for at least some of their judges. Judicial elections are controversial, however. Supporters argue that they give people a voice, while holding judges accountable and keeping them in line with public opinion. Critics, however, say judicial elections can create a conflict of interest. For example, in 2002 the U.S. Chamber of Commerce and the Business Roundtable, two organizations that regularly appear in court, spent $25 million to influence judicial elections across the country.[20] Others argue that few people are able to cast educated votes in judicial elections and that the threat of defeat may influence judges' rulings.

FEDERAL COURTS

The federal system is also three-tiered. There is an entry-level tier, called the district courts, an appellate level, and the Supreme Court at the very top (see Figure 10.1). In this section, we discuss the lower two tiers and how the judges for those courts are chosen. Given the importance of the Supreme Court in the American political system, we discuss it separately in the following section.

District Courts The lowest level of the federal judiciary hierarchy consists of ninety-four U.S. federal district courts. These courts are distributed so that each state has at least one and the largest states each have four. The district courts have original jurisdiction over all cases involving any question of a federal nature or any issue that involves the Constitution, Congress, or any other aspect of the federal government. Such issues are wide-ranging but might include, for example, criminal charges resulting from a violation of the federal anti-carjacking statute or a lawsuit against the Environmental Protection Agency.

The district courts hear both criminal and civil law cases. In trials at the district level, evidence is presented, and witnesses are called to testify and are questioned and cross-examined by the attorneys representing both sides. In criminal cases the government is always represented by a U.S. attorney. U.S. attorneys, one per district, are appointed by the president, with the consent of the Senate. In district courts, juries are responsible for returning the final verdict.

U.S. Courts of Appeals Any case appealed beyond the district court level is slated to appear in one of the U.S. courts of appeals. These courts are arranged in twelve circuits, essentially large superdistricts that encompass several of the district court territories, except for the twelfth, which covers just Washington, D.C. (see Figure 10.2). This twelfth circuit court hears all appeals involving government agencies, and so its caseload is quite large even though its territory is small. (A thirteenth Federal Circuit court hears cases on such specialized issues as patents and copyrights.) Cases are heard in the circuit that includes the district court where the case was originally heard. Therefore, a case that was initially tried in Miami, in the southern district in Florida, would be appealed to the court of appeals in the Eleventh Circuit, located in Atlanta, Georgia.

The jurisdiction of the courts of appeals, as their name suggests, is entirely appellate in nature. The sole function of these courts is to hear appeals from the lower federal district courts and to review the legal reasoning behind the decisions reached there. As a result, the proceedings involved in the appeals process differ markedly from those at the district court level. No evidence is presented, no new witnesses called, and no jury impaneled. Instead, the lawyers for both sides present written briefs summarizing their arguments and make oral arguments as well. The legal reasoning used to reach the decision in the district court is scrutinized, but the facts of the case are assumed to be the truth and are not debated.

FIGURE 10.2
The Federal Judicial Circuits

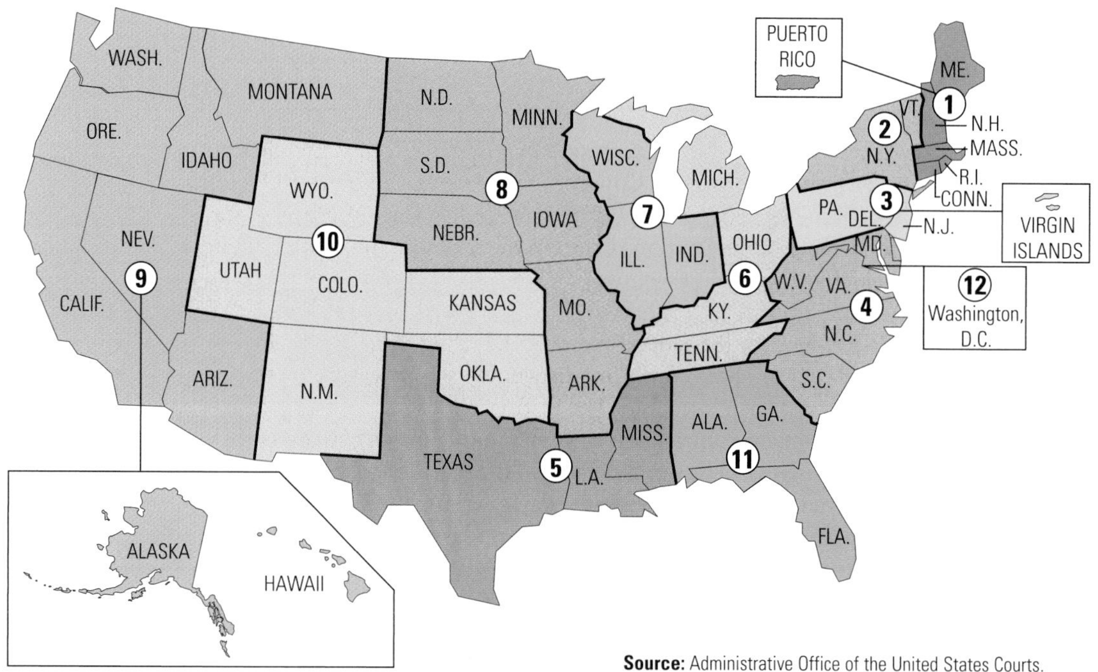

Source: Administrative Office of the United States Courts.

The decisions in the courts of appeals are made by a rotating panel of three judges who sit to hear the case. Although many more than three judges are assigned to each federal appeals circuit (the Court of Appeals for the Ninth Circuit, based in San Francisco, has forty-seven), the judges rotate in order to provide a decision-making body that is as unbiased as possible. In rare cases where a decision is of crucial social importance, all the judges in a circuit will meet together, or *en banc*, to render a decision. Having all the judges present, not just three, gives a decision more legitimacy and sends a message that the decision was made carefully.

Selection of Federal Judges The Constitution is silent about the qualifications of federal judges. It specifies only that they shall be appointed by the president, with the advice and consent of the Senate, and that they shall serve lifetime terms under good behavior. They can be removed from office only if impeached and convicted by the House of Representatives and the Senate, a process that has resulted in only thirteen impeachments and seven convictions in more than two hundred years.

Traditionally, federal judgeships have been awarded on the basis of several criteria, not the least of which has been to reward political friendship and support and to cultivate future political support, whether of a particular politician or an entire gender or ethnic or racial group. An increasingly important qualification for the job of federal judge is the ideological or policy positions of the appointee. Since the 1970s, politicians have become more aware of the political influence of these courts.

Consequently, politicians can have quite an impact in shaping the U.S. judicial system by the appointments they make, and as they have taken advantage of that opportunity, the Senate confirmation process has become more rancorous (see Figure 10.3). Together, Republican presidents Ronald Reagan and George H. W. Bush appointed more than 60 percent of all federal judges, and they made a conscious effort to redirect what they saw as the liberal tenor of court appointments in the years since the New Deal. Even though Democratic president Bill Clinton appointed many judges as well, the moderate ideology of most of his appointees means that the courts have not swung back in a radically liberal direction.[21] He renewed a commitment made by President Jimmy Carter to create diversity on the federal bench. Nearly half of Clinton's appointees were women and minorities, compared to 35 percent under Carter, 14 percent under Reagan, and 27 percent under Bush.[22] Clinton's appointees also were what one observer called "militantly moderate"—more liberal than Reagan's and Bush's, but less liberal than Carter's, and similar ideologically to the appointments of Republican president Gerald Ford.[23]

President George W. Bush's appointees look similar to those of his father in terms of race, gender, and ideology.[24] Bush has especially made a point of solidifying the conservative balance on the courts. As of 2005, 94 of the current 162 judges on the U.S. Court of Appeals were appointed by Republican presidents; and Republican appointees are a majority on ten of the thirteen circuit courts.[25]

Nonetheless, as we saw in Chapter 7, conservative critics who deplore what they call the "activist" nature of the current courts are pushing President Bush to make nominations that are even more conservative, and in 2005 strongly urged the Senate to eliminate the judicial filibuster so that Democrats could not block Bush's more conservative appointments. Although moderates in both parties agreed to a compromise to allow votes on three of Bush's stalled nominees, it is not clear that this bipartisan agreement will lessen the hostile nature of the nomination process.[26]

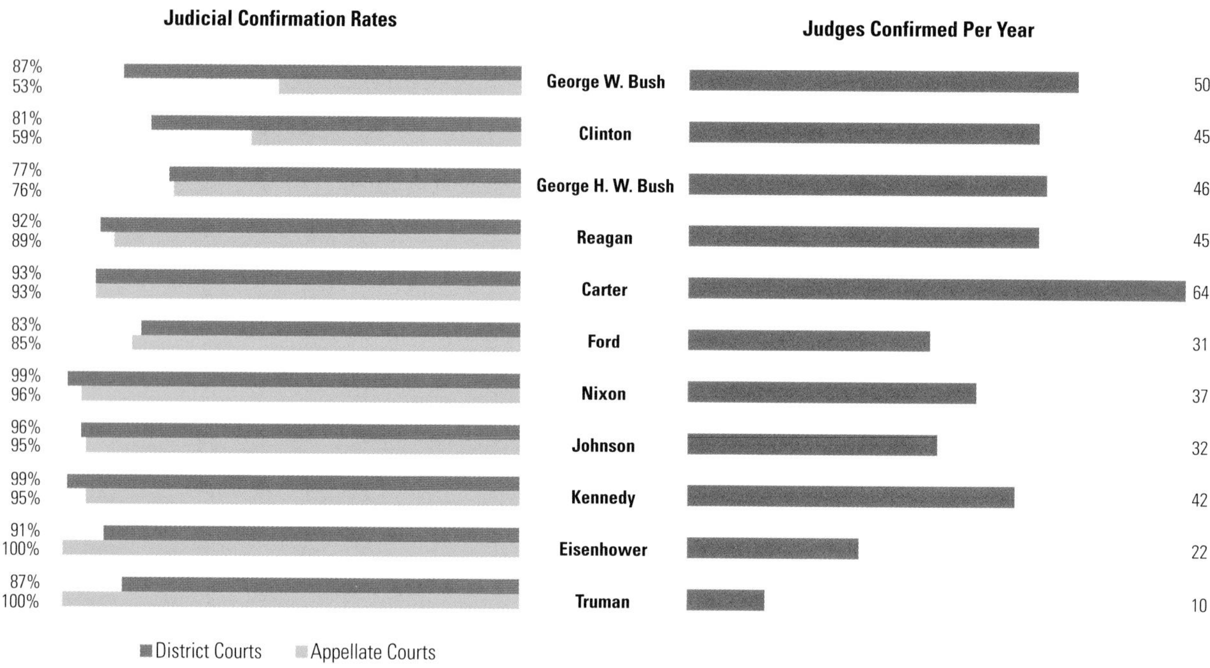

FIGURE 10.3

Number and Percentage of Judges Confirmed, Truman–George W. Bush

Source: Sarah Binder, Forrest Maltzman, and Alan Murphy, "Op-Chart; History's Verdict," *New York Times*, May 19, 2005, A27.

senatorial courtesy tradition of granting senior senators of the president's party considerable power over federal judicial appointments in their home states

Another influence on the appointment of federal judges is the principle of **senatorial courtesy**, which we discussed in Chapter 8. In reality, senators do most of the nominating of district court judges, often aided by applications made by lawyers and state judges. Traditionally, a president who nominated a candidate who failed to meet with the approval of the state's senior senator was highly unlikely to gain Senate confirmation of that candidate, even if he was lucky enough to get the Senate Judiciary Committee to hold a hearing on the nomination. In recent years the practice of senatorial courtesy has been weakened somewhat by the Bush administration and Senate Republicans who have forced confirmation hearings despite the objections of Democratic home state senators.[27]

The growing influence of politics in the selection of federal judges does not mean that merit is unimportant. As the nation's largest legal professional association, the American Bar Association (ABA) has had the informal role since 1946 of evaluating the legal qualifications of potential nominees. While poorly rated candidates are occasionally nominated and confirmed, perhaps because of the pressure of a senator or a president, most federal judges receive the ABA's professional blessing. The ABA's role has become more controversial in recent years, as Republicans are convinced that it has a liberal bias, and in 2001 the Bush administration announced that it would no longer seek the ABA's ratings of its nominees, breaking a tradition that goes back to Eisenhower. The ABA continues to rate the nominees (and the Bush White House boasts that 99 percent of its nominees have been rated qualified or well qualified), but it does so independently.[28]

TABLE 10.1 Characteristics of Presidential Appointees to U.S. District Court Judgeships (by presidential administration, 1963–2003)

	LYNDON JOHNSON (1963–1968) (*N* = 122)	RICHARD NIXON (1969–1974) (*N* = 179)	GERALD FORD (1974–1976) (*N* = 52)	JIMMY CARTER (1977–1980) (*N* = 202)	RONALD REAGAN (1981–1988) (*N* = 290)	GEORGE H. W. BUSH (1989–1992) (*N* = 148)	BILL CLINTON (1993–2000) (*N* = 305)	GEORGE W. BUSH (2001–2003) (*N* = 83)
Sex								
Male	98.4%	99.4%	98.1%	85.6%	91.7%	80.4%	71.5%	79.5%
Female	1.6	0.6	1.9	14.4	8.3	19.6	28.5	20.5
Ethnicity								
White	93.4	95.5	88.5	78.7	92.4	89.2	75.1	85.5
Black	4.1	3.4	5.8	13.9	2.1	6.8	17.4	7.2
Hispanic	2.5	1.1	1.9	6.9	4.8	4.0	5.9	7.2
Asian	0.0	0.0	3.9	0.5	0.7	0.0	1.3	0.0
Native American	n/a	n/a	n/a	n/a	n/a	n/a	0.3	0.0
Religion								
Protestant	58.2	73.2	73.1	60.4	60.3	64.2	n/a	n/a
Catholic	31.1	18.4	17.3	27.7	30.0	28.4	n/a	n/a
Jewish	10.7	8.4	9.6	11.9	9.3	7.4	n/a	n/a
Political Party								
Democrat	94.3	7.3	21.2	91.1	4.8	6.1	87.5	7.2
Republican	5.7	92.7	78.8	4.5	91.7	88.5	6.2	83.1
Independent/Other	0.0	0.0	0.0	4.5	3.4	5.4	6.2	9.6
ABA Rating								
Exceptionally well/ well qualified	48.4	45.3	46.1	50.9	54.1	57.4	63.9	66.0
Qualified	49.2	54.8	53.8	47.5	45.9	42.6	34.4	33.0
Not qualified	2.5	0.0	0.0	1.5	0.0	0.0	1.8	1.0

Note: Percentages may not add to 100 because of rounding. ABA = American Bar Association; n/a = not available.

Source: Sheldon Goldman, "Reagan's Judicial Legacy: Completing the Puzzle and Summing Up," *Judicature* 72 (April–May 1989): 320, 321, Table 1; and Sheldon Goldman and Elliot Slotnick, "Clinton's First Term Judiciary: Many Bridges to Cross," *Judicature* 80 (May–June 1997): 261. Table adapted by Sourcebook staff, Bureau of Justice Statistics, *Sourcebook of Criminal Justice Statistics, 1996* (Washington, D.C.: U.S. Dept. of Justice, 1996), Table 1.77, p. 62; Harold W. Stanley and Richard G. Niemi, *Vital Statistics on American Politics, 2003–2004* (Washington, D.C.: CQ Press, 2004), 281–282; American Bar Association, www.abanet.org/scfedjud/ratings107.pdf, compiled by authors for George W. Bush ABA ratings.

WHO, WHAT, HOW The dual court system in America is shaped by rules that ultimately determine who will win and lose in legal disputes. Because our common law tradition gives the judge a great deal of power to interpret what the law means, the selection of judges is critical to how the rules are applied. Both the president and the Senate are involved in the selection of federal judges, and both have a stake in creating a federal judiciary that reflects the views they think are important—and rewards the people they feel should be rewarded. The rules that determine whether the president or the Senate is successful come partly from the Constitution (the nomination and confirmation processes) and partly from tradition (senatorial courtesy).

POLITICS AND THE SUPREME COURT

At the very top of the nation's judicial system reigns the Supreme Court. While the nine justices do not wear the elaborate wigs of their British colleagues in the House of Lords, the highest court of appeals in Britain, they do don long black robes to hear their cases and sit against a majestic background of red silk, perhaps the closest thing to the pomp and circumstance of royalty that we have in American government. Polls show that even after its role in the contested presidential election of 2000, the Court gets higher ratings from the public than does Congress or the president, and that it doesn't suffer as much from the popular cynicism about government that afflicts the other branches.[29]

The American public seems to believe that the Supreme Court is indeed above politics, as the founders wished it to be. Such a view, while gratifying to those who want to believe in the purity and wisdom of at least one aspect of their government, is not strictly accurate. The members of the Court themselves are preserved by the rule of lifetime tenure from continually having to seek reelection or reappointment, but they are not removed from the political world around them. It is more useful, and closer to reality, to regard the Supreme Court as an intensely political institution. In at least four critical areas—how its members are chosen, how those members choose which cases to hear, how they make decisions, and the effects of the decisions they make—the Court is a decisive allocator of who gets what, when, and how. Reflecting on popular idealizing of the Court, scholar Richard Pacelle says that "not to know the Court is to love it."[30] In the remainder of this chapter, we get to know the Court, not to stop loving it but to gain a healthy respect for the enormously powerful political institution it is.

HOW MEMBERS OF THE COURT ARE SELECTED

In a perfect world, the wisest and most intelligent jurists in the country would be appointed to make the all-important constitutional decisions faced by members of the Supreme Court. In a political world, however, the need for wise and intelligent justices needs to be balanced against the demands of a system that makes those justices the choice of an elected president, and confirmed by elected senators. The need of these elected officials to be responsive to their constituencies means that the nomination process for Supreme Court justices is often a battleground of competing views of the public good. Merit is certainly important, but it is tempered by other considerations resulting from a democratic selection process.

On paper, the process of choosing justices for the Supreme Court is not a great deal different from the selection of other federal judges, though no tradition of senatorial courtesy exists at the high court level. Far too much is at stake in Supreme Court appointments to even consider giving any individual senator veto power. Because the job is so important, the president himself gets much more involved than he does in other federal judge appointments. As the box "Packing the Courts" highlights, the composition of the Court has serious political consequences.

The Constitution, silent on so much concerning the Supreme Court, does not give the president any handy list of criteria for making these critical appointments. But the demands of his job suggest that merit, shared ideology, political reward, and demo-

Farewell to the Chief
When Sandra Day O'Connor announced her retirement from the Supreme Court in June 2005, President Bush nominated John Roberts to replace her. But in early September, before Roberts's confirmation hearings had even begun, Chief Justice William Rehnquist died and Bush converted Roberts's nomination to Chief Justice. This photo shows Rehnquist's body being brought to the Supreme Court. Roberts, a former law clerk of Rehnquist's, is the second pallbearer from the front, on the left. Along the right, six of the remaining justices pay their respects: (from the top) Justices Stevens, O'Connor, Scalia, Thomas, Ginsburg, and Breyer.

graphic representation all play a role in this choice.[31] We can understand something about the challenges that face a president making a Supreme Court appointment by examining each of these criteria briefly.

Merit The president will certainly want to appoint the most qualified person and the person with the highest ethical standards who also meets the other prerequisites. Scholars agree that most of the people who have served the Court over the years have been among the best legal minds available, but they also know that sometimes presidents have nominated people whose reputations have proved questionable.[32] The ABA passes judgment on candidates for the Supreme Court, as it does for the lower courts, issuing verdicts of "well qualified," "qualified," "not opposed," and "not qualified." The Federal Bureau of Investigation (FBI) also checks out the background of nominees, although occasionally critical information is missed. In 1987 the Reagan administration, which had widely publicized its Just Say No campaign against drug use, was deeply embarrassed when National Public Radio reporter Nina Totenberg broke the story that its Supreme Court nominee, appeals court judge Douglas Ginsburg, had used marijuana in college and while on the Harvard Law School faculty. Ginsburg withdrew his name from consideration. More controversial was the 1991 case of Clarence Thomas, already under attack for his lack of

Packing the Courts

The Supreme Court was a thorn in President Franklin Roosevelt's side. Faced with the massive unemployment and economic stagnation that characterized the Great Depression of the 1930s, Roosevelt knew he would have to use the powers of government creatively, but he was hampered by a Court that was ideologically opposed to his efforts to regulate business and industry and skeptical of his constitutional power to do so. In Roosevelt's view, he and Congress had been elected by the people, and public opinion favored his New Deal policies, but a majority of the "nine old men," as they were called, on the Supreme Court consistently stood in his way. Six of the justices were over age seventy, and Roosevelt had appointed none of them.

Roosevelt proposed to change the Court that continually thwarted him. The Constitution allows Congress to set the number of justices on the Supreme Court, and indeed the number has ranged from six to ten at various times in our history. Roosevelt's answer to the recalcitrant Court was to ask Congress to allow him to appoint a new justice for every justice over age seventy who refused to retire, up to a possible total of fifteen. Thus he would create a Court whose majority he had chosen and that he confidently believed would support his New Deal programs.

Most presidents try to pack the Court, building their own legacies with appointees who they hope will perpetuate their vision of government and politics. But Roosevelt's plan was dangerous because it threatened to alter the two constitutional principles of separation of powers and checks and balances. Roosevelt would have made into a truism Hamilton's claim that the judiciary was the least dangerous branch of government, while raising the power of the presidency to a height even Hamilton had not dreamed of. The American people reacted with dismay. Public opinion may have backed his policies, but it turned on him when he tried to pack the Court.

Precedent for the President

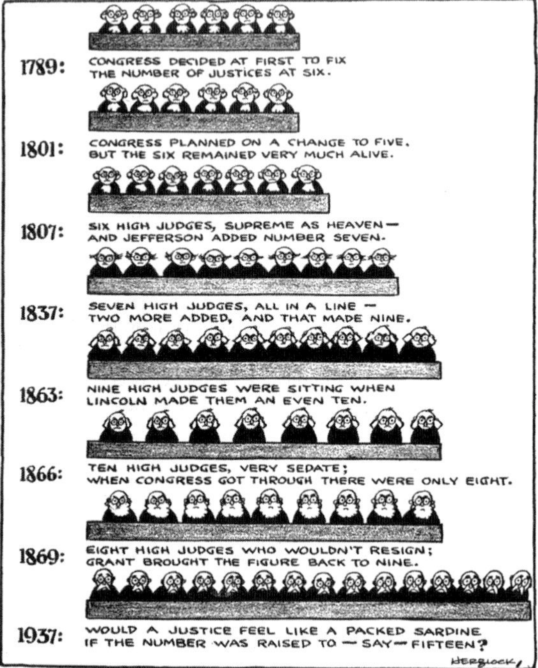

HISTORICAL FIGURES—from *Herblock: A Cartoonist's Life* (Times Books, 1998).

No other president has attempted to pack the Court as blatantly as Roosevelt did, and none has failed so ignominiously. The public backlash may have contributed to the slowing of the New Deal and the Republican victories in 1938 that left Roosevelt with a weakened Democratic majority in Congress. His audacious plan had risked the very policy success he was trying so hard to achieve.

In the end, Roosevelt was reelected two more times. The Court, ironically, did an about-face. One justice started voting with the Roosevelt supporters; another retired. Eventually he made eight appointments to the Supreme Court, putting his stamp on it more effectively than any other president since Washington. The Court was, in essence, packed by Roosevelt after all.

judicial experience and low ABA rating, who was accused of sexual harassment by a former employee, law professor Anita Hill. Although Thomas was confirmed, the hearings brought ethical questions about Court nominees to center stage.

Political Ideology Although a president wants to appoint a well-qualified candidate to the Court, he is constrained by the desire to find a candidate who shares his views on politics and the law. Political ideology here involves a couple of dimensions. One is the traditional liberal–conservative dimension. Supreme Court justices, like all other human beings, have views on the role of government, the rights of individuals, and the relationship between the two. Presidents want to appoint justices who look at the world the same way they do, although they are occasionally surprised when their nominee's ideological stripes turn out to be different than they had anticipated. Republican president Dwight Eisenhower called the appointment of Chief Justice Earl Warren, who turned out to be quite liberal in his legal judgments, "the biggest damn fool mistake I ever made."[33] Although there have been notable exceptions, most presidents appoint members of their own party in an attempt to get ideologically compatible justices. Overall, roughly 90 percent of Supreme Court nominees belong to the president's party.

But ideology has another dimension when it refers to the law. Justices can take the view that the Constitution means exactly what it says it means and that all interpretations of it must be informed by the founders' intentions. This approach, called **strict constructionism**, holds that if the meaning of the Constitution is to be changed, it must be done by amendment, not by judicial interpretation. Judge Robert Bork, a Reagan nominee who failed to be confirmed by the Senate, is a strict constructionist. During his confirmation hearings, when he was asked about the famous reapportionment ruling in *Baker v. Carr* that the Constitution effectively guarantees every citizen one vote, Bork replied that if the people of the United States wanted their Constitution to guarantee "one man one vote," they were free to amend the document to say so. In Bork's judgment, without that amendment, the principle was simply the result of justices' rewriting the Constitution. When the senators asked him about the right to privacy, another right enforced by the Court but not specified in the Constitution, Bork simply laughed.[34] The opposite position to strict constructionism, what might be called **judicial interpretivism**, holds that the Constitution is a living document, that the founders could not possibly have anticipated all possible future circumstances,

strict constructionism a judicial approach holding that the Constitution should be read literally, with the framers' intentions uppermost in mind

judicial interpretivism a judicial approach holding that the Constitution is a living document and that judges should interpret it according to changing times and values

and that justices should interpret the Constitution in light of social changes. When the Court, in *Griswold v. Connecticut*, ruled that while there is no right to privacy in the Constitution, the Bill of Rights can be understood to imply such a right, it was engaging in judicial interpretation. Strict constructionists would deny that there is a constitutional right to privacy.

While interpretivism tends to be a liberal position because of its emphasis on change, and strict constructionism tends to be a conservative position because of its adherence to the status quo, the two ideological scales do not necessarily go hand in hand. For instance, even though the Second Amendment refers to the right to bear arms in the context of militia membership, many conservatives would argue that this needs to be understood to protect the right to bear arms in a modern context, when militias are no longer necessary or practical—not a strict constructionist reading of the Constitution. Liberals, on the other hand, tend to rely on a strict reading of the Second Amendment to support their calls for tighter gun controls.

Even though it is often hard for a president to know where a nominee stands on the strict constructionist–interpretivist scale, especially if that nominee does not have a large record of previous decisions in lower courts, this ideological placement can be very important in the decision-making process. This was the case, for instance, with President Richard Nixon, who was convinced that interpretivist justices were rewriting the Constitution to give too many protections to criminal defendants, and with President Reagan, who faulted interpretivist justices for the *Roe v. Wade* decision legalizing abortion on the grounds of the right to privacy. But in neither case have all of these presidents' appointees adhered to the desired manner of interpreting the Constitution.

Reward More than half of the people who have been nominated to the Supreme Court have been personally acquainted with the president.[35] Often nominees are either friends of the president, or his political allies, or other people he wishes to reward in an impressive fashion. Harry Truman knew and had worked with all four of the men he appointed to the Court, Franklin Roosevelt appointed people he knew (and who were loyal to his New Deal), John Kennedy appointed his long-time friend and associate Byron White, and Lyndon Johnson appointed his good friend Abe Fortas.[36] While several FOBs (Friends of Bill) appeared on Clinton's short lists for his appointments, none was actually appointed.

Representation Finally, the president wants to appoint people who represent groups he feels should be included in the political process, or whose support he wants to gain. Lyndon Johnson appointed Thurgood Marshall at least in part because he wanted to appoint an African American to the Court. After Marshall retired, President George H. W. Bush appointed Clarence Thomas to fill his seat. While he declared that he was making the appointment because Thomas was the person best qualified for the job, and not because he was black, few believed him. In earlier years, presidents also felt compelled to ensure that there was at least one Catholic and one Jew on the Court. This necessity has lost much of its force today as interest groups seem more concerned with the political than the denominational views of appointees.

Table 10.2 shows the composition of the Supreme Court after John Roberts was confirmed but before Sandra Day O'Connor's replacement had been confirmed. There are seven men on the Court and two women (the only two ever to have been appointed). Four justices are Catholic, three Protestant, and two Jewish; only Judeo-

Christian religions have been represented on the Court so far. Seven of the justices are Republicans, primarily a reflection of appointments by Reagan and Bush, and two, appointed by Clinton, are Democrats. They have attended an elite array of undergraduate institutions and law schools. In early 2005 their ages ranged from 50 to 85, with the average 68, although at least one retirement was expected that summer. There have never been any Hispanics, Native Americans, or Asian Americans on the Court, and only a total of two African Americans, whose terms did not overlap. The overwhelmingly elite white male Christian character of the Court raises interesting questions. We naturally want our highest judges to have excellent legal educations (although John Marshall barely had any). But should the nation's highest court represent demographically the people whose Constitution it guards? Some observers have suggested that women judges may be sensitive to issues that have not been salient to men and may alter behavior in the courtroom; the same may be true of minority judges as well. In a different vein, what message is sent to citizens when the custodians of national justice are composed primarily of a group that is itself fast becoming a minority in America?

Confirmation by the Senate As with the lower courts, the Senate must approve presidential appointments to the Supreme Court. Here again, the Senate Judiciary Committee plays the largest role, holding hearings and inviting the nominee, colleagues, and concerned interest groups to testify. Sometimes the hearings, and the subsequent vote in the Senate, are mere formalities, but increasingly, as the appointments have become more ideological and when the Senate majority party is not the party of the president, the hearings have had the potential to become political battlefields. Even when the president's party controls the Senate, the minority party can still influence the choice through the filibuster unless the Senate Republicans renew their 2005 effort to halt this tradition. The Bork and Thomas hearings are excellent examples of what

TABLE 10.2 **Composition of the Supreme Court, 2005**

JUSTICE	YEAR BORN	YEAR APPOINTED	POLITICAL PARTY	APPOINTING PRESIDENT	HOME STATE	COLLEGE/LAW SCHOOL	RELIGION	POSITION WHEN APPOINTED
John G. Roberts	1955	2005	Rep.	W. Bush	Maryland	Harvard/Harvard	Catholic	U.S. Appeals Court Judge
John Paul Stevens	1920	1975	Rep.	Ford	Illinois	Chicago/ Northwestern	Non-denominational Protestant	U.S. Appeals Court Judge
Sandra Day O'Connor*	1930	1981	Rep.	Reagan	Arizona	Stanford/Stanford	Episcopalian	State Appeals Court Judge
Antonin Scalia	1936	1986	Rep.	Reagan	D.C.	Georgetown/ Harvard	Catholic	U.S. Appeals Court Judge
Anthony M. Kennedy	1936	1988	Rep.	Reagan	California	Stanford/Harvard	Catholic	U.S. Appeals Court Judge
David H. Souter	1939	1990	Rep.	Bush	New Hampshire	Harvard/Harvard	Episcopalian	U.S. Appeals Court Judge
Clarence Thomas	1948	1991	Rep.	Bush	Georgia	Holy Cross/Yale	Catholic	U.S. Appeals Court Judge
Ruth Bader Ginsburg	1933	1993	Dem.	Clinton	New York	Cornell/Columbia	Jewish	U.S. Appeals Court Judge
Stephen G. Breyer	1938	1994	Dem.	Clinton	California	Stanford, Oxford/Harvard	Jewish	U.S. Appeals Court Judge

* Announced retirement June 2005, pending confirmation of her replacement.

Sandra Day O'Connor

Even though she's told the story many times, her voice still echoes with the frustration of that first job hunt. But there is irony in her voice too—after all, the story has a happy ending, though it's one she never imagined when she graduated from law school back in 1952.

Really, all she wanted then was to work as a lawyer. She was getting married that summer and her husband-to-be still had a year left in law school. Since, she says dryly, they both liked to eat, she thought getting a job would be a good idea.

"[E]very new generation has to learn all over again the foundations of our government and every individual's role in it."

But she reckoned without the prejudice against hiring women that pervaded the country in those days. There were positions galore posted on the jobs board at Stanford Law School, where she'd graduated third in her class of 102, but none of the firms was willing to hire a woman. She'd even parlayed an undergraduate friendship into an interview at the friend's father's firm, but all that resulted were questions about her office skills.

Her story sounds both ludicrous and poignant today, as she recalls it in her impressive law chambers, with their rich polished woods and warm leather furniture, the walls lined with thick volumes of legal wisdom. As this most distinguished of American women recounts that long-ago interview in her precise, forceful voice, her snowy white hair and soft blue suit not blunting at all the effect of the power she radiates, it's hard not to find the incongruity a little amusing, even as one imagines the bitter disappointment of the young lawyer she once was.

"Well, Miss Day, how do you type?" asked the partner who interviewed her. Just so-so, she replied. "If you can type well enough, maybe I can get you a job here as a legal secretary," he suggested. "But, Miss Day, our firm has never hired a woman as a lawyer. I don't see the day when we will—our clients wouldn't accept it."

Having run into a brick wall in the private sector, Sandra Day, soon to be Sandra Day O'Connor, set to work convincing the San Mateo county attorney to hire her; because he was engaged in public law, "he wasn't afraid to have a woman in his office." With that first job—initially undertaken without pay and in a shared office—she launched herself on a public career that coursed through years in the state attorney general's office in Arizona, the Arizona state Senate, and the state bench and would finally hit its dramatic peak twenty-nine years later, when President Ronald Reagan appointed her as the first female justice on the U.S. Supreme Court.

Don't you just wish you could have seen her girlfriend's father's partner's face when that announcement was made?

can happen when interest groups and public opinion get heavily involved in a controversial confirmation battle. These political clashes are so grueling because so much is at stake. No sooner had Justice Sandra Day O'Connor announced her retirement in June 2005, than both sides were on high alert, rallying supporters, faxing information to the press, and making public statements about what kinds of nominees would be acceptable—and that before President Bush ever made a nomination. Conservatives were determined to replace O'Connor's moderate vote with a solidly conservative justice who would help overturn *Roe v. Wade* and allow government to accommodate religion in the public realm; liberals insisted that Bush find another moderate conservative who had an open mind on abortion rights and kept church and state separate.[37]

But maybe it's too easy to blame Sandra Day O'Connor's extraordinary career in public law on the stubborn sexism of the private legal profession in 1950s America. She might have taken that path anyway—her decision to go to law school in the first place was in part idealistic, inspired by a professor she'd taken a law class from as an undergraduate. "He was the first one who persuaded me that the individual could make a difference in this big world of ours," she remembers. By "the individual" he meant not just a president or governor or other person with power, but even someone "at the bottom of the totem pole." "The person at the bottom will sometimes have the best understanding of how to make something work. If you are sincere about it and determined enough, you can hang in there and see to it that it happens."

And those are the recurring themes in the life of Sandra Day O'Connor: sincerity in her efforts, determination to make a difference, persistence in the face of opposition, and independence in charting her path.

Perhaps all these qualities were honed from an early age, as she grew up on her family's Lazy B Ranch on the border of New Mexico and Arizona. There the fact that their herd grazed on federal land taught her early about the interrelationship between citizens and government. The harsh, isolated beauty of the land taught her other things as well. As she has written, the ranch was "a place where the wind always blows, the sky forms a dome overhead, and the clouds make changing patterns against the blue, and where the stars at night are brilliant and constant, a place to see the sunrise and sunset, and always to be reminded how small we are in the universe but, even so, how one small voice can make a difference."[1]

And there is that idealism again, an optimism about the potential of human beings that is tempered, when she talks, with a strong no-nonsense manner and a brisk practicality, a moderation and pragmatism that is reflected in her judgments on the Court. She clearly doesn't suffer fools gladly but at the same time is not without hope that we can save ourselves from foolishness. Here is some of her advice:

On what she'd tell today's students about how one person can make a difference:

> Of course [you] have to have courage, you have to learn to believe in yourself, and to do that you have to develop some skills. So learn to read fast, and to write well, that's what you need to learn to do as a student. I have to read something like 1,500 pages a day. Now I couldn't do that if I hadn't taken speed reading. And that's important. I'm serious. You don't realize how important it is to be able to read fast. Because if you can read fast, think of all you can learn. . . . And then have courage to believe that, yes, you are equipped to do something, and go do it.

On keeping the republic:

> You know, I've always said that we don't inherit our knowledge and understanding through the gene pool. And every new generation has to learn all over again the foundations of our government, how it was set up and why, and what is every individual's role in it. And we have to convey that to every generation . . . [i]f every young generation of citizens [doesn't] have an understanding of this, we can't keep our nation in decent order for the future.

1. Sandra Day O'Connor and H. Alan Day, *Lazy B: Growing Up on a Cattle Ranch in the American Southwest* (New York: Random House. 2002), 302.

Source: Sandra Day O'Connor talked with Christine Barbour on March 3, 2005.

CHOOSING WHICH CASES TO HEAR

The introduction of political concerns into the selection process makes it almost inevitable that political considerations will also arise as the justices make their decisions. Politics makes an appearance at three points in the decision-making process, the first of which is in the selection of the cases to be heard.

The Supreme Court could not possibly hear the roughly eight thousand petitions it receives each year.[38] Intensive screening is necessary to reduce the number to the more manageable 90 to 120 that the Court finally hears (see Figure 10.4). This screening process is a political one; having one's case heard by the Supreme Court is

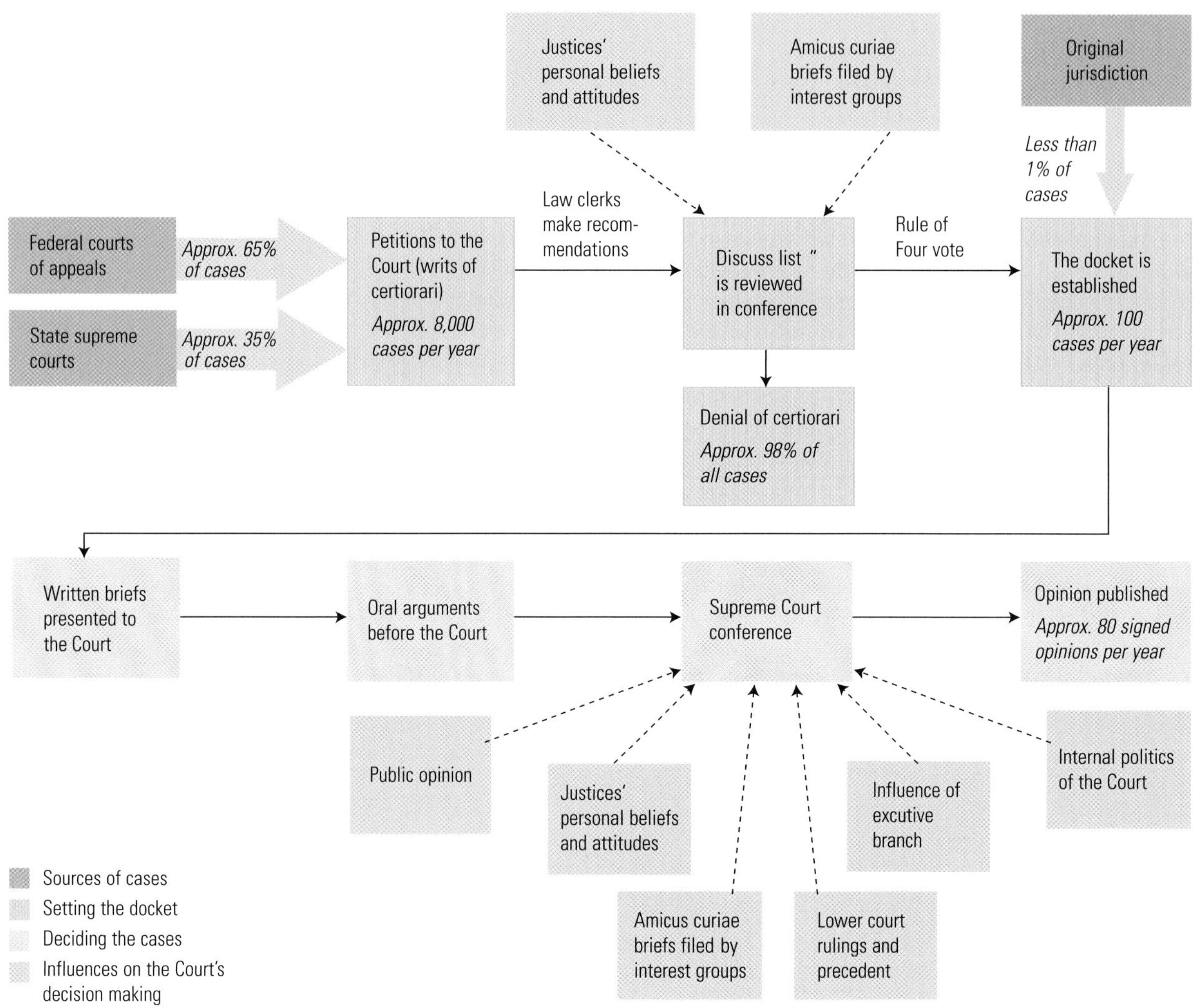

FIGURE 10.4
Pathway to and through the Supreme Court
Source: Administrative Office of the United States Courts.

a scarce resource. What rules and which people determine who gets this resource and who doesn't?

writ of certiorari formal request by the U.S. Supreme Court to call up the lower court case it decides to hear on appeal

Petitioning the Supreme Court Almost all the cases heard by the Court come from its appellate, not its original, jurisdiction, and of these virtually all arrive at the Court in the form of petitions for **writs of certiorari**, in which the losing party in a lower court case explains in writing why the Supreme Court should hear its case. Petitions to the Court are subject to strict length, form, and style requirements and must be accompanied by a $200 filing fee (which increases to $300 if the justices decide to hear the case). Those too poor to pay the filing fee are allowed to petition the Court *in forma pauperis,* which exempts them not only from the filing fee but also from the stringent style and form rules. In the 2003 term, 6,092 of the 7,814 case filings were *in forma pauperis.*[39] The Court's jurisdiction here is discretionary; it can either grant or deny a writ of certiorari. If it decides to grant certiorari and review the case, then the records of the case will be called up from the lower court where it was last heard.

For a case to be heard by the Court, it must be within the Court's jurisdiction, and it must present a real controversy that has injured the petitioner in some way, not just request the Court's advice on an abstract principle. In addition, it must be an appropriate question for the Court—that is, it must not be the sort of "political question" usually dealt with by the other two branches of government. This last rule is open to interpretation by the justices, however, and they may not all agree on what constitutes a political question. But these rules alone do not narrow the Court's caseload to a sufficiently small number of cases, and an enormous amount of work remains for the justices and their staffs, particularly their law clerks.

The Role of Law Clerks Law clerks, usually recent graduates from law school who have served a year as clerk to a judge on a lower court, have tremendous responsibility over certiorari petitions, or "cert pets," as they call them. They must read all the petitions (thirty pages in length plus appendixes) and summarize each in a two- to five-page memo that includes a recommendation to the justices on whether to hear the case, all with minimal guidance or counsel from their justices.[40] Some justices join a "cert pool"—each clerk reads only a portion of the whole number of submitted petitions and shares his or her summaries and evaluations with the other justices. Currently eight of the nine justices of the Court are in a pool; one justice, Justice John Paul Stevens, requires his clerks to read and evaluate all the petitions.

The memos are circulated to the justices' offices, where clerks read them again and make comments on the advisability of hearing the cases. The memos, with the clerks' comments, go on to the justices, who decide which cases they think should be granted cert and which denied. The chief justice circulates a weekly list of the cases he thinks should be discussed, which is known unimaginatively as the "discuss list." Other justices can add to that list the cases they think should be discussed in their Friday afternoon meetings.

The Rule of Four Once a case is on the discuss list, it takes a vote of four justices to agree to grant it certiorari. This **Rule of Four** means that it takes fewer people to decide to hear a case than it will eventually take to decide the case itself, and thus it gives some power to a minority on the Court. The denial of certiorari does not necessarily signal that the Court endorses a lower court's ruling. Rather, it simply means that the case was not seen as important or special enough to be heard by the highest court. Justices who believe strongly that a case should not be denied have, increasingly in recent years, engaged in the practice of "dissenting from the denial," in an effort to persuade other justices to go along with them (since dissension at this stage makes the Court look less consensual) and to put their views on record. Fewer than 5 percent of cases appealed to the Supreme Court survive the screening process to be heard by the Court.

Rule of Four the unwritten requirement that four Supreme Court justices must agree to grant a case certiorari in order for the case to be heard

Other Influences The decisions to grant cert, then, are made by novice lawyers without much direction, who operate under enormous time and performance pressures, and by the justices, who rely on the evaluations of these young lawyers, while bringing to the process the full array of values and ideologies for which they were, in part, chosen.

Naturally the product of this process will reflect these characteristics, but there are other influences on the justices and the decision-making process at this point as well.

One factor is whether the United States, under the representation of its lawyer, the **solicitor general**, is party to any of the cases before them. Between 70 and 80 percent of the appeals filed by the federal government are granted cert by the justices, a far greater proportion than for any other group.[41] Researchers speculate that this is because of the stature of the federal government's interests, the justices' trust in the solicitor general's ability to weed out frivolous lawsuits, and the experience the solicitor general brings to the job.[42] Justices are also influenced by **amicus curiae briefs**, or "friend of the court" documents, that are filed in support of about 8 percent of petitions for certiorari by interest groups that want to encourage the Court to grant or deny cert. The amicus briefs do seem to affect the likelihood that the Court will agree to hear a case, and since economic interest groups are more likely to be active here than are other kinds of groups, it is their interests that most often influence the justices to grant cert.[43] As we will see, amicus curiae briefs are also used further on in the process.

solicitor general Justice Department officer who argues the government's cases before the Supreme Court

amicus curiae briefs "friend of the court" documents filed by interested parties to encourage the court to grant or deny certiorari or to urge it to decide a case in a particular way

DECIDING CASES

Once a case is on the docket, the parties are notified and they prepare their written briefs and oral arguments for their Supreme Court appearance. Lawyers for each side get only a half-hour to make their cases verbally in front of the Court, and they are often interrupted by justices who seek clarification, criticize points, or offer supportive arguments. The half-hour rule is generally followed strictly. In one case, two justices got up and walked out as the oral argument cut into their lunch hour, even though the lawyer who was speaking had been granted an extension by the chief justice.[44]

The actual decision-making process occurs before and during the Supreme Court conference meeting. Conference debates and discussions take place in private, although justices have often made revealing comments in their letters and memoirs that give insight into the dynamics of conference decision making. A variety of factors affect the justices as they make decisions on the cases they hear. Some of those factors come from within the justices—their attitudes, values, and beliefs—and some are external.

Judicial Attitudes Justices' attitudes toward the Constitution and how literally it is to be taken are clearly important, as we saw earlier in our discussion of strict constructionism and interpretivism. Judges are also influenced by the view they hold of the role of the Court: whether it should be an active law- and policymaker, or should keep its rulings narrow and leave lawmaking to the elected branches of government. Those who adhere to **judicial activism** are quite comfortable with the idea of overturning precedents, exercising judicial review, and otherwise making decisions that shape government policy. Practitioners of **judicial restraint**, on the other hand, believe more strongly in the principle of *stare decisis* and reject any active lawmaking by the Court as unconstitutional.

These positions seem at first to line up with the positions of interpretivism and strict constructionism, and often they do. But exceptions exist, as when liberal justice Thurgood Marshall, who had once used the Constitution in activist and interpretivist ways to change civil rights laws, pleaded for restraint among his newer and more

judicial activism view that the courts should be lawmaking, policymaking bodies

judicial restraint view that the courts should reject any active lawmaking functions and stick to judicial interpretations of the past conservative colleagues who were eager to roll back some of the earlier decisions by overturning precedent and creating more conservative law.[45]

In recent years, especially in the wake of a Massachusetts Supreme Court decision that said forbidding gays the right to marry violates the Massachusetts constitution, conservatives have lambasted what they call the activism or "legislating from the bench" of courts who they say take decision making out of the hands of the people. But activism is not necessarily a liberal stance, and restraint is not necessarily conservative. Activism or restraint often seems to be more a function of whether a justice likes the status quo than it does of any steady point of principle.[46] A justice seeking to overturn the *Roe v. Wade* ruling allowing women to have abortions during the first trimester of pregnancy would be an activist conservative justice; Justice Thurgood Marshall ended his term on the Court as a liberal restraintist.

In addition to being influenced by their own attitudes, justices are influenced in their decision making by their backgrounds (region of residence, profession, place of education, and the like), their party affiliations, and their political attitudes, all of which the president and the Senate consider in selecting future justices.[47]

External Factors Justices are also influenced by external factors.[48] Despite the founders' efforts to make justices immune to politics and the pressures of public opinion by giving them lifetime tenure, political scientists have found that they usually tend to make decisions that are consistent with majority opinion in the United States. Of course, this doesn't mean that justices are reading public opinion polls over breakfast and incorporating their findings into judicial decisions after lunch. Rather, the same forces that shape public opinion also shape the justices' opinions, and people who are elected

Factors Beyond the Water's Edge
Justice Anthony Kennedy, shown here addressing a law class at the New England School of Law in Boston, made a rare reference to other countries' standards in his opinion in the juvenile death penalty case, *Roper v. Simmons.* He feared that the United States would be isolated in the international community if it allowed minors to be executed. The suggestion that the United States should follow the lead of other countries infuriated conservative critics, some of whom called for Kennedy's impeachment.

by the public choose the justices they hope will help them carry out their agenda, usually one that is responsive to what the public wants.

Other political forces than public opinion exert an influence on the Court, however. The influence of the executive branch, discussed earlier, contributes to the high success rate of the solicitor general. Interest groups also put enormous pressure on the Supreme Court, although with varying success. Interest groups are influential in the process of nomination and confirmation of the justices, they file amicus curiae briefs to try to shape the decisions on the certiorari petitions, and they file an increasingly large number of briefs in support of one or the other side when the case is actually reviewed by the Court. According to one scholar, the number of amicus briefs filed by interest groups is increasing. In the 2001 term the average number of such briefs in cases with oral arguments was 5.47 compared to 4.23 during the 1986–1995 terms.[49] Some 149 briefs were filed in connection with the University of Michigan affirmative action cases discussed in Chapter 6.[50] Interest groups also have a role in sponsoring cases when individual petitioners do not have the resources to bring a case before the Supreme Court. The National Association for the Advancement of Colored People (NAACP), the American Civil Liberties Union (ACLU), and the Washington Legal Foundation are examples of groups that have provided funds and lawyers for people seeking to reach the Court. While interest group activity has increased tremendously since the 1980s, researchers are uncertain whether it has paid off in court victories. Their support does seem to help cases get to the Court, however, and they may reap other gains, such as publicity.

A final influence on the justices worth discussing here is the justices' relationships with each other. While they usually (at least in recent years) arrive at their conference meeting with their minds already made up, they cannot afford to ignore one another. It takes five votes to decide a case, and the justices need each other as allies. One scholar who has looked at the disputes among justices over decisions, and who has evaluated the characterization of the Court as "nine scorpions in a bottle," says that the number of disagreements is not noteworthy.[51] On the contrary, what is truly remarkable is how well the justices tend to cooperate, given their close working relationship, the seriousness of their undertaking, and the varied and strong personalities and ideologies that go into the mix.

opinion the written decision of the court that states the judgment of the majority

concurring opinions documents written by justices expressing agreement with the majority ruling but describing different or additional reasons for the ruling

Writing Opinions Once a decision is reached, or sometimes as it is being reached, the writing of the opinion is assigned. The **opinion** is the written part of the decision that states the judgment of the majority of the Court; it is the lasting part of the process, read by law students, lawyers, judges, and future justices. As the living legacy of the case, the written opinions are vitally important for how the nation will understand what the decision means. If, for instance, the opinion is written by the least enthusiastic member of the majority, it will be weaker and less authoritative than if it is written by the most passionate member. The same decision can be portrayed in different ways, can be stated broadly or narrowly, with implications for many future cases or for fewer. If the chief justice is in the majority, it is his or her job to assign the opinion-writing task. Otherwise, the senior member in the majority assigns the opinion. So important is the task that chief justices are known to manipulate their votes, voting with a majority they do not agree with in order to keep the privilege of assigning the opinion to the justice who would write the weakest version of the majority's conclusion.[52] Those justices who agree with the general decision, but for reasons other than or in addition to those stated in the majority opinion, may write **concurring opin-**

ions, and those who disagree may write **dissenting opinions**. These other opinions often have lasting impact as well, especially if the Court changes its mind, as it often does over time and as its composition changes. When such a reversal occurs, the reasons for the about-face are sometimes to be found in the dissent or the concurrence for the original decision.

dissenting opinions documents written by justices expressing disagreement with the majority ruling

THE POLITICAL EFFECTS OF JUDICIAL DECISIONS

The last area in which we can see the Supreme Court as a political actor is in the effects of the decisions it makes. These decisions, despite the best intentions of those who adhere to the philosophy of judicial restraint, often amount to the creation of public policies as surely as do acts of Congress. Chapters 5 and 6, on civil liberties and the struggle for equal rights, make clear that the Supreme Court, at certain points in its history, has taken an active lawmaking role. The history of the Supreme Court's policymaking role is the history of the United States, and we cannot possibly recount it here, but a few examples should show that rulings of the Court have had the effect of distributing scarce and valued resources among people, affecting decisively who gets what, when, and how.[53]

It was the Court, for instance, under the early leadership of John Marshall, that greatly enhanced the power of the federal government over the states by declaring that the Court itself has the power to invalidate state laws (and acts of Congress as well) if they conflict with the Constitution;[54] that state law is invalid if it conflicts with national law;[55] that Congress's powers go beyond those listed in Article I, Section 8, of the Constitution;[56] and that the federal government can regulate interstate commerce.[57] In the early years of the twentieth century, the Supreme Court was an ardent defender of the right of business not to be regulated by the federal government, striking down laws providing for maximum working hours,[58] regulation of child labor,[59] and minimum wages.[60] The role of the Court in making civil rights policy is well known. In 1857 it decided that slaves, even freed slaves, could never be citizens;[61] in 1896 it decided that separate accommodations for whites and blacks were constitutional;[62] and then it reversed itself, declaring separate but equal to be unconstitutional in 1954.[63] It is the Supreme Court that has been responsible for the expansion of due process protection for criminal defendants,[64] for instituting the principle of one person–one vote in drawing legislative districts,[65] and for establishing the right of a woman to have an abortion in the first trimester of pregnancy.[66] Each of these actions has altered the distribution of power in American society in ways that some would argue should be done only by an elected body.

WHO, WHAT, HOW The Supreme Court is a powerful institution, and all Americans have a great stake in what it does. Citizens want to respect the Court and to believe that it is the guardian of American justice and the Constitution.

The president wants to create a legacy and to build political support with respect to his Supreme Court appointments, and he wants to place justices on the Court who reflect his political views and judicial philosophy. Occasionally he also wants to influence the decisions made by the Court.

Members of the Senate also have an interest in getting justices on the Court who reflect their views and the views of their parties. They are also responsive to the wishes of their constituents and to the interest groups that support them. Confirmation hearings can consequently be quite divisive and acrimonious. Interest groups, which want members on the Court to reflect their views, can lobby the Senate before and during the confirmation hearings, and can prepare amicus curiae briefs in support of the parties they endorse in cases before the Court.

Finally, the justices themselves have a good deal at stake in the politics of the Supreme Court. They want a manageable caseload and are heavily reliant on their law clerks and the rules of court procedure. They want to make significant and respected decisions, which means that they have to weigh their own decision-making criteria carefully.

THE CITIZENS AND THE COURTS

In this chapter we have been arguing that the legal system and the American courts are central to the maintenance of social order and conflict resolution and are also a fundamental component of American politics—who gets what, and how they get it. This means that a crucial question for American democracy is, Who takes advantage of this powerful system for allocating resources and values in society? An important component of American political culture is the principle of equality before the law, which we commonly take to mean that all citizens should be treated equally *by* the law, but which also implies that all citizens should have equal access *to* the law. In this concluding section we look at the questions of equal treatment *and* equal access.

EQUAL TREATMENT BY THE CRIMINAL JUSTICE SYSTEM

In Chapter 6, on civil rights, we examined in depth the issue of equality before the law in a constitutional sense. But what about the day-to-day treatment of citizens by the law enforcement and legal systems? Citizens *are* treated differently by these systems according to their race, their income level, and the kinds of crimes they commit. That African Americans and whites have very different views of their treatment by law enforcement and the courts was brought home to Americans by their very different reactions to the verdict in the first, criminal trial of O. J. Simpson. When the "not guilty" verdict was read, a camera caught the faces of black and white students watching television together on a college campus (see photo on page 449). The black faces were elated, the white faces stunned. On reflection, the difference seemed to be this: Blacks have become so used to a law enforcement system that treats them with suspicion and hostility, and some of the Los Angeles police who arrested Simpson were, in fact, so obviously racist, that blacks had no difficulty believing that the evidence against Simpson was trumped up and that the system was out to bring him down simply for being a successful African American man. Whites, on the other hand, who have had far less reason to distrust the police and the courts, saw in the Simpson case a straightforward instance of violent spousal abuse that ended in murder. The "disconnect" on the issue between the races was huge and highlights a compelling truth about our criminal justice system.

African Americans and white Americans do not experience our criminal justice system in the same ways, beginning with what is often the initial contact with the sys-

The Verdict
Reactions of black and white college students in Rock Island, Illinois, to the O. J. Simpson criminal trial verdict announced on October 3, 1995, contrasted sharply, indicating still-potent tensions around the issue of race relations.

tem, the police. In a poll taken during the O. J. Simpson criminal trial, months before the verdict was reached, only 33 percent of blacks said they believed the police testify truthfully, and only 18 percent said they would believe the police over other witnesses at a trial. Sixty-six percent of blacks said they think the criminal justice system is racist, as opposed to only 37 percent of whites.[67] Blacks are often harassed by police or treated with suspicion simply because they are black, and they tend to perceive the police as persecutors rather than protectors.

In fact, blacks are more likely to be arrested than whites, and they are more likely to go to jail, where they serve harsher sentences. In part, this is because blacks are more likely to be poor and urban, and to belong to a socioeconomic class where crime not only doesn't carry the popular sanctions that it does for the middle class, but where it may provide some of the only opportunities for economic advancement. But studies show that racial bias and stereotyping also play a role in the racial disparities in the criminal justice system.[68]

Race is not the only factor that divides American citizens in their experience of the criminal justice system. Income also creates a barrier to equal treatment by the law. Over half of those accused of felonies in the United States have court-appointed lawyers. These lawyers are likely to be less than enthusiastic about these assignments: pay is modest and sometimes irregular. Many lawyers do not like to provide free services *pro bono publico* ("for the public good") because they are afraid it will offend their regular corporate clients. Consequently the quality of the legal representation available to the poor is not the same standard available to those who can afford to pay well. Yale law professor John H. Langbein is scathing on the role of money in determining the legal fate of Americans. He says, "Money is the defining element of our modern American criminal-justice system." The wealthy can afford crackerjack lawyers who can use the "defense lawyer's bag of tricks for sowing doubts, casting aspersions, and coaching witnesses," but "if you are not a person of means, if you cannot afford to engage the elite defense-lawyer industry—and that means most of us—you will be cast into a different system, in which the financial advantages of the state will overpower you and leave you effectively at the mercy of prosecutorial whim."[69]

EQUAL ACCESS TO THE CIVIL JUSTICE SYSTEM

While the issue with respect to the *criminal* justice system is equal treatment, the issue for the *civil* justice system is equal access. Most of us in our lifetimes will have some legal problems. While the Supreme Court has ruled that low-income defendants must be provided with legal assistance in state and federal criminal cases, there is no such guarantee for civil cases. That doesn't mean, however, that less affluent citizens have no recourse for their legal problems. Both public and private legal aid programs exist. Among others, the Legal Services Corporation (LSC), created by Congress in 1974, is a nonprofit organization that provides resources to over 260 legal aid programs around the country. The LSC helps citizens and some immigrants with legal problems such as those concerning housing, employment, family issues, finances, and immigration. This program has been controversial, as conservatives have feared that it has a left-wing agenda. President Reagan tried to phase it out but was rebuffed by Congress. Now under Republican control, Congress has more recently acted to limit the eligibility for LSC aid for immigrants and prisoners.

Does the fact that these services exist mean that more citizens get legal advice? Undoubtedly it does. In 2001, over one million cases were handled by the LSC alone.[70] Still, there is no question that many of the legal needs of the less affluent are not being addressed through the legal system.[71]

Clearly, a bias in the justice system favors those who can afford to take advantage of lawyers and other means of legal assistance. And since people of color and women are much more likely to be poor than are white males (although white men are certainly represented among the poor), the civil justice system ends up discriminating as well.

These arguments do not mean that the U.S. justice system has made no progress toward a more equal dispensation of justice. Without doubt, we have made enormous strides since the days of *Dred Scott*, when the Supreme Court ruled that blacks did not have the standing to bring cases to court, and since the days when lynch mobs dispensed their brand of vigilante justice in the South. The goal of equal treatment *by* and equal access *to* the legal system in America, however, is still some way off.

WHAT'S AT STAKE REVISITED

Since the divisive outcome of *Bush v. Gore*, the nation has calmed down. The pickets and the angry voices are quiet. The stunning national crisis that began with the terrorist attacks on September 11, 2001, has put things into a broader perspective, and a Court-decided election no longer seems as great a danger as the possibility of being caught without any elected leader at all at a critical time. Public opinion polls show that trust in all institutions of government, including the Supreme Court, ran high after September 11, and Bush's legitimacy no longer rests with the Court's narrow majority but rather with the approval ratings that hit unprecedented heights in the aftermath of the terrorist attacks and with his successful reelection in 2004.

But changed national circumstances and subsequent elections do not mean that the Court's unusual and controversial move in resolving the 2000 election should go unanalyzed. What was at stake in this extraordinary case?

First, as Justice Stevens pointed out, the long-term consequences of people's attitudes toward the Court are unknown. The Court, as we have seen, has often engaged in policymaking, and to believe that it is not a political institution would be a serious mistake. But part of its own legitimacy has come from the fact that most people do not perceive it as political, and it is far more difficult now to maintain that illusion. In the immediate aftermath of the decision, the justices, speaking around the country, tried to contain the damage and reassure Americans; some of the dissenting justices emphasized that the decision was not made on political or ideological grounds. Only in the longer term will we see if that case was persuasive to the American public. It would be ironic indeed if the Court moved to ensure Bush's legitimacy at the expense of its own.

Also at stake in such a deeply divided decision was the Court's own internal stability and ability to work together. While the confidentiality of the justices' discussions in arriving at the decision has been well guarded, the decision itself shows that they were acrimonious. Again, in the aftermath, the justices have tried to put a unified front on what was clearly a bitter split. Members of the majority have continued to socialize with dissenters, and as Justice Scalia himself told one audience, "If you can't disagree without hating each other, you better find another profession other than the law."[72] While the stakes in this case may have been more directly political than in most other cases, the members of the Supreme Court are used to disagreeing over important issues and probably handle the level of conflict more easily than do the Americans who look up to them as diviners of truth and right.

Another stake in the pivotal decision was the fundamental issue of federalism itself. The federal courts, as Justice Ruth Bader Ginsburg wrote in her dissent, have a long tradition of deferring to state courts on issues of state law. Indeed, many observers were astounded that the Court agreed to hear the case in the first place, assuming that the justices would have sent it back to be settled

continued

Thinking Outside the Box

- Is justice a matter of enduring principles or the product of a political process?
- What would American politics look like today if Chief Justice John Marshall hadn't adopted the power of judicial review?
- How would the federal judiciary be different if judges were elected rather than appointed?

WHAT'S AT STAKE REVISITED *(continued)*

in Florida. Normally it would have been the ardent conservatives on the Court—Rehnquist, Scalia, and Thomas—whom one would have expected to leap to the defense of states' rights. It has been made clear, however, that the *Bush v. Gore* decision did not signal a reversal on their part. If the opinions of the Court about federalism have changed at all since 2000, it will probably be due more to the imperatives of the war on terrorism, as we suggested in Chapter 4, than to the dictates of the election case.

Some observers argue that the majority of the Court saw something else at stake that led them to set aside their strong beliefs in states' rights and to run the risk that they might be seen as more Machiavelli than King Solomon, more interested in power than wisdom. The majority saw the very security and stability of the nation at stake. Anticipating a long recount of the votes that might even then be inconclusive, they thought it was better to act decisively at the start rather than to wait until a circus-like atmosphere had rendered impossible the most important decision a voting public can make. Whether they were right in doing so, and whether the stakes justified the risks they took, politicians, partisans, and historians will be debating for years to come.

To Sum Up

KEY TERMS

college.cqpress.com/ktr

Key terms, chapter summaries, practice quizzes, Internet links, and other study aids are available on the companion Web site at: republic.cqpress.com.

SUMMARY

republic.cqpress.com

- Laws serve five main functions in a democratic society. They offer security, supply predictability, provide for conflict resolution, reinforce society's values, and provide for the distribution of social costs and benefits.
- American law is based on legislation, but its practice has evolved from a tradition of common law and the use of precedent by judges.
- The American legal system is considered to be both adversarial and litigious in nature. The adversarial nature of our system implies that two opposing sides advocate their position with lawyers in the most prominent roles, while the judge has a relatively minor role in comparison.
- Laws serve many purposes and are classified in different ways. *Substantive laws* cover what we can or cannot do, while *procedural laws* establish the procedures used to enforce law generally. *Criminal laws* concern specific behaviors considered undesirable by the government, while *civil laws* cover interactions between individuals. *Constitutional law* refers to laws included in the Constitution as well as the precedents established over time by judicial decisions relating to these laws. *Statutory laws, administrative laws,* and *executive orders* are established by Congress and state legislatures, the bureaucracy, and the president, respectively.
- The founders were deliberately vague in setting up a court system so as to avoid controversy during the ratification process. The details of design were left to Congress, which established a layering of district, state, and federal courts with differing rules of procedure.
- The Constitution never stated that courts could decide the constitutionality of legislation. The courts gained the extraconstitutional power of judicial review when Chief Justice John Marshall created it in *Marbury v. Madison.*
- The political views of the judge and the jurisdiction of the case can have great impact on the verdict. The rules of the courtroom may vary from one district to another, and the American dual court system often leads to more than one court having authority to deliberate.
- The U.S. Supreme Court reigns at the top of the American court system. It is a powerful institution, revered by the American public but as political an institution as the other two branches of government. Politics is involved in how the Court is chosen and how it decides a case, and in the effects of its decisions.
- While the U.S. criminal justice system has made progress toward a more equal dispensation of justice, minorities and poor Americans have not always experienced equal treatment by the courts or had equal access to them.

PRACTICE QUIZ

republic.cqpress.com

1. According to this chapter, one purpose of courts in a democracy is to

a. make laws that are fair to all.
b. ensure that no innocent person goes to jail.
c. protect the values of democracy.
d. resolve conflicts.
e. protect citizens from the government.

2. In *Federalist* No. 78, Alexander Hamilton argued for establishing an independent judiciary by referring to the judiciary as

a. potentially dangerous to the liberties of citizens.
b. the most important branch of government.
c. the smallest branch of government.
d. the least dangerous branch of government.
e. the most powerful branch of government.

3. The importance of judicial review is that it

a. significantly expanded the power of the courts.
b. established the dual court system.
c. keeps unelected officials from making laws.
d. limits the ability of judges to let their personal opinions guide their rulings.
e. increases the courts' dockets because they now must review all laws.

4. The American dual court system is an application of

a. the English legal system.
b. federalism.
c. checks and balances.
d. separation of powers.
e. judicial review.

5. Concerning equal treatment of citizens by the U.S. criminal justice system,

a. enormous strides have been made since the days of *Dred Scott,* but the goal of equality is still some way off.
b. despite the court reform efforts since the days of *Dred Scott,* little progress has been made toward the goal of equality in our courts.
c. as long as white men are the majority of judges in the American courts, women and minorities can expect little help from the courts in their quest for equality.
d. the efforts to reform our justice system ensure equal justice for all today.
e. the courts have made great strides toward ensuring equality for African Americans but not for women.

SUGGESTED RESOURCES

republic.cqpress.com

Books

Baum, Lawrence. 1998. *American Courts: Process and Policy,* 4th ed. Boston: Houghton Mifflin. An extremely informative text on the American court system and how it influences policy.

Baum, Lawrence. 2004. *The Supreme Court,* 8th ed. Washington, D.C.: CQ Press. The definitive book for understanding the Supreme Court as a political institution.

Bork, Robert H. 1990. *The Tempting of America: The Political Seduction of the Law.* New York: Free Press. One of the country's most controversial Supreme Court nominees discusses his interpretations of the Constitution as well as the events that led to his unsuccessful attempt to sit on the Supreme Court.

Carp, Robert A., Ronald Stidham, and Kenneth L. Manning. 2004. *Judicial Processes in America*, 6th ed. Washington, D.C.: CQ Press. The Constitution was written so that judges would be impartial observers and not be influenced by politics. The authors, however, argue that justices are actually quite involved in the policymaking process.

O'Brien, David M. 1999. *Storm Center: The Supreme Court in American Politics*, 5th ed. New York: Norton. A wonderful narrative on the workings of the Supreme Court in the past as well as the present.

Pacelle, Richard L. 2001. *The Supreme Court in American Politics: The Least Dangerous Branch.* Boulder: Westview Press. Focusing on the role of the Court as a nonelected institution within a representative democracy, Pacelle examines the ways in which appointed judges shape national law.

Rosenberg, Gerald N. 1991. *The Hollow Hope: Can Courts Bring About Social Change?* Chicago: University of Chicago Press. A powerful and somewhat controversial book about the inability of many court rulings to bring significant change to people's lives.

Tushnet, Mark V., ed. 2001. *Thurgood Marshall: His Speeches, Writings, Arguments, Opinions, and Reminiscences.* Chicago: Lawrence Hill Books. A collection of writings and speeches from the trailblazing NAACP lawyer and the first African American Supreme Court justice.

Web Sites

CQ Supreme Court Collection. library.cqpress.com/scc. Have a question about the Supreme Court? You will find your answer here. This is a wonderful collection of information regarding the history of the court, justices, and cases. The site is password-protected, but many schools' libraries have a subscription.

FindLaw. www.findlaw.com. This site is an exceptional source for information on federal court decisions.

U.S. Court. www.uscourts.gov. This Web site offers a plethora of information on the federal courts.

Movies

***First Monday in October.* 1981.** A romantic comedy about the first woman appointed to the Supreme Court. This movie was released the same year that Sandra Day O'Connor became the first woman to sit on the Court.

***Twelve Angry Men.* 1957.** A classic movie about the tough decisions that a jury has to make as it deliberates the verdict in a murder trial.

Who decides? If the U.S. Constitution allowed direct democracy, citizens could vote on public policy at the national level. France, for example, held a national referendum on whether to ratify the European Union constitution (right). But American public policy is decided primarily by Congress, typically with the options discussed and narrowed in committees, like this meeting of the House Government Reform Committee (below), before legislation is decided by roll calls of members of the House and Senate, but not the American voter.

PUBLIC OPINION

11

WHAT'S AT STAKE?

How much responsibility do you want to take for the way you are governed? Most of us are pretty comfortable with the idea that we should vote for our *rulers* (although we don't all jump at the chance to do it), but how about voting on the *rules*? As we saw in Chapter 4, citizens of some states—California, for instance—have become used to being asked for their votes on new state laws. But what about national politics—do you know enough or care enough to vote on laws for the country as a whole, just as if you were a member of Congress or a senator? Should we be governed more by public opinion than by the opinions of our elected leaders? This is the question that drives the debate about whether U.S. citizens should be able to participate in such forms of direct democracy as the national referendum or initiative.

Not only do many states (twenty-seven out of fifty) employ some form of direct democracy, but many other countries do as well. In the past several years alone, voters in Ireland were asked to decide about the legality of divorce and abortion, in Bermuda about national independence, in Norway and Sweden about joining the European Union, in Iraq about supporting Saddam Hussein (there was no real freedom of choice in this vote), and in Bosnia about peace.

In 1995, former senator Mike Gravel, D-Alaska, proposed that the United States join many of the world's nations in adopting a national *plebiscite,* or popular vote on policy. He argued that Americans should support a national initiative he called "Philadelphia II" (to evoke "Philadelphia I," which was, of course, the Constitutional Convention), which would set up procedures for direct popular participation in national lawmaking.[1] Such participation could take place through the ballot box (the Swiss go to the polls four times a year to vote on national policy) or even electronically, as some have suggested, with people voting on issues by computer at home. Experts agree that the technology exists for at-home participation in government. And public opinion is overwhelmingly in favor of proposals to let Americans vote for or against major national issues before they become law.[2]

Do you agree with Gravel and the roughly three-quarters of Americans who support more direct democracy at the national level? Should we have rule by public opinion in the United States? How would the founders have responded to this proposal? And what would be the consequences for American government if a national plebiscite were passed? Just what is at stake in the issue of direct democracy at the national level?

It is fashionable these days to denounce the public opinion polls that claim to tell us what the American public thinks about this or that political issue. The American people themselves are skeptical—65 percent of them think that the polls are "right only some of the time" or "hardly ever right."[3] (You might believe that finding, or you might not.) Politicians can be leery of polls, too—or even downright scornful of them. Disdainful of the Clinton years, when the president's team of pollsters openly tested the public on various issues, including his approval ratings, the Bush administration has been cagey about the fact that they watch polls at all. Bush himself frequently says things like "I really don't worry about polls or focus groups; I do what I think is right."[4] Matthew Dowd, the Bush administration's chief of polling at the Republican National Committee, echoed that stance with an emphatic "We don't poll policy positions. Ever."[5]

Of course, the Bush administration does look at polls, and conducts them too, just like every other administration since the advent of modern polling. They are just better at distancing Bush from them, but the polls are inevitable. When in 2002 a reporter visited Karl Rove, Bush's chief political adviser, and asked about the impact of the corporate scandals of the time on Bush's effectiveness as president, Rove pulled out a bundle of polls and started reading off data to support his claim that people continued to support Bush. Then he caught the reporter's quizzical look. "'Not that we spend a lot of time on these,' he said quickly. . . ."[6]

These reactions to public opinion raise an interesting question. What is so bad about being ruled by the polls in a democracy, which, after all, is supposed to be ruled by the people? If politics is about who gets what, and how they get it, shouldn't we care about what the "who" thinks? **Public opinion** is just what the public thinks. It is the aggregation, or collection, of individual attitudes and beliefs on one or more issues at any given time. **Public opinion polls** are nothing more than scientific efforts to measure that opinion—to estimate what an entire group of people think about an issue by asking a smaller sample of the group for their opinions. If the sample is large enough and chosen properly, we have every reason to believe that it will provide a reliable estimate of the whole. Today's technology gives us the ability to keep a constant finger on the pulse of America, and to know what its citizens are thinking at almost any given time. And yet, at least some Americans seem torn about the role of public opinion in government today. On the one hand, we want to believe that what we think matters, but on the other hand, we'd like to think that our elected officials are guided by unwavering standards and principles.

public opinion the collective attitudes and beliefs of individuals on one or more issues

public opinion polls scientific efforts to estimate what an entire group thinks about an issue by asking a smaller sample of the group for its opinion

In this chapter we argue that public opinion *is* important for the proper functioning of democracy, that the expression of what citizens think and what they want is a prerequisite for their ability to use the system and its rules to get what they want from it. But the quality of the public's opinion on politics, and the ways that it actually influences policy, may surprise us greatly. Specifically, in this chapter you will learn about

- the role of public opinion in a democracy
- how public opinion can be measured
- where our opinions come from
- what our opinions are—do we think like the "ideal democratic citizen"?
- the relationship of citizenship to public opinion

THE ROLE OF PUBLIC OPINION IN A DEMOCRACY

Public opinion is important in a democracy for at least two reasons. The first reason is normative: we believe public opinion *should* influence what government does. The second is empirical: a lot of people actually behave as though public opinion does matter, and to the degree that they measure, record, and react to it, it does indeed become a factor in American politics.

WHY PUBLIC OPINION *OUGHT* TO MATTER

The presence of "the people" is pervasive in the documents that create and support the American government. In the Declaration of Independence, Thomas Jefferson wrote that a just government must get its powers from "the consent of the governed." Our Constitution begins, "We, the People. . . ." And Abraham Lincoln's Gettysburg Address hails our nation as "government of the people, by the people, and for the people." What all of this tells us is that the very legitimacy of the U.S. government, like that of all other democracies, rests on the idea that government exists to serve the interests of its citizens.

Since the beginning of the Republic, there has been a shift in our institutions toward a greater role for the citizenry in politics. We can see this in the passage of the Seventeenth Amendment to the Constitution (1913), which took the election of the U.S. Senate from the state legislatures and gave it to the citizens of the states. We can see it in the altered practice of the electoral college. Once supposed to be a group of enlightened citizens who would exercise independent judgment, in recent decades it almost always follows the vote of the people (with the dramatic exception of the 2000 election). We can see it in state politics, where the instruments of direct democracy—the initiative, referendum, and recall—allow citizens to vote on policies and even remove officials from office before their terms are up. These changes reflect views like those of political scientist V. O. Key, who observed, "Unless mass views have some place in the shaping of policy, all talk about democracy is nonsense."[7]

But how to determine whose views should be heard? As we saw in Chapter 1, different theories of democracy prescribe different roles for "the people," in part because these theories disagree about how competent the citizens of a country are to govern themselves. Elitists suspect that citizens are too ignorant or ill informed to be trusted with major political decisions; pluralists trust groups of citizens to be competent on those issues in which they have a stake, but they think that individuals may be too busy to gather all the information they need to make informed decisions, and proponents of participatory democracy have faith that the people are both smart enough and able to gather enough information to be effective decision makers.

As Americans, we are also somewhat confused about what we think the role of the democratic citizen should be. We introduced these conflicting notions of citizenship in Chapter 1. One view, which describes what we might call the *ideal democratic citizen,* is founded on the vision of a virtuous citizen activated by concern for the common good, who recognizes that democracy carries obligations as well as rights. In this familiar model, a citizen should be attentive to and informed about politics; have reasonably formed, stable opinions on the issues; exhibit political tolerance and a willingness to compromise; and practice high levels of participation in civic activities.

A competing view of American citizenship holds that Americans are *apolitical, self-interested actors.* According to this view, Americans are almost the opposite of the ideal citizen: inattentive and ill informed, easily manipulated, politically intolerant and rigid, and unlikely to get involved in political life.

We argue in this chapter, as we have earlier, that the American public displays both of these visions of citizenship. But we also argue that there are mechanisms in American politics that buffer the impact of apolitical, self-interested behavior, so that government by public opinion does not have disastrous effects on the American polity. Although it may seem like some kind of magician's act, we show that Americans as a *group* often behave as ideal citizens, even though as *individuals* they do not.

WHY PUBLIC OPINION *DOES* MATTER

Politicians and media leaders act as though they agree with Key's conclusion, which is the practical reason public opinion matters in American politics. Elected politicians, for example, overwhelmingly believe that the public is keeping tabs on them. When voting on major bills, members of Congress worry quite a lot about public opinion in their districts.[8] Presidents, too, pay close attention to public opinion. In fact, recent presidents have invested major resources in having an in-house public opinion expert whose regular polls are used as an important part of presidential political strategies. And, indeed, the belief that the public is paying attention is not totally unfounded. Although the public does not often act as if it pays attention or cares very much about politics, it can change its mind and act decisively if the provocation is sufficient. In the 1998 midterm election, after Republicans repeatedly flew in the face of public opinion polls and proceeded with plans to impeach President Clinton, they suffered unexpected losses.

Keeping in Touch
Members of Congress regularly face the problem that voters feel they have "lost touch" with their districts. They work hard to counter this perception with speeches, town hall meetings, and other appearances in their districts. Here, Rep. Loretta Sanchez (center) gets an earful from one of her constituents while making the rounds in Santa Ana, one of the cities in her Orange County, California, district.

Politicians are not alone in their tendency to monitor public opinion as they do their jobs. Leaders of the media also focus on public opinion, making huge investments in polls and devoting considerable coverage to reporting what the public is thinking. Polls are used to measure public attitudes toward all sorts of things. Of course, we are familiar with "horse race" polls that ask about people's voting intentions and lend drama to media coverage of electoral races. Sometimes these polls themselves become the story the media covers. With the availability of a twenty-four-hour news cycle and the need to find something to report on all the time, it is not surprising that the media have fastened on their own polling as a newsworthy subject. Public opinion, or talk about it, seems to pervade the modern political arena.

WHO, WHAT, HOW Public opinion is important in theory—in our views about how citizens and politicians *should* behave—and in practice—how they actually *do* behave. American political culture contains two views of citizenship, an idealized view and a self-interested view. These two views seem to be at odds, and

Americans are ambivalent about the role public opinion should play in politics. The founders of the American polity developed constitutional rules to hold the power of citizens in check. Many of those rules, however, have changed over the intervening two hundred years as consensus has grown that citizens should play a stronger role in government.

Politicians and the media act as if they think the public is very powerful indeed. Politicians usually try to play it safe by responding to what the public wants, or what they think it will want in the future, while the media often cover public opinion as if it were a story in itself, and not just the public's reaction to a story.

MEASURING AND TRACKING PUBLIC OPINION

While public opinion polls are sometimes discounted by politicians who don't like their results, the truth is that today most social scientists and political pollsters conduct public opinion surveys according to the highest standards of scientific accuracy, and their results are for the most part reliable. In this section we look at the process of scientific polling and examine how we can tell when polls are flawed. We also acknowledge an approach to measuring public opinion that politicians were using long before the beginning of modern scientific polling: direct experience. Today, many politicians still base their reading of the public's will on their own experience, using scientific surveys or polls only to supplement these findings.

LEARNING ABOUT PUBLIC OPINION WITHOUT POLLS

You undoubtedly know what your friends and family think about many issues, even though you have never conducted an actual poll on their beliefs. We all reside in social communities that bring us into contact with various types of people. Simply by talking with them, we get a sense of their ideas and preferences. Politicians, whose careers depend on voters, are necessarily good talkers and good listeners. They learn constituent opinion from the letters, phone calls, and email they receive. They visit constituents, make speeches, attend meetings, and talk with community leaders and interest group representatives. Elected politicians also pick up signals from the size of the crowds that turn out to hear them speak and from the way those crowds respond to different themes. All of these interactions give them a sense of what matters to people and how citizens are reacting to news events, economic trends, and social changes. Direct contact with people puts politicians in touch with concerns that could be missed entirely by a scientifically designed public opinion poll. That poll might focus on issues of national news that are on the minds of national politicians or pollsters, while citizens may be far more concerned about the building of a dam upriver from their city or about teacher layoffs in their school district.

Thus politicians are fond of saying that they do not believe in polls or that they do not trust them. Perhaps what they are actually saying is that polls are no substitute for their own sampling of what is on their constituents' minds. It is natural to want to rely on our personal experiences with people (see Figure 11.1).

While informal soundings of public opinion may be useful to a politician for some purposes, they are not very reliable for gauging how everyone in a given population thinks because they are subject to sampling problems. A **sample** is the portion of the

sample the portion of the population that is selected to participate in a poll

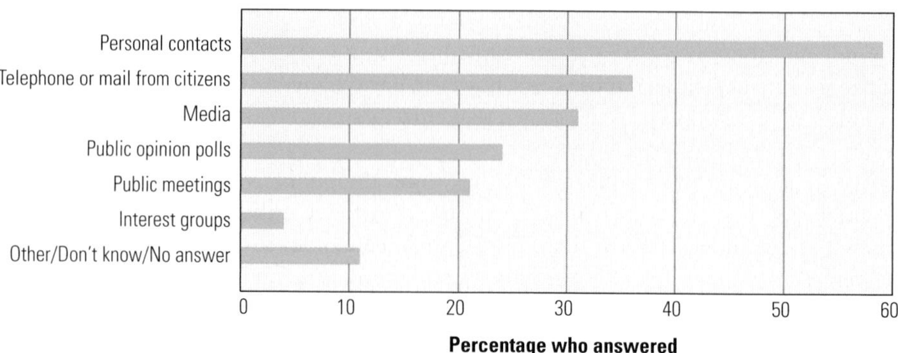

FIGURE 11.1

Congressional Sources of Public Opinion Information

A survey of members of Congress found that they use a mix of sources to learn about public opinion, with opinion polls being fairly far down the list.

Note: Eighty-one members of Congress were asked, "What is your principal source of information about the way the public feels about issues?"

Source: Data from the Pew Research Center for the People and the Press, Trust in Government Study, October 1997 and February 1998.

population a politician or pollster surveys on an issue. Based on what that sample says, the surveyor then makes an estimation of what everyone else thinks. This may sound like hocus-pocus, but if the sample is scientifically chosen to be representative of the whole population, sampling actually works very well. Pollsters are trained in how to select a truly random sample—that is, one that does not overrepresent any portion of the population and whose responses can therefore be safely generalized to the whole. When a sample is not chosen scientifically and has too many people in it from one portion of the population, we say it has a problem of **sample bias**. When trying to judge public opinion from what they hear among their supporters and friendly interest groups, politicians must allow for the bias of their own sampling. If they are not effective at knowing how those they meet differ from the full public, they will get a misleading idea of public opinion.

sample bias the effect of having a sample that does not represent all segments of the population

THE DEVELOPMENT OF MODERN PUBLIC OPINION POLLS

The scientific poll as we know it today was developed in the 1930s. However, newspapers and politicians have been trying to read public opinion as long as we have had democracies. The first efforts at actually counting opinions were the **straw polls**, dating from the first half of the nineteenth century and continuing in a more scientific form today.[9] The curious name for these polls comes from the fact that a straw, thrown up into the air, will indicate which way the wind is blowing.[10] These polls were designed to help politicians predict which way the political winds were blowing and, more specifically, who would win an upcoming election. Before the modern science of sampling was well understood, straw polls were conducted by a variety of hit-or-miss methods, and though their results were often correct, they were sometimes spectacularly wrong.

straw polls polls that attempt to determine who is ahead in a political race

The experience of the *Literary Digest* illustrates this point dramatically. The *Literary Digest* was a highly popular magazine that conducted straw polls in the 1920s and

1930s. It mailed millions of questionnaires during presidential election campaigns asking recipients who they planned to vote for and then tabulated the mailed-in results. The *Digest* polls were quite successful in predicting the election winners in 1920 through 1932 and received wide recognition and publicity. However, in 1936 the magazine predicted that President Franklin Roosevelt would be defeated by Alf Landon by a wide margin. Of course, Roosevelt won handily. The poll was wrong for several reasons. First, people change their minds often during an election campaign, with some remaining undecided until the final days, but the *Digest* poll was unable to record last-minute voting decisions. Second, there was a clear (in retrospect) sample bias; the *Digest* poll had included too many Republican voters in its sample because it drew names from lists of automobile registrations, telephone directories, and different clubs and organizations. The sample thus overrepresented the middle-class, financially well-off population, since at that time most families could not afford cars or telephones. Although this bias had not been a problem in the past, by 1936 these voters were becoming more identified with the Republican Party.[11] The sample bias was compounded because respondents had to mail in their questionnaires. Not only were they not representative to begin with, but the more political, intense, and involved voters who self-selected themselves by mailing back the questionnaire further skewed the results.

Polling errors led to an even more well-known polling fiasco in 1948, one whose results were captured in a photograph of a smiling and victorious President Harry S. Truman holding up a copy of the *Chicago Daily Tribune,* whose headline declared "Dewey Defeats Truman." By this time, pollsters had learned more about sampling requirements but not enough about changing voter minds. Having polled the public early on and established that Dewey held a substantial lead, few polling organizations bothered to follow up. The *Tribune* used old data, and polls again failed to capture last-minute changes in voters' decisions.

Oops!
Harry S. Truman laughed last and loudest after one of the biggest mistakes in American journalism. The *Chicago Daily Tribune* relied on a two-week-old Gallup poll to predict the outcome of the 1948 presidential race, damaging polling's image for decades. With polls today conducted all the way up to election day—and exit polls tracking how ballots are actually cast—similar goofs are highly unlikely.

THE QUALITY OF OPINION POLLING TODAY

Today, polling is big business and a relatively precise science. Political polls are actually a small portion of the marketing business, which tries to gauge what people want and are willing to buy. Many local governments also conduct surveys to find out what their citizens want and how satisfied they are with various municipal services. All polls face the same two challenges, however: (1) getting a good sample, which entails both sampling the right number of people and eliminating sample bias, and (2) asking questions that yield valid results.

How Big Does a Sample Need to Be? No sample is perfect in matching the population from which it is drawn, but it should be close. Confronted with a critic who did not trust the notion of sampling, George Gallup is said to have responded, "Okay, if you do not like the idea of a sample, then the next time you go for a blood test, tell them to take it all!" While it might seem counterintuitive, statisticians have determined that a sample of only 1,000 to 2,000 people can be very representative of the entire 300 million residents of the United States.

sampling error a number that indicates within what range the results of a poll are accurate

Sampling error is a number that indicates how reliable the poll is; based on the size of the sample, it tells within what range the actual opinion of the whole population would fall. Typically a report of a poll will say that its "margin of error" is plus or minus 3 percent. That means that, based on sampling theory, there is a 95 percent chance that the real figure for the whole population is within 3 percent of that reported. For instance, when a poll reports a presidential approval rating of 60 percent and a 3 percent margin of error, this means that there is a 95 percent chance that between 57 and 63 percent of the population approve of the president's job performance. A poll that shows one candidate leading another by 2 percent of the projected vote is really too close to call since the 2 percent might be due to sampling error. The larger the sample, the smaller the sampling error, but samples larger than 2,000 add very little in the way of reliability. Surveying more people, say 5,000, is much more expensive and time-consuming, but does not substantially reduce the sampling error.

random samples samples chosen in such a way that any member of the population being polled has an equal chance of being selected

Dealing With the Problem of Sample Bias Because of fiascos like the *Literary Digest* poll, modern polls now employ systematic **random samples** of the populations whose opinions they want to describe. In a systematic random sample, everyone should have the same chance to be interviewed. Since almost all households now have telephones, it is possible to get a representative sample in telephone polls. Some pollsters argue that respondents are more candid and cooperative when they are interviewed in person. But achieving a representative sample for in-person interviewing is much more difficult since it requires interviewers to make personal contact with specific individuals chosen in advance.

Because reputable survey firms use scientific sampling strategies, sampling bias is not generally a problem that plagues modern pollsters, but there is one way it can sneak in through the back door. The chief form of sample bias in current surveys is nonresponse. Over the years, response rates to telephone surveys have dropped a good deal so that in current surveys sometimes as few as one-quarter of those intended to be included in surveys actually participate. The reasons for this drop include hostility to telemarketers; the increasing use of Caller ID; the increasingly common use of cell phones (which by law pollsters are banned from calling); and the simple fact that people are busier, are working more, and have less time and inclination to talk to strangers on the phone.[12] Surprisingly, studies of the decreasing response rates, which one might think would cause serious sample biases, find that well-constructed telephone polls continue to provide accurate information on citizens' responses to most questions about politics and issues. The major difference found is that the most reluctant respondents—those likely to be missed in a typical survey—seem to be less racially tolerant than the average population, meaning that a standard survey might yield responses that are slightly more liberal on racial matters than the population as a whole.[13]

The Importance of Asking the Right Questions Asking the right questions in surveys is a surprisingly tricky business. Researchers have emphasized three main points with respect to constructing survey questions.

- *Respondents should be asked about things they know and have thought about.* Otherwise, they will often try to be helpful but will give responses based on whatever cues they can pick up from the context of the interview or the particular question. For example, some researchers from the University of Cincinnati did a local survey in which they asked respondents whether they favored a nonexistent "Public Affairs Act of 1974." Almost a quarter of the respondents were willing to give an opinion![14] However, researchers also have found that if questions provide a "don't know" option, only about 10 percent of respondents will choose it.[15]
- *Questions should not be ambiguous.* One highly controversial example comes from a 1992 survey that reported that over a third of the American public either did not believe or doubted that the Holocaust had even happened.[16] One newspaper called the American public "willfully stupid"; Holocaust survivor, author, and Nobel laureate Elie Wiesel was "shocked" by the results.[17] The uproar was largely the product of a bad question, however. Respondents were asked, "Does it seem possible or does it seem impossible to you that the Nazi extermination of the Jews never happened?" To say that one believed the Holocaust happened, the respondent had to agree to a double negative—that it was "impossible" that it "never" happened. There was plenty of room for confusion. Other respondents were asked a more straightforward version of the question: "The term *Holocaust* usually refers to the killing of millions of Jews in Nazi death camps during World War II. Do you doubt that the Holocaust actually happened, or not?" With this wording, only 9 percent doubted the Holocaust and 4 percent were unsure.[18]
- *Beware of questions that use words with loaded meaning.* For instance, do a majority of Americans support affirmative action? It depends on how you ask the question. Notice how modest changes in question wording in Figure 11.2 result in

Doonesbury BY GARRY TRUDEAU

Comparison of results from two versions of affirmative action questions

Version A

Question: Do you favor or oppose affirmative action programs to help blacks, women, and other minorities get better jobs and education?

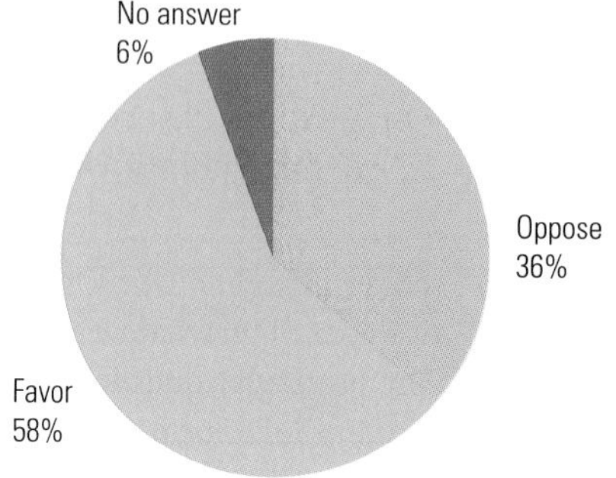

Version B

Question: Do you favor or oppose affirmative action programs which give special preferences to qualified blacks, women, and other minorities?

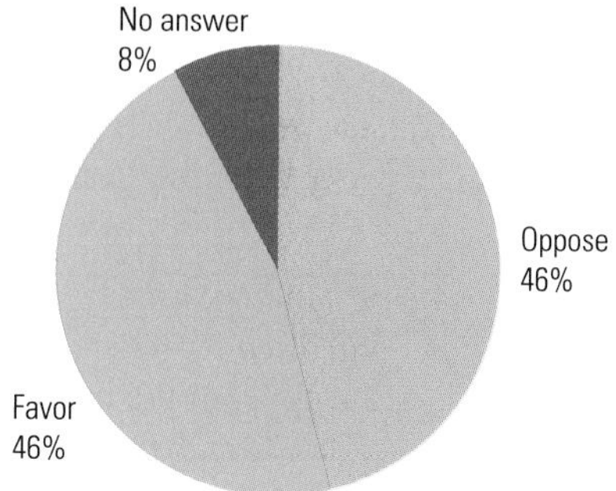

FIGURE 11.2
Asking the Right Question

Source: Data from the Pew Research Center for the People and the Press, August 24, 1995.

different answers. A majority is favorable to affirmative action when it is defined as helping minorities to get better jobs and education, but not when the phrase "special preferences" is used. "Special preferences" signals to Americans that people will be treated differently, and thus perhaps unfairly. Even though the goal of affirmative action is usually to ensure equal treatment, the "special preferences" wording tapped into deep cultural values about fairness and caused Americans to reject a policy they might otherwise have approved. Sometimes even subtle changes in question wording can produce significant apparent differences in public opinion.

There are still other considerations that pollsters should take into account. Studies have shown, for instance, that the order in which questions are asked can change the results, as can even such a simple factor as the number of choices offered for responses. Clearly, good surveys can tell us a good deal about public opinion, but they will hardly ever produce a final word. And, of course, just as soon as they might, public opinion would probably shift again in any case.

TYPES OF POLLS

Many people and organizations report the results of what they claim are measures of public opinion. To make sense of this welter of claims, it is useful to know some basic polling terminology and the characteristics of different types of polls.

National Polls National polls are efforts to measure public opinion within a limited period of time using a national representative sample. The time period of interviewing may be as short as a few hours, with the results reported the next day, or extended over a period of weeks, as in academic polls. The underlying goal, however, is the same: to achieve scientifically valid measures of the knowledge, beliefs, or attitudes of the adult population.

Many national polls are conducted by the media in conjunction with a professional polling organization. These polls regularly measure attitudes on some central item, such as how the public feels about the job that the president or Congress is doing. Several of these organizations make their polls available through the Internet.[19] Some of the polls that regularly collect data in large national samples include the following: the ABC News/*Washington Post* poll, the CBS News/*New York Times* poll, the NBC News/*Wall Street Journal* poll, the CNN/*USA Today*/Gallup poll, and the *Los Angeles Times* poll. Other polling organizations provide more in-depth surveys than these media polls. Some are designed to see how people feel about particular topics or to find out how people develop attitudes and evaluate politics more generally. Two of these in particular, the General Social Survey and the National Election Studies, provide much of the data for academic research on public opinion in America (and much of what we say in this chapter about public opinion).

Campaign Polls A lot of polling is done for candidates in their efforts to win election or reelection. Most well-funded campaigns begin with a **benchmark poll**, taken of a sample of the population, or perhaps just of the potential voters, in a state or district to gather baseline information on how well the candidate is known, what issues people associate with the candidate, and what issues people are concerned about, as well as assessments of the opposition, especially if the opponent is an incumbent. Benchmark polls are instrumental in designing campaign strategy.

benchmark poll initial poll on a candidate and issues on which campaign strategy is based and against which later polls are compared

Presidential campaigns and a few of the better-funded statewide races (for example, those for governor or U.S. senator) conduct **tracking polls**. These follow changes in attitudes toward the candidates by having ongoing sets of interviews. Such daily samples are too small to allow reliable generalization, but groups of these interviews averaged over time are extremely helpful. The oldest interviews are dropped as newer ones are added, providing a dynamic view of changes in voters' preferences and perceptions. A sudden change in a tracking poll might signal that the opponent's new ads are doing damage or that interest group endorsements are having an effect. Campaign strategies can be revised accordingly. More recently the news media have undertaken tracking polls as part of their election coverage. In the 2004 presidential election, tracking polls were conducted by several polling organizations and were reported widely in the media. Several tracking polls showed a very close race with none quite anticipating the size of Bush's three-percentage-point victory on election night.

tracking polls ongoing series of surveys that follow changes in public opinion over time

On election night the media commentators often "call" a race, declaring one candidate a winner, sometimes as soon as the voting booths in a state are closed but well before the official vote count has been reported. These predictions are made, in part, on the basis of **exit polls**, which are short questionnaires administered to samples of voters in selected precincts after they vote. Exit polls focus on vote choice, a few demographic questions, some issue preferences, and evaluations of candidates. In addition to helping the networks predict the winners early, exit polls are used by network broadcasters and journalists to add explanatory and descriptive material to their election coverage. Because exit polls are expensive to conduct, in recent years media organizations have banded together to share the costs of conducting national exit polls.

exit polls election-related questions asked of voters right after they vote

Exit polls, however, have proved embarrassingly faulty in recent elections, leading news agencies to become very cautious in how the results are used. In 2000, flawed data led the networks to mistakenly "call" Florida for Vice President Al Gore (which

Andrew Kohut

Andrew Kohut knows what you're thinking. In fact, he knows what we're all thinking, and it's a little disconcerting to sit across the desk from him and realize you haven't got a clue what *he's* thinking. Dapper and reserved, this reader of the nation's mind doesn't give away much himself, though no one who has heard his grave, scholarly voice on National Public Radio explaining us to ourselves can doubt his fascination with the way Americans view politics.

"One of the many lessons of the war in Vietnam is you can't run a war without public support."

That's because Kohut is the president of the Pew Research Center, an independent research organization that studies public opinion. He's been with Pew for over ten years, but he's been involved with public opinion far longer than that. He "grew up" in the Gallup organization, he says, and was president there from 1979 to 1989.

George Gallup, Gallup's founder, was unapologetic about the mission of his organization—"The best guarantee for the maintenance of a vigorous democratic life lies not in concealing what people think, but in trying to find out what their ultimate purposes are, and in seeking to incorporate these purposes into legislation."[1] They've been trying to uncover the people's "ultimate purposes" for more than seventy years. Kohut saw Gallup as playing a great public role and providing a great service, and it's clear he sees his own role in a similar light.

He says of the connection between public opinion and governance: "Giving the voice to how people feel about things, I think, is of extraordinary importance, for leaders to have a better understanding as to how to get their ideas across and to get a different view of, a better view of, how the public sees things. In part I think I was influenced by when I grew up. I came of age in the Vietnam era. And Vietnam was one of those classic cases where public opinion was ignored. And one of the many lessons of the war in Vietnam is you can't run a war without public support. And that war as much as anything was lost because the battle for public support was lost."

would have meant that he'd won the presidency), then to switch the call to George W. Bush, and finally, late in the evening, to conclude that the state was too close to call at all. In 2002 a software malfunction meant that no exit poll results were available for election night coverage. Finally, in 2004, early exit polls leaked by bloggers on the Internet erroneously suggested that Sen. John Kerry was winning the election, and even the final exit polls showed a Kerry bias larger than expected from sampling error—apparently because Kerry voters were more eager to participate in the exit polls.

Exit poll defenders argue that these polls are being misused by the public and the media; they are not intended to predict the elections in progress but to explain the vote after the election by providing information on what groups voted for which candidates. The challenges faced by those conducting exit polls are the same as those the preelection pollsters must contend with: it is very difficult to obtain a fully representative sample of voters, especially when one candidate's supporters disproportionately refuse to be interviewed. As a result of these problems, networks are now relatively cautious in declaring winners without corroborating evidence from the actual vote returns; there were no mistakes in "calling" the states in the 2004 presidential election.[20]

His conviction that the study of public opinion is an essential public service is reflected in his involvement in the *Los Angeles Times*'s effort in the 1980s to show the journalistic community how the public felt about "the so-called emerging crisis of confidence in the media." That poll expanded and turned into the Times Mirror Center for the People and the Press, where Kohut stayed until 1995. Moving the organization to the nonpartisan Pew Center broadened its mission and extended its reach to news outlets that might have felt constrained to use the services of a competitor.

His work now is founded on two ideas: that public opinion plays an important role in the course of the country's events and that, to understand what the public feels, more than one or two questions need to be asked on an issue. "You wouldn't try to judge me or I wouldn't try to judge you on the basis of a one- or two-question conversation about a subject. We want to go into a little more depth." And so he dips deeply into the national psyche. "What's fun about what I do, I think, is discovering some new truths about things. Things that surprise me, and [make me] say, 'Wow, look at that! Isn't that surprising?' And also telling a good story about the way the public is reacting to what's happening in the world." Here are some of his other thoughts:

On how he got started in public service:

I think people who achieve things look for opportunities and when they see these opportunities they seize them. And the early part of my career was building the Gallup organization, a commercial enterprise. It wasn't necessarily public service. I got to a certain point in my career when I thought this would be a marvelous thing to do. And part of it was that I didn't have a great economic imperative, I certainly needed a salary and needed money but I didn't need to get rich, didn't want to get rich—that wasn't my objective.

On keeping the republic:

Well, I think the most important thing to do is to not take [our] democracy and rights for granted. They were hard fought and we are a very distinctive, we remain a distinctive society—far from a perfect society—but the amount of personal freedom that we have, the amount of opportunity that we have, is a consequence of a lot of sacrifice and a system that works remarkably well. Respect that. Participate in it and don't think it's something that we're owed.

1. George Horace Gallup and Saul Forbes Rae, *The Pulse of Democracy* (New York: Simon & Schuster, 1940).

Source: Andrew Kohut spoke with Christine Barbour on March 11, 2005.

Pseudo-Polls A number of opinion studies are wrongly presented as polls. More deceptive than helpful, these pseudo-polls range from potentially misleading entertainment to outright fraud. Self-selection polls are those, like the *Literary Digest*'s, in which respondents, by one mechanism or another, select themselves into a survey rather than being chosen randomly. Examples of self-selection polls include viewer or listener call-in polls and Internet polls. These polls tell you only how a portion of the media outlet's audience (self-selected in the first place by their choice of a particular outlet) who care enough to call in or click a mouse (self-selected in the second place by their willingness to expend effort) feel about an issue.

When the CNN web site asks users to record their views on whether the United States should engage in military action with Iraq, for instance, the audience is limited, first, to those who own or have access to computers; second, to those who care enough about the news to be on the CNN site; and third, to those who want to pause in their news reading for the short time it takes for their vote to be counted and the results to appear on the screen. Further, nothing stops individuals from recording multiple votes to make the count seem greater than it is. Results of such polls are likely to be highly unrepresentative of the population as a whole; they should be presented with caution and interpreted with a great deal of skepticism.

push polls polls that ask for reactions to hypothetical, often false, information in order to manipulate public opinion

A second and increasingly common kind of pseudo-poll is the push poll, which poses as a legitimate information-seeking effort but is really a shady campaign trick to change people's attitudes. **Push polls** present false information, often in a hypothetical form, and ask respondents to react to it. The false information, presented as if true or at least possible, can raise doubts about a candidate and even change a person's opinion about him or her. Insofar as they have a legitimate function, "push questions" are used on a limited basis by pollsters and campaign strategists to find out how voters might respond to negative information about the candidate or the opposition. This is the kind of information that might be gathered in a benchmark poll, for example. Less scrupulous consultants, working for both political parties, however, sometimes use the format as a means of propaganda. As an example, a pollster put this question to Florida voters:

> Please tell me if you would be more likely or less likely to vote for Lt. Governor Buddy MacKay if you knew that Lt. Gov. Buddy MacKay plans to implement a new early-release program for violent offenders who have served a mere 60 percent of their sentences if he is elected governor?[21]

MacKay had no such plans, and to imply that he did was false. Moreover, the goal of this "poll" was not to learn anything but rather to plant negative information in the minds of thousands of people. By posing as a legitimate poll, the push poll seeks to trick respondents into accepting the information as truthful and thereby to influence the vote. Such polls are often conducted without any acknowledgment of who is sponsoring them (usually the opponents of the person being asked about). The target candidate often never knows that such a poll is being conducted, and because push polls frequently pop up the weekend before an election, he or she cannot rebut the lies or half-truths. A key characteristic of push polls is that they seek to call as many voters as they can with little regard to the usual care and quality of a legitimate representative sample. "Push polling for me is marketing," said Floyd Ciruli, a Denver-based pollster. "You call everybody you can call and tell them something that may or may not be true."[22]

Legislation against push polling has been introduced in several state legislatures, and the practice has been condemned by the American Association of Political Consultants.[23] There is a real question, however, about whether efforts to regulate push polls can survive a First Amendment test before the Supreme Court.

HOW ACCURATE ARE POLLS?

For many issues, such as attitudes toward the environment or presidential approval, we have no objective measure against which to judge the accuracy of public opinion polls. With elections, however, polls do make predictions, and we can tell by the vote count whether the polls are correct. The record of most polls is, in general, quite good. For example, all of the major polls have predicted the winner of presidential elections correctly since 1980, except in the incredibly close 2000 election. They are not correct to the percentage point, nor would we expect them to be, given the known levels of sampling error, preelection momentum shifts, and the usual 15 percent of voters who claim to remain "undecided" up to the last minute. Polls taken closer to Election Day typically become more accurate as they catch more of the late deciders.[24] Even in the 2000 presidential election, most of the polls by election eve had done a fairly good job of predicting the tightness of the race. Read "*Consider the Source:* How to Be a Critical Poll Watcher" for some tips on how you can gauge the reliability of poll results you come across.

WHO, WHAT, HOW Citizens, politicians and their staffs, the media, and professional polling organizations are all interested in the business of measuring and tracking public opinion. Citizens rely on polls to monitor elections and get a sense of where other Americans stand on particular issues. Their interest is in fair polling techniques that produce reliable results.

In order to win elections, politicians must know what citizens think and what they want from their officials. They need to know how various campaign strategies are playing publicly and how they are faring in their races against other candidates. Politicians and their campaign consultants evaluate face-to-face contact with voters and their correspondence and calls, but they also pay attention to national media and party or campaign polls.

The media want current and accurate information on which to base their reporting. They also have an interest in keeping and increasing the size of their audiences. To build their markets, they create and publish polls that encourage their audiences to see elections as exciting contests.

Finally, professional pollsters have an interest in producing accurate information for their clients. The quality of their surveys rests with good scientific polling techniques.

CITIZEN VALUES: HOW DO WE MEASURE UP?

At the beginning of this chapter we reminded you of the two competing visions of citizenship in America: one, the ideal democratic citizen who is attentive and informed, holds reasoned and stable opinions, is tolerant and participates in politics, and two, the apolitical self-interested actor who does not meet this ideal. As we might expect from the fact that Americans hold two such different views of what citizenship is all about, our behavior falls somewhere in the middle. For instance, some citizens tune out political news but are tolerant of others and vote regularly. Many activist citizens are informed, opinionated, and participatory but are intolerant of others' views, which can make the give and take of democratic politics difficult. We are not ideal democratic citizens, but we know our founders did not expect us to be. As we will see by the end of this chapter, our democracy survives fairly well despite our lapses.

Consider the Source

How to Be a Critical Poll Watcher

In the heat of the Clinton impeachment hearings, angry conservative Republicans could not believe the polls: over 65 percent of Americans still approved of the job the president was doing and did not want to see him removed from office. Their conclusion? The polls were simply wrong. "The polls are targeted to get a certain answer," said one Floridian. "There are even T-shirts in South Florida that say 'I haven't been polled.'"[1]

Do we need to know people personally who have been polled in order to trust poll results? Of course not. But there are lots of polls out there, not only those done carefully and responsibly by reputable polling organizations but also polls done for marketing and overtly political purposes—polls with an agenda, we might say. How are we, as good scholars and citizens, to know which results are reliable indications of what the public thinks, and which are not? One thing we can do is bring our critical thinking skills to bear by asking some questions about the polls reported in the media. Try these.[2]

1. **Who is the poll's sponsor?** Even if the poll was conducted by a professional polling company, it may still have been commissioned on behalf of a candidate or company. Does the sponsor have an agenda? How might that agenda influence the poll, the question wording, or the sponsor's interpretation of events?
2. **Is the sample representative?** That is, were proper sampling techniques followed? What is the margin of error?
3. **From what population was the sample taken?** There is a big difference, for instance, between the preference of the *general public* for a presidential candidate and the preference of *likely voters,* especially if one is interested in predicting the election's outcome! Read the fine print. Sometimes a polling organization will weight responses according to the likelihood that the respondent will actually vote in order to come up with a better prediction of the election result. Some polls survey only the members of one party, or the

POLITICAL KNOWLEDGE

The ideal democratic citizen understands how government works, who the main actors are, and what major principles underlie the operation of the political system. Public opinion pollsters periodically take readings on what the public actually knows about politics, and the conclusion is always the same: Americans are not very well informed about their political system.[25]

Knowledge of key figures in politics is important for knowing whom to thank—or blame—for government policy, key information if we are to hold our officials accountable. Virtually everyone (99 percent of Americans) can name the president, but knowledge falls sharply for less central offices.[26] Only about one-quarter of the public can name both senators of their state, and before the Supreme Court's decisive role in resolving the 2000 election, only 16 percent could name the chief justice (the percentage rose to 31 percent afterward). Americans have a reasonable understanding of the most prominent aspects of the governmental system and the most visible leaders but are ignorant about other central actors and key principles of American political life.

IDEOLOGY

Ideologies are the sets of ideas about politics, the economy, and society that help us deal with the political world. They provide citizens with an organizational framework for analyzing the political world and directing their actions. In Chapter 2 we pointed readers of a particular magazine, or people of a certain age, depending on the information they are seeking to discover. Be sure the sample is not self-selected. Always check the population being sampled, and do not assume it is the general public.

4. **How are the questions worded?** Are loaded, problematic, or vague terms used? Could the questions be confusing to the average citizen? Are the questions available with the poll results? If not, why not? Do the questions seem to lead you to respond one way or the other? Do they oversimplify issues or complicate them? If the survey claims to have detected change over time, be sure the same questions were used consistently. All these things could change the way people respond.

5. **Are the survey topics ones that people are likely to have information and opinions about?** Respondents rarely admit that they don't know how to answer a question, so responses on obscure or technical topics are likely to be more suspect than others.

6. **What is the poll's response rate?** A lot of "don't knows," "no opinions," or refusals to answer can have a decided effect on the results.

7. **Do the poll results differ from those of other polls, and if so, why?** Don't necessarily assume that public opinion has changed. What is it about this poll that might have caused the discrepancy?

8. **What do the results mean?** Who is doing the interpreting? What are that person's motives? For instance, pollsters who work for the Democratic Party will have an interpretation of the results that is favorable to Democrats, and Republican interpretation will favor Republicans. Try interpreting the results yourself.

1. Melinda Henneberger, "Where G.O.P. Gathers, Frustration Does Too," *New York Times,* February 1, 1999, 3.

2. Some of these questions are based in part on similar advice given to poll watchers in Herbert Asher, *Polling and the Public: What Every Citizen Should Know,* 6th ed. (Washington, D.C.: CQ Press, 2004), 190–193.

out that, for some people, liberalism and conservatism represent fundamental philosophical positions, but few of us walk around with whole political philosophies in our heads. For many Americans today, liberalism stands for faith in government action and social tolerance, conservatism for the belief that government should be limited and that its policies should emphasize "family values." A whole host of other issue positions follows from these central tenets.

In what became a landmark work in the study of American political behavior, political scientist Philip Converse developed a scheme for classifying people's belief systems according to how well they were organized along the dimensions of liberalism and conservatism. For Converse, those citizens who thought about politics in liberal or conservative terms and whose ideas were internally consistent (that is, they didn't combine liberal and conservative elements in an inconsistent way) were more politically sophisticated.[27] This is similar to what we mean when we say that the ideal democratic citizen would have well-reasoned and stable opinions.

To determine people's political ideologies, pollsters ask their respondents to "self-identify"—that is, to place themselves on a liberal–conservative scale. In the United States for more than thirty years, there have been more self-identified conservatives than liberals, but more people call themselves moderate than either liberal or conservative. Over this time period the percentages of self-proclaimed liberals, moderates, and conservatives have been quite steady with only modest increases in the number saying they are moderates. Not everyone thinks of him or herself in ideological terms; about one in five Americans is either unwilling or unable to self-identify in these ideological terms.[28]

Learning About Politics the Easy Way
Quite a few people have decided that learning about politics can be more entertaining than watching the talking heads of network news or listening to noisy verbal jousting matches of the left and right seen on some political talk shows. One example is Comedy Central's wildly popular mock news program, *The Daily Show with John Stewart.* Stewart "reports" current political news with biting satire, hilarious correspondents, and interviews with major figures on the arts and politics (here, with Sen. Arlen Specter, R-Penn.). One survey showed that the viewers of *The Daily Show* were better informed about the facts of the Iraq War than those getting their news from the traditional networks.

In practical policy terms, those who identify themselves as liberals and conservatives tend to take different positions on an array of economic and social issues. It is important to note that not all liberals automatically take the liberal side on every issue, nor do conservatives consistently take conservative positions. One can care intensely about equal rights and the environment, and thus call oneself a liberal, and at the same time maintain more conservative positions on, say, abortion and government spending. Converse found, however, that among those who are highly informed and active in politics, ideological consistency is quite high—that is, they tend to be liberal on most issues or conservative on most issues. As information and political activity levels drop, so does the level of ideological consistency.[29] From this we draw a clear lesson: those most involved and knowledgeable about politics tend to think in ideological terms and to take ideologically consistent positions across different issues. Such ideological consistency fits with the reasoned and stable opinion holding of the ideal democratic citizen.

TOLERANCE

A key democratic value is tolerance. In a democracy, with many people jockeying for position and many competing visions of the common good, tolerance for ideas different from one's own and respect for the rights of others provide oil to keep the democratic machinery running smoothly. It is also a prerequisite for compromise, an essential component of politics generally, and democratic politics particularly.

How do Americans measure up on the important democratic requirement of respect for others' rights? The record is mixed. As we saw in Chapters 5 and 6, America has a history of denying basic civil rights to some groups, but clearly tolerance is on the increase since the civil rights movement of the 1960s. Small pockets of intolerance persist, primarily among such extremist groups as those who advocate violence against doctors who perform abortions, the burning of black churches in the South, or anti-Arab and anti-Muslim incidents following the terrorist attacks on the World Trade Center and the Pentagon on September 11, 2001.[30] Such extremism, however, is the exception rather than the rule in contemporary American politics.

In terms of general principles, almost all Americans support the values of freedom of speech, religion, and political equality. For instance, 90 percent of respondents told researchers that they believed in "free speech for all, no matter what their views might be." However, when citizens are asked to apply these principles to particular situations in which specific groups have to be tolerated (especially unpopular groups like the American Nazi Party preaching race hatred or atheists preaching against God and religion), the levels of political tolerance drop dramatically.[31]

In studies of political tolerance, the least politically tolerant are consistently the less educated and less politically sophisticated. For example, one study found that on a civil liberties scale designed to measure overall support for First Amendment rights, only 24 percent of high school graduates earned high scores, compared with 52 percent of college graduates.[32]

Many such findings have led some observers to argue that elites are the protectors of our democratic values. According to this view, the highly educated and politically active are the ones who guard the democratic process from the mass of citizens who would easily follow undemocratic demagogues (like Adolf Hitler). Critics of this theory, however, say that educated people simply know what the politically correct responses to polls are and so can hide their intolerance better. In practice, the mass public's record has not been bad, and some of the worst offenses of intolerance in our history, from slavery to the incarceration of the Japanese in America during World War II, were led by elites, not the mass public. Nevertheless, the weight of the evidence does indicate that democratic political tolerance increases with education.

PARTICIPATION

One of the most consistent criticisms of Americans by those concerned with the democratic health of the nation is that we do not participate enough. And indeed, as participation is usually measured, the critics are right. Figure 11.3 shows that for voter turnout in national elections, the United States ranks last among industrialized nations. Various explanations have been offered for the low U.S. turnout, including the failure of parties to work to mobilize turnout and obstacles to participation such as restrictive registration laws, limited voting hours, and the frequency of elections. We discuss the problem of declining voter turnout in Chapter 14.

Political participation in the United States is also unusual in other ways. For example, unlike in many European countries, political participation in the United States is quite highly correlated with education and measures of socioeconomic achievement. This means that there is a much higher class bias to political participation in the United States, with greater portions of the middle and upper classes participating than the working and lower classes.[33]

Table 11.1 shows that turnout in the 2004 election varied greatly with age, race, education, and employment status. Turnout was the lowest among the youngest voters, the unemployed, and those without a high school education, and higher among older citizens and those with better educations. In large part because of lower education levels, minorities have lower participation rates than do whites. Turnout among young

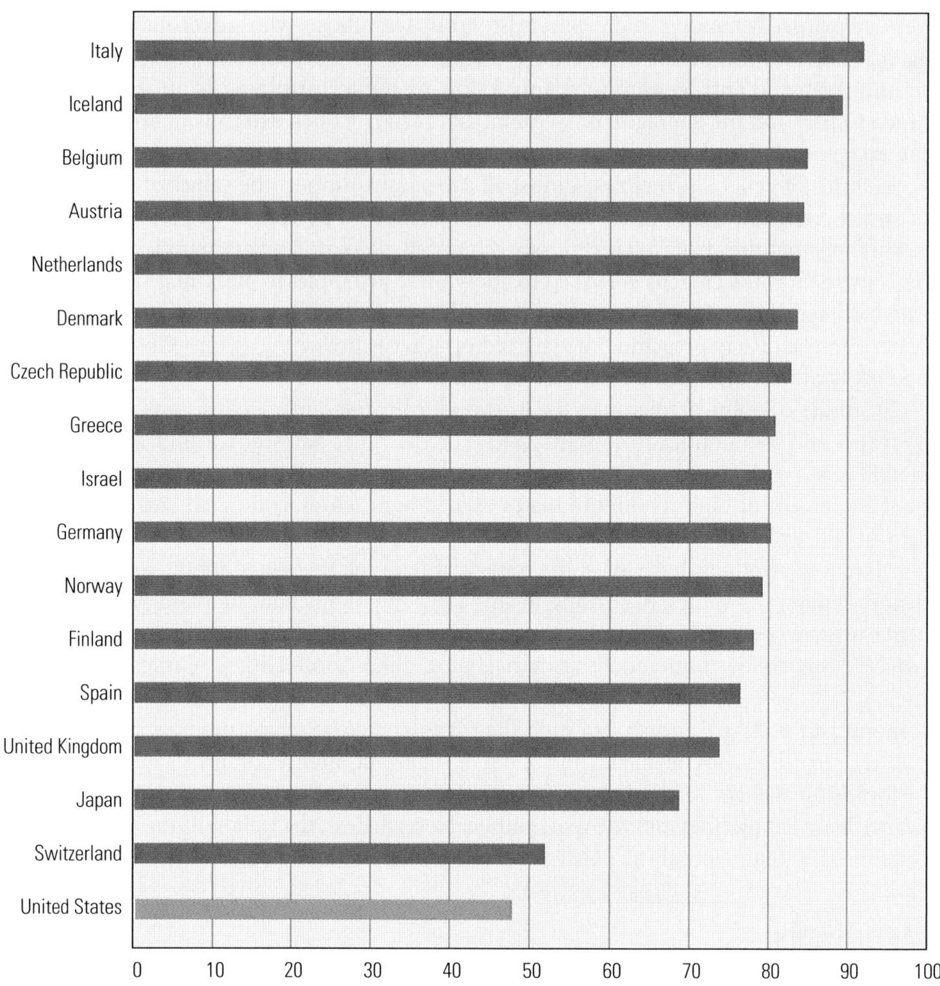

FIGURE 11.3
Comparison of Voter Turnout Among Industrialized Nations

Source: Data from the Institute for Democracy and Electoral Assistance.

people was higher than usual in 2004, but other age groups voted in larger numbers as well so that the difference in participation between age groups was consistent with past patterns.

Notice also that the levels of voting reported in the data in Table 11.l, which are based on responses to surveys taken after the election, are higher than the official turnout rate for the nation shown in Figure 11.3. There are several reasons for this discrepancy, including differences in samples—surveys do not include the low voting populations of adults in institutions, for example—and the tendency for some people to report voting when they did not. Some misreporters may have thought they voted, and others may have reported what they felt they "should" have done or what they intended to do.[34]

WHO, WHAT, HOW In a nation that claims to be ruled by the people, all American citizens have a stake in ensuring that "the people" are as close to being public-spirited ideal democratic citizens as they can be. It is also the case, however, that the primary incentive that drives each citizen is concern for his or her own interests, and that although many citizens do exhibit some of the characteristics of the ideal democratic citizen, they rarely exhibit all of them. Consequently, most citizens do not fit the model of the theoretical ideal. Those who do fit the model achieve that status through political education, the development of ideological thinking about politics, the practice of toleration, and political participation.

TABLE 11.1 **Percentage Reporting Voting in the 2004 Presidential Election**

	PERCENTAGE REPORTING THEY VOTED
Total	76.3%
Age	
18–24 years old	59.8
25–34 years old	71.7
35–44 years old	76.4
45–64 years old	81.9
65–74 years old	87.0
75 years old and over	75.0
Sex	
Male	74.6
Female	78.0
Race and Ethnicity	
White	79.4
Black	69.9
Hispanic/Latino	62.8
Education	
Less than high school graduate	53.1
High school graduate	70.7
Some college	79.5
4-year degree or more	92.7
Employment	
Employed	78.6
Unemployed	48.1
Not in labor force	75.2

Source: National Election Studies, 2004. Calculated by the authors.

WHAT INFLUENCES OUR OPINIONS ABOUT POLITICS?

So far, we have learned that many, but by no means all, Americans exhibit the characteristics of our so-called ideal democratic citizen, and we have discovered that the traits of ideal democratic citizenship are not distributed equally across the population. The implication of our analysis, that education and socioeconomic status have something to do with our political opinions and behaviors, still does not tell us where our opinions come from. In this section we look at several sources of public opinion: political socialization, economic self-interest, religion, age, race, gender, and geographic region of residence. All of these things affect the way we come to see politics, what we believe we have at stake in the political process, and the kind of citizenship we practice.

LEARNING THE RULES OF THE GAME

Democracies and, indeed, all other political systems depend for their survival on each new generation picking up the values and allegiances of previous generations—beliefs in the legitimacy of the political system and its leaders, and a willingness to obey the laws and the commands of those leaders. You can well imagine the chaos that would result if each new generation of citizens, freshly arrived at adulthood, had to be convinced from scratch to respect the system and obey its laws. In fact, that doesn't happen because we all learn from our cradles to value and support our political systems, which is why the children in France or China support their leaders as surely as the children of the United States support theirs. The process by which we learn our political orientations and allegiances is called **political socialization**, and it works through a variety of agents, including family, schools, group memberships, and the major public events of our lives.

political socialization the process by which we learn our political orientations and allegiances

Family The family, of course, has a tremendous opportunity to influence political development. Children typically develop an emotional response to some fundamental objects of government before they really understand much about those objects. Thus one of the important orientations that develops in the preschool years is nationalism, a strong emotional attachment to the political community. Children saluting the flag or watching fireworks at Independence Day celebrations easily absorb the idea that being American is something special. The greatest impact of the family—though one that has weakened somewhat in recent years—is on party identification.[35] Children tend to choose the same political party as their parents.[36] Interestingly, when parents disagree in their partisanship, the child identifies more often with the party affiliation of the mother. The family has a weaker effect on attitudes such as racial relations or welfare.

Little Patriots
Early political socialization can happen unintentionally. Parents take youngsters to parades to enjoy the music and the colorful pageantry. Once there, though, children begin to develop an emotional response to political celebrations (like the Fourth of July) and national symbols (like the American flag).

Schools and Education Schools, where many children begin their day with the Pledge of Allegiance, and where schoolbooks emphasize stories of patriotism and national heroes, are an important agent of political learning and the development of citizen orientations. Most school districts include as part of their explicit mission that the schools should foster good citizenship.[37] In many districts, U.S. history or civics is a required course, and some state legislatures require a course or two in U.S. and state politics for all college students in the state system.

Early on in school, children develop basic citizenship skills, such as learning fundamental civic precepts—like "Always obey the laws" and "Be helpful to others."[38] Political training also continues in the schools with the establishment of class officers, mock presidential elections, and, at the upper grades, a widening array of clubs and extracurricular activities whose byproducts include training in leadership and group skills, group decision making, cooperation, and problem solving. All of these experiences help foster essential citizenship skills in a society that depends largely on grassroots organization and voluntary compliance with political decisions.

Groups Shared values and experiences help define families, friends, and social groups, and research backs up the common notion that peer groups have a lot of influence on individuals' social and political attitudes. People who attend the same church tend to have similar political attitudes, as do individuals who live in the same neighborhoods. These tendencies can be traced in part to the ways people select themselves into groups, but they are reinforced by social contacts. The processes of talking, working, and worshiping together lead people to see the world similarly.[39]

Groups can also influence members by simple peer pressure. Researchers have documented the effects of peer pressure as a phenomenon they call the **spiral of silence**, a process by which a majority opinion becomes exaggerated.[40] In many contexts, when there is a clearly perceived majority position, those holding minority positions tend not to speak up or defend their views. This relative silence tends to embolden the advocates of the majority opinion to speak even more confidently. Thus what may begin as a bare majority for a group's position can become the overwhelming voice of the group through this spiral of silence.

spiral of silence the process by which a majority opinion becomes exaggerated because minorities do not feel comfortable speaking out in opposition

Political and Social Events Major political and social events can have a profound socializing influence on the political orientations of the public and, because most of us experience these events largely, if not exclusively, through the filter of the media, those in the news and entertainment business have a potentially strong influence over how our views are shaped.

Divisive political events can cause levels of trust in government to decline; unifying events can cause them to rise. For example, coming out of World War II and into the prosperity of the 1950s, many Americans had a rosy picture of the United States; their good feelings were manifested as strong approval of government. However, the divisive events of the 1960s, including the civil rights movement and the unpopular Vietnam War, followed by the scandal of Watergate and the resignation of President Richard Nixon in the 1970s had visible consequences in declining levels of trust in government, as Figure 11.4 shows.[41]

The partisan politics of the 1990s, including the impeachment of President Bill Clinton and the contested presidential election of 2000, should have caused levels of trust to fall even further. That they did not probably reflects citizens' generally positive assessment of government's role in the economic prosperity of the era. The events of September 11, 2001, and the ensuing war on terror caused Americans to see their government in an even more positive light. As is evident from the graph, however, as Americans' attention focused on domestic issues and partisan politics returned to business as usual, expressions of trust fell to their pre–September 11 level.

SOURCES OF DIVISIONS IN PUBLIC OPINION

Political socialization produces a citizenry that largely agrees with the rules of the game and accepts the outcomes of the national political process as legitimate. That does not mean, however, that we are a nation in agreement on most or even very many things. There is a considerable range of disagreement in the policy preferences of Americans, and those disagreements stem in part from citizens' interests, education, age, gender, race, and religion—even the area of the country in which they live.

Self-Interest People's political preferences often come from an assessment of what is best for them economically, from asking, "What's in it for me?" So, for instance, as

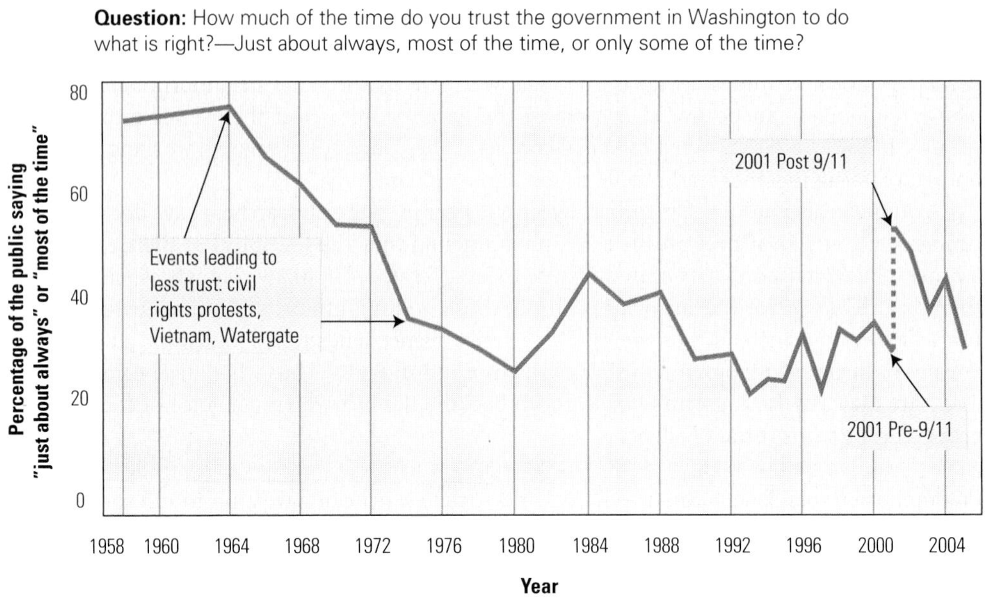

Question: How much of the time do you trust the government in Washington to do what is right?—Just about always, most of the time, or only some of the time?

FIGURE 11.4

Trust in Government, 1958–2004

Public levels of trust in government respond to major political events.

Source: National Election Studies, 1958–2000; various polls from the Roper Center, 1994–2004. Yearly averages calculated by the authors with separate averages for 2001 (before and after September 11).

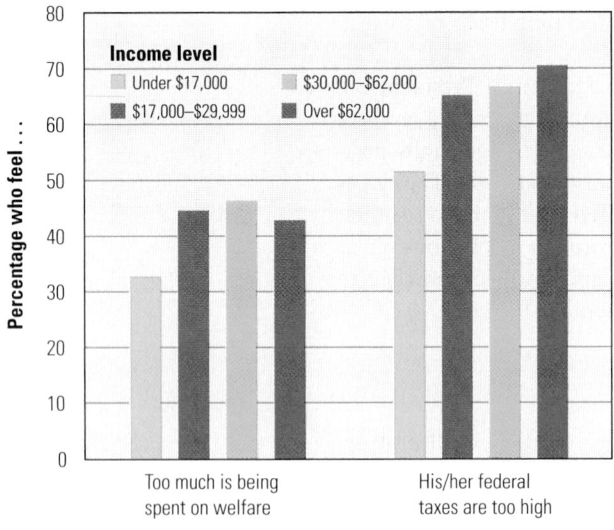

FIGURE 11.5

Attitudes Toward Welfare Spending and Taxes by Income

Source: General Social Survey, 2002.

Figure 11.5 shows, those in the lowest income brackets are the least likely to agree that too much is being spent on welfare, while those with more income are more likely to agree. Similarly, as incomes increase so does the feeling that one is paying too much in taxes. These patterns are only tendencies, however. Some wealthy people favor the redistribution of wealth and more spending on welfare; some people living in poverty oppose these policies. Even on these straightforward economic questions, other factors are at work. Similarly, those with lower incomes are generally more favorable than the wealthy are to government attempts to narrow the income gap between rich and poor.

Education As we suggested earlier in our discussion of the ideal democratic citizen, a number of political orientations change as a person attains more education. One important study looked in depth at how education influences aspects of citizenship, separating citizen values into "democratic enlightenment" and "democratic engagement."[42] *Democratic enlightenment* refers to a citizen's ability to hold democratic beliefs, including the acceptance that politics is about compromise and that sometimes the needs of the whole community will conflict and override one's individual preferences. *Democratic engagement* refers to a citizen's ability to understand his or her own interests and how to pursue those interests in politics. Both democratic dimensions are tied to education: better-educated citizens are more likely to be tolerant and committed to democratic principles and are more likely to vote, to be informed about politics, and to participate at all levels of the political system (see Figure 11.6).[43] In short, those who graduate from college have many more of the attributes of the idealized active democratic citizen than do those who do not graduate from high school.

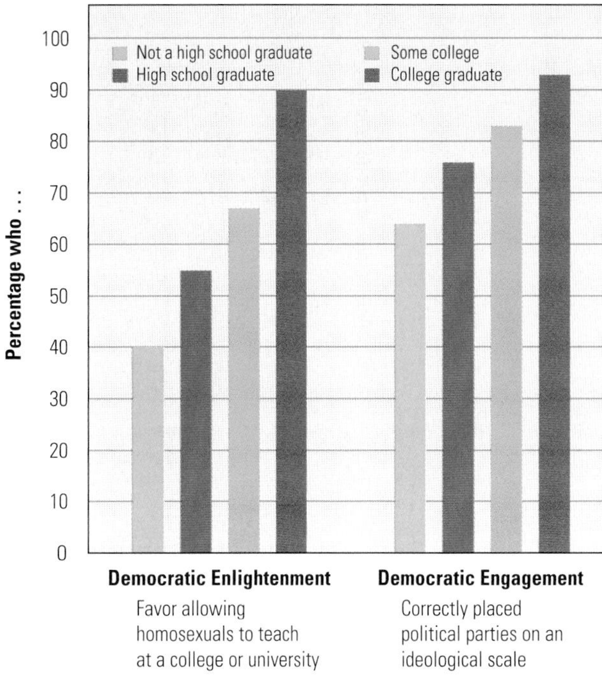

FIGURE 11.6
The Effects of Education on Democratic Enlightenment and Engagement

Source: National Election Studies, 2004; General Social Survey, 2002.

Age We might expect that people change their opinions as they age, that our experiences over time affect how we see the political world. There is, however, precious little evidence for the common view that masses of people progress from youthful idealism to mature conservatism.

Indeed, extensive research shows that on most political issues, there are only small differences in policy preferences related to age.[44] One exception is the finding that there are consistent age differences in political engagement. Middle-age and older citizens are typically more attentive to and more active in politics: they report more frequent efforts to persuade others, they vote more often, and they are more likely to write letters to public officials and to contribute to political campaigns. It seems that acting out one's political role may be part and parcel of the array of activities that we associate with "settling down," such as marrying, having children, and establishing a career.

Another area in which age plays a role in public opinion is in the creation of **political generations**, groups of citizens who have been shaped by particular events, usually in their youth, and whose shared experience continues to identify them throughout their lives. One of the most distinctive of such groups is the New Deal generation—those who came of age during the Great Depression. They are distinctly more Democratic in their party orientations than preceding generations.[45] Young people are likely to be more influenced by current political trends since they carry less political baggage to offset new issues that arise. Thus, for example, environmental issues and gay rights are currently prominent on the political agenda. On both of these issues, as we can see in Figure 11.7, younger citizens are markedly more liberal than their elders, for whom accepted attitudes on these issues were rather different when they came of age politically. Thus political events and age intersect, forming lasting imprints on younger groups, who tend to continue with the attitudes formed as they entered the electorate. As older groups die, overall opinion among the citizenry changes. This is the process of generational replacement.

political generations groups of citizens whose political views have been shaped by the common events of their youth

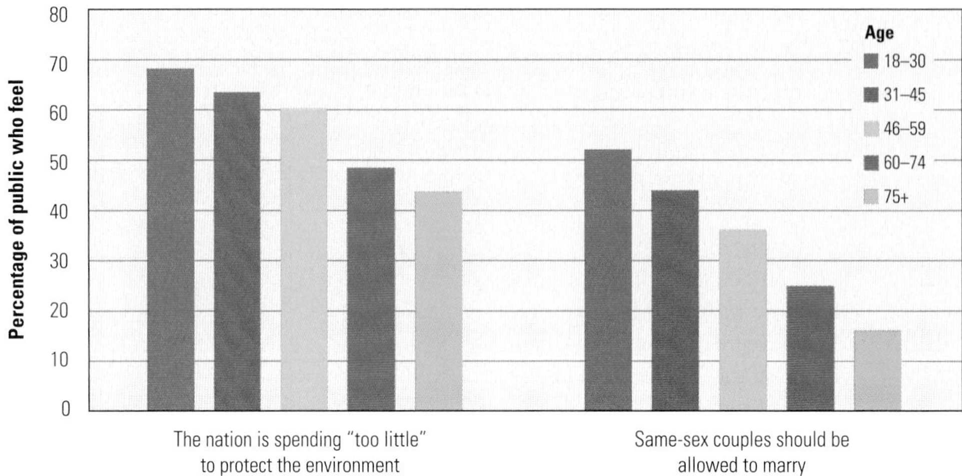

FIGURE 11.7
The Effect of Age on Political Orientation

Source: General Social Survey, 2002; National Election Studies, 2004.

Gender For many years, one's gender had almost no predictive power in explaining opinions and behavior—except that women were less active in politics and usually less warlike in their political attitudes. Just after World War II in the United States, there was a strong presumption that the man was the breadwinner and the woman's place was in the home (see Table 11.2). Since the 1960s, however, there has been something of a revolution in our expectations about the role of women in society and in politics. As women gained more education and entered the work force, they also increased their levels of participation in politics. Whereas in the 1950s women trailed men in voter turnout by over 12 percent,[46] by 2004 women voted at a slightly higher rate than did men (see Table 11.1).

Interestingly, in the last quarter of the twentieth century, as men and women approached equality in their levels of electoral participation, their attitudes on issues diverged. This tendency for men and women to take different issue positions or to evaluate political figures differently is called the **gender gap**. In almost all cases, it means that women are more liberal than men. The ideological stances of women overall have not changed significantly since the 1970s, but those of men have shifted steadily, as more call themselves conservatives (see Figure 11.8). The gap is substantial (10 percent or larger) on the death penalty and spending on space exploration (see Table 11.3). In general, the gender gap has been found to be especially large on issues that deal with violence.[47] The gender gap also has electoral consequences. Women are more likely than men to vote for Democratic candidates. In fact, had it not been for women voters, President Bill Clinton would have lost the presidency to Sena-

gender gap the tendency of men and women to differ in their political views on some issues

TABLE 11.2 **Postwar Attitudes, 1945**

QUESTION ASKED OF THE GENERAL PUBLIC:	
Do you think married women whose husbands earn enough to support them should or should not be allowed to hold jobs if they want to?	
Should be allowed	24%
Should not be allowed	60
Depends (volunteered)	13

Source: Roper Polls reported in Sally Daniels, Bradford Fay, and Nicholas Tortorello, "Americans' Changing Attitudes Toward Women and Minorities," *Public Perspective* (Dec. 1997–Jan. 1998), 47–48. Reprinted by permission.

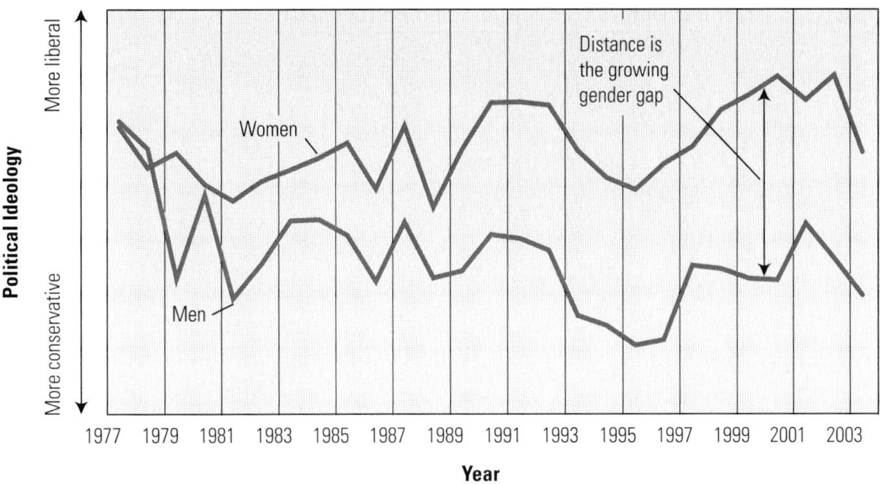

FIGURE 11.8
The Effect of Gender on Political Ideology

Source: Data from CBS/*New York Times* polls.

tor Robert Dole in 1996, and the 2000 presidential election, which was eventually decided by the Supreme Court, would have been won handily by George W. Bush.[48]

The differences between men and women might be explained by their different socialization experiences and by the different life situations they face. The impact of one's life situation has recently emerged in what observers are calling the **marriage gap**. This refers to the tendency for different opinions to be expressed by those who are married or widowed versus those who have never been married. "Marrieds" tend toward more traditional and conservative values; "never marrieds" tend to have a more liberal perspective. The "never marrieds" are now sufficiently numerous that in many localities they constitute an important group that politicians must heed in deciding which issues to support. The effect of the marriage gap in terms of specific issues in shown in Table 11.4.

marriage gap the tendency for married people to hold political opinions that differ from those of people who have never married

Race and Ethnicity Race has been a perennial cleavage in American politics. Only in recent decades have blacks achieved the same political rights as the white majority, and yet disparity in income between whites and blacks continues. When we compare by race the answers to a question about spending to improve the condition of blacks, the responses are quite different. African Americans are more favorable to such spending than are whites. We see a similar pattern in whether respondents would support a community bill to bar discrimination in housing. African Americans tend to favor such a law; whites are more likely to side with the owner's right to sell a house to whomever he or she chooses. These differences, some of which are shown in Figure 11.9, are typical of a general pattern. On issues of economic policy and race, African Americans are substantially more liberal than whites. However, on social issues like abortion and prayer in schools, the racial differences are more muted.

The root of the differences between political attitudes of blacks and whites most certainly lies in the racial discrimination historically experienced by African Ameri-

TABLE 11.3 Gender Differences on Selected Political Issues

ISSUE	MEN	WOMEN	GAP *
Favor allowing abortion for any reason	44.4%	41.3%	–3.1%
Oppose death penalty for murder	24.7	37.4	12.7
Agree government spends "Too much" on space exploration	30.9	43.5	12.6
Agree that employers should hire and promote women because of past discrimination	58.9	75.2	16.3
Vote for Clinton 1996	46.2	60.1	13.9
Vote for Gore 2000	46.9	57.3	10.4
Vote for Kerry 2004	45.1	52.6	7.5

*Gap is positive for more liberal response among women.

Source: General Social Survey, 2002; National Election Studies, Cumulative File.

TABLE 11.4 Policy Positions by Marital Status

	MARRIED	WIDOWED	DIVORCED	SEPARATED	NEVER MARRIED
Favor death penalty	73.5%	64.6%	67.6%	59.6%	61.7%
Allow homosexuals to teach in colleges and universities	78.6	71.0	81.7	83.1	84.8
Allow women to have an abortion for any reason	39.2	35.2	48.9	44.3	45.5
Approve of Bible prayer in public schools	63.2	80.8	62.8	61.7	52.9
"Too little" spent on improving and protecting environment	58.7	52.2	64.1	61.0	69.6
Ideology					
Liberal (all categories)	23.4	17.2	27.3	25.5	33.6
Moderate	38.2	37.7	43.1	47.1	38.1
Conservative (all categories)	38.5	45.1	29.7	27.5	28.2

Source: General Social Survey, 2002, 2004.

cans. Blacks tend to see much higher levels of discrimination and racial bias in the criminal justice system, in education, and in the job market. There is undeniably a very large gulf between the races in their perceptions about the continuing frequency and severity of racial discrimination.[49]

Finally, reflecting the very different stands on racial and economic issues the parties have taken, African Americans are the most solidly Democratic group in terms of both party identification and voting. Interestingly, as income and other status indicators rise for whites, they become more conservative and Republican. This does not happen among African Americans. Better-educated and higher-income blacks actually have stronger racial identifications, which results in distinctly liberal positions on economic and racial issues and solid support for Democratic candidates.[50]

Some signs indicate that this may be changing, however. Declaring that the Democratic Party should not be able to take for granted the support of African Americans, former chairman of the Joint Chiefs of Staff (and later secretary of state) Colin Pow-

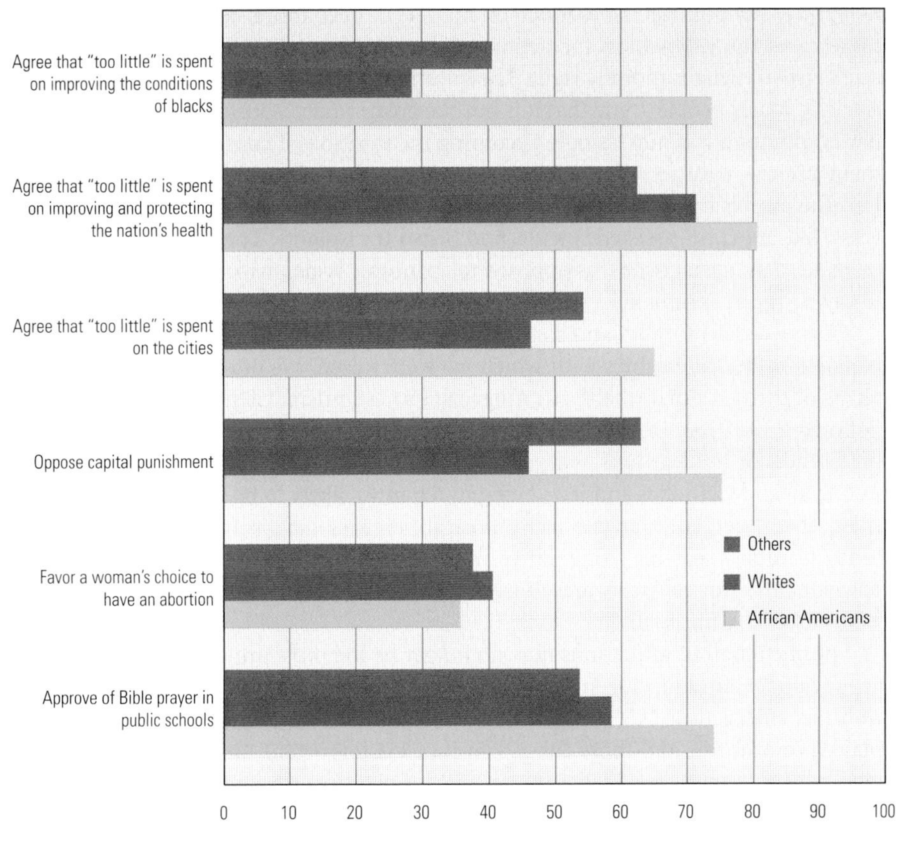

FIGURE 11.9
The Effect of Race on Political Views Held

Source: Data from General Social Survey, 1998–2002.

ell broke with convention in 1996 to align himself with the Republicans. While his stances on some controversial issues like abortion and affirmative action reflect more liberal positions, on other issues he is truly conservative. The increasing number of black conservatives, exemplified perhaps by the current secretary of state, Condoleezza Rice (see the *Profiles in Citizenship* in Chapter 8), Supreme Court Justice Clarence Thomas, and former California Board of Regents member Ward Connerly (see the *Profiles in Citizenship* in Chapter 6), show that the assumptions once made about African Americans and the Democratic Party are no longer universally true, and that the shape of race politics in the United States may be changing.

Blacks are not, of course, the only minority group in the country. When it comes to public opinion, many other groups, like Hispanics and Asian Americans, do not turn out to be dramatically different from the majority-non-Hispanic whites on most issues (see the general behavior of the "Others" bar in figure 11.9). There is so much diversity of opinion within these broad groupings that it can be misleading to talk about a "Hispanic" or an "Asian" opinion.[51]

Religion Many political issues touch on matters of deep moral conviction or values. In these cases the motivation for action or opinion formation is not self-interest but one's view of what is morally right. The question of morals and government, however, is tricky. Many people argue that it is not the government's business to set moral standards, although it is increasingly becoming the position of conservatives that government policy ought to reflect traditional moral values. In addition, government gets into the morals business by virtue of establishing policies on issues of moral controversy, like abortion, assisted suicide, and organ transplants. These questions are often referred to as "social issues" as opposed to economic issues, which center more on how to divide the economic pie.

Our views of morality and social issues are often rooted in our differing religious convictions and the values with which we were raised. We often think of religion in terms of the three major faiths in America: Protestantism, Catholicism, and Judaism. Following the New Deal realignment, there were major political differences in the preferences of these groups, with non-southern Protestants being predominantly Republican, and Catholics and Jews being much more likely to be Democrats and to call themselves liberals. Over the years those differences have softened quite a bit, but today Catholics are less conservative than Protestants, and more Democratic, while Jews and the not religious are clearly more liberal and Democratic than the other groups (see Figure 11.10).

Specific religious affiliations may no longer be the most important religious cleavage for understanding citizen opinions on social issues. Since the 1970s a new distinction has emerged in U.S. politics, between those in whose lives traditional religion plays a central role and those for whom it is less important. In this alignment, those who adhere to traditional religious beliefs and practices (frequent churchgoers, regular Bible readers, "born-again Christians") tend to take conservative positions on an array of social issues (like homosexuality and abortion), compared with more liberal positions taken on those issues by what may be called "seculars." This tendency is

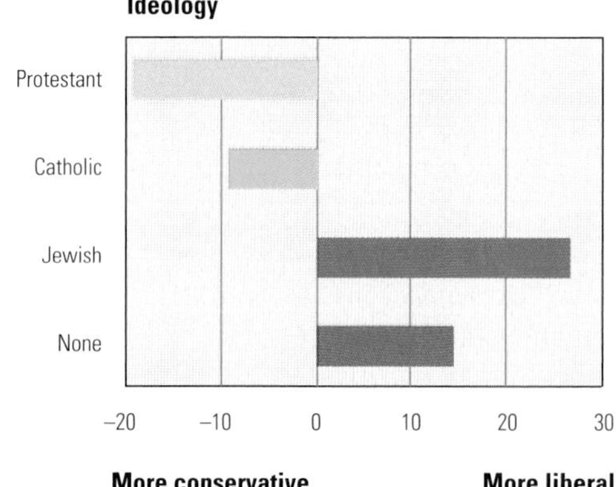

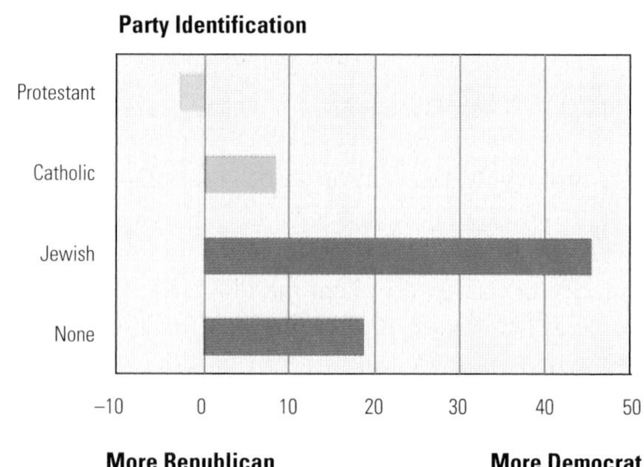

FIGURE 11.10

Ideological and Party Identification by Major Religious Denominations

Note: Ideology is calculated as percent liberal minus percent conservative; party identification is shown as percent Democrats minus percent Republican.

Source: CBS/*New York Times* polls, 2000–2004. Calculated by authors.

suggested in Figure 11.10; among those who say they are not religious, Democrats outnumber Republicans and liberals outnumber conservatives.

Geographical Region Where we live matters in terms of our political beliefs. People in the Farm Belt talk about different things than do city dwellers on the streets of Manhattan. Texans appreciate subtle assumptions that are not shared by Minnesotans. Politicians who come from these areas represent people with different preferences, and much of the politics in Congress is about being responsive to differing geography-based opinions.[52] For instance, scholars have long argued that "the South is different." The central role of race and its plantation past for a long time gave rise to different patterns of public opinion compared to the non-southern states. The South today is not the Old South, but the region does retain some distinctive values. Opinions in the South—by which we mean the eleven states of the Confederacy—remain more conservative on civil rights but also on other social issues. (See the "*Who Are We?*" feature in Chapter 4, which shows how the states vary in terms of political ideology.)

Whether we live in the city, the suburbs, or the country also has an effect on our opinions. City dwellers are more Democratic in their political preferences and more liberal on issues like spending to help minorities and to improve education. On other issues, such as the environment, abortion, and a proposed constitutional amendment to ban same-sex marriages, rural residents stand out as distinctly conservative compared to other residential groups (see Table 11.5).

WHO, WHAT, HOW Political socialization helps to fuel and maintain the political system by transferring fundamental democratic values from one generation to the next. More specific values come from demographic characteristics—our age, race, and gender—and from our life experiences—education, religious affiliation, and where we live.

As citizens find themselves in different circumstances, with differing political ideas, these differences are mined by interest groups, political parties, and candidates for

TABLE 11.5 **Where We Live Makes a Difference**

	BIG CITY	SUBURBS	SMALL TOWN	RURAL
Party identification				
Democrat	54.6%	44.3%	42.4%	39.6%
Republican	23.1	37.1	33.9	42.0
Ideology				
Liberal	31.8	30.4	24.7	13.3
Conservative	30.1	36.7	31.9	52.9
Policy (percent taking each response)				
Too little spending to help blacks	44.5	38.0	36.1	18.8
Too little spending on education	77.0	70.8	71.3	67.5
Too little spending on environment	63.9	62.7	60.5	48.8
Allow abortion for any reason	44.8	50.0	37.1	27.6
Favor constitutional amendment to prevent homosexual couples from marrying.	41.7	36.1	42.4	61.7

Note: The middle categories of "moderate" and "independent" have been omitted for Party identification and Ideology.

Source: General Social Survey, 2000, except the item on gay marriage, which is from the ABC News/*Washington Post* poll, March 2004.

office who are looking for support, either to further their causes or to get elected. Thus the differences in policy preferences that a complex society inevitably produces become the stuff of political conflict.

THE CITIZENS AND PUBLIC OPINION

We have seen ample evidence that although politicians may act as if citizens are informed and attentive, only some Americans live up to our model of good citizenship, and those who do often belong disproportionately to the ranks of the well educated, the well-off, and the older portions of the population. This disparity between our ideal citizen and reality raises some provocative questions about the relationship between citizens, public opinion, and democracy. Were the founders right to limit the influence of the masses on government? Do we want less informed and coherent opinions represented in politics? Can democracy survive if it is run only by an educated elite?

Earlier in this chapter we suggested that all would not be lost for American democracy if only some of us turned out to be ideal citizens, and that it was possible to argue that although Americans as individuals might not fit the ideal, Americans as a group might behave as that ideal would predict. How is such a trick possible? The argument goes like this.

It may not be rational for all people to be deeply immersed in the minutiae of day-to-day politics. Our jobs, families, hobbies, and other interests leave us little time for in-depth study of political issues, and unless we get tremendous satisfaction from keeping up with politics (and some of us certainly do), it might be rational for us to leave the political information gathering to others. Social scientists call this idea **rational ignorance**.

rational ignorance the state of being uninformed about politics because of the cost in time and energy

This does not mean that we are condemned to make only ignorant or mistaken political decisions. Citizens are generally pretty smart. In fact, studies show that voters can behave much more intelligently than we could ever guess from their answers to surveys about politics. A great many of us use shortcuts to getting political information that serve us quite well, in the sense that they help us make the same decisions we might have made had we invested considerable time and energy in collecting that political information ourselves.[53]

SHORTCUTS TO POLITICAL KNOWLEDGE

on-line processing the ability to receive and evaluate information as events happen, allowing us to remember our evaluation even if we have forgotten the specific events that caused it

One shortcut is the **on-line processing** of information.[54] (*On-line* here does not refer to time spent on the Internet, as you will see.) Many of the evaluations we make of people, places, and things in our lives (including political figures and ideas) are made on the fly. We assemble impressions and reactions while we are busy leading our lives. When queried, we might not be able to explain why we like or dislike a thing or a person, and we might sound quite ignorant in the sense of not seeming to have reasons for our beliefs. But we do have reasons, and they may make a good deal of sense, even if we can't identify what they are.

two-step flow of information the process by which citizens take their political cues from more well-informed opinion leaders

A second important mental shortcut that most of us use is the **two-step flow of information**. Politicians and the media send out massive amounts of information. We can absorb only a fraction of it, and even then it is sometimes hard to know how to interpret it. In these circumstances, we tend to rely on **opinion leaders**, who are more or less like ourselves but who know more about the subject than we do.[55] Opinion leaders and followers can be identified in all sorts of realms besides politics. When we make an important purchase, say, a computer or a car, most of us do not research all the scientific data and technical specifications. We ask people who are like us, who we think should know, and whom we can trust. We compile their advice, consult our own intuition, and buy. The result is that we get pretty close to making an optimal purchase without having to become experts ourselves. The two-step flow allows us to behave as though we were very well informed without requiring us to expend all the resources that actually being informed entails.

opinion leaders people who know more about certain topics than we do and whose advice we trust, seek out, and follow

THE RATIONAL ELECTORATE

Politicians deal with citizens mostly in groups and only rarely as individuals. Elected officials think about constituents as whole electorates ("the people of the great state of Texas") or as members of groups (women, environmentalists, developers, workers, and so forth). Groups, it turns out, appear to be better behaved, more rational, and better informed than the individuals who make up the groups, precisely because of the sorts of shortcuts we discussed in the previous section. This doesn't seem to make sense, so perhaps a nonpolitical example will clarify what we mean.

Consider the behavior of fans at a football game. People seem to cheer at the appropriate times; they know pretty much when to boo the referees; they oooh and aaaah more or less in unison. We would say that the crowd understands the game and participates effectively in it. However, what do the individual spectators know? If we were to do a football survey, we might ask about the players' names, the teams' win-loss records, the different offensive and defensive positions, the meaning of the referees' signals, and so forth. Some fans would do well, but many would probably get only a few questions right. From the survey, we might conclude that many people in this crowd do not know football at all. But because they take their cues from others, following the behavior of those who cheer for the same team, they can act as if they know what they are doing. Despite its share of football-ignorant individuals, in the aggregate—that is, as a group—the crowd acts remarkably football-intelligent.

Similarly, if we were to ask people when national elections are held, for instance, only a handful would be able to say it is the Tuesday after the first Monday in November of evenly numbered years. Some people would guess that they occur in November, others might say in the fall sometime, and others would admit they don't know. Based on the level of individual ignorance in this matter, it would be surprising if many people ever voted at all, since you can't vote if you don't know when Election Day is. But somehow, as a group, the electorate sorts it out, and almost everyone who is registered and wants to vote finds his or her way to the polling place on the right day. By using shortcuts and taking cues from others, the electorate behaves just as if it knew all along when the election was. More substantively, even though many voters may be confused about which candidates stand where on specific issues, groups of voters do a great job of sorting out which party or candidate best represents their interests. Members of the religious right vote for Republicans, and members of labor unions vote for Democrats, for instance. Even though there are undoubtedly quite a few confused voters in the electorate in any particular election, they tend to cancel each other out in the larger scheme of things. As a whole, from the politician's point of view, the electorate appears to be responsive to issues and quite rational in evaluating an incumbent's performance in office.[56]

So even though citizens do not spend a lot of time learning about politics, politicians are smart to assume that the electorate is attentive and informed. In fact, this is precisely what most of them do. For example, studies have shown that state legislators vote in accordance with the ideological preferences of their citizens, just as if the citizens were instructing them on their wishes.[57] The states with the most liberal citizens—for example, New York, Massachusetts, and California—have the most liberal policies. And the most conservative states, those in the South and the Rocky Mountains, have the most conservative policies. Other studies confirm a similar pattern in national elections.[58]

We began this chapter by asking why polling is routinely disparaged by politicians. Why don't we have more confidence in being ruled by public opinion? After all, in a democracy where the people's will is supposed to weigh heavily with our elected officials, we have uncovered some conflicting evidence. Many Americans do not model the characteristics of the ideal democratic citizen, but remember that the United States has two traditions of citizenship—one much more apolitical and self-interested than the public-spirited ideal. The reality in America is that the ideal citizen marches side by side with the more self-interested citizen, who, faced with many demands, does not put politics ahead of other daily responsibilities. But we have also argued that there are mechanisms and shortcuts that allow even some of the more apolitical and self-interested citizens to cast intelligent votes and to have their views represented in public policy. This tells us that at least one element of democracy—responsiveness of policies to public preferences—is in good working order.

We should not forget that political influence goes hand in hand with opinion formation. Those who are opinion leaders have much more relative clout than do their more passive followers. And opinion leaders are not distributed equally throughout the population. They are drawn predominantly from the ranks of the well educated and the well-off. Similarly, even though the shortcuts we have discussed allow many people to vote intelligently without taking the time to make a personally informed decision, many people never vote at all. Voters are also drawn from the more privileged ranks of American society. The poor, the young, and minorities—all the groups who are underrepresented at the voting booth—are also underrepresented in policymaking. There cannot help but be biases in such a system.

WHAT'S AT STAKE REVISITED

We have argued in this chapter that public opinion is important in policymaking and that politicians respond to it in a variety of ways. But what would happen if we more or less bypassed elected officials altogether and allowed people to participate directly in national lawmaking through the use of a national referendum or initiative? What is at stake in rule by public opinion?

On the one hand, voters would seem to have something real to gain in such lawmaking reform. It would give new meaning to government "by the people," and decisions would have more legitimacy with the public. Certainly it would be harder to point the finger at those in Washington as being responsible for bad laws. In addition, as has been the experience in states with initiatives, citizens might succeed in getting legislation passed that legislators themselves refuse to vote for. Prime examples are term limits and balanced budget amendments. Term limits would cut short many congressional careers and balanced budget amendments force politicians into hard choices about taxation and spending cuts that they prefer to avoid.

On the other side of the calculation, however, voters might be worse off. While policies like the two mentioned above clearly threaten the jobs of politicians, they also carry unintended consequences that might not be very good for the nation as a whole. Who should decide—politicians who make a career out of understanding government, or people who pay little attention to politics and current events and who vote from instinct and outrage? Politicians who have a vested interest in keeping their jobs, or the public who can provide a check on political greed and self-interest? The answer changes with the way you phrase the question, but the public might well suffer if left to its own mercy on questions of policy it does not thoroughly understand.

There is no doubt that the founders of the Constitution, with their limited faith in the people, would have rejected such a referendum wholeheartedly. Not only does it bring government closer to the people, but it wreaks havoc with their system of separation of powers and checks and balances. Popular opinion was supposed to be checked by the House and the Senate, which were in turn to be checked by the other two branches of government. Bringing public opinion to the fore upsets this delicate balance.

In addition, many scholars warn that the hallmark of democracy is not just hearing what the people want, but allowing the people to discuss and deliberate over their political choices. Home computer voting or trips to the ballot box do not necessarily permit such key interaction.[59] Majority rule without the tempering influence of debate and discussion can quickly deteriorate into majority tyranny, with a sacrifice of minority rights.

The flip side may also be true, however. Since voters tend to be those who care more intensely about political issues, supporters of a national referendum also leave themselves open to the opposite consequence of majority tyranny:

continued

Thinking Outside the Box

- Do frequent option polls enhance or diminish democracy?
- Of the four traits of the ideal citizen we discuss here—knowledge, ideology, tolerance, and participation—which is most important for the health of democracy?
- Is a democracy that depends on citizen "shortcuts" weaker than one that does not?

WHAT'S AT STAKE REVISITED *(continued)*

the tyranny of an intense minority who care enough to campaign and vote against an issue that a majority prefer but only tepidly.

Finally, there are political stakes for politicians in such a reform. As we have already seen, the passage of laws they would not have themselves supported would make it harder for politicians to get things done. But on the positive side, a national referendum would allow politicians to avoid taking the heat for decisions that are bound to be intensely unpopular with some segment of the population. One of the reasons that national referenda are often used in other countries is to diffuse the political consequences for leaders of unpopular or controversial decisions.

Direct democracy at the national level would certainly have a major impact on American politics, but it is not entirely clear who the winners and losers would be, or even if there would be any consistent winners. The new rules would benefit different groups at different times. The American people believe they would enjoy the power, and various groups are confident they would profit, but in the long run the public interest might be damaged in terms of the quality of American democracy and the protections available to minorities. Politicians have very little to gain. If such a reform ever does come about, it will be generated not by the elite but by public interest groups, special interest groups, and reformers from outside Washington.

KEY TERMS
republic.cqpress.com

benchmark poll (p. 467)
exit polls (p. 467)
gender gap (p. 482)
marriage gap (p. 483)
on-line processing (p. 488)
opinion leaders (p. 489)
political generation (p. 481)
political socialization (p. 478)
public opinion (p. 458)
public opinion polls (p. 458)
push polls (p. 470)
random samples (p. 464)
rational ignorance (p. 488)
sample (p. 461)
sample bias (p. 462)
sampling error (p. 464)
spiral of silence (p. 479)
straw polls (p. 462)
tracking polls (p. 467)
two-step flow of information (p. 488)

Key terms, chapter summaries, practice quizzes, Internet links, and other study aids are available on the companion Web site at: republic.cqpress.com.

SUMMARY
republic.cqpress.com

- The role of public opinion in politics has been hotly debated throughout American history. The founders devised a Constitution that would limit the influence of the masses. Today, some changes in the rules have given the public a greater role in government.
- Politicians and the media both watch public opinion very closely. Elected officials look for job security by responding to immediate public desires or by skillfully predicting future requests. The media make large investments in polls, sometimes covering public attitudes on a candidate or issue as a story in itself.
- While most politicians pay attention to their own informal samplings of opinion, they have also come to rely on professional polling. Such polls are based on scientific polling methods that focus on getting a good sample and asking questions that yield valid results.
- There are two competing visions of citizenship in America. The ideal democratic citizen demonstrates political knowledge, possesses an ideology (usually liberal or conservative), tolerates different ideas, and votes consistently. At the other extreme lies the apolitical, self-interested citizen. Most Americans fall somewhere between these extremes, but factors such as age, higher education, and improved socioeconomic status seem to contribute to behavior that is closer to the ideal.
- Political socialization—the transfer of fundamental democratic values from one generation to the next—is affected by demographic characteristics such as race and gender, and by life experiences such as education and religion. Interest groups, political parties, and candidates all attempt to determine the political ideas shared by various groups in order to gain their support.
- Even though Americans do not measure up to the ideal of the democratic citizen, there is much evidence to support the idea that public opinion does play a large role in government policy. While some citizens may seem apolitical and disinterested, many use rational information shortcuts to make their voting decisions. Policymakers have responded by staying generally responsive to public preferences.

PRACTICE QUIZ

republic.cqpress.com

1. According to supporters of pluralist democracy, citizens' opinions

a. should be ignored by politicians because the people are too uninformed to make important political decisions.

b. should be reflected through groups that fight for their members' interests.

c. should influence politicians on local issues, but not national issues.

d. should be followed closely by politicians because individuals are informed enough to be effective decision makers.

e. should influence politicians only on domestic policy, but not on foreign policy.

2. An ongoing series of surveys that follow public opinion over time are known as _______ polls.

a. exit

b. straw

c. following

d. benchmark

e. tracking

3. Which of the following is NOT true regarding political participation?

a. Minorities have lower participation rates than do whites.

b. The older someone is, the more likely he or she is to participate.

c. Compared to other industrialized countries, the United States ranks toward the bottom regarding voter turnout.

d. Women are less likely to vote than are men.

e. The more education one has, the more likely he or she is to vote.

4. Which of the following is NOT true about political socialization?

a. The spiral of silence can occur because of peer pressure.

b. Children develop nationalism before they enter school.

c. Children generally learn their basic citizenship skills from the family.

d. Political events, such as the Clinton impeachment, can significantly influence people's political orientations.

e. One area where the family has a weaker effect on attitudes is race relations.

5. People who know more about certain topics than we do and whose advice we trust, seek out, and follow are known as

a. opinion formers.

b. opinion leaders.

c. rational cue providers.

d. on-line processors.

e. opinion elites.

SUGGESTED RESOURCES

republic.cqpress.com

Books

Asher, Herbert. 2004. *Polling and the Public: What Every Citizen Should Know,* 6th ed. Washington, D.C.: CQ Press. An easy-to-understand and extremely informative source on the problems with public opinion polling undertaken by both candidates and the news media.

Delli Carpini, Michael X., and Scott Keeter. 1996. *What Americans Know About Politics and Why It Matters.* New Haven: Yale University Press. In this in-depth analysis of the American public's political knowledge, the authors discuss the problems that can exist in a democracy when the vast majority of the public are uninformed and disinterested in the political process.

Erikson, Robert S., and Kent L. Tedin. 2005. *American Public Opinion: Its Origins, Content, and Impact,* 7th ed. New York: Pearson Longman. The authors examine how the public thinks, why they think this way, what kinds of differences exist among Americans with different demographic backgrounds, and what influence public opinion has on public policy.

Gallup, George, and Saul Forbes Rae. 1940. *The Pulse of Democracy.* New York: Simon & Schuster. This is a hopeful account of the processes and promise of polling by perhaps the most important figure behind the development of the polling industry as we know it today. Gallup provides an insightful and candid view of polling in its infancy and with it wonderful insights into the politics of the early days of the New Deal era.

Key, V. O., Jr. 1961. *Public Opinion and American Democracy.* New York: Knopf. A classic work by one of America's most influential political scientists. Key challenges the conventional wisdom and argues that the public is capable of making tough political decisions.

McClosky, Herbert, and Alida Brill. 1983. *Dimensions of Tolerance: What Americans Believe About Civil Liberties.* New York: Russell Sage. A heavily empirical but engaging analysis of both the mass public's and the elites' support for unpopular minorities.

Page, Benjamin I., and Robert Y. Shapiro. 1992. *The Rational Public: Fifty Years of Trends in Americans' Policy Preferences.* Chicago: University of Chicago Press. A comprehensive examination of American public opinion over time and across various demographic groups. Page and Shapiro argue that—contrary to popular belief—public opinion is quite stable, and when changes do occur, they do so for rational reasons.

Pew Research Center. 2005. *Trends 2005.* Washington, D.C.: Pew Research Center. This annual report from Andrew Kohut and the people at Pew summarizes the year's findings on their major research projects: The American Public, Religion and Public Life, Media, Internet, Hispanics, and The States and Global Opinion.

Stimson, James A. 1999. *Public Opinion in America: Moods, Cycles, and Swings,* 2d ed. Boulder: Westview Press. This path-breaking work takes a new approach in public opinion research by constructing an overall measure of the public "mood" for more or less government activism and tracing these changes over the last half of the twentieth century.

Internet Sites

ABC News/*Washington Post* Polls. abcnews.go.com/US/PollVault/ and www.washingtonpost.com/wp-dyn/content/politics/polls/. Analysis of the most recent ABC News/*Washington Post* polls.

The Gallup Organization. www.gallup.com. The home page for the world's most famous polling company.

***Los Angeles Times* Polls.** www.latimes.com/news/custom/timespoll. Descriptions and analyses of polls about current issues and elections.

***New York Times*/CBS News Polls.** www.nytimes.com/library/politics/newspoll.html. Analysis of the most recent *New York Times*/CBS News polls.

Two great sites, **The Pew Research Center for the People and the Press** (www.people-press.org) and **Public Agenda** (www.publicagenda.org), provide information about polls dealing with a variety of issues.

PollingReport.com. An independent, nonpartisan resource on public opinion trends. Summarizes results from major public opinion surveys, including national and congressional elections.

The Roper Center for Public Opinion Research. www.ropercenter.uconn.edu. Provides access to hundreds of public opinion datasets about many current topics.

Ralph Nader ran as an anti-Corporate America candidate on the Reform Party ticket in 2000. The bitter lesson for Al Gore (shown below at his concession speech with his vice presidential nominee, Joe Lieberman) is that third-party candidates do more electoral harm to the party to which they are closest. Because his candidacy helped to elect George W. Bush in 2000, Nader was unable to generate much support for his 2004 run. In Oregon (at right) he failed to garner the required signatures to even get on the 2004 ballot.

POLITICAL PARTIES

12

WHAT'S AT STAKE?

Even many of Ralph Nader's best friends left him high and dry in his 2004 run for the presidency. The liberal journal *The Nation* published an open letter to him titled "Ralph, Don't Run."[1] Left-wing activist Michael Moore and libertarian television host Bill Maher got down on their knees on Maher's show to beg him to drop out of the race. Why was Nader so unpopular, even with those who supported many of the things he stood for? Much as they might have liked Nader, they disliked George W. Bush more, and they were having nightmares about Nader's role in the 2000 election, which they believed had made the Bush presidency possible.

Of course, no one had really thought Ralph Nader had a chance of winning the 2000 presidential election, including Nader himself. Running as the candidate of the Green Party, he was polling only about 4 percent of the vote, well behind both of the two major-party candidates, Democrat Al Gore and Republican George W. Bush. Under normal circumstances, his campaign would have drawn the usual nominal media attention that most third-party candidacies draw in the traditional American two-party system.

But very little about the 2000 election would prove to be normal. In fact, the electorate was so closely split between Bush and Gore that polls often showed the two men less than four percentage points apart, and the final election results would show that they essentially were tied for the win. Because of the electoral college, what really mattered was the vote in the states. In some states, most notably Florida, Nader's support was clearly enough to affect the election outcome. In an election that close, even Nader's minuscule support took on crucial importance to the two parties.

Polls showed that Nader was most likely drawing his support from the ranks of Gore voters, although some undoubtedly came from Bush supporters as well and some were first-time voters or people who otherwise would not have voted at all. As the election approached and neither major candidate maintained a commanding lead, Gore supporters began a vigorous campaign to convince Nader's supporters that voting for Nader was really voting for Bush, ensuring a Bush victory by taking crucial votes from Gore. Since Nader could not win, they argued, why not vote for Gore, who, while not taking positions as liberal as Nader's, was still closer to the values of most

Nader voters than Bush was. They accused Nader of playing the role of the spoiler, taking enough votes from one candidate to spoil his chances and throw the election to the other.

Confronted with this argument, Nader often laughed. Asked by commentator Tim Russert if he would care whether his candidacy helped to elect Bush, he responded, "Not at all. I mean, you're dealing with Democratic do-littles and Republican do-nothings, and that's just not enough for the American people."[2] Since he said he believed that there were no significant differences between the Democratic and Republican Parties, it mattered little to him which one actually won. In addition, he claimed that much of his support came from people who would not have otherwise voted, so that he wasn't really a spoiler at all.[3] His goal was to win at least 5 percent of the vote so that the Green Party could receive federal matching funds in the next election and have a better chance of promoting its agenda.

Some of his supporters were conflicted, however. Many engaged in elaborate on-line vote-swapping exchanges whereby they would promise to vote for Gore in states where the election was close in return for having someone vote for Nader in a state where Gore was well ahead. This would allow Nader to try to achieve the 5-percent threshold nationally while preserving a Gore victory in crucial states.

Was Nader right to argue that the two major parties were essentially the same? Was he in fact playing the spoiler to Al Gore's chances? Were his supporters fooling themselves to believe that their votes for Nader would not propel Bush into the presidency? That was surely what many of those supporters had come to believe by 2004. What is really at stake for all concerned in a third-party run for the White House? We return to this question at the end of this chapter, after we look more closely at the American two-party system, third-party movements, and what the Republicans and Democrats actually stand for. *

political gridlock the stalemate that occurs when political rivals, especially parties, refuse to budge from their positions to achieve a compromise in the public interest

Americans have always been of two minds about political parties. While partisan passions can burn long and brightly, fueling public service and civic action, we are also cynical about partisan bickering and the **political gridlock**, or stalemate, that can result when rival parties stubbornly refuse to budge from their positions to achieve a compromise in the public interest. Skepticism about political parties, in fact, has been a major feature of American politics since the drafting of the Constitution. When James Madison wrote in *Federalist* No. 10 that "liberty is to faction what air is to fire," he conceded that factions, whether in the form of interest groups or political parties, are a permanent fixture within our representative system, but he hoped to have limited their effects by creating a large republic with many and varied interests. President George Washington echoed Madison's concerns when he warned "against the baneful effects of the spirit of party generally," in his farewell address as president in 1796.

But it was already too late. In the presidential election of 1796, Washington's vice president, John Adams, was backed by the Federalist Party, and his opponent, Thomas Jefferson, was supported by the Democratic-Republicans. The degree to which Madison, as primary author of the Constitution, overestimated the new Republic's ability to contain the effects of faction is shown by the fact that the Constitution originally awarded the presidency to the top electoral college vote-getter, and the vice presidency to the runner-up. In 1796 this meant that Federalist John Adams found himself with Democratic-Republican Jefferson as his vice president. (The Constitution was amended in 1804 to prevent this unhappy partisan consequence from becoming a regular occurrence.) Parties have been entrenched in American politics ever since.

Political scientists began charting a decline in the public's perceptions of political parties in the mid-1960s.[4] But despite popular disenchantment with political parties and politicians' occasional frustration with them, most political observers and scholars believe that parties are essential to the functioning of democracy in general, and American democracy in particular. Despite Madison's opinion of factions, parties have not damaged the Constitution. They provide an extraconstitutional framework of rules and institutions that enhance the way the Constitution works. Who wins and who loses in American politics are determined not just by the Constitution but also by more informal rules, and chief among these are the rules produced by the political parties.

We can define a **political party** as a group of citizens united under a label to promote their ideas and policies by recruiting, nominating, promoting, and electing candidates for office in order to control the government. In this chapter you learn more about parties themselves, their role in American politics, their history, and the peculiar nature of American parties. Specifically, you will learn about

political party a group of citizens united by ideology and seeking control of government in order to promote their ideas and policies

- what political parties are, and whether they live up to our expectations of their role in a democracy
- what parties stand for in America, and whether they offer us a choice
- the history of political parties in America
- how the functions of parties developed in the American context and what they do today—how they conduct two central functions of democratic politics: electioneering and governing
- characteristics of the American party system, and how it compares to party systems in other countries
- the relationship of citizens to parties, in particular the popular unhappiness with partisanship and parties in the United States

WHAT ARE POLITICAL PARTIES?

Probably because Madison hoped that they would not thrive, political parties, unlike Congress, the presidency, the Supreme Court, and even the free press, are not mentioned in the Constitution. As we will see, in fact, many of the rules that determine the establishment and role of the parties have been created by party members themselves. Although the founding documents of American politics are silent on the place of political parties, keen political observers have long appreciated the fundamental role that political parties play in our system of government.[5] According to one scholar, "Political parties created democracy, and . . . democracy is unthinkable save in terms of parties."[6]

THE ROLE OF PARTIES IN A DEMOCRACY

Our definition of parties—that they are organizations that seek, under a common banner, to promote their ideas and policies by gaining control of government through the nomination and election of candidates for office—underscores a key difference between parties and interest groups. While both interest groups and parties seek to influence governmental policies, only parties gain this influence by sponsoring candidates in competitive elections. For political parties, winning elections represents a means to the end of controlling democratic government. Parties are crucial to the maintenance of democracy for three reasons:

- *Political linkage.* Parties provide a linkage between voters and elected officials, helping to tell voters what candidates stand for and providing a way for voters to hold their officials accountable for what they do in office, both individually and collectively.
- *Unification of a fragmented government.* Parties help overcome some of the fragmentation in government that comes from separation of powers and federalism. The founders' concern, of course, was to prevent government from becoming too powerful. But so successful were they in dividing up power that without the balancing effect of party to provide some connection between state and national government, for instance, or between the president and Congress, American government might find it very hard to achieve anything at all. Parties can lend this coherence, however, only when they control several branches or several levels of government.
- *A voice for the opposition.* Parties provide an articulate opposition to the ideas and policies of those elected to serve in government. Some citizens and critics may decry the **partisanship**, or taking of political sides, that sometimes seems to be motivated by possibilities for party gain as much as by principle or public interest. Others, however, see partisanship as providing the necessary antagonistic relationship that, like our adversarial court system, keeps politicians honest and allows the best political ideas and policies to emerge.

partisanship loyalty to a political cause or party

To highlight the multiple tasks that parties perform to make democracy work and make life easier for politicians, political scientists find it useful to divide political parties into three separate components: the party organization, the party-in-government, and the party-in-the-electorate.[7]

party organization the official structure that conducts the political business of parties

Party Organization The **party organization** is what most people think of as a political party. The party organization represents the system of central committees at the national, state, and local levels. At the top of the Democratic Party organization is the Democratic National Committee, and the Republican National Committee heads the Republican Party. Underneath these national committees are state-level party committees, and below them are county-level party committees, or county equivalents (see Figure 12.1). These party organizations raise money for campaigns, recruit and nominate candidates, organize and facilitate campaigns, register voters, mobilize voters to the polls, conduct party conventions and caucuses, and draft party platforms. This may seem like a lot; however, this is only a fraction of what party organizations do, as we will see at the end of this chapter.

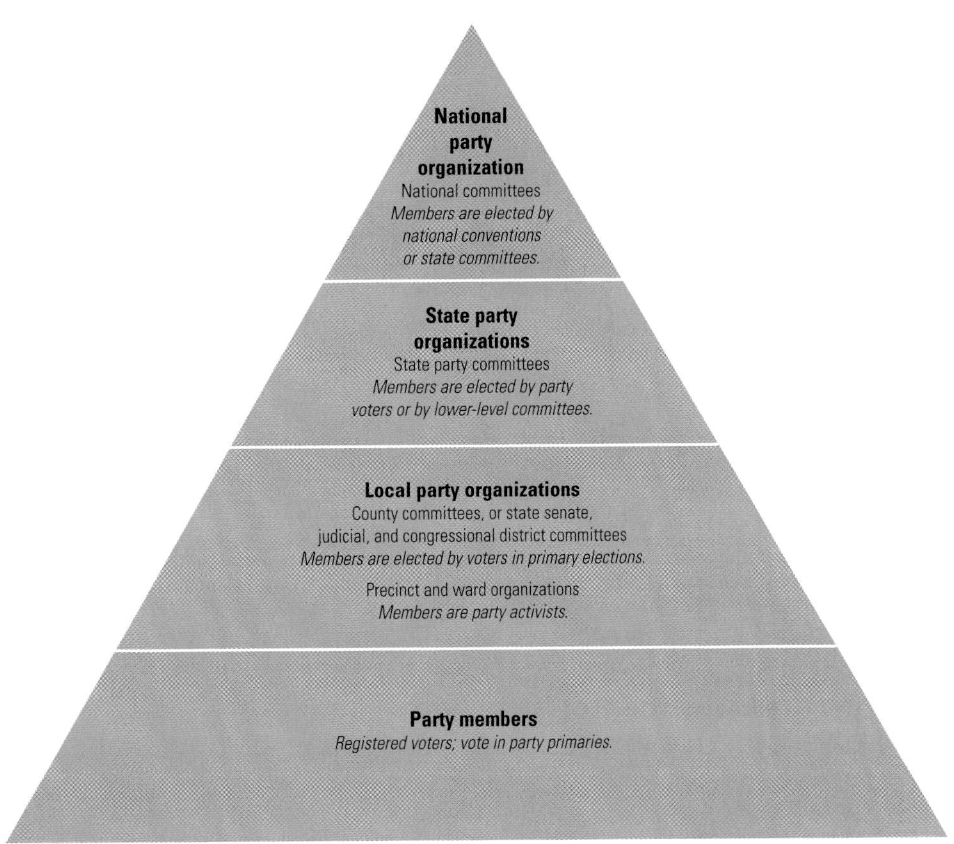

FIGURE 12.1
Organizational Structure of the Party System

Party-in-Government The **party-in-government** comprises all the candidates for national, state, and local office who have been elected. The president, as the effective head of his party, the Speaker of the House of Representatives, the majority and minority leaders in the House and Senate, the party whips in Congress, and state governors are all central actors in the party-in-government, which plays an important role in organizing government and in translating the wishes of the electorate into public policies.

party-in-government members of the party who have been elected to serve in government

Party-in-the-Electorate The **party-in-the-electorate** represents ordinary citizens who identify with or have some feeling of attachment to one of the political parties. Public opinion surveys determine **party identification**, or party ID, by asking respondents if they think of themselves as Democrats, Republicans, or independents. You can see two clear trends in party identification over time in Figure 12.2. Overall, voter attachments to the parties have declined; the percentages identifying as independents increased in the 1960s and the 1970s so that today more people consider themselves independents than identify with either of the political parties. The second trend to note in Figure 12.2 is the loss of the large numerical advantage the Democratic Party had among identifiers in the 1950s so that now the parties are about even.

party-in-the-electorate ordinary citizens who identify with the party

party identification voter affiliation with a political party

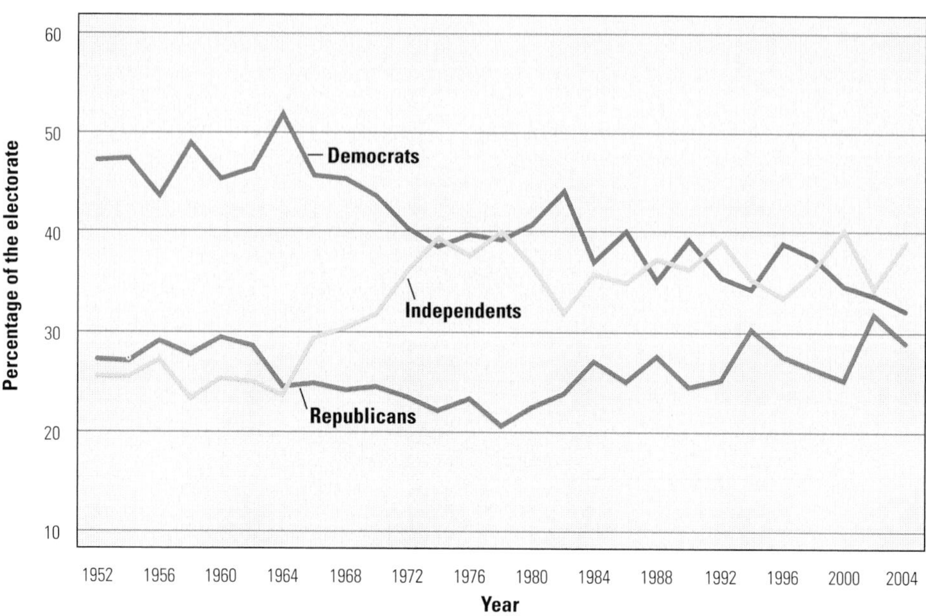

FIGURE 12.2
Party Identification, 1952–2004

Source: Calculated by the authors from American National Election Studies data.

Most voters who identify with one of the political parties "inherit" their party IDs from their parents, as we suggested in our discussion of political socialization in Chapter 11.[8] Party identifiers generally support the party's basic ideology and policy principles. These policy principles usually relate to each party's stance on the use of government to solve various economic and social problems.

Voters in most states can choose to register their party preferences for the purpose of voting in party primaries (elections to choose candidates for office). These voters are not required to perform any special activities, to contribute money to the political party, or for that matter, even to vote in the primaries. However, while voters do not have a strong formal role to play in the party organization, parties use identifiers as a necessary base of support during elections. In the 2004 presidential election, both John Kerry and George W. Bush won the votes of an overwhelming percentage of those who identified with their respective parties. But just capturing one's **party base** is not sufficient to win a national election since neither party has a majority of the national voters. As we will see later in this chapter, candidates are often pulled between the ideological preferences of their base and the more moderate preferences of independents. Usually they try to capture those moderates during the general election campaign, but in 2004 George W. Bush took the opposite tack, focusing on appeals to his conservative activist base. Although John Kerry won more of the independent vote, the much higher turnout rate and very small number of defections among Republicans were enough to return Bush to the White House.

party base members of a political party who consistently vote for that party's candidates

THE RESPONSIBLE PARTY MODEL

Earlier we said that one of the democratic roles of parties is to provide a link between the voters and elected officials, or, to use the terms we just introduced, between the party-in-the-electorate and the party-in-government. There are many ways in which parties can link voters and officials, but for the link to truly enhance democracy— that is, the control of leaders by citizens—certain conditions have to be met. Political scientists call the fulfillment of these conditions the responsible party model.[9] Under the **responsible party model**

- Each party should present a coherent set of programs to the voters, consistent with its ideology and clearly different from those of the other party.
- The candidates for each party should pledge to support their party's platform and to implement their party's program if elected.
- Voters should make their choices based on which party's program most closely reflects their own ideas and hold the parties responsible for unkept promises by voting their members out of office.
- While governing, each party should exercise control over its elected officials to ensure that party officials are promoting and voting for its programs, thereby providing accountability to the voters.

responsible party model
party government when four conditions are met: clear choice of ideologies, candidates pledged to implement ideas, party held accountable by voters, and party control over members

The responsible party model proposes that democracy is strengthened when voters are given clear alternatives and hold the parties responsible for keeping their promises. Voters can, of course, hold officials accountable without the assistance of parties, but it takes a good deal more of their time and attention. Furthermore, several political scientists have noted that while individuals can be held accountable for their own actions, many, if not most, government actions are the product of many officials. Political parties give us a way of holding officials accountable for what they do collectively as well as individually.[10]

Responsible Revolutionaries?
For the first time in forty years, Republicans assumed control of the House of Representatives in 1994. They did so, in part, by a change in strategy: rather than running as isolated individuals, GOP candidates ran on a national program that included a set of promises known as the "Contract with America." While many observers referred to the 1994 election as a "Republican revolution," we can also see it as a step in moving America closer to the responsible party model.

The responsible party model reflects an ideal party system, one that the American two-party system rarely measures up to in reality (although other countries, notably Great Britain, do come close to the model). For example, even though voters theoretically make decisions based on each party's programs, as we will see in Chapter 14, a host of other factors, such as candidate image or evaluations of economic conditions, also influence voting behavior.[11] In addition, parties themselves do not always behave as the model dictates. For instance, as we will see, American parties cannot always control candidates who refuse to support the party's program. Despite these problems, the responsible party model is valuable because it underscores the importance of voters holding the parties accountable for governing. Even if the responsible party model is not an accurate description of party politics in America, it provides a useful yardstick for understanding the character of the U.S. two-party system.

WHO, WHAT, HOW Political parties seek to control government and to promote their ideologies and policies. They do this by creating rules that allow them to control the nomination, campaign, and election processes and by trying to control the actions of their members elected to office. Politicians obviously have something at stake here, too. Parties provide a mechanism that helps them get nominated for office, win elections, and run government—but winning requires the support of nonparty members as well.

American citizens also have a big stake in what political parties do. Parties provide a link between citizens and government, cohesion among levels and branches of government, and an articulate opposition to government policy.

DO AMERICAN PARTIES OFFER VOTERS A CHOICE?

A key feature of the responsible party model is that the parties should offer voters a choice between different visions of how government should operate. Barry Goldwater, the 1964 Republican presidential nominee, stated this more bluntly: political parties, he said, should offer "a choice, not an echo." Offering voters a choice is the primary means through which parties make representative democracy work. In many countries, particularly those with more than two parties, the choices offered by parties can range from radical communist to ultraconservative.

In America, however, the ideological range of the two major parties, the Democrats and the Republicans (often also called the GOP for "Grand Old Party"), is much narrower. In fact, among many American voters there is a perception that the two parties do *not* offer real choices. For example, in 2000, when people were asked which party could handle the most important problem they thought the country faced, 50 percent said it did not make much difference.[12] In this section we investigate the widespread perception that the parties do not offer meaningful choices to voters, by examining, first, what the two major parties stand for and, second, the forces that draw the parties together and those that keep them ideologically distinct.

WHAT DO THE PARTIES STAND FOR?

Although it may seem to voters that members of the two parties are not very different once they are elected to office, the parties can be considered quite distinct in three areas: their ideologies, their memberships, and the policies they stand for.

Party Ideology In theory, each major party represents a different ideological perspective about the way that government should be used to solve problems. Ideologies, as we have said before, are broad sets of ideas about politics that help to organize our views of the political world, the information that regularly bombards us, and the positions we take on various issues. As we saw in Chapter 2, liberalism and conservatism today are ideologies that divide the country sharply over issues such as the role of government in the economy, in society, and in citizens' private lives. In general, conservatives look to government to provide social and moral order, but they want the economy to remain as unfettered as possible in the distribution of material resources. Liberals encourage government action to solve economic and social problems but want government to stay out of their personal, religious, and moral lives, except as a protector of their basic rights.

At least since the New Deal of the 1930s, the Democratic Party, especially outside the South, has been aligned with a liberal ideology and the Republican Party with a conservative perspective.[13] Since the 1960s the parties have become more consistent internally with respect to their ideologies. The most conservative region in the country is the South, but because of lingering resentment of the Republican Party for its role in the Civil War, the South was for decades tightly tied to the Democratic Party. In the 1960s, however, conservative southern Democratic voters began to vote for the Republican Party, and formerly Democratic politicians were switching their allegiances as well. By the 1990s the South had become predominantly Republican. This swing made the Democratic Party more consistently liberal and the Republicans more consistently conservative, and gave the party activist bases more power within each party because they did not have to do battle with people of different ideological persuasions. The stronger activist core has been able to exert more internal pressure within the parties, nominating candidates through primaries but also calling for ideological conformity in the parties in Congress. That is not to say, however, that all Democrats think the same or that all Republicans think the same. We saw earlier that the Republican Party includes both economic conservatives, who take the more libertarian stance of wanting to keep government limited in all spheres of life, and social or religious conservatives, who argue that government ought to take an active role in regulating the personal moral decisions that individuals make, for instance, with respect to abortion, stem cell research, end-of-life treatment, and sexual orientation. While the Democratic Party has members who are economically liberal as well as socially liberal, the combination is not as difficult for party leaders to juggle since the social liberals are currently a much smaller group.[14] Table 12.1 shows how party ID matches up with a number of issue positions.

Party Membership Party ideologies attract and are reinforced by different coalitions of voters. This means that the Democrats' post–New Deal liberal ideology reflects the preferences of its coalition of working- and lower-class voters, including union members, minorities, women, the elderly, and urban dwellers. The Republicans' conservative ideology, on the other hand, reflects the preferences of upper- to middle-class whites, those who are in evangelical and Protestant religions, and suburban voters. Table 12.2 shows how each party's coalition differs based on group characteristics. There is nothing inevitable about these coalitions, however, and they are subject to change as the parties' stances on issues change and as the opposing party offers new alternatives. Differences between men and women used to be insignificant, but the gender gap has grown and endured as the parties have taken contrasting positions on

TABLE 12.1 Party Identification and Issue Positions, 2004

ISSUE POSITION	DEMOCRATS	INDEPENDENTS	REPUBLICANS
Ideological Self-Identification			
Liberal	41%	25%	4%
Moderate	50	52	29
Conservative	9	24	67
Gay Marriage			
Agree gays and lesbians should be allowed to marry	40	45	14
Health Care Policy			
Government should provide health insurance for all	54	46	24
Defense Spending			
Defense spending should be increased	34	53	76
Abortion			
Oppose use of government funds to help pay for the costs of abortion for women who cannot afford them	47	55	76
Social Spending			
Prefer more services in health and education even if it means an increase in spending	52	42	21
Interventionism			
Must be ready to use force versus diplomacy to solve international problems	23	33	60

Note: Compare across columns. For example, 41 percent of Democrats compared to only 4 percent of Republicans considered themselves liberal.

Source: Calculated by the authors from the 2004 National Election Studies data set.

a series of issues on which men and women tend to feel differently (see discussion of the gender gap in Chapter 11).

party platform list of policy positions a party endorses and pledges its elected officials to enact

Policy Differences Between the Parties When the parties run slates of candidates for office, those candidates run on a **party platform**—a list of policy positions the party endorses and pledges its elected officials to enact as policy. A platform is the national party's campaign promises, usually made only in a presidential election year. If the parties are to make a difference politically, then the platforms have to reflect substantial differences that are consistent with their ideologies. The responsible party model requires that the parties offer distinct platforms, that voters know about them and vote on the basis of them, and that the parties ensure that their elected officials follow through in implementing them.

The two major parties' stated positions on some key issues from their 2004 platforms appear in "*Consider the Source:* How to Be a Critical Reader of Political Party Platforms." These differences between the Democratic and Republican platforms in 2004 are typical. Moreover, the variations between the parties' platforms become greater during times of social change when each party's coalition of voters is changing. This means that during times when the potential for political change is greatest,

TABLE 12.2 **Party Identification by Groups**

SOCIAL GROUPS	DEMOCRATS	INDEPENDENTS	REPUBLICANS	PARTY DIFFERENCE
Religious Group				
Protestants	27%	35%	38%	−11%
Catholics	32	38	30	−2
Jews	58	25	17	+41
Other	39	40	22	+17
Sex				
Men	26	44	30	−4
Women	37	35	28	+9
Race/Ethnicity				
Whites	26	38	37	−11
Blacks	61	37	3	+58
Hispanics	37	48	14	+23
Asians	23	46	31	−8
Household Income				
Less than $30,000	38	43	19	+19
$30,000–89,999	30	37	32	−2
$90,000+	27	35	39	−12

Note: In each row, the cell entries for the three party identifications sum to 100 percent. For example, 27 percent of the Protestants are Democrats, 35 percent are Independents, and 38 percent are Republican. The figures in the last column show the relative partisan balance for each group with positive values indicating more Democrats among that group.

Source: Calculated by the authors from the 2004 National Election Studies data set. The figures for Asians are based on the 2000–2004 surveys for enough cases for a reliable estimate.

the parties are most likely to provide voters with distinctly different ideologies and policy agendas.[15]

FORCES DRAWING THE PARTIES TOGETHER AND PUSHING THEM APART

As we have seen, there are clear differences between the parties in terms of their ideologies, their members, and their platforms. That does not guarantee that the parties will really seem different, however, especially when their candidates are running for national office. There are important electoral forces that draw the parties together as well as internal forces that drive them apart. These forces are central to understanding electoral politics in America today. In this section we look more closely at these complex relationships.

The Pull Toward Moderation Obviously, if a candidate is going to win an election, he or she must appeal to more voters than the opposing candidate does. On any policy or set of policies, voters' opinions range from very liberal to very conservative; however, in the American two-party system, most voters tend to be in the middle, holding a moderate position between the two ideological extremes (see Figure 12.3, top, on page 510). The party that appeals best to the moderate voters usually wins most of the votes. Thus, even though the ideologies of the parties are distinct, the pressures related to winning a majority of votes can lead both parties to campaign on the same issue positions, thus making them look similar to voters.[16] As a result, Republicans moved from their initial opposition to join the majority of voters in supporting Social Security, Medicare, and Medicaid. Similarly, the Democrats have dropped their resistance to become strong supporters of a balanced federal budget.

Consider the Source

How to Be a Critical Reader of Political Party Platforms

Think of it as an invitation to a party—so to speak. In their platforms, political parties make a broad statement about who they are and what they stand for in the hope that you will decide to join them. The excerpts below from the Democratic and Republican platforms of 2004 show differing positions on several key issues. The full text of these platforms can be found on the Web sites of the parties' national committees. Platforms of various third parties can also be found on the Web. Should you be interested enough to pursue your acquaintance with any or all of these parties, go armed with these questions:

1. **Whose platform is it, and what do you know about that party's basic political positions?** Understanding the basics will help you to interpret key phrases. For instance, how might the terms "family values" and "religious freedom" be defined differently in the Democratic and Republican platforms?

2. **Who is the audience?** Parties direct their platforms to two different groups—the party faithful and potential new supporters. For example, Democrats want to keep their traditional supporters, like union members, but they also want to broaden their appeal to the middle class and to small business owners. Republicans want to keep their base (including pro-life activists) happy but also want to attract more women in an effort to close the gender gap. How does this dual audience affect how parties portray themselves?

3. **Which statements reflect values, and which are statements of fact?** First, get clear about the values you are being asked to support. Parties tend to sprinkle their platforms liberally with phrases like "fundamental rights." Everybody is in favor of fundamental rights. Which ones do they actually mean, and do you consider them fundamental rights? What are the costs and benefits of agreeing to their value claims? Then evaluate the facts. Are they accurate? Check out statistics. Do they seem reasonable? If not, look them up.

4. **Do you think the party can deliver on its policy proposals?** What resources (money, power, and so on) would it need? Can it get them? What if the party does enact the promised policies? Would it achieve what the party claims it would achieve? Who would be the winners, and who the losers?

5. **What is your reaction to the platform?** Could you support it? How does it fit with your personal values and political beliefs? Is the appeal of this platform emotional? Intellectual? Ideological? Moral? Remember that party platforms are not just statements of party principles and policy proposals; they are also advertisements. Read them with all the caution and suspicion you would bring to bear on any other ad that wants to convince you to buy, or buy into, something. *Caveat emptor*! (Let the buyer beware!)

DEMOCRATIC PLATFORM

Adopted by the Democratic National Convention:
July 27, 2004
Title: *Strong at Home, Respected in the World*

Affirmative Action and Civil Rights

We support affirmative action to redress discrimination and to achieve the diversity from which all Americans benefit. . . . We will enact the bipartisan legislation barring workplace discrimination based on sexual orientation. We are committed to equal treatment of all service members. . . . We support the appointment of judges who will uphold our laws and constitutional rights, not their own narrow agendas.

Gay Rights

We support full inclusion of gay and lesbian families in the life of our nation. . . . We repudiate President Bush's divisive effort to politicize the Constitution by pursuing a "Federal Marriage Amendment."

REPUBLICAN PLATFORM

Adopted by the Republican National Convention:
August 26, 2004
Title: *A Safer World and a More Hopeful America*

Affirmative Action and Civil Rights

The Republican Party favors. . .measures to ensure that no individual is discriminated against on the basis of race, national origin, gender, or other characteristics covered by our civil rights laws. . . . We believe in . . . taking steps to ensure that disadvantaged individuals of all colors and ethnic backgrounds have the opportunity to compete economically and that no child is left behind educationally.

Gay Rights

We . . . believe that legal recognition and the accompanying benefits afforded couples should be preserved for that unique and special union of one man and one woman which has historically been called marriage. [We] defend the Defense of Marriage Act,

DEMOCRATIC PLATFORM (*continued*)

Abortion
We stand proudly for a woman's right to choose, consistent with *Roe v. Wade,* and regardless of her ability to pay. . . . At the same time, we strongly support family planning and adoption incentives. Abortion should be safe, legal, and rare.

Education
We believe in an America where . . . every qualified young person who wants to go to college can afford it. And where every adult who needs additional job training can get it. In President George Bush's America, our government ignores the shameful truth that the quality of a child's education depends on the wealth of that child's neighborhood. . . . When President Bush signed the No Child Left Behind Act, . . . he promptly broke his word, providing schools $27 billion less than he had promised, literally leaving millions of children behind.

Gun Control
We will keep guns out of the hands of criminals and terrorists by fighting gun crime, reauthorizing the assault weapons ban, and closing the gun show loophole.

National Defense/Terrorism
Despite his tough talk, President Bush's actions against terrorism have fallen far short. He still has no comprehensive strategy for victory. After allowing bin Laden to escape from our grasp at Tora Bora, he diverted crucial resources from the effort to destroy al Qaeda in Afghanistan. His doctrine of unilateral preemption has driven away our allies and cost us the support of other nations. . . . The only possible path to victory will be found in the company of others, not walking alone. . . . We must enlist those whose support we need for ultimate victory.

Budget
We will roll back the Bush tax cuts for those making more than $200,000. . . . We will commit to living within tough budget caps—real and enforceable limits on what the government can spend.

Taxes
We should set taxes for families making more than $200,000 a year at the same level as in the late 1990s. . . . We will cut taxes for 98 percent of Americans and . . . end deferral that encourages companies to ship jobs overseas. . . .

Source: www.democrats.org/pdfs/2004platform.pdf

REPUBLICAN PLATFORM (*continued*)

which . . . reaffirms the right of states not to recognize same-sex marriages licensed in other states. . . . We affirm that homosexuality is incompatible with military service.

Abortion
We support a human life amendment to the Constitution and we endorse legislation to make it clear that the Fourteenth Amendment's protections apply to unborn children. . . . We oppose using public revenues for abortion and will not fund organizations which advocate it. We support the appointment of judges who respect traditional family values and the sanctity of innocent human life.

Education
Strong schools will also produce a workforce with the skills to compete in the 21st century economy. . . . The No Child Left Behind Act of 2001 . . . was the most significant overhaul of federal education policy since 1965. And it became a promise kept to parents, students, teachers, and every American. Public education, access for every child to an excellent education, is a foundation of a free, civil society.

Gun Control
[We] strongly support an individual right to own guns. . . . We oppose federal licensing of law-abiding gun owners and national gun registration. . . . We support efforts . . . to enhance the instant background check system for gun purchases and to ensure that records of lawful transactions are destroyed in a timely manner.

National Defense/Terrorism
We are going after terrorists wherever they plot and plan and hide. . . . We will extend the peace by supporting the rise of democracy, . . . as the alternative to hatred and terror in the broader Middle East. We will not allow the world's most dangerous regimes to possess the world's most dangerous weapons. . . . Today, . . . the forces of terror and tyranny have suffered defeat after defeat, and America and the world are safer.

Budget
[Bush's] top budgetary priority is to protect America and win the War on Terror. He also remains committed to . . . education reforms. . . . All discretionary spending must be kept in check and taxes must remain low to stimulate economic growth.

Taxes
Making the tax cuts permanent is a crucial first step toward expanding ownership and ensuring that America turns economic growth into lasting prosperity. We support extending the pay-as-you-go[1] requirement for mandatory spending only.

Source: www.gop.com/media/2004platform.pdf

1. Pay-as-you-go is a requirement that was in place in the Senate from 1991 to 1997. It required anyone proposing a new tax cut or entitlement expansion to come up with a way to pay for it without enlarging the deficit, or with sixty votes in the Senate to bypass the bill. Without pay-as-you-go, members of Congress are free to introduce tax cuts or entitlement expansions, leaving the added cost to accumulate in the national deficit. See Richard Kogan, "The Need to Restore Pay-as-You-Go Budget Enforcement for Tax Cuts and Entitlements," Center on Budget and Policy Priorities, www.cbpp.org/3-14-05bud.htm.

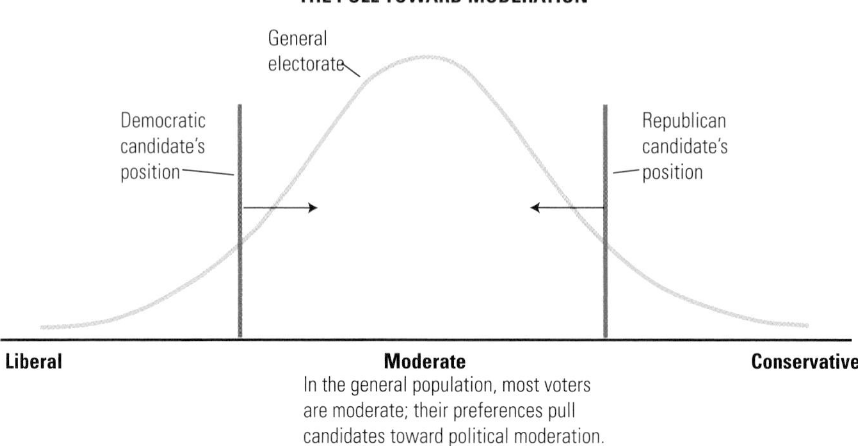

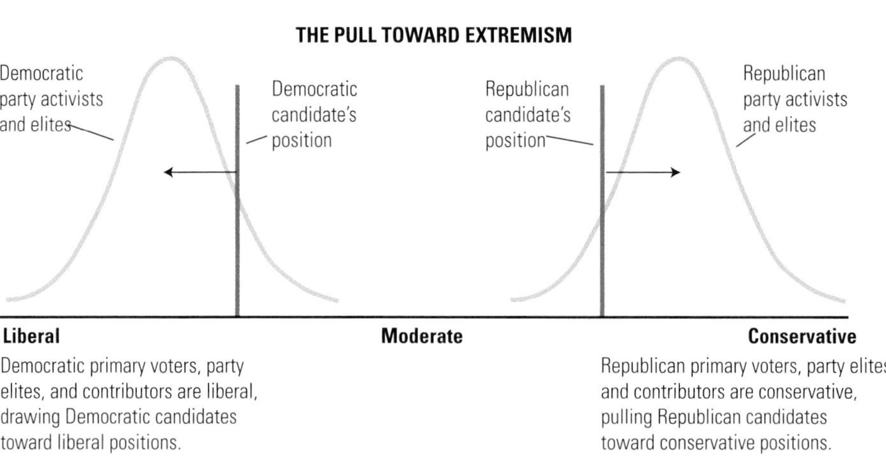

FIGURE 12.3
External and Internal Forces on the Parties

The parties can deal with the tension between activists and the larger body of moderates in ways other than by changing the party positions. One strategy is to simply emphasize issues that are popular with moderates. Republicans routinely claimed that President Bill Clinton kept stealing their ideas and policies, because as a moderate Democrat, he had some ideas and policies on the economy and social programs that were not far removed from those of the Republicans. In turn, Democrats protested after the 2000 Republican convention that Republicans, with their display of diversity and concern for the poor, were turning into Democrats. In the 2004 election, George W. Bush focused on the dangers inherent in the war on terror, on which moderates favored him strongly over John Kerry.

Another way parties can make their programs attractive to moderates while keeping their bases happy is to reframe the issues in ways that are palatable to more voters. When, in early 2005, polls showed that a majority of Americans did not support President Bush's proposals to privatize Social Security, the same proposals were recast as "creating personal accounts" to connote more independence and individual control.[17]

Building and Securing the Base
Here, the majority leader of the U.S. Senate, Bill Frist, addresses a crowd via teleconferencing at an evangelical Christian rally called "Justice Sunday." The Republican Party has gained identifiers through its appeals to the Christian right. However, one of the consequences of bringing such new groups into a party is that they then, understandably, make new demands on the party and its leaders, and thus help to redefine what the party stands for.

Similarly, a tax cut that rewarded those with higher incomes was presented as a "jobs bill" rather than a tax cut for the very rich.[18] Both parties, of course, attempt to present their policies in ways that will get the widest possible acceptance among the public.

The Pull Toward Extremism On key issues, presidents will seek to portray their proposals as serving the interests of the general public, but in fact the specific policy solutions are almost always consistent with their party's ideological perspective and policy agenda. Even though the necessity of appealing to the many moderate voters in the middle of the American political spectrum draws the two major parties together, there are also major forces within the parties that keep them apart: the need to placate party activists and the need to raise money.

The main players in political parties are often called the "party faithful," or **party activists**, people who are especially committed to the values and policies of the party, and who devote more of their resources, both time and money, to the party's cause. Although these party activists are not an official organ of the party, they certainly represent a party's lifeblood. A typical party activist is a person with a strong attachment to the party who often takes a vigorous role in campaign activities or other types of party functions. Compared to the average voter, party activists tend to be more ideologically extreme (more conservative or more liberal even than the average party identifier) and to care more intensely about the party's issues. Their influence can have significant effects on the ideological character of both parties.[19]

party activists the "party faithful"; the rank-and-file members who actually carry out the party's electioneering efforts

Party activists play a key role in keeping the parties ideologically distinct because one of their primary purposes in being active in the party is to ensure that the party advocates their issue positions. Because they tend to be concerned with keeping the party pure, they are reluctant to compromise on their issues, even if this means losing the election.[20] Liberal activists kept the Democratic Party to the left of most Americans during the 1970s and 1980s; the only Democratic candidate who won a presidential election during that time was Jimmy Carter, in the immediate aftermath of the Watergate scandal that drove Republican Richard Nixon from office. Republicans sought to keep alive the impression that the Democrats were a party of crazed left-wing activists in 1988 by making *liberal,* or "the L-word" as they referred to it, such a derogatory term that the Democrats could not use it to describe themselves without turning off voters. While Democrats dealt with the problem by restructuring their internal politics and giving more weight to moderate Democrats like Bill Clinton and Al Gore, the Republicans fell into the same difficulty of appearing to be as conservative as their most activist members in the religious right. The Democrats were consequently able to capture the presidency by appealing to the moderate middle—focusing on the economic problems of Americans in 1992 and appropriating and giving less extreme meaning to the label of "family values" in 1996. The Republicans, in turn, regrouped in 2000 and chose in George W. Bush a presidential candidate who could appeal to moderate voters.

Party activists are able to exert considerable influence on candidates because they are the party's chief campaign workers and fundraisers, and they make up the bulk of the voters who bother to vote in the party's primaries, in which the party's nominees are chosen. This puts the candidates in a bind. Even though in the general election candidates must appeal to the middle voters, who tend to be moderate, they must first win their party's primary. This requires them to appeal to party activists to contribute their time, energy, and resources to their primary campaigns and to attract a majority of the party's primary voters.

An excellent example of the political dilemma this creates is the decision faced by House Republicans on the impeachment of President Clinton in 1998. Even though public opinion ran strongly in favor of the president, about a third of the voters, largely the Republican base, wanted to see him impeached. Conservative Republicans from conservative districts faced no problems in voting for impeachment. Moderate Republicans, on the other hand, who needed the votes of some Democrats to win reelection in their less conservative districts, had to choose between (1) obeying the dictates of their constituencies and voting against impeachment while alienating their party activists and (2) doing what their party activists wanted by voting for impeachment, securing their party's nomination, and hoping the majority of their constituents' memories would be short. Almost all chose the latter course of action. The dilemma was less severe for senators who had to vote for or against conviction of the president shortly afterward because, as representatives of whole states, their constituents were more diverse.

The need to please party activists gives candidates a powerful incentive to remain true to the party's causes. Activists are poised to work hard for candidates who promote their political, social, economic, or religious agendas and, conversely, to work just as hard against any candidate who does not pass their litmus test.[21] This means that candidates who moderate too much or too often risk alienating the activists who are a key component of their success. Moreover, because activists are tied more to a cause than a candidate, many activists will work fervently to purge the party of those candidates whom they perceive to have sold out their cause.[22]

The central role of money in campaigning today reinforces the effects of the party activists and primary voters. Most of the money used to fund campaigns comes from two sources: individual donors, who many times are also party activists contributing to the efforts of a candidate; and political action committees, or PACs. PACs are the fundraising arms of interest groups that unite to influence the government to support their political goals. But unlike parties, PACs do not control the government directly. Even though there are numerous kinds of PACs, many have a strong ideological bent.

For example, PACs representing labor, teachers, and environmentalists are more liberal in orientation, whereas PACs representing business and industry tend to be more conservative. Being beholden to an interest group with an ideological agenda helps to keep politicians true to their ideological roots.[23]

Together these factors help to keep candidates from converging to the moderate voter (see Figure 12.3, bottom). Thus the likely winner of most Democratic primaries is going to be more liberal than the average voter in the general election, and the likely winner of most Republican primaries will be more conservative. Even though candidates do win some votes by taking more moderate stands, they are nevertheless mindful of their bases and tend not to stray very far from their roots once in office.[24] This means that few politicians are willing to be truly moderate and work with the other side. Since the 1980s, there has been an increased ideological polarization between the parties that has yielded more intense partisan conflict and sometimes policy gridlock.

WHO, WHAT, HOW While the rules of electoral politics create incentives for the parties to take moderate positions that appeal to the majority of voters, party activists, primary voters, and big-money donors, who tend to be more ideological and issue oriented, pull party policy agendas back toward their extremes. As a consequence, parties and their candidates tend to remain true to their respective party's ideological perspective, promoting policy solutions that are consistent with the party's ideology. Thus Democratic candidates espouse a policy agenda that reflects the liberal interests of the coalition of groups that represent their most ardent supporters. Likewise, Republican candidates advocate a policy agenda that reflects the conservative interests of the coalition of groups that are *their* most ardent supporters. In this way, both parties, in most elections, offer voters "a choice, not an echo," but they also contribute to the growing partisanship of American politics. The real losers in this situation may be the party moderates and independents who, less intense and active than the party base, find themselves poorly represented at the end of the day.

THE HISTORY OF PARTIES IN AMERICA

For James Madison, parties were just an organized version of that potentially dangerous political association, the faction. He had hopes that their influence on American politics would be minimal, but scarcely was the ink dry on the Constitution before the founders were organizing themselves into groups to promote their political views. In the 1790s a host of disagreements among these early American politicians led Alexander Hamilton and John Adams to organize the Federalists, the group of legislators that supported their views. Later, Thomas Jefferson and James Madison would do the same with the Democratic-Republicans. Over the course of the next decade, these organizations expanded beyond their legislative purposes to include recruiting candidates to run as members of their party for both Congress and the presidency. The primary focus, however, was on the party-in-government and not on the voters.[25]

THE EVOLUTION OF AMERICAN PARTIES

The history of political parties in the United States is dominated by ambitious politicians who have shaped their parties in order to achieve their goals.[26] Chief among those goals, as we have seen, are getting elected to office and running government once there. In 1828, Martin Van Buren and Andrew Jackson turned the Democratic Party away from a focus on the party-in-government, creating the country's first mass-based party and setting the stage for the development of the voter-oriented party machine. **Party machines** were tightly organized party systems at the state, city, and county levels that kept control of voters by getting them jobs, helping them out financially when necessary, and in fact becoming part of their lives and their communities. This mass organization was built around one principal goal: taking advantage of the expansion of voting rights to all white men (even those without property) to elect more Democratic candidates.[27]

party machines mass-based party systems in which parties provided services and resources to voters in exchange for votes

The Jacksonian Democrats enacted a number of party and governmental reforms designed to enhance the control of party leaders, known as **party bosses**, over the candidates, the officeholders, and the campaigns. During the nomination process the party bosses would choose the party's candidates for the general election. The most common means for selecting candidates was the party caucus, a special meeting of hand-picked party leaders who appointed the party's nominees. Any candidate seeking elective office (and most offices were elective) would have to win the boss's approval by pledging his loyalty to the party boss and supporting policies that the party boss favored.

party bosses party leaders, usually in an urban district, who exercised tight control over electioneering and patronage

Winning candidates were expected to hire only other party supporters for government positions and reward only party supporters with government contracts. This largesse expanded the range of people with a stake in the party's electoral success. The combination of candidates and people who had been given government jobs and contracts meant that the party had an army of supporters to help recruit and mobilize voters to support the party. Moreover, because party bosses controlled the nomination process, any candidate who won elective office but did not fulfill his pledges to the party boss would be replaced by someone who would. This system of **patronage**, which we discussed in Chapter 9, on bureaucracy, rewarded faithful party supporters with public office, jobs, and government contracts and ensured that a party's candidates were loyal to the party or at least to the party bosses.

patronage system in which successful party candidates reward supporters with jobs or favors

Because the Democratic Party machine was so effective at getting votes and controlling government, the Whig Party (1830s through 1850s), and later the Republican Party (starting in the mid-1850s), used these same techniques to organize. Party bosses and their party machines were exceptionally strong in urban areas in the East and Midwest. Boss Tweed in New York City, the Pendergasts in Kansas City, Frank Hague (who was quoted as saying "I am the law") in Jersey City, James Michael Curley in Boston, and "Big Bill" Thompson in Chicago represent just a partial list of the party bosses who dominated the urban landscape in the nineteenth and early twentieth centuries.

The urban machines, while designed to further the interests of the parties themselves, had the important democratic consequence of integrating into the political process the masses of new immigrants coming into the urban centers at the turn of the twentieth century. Because parties were so effective at mobilizing voters, the average participation rate exceeded 80 percent in most U.S. elections prior to the 1900s.

However, the strength of these party machines was also their weakness. In many cases, parties would do almost anything to win, including directly buying the votes of people, mobilizing new immigrants who could not speak English and were not U.S. citizens, and resurrecting dead people from their graves to vote in the elections. In addition, the whole system of patronage, based on doling out government jobs, contracts, and favors, came under attack by reformers in the early 1900s as representing favoritism and corruption. Political reforms such as the **party primary**, in which the

party primary nomination of party candidates by registered party members rather than party bosses

Taking on the Political Machine
This 1871 Thomas Nast cartoon was part of an outcry at the abuses of power and corruption of Tammany Hall, the name of the Manhattan political machine controlled by William "Boss" Tweed in the years following the Civil War. Tweed went to jail but Tammany Hall continued to control New York City politics into the Great Depression.

"THAT'S WHAT'S THE MATTER."
Boss Tweed. "As long as I count the Votes, what are you going to do about it? say?"

party-in-the-electorate rather than the party bosses chose between competing party candidates for a party's nomination, and civil service reform, under which government jobs were filled on the basis of merit instead of party loyalty, did much to ensure that party machines went the way of the dinosaur.

A BRIEF HISTORY OF PARTY ERAS

A striking feature of American history is that, while we have not had a revolutionary war in America since 1776, we have several times changed our political course in rather dramatic ways. One of the many advantages of a democratic form of government is that dramatic changes in policy direction can be effected through the ballot box rather than through bloody revolution. Over the course of two centuries, the two-party system in the United States has been marked by twenty-five to forty-year periods of relative stability, with one party tending to maintain a majority of congressional seats and controlling the presidency. These periods of stability are called **party eras**. Short periods of large-scale change—peaceful revolutions, as it were, signaled by one major **critical election** in which the majority of people shift their political allegiance from one party to another—mark the end of one party era and the beginning of another. Scholars call such shifts in party dominance a **realignment**. In these realignments the coalitions of groups supporting each of the parties change to a new alignment of groups. Though it is not always the case, realignments generally result in parallel changes in governmental policies, reflecting the policy agenda of each party's new coalition. Realignments have been precipitated by major critical events like the Civil War and the Great Depression. The United States has gone through six party eras in its two-hundred-years-plus history. In the following sections we look at each of these eras briefly. (Figure 12.4 shows the six party eras and the realigning elections associated with the transitions between them.)

party eras extended periods of relative political stability in which one party tends to control both the presidency and Congress

critical election an election signaling a significant change in popular allegiance from one party to another

realignment substantial and long-term shift in party allegiance by individuals and groups, usually resulting in a change in policy direction

The First Party Era The First Party Era began in the 1790s and early 1800s and lasted until 1824. During this period the party system was primarily an elite phenomenon and, like the national government itself, was in a process of formation. One major issue—the power of the national government versus the states—provided a central

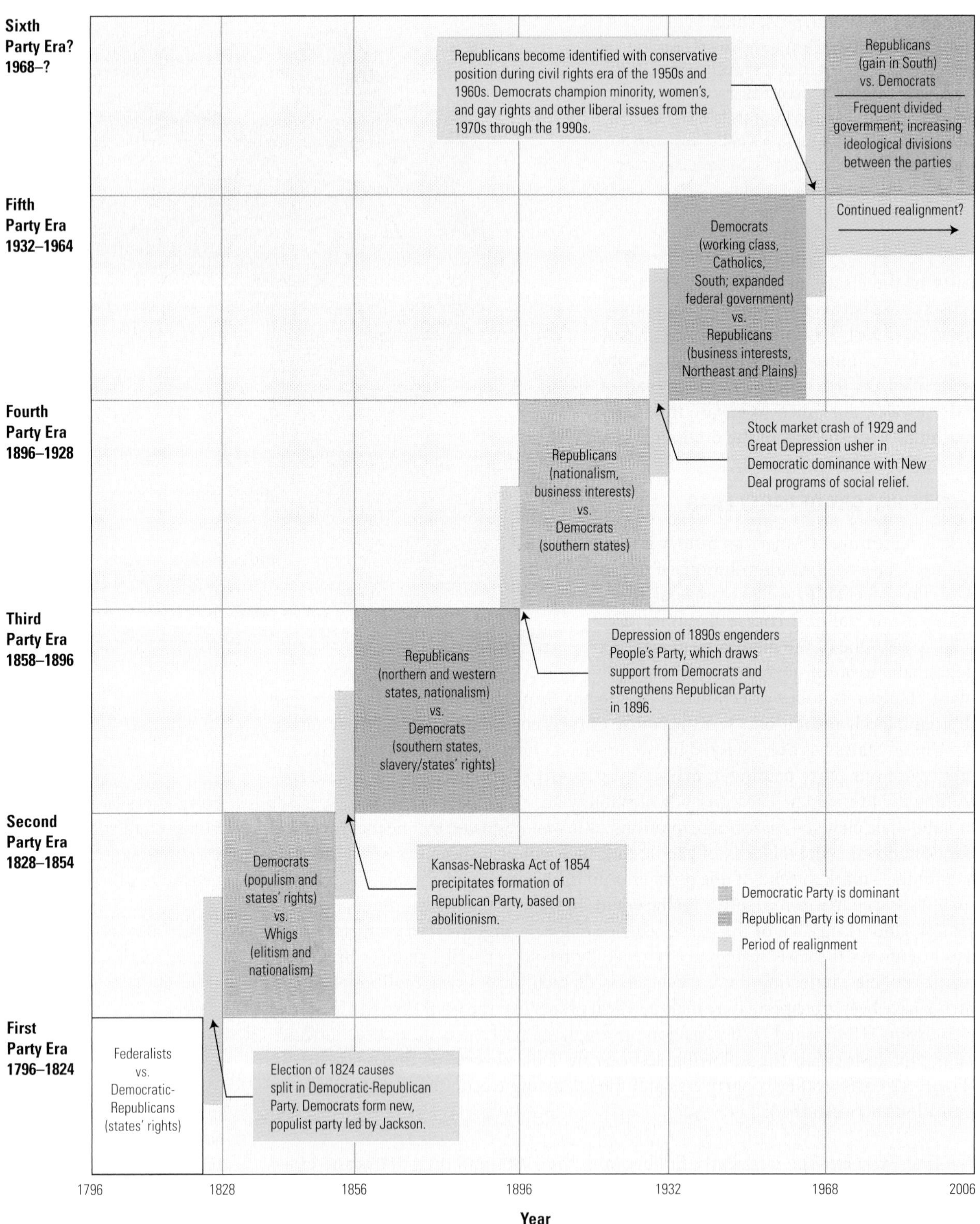

FIGURE 12.4
Party Eras and Realignments

core around which coalitions formed. On one side of the issue supporting a stronger national government were the Federalists, led by John Adams and Alexander Hamilton, and on the states' rights side were the Democratic-Republicans (also called Jeffersonian Republicans), led by Thomas Jefferson and James Madison.

The Second Party Era The Second Party Era began after the election of 1824, a four-way struggle that ended up in the House of Representatives because no candidate received a majority of the 261 electoral college votes. (Recall that the Twelfth Amendment requires the House to select the president from among the electoral vote leaders when no person wins the majority of votes.) While first-time candidate Andrew Jackson led in both the popular vote (43 percent) and the electoral college vote (38 percent, or 99 of 261 votes), the House instead chose his closest competitor, John Quincy Adams (with 31 percent of the popular vote and 32 percent of the electoral vote) to be the next president. Fueled by their outrage over this seemingly unfair outcome, Jackson's supporters immediately began planning his campaign for 1828. The Democratic-Republican Party split, with the Jacksonians eventually becoming the Democratic Party and the Adams wing emerging as the National Republican Party. Jackson prevailed in 1828 in a bitter election.

The election of 1828 is most notable, however, for its demonstration of a new feature in electoral politics: mass participation. Jackson's belief in popular government and his criticism of elitist attitudes, combined with the changes in state voting requirements extending the suffrage to many non–property-owning white males, created an explosion in the number of voters. Voter turnout, only 350,000 in 1824, had swelled to well over a million by 1828.

Jackson's election solidified the coalition of politicians and voters who supported states' rights (lower classes and southern states) over the power of the national government (business interests and northern states). From the ashes of Adams's failed candidacy came a new party to oppose the Democrats, the Whigs, led by Henry Clay and Daniel Webster. From the late 1830s until the mid-1850s, the Democrats and Whigs actively competed against each other in the North, South, and newly emerged midwestern and far western states. In 1854 the Kansas-Nebraska Act, which gave each territory the right to decide the slavery issue, galvanized the abolitionists in the North and the pro-slavery movement in the South. That year a new party, the Republicans, formed primarily based on its opposition to slavery.

The Third Party Era The Third Party Era dates from 1858, when the Republicans took control of the House of Representatives. By 1860 its presidential candidate, Abraham Lincoln, had won the presidency as well. After the Civil War, regionalism defined the new party era, with the Democrats dominating the states of the old Confederacy and proslavery states, and the Republicans dominating northern and western states. On the national level, presidential elections were closely contested, but the Republicans tended to hold the edge.

The Fourth Party Era The Fourth Party Era started in the 1890s, when the United States was in the midst of a depression that hit farmers in the South and the Great Plains particularly hard. A third party, the People's Party, formed in response to this economic crisis. In the presidential elections in 1896, William Jennings Bryan, a Nebraska Democrat, attempted to merge the Democratic Party with the People's Party but failed to amass enough farmers and industrial labor voters to win.[28] As the depression ended in the late 1890s, the issues surrounding the formation of the People's Party died, and the regional basis of the other two parties became more intense. The Democrats solidified their control of the southern states, and the Republicans did the same over the other parts of the country.

The Fifth Party Era The Fifth Party Era was a political response to the Great Depression, which began with the stock market crash in October 1929 and produced massive unemployment, property foreclosures, and bank failings. Desperate people looked to the federal government for relief, and in 1932, Franklin D. Roosevelt and the Democrats, campaigning on the promise of a New Deal, swept the Republicans out of office. The coalition of voters supporting the Democrats' New Deal included Southern Democrats, Catholic immigrants (Italians and Irish), blue collar workers, and farmers. Republicans maintained support among business owners and industrialists, and strengthened their regional support in the Northeast and the Plains states.

A Sixth Party Era? Most analysts agree that the New Deal coalition supporting the Fifth Party Era has changed, but there is much controversy about the timing and character of that change and, in fact, about whether we have entered a new partisan era at all.[29] The controversy is hard to resolve because no single critical election has marked the realignment, although incremental changes have occurred that are large and seemingly long lasting. Among these are the massive migration of white southerners to the Re-

Mudslinging Back in the Fourth Party Era

Tough campaigns aren't new to American politics. During the 1896 presidential race one very partisan novelty item attempted to show what a vote for either candidate would mean: a vote for William McKinley "Protecting American Industries"; a vote for William Jennings Bryan, "Repudiation Bankruptcy, and Dishonor."

publican Party and the less massive but still notable trend for Catholics to be less solidly Democratic than they were at the formation of the New Deal. Similarly, African Americans have shifted from somewhat favoring the Democratic Party to overwhelming Democratic identification. The geographic bases of the parties have changed: the South used to be referred to as the "Solid South," meaning solidly Democratic; it is now the most dependable region for the Republican Party in presidential elections (see Figure 12.5). In recent elections, Democrats have been more likely to win in New England and the mid-Atlantic states—areas where the Republicans were stronger in the 1940s. In recent years these changes have been labeled as differences between "Red" and "Blue" America, which refers to the southern, Midwestern, and mountain support for the Republican Party set against a pattern of coastal and industrial Northeast support for Democrats (see "*Who Are We?* Red vs. Blue, or Purple All Over?" in Chapter 14).

These coalition changes have fundamentally changed the character of the old New Deal party system; however, they have not resulted in a solid new majority, which some scholars feel signals a realignment and a new party era.[30] It is true that the Republicans have recently had control of the White House as well as the House of Representatives and the Senate, but their majorities are still narrow and the presidential race margins have been razor thin. Unlike the overwhelming Democratic majorities that ushered in the Fifth Party Era, the current era is characterized by a narrowly divided nation, intense party competition, and a large number of independents whose votes are up for grabs in any election.

This pattern of change is illustrated in Figure 12.2 on page 502; those who focus on this change as particularly significant argue for a period of **dealignment**. This refers to a dissolving of the old era of party dominance in which older party loyalties are

dealignment a trend among voters to identify themselves as independents rather than as members of a major party

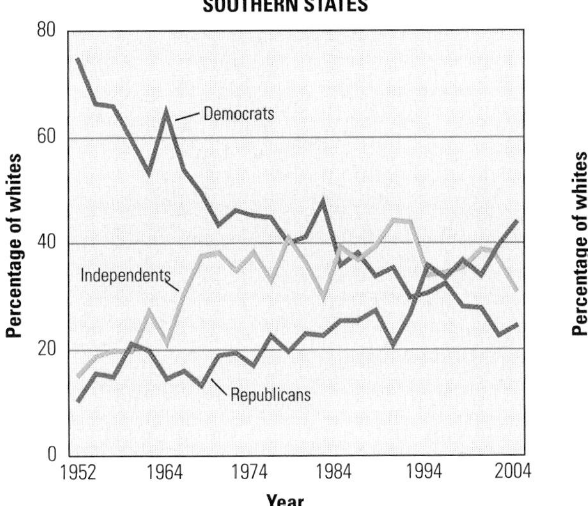

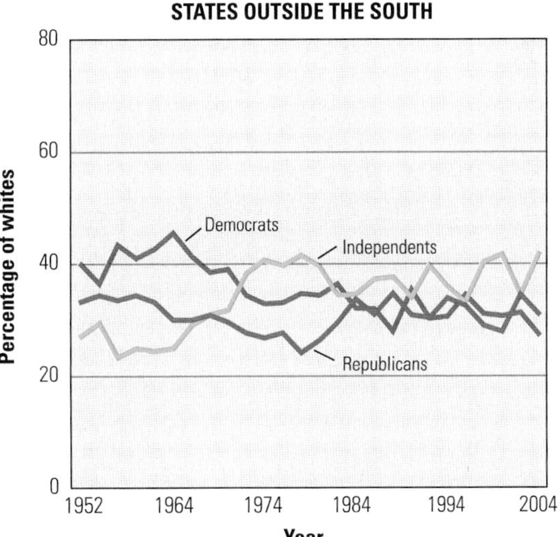

FIGURE 12.5

Changing Party Identification of White Voters In and Outside the South, 1952–2004

Has there been a realignment from the New Deal? Party identification among white southerners shows clear evidence of a fundamentally changed system over the past 50 years, from clear dominance by Democrats to near equality for the major parties. Outside the South, the parties are now highly competitive as well, but this came about with much less change than occurred in the southern states.

Source: Calculated by the authors from National Election Studies data.

weakened and voters are more likely to call themselves independents.[31] However, since the 1980s, party identification has shown some signs of strengthening, but along more consistent ideological and less regional lines.[32] What no one knows is whether this period of highly competitive parties is one of transition to a new party era, or whether it is its own era, breaking with the patterns of clear party dominance that have defined such periods in the past.

Current American party politics is thus characterized by both a realigning process, which has mobilized blacks and other minorities into the Democratic Party and southern whites into the Republican Party, and a dealigning process, which has led to an increase in the number of voters who are independent of either major party, and a system in which neither party has a clear, enduring majority. These phenomena have led to a much higher incidence of divided government at the national and state levels, with the executive and legislative branches in the hands of different parties. One of the hallmarks of divided government is the gridlock we mentioned earlier, as each party moves to prevent the other from enacting its policy goals. Gridlock and even the unified government with tiny governing majorities, such as President George W. Bush has had for most of his administration, make it much harder for the presidential party to achieve its agenda because it is easily blocked by the other party. Citizens, as a consequence, do not know which party to hold accountable if they are dissatisfied with government policy or inaction.

WHO, WHAT, HOW Early political leaders designed parties as elite-driven institutions that served their own interests in governing. Laws that gave the vote to all white males, however, meant that politics was less of an elite activity and inspired leaders to create the mass-based political machine. These machines continued to allow leaders total control over the party but with the perhaps unexpected consequence of politicizing new generations of American immigrants and strengthening American democracy.

Reformers wanted more political accountability—more power for the voters and less for the party bosses. They broke the machines with civil service reform and primary elections. The American party system, although it is not perfect, has allowed citizens to repeatedly change their government, at times radically, without resort to violence or bloodshed.

WHAT DO PARTIES DO?

We have said that, in general, parties play an important role in American democracy by providing a link between citizens and government, coherence in government, and a vocal opposition. These roles are closely tied to the two main activities of parties: electioneering and governing. Generally, party organizations handle tasks related to electioneering, and the party-in-government handles tasks related to governing. In this section we look at each of these two party functions.

ELECTIONEERING

electioneering the process of getting a person elected to public office

Electioneering involves recruiting and nominating candidates, defining policy agendas, and getting candidates elected. According to an old saying in politics, "before you can save the world, you must save your seat." One of the primary reasons for the existence of party organizations is to help candidates get and save their seats.

By Invitation Only
As part of his 2004 reelection campaign, President George W. Bush frequently held town meetings taking questions from members of the public. Meetings using this format are typically staged for television to present the candidate dealing with real people and their concerns. The twist developed by the Bush campaign was to carefully screen the "public" allowed into the events, which effectively prevented the president from having to deal with embarrassing questions of contentious issues.

Who Should Run? Recruiting Candidates Each party's electioneering activities begin months before the general election with the first step of finding candidates to run. There is usually no shortage of ambitious politicians eager to run for high-profile offices like state governor and U.S. senator, but the local parties have to work hard to fill less visible and desirable elective offices like those in the state legislature and county government. It is especially difficult to recruit candidates to run against a current officeholder because incumbents enjoying the advantages of having previously assembled a winning coalition and having a name voters recognize are hard to beat. Incumbents also tend to have a financial advantage; donors and interest groups are more likely to give money to candidates who have proven themselves by winning than to challengers who are largely untested. Unless there is a strong indication that an incumbent is vulnerable, it is hard to recruit opposing candidates.[33]

In response to this reality, parties have begun to target races they think they can win and to devote their resources to those elections. Although they generally try to run candidates in most races, they will target as especially winnable those contests where the seat is open (no incumbent is running), or where the incumbent has done something to embarrass himself or herself (perhaps a scandal), or where strong electoral indicators suggest that the party has a good chance of winning the seat (perhaps the party's previous gubernatorial candidate won a strong majority of votes in the district). In these targeted races the party attempts to recruit quality candidates—perhaps known community leaders—and to direct campaign contributions and aid to the targeted contests.[34]

Nominating Candidates The nomination phase is a formal process through which the party chooses a candidate for each elective office to be contested that year. The nomination phase can unite the party behind its candidates, or it can lead to division within the party among the competing factions that support different candidates and different policy agendas. For this reason the nomination phase is one of the most difficult and important tasks for the party.

Today, as we have seen, party primaries are the dominant means for choosing candidates for congressional, statewide, state legislative, and local offices. In most states the primary election occurs three to four months prior to the general election. In these primaries, party members select their party's nominees for the offices on the ballot. There are a number of different types of primaries. Generally, in **closed primaries**, only voters who have registered as a member of that party are allowed to vote in that party's primary. In **open primaries**, voters simply request one party's ballot on the day of the primary or choose which party's primary they wish to participate in after they enter the polling booth.[35]

closed primaries primary elections in which only registered party members may vote

open primaries primary elections in which eligible voters do not need to be registered party members

Many party officials complain about the open primary system because it permits members of the other party to get involved in the nomination process, as some

Democrats did when they crossed party lines to vote for Senator John McCain, R-Ariz., in the 2000 Republican primaries. Because voters who are not necessarily loyal to a party are allowed to vote, open primaries can weaken political parties.[36]

In presidential primaries, voters do not choose the actual candidates they want to run for president; rather, they elect delegates. Delegates are usually party activists who support a candidate and run for the opportunity to go to the party's national **nominating convention** the summer before the election and cast a vote for him or her. We discuss the mechanics of presidential election nominating conventions in more detail in Chapter 14.

nominating convention formal party gathering to choose candidates

In addition to nominating candidates, party conventions have the important function of bringing the party faithful together to set the policy priorities of the party, to elect party officers, and, not least, to provide a sense of solidarity and community for the activists. After working long and hard all year in their communities, party activists find it restoring and rejuvenating to come together with like-minded people to affirm the principles and policies they hold in common.

The primary process and the practice of televising convention proceedings have dramatically changed the nature of these national conventions. Before reforms in the late 1960s that ensured that candidates would be chosen by elected delegates rather than party bosses, national conventions were filled with political bargaining and intrigue and conflict over platform issues. Delegates going into the convention did not always know who would be the party's nominee.[37] For instance, in 1952, Democratic senator Estes Kefauver, who won every primary election that year, was passed over by the party when it nominated Adlai Stevenson, who had not campaigned at all in the primaries. By 1972, when many states had adopted the primary system, delegates were committed to presidential candidates before the convention began, meaning that there was little question about who would get the nomination. Usually presidential nominating conventions today merely rubber-stamp the primary victor.

The National Party Nominating Conventions: News or Media Events? The national presidential nominating conventions have evolved into full-blown spectacles, complete with balloons, confetti, and upbeat delegates decked out in full party regalia. Because they are choreographed for television to present positive images without conflict and surprises that could embarrass the parties, the networks have deemed them less "newsworthy" and have cut back coverage of recent conventions. Nevertheless, the job of the nominating conventions—naming the nominees and defining the future directions of the political parties—remains as significant as ever.

Television's influence on the national conventions has been considerable as well. In the 1950s the new medium of television began covering the national conventions. With a national audience watching, the parties began to use these conventions as a public springboard for the presidential campaign. It was important that the party appear to be strong and unified, to maximize its electoral chances. The riot-torn 1968 Democratic convention in Chicago highlights the importance of party unity: young people, most of them Democrats, protested the Vietnam War and the selection process that led to the nomination of Vice President Hubert H. Humphrey, a supporter of U.S. involvement in the war. The protests, conflict, and disarray of the Democratic convention, which television brought into America's living rooms, may have played a role in Humphrey's loss to Richard Nixon in the general election.

Even though skirmishes between the ideological wings within both parties occasionally flare up, for the most part, conventions have turned into choreographed events, designed to show, in prime time, that the party is unified behind its presidential candidate. In fact, conventions have become so routine and predictable that the television networks have cut back on their coverage of the national conventions in recent years. In 1996 the Republicans were outraged when ABC's *Nightline* packed up and went home halfway through their convention, concluding that there was nothing newsworthy going on and that the Republicans were just using network coverage as an extended (and free) campaign commercial. In 2000 and 2004 the networks devoted very little prime-time coverage to the conventions.

Defining Policy Agendas After a political party nominates its candidates, one of the party's main roles is to develop a policy agenda, which represents policies that a party's candidates agree to promote when campaigning and to pursue when governing. The development of such an agenda involves much politicking and gamesmanship as each faction of the party tries to get its views written into the party platform, which we discussed earlier. Whoever wins control over the party platform has decisive input on how the campaign proceeds.

General Elections In the election phase the role of the party changes from choosing among competing candidates within the party and developing policy agendas to getting its nominated candidates elected. Traditionally the parties' role here was to "organize and mobilize" voters, but increasingly they are becoming the providers of extensive services to candidates.

The advent of mass communication—radio and television—has changed the way a party and its candidates relate to voters. When party organizations were the major source of information about a candidate, elections were party centered. Now, with mass communication, elections are more candidate centered. Candidates can effectively run their own campaigns—buying television and radio ad time and presenting themselves on their own terms—and party affiliation is just one of the many characteristics of a candidate, not the sole identifying feature. This shift toward candidate-centered politics is part of a larger transformation in campaigning from the labor-intensive campaigns of the past, which depended on party workers getting out the vote for the party's candidates, to today's capital-intensive campaigns, which depend on the tools of mass communication and money to buy airtime.[38]

Consistent with this change toward capital-intensive campaigns, today's political parties primarily offer candidate services, including fundraising and training in campaign tactics, instruction on compliance with election laws, and public opinion polling and professional campaign assistance for candidates.[39]

Money, of course, is central in a capital-intensive campaign, and the parties are major fundraising organizations. Because of a loophole in the campaign finance laws that allowed parties to collect contributions of unlimited size from donors, parties became major banks for candidates in the 1990s (see Chapter 14). These unlimited funds, called "soft money," were used by the parties for party-building efforts such as voter registration and issue development activities, and amounted to as much as $500 million in 2000.[40] Both parties distributed money to candidates either by giving cash directly to the candidates or by supplementing the campaign efforts of candidates with television and radio issue advertising. Although this issue advertising was supposed to represent an "independent" expenditure of money—candidates were not allowed to participate in the decisions about how the money was spent or direct the content of the issue ads—in practice, there was generally much correspondence between the issue ads of the party and the campaign ads of the candidates, because parties simply mimicked the ads of their candidates.

Soft money raising was seriously limited by campaign finance reform legislation passed in 2002 called the Bipartisan Campaign Reform Act, or BCRA. Especially important to the parties was the provision that did away with their ability to collect unlimited soft money contributions. Nevertheless, bundling of individual contributions by PACs to make larger donations and other apparent loopholes allow the parties to continue their role as major providers of campaign services to candidates.[41]

Both parties spend a great deal of money on the targeted contests we discussed earlier.[42] For targeted seats the parties supplement their issue ads by sending party leaders into the district to raise money for the candidate. This move has the added benefit of giving the candidate greater media visibility. For the party that does not control the presidency, congressional leaders and presidential hopefuls (sometimes one and the same) usually fill this void. For the party in control of the presidency, the president, vice president, and even their spouses perform these duties. In the 1998 elections, when President Clinton was embroiled in the impeachment proceedings and few candidates wanted to risk their political futures by being seen with him, it was Hillary Clinton who stepped in and campaigned for Democratic candidates, raising millions in contributions for them.[43] Of course, if the party is successful in its efforts to win a targeted seat, the winning candidate feels an even greater sense of loyalty to the party. In 2002, President Bush put his political credibility on the line when he campaigned hard in a successful effort to ensure that he had a Republican House and Senate to work with in 2003. His efforts helped to reverse the usual tendency for the presidential party to lose seats in midterm contests, and he earned a high level of support from grateful congressional Republicans.[44]

GOVERNING

governing activities directed toward controlling the distribution of political resources by providing executive and legislative leadership, enacting agendas, mobilizing support, and building coalitions

Once a party's candidates have been elected to office, attention turns to the matter of governance. **Governing** involves the two major jobs of controlling government by organizing and providing leadership for the legislative and/or executive branches and enacting the party's policy agendas. Party governance gives voters a means to make officeholders accountable for failed and successful governing policies,[45] and it can provide an extraconstitutional framework that can lend some coherence to the fragmentation produced by separation of powers and federalism.

Controlling Government When parties "control" government at the national level and in the states, it means that the party determines who occupies the leadership positions in the branch of government in which the party has a majority. Thus, when George W. Bush won the presidency in 2000, Bush—and, by extension, the Republicans—controlled the top leadership positions in the executive branch of the government (cabinet secretaries and undersecretaries of agencies and the White House staff). For the first six months of Bush's administration, his party also controlled the legislative branch. When Vermont senator Jim Jeffords left the Republican Party in the summer of 2001, however, Democrats gained the majority in the Senate and the right to organize that chamber. After the 2002 midterm elections, the Republicans controlled both houses—this means selecting the majority leader in the Senate and the Speaker of the House, controlling committee assignments, selecting chairs of legislative committees, and having a majority of seats on each committee. Controlling government also means that the legislative leadership controls the legislative calendar and the rules governing legislative debate and amendments (especially in the House).

Execution of Policy Agendas and Accountability Of course the ultimate goal of a political party is not only to choose who occupies the leadership positions in government but also to execute its policy agenda—the party's solutions to the nation's problems. Whether the problem is defined as a lack of affordable health care, insufficient national security, high taxes, distressed communities, unemployment, illegal immigration, or a failing economy, each party represents an alternative vision for how to approach and solve problems.

We have already noted that significant differences exist between the platforms and policy agendas of the two major parties. The question here is whether the parties actually implement their policy agendas. On this score, parties do fairly well. About two-thirds of the platform promises of the party that controls the presidency are implemented, while about half of the platform promises of the party that does not control the presidency are implemented.[46]

The classic example of a party fulfilling its campaign promises was the first hundred days of the New Deal under the Democratic Party. Running on a platform that called for an activist national government, Franklin Roosevelt and the congressional Democrats were elected in a landslide in 1932. Under Roosevelt's leadership, Congress proceeded to pass New Deal legislation designed to regulate the economy and banking industry, and to provide government programs to help farmers and the unemployed. After maintaining control of Congress in 1934, the Democrats went on to pass one of the most important pieces of legislation in American history, the Social Security Act (1935).

Through most of our history, until the latter half of the twentieth century, when a party was elected to power, it usually controlled not just one branch of government but both the

The Outs Want to Be In
The goal of both parties is to gain control of government to make their policies national policy. The party out of power, of course, wants back in. Here, Rep. Nancy Pelosi and Sen. Harry Reid, the Democratic leaders in the House and Senate, prepare for their joint response to President George W. Bush's February 2005 State of the Union Address. The questioning and critical assessment of those in power by the out party is one of the vital functions for a healthy democracy.

Profiles in Citizenship

Rahm Emanuel

The clock on the wall is buzzing intermittently, signifying an imminent vote in the U.S. House of Representatives. Congressman Rahm Emanuel doesn't want to miss it, and he is alert to the time, one part of his mind calculating exactly how much longer he can talk before heading to the House floor from his office in the Longworth House Office Building.

But part of his attention is wholly focused on his visitors, and on recounting the course his career in public life has taken, this son of an immigrant doctor in Chicago who became a student of child psychology in college, then a player in Chicago politics, a fundraiser for the Clinton campaign in 1992, a senior presidential adviser with an office next to the Oval Office (and, reportedly, the model for Josh Lyman in the television show *The West Wing*), an investment banker, and now a member of Congress and chair of the DCCC—the Democratic Congressional Campaign Committee.

"I don't think that every disagreement is partisan"

And all this before he turned forty-five years old. It should be astounding, but it's not. Emanuel seems to live his life at a faster pace than the rest of us, packing more in and pushing more limits in his impatience and fervor to get things done. He even talks fast, answering questions by telling stories, leaving his listeners to draw their own conclusions as he moves quickly on to his next idea.

Maybe that passion and drive come from his Chicago childhood, where he and his two brothers would read the newspapers to prepare for dinner-table conversation with their parents. The family went to civil rights rallies (his mom ran Chicago CORE—the Congress for Racial Equality), they went to cultural events, and they argued politics at the top of their lungs. (It's an Eastern European–Jewish family thing, Emanuel says. "The decibel level of eight is probably your normal conversation mode.")

In one memorable high-octane family debate in the sixties, Emanuel's mother and maternal grandfather got into a huge argument over a man named Wallace, who young Rahm took to be Alabama governor George Wallace. Nope, his Dad told him, the argument was over Henry Wallace, circa 1948. His family was arguing passionately over a political controversy twenty years old.

Those are some serious political genes, and they propelled Emanuel into Chicago politics, where he worked closely with Mayor Richard Daley and Sen. Paul Simon, and then into Clinton's 1992 campaign for the presidency.

executive and the legislature (which also made it easy to control significant judicial appointments as well). In this sense, parties were able to overcome some of the checks provided by separation of powers and to operate much more like the parliamentary systems of Europe, engaging in smooth and efficient policymaking. The increased incidence of split-ticket voting in more recent years has resulted in frequent divided government, which makes the enactment of policy agendas by either party much more difficult. The experience of the Clinton administration provides a telling illustration. In his first two years in office—when the Democrats still held the majority in Congress—President Clinton accomplished far more of his policy agenda than most of his immediate predecessors, successfully shepherding the Family and Medical Leave Act, the Crime Bill, his budget plan, and the North American Free Trade Agreement (NAFTA) through Congress. However, once the Republicans took control of Congress in 1994, Clinton faced the same difficulties as most of his Republican predecessors and was much less successful in getting his presidential agenda through Congress. As we

How did he get to the White House while still in his thirties? "I was thirty, thirty-one, single, and I figured you want to do politics and you want to play for the big leagues, the presidential is it. . . . I wanted to be in the White House." So he signed on as a fundraiser for the campaign, and when, against all odds, Clinton won, Emanuel found himself right where he wanted to be.

Okay, so he's clearly driven and goal oriented and ambitious, but it does not appear to be power or, at least, not power for its own sake that drives him. He is dedicated to bringing about a certain community-based vision of society, and the White House was the best platform from which to do it. "In politics and policy [being in the White House] is the Super Bowl. And so there are things that I care about and if you want to make an impact, that's a place you can make a big impact." And a big impact is exactly what he had as he worked on welfare reform, children's health insurance, the Crime Bill, the assault weapons ban, NAFTA, and the balanced budget.

He's making the same impact today, as a representative from Illinois and the guy who has taken on the job, via the DCCC, of increasing his party's representation in Congress. But though it is his job to strengthen the Democratic Party, Emanuel is cautious about using the word *partisanship*, believing that the media is too quick to chalk up differences to party conflict rather than honest debate and diversity of opinion. It's natural for democracy to be messy and for people to have huge debates about what government should do, but all too often we treat it as pathology rather than a sign of a healthy, functioning democratic system.

Before he can develop this final theme very far, the buzzing of the clock gets more insistent, and Emanuel has to leave. Getting up from his chair with energy and grace, he shrugs on an impeccably cut jacket. Dapper and elegant, he heads out the door, his mind already on the vote he is going to cast. Here are some of his other thoughts:

On the difference between partisanship and honest political disagreement:

I don't think that every disagreement is partisan. . . . [Politics is] how we settle our differences. And through homogenization of debate, we're saying every debate is a partisan debate. It isn't. It's a political debate about political differences.

On keeping the republic:

Get involved in public service. That could mean a community group, that could be a neighborhood group, that could mean an interest group on some issue, that could mean public office. A campaign. But get involved in your public life. We spend enough time with our iPods, TVs, computers—being individuals. Somewhere else in your life find a way to be part of your community . . . and I think you'll find something that's enriching and also something that allows you to contribute. That's different from anything else you're ever going to do in your life.

Source: Rahm Emanuel spoke with Christine Barbour and Gerald Wright on May 17, 2005.

saw in Chapter 8, divided government makes policymaking a potential minefield for both parties involved.

Within the context of the responsible party model, the ability of a party to accomplish its stated agenda is extremely important for voter accountability. As the party in power promotes its policy agenda and its ideas for how government should solve problems, it provides voters with an opportunity to hold the party responsible for its successes or failures. Voters then determine if a party's candidates should be rewarded through reelection or punished by "throwing the rascals out." In 1932 the persistence of the Depression convinced voters that the GOP policies had failed and led them to replace the Republicans with the Democrats and their solutions. After seeing Democrats implement the New Deal in 1933 and 1934, the voters cast their ballots to keep Roosevelt and his party in power, thus rewarding the party for its efforts to deal with the Great Depression. As we have pointed out, such clear accountability is more difficult under divided government, when voters do not know which party to hold accountable.

WHO, WHAT, HOW It is hard to imagine any actors in American politics *not* having a stake in the activities of electioneering and governing. For political parties, the stakes are high. They want electoral victory for their candidates and control of government. They try to achieve these goals by using the rules they themselves have created, as well as the electoral rules imposed by the state and federal governments.

Candidates seeking to get elected to office, and to build a reputation once there, engage in candidate-centered campaigns with the assistance of the party organization and the party-in-the-electorate. They also encourage the election of other members of their party.

Party activists want to gain and keep control of the party's agenda, to ensure that it continues to serve the causes they believe in. They participate in primaries and hold the elected officials accountable.

Citizens value their limited government, but paradoxically they also get impatient when government seems to grind to a halt in a morass of partisan bickering. The policy efficiency and coherence that parties can create can dissolve the gridlock, but this comes at the potential cost of a more powerful government. When voters split their tickets and elect a divided government, gridlock is almost inevitable.

CHARACTERISTICS OF THE AMERICAN PARTY SYSTEM

Party systems vary tremendously around the world. In some countries, only one major party exists in the governmental structure. This single party usually maintains its power through institutional controls that forbid the development of opposition parties (totalitarian states like China and the old Soviet Union), or through corruption and informal means of physical coercion (Mexico, until recently), or through military control (Burma, Libya, and Sudan). These systems essentially prevent any meaningful party competition. Without choices at the ballot box, democracy is eliminated. Some countries, on the other hand, have so many parties that often no single party can amass enough votes to control government. When that happens, the parties may try to cooperate with other parties, governing together as a coalition. Parties can represent ideological positions, social classes, or even more informal group interests. Parties can put tight constraints on what elected leaders can do, making them toe the "party line," or they can give only loose instructions that leaders can obey as they please. The truth is, there is no single model of party government.

Among all the possibilities, the American party system is distinctive, but it too fails to fit a single model. It is predominantly a two-party system, although third-party movements have come and gone throughout our history. The American system also tends toward ideological moderation, at least compared with other multiple-party countries. And finally, it has decentralized party organizations and fluctuating levels of party discipline. We explore each of these characteristics in this section.

TWO PARTIES

As we have seen, the United States has a two-party system. Throughout most of the United States's history, in fact, two specific parties, the Democrats and the Republicans, have been the only parties with a viable chance of winning the vast majority of elective offices. As a consequence, officeholders representing these two parties tend to dominate the governing process at the national, state, and local levels.

Why a Two-Party System? The United States—along with countries like Great Britain and New Zealand—stands in sharp contrast to other democratic party systems around the world, such as those found in Sweden, France, Israel, and Italy, which have three, four, five, or more major political parties, respectively. The United States has experienced few of the serious political splits—stemming from such divisive issues as language, religion, or social conflict—that are usually responsible for multiple parties. The lack of deep and enduring cleavages among the American people is reinforced by the longevity of the Democratic and Republican Parties themselves. Both parties predate the industrial revolution, the urbanization and suburbanization of the population, and the rise of the information age, and they have weathered several wars, including the Civil War and two world wars, as well as numerous economic recessions and depressions. One scholar compared each party to a "massive geological formation composed of different strata, with each representing a constituency or group added to the party in one political era and then subordinated to new strata produced in subsequent political eras." Proponents from one era may continue to support a political party even if it undergoes changes in issue positions. These political parties persist not just because of the support they can attract today but because of the accumulation of support over time.[47]

But the most important reason that the United States maintains a two-party system is that the rules of the system, in most cases designed by members of the two parties themselves, make it very difficult for third parties to do well on a permanent basis.[48] As we saw in Chapter 4, for instance, democracies that have some form of proportional representation are more likely to have multiple parties. These governments distribute seats in the legislature to parties by virtue of the proportion of votes that each party receives in the election. For example, if a party receives 20 percent of the vote, it will receive roughly 20 percent of the seats in the legislature. Countries with proportional representative systems tend to have more parties than those with single-member plurality-vote systems, simply because small parties can still participate in government even though they do not get a majority of the votes. The U.S. Constitution, on the other hand, prescribes a single-member district electoral system. This means that the candidate who receives the most votes in a defined district (generally with only one seat) wins that seat, and the loser gets nothing, except perhaps some campaign debt. This type of winner-take-all system creates strong incentives for voters to cast their ballots for one of the two established parties because many voters believe they are effectively throwing their votes away when they vote for a third-party candidate.

The United States has other legal barriers that reinforce the two-party system. In most states, legislators from both parties have created election laws that regulate each major party's activities, but these laws also protect the parties from competition from other parties. For example, state election laws ensure the place of both major parties on the ballot and make it difficult for third parties to gain ballot access. Many states require that potential independent or third-party candidates gather a large number of signature petitions before their names can be placed on the ballot. Another common state law is that before a third party can conduct a primary to select its candidate, it must have earned some minimum percentage of the votes in the previous election.

Third parties are also hampered by existing federal election laws. These laws regulate the amount of campaign contributions that presidential candidates can receive from individuals and PACs and provide dollar-for-dollar federal matching money for both major parties' presidential campaigns, if the candidates agree to limit their spending to a predetermined amount. However, third-party candidates cannot claim federal campaign funds until after the election is over, and even then their funds are limited by the percentage of past and current votes they received. As an additional hurdle, they need to have gained about 5 percent or more of the national vote in order to be eligible for federal funds.[49]

Access to the national media can also be a problem for third parties. Even though regulations are in place to ensure that the broadcast media give candidates equal access to the airwaves, Congress has insisted on a special exception that limits participation in televised debates to candidates from the two major parties, which kept Ross Perot out of the debates in 1996,[50] Ralph Nader and Patrick Buchanan in 2000, and Nader again in 2004.

Third-Party Movements Just because the Democrats and the Republicans have dominated our party system does not mean that they have gone unchallenged. Over the years, numerous third-party movements have tried to alter the partisan makeup of American politics. These parties have usually arisen either to represent specific issues that the parties failed to address, like prohibition in 1869, or to promote ideas that were not part of the ideological spectrum covered by the existing parties, like socialist parties, never very popular here, or the Libertarian Party. In general, third parties have sprung up from the grassroots or have broken off from an existing party (the latter are referred to as splinter parties). In many cases they have been headed up by a strong leader who carries much of the momentum for the party's success on his or her own shoulders (for example, Teddy Roosevelt, George Wallace, Ross Perot). Table 12.3 shows some key third-party movements that have made their mark on U.S. history.

Third parties can have a dramatic impact on presidential election outcomes. For example, in 2000, Ralph Nader pulled crucial support from Democrat Al Gore in Oregon, Florida, and New Hampshire that some analysts argue could have won the election for Gore. A similar fate befell William Howard Taft in the 1912 presidential election, when Teddy Roosevelt's Bull Moose Party pulled enough Republican votes from him that Democrat Woodrow Wilson won the election. In playing the role of a spoiler, third parties show the major parties the painful significance of dissatisfied voters whose issues they have ignored or suppressed. In this sense, third parties provide a platform through which these issues can be publicly debated and put on the public agenda, and they represent an important pressure release valve for the party system. Thus, although third parties are, in most cases, short-lived, they nonetheless fill a significant role in the American party system.

IDEOLOGICAL MODERATION

Compared with many other party systems—for instance, the Italian system, which offers voters a variety of choices ranging from the communist-based Democratic Left Party to the ultraconservative neo-Fascist National Alliance Party—the United States has a fairly limited menu of viable parties: the moderately conservative Republican Party and the moderately liberal Democratic Party. Neither the Democrats nor the Republicans promote vast changes to the U.S. political and economic systems. Both

TABLE 12.3 **Third-Party Movements in America**

THIRD PARTY	YEAR EST.	MOST SUCCESSFUL PRESIDENTIAL CANDIDATE	HISTORY AND PLATFORM
National Republican Party	1824	John Quincy Adams	Split off from Democratic-Republicans to oppose Andrew Jackson's campaign for the presidency.
Anti-Masonic Party	1826	William Wirt	Held the first American party convention in 1831. Opposed elite organizations (the Masons in particular), charging they were antidemocratic.
Free Soil Party	1848	Former President Martin Van Buren	Fought for cheap land and an end to slavery. The antislavery members eventually became supporters of Lincoln's Republican Party.
Know-Nothing Party	1849	Millard Fillmore	Promoted native-born Protestants' interests, claiming that Catholics were more loyal to the pope than to the United States.
Prohibition Party	1869	James Black	Advocated the prohibition of alcohol manufacture and use. The party continues to run candidates.
Populist Party	1891	James Weaver	Appealed to farmers during the depressed agricultural economy period by blaming railroads and eastern industrialists for unfair prices.
Socialist Party of America	1901	Eugene V. Debs	Fought for an end to the capitalist economic system in the United States. When jailed for sedition in 1920, Debs ran for president from prison and received 3.4% of the popular vote.
Bull Moose Party (Progressive Party)	1912	Former President Teddy Roosevelt	As the most successful third-party candidate in American presidential election history, Roosevelt campaigned as a progressive crusader and received 27.4% of the vote.
States' Rights Party (Dixiecrats)	1948	Strom Thurmond (later 8-term senator from S.C.)	Split from the Democratic Party in 1948 over civil rights; advocated segregation and used the Democratic Party infrastructure in southern states to gain 2.4% of the vote.
American Independent Party	1968	George Wallace	Former Democrat Wallace began his own party, which attacked civil rights legislation and Great Society programs. He received 13.5% of the vote.
Libertarian Party	1971	Ed Clark	Fights for personal liberties and opposes all welfare state policies. Clark won 1.1% of the vote in 1980.
Reform Party	1995	Ross Perot	Perot received 19% of the presidential vote as an independent in 1992, and he began this party to formalize a third-party challenge. Perot won 8% of the vote in 1996. Reform candidate Jesse Ventura was elected governor of Minnesota in 1998.
Green Party	1984/ 1996	Ralph Nader	Really two parties. Green Party USA was founded on a platform of eliminating the Senate and breaking up the nation's 500 largest corporations. The Association of State Green Parties (ASGP) broke off in the mid-1990s to promote more mainstream social justice and environmental issues. Nader, a member of neither, ran as the ASGP candidate in 2000, winning less than 3% of the vote. The ASGP backed another candidate in 2004.

Why Are These Men Laughing?
Third-party candidates have a tough time in American politics. Major-party candidates Bill Clinton and George Bush were guaranteed a place in the 1992 presidential debates, but Ross Perot had to overcome major resistance before he was allowed to participate. In 1996, believing Perot had little chance of winning the election, debate sponsors didn't offer him a return invitation, and both Pat Buchanan and Ralph Nader were excluded in 2000, and Nader again in 2004.

parties support the Bill of Rights, the Constitution and its institutions (presidency, Congress, the courts, and so on), the capitalist free-enterprise system, and even basic governmental policies like Social Security and the Federal Reserve system. This broad agreement between the two parties in major areas is a reflection of public opinion. Surveys show broad public support for the basic structure and foundations of the U.S. political and economic systems.

DECENTRALIZED PARTY ORGANIZATIONS

In American political parties, local and state party organizations make their own decisions. They have affiliations with the national party organization but no obligations to obey its dictates other than selecting delegates to the national convention. Decision making is dispersed across the organization rather than centralized at the national level; power tends to move from the bottom up instead of from the top down. This means that local concerns and politics dominate the lower levels of the party, molding its structure, politics, and policy agendas. Local parties and candidates can have a highly distinctive character and may look very different from the state or national parties. Political scientists refer to this as a *fragmented party organization.*

American parties are organized into several major divisions:

- Each party has a *national committee,* the Republican National Committee (RNC) and the Democratic National Committee (DNC), whose members come from each state. Each elects a chair, vice chair, secretary, fundraising chair, and other officers. When the party wins the White House, the president chooses the chair. While the national presidential nominating conventions draft the platforms and determine the rules of delegate selection, the national committees run the party business in between conventions. Increasingly, in an effort to tie candidates and state parties to the national party, the committees focus on candidate-centered activities like polling, candidate training, development of databases of party supporters, and direct-mail fundraising. We have already seen that in the past the RNC and the DNC expended enormous sums of so-called soft money to get their candidates elected.
- The *congressional campaign committees* are formed by each party for the sole purpose of raising and distributing campaign funds for party candidates in the House and the Senate (see *Profiles in Citizenship:* Rahm Emanuel on page 526). These committees are strongly tied to the leadership in each chamber, and the expectation is that if the leadership, through the committee, helps get a member elected, then the member will be more supportive of those particular party leaders. Traditionally, the congressional campaign committees have been at odds with the national committees because they are competing for money from the same sources.
- *State party committees,* like the national committees, are increasingly candidate centered and tend to focus their efforts on statewide races and to a lesser extent on

state legislative contests. The state committees are elected in party primaries or at the state conventions, and the committees in turn elect the state party chairs. The election of the chairs is generally heavily influenced by the parties' candidates for governor, thus reinforcing the strong state focus of the activities of the state committees. Since the mid-1970s there has been a rapid growth in state legislative campaign committees. These are usually controlled by the leadership of each party in the legislature and are devoted to electing more of their people to the legislatures.[51]

- *Local party organizations* come together when an election approaches but are not permanently organized. If they have formal party headquarters at all, these are usually set up just two or three months prior to an election. Local party officials usually are unpaid volunteers. Because most city and school board offices are nonpartisan, local parties tend to organize at the county level.

The decentralized nature of the party organization structure just described can be seen in the rise of the Christian Right in the Republican Party. Motivated by Pat Robertson's 1988 bid for the Republican nomination, members of the Christian Right began a concerted effort to exert their influence within the Republican parties in many states and localities. Taking advantage of the decentralized nature of the party system, the Christian Right first recruited people to run for GOP positions at the local precinct or ward levels. Often its candidate would go unchallenged for these party positions. Next, it mobilized other members of its group to turn out and vote in the GOP primaries. Not only did these primary voters start to exert considerable influence over who was selected into party leadership roles, but the Christian Right also influenced the nomination process. Republican candidates who were willing to pledge their support for the Christian Right's agenda also received the benefits of a large number of volunteers who were willing to campaign actively for them. As the Christian Right took control of county-level party organizations, their influence within the state parties also grew. Today the Christian Right is a major force within the Republican Party in many states.

There are several reasons for the decentralized structure of the American parties. One is that the federal electoral structure makes it difficult for any national coordinating body to exercise control. For example, in some states, local and state elections occur on different schedules from national and congressional elections. Sometimes this has been done intentionally to disconnect the state and local elections from national influences. Federalism also leads to decentralized parties because state laws have historically dictated the organizational structure and procedures of the state and local parties. Even though some of this state regulation has been rolled back recently,[52] the state and local parties still reflect this legislatively dictated structure, as opposed to one laid out by the national organization.

In addition, U.S. parties lack strong organizational tools to exercise centralized control of candidates for office. Many parties in Europe exercise some form of centralized control of the nomination process. That is, all candidates who run under the party banner, no matter what the level, have been approved by the party. If the party does not approve of the candidate, this person does not receive the party's nomination. In most cases in the United States, however, each party's candidates are chosen in direct primaries, in which local party voters rather than party leaders control the nomination process, making strong centralized control an almost impossible task. For example, when former Ku Klux Klan member David Duke ran for governor of Louisiana as a Republican in 1992, Republican leaders were outraged but powerless to stop him (he lost

the election). Similarly, when the scandal-tainted California representative Gary Condit filed for reelection in 2001, disappointed Democratic officials could only watch, despite their belief that his candidacy would lose the seat for their party.[53] Fortunately (from their perspective), he did not survive his primary election battle.

Decentralization, however, does not mean that local parties are necessarily different from their national counterparts. Consider the possible effect of party activists. While their influence means that the base may control the leadership (decentralization) rather than the other way around, power may actually be less fragmented as the base strengthens its hold on the entire party. The more conservative base of the Republican Party has long had greater control at the local level, but national Republican policy was tempered by the need to get along with Democrats in Congress and to appeal to the moderate voter in national elections. When the party took control of Congress in 1994, however, members of Congress were better able to impose their more ideological perspective at the upper levels of the party.

CHANGES IN PARTY DISCIPLINE OVER TIME

Historically, American party organizations have been notable for their lack of a hierarchical (top-down) power structure, and the officials elected to government from the two parties have not felt compelled to take their orders from the top. This looseness within the parties was a continuing source of frustration for the advocates of the responsible party model of government. They wished for greater **party discipline**—the ability of party leaders to keep members voting together in a cohesive way—which was more typical of European parliamentary parties. This lack of party unity among legislators in the United States reflected the diversity of opinions within the parties, both among activists and among rank-and-file identifiers. We have seen, however, that

party discipline ability of party leaders to bring party members in the legislature into line with the party program there have been significant changes in the parties' base coalitions, especially in the movement of southern conservatives from the Democratic to the Republican Party. This shift, with similar but less dramatic ideological alignment in the non-southern states, has resulted in a party system in which we have greater ideological agreement within the parties and greater ideological distance between them.

At the same time that these changes in the electoral environment of Congress have helped create the conditions for higher levels of party discipline,[54] more powerful party leaders who can withhold privileges and benefits from members who do not toe the party line have also increased the level of party loyalty. Changes in the rules in the House of Representatives in the 1970s paved the way for the very strong House party leadership that we see today. Although the current speaker, Dennis Hastert, has a less ideologically intense demeanor than his predecessor, Newt Gingrich, who led the Republican takeover of the House in 1994, he is backed up by the current, take-no-prisoners majority leader of the House Republicans, Tom DeLay, whose nick-name, "The Hammer," signals his approach and effectiveness at keeping his party members in line.

WHO, WHAT, HOW The United States's two-party system is a direct result of, first, the kind of electoral system that the founders designed and, second, the rules that lawmakers in the two parties have put into place to make it difficult for third parties to thrive. This does not stop the drive for third parties, however, when dissatisfied voters seek representation of ideas and issues that the two major parties do not address.

The American parties are, in general, ideologically moderate. Activists want parties to take more extreme stances and to act on their principles. Voting in primaries has enabled them to pull the parties in a more extreme, but also more disciplined, direction. The losers here are the general voting public, who cannot always find a moderate alternative to vote for. Some scholars argue that these voters may register their wishes for moderation by splitting their tickets, resulting in a divided government that is less able to act decisively.[55]

THE CITIZENS AND POLITICAL PARTIES

We began this chapter by noting that, for all their importance to the success of democracy, political parties have been perennially unpopular with the public. Scholars tell us that one reason for this unpopularity is that voters are turned off by partisan bickering and each party's absorption with its own ideological agenda instead of a concern for the public interest.[56] In this section we suggest the possibility that politics is *about* bickering, and that bickering may itself be a major safeguard of American democracy.

We defined politics at the start of this book as the struggle over who gets what and how they get it in society, a process that involves cooperation, bargaining, compromise, and tradeoffs. We remarked at the outset that politics is often seen as a dirty business by Americans, but that it is really our saving grace since it allows us to resolve conflict without violence. The difficulty is that Americans do not see politics as our saving grace. Perhaps we have enjoyed relative domestic tranquility for so long that we do not know what it is like to have to take our disagreements to the streets and the battlefields to resolve them. Some researchers have found that when Americans look at government, they do not focus primarily on the policy *outcomes* but on the political *process* itself. Although policies themselves are increasingly complex and difficult to grasp, most of us are able to understand the way in which the policies are created, the give and take, the influence of organized interests, and the rules of the game. In other words, finding the *what* of politics to be complicated, most citizens focus their attention and evaluation on the *how*. We are not helped out here by the media, which, rather than explaining the substance of policy debate to American citizens, instead treat politics like one long, bitterly contested sporting event.

Given citizen dissatisfaction with partisan politics in America, where do we go from here? What is the citizens' role in all this, if it is not to stand on the sidelines and be cynical about partisan politics? Political scientists John Hibbing and Elizabeth Theiss-Morse argue that the problem lies with a lack of citizen education—education not about the facts of American government but about the process. "Citizens' big failure," they claim, "is that they lack an appreciation for the ugliness of democracy."[57] Democratic politics is messy by definition; it is authoritarian government that is neat, tidy, and efficient. Perhaps the first thing we as citizens should do is to recognize that partisanship is not a failure of politics; it is the heart of politics.

At the beginning of this chapter, we said there were three ways in which parties enhanced democracy in America. We have given considerable attention to the first two: the linkage between citizen and government and the coherence among the branches of government that parties can provide. The third way parties serve democracy is in providing for a vocal opposition, an adversarial voice that scrutinizes and critiques the opposite side, helping to keep the process and the people involved honest. This is akin to the watchdog function the media is said to serve, but it is more institutionalized, a self-monitoring process that keeps both parties on their toes. To be sure, this self-monitoring certainly can, and does, deteriorate into some of the uglier aspects of American democracy, but it also serves as the guardian of political freedom. Where such partisan squabbling is not allowed, political choice and democratic accountability cannot survive either.

There are three things citizens can do to offset their frustration with the partisan course of American politics.

1. *Get real.* Having realistic expectations of the process of democratic government can certainly help head off disillusionment when those expectations are not met.
2. *Get involved.* Parties, because of their decentralized nature, are one of the places in American politics to which citizens have easy access. The only reason the more extreme ideologues hold sway in American politics is that the rest of us allow them to, by leaving the reins in their hands.
3. *Don't split your ticket.* If you are truly disturbed at what you see as government paralysis, try voting for a straight party ticket. Even if you vary the party from election to election, you will be able to hold the party accountable for government's performance.

WHAT'S AT STAKE REVISITED

As we have seen in this chapter, the issue of third parties is a complex one in the U.S. system. The Democratic and Republican Parties do offer voters real choices, and the enthusiastic involvement of their party activists ensures that they will continue to do so, but as an election approaches, there is every incentive for the parties to move closer together. Almost always, third parties are established to run against the two-party system itself, challenging it to reform, to respond to new issues, or to present deeper choices to the electorate. The end of this chapter is an appropriate place to reflect on what is really at stake in a third-party run for the presidency. We can look at this question from the perspectives of the third parties themselves, the major-party candidates, the two-party system, and the voters.

What is at stake for third parties, when many of them acknowledge from the start that they have little or no chance of winning an election? Ralph Nader's goal in the 2000 presidential election was more than victory; he wanted to "start a long-range political reform movement . . . [a]nd to become a watchdog for people who feel they have been taken for granted."[58] He wanted to highlight his contention that there was no fundamental difference between the Republicans and the Democrats on the most important issues, and he believed that if Bush won, he would be a lightning rod for angry liberals, who would be energized by dislike of his agenda. Indeed, Nader said that "there's a dynamic involved, there's a reawakening involved, there's a churning."[59] From this perspective, even though he failed to get the 5 percent of the national vote he wanted, the more media attention and public awareness he raised—even, or perhaps especially, if it included the anger of Democrats—the more successful he was. If his goal was to upset the system itself, he could not really lose unless he was ignored.

Thinking Outside the Box

- Can you have a democracy without political parties?
- Does partisanship have to lead to devisiveness?
- Are the American people well represented by a two-party system?

The major-party candidates also have a real stake in third-party candidacies. When the winning margins are large, third parties may be merely a blip on the screen, but when the electorate is narrowly divided, the presence of third-party candidates is fraught with peril for Democrats and Republicans. After he voted for Nader in 2000, Green Party member Matt Duss got telephone calls from Democrats. "Are you !#%!b GREENS out of your !# minds?" they screamed into his ear.[60] Some joked that GREEN stood for "Get Republicans Elected Every November." Did Ralph Nader cost Al Gore the election? Perhaps he did, but that oversimplifies a complex event. As one analyst put it, Nader undoubtedly cost Gore many votes, but Pat Buchanan's Reform Party candidacy cost Bush as well. Although Buchanan won only 450,000 votes overall, had he not been in the race, Bush arguably could have won narrow victories in Iowa, New Mexico, Oregon, and Wisconsin and won the electoral college without the help of Florida.[61] Many Republicans believe that Bush's father was also hurt in his 1992 reelection bid against Bill Clinton by the candidacy of Ross Perot. Third-party challenges are not just a lose-lose proposition for the major parties, however. In an effort to

continued

WHAT'S AT STAKE REVISITED
(continued)

prevent third parties from taking crucial support away from them, many major-party candidates, as we saw earlier, try to appropriate their issues, thereby broadening their base of support.

In a way, then, the two-party system stands to gain favorably from third-party candidacies. Although it is stable enough in most cases to minimize the effects of third-party candidates, it is strengthened by the influx of new issues and demands that third parties bring in. Oddly, while the goal of third parties may be to topple the two-party system, they may have the perverse effect of strengthening it if the parties respond in a positive way.

Finally, what is at stake for voters in a third-party candidacy for office? For many voters, it is a chance to support a candidate they can truly believe in, or to support an ideal or vent their frustration with the system. Often we think of voting simply as a way to choose among competing candidates for office, but if we view it as a way of expressing ourselves or giving voice to our consciences, then clearly the more choices we have the better, and it doesn't really matter who wins or who loses. What matters is the expressive benefits that flow to us. Certainly, Nader voters in 2000 indicate that this was the case. One Florida woman said, "Some people tell me my vote cost Gore the election, but I reject that argument. It's arrogant. I didn't vote for George Bush. I voted for greater democracy. I voted for taking immediate steps to end the crisis of the environment and the corporate dominance of our government and our culture." Similarly, another Florida Nader supporter said, "I haven't doubted my vote for a second, even being yelled at. I had to take a chance and assume that if our Nader votes threw the election to Bush, the country wouldn't dissolve overnight." Besides, he adds, "For years I've equated politics with terminally boring dullness. This is fun."[62]

To Sum Up

KEY TERMS
republic.cqpress.com

closed primaries (p. 521)
critical election (p. 515)
dealignment (p. 519)
electioneering (p. 520)
governing (p. 524)
nominating convention (p. 522)
open primaries (p. 521)
partisanship (p. 500)
party activists (p. 511)
party base (p. 502)
party bosses (p. 514)
party discipline (p. 534)
party eras (p. 515)
party identification (p. 501)
party-in-government (p. 501)
party-in-the-electorate (p. 501)
party machines (p. 514)
party organization (p. 500)
party platform (p. 506)
party primary (p. 514)
patronage (p. 514)
political gridlock (p. 498)
political party (p. 499)
realignment (p. 515)
responsible party model (p. 503)

Key terms, chapter summaries, practice quizzes, Internet links, and other study aids are available on the companion Web site at: republic.cqpress.com.

SUMMARY
republic.cqpress.com

- Political parties make a major contribution to American government by linking citizens and government, overcoming some of the fragmentation of government that separation of powers and federalism can produce, and creating an articulate opposition.
- American political parties offer the average voter a choice in terms of ideology, membership, and policy positions (platform). The differences may not always be evident, however, because electoral forces create incentives for parties to take moderate positions, drawing the parties together. At the same time, party activists who are committed to the values and policies of a particular party play a key role in pushing the parties apart and keeping them ideologically distinct.
- The two primary activities of parties are electioneering (getting candidates elected) and governing (all the activities related to enacting party policy agendas in government).
- American history reveals at least five distinct party eras. These are periods of political stability when one party has a majority of congressional seats and controls the presidency. A realignment, or new era, occurs when a different party assumes control of government. Party politics today may be undergoing both a realignment and a dealignment, resulting in greater numbers of voters identifying themselves as independents.
- America's two-party system is relatively moderate, decentralized, and increasingly disciplined. Although the rules are designed to make it hard for third parties to break in, numerous third-party movements have arisen at different times to challenge the two dominant parties.
- While public disenchantment with political parties may be on the increase, parties remain one of the most accessible avenues for citizen participation in government.

PRACTICE QUIZ

republic.cqpress.com

1. Which of the following is NOT a condition of the responsible party model?

a. The parties offer a clear choice of ideologies.

b. The candidates pledge to implement their parties' programs.

c. The party is held accountable by voters.

d. The party has control over its elected officials.

e. The party gives campaign contributions to all of its candidates.

2. ___________are least likely to be members of the Democratic Party.

a. Women

b. African Americans

c. Jews

d. Protestants

e. Union members

3. A __________is a trend among voters to identify themselves as independent rather than as members of a major party.

a. dealignment

b. critical election

c. party era

d. realignment

e. partisan reshuffling

4. The Bipartisan Campaign Reform Act limited the power of parties because it

a. eliminated bundling.

b. eliminated a party's ability to collect unlimited soft money donations.

c. made it harder for parties to handpick their nominees.

d. increased the power of interest groups by making issue advocacy ads subject to fewer regulations.

e. prohibited parties from running television commercials in support of their candidates.

5. According to researchers, most American citizens focus on the _________ of politics rather than on the _________.

a. how, what

b. who, how

c. how, who

d. who, what

e. what, how

SUGGESTED RESOURCES

republic.cqpress.com

Books

Aldrich, John H. 1995. *Why Parties? The Origin and Transformation of Political Parties in America.* Chicago: University of Chicago Press. In one of the most insightful books written in recent years on political parties in America, Aldrich argues that parties are still quite strong and remain so because of their ability to overcome collective action problems.

Cohen, Jeffrey E., Richard Fleisher, and Paul Kantor. 2001. *American Political Parties: Decline or Resurgence?* Washington, D.C.: CQ Press. This book of readings by noted experts looks at parties in the electorate as organizations and at their role in governing. The book describes changes in the political parties and assesses how these changes have affected the contributions of political parties to democratic government in America.

Hershey, Marjorie Randon, and Paul Allen Beck. 2004. *Party Politics in America,* 11th ed. New York: Pearson Longman. A comprehensive text on parties in America. Earlier editions elucidated the distinction among party-in-government, party-in-the-electorate, and party organization.

Jewel, Malcolm, and Sarah Morehouse. 2001. *Political Parties and Elections in American States,* 4th ed. Washington, D.C.: CQ Press. Two distinguished scholars of state politics present a unique view of the party system with their focus on differences across the fifty states in the roles of the political parties in the electoral process for the state legislatures and governorships. The authors consider campaign finance, rules governing the parties and elections, and state political cultures to conclude that the parties are alive and well in states, and that competition between the parties is increasing in several of the states.

Key, V. O., Jr. 1949. ***Southern Politics in State and Nation.*** **New York: Random House.** A seminal work on the one-party South. Key is a *must-read* for anyone interested in understanding the current state of southern politics.

Nader, Ralph. 2002. *Crashing the Party: How to Tell the Truth and Still Run for President.* New York: St. Martin's Press. The vigilant muckraker and Green Party candidate gives a blow-by-blow account of his 2000 run for the White House and offers theories on what he sees as the failure of the two-party system.

Schattschneider, E. E. 1942. *Party Government.* New York: Holt, Rinehart, and Winston. A classic book on the need for strong, centralized parties in order for democracy to prosper.

Wattenberg, Martin P. 1996. *The Decline of American Political Parties, 1952–1994.* Cambridge: Harvard University Press. Wattenberg presents an interesting argument about how the rise of candidate-centered elections has severely limited the influence and power of political parties.

Internet Sites

National Republican Senatorial Committee, National Republican Congressional Committee, Democratic Senatorial Campaign Committee, and Democratic Congressional Campaign Committee. www.nrsc.org, www.nrcc.org, www.dscc.org, and www.dccc.org. Want to know how policy issues are being framed in congressional campaign and fundraising efforts? These four sites give you the partisan line.

Republican and Democratic National Committees. www.rnc.org and www.democrats.org. These two sites will answer all your questions about the two major parties.

The passage of the McCain-Feingold campaign finance reform bill in March 2002 naturally cheered its sponsors (below), who claimed it as a victory for average citizens' freedom to give money to candidates. A loophole in the bill allowed issue advocacy groups, like the Swift Boat Veterans for Truth, to spend millions of unregulated dollars on damaging television ads attacking the war record of John Kerry, the Democratic nominee for president in 2004 (right). Such groups have multiplied both on the left and the right.

INTEREST GROUPS

13

WHAT'S AT STAKE?

In the end, Senator John Kerry's 2004 presidential aspirations may have been shot down by some not-so-friendly fire from his fellow Vietnam vets. A group of veterans organized themselves under the name Swift Boat Veterans for Truth to run television commercials accusing Kerry of lying about his war record and betraying American interests. The group's commercials, funded by a Republican supporter of President George W. Bush to the tune of $4,450,000 as well as by public contributions, got tremendous coverage in the mainstream media, multiplying their effect.[1] Kerry's public opinion ratings fell, and while they eventually recovered somewhat, he was never again perceived as a military hero who could keep the nation secure in time of war.[2]

Where did this media attack come from? Swift Boat Veterans for Truth, like MoveOn.org and other liberal groups that ran commercials against Bush, were so-called 527 groups, named for the loophole in the U.S. tax code that allowed them to organize without being subject to the regulations of the newly passed McCain-Feingold campaign finance reform bill. One of the main goals of that bill had been to limit the contributions of interest groups to political campaigns. Supporters of campaign finance reform were angered and frustrated by the sudden appearance of 527 groups. Having finally won passage of legislation that was supposed to limit the ability of interest groups to pour unlimited money into campaigns, the reformers felt like they were back at square one.

The battle to reform the campaign finance laws had been long and hard, but in the spring of 2002 it appeared to have been won, due in no small part to public pressure following the spectacular flameout of the energy company Enron. In the ten years before it collapsed, Enron had given over $6.5 million to the two major political parties in the form of "soft money" donations: money that could be given without limit to parties for "party-building activities" as long as they didn't spend it to support particular candidates. Although election laws passed in 1974 limited direct contributions to candidates, soft money was perfectly legal and was a favorite way for interest groups, including corporations like Enron, to ensure that those elected to public office would be people who favored their interests and would listen to their concerns. Enron probably counted the money well spent. Although the Bush administration refused to intervene to save the company from ultimate collapse, Enron was among those consulted extensively by Vice President Dick Cheney as he put together the administration's energy bill, and the tax cut passed in the first year of the Bush administration contained a tax break that saved Enron an estimated $250 million.

In the 2000 election cycle, the two major parties had brought in almost $500 million in soft money donations, capping a dramatic rise from the $86 million in 1992 and $263.5 million in 1996. But soft money was not the only way that interest groups could get around the limits on direct contributions to candidates and still find their way to a candidate's heart. In the days leading up to an election, they could run unlimited issue advocacy ads. These commercials, run ostensibly to push a particular issue position (and, like soft money, perfectly legal if they did not directly support a candidate by instructing voters on whom to vote for), were often little more than thinly veiled attack ads on their candidate's opponent.

At one time caught himself in a campaign finance scandal, Sen. John McCain, R-Ariz., along with Sen. Russell Feingold, D-Wis., had been sponsoring legislation for nearly ten years that would end soft money contributions and limit issue advocacy ads. Their reforms proved popular with the public, and McCain's support for campaign finance reform was partly responsible for his surprising success in the 2000 Republican primaries. By the spring of 2002, prospects for passing the McCain-Feingold bill were finally bright—partly because of the Enron scandal and partly because the Democrats, who were more supportive of reform on the whole than were the Republicans, now controlled the Senate.

The impending passage drove interest groups into a frenzy of activity. Some were supportive. Groups like Common Cause, Public Citizen, People for the American Way, and MoveOn.org favored the reform, and asked their members to call, write, or email senators urging them to vote for the bill. They argued that the massive influx of money into politics in recent years tarnished the democratic process, dwarfed the power of the individual citizen, and put elected officials in debt to powerful interests. On the other side, groups that do not often find themselves on the same side of an issue—like the National Rifle Association (NRA), the Christian Coalition, the labor unions, and the American Civil Liberties Union (ACLU)—strenuously opposed reform, declaring that it didn't expand the freedom of citizens but rather limited the freedom of those wishing to express themselves through their campaign contributions.

The bill passed, and a reluctant but realistic President Bush signed the Bipartisan Campaign Reform Act of 2002. Immediately many of the groups opposed, like the NRA and the ACLU, joined critics like Sen. Mitch McConnell, R-Ky., in planning a lawsuit to challenge the bill in federal court, arguing that the reform measure, especially the prohibition on issue ads, was an unconstitutional restriction on free speech. The Supreme Court rebuffed the free speech argument, however, and the reforms kicked in for the 2004 election cycle.[3] Other interest groups got busy trying to find a way around the new legislation, focusing on section 527 of the U.S. tax code that would allow groups like the Swift Boat Veterans for Truth to organize without regulation.

What was going on here? Was campaign finance reform a giant step forward for American democracy, a civil liberties debacle, or nothing more than a legislative joke that would have the so-called 527 groups laughing all the way to the bank? What was really at stake for interest groups and American democracy in the issue of campaign finance reform? *

French observer Alexis de Tocqueville, traveling in America in the early 1830s, noted a peculiar (he thought) tendency of Americans to join forces with their friends, neighbors, and colleagues. He said, "Americans of all ages, all conditions, and all dispositions, constantly form associations. They have not only commercial and manufacturing companies, in which all take part, but associations of a thousand other kinds—religious, moral, serious, futile, general or restricted, enormous or diminutive."[4] Figure 13.1 shows that Americans are indeed among the top "joiners" in the world.

While Tocqueville's remarks did not refer specifically to political groups, James Madison was concerned about the American propensity to form political associations, or what he called factions. As we saw in Chapter 3, Madison defined a **faction** as a group of citizens united by some common passion or interest, and opposed to the rights of other citizens or to the interests of the whole community.[5] He feared that factions would weaken and destabilize a republic, but he also believed, as he argued in *Federalist* No. 10, that a large republic could contain the effects of factions by making it hard for potential members to find one another and by providing for so many potential political groups that if they did find each other and organize, their very numbers would cancel each other out.

faction a group of citizens united by some common passion or interest and opposed to the rights of other citizens or to the interests of the whole community

Modern political scientists have a different take on factions, which they call by the more neutral term *interest groups*. An **interest group** is an organization of individuals who share a common political goal and unite for the purpose of influencing public policy decisions.[6] (Parties, as you may recall from the previous chapter, also seek to influence policy, but they do so by sponsoring candidates in elections.) The one major difference between this definition and Madison's is that many political scientists do not believe that all interest groups are opposed to the broad public interest. Rather, they hold that interest groups play an important role in our democracy, ensuring that the views of organized interests are heard in the governing process.[7] We saw in Chapter 1 that interest groups play a central role in the pluralist theory of democracy, which argues that democracy is enhanced when citizens' interests are represented through group membership. The group interaction ensures that member interests are represented but also that no group can become too powerful.

interest group an organization of individuals who share a common political goal and unite for the purpose of influencing government decisions

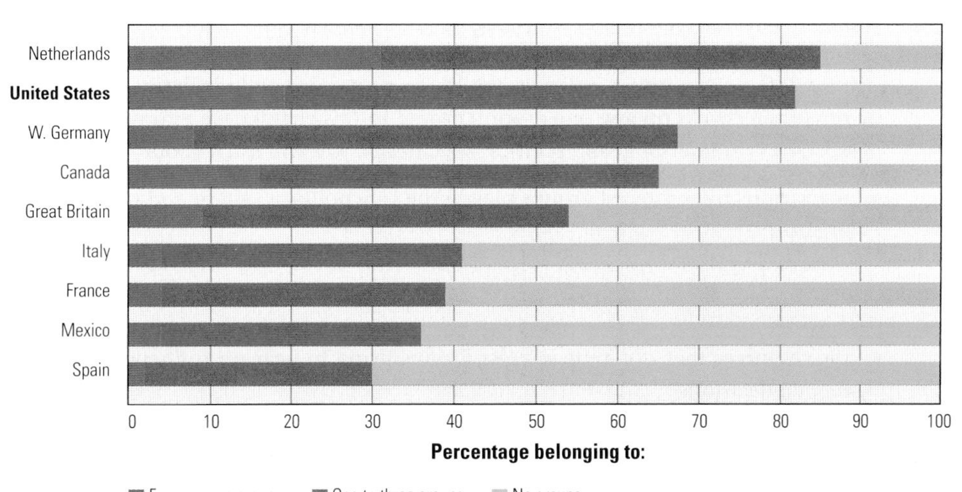

FIGURE 13.1
Americans Like to Belong

Source: Data from *The Public Perspective*, April/May 1995.

Although they have long existed, interest groups, unlike political parties, were not a major force in American politics until the beginning of the twentieth century. When the Progressive reformers at the turn of the century opened up the political process to the people, political parties were weakened and interest groups were correspondingly strengthened. By the 1960s, Washington, D.C., was awash in interest group activity as the federal government continued to expand its New Deal and Great Society programs,[8] and the growth has continued to the present day. While precise data on the number of interest groups do not exist, according to one author, from 1970 to 1990, an average of ten interest groups were formed every week.[9]

The increase in the number of interest groups accelerated after 1974, when the Federal Election Campaign Act was passed in an effort to curb campaign spending abuses. Seeking to regulate the amount of money an interest group could give to candidates for federal office, the law provided for **political action committees (PACs)** to serve as fundraisers for interest groups. As we will see later in this chapter, PACs are limited in how much money they can donate to a candidate, but a number of loopholes allow them to get around some of the restrictions. Although many PACs are creatures of interest groups, others are independent and act as interest groups in their own right. Though their activities are limited to collecting and distributing money, PACs have become extremely powerful players in American politics. Today there are about 4,500 PACs, and they contribute a substantial portion of candidates' campaign funds.[10]

political action committee (PAC) the fundraising arm of an interest group

The explosion of interest group activity has probably caused Madison and the other founders to roll over in their graves. After all, Madison believed that he had secured the republic against what he called the "mischiefs of faction." He could not have envisioned a day when mass transportation and communication systems would virtually shrink the large size of the republic that he had believed would isolate interest groups. In today's world, dairy farmers in Wisconsin can easily form associations with dairy farmers in Pennsylvania; coal producers in the East can organize with coal producers in the Midwest; citrus growers in Florida can plan political strategy with citrus growers in California. Nor would Madison have foreseen the development of the Internet, which allows hundreds of thousands of people to organize and to voice their concerns to their representatives almost instantaneously.

Critics argue that interest groups have too much power, that they don't effectively represent the interests of groups that don't organize (the poor, the homeless, or the young, for instance), and that they clog up the vital arteries of American democracy, leading to gridlock and stagnation.[11] Supporters echo Madison's pluralist hopes—that group politics can preserve political stability by containing and regulating conflict and by providing checks on any one group's power. In this chapter, we examine these two perspectives on interest group politics. Specifically, you will learn about

- the various roles interest groups play in the U.S. political system and the ways they organize
- the many types of interest groups and the kinds of interests they represent
- how interest groups attempt to exert their influence through lobbying and campaign activities
- the resources that different interest groups bring to bear on influencing governmental decisions
- the relationship of citizens to interest groups in American politics—and the question of whether interest group politics is biased in favor of certain groups in society

THE ROLE AND FORMATION OF INTEREST GROUPS

Whether we approve or disapprove of the heavy presence of interest groups in the United States, it is undeniable that they play a significant role in determining who gets what in American politics. In this section we consider the various political roles that interest groups play, and the conditions and challenges they have met in order to organize in the first place.

ROLES OF INTEREST GROUPS

Negative images of interest groups abound in American politics and the media. Republicans speak of the Democrats as "pandering" to special interest groups like labor unions and trial lawyers; in their turn, the Democrats claim that the Republican Party has been captured by big business and the religious right. In both cases, the parties charge each other with giving special treatment to some groups at the expense of the public good. The truth is that, as Madison guessed, interest groups have become an integral part of American politics, and neither party can afford to ignore them. In this section we go beyond the negative stereotypes of interest groups to discuss the important roles they play in political representation, participation, education, agenda building, provision of program alternatives, and program monitoring.[12]

- *Representation.* Interest groups play an important role in representing their members' views to Congress, the executive branch, and administrative agencies. Whether they represent teachers, manufacturers of baby food, people concerned with the environment, or the elderly, interest groups ensure that their members' concerns are adequately heard in the policymaking process. The activity of persuading policymakers to support their members' positions is called **lobbying**. Lobbying is the central activity of interest groups.

lobbying interest group activities aimed at persuading policymakers to support the group's positions

- *Participation.* Interest groups provide an avenue for citizen participation in politics that goes beyond voting in periodic elections. They are a mechanism for people sharing the same interests or pursuing the same policy goals to come together, pool resources, and channel their efforts for collective action. Whereas individual political action might seem futile, participation in the group can be much more effective.
- *Education.* One of the more important functions of interest groups is to educate policymakers regarding issues that are important to the interest group. Members of Congress must deal with many issues and generally cannot hope to become experts on more than a few. Consequently they are often forced to make laws in areas where they have scant knowledge. Interest groups can fill this void by providing details on issues about which they are often the experts. (See the box on page 548, "Think Tanks and the Power of Ideas" for ways that one kind of interest group provides this knowledge.) In addition, sometimes interest groups must educate their members about important issues that may affect them.
- *Agenda building.* We can think of those issues that Congress, the executive branch, or administrative agencies will address as an informal political agenda. It is the role of an interest group to alert the proper government authorities about its issue, get the issue on the political agenda, and, finally, make the issue a high priority for action.

Think Tanks and the Power of Ideas

Interest groups give people a chance to maximize their clout by pooling their resources, perhaps their voices, their dollars, their energy, or their expertise. One important interest group resource is knowledge, and although all groups try to accumulate and use it, some groups specialize in it. These "knowledge factories," called *think tanks*, focus on putting smart people together to generate important ideas, and those ideas can be enormously powerful. Knowledge and ideas can bolster one's political position or undermine an enemy's, they can change minds and inspire supporters, they can help set the agenda of what government does. Money and leadership ring hollow unless they command compelling ideas.

Think tanks, funded mostly by private sources such as foundations, corporations, unions, and other interests that want to influence government policy, are research institutions that craft political positions, highlight political problems, and suggest policy solutions. Because their influence stems from research rather than lobbying, they remain tax-exempt, nonprofit institutions even though the fruits of their efforts may have the same effect as vigorous lobbying. The most influential think tanks, not surprisingly, are headquartered in Washington, D.C., or have a heavy presence there. They employ academics, journalists, and former government officials who research issues, present findings, provide policy proposals, and sometimes even draft legislation.[1]

As with other interest groups, there is often a revolving door between high-level government positions and think tank employment, especially for former officials whose party does not control the White House. In some ways they become holding tanks for those out of power to continue to hone new ideas and positions while they counter the positions and policies of the current administration, staying intellectually fit for the job of governing once again. After Republicans had been out of power for eight years, President George W. Bush turned to conservative think tanks for staff, political appointees, and even some cabinet secretary positions, often from the ranks of those who had served in his father's administration.[2] On issues ranging from missile defense, to tax policy, to the Iraq invasion, the work these officials had been doing in think tanks provided a blueprint for policy action by the Bush administration.

Think tanks have not always been so political. Older think tanks like the Brookings Institution undertook in-depth, nonpartisan research projects or government contract work.[3] A major change in the nature of think tanks began in the 1970s, when conservative foundations and corporations began to fund conservative think tanks to produce research they hoped would reinvigorate conservatism and redefine policy debates.[4] Influential conservatives felt that they were losing the battle of ideas in Washington and that public policy debates had become dominated by what they perceived to be overly liberal academic research and media coverage.[5] To remedy this, conservative think tanks such as the Heritage Foundation have worked to provide briefer, more focused, media-friendly research results.[6] Heritage and other conservative think tanks like the American Enterprise Institute (see the "Profiles in Citizenship" with AEI scholar Newt Gingrich, pages 96–97) have systematically worked to get their views heard in the American media, whether by supplying research findings for news stories that cite their work, by writing opinion columns in newspapers, or by providing media commentary on television.

So successful have these conservative think tanks been in conveying their message through the media over the last three decades that they have helped shift public debate on policy in a conservative direction.[7] Some powerful Democrats now feel that they are losing the battle of ideas and have recently scrambled to improve or develop new liberal think tanks in the mirror image of their conservative counterparts.[8] The war of the think tanks demonstrates as well as anything the fact that power in Washington comes as much from ideas as it does from pouring resources into lobbying and twisting people's arms.

1. Jeffrey Berry, *The Interest Group Society*, 3d ed. (New York: Longman, 1997), 126–128.
2. Gary Strauss. "Why the Bush Administration Means Business," *USA Today*, January 19, 2001, 3B.
3. R. Kent Weaver, "The Changing World of Think Tanks," *PS: Political Science & Politics* (September 1989): 563–578.
4. Weaver, 1989; Berry, 1997.
5. Mark A. Smith. *American Business and Political Power* (Chicago: University of Chicago Press, 2000), 172–173.
6. Berry, 1997.
7. Smith, 2000, 183–186; 189–194.
8. Matt Bai, "Notion Building," *New York Times Magazine*, October 12, 2003, 82.

- *Provision of program alternatives.* Interest groups can be effective at supplying alternative suggestions for how issues should be dealt with once they have been put on the agenda. From this mix of proposals, political actors choose a solution.[13]
- *Program monitoring.* Once laws are enacted, interest groups keep tabs on their consequences, informing Congress and the regulatory agencies about the effects, both expected and unexpected, of federal policy. For example, the Children's Defense Fund has been active in drawing the attention of the national government to the effect of federal policies on the well-being of children.[14] Program monitoring helps the government decide whether to continue or change a policy, and it also helps to keep politicians accountable by ensuring that someone is paying attention to what they do.

WHY DO INTEREST GROUPS FORM?

Many of us can imagine public problems that we think need to be addressed. But despite our country's reputation as a nation of joiners, most of us never act, never organize a group, and never even join one. Social scientists call this the *problem of collective action*: the difficulty of getting people to work together to achieve a common goal. The problem of collective action can be overcome, in part, by the shared perception of a serious common problem or threat, an abundance of time and money to support a cause, and effective leadership.

Common Problem or Threat Most interest groups seem to be organized around shared interests, but many people who share interests never come together at all. What causes some groups to organize? For one noted scholar, the key triggering mechanism for interest group formation is a disturbance in the political, social, or economic environment that threatens the members of a group—for instance, governmental action to regulate businesses and professions.[15] This threat alerts the group's members that they need to organize to protect their interests through political action.

Persuasive Widows
Influence in Washington is not always rooted in money and votes; sometimes the cause of a group is so compelling that even hardened politicians cannot resist its demands. These four New Jersey widows whose husbands were killed in the 9/11 attack on the World Trade Center organized protests and lobbied Congress to authorize and then adequately fund the commission that investigated why the attacks were not prevented.

Resource Advantage While this explanation helps us understand interest group formation, it focuses on the external threats to a group rather than the internal resources that the potential group has. Researchers have long observed that some interest groups organize more easily than others and that some interest groups have formed without an external threat.[16] The resources available to prospective interest group members seem to be the key. Those with more money can pay for the direct-mail campaigns, publicity, legal assistance, and professional lobbying help that get the message to Washington and the public that the group means business. Perhaps just as important, those with greater resources are more likely to understand the political process, to have the confidence to express their views, and to appreciate the value of organizing into an interest group to push their policy positions.[17] This suggests that individuals with more wealth and more knowledge of the political system have a natural advantage in using the interest group process to pursue their policy goals. This also can explain why business and professional groups are more prevalent than those that represent the homeless, welfare recipients, and the unemployed.

Effective Leadership But even though wealthy groups have an advantage over groups whose pockets are not as well lined, an effective and charismatic leader can help redress the balance. The strong, effective leadership of what one scholar has called **interest group entrepreneurs** can be crucial to a group's ability to organize no matter what its resources are.[18] These entrepreneurs have a number of important characteristics, among them that they shoulder much of the initial burden and costs of organizing the group, and that they can convince people that the interest group will be able to promote the group's interests and influence the policies that affect it.[19] Such inspirational leaders have included César Chavez, who organized the United Farm Workers; Ralph Nader, who began a number of consumer interest groups; and Candy Lightner, who established Mothers Against Drunk Driving (MADD).

interest group entrepreneur an effective group leader who is likely to have organized the group and can effectively promote its interests among members and the public

THE FREE RIDER PROBLEM

External threats, financial resources, and effective leadership can all spur interest group formation, but they are usually not enough to overcome what we called earlier the problem of collective action. Another name for this is the **free rider problem**: why should people join you to solve the problem when they can free ride—that is, reap the benefits of your action whether they join or not?[20] The free rider problem affects interest groups because most of the policies that interest groups advocate involve the distribution of a collective good. A **collective good** is a good or benefit that, once provided, cannot be denied to others. Public safety, clean air, peace, and lower consumer prices are all examples of collective goods that can be enjoyed by anyone. When collective goods are involved, it is difficult to persuade people to join groups because they are going to reap the benefits anyway. The larger the number of potential members involved, the more this holds true, because each will have trouble seeing that his or her efforts will make a difference.

free rider problem the difficulty groups face in recruiting when potential members can gain the benefits of the group's actions whether they join or not

collective good a good or service that, by its very nature, cannot be denied to anyone who wants to consume it

Let's say, for instance, that in response to a number of rapes and muggings on campus, you decide to organize a group that advocates for better campus security. After a month of going to student organizations, dorms, and cafeterias, you have had little luck. Students for a Safer Campus still has only a handful of members. Your lack of organizational success can probably be chalked up to the free rider problem. The student who sits next to you in your American government class will benefit from better light-

Breaking the Fast
Inspirational leaders attract attention to their causes, making their appeals difficult to ignore. César Chavez, founder of the United Farm Workers, went on a twenty-five-day fast in 1968 to reaffirm the importance of nonviolence in union organizing. The bread-breaking ceremony that ended his fast drew a crowd of 4,000 farm workers, supporters like Sen. Robert F. Kennedy, and widespread media coverage.

ing and patrols if you are successful in your campaign, whether she joins or not. This makes it much harder to recruit members.

Many groups overcome the free rider problem by supplying **selective incentives**—benefits available to their members that are not available to the general population. There are three types of these incentives.[21]

selective incentives benefits that are available only to group members as an inducement to get them to join

- **Material benefits** are tangible rewards that members can use. One of the most common material benefits is information. For example, many groups publish a magazine or a newsletter packed with information about issues important to the group and pending legislation relevant to the group's activities. The American Bankers Association provides two publications (*Banking Journal* and *Banking News*) as well as email and fax service to select members who desire immediate information about banking issues that develop in Washington (*ABA Insider*). In addition to information, interest groups often offer material benefits in the form of group activities or group benefit policies. The NRA sponsors hunting and shooting competitions and offers discounted insurance policies. The Sierra Club offers a package of benefits that includes over 250 nature treks throughout the United States.

material benefits selective incentives in the form of tangible rewards

- **Solidary benefits** come from interaction and bonding among group members. For many individuals, politics is an enjoyable activity, and the social interactions occurring through group activities provide high levels of satisfaction and, thus, are a strong motivating force. Solidary incentives can come from local chapter meetings, lobbying missions to Washington or the state capital, or group-sponsored activities. The significant point is that the interest group provides the venue through which friendships are made and social interactions occur.

solidary benefits selective incentives related to the interaction and bonding among group members

- **Expressive benefits** are those rewards that come from doing something that you strongly believe in, from affiliating yourself with a purpose to which you are deeply committed—essentially from the *expression* of your values and interests. Many

expressive benefits selective incentives that derive from the opportunity to express values and beliefs and to be committed to a greater cause people, for example, are attracted to the ACLU because they passionately believe in protecting individual civil liberties. People who join the National Right to Life Committee believe strongly in making all abortions illegal in the United States. Their membership in the group is a way of expressing their views and ideals.

It is important to note that group leaders often use a mixture of incentives to recruit and sustain members. Thus the NRA recruits many of its members because they are committed to the cause of protecting an individual's right to bear arms. The NRA reinforces this expressive incentive with material incentives like its magazine and with solidary incentives resulting from group fellowship. The combination of these incentives helps make the NRA one of the strongest interest groups in Washington.

The provision of selective incentives can help to solve your problem of low membership in Students for a Safer Campus. As an entrepreneurial leader, you can provide a mix of benefits to those who sign on: discounted bus passes, free rides to and from the library after dark, and admission to a campus rock concert held to benefit your cause (material benefits); the opportunity for students to meet others and get involved in campus political life (solidary benefits); or the means to express the belief that the campus should be safe for all people at all times (expressive benefits). Your lagging membership drive should quickly revive when you follow the selective incentive strategy.

WHO, WHAT, HOW While they may have any number of goals, interest groups primarily want to influence policy. To accomplish this goal, they employ representation, participation, education, agenda building, alternative policy proposals, and program monitoring. In order to get anything done at all, however, they must organize and convince members to join. If all of the benefits of membership are collective goods, then potential members may free ride on the efforts of others, while still enjoying the product of the group's success. Thus interest groups offer selective benefits to entice members: material benefits, solidary benefits, and expressive benefits.

TYPES OF INTEREST GROUPS

There are potentially as many interest groups in America as there are interests, which is to say the possibilities are unlimited. Therefore, it is helpful to divide them into different types, based on the kind of benefit they seek for their members. Here we distinguish between economic, equal opportunity, public, and government (both foreign and domestic) interest groups. Depending on the definitions that they use, scholars have come up with different schemes for classifying interest groups, so do not be too surprised if you come across these groups with different labels at various times.

ECONOMIC INTEREST GROUPS

economic interest groups groups that organize to influence government policy for the economic benefit of their members

Economic interest groups seek to influence government for the economic benefit of their members. Generally these are players in the productive and professional activities of the nation—businesses, unions, other occupational associations, agriculturalists, and so on. The economic benefits they seek may be higher wages for a group or industry, lower tax rates, bigger government subsidies, or more favorable regulations. What all economic interest groups have in common is that they are focused primarily on pocketbook issues.

Corporations and Business Associations Given that government plays a key role in regulating the economy and defining the ground rules for economic competition, it should not surprise us that corporations and business groups are the most numerous and the most powerful of all interest groups. About 70 percent of all the interest groups that have their own lobbies in Washington, D.C., or hire professionals there, are business related.[22] The primary issues that they pursue involve taxes, labor, and regulatory issues. However, business interests have also been active in the areas of education, welfare reform, and health insurance.

Economic interest groups may be corporations like Enron or General Electric, which lobby government directly. More than six hundred corporations keep full-time Washington offices to deal with government relations, and that doesn't count the companies that hire out this function to independent lobbyists, or whose attempts to influence policy are made in cooperation with other businesses.[23] Such cooperation may take the form of industry associations, like the Tobacco Institute, the American Sportfishing Association, or the National Frozen Pizza Institute.

At a more general level, businesses may join together in associations like the National Association of Manufacturers, representing 14,000 manufacturers, or the Business Roundtable, representing major corporations.[24] The most diverse of these major business lobbies is the Chamber of Commerce, which represents a whole host of businesses (three million) ranging from small mom-and-pop stores to large employers.[25]

Unions and Professional Associations Interest groups often organize in response to each other. The business groups we just discussed organized not only as a way to deal with the increased regulatory powers of the federal government but also because labor was organized. Although labor organizations do not represent the force in society that they once did (membership has declined dramatically since the early 1950s, when over 35 million workers were unionized),[26] they can still be a formidable power when they decide to influence government, especially at the state level. The American Federation of Labor–Congress of Industrial Organizations (AFL-CIO) is by far the largest American union organization. At the start of 2005, the year of its fiftieth anniversary, it had more than 13 million members from fifty-eight trade and industrial unions. That same year, however, two of its most influential member unions, the Brotherhood of Teamsters (1.4 million members) and Service Employees International Union (1.8 million members), left the AFL-CIO with two other unions, depriving the organization of one-third of its members.[27] The United Auto Workers (710,000 members) and the United Mine Workers of America (240,000 members) also represent major segments of the labor force.[28]

Another large segment of America's workforce represented by unions are public employees. The American Federation of Government Employees represents federal workers, while the American Federation of State, County and Municipal Employees represents workers at lower levels of government. Teachers, firefighters, police, and postal workers, among others, also have large unions that wield significant influence on matters of policy in their particular areas of interest.

Unions are not the only organizations to represent economic interests along occupational lines. Many occupations that require much training or education have

Divided We Fall. . .
Despite the efforts of AFL-CIO leaders—shown here at a solidarity rally in Chicago are Linda Chavez-Thompson, Rich Trumka, and John Sweeney—four of the major unions of the AFL-CIO split off from the parent group in 2005 in a disagreement about the best tactics to stem organized labors' declining numbers and influence. Whereas most commentators feel that labor will be less effective, some believe that the breakup could lead to the adoption of new, innovative strategies that might actually help workers.

formed professional associations. Their basic purposes are to protect the profession's interests and to promote policies that enhance its position. For example, the American Medical Association has vigorously lobbied to lower the amount of medical malpractice awards.[29] The American Bar Association not only represents attorneys' interests (as do groups like the Association of Trial Lawyers of America) but, over the years, also has actively promoted structural and procedural reforms of the courts.

Agricultural Interest Groups Farming occupies an unusual place in American labor politics. It is the one occupation on which everyone in the nation depends for food, but it is also the one most subject to the vagaries of climate and other forces beyond human control. To keep farmers in business and the nation's food supply at affordable levels, the U.S. government has long regulated and subsidized agriculture. Consequently, although less than 2 percent of the U.S. work force is involved in farming, a large network of interest groups has grown up over the years to pursue policies favorable to agriculture. These include the American Farm Bureau, the largest national organization representing farmers (five million), and other groups like the American Agriculture Movement and the National Farmers Union, which represents small farmers.[30]

The agricultural community has evolved over the years to include agribusiness interests ranging from growers' associations (wheat, corn, fruit) to large multinational corporations like Archer Daniels Midland (ADM is a major grain processor), Altria (made up of the Philip Morris tobacco company and Kraft Foods), and ConAgra Foods, Inc. These agribusiness interests are not very different from the corporate interests we discussed earlier, even though their business is agriculture.

EQUAL OPPORTUNITY INTEREST GROUPS

equal opportunity interest groups groups that organize to promote the civil and economic rights of underrepresented or disadvantaged groups

Equal opportunity interest groups organize to promote the civil rights of groups that do not believe that their members' interests are being adequately represented and protected in national politics through traditional means. Because in many cases these groups are economically disadvantaged, or are afraid that they might become disadvantaged, these groups also advocate economic rights for their members. Equal opportunity groups believe that they are underrepresented not because of *what they do* but because of *who they are.* They may be the victims of discrimination, or see themselves as threatened. These groups have organized on the basis of age, race, ethnic group, gender, and sexual orientation. Membership is not limited to people who are part of the demographic group because many people believe that promoting the interests and rights of various groups in society is in the broader interest of all. For this reason, some scholars classify these groups as public interest groups, a type we explore in the next section.

Age One of the fastest growing segments of the U.S. population is composed of people over the age of sixty-five, as we saw in Chapter 2. Established in 1961, the American Association of Retired Persons (now known simply as the AARP) has a membership of more than 35 million Americans, more than one-half of all Americans over fifty years old. Despite its name, ironically, almost half of AARP's members still work.[31] Why does a group that claims to represent retired Americans have so many workers? Because a mere $12.50 a year is all it takes to become a member of AARP and to enjoy its numerous material benefits, like reduced health insurance rates and travel discounts.

With the motto of "Leave No Child Behind," the Children's Defense Fund (CDF) stands in sharp contrast to AARP. The CDF is funded from foundation grants and private donations. Indeed, because its constituents are not adults, it does not have any formal members. To combat this, the CDF regularly holds media events in which it issues reports and displays the results of its sponsored research. Through these media events, the CDF hopes to draw the public's attention to the plight of children in poverty and enhance the public's support for programs that address their needs.[32] However, unlike AARP, the CDF does not have the support of a legion of dues-paying members to get its proposed legislation passed. Supporters of children's rights and well-being suggest that this lack of effective advocates is precisely the reason that children are the largest group in the United States living in poverty.

Race and Ethnicity Many equal opportunity groups promote the interests of racial or ethnic minorities. Among such groups, none can match the longevity and success of the National Association for the Advancement of Colored People (NAACP). Founded in 1909 in response to race riots in Springfield, Illinois (the home of Abraham Lincoln), the NAACP has had a long history of fighting segregation and promoting the cause of equal opportunity and civil rights for African Americans. Its Legal Defense and Educational Fund is responsible for litigating most of the precedent-setting civil rights cases, including the famous *Brown v. Board of Education.* (See Chapter 6 for details on the struggle for equal rights.) Today the NAACP is by far the largest race-based equal opportunity group, with a membership of over 500,000.[33]

Many other equal opportunity interest groups are similar to the NAACP but focus on the civil rights of other races or ethnic minorities. The League of United Latin

American Citizens (LULAC) has worked for over seventy-five years to advocate the rights of Hispanics in the United States with respect to such issues as education, employment, voter registration, and housing.[34] The Mexican American Legal Defense and Educational Fund (MALDEF) is dedicated to the protection of Latinos in the United States, working through the courts and the legislatures on issues of language, immigration, employment, and education.[35] In a similar vein the American Indian Movement (AIM) has for over thirty-five years promoted and protected the interests of Native Americans. Founded on a philosophy of self-determination, AIM has worked to support legal rights, educational opportunities, youth services, job training, and other programs designed to eliminate the exploitation and oppression of Native Americans.[36] Likewise, numerous groups represent the concerns of Asian Americans. For example, the Southeast Asia Resource Action Center (SEARAC)is an umbrella organization coordinating the efforts of several networks supporting Asian Americans. SEARAC is a national and regional advocate for Cambodian, Laotian, and Vietnamese Americans on public policies concerning health care, economic growth, civil rights, and increased political participation.[37]

Gender Issues dealing with the equal treatment of women are a major feature of the American political landscape. Among women's groups, the National Organization for Women (NOW) is the largest, with over 500,000 members nationwide.[38] Funded by membership dues, NOW maintains an active lobbying effort in Washington and in many state capitals, builds coalitions with other women's rights groups, and conducts leadership training for its members. However, NOW has been a lightning rod for controversy among women because of its strong support for women's reproductive rights. Other groups that have drawn fire for having a feminist ideological agenda include EMILY's List, which stands for Early Money Is Like Yeast (it makes the dough rise). EMILY's List is a PAC that contributes money to Democratic women candidates.

While NOW and groups like EMILY's List have ties to liberal interests, other groups like the National Women's Political Caucus have sprung up to support the efforts of all women to be elected to public office, no matter what their partisan affiliation. Still others are conservative. For every group like NOW or EMILY's List, there is a conservative counterpart that actively opposes most, if not all, of what is seen as a liberal feminist agenda. For instance, Republican women have formed WISH (Women in the Senate and House). Another prominent conservative women's group is the Eagle Forum, led by Phyllis Schlafly. Since 1972 the Eagle Forum has campaigned against reproductive rights, the Equal Rights Amendment, and the societal trend of women working outside the home.[39]

In addition to these women's groups, there are groups that promote equal opportunity for men. The American Coalition for Fathers and Children and the National Congress for Fathers and Children have formed around the issue of promoting divorced men's custodial rights.[40] These men's groups pale in comparison, however, to the women's groups when it comes to funding, membership, and national exposure.

Sexual Orientation With the sexual revolution of the late 1960s and early 1970s, a number of gay and lesbian groups formed to fight discriminatory laws and practices based on sexual orientation. Their activities represent a two-tier approach to advocating equal opportunities for gays and lesbians. First, there is a focus on local and state governments to pass local ordinances or state laws protecting the civil rights of gays and lesbians. Groups that have made efforts at the local and state levels include the Gay and Lesbian Activists Alliance, which has been active in the mid-Atlantic states around Washington, D.C., since 1971, and the Gay and Lesbian Advocates and Defenders, a group composed of individuals from New England. On the national level, groups like the National Gay and Lesbian Task Force tend to focus their efforts on opposing federal policies that are intolerant of gays and lesbians (for example, exclusion of gays and lesbians from the military or a constitutional amendment to ban gay marriage) and on promoting funding for AIDS research.

While most gay and lesbian groups are officially nonpartisan, many have close ties to the Democratic Party. To promote gay and lesbian issues within the Republican Party, activists within the GOP have formed groups like the Log Cabin Republicans, to provide campaign contributions to GOP candidates who support equal opportunity for gays and lesbians, and lobby Republican representatives and senators on gay and lesbian issues.[41]

PUBLIC INTEREST GROUPS

A **public interest group** tries to influence government to produce noneconomic benefits that cannot be restricted to the interest group's members or denied to any member of the general public. The benefits of clean air, for instance, are available to all, not just the members of the environmental group that fought for them. In a way, all interest group benefits are collective goods that all members of the group can enjoy, but public interest groups seek collective goods that are open to all members of society or, in some cases, the entire world.

public interest group group that organizes to influence government to produce collective goods or services that benefit the general public

Public interest group members are usually motivated by a view of the world that they think everyone would be better off to adopt. They believe that the benefit they seek is good for everyone, even if individuals outside their group may disagree or even reject the benefit. While few people would dispute the value of clean air, peace, and the protection of human rights internationally, there is no such consensus about protecting the right to an abortion, or the right to carry concealed weapons, or the right to smoke marijuana. Yet each of these issues has public interest groups dedicated to procuring and enforcing these rights for all Americans. Because they are involved in the production of collective goods for very large populations and the individual incentive to contribute may be particularly difficult to perceive, public interest groups are especially vulnerable to the free rider problem. That has not stopped them from organizing, however. There are over 2,500 public interest groups in the United States.[42] The number of these groups grew dramatically in the 1960s and again in the 1980s.

People are drawn to public interest groups because they support the groups' values and goals; that is, expressive benefits are the primary draw for membership. Often when events occur that threaten the goals of a public interest group, membership increases. For example, fearing that the Republicans would dismantle environmental laws after Ronald Reagan was elected president, new members flocked to environmental interest groups like the Sierra Club and the National Wildlife Federation; these organizations gained about 150,000 members from 1980 to 1985.[43] Likewise, after President Clinton signed the Brady Bill in 1993, requiring a waiting period before gun purchases, among other regulations, the NRA saw its membership increase by half a million.

While many members are initially attracted by expressive benefits, public interest groups seek to keep them active by offering material benefits and services ranging from free subscriptions to the group's magazine to discount insurance packages.

Environmental Groups Starting with Earth Day in 1970, environmentally based interest groups have been actively engaged in promoting environmental policies. The Clean Air and Water Acts, the Endangered Species Act, and the creation of the Environmental Protection Agency all represent examples of their successes during the 1970s. Today the Sierra Club, National Audubon Society, and Natural Resources Defense Council maintain active and professional lobbying efforts in Washington, as do environmental groups such as Greenpeace. On the extreme fringes of the environmental movement are more confrontational groups like Earth First! Their members take a dim view of attempts to lobby members of Congress for "green" laws. Instead, their calls for direct action have included building and living in aerial platforms in old-growth redwood forests in California so as to dissuade the timber industry from felling the trees. Activists have also protested by taking over the offices of local members of Congress.[44]

Consumer Groups The efforts of Ralph Nader and his public interest group Public Citizen have become synonymous with the cause of consumer protectionism. Since his path-breaking book *Unsafe at Any Speed* (1965) documented the safety problems with Chevrolet's Corvair, Nader has been exposing the hazards of a variety of other consumer products and addressing unsafe practices in the nuclear power, airline, and health care industries.[45] Another consumer advocacy group is Consumers Union, the nonprofit publisher of *Consumer Reports* magazine. Consumers Union testifies before state and federal government agencies, petitions government, and files lawsuits to protect consumer interests.[46]

Religious Groups Religious groups in America have had a long history of interest group activity, dating back to the abolitionist movement. In more recent times, religious groups have developed and grown in response to what they describe as the moral decay and decadence of American society. The Christian Coalition, for example, with two million members the most powerful religious fundamentalist group in American politics,[47] lobbies on political issues and provides members with voters' guides. Pat Robertson, who had been chairman of the Christian Coalition's board, also developed the Christian Broadcasting Network in 1976, which, along with other large Christian media sources like Dr. James Dobson's *Focus on the Family* radio broadcast, helps to educate and mobilize evangelical Christians on political issues nationwide. These groups have become a major force in national politics and an important part of the coalition supporting the Republican Party.[48]

Fundamentalist Christian groups are not the only religiously affiliated interest groups. The United States Conference of Catholic Bishops also lobbies on particular issues, and the Anti-Defamation League promotes a broad set of foreign, domestic, and legal issues that combat worldwide anti-Semitism and discrimination against Jewish Americans.

Second Amendment Groups Based on its interpretation of the Second Amendment to the Constitution, the NRA is opposed to almost any effort to control and regulate the sale and distribution of firearms. Overall, the NRA has had considerable policy success. Despite public opinion polls that show a clear majority of Americans favoring gun control, the level of regulation of gun purchases remains minimal. The NRA's success can be credited to its highly dedicated members who are willing to contribute their time, resources, and votes to those candidates who support the NRA's positions—and, conversely, to a credible threat of retribution to officeholders who cross the NRA. In the 1994 elections, one year after passage of the Brady Bill, NRA voters contributed to the coalition of voters who ousted moderate Democratic representatives, and Brady supporters, across the South.[49]

One group that has challenged the power of the NRA is Handgun Control, Inc., an interest group founded by Brady Bill namesake James Brady, who was severely wounded in the 1981 attempted assassination of President Reagan, and his wife, Sarah. Handgun Control, Inc., now known as the Brady Campaign to Prevent Gun Violence, was instrumental in getting the waiting-period legislation passed in 1993. In 1994, Congress followed the Brady Bill with the Violent Crime Control and Law Enforcement Act, which banned nineteen types of automatic or semiautomatic assault rifles.[50] With the election of a Republican majority in 1994, gun control efforts had less success in Congress and when the assault weapons ban lapsed in 2004, they were able to keep it from being renewed.[51]

Reproductive Rights Groups The Supreme Court's decision in *Roe v. Wade* (1973) granting women the right to an abortion generated a number of interest groups. On the pro-choice side of this debate are the National Abortion Rights Action League (NARAL) and Planned Parenthood. These groups have mounted a public relations campaign aimed at convincing policymakers that a majority of Americans want women to have the right to choose safe and legal abortions.[52]

On the pro-life side of the debate is the National Right to Life Committee and its more confrontational partner, Operation Rescue. The National Right to Life Committee lobbies Congress and state legislatures to limit abortions, hoping ultimately to secure the passage of a constitutional amendment banning them altogether. Operation Rescue attempts to prevent abortions by blocking access to abortion clinics, picketing clinics, and intercepting women who are considering abortions. In recent years, pro-life groups have shifted from a single focus on abortion to other issues they see as similar, such as opposing stem cell research and, in 2005, protesting the removal of a feeding tube from a brain-damaged woman.

Other Public Interest Groups Other public interest groups target the issue of human rights. The ACLU is a nonprofit, nonpartisan defender of individual rights against the encroachment of a powerful government. The ACLU supports the rights of disadvantaged minorities and claims to be the "nation's guardian of liberty."[53] Another human rights group, Amnesty International, promotes human rights worldwide, with over 1.5 million members in 150 countries. In the United States, Amnesty International lobbies on issues such as the death penalty, arms control, and globalization.[54]

Interest groups have also taken up the cause of animal rights. The most well-known of these groups is the Humane Society. Beyond providing local animal shelters, the Humane Society researches animal cruelty and lobbies governments at all levels on issues ranging

The Politics of Abortion
Few political issues produce the kind of heated reactions that the debate over a woman's right to terminate a pregnancy provokes. Interest groups on both sides of this controversy use disturbing, graphic displays and sometimes confrontational tactics to influence members of the public as well as policymakers. Here, pro-life and pro-choice activists clash at a rally in front of the Supreme Court in Washington, D.C.

from domestic pet overpopulation and adoption to farm animal treatment and wildlife habitat protection (see "*Profiles in Citizenship:* Wayne Pacelle"). In recent years a number of actors and actresses have used their celebrity status to protect animals. People for the Ethical Treatment of Animals (PETA) is a leading national interest group promoting the rights of animals. Its grassroots campaigns include attacking major health and beauty corporations like Procter & Gamble for using animals for product testing, assailing circuses and rodeos for using animals as entertainment, and condemning fur coat manufacturers for the cruel ways they kill animals.[55] Other groups like the Animal Rights Law Project at Rutgers University and the Animal Liberation Front also advocate animal rights. Animal rights activists often use civil disobedience in their attempts to stop hunting and end the use of animals for biomedical and product safety tests.[56]

GOVERNMENT INTEREST GROUPS

Foreign governments also lobby Congress and the president. Typically some lobbyists' most lucrative contracts come from foreign governments seeking to influence foreign trade policies. The Japanese government maintains one of the more active lobbying efforts in Washington, hiring former members of Congress and bureaucrats to aid in their efforts to keep U.S. markets open to Japanese imports.[57] In recent years, ethics rules have been initiated to prevent former government officials from working as foreign government lobbyists as soon as they leave office, but lobbying firms continue to hire them when they can because of their contacts and expertise.[58]

Domestic governments have also become increasingly involved in the business of influencing federal policy. With the growing complexities of American federalism, state and local governments have an enormous stake in what the federal government does, and often try to gain resources, limit the impact of policy, and otherwise alter the effects of federal law. All fifty states have government relations offices in Washington to attempt to influence federal policy directly. In addition, the "Big Seven" major intergovernmental interest groups—the National Governors Association, the Council of State Governments, the National Conference of State Legislatures, the National League of Cities, the National Association of Counties, the United States Conference of Mayors, and the International City/County Management Association—all either lobby for benefits for subnational governments or otherwise represent the interests of intergovernmental actors.[59]

WHO, WHAT, HOW All citizens stand to win or lose a great deal from government action. If it goes their way, producing policy that benefits them, they win. But if it produces policy that helps other citizens at their expense, or passes the cost of expensive policy on to them, or reduces their ability to use the system to get what they want, then they lose. Economic actors want to protect their financial interests; members of disadvantaged or threatened groups want to protect their legal and economic interests; ideologically motivated people want to promote their vision of the good society; and governments want a good relationship with the U.S. federal government. All these citizens promote their goals through the formation of different types of interest groups.

INTEREST GROUP POLITICS

The term *lobbying* comes from seventeenth-century England, where representatives of special interests would meet members of the English House of Commons in the large anteroom, or lobby, outside the Commons floor to plead their cases.[60] Contemporary lobbying, however, reaches far beyond the lobby of the House or Senate. Interest groups do indeed contact lawmakers directly, but they no longer confine their efforts to chance meetings in the legislative lobby or to members of the legislature.

Today, lobbyists target all branches of government and the American people as well. The ranks of those who work with lobbyists have also swelled. Beginning in the 1980s, interest groups, especially those representing corporate interests, have been turning to a diverse group of political consultants, including professional Washington lobbyists, campaign specialists, advertising and media experts, pollsters, and academics. Lobbying today is a big business in its own right.

There are two main types of lobbying. **Direct lobbying** is interaction with actual decision makers within government institutions. While we tend to think of Congress as the typical recipient of lobbying efforts, the president, the bureaucracy, and even the courts are also the focus of heavy efforts to influence policy. **Indirect lobbying** attempts to influence policymakers by mobilizing interest group members or the general public to contact elected representatives on an issue. Some groups have resorted to more confrontational indirect methods, using political protests, often developing into full-blown social movements, to make their demands heard by policymakers. Recently, corporations and other more traditional interest groups have been combining tactics—joining conventional lobbying methods with the use of email, computerized databases, talk radio, and twenty-four-hour cable television—to bring unprecedented pressure to bear on the voting public to influence members of government.

direct lobbying direct interaction with public officials for the purpose of influencing policy decisions

indirect lobbying attempts to influence government policymakers by encouraging the general public to put pressure on them

DIRECT LOBBYING: CONGRESS

When interest groups lobby Congress, they rarely concentrate on all 435 members of the House or all 100 members of the Senate. Rather, lobbyists focus their efforts on congressional committees, where most bills are written and revised. Because the committee leadership is relatively stable from one Congress to the next (unless a different party wins a majority), lobbyists can develop long-term relationships with committee members and their staffs.

Strategies for Congressional Lobbying Interest groups use many strategies to influence members of Congress:

- *Personal contacts.* Personal contacts, including appointments, banquets, parties, lunches, or simply casual meetings in the hallways of Congress, are the most common and the most effective form of lobbying.
- *Use of professional lobbyists.* Much of modern lobbying involves the use of professional lobbyists, many of them former government officials, put on retainer by a client to lobby for that client's interests. Rotating into lobbying jobs from elected or other government positions is known as passing through the **revolving door**, a concept we meet again in Chapter 15. It refers to public officials who leave their posts to become interest group representatives (or media figures), parlaying the

revolving door the tendency of public officials, journalists, and lobbyists to move between public and private sector (media, lobbying) jobs

Profiles in Citizenship

Wayne Pacelle

In the midst of one of his finest moments, Wayne Pacelle got himself thrown out of the gallery of the House of Representatives.

He was watching the vote on a budget amendment he had lobbied hard for, an amendment to cut millions of dollars of taxpayer money spent to promote the sale of U.S.-made mink coats in Italy, China, and France. He needed 218 votes to win, and everyone thought they were going to be trounced. He watched the scoreboard light up with vote after vote. When they got to 232, he couldn't help it. He let out a yell and pumped his fist. But the House frowns on emotional displays in the gallery, and out he went. Was he abashed? Hardly. "It didn't take the smile off my face," he says, grinning even now at the memory.

". . .making the world a better place—that's the bottom line."

It was a great win, but every single triumph matters to Pacelle—it's how he feeds his spirit and keeps himself going in the face of the often daunting odds and unimaginable stories of animal abuse he confronts daily in his job as CEO of the Humane Society of the United States. Each law enacted by Congress to protect animals (fifteen in the past few years), each state bill passed (more than 150), each statewide ballot measure approved (fifteen so far), each animal life saved, each creature relieved of pain and suffering—he tallies them all. "I celebrate the positive action because it's easy to get burned out," he says. "It's easy to get demoralized. . . . And for me, I just tell people you've got to celebrate every little victory, it makes a big difference."

"For us, it's not an all-or-nothing game," he explains. "We can't solve all of the issues in the world, we never will. . . . But if we solve it for a million, or ten million, or a billion creatures, that's a 100-percent victory for each of those animals. And just that one act of merciful behavior or the shielding of an animal from abuse or cruelty can mean all the difference between a good quality of life and a miserable tormented existence for that creature."

Pacelle has felt that kind of enormous compassionate connection to animals ever since he was two or three years old. "It was a purely emotional, altruistic response that I had toward other creatures. I just saw them as powerless and I saw them as peers at that age, and they looked to me like they were composed of the same spark of life that people were."

He carried that empathy and awareness with him as he got older and, as he read philosophy and learned more about the world, he began to fit it into a broader context of what it meant to him to be a responsible citizen. He started an animal rights group in college in the

special knowledge and contacts they gathered in government into lucrative salaries in the private sector. Current law requires that employees of the federal government wait only one year before lobbying their former agencies.[61]

Many officials are too impatient to wait. Less than six months after his retirement, Rep. Gerald Solomon of New York, known as the congressman from General Electric for his consistent support of business interests while in office, became a lobbyist for GE. Solomon made no bones about his motives, saying that after twenty years on a representative's salary ($136,700 a year when he left office), he wanted to leave a large estate to his children and grandchildren.[62]

Professional lobbying has been one of the nation's growth industries, with the number of registered lobbyists in Washington more than doubling between 2000 and 2005. Businesses especially see opportunities to influence the government in the corporate-friendly Republican-controlled Congress and White House, but trade associa-

1980s, at the same time that he was active in the anti-apartheid movement to limit U.S. investment in South Africa and in protests of U.S. involvement in Central America. Ask him what the common thread is and he is clear: "I'm broadly interested in making the world a better place," he says. "That's the bottom line. Public policy is just the means to achieve the end of a more fair, a more just society."

A huge and saintly ambition, but Pacelle doesn't look like a zealot or a crusader when he says it. Actually, he looks like, well, a movie star, or a relative of a famous American political family (possessing what the *Washington Post* once called "John Kennedy, Jr. good looks"). He is polished, articulate, and funny (it must run in the family—his brother, Richard, is the funniest political scientist we know), and the animals couldn't ask for a more dedicated or committed advocate.

How has he kept that idealism and commitment in the face of the giant sums of money that Washington lobbyists traffic in these days? He may be an optimist, but he's a realist, too. "You'd be naive to think money doesn't have an impact," he says. "It does. It gains access, and it builds loyalty. But, ultimately, money is a means to an end. Money is there to have resources to deliver a message to influence voting behavior. So if you've got people who can organize around a principle and you can deliver votes based on that set of ideas, then you don't need money." Well, maybe not as much, anyway. Here are some of his thoughts:

On the positive side of lobbying:

There's a reason in Washington, D.C., that there are thousands of lobbyists and thousands of interest groups. They're not here for fun; it's not just a big party. They're here because it does make a difference and participation can have a measurable impact on public policy. I think for me, just being determined and dogged about it, just not relenting, just basically treating this as if it's a full court press all the time. . . . I mean when we're not on defense, we're on the offense. It's almost a very crusading sort of attitude. I don't like to infuse it with religious sorts of notions, but it's a powerful, ethical construct. And having enough imagination to see that things can be different. That we're not just locked into our present set of social relationships and circumstance, that we can aspire to do things better.

On keeping the republic:

No one's going to hand you a key to change everything, but if you're smart and if you're determined you can make a real difference in the world. I've seen it happen thousands and thousands of times. And anybody who tells me differently just isn't paying attention to what's going on. And don't count on somebody else to do it, you know, don't count on a group like the Humane Society of the United States to do it. When I go around and I talk to people I say, "Listen, we can help." And our staff of four hundred, we've got great experts and we do a lot of amazing stuff, but you make the difference. It's the collective action of people of conscience that really can have a meaningful impact on society. And again, the history is of people stepping up and calling themselves to action. And leadership and citizenship are such important values in this culture. And if not them, who?

Source: Wayne Pacelle talked with Christine Barbour on March 10, 2005.

tions and other interest groups need professional help to navigate the increasingly complex world of government regulations and benefits.[63]

For example, one Washington lobbying firm employs former Republican senator Bob Dole and former Democratic senator Tom Daschle. Although neither of the retired senators actually goes to the Hill to lobby directly for clients, they are available to dispense political wisdom; to share their experience, knowledge, and contacts; and to provide access to their one-time colleagues. Such assistance can be so invaluable to their clients that even legislative aides can make their fortune lobbying, commanding starting salaries of upwards of $300,000 a year in 2005.[64]

Revolving-door activity is subject to occasional attempts at regulation, and frequent ethical debate, because it raises questions about whether people should be able to convert public service into private profit, and whether such an incentive draws people into public office for motives other than serving the public interest.

- *Providing expert testimony.* Interest groups lobby decision makers by providing testimony and expertise and sometimes even draft legislation on the many issue areas in which policymakers cannot take the time to become expert.[65] Information is one of the most important resources lobbyists can bring to their effort to influence Congress. Providing valid information to representatives and staffers becomes a tool that lobbyists use to build long-term credibility with members of Congress.

  For example, with support from a president and vice president who are former energy company executives, Republicans in Congress worked closely with energy companies to develop legislation that would increase oil exploration, coal mining, and nuclear plant development in 2003. One industry lobbyist said of the energy bill: "This is the mother lode."[66] Democrats, locked out of the conference committee that was considering the bill, were so frustrated by the influence of the energy lobbyists that then-senator Bob Graham, D-Fla., fumed, "at this point, industry lobbyists are effectively writing this bill."[67] Of course, in their turn energy companies had been frustrated with the Clinton administration's pro-environmental positions on energy exploration, claiming that they listened only to conservationists and environmental groups.[68]

- *Campaign contributions.* Giving money to candidates is another lobbying technique that helps interest groups gain access and a friendly ear. The 1974 Federal Election Campaign Act that was passed in an effort to curb campaign spending abuses was aimed at regulating the amount of money an interest group could give to candidates for federal office, by providing for PACs to serve as fundraisers for interest groups. Despite strict limitations on how much money PACs can donate to a candidate, they have found a number of loopholes that let them circumvent the restrictions. Figure 13.2 shows how the major types of interest groups divide their money between the Democratic and Republican Parties.

- *Coalition formation.* Interest groups attempt to bolster their lobbying efforts by forming coalitions with other interest groups. While these coalitions tend to be based on single issues, building coalitions in favor of or against specific issues has become an important strategy in lobbying Congress.

Attempts at Lobbying Reform Many attempts have been made to regulate the tight relationship between lobbyist and lawmaker. The difficulty, of course, as the battle over campaign finance reform that we talk about in this chapter's *What's at Stake?* makes clear, is that lawmakers benefit from the relationship with lobbyists in many ways and are not enthusiastic about curtailing their opportunities to get money and support. In 1995, Congress completed its first attempt in half a century to regulate lobbying when it passed the Lobbying Disclosure Act. The act requires lobbyists to report how much they are paid, by whom, and what issues they are promoting.[69]

Also in 1995, both the Senate and the House passed separate resolutions addressing gifts and travel given by interest groups to senators and representatives.[70] The House ban, which had been more restrictive than the Senate's, was eased in 1999 to match the Senate's rules on the acceptance of gifts from lobbyists.[71] In 2003 the House reversed its strict prohibition against the funding of representatives' travel to charity events by lobbyists.[72] The following provisions currently govern gift and travel rules:[73]

- Senators, members of the House, and their aides are prohibited from receiving any gift or meal of $50 or more, and they cannot receive gifts or meals amounting to $100 or more over the course of a year from a particular lobbyist.

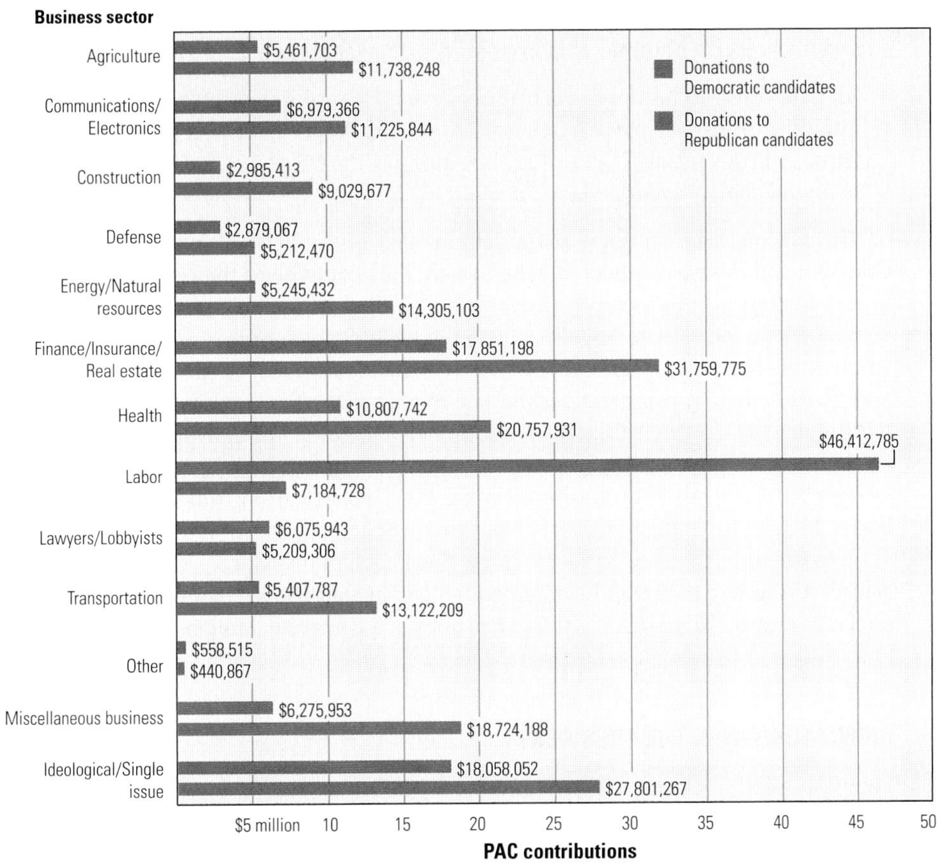

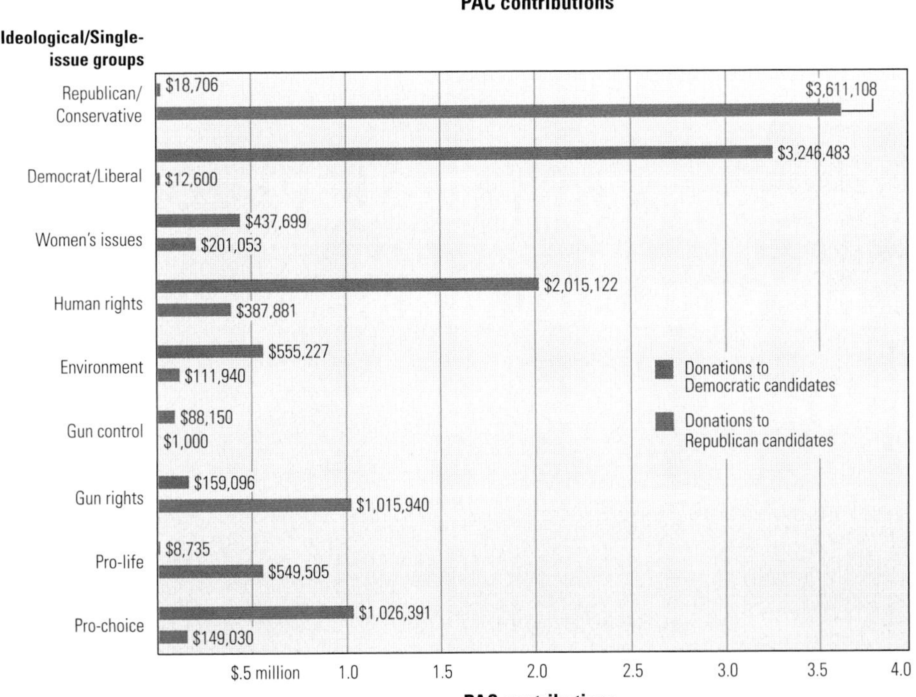

FIGURE 13.2

How Interest Groups Spent Their Money in the 2004 Campaign

These two figures show the breakdown of contributions made to Democratic and Republican candidates by interest groups in different sectors. The bottom figure itemizes the Ideological Groups category (most of which we call public interest groups) even further, according to the focus of their efforts.

Source: Data from Center for Responsive Politics, 2005, www.opensecrets.org/pacs/list.asp.

- House members, senators, and their aides may accept gifts from family and friends and may receive nominal gifts like plaques or awards.
- All paid travel to leisure or recreational events is prohibited to senators, although interest groups can pay for senators to attend events like speeches, fact-finding trips, and conventions. Interest groups may pay the travel fees for House members to attend charity events.

The 1995 reforms initially cast a definite chill on lobbyist activity.[74] Members of Congress and lobbyists quickly learned where they could bend the rules, however, allowing interest groups to fund speeches, fact-finding trips, and conferences in exotic places.[75] In any case, loosening the rules to allow fifty-dollar gifts is not necessarily restrictive where creative members of Congress are concerned. For instance, the House and Senate ethics committees set the fair-market value for seats in luxury suites at Washington, D.C.'s MCI Center at just under $50 (even though nearby seats with fewer amenities go for $90), allowing members to "legally" enjoy sporting events in a lobbyist's luxury box.[76] In addition, as the 2005 investigation into House majority leader Tom DeLay's acceptance of an expensive Scottish golf trip illustrates, there are many more ways to get around the rules. The problem for which DeLay was investigated was not so much that he accepted the trip as that it was charged to a lobbyist's own credit card.[77] Clearly the gift ban has not put a complete damper on lobbyists' attempts to woo congressional support with fancy perks.

DIRECT LOBBYING: THE PRESIDENT

Lobbyists also target the president and the White House staff in order to try to influence policy. As with Congress, personal contacts within the White House are extremely important, and the higher up in the White House, the better. For instance,

Crossing the Line
Lobbyist Jack Abramoff, representing American Indian gambling interests, pushed the limits of the law in paying for foreign travel, including golf trips, for House Majority Leader Tom DeLay (R-Texas) and others. In 2005, Abramoff was indicted and also being investigated for defrauding his clients. Meanwhile, DeLay was unable to get past rumors and reports about his questionable dealings with the lobbyist. Here an anti-DeLay group draws his constituents' attention to the controversy with this Houston-area billboard.

Vice President Cheney consulted with executives from energy companies, including the ill-fated Enron, to get their input on the administration's energy proposals that would have a direct impact on the energy companies' financial prospects. Nor has the White House been exempt from the revolving-door phenomenon. At least two Clinton cabinet members, the late secretary of commerce Ron Brown and trade representative Mickey Kantor, had been professional lobbyists, and this despite Clinton's unusually tough stance against lobbying.[78]

The official contact point between the White House and interest groups is the Office of Public Liaison. Its basic purpose is to foster good relations between the White House and interest groups in order to mobilize these groups to support the administration's policies. Given the highly partisan and ideologically charged nature of most presidencies, it should not be surprising that the groups each White House administration cultivates are those it feels most ideologically comfortable with.

DIRECT LOBBYING: THE BUREAUCRACY

While opportunities for lobbying the president may be somewhat limited, opportunities for lobbying the rest of the executive branch abound. Interest groups know that winning the legislative battle is only the first step. The second, and sometimes most important, battle takes place in the bureaucracy, where Congress has delegated rulemaking authority to federal agencies that implement the law.[79] When, for instance, the Occupational Safety and Health Administration (OSHA) decreed that workplace design must take into account the physical abilities of workers in order to avoid repetitive motion injuries, groups like organized labor supported the effort, although they believed the new standards did not go far enough, while business groups lobbied heavily against it, claiming that the standards were unnecessary, unsupported by medical evidence, and expensive to implement.[80]

Interest groups often try to gain an advantage by developing strong relations with regulating agencies. Because many of the experts on a topic are employed by the interests being regulated, it is not unusual to find lobbyists being hired by government agencies, or vice versa, in an extension of the revolving-door situation we just discussed. The close relationships that exist between the regulated and the regulators, along with the close relationships between lobbyists and congressional staffers, leads to the creation of the iron triangles we talked about in Chapter 9 (see especially Figure 9.2 on page 403). Iron triangles not only work against an open policymaking environment by limiting the participation of actors not in the triangle, but they also have the potential for presenting conflicts of interest. Although recent laws prevent former government employees from lobbying their former agencies for five years after they leave their federal jobs, government agencies are sometimes forced to recruit personnel from within the businesses they are regulating because that is often where the experts are to be found.

DIRECT LOBBYING: THE COURTS

Interest groups also try to influence government policy by challenging the legality of laws or administrative regulations in the courts. These legal tactics have been used by groups like the NAACP (challenging segregation laws), the ACLU (freedom of speech, religion, and civil liberties cases), the Sierra Club (environmental enforcement), and

Common Cause (ethics in government). As soon as campaign finance reform was passed in 2002, the NRA, the ACLU, the AFL-CIO, and other groups immediately went into action to challenge the new law in court. Sometimes groups bring cases directly, and sometimes they file amicus curiae ("friend of the court") briefs asking the courts to rule in ways favorable to their positions.

INDIRECT LOBBYING: THE PUBLIC

One of the most powerful and fastest-growing kinds of lobbying is indirect lobbying, in which the lobbyists use public opinion to put pressure on politicians to do what they want.[81] In this section we examine the various ways in which interest groups use the public to lobby and influence government decision makers. These efforts include educating the public by disseminating information and research, mobilizing direct citizen lobbying efforts, and organizing demonstrations or protests.

Educating the Public Interest groups must get their issues onto the public's agenda before they can influence how the public feels about them. Many interest group leaders are sure that the public will rally to their side once they know "the truth" about their causes.[82] Interest groups often begin their campaigns by using research to show that the problem they are trying to solve is a legitimate one. For example, the Tax Foundation is a conservative group promoting tax cuts. To dramatize its point that American taxes are too high, every year the foundation announces "Tax Freedom Day"—the day on which the average wage earner finishes paying the amount of taxes he or she will owe and starts working for his or her own profit. In 2005, that day was April 17.[83] The foundation believes that this information is so compelling that it will convince the public to share its view that taxes are too high.

Of course, all the research in the world by the Tax Foundation, or any other interest group, does no good if the public is unaware of it. For this reason, interest groups cultivate press coverage. They know that people are more likely to take their research seriously if it is reported by the media as legitimate news. Thus the Tax Foundation, which could simply post Tax Freedom Day on its Web site, uses that Web site to announce a press conference held by its director at the National Press Club in an effort to gain maximum attention for the cause. Getting news coverage can be difficult for interest groups because they are in competition with every other interest group, not to mention news stories generated by current events in the nation and the world. Many of them turn to expensive public relations firms to help them get their message out, using tactics ranging from TV commercials to direct-mail campaigns. (See "*Consider the Source:* How to Be a Critical Consumer of Direct Mail.")

issue advocacy ads advertisements that support issues or candidates without telling constituents how to vote

An increasingly popular way for interest groups to get out their message is through the use of **issue advocacy ads**. These commercials encourage constituents to support or oppose a certain policy or candidate without directly telling citizens how to vote. In the past, as long as these ads did not specifically promote the election or defeat of a particular candidate, issue advocacy ads were not subject to any limitations, meaning a PAC could spend all the money it wanted on ads promoting an issue and, by implication, the candidates of its choice. With the passage of the 2002 Bipartisan Campaign Reform Act (also called the McCain-Feingold Act), however, these ads are forbidden thirty days before primary elections and sixty days before general elections. A strange mixture of ideologically opposed interest groups challenged the McCain-

How to Be a Critical Consumer of Direct Mail

The NRA knows where you live—but it is not gunning for you; it is after your money. So are the Brady Campaign to Prevent Gun Violence, Mothers Against Drunk Driving, the Sierra Club, and the Children's Defense Fund. You can only be glad that you are probably too young for AARP to take an interest in you yet. Our mailboxes, once a repository for letters from mom and a handful of bills, have become a battleground for interest groups after our hard-earned cash. Welcome to the age of direct-mail solicitations.

If it hasn't happened to you yet, no doubt as you become gainfully employed, give money to a cause or two you admire, and become integrated into your community, you too will become the target of "personalized" written requests from interest groups for the donations that they need to keep financially afloat. Direct mail is big business, run by professionals whose job it is to design the impassioned pleas that encourage you to open your wallet or write that check. Because interest groups have so much at stake in their direct-mail solicitations (in many cases, their very survival depends on it), they pull out all the stops in their letters to you. How can you evaluate these dramatic requests so that you can in fact support the legitimate groups whose causes you believe in, but not fall (as they hope you will) for over-the-top exaggeration and provocatively embellished prose? When presented with a plea for funds, ask yourself the following questions:

1. **What is this group? What do they stand for?** Sometimes direct-mail writers spend the majority of their time telling you what they are against, or whom they oppose, in the hopes that you will share their animosities and therefore support them. Many groups give a web address. Check them out, but remember that the web site is also written by supporters and may not give you a full or unbiased view. Look them up in a newspaper archive and get some objective information (that is, information not written by the group itself!).

2. **How did they get your address?** Do they treat you as a long-lost friend? Often a group will buy a mailing list from some other group. You can occasionally trace your name by the particular spelling (or misspelling), use of a maiden name or nickname, or some other characteristic that does not appear on your standard mailing address. Knowing how a group got your name can sometimes tell you what its connections are and what it is about. A simple mail order purchase of hiking boots can get you on the mailing lists of sports outfitters, and a short step later onto the lists of the NRA, which hopes that outdoorsy people will hunt and thus support its cause. In addition, as mailing techniques get more sophisticated, interest groups are able to personalize their requests for support. If you belong to the local humane society and other groups that would indicate your love for animals, and if the interest group got your name from their lists, it can target you with a fundraising letter that plays on your concern for animal life. If the letter seems to be directed to your deepest values, harden your heart until you have checked out the group independently.

3. **What claims do they make?** Direct mail is designed to make you sit down and write a check *now*. From some letters, you get the sense that Armageddon is at hand and the world will soon self-destruct without your donation. Do *not* believe everything you read in a fundraising letter. Verify the facts before you send any money. The more persuasive and amazing the claim appears to be, the more it requires verification!

4. **What are they asking for?** It is almost always money, but a group may also ask you to write your congressperson, make a phone call, wear a ribbon, or otherwise show support for a cause. Be clear about what you are being asked to do and what you are committing to do. If possible, check out the interest group's record for effective action. If most of the money it gets goes to administrative costs, you won't be furthering your cause much by contributing your dollars.

5. **What do you get for your money?** What material benefits does the group offer? Do you receive a newsletter? Discounts on products or services? Special offers for the group? We are not advising free-ridership here, but it is wise to know exactly what you are getting before you part with your cash.

Feingold reforms as unfair limitations on their free speech, but the Supreme Court ruled that the limitations were constitutional.[84]

As we saw in the *What's at Stake?* feature that opened this chapter, however, the campaign finance reforms did not limit all advertising by special interests. So-called **527 groups** like the Swift Boat Veterans for Truth can raise unlimited amounts of money from labor unions, corporations, and interest groups to mobilize voters with issue advocacy ads on television and radio, so long as they do not directly advocate the election or defeat of a candidate.[85] Organized under section 527 of the Internal Revenue Code, they are not subject to laws that the Federal Election Commission regulates.[86] Senator McCain and other advocates of reform have called on the Federal Election Commission to regulate these groups and on Congress to close this loophole, but the long history of the Bipartisan Campaign Reform Act shows just how long it can take to pass reforms that powerful interest groups want to prevent.[87]

527 groups groups that mobilize voters with issue advocacy advertisements on television and radio but may not directly advocate the election or defeat of a particular candidate

Mobilizing the Public The point of disseminating information, hiring public relations firms, and running issue ads is to motivate the public to lobby politicians themselves. On most issues, general public interest is low, and groups must rely on their own members for support. As you might suspect, groups like AARP, the Christian Coalition, and the NRA, which have large memberships, have an advantage because they can mobilize a large contingent of citizens from all over the country to lobby representatives and senators. Generally this mobilization involves encouraging members to write letters, send emails or faxes, or make phone calls to legislators about a pending issue. Of course, lobbyists try to target members from the representative's constituency. Professional lobbyists freely admit that their efforts are most effective when the people "back home" are contacting representatives about an issue.[88]

To generate support, interest groups have computerized lists of their members, broken down by state and congressional district to allow them to plan strategic responses to specific politicians on select issues. Some groups try to reach beyond their members to citizens more generally or to the customers who use their services.

In activating public support, interest groups make the critical assumption that legislators listen to their constituents and respond to their needs, if for no other reason than that they want to be reelected. While considerable evidence indicates that members of Congress do monitor their mail and respond to the wishes of their constituents, there is also some evidence that as these tactics have become more prevalent, they are being met with increasing skepticism and resistance on Capitol Hill.[89] To combat congressional skepticism, many interest groups have begun to deliver on their threats to politicians by mobilizing their members to vote. For instance, in the 1998 midterm elections, labor unions reversed their previous pattern of spending priorities, reserving less for issue ads and more for the "ground war" of getting out the vote, and Democrats picked up congressional seats. The Christian Coalition learned from the unions' 1998 success and employed a similar grassroots effort for the 2002 elections, which netted upsets in congressional and gubernatorial elections.[90] In 2004 the Bush-Cheney reelection campaign talked weekly with conservative religious groups, and many observers credit these groups' mobilization of social conservatives with Bush's victory.[91]

social protest public activities designed to bring attention to political causes, usually generated by those without access to conventional means of expressing their views

Unconventional Methods, Social Protest, and Mass Movements A discussion of interest group politics would not be complete without mention of the unconventional technique of social protest. Throughout our history, groups have turned to **social protest**—activities ranging from planned, orderly demonstrations to strikes and boy-

Lobbying the Media
Antiwar activist Cindy Sheehan, whose son was killed in the Iraq war, staged a protest near President George W. Bush's ranch in Crawford, Texas, in the summer of 2005. President Bush refused her requests for a meeting, which provided a focus for her protests. Having little else to do while Bush was secluded on his ranch, the national media crews happily gave sustained national exposure to Sheehan and her criticism of the president and the war.

cotts, to acts of civil disobedience—when other techniques have failed to bring attention to their causes. The nonviolent civil rights protests beginning with the Montgomery, Alabama, bus boycott discussed in Chapter 6 illustrate the types of actions such groups have used to bring their concerns to national attention.

Like other grassroots lobbying techniques, the techniques of social protest provide a way for people to express their disagreement publicly with a government policy or action. At the same time, their use often signals the strength of participants' feelings on an issue—and, often, outrage over being closed out from more traditional avenues of political action. Thus demonstrations and protests have frequently served an important function for those who have been excluded from the political process because of their minority, social, or economic status. While social protest may have the same objective as other types of indirect lobbying—that is, educating the public and mobilizing the group's members—demonstrations and spontaneous protests also aim to draw in citizens who have not yet formed an opinion or to change the minds of those who have. Such actions may turn a political action into a mass movement, attracting formerly passive or uninterested observers to the cause.

Social protest in the United States did not begin with the civil rights movement, although many activists since then have followed the strategies used by civil rights leaders. The labor movement of the late nineteenth century used demonstrations and strikes to attract more members to unions, with the goal of improving working conditions and wages. The women's suffrage movement of the late nineteenth and early twentieth centuries, discussed in Chapter 6, used social protest to fight for voting rights for women. Social movements have been used to change both private and government behavior. The prohibition (or temperance) movement of the late nineteenth and early twentieth centuries, for example, was aimed at stopping one particular behavior: the drinking of alcohol.

Modern mass movements employ many of the same tactics as those used in earlier days, but they have also benefited greatly from the opportunities offered by the modern media. The increasingly widespread medium of television was important to the success of the civil rights movement in the 1950s and early 1960s, as the protests and demonstrations brought home the plight of southern blacks to other regions of the country. Especially significant to the TV audience was the coverage of police brutality. Viewers were shocked by the beatings with nightsticks and the use of high-pressure hoses on demonstrators. In the 1970s, mass demonstration was effectively used by peace groups protesting American involvement in the Vietnam War. Americans at home could not help but be impressed by the huge numbers of students gathered at such protests—burning draft cards, marching on the Pentagon, or staging college sit-ins or teach-ins to protest the government's policy. Month after month, a complete recap of the day's major protest activities on the evening news forced most people to at least confront their own views on the situation.

The possibilities for using the media to support mass movements have exploded with the advent of the Internet. High-tech flash campaigns have helped groups like Censure and Move On (now MoveOn.org, a citizen action group originally formed in 1998 to pressure Congress not to impeach President Clinton) mobilize hundreds of thousands of citizens to lobby Congress by setting up relatively inexpensive and efficient "cyberpetitions" on their Web sites.[92]

Napping for Trees
Citizens engage in political actions both conventional and unconventional. Here, an Earth First! activist passes the time in a northern California forest, suspended from a tree he is trying to protect from being harvested.

Other groups, less mainstream but hoping to turn what are currently fringe movements into mass movements by reaching followers in far-flung places, have taken advantage of the Internet as well. When Barnett Slepian, a New York doctor who performed abortions, was shot and killed by a sniper in his home in 1998, investigators found that he had been receiving death threats from antiabortion activists since the 1980s. A right-to-life Web site was found to have posted a list of potential targets, including Slepian, for removal by zealous advocates. Despite concerns by some analysts that it violated the First Amendment's protection of speech, a federal appellate court upheld a lower court judgment that awarded a group of doctors extensive damages from the antiabortion Web site's creators.[93] Social analysts have observed that the Internet has facilitated the growth of groups like militias and white supremacist organizations that previously dwelled on the fringes.[94]

Today a number of groups continue in the tradition of unconventional social protest. Operation Rescue, which opposes abortion rights, tends to be the most active in using unconventional techniques to influence public opinion, and, through harassment and intimidation, to discourage both providers and those seeking abortions. More recently, as we indicated earlier, they extended their tactics to protest the termination of medical treatment to a brain-damaged woman.[95] Although Operation Rescue's tactics tend to be the most extreme, even more traditional mainstream abortion groups like the National Right to Life Committee (on the pro-life side) and NOW (a pro-choice group) take an active role in organizing annual marches in Washington to promote their respective causes.

In recent years, street theater has also become a popular form of protest, particularly in response to the Bush administration's Iraq war policies. Some protesters literally hit the streets by lying down in a "die-in," while more colorful demonstrators protested Bush's postwar policies by stripping to their underwear and recreating the infamous naked prisoner pyramid that had been at the center of the Abu Ghraib Iraqi prison scandal.[96]

"ASTROTURF" POLITICAL CAMPAIGNS AND THE STATE OF LOBBYING TODAY

Lobbying the public is often called **grassroots lobbying**, meaning that it addresses people in their roles as ordinary citizens. It is the wielding of power from the bottom (roots) up, rather than from the top down. Most of what we refer to as grassroots lobbying, however, does not spring spontaneously from the people but is orchestrated by elites, leading some people to call it **astroturf lobbying**—indicating that it is not really genuine. Often the line between real grassroots and astroturf lobbying is blurred, however. A movement may be partly spontaneous but partly orchestrated. After MoveOn.org's success as a spontaneous expression of popular will spread by "word of mouse" over the Internet, its organizers began other flash campaigns, notably one called "Gun Safety First," urging people to support gun control measures. This was less clearly a spontaneous popular movement, but it still involved mobilizing citizens to support a cause they believed in. At the astroturf extreme, there was nothing spontaneous at all about the pharmaceutical industry's 2003 efforts to oppose the importation of cheaper drugs from Canada. The Pharmaceutical Research and Manufacturers Association (PhRMA), the industry's lobbying group, spent over $4 million on such tactics as persuading seniors that their access to medicine would be limited if reimportation of these American-made drugs were allowed and convincing members of a

grassroots lobbying indirect lobbying efforts that spring from wide-spread public concern

astroturf lobbying indirect lobbying efforts that manipulate or create public sentiment, "astroturf" being artificial grassroots

Christian advocacy group that prescription drug importation might lead to easier access to the controversial morning-after pill.[97] Concerned citizens were then coached by a PhRMA-hired public relations firm on how to contact legislators to weigh in against the proposed law. Such a strategy is obviously an attempt to create an opinion that might not otherwise even exist, playing on popular fears about drug availability and sentiments about abortion to achieve corporate ends.

While pure grassroots efforts are becoming increasingly rare, a good deal of indirect lobbying is done to promote what a group claims is the public interest, or at least the interest of the members of some mass-based group like AARP. More often than not, astroturf lobbying uses the support of the public to promote the interest of a corporation or business. In many cases the clients of astroturf lobbying efforts are large corporations seeking tax breaks, special regulations, or simply the end of legislation that may hurt the corporation's interest. To generate public support, clients employ armies of lobbyists, media experts, and political strategists to conduct polls, craft multimedia advertising campaigns, and get the message out to "the people" through cable and radio news talk shows, the Internet, outbound call centers, fax machines, or some combination of these. Astroturf campaigns are very expensive.

One of the more interesting astroturf campaigns was sponsored in 1994 by the Health Insurance Association of America (HIAA), an interest group representing small- to medium-size insurance companies, whose president, Bill Gradison, is a former congressman from Ohio. Convinced that President Clinton's national health care legislation would hurt their businesses, the HIAA launched a $15 million national television campaign. The TV spots featured "Harry and Louise," a forty-something couple sitting at their kitchen table, discussing their concerns about big government and the major changes that would result from national health insurance. Although public opinion had initially supported national health care, by the end of the Harry and Louise campaign, national sentiment had turned against it. Analysts are split over whether the ads themselves changed public opinion directly or whether they were more effective in shaping the views of the opinion leaders that the public responds to.[98] That supporters of the health care plan believed that the ads were instrumental in defeating their proposal was clear from their response: the Democratic National Committee launched its own Harry and Louise commercial, showing a bedridden Harry in a full body cast, out of work and uninsured, regretting his stance against the Clinton health care plan.[99]

Significantly, the insurance and pharmaceutical industries are not the only entities engaging in astroturf campaigns. Such campaigns can make it easy for citizens to register their views by calling a toll-free number. Many of these campaigns offer to write a letter to the caller's congressperson on his or her behalf, even going so far as to vary the stationery, envelopes, and stamps so that the representatives who receive the mail might not realize that it is generated professionally.[100] When the Competitive Long Distance Coalition used these techniques to try to defeat telecommunications legislation in 1995, half of the telegrams that swamped House members turned out to have been sent without the consent of the people who appeared to have signed them.[101] One observer who works for a public interest group says, "Grassroots politics has become a top-down corporate enterprise," and speculates that there is very little genuine grassroots-type lobbying left.[102]

One prominent campaign media consultant predicted that direct lobbying will become less important as indirect lobbying gains in effectiveness and popularity.[103] While indirect lobbying seems on its face to be more democratic, to the extent that it manipulates public opinion, it may in fact have the opposite effect. And as multimedia campaigns get more and more expensive, the number of groups that can afford to participate will undoubtedly decline. Ironically, as lobbying moves away from the closed committee rooms of Congress and into the realm of what appears to be popular politics, it may not get any more democratic than it has traditionally been.

WHO, WHAT, HOW Interest groups exist to influence policy. Because of the complexity of the American system, these groups can accomplish their goals in a number of ways. They can engage in direct lobbying, by working from inside the government to influence what the government does, or by working on the public rather than on government officials to influence policy. Sometimes interest group organizers will inspire their members to use unconventional methods to try to influence government, including social protests, mass resistance or demonstrations, and Internet communication. Increasingly, lobbyists are combining strategies and taking advantage of the new communication technologies to create innovative, expensive, and often successful campaigns to influence public policy.

INTEREST GROUP RESOURCES

Interest group success depends in large part on the resources a group can bring to the project of influencing government. The pluralist defense of interest groups is that all citizens have the opportunity to organize, and thus all can exercise equal power. But all interest groups are not created equal. Some have more money, more effective leadership, more members, or better information than others, and these resources can translate into real power differences. Table 13.1 lists the top twenty-five Washington interest groups in 2001 according to a survey of members of Congress, their staffs, White House aides, and major interest groups and lobbying firms. Those twenty-five groups have a better chance of influencing government policy than, say, the Children's Defense Fund. In this section we examine the resources that interest groups can draw on to exert influence over policymaking: money, leadership, membership, and information.

MONEY

Interest groups need money to conduct the business of trying to influence governmental policymakers. Money can buy an interest group the ability to put together a well-trained staff, to hire outside professional assistance, and to make campaign contributions in the hopes of gaining access to government officials. Having money does not guarantee favorable policies, but not having money just about guarantees failure.

Staff One of the reasons money is important is that it enables an interest group to hire a professional staff, usually an executive director, assistants, and other office support staff. The main job of this professional staff is to take care of the day-to-day operations of the interest group, including pursuing policy initiatives, recruiting and maintaining membership, providing membership services, and, of course, getting more money through direct mailings, telemarketing, Web site donations, and organizational functions. Money is important for creating an organizational infrastructure that can in turn be used to raise additional support and resources.

TABLE 13.1 **The Lobbying Groups With the Most Clout in Washington**

LOBBYING GROUP	RANK
National Rifle Association	1
AARP	2
National Federation of Independent Business	3
American Israel Public Affairs Committee	4
Association of Trial Lawyers	5
AFL-CIO	6
Chamber of Commerce	7
National Beer Wholesalers Association	8
National Association of Realtors	9
National Association of Manufacturers	10
National Association of Home Builders	11
American Medical Association	12
American Hospital Association	13
National Education Association	14
American Farm Bureau Federation	15
Motion Picture Association of America	16
National Association of Broadcasters	17
National Right to Life Committee	18
Health Insurance Association of America	19
National Restaurant Association	20
National Governors Association	21
Recording Industry Association	22
American Bankers Association	23
Pharmaceutical Research and Manufacturers Association	24
International Brotherhood of Teamsters	25

Source: Jeffrey Birnbaum and Russell Newell, "Fat & Happy in D.C.," *Fortune*, May 28, 2001, 94.

Professional Assistance Money also enables the interest group to hire the services of professionals, such as a high-powered lobbying firm. These firms have invested heavily to ensure that they have connections to members of Congress.[104] A well-endowed group can also hire a public relations firm to help shape public opinion on a policy, as was done with the Harry and Louise campaign discussed earlier.

Campaign Contributions Interest groups live by the axiom that to receive, one must give—and give a lot to important people. The maximum that any PAC can give to a congressional campaign is $5,000 for each separate election. In the 2003–2004 cycle, PACs gave a total of $292.1 million to congressional candidates up for election.[105] Figure 13.3 shows that this is an all-time high for PAC contributions, up 10 percent from the 2001–2002 cycle. While some PACs give millions to campaigns, most PACs give less than $50,000 to candidates for each election cycle, focusing their contributions on members of the committees responsible for drafting legislation important to their groups.[106]

PAC spending is usually directed toward incumbents of both parties, with incumbents in the majority party, especially committee chairs, getting the greatest share. For the 2004 elections, about 79 percent of PAC contributions went to incumbent members of Congress, the bulk landing in Republican campaign coffers.[107] However, when the Democrats controlled Congress prior to 1994, they obtained the lion's share of PAC contributions. While most PACs want to curry favor with incumbents of either party, some tend to channel their money to one party. For instance, business interests, the American Medical Association, pro-life groups, Christian groups, and the NRA tend to support Republican candidates; and labor groups, the Association of Trial Lawyers of America, the National Education Association, and environmental and pro-choice groups give primarily to Democrats.

The ability to make sizable and strategically placed campaign contributions buys an interest group access to government officials.[108] Access gives the interest group the ability to talk to a representative and members of his or her staff and to present information relevant to the policies they seek to initiate, change, or protect. Access is important because representatives have any number of competing interests vying for their time. Money is meant to oil the door hinge of a representative's office so that it swings open for the interest group. For instance, a $175,000 donation to the Republican National Committee over four years yielded a three-day private event between the donors and the Republican leadership of Congress.[109] The Clinton administration was well known in its early years for allowing major donors to stay in the Lincoln bedroom of the White House. The access bought by campaign contributions is usually less blatant, but officials know who has supported their campaigns, and they are unlikely to forget it when the interest group comes knocking at their doors.

The relationship between money and political influence is extremely controversial. Many critics argue that this money buys more than just access; rather, they charge, it buys votes. The circumstantial evidence is strong. For instance, on a Senate vote to allow the timber industry to harvest dead and dying trees from public lands, the fifty-four senators voting in favor had received almost $20,000 on average in campaign contributions from the timber industry. The forty-two who voted against had received less than $3,000 on average.[110]

However, in the matter of vote buying, systematic studies of congressional voting patterns are mixed. These studies show that the influence of campaign contributions is strongest in committees, where most bills are drafted. However, once the bill reaches the floor of the House or the Senate, there is no consistent link between campaign contributions and roll-call voting.[111] This suggests that campaign contributions influence the process of creating and shaping the legislation, and thus defining the policy alternatives. Nonetheless, the final outcome of a bill is determined by political circumstances that go beyond the campaign contributions of interest groups.

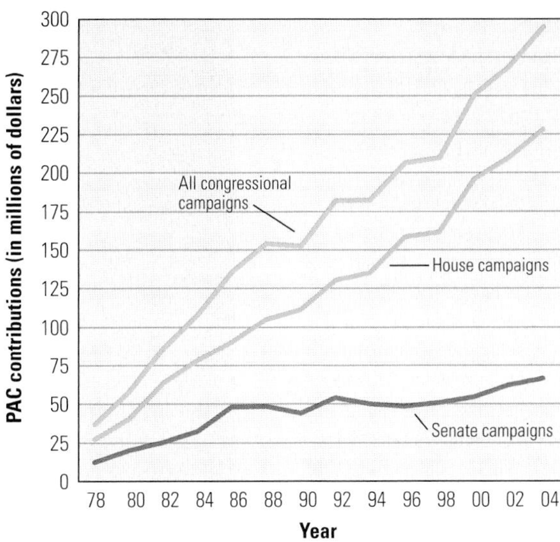

FIGURE 13.3 **Increased PAC Contributions for Congressional Campaigns, 1978–2004**

Source: Federal Election Commission, "PAC Activity Increases for 2004 Election," April 13, 2005, www.fec.gov/press/press2005/20050412pac/PACFinal2004.html.

LEADERSHIP

Leadership is an intangible element in the success or failure of an interest group. We mentioned earlier that an effective and charismatic leader or interest group entrepreneur can help a group organize even if it lacks other resources. In the same way, such a leader can keep a group going when it seems to lack the support from other sources. Candy Lightner's role in MADD and César Chavez's leadership of the United Farm Workers are excellent cases in point.

The importance of effective leadership can also be seen by the chaos that often follows from its absence. For example, in 1997 the NRA, long known as one of the richest and most powerful interest groups in Washington, was beset by a bitter power struggle between moderates and extremists. The moderates were led by the NRA's executive vice president, Wayne R. LaPierre Jr., who initiated a shift in NRA tactics toward emphasizing crime prevention and gun safety. Under his leadership the NRA's membership had grown to 3.5 million members by 1995. However, negative public reaction to the violence of the Oklahoma City bombings and its connection to an NRA member, along with internal disputes, led to trouble, which peaked when former president George H. W. Bush resigned from the group because of an NRA fundraising letter's reference to federal agents as "jack-booted thugs." By 1997 the group's membership had plummeted to 2.8 million members.[112] An extreme conservative, Neal Knox, challenged LaPierre's leadership. LaPierre and his supporters won, although the votes were extremely close. Hoping once again to appeal to the mainstream, the board selected popular movie star Charlton Heston as first vice president in 1997, and Heston won the NRA presidency a year later. With Heston and LaPierre's steady leadership, the group survived the severe criticism and negative publicity that followed the 1999

"Bruce Who?"
That was the response of many when learning that Bruce S. Gordon had been named the new president of the National Association for the Advancement of Colored People (NAACP). Turning to a businessman—a retired Verizon executive—to lead the nation's largest and oldest civil rights group, the NAACP's board of directors departed from a tradition of selecting its leadership from the ranks of civil rights activists. Gordon is expected to provide leadership and strategies adapted to the current era, focusing on attacking the problems of economic inequality that have endured long after the era of legal segregation.

shooting deaths of 15 people at Columbine High School in Littleton, Colorado.[113] Indeed, less than a year after Columbine, the NRA's membership grew by 900,000. With membership at record levels the NRA was named the most powerful lobbying group in Washington in 2001, as illustrated in Table 13.1.[114]

MEMBERSHIP: SIZE AND INTENSITY

The membership of any interest group is an important resource in terms of its size, but the level of intensity that members exhibit in support of the group's causes is also critical. Members represent the lifeblood of the interest group because they generally fund its activities. When an interest group is trying to influence policy, it can use its members to write letters, send emails, and engage in other forms of personal contact with legislators or administrative officials. Often interest groups try to reinforce their PAC contributions by encouraging their members to give personal campaign contributions to favored candidates.

Larger groups generally have an advantage over smaller ones. For instance, with more than 35 million members, AARP can mobilize thousands of people in an attempt to influence elected officials' decisions regarding issues like mandatory retirement, Social Security, or Medicare. In addition, if an interest group's members are spread throughout the country, as are AARP's, that group can exert its influence on almost every member of Congress.

If a group's members are intensely dedicated to the group's causes, then the group may be far stronger than its numbers would indicate. Intense minorities, because of their willingness to devote time, energy, and money to a cause they care passionately about, can outweigh more apathetic majorities in the political process. For instance, despite the fact that a majority of Americans favor some form of gun control, they are outweighed in the political process by the intense feeling of the four million members of the NRA, who strongly oppose gun control.[115]

INFORMATION

Information is one of the most powerful resources in an interest group's arsenal. Often the members of the interest group are the *only* sources of information on the potential or actual impact of a law or regulation. The long struggle to regulate tobacco is a case in point. While individuals witnessed their loved ones and friends suffering from lung diseases, cancer, and heart problems, it took public health interest groups like the American Cancer Society, the Public Health Cancer Association, and the American Heart Association to conduct the studies, collect the data, and show the connection between these life-threatening illnesses and smoking habits. Of course the tobacco industry and its interest group, the Tobacco Institute, presented their own research to counter these claims. Not surprisingly, the tobacco industry's investigations showed "no causal relationship" between tobacco use and these illnesses.[116] Eventually, the volume of information showing a strong relationship overwhelmed industry research suggesting otherwise. In 1998 the tobacco industry reached a settlement with states to pay millions of dollars for the treatment of tobacco-related illnesses.

WHO, WHAT, HOW Again, there is no mystery about what interest groups want: they seek to influence the policymaking process. Some interest groups are clearly more successful than others because the rules of interest group politics reward some group characteristics—such as size, intensity, money, effective leadership, and the possession of information—more than others (perhaps social conscience or humanitarianism). It is certainly possible to imagine reforms or rule changes that would change the reward structure and, in so doing, change the groups that would be successful.

THE CITIZENS AND INTEREST GROUPS

Defenders of pluralism believe that interest group formation helps give more power to more citizens, and we have seen that it certainly can enhance democratic life. Interest groups offer channels for representation, participation, education, defining policy solutions, and public agenda building, and they help to keep politicians accountable. Pluralists also believe that the system as a whole benefits from interest group politics. They argue that if no single interest group commands a majority, interest groups will compete with one another and ultimately must form coalitions to create a majority. In the process of forming coalitions, interest groups compromise on policy issues, leading to final policy outcomes that reflect the general will of the people as opposed to the narrow interests of specific interest groups.[117] In this final section we examine the claims of critics of interest group politics who argue that it skews democracy—gives more power to some people than to others—and particularly discriminates against segments of society that tend to be underrepresented in the first place (the poor and the young, for instance).

We have seen in this chapter that a variety of factors—money, leadership, information, intensity—can make an interest group successful. But this raises red danger flags for American democracy. In American political culture, we value political equality, which is to say the principle of one person, one vote. And as far as voting goes, this is how we practice democracy. Anyone who attempts to visit the polls twice on Election Day is turned away, no matter how rich that person is, how intensely she feels about the election, or how eloquently she begs for another vote. But policy is made not only at the ballot box. It is also made in the halls and hearing rooms of Congress; in the conference rooms of the bureaucracy; and in corporate boardrooms, private offices, restaurants, and bars. In these places interest groups speak loudly, and since some groups are vastly more successful than others, they have the equivalent of extra votes in the policymaking process.

We are not terribly uncomfortable with the idea that interest groups with large memberships should have more power. After all, democracy is usually about getting the most votes in order to win. But when it comes to the idea that the wealthy have an advantage, or those who feel intensely, or those who have more information, we start to balk. What about the rest of us? Should we have relatively less power over who gets what because we lack these resources?

It is true that groups with money, and business groups in particular, have distinct advantages of organizational access. Many critics suggest that business interests represent a small, wealthy, and united set of elites who dominate the political process,[118] and there is much evidence to support the view that business interests maintain a special relationship with government and tend to unite behind basic conservative issues (less government spending and lower taxes). Other evidence, however, suggests that business interests are often divided regarding governmental policies and that other factors can counterbalance their superior monetary resources.

Because business interests are not uniform and tightly organized, groups with large memberships can prevail against them. While corporate money may buy access, politicians ultimately depend on votes. Groups with large memberships have more voters. A good example of this principle occurred in 1997 when President Clinton proposed trimming $100 billion in Medicare spending over five years. Instead of raising premiums on the elderly, the Clinton administration proposed cuts in Medicare reimbursements to hospitals and doctors. This proposal sparked an intensive lobbying campaign pitting the American Medical Association and the American Hospital Association, two of the most powerful and well-financed lobbies in Washington, against AARP, representing more than 35 million older Americans. Fearing the voting wrath of AARP, the Republican-led Congress struck a deal with the administration to cut Medicare reimbursements for hospitals and doctors.[119] As this example suggests, when a group's membership is highly motivated and numerous, it can win despite the opposition's lavish resources.[120]

While interest group politics today in America clearly contains some biases, it is not the case that any one group or kind of group always gets its way. After years of collecting government subsidies and benefiting from favorable policies, the tobacco industry has at last been stripped of its privilege, illustrating that even corporate giants can be brought low.[121] Similarly the less wealthy but very intense NRA, which kept gun control off the American law books for decades, has finally been confronted by angry citizens' groups that have put the issue of gun control firmly on the public's agenda.[122]

What has helped to equalize the position of these groups in American politics is the willingness on the part of citizens to fight fire with fire, politics with politics, organization with organization. It is, finally, the power of participation and democracy that can make pluralism fit the pluralists' hopes. For some groups, such as the poor, such advice may be nearly impossible to follow. Lacking the knowledge of the system and the resources to organize in the first place, poor people are often the last to be included in interest group politics. Neighborhood-level organizing, however, such as that done by the Southwest Voter Registration Education Project and Hermandad Mexicana Latinoamericano, can counteract this tendency. Other groups left out of the system, such as the merely indifferent, or young people who regard current issues as irrelevant, will pay the price of inattention and disorganization when the score cards of interest group politics are finally tallied.

WHAT'S AT STAKE REVISITED

We have seen that interest groups wield considerable power on the American political scene. One of the chief sources of that power is money, and particularly money given to candidates to influence the outcome of elections and gain the ear of officials once they are elected. Unequal access to money helps create unequal representation of interests in American politics, and it is one of the reasons that Madison's sanguine confidence that his large republic would be resistant to the power of factions turns out to have been misplaced.

So what is at stake for interest groups in campaign finance reform? Critics argue that freedom of speech is at stake, especially in the limits on issue advocacy ads. They say that people with money have a right to use it in any way they please, especially to support views that are near to their hearts, and that these reforms take their political freedom and power away.

Many of the opponents of the McCain-Feingold bill are slightly disingenuous in their criticism, however. They are not just concerned with freedom of speech purely as a matter of principle. Some of them recognize that the changed campaign finance laws will force them to find another way to exercise their financial leverage on candidates, or suffer from reduced power and influence. In a political world where no one wants to lose power, they have a tremendous amount of real clout at stake.

Reform opponents also predicted that the reforms as passed would not really change the system but would merely force interest groups to exploit as yet undiscovered loopholes to get their money into the pockets of those they want to influence. Just as a loophole in the 1974 election law gave rise to the soft money problem, new loopholes will make the system more inequitable than ever. These predictions came true for the 2004 elections. First, more money was spent than ever before—in fact the total spent on the presidential campaign doubled despite the strict bans put in place by McCain-Feingold. Second, 527

continued

Thinking Outside the Box

- Does it distort democracy for interest groups to bring different resources to the political process?
- Are there ways to get people to pay for collective goods?
- Are there any lobbying techniques that should be off limits in a democracy?

WHAT'S AT STAKE REVISITED *(continued)*

groups took advantage of a loophole and continued to spend soft money. Since they are regulated by the Internal Revenue Code rather than the Federal Election Commission, the McCain-Feingold law does not affect 527s. This loophole meant that 527s were able to raise and spend unlimited amounts on issue advocacy ads sixty days prior to the election. Even more, it wasn't just those opposed to McCain-Feingold who used the 527 loophole. Indeed, even MoveOn.org, which had pushed vigorously for McCain-Feingold, took advantage of the 527 loophole and raised over $20 million to run issue advocacy ads against President Bush.

Those who support the bill want to argue that in a democracy, political equality ought to be paramount, and that where economic resources are unequally distributed from the start, unequal campaign contributions do not reflect people's desire to support candidates or an issue but their ability to do so. For these supporters, reduced freedom for some is not too high a price to pay for increased political equality.

The Supreme Court sided with this last argument. Despite the precedent set by *Buckley v. Valeo* (1976) that giving money is a constitutionally protected form of political expression, the Supreme Court decision claimed that the government was right to curb the influence of money on politicians' decision making, or to avoid the appearance that it has an influence. Even though reformers achieved an enormous victory curbing the influence of interest groups through campaign finance, large questions remain over whether 527s can be regulated as tightly.[123]

To Sum Up

KEY TERMS

republic.cqpress.com

astroturf lobbying (p. 573)
collective good (p. 550)
direct lobbying (p. 561)
economic interest groups (p. 552)
equal opportunity interest groups (p. 555)
expressive benefits (p. 551)
faction (p. 545)
527 groups (p. 570)
free rider problem (p. 550)
grassroots lobbying (p. 573)
indirect lobbying (p. 561)
interest group (p. 545)
interest group entrepreneurs (p. 550)
issue advocacy ads (p. 568)
lobbying (p. 547)
material benefits (p. 551)
political action committee (PAC) (p. 546)
public interest group (p. 557)
revolving door (p. 561)
selective incentives (p. 551)
social protest (p. 570)
solidary benefits (p. 551)

Key terms, chapter summaries, practice quizzes, Internet links, and other study aids are available on the companion Web site at: republic.cqpress.com.

SUMMARY

republic.cqpress.com

- Government will always distribute resources in ways that benefit some at the expense of others. People who want influence on the way that government policy decisions are made form interest groups. To accomplish their goals, interest groups lobby elected officials, rally public opinion, offer policy suggestions, and keep tabs on policy once enacted. Interest groups also must organize and convince others to join, often offering selective benefits to members.
- Interest groups come in all different types. Economic groups like business associations or trade unions want to protect and improve their status. Public interest groups advocate their vision of society, and equal opportunity groups organize to gain, or at least improve, economic status and civil rights. Governments form associations to improve relations among their ranks.
- Lobbyists are the key players of interest groups. They influence public policy either by approaching the three branches of government (direct lobbying) or by convincing the people to pressure the government (indirect lobbying).
- The success of individual interest groups is often affected by factors like funding, quality of leadership, membership size and intensity, and access to information.
- Critics of interest groups fear that the most powerful groups are simply those with the most money, and that this poses a danger to American democracy. However, interest group formation may also be seen as a way to give more power to more citizens, offering a mechanism to keep politicians accountable by offering additional channels for representation, participation, education, creation of policy solutions, and public agenda building.

PRACTICE QUIZ

republic.cqpress.com

1. Which of the following is NOT a role played by interest groups?

a. Education
b. Contesting elections
c. Providing program alternatives
d. Agenda building
e. Program monitoring

2. The free rider problem is

a. a good or service that, by its very nature, cannot be denied to anyone who wants to consume it.

b. a problem arising when an interest group rides on the coattails of its patron political party when passing legislation.

c. a benefit that is available only to group members as an inducement to get them to join.

d. the difficulty groups face in recruiting when potential members can gain the benefits of the group's actions whether or not they join.

e. the difficulty groups face when an interest group entrepreneur uses a group to benefit financially.

3. Which of the following is a type of interest group that organizes to influence government to produce collective goods or services that benefit the general public?

a. Public interest groups

b. Equal opportunity interest groups

c. Economic interest groups

d. Economic interest groups, except for unions and professional organizations

e. Government interest groups

4. What is the key difference between direct lobbying and indirect lobbying?

a. Direct lobbying involves interest groups interacting with the legislative branch, whereas indirect lobbying involves interest groups interacting with the executive branch.

b. Direct lobbying involves interest groups interacting with public officials, whereas indirect lobbying involves interest groups giving campaign contributions to public officials.

c. Direct lobbying involves interest groups interacting with public officials, whereas indirect lobbying involves interest groups trying to influence government policymakers by encouraging the general public to put pressure on them.

d. Direct lobbying involves interest groups funding a lawmaker's travel on fact-finding trips, whereas indirect lobbying involves interest groups funding a lawmaker's reelection with campaign contributions.

e. Direct lobbying involves interest groups lobbying a congressperson in her office, while indirect lobbying involves interest groups providing testimony at a hearing.

5. Which of the following is NOT an important resource for interest groups?

a. Money

b. Leadership

c. Intensity of membership

d. Information

e. Contacts with political parties

SUGGESTED RESOURCES

republic.cqpress.com

Books

Berry, Jeffrey M. 1997. *The Interest Group Society,* 3d ed. New York: Longman. In one of the most comprehensive books on interest groups available, Berry covers all the bases, including PACs, lobbying, and the problems that interest groups bring to the policymaking process.

Birnbaum, Jeffrey. 1992. *The Lobbyists: How Influence Peddlers Work Their Way in Washington.* New York: Random House. A journalist takes the reader into the halls of the Capitol and examines the role that lobbyists play in the political arena.

Cigler, Allan J., and Burdett A. Loomis, eds. 2002. *Interest Group Politics,* 6th ed. Washington, D.C.: CQ Press. A noteworthy collection dealing with the many facets of interest group politics.

Foundation for Public Affairs. 2004. *Public Interest Group Profiles, 2004–2005.* Washington, D.C.: CQ Press. Provides membership information, interests, goals, addresses, media quotes, and other key information about numerous interest groups covering multiple interest areas.

Olson, Mancur, Jr. 1971. *The Logic of Collective Action: Public Goods and the Theory of Groups.* Cambridge: Harvard University Press. The classic work on collective action problems. Olson argues that groups must offer selective incentives in order to attract members, but they remain vulnerable to free rider problems.

Rauch, Jonathan. 1994. *Demosclerosis: The Silent Killer of American Government.* New York: Crown. This fascinating book argues that the recent growth in interest groups has had negative effects on the development of public policy.

Truman, David B. 1971. *The Governmental Process: Political Interests and Public Opinion,* 2d ed. New York: Knopf. A classic work on the formation of pluralist theory.

Walker, Jack L. 1991. *Mobilizing Interest Groups in America: Patrons, Professions, and Social Movements.* Ann Arbor: University of Michigan Press. An engaging study of how interest groups originate, prosper, and work with other interest groups and government actors.

Web Sites

See the book's companion Web site at **republic.cqpress.com** for links to many of the specific interest groups mentioned in this chapter.

Center for Responsive Politics. www.opensecrets.org. This excellent source of up-to-the-minute data on money and politics contains a wealth of information on lobbyists and PACs, politician and congressional committee profiles, campaign donation lists, and much more.

Federal Election Commission. www.fec.gov. This Web site lists the official reports regarding campaign finance. With a little research, the user can gain access to how much PAC money was spent in recent as well as past elections.

Senate Office of Public Records. sopr.senate.gov. This Web site for the Senate's lobby filing disclosure program provides a searchable function that allows the researcher to read the midyear and year-end Lobbying Disclosure Reports for all of the interests that have lobbied Congress. Specifically, one can see how much each interest group spent lobbying Congress.

Other Media

***K Street.* 2003.** There are so many lobbying firms on Washington, D.C.'s K Street that the street name has become synonymous with the activity. This one-season HBO series delved into the relationships between lobbyists—some real and some fictional—and the government.

"Dangerous Prescription." 2003. *Frontline* (Boston: WGBH). This is an interesting documentary on the Food and Drug Administration's difficulty regulating medicines. The pharmaceutical industry's lobbying strengths and influence are highlighted.

Both of George W. Bush's presidential elections were close. The 2004 outcome was more typical in that it provided a clear winner, allowing the president and First Lady to attend their victory celebration party on election eve (right). The 2000 election, however, which hinged on an inconclusive Florida outcome, dragged on for weeks. Attention was focused on recounts and recounts of recounts by officials like this Broward County canvasser who attempted to figure out voter intent (below).

VOTING, CAMPAIGNS, AND ELECTIONS

14

WHAT'S AT STAKE?

In the weeks before an election, nervous campaign officials fret about the possibility of an "October surprise," a last-minute event that would suddenly influence wavering voters. What neither Bush nor Gore officials foresaw in the fall of 2000, however, was the possibility of a nearly unprecedented *November* surprise—an undecided presidential election on election night itself.

As election tracking polls had indicated before Tuesday, the election was going to be a close one. Texas governor George W. Bush had had a very small lead in the polls in the weeks preceding the election, but immediately before the vote, Vice President Al Gore had edged ahead in some polls. On election night, the media first indicated that Al Gore might be winning the election after he had apparently captured Florida's twenty-five electoral college votes. Later Tuesday evening, however, the networks found errors in the Florida data and declared that state too close to call. Very early Wednesday morning, the networks put Florida's votes in Bush's column and projected him the winner of the presidency. But when Bush's lead dwindled to a few hundred votes, the media changed their minds again and declared the entire presidential race too close to call. After phoning the Texas governor to concede defeat, Vice President Gore, on his way to make a speech to disappointed supporters, got the word that the race was still up in the air. The vice president called Bush to retract his concession and returned to his hotel. By the time the sun rose on Wednesday, Al Gore was ahead in the national popular vote by about 200,000 votes. Gore also led in the electoral college, but with Florida still undecided, neither candidate had won the required 270 electoral votes.

What was the problem? George W. Bush led at the end of the night in Florida by something less than two thousand votes, triggering a Florida state law that requires an automatic electronic recount when the winning margin is less than one-half of 1 percent. At the end of the recount, several days later, Bush's lead had been cut to three hundred votes, with up to two thousand absentee ballots from overseas still to be counted. Adding to the sense of chaos was the impression that (amid other claims of voting irregularities in Florida) voting in Palm Beach County, a largely Democratic district, had gone awry. The format of the ballot (determined under Florida law by local officials) was confusing to some voters, perhaps leading many who wanted to vote for the Democratic ticket to vote instead for Reform Party candidate Pat Buchanan or to mistakenly vote for multiple candidates.

A political firestorm ensued. Newspaper editorials begged for caution and statesmanlike behavior from both sides. Republican George W. Bush held meetings to begin his transition to the White House, while Democrats accused him of trying to assume the mantle of the presidency without waiting for the official results. Private individuals in Florida filed lawsuits claiming their rights to vote had been denied, and citizens demonstrated in the streets, asking for a new vote in Palm Beach County. Democrats suggested they might pursue legal recourse and in the meantime asked for a manual count of the ballots, a possibility allowed under Florida law to help determine the intention of the voters. At the same time, Republicans accused Gore of trying to steal the election and criticized the Democrats for bringing the election into the courts.

Public opinion polls showed that Americans generally had cooler heads than their leaders, and over half were reported to be willing to wait for a fair resolution. Two-thirds said that the federal government should move to make the ballot procedure consistent from state to state, and nearly as many said that the electoral college should be abolished. Foreign observers watched disbelievingly as the electoral college, an institution that many had never heard of and fewer understood, seemed to stand in the way of a popularly elected president taking office.

A contested election was not unheard of in the United States, but not since 1888 had the winner of the electoral college lost the popular vote. Was the United States in constitutional crisis? Had the will of the people been thwarted? Could the new president, whomever he turned out to be, govern under such a cloud? Are elections a state matter, as the Constitution decrees, or should they be turned over to the federal government? And what about that seemingly arcane institution, the electoral college? Just what is at stake in a contested presidential election? *

Although we pride ourselves on our democratic government, Americans seem to have a love-hate relationship with the idea of campaigns and voting. On the one hand, many citizens believe that elections do not accomplish anything, that elected officials ignore the wishes of the people, and that government is run for the interests of the elite rather than the many. Voters in 2004 were unusually motivated and turned out at the rate of 60 percent, but typically only about half of the eligible electorate votes.

On the other hand, however, when it is necessary to choose a leader, whether the captain of a football team, the president of a dorm, or a local precinct chairperson, the first instinct of most Americans is to call an election. Even though there are other ways to choose leaders—picking the oldest, the wisest, or the strongest; holding a lottery; or asking for volunteers—Americans almost always prefer an election. We elect over half a million public officials in America.[1] This means we have a lot of elections—more elections more often for more officials than in any other democracy.

In this chapter we examine the complicated place of elections in American politics and American culture. You will learn about

- what the founders were thinking when they established a role for elections, and the potential roles that elections can play in a democracy
- Americans' ambivalence about the vote and the reasons that only about half of the citizenry even bother to exercise what is supposed to be a precious right
- how voters go about making decisions, and how this in turn influences the character of presidential elections
- the organizational and strategic aspects of running for the presidency
- what elections mean for citizens

VOTING IN A DEMOCRATIC SOCIETY

Up until the last couple hundred years, it was virtually unthinkable that the average citizen could or should have any say in who would govern. Rather, leaders were chosen by birth, by the church, by military might, by the current leaders, but not by the mass public. Real political change, when it occurred, was usually ushered in with violence and bloodshed.

Today, global commitment to democracy is on the rise. Americans and, increasingly, other citizens around the world believe that government with the consent of the governed is superior to government imposed on unwilling subjects and that political change is best accomplished through the ballot box rather than on the battlefield or in the streets. The mechanism that connects citizens with their governments, by which they signify their consent and through which they accomplish peaceful change, is elections. Looked at from this perspective, elections are an amazing innovation—they provide a method for the peaceful transfer of power. Quite radical political changes can take place without blood being shed, an accomplishment that would confound most of our political ancestors.

As we saw in Chapter 1, however, proponents of democracy can have very different ideas about how much power citizens should exercise over government. Elite theorists believe that citizens should confine their role to choosing among competing elites; pluralists think citizens should join groups that fight for their interests in government on their behalf; and participatory democrats call for more active and direct citizen involvement in politics. Each of these views has consequences for how elections should be held. How many officials should be chosen by the people? How often should elections be held? Should people choose officials directly, or through representatives whom they elect? How accountable should officials be to the people who elect them?

We have already seen, in Chapter 11, that though Americans hardly resemble the informed, active citizens prescribed by democratic theory, that does not mean they are unqualified to exercise political power. At the end of this chapter, when we have a clearer understanding of the way that elections work in America, we will return to the question of how much power citizens should have and what different answers to this question mean for our thinking about elections. We begin our study of elections, however, by examining the functions that they can perform in democratic government. First we look at the very limited role that the founders had in mind for popular elections when they designed the American Constitution, and then we evaluate the claims of democratic theorists more generally.

A Hard-Won Right
Democracy is nothing if it is not about citizens choosing their leaders. In 1966, black voters in Peachtree, Alabama, line up to vote for the first time since passage of the Voting Rights Act of 1965.

THE FOUNDERS' INTENTIONS

The Constitution reflects the founding fathers' fears that people could not reliably exercise wise and considered judgment about politics, that they would band together with like-minded people to fight for their interests, and that their political role should therefore be limited. Consequently the founders built a remarkable layer of insulation between the national government and the will of the people. The president was to be elected by an electoral college, not directly by the people, lest they be persuaded by some popular but undesirable leader. The electoral college was expected to be a group of wiser-than-average men who would use prudent judgment. In fact, only the House of Representatives, one-half of one-third of the government, was to be popularly elected. The Senate and the executive and judicial branches were to be selected by different types of political elites who could easily check any moves that might arise from the whims of the masses. In the founders' view, the government needed the support of the masses, but it could not afford to be led by what they saw as the public's short-sighted and easily misguided judgment.

THE FUNCTIONS OF ELECTIONS

Despite the founders' reluctance to entrust much political power to American citizens, we have since altered our method of electing senators to make these elections direct, and the electoral college, as we shall see, almost always endorses the popular vote for president. As we said in the introduction to this chapter, elections have become a central part of American life, even if our participation in them is somewhat uneven. Theorists claim that elections fulfill a variety of functions in modern democratic life: selecting leaders, giving direction to policy, developing citizenship, informing the public, containing conflict, and legitimating and stabilizing the system. Here we examine and evaluate how well elections fill some of those functions.

Selection of Leaders Like our founders, many philosophers and astute political observers have had doubts about whether elections are the best way to choose wise and capable leaders. Plato, for example, likened choosing the head of state to choosing the captain of a ship. To safely guide a ship to its destination requires experience, wisdom, good judgment, and keenly developed skills. He argued that as we would never elect the captains of our ships, neither should we be entrusted with the difficult job of finding suitable leaders to guide us politically. John Stuart Mill, often regarded as a proponent of democracy, argued that the "natural tendency of representative government . . . is toward collective mediocrity; and this tendency is increased by all reductions and extensions of the franchise, their effect being to place the principal power in the hands of classes more and more below the highest level of instruction in the community."[2] In short, the argument is that you cannot trust the average citizen to make wise choices in the voting booth.

Some critics say democratic elections often fail to produce the best leaders because the electoral process scares off many of the most capable candidates. Running for office is a hard, expensive, and bruising enterprise. A lot of qualified people are put off by the process, though they might be able to do an excellent job and have much to offer through public service. Colin Powell, the chairman of the Joint Chiefs of Staff under Presidents George H. W. Bush and Bill Clinton before becoming George W. Bush's first secretary of state, was clearly one of the most popular candidates going into the 1996 presidential election; polls showed him well ahead of the competition. But he looked at what the process demanded and decided not to run. Indeed, many of the most obvious possible contenders for the presidency regularly decide not to run.

The simple truth is that elections only ensure that the leader chosen is the most popular on the ballot. There is no guarantee that the best candidate will run, or that the people will choose the wisest, most honest, or most capable leader from the possible candidates.

Policy Direction Democracy and elections are only partially about choosing able leadership. The fears of the founders notwithstanding, today we also expect that the citizenry will have a large voice in what the government actually does. Competitive elections are intended in part to keep leaders responsive to the concerns of the governed, since they can be voted out of office if voters are displeased.

The policy impact of elections, however, is indirect. For instance, at the national level, we elect individuals, but we do not vote on policies. Although citizens in about half the states can make policy directly through initiatives and referenda, the founders left no such option at the national level. Rather, they provided us with a complicated system in which power is divided and checked. Those who stand for election have different constituencies and different terms of office. Thus the different parts of the national government respond to different publics at different times. The voice of the people is muted and modulated. At times, however, especially when there is a change in the party that controls the government, elections do produce rather marked shifts in public policy.[3] The New Deal of the 1930s is an excellent case in point. The election of a Democratic president and Congress allowed a sweeping political response to the Depression, in sharp contrast to the previous Republican administration's hands-off approach to the crisis.

The electoral process actually does a surprisingly good job of directing policy in less dramatic ways as well. A good deal of research demonstrates, for example, that in the states, elections achieve a remarkable consistency between the general preferences of citizens and the kinds of policies that the states enact.[4] At the congressional level, members of the House and the Senate are quite responsive to overall policy wishes of their constituents, and those who are not tend to suffer at the polls.[5] At the presidential level, through all of the hoopla and confusion of presidential campaigns, scholars have found that presidents do, for the most part, deliver on the promises that they make and that the national parties do accomplish much of what they set out in their platforms.[6] Finally, elections speed up the process by which changes in public preferences for a more activist or less activist (more liberal or more conservative) government are systematically translated into patterns of public policy.[7]

Citizen Development Some theorists argue that participation in government in and of itself—regardless of which leaders or policy directions are chosen—is valuable for citizens and that elections help citizens feel fulfilled and effective.[8] When individuals are unable to participate in political affairs, or fail to do so, their sense of *political efficacy,* of being effective in political affairs, suffers. Empirical evidence supports these claims. In studies of the American electorate, people who participate more, whether in elections or through other means, have higher senses of political efficacy.[9] From this perspective, then, elections are not just about picking leaders and promoting a preferred set of policies; they are also about realizing and developing essential human characteristics. They provide a mechanism by which individuals can move from passive subjects who see themselves pushed and pulled by forces larger than themselves to active citizens fulfilling their potential to have a positive effect on their own lives.

Informing the Public When we watch the circus of the modern presidential campaign, it may seem a bit of a stretch to say that an important function of elections, and the campaigns that go along with them, is to educate the public. But they actually do. Ideally the campaign is a time of deliberation when alternative points of view are openly aired so that the citizenry can judge the truth and desirability of competing claims and the competence of competing candidates and parties. The evidence is that campaigns do in fact have this impact. People learn a good deal of useful political information from campaign advertisements and for the most part choose the candidates who match their value and policy preferences.[10] As citizens, we probably know and understand a lot more about our government because of our electoral process than we would without free and competitive elections.

Containing Conflict Elections help us influence policy, but in other ways they also limit our options for political influence.[11] When groups of citizens are unhappy about their taxes, or the quality of their children's schools, or congressional appropriations for AIDS research, or any other matter, the election booth is their primary avenue of influence. Of course, they can write letters and sign petitions, but those have an impact only because the officials they try to influence must stand for reelection. Even if their candidate wins, there is no guarantee that their policy concerns will be satisfied. And those who complain are likely to hear the systemwide response: If you don't like what's going on, vote for change.

If elections help reduce our political conflicts to electoral contests, they also operate as a kind of safety valve for citizen discontent. There is always a relatively peaceful mechanism through which unhappy citizens can vent their energy. Elections can change officials, replacing Democrats with Republicans or vice versa, but they do not fundamentally alter the underlying character of the system. Without the electoral vent, citizens might eventually turn to more threatening behaviors like boycotts, protests, civil disobedience, and rebellion.

Legitimation and System Stability A final important function of elections is to make political outcomes acceptable to participants. By participating in the process of elections, we implicitly accept, and thereby legitimize, the results. The genius here is that participation tends to make political results acceptable even to those who lose in an immediate sense. They do not take to the streets, set up terrorist cells, or stop paying their taxes. Rather, in the overwhelming majority of instances, citizens who lose in the electoral process shrug their shoulders, obey the rules made by the winning representatives, and wait for their next chance to achieve candidates and policies more to their liking. Even many supporters of Al Gore in 2000 came to accept Bush's electoral college victory as conferring legitimacy on him, despite his loss of the popular vote. Change occurs in a democracy but without grave threats to the stability of the system.

WHO, WHAT, HOW Those with the greatest stake in the continued existence of elections in America are the citizens who live under their rule. At stake for citizens is, first, the important question of which candidates and parties will govern. However, by viewing elections in a broader perspective, we can see that elections also contribute to the quality of democratic life: they help to define a crucial relationship between the governed and those they choose as leaders, to influence public policy, to educate the citizenry, to contain conflict, and to legitimize political outcomes and decisions.

EXERCISING THE RIGHT TO VOTE IN AMERICA

We argued in Chapter 11 that even without being well informed and following campaigns closely, Americans can still cast intelligent votes reflecting their best interests. But what does it say about the American citizen that, in a typical presidential election, barely half of the adult population votes? In off-year congressional elections, in primaries, and in many state and local elections held at different times from the presidential contest, the rates of participation drop even lower.

How do we explain this low voter turnout? Is America just a nation of political slackers? This is a serious and legitimate question in light of the important functions of democracy we have just discussed, and in light of the tremendous struggle many groups have had to achieve the right to vote. Indeed, as we saw in Chapter 6, the history of American suffrage—the right to vote—is one struggle after another for access to the ballot box.

Voting varies dramatically in its importance to different citizens. For some, it is a significant aspect of their identities as citizens. Eighty-seven percent of American adults believe that voting in elections is a "very important obligation" for Americans.[12] Thus many people vote because they believe they should and because they believe the vote gives them a real influence on government. However, only about half the electorate has felt this way strongly enough to vote in recent presidential elections.

WHO VOTES AND WHO DOESN'T?

Many political observers, activists, politicians, and political scientists worry about the extent of nonvoting in the United States.[13] When people do not vote, they have no voice in choosing their leaders, their policy preferences are not registered, and they do not develop as active citizens. Some observers fear that their abstention signals an alienation from the political process.

We know quite a lot about who votes and who doesn't in America in terms of their age, income, education, and racial and ethnic makeup from survey data. (Recall from Chapter 11 that reported turnout from survey data is always higher than actual turnout.)

- *Age.* Sixty-nine percent of those aged eighteen to twenty-nine reported voting in the 2004 election (only 54 percent of that group voted in 2000). Turnout increases with age, so that among those forty and over, reported turnout runs above 83 percent.[14]
- *Income.* Turnout among the relatively wealthy (income above $70,000) was 90 percent in 2004 and dropped with income; only 60 percent of those with incomes less than $15,000 reported voting (up from 48 percent in 2000).[15]
- *Education.* Education is consistently one of the strongest predictors of voter turnout. In 2004, 67 percent of those with a high school education or less reported voting, compared to 92 percent of college graduates.[16]

- *Race and ethnicity.* In most elections, minority group members are less likely to report having voted than are whites. This was true in 2004 for African Americans (75 percent) and Hispanics (67 percent) compared to whites (81 percent).[17]

When we add these characteristics together, the differences are quite substantial. Wealthy, college-educated, older whites voted at a rate of 95 percent in 2004, whereas poor, young, minority group members who went no further than high school were estimated to vote at a rate of 54 percent.[18] The clear implication is that the successful white middle class is substantially overrepresented in the active electorate and their interests get a disproportionate amount of attention from politicians.

WHY AMERICANS DON'T VOTE

As we have noted elsewhere, compared with other democratic nations, our voter turnout levels are low (see Figure 11.3 on page 476). Despite overall increases in education, age, and income, which generally increase the number of voters, presidential election turnout rates have stayed stubbornly under the 60-percent mark for more than thirty years (and midterm congressional turnout rates have been much lower).[19] (See Figure 14.1.) What accounts for such low turnout rates in a country where 82 percent of adults say voting is important to democracy[20]—indeed, in a country that often prides itself on being one of the best and oldest examples of democracy in the world? The question of low and declining voter turnout in the United States poses a tremendous puzzle for political scientists, who have focused on six factors to try to explain this mystery.

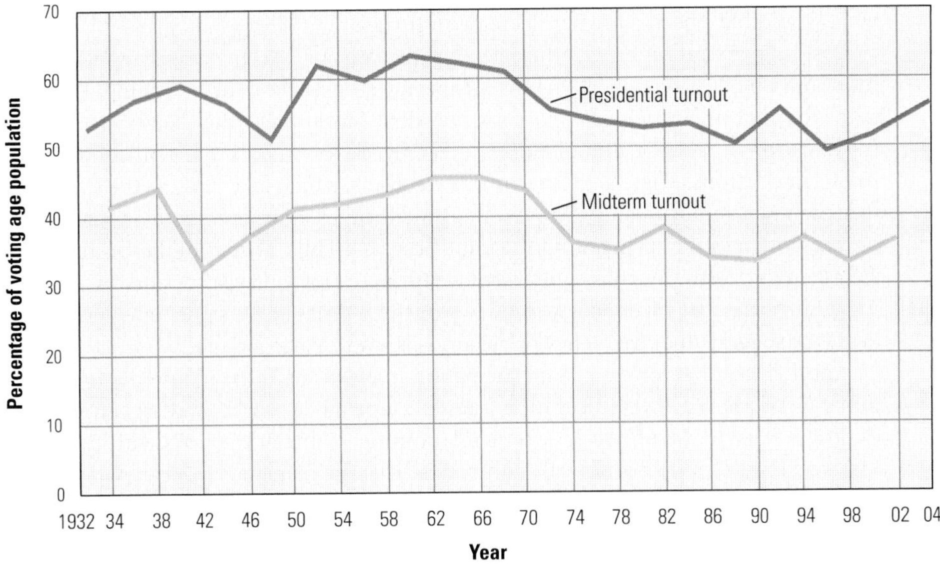

FIGURE 14.1
Voter Turnout in Presidential and Midterm House Elections, 1932–2004

Source: Presidential data through 2000 from 2005. *The New York Times Almanac*, p. 114; midterm data through 1998 from U.S. Census Bureau, *2000 Statistical Abstract*, 291; 2004 presidential data from United States Election Project, "2004 Voting-Age and Voting-Eligible Population Estimates and Voter Turnout," elections.gmu.edu/voter_turnout_2004.htm; 2002 midterm data from United States Election Project, "2002 Voting-Age and Voting-Eligible Population Estimates and Voter Turnout," elections.gmu.edu/voter_turnout_2002.htm.

Legal Obstacles Voter turnout provides a dramatic illustration of our theme that rules make a difference in who wins and who loses in politics. The rules that govern elections vary in democracies around the world, yielding very different rates of turnout. Several election rules in the United States contribute to low turnout by making it more difficult for voters to exercise their right to vote. The low turnout may be an accidental consequence of laws intended for other purposes, but in some cases it is a deliberate goal of politicians who believe that high turnout will benefit the other party or be harmful to stable government.

One U.S. election law that lowers voter turnout is the requirement that citizens register before they vote. Usually voters must register well before the campaign has even begun and before they are engaged enough in the issues or personalities to think they might want to vote. About a third of the electorate never registers and is therefore ineligible to vote on Election Day. Estimates suggest that this decreases participation by 10 to 14 percent.[21] In many other democracies, it is government, not the individual voter, that bears the responsibility for registering citizens, and if voters do not vote, it is not because they neglected to register months before. In a number of countries—Australia, Belgium, and Italy, for example—voting is actually required by law. Turnout rates in these countries are 84 percent, 85 percent, and 93 percent, respectively.[22] The National Voter Registration Act of 1993, or the **Motor Voter Bill** as it is more commonly called, requires that the states take a more active role in registering voters, allowing them to register when they apply for a driver's license, welfare, or other state benefits. It is not clear that the legislation has had much effect on participation because in two of the three presidential elections since 1993 turnout on Election Day has remained around 50 percent even though the number of registered voters has increased. Some scholars argue, however, that the Motor Voter Bill has actually slowed what would have been a greater decrease in turnout.[23]

Motor Voter Bill legislation allowing citizens to register to vote at the same time they apply for a driver's license or other state benefit

Besides registration rules, other election regulations also make voting in America more difficult than it typically is in European democracies. For one thing, U.S. laws allow for a lot of elections. We vote for president (and other offices) every four years. In between, we choose our members of Congress as well as state officeholders in midterm elections. There are also primary elections, which take place in the spring before each November election. Most states hold local elections and vote on local issues or taxes, often in the spring of odd-numbered years. Thus citizens in the United States are asked to trek to the polls eight to twelve times over a four-year period. In contrast, most Europeans are asked to vote only two or three times in the same time period. The evidence suggests that frequency of elections leads to voter fatigue.

Another law that lowers U.S. participation in elections is the requirement that national elections are always held on a Tuesday, typically a workday. Many Americans, finding it hard to get off work or to juggle waiting in line at the polls with their normal weekday tasks, do not vote. By contrast, a large majority of European nations have weekend voting, which contributes to their higher turnout levels. The research suggests that switching to weekend voting would increase turnout by 5 to 6 percent.[24]

In an effort to save money on electoral administration and also to make it easier for citizens to vote, Oregon conducts all of its elections completely by mail. Studies indicate that this system is popular and increases turnout in the state by 6 to 9 percent.[25] More generally, estimates are that vote-by-mail can increase participation by around 4 percent.[26]

Politicians have been reluctant to pass major electoral reforms because of fears about whom the beneficiaries of such changes might be. The conventional wisdom is that Democrats would benefit from efforts to increase turnout because Republicans are already motivated enough to turn out under current laws, but this expectation (or fear) does not seem to have been borne out by our experience with the Motor Voter Bill. In the wake of the 2000 presidential election, and after reports of voting irregularities and long lines at the polls in the 2004 presidential election, calls for various sorts of reform are louder and more widespread than ever, and state legislators around the country are now grappling with the issue. See the box "Electoral Reform."

"It's in the Mail" This is an excuse that won't help with Oregon's mail-in ballot. Oregon became the only state in the nation to use mail-in ballots exclusively. The process is intended to make it easier to vote and is very popular in the state. For the procrastinators among us, Oregon supplies official drop-off sites for those whose ballots would not reach election centers if mailed on or just before election day.

Attitude Changes Political scientists have found that some of the low voter turnout we can see in Figure 14.1 is accounted for by changes over time in psychological orientations or attitudes toward politics.[27] For one thing, if people feel that they do not or cannot make a difference and that government is not responsive to their wishes, they often don't bother to vote. Lower feelings of political efficacy lead to less participation.

A second orientation that has proved important in explaining low turnout is partisanship. There was a distinct decline in Americans' attachments to the two major political parties in the 1960s and 1970s. With a drop in party identification came a drop in voting levels. This decline, however, has leveled off, and in recent years there has even been a slight increase in the percentage of citizens saying they identify as Democrats or Republicans. This slight increase in partisanship may have stemmed the decline in turnout that was apparent from the late 1960s through the 1980s.

Attitudes, of course, do not change without some cause; they reflect citizens' reactions to what they see in the political world. It is easy to understand why attitudes have changed since the relatively tranquil 1950s. From Vietnam to Watergate to the Iran-contra affair and the sex scandals that haunted the Clinton administration—the public airwaves were dominated by negative information and images about the leadership of the national government. Even though George W. Bush came into office promising to change the partisan tone of Washington, scandals like Enron, the alleged exposure by administration officials of an undercover CIA agent, and the controversy over the war in Iraq have done nothing to alleviate negative attitudes about government. A post–September 11 era of good feeling about government soon dissipated as politics in Washington got back to usual.

Voter Mobilization Another factor that political scientists argue has led to lower turnout from the 1960s into the 1990s is a change in the efforts of politicians, interest groups, and especially political parties to make direct contact with people during election campaigns.[28] **Voter mobilization** includes contacting people—especially supporters—to inform them about the election and to persuade them to vote. It can take the form of making phone calls, knocking on doors, or even supplying rides to the

voter mobilization a party's efforts to inform potential voters about issues and candidates and persuade them to vote

Election Reform in the Aftermath of 2000

A national cry for electoral reform followed the long, drawn-out ordeal of the 2000 presidential contest. Multiple study commissions concluded that reform was necessary—that much of the nation's voting equipment was outmoded, that the worst equipment was used in the poorest areas of the country (which were disproportionately minority areas), and that there was no consistency in how elections were run from state to state, or even within states. There was no shortage of ideas for change. Legislation for reform was submitted in virtually every state legislature as well as in Congress, amounting to a mind-boggling 3,561 bills. However, only a fraction of these were passed. Major changes were achieved in Florida, the focus of the 2000 election debacle, as well as in Georgia and Maryland, but in most states, reform only inched along or did not move at all as the states waited to see what action Congress would take. In the 2002 midterm elections, most Americans voted using the same equipment and widely varying procedures that were in place in 2000.

Congress eventually passed the Help America Vote Act, which was signed by President Bush in October 2002. The bill addressed the Democrats' main concern over open and equal access as well as Republican concerns about safeguarding against voter fraud.

The bill includes the following provisions:

- *Improved voting machines.* The old punch card systems, and the even older 1950s-era lever voting machines will be replaced by (1) the somewhat more reliable and relatively inexpensive optical scan technology, similar to that used for multiple-choice tests in schools, and (2) the electronic touchscreen machines that are easier to use and less error prone, but more expensive. A number of states will continue to use inferior technologies for a period of time, however. The obstacle here? New technology is expensive, and most states will wait for Congress to pay for the equipment. The bill includes funds for training poll workers, upgrading equipment and technology, and programs to get young people involved in the electoral process. Ultimately, however, this is not just a matter of upgrading technology. Studies have shown that, when tested, even the most modern machines have troubling glitches. Further, many observers complain that the touchscreen machines may be open to software tampering and often do not provide a backup paper record.[1] Although there is no evidence of malfeasance, Democratic critics raised questions when one voting machine manufacturer and another company that tests touchscreen machine accuracy had given money to Republican political candidates.[2]
- *Better voter identification.* In the 2000 election, registration and polling place mix-ups caused up to four million voters to be turned away from the polls or have their votes go uncounted. The bill provides that identification must be provided at registration and the first time one votes. Voters will be checked against statewide voter databases the states will set up and maintain. These provisions are the product of a compromise between Republicans, who were most concerned about fraud and favored systems

polls. As the technology of campaigns, especially the use of television, developed and expanded in the 1980s and 1990s, fewer resources were used for the traditional shoe-leather efforts of direct contact with voters. While television is certainly useful for reaching large numbers of citizens with a campaign message, it is less effective at motivating people to vote. As television grew so did the use of negative attack ads, which turn people off and hurt turnout.[29] In recent campaigns, both Democrats and Republicans have increased their efforts at voter mobilization. They and a growing number of interest groups are combining computer technology with personal contacts as an integral part of their overall campaigns.[30] The increases in turnout that we have seen that provided more safeguards, and Democrats, who worried that such safeguards would amount to voter harassment and have a negative effect on turnout, especially among minorities, the less educated, and the elderly (all of whom tend to vote Democratic).

- *Implementation of standard procedures.* The Supreme Court's decision in *Bush v. Gore* held that different procedures for recounting ballots in Florida's counties amounted to a denial of citizens' equal protection under the law. The bill calls for a number of standardized procedures. Areas of reform include increasing polling place accessibility and establishing maximum acceptable error rates and nondiscriminatory state definitions of what constitutes a legal vote. The obstacle to these reforms is meeting the challenge of achieving an acceptable level of standardization without giving up the principles of state and local control. For example, one standard procedure required of all states by the Help America Vote Act is that anyone who does not appear on official voter rolls may fill out a provisional ballot that could be counted later if the registration proves valid. Yet some states ran out of provisional ballots on election night 2004, and, while all states must provide such ballots, they have very different standards for using and counting them.[3] Whether these differing standards provide equal protection is unclear.

On a related front, following the 2000 census, the Justice Department, carrying out provisions of the Voting Rights Act, began notifying some localities that changes in the ethnic makeup of their constituencies meant they must accommodate different language groups. Spanish-language ballots were already required in areas with large Hispanic populations, but Miami–Dade County now has to provide language access for Creole-speaking Haitians, and other jurisdictions must make voting accessible for Vietnamese speakers.

Achieving widespread election reform is difficult because it involves three key political questions:

1. Who will have more power—national, state, or local government—in making the rules and administering elections?
2. What groups of voters will be negatively or positively affected by proposed changes? Changes are not neutral; some help Democrats, and others aid Republicans.
3. Who will pay for changes in technology and training to implement reforms? Even as states quickly wrestle with upgrading standards so that they can meet deadlines to receive funding from the Help America Vote Act, some in Congress, including senators John Kerry, Hillary Clinton, and Barbara Boxer, are not satisfied and have pushed for more reforms and higher standards under what has been called the Count Every Vote Act.

1. Ted Selker, "Fixing the Vote," *Scientific American,* October 2004.
2. Roger Fillion, "Workers at Voting Firm Gave to GOP," *Rocky Mountain News,* August 21, 2004, 1C.
3. Jerome Sherman and Steve Levine, "Provisional Voters Run Into Delays," *Pittsburgh Post Gazette,* November 3, 2004; Erin Cox and Susan Greene, "Provisional Votes Faced Higher Bar," *Denver Post,* November 17, 2004, A1.

in the last couple of presidential elections (see Figure 14.1) are attributable, at least in part, to these efforts.[31]

Decrease in Social Connectedness Some of the overall decline in voter turnout toward the end of the last century is due to larger societal changes rather than to citizen reactions to parties and political leaders. **Social connectedness** refers to the number of organizations people participate in and how tightly knit their communities and families are—that is, how well integrated they are into the society in which they live. The evidence is that people are increasingly likely to live alone and to be single, new to their

social connectedness citizens' involvement in groups and their relationships to their communities and families communities, and isolated from organizations. As individuals loosen or altogether lose their ties to the larger community, they have less stake in participating in communal decisions—and less support for participatory activities. Lower levels of social connectedness have been an important factor in accounting for the low turnout in national elections.[32]

Generational Changes Events occurring in the formative years of a generation continue to shape its members' orientation toward politics throughout their lives, and can account for varying turnout levels. This is different from the observation that people are more likely to vote as they get older. For instance, those age groups (cohorts) that came of age after the 1960s show much lower levels of attachment to politics, and they vote at lower rates than do their parents or grandparents. Some research suggests that generational differences account for much or most of turnout decline at the end of the 1900s. That is, people who once voted have not stopped voting; rather they are dying and are being replaced by younger, less politically engaged voters. The result is lower turnout overall.[33]

The Rational Nonvoter A final explanation for the puzzle of low voter turnout in America considers that, for some people, not voting may be the rational choice. This suggests that the question to ask is not "Why don't people vote?" but rather "Why does anyone vote?" The definition of *rational* means that the benefits of an action outweigh the costs. It is rational for us to do those things from which we get back more than we put in. Voting demands our resources, time, and effort. Given those costs, if someone views voting primarily as a way to influence government and sees no other benefits from it, it becomes a largely irrational act.[34] That is, no one individual's vote can change the course of an election unless the election would otherwise be a tie, and the

The Greatest Generation
Whether or not one agrees with Tom Brokaw's characterization of the 16 million men and women who fought in World War II, there is no doubt that that generation, including this veteran shown at the dedication of the World War II memorial in Washington, D.C., experienced a different political world than eighteen- to twenty-year-olds today. Those experiences shape subsequent political behavior.

probability of that happening in a presidential election is small (though as the 2000 election showed, it is not impossible).

For many people, however, the benefits of voting go beyond the likelihood that they will affect the outcome of the election. In fact, studies have demonstrated that turnout decisions are not really based on our thinking that our votes will determine the outcome. Rather, we achieve other kinds of benefits from voting. It feels good to do what we think we are supposed to do or to help, however little, the side or the causes we believe in. Plus, we get social rewards from our politically involved friends for voting (and avoid sarcastic remarks for not voting). All of these benefits accrue no matter which side wins.

DOES NONVOTING MATTER?

What difference does it make that some people vote and others do not? There are two ways to tackle this question. One approach is to ask whether election outcomes would be different if nonvoters were to participate. The other approach is to ask whether higher levels of nonvoting indicate that democracy is not healthy. Both, of course, concern important potential consequences of low participation in our elections.

Consequences for Outcomes Studies of the likely effects of nonvoting come up with contradictory answers. A traditional, and seemingly logical, approach is to note that nonvoters, being disproportionately poor and less educated, have social and economic characteristics that are more common among Democrats than among Republicans. Therefore, were these people to vote, we could expect that Democratic candidates would do better. Some polling results from the 1998 elections support this thinking. Pollsters asked registered voters a number of questions to judge how likely it was that they would actually vote in elections for House members. When the voting intentions of all registered voters and the subset of likely voters were compared, the likely voters were distinctly more Republican. If this were to hold true generally, we could conclude that nonvoting works to the disadvantage of Democratic candidates. One political scholar found some evidence of this for the 1980 presidential election and concluded that a much higher turnout among nonvoters would have made the election closer and that Carter might even have won reelection.[35]

Undermining this interpretation are findings from most other presidential elections. There we find that nonvoters' preferences are quite responsive to short-term factors, so they go disproportionately for the winning candidate. Because they are less partisan and have less intensely held issue positions, they are moved more easily by the short-term campaign factors favoring one party or the other. In most presidential elections, nonvoters' participation would have increased the winner's margin only slightly or not changed things at all.[36] In 2004, surveyed nonvoters were only 1 percent more likely to have supported Bush than were surveyed voters.[37] The potential effects of nonvoters being mobilized, therefore, are probably not as consistently pro-Democratic as popular commentary suggests.

Consequences for Democracy Although low turnout might not affect who actually wins an election, we have made it clear that elections do more than simply select leaders. How might nonvoting affect the quality of democratic life in America? Nonvoting can influence the stability and legitimacy of democratic government. The victor in close presidential elections, for example, must govern the country, but as critics often point out, as little as 25 percent of the eligible electorate may have voted for the winner. When a majority of the electorate sits out of an election, the entire governmental process may begin to lose legitimacy in society at large. Nonvoting can also have consequences for the nonvoter. As we have noted, failure to participate politically can aggravate already low feelings of efficacy and produce higher levels of political estrangement. To the extent that being a citizen is an active pursuit, unhappy, unfulfilled, and unconnected citizens seriously damage the quality of democratic life for themselves and for the country as a whole.

WHO, WHAT, HOW All political actors are not equal on Election Day. Some reduce their power considerably by failing to turn out to vote. Two things are at stake in these turnout patterns. The first is a question of representation and political power: while many politicians would like to attend to the needs of all constituents equally, when push comes to shove and they have to make hard choices, voters are going to be heeded more than silent nonvoters. A second issue at stake in low and declining turnout rates is the quality of democratic life we spoke of earlier—and the stability and legitimacy of the system. Nonvoting is tied to citizen estrangement from the political process, and, in this view, the quality of democratic life itself depends on active citizen participation.

HOW THE VOTER DECIDES

Putting an X next to a name on a ballot or pulling a lever on a voting machine to register a preference would seem like a pretty simple act. But although the action itself may be simple, the decision process behind the choice is anything but. A number of considerations go into our decision about how to vote, including our partisan identification and social group membership, our stance on the issues, our evaluation of the job government has been doing generally, and our opinions of the candidates. In this section we examine how these factors play out in the simple act of voting.

PARTISANSHIP AND SOCIAL GROUP MEMBERSHIP

The single biggest factor accounting for how people decide to vote is *party identification,* a concept we discussed in Chapter 12. For most citizens, party ID is stable and long term, carrying over from one election to the next in what one scholar has called "a standing decision." [38] In 2004, for example, 90 percent of those identifying with the Democratic Party voted for John Kerry, and 93 percent of those identifying with the Republican Party voted for George W. Bush.[39]

Clearly, party ID has a strong and direct influence on identifiers' voting decisions. Scholars have demonstrated that party ID also has an important indirect influence on voting decisions, because voters' party ID also colors their views on policy issues and their evaluation of candidates, leading them to judge their party's candidate and issue positions as superior.[40]

Under unusual circumstances, social group characteristics can exaggerate or override traditional partisan loyalties. The 1960 election, for instance, was cast in terms of whether the nation would elect its first Catholic president. In that context, religion was especially salient, and fully 82 percent of Roman Catholics supported John Kennedy, compared to just 37 percent of Protestants—a difference of 45 percentage points. Compare that to 1976, when the Democrats ran a devout Baptist, Jimmy Carter, for president. The percentage of Catholics voting Democratic dropped to 58 percent, while Protestants voting Democratic increased to 46 percent. The difference shrank to just 12 percent.

In 2000 Al Gore chose Connecticut senator Joseph Lieberman, an orthodox Jew, as his running mate. Lieberman's run as the first Jew on a major-party ticket did not have as dramatic an effect on Democratic support as did Kennedy's nomination, since Jews generally turn out for Democrats in large numbers. President Bush's strong display of his born-again Protestant faith has paid off significantly for him among the growing ranks of American evangelicals. A key to his 2004 victory was his ability to capture 78 percent of white evangelical voters.[41]

ISSUES AND POLICY

An idealized view of elections would have highly attentive citizens paying careful attention to the different policy positions offered by the candidates and then, perhaps aided by informed policy analyses from the media, casting their ballots for the candidates who best represent their preferred policy solutions. In truth, as we know by now, American citizens are not "ideal," and the role played by issues is less obvious and more complicated than the ideal model would predict. The role of issues in electoral decision making is limited by the following factors:

- People are busy and, in many cases, rely on party labels to tell them what they need to know about the candidates.[42]
- People know where they stand on "easy" issues like capital punishment or prayer in schools, but some issues, like economic policy or health care reform, are very complicated, and many citizens tend to tune them out.[43]
- The media do not generally cover issues in depth. Instead, they much prefer to focus on the horse-race aspect of elections, looking at who is ahead in the polls rather than what substantive policy issues mean for the nation.[44]
- As we discussed in Chapter 11, people process a lot of policy-relevant information in terms of their impressions of candidates (on-line processing) rather than as policy information. They are certainly influenced by policy information, but they cannot necessarily articulate their opinions and preferences on policy.

Although calculated policy decisions by voters are rare, policy considerations do have a real impact on voters' decisions. To see that, it is useful to distinguish between prospective and retrospective voting. The idealized model of policy voting with which we opened this section is **prospective voting**, in which voters base their decisions on what will happen in the future if they vote for a candidate—what policies will be enacted, what values will be emphasized in policy. Prospective voting requires a good deal of information that average voters, as we have seen, do not always have or even want. While all voters do some prospective voting and, by election time, are usually aware of the candidates' major issue positions, it is primarily party activists and political elites who engage in the full-scale policy analysis that prospective voting entails.

prospective voting basing voting decisions on well-informed opinions and consideration of the future consequences of a given vote

Instead, most voters supplement their spotty policy information and interest with their evaluation of how they think the country is doing, how the economy is performing, and how well the incumbents are carrying out their jobs. They engage in **retrospective voting**, casting their votes as signs of approval or to signal their desire

retrospective voting basing voting decisions on reactions to past performance; approving the status quo or signaling a desire for change for change.[45] In presidential elections, this means that voters consistently look back at the state of the economy, at perceived successes or failures in foreign policy, and at domestic issues like education, gun control, or welfare reform. In 1980 the economy was suffering from a high rate of inflation. Ronald Reagan skillfully focused on voter frustration in the presidential debate by asking voters this question: "Next Tuesday, all of you will go to the polls, and stand there in the polling place and make a decision. I think when you make that decision it might be well if you would ask yourself, are you better off than you were four years ago?"[46] Bill Clinton pointedly borrowed the same theme in his 1996 campaign, after the economy had improved during his first term as president.[47] It worked; those who voted on the basis of the economy strongly supported the Clinton administration.

Retrospective voting is considered to be "easy" decision making as opposed to the more complex decision making involved in prospective voting. Why? Because one only has to ask, "How have things been going?" as a guide to whether to support the current party in power. Retrospective voting is also seen as a useful way of holding politicians accountable, not for what they said or are saying in a campaign, but for what they or members of their party in power *did.* Some scholars believe that, realistically, this type of voting is all that is needed for democracy to function well.[48]

Our idealized model has voters listening as candidates debate the issues through the campaign. More realistic is a model that views voters as perhaps listening to policy debates with one ear and getting information through their party or their friends and families (the opinion leaders we discussed in Chapter 11) but also evaluating the past performance of candidates, particularly as those performances have affected their lives. Thus voters decide partly on what candidates promise to do and partly on what incumbents have done.

THE CANDIDATES

When Americans vote, they are casting ballots for people. In addition to considerations of party and issues, voters also base their decisions on judgments about candidates as individuals. What goes into voters' images of candidates?

Some observers have claimed that voters view candidate characteristics much as they would a beauty or personality contest. There is little support, however, for the notion that voters are won over merely by good looks or movie-star qualities. Consider, for example, that Richard Nixon almost won against John Kennedy, who had good looks, youth, and a quick wit in his favor. Then, in 1964, the awkward, gangly Lyndon Johnson defeated the much more handsome and articulate Barry Goldwater in a landslide. In contrast, there is ample evidence that voters form clear opinions about candidate qualities that are relevant to governing. These include trustworthiness, competence, experience, and sincerity. Citizens also make judgments about the ability of the candidates to lead the nation and to withstand the pressures of the presidency. Ronald Reagan, for example, was widely admired for his ability to stay above the fray of Washington politics and to see the humor in many situations. He appeared, to most Americans, to be in control. By contrast, his predecessor, Jimmy Carter, seemed overwhelmed by the job.

By the end of the 2004 campaign, voters had quite distinctive images of George W. Bush and John Kerry. According to Pew Research Center data, more people saw Bush as willing to take a stand (63 percent vs. Kerry's 27 percent), as a strong leader (50 percent vs. 36 percent), as someone who would use good judgment in a crisis (48 percent vs. 41 percent), and slightly more honest and truthful than Kerry (40 percent vs. 37 percent). Kerry was seen to care more about "people like me" (48 percent vs. Bush's 38 percent). On issues, the public thought Bush would "do a better job of" making wise decisions about Iraq (47 percent vs. Kerry's 41 percent) and defending the country from future terrorist attacks (53 percent vs. 35 percent). Kerry, on the other hand, was projected to do a better job at improving the health care system (50 percent vs. Bush's 34 percent) and improving economic conditions (47 percent vs. 40 percent).[49] Not surprisingly, Bush focused his campaign on his leadership role after September 11, whereas Kerry concentrated on the poor economic conditions the country faced.

WHO, WHAT, HOW Citizens have a strong interest in seeing that good and effective leaders are elected and that power transfers peacefully from losers to winners. By the standard of highly informed voters carefully weighing the alternative policy proposals of competing candidates, the electorate may seem to fall short. However, by a realistic standard that considers the varying abilities of people and the frequent reluctance of candidates and the media to be fully forthcoming about policy proposals, the electorate does not do too badly. Voters come to their decisions through a mix of partisan considerations, membership in social groups, policy information, and candidate image.

PRESIDENTIAL CAMPAIGNS

Being president of the United States is undoubtedly a difficult challenge, but so is getting the job in the first place. In this section we examine the long, expensive, and grueling "road to the White House," as the media like to call it.

GETTING NOMINATED

Each of the major parties (and the minor parties, too) needs to come up with a single viable candidate from the long list of party members with ambitions to serve in the White House. How the candidate is chosen will determine the sort of candidate chosen. Remember, in politics the rules are always central to shaping the outcome. Prior to 1972, primary election results were mostly considered "beauty contests" because their results were not binding. But since 1972, party nominees for the presidency have been chosen in primaries, taking the power away from the party elite and giving it to the activist members of the party who care enough to turn out and vote on Election Day.

The Shake That Launched a Dream?
What inspires a person to want to become president? Having the opportunity to shake the hand of a sitting president—especially one he particularly admired—clearly meant a lot to the teenaged Bill Clinton.

The Pre-primary Season It is hard to say when a candidate's presidential campaign actually begins. Potential candidates may begin planning and thinking about running for the presidency in childhood. Bill Clinton is said to have wanted to be president since high school, when he shook President Kennedy's hand. At one time or another, many people in politics consider going for the big prize, but there are several crucial steps between wishful thinking and actually running for the nomination. Candidates vary somewhat in their approach to the process, but most of those considering a run for the White House go through the following steps:

1. Potential candidates usually test the waters unofficially. They talk to friends and fellow politicians to see just how much support they can count on, and they often leak news of their possible candidacy to the press to see how it is received in the media. Scarcely a year or two into George W. Bush's presidency, Democrats were lining up to test the viability of a presidential run in 2004. Since Bush cannot run again in 2008, many Republicans as well as Democrats are testing the waters for a possible candidacy.
2. If the first step has positive results, candidates file with the Federal Election Commission (FEC) to set up a committee to receive funds so that they can officially explore their prospects. The formation of an *exploratory committee* can be exploited as a media event by the candidate, using the occasion to get free publicity for the launching of the still-unannounced campaign.
3. Candidates then need to acquire a substantial war chest to pay for the enormous expenses of running for the nomination. Some well-positioned candidates, like Vice President Al Gore in 1999, are able to raise large amounts of money before they officially enter the race. Others are forced to scramble to catch up. It takes money to be taken seriously. Because of the way the primaries were structured for 2000, commentators were agreeing that a credible candidacy in the primaries would take over $20 million *before the first caucus or primary.* For most candidates, this required an enormous effort: achieving the target figure of $20 million meant raising an average of about $55,000 a day for a year![50] Before the first caucus in 2004, four Democratic contenders had raised over $16 million, with John Kerry ($25 million) and Howard Dean ($41 million) leading the way.[51] The very wealthy, of course, can ignore this step. Steve Forbes ran for the Republican nomination in 1996 and again in 2000 using his own wealth.
4. The potential candidate must use the pre-primary season to position himself or herself as a credible prospect with the media. It is no coincidence that in the last eight elections, the parties' nominees have all held prominent government offices and have entered the field with some media credibility. Incumbents especially have a huge advantage here.

Putting out Feelers
One of the first steps candidates take in the pre-primary season is to test the political waters to see if they have enough support to run for office. George W. Bush's exploratory committee, formed in March 1999, consisted entirely of members of Congress and other prominent Republicans, many of whom went on to become key players in his administration.

5. The final step of the pre-primary season is the official announcement of candidacy. Like the formation of the exploratory committee, this statement is part of the campaign itself. Promises are made to supporters, agendas are set, media attention is captured, and the process is under way.

Primaries and Caucuses The actual fight for the nomination takes place in the state party caucuses and primaries in which delegates to the parties' national conventions are chosen. In a **party caucus**, grassroots members of the party in each community gather in selected locations to discuss the current candidates. They then vote for delegates from that locality who will be sent to the national convention, or who will go on to larger caucuses at the state level to choose the national delegates. Attending a caucus is time-consuming, and other than in the 2004 Iowa caucus, where the turnout doubled from its 2000 level, participation rates are frequently in the single digits.[52] While most states still hold primary elections, in recent years there has been a trend toward caucuses, the method used in fifteen states.[53]

party caucus local gathering of party members to choose convention delegates

The most common device for choosing delegates to the national conventions is the **presidential primary**. Primary voters cast ballots that send delegates committed to voting for a particular candidate to the conventions. Presidential primaries can be either open or closed, depending on the rules the state party organizations adopt, and these can change from year to year. Any registered voter may vote in an **open primary**, regardless of party affiliation. At the polling place, the voter chooses the ballot of the party whose primary he or she wants to vote in. Only registered party members may vote in a **closed primary**. A subset of this is the independent primary, open only to registered party members and those not registered as members of another party.

presidential primary an election by which voters choose convention delegates committed to voting for a certain candidate

open primary primary election in which eligible voters do not need to be registered party members

closed primary primary election in which only registered party members may vote

Most primaries are closed. Democrats generally favor closed primaries, while Republican rules vary. In addition to the delegates chosen by the state's preferred method, the Democrats also send elected state officials, including such people as Democratic members of Congress and governors, to their national conventions. Some of these officials are "superdelegates," able to vote as free agents, but the rest must reflect the state's primary vote.[54]

In addition to varying in terms of whom they allow to vote, the parties' primary rules also differ in how they distribute delegates among the candidates. The Democrats generally use a method of proportional representation, in which the candidates get the percentage of delegates equal to the percentage of the primary vote they win (provided they get at least 15 percent). Republican rules run from proportional representation, to winner take all (the candidate with the most votes gets all the delegates, even if he or she does not win an absolute majority), to direct voting for delegates (the delegates are not bound to vote for a particular candidate at the convention), to the absence of a formal system (caucus participants may decide how to distribute the delegates).

front-loading the process of scheduling presidential primaries early in the primary season

State primaries also vary in the times at which they are held, with various states engaged in **front-loading**, vying to hold their primaries first in order to gain maximum exposure in the media and power over the nomination. By tradition and state law, the Iowa caucus and the New Hampshire primary are the first contests for delegates. As a result, they get tremendous attention, from both candidates and the media—much more than their contribution to the delegate count would justify. This is why other states have been moving their primaries earlier in the primary season. In 1988, eleven southern states, seeking to boost their clout, agreed to have their primaries on the second Tuesday in March, a day they called Super Tuesday. In an attempt to highlight his state's role in the process, Gov. Pete Wilson signed a bill in the fall of 1998 moving California's primary from the end of March to the first Tuesday in March.

The Republicans moved their primaries earlier in the season in 2000, allowing them to capture the media's attention without competition from the Democrats, who began a month later. In order to give their candidate maximum time to campaign against President Bush rather than against other Democrats, the Democrats allowed states to move up their primary dates in 2004. So many states did so that by five weeks into the 2004 primaries, a quarter of the Democratic delegates had been selected compared to only 1 percent at the same point in 2000.[55]

The consequence of such front-loading is that candidates must have a full war chest and be prepared to campaign nationally from the beginning. Traditionally, winners of early primaries could use that success to raise more campaign funds to continue the battle. With the primaries stacked at the beginning, however, this becomes much harder. When the winner can be determined within weeks of the first primary, it is less likely that a dark horse, or unknown candidate, can emerge. The process favors well-known, well-connected, and especially well-funded candidates. Again, incumbents have an enormous advantage here.

The heavily front-loaded primary has almost no defenders, but it presents a classic example of the problems of collective action that politics cannot always solve.[56] No single state has an incentive to hold back and reduce its power for the good of the whole; each state is driven to maximize its influence by strategically placing its primary early in the pack. Since states make their own laws, subject to only a few regulations laid down by the parties, they are able to schedule the primary season pretty much as they want, regardless of what system would produce the best nominees for national office.

The vagaries of primary scheduling and state rules mean that candidates negotiating the primary season need to have a very carefully thought-out strategy, especially as the primaries become increasingly front-loaded and the time to correct campaign errors is correspondingly reduced. In the fierce battle that the primaries have become, incumbents, of course, have a tremendous advantage. No incumbent has been

TABLE 14.1 **Highest Previously Held Offices of Presidential Nominees**

YEAR	DEMOCRATIC NOMINEE	PREVIOUS OFFICE	REPUBLICAN NOMINEE	PREVIOUS OFFICE
1968	Hubert Humphrey	Incumbent vice president	Richard Nixon	Former vice president
1972	George McGovern	U.S. senator	Richard Nixon	Incumbent president
1976	Jimmy Carter	Governor (Georgia)	Gerald Ford	Incumbent president
1980	Jimmy Carter	Incumbent president	Ronald Reagan	Governor (California)
1984	Walter Mondale	Former vice president	Ronald Reagan	Incumbent president
1988	Michael Dukakis	Governor (Massachusetts)	George H. W. Bush	Incumbent vice president
1992	Bill Clinton	Governor (Arkansas)	George H. W. Bush	Incumbent president
1996	Bill Clinton	Incumbent president	Bob Dole	U.S. senator
2000	Al Gore	Incumbent vice president	George W. Bush	Governor (Texas)
2004	John Kerry	U.S. senator	George W. Bush	Incumbent president

seriously challenged since Ronald Reagan gave Gerald Ford a good scare in 1976. While the incumbent's advantage is most powerful here, most serious presidential contenders have at least held some major elected office. As Table 14.1 shows, of the two major parties' nominees over the last ten presidential elections, seven were incumbent presidents, three were incumbent vice presidents, three were senators, and five were governors. Governors, with executive experience and the ability to claim that they are untainted by the gridlock politics of Washington, have recently had the edge, with four of those five former governors going on to win the presidency.

In most of the crowded primaries in recent years there has been a clear **front-runner**, a person whom many assume will win the nomination before the primaries even begin. Early front-runner status is positive because it means the candidate has raised significant money, has a solid organization, and receives more media coverage than his or her opponents. But success in primaries comes not just from getting a majority of the votes but also from being perceived as a winner, and front-runners are punished if they fail to live up to lofty expectations. The goal for all of the other candidates is to attack the front-runner so as to drive down his or her support, while maneuvering into position as the chief alternative. Then if the front-runner stumbles, as often happens, each of the attacking candidates hopes to emerge from the pack.

front-runner the leading candidate and expected winner of a nomination or an election

Generally a candidate's campaign strategy becomes focused on developing **momentum**, the perception by the press, the public, and the other candidates in the field that one is on a roll, and that polls, primary victories, endorsements, and funding are all coming one's way. Since all candidates in a primary are from the same party, voters cannot rely on partisanship as a cue in making up their minds. Considerations of electability—which candidate has the best chance to triumph in November—are important as voters decide whom to support, and here candidates who seem to have momentum can have an advantage. Developing momentum helps to distinguish one's candidacy in a crowded field and is typically established in the early primaries.

momentum the widely held public perception that a candidate is gaining electoral strength

Consequently, who actually "wins" in the primaries is not always the candidate who comes in first in the balloting. An equally critical factor is whether the candidate is seen to be improving or fading—the matter of momentum and expectations. Much of the political credit that a candidate gets for an apparent "win" depends on who else is running in that primary and what the media expectations of that candidate's performance were. Table 14.2 shows the fate of former Vermont governor Howard Dean, the Democrats' 2004 front-runner heading into the primaries, due largely to Democratic activists' enthusiasm for his strong stand against Bush and the war in Iraq. Voters in Iowa, however, had qualms about whether that antiwar stance could beat Bush in the general election, and Dean came in third in the Iowa caucuses. This disappointing showing caused his support among Democrats to plummet. John Kerry, on the other hand, perceived as a war hero who could take on Bush, won in Iowa (where he had been expected to do badly), picked up momentum, and saw his national fortunes soar. The perception that in Kerry the Democratic Party had a candidate who could beat Bush clinched the nomination for him. John Edwards's second-place finish in Iowa also beat expectations, doubled his support, and made him the front-runner to be Kerry's vice-presidential choice.

The Convention Since 1972, delegates attending the national conventions have not had to decide who the parties' nominees would be. However, two official actions continue to take place at the conventions. First, as we discussed in Chapter 12, the parties hammer out and approve their platforms, the documents in which parties set out their distinct issue positions. Second, the vice-presidential candidate is officially named. The choice of the vice president is up to the presidential nominee. Traditionally the choice was made to balance the ticket (ideologically, regionally, or even, when Democrat Walter Mondale chose Geraldine Ferraro in 1984, by gender). Bill Clinton's choice of Al Gore was a departure from this practice, as he tapped a candidate much like himself—a Democratic moderate from a southern state. In 2000, George W. Bush picked Dick Cheney, a man whose considerable experience in the federal government could be expected to offset Bush's relative lack of it. In 2004, liberal Bostonian Kerry returned to the regional and ideological balancing principle, choosing moderate North Carolina senator John Edwards as his running mate, though he broke with tradition by

TABLE 14.2
Candidate Support Momentum Swings in the 2004 Democratic Primary Season

DATE	KERRY	DEAN	EDWARDS	CLARK
December 11, 2003	10%	31%	4%	10%
December 25, 2003	7	27	6	12
January 2, 2004	11	24	6	20
January 9, 2004	9	26	7	20
January 19, 2004	Iowa caucus: Kerry wins, Edwards comes in second.			
January 22, 2004	29	17	13	11
January 27, 2004	New Hampshire primary: Kerry wins, Edwards comes in second.			
January 29, 2004	49	14	13	9
February 6, 2004	52	14	13	10
February 16, 2004	65	8	19	Dropped out

Note: Data show changes in Democrats' support for their party's nominee in the early 2004 primary season.

Source: CNN/*USA Today*/Gallup poll results. Respondents were Democrats or those who leaned toward the Democratic Party nationwide who were registered to vote. Full question: "After I read the names, please tell me which of those candidates you would be most likely to support for the Democratic nomination for president in the year 2004." Results from January 22, 2004, come from Fox News/Opinion Dynamics poll, January 21–22, 2004. Question: "If a 2004 Democratic primary for president were held today, which one of the following candidates would you most likely vote for?"

announcing his choice three weeks before his party's convention. There is no clear evidence that the vice-presidential choice has significant electoral consequences, but the presidential nominees weigh it carefully nonetheless. If nothing else, the caliber of the decision about who the vice president should be is held to be an indication of the kind of appointments the nominee would make if elected.

Although their actual party business is limited, the conventions still provide the nominee with a "convention bump" in the polls. The harmonious coverage, the enthusiasm of party supporters, and even the staged theatrics seem to have a positive impact on viewers. The result is that candidates have usually, though not always, experienced a noticeable rise in the polls immediately following the conventions.

THE GENERAL ELECTION CAMPAIGN

After the candidates are nominated in late summer, there is a short break, at least for the public, before the traditional campaign kickoff after Labor Day. When the campaign begins, the goal of each side is to convince supporters to turn out and to get undecided voters to choose its candidate. Most voters, the party identifiers, will usually support their party's candidate, although they need to be motivated by the campaign to turn out and cast their ballots. Most of the battle in a presidential campaign is for the **swing voters**, the one-third or so of the electorate who have not made up their minds at the start of the campaign and who are open to persuasion by either side. As one would expect given the forces described in Chapter 12 (see Figure 12.3), this means that for both parties, the general election strategy differs considerably from the strategy used to win a primary election. To win the general election, the campaigns move away from the sharp ideological tone used to motivate the party faithful in the primaries and "run to the middle" by making less ideological appeals.

swing voters the approximately one-third of the electorate who are undecided at the start of a campaign

In the general campaign, each side seeks to get its message across, to define the choice in terms that give its candidate the advantage. This massive effort to influence the information citizens are exposed to requires a clear strategy, which begins with a plan for winning the states where the candidate will be competitive.

The Electoral College The presidential election is not a national race; it is a race between the candidates in each of the fifty states and the District of Columbia (see "*Who Are We?* Red vs. Blue, or Purple All Over?"). The reasons for the electoral college's existence may seem outdated sometimes, but it nevertheless drives campaign strategy. Because our founders feared giving too much power to the volatile electorate, we do not actually vote for the president and vice president in presidential elections. Rather, we cast our votes in November for electors (members of the electoral college), who in turn vote for the president in December. The Constitution provides for each state to have as many electoral votes as it does senators and representatives in Congress. Thus Alaska has three electoral votes (one for each of the state's U.S. senators and one for its sole member of the House of Representatives). By contrast, California has fifty-five electoral votes (two senators and fifty-three representatives). In addition, the Twenty-third Amendment gave the District of Columbia three electoral votes. There are 538 electoral votes in all; 270 are needed to win the presidency. Figure 14.2 shows the distribution of electoral votes among the states today.

Electors are generally activist members of the party whose presidential candidate carried the state. In December, following the election, the electors meet and vote in their state capitals. In the vast majority of cases, they vote as expected, but there are

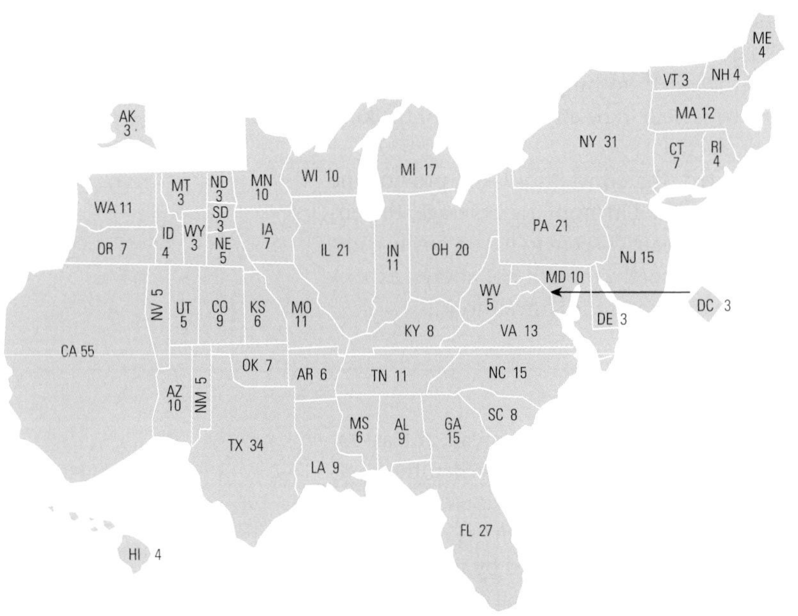

FIGURE 14.2
Electoral College, 2001–2010

Note: This distorted map, in which the states are sized according to their number of electoral votes, demonstrates the electoral power of the more populous states. Total electoral votes = 538.

occasional "faithless electors" who vote for their own preferences. The results of the electors' choices in the states are then sent to the Senate, where the ballots are counted when the new session opens. If no candidate achieves a majority in the electoral college, the Constitution calls for the House of Representatives to choose from the top three electoral vote winners. In this process, each state has one vote. Whenever the vote goes to the House, the Senate decides on the vice president, with each senator having a vote. This has happened only twice (the last time was in 1824), although some observers of the 2000 election speculated that that election, too, could have been decided in the House of Representatives if Florida's election had not been decided in the courts.

The importance of the electoral college is that all the states but Maine and Nebraska operate on a winner-take-all basis. Thus the winner in California, even if he or she has less than a majority of the popular vote, wins all of the state's fifty-five electoral votes. The loser in California may have won 49 percent of the popular vote but gets nothing in the electoral college. It is possible, then, for the popular vote winner to lose in the electoral college. This has happened only three times in our history, most recently in 2000, when Bush received an electoral college majority even though Gore won the popular vote by more than half a million votes.

Usually, however, the opposite happens: the electoral college exaggerates the candidate's apparent majority. In 1992 and 1996, Bill Clinton received only 43.2 and 49 percent of the popular vote, but his electoral majorities were 69 and 70 percent, respectively. This exaggeration of the winning margin has the effect of legitimizing the winner's victory and allowing him to claim that he has a *mandate*—a broad popular endorsement—even if he won by a small margin of the popular vote.

The rules of the electoral college give greater power to some states over others. The provision that all states get at least three electoral votes in the electoral college means that citizens in the smaller states get proportionately greater representation in the electoral college. Alaska, for example, sent one elector to the electoral college for every 209,000 people, while California had one elector for every 627,000 residents.

However, this "advantage" is probably offset by the practice of winner take all, which focuses the candidates' attention on the largest states with the biggest payoff in electoral votes. The swing voters who will help the candidate win a large state, and hence the full pot of the state's electoral votes, become much more important to a candidate than all the voters in a small state. Thus small states receive very few campaign visits from presidential candidates. Similarly, voters in competitive states (where the race is tight) are much more important to the candidates than are the voters in a state where the winner can be safely predicted. The state of Indiana, for instance, almost

Red vs. Blue, or Purple All Over?

In our electoral college system, presidential elections are won state by state. In election night coverage, the networks light up the states red as they go for the Republican candidate and blue as they go for the Democrat. Because support for Republicans in the last several elections has tended to come from the southern and plains states and the Democrats have been successful in the coastal and upper Midwest regions, it has become popular to speak of a red and blue America—an America closely but irreconcilably split between conservative and liberal states.

Critics of this view point out that in twenty-four of the fifty states the winning candidate got less than 55 percent of the vote. When you break down the presidential vote by county instead of by state, you can see that pockets of red and blue are interspersed with varying shades of purple, indicating a county that may lean Democrat or Republican but is not decisively either. A map of red and blue America, these critics say, oversimplifies the cultural, social, and political divisions in this country.

So who are we: two separate countries, bound by geography but not much else, or a diverse and integrated nation of many opinions? What difference does it make how you answer that question?

Red vs. Blue America

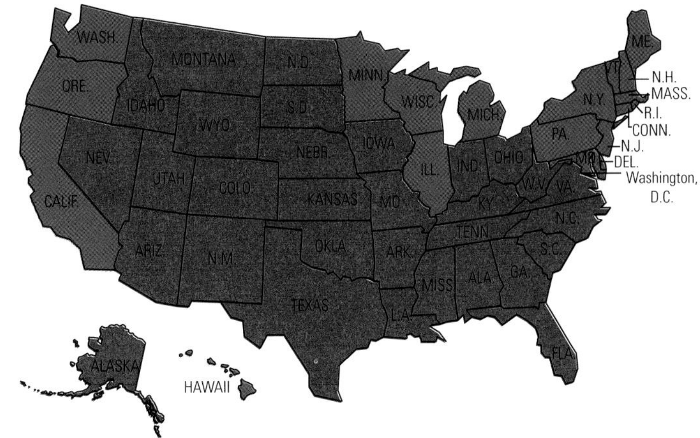

Source: Michael Gastner, Cosma Shalizi, and Mark Newman, "Maps and cartograms of the 2004 U.S. presidential election results," www-personal.umich.edu/~mejn/election.

Purple America

Source: Robert J. Vanderbei, "Election 2004 Results," www.princeton.edu/~rvdb/JAVA/election2004. Used by permission.

always votes Republican. Consequently, Hoosiers are rarely visited by presidential campaigns, and candidates do not bother to spend their advertising dollars there. It is not worthwhile for the Democrats to go to Indiana, and the Republicans don't need to bother. Candidates tend to spend the lion's share of their time, resources, and media efforts in the large competitive states. In 2004, over 60 percent of the general election campaign trips made by the two major-party presidential candidates were to five states: Florida, Iowa, Ohio, Pennsylvania, and Wisconsin.[57] Because of this aspect of the electoral college, not all citizens experience the same political campaign.

Hundreds of bills have been introduced in Congress to reform or abolish the electoral college, an especially urgent project for many Democrats after the 2000 election.[58] Major criticisms of the current system include the following:

- The electoral college is undemocratic because it is possible for the popular winner not to get a majority of the electoral votes.
- In a very close contest, the popular outcome could be dictated by a few "faithless electors" who vote their consciences rather than the will of the people of their states.
- The electoral college distorts candidates' campaign strategies. The winner-take-all provision in all but two states puts a premium on a few large competitive states, which get a disproportionate share of the candidates' attention.

Few people deny the truth of these charges, and hardly anyone believes that if we were to start all over, the current electoral college would be chosen as the best way to elect a president. Nevertheless, all the proposed alternatives also have problems, or at least serious criticisms. See *What's at Stake Revisited* at the end of this chapter for a discussion of whether the 2000 election is likely to finish off the electoral college.

Who Runs the Campaign? Running a modern presidential campaign has become a highly specialized profession. Most presidential campaigns are led by an "amateur," a nationally prestigious chairperson who may serve as an adviser and assist in fundraising. However, the real work of the campaign is done by the professional staff the candidate hires. These may be people the candidate knows well and trusts, or they may be professionals who sign on for the duration of the campaign and then move on to another. Clinton strategist James Carville (interestingly, married to former president George H. W. Bush's deputy campaign manager and Dick Cheney's former spokesperson, Mary Matalin) became a loyal Clinton friend and defender but has gone to work for other candidates, including Ehud Barak, who won the 1999 election as prime minister of Israel. (See the *Profiles in Citizenship* feature on pages 616–617.) Karl Rove was in charge of both of George W. Bush's election campaigns and continues to work in the Bush White House as a trusted political adviser.

Campaign work at the beginning of the twenty-first century is big business. Some of the jobs include not only the well-known ones of campaign manager and strategist but also more specialized components tailored to the modern campaign's emphasis on information and money. For instance, candidates need to hire research teams to prepare position papers on issues so that the candidate can answer any question posed by potential supporters and the media. But researchers also engage in the controversial but necessary task of **oppo research**—delving into the background and vulnerabilities of the opposing candidate with an eye to exploiting his or her weaknesses. Central to the modern campaign's efforts to get and control the flow of information are pollsters and focus group administrators, who are critical for testing the public's reactions to issues and strategies. Media consultants try to get free coverage of the campaign whenever possible and to make the best use of the campaign's advertising dollars by designing commercials and print advertisements.

oppo research investigation of an opponent's background for the purpose of exploiting weaknesses or undermining credibility

Candidates also need advance teams to plan and prepare their travel agendas, to arrange for crowds (and the signs they wave) to greet the candidates at airports, and even to reserve accommodations for the press. Especially in the primaries, staff devoted to fundraising are essential to ensure the constant flow of money necessary to grease the wheels of any presidential campaign. They work with big donors and

engage in direct-mail campaigns to solicit money from targeted groups. Finally, of course, candidates need to hire a legal team to keep their campaigns in compliance with the regulations of the FEC and to file the required reports. In general, campaign consultants are able to provide specialized technical services that the parties' political committees cannot.[59]

Presenting the Candidate An effective campaign begins with a clear understanding of how the strengths of the candidate fit with the context of the times and the mood of the voters. To sell a candidate effectively, the claims to special knowledge, competence, or commitment must be credible.[60] In 1992, voters were getting pretty tired of politics and inaction in Washington, D.C., particularly the seeming inaction on what many people perceived to be a worsening economy. Thus the Clinton campaign emphasized the elements of the candidate (young, articulate, intelligent, and energetic with a record as an effective governor) that contrasted with the public's perceptions of the familiar incumbent, President George H. W. Bush, who appeared to lack a clear policy direction or vision. The Clinton campaign headquarters (which staffers called "The War Room") prominently displayed a sign—"It's the Economy, Stupid"—to help keep the campaign on track.

Al Gore's 2000 presidential campaign stumbled when it lost sight of that same message. Seeking to distance himself from the scandals that plagued President Clinton, Gore also distanced himself from Clinton's successful economic record and did not focus on the message that "prosperity is on the ballot" until the closing days of his

Politics Makes Strange Bedfellows
Each of the political parties hires professional campaign consultants whose fortunes rise and fall with the victories and losses of the candidates whose campaigns they run. Among the most famous of these in recent years is the defiantly liberal James Carville, who ran Bill Clinton's successful 1992 presidential campaign. Carville is married to Mary Matalin, who was deputy campaign manager in George H. W. Bush's failed 1992 reelection bid, a conservative commentator on CNN, and from January 2001 through the end of 2002, Vice President Dick Cheney's top public relations strategist. The two are regular guests on NBC's *Meet the Press.*

Profiles in Citizenship

James Carville

James Carville found his calling and his salvation in his love affair with politics. "You know, I was never that great at anything," he says in that manic Louisiana drawl familiar to anyone who has watched the movie *The War Room* or seen him on CNN. "The only thing I was great at was being kind of, you know, a horrible student—a worse than bad lawyer. I sat in my office one day and said if I had to hire a lawyer I wouldn't hire me."

". . . don't confuse the right to do something with the right thing to do."

But the man loved politics—had done so since he was a kid, when larger-than-life figures walked the Louisiana landscape of his youth, people like Gov. Earl Long ("There's a great man! He's my guy!") and characters called "Pinhead Willie," "Coozan Dud," and "Wild Bill, Big Bad Bill Dodd." Ask him if politics was a big deal in his family when he was growing up in Carville, Louisiana (a town named for his postmaster grandfather), and he gives a single-word answer: "Huge."

So politics was the path he chose to get himself away from lawyering. He set up as a political consultant, finding the pace of electoral politics perfectly suited to his personal occupational challenges ("I have pretty serious attention problems and dyslexia and the whole dictionary of fashionable childhood diseases"). It was a life made to measure for him: "You're really determining something that profoundly matters to people all across the spectrum and it's something that, if you're like me and you've got a lot of energy left over—if you're a sprinter, not a distance runner—it's perfect. And you know at the end of the day if you've won or lost. How can you beat it? There's nothing that could be more fun."

With his brilliant mind and intuitive understanding of politics, Carville ran a couple of winning Pennsylvania campaigns and caught the attention of Bill Clinton in his 1992 run for the presidency. Carville headed up the Little Rock "War Room" and kept attention focused on the campaign's famous mantra—"It's the Economy, Stupid." Of course, Clinton won—and now Carville was at the top of his game. "And there was a time—it certainly passed—there was a time in my life where if I had to hire a political consultant I would have hired me. Now that's a great feeling. . . . And it was particularly great on the heels of knowing that I was a bad lawyer. It's not a very satisfying way to go through life, being bad and not liking what you do."

Carville's life must be superbly satisfying now. No longer running campaigns (he says he has become a victim of his own success, drawing more attention than the candidates he would work for), he is still active in the Democratic Party, appearing frequently as a commentator on television and with his wife, Republican Mary Matalin, on the lecture circuit.

Matalin was working for the first president Bush when she and Carville met (they ran opposing campaigns in

campaign. John Kerry was also perceived as failing to articulate a clear message for his campaign. Awkward statements like "I voted for the $87 billion before I voted against it," and his inability to stake a clear position on the Iraq war until well into the campaign left many voters unclear about what he stood for. When a campaign fails to present its candidate in a positive light, it gives the opposition an opening to paint a negative caricature of him. For example, George W. Bush's team seized on Kerry's qualified statements as illustrations that Kerry "flip-flopped" on issues.

As the campaigns struggle to control the flow of information about their candidates and influence how voters see their opponent, oppo research comes into play, sometimes complete with focus groups and poll testing. In fact, oppo research has become a central component in all elections, leading to the negative campaigning so

1992), and she has worked for Vice President Dick Cheney since that time. If you think "politics makes strange bedfellows," read their book, *All's Fair: Love, War and Running for President*, to see just how strange. With the high-octane life their parents lead, it would seem that politics could hardly help being as "huge" for their two kids as it was for Carville (although he says since it's "the family business," they are not too impressed).

But it's hard to imagine that they will remain wholly unmoved by their father's powerful feelings about politics. Nobody could be. Leafing though a book of photographs of his beloved Louisiana, James Carville talks about politics with the passion and reverence of a man recalling a first love. His voice gets hushed with the intensity of his memories, reading passages out loud and getting so eager to share the stories that he impulsively gives us the book to keep.

Impulsive and emotional, Carville may be, but when it comes to assessing the day-to-day stake of politics, he is a sharp-eyed realist. He knows powerful people would prefer us to check out and let them have their way. "All these decisions are going to get made—doesn't matter whether you're involved in them," he says. "The school's going to go on, somebody's going to have the hiring policy, somebody's going to decide the curriculum, the hospitals are going to get built, somebody's going to have to decide where they are, who gets served, etc., etc. . . . the taxes are going to get collected. Whatever. Okay. Now what a lot of powerful people would like to tell you is, you don't worry your pretty little head with that. We'll take care of all these things and you don't need to, you know, you just have a couple of beers and eat some Doritos and watch the game."

He is amazed that people fall for the idea that they can't figure out complex issues. "None of this stuff is impenetrable. The only way that the political golden rule operates—that those who have got the gold make the rules—is if it's by default," that is, if people fail to pay attention. More Carville wisdom:

On why politics matters:

> There's a lot of things you can say about politics and politicians . . . some are corrupt and some are liars . . . but the one thing you can't say is that what they do doesn't matter. Because it matters profoundly. From where you put the intersection, to the park, to the taxes, to the bonds, you name it. Abortion, euthanasia, it doesn't matter. On a sliding scale of does the bridge get built or not, all of this is decided by politicians. So every criticism that a young person has of politics is valid until they get to the point that it doesn't matter. Then that's where the whole argument completely falls apart. Right on its face.

On keeping the republic:

> The first thing we need to do is remove this thing that participating in public affairs in whatever form you want to is some kind of chore. I don't think it really is. I think it's kind of a privilege and it's fun. . . . I tell young people you have the right not to participate, but don't confuse the right to do something with the right thing to do. They are two distinct things. I think the biggest thing that young people can do is, when it comes to this, be guided by your passion. . . . It's a hell of a lot of fun. And it's a really fascinating thing. And you learn a lot. But the biggest thing you do is you actually get to make a difference.

Source: James Carville spoke with Christine Barbour and Gerald Wright June 21, 2005.

prevalent in recent years.[61] Astute candidates also have oppo research done on themselves; knowing that their opponent will be studying them, they hope to forestall any unpleasant surprises. With his checkered youth in mind, Texas governor George W. Bush hired people to do oppo research on him twice during his runs for governor. The benign results then convinced him later that he had nothing to fear from the close scrutiny of a national campaign.

The Issues Earlier we indicated that voters do consider issues as they decide how to vote. This means that issues must be central to the candidate's strategy for getting elected. From the candidate's point of view, there are two kinds of issues to consider when planning a strategy: valence issues and position issues.

valence issues issues on which most voters and candidates share the same position

Valence issues are policy matters on which the voters and the candidates all share the same preference. These are what we might call "motherhood and apple pie" issues, because no one opposes them. Everyone is for a strong, prosperous economy; for America having a respected leadership role in the world; for fighting terrorism; for thrift in government; and for a clean environment. Similarly, everyone opposes crime and drug abuse, government waste, political corruption, and immorality.

position issues issues on which the parties differ in their perspectives and proposed solutions

Position issues have two sides. On abortion, there are those who are pro-life and those who are pro-choice. On Vietnam, there were the hawks who favored pursuing a military victory and the doves who favored just getting out. Many of the hardest decisions for candidates are on position issues—although a clear stand means that they will gain some friends, it also guarantees that they will make some enemies. Realistic candidates, who want to win as many votes as possible, try to avoid being clearly identified with the losing side of important position issues. One example is abortion. Activists in the Republican Party fought to keep their strong pro-life plank in the party platform in 2000. However, because a majority of the electorate are opposed to the strong pro-life position, George W. Bush seldom mentioned the issue during the campaign, even though one of his first acts as president was to cut federal funding to overseas groups that provide abortions or abortion counseling.

wedge issue a controversial issue that one party uses to split the voters in the other party

When a candidate or party does take a stand on a difficult position issue, the other side often uses it against them as a wedge issue. A **wedge issue** is a position issue on which the parties differ and that proves controversial within the ranks of a particular party. For a Republican, an anti–affirmative action position is not dangerous, since few Republicans actively support affirmative action. For a Democrat, though, it is a very dicey issue, because liberal party members endorse it but more moderate members do not. An astute strategy for a Republican candidate is to raise the issue in a campaign, hoping to drive a wedge between the Democrats and to recruit to his or her side the Democratic opponents of affirmative action.

issue ownership the tendency of one party to be seen as more competent in a specific policy area

The idea of **issue ownership** helps to clarify the role of policy issues in presidential campaigns. Because of their past stands and performance, each of the parties is widely perceived as better able to handle certain kinds of problems. For instance, the Democrats may be seen as better able to deal with education matters, and the Republicans more effective at solving crime-related problems. The voter's decision then is not so much evaluating positions on education and crime, but rather deciding which problem is more important. If education is pressing, a voter might go with the Democratic candidate; if crime is more important, the voter might choose the Republican.[62] From the candidate's point of view, the trick is to convince voters that the election is about the issues that his or her party "owns."

An example of how issue ownership operated in the 2004 presidential election can be seen in exit poll data. Voters were asked which of seven issues was most important in their vote decision. Table 14.3 shows that four of those issues (economy/jobs, health care, education, and Iraq) clearly worked to the advantage of John Kerry. Two of those issues, economy/jobs and health care, are Democratic-owned issues, and Kerry received about eight in ten votes from the 28 percent of Americans who felt that they were the most important issues. George W. Bush had the edge on three Republican-owned issues (taxes, terrorism, and moral values). Moral values and terrorism were the most important overall, and Bush held a whopping advantage, 79 percent and 86 percent, respectively, on these issues. Sometimes a party will try to take an issue that is "owned" by the other party and redefine it in order to claim ownership of it. Bush

TABLE 14.3 Issue Ownership in the 2004 Election

"WHICH ISSUE MATTERED THE MOST IN HOW YOU VOTED FOR PRESIDENT?"	NAMING ISSUE MOST IMPORTANT	VOTED FOR KERRY	VOTED FOR BUSH
Kerry's Issues			
Economy/jobs	20%	80%	18%
Health care	8	78	22
Total concerned about Kerry's issues	28		
Bush's Issues			
Moral values	22	18	79
Terrorism	19	14	86
Taxes	5	44	56
Total concerned about Bush's issues	46		
Claimed by Both Candidates			
Education	4	75	25
Iraq	15	74	25
Total concerned about issues claimed by both candidates	19		

Source: Data are from National Election Pool exit polls cited in Gerald Pomper, "The Presidential Election: The Ills of American Politics After 9/11," in *The Elections of 2004*, ed. Michael Nelson (Washington, D.C.: CQ Press, 2005), 56.

did this successfully in 2000 with the education issue, just as Clinton reversed the advantage Republicans usually held on crime.[63]

Because valence issues are relatively safe, candidates stress them at every opportunity. They also focus on the position issues that their parties "own" or on which they have majority support. What this suggests is that the real campaign is not about debating positions on issues—how to reduce the deficit or whether to restrict abortion—but about which issues should be considered. Issue campaigning is to a large extent about setting the agenda.

The Media It is impossible to understand the modern political campaign without appreciating the pervasive role of the media. Even though many voters tend to ignore campaign ads—or at least they tell survey interviewers that they do—we know that campaign advertising matters. It has increased dramatically with the rise of television as people's information source of choice. Studies show that advertising provides usable information for voters. Political ads can heighten the loyalty of existing supporters, and they can educate the public about what candidates stand for and what issues candidates believe are most important. Ads also can be effective in establishing the criteria on which voters choose between candidates.

One of the best examples of this effective advertising came from the 1988 presidential campaign. Because George H. W. Bush was behind in the polls and perceived as not very sympathetic to average citizens, his campaign sought to change the way people were thinking about him and his opponent, Michael Dukakis. They came up with an effective ad showing criminals walking in and out of a prison through a turnstile. A voice-over claimed that Dukakis's "revolving door prison policy" had permitted first-degree murderers to leave on weekend furloughs. At the same time, a pro-Bush group called the National Security PAC ran the more controversial Willie

Horton ad, which focused on the mug shot of Horton, showing (without saying so) that he was African American. Implying that Dukakis bore some responsibility for it, the commercial coolly told how Horton, who was serving a life sentence for murder, had stabbed a man and raped his girlfriend while on a weekend pass.[64] The Dukakis campaign failed to respond to this one-two punch, and subsequent surveys showed that those who saw the commercials came to think of crime as an important issue in the campaign. Bush's standings began to climb, and of course he went on to win the election.[65] (See "*Consider the Source:* Interpreting Campaign Advertising" for some advice on how to critically evaluate the political ads that come your way.) And while **negative advertising** may turn off some voters and give the perception that politics is an unpleasant business, the public accepts accurate attacks on the issues. As long as it does not go too far, an attack ad that highlights negative aspects of an opponent's record actually registers more quickly and is remembered more frequently and longer by voters than are positive ads.[66] Experts suggested that requiring candidates to appear in their own ads would discourage negativity in the 2004 election, but 40 percent of Kerry's ads still criticized Bush while a whopping 75 percent of Bush's ads took on Kerry.[67]

negative advertising campaign advertising that emphasizes the negative characteristics of opponents rather than one's own strengths

Because paid media coverage is so expensive, a campaign's goal is to maximize opportunities for free coverage. The major parties' presidential candidates are accompanied by a substantial entourage of reporters who need to file stories on a regular basis. As a result, daily campaign events are planned more for the press and the demands of the evening news than for the personal audiences, who often seem to function primarily as a backdrop for the candidates' efforts to get favorable airtime each day. Although the candidates want the regular exposure, they do not like the norms of broadcast news, which they see as perpetuating horse-race journalism.[68] The exhausting nature of campaigns, and the mistakes and gaffes that follow, are a source of constant concern because of the media's tendency to zero in on them. The relationship between the campaigns and the media is testy. They need each other, but the candidates want to control the message, and the media want stories that are "news"—controversies, changes in the candidates' standings, or stories of goofs and scandals. We discuss the complex relationship between the media and the candidates at greater length in Chapter 15.

Traditionally, most citizens got information from "hard news" sources like the television networks' evening newscasts. Candidates in recent elections, however, have turned increasingly to "soft news" and entertainment programming to get their messages across. *Larry King Live* was the site where third-party presidential hopeful Ross Perot announced his candidacy in 1992 and 1996. Bill Clinton did a stint on MTV to appeal to younger voters and played his sax on the *Arsenio Hall Show.* Following this example, in 2004 both Bush and Kerry appeared separately with their wives on the *Dr. Phil* show, and Kerry also went on *Live With Regis and Kelly,* the *Late Show With David Letterman,* and *The Daily Show With Jon Stewart.* Such appearances give the candidates more unedited airtime and allow them to evade the hard news tendency to interpret all events in horse-race terms.

Since 1976 the presidential debates have become one of the major focal points of the campaign. The first televised debate was held in 1960 between Sen. John Kennedy and Vice President Richard Nixon. The younger and more photogenic Kennedy came out on top in those televised debates, but interestingly, those who heard the debates on the radio thought that Nixon did a better job.[69] In general, leading candidates find it less in their interest to participate in debates because they have more to lose and less to win, and so for years debates took place on a sporadic basis.

In the past twenty-five years, however, media and public pressure have all but guaranteed that at least the major-party candidates will participate in debates, although the number, timing, and format of the debates are renegotiated for each presidential election season. Recent elections have generated two or three debates, with a debate among the vice-presidential contenders worked in as well. Third-party candidates, who have the most to gain from the free media exposure and the legitimacy that debate participation confers on a campaign, lobby to be included but rarely are. Ross Perot was invited in 1992 because both George Bush and Bill Clinton hoped to woo his supporters. Ralph Nader and Pat Buchanan were shut out of all three debates in 2000.

Presidential Politics Enters the Media Age
The first televised debates were held in 1960 between then Vice President Richard Nixon and the younger and less experienced Sen. John F. Kennedy. Many believe that television made the difference in Kennedy's razor-thin victory margin. Kennedy appeared relaxed and charismatic compared with the brooding Nixon—reinforced by the latter's unfortunate five o'clock shadow. Today, the presidential debates are an expected and anticipated feature of presidential campaigns.

Do the debates matter? Detailed statistical studies show, not surprisingly, that many of the debates have been standoffs. However, some of the debates, especially those identified with significant candidate errors or positive performances, have moved vote intentions 2 to 4 percent, which in a close race could be significant.[70] After trailing in the polls following the 2004 Republican convention, John Kerry's solid performance in the debates drew him within the margin of error with President Bush and the race remained tight thereafter. In addition, there is a good deal of evidence, including from 2004, that citizens learn about the candidates and their issue positions from the debates.[71] Interest in the debates varies with how much suspense surrounds the outcome of the election. When the seat is open or the candidates are less well known, more people are likely to watch the debates.[72]

Money Winning—or even losing—a presidential campaign involves serious money. The presidential candidates in 2004 spent a total of almost $718 million, more than double what was spent by the presidential candidates in 2000 and, as the data in Figure 14.3 show, clearly part of an upward trend. This increase in spending came about despite significant fundraising limits put into place by the Bipartisan Campaign Reform Act of 2002 (BCRA), also known as the McCain-Feingold Act.

This torrent of cash is used to cover the costs of all of the activities just discussed: campaign professionals, polling, travel for the candidates and often their wives (along with the accompanying staff and media), and the production and purchase of media advertising. The campaign costs for all federal offices in 2004 came in at about $4 billion, or almost $13.60 for every man, woman, and child in the country.[73]

Where does all this money come from? To make sense of the changing world of election campaign finance, we need to start by defining the different kinds of campaign contributions, each with different sources and regulations.

government matching funds money given by the federal government to qualified presidential candidates in the primary and general election campaigns

- **Government matching funds** are given to qualified presidential candidates in the primary and general election campaigns. This money comes from citizens who have checked the box on their tax returns that sends $3 ($6 on joint returns) to fund presidential election campaigns. The idea behind the law is to more easily

Consider the Source

Interpreting Campaign Advertising

"Sticks and stones may break my bones," goes the old childhood rhyme, "but words can never hurt me." Try telling that to the innumerable targets of negative advertising, sloganeering that emphasizes the negative characteristics of one's opponents rather than one's own strengths. Negative advertising has characterized American election campaigns since the days of George Washington. George Washington? His opponents called him a "dictator" who would "debauch the nation."[1] Thomas Jefferson was accused of having an affair with a slave, a controversy that has outlived any of the people involved; Abraham Lincoln was claimed to have had an illegitimate child; and Grover Cleveland, who admitted to fathering a child out of wedlock, was taunted with the words, "Ma, Ma, where's my Pa?"[2] (His supporters had the last laugh, however: "Gone to the White House, ha, ha, ha.")

Like it or not (and most Americans say they do not), the truth is that negative campaign advertising works, and in the television age it is far more prevalent than anything that plagued Washington, Jefferson, or Lincoln. People remember it better than they do positive advertising; tracking polls show that after a voter has seen a negative ad eight times, he or she begins to move away from the attacked candidate.[3] Some candidates claim that their advertising is not really negative but rather "comparative," and indeed a candidate often needs to compare her record with another's in order to make the case that she is the superior choice. Negative advertising is nonetheless unpopular with voters, who often see it as nasty, unfair, and false. In fact, advertising that is proved to be false can frequently backfire on the person doing the advertising. But how is a savvy media consumer to know what to believe? Be careful, be critical, and be fair in how you interpret campaign ads. Here are some tips. Ask yourself these questions:

1. **Who is running the ad?** What do they have to gain by it? Look to see who has paid for the ad. Is it the opponent's campaign? An interest group? A political action committee (PAC) or a 527 group? What do they have at stake, and how might that affect their charges? If the ad's sponsors do not identify themselves, what might that tell you about the source of the information? About the information itself?
2. **Are the accusations relevant to the campaign or the office in question?** If character is a legitimate issue, questions of adultery or drug use might have bearing on the election. If not, they might just be personal details used to smear this candidate's reputation. Ask yourself, What kind of person should hold the job? What kinds of qualities are important?
3. **Is the accusation or attack timely?** If a person is accused of youthful experimentation with drugs or indiscreet behavior in his twenties but has been an upstanding lawyer and public servant for twenty-five

regulate big money influence on campaign finances, ensure a fair contest, and free up candidates to communicate with the public. For primary elections, if a candidate raises at least $5,000 in each of twenty states and agrees to abide by overall spending limits (about $45 million in 2004), as well as state-by-state limits, the federal government matches every contribution up to $250. The total a candidate could have received in public funding for primaries in 2004 was $18.7 million.

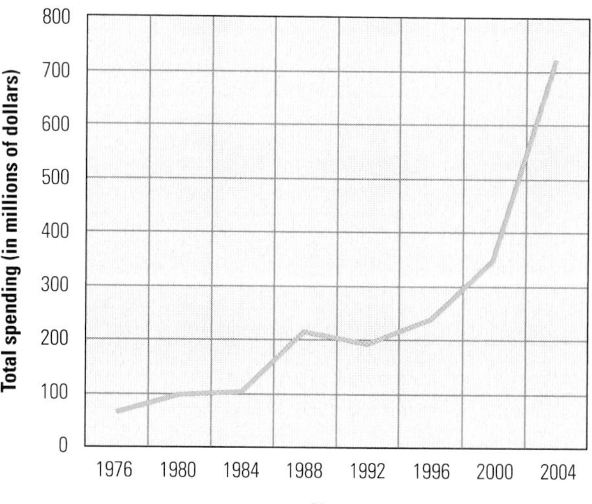

FIGURE 14.3
Increase in Total Spending in Presidential Campaigns, 1976–2004

Source: Center for Responsive Politics, 2004 Presidential Election, 2005, www.opensecrets.org/presidential/index.asp?graph=spending.

Whichever Way the Wind Blows
Windsurfing off Nantucket during the 2004 presidential campaign, John Kerry probably thought he was projecting an athletic image. The Bush campaign, however, seized the opportunity to air an ad that equated Kerry's zig-zagging through the surf with "flip-flopping" on issues, a claim that dominated much of the campaign's negative advertising. The ad ends with the narrator saying, "John Kerry: whichever way the wind blows."

years, do the accusations have bearing on how the candidate will do the job?

4. **Does the ad convey a fair charge that can be answered, or does it evoke unarticulated fears and emotions?** A 1964 ad for Lyndon Johnson's presidential campaign showed a little girl counting as she plucked petals from a daisy. An adult male voice gradually replaced hers, counting down to an explosion of a mushroom cloud that obliterated the picture. The daisy commercial never even mentioned Johnson's opponent, Barry Goldwater, though the clear implication was that the conservative, promilitary Goldwater was likely to lead the nation to a nuclear war. Amid cries of "Foul!" from Goldwater's Republican supporters, the ad was aired only once, but it became a classic example of the sort of ad that seeks to play on the fears of its viewers.

5. **Is the ad true?** FactCheck.org, a project of the Annenberg Public Policy Center, is an excellent resource for monitoring factual accuracy in campaign ads. Other media outlets like the *New York Times* will often run "ad watches" to help viewers determine if the information in an advertisement is true. If it is not (and sometimes even if it is), you can usually count on hearing a response from the attacked candidate rebutting the charges. Occasionally candidates have chosen not to respond, claiming to take the high road, but as Michael Dukakis's dismal performance in the 1988 election showed, false attacks left unanswered can be devastating. Try to conduct your own "ad watch." Study the campaign ads and evaluate their truthfulness.

1. Alexandra Marks, "Backlash Grows Against Negative Political Ads," *Christian Science Monitor*, September 28, 1995, 1.
2. Roger Stone, "Positively Negative," *New York Times*, February 26, 1996, 13.
3. Ibid.

This same fund fully finances both major-party candidates' general election campaigns. After they accepted their parties' nominations in 2004, John Kerry and George W. Bush each received $74.6 million to subsidize their entire fall campaign. If presidential candidates accept this public funding, which so far all major-party candidates have done for the general election campaign, they may not raise any other funds or use any leftover funds raised during the primary campaign. Third parties that received at least 5 percent of the vote in the previous presidential campaign may also collect public financing. Unlike the two major parties, however, the money a third party receives depends on the number of votes the party received in the previous election. Ross Perot was eligible to receive $29 million for his 1996 presidential campaign after his party won 19 percent of the vote in 1992, while the two major parties received $61.8 million each.[74]

- **Hard money** refers to the funds given *directly* to candidates by individuals, political action committees (PACs), the political parties, and the government. The spending of hard money is under the control of the candidates, but its collection is governed by the rules of the Federal Election Campaign Act (FECA) of 1972,

hard money campaign funds donated directly to candidates; amounts are limited by federal election laws

1974, and its various amendments. This act established the FEC and was intended to stop the flow of money from, and the influence of, large contributors by outlawing contributions by corporations and unions, and by restricting contributions from individuals. The campaign finance reform bill passed in 2002 actually raised the hard money limits. Under that law, individuals can give a federal candidate up to $2,000 per election and can give a total of $95,000 to all federal candidates and parties in a two-year election cycle. The limit on the parties' hard money contributions to candidates was held to be unconstitutional in a 1999 Colorado district federal court decision, but was later upheld in a five-to-four Supreme Court decision.[75]

soft money unregulated campaign contributions by individuals, groups, or parties that promote general election activities but do not directly support individual candidates

issue advocacy ads advertisements paid for by soft money, and thus not regulated, that promote certain issue positions but do not endorse specific candidates

- **Soft money** is unregulated money collected by parties and interest groups in unlimited amounts to spend on party-building activities, get-out-the-vote drives, voter education, or issue position advocacy. Prior to the passage of campaign finance reform in 2002, as long as the money was not spent to tell people how to vote or coordinated with a specific candidate's campaign, the FEC could not regulate soft money. This allowed corporate groups, unions, and political parties to raise unlimited funds often used for television and radio advertising, especially in the form of issue advocacy ads. As we discussed in Chapter 13, **issue advocacy ads** are television or radio commercials run during an election campaign that promote a particular issue, usually by attacking the character, views, or position of the candidate the group running the ad wishes to defeat. The courts have considered these ads protected free speech and have held that individuals and organizations could not be stopped from spending money to express their opinions about issues, or even candidates, so long as they did not explicitly tell viewers how to vote.

Most observers thought that BCRA would remove unregulated money from campaigns and curb negative advertising. While it limited the spending of PACs and parties, new groups, called 527 groups after the loophole (section 527) in the Internal Revenue Code that allows them to avoid the regulations imposed by BCRA, have sprung up in their stead (see Chapter 13). Like groups that raised and spent soft money prior to BCRA, 527s may raise unlimited funds for issue advocacy or voter mobilization so long as they do not openly promote any candidate or openly try to defeat any particular candidate. BCRA does forbid all groups, even 527s, from running such ads funded by soft money within 60 days of a general election, or 30 days of a primary election.

In the 2004 election, liberal 527 groups like America Coming Together and MoveOn.org, and conservative 527 groups like the Club for Growth and Swift Boat Veterans for Truth, spent enormous amounts of money negatively targeting presidential and congressional candidates.

get-out-the-vote (GOTV) drives efforts by political parties, interest groups, and the candidate's staff to maximize voter turnout among supporters

Getting Out the Vote **Get-out-the-vote (GOTV) drives** refer to the voter mobilization efforts we discussed earlier in this chapter, an increasingly important part of any presidential campaign. As we noted, in the 1980s and 1990s, such efforts concentrated mostly on television advertising. The expense of these "air wars" meant that parties and campaigns worried less about knocking on doors and the shoe-leather efforts associated with a campaign's "ground war." Parties mistakenly associated GOTV with "get on television" rather than its traditional meaning of "get-out-the-vote."[76] In the 1998 and 2000 elections, however, Democrats and unions concentrated more effort and money on voter mobilization and it paid off. Republicans, chalking up their loss of the 2000 presidential popular vote to a lack of mobilization, retooled and followed suit in 2002 and 2004.[77]

Parties have not decreased their television advertising, but they have found that increasing their volunteer corps on the ground, in conjunction with the efforts of sympathetic interest groups (unions and liberal groups for Democrats, Christian conservative groups for Republicans) is a successful strategy for mobilizing voters. In an analysis of the 2002 midterm elections, Republicans found that they could turn out 2 to 3 percent more of their voters by having precinct chairs knock on doors than by using advertising and phone calling alone.[78] Both parties conducted impressive ground wars in 2004. In Ohio alone, one liberal group claimed to have knocked on 3.7 million Ohioans' doors and the Republican Party claimed it had over 78,000 volunteers.[79]

What is particularly interesting about these grassroots efforts is that they are not just a return to a by-gone era. Rather, mobilization efforts combine old-school door-to-door campaigning with modern technology.[80] Vast computer databases tell volunteers whose doors to knock on, and these volunteers often have hand-held personal electronic devices that have detailed information on each voter.[81] This allows parties and groups to target swing voters and their base voters. Campaigns and interest groups also flood supporters' email in-boxes and tie up the phone lines. Seventy-six percent of voters in battleground states reported that they had been contacted and urged to vote a particular way.[82] In their zeal to seek out all possible voters, parties have reached out to poorer voters in both urban and rural areas who have not received either party's attention in recent decades.[83]

INTERPRETING ELECTIONS

After the election is over, when the votes are counted, and we know who won, it would seem that the whole election season is finally finished. In reality, the outcomes of our collective decisions cry for interpretation. Probably the most important interpretation is the one articulated by the victor. The winning candidate in presidential elections inevitably claims an **electoral mandate**, maintaining that the people want the president to do the things he campaigned on. Thus the winner casts the election as a preference for his leadership and his policies. Presidents who can sell the interpretation that their election to office is a ringing endorsement of their policies can work with Congress from a favored position. To the extent that the president is able to sell his interpretation, he will be more successful in governing. In contrast, the losing party will try to argue that its loss was due to the characteristics of its candidate or specific campaign mistakes. Party members will, predictably, resist the interpretation that the voters rejected their message and their vision for the nation. The parties interpreted the 2004 election as we might expect. Republicans claimed that by receiving more votes than any candidate ever, winning a majority of the popular vote, and picking up seats in Congress, Bush had a mandate to pursue his foreign policy vision, reform Social Security, and appoint conservative federal judges. Democrats countered that Kerry had also received more votes than any previous candidate, and that because Bush's reelection was the smallest margin of any recently reelected president, no mandate existed.

electoral mandate the perception that an election victory signals broad support for the winner's proposed policies

The media also offer their interpretations. In fact, research shows that of the many possible explanations that are available, the media quickly—in just a matter of weeks—hone in on an agreed-upon standard explanation of the election.[84] Thus in 1992, Bill Clinton was said to have won because of George H. W. Bush's ineffectual dealing with the recession, while the 1996 election was interpreted in terms of Clinton's superior appeal to "soccer moms" and his challenger Bob Dole's inability to expand effectively from his conservative base. In 2000 the media, in explaining the closeness of the race, focused on how much more likable voters found George W. Bush, despite the majority's agreement with Al Gore on the issues, and on what they claimed to be Gore's badly run campaign. In 2004 the media quickly decided that though the nation was closely divided, moral-values voters in red states put Bush over the top. All of these explanations offer parts of the truth, but they do not give us a complete understanding of the complex decisions made by the American electorate.

WHO, WHAT, HOW In the matter of presidential elections, the parties, their elites, party activists, and the candidates all have something vital at stake. The traditional party leaders fared best under the old rules and closed-door decision making that yielded seasoned and electable politicians as the parties' nominees. Activists, with a broader agenda than simply winning power, seek control of the platform and the nomination, and may well have other goals than electability in mind. The primary system allows them to reap the fruits of the considerable time and resources they are willing to invest in politics.

Candidates seeking the nomination must answer to both the traditional party leaders and the activist members. This often puts them in a difficult position. Once nominated and pursuing a national bipartisan victory, the candidate needs to hold on to party supporters while drawing in those not already committed to the other side. Here the candidate makes use of the rules of the electoral college, professional staff, strategic issue positions, the media, fundraising, and voter mobilization.

THE CITIZENS AND ELECTIONS

At the beginning of this chapter we acknowledged that the American citizen does not look like the ideal citizen of classical democratic theory. Nothing we have learned in this chapter has convinced us otherwise, but that does not mean that Americans are doomed to an undemocratic future. In the first chapter of this book we considered three models of citizen activity in democracies, which we revisit here.

The first model we discussed is the elite model, which argues that as citizens we can do no more (or are fitted to do no more) than choose the elites who govern us, making a rather passive choice from among remote leaders. The second model of democratic politics, the pluralist model, sees us as participating in political life primarily through our affiliation with different types of groups. Finally, the participatory model of democracy is perhaps more prescriptive than the other two models, which it rejects because it believes that it is unsatisfactory for the majority of the citizenry to play a largely passive role in the political system. This model holds that we grow and develop as citizens through being politically active. In fact, rather than fitting any of these models exclusively, the American citizen's role in elections seems to borrow elements from all three models in a way that might be called a fourth model. As we shall see, American citizens, though they do not meet the ideals of democratic theory, do make a difference in American politics through the mechanism of elections.

A FOURTH MODEL?

The early studies of voting that used survey research found that most citizens had surprisingly low levels of interest in presidential election campaigns. These studies of the 1944 and 1948 presidential elections found that most citizens had their minds made up before the campaigns began and that opinions changed only slightly in response to the efforts of the parties and candidates. Instead of people relying on new information coming from the campaigns, people voted according to the groups they belonged to. That is, income, occupation, religion, and similar factors structured who people talked to, what they learned, and how they voted.

The authors of these studies concluded that democracy is probably safer without a single type of citizen who matches the civics ideal of high levels of participation, knowledge, and commitment.[85] In this view, such high levels of involvement would indicate a citizenry fraught with conflict. Intense participation comes with intense commitment and strongly held positions, which make for an unwillingness to compromise. This revision of the call for classic "good citizens" holds that our democratic polity is actually better off when it has lots of different types of citizens: some who care deeply, are highly informed, and participate intensely; many more who care moderately, are a bit informed, and participate as much out of duty to the process as commitment to one party or candidate; and some who are less aware of politics until some great issue or controversy awakens their political slumber.

The virtue of modern democracy in this *political specialization view* is that citizens play different roles and that together these roles combine to form an electoral system that has the attributes we prefer: it is reasonably stable; it responds to changes of issues and candidates, but not too much; and the electorate as a whole cares but not so intensely that any significant portion of the citizenry will challenge the results of an election. Its most obvious flaw is that it is biased against the interests of those who are least likely to be the activist or pluralist citizens—the young, the poor, the uneducated, and minorities.

DO ELECTIONS MAKE A DIFFERENCE?

If we can argue that most Americans do take more than a passive role in elections and that, despite being less-than-ideal democratic citizens, most Americans are involved "enough," then we need to ask whether the elections they participate in make any difference. We would like to think that elections represent the voice of the people in charting the directions for government policy. Let us briefly discuss how well this goal is attained. At a minimal but nevertheless important level, elections in the United States do achieve electoral accountability. By this we mean only that by having to stand for reelection, our leaders are more or less constantly concerned with the consequences of what they do for their next election. The fact that citizens tend to vote retrospectively provides incumbent administrations with a lot of incentive to keep things running properly and certainly to avoid policies that citizens may hold against them. Thus we begin by noting that elections keep officeholders attentive to what they are doing.

We can also ask if elections make a difference in the sense that it matters who wins. The answer is yes. Today the parties stand on opposite sides of many issues, and given the chance, they will move national policy in the direction they believe in. Thus, in 1980 the election of Ronald Reagan ushered in conservative policies, especially his tax cuts and domestic spending reductions, that Jimmy Carter, whom Reagan defeated, would never have even put on the agenda. Looking at elections over time, scholars Erikson, MacKuen, and Stimson observe a direct relationship between national elections and the policies that government subsequently enacts. Electing Democrats results in more liberal policies; electing Republicans results in more conservative policies.[86] This same generalization can be seen in the politics of the American states, where we find that more liberal states enact more liberal policies and more conservative states enact more conservative policies. Policy liberalism, which is a composite measure of things like the tax structure, welfare benefits, educational spending, voting for the Equal Rights Amendment, and so forth, is higher as the states become more liberal.[87] There is much solid evidence that elections are indeed crucial in bringing about a degree of policy congruence between the electorate and what policymakers do.

Just because elections seem to work to bring policy into rough agreement with citizen preferences does not mean that all citizens know what they want and that candidates know this and respond. Some citizens do know what they want; others do not. Some candidates heed the wishes of constituents; others pay more attention to their own consciences or to the demands of ideological party activists and contributors. Averaged over all of these variables, however, we do find that policy follows elections. Citizens, even with the blunt instrument of the ballot, can and do change what government does.

WHAT'S AT STAKE REVISITED

When George W. Bush won the presidency in 2000 with the eleventh-hour intervention of the Supreme Court, much of the heat of the weeks following the election was forgotten. But the issues generated by the messy election of 2000 remain. Commentators and scholars suggested a number of things that might be at stake in a contested presidential election.

Many observers hinted direly, with vague references to "constitutional crisis," that the very Constitution is at stake. It is quite true, as we discussed in Chapter 1, that when governments are perceived as illegitimate, they lose their authority. Peaceful transitions of power require that people trust the system and accept the results of that system as legitimate. Although there were calls for a constitutional amendment, for lawsuits, for recounts, and even for new elections, these were all potential remedies *within* the constitutional framework. No one called for revolution, or for a military coup, or for any of the other radical remedies that would signal a constitutional crisis. In fact, the U.S. Constitution allows for different winners of the popular vote and the electoral college vote, and state laws contain provisions for close elections precisely because they do happen. The rarity of these circumstances coinciding shouldn't confuse us into thinking that they are necessarily unacceptable.

Still other observers suggested that what's at stake is whether a contested winner's presidency can be effective—that no one can lead who is believed to have "squeaked through" with a victory, or who may not have won a majority of the popular votes cast. As we have said, presidents need to convincingly claim a mandate to lead in order to gather popular and congressional support for their proposals. History suggests that strong leadership may be hard to achieve after a contested election. Previous presidents who have won the electoral college but lost the popular vote have found governing difficult and have lasted only one term. However, history has treated none of those presidents as it has treated George W. Bush. Within a year of his taking office, the nation was hit with the September 11 terrorist attacks and found itself at war. Bush's unusually high opinion polls meant that all bets were off in predicting the outcome of the 2004 election, and while in fact that election was quite close, he did win a second term.

We should also consider the issue of federalism here. The Constitution gives states the power to conduct elections. Appeals to federal courts to settle election disputes within states, particularly before state courts have been allowed to resolve the issues, seriously challenge the balance of power between nation and states. Similarly, appeals for a national ballot and a uniform system of voting would require a federal law to override the Constitution, and such a law would be challenged in the courts as unconstitutional. At the same time, the Fifteenth, Nineteenth, Twenty-fourth, and Twenty-sixth Amendments put limits on how states conduct elections and determine eligible voters, and the Fourteenth Amendment says that no state can deny its citizens the equal protection of the laws. Challenges to state election law on these grounds are constitutional.

Clearly at stake in contested elections like the one in 2000 is the future of the electoral college. Although, as we have seen, there have been many calls for reform of this institution over the years, the public may not become truly aware of the institution until faced with its potentially negative consequences: a divergence between the popular-vote winner and the electoral college winner. Sen. Hillary Rodham Clinton, for instance, lost no time after winning her own election in declaring that the electoral college should be abolished. Supporters of the institution pointed out what havoc would be visited on the nation in a close election *without* an electoral college. Instead of recounting the votes only in contested or close states, the entire national vote would likely have been contested. A recount on that scale would take months and would leave the nation in limbo for a far longer time than a recount in a few states. Furthermore, the electoral college goes to the heart of the federalism issue, giving states as well as citizens a role in electing the president. We should consider the benefits of that arrangement before we rush to dismantle it.

Thinking Outside the Box

- Are elections the best way to choose our leaders?
- Should there be penalties for those who don't vote?
- Is our democracy stronger if more Americans vote?

The fate of third parties, as we discussed in Chapter 12, if not actually at stake, was certainly questioned after an election like 2000's. People who voted for Ralph Nader were divided between those who were happy to have thrown the system into a tailspin and those who regretted contributing to the confusion. What does seem clear is that the old maxim that voting for a third party

continued

WHAT'S AT STAKE REVISITED *(continued)*

is just throwing a vote away has been proved to be untrue. No one can argue that Nader voters did not make a difference in 2000—although perhaps not the type of difference they had hoped to make.

A number of observers, both foreign and domestic, argue that America's standing in the world was at stake in the close election of 2000—that we who have been telling the world how to run a democratic government looked a bit like a fledgling third-world democracy ourselves, with people denied the right to vote and demonstrating in the streets. These fears may have been allayed by the high turnout and relatively controversy-free 2004 election results. Far from revealing a weakness in American democracy, the aftermath of this election shows that the system works as well as ever. Citizens express their views vocally, courts handle legal challenges, politicians negotiate compromises, and the Constitution provides a framework of stability, just as the founders intended.

Finally, we need to think about what is at stake for American political culture in light of the unusual election of 2000. We noted in Chapter 2 that the United States is more committed to procedural than to substantive values—that is, we are committed more to following the rules and trusting the outcome of those rules than to evaluating the outcome by independent criteria. Although to the rest of the world it may seem insane that a candidate preferred by a majority of voters could lose to a candidate who wins the electoral college, Americans have less difficulty accepting that outcome. Many Americans, however, did rebel at the notion, and this contested election shows the cracks in consensus on national political norms. Another aspect of our political culture that is at stake is our desire to believe that democracy is a neat and tidy form of governance. As we discussed in Chapter 7, on Congress, democracy is notoriously messy, something many Americans find objectionable. Contested elections put our distaste for partisanship and political disagreement on the line.

To Sum Up

KEY TERMS
republic.cqpress.com

closed primary (p. 607)
electoral mandate (p. 625)
front-loading (p. 608)
front-runner (p. 609)
get-out-the-vote (GOTV) drives (p. 624)
government matching funds (p. 621)
hard money (p. 623)
issue advocacy ad (p. 624)
issue ownership (p. 618)
momentum (p. 609)
Motor Voter Bill (p. 596)
negative advertising (p. 620)
open primary (p. 607)
oppo research (p. 614)
party caucus (p. 607)
position issues (p. 618)
presidential primary (p. 607)
prospective voting (p. 603)
retrospective voting (p. 603)
social connectedness (p. 599)
soft money (p. 624)
swing voters (p. 611)
valence issues (p. 618)
voter mobilization (p. 597)
wedge issue (p. 618)

Key terms, chapter summaries, practice quizzes, Internet links, and other study aids are available on the companion Web site at: republic.cqpress.com.

SUMMARY
republic.cqpress.com

- Elections represent the core of American democracy, serving several functions: selecting leaders, giving direction to policy, developing citizenship, informing the public, containing conflict, and stabilizing the political system.
- Voting enhances the quality of democratic life by legitimizing the outcomes of elections. However, American voter turnout levels are typically among the lowest in the world and may endanger American democracy. Factors such as age, income, education, and race affect whether a person is likely to vote.
- Candidates and the media often blur issue positions, and voters realistically cannot investigate policy proposals on their own. Therefore, voters make a decision by considering party identification and peer viewpoints, prominent issues, and campaign images.
- The "road to the White House" is long, expensive, and grueling. It begins with planning and early fundraising in the pre-primary phase and develops into more active campaigning during the primary phase, which ends with each party's choice of a candidate, announced at the party conventions. During the general election the major-party candidates are pitted against each other in a process that relies increasingly on the media and getting out the vote. Much of the battle at this stage is focused on attracting voters who have not yet made up their minds.
- The electoral college demonstrates well the founders' desire to insulate government from public whims. Citizens do not vote directly for president or vice president but rather for an elector who has already pledged to vote for that candidate. Except in Maine and Nebraska, the candidate with the majority of votes in a state wins all the electoral votes in that state.
- Although American citizens do not fit the mythical ideal of the democratic citizen, elections still seem to work in representing the voice of the people in terms of citizen policy preferences.

PRACTICE QUIZ
republic.cqpress.com

1. Which of the following groups of people are generally LEAST likely to vote?

a. 18–30 year-olds
b. Women
c. The wealthy
d. Those with advanced degrees
e. Whites

2. Which of the following is the single biggest factor accounting for how people decide to vote?

a. The issue positions of the candidates
b. A candidate's personal characteristics
c. Whether the candidate is an incumbent
d. The candidate's party affiliation
e. The candidate's experience

3. Scholars usually refer to a candidate gaining "momentum" during the

a. pre-primary season.
b. primary season.
c. national convention.
d. presidential debates.
e. general election.

4. A position issue is

a. an issue on which most voters and candidates share the same position.
b. a controversial issue that one party uses to split the voters in the other party.
c. the tendency of one party to be seen as more competent in a specific policy area.
d. an issue that is perceived to be unimportant by the electorate.
e. an issue on which the parties differ in their perspectives and proposed solutions.

5. Which of the following is NOT a key function of elections?

a. They provide legitimacy to the government.
b. They allow government to change policy direction or keep with current policy direction.
c. They allow disaffected citizens to remove all of their representatives at one time.
d. They educate the public.
e. They increase political efficacy.

SUGGESTED RESOURCES

republic.cqpress.com

Books

Anonymous (Joe Klein). 1996. *Primary Colors: A Novel of Politics.* New York: Random House. A "fictional" account of a southern governor running for president whose campaign is constantly plagued by scandal. Fun to read!

Campbell, Angus, Philip E. Converse, Warren E. Miller, and Donald E. Stokes. 1960. *The American Voter.* New York: Wiley. This classic in voting studies shows the importance of party identification in electoral behavior. These surveys developed into the National Election Studies, which continue to serve as the chief source of data for academic electoral research in the United States.

Conway, M. Margaret, Gertrude A. Steuernagel, and David W. Ahern. 2005. *Women and Political Participation: Cultural Change in the Political Arena,* 2d ed. Washington, D.C.: CQ Press. A succinct overview of the various ways in which women participate in politics.

Fiorina, Morris P. 1981. *Retrospective Voting in American National Elections.* New Haven: Yale University Press. In an intriguing analysis of voting behavior, Fiorina argues that citizens vote based on retrospective evaluations of the incumbent and, if the issues are clear, prospective evaluations of the candidates' positions.

Polsby, Nelson W., and Aaron Wildavsky. 2004. *Presidential Elections: Strategies and Structures of American Politics,* 11th ed. Lanham, Md.: Rowman & Littlefield. A great text on presidential elections.

Nelson, Michael, ed. 2005. *The Elections of 2004.* Washington, D.C.: CQ Press. A strong collection of chapters that analyze key aspects and dynamics of the 2004 presidential and congressional elections.

Rosenstone, Steven, and John Mark Hansen. 1993. *Mobilization, Participation, and Democracy in America.* New York: Macmillan. A well-written account of why some people participate in politics and others do not, with a special emphasis on the factors that have led to voter turnout decline.

Toobin, Jeffrey. 2001. *Too Close to Call: The Thirty-six Day Battle to Decide the 2000 Election.* New York: Random House. This in-depth, dramatic account of the 2000 election mess follows the activities of the Bush and Gore camps from election night through the U.S. Supreme Court's decision to stop the recount in Florida thirty-six days later.

Wattenberg, Martin P. 1991. *The Rise of Candidate-Centered Politics: Presidential Elections of the 1980s.* Cambridge: Harvard University Press. Wattenberg examines the weakened role of parties in presidential elections and argues that candidates now play a more central role in the campaigns.

Wolfinger, Raymond, and Steven Rosenstone. 1980. *Who Votes?* New Haven: Yale University Press. An empirical study of what types of people are likely to go to the polls.

Web Sites

AllPolitics. www.cnn.com/politics. A great source for up-to-the-minute analysis of current elections.

Center for Responsive Politics. www.opensecrets.org. This Web site keeps tabs on campaign finance, offering multiple ways to research contributions to candidates and the spending patterns in presidential elections.

Electoral College Home Page. www.archives.gov/federal_register/electoral_college. A fascinating compendium of information on the electoral college, including history, procedures, and presidential/vice presidential "box scores" for 1789 through 2004.

The Living Room Candidate: Presidential Campaign Commercials. livingroomcandidate.movingimage.us/index.php. This is an excellent site from which to view old and new presidential campaign commercials. The historical value of comparing past commercials to current commercials is especially useful.

Project Vote Smart. www.vote-smart.org. This useful site will answer just about any question you might have about current elections and candidates.

Movies

The Candidate. 1972. The son of a former California politician is persuaded by his party to challenge a popular incumbent senator. The candidate speaks his mind and surprises everyone in the polls.

Journeys With George. 2003. Comical Emmy-winning documentary of a reporter (and filmmaker) and the presidential candidate—George W. Bush—with whom she travels during the 2000 campaign.

The Perfect Candidate. 1996. A superb documentary on the 1994 Virginia Senate race between Oliver North and Charles Robb. The cameras take you on the campaign trail for a behind-the-scenes look at how campaigns are run.

The War Room. 1992. This excellent documentary puts you at the heart of Clinton's 1992 presidential campaign.

Journalists have a long tradition of risking their lives in search of truth, especially in times of war. Ernie Pyle (right), an acclaimed frontline reporter and "friend of the G.I." during World War II, was killed by a sniper's bullet in 1945. More than sixty years later, Danny Pearl became a casualty of the U.S. war on terrorism. Pearl (below) was kidnapped and murdered well behind the frontlines by would-be informants who claimed that he was an American spy; his effort to keep people informed was hampered by the rules of a new kind of war.

THE MEDIA

15

WHAT'S AT STAKE?

Once the stuff of danger, heroism, and romance, wartime reporting was the province of legendary figures like Edward R. Murrow, broadcasting from the rooftops of London during the Blitz, and Ernie Pyle, killed near the end of World War II by Japanese sniper fire—dedicated professionals risking their all on the frontlines to bring the story of war to the folks back home. Wartime reporting remains a highly dangerous activity—in 2004, the deadliest year for journalists in a decade, twenty-three of the fifty-six journalists who were killed worldwide died in Iraq.[1] Still, modern reporting technology and high-tech warfare have dramatically changed the terms of wartime news coverage. The most notable journalistic figure to emerge early in the war on terrorism was Daniel Pearl, a reporter for the *Wall Street Journal* killed not on the frontlines but well behind them, lured to a hostage's death by a treacherous story source.

In today's wartime reporting, the frontlines are often hard to determine, or too dangerous to get to, or off limits to journalists altogether, and access to information about the war is consequently tightly controlled, either because the information is denied, or because reporters are dependent on official reports. One *Washington Post* reporter, in pursuit of a story that American missiles had hit Afghan villagers rather than suspected terrorists, was stopped at gunpoint by U.S. soldiers who, he claims, told him, "If you go further, you would be shot."[2] In fact, one author argues that "journalists have been denied access to American troops in the field in Afghanistan to a greater degree than in any previous war involving U.S. military forces."[3]

When the Iraq war began in March 2003, American reporters were "embedded" in military units—gaining protection in exchange for restrictions on their access to information. When President Bush declared major combat in Iraq over in May of that year, the danger for reporters only got worse; as high-profile foreigners they have been abducted and killed in increasing numbers by insurgents. Traveling only rarely in pursuit of a story, American journalists become more reliant on military reports and hired Iraqi reporters. Independent, objective reporting becomes almost impossible under such circumstances.

Wartime reporters are hindered in our modern wars not only by danger and limited government access but also by intense pressure from some groups not to be critical of the government's war effort or, indeed, of the government at all because these groups view such criticism as unpatriotic. The Media Research Center, for instance, a conservative media watchdog, issued a report that documented the amount of time the different major networks spent covering civilian deaths in Afghanistan, with the clear implication that such coverage ran counter to American interests. When Fox News correspondent Brit Hume, citing the findings, reported that ABC had devoted the most airtime to civilian casualties, he also mentioned that ABC had forbidden its anchors to wear flag lapel pins in an effort to appear more objective in their nightly broadcasts. The unspoken subtext was that objectivity spelled un-Americanism. The Media Research Center made its purpose clear: "We are training our guns on any media outlet or reporter interfering with America's war on terrorism or trying to undermine the authority of President Bush." While the network reporters try to ignore such partisan criticism, one news editor at ABC said, "I suppose in a subtle way it's in the back of your mind."[4]

The motive for such censorship of course is understandable; we all want to support our country during times of threat. It is a challenge, however, to provide that support while ensuring that citizens have the information about the conduct and costs of war that they need to keep the democratic process working well, especially when that information opens the nation's leaders to criticism. Even coverage of the coffins of America's war dead returning home has been banned by the Pentagon since 1991. The Pentagon claims that the pictures were restricted for privacy reasons, but critics argued that it was really to keep Americans from graphically seeing the consequences of the war. When photos of the flag-draped coffins of American soldiers were obtained by an advocate of press freedom under the Freedom of Information Act in April 2004 and posted on the Web, the Pentagon moved to withhold further release of the photos. It was not until April 2005 that all the pictures of the soldiers' coffins were quietly released.

As we will see in this chapter, the American media are constrained in the best of times by their own professional imperatives, by enormous corporate pressures to turn a profit, and by the skilled manipulation of politicians who seek to control the media through which their message is carried. In wartime, however, more pressures are piled on—official pressure to protect the security of the troops on the battlefield and the vulnerable population back home, and ideological pressure to report the "home team" in a favorable, patriotic light. At the same time that the media face these additional constraints on doing the job of informing the citizenry and checking the government, the stakes are higher than they have ever been. After we examine the purpose and power of the media in this country, we return to the question of what is at stake in open, free, and critical wartime reporting. *

It's hard to imagine today, but most of those who voted for George Washington for president, or for Abraham Lincoln, never heard the voice of the candidate they chose. While photographs of Lincoln were available, only portraits, sketches, or cartoons of Washington could reach voters. And while Franklin Roosevelt's voice reached millions in his radio "fireside chats," and his face was widely familiar to Americans from newspaper and magazine photographs, his video image was restricted to newsreels that had to be viewed in the movie theater. Not until the advent of television in the mid–twentieth century were presidents, congressmen, and senators beamed into the living rooms of Americans, and their smiling, moving images made a part of the modern culture of American politics.

Today we cannot conceive of politics without the accompanying brouhaha of the electronic media. Campaign commercials, State of the Union messages, nightly sound bites, talk shows, and endless commentary help shape our political perceptions. C-SPAN even allows us to watch politics on television around the clock. Indeed, the advent of television has shaped American politics in distinctive ways. But that fact should not obscure the truth that modern democracy itself would not be possible without some form of mass communication. Nor should the speed with which technology cranks out new ways of communicating overshadow the fact that, in terms of making democracy possible, the most marvelous technological development of all may have been the printing press, which for the first time made communication affordable on a broad scale.

Democracy demands that citizens be informed about their government, that they be able to criticize it, deliberate about it, change it if it doesn't do their will. Information, in a very real sense, is power. Information must be available, and it must be widely disseminated. This was fairly easy to accomplish in the direct democracy of ancient Athens, where the small number of citizens were able to meet together and debate the political issues of the day. Because their democracy was direct and they were, in effect, the government, there was no need for anything to mediate *between* them and government, to keep them informed, to publicize candidates for office, to identify issues, and to act as a watchdog for their democracy.

But today our democratic political community is harder to achieve. We don't know many of our fellow citizens, we cannot directly discover the issues ourselves, and we have no idea what actions our government takes to deal with issues unless the media tell us. The mass media create a political community, connecting us to our government, and creating the only real space we have for public deliberation of issues. Increasing technological developments make possible ever-newer forms of political community. Ross Perot, third-party presidential candidate in 1992 and 1996, talked of the day when we would all vote electronically on individual issues from our home computers. If we have not yet arrived at that day of direct democratic decision making, we can certainly meet like-minded citizens and share our political views on the Internet, which is revolutionizing the possibilities of democracy, much as the printing press and television both did earlier, bringing us closer to the Athenian ideal of political community in cyberspace, if not in real space.

In this chapter you will learn about this powerful entity called the media by focusing on

- the sources of our news
- the historical development of the ownership of the American media and its implications for the political news we get

- the role of journalists themselves—who they are and what they believe
- the link between the media and politics
- the relationship of citizens to the media

WHERE DO WE GET OUR NEWS?

mass media means of conveying information to large public audiences cheaply and efficiently

Media is the plural of *medium,* meaning in this case an agency through which communication between two different entities can take place. Just as a medium can be a person who claims to transmit messages from the spiritual world to earth-bound souls, today's **mass media**, whether through printed word or electronic signal, convey information from the upper reaches of the political world to everyday citizens cheaply and efficiently. And what is just as important in a democratic society, the media help carry information back from citizens to the politicians who lead, or seek to lead, them.

The news media in the twenty-first century increasingly rely on new technology. The printing press may have been invented over a thousand years ago (in China), but almost all of the truly amazing innovations in information technology—telegraphs, telephones, photography, radio, television, computers, faxes, and the Internet—have been developed in the past two hundred years, and most of them have come into common use only in the past fifty. What that means is that our technological capabilities sometimes outrun our sophistication about how that technology ought to be used or how it may affect the news it transfers.

Understanding who gets information, where it comes from, and how that information is affected by the technol-

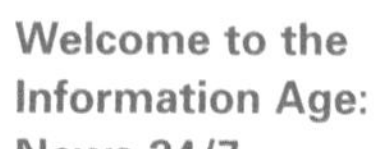

Welcome to the Information Age: News 24/7

In 1968 President Lyndon Johnson was able to watch all of the national news (in this case, a rocket launch) with three television sets tuned to the three networks, ABC, CBS, and NBC. Today, twenty-four-hour news programming comes from many more sources—including the Internet—providing information around the clock.

ogy that brings it to us is crucial to being a knowledgeable student of politics, not to mention an effective democratic citizen. In this section we examine the sources that we in America turn to for the news and the consequences that follow from our choices.

WHO GETS WHAT NEWS FROM WHERE?

Americans are increasingly indifferent to news about the world around them. Although this figure changed dramatically, if temporarily, with the terrorist attacks on the United States in September 2001, in 2000 only 45 percent of Americans said they enjoyed keeping up with the news a great deal, and only 48 percent said they followed it closely. Young people were less likely than older Americans to feel this way: fewer than a third of those aged eighteen to twenty-nine enjoyed the news, compared to nearly two-thirds of those aged fifty and over. The disenchantment of Americans, especially young Americans, with the news grew throughout the 1990s.[5]

Americans' exposure to the events of the world is reflected in this 2004 snapshot: When asked about where they get their news, 51 percent of Americans said they watch local television news every day; only 39 percent watch cable news channels, and 36 percent watch the network news shows that cover national and international events. Forty-four percent said they read a local paper daily, 7 percent read a national newspaper such as the *New York Times*, and 20 percent read their news on-line.[6] Like their elders, about 20 percent of young people get their news from the Internet; despite the assumption that they are more technologically advanced, they too are more likely to watch the local news or read the paper. In 2004, 21 percent of young people said that they regularly learned something about the presidential election campaign from late-night comedy shows like *Saturday Night Live* and *The Daily Show With Jon Stewart*.[7]

Despite the fact that most of the American public is exposed to some news, and some people are exposed to quite a lot of it, levels of political information in this country are not high. In one study, an average of only 43 percent of the public answered questions about news events and public figures correctly.[8] These politically informed people are not evenly distributed throughout the population either. Young people were less likely than older Americans to answer the questions correctly, and men were more likely than women to get the correct answers to questions dealing with domestic policy, public figures, and international news. This reflects the fact that women say they pay more attention to news about disasters, court rulings, crime, and celebrity scandal, whereas men focus on the military, international politics, the economy, and sports.

NEWSPAPERS AND MAGAZINES

American newspaper readership is currently at a historical low (see Figure 15.1), and as Figure 15.2 shows, it is also lower than in most other industrialized nations.[9] Today only about a dozen cities have more than one daily paper. But several major newspapers—the *Wall Street Journal, USA Today,* the *New York Times,* the *Christian Science Monitor,* the *Washington Post,* and the *Los Angeles Times*—have achieved what amounts to national circulation, providing even residents of single-daily cities with an alternative. Those major papers gather their own news, and some smaller papers that cannot afford to station correspondents around the world can subscribe to their news

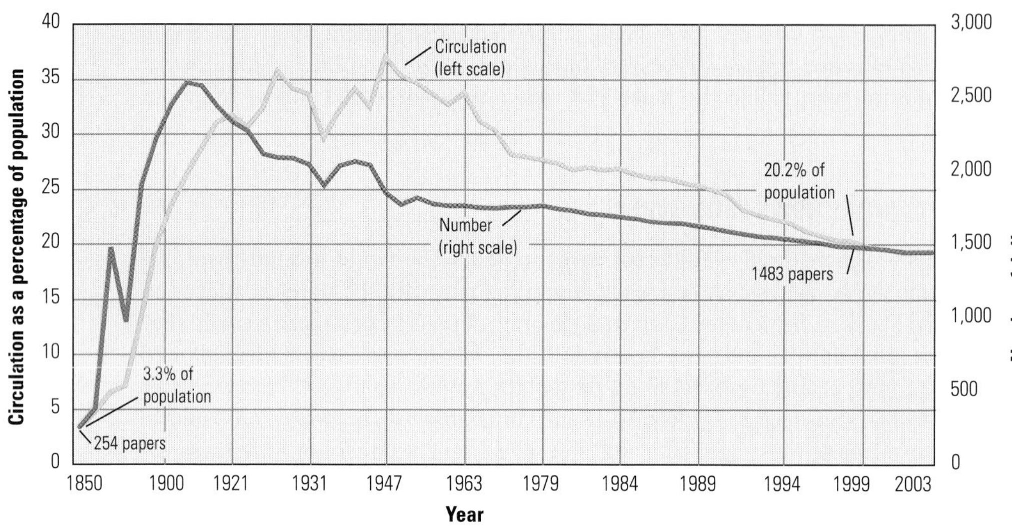

FIGURE 15.1

Newspaper Circulation as a Percentage and Number of Newspapers, 1850–2004

Source: Harold W. Stanley and Richard G. Niemi, *Vital Statistics on American Politics, 2005–2006* (Washington, D.C.: CQ Press, 2005), 174–175.

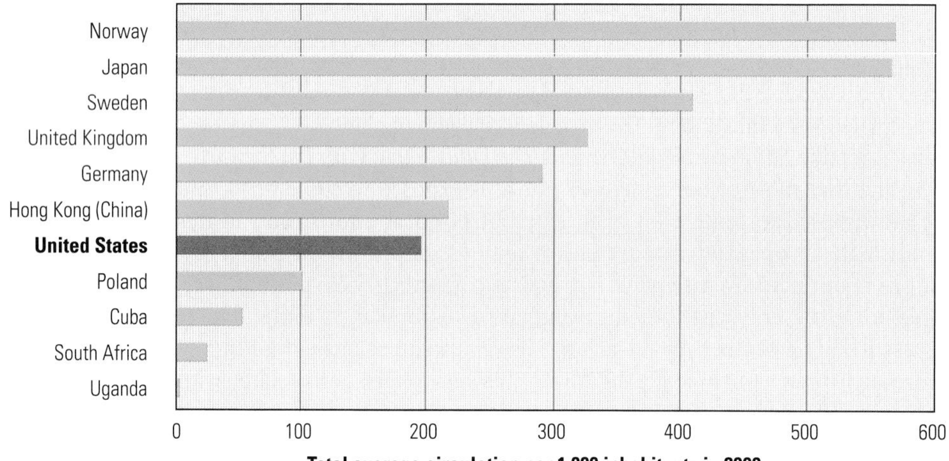

FIGURE 15.2

U.S. Newspaper Circulation Compared to Other Countries

Source: Harold W. Stanley and Richard G. Niemi, *Vital Statistics on American Politics, 2005–2006* (Washington, D.C.: CQ Press, 2005), 174–175.

services. Practically speaking, this means that most of the news that Americans read on a daily basis comes from very few sources: these outlets or wire services like the Associated Press (AP) or Reuters.

Newspapers cover political news, of course, but many other subjects also compete with advertising for space in a newspaper's pages. Business, sports, entertainment (movies and television), religion, weather, book reviews, comics, crossword puzzles, advice columns, classified ads, and travel information are just some of the kinds of content that most newspapers provide in an effort to woo readers. Generally the front section and especially the front page are reserved for major current events, but these need not be political in nature. Business deals, sporting events, and even sensational and unusual weather conditions can push politics farther back in the paper.

Magazines can often be more specialized than newspapers. While the standard weekly news magazines (*Newsweek, Time,* and *U.S. News and World Report*) carry the same eclectic mix of subjects as major newspapers, they can also offer more comprehensive news coverage because they do not need to meet daily deadlines, giving them more time to develop a story. These popular news magazines tend to be middle of the road in their ideological outlook. Other magazines appeal specifically to liberal readers—for instance, the *American Prospect* and *Nation*—and to conservatives—for instance, the *National Review* and the *American Spectator.*

RADIO

The decline in the number of newspapers that began in the early 1900s was probably due in part to the emergence of radio. Although radios were expensive at first, one in six American families owned one by 1926,[10] and the radio had become a central part of American life. Not only was radio news more up-to-the-minute, it was also more personal. Listeners were able to hear a session of Congress for the first time in 1923 and a presidential inauguration in 1925.[11] Disasters such as the 1937 crash of the airship *Hindenberg* were brought into Americans' homes with an immediacy that newspapers could not achieve. Franklin Roosevelt used his "fireside chats" to sell his New Deal policies directly to the public, without having to go through the reporters he viewed as hostile to his ideas.[12]

Today, 99 percent of American households own at least one radio,[13] and more than 11,000 radio stations offer entertainment and news shows through commercial networks and their local affiliates. There are also two noncommercial networks, National Public Radio and Public Radio International, funded in small part by the U.S. government but also by private donations from corporations and individuals. Since the 1980s the radio call-in talk show has grown in popularity, allowing the radio hosts and their guests, as well as the audience, to air their opinions on politics and creating a sense of political community among their primarily conservative listeners.

Fighting Fire with Fire
While many of us go to the radio for music or the news, political talk shows have proven to be popular and effective. Conservatives, led by Rush Limbaugh, have dominated the talk show airwaves, but in 2004 comedian Al Franken started the liberal talk program *Air America* to provide a left-of-center answer in this medium. Taking aim at the popular right wing talk radio star, Franken also wrote a book, *Rush Limbaugh is a Big Fat Idiot.*

TELEVISION

The impact of radio on the American public, however dramatic initially, cannot compare with the effects of television. American ownership of television sets skyrocketed from 9 percent of households in 1950 to 98 percent in 1975, a statistic that continues to hold firm. In fact, 40 percent of American households today own three or more television sets, and two-thirds receive cable transmission. When television was introduced, it grew into a national medium almost immediately thanks to the previously established radio networks.

Politicians were quick to realize that, like radio, television allowed them to reach a broad audience without having to deal with print reporters and their adversarial questions. The Kennedy administration was the first to make real use of television, a medium that might have been made for the young telegenic president. And it was television that brought the nation together in a community of grief when Kennedy was assassinated.

Television carried the Vietnam War (along with its protesters) and the civil rights movement into Americans' homes, and the images that it created helped build popular support to end the war abroad and segregation at home. Television can create global as well as national communities, an experience many Americans shared as they sat captive before their television sets in the days following the terrorist attacks on New York and Washington, D.C., in 2001.

Americans turn their televisions on for an average of seven hours a day.[14] Given that most Americans spend six to eight hours a day at school or at work, this is an astounding figure, accounting for much of America's leisure time. Television is primarily an entertainment medium; news has always been a secondary function. While the earliest news offerings consisted simply of "talking heads" (reporters reading their news reports), many newscasts now fall into the category of "infotainment," news shows dressed up with drama and emotion to entice viewers to tune in. Once given a choice of only three networks, in 2003 the typical American home received one hundred television channels.[15] Rather than pursuing broad markets, stations are now often focusing on specific audiences such as people interested in health and fitness, sports, or travel. This practice of targeting a small, specialized broadcast market is called **narrowcasting**.[16] The competition for viewers is fierce, and as we will see, the quality of the news available can suffer as a consequence.

narrowcasting the targeting of specialized audiences by the media

There are many television shows whose primary subject is politics. Many cable stations and C-SPAN, sometimes called "America's Town Hall," offer news around the clock, although not all the news concerns politics. Weekend shows like *Meet the Press* highlight the week's coverage of politics, and shows like *The Capital Gang* showcase debates between liberals and conservatives on current issues. Some stations, such as the music channel MTV, direct their political shows to a specific age group (here, young people), and others, like *America's Voice,* to those holding particular ideologies (conservatism, in this case).

Like radio, television has its call-in talk shows, the most prominent being CNN's *Larry King Live.* And politics is often the subject of the jokes on such shows as *Late Show With David Letterman,* Jay Leno's *Tonight Show, Saturday Night Live,* and *The Daily Show With Jon Stewart.* Sometimes the line between fun and fact gets blurred, as when in 2003 Democratic senator John Edwards announced his candidacy for the presidency on Stewart's show, prompting Stewart to say, "I guess I should probably tell you now that we're a fake show. So, I want you to know that this may not count." In both 2000 and 2004 the major presidential candidates and their wives regularly sat down to chat with Larry King, Leno, Letterman, and even Oprah Winfrey.

THE INTERNET

The most recent new medium to revolutionize the way we get political news is the Internet, or the Web (for World Wide Web), which connects home or business computers to a global network of sites that provide printed, audio, and visual information on any topic you can imagine. In 2004, some 63 percent of Americans aged eighteen and older accessed the Web at least occasionally, and a whopping 81 percent of those aged twelve to seventeen went on-line. On an average day that year, 70 million adults logged on to the Internet, an increase of 37 percent from 2000.[17] It is not too much to say that the Internet is revolutionizing the way we get information.

The mainstream media take advantage of the Web but mostly to replicate or supplement the information that they publish through traditional means. All the major newspapers and the AP have Web sites, usually free, where all or most of the news in their print versions can be found. (Visit republic.cqpress.com and choose Chapter 15 for links to major news sites.) Many magazines and journals are also available on-line. By searching for the topics we want and connecting to links with related sites, we can customize our Web news. Politics buffs can bypass nonpolitical news, and vice versa. True politics junkies can go straight to the source: the federal government makes enormous amounts of information available at its www.whitehouse.gov and www.senate.gov sites.

In addition to traditional media outlets that provide on-line versions, there are myriad other Web sources of information. On-line magazines like *Slate, Salon,* and the *Drudge Report* exist solely on the Internet and may or may not adopt the conventions, practices, and standards of the more traditional media. Web logs, or **blogs**, have become increasingly popular as well. Blogs—on-line journals that can be set up by anyone with a computer and an Internet connection—can be personal, political, cultural, or anything in between; they run the gamut from individual diaries to investigative journalism. In fact, anyone can put up a blog or a Web page and distribute information on any topic. This makes the task of using the information on the Web challenging. It gives us access to more information than ever before, but the task of sorting and evaluating that information is solely our own responsibility (see *Consider the Source* in Chapter 5).

blogs Web logs, or on-line journals, that can cover any topic, including political analysis

Not only does the Web provide information, but it is also interactive to a degree that far surpasses talk radio or television. Many Web sites and blogs have chatrooms or discussion opportunities where all sorts of information can be shared, topics debated, and people met. Although this can allow the formation of communities based on specialized interests or similar views, it can also make it very easy for people with fringe or extreme views to find each other and organize.[18] And even though the Internet has the potential to increase the direct participation of citizens in political communities and political decisions, the fact that not all Americans have access to the Web means that multiple classes of citizenship could form.

WHO, WHAT, HOW From newspapers to radio, television, and, most recently, the Internet, Americans have moved eagerly to embrace the new forms of technology that entertain them and bring new ways of communicating information. But the deluge of political information requires consumers to sort through and critically analyze the news they get, often a costly exercise in terms of time, effort, and financial resources. Consequently, while the amount of political information available to Americans has increased dramatically, Americans do not seem to be particularly well informed about their political world.

Citizen Journalism

Andrew Sullivan argues that "blogs could well be a milestone in the long history of journalism. By empowering individual writers, by reducing the costs of entry into publishing to close to zero, the blog revolution has only begun to transform the media world." In his words:

"In October of 2000, I started my fledgling site, posting pieces I had written, and then writing my own blog, publishing small nuggets of opinion and observation at least twice a day about this, that and the other. I thought of it as a useful vanity site—and urged my friends and their friends to read it. But within a couple of weeks, something odd started happening. With only a few hundred readers, a few started writing back. They picked up on my interests, and sent me links, ideas, and materials to add to the blog. Before long, around half the material on my site was suggested by readers. Sometimes, these readers knew far more about any subject than I could. I remember trying to fathom some of the complexities of the Florida election nightmare when I got an email from a Florida politics professor explaining every detail imaginable. If I'd been simply reporting the story in the traditional way, I'd have never found this font of information. As it was, I found myself scooping major news outlets on arcane electoral details about chads and voting machines. Peer-to-peer journalism, I realized, had a huge advantage over old-style journalism. It could marshal the knowledge and resources of thousands, rather than the certitudes of the few.

"And as the blog developed into round-the-clock musing and reporting, its audience grew. I had no advertising or marketing budget to promote it—so I simply put it in my regular bylines, and went on television a lot to have the site's name—www.andrewsullivan.com—put prominently on the screen. My readers did the rest. Within six months, I was amazed to find I was pulling in close to 5,000 individual visits a day, from a couple of thousand separate people. From being a fixed piece of written journalism, the blog gradually developed into something much more like a 24-hour broadcast. When we got technical glitches (the 'we' refers to my web-partner and business adviser), it was less like a breakdown in a printing machine than a screw-up on television. We had to fix the problem—and fast. I also noticed, as many other bloggers do, that the site was beginning to take over my life. If I didn't post for a day or

WHO OWNS THE MEDIA, AND HOW DOES THAT AFFECT OUR NEWS?

The ownership structure of the American media has changed dramatically since the days of the nation's founding. The media have gone from dependence on government for their very existence to massive corporate ownership that seems to rival government for its sheer power and influence on the citizenry. In this section we look at the ways in which the ownership of those media has changed the kind of news we get.

THE EARLY AMERICAN PRESS: DEPENDENCE ON GOVERNMENT

In its earliest days, the press in America was dependent on government officials for its financial, and sometimes political, survival. Under those circumstances, the press could hardly perform either the watchdog function of checking up on government or the democratic function of empowering citizens. It served primarily to empower government or, during the Revolution, the patriots who had seized control of many of the colonial presses.

so, I'd get emails asking me if I were ill. This was getting to be a performance as much as a job.

"But there was instant gratification. With each month, the numbers grew. Unlike regular journalism, where you write a column in a newspaper or magazine, and the only feedback you really get is a few nice (or rough) comments from friends or outraged letters to the editor, each morning I would get up to a hundred emails about something I'd written just a few hours before—and a statistical report telling me how many people had dropped by in the previous 24 hours. All the familiar writer's anxiety about his work was overwhelmed by a sea of instant response. I added a letters page. Soon emails were flooding in responding to other emails. Again, the numbers rose till by last summer I was getting close to 8,000 visits a day.

"And then the war broke out. Suddenly, it felt as if this event were not just happening to me—but to all of the little community the weblog had pioneered. I started writing about my feelings, and readers responded with an intensity I've never felt in any other journalistic form. For a few months, the site was entirely about the war, a place where every possible argument about the conflict could be grappled with. People sent in poems, stories, first-person accounts, until the site became a clearing house for September 11 reflection. The blog almost seemed designed for this moment. In an instant, during the crisis, the market for serious news commentary soared. But people were not just hungry for news, I realized. They were hungry for communication, for checking their gut against someone they had come to know, for emotional support and psychological bonding. In this world, the very personal nature of blogs had far more resonance than more impersonal corporate media products. Readers were more skeptical of anonymous news organizations anyway, and preferred to supplement them with individual writers they knew and liked. The audience doubled literally over night. By last November, the site was getting over half a million visits a month."

Sullivan's conclusions on blogging?

"[I]t harnesses the web's real genius—its ability to empower anyone to do what only a few in the past could genuinely pull off. In that sense, blogging is the first journalistic model that actually harnesses rather than merely exploits the true democratic nature of the web. It's a new medium finally finding a unique voice. Stay tuned as that voice gets louder and louder."

Source: Andrew Sullivan, "A Blogger Manifesto: Why online Weblogs are one future for journalism," *The Sunday Times of London* (February 24, 2002). Copyright © 2002 Andrew Sullivan, reprinted with the permission of the Wylie Agency.

During colonial times, printers were required to obtain government approval and thus tended to avoid controversial political reporting so that they could stay in business. But the radical patriot movement was aggressive and violent in its methods of securing a supportive press. As public opinion swung toward independence, printers who favored British rule or aimed to treat both sides objectively were targeted with letters and criticism, and their print shops were raided, vandalized, and burned. Angry mobs burned the loyalist printers in effigy and frequently forced them to change their viewpoints or shut down their presses.

After the American Revolution, with independence firmly in hand, Americans celebrated their "freedom of the press," which they enshrined in the First Amendment to the Constitution. The debates over the Constitution itself took place in newspapers and pamphlets, producing works such as the *Federalist Papers.* Most revolutionaries concluded that without the press, independence could not have been won and that liberty could not survive. It is ironic that the victory they celebrated was founded on the vigorous suppression of their opponents' freedom of the press.

The press that grew up in the early American republic continued to be anything but free and independent. Because the newspaper business was still a risky financial proposition, it was an accepted practice for a politician or a party to set up a newspaper and support it financially—and expect it to support the appropriate political causes in return. Andrew Jackson, elected in 1828, carried the patronage of the press to new lengths. Like his predecessors, he offered friendly papers the opportunity to print government documents and denied it to his critics. But Jackson's administration heralded an age of mass democracy. Voter turnout doubled between 1824 and 1828.[19] People were reading newspapers in unheard of numbers, and those papers were catering to their new mass audiences with a blunter and less elite style than they had used in the past.

GROWING MEDIA INDEPENDENCE

The newspapers after Jackson's day were characterized by larger circulations, which drew more advertising and increased their financial independence. As newspapers sought to increase their readership, they began to offer more politically impartial news coverage in the hope that they would not alienate potential readers. This effort to be objective, which we see as a journalistic virtue today, came about at least partly as the result of the economic imperatives of selling newspapers to large numbers of people who do not share the same political views.

Prior to 1833, newspapers had been expensive; a year's subscription cost more than the average weekly wages of a skilled worker.[20] But in that year, the *New York Sun* began selling papers at only a penny a copy. Its subject matter was not an intellectual treatment of complex political and economic topics but rather more superficial political reporting of crime, human interest stories, humor, and advertising. As papers began to appeal to mass audiences rather than partisan supporters, they left behind their opinionated reporting and strove for more objective, "fairer" treatment of their subjects that would be less likely to alienate the readers and the advertisers on whom they depended for their livelihood. This isn't to say that newspaper editors stayed out of politics, but they were not seen as being in the pocket of one of the political parties, and the news they printed was seen as evenhanded. In 1848 the Associated Press was organized as a wire service to collect foreign news and distribute it to member papers in the United States. This underscored the need for objectivity in political reporting so that the news would be acceptable to a variety of papers.[21]

After the Civil War, the need for newspapers to appeal to a mass audience resulted in the practice of *yellow journalism,* the effort to lure readers with sensational reporting on topics like sex, crime, gossip, and human interest. With the success of such techniques, newspapers became big business in the United States. Newspaper giant Joseph Pulitzer's *World* was challenged by William Randolph Hearst's New York *Journal,* and the resulting battle for circulation drew the criticism that there were no depths to which journalists wouldn't sink in their quest for readers. The irony, of course, is that sensationalism did win new readers and allowed papers to achieve independence from parties and politicians, even as they were criticized for lowering the standards of journalism.

THE MEDIA TODAY: CONCENTRATED CORPORATE POWER

Today the media continue to be big business but on a scale undreamed of by such early entrepreneurs as Pulitzer and Hearst. No longer does a single figure dominate a paper's editorial policy; rather, all but one of the major circulation newspapers in this country (the *Christian Science Monitor*), as well as the national radio and television stations, are owned by major conglomerates. Often editorial decisions are matters of corporate policy, not individual judgment. And if profit was an overriding concern for the editor-entrepreneurs, it is gospel for the conglomerates. Interestingly, journalists freed themselves from the political masters who ruled them in the early years of this country, only to find themselves just as thoroughly dominated by the corporate bottom line.

Media Monopoly The modern media get five times as much of their revenue from advertising as from circulation. Logic dictates that the advertisers will want to spend their money where they can get the biggest bang for their buck: the papers with the most readers and the stations with the largest audiences. Because advertisers go after the most popular media outlets, competition is fierce, and outlets that cannot promise advertisers wide enough exposure fail to get the advertising dollars and go out of business. Competition drives out the weaker outlets, corporations seeking to maximize market share gobble up smaller outlets, and to retain viewers, they all stick to the formulas that are known to produce success. What this means for the media world today is that there are fewer and fewer outlets, they are owned by fewer and fewer corporations, and the content they offer is more and more the same.[22]

In fact, today, ten corporations, among them Time-Warner, Disney, Viacom, News Corporation Limited, and General Electric, own the major national newspapers, the leading news magazines, the national television networks including CNN and other cable stations, as well as publishing houses, movie studios, telephone companies, entertainment firms, and other multimedia operations. Most of these corporations are also involved in other businesses, as their familiar names attest. Figure 15.3 shows in detail the media empires that own the five major television networks. These giant corporations cross national lines, forming massive global media networks, controlled by a handful of corporate headquarters. Media critic Ben Bagdikian calls these media giants a "new communications cartel within the United States," with the "power to surround every man, woman, and child in the country with controlled images and words, to socialize each new generation of Americans, to alter the political agenda of the country."[23] What troubles him and other critics is that many Americans don't know that most of the news and entertainment comes from just a few corporate sources and are unaware of the consequences that this corporate ownership structure has for all of us.

Implications of Corporate Ownership for the News We Get What does the concentrated corporate ownership of the media mean to us as consumers of the news? We should be aware of at least four major consequences:

- There is a **commercial bias** in the media today toward what will increase advertiser revenue and audience share. People tune in to watch scandals and crime stories, so extensive coverage of nonnewsworthy events like the Scott Peterson murder trial and Michael Jackson's trial for child molestation appear relentlessly on the front pages of every newspaper in the country, not just the gossip-hungry tabloids but also the more sober *New York Times, Christian Science Monitor,* and *Wall Street Journal.* It may not be because an editor has decided that the American people need to know the latest developments, but because papers that don't reveal those developments may be passed over by consumers for those that do. Journalistic judgment and ethics are often at odds with the imperative to turn a profit.

commercial bias the tendency of the media to make coverage and programming decisions based on what will attract a large audience and maximize profits

- The effort to get and keep large audiences, and to make way for increased advertising, means a reduced emphasis on political news. This is especially true at the local level, which is precisely where the political events that most directly affect most cit-

THE WALT DISNEY COMPANY

Television

Stations
– 10 owned and operated stations

Networks
– **ABC Television Network,** ABC Family, The Disney Channel, Toon Disney, SoapNet, ESPN Inc. (80% - Hearst Corporation owns the remaining 20%) includes ESPN, ESPN2, ESPN News, ESPN Now, ESPN Extreme, Classic Sports Network, A&E Television (partial), The History Channel (partial), Lifetime Television (partial), Lifetime Movie Network (partial), E! Entertainment (with Comcast and Liberty Media), Disney Channel International (UK, Taiwan, Australia, Malaysia, France, Middle East, Italy, Spain), ESPN Inc. International Ventures, ESPN Brazil (50%), ESPN STAR (50% - sports programming throughout Asia), Net STAR (33% - The Sports Network of Canada)

Buena Vista Television
Touchstone Television
Walt Disney Television
Walt Disney Television Animation (has three wholly owned production facilities outside the United States - Japan, Australia, Canada)

Film

Walt Disney Pictures
Touchstone Pictures
Hollywood Pictures
Caravan Pictures
Miramax Films
Buena Vista Home Video
Buena Vista Home Entertainment
Buena Vista International

Theme Parks & Resorts

Over a dozen including:
Disneyland - Anaheim, CA
Walt Disney World - Orlando, FL
Disney - MGM Studios, Disneyland Paris, Tokyo Disneyland
Disney Cruise Line

Publishing

Books
– Hyperion (Miramax Books, ESPN Books, ABC Daytime Press, Hyperion Audiobooks, Hyperion East), Disney Publishing Worldwide (Cal Publishing Inc., CrossGen), Disney Global Children's Books

Magazines
– Automotive Industries, Biography (with GE and Hearst), Discover, Disney Adventures, Disney Magazine, ECN News, ESPN Magazine (distributed by Hearst), Family Fun, Institutional Investor, JCK, Kodin, Top Famille (French family magazine), US Weekly (50%), Video Business, Quality

Other

Sid R. Bass (partial interest - crude petroleum and natural gas production)
Walt Disney Theatrical Productions
Buena Vista Music Group
Hollywood Records (popular music and soundtracks for motion pictures)
Lyric Street Records (Nashville based country music label)
Mammoth Records (popular and alternative music label)
Walt Disney Records
Mighty Ducks of Anaheim (NHL)
Anaheim Sports, Inc.
TiVo (partial investment)

Online/Multimedia

ABC Internet Group, ABC.com, ABCNEWS.com, Oscar.com, Mr. Showbiz, Disney Online (Web sites and content), Family.com, ESPN Internet Group, Soccernet.com (60%), NBA.com, NASCAR.com, Skillgames, Disney Interactive, Wall of Sound, Go Network, Toysmart.com

Radio

64 radio stations
Radio Disney
ESPN Radio (syndicated programming)

NEWS CORPORATION

Radio

Fox Sports Radio Network
Sky Radio Denmark
Sky Radio Germany
Classic FM

Film

20th Century Fox
Fox Searchlight Pictures
Blue Sky Studios

Publishing

Newspapers
– New York Post
– United Kingdom - 6 papers
– Australia - 20 papers

Magazines
InsideOut, donna hay, SmartSource, The Weekly Standard, TV Guide (partial)

Books
HarperMorrow (Avon, HarperCollins, Quill, ReganBooks, William Morrow, Trophy)

Television

Stations
35 Fox Stations

Networks
– **Fox Television Network,** BskyB, Sky Italia, Fox News Channel, Fox Movie Channel, FX, FUEL, National Geographic Channel, SPEED Channel, Fox Sports Net, FSN New England (50%), FSN Ohio, FSN Florida, National Advertising Partners, Fox College Sports, Fox Soccer Channel,
– Stats, Inc.

DirecTV
Fox Television Studios

Other

Los Angeles Kings (NHL, 40% option) Los Angeles Lakers (NBA, 9.8% option)
Staples Center (40% owned by Fox/Liberty)
News Interactive
Broadsystem
Festival Records
Fox Interactive
Mushroom Records
National Rugby League
NDS
News Outdoor
Nursery World

FIGURE 15.3 **Who Owns the Network News?**

Source: Data from the Project for Media Ownership (www.promo.org) and from the *Columbia Journalism Review* (www.cjr.org/owners).

GENERAL ELECTRIC

NBC Universal (80%-owned by GE, 20% controlled by Vivendi Universal)

Television

Stations
- 14 NBC Stations
- 14 Telemundo Stations
- Paxson Communications (30%)

Networks
- **NBC Television Network,** CNBC, MSNBC, Bravo, Mun2TV, Sci-Fi, Trio, USA, ShopNBC, A&E Television (partial), The History Channel (partial)
- NBC Universal Television Studio
- NBC Universal Television Distribution

Film

Universal Pictures
Focus Features

Other

Commercial Finance - loans, operating leases, financing programs, commercial insurance

Consumer Finance - credit services to consumers, retailers and automotive dealers

Industrial - appliances, aircraft engines, lighting and industrial products; factory automation systems, plastics, silicones and quartz products, security and sensors technology, and equipment financing, management, and operating services

Infrastructure - energy, oil and gas, and water process technologies

Healthcare - financing, facility operation, power solutions, and new diagnostic imaging technology

Theme Parks/Resorts

Universal Parks & Resorts

TIME WARNER

Television

Networks
- The WB Television Network, HBO, **CNN,** CNN Headline News, CNN fn, Court TV (with Liberty Media), TBS Superstation, Turner Network Television (TNT), Turner South, Cartoon Network, Turner Classic Movies, The Warner Channel (Latin America, Asia - Pacific, Australia, Germ.)

Cable Systems
- Time Warner Cable
- Kablevision (53.75% - cable television in Hungary)

Warner Bros. Television (production)
Warner Bros. Television Animation
Hanna - Barbera Cartoons

Film

Warner Bros. Studios
Castle Rock Entertainment Telepictures Production
New Line Cinema
Fine Line Features
Turner Original Productions

Warner Bros. International Theaters (owns/operates multiplex theaters in over 12 countries)

Other

Atlanta Braves (MLB)
CNN Newsroom (daily news program for classrooms)
Turner Adventure Learning (electronic field trips for schools)
Turner Home Satellite
Turner Network Sales
AOL MovieFone

Publishing

Books
- Warner Books, Little, Brown and Company, Time Inc.

Magazines
- Over 75 magazines, including Time, Fortune, Sports Illustrated, Golf Magazine, Outdoor Life, Popular Science, Food & Wine, DC Comics

Online/Multimedia

CompuServe Interactive Services
AOL Instant Messenger
AOL.com portal
Digital City
AOL Europe
ICQ
MapQuest.com
Spinner.com
Winamp
Legend (49% - Internet service in China)
Netscape Netcenter portal
Amazon.com (partial)
Quack.com
Streetmail (partial)
iAmaze
Netscape Communications

Theme Parks /Resorts

Warner Brothers Recreation Enterprises (owns/operates international theme parks)

VIACOM

Television

Stations
- 17 CBS stations
- 18 UPN Stations
- 5 other

Networks
- **CBS Television Network,** UPN, MTV, MTV2, Nickelodeon, BET, Nick at Nite, TV Land, NOGGIN, VH1, Spike TV, CMT, Comedy Central, Showtime, The Movie Channel, Flix, Sundance Channel

Spelling Television
Big Ticket Television
King World Productions

Radio

Infinity Broadcasting (177 stations)
TDI Worldwide
Westwood One

Film

Paramount Pictures
Paramount Home Entertainment

Publishing

Simon & Schuster (Kaplan, Pocket Books, The Free Press, Touchstone, Fireside Group, Aladdin Paperbacks, MTV Books)

izens occur. More Americans watch local television news than watch national news, and yet one political scientist, drawing on his research of local news in North Carolina, has shown that local news shows spend an average of only six out of thirty minutes on political news, compared with hot topics like weather, sports, disasters, human interest stories, and "happy talk" among the newscasters.[24]

- The content of the news we get is lightened up and dramatized to keep audiences tuned in.[25] As in the days of yellow journalism, market forces encourage sensational coverage of the news. Television shows often capitalize on the human interest in dramatic reenactments of news events, with a form of journalism that has come to be called *infotainment* because of its efforts to make the delivery of information more attractive by dressing it up as entertainment. To compete with such shows, the mainstream network news broadcasts increase the drama of their coverage as well. Sensational newscasts focus our attention on scandalous or tragic events rather than the political news that democratic theory argues citizens need.
- The corporate ownership of today's media means that the media outlets frequently face conflicts of interest in deciding what news to cover or how to cover it. As one critic asks, how can NBC's anchor report critically on nuclear power without crossing the network's corporate parent, General Electric, or ABC give fair treatment to Disney's business practices?[26] The question is not hypothetical: after Disney acquired ABC, several ABC employees, including a news commentator, who had been critical of Disney in the past were fired.[27] In fact, 33 percent of newspaper editors in America said they would not feel free to publish news that might harm their parent company,[28] a statistic that should make us question what is being left out of the news we receive. A further conflict of interest arises in advertising matters. Note, as just one example, the media's slowness to pick up on stories critical of the tobacco industry, a major advertiser.[29]

Alternatives to the Corporate Media The corporate media monopoly affects the news we get in serious ways. Citizens have some alternative news options, but none is truly satisfactory as a remedy, and all require more work than switching on the television in the evening. One alternative is public radio and television. Americans tend to assume that media wholly owned or controlled by the government serve the interests of government rather than the citizens. This was certainly true in our early history and is true in totalitarian countries such as the former Soviet Union or today's China. But as we have seen, privately owned media are not necessarily free either.

And, in fact, government-controlled media are not necessarily repressive. Great Britain and other European countries have long supported a media system combining privately owned (and largely partisan) newspapers with publicly owned radio and television stations. Although such stations now find themselves competing with cable rivals, some, including the British Broadcasting Company (BBC), are renowned for their programming excellence. Sometimes, then, publicly owned media may be even "freer" than privately owned media if they allow producers to escape the commercial culture in which most media shows exist. The United States has public radio and television networks, but they are not subsidized by the government at sufficient levels to allow them complete commercial freedom. Rather, they are funded by a combination of government assistance and private or corporate donations. These donations sound very much like commercials when announced at the start and finish of programming and could arguably affect the content of the shows.

Another choice for citizens is the *alternative press.* Born of the counterculture and antiwar movement in the 1960s, these local weekly papers, like the (New York) *Village Voice* and the *SF* (San Francisco) *Weekly* were intended to offer a radical alternative to the mainstream media. Usually free and dependent on advertising, these papers have lost their radical edge and become so profitable that, in an ironic turn of events, they themselves are now getting bought up by chains like New Times, Inc.[30] Rejecting the alternative press as too conventional, there is now even an "alternative to the alternative press" aimed at a younger audience and coveted by advertisers. This Generation X–focused press is cynical and critical but not, in general, political, and so it does not offer a real alternative for political news.[31]

Nevertheless, an independent press does continue to thrive without the support of corporate owners. A few investigative magazines, like *Mother Jones* (published by the Foundation for National Progress) and *Consumer Reports* (published by Consumers Union) rely on funding from subscribers and members of their nonprofit parent organizations. However, unless they are completely free from advertising (as is *Consumer Reports*), even these independent publications are not entirely free from corporate influence. Other alternative newsletters and magazines, such as the liberal *Nation* or the conservative *National Review,* cover issues and policies often ignored by the mainstream press, but they do so from a perspective that supports their own political agendas.

A final alternative to the mainstream corporate media is the Internet. Certainly the Internet offers myriad sources for political news. But as we saw in *Consider the Source* in Chapter 5, it takes time and effort to figure out which of these sources are accurate and trustworthy, and in many cases the news options on the Web are dominated by the same corporate interests as are the rest of the media. The use of the Web is inexpensive to those who own a computer, but it may not be long before corporate America figures out a way to charge for access to individual media sites on the Web. On the other hand, the growing number of blogs presents news readers with a new and independent option for finding news on-line—one that allows them to go around the corporate barriers in their quest for news. Although in 2005 only 32 percent of Internet users said they were familiar with blogs, and only 12 percent read political blogs regularly, that is still a huge number of Americans who are logging on to get their political news from this alternative source.[32] The fact that these blog readers are disproportionately young suggests that America's news-reading habits may be changing dramatically, and that the Web may come closer to realizing its potential for offering a truly democratic, practical, and "free" alternative to the corporate-produced news we now receive.

REGULATION OF THE BROADCAST MEDIA

The media in America are almost entirely privately owned, but they do not operate without some public control. Although the principle of freedom of the press keeps the print media almost free of restriction (see Chapter 4), the broadcast media have been treated differently. In the early days of radio, great public enthusiasm for the new medium resulted in so many radio stations that signal interference threatened to damage the whole industry. Broadcasters asked the government to impose some order, which it did with the passage of the Federal Communications Act, creating the Federal Communications Commission (FCC), an independent regulatory agency, in 1934.

Because access to the airwaves was considered a scarce resource, the government acted to ensure that radio and television serve the public interest by representing a variety of viewpoints. Accordingly, the 1934 bill contained three provisions designed to ensure fairness in broadcasting:

- *The equal time rule.* The *equal time rule* means that if a station allows a candidate for office to buy or use airtime outside of regular news broadcasts, it must allow all candidates that opportunity. On its face, this provision seems to give the public a chance to hear from candidates of all ideologies and political parties, but in actuality, it often has the reverse effect. Confronted with the prospect of allowing every candidate to speak, no matter how slight the chance of his or her victory and how small an audience is likely to tune in, many stations instead opt to allow none to speak at all. This rule has been suspended for purposes of televising political debates. Minor-party candidates may be excluded and may appeal to the FCC if they think they have been unfairly left out.
- *The fairness doctrine.* The *fairness doctrine* extended beyond election broadcasts; it required that stations give free airtime to issues that concerned the public and to opposing sides when controversial issues were covered. Like the equal time rule, this had the effect of encouraging stations to avoid controversial topics. The FCC ended the rule in the 1980s, and when Congress tried to revive it in 1987, President Reagan vetoed the bill, claiming it led to "bland" programming.[33]
- *The right of rebuttal.* The *right of rebuttal* says that individuals whose reputations are damaged on the air have a right to respond. This rule is not strictly enforced by the FCC and the courts, however, for fear that it would quell controversial broadcasts, as the other two rules have done.

All of these rules remain somewhat controversial. Politicians would like to have them enforced because they help them to air their views publicly. Theoretically, the rules should benefit the public, though as we have seen, they often do not. Media owners see these rules as forcing them to air unpopular speakers who damage their ratings and as limiting their abilities to decide station policy. They argue that given all the cable and satellite outlets, access to broadcast time is no longer such a scarce resource and that the broadcast media should be subject to the same legal protections as the print media.

Many of the limitations on station ownership that the original act established were abolished with the 1996 Telecommunications Act, which now permits ownership of multiple stations as long as they do not reach more than 35 percent of the market. Nothing prevents the networks themselves from reaching a far larger market, though, through their collective affiliates. The 1996 legislation also opened up the way for ownership of cable stations by network owners, and it allows cable companies to offer many services previously supplied only by telephone companies. The overall effect of this deregulation is to increase the possibilities for media monopoly.

WHO, WHAT, HOW The ownership of the media has historically influenced whether the news is objective, and thus serves the public interest, or is slanted to serve a particular political or economic interest. Democratic theory and American political tradition tell us that democracy requires a free press to which all citizens have access. We have a free press in this country, and we also have a free market, and these two worlds produce clashing rules in which the press has largely been the loser to economic imperative.

WHO ARE THE JOURNALISTS?

Corporate ownership does not tell the whole story of modern journalism. Although the mass media are no longer owned primarily by individuals, individuals continue to be the eyes, ears, nose, and, in fact, legs of the business. Journalists are the people who discover, report, edit, and publish the news in newspapers and magazines and on the radio, television, and the Internet. To understand the powerful influence the media exert in American politics, we need to move beyond the ownership structure to the question of who American journalists are and how they do their job.

WHAT ROLES DO JOURNALISTS PLAY?

Journalism professors David Weaver and Cleveland Wilhoit have asked journalists about their perceptions of the roles they play in American society. Based partly on their work, we can distinguish four journalistic roles: the gatekeeper, the disseminator, the interpretive/investigator, and the public mobilizer.[34] Often these roles coexist in a single journalist.

- **Gatekeepers** decide, in large part, the details about what news gets covered (or not) and how. Not all journalists share this enormous power of gatekeeping equally. Managers of the wire services, which determine what news gets sent on to member papers, editors who decide what stories should be covered or what parts of a story should be cut, and even reporters who decide how to pitch a story are all gatekeepers, though to varying degrees.

gatekeepers journalists and media elite who determine which news stories are covered and which are not

- *Disseminators* confine their role to getting the facts of the story straight and moving the news out to the public quickly, avoiding stories with unverified content, and reaching as wide an audience as possible. The disseminator role is open to the criticism that in a complex society, simple dissemination does nothing to help citizens understand the news. In the words of veteran journalist Eric Sevareid, in merely reporting the facts, journalists "have given the lie the same prominence and impact the truth is given."[35]
- *Interpretive/investigators* developed their role in reaction to this criticism and to the growing sophistication of the issues confronting the American public. This role combines the functions of investigating government's claims, analyzing and interpreting complex problems, and discussing public policies in a timely way. Such interpretation is related to investigation, or the actual digging for information that is not readily apparent or available. Such a role is not new to journalism. The **muckrakers** of the early twentieth century exposed abuses of public and private power ranging from corporate monopolies, to municipal corruption, to atrocious conditions in meatpacking plants, to political dishonesty, and their work inspired a wide array of political reforms. Bob Woodward and Carl Bernstein, the two young reporters for the *Washington Post* who uncovered the Watergate scandal in the 1970s, brought the spirit of investigative journalism to the present day. The public legacy of muckraking is alive in journalism today as reporters uncover shameful migrant worker conditions, toxic waste dumps near residential areas, and corruption in local officials.

muckrakers investigative reporters who search for and expose misconduct in corporate activity or public officials

- *Public mobilizers* develop the cultural and intellectual interests of the public, set the political agenda, and let the people express their views. This role is closely aligned

civic journalism a movement among journalists to be responsive to citizen input in determining what news stories to cover

with a contemporary movement in the American media called public or civic journalism. **Civic journalism** is a movement among journalists to be responsive to citizen input in determining what news stories to cover. It is a reaction to the criticism that the media elite report on their own interests and holds that, instead, the media ought to be driven by the people and their interests. The movement is controversial in American journalism because while on its face it is responsive to the citizens, it is also seen as condescending to them, with the potential for manipulation. We return to this topic at the end of the chapter.

WHO CHOOSES JOURNALISM?

The vast majority of journalists in this country (just over two-thirds) work in the print media, and about one-third are in broadcast journalism. Journalists live throughout the country, although those with more high-powered jobs tend to be concentrated in the Northeast. The gender, education, ethnic backgrounds, and religious affiliations of American journalists are examined in "*Who Are We?* U.S. Journalists."

Does this demographic profile of journalism make any difference? Does a population need to get its news from a group of reporters that mirrors its own gender, ethnic, and religious characteristics in order to get an accurate picture of what is going on? Not surprisingly, this question generates controversy among journalists. Some insist that the personal profile of a journalist is irrelevant to the quality of his or her news coverage, but some evidence suggests that the life experiences of journalists do influence their reporting. For instance, most mainstream media focus on issues of concern to white middle-class America and reflect the values of that population, at the expense of minority issues and the concerns of poor people. General reporting also emphasizes urban rather than rural issues and concentrates on male-dominated sports. Women journalists, on the other hand, tend to report more on social issues that are of more concern to women.[36]

A Press Crusader
The role of the press to expose wrongdoing in American politics is well established. Early in the twentieth century, muckraker Ida Tarbell exposed corruption in companies like John D. Rockefeller's Standard Oil. The efforts fed the public appetite for scandal and often led to successful public calls to clean up corruption in government.

WHAT JOURNALISTS BELIEVE: IS THERE A LIBERAL BIAS IN THE MEDIA?

It is not the demographic profile of journalists, but their ideological profile—that is, the political views that they hold—that concerns many observers. Political scientists know that the more educated people are, the more liberal their views tend to be, and journalists are a well-educated lot on the whole. But even so, their views tend to be more liberal, particularly on social issues, than the average educated American's,[37] raising the question of whether these views slant the news that Americans get in a liberal direction.

There is no question that members of the media are more liberal than the rest of America. Table 15.1 shows how the political leanings of journalists compare with those of the U.S. adult population. This ideological gap is mirrored by party membership. Journalists are more likely to be Demo-

TABLE 15.1 Political Leanings of U.S. Journalists Compared With U.S. Adult Population (percentage in each group)

POLITICAL LEANINGS	JOURNALISTS 1971	1982–1983	1992	U.S. ADULT POPULATION 1982	1992
Pretty far to left	7.5	3.8	11.6	–	–
A little to left	30.5	18.3	35.7	21.0	18.0
Middle of the road	38.5	57.5	30.0	37.0	41.0
A little to right	15.6	16.3	17.0	32.0	34.0
Pretty far to right	3.4	1.6	4.7	–	–
Don't know/refused	4.5	2.5	1.0	10.0	7.0
Total	100.0	100.0	100.0	100.0	100.0

Source: Data from John W. C. Johnstone, Edward J. Slawski, and William W. Bowman, *The News People* (Champaign: University of Illinois Press, 1976), 93; David H. Weaver and G. Cleveland Wilhoit, *The American Journalist in the 1990s* (Mahwah, N.J.: Lawrence Erlbaum Associates, 1996), 26; George H. Gallup, *The Gallup Poll: Public Opinion, 1983* (Wilmington, Del.: Scholarly Resources, 1984), 82; Gallup Organization national telephone surveys of 1,307 U.S. adults, July 6–8, 1992, and 955 U.S. adults, July 17, 1992. Table from D. Weaver and G. Wilhoit, *The American Journalist in the 1990s: U.S. News People at the End of an Era*, © 1996 (Hillsdale, N.J.: Lawrence Erlbaum Associates, Inc., Publishers). Reprinted by permission.

TABLE 15.2 Political Party Identification of U.S. Journalists Compared With U.S. Adult Population (percentage in each group)

POLITICAL LEANINGS	JOURNALISTS 1971	1982–1983	1992	2002	U.S. ADULT POPULATION 1971	1982–1993	1992	2002
Democrat	35.5	38.5	44.1	37.0	43.0	45.0	34.0	32.0
Republican	25.7	18.8	16.4	18.6	28.0	25.0	33.0	31.0
Independent	32.5	39.1	34.4	33.5	29.0	30.0	31.0	32.0
Other/don't know/refused	6.3	3.7	5.1	10.5	–	–	3.0	5.0

Source: See Table 15.1.; David H. Weaver et al., *The American Journalist in the 21st Century* (Mahwah, N.J.: Lawrence Erlbaum Associates, forthcoming); Gallup/CNN/*USA Today* survey, July 29–31, 2002.

crats than the average American. This is especially true of women and minority journalists (see Table 15.2).[38]

What influence does this have on the news we get? Most journalists, aware that their values are more liberal than the average American's, try hard to keep their coverage of issues balanced. Some Democratic candidates for president have even accused the press of being harder on them to compensate for their personal preferences. Ben Bradlee, executive editor of the *Washington Post,* said that when Ronald Reagan became president, the journalists at the *Post* thought, "Here comes a true conservative. . . . And we are known—though I don't think justifiably—as the great liberals. So [we thought] we've got to really behave ourselves here. We've got to not be arrogant, make every effort to be informed, be mannerly, be fair. And we did this. I suspect in the process that this paper and probably a good deal of the press gave Reagan not a free ride, but they didn't use the same standards on him that they used on Carter and Nixon."[39] In addition to this sort of self-restraint, the liberal tendencies of many journalists are tempered by the undoubtedly conservative nature of news ownership and management we have already discussed. The editorial tone of many papers is conservative; for instance, generally more papers endorse Republican candidates for president than they do Democrats (see Figure 15.4). However, in the run-up to the 2004 presidential election, John Kerry received endorsements from the majority of the nation's daily newspapers, including forty-three papers that had backed Bush four years earlier.[40]

Who Are We?

U.S. Journalists

Do American journalists mirror the American population? In terms of race and ethnic background, journalists do not reflect the general labor force, although they do come closer to reflecting the demographics of the labor force who hold college degrees. How might this lack of representation in journalism affect the news we receive?

AGE (YEARS)	**PERCENTAGE OF JOURNALISTS IN AGE GROUP**	**PERCENTAGE OF CIVILIAN LABOR FORCE IN AGE GROUP**
20–24	4.4%	10.2%
25–34	29.3	22.1
35–44	27.9	25.0
45–54	28.3	22.7
55–64	7.8	11.8
65+	2.3	3.3
GENDER	**GENDER OF JOURNALISTS**	**GENDER OF U.S. CIVILIAN LABOR FORCE**
Male	67%	53.4%
Female	33.0	46.6
ETHNIC ORIGIN	**ETHNIC ORIGINS OF U.S. JOURNALISTS**	**ETHNIC ORIGINS OF U.S. POPULATION**
African American	3.7%	12.7%
Hispanic	3.3	13.4
Asian American	1.0	4.2
American Indian	0.4	0.9
White (non-Hispanic)	85.4	67.0
RELIGION	**JOURNALISTS' RELIGIONS**	**RELIGIONS OF U.S. ADULT POPULATION**
Protestant	46.2%	53.0
Catholic	32.7	25.0
Jewish	6.2	2.0
Other/none	14.8	20.0

Note: Column totals may not add to 100 percent due to rounding. Persons of Hispanic or Latino origin may be of any race.

Source: For data on U.S. journalists: David H. Weaver, Randal A. Beam, Bonnie J. Brownlee, Paul S. Voakes, and G. Cleveland Wilhoit, *The American Journalist in the 21st Century* (Mahwah, N.J.: Lawrence Erlbaum Associates, forthcoming); for data on the U.S. adult population: U.S. Census Bureau, *Statistical Abstract of the U.S. 2004–2005*, Tables No. 15, 67, 570, 572.

Until the mid-1980s, citizens themselves were not convinced that there was an ideological bias in the media—55 percent believed that the media were basically accurate and only 45 percent thought the press was biased in its reporting. Today only 36 percent think that the press gets its facts straight, and 53 percent say that it is biased. Of those, 51 percent say the bias is liberal, 26 percent say conservative, and 14 percent say neither.[41] Not surprisingly, the rise in the perception that the media are biased coincides with the growth of a more partisan tone in the media. A concerted conservative effort to bring what they believe is a much needed balance to the news has resulted in a host of talk radio shows, the Fox News Channel, the on-line *Drudge Report,* and the *Wall Street Journal Editorial Report* on PBS. In response, liberals have launched efforts like *Air America,* which claims to be in the business of "debunking the right-wing media," and the on-line "Huffington Post." No wonder people perceive the media as biased in one direction or another.

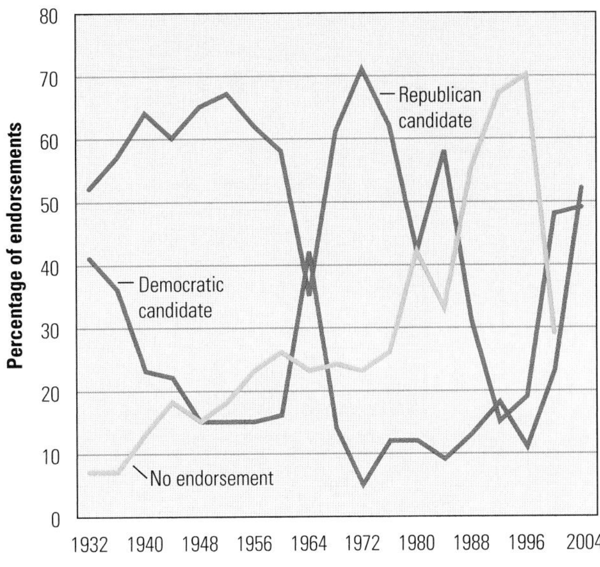

FIGURE 15.4
Newspaper Endorsements of Presidential Candidates, 1932–2004

Source: Harold W. Stanley and Richard G. Niemi, *Vital Statistics on American Politics, 2005–2006* (Washington, D.C.: CQ Press, 2005), Table 14.7.

THE GROWTH OF THE WASHINGTON PRESS CORPS

From a news-gathering perspective, America is organized into beats, identifiable areas covered by reporters who become familiar with their territories, get to know the sources of their stories, and otherwise institutionalize their official bit of journalistic "turf." Typical beats include the police, politics, business, education, and sports, and these can be broken down into even more specialized areas, such as the White House, Congress, and the Supreme Court. News that doesn't fit neatly into a preexisting beat may not get well covered or may turn up in unexpected places. For instance, in the 1960s, political news about women was rare. When the National Organization for Women was formed in 1966, the *Washington Post* did not mention it and the *New York Times* ran its story on the "Food, Fashion, Family, and Furnishings" page under a recipe for roasting turkey.[42]

The beat system, however, is well entrenched in American journalism, and at the top echelon of American journalists are those who cover the national political beat in Washington. National politics takes place in Washington—not just the interactions of Congress, the president, and the courts but also the internal workings of political parties and the rival lobbying of interest groups, including states, major corporations, and other national organizations. For a political reporter, Washington is the coveted place to be.

The Revolving Door As the *Washington Post*'s David Broder points out, the concentration of politics, politicians, and reporters in Washington leads to "a complex but cozy relationship between journalists and public officials."[43] Washington journalists share an interest in politics with politicians, they have similar educations, they often make about the same amount of money, and they are in many ways natural colleagues and friends. So much do journalists and politicians have in common that they often exchange jobs with ease, in a trend that Broder calls the "revolving door."

The **revolving door**, like the practice we discussed in Chapter 13, refers to the practice of journalists taking positions in government and then returning to journalism again, perhaps several times over. The number of prominent journalists who have gone through this revolving door is legion, including such notables as William Safire, the former Nixon speechwriter who went on to become a columnist for the *New York Times*; Dee Dee Meyers, former Clinton press secretary and frequent guest on *Larry King Live*; and George Stephanopoulos, a Clinton adviser who now anchors *This Week* on ABC, to name only a few.[44]

revolving door the tendency of public officials, journalists, and lobbyists to move between public and private sector (media, lobbying) jobs

The Rise of the Pundit Many of those who return to the media through the revolving door find themselves joining the ranks of the journalists and academics who have earned the unofficial and slightly tongue-in-cheek title of **pundit**. A pundit is tradi-

pundit a professional observer and commentator on politics

tionally a learned person, someone professing great wisdom. In contemporary media parlance, it has come to mean a professional observer and commentator on politics—a person skilled in the ways of the media and of politics who can make trenchant observations and predictions about the political world and help us untangle the complicated implications of political events. Because of the media attention they get, many pundits join the unofficial ranks of the celebrity journalists who cross over from reporting on public figures to being public figures themselves, thus raising a host of questions about whether they themselves should be subject to the same standards of criticism and scrutiny that they apply to politicians. Because they receive wide media coverage from their fellow journalists, the pronouncements of the punditry carry considerable power. The pundits, as journalists, are meant to be a check on the power of politicians, but who provides a check on the pundits?

WHO, WHAT, HOW American journalists do not mirror American society; they are more male, more white, and more liberal than the average population, although some elements of that picture are changing. It is not clear, however, how much difference this profile makes in the public's perception of the news it gets. In the high-stakes world of Washington journalism, the tight relationship between journalists and politicians provides citizens with more information and a more complete context in which to understand it. But the link also requires citizens to be skeptical about what they hear and who they hear it from.

THE MEDIA AND POLITICS

As we have seen, the American media make up an amazingly complex institution. Once primarily a nation of print journalism, the United States is now in the grip of the electronic media. Television has changed the American political landscape, and now the Internet promises, or threatens, to do the same. Privately owned, the media have a tendency to represent the corporate interest, but that influence is countered to some extent by the professional concerns of journalists. Still, some of those at the upper levels of the profession, those who tend to report to us on national politics, have very close links with the political world they cover, and this too influences the news we get. What is the effect of all this on American politics? In this section we look at four major areas of media influence on politics: the shaping of public opinion, the portrayal of politics as conflict and image, the use of public relations strategies by politicians, and the reduction in political accountability.

THE SHAPING OF PUBLIC OPINION

As we saw in Chapter 11, the media are among the main agents of political socialization: they help to transfer political values from one generation to the next and to shape political views in general. We have already looked at the question of bias in the media and noted that not only is there a corporate or commercial bias, but that Americans are also increasingly convinced that the news media are ideologically biased. Political scientists acknowledge that ideological bias may exist, but they conclude that it isn't so much that the media tell us what to think as that they tell us what to think *about.* These scholars have documented four kinds of media effects on our thinking: agenda setting, priming, framing, and persuasion by professional communicators.[45]

Agenda Setting Most of us get most of our news from television, but television is limited in which of the many daily political events it can cover. As political scientists Shanto Iyengar and Donald Kinder say, television news is "news that matters,"[46] which means that television reporters perform the function of agenda setting. When television reporters choose to cover an event, they are telling us that out of all the events happening, this one is important, and we should pay attention. A classic example of agenda setting in television news concerns the famine in Ethiopia that hit the American airwaves in 1984 in the form of a freelance film that NBC's Tom Brokaw insisted on showing on *The Nightly News.* Although the Ethiopian famine had been going on for over a decade, it became news only after NBC chose to make it news, and the famine was a major concern for the American public for almost a year. U.S. government food aid rose from $23 million in 1984 to $98 million after the NBC broadcast.[47]

The agenda-setting role of the media is not the last word, however. When Americans lost interest in the famine, the network coverage ceased, although the famine itself did not. Often the media will be fascinated with an event that simply fails to resonate with the public. Despite extensive media coverage of President Clinton's affair with White House intern Monica Lewinsky in 1998, public opinion polls continued to show that the public did not think it was an issue worthy of the time the media spent on it.

Priming Closely related to agenda setting, **priming** refers to the ways that the media influence how people and events should be evaluated by things that they emphasize as important. The theory of priming says that if the media are constantly emphasizing crime, then politicians, and particularly the president, will be evaluated on how well they deal with crime. If the media emphasize the environment, then that will become the relevant yardstick for evaluation. During George W. Bush's presidential campaign, the media emphasized the intelligence of the candidates, causing many of Bush's verbal gaffes to be seen as indications of his intelligence. He continued to misspeak in the same ways after he became president, but once the war on terrorism began, those in the media chose to emphasize different yardsticks—such as leadership and calmness—for evaluating Bush's performance, and his intelligence was no longer seen as an issue. In effect, according to this concept, the media not only tell us what to think about but how to think about those things. Priming has been supported with empirical evidence,[48] although it is clearly not in effect all the time on all the issues.

priming the way in which the media's emphasis on particular characteristics of people, events, or issues influences the public's perception of those people, events, or issues

Framing A third media effect on our thinking is called **framing**. Just as a painting's appearance can be altered by changing its frame, a political event can look different to us depending on how the media frame it—that is, what they choose to emphasize in

framing process through which the media emphasize particular aspects of a news story, thereby influencing the public's perception of the story their coverage. For example, people view a war differently depending on whether the coverage highlights American casualties or military victories. Similarly, the story of a mother on welfare can emphasize the circumstances of her personal life, leading to the conclusion that she is responsible for her plight, or national data on education, poverty levels, and unemployment, implying that social forces are to blame. The important point about framing is that how the media present a political issue or event may affect how the public perceives that issue, whether they see it as a problem, and who they view as responsible for solving it.

Persuasion by Professional Communicators Finally, some political scientists argue that the media affect public opinion because viewers, who often don't have the time or background to research the issues themselves, sometimes change their minds to agree with trusted newscasters and expert sources.[49] Familiar with this phenomenon, when President Lyndon Johnson heard popular CBS news anchor Walter Cronkite take a stand against American involvement in Vietnam, he told an aide it was "all over." Predicting that the public would follow the lead of one of the most trusted figures in America, he knew there would be little support for a continued war effort. Often, however, especially in the age of cable news and multiple broadcast choices, the communicators on whom the media rely are not revered figures like "Uncle Walter," but people who regularly pass through the revolving door and whose objectivity cannot be taken for granted.

Do Media Effects Matter? The effects of agenda setting, priming, framing, and expert persuasion should not be taken to mean that we are all unwitting dupes of the media. In the first place, these are not iron-clad rules; they are tendencies that scholars have discovered and confirmed with experimentation and public opinion surveys. That means that they hold true for many but not all people. Members of the two major political parties, for instance, are less affected by agenda setting than are independents, perhaps because the latter do not have a party to rely on to tell them what is important.[50]

Second, we bring our own armor to the barrage of media effects we face regularly. We all filter our news watching through our own ideas, values, and distinct perspectives. Scholars who emphasize that audiences are active, not passive, consumers of the media say that people counter the effects of the media by setting their own agendas and processing the news in light of those agendas. That is, viewers exercise **selective perception**; they filter information through their own values and interests, thereby determining the news items they will pay attention to, the items they will remember, and the items they will forget.[51] If people do not seem to be well informed on the issues emphasized by the media, it may be that they do not see them as having an effect on their lives. The point is that as consumers, we do more than passively absorb the messages and values provided by the media.

selective perception the phenomenon of filtering incoming information through personal values and interests

This same point can be made with respect to ideological bias in the news. While researchers have tried to look at whether the ideological slant of a news source makes a difference to one's perception of the news, it is a difficult question to answer since people seem to gravitate to the sources that they agree with. Are their views shaped by bias in the news, or do they choose the bias they prefer to be exposed to? One recent study looking at misperceptions about the Iraq war (specifically, beliefs that there was evidence of links between al Qaeda and Saddam Hussein, that weapons of mass destruction had been found in Iraq, and that world opinion favored U.S. action in Iraq) concluded that the frequency with which those beliefs were held varied dramatically with the primary source of a person's news, with watchers of the Fox News Channel (which tends to be more supportive of the Bush administration) holding those misperceptions much more frequently than those who got their news from other sources.[52] (See the box, "Media and Misperception.")

THE PORTRAYAL OF POLITICS AS CONFLICT AND IMAGE

In addition to shaping public opinion, the media also affect politics by their tendency to portray complex and substantive political issues as questions of personal image and contests between individuals. Rather than examining the details and nuances of policy differences, the media tend to focus on image and to play up personalities and conflicts even when their readers and viewers say they want something quite different. The effect of this, according to some researchers, is to make politics seem negative and to increase popular cynicism.

Media and Misperception

Where you get your news matters. One of the more interesting media studies done in recent years showed a clear relationship between where people get their news and the accuracy of their beliefs about the war in Iraq. A series of three polls taken from June through September 2003 found that a surprising number of U.S. adults had the following misperceptions on aspects of the situation in Iraq:

- Evidence of links between Iraq and al Qaeda has been found. [No evidence has been found.]
- Weapons of mass destruction have been found in Iraq. [No such weapons have been found.]
- World public opinion favored the United States going to war with Iraq. [World opinion was strongly opposed to the U.S. invasion of Iraq.]

The figure shows the relationship between having misperceptions on these issues and respondents' primary media sources. The highest rates of misperceptions occurred among Fox News viewers, among whom 80 percent had at least one of the above items wrong. The most accurate perceptions were among the Public Broadcasting System (PBS) and National Public Radio (NPR) audience, in which just 23 percent had any misperceptions on the above items. Interestingly, these media source effects held up even when levels of education and partisanship were taken into account. Researchers have not been able to determine causality here. That is, they do not know whether Fox's support of the Bush administration's war effort led to the misperceptions being held, or whether supporters of the president who already held the misperceptions decided to watch Fox.

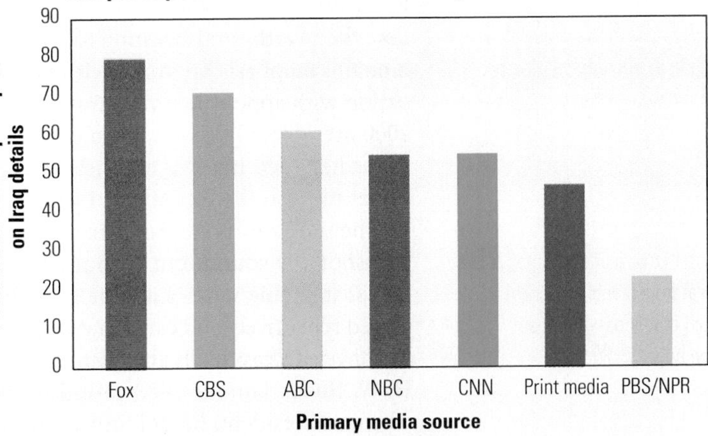

Source: Steve Kull "Misperceptions, the Media and the Iraq War," the PIPA/Knowledge Networks Poll (October 2, 2003), www.pipa.org.

horse-race journalism the media's focus on the competitive aspects of politics rather than on actual policy proposals and political decisions

Horse-race Journalism **Horse-race journalism** refers to the media's tendency to see politics as competition between individuals. Rather than report on the policy differences between politicians or the effects their proposals will have on ordinary Americans, today's media tend to report on politics as if it were a battle between individual gladiators or a game of strategy and wit but not substance. This sort of journalism not only shows politics in the most negative light, as if politicians cared only to score victories off one another in a never-ending fight to promote their own self-interests, but it also ignores the concerns that citizens have about politics.

As journalist James Fallows points out, when citizens are given a chance to ask questions of politicians, they focus on all the elements of politics that touch their lives: taxes, wars, social security, student loans, education, and welfare.[53] But journalists focus on questions of strategy, popularity, and relative positioning in relation to real or imagined rivals. Fallows gives the following example of coverage of the 1996 presidential campaign. When interviewed by former CBS anchor Dan Rather about Bill Clinton's reelection campaign, Sen. Edward Kennedy, D-Mass., started to speak about the balanced budget amendment, which was supported by many Americans but not by the president. Rather responded, "Senator, you know I'd talk about these things the rest of the afternoon, but let's move quickly to politics. Do you expect Bill Clinton to be the Democratic nominee for reelection in 1996?"[54] The obsession with who is winning makes the coverage of campaigns, or of partisan battles in Congress, or of disputes between the president and Congress far more trivial than it needs to be, and far less educational to the American public. ("*Consider the Source:* Becoming a Savvy Media Consumer" will help you get beyond the horse-race coverage in much of today's media.)

The Emphasis on Image Television is primarily an entertainment medium and, by its nature, one that is focused on image: what people look like, what they sound like, and how an event is staged and presented. Television, and to some extent its competitors in the print media, concentrates on doing what it does well: giving us pictures of politics instead of delving beneath the surface. This has the effect of leading us to value the more superficial aspects of politics, even if only subconsciously. An early and telling example was the 1960 presidential debate between Richard Nixon and John Kennedy, when the young and telegenic Kennedy presented a more presidential image than the swarthy and sweating Nixon and won both the debate and the election. Combine this emphasis on image with horse-race journalism, and the result is a preoccupation with appearance and strategy at the cost of substance. In their coverage of the 2000 presidential debates, the media focused on candidate Al Gore's impatient behavior as he rolled his eyes and heaved sighs of exasperation while Bush was speaking, rather than on the substance of what either candidate had to say.

sound bite a brief, snappy excerpt from a public figure's speech that is easy to repeat on the news

The words of politicians are being similarly reduced to the audio equivalent of a snapshot, the **sound bite**. A sound bite is a short block of speech by a politician that makes it on the news. Like the film clips of Gore's debate behavior, these are often played repetitively and can drown out the substance of the message a politician wishes to convey. Occasionally they can come back to haunt a politician, too, as did George H. W. Bush's famous 1988 promise, "Read my lips, no new taxes," broken in 1992 when, as president, he did, in fact, support a tax hike. The amount of time that the electronic media devote to the actual words a politician utters is shrinking. In 2000 the average length for a sound bite from a presidential candidate on the nightly network news was 7.3 seconds, down from 10 seconds in 1992 and 42 seconds in 1968.[55] Journalists use the extra time to interpret what we have heard and often to put it into the horse-race metaphor we just discussed.[56]

The emphasis on superficial image is exacerbated by the competition among media outlets. Ratings wars have led television news shows to further reduce the substance of their coverage under the assumption that audiences want more "light" news. To make way for the human interest features—such as medical advances, pet stories, and scandals—that they believe will attract viewers, networks must reduce the time available for the major news events of the day—what one critic calls an effort to "dumb down the content" of news.[57]

Scandal Watching Reporters also tend to concentrate on developing scandals to the exclusion of other, possibly more relevant, news events. The 1998 revelations about President Clinton's affair with Monica Lewinsky are a case in point. During the period of daily revelations, allegations, and investigations, almost nothing else Clinton did got media attention. Even when visiting British prime minister Tony Blair held a joint press conference with Clinton, many of the questions the media asked focused on Lewinsky. Political scientist Larry Sabato refers to this behavior as a **feeding frenzy**: "the press coverage attending any political event or circumstance where a critical mass of journalists leap to cover the same embarrassing or scandalous subject and pursue it intensely, often excessively, and sometimes uncontrollably."[58] Many such feeding frenzies have been over scandals that have proved not to be true or seemed insignificant with the passing of time, and yet the media have treated them with the seriousness of a world crisis. Reputations have been shredded, justly or unjustly, but once the frenzy has begun, it is difficult to bring rational judgment to bear on the case. After such attacks, the media frequently indulge in introspection and remorse, until the next scandal starts to brew.

feeding frenzy excessive press coverage of an embarrassing or scandalous subject

Growing Negativism, Increased Cynicism Political scientist Thomas Patterson attributes the phenomenon of the feeding frenzy to an increased cynicism among members of the media. He argues that it is not a liberal or a conservative bias among reporters that we ought to worry about. Rather, it is their antigovernment views, focusing on the adversarial and negative aspects of politics to the exclusion of its positive achievements, that foster a cynical view of politics among the general public. Most presidents and presidential candidates are treated by the press as fundamentally untrustworthy, when in fact most do precisely what they say they are going to do. Clinton, in his first year, was plagued by press criticism despite the fact that he kept a majority of his campaign promises and was more successful in getting his legislative packages through Congress that year than Kennedy, Nixon, Ford, Carter, Reagan, or Bush had been in their best years. Yet in the first six months of his presidency, 66 percent of his news evaluations were negative.[59] Since it takes time and energy to investigate all the claims that a president or a candidate makes, the media evaluate political claims not with their own careful scrutiny but with statements from political opponents. This makes politics appear endlessly adversarial and, as Patterson says, replaces investigative journalism with attack journalism.[60]

Consequences of the Emphasis on Conflict and Image A consequence of the negative content of political coverage is that voters' opinions of candidates have sunk, and citizen dissatisfaction with the electoral process has risen.[61] Not only is the public becoming more cynical about the political world, but it is also becoming more cynical

Consider the Source

Becoming a Savvy Media Consumer

As we have seen in this chapter, many forces are working to make the citizen's job difficult when it comes to getting, following, and interpreting the news. But forewarned is forearmed, and the knowledge you have gained can turn you into the savviest of media consumers. Journalist Carlin Romano says, "*What* the press covers matters less in the end than *how* the public reads. Effective reading of the news requires not just a key—a Rosetta stone by which to decipher current cliches—but an activity, a regimen."[1] When you read the paper, watch the news, listen to the radio, or surf the Internet, try to remember to ask yourself the following questions. This will be a lot more work than just letting the words wash over you or pass before your eyes, but as a payoff you will know more and be less cynical about politics; you will be less likely to be manipulated, either by the media or by more knowledgeable friends and family; and, as a bonus, you will be a more effective, sophisticated, and satisfied citizen. Here are the questions. Keep a copy in your wallet.

1. **Who owns this media source?** Look at the page in newspapers and magazines that lists the publisher and editors. Take note of radio and television call letters. Check out Figure 15.3 and see if the source is owned by one of the media conglomerates shown there. Look to see who takes credit for a web site. What could be this owner's agenda? Is it corporate, political, ideological? How might that agenda affect the news?
2. **Who is this journalist (reporter, anchor person, webmaster, etc.)?** Does he or she share the characteristics of the average American or of the media elite? How might that affect his or her perspective on the news? Has he or she been in politics? In what role? How might that affect how he or she sees current political events? Some of this information might be hard to find at first, but if a particular journalist appears to have a special agenda, it might be worth the extra research to find out.
3. **What is the news of the day?** How do the news stories covered by your source (radio, TV, newspaper, magazine, or web) compare to the stories covered elsewhere? Why are these stories covered and not others? Who makes the decisions? How are the stories framed? Are positive or negative aspects emphasized? What standards do the journalists suggest you use to evaluate the story—that is, what standards do they seem to focus on?
4. **What issues are involved?** Can you get beyond the "horse race?" For instance, if reporters are focusing on the delivery of a politician's speech and her opponent's reactions to it, try to get a copy of the speech to read for yourself. Check the web or a source like the *New York Times*. Similarly, when the media emphasize conflict, ask yourself what underlying issues are involved. Look for primary (original) sources

about the media. A recent public opinion poll shows that half or more of the American public now thinks that the news is too biased, sensationalized, and manipulated by special interests and that reporters offer too many of their own opinions, quote unnamed sources, and are negative.[62] Two scholars argue that the "conflict-driven sound-bite oriented discourse of politicians," in conjunction with the "conflict-saturated strategy-oriented structure of press coverage," creates a mutually reinforcing lack of confidence in the system that they call the "spiral of cynicism."[63] But as we argued at the beginning of this chapter, the media have a real and legitimate role to play in a democracy: disseminating information, checking government, and creating political community. If people cease to trust the media, the media become less effective in playing their legitimate roles as well as their more controversial ones, and democracy becomes more difficult to sustain.

Another consequence, and one that may somewhat alleviate the first, is that new forms of the media are opening up to supplement or even replace the older ones. Television talk shows, radio call-in shows, and other outlets that involve public input and bypass the adversarial questions and negative comments of the traditional media allow the public, in some ways, to set the agenda. In fact, a study of the 1992 election showed whenever possible, ones that have not been processed by the media for you. If conflicts are presented as a choice between two sides, ask yourself if there are other sides that might be relevant.

5. **Who are the story's sources?** Are they "official" sources? Whose point of view do they represent? Are their remarks attributed to them, or are they speaking "on background" (anonymously)? Such sources frequently show up as "highly placed administration officials" or "sources close to the senator." Why would people not want their names disclosed? How should that affect how we interpret what they say? Do you see the same sources appearing in many stories in different types of media? Have these sources been through the "revolving door?" Are they pundits? What audience are they addressing?
6. **Is someone putting spin on this story?** Is there visible news management? Is the main source the politician's press office? Is the story based on a leak? If so, can you make a guess at the motivation of the leaker? What evidence supports your guess? What is the spin? That is, what do the politician's handlers want you to think about the issue or event?
7. **Who are the advertisers?** How might that affect the coverage of the news? What sorts of stories might be affected by the advertisers' presence? Are there potential stories that might hurt the advertiser?
8. **What are the media doing to get your attention?** Is the coverage of a news event detailed and thorough, or is it "lightened up" to make it faster and easier for you to process? If so, what are you missing? What is on the cover of the newspaper or magazine? What is the lead story on the network? How do the media's efforts to get your attention affect the news you get? Would you have read or listened to the story if the media had not worked at getting your attention?
9. **What values and beliefs do you bring to the news?** What are your biases? Are you liberal? Conservative? Do you think government is too big, or captured by special interests, always ineffective, or totally irrelevant to your life? Do you have any pet peeves that direct your attention? How do your current life experiences affect your political views or priorities? How do these values, beliefs, and ideas affect how you see the news, what you pay attention to, and what you skip? List all the articles or stories you tuned out, and ask yourself why you did so.
10. **Can you find a news source that you usually disagree with, that you think is biased or always wrong?** Read it now and again. It will help you keep your perspective and ensure that you get a mix of views that will keep you thinking critically. We are challenged not by ideas we agree with but by those that we find flawed. Stay an active media consumer.

that television talk shows focused more on substantive policy issues and presented more balanced and positive images of the candidates than did the mainstream media.[64]

POLITICS AS PUBLIC RELATIONS

There is no doubt that the media portray politics in a negative light, that news reporting emphasizes personality, superficial image, and conflict over substantive policy issues. Some media figures argue, however, that this is not the media's fault, but rather the responsibility of politicians and their press officers who are so obsessed with their own images on television that they limit access to the media, speak only in prearranged sound bites, and present themselves to the public in carefully orchestrated "media events."[65] Media events are designed to limit the ability of reporters to put their own interpretation on the occasion. The rules of American politics mean that politicians have to try to get maximum exposure for their ideas and accomplishments while limiting the damage the media can do with their intense scrutiny, investigations, and critical perspectives.

"...Political campaigns have become so simplistic and superficial... In the 20 seconds we have left, could you explain why?..

news management the efforts of a politician's staff to control news about the politician

spin an interpretation of a politician's words or actions, designed to present a favorable image

News Management **News management** describes the efforts of a politician's staff—media consultants, press secretaries, pollsters, campaign strategists, and general advisers—to control the news about the politician. The staff want to put their own issues on the agenda, determine for themselves the standards by which the politician will be evaluated, frame the issues, and supply the sources for reporters, so that they will put their client, the politician, in the best possible light. In contemporary political jargon, they want to put a **spin**, or an interpretation, on the news that will be most flattering to the politician whose image is in their care. To some extent, modern American politics has become a battle between the press and the politicians and among the politicians themselves to control the agenda and the images that reach the public. It has become a battle of the "spin doctors."

The classic example of news management is the rehabilitation of the image of Richard Nixon after he lost the 1960 election to the more media-savvy Kennedy campaign. Inspired by the way the Kennedy administration had managed the image of Kennedy as war hero, patriot, devoted father, and faithful husband, when at least one of those characterizations wasn't true, Nixon speechwriter Ray Price saw his mission clearly. Noting that Nixon was personally unpopular with the public, he wrote in a 1967 memo, "We have to be very clear on this point: that the response is to the image, not to the man, since 99 percent of the voters have no contact with the man. It's not what's there that counts, it's what's projected—and it's not what he projects but rather what the voter receives. It's not the man we have to change, but rather the received impression."[66] With the help of an advertising executive and a television producer, among others, Nixon was repackaged and sold to voters as the "New Nixon." He won election as president in 1968 and 1972, and that he had to resign in 1974 is perhaps less a failure of his image makers than the inevitable revelation of the "real" Nixon underneath.

News Management Techniques The techniques that Nixon's handlers developed for managing his image have become part of the basic repertoire of political staffs, particularly in the White House but even to some extent for holders of lesser offices. They can include any or all of the following:[67]

- *Tight control of information.* Staffers pick a "line of the day"—for instance, a focus on education or child care—and orchestrate all messages from the administration around that theme. This frustrates journalists who are trying to follow independent stories. But this strategy recognizes that the staff must "feed the beast" by giving the press something to cover, or they may find the press rebelling and covering stories they don't want covered at all.[68]
- *Tight control of access to the politician.* If the politician is available to the press for only a short period of time and makes only a brief statement, the press corps is forced to report the appearance as the only available news.
- *Elaborate communications bureaucracy.* The Nixon White House had four offices handling communications. In addition to the White House press secretary, who was frequently kept uninformed so that he could more credibly deny that he knew the answers to reporters' questions, there was an Office of Communications, an Office of Public Liaison, and a speechwriting office.
- *A concerted effort to bypass the White House press corps.* During Nixon's years this meant going to regional papers that were more easily manipulated. Today it can also include the so-called new media of television talk shows and late-night television, and other forums that go directly to the public, such as town hall meetings. Part and parcel of this approach is the strategy of rewarding media outlets that provide friendly coverage and punishing those that do not.
- *Prepackaging the news in sound bites.* If the media are going to allow the public only a brief snippet of political language, the reasoning goes, let the politician's staff decide what it will be. In line with this, the press office will repeat a message often, to be sure the press and the public pick up on it, and it will work on phrasing that is catchy and memorable.
- *Leaks.* A final and effective way that politicians attempt to control the news is with the use of leaks, secretly revealing confidential information to the press. **Leaks** can serve a variety of purposes. For instance, a leak can be a **trial balloon**, in which an official leaks a policy or plan in order to gauge public reaction to it. If the reaction is negative, the official denies he or she ever mentioned it, and if it is positive, the policy can go ahead without risk. Bureaucrats who want to anonymously stop a practice they believe is wrong may use a "whistle blower leak." Information can be leaked to settle grudges, or to curry favor, or just to show off.[69]

leaks confidential information secretly revealed to the press

trial balloon an official leak of a proposal to determine public reaction to it without risk

A classic and recent example of the extent to which information is passed under the table in Washington occurred in 2003, when Democrats accused Republicans of leaking the identity of an undercover CIA agent to the press in order to discredit her husband, who was highly critical of President Bush's reasons for going to war with Iraq. Because it is illegal to reveal the identity of a covert agent of the U.S. government, the Justice Department has been conducting an investigation of the leak, which has so far revealed that Bush adviser Karl Rove was one of the sources who provided information on the agent's identity. Interestingly, we know that much because of leaks to the

The Man Behind the President
Karl Rove is the president's chief political adviser and deputy chief of staff (shown here seated behind the president as he fields questions from reporters). Rove, who ran both of Bush's campaigns, is influential in many aspects of Bush's administration including political strategy and directing the administration's very effective news management efforts.

media about the progress of the investigation. Some leaks may help an administration control the information that gets to the press, but others, clearly, can work against the administration; these are frequently the bane of a politician's existence.

Not all presidential administrations are equally accomplished at using these techniques of news management, of course. Nixon's was successful, at least in his first administration, and Reagan's has been referred to as a model of public relations.[70] President Clinton did not manage the media effectively in the early years of his first administration, and he was consequently at the mercy of a frustrated and annoyed press corps. Within a couple of years, however, the Clinton staff had become much more skilled and, by his second administration, was adeptly handling scandals that would have daunted more seasoned public relations experts.

News Management in the Bush Administration The George W. Bush administration has done a superb job of news management. The administration's attitude toward the media is summed up in this 2003 statement by President Bush: "I'm mindful of the filter through which some news travels, and somehow you just got to go over the heads of the filter and speak directly to the people."[71] Some elements of the Bush administration's strategy of getting around the "filter" of the media have been particularly noteworthy, both for their effectiveness and for their tendency to draw strong criticism:

- Most of Bush's public events are open only to Bush supporters; where there is audience interaction, he receives questions only from those who endorse his programs and goals. When these events are covered by the news media, there is only positive news to report, and on the accompanying videos the president is cheerful and relaxed.
- In 2005 it was revealed that the Bush administration had paid several journalists to report favorably on the president's policies, including a $240,000 payment to conservative columnist Armstrong Williams to promote the No Child Left Behind Act. Bush later said the practice was wrong.
- Still in effect, however, is an administration publicity effort that expands on a Clinton-era program of government-produced videos touting administration achievements that are distributed to local television stations, which show them as actual news. Local stations, under budgetary constraints, welcome the free footage, but viewers are generally unaware that the favorable coverage of the Iraq war, or the administration's agricultural policy, or a recently passed Medicare bill is paid for by the people it praises.[72] The Government Accountability Office has said that such videos may be "covert propaganda" and cannot be made if they do not disclose who made them, but the Department of Justice and the Office of Management and Budget has said that the agencies may ignore that finding.[73] Bush has said that this practice is deceptive if the source of the videos is not disclosed but that the re-

sponsibility is with the news organization to disclose it, not the administration to stop producing the videos.[74]

- Reporters who can be trusted to ask supportive questions are favored in White House news briefings and press conferences. One such preferred questioner turned out to be in the employ of a partisan Internet news agency run by Republican volunteers, and owned by a Texas Republican operative. The "reporter," who was issued a White House press pass under an assumed name, asked what reporters call "softball questions," one of which brought him to the attention of bloggers in February 2005. When, referring to Senate Democrats, he asked the president, "How are you going to work with people who seem to have divorced themselves from reality?" Irate liberal bloggers started to investigate and discovered his journalistic credentials were not tied to a legitimate news outlet.[75]

Supporters defend the Bush White House's news management strategy as efficient and praiseworthy. Former Bush press secretary Ari Fleischer told one news outlet, "In terms of getting the message out, there is no difference between the Bush administration and other administrations. . . . All administrations use all the tools of modern technology to put their programs in the best light. What is different is that this is a much more disciplined, tight-lipped administration, and that frustrates reporters."[76] Critics, on the other hand, claim that the White House has become a "propaganda machine" to serve the president's political goals.[77] "George W. Bush doesn't really want people to get the news unfiltered. He wants people to get the news filtered by George W. Bush," says one.[78]

There is a real cost to the transformation of politics into public relations, no matter whose administration is engaging in the practice (and Fleischer is right that, with varying degrees of expertise, they all do). Not only does the public suffer from not getting the straight story to evaluate government policies that affect their lives, but politicians must spend time and energy on image considerations that do not really help them serve the public. And the people who are skilled enough at managing the press to get elected to office have not necessarily demonstrated any leadership skills. The skills required by an actor and a statesperson are not the same, and the current system may encourage us to choose the wrong leaders for the wrong reasons and discourage the right people from running at all.

REDUCTION IN POLITICAL ACCOUNTABILITY

A final political effect of the media, according to some scholars, is a reduction in political accountability. **Political accountability** is the very hallmark of democracy: political leaders must answer to the public for their actions. If our leaders do something we do not like, we can make them bear the consequences of their actions by voting them out of office. The threat of being voted out of office is supposed to encourage them to do what we want in the first place.

political accountability the democratic principle that political leaders must answer to the public for their actions

Some political scientists, however, argue that Americans' reliance on television for their news has weakened political accountability, and thus democracy as well.[79] Their arguments are complex but compelling.

First, they say that television has come to reduce the influence of political parties, since it allows politicians to take their message directly to the people. Parties are no longer absolutely necessary to mediate politics—that is, to provide a link between leaders and the people—but parties have traditionally been a way to keep politicians accountable.

Second, television covers politicians as individuals, and as individuals, they have incentives to take credit for what the public likes and to blame others for what the public doesn't like. And because they are covered as individuals, they have little reason to form coalitions to work together.

Third, television, by emphasizing image and style, allows politicians to avoid taking stances on substantive policy issues; the public often does not know where they stand and cannot hold them accountable.

Finally, the episodic way in which the media frame political events makes it difficult for people to discern what has really happened politically and whose responsibility it is.

The result is that the modern media, and especially television, have changed the rules of politics. Today it is harder for citizens to know who is responsible for laws, policies, and political actions and harder to make politicians behave responsibly.

WHO, WHAT, HOW Where the worlds of politics and the media intersect, there are many actors with something serious at stake. Journalists, of course, want bylines or airtime, the respect of their peers, and professional acclaim, at the same time that they want to help keep their news organizations competitive and profitable. Their goals and rules clash with those of politicians, who need to communicate with the public, to present themselves as attractive, effective leaders, and to make their ideas and proposed policies clear to voters. The clash of journalists' and politicians' goals means that each side often feels exploited or treated unfairly by the other, making for an uneasy relationship between the two.

What is at stake for citizens is not only their ability to get information on which to base their political decisions, but also their ability to see good as well as bad in government, to know their leaders as they really are and not just their public relations images, and to hold them accountable. The rules put the burden of responsibility on citizens to be critical consumers of the media.

THE CITIZENS AND THE MEDIA

We have been unable to talk about the media in this chapter without talking about citizenship. Citizens have been a constant "who" in our analysis because the media exist, by definition, to give information to citizens and to mediate their relationship to government. But if we evaluate the traditional role of the media with respect to the public, the relationship that emerges is not a particularly responsive one. Almost from the beginning, control of the American media has been in the hands of an elite group, whether party leaders, politicians, wealthy entrepreneurs, or corporate owners. Financial concerns have meant that the media in the United States have been driven more by profit motive than by public interest. Not only are ownership and control of the media far removed from the hands of everyday Americans, but the reporting of national news is done mostly by reporters who do not fit the profile of those "average" citizens and whose concerns often do not reflect the concerns of their audience.

What's a Citizen to Do? From administration reports of weapons of mass destruction in Iraq that did not exist, to opponents' forged "proof" of Bush's not fulfilling his duties as a member of the Air National Guard, citizens have been hit with a barrage of claims that later prove to be false. It is understandable that many people become frustrated with politics, but citizen attentiveness is of vital importance since government continues to affect our lives in profound ways, even for those who try to ignore it.

Citizens' access to the media is correspondingly remote. The primary role available to them is passive: that of reader, listener, or watcher. The power they wield is the power of switching newspapers or changing channels, essentially choosing among competing elites, but this is not an active participatory role. While freedom of the press is a right technically held by all citizens, there is no right of access to the press; citizens have difficulty making their voices heard, and, of course, most do not even try. Members of the media holler long and loud about their right to publish what they want, but only sporadically and briefly do they consider their obligations to the public to provide the sort of information that can sustain a democracy. If active democracy requires a political community in which the public can deliberate about important issues, it would seem that the American media are failing miserably at creating that community.

Two developments in the American media we have already touched on, the rise of new media and civic journalism, offer some hope that the media can be made to serve the public interest more effectively.

THE NEW MEDIA

As we have indicated, the term *new media* refers to the variety of high-tech outlets that have sprung up to compete with traditional newspapers, magazines, and network news. Some of these, such as cable news, specialized television programs, and Internet news, allow citizens to get fast-breaking reports of events as they occur and even to customize the news that they get. Talk radio and call-in television shows—new uses of the "old" media—allow citizen interaction, as do Internet chatrooms and other on-line forums. Already, many Web sites allow users to give their opinions of issues in unscientific straw polls. Some analysts speculate that it is only a matter of time until

Profiles in Citizenship

Markos Moulitsas

Markos Moulitsas Zúniga is a man of, shall we say, strong opinions, and his penchant for voicing them in the workplace was making his San Francisco colleagues crazy. "And so this," he says, "this" being his incredibly popular Web log, "became a way to get [things] off my chest without really driving everybody around me nuts because I was always in a rampage."

"To me, dissenting by itself is an act of patriotism."

What started small, as an outlet for venting Moulitsas's spleen, is now *The Daily Kos* (www.dailykos.com), one of the top-rated blogs in the country, getting 650,000 visits a day even in a nonelection year. The blog has gone from being a safe place for Moulitsas and like-minded friends to air their views to a cyber-hotbed of political activism—one that Moulitsas hopes can provide a liberal counterpoint to what he sees as a well-coordinated conservative media machine that reports and amplifies the Republican message.

His hopes are not unfounded. In the 2004 election, liberal readers flocked to *The Daily Kos* to have their say, exchange information about candidates, and monitor the mainstream media coverage. So effective were they in engaging large numbers of readers that Moulitsas and his partner-in-liberal-blogging, Jerome Armstrong (www.mydd.com), became consultants to Howard Dean's maverick presidential campaign, providing the expertise that helped that campaign reach the cutting edge of Internet organization. Later, when Dean's effort failed, they helped launch the movement to draft General Wesley Clark as a presidential candidate. Moulitsas's fundraising efforts aren't shabby either. Overall in 2004, his readers contributed more than half a million dollars to congressional candidates he had tagged as worthy, and nearly as much to John Kerry and the Democratic National Committee.

Moulitsas has become, if not exactly a king maker, certainly a player. He and Armstrong are the authors of a book, *This Ain't No Party*, detailing the decline of the Democratic Party and what they think can be done to get it back on its feet. Given the size of their readership, it will be a book that the traditional elite in the Democratic Party ignore at their own peril.

Sitting in his comfortable Berkeley, California, living room, Moulitsas marvels at the democratizing power of the Internet that could have brought him, the son of poor war refugees from El Salvador, to what he calls "a place at the table" of Democratic politics—a table that has traditionally been reserved for people with money and the heads of major, well-funded interest groups. It has happened without scoring a job at a mainstream media outlet, without printing or broadcasting a word—just Moulitsas himself, at home on the couch with his laptop computer, tapping the keys in a direct line to hundreds of thousands of readers.

Of course, it wasn't the Internet alone that propelled Moulitsas into national prominence. Many bloggers put in endless hours without achieving his numbers or his fame. The force of his own personality—his intensity, determination, and charisma—has had something to do with it as well. That, and his obsessive, abiding interest in the details, big and small, of the political world.

we can all vote on issues from our home computers. The one thing that these new forms of media have in common is that they bypass the old, making the corporate journalistic establishment less powerful than it was but perhaps giving rise to new elites and raising new questions about participation and how much access we really want citizens to have.

One of the most significant developments in the new media is the proliferation of Web logs, or blogs (see *Profiles in Citizenship:* Markos Moulitsas), which we mentioned earlier. It is truly citizen journalism—the cyber-equivalent of giving everyday people their own printing presses and the means to publish their views. While blogs can be on any subject, the ones that interest us here are the ones that focus on politics

That interest started early. Although Moulitsas was born in Chicago, his family moved to his El Salvadoran mother's home when he was four, only to return when civil war threatened their safety. Moulitsas grew up "where politics was literally a life-or-death situation," and he found it hard to take lightly. Safely in the United States in 1980, he remembers watching the Solidarity protests in Poland on television and asking his dad what was going on. "And my father said, 'ah, it's just politics.' And so I was like, okay, this is politics. This looks interesting. Politics is interesting. . . . And I forced my parents, because we didn't have a lot of money, but I had them subscribe to both the *Sun Times* and the *Chicago Tribune* because one wasn't good enough apparently. I needed to get both. It was just never enough. And I can't imagine what it would have been like then had I had access to the kind of things that we have now. . . . I can't imagine. I mean I was already a nerd. I think I would have been hopelessly lost."

The young news junkie was also a Reagan Republican at the time, sold by virtue of his own innate fiscal conservatism and Reagan's hawkish stance on aid to El Salvador. Moulitsas still calls himself a "military hawk"—"I think military force can be a force of good if it's used to prevent bloodshed or halt bloodshed or prevent a greater harm." Believing that holding such views meant he should be willing to put his own life on the line, he enlisted in the army and, in the process, turned his political views upside down.

For the first time, he says, "I was in close quarters with people from pretty much every state in the union, from all different socioeconomic status[es]. So you start realizing that my world is a little bigger than me. And there's a lot of people, and these are people who are good people, they work hard, they do what they can and sometimes that's just not good enough. And that's why certain government involvement can be for the common good." He was (and is) still a fiscal conservative, and still a hawk, but he belongs to the Democratic Party now. No conventional Democrat, he is eager to turn his party away from the entrenched power elite that he believes is strangling it, and toward something closer to what he calls "the netroots"—the vital Internet community that represents a new dimension of the grassroots of American democracy. Here are some of his thoughts:

On patriotism:

Patriotism to me is being proud to live in a country where you can either toe the majority line or oppose it and dissent. And either way it's allowed because the laws and the constitution encourage that kind of behavior. It's a lot different from a lot of places where dissenting gets you killed. Or gets you ostracized or exiled. And to me, dissenting by itself is an act of patriotism. It's a validation and a confirmation of everything that America stands for.

On keeping the republic:

You know, everybody has talents. Everybody has skills. And those skills always have some sort of political application. And I think what's important is to understand what the issues are, understand what's at stake. I think it's important to take a side. Any side. And use those skills—technology allows people to use those skills if you get plugged into the right communities. . . . I think what's key, and it doesn't have to be Democratic Party and Republican Party either, it can be if you believe strongly in the arts and it's defending funding for the arts or volunteering with your local theater arts group or artist colony. It could be advocating for stem cell research. . . . It's [important to] find something that you believe in and tap into that community. And the way technology is developing, there's a community for everything out there.

Source: Markos Moulitsas talked with Christine Barbour and Gerald Wright on July 5, 2005.

and media criticism. As is true of any unregulated media source, there is a good deal of inaccurate and unsubstantiated information in the so-called blogosphere. There is no credentialing process for bloggers, they are not usually admitted to the White House or other official news conferences unless they also report for a more traditional media outlet, and they generally lack the resources required to do a great deal of investigative reporting.

But blogs can also do many things their more mainstream brethren cannot and there is some truly first-rate journalism to be found on blogs. Since bloggers are not (usually) indebted to deep corporate pockets, they can hold the mainstream media accountable. For example, when CBS's Dan Rather reported in the fall of 2004 on documents that seemed to support the claim that President Bush had used influence to escape the draft, it was bloggers who discovered that the evidence was fraudulent. It is the job of the consumer to scrutinize the reporting of bloggers as scrupulously as they do the rest of the media, however. When bloggers argued that an ABC broadcast memo reportedly circulated by Republicans to detail how they could make political use of the Terri Schiavo case was also fraudulent, they turned out to be wrong. There is no substitute for critical evaluation of the news, but blogs are a media form that is truly independent, open, and democratic in a way that no other media source can be.

CIVIC JOURNALISM

A second noteworthy development in the American media has emerged from a crisis of conscience on the part of some journalists themselves. These reformers have been drawn by increasing levels of public cynicism about the press and politics and by relentless criticism of the media to reconsider the principles that guide their profession. Many of them advocate civic journalism, a journalistic movement to be responsive to citizen input in determining what news to cover. Under the banner of civic journalism, a wide range of projects and experiments focused on bringing citizens' concerns and proposed solutions into the reporting process have been carried out.

A 1992 study of these efforts found them to be widespread—322 of the 1,500 daily papers in the United States experimented with some form of civic journalism between 1994 and 2001. Two main strategies the papers followed was to provide explanations of events rather than focusing on conflicting viewpoints about them, and to provide space for citizen perspectives on the day's news. The study found positive effects of such practices on the capacity of communities to deliberate on issues, on the development of individuals' citizenship skills, and even, to a lesser degree, on pubic policy itself.[80]

But while civic journalism practices are popular with readers and seem to be effective at reaching their goals, they are not without critics who claim that efforts to involve the public more fully in the reporting process are unnecessary since good journalists already do so. Critics also warn that some efforts may confuse journalists with social workers or turn journalists into advocates rather than neutral observers; that the experiments are just marketing gimmicks; that the movement lets consumers, rather than the professional judgment of journalists, control the content of newspapers.[81] What is at stake here is a vision of journalism, and of the ideal journalist as a detached recorder of events, but also a vision of democracy. The democracy reinforced by the traditional media is an elite version; the democracy suggested by these reforms is far more participatory, although even these reforms come from the top down rather than from the grassroots up.

WHAT'S AT STAKE REVISITED

We have seen in this chapter that free media have a vital role to play in a democracy but that many forces conspire to limit their ability to play that role. Pressures within the profession of journalism itself; corporate pressures from owners and advertisers; and political pressures from candidates, officials, and their staff all make the job of honest, objective reporting in the public interest difficult to pull off. During wartime, those pressures are joined by physical threats that limit where journalists can go, by official pressure from government to restrict information, and by ideological pressure from those who want to silence criticism of government in the name of patriotism.

In time of war, democracies have an even greater stake in having a free and responsible media. When passions run high and emotions are near the surface, when love of one's country makes one want to cast objectivity to the winds and leap to its defense, when the government has called out its military and is wielding huge and unprecedented power, administering justice and killing people without all the usual democratic safeguards of due process and democratic deliberation, it is more important than ever that checks, including the check of a free press, be placed on the power of that government. Ironically, that is the time when those checks are least likely to be forthcoming.

Journalist Neil Hickey argues that the press and the government can rarely be on "cozy" terms because their interests are inevitably opposed and their cultures are very different.[82] The Pentagon wants to control war news because it has an obligation to protect its troops on the ground and to keep its military strategy confidential. Much of the war on terrorism is waged in unconventional and clandestine ways, not suitable for traditional media coverage. In fact, the military sometimes has an interest not just in keeping true information from the enemy, but in distributing false information—information that would reach American enemies and citizens alike. At home, the threat to domestic security is real. The administration is reluctant to release information about potential attacks because it does not want to cause panic and because it needs to protect its intelligence sources to guard against future attacks. Sensitive information is withdrawn from the public realm because terrorists have shown their taste for turning American technology against us, and to limit their access to harmful information is to limit ours as well.

Weighed against the interests of the government in maintaining control of information is the media's interest in gaining access. There is no getting around the fact that, in a democracy, people make decisions about their leaders that they can make only if they know what those leaders are doing. Information is essential for a functioning democracy. To suppress that information gives politicians a free pass from democratic scrutiny and from accountability to the public. Power wielded in secret is subject to abuse in ways that power wielded

continued

Thinking Outside the Box

- Should the media be driven by what consumers want to know or what they need to know?
- Can a corporately owned press be a free press?
- Should journalists rely on anonymous sources?

WHAT'S AT STAKE REVISITED *(continued)*

in sunlight is not. To claim that information is not necessary is to trust in elected officials to a degree that our founders warned against and to risk the loss of freedoms that, once lost, would be very hard to regain. It is ironic that the administration's goal in the current war in Iraq is to gain a foothold for democracy in the Middle East, when critics at home claim that democracy at home is endangered by that effort.

Hickey argues that the conflicting agendas of the government and of the press are equally valid. It is in the tension between the two, he claims, that the public is best served; they each, essentially, help to keep the other side honest. What that requires is that public opinion supports the media's ability to do their job. Those who try to rally the public against the media and claim that censorship in the name of "patriotic policing" is in the national interest may be advocating the very policy that could ultimately bring this country to its knees.

To Sum Up

KEY TERMS

republic.cqpress.com

blogs (p. 643)
civic journalism (p. 654)
commercial bias (p. 647)
feeding frenzy (p. 663)
framing (p. 659)
gatekeepers (p. 653)
horse-race journalism (p. 662)
leaks (p. 667)
mass media (p. 638)
muckrakers (p. 653)
narrowcasting (p. 642)
news management (p. 666)
political accountability (p. 669)
priming (p. 659)
pundit (p. 657)
revolving door (p. 657)
selective perception (p. 660)
sound bite (p. 662)
spin (p. 666)
trial balloon (p. 667)

Key terms, chapter summaries, practice quizzes, Internet links, and other study aids are available on the companion Web site at: republic.cqpress.com.

SUMMARY

republic.cqpress.com

- Mass media are forms of communication—such as television, radio, the Internet, newspapers, and magazines—that reach large public audiences. More media outlets and more information mean that Americans must devote ever-increasing time, effort, and money to sort out what is relevant to them.
- Media ownership can influence the kind of news we get. Early political parties and candidates created newspapers to advocate their issues. When newspapers suddenly became cheap and thus accessible to the general public in the 1830s, papers aimed for objectivity as a way to attract more readers. Later, newspaper owners used sensationalist reporting to sell more newspapers and gain independence from political interests. Today's media, still profit driven, are now owned by a few large corporate interests.
- The 1934 Federal Communications Act, which created the Federal Communications Commission, imposed order on multiple media outlets and attempted to serve the public interest through three provisions: the equal time rule, the fairness doctrine, and the right of rebuttal.
- Journalists, playing four roles, have great influence over news content and presentation. Gatekeepers decide what is news and what is not. Disseminators determine relevant news and get it out to the public quickly. The investigator role involves verifying the truth of various claims or analyzing particular policies. Finally, as public mobilizers, journalists try to report the peoples' interests rather than their own.
- Public skepticism of the media has increased in recent decades. Some critics believe the homogeneous background of journalists—mostly male, white, well educated, with northeastern roots—biases the press, as does their predominantly liberal ideology. Others claim that the revolving door, the practice of journalists taking government positions but later returning to reporting, severely damages news objectivity.
- Citizen access to the media has been primarily passive, but the rise of new, interactive media and the growth of the civic journalism movement may help to transform citizens into more active media participants.

PRACTICE QUIZ

republic.cqpress.com

1. Compared to most industrialized countries,

a. American newspapers are more ideological.
b. newspaper circulation is much lower in the United States.
c. newspaper circulation is much higher in the United States.
d. U.S. cities are more likely to have two major newspapers.
e. Americans rely more on newspapers to receive their news.

2. The increase in the use of blogs is significant because

a. the news communicated through blogs is much more accurate than other news sources.
b. the web may realize its potential for offering a truly democratic and "free" alternative to the corporate-produced news we now receive.
c. it is easier for the poor to obtain political news.
d. it will lessen the effects of feeding frenzy.
e. it is a strictly regulated news source.

3. The journalistic reporting of Bob Woodward and Carl Bernstein in uncovering the Watergate scandal is an example of

a. muckraking.
b. yellow journalism.
c. civic journalism.
d. exploitation.
e. investigative journalism.

4. Civic journalism is the

a. belief that it is a journalist's job to teach the public basic facts about government.
b. movement among journalists to be responsive to citizen input in determining what news stories to cover.
c. movement toward making news coverage more positive.
d. movement toward making news coverage more objective.
e. movement toward increasing the number of blogs.

5. The process through which the media emphasize particular aspects of a news story, thereby influencing the public's perception of the story is

a. priming.
b. agenda setting.
c. news management.
d. selective perception.
e. framing

SUGGESTED RESOURCES

republic.cqpress.com

Books

Alterman, Eric. 2004. *What Liberal Media? The Truth About Bias and the News.* New York: Basic Books. Alterman takes Goldberg (see below) to task and argues that the real problems with the media are corporate ownership and a conservative "punditocracy."

Bagdikian, Ben H. 2004. *The New Media Monopoly.* Boston: Beacon Press. Bagdikian provides an engaging analysis of the evils of large media corporations and their domination of American news, entertainment, and popular culture.

Crouse, Timothy. 1973. *The Boys on the Bus: Riding With the Campaign Press Corps.* New York: Ballantine. One of the most exciting books you'll find on media coverage of political campaigns. The author takes you behind the scenes during the 1972 presidential election.

Downie, Leonard, Jr., and Robert G. Kaiser. 2002. *The News About the News: American Journalism in Peril.* New York: Knopf. Two *Washington Post* veterans share their take on what is wrong with the American news media. Among their targets: television news, civic journalism, and corporately owned media outlets.

Goldberg, Bernard. 2003. *Bias: A CBS Insider Exposes How the Media Distort the News.* New York: Perennial. CBS news veteran Goldberg claims that the media are overwhelmingly liberally biased, shares stories from his days at CBS, and goes after Dan Rather.

Graber, Doris A. 2006. *Mass Media and American Politics,* 7th ed. Washington, D.C.: CQ Press. Graber argues that the mass media have become increasingly important and powerful players in the American political process.

Hertsgaard, Mark. 1988. *On Bended Knee: The Press and the Reagan Presidency,* New York: Farrar Straus & Giroux. In crafting this wonderful account of Reagan's relationship with the press, Hertsgaard interviewed 175 senior Reagan officials, journalists, and news executives to get an in-depth look at the Great Communicator's dealings with the media.

Iyengar, Shanto, and Donald R. Kinder. 1987. *News That Matters: Television and American Opinion.* Chicago: University of Chicago Press. A relatively short book with a compelling message: that television news educates the American public and shapes our perception of political life.

Sabato, Larry J. 1991. *Feeding Frenzy: How Attack Journalism Has Transformed American Politics.* New York: Free Press. A thought-provoking analysis of how the press's preference for sensationalized news has changed the way politics is played.

Walsh, Kenneth T. 1996. *Feeding the Beast: The White House Versus the Press.* New York: Random House. A well-known White House reporter's engaging account of how the White House and the press use each other to achieve their goals.

West, Darrell M. 2005. *Air Wars: Television Advertising in Election Campaigns, 1952–2004,* 4th ed. Washington, D.C.: CQ Press. A comprehensive and informative source on the use of television advertising in campaigns and how political ads have changed over time.

Web Sites

A lengthy compilation of media sites that cover political news, including the Web sites of daily newspapers, blogs, and other outlets, appears on this book's companion Web site, at **republic.cqpress.com.** Here we highlight only a few:

Columbia Journalism Review. www.cjr.org. An outlet for the media to report on the media.

www.drudgereport.com and **www.buzzflash.com.** Conservative Drudge and liberal Buzzflash provide up-to-the-minute summaries of a variety of political stories, events, and rumors.

Poynter Online. www.poynter.org. The Web site for the Poynter Institute, a nonprofit school for journalists and teachers of journalists, offers useful information on issues of diversity, ethics, and interpreting the media.

Movies

***All the President's Men.* 1976.** The story of how two young *Washington Post* journalists' investigative reporting led to the downfall of Richard Nixon. After the movie (as well as the book) was released, the number of people entering the field of journalism increased dramatically.

***Wag the Dog.* 1998.** The president "creates" a war on television to distract the public from a recent scandal, raising interesting questions about the strength of our democracy given the enormous influence of the media and other elites.

Television for suggested viewing: **The Daily Show With Jon Stewart** (Comedy Central). A hip, irreverent, and smart comedic take on the media and politics.

APPENDIX MATERIAL

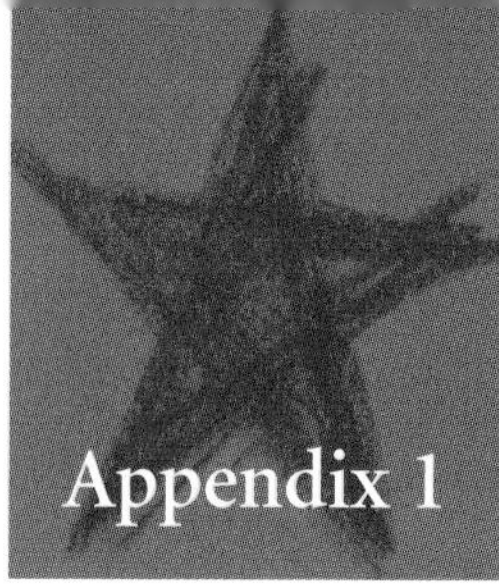

Appendix 1

ARTICLES OF CONFEDERATION

To all to whom these Presents shall come, we the under-signed Delegates of the States affixed to our Names send greeting.

Articles of Confederation and perpetual Union between the states of New Hampshire, Massachusetts-bay Rhode Island and Providence Plantations, Connecticut, New York, New Jersey, Pennsylvania, Delaware, Maryland, Virginia, North Carolina, South Carolina and Georgia.

ARTICLE I

The Stile of this Confederacy shall be "The United States of America".

ARTICLE II

Each state retains its sovereignty, freedom, and independence, and every power, jurisdiction, and right, which is not by this Confederation expressly delegated to the United States, in Congress assembled.

ARTICLE III

The said States hereby severally enter into a firm league of friendship with each other, for their common defense, the security of their liberties, and their mutual and general welfare, binding themselves to assist each other, against all force offered to, or attacks made upon them, or any of them, on account of religion, sovereignty, trade, or any other pretense whatever.

ARTICLE IV

The better to secure and perpetuate mutual friendship and intercourse among the people of the different States in this Union, the free inhabitants of each of these States, paupers, vagabonds, and fugitives from justice excepted, shall be entitled to all privileges and immunities of free citizens in the several States; and the people of each State shall free ingress and regress to and from any other State, and shall enjoy therein all the privileges of trade and commerce, subject to the same duties, impositions, and restrictions as the inhabitants thereof respectively, provided that such restrictions shall not extend so far as to prevent the removal of property imported into any State, to any other State, of which the owner is an inhabitant; provided also that no imposition, duties or restriction shall be laid by any State, on the property of the United States, or either of them.

If any person guilty of, or charged with, treason, felony, or other high misdemeanor in any State, shall flee from justice, and be found in any of the United States, he shall, upon demand of the Governor or executive power of the State from which he fled, be delivered up and removed to the State having jurisdiction of his offense.

Full faith and credit shall be given in each of these States to the records, acts, and judicial proceedings of the courts and magistrates of every other State.

ARTICLE V

For the most convenient management of the general interests of the United States, delegates shall be annually appointed in such manner as the legislatures of each State shall direct, to meet in Congress on the first Monday in November, in every year, with a power reserved to each State to recall its delegates, or any of them, at any time within the year, and to send others in their stead for the remainder of the year.

No State shall be represented in Congress by less than two, nor more than seven members; and no person shall be capable of being a delegate for more than three years in any term of six years; nor shall any person, being a delegate, be capable of holding any office under the United States, for which he, or another for his benefit, receives any salary, fees or emolument of any kind.

Each State shall maintain its own delegates in a meeting of the States, and while they act as members of the committee of the States.

In determining questions in the United States in Congress assembled, each State shall have one vote.

Freedom of speech and debate in Congress shall not be impeached or questioned in any court or place out of Congress, and the members of Congress shall be protected in their persons from arrests or imprisonments, during the time of their going to and from, and attendence on Congress, except for treason, felony, or breach of the peace.

ARTICLE VI

No State, without the consent of the United States in Congress assembled, shall send any embassy to, or receive any embassy from, or enter into any conference, agreement, alliance or treaty with any King, Prince or State; nor shall any person holding any office of profit or trust under the United States, or any of them, accept any present, emolument, office or title of any kind whatever from any King, Prince or foreign State; nor shall the United States in Congress assembled, or any of them, grant any title of nobility.

No two or more States shall enter into any treaty, confederation or alliance whatever between them, without the consent of the United States in Congress assembled, specifying accurately the purposes for which the same is to be entered into, and how long it shall continue.

No State shall lay any imposts or duties, which may interfere with any stipulations in treaties, entered into by the United States in Congress assembled, with any King, Prince or State, in pursuance of any treaties already proposed by Congress, to the courts of France and Spain.

No vessel of war shall be kept up in time of peace by any State, except such number only, as shall be deemed necessary by the United States in Congress assembled, for the defense of such State, or its trade; nor shall any body of forces be kept up by any State in time of peace, except such number only, as in the judgement of the United States in Congress assembled, shall be deemed requisite to garrison the forts necessary for the defense of such State; but every State shall always keep up a well-regulated and disciplined militia, sufficiently armed and accoutered, and shall provide and constantly have ready for use, in public stores, a due number of filed pieces and tents, and a proper quantity of arms, ammunition and camp equipage.

No State shall engage in any war without the consent of the United States in Congress assembled, unless such State be actually invaded by enemies, or shall have received certain advice of a resolution being formed by some nation of Indians to invade such State, and the danger is so imminent as not to admit of a delay till the United States in Congress assembled can be consulted; nor shall any State grant commissions to any ships or vessels of war, nor letters of marque or reprisal, except it be after a declaration of war by the United States in Congress assembled, and then only against the Kingdom or State and the subjects thereof, against which war has been so declared, and under such regulations as shall be established by the United States in Congress assembled, unless such State be infested by pirates, in which case vessels of war may be fitted out for that occasion, and kept so long as the danger shall continue, or until the United States in Congress assembled shall determine otherwise.

ARTICLE VII

When land forces are raised by any State for the common defense, all officers of or under the rank of colonel, shall be appointed by the legislature of each State respectively, by whom such forces shall be raised, or in such manner as such State shall direct, and all vacancies shall be filled up by the State which first made the appointment.

ARTICLE VIII

All charges of war, and all other expenses that shall be incurred for the common defense or general welfare, and allowed by the United States in Congress assembled, shall be defrayed out of a common treasury, which shall be supplied by the several States in proportion to the value of all land within each State, granted or surveyed for any person, as such land and the buildings and improvements thereon shall be estimated according to such mode as the United States in Congress assembled, shall from time to time direct and appoint.

The taxes for paying that proportion shall be laid and levied by the authority and direction of the legislatures of the several States within the time agreed upon by the United States in Congress assembled.

ARTICLE IX

The United States in Congress assembled, shall have the sole and exclusive right and power of determining on peace and war, except in the cases mentioned in the sixth article— of sending and receiving ambassadors—entering into treaties and alliances, provided that no treaty of commerce shall be made whereby the legislative power of the respective States shall be restrained from imposing such imposts and duties on foreigners, as their own people are subjected to, or from prohibiting the exportation or importation of any species of goods or commodities whatsoever—of establishing rules for deciding in all cases, what captures on land or water shall be legal, and in what manner prizes taken by land or naval forces in the service of the United States shall be divided or appropriated—of granting letters of marque and reprisal in times of peace—appointing courts for the trial of piracies and felonies commited on the high seas and establishing courts for receiving and determining finally appeals in all cases of captures, provided that no member of Congress shall be appointed a judge of any of the said courts.

The United States in Congress assembled shall also be the last resort on appeal in all disputes and differences now subsisting or that hereafter may arise between two or more States concerning boundary, jurisdiction or any other causes whatever; which authority shall always be exercised in the manner following. Whenever the legislative or executive authority or lawful agent of any State in controversy with another shall present a petition to Congress stating the matter in question and praying for a hearing, notice thereof shall be given by order of Congress to the legislative or executive authority of the other State in controversy, and a day assigned for the appearance of the parties by their lawful agents, who shall then be directed to appoint by joint consent, commissioners or judges to constitute a court for hearing and determining the matter in question: but if they cannot agree, Congress shall name three persons out of each of the United States, and from the list of such persons each party shall alternately strike out one, the petitioners beginning, until the number shall be reduced to thirteen; and from that number not less than seven, nor more than nine names as Congress shall direct, shall in the presence of Congress be drawn out by lot, and the persons whose names shall be so drawn or any five of them, shall be commissioners or judges, to hear and finally determine the controversy, so always as a major part of the judges who shall hear the cause shall agree in the determination: and if either party shall neglect to attend at the day appointed, without showing reasons, which Congress shall judge sufficient, or being present shall refuse to strike, the Congress shall proceed to nominate three persons out of each State, and the secretary of Congress shall strike in behalf of such party absent or refusing; and the judgement and sentence of the court to be appointed, in the manner before prescribed, shall be final and conclusive; and if any of the parties shall refuse to submit to the authority of such court, or to appear or defend their claim or cause, the court shall nevertheless proceed to pronounce sentence, or judgement, which shall in like manner be final and decisive, the judgement or sentence and other proceedings being in either case transmitted to Congress, and lodged among the acts of Congress for the security of the parties concerned: provided that every commissioner, before he sits in judgement, shall take an oath to be administered by one of the judges of the supreme or superior court of the State, where the cause shall be tried, 'well and truly to hear and determine the matter in question, according to the best of his judgement, without favor, affection or hope of reward': provided also, that no State shall be deprived of territory for the benefit of the United States.

All controversies concerning the private right of soil claimed under different grants of two or more States, whose jurisdictions as they may respect such lands, and the States which passed such grants are adjusted, the said grants or either of them being at the same time claimed to have originated antecedent to such settlement of jurisdiction, shall on the petition of either party to the Congress of the United States, be finally determined as near as may be in the same manner as is before prescribed for deciding disputes respecting territorial jurisdiction between different States.

The United States in Congress assembled shall also have the sole and exclusive right and power of regulating the alloy and value of coin struck by their own authority, or by that of the respective States—fixing the standards of weights and measures throughout the United States—regulating the trade and managing all affairs with the Indians, not members of any of the States, provided that the legislative right of any State within its own limits be not infringed or violated—establishing or regulating post offices from one State to another, throughout all the United States, and exacting such postage on the papers passing through the same as may be requisite to defray the expenses of the said office—appointing all officers of the land forces, in the service of the United States, excepting regimental officers—appointing all the officers of the naval forces, and commissioning all officers whatever in the service of the United States—making rules for the government and regulation of the said land and naval forces, and directing their operations.

The United States in Congress assembled shall have authority to appoint a committee, to sit in the recess of Congress, to be denominated 'A Committee of the States', and to consist of one delegate from each State; and to appoint such other committees and civil officers as may be necessary for managing the general affairs of the United States under their direction—to appoint one of their members to preside, provided that no person be allowed to serve in the office of president more than one year in any term of three years; to ascertain the necessary sums of money to be raised for the service of the United

States, and to appropriate and apply the same for defraying the public expenses—to borrow money, or emit bills on the credit of the United States, transmitting every half-year to the respective States an account of the sums of money so borrowed or emitted—to build and equip a navy—to agree upon the number of land forces, and to make requisitions from each State for its quota, in proportion to the number of white inhabitants in such State; which requisition shall be binding, and thereupon the legislature of each State shall appoint the regimental officers, raise the men and cloath, arm and equip them in a solid-like manner, at the expense of the United States; and the officers and men so cloathed, armed and equipped shall march to the place appointed, and within the time agreed on by the United States in Congress assembled. But if the United States in Congress assembled shall, on consideration of circumstances judge proper that any State should not raise men, or should raise a smaller number of men than the quota thereof, such extra number shall be raised, officered, cloathed, armed and equipped in the same manner as the quota of each State, unless the legislature of such State shall judge that such extra number cannot be safely spread out in the same, in which case they shall raise, officer, cloath, arm and equip as many of such extra number as they judge can be safely spared. And the officers and men so cloathed, armed, and equipped, shall march to the place appointed, and within the time agreed on by the United States in Congress assembled.

The United States in Congress assembled shall never engage in a war, nor grant letters of marque or reprisal in time of peace, nor enter into any treaties or alliances, nor coin money, nor regulate the value thereof, nor ascertain the sums and expenses necessary for the defense and welfare of the United States, or any of them, nor emit bills, nor borrow money on the credit of the United States, nor appropriate money, nor agree upon the number of vessels of war, to be built or purchased, or the number of land or sea forces to be raised, nor appoint a commander in chief of the army or navy, unless nine States assent to the same: nor shall a question on any other point, except for adjourning from day to day be determined, unless by the votes of the majority of the United States in Congress assembled.

The Congress of the United States shall have power to adjourn to any time within the year, and to any place within the United States, so that no period of adjournment be for a longer duration than the space of six months, and shall publish the journal of their proceedings monthly, except such parts thereof relating to treaties, alliances or military operations, as in their judgement require secrecy; and the yeas and nays of the delegates of each State on any question shall be entered on the journal, when it is desired by any delegates of a State, or any of them, at his or their request shall be furnished with a transcript of the said journal, except such parts as are above excepted, to lay before the legislatures of the several States.

ARTICLE X

The Committee of the States, or any nine of them, shall be authorized to execute, in the recess of Congress, such of the powers of Congress as the United States in Congress assembled, by the consent of the nine States, shall from time to time think expedient to vest them with; provided that no power be delegated to the said Committee, for the exercise of which, by the Articles of Confederation, the voice of nine States in the Congress of the United States assembled be requisite.

ARTICLE XI

Canada acceding to this confederation, and adjoining in the measures of the United States, shall be admitted into, and entitled to all the advantages of this Union; but no other colony shall be admitted into the same, unless such admission be agreed to by nine States.

ARTICLE XII

All bills of credit emitted, monies borrowed, and debts contracted by, or under the authority of Congress, before the assembling of the United States, in pursuance of the present confederation, shall be deemed and considered as a charge against the United States, for payment and satisfaction whereof the said United States, and the public faith are hereby solemnly pleged.

ARTICLE XIII

Every State shall abide by the determination of the United States in Congress assembled, on all questions which by this confederation are submitted to them. And the Articles of this Confederation shall be inviolably observed by every State, and the Union shall be perpetual; nor shall any alteration at any time hereafter be made in any of them; unless such alteration be agreed to in a Congress of the United States, and be afterwards confirmed by the legislatures of every State.

And Whereas it hath pleased the Great Governor of the World to incline the hearts of the legislatures we respectively represent in Congress, to approve of, and to authorize us to ratify the said Articles of Confederation and perpetual Union. Know Ye that we the undersigned delegates, by virtue of the power and authority to us given for that purpose, do by these presents, in the name and in behalf of our respective constituents, fully and entirely ratify and confirm each and every of the said Articles of Confederation and perpetual Union, and all and singular the matters and things therein contained: And we do further solemnly plight and engage the faith of our respective constituents, that they shall abide by the determinations of the United States in Congress assembled, on all questions, which by the said Confederation are submitted to them. And that the Articles thereof shall be inviolably observed by the States we respectively represent, and that the Union shall be perpetual.

In Witness whereof we have hereunto set our hands in Congress. Done at Philadelphia in the State of Pennsylvania the ninth day of July in the Year of our Lord One Thousand Seven Hundred and Seventy-Eight, and in the Third Year of the independence of America.

Agreed to by Congress 15 November 1777
In force after ratification by Maryland, 1 March 1781

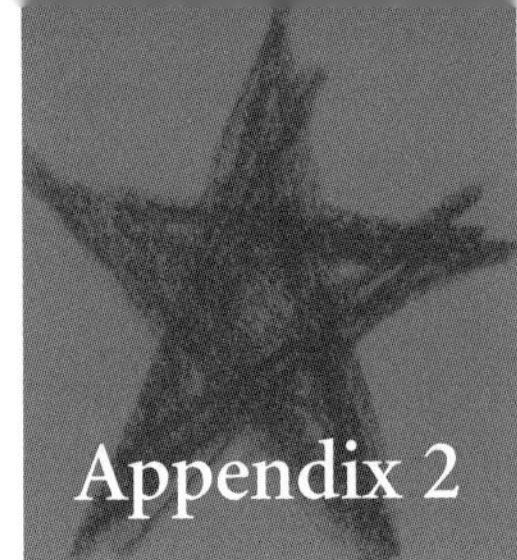

DECLARATION OF INDEPENDENCE

In Congress, July 4, 1776,
The Unanimous Declaration of
the Thirteen United States of America,

On June 11, 1776, the responsibility to "prepare a declaration" of independence was assigned by the Continental Congress, meeting in Philadelphia, to five members: John Adams, Benjamin Franklin, Thomas Jefferson, Robert Livingston, and Roger Sherman. Impressed by his talents as a writer, the committee asked Jefferson to compose a draft. After modifying Jefferson's draft the committee turned it over to Congress on June 28. On July 2 Congress voted to declare independence; on the evening of July 4, it approved the Declaration of Independence.

When in the Course of human events, it becomes necessary for one people to dissolve the political bands which have connected them with another, and to assume among the Powers of the earth, the separate and equal station to which the Laws of Nature and of Nature's God entitle them, a decent respect to the opinions of mankind requires that they should declare the causes which impel them to the separation.

We hold these truths to be self-evident, that all men are created equal, that they are endowed by their Creator with certain unalienable Rights, that among these are Life, Liberty and the pursuit of Happiness. That to secure these rights, Governments are instituted among Men, deriving their just powers from the consent of the governed. That whenever any form of Government becomes destructive of these ends, it is the Right of the People to alter or to abolish it, and to institute new Government, laying its foundation on such principles and organizing its powers in such form, as to them shall seem most likely to effect their Safety and Happiness. Prudence, indeed, will dictate that Government long established should not be changed for light and transient causes; and accordingly all experience hath shown, that mankind are more disposed to suffer, while evils are sufferable, than to right themselves by abolishing the forms to which they are accustomed. But when a long train of abuses and usurpations, pursuing invariably the same Object evinces a design to reduce them under absolute Despotism, it is their right, it is their duty, to throw off such Government, and to provide new Guards for their future security. Such has been the patient sufferance of these Colonies; and such is now the necessity which constrains them to alter their former Systems of Government. The history of the present King of Great Britain is a history of repeated injuries and usurpations, all having in direct object the establishment of an absolute Tyranny over these States. To prove this, let Facts be submitted to a candid world.

He has refused his Assent to Laws, the most wholesome and necessary for the public good.

He has forbidden his Governors to pass Laws of immediate and pressing importance, unless suspended in their operation till his Assent should be obtained; and when so suspended, he has utterly neglected to attend to them.

He has refused to pass other Laws for the accommodation of large districts of people, unless those people would relinquish the right of Representation in the Legislature, a right inestimable to them and formidable to tyrants only.

He has called together legislative bodies at places unusual, uncomfortable, and distant from the depository of their Public Records, for the sole purpose of fatiguing them into compliance with his measures.

He has dissolved Representative Houses repeatedly, for opposing with manly firmness his invasions on the rights of the people.

He has refused for a long time, after such dissolutions, to cause others to be elected; whereby the Legislative Powers, incapable of Annihilation, have returned to the People at large for their exercise; the State remaining in the mean time exposed to all the dangers of invasion from without, and convulsions within.

He has endeavored to prevent the population of these States; for that purpose obstructing the Laws of Naturalization of Foreigners; refusing to pass others to encourage their migration hither, and raising the conditions of new Appropriations of Lands.

He has obstructed the Administration of Justice, by refusing his Assent to Laws for establishing Judiciary Powers.

He has made Judges dependent on his Will alone, for the tenure of their offices, and the amount and payment of their salaries.

He has erected a multitude of New Offices, and sent hither swarms of Officers to harass our People, and eat out their substance.

He has kept among us, in times of peace, Standing Armies without the Consent of our legislature.

He has affected to render the Military independent of and superior to the Civil Power.

He has combined with others to subject us to a jurisdiction foreign to our constitution, and unacknowledged by our laws; giving his Assent to their acts of pretended legislation:

For quartering large bodies of armed troops among us:

For protecting them, by a mock Trial, from Punishment for any Murders which they should commit on the Inhabitants of these States:

For cutting off our Trade with all parts of the world:

For imposing taxes on us without our Consent:

For depriving us in many cases, of the benefits of Trial by Jury:

For transporting us beyond Seas to be tried for pretended offences:

For abolishing the free System of English Laws in a neighbouring Province, establishing therein an Arbitrary government, and enlarging its Boundaries so as to render it at once an example and fit instrument for introducing the same absolute rule into these Colonies:

For taking away our Charters, abolishing our most valuable Laws, and altering fundamentally the Forms of our Governments:

For suspending our own Legislature, and declaring themselves invested with Power to legislate for us in all cases whatsoever.

He has abdicated Government here, by declaring us out of his Protection and waging War against us.

He has plundered our seas, ravaged our Coasts, burnt our towns, and destroyed the lives of our people.

He is at this time transporting large armies of foreign mercenaries to compleat the works of death, desolation and tyranny, already begun with circumstances of Cruelty & perfidy scarcely parallel in the most barbarous ages, and totally unworthy the Head of a civilized nation.

He has constrained our fellow Citizens taken Captive on the high Seas to bear Arms against their Country, to become the executioners of their friends and Brethren, or to fall themselves by their Hands.

He has excited domestic insurrections amongst us, and has endeavoured to bring on the inhabitants of our frontiers, the merciless Indian Savages, whose known rule of warfare, is an undistinguished destruction of all ages, sexes and conditions.

In every stage of these Oppressions We have Petitioned for Redress in the most humble terms: Our repeated Petitions have been answered only by repeated injury. A Prince, whose character is thus marked by every act which may define a Tyrant, is unfit to be the ruler of a free People.

Nor have We been wanting in attention to our British brethren. We have warned them from time to time of attempts by their legislature to extend an unwarrantable jurisdiction over us. We have reminded them of the circumstances of our emigration and settlement here. We have appealed to their native justice and magnanimity, and we have conjured them by the ties of our common kindred to disavow these usurpations, which would inevitably interrupt our connections and correspondence. They too have been deaf to the voice of justice and of consanguinity. We must, therefore, acquiesce in the necessity, which denounces our Separation, and hold them, as we hold the rest of mankind, Enemies in War, in Peace Friends.

We, therefore, the Representatives of the United States of America, in General Congress, Assembled, appealing to the Supreme Judge of the world for the rectitude of our intentions, do, in the Name, and by Authority of the good People of these Colonies, solemnly publish and declare, That these United Colonies are, and of Right ought to be Free and Independent States; that they are Absolved from all Allegiance to the British Crown, and that all political connection between them and the State of Great Britain, is and ought to be totally dissolved; and that as Free and Independent States, they have full Power to levy War, conclude Peace, contract Alliances, establish Commerce, and to do all other Acts and Things which Independent States may of right do. And for the support of this Declaration, with a firm reliance on the Protection of Divine Providence, we mutually pledge to each other our Lives, our Fortunes and our sacred Honor.

John Hancock.

New Hampshire:
Josiah Bartlett,
William Whipple,
Matthew Thornton.

Massachusetts-Bay:
Samuel Adams,
John Adams,
Robert Treat Paine,
Elbridge Gerry.

Rhode Island:
Stephen Hopkins,
William Ellery.

Connecticut:
Roger Sherman,
Samuel Huntington,
William Williams,
Oliver Wolcott.

New York:
William Floyd,
Philip Livingston,
Francis Lewis,
Lewis Morris.

Pennsylvania:
Robert Morris,
Benjamin Harris,
Benjamin Franklin,
John Morton,
George Clymer,
James Smith,
George Taylor,
James Wilson,
George Ross.

Delaware:
Caesar Rodney,
George Read,
Thomas McKean.

Georgia:
Button Gwinnett,
Lyman Hall,
George Walton.

Maryland:
Samuel Chase,
William Paca,
Thomas Stone,
Charles Carroll of Carrollton.

Virginia:
George Wythe,
Richard Henry Lee,
Thomas Jefferson,
Benjamin Harrison,
Thomas Nelson Jr.,
Francis Lightfoot Lee,
Carter Braxton.

North Carolina:
William Hooper,
Joseph Hewes,
John Penn.

South Carolina:
Edward Rutledge,
Thomas Heyward Jr.,
Thomas Lynch Jr.,
Arthur Middleton.

New Jersey:
Richard Stockton,
John Witherspoon,
Francis Hopkinson,
John Hart,
Abraham Clark.

Appendix 3

CONSTITUTION OF THE UNITED STATES

The United States Constitution was written at a convention that Congress called on February 21, 1787, for the purpose of recommending amendments to the Articles of Confederation. Every state but Rhode Island sent delegates to Philadelphia, where the convention met that summer. The delegates decided to write an entirely new constitution, completing their labors on September 17. Nine states (the number the Constitution itself stipulated as sufficient) ratified by June 21, 1788.

The Framers of the Constitution included only six paragraphs on the Supreme Court. Article III, Section 1, created the Supreme Court and the federal system of courts. It provided that "[t]he judicial power of the United States, shall be vested in one supreme Court," and whatever inferior courts Congress "from time to time" saw fit to establish. Article III, Section 2, delineated the types of cases and controversies that should be considered by a federal—rather than a state—court. But beyond this, the Constitution left many of the particulars of the Supreme Court and the federal court system for Congress to decide in later years in judiciary acts.

We the People of the United States, in Order to form a more perfect Union, establish Justice, insure domestic Tranquility, provide for the common defence, promote the general Welfare, and secure the Blessings of Liberty to ourselves and our Posterity, do ordain and establish this Constitution for the United States of America.

ARTICLE I

Section 1. All legislative Powers herein granted shall be vested in a Congress of the United States, which shall consist of a Senate and House of Representatives.

Section 2. The House of Representatives shall be composed of Members chosen every second Year by the People of the several States, and the Electors in each State shall have the Qualifications requisite for Electors of the most numerous Branch of the State Legislature.

No Person shall be a Representative who shall not have attained to the age of twenty five Years, and been seven Years a Citizen of the United States, and who shall not, when elected, be an Inhabitant of that State in which he shall be chosen.

[Representatives and direct Taxes shall be apportioned among the several States which may be included within this Union, according to their respective Numbers, which shall be determined by adding to the whole Number of free Persons, including those bound to Service for a Term of Years, and excluding Indians not taxed, three fifths of all other Persons.][1] The actual Enumeration shall be made within three Years after the first Meeting of the Congress of the United States, and within every subsequent Term of ten Years, in such Manner as they shall by Law direct. The Number of Representatives shall not exceed one for every thirty Thousand, but each State shall have at Least one Representative; and until such enumeration shall be made, the State of New Hampshire shall be entitled to chuse three, Massachusetts eight, Rhode-Island and Providence Plantations one, Connecticut five, New-York six, New Jersey four, Pennsylvania eight, Delaware one, Maryland six, Virginia ten, North Carolina five, South Carolina five, and Georgia three.

When vacancies happen in the Representation from any State, the Executive Authority thereof shall issue Writs of Election to fill such Vacancies.

The House of Representatives shall chuse their Speaker and other Officers; and shall have the sole Power of Impeachment.

Section 3. The Senate of the United States shall be composed of two Senators from each State, [chosen by the Legislature thereof,][2] for six Years; and each Senator shall have one Vote.

Immediately after they shall be assembled in Consequence of the first Election, they shall be divided as equally as may be into three Classes. The Seats of the Senators of the first Class shall be vacated at the Expiration of the second Year, of the second Class at the Expiration of the fourth Year, and of the third Class at the Expiration of the sixth Year, so that one third may be chosen every second Year; [and if Vacancies happen by Resignation, or otherwise, during the Recess of the Legislature of any State, the Executive thereof may make temporary Appointments until the next Meeting of the Legislature, which shall then fill such Vacancies.][3]

No Person shall be a Senator who shall not have attained to the Age of thirty Years, and been nine Years a Citizen of the United States, and who shall not, when elected, be an Inhabitant of that State for which he shall be chosen.

The Vice President of the United States shall be President of the Senate, but shall have no Vote, unless they be equally divided.

The Senate shall chuse their other Officers, and also a President pro tempore, in the Absence of the Vice President, or when he shall exercise the Office of President of the United States.

The Senate shall have the sole Power to try all Impeachments. When sitting for that Purpose, they shall be on Oath or Affirmation. When the President of the United States is tried, the Chief Justice shall preside: And no Person shall be convicted without the Concurrence of two thirds of the Members present.

Judgment in Cases of Impeachment shall not extend further than to removal from Office, and disqualification to hold and enjoy any Office of honor, Trust or Profit under the United States: but the Party convicted shall nevertheless be liable and subject to Indictment, Trial, Judgment and Punishment, according to Law.

Section 4. The Times, Places and Manner of holding Elections for Senators and Representatives, shall be prescribed in each State by the Legislature thereof; but the Congress may at any time by Law make or alter such Regulations, except as to the Places of chusing Senators.

The Congress shall assemble at least once in every Year, and such Meeting shall [be on the first Monday in December],[4] unless they shall by Law appoint a different Day.

Section 5. Each House shall be the Judge of the Elections, Returns and Qualifications of its own Members, and a Majority of each shall constitute a Quorum to do Business; but a smaller Number may adjourn from day to day, and may be authorized to compel the Attendance of absent Members, in such Manner, and under such Penalties as each House may provide.

Each House may determine the Rules of its Proceedings, punish its Members for disorderly Behaviour, and, with the Concurrence of two thirds, expel a Member.

Each House shall keep a Journal of its Proceedings, and from time to time publish the same, excepting such Parts as may in their Judgment require Secrecy; and the Yeas and Nays of the Members of either House on any question shall, at the Desire of one fifth of those Present, be entered on the Journal.

Neither House, during the Session of Congress, shall, without the Consent of the other, adjourn for more than three days, nor to any other Place than that in which the two Houses shall be sitting.

Section 6. The Senators and Representatives shall receive a Compensation for their Services, to be ascertained by Law, and paid out of the Treasury of the United States. They shall in all Cases, except Treason, Felony and Breach of the Peace, be privileged from Arrest during their Attendance at the Session of their respective Houses, and in going to and returning from the same; and for any Speech or Debate in either House, they shall not be questioned in any other Place.

No Senator or Representative shall, during the Time for which he was elected, be appointed to any civil Office under the Authority of the United States, which shall have been created, or the Emoluments whereof shall have been encreased during such time; and no Person holding any Office under the United States, shall be a Member of either House during his Continuance in Office.

Section 7. All Bills for raising Revenue shall originate in the House of Representatives; but the Senate may propose or concur with Amendments as on other Bills.

Every Bill which shall have passed the House of Representatives and the Senate, shall, before it become a Law, be presented to the President of the United States; If he approve he shall sign it, but if not he shall return it, with his Objections to that House in which it shall have originated, who shall enter the Objections at large on their Journal, and proceed to reconsider it. If after such Reconsideration two thirds of that House shall agree to pass the Bill, it shall be sent, together with the Objections, to the other House, by which it shall likewise be reconsidered, and if approved by two thirds of that House, it shall become a Law. But in all such Cases the Votes of both Houses shall be determined by yeas and Nays, and the Names of the Persons voting for and against the Bill shall be entered on the Journal of each House respectively. If any Bill shall not be returned by the President within ten Days (Sundays excepted) after it shall have been presented to him, the Same shall be a

Law, in like Manner as if he had signed it, unless the Congress by their Adjournment prevent its Return, in which Case it shall not be a Law.

Every Order, Resolution, or Vote to which the Concurrence of the Senate and House of Representatives may be necessary (except on a question of Adjournment) shall be presented to the President of the United States; and before the Same shall take Effect, shall be approved by him, or being disapproved by him, shall be repassed by two thirds of the Senate and House of Representatives, according to the Rules and Limitations prescribed in the Case of a Bill.

Section 8. The Congress shall have Power To lay and collect Taxes, Duties, Imposts and Excises, to pay the Debts and provide for the common Defence and general Welfare of the United States; but all Duties, Imposts and Excises shall be uniform throughout the United States;

To borrow Money on the credit of the United States;

To regulate Commerce with foreign Nations, and among the several States, and with the Indian Tribes;

To establish an uniform Rule of Naturalization, and uniform Laws on the subject of Bankruptcies throughout the United States;

To coin Money, regulate the Value thereof, and of foreign Coin, and fix the Standard of Weights and Measures;

To provide for the Punishment of counterfeiting the Securities and current Coin of the United States;

To establish Post Offices and post Roads;

To promote the Progress of Science and useful Arts, by securing for limited Times to Authors and Inventors the exclusive Right to their respective Writings and Discoveries;

To constitute Tribunals inferior to the supreme Court;

To define and punish Piracies and Felonies committed on the high Seas, and Offences against the Law of Nations;

To declare War, grant Letters of Marque and Reprisal, and make Rules concerning Captures on Land and Water;

To raise and support Armies, but no Appropriation of Money to that Use shall be for a longer Term than two Years;

To provide and maintain a Navy;

To make Rules for the Government and Regulation of the land and naval Forces;

To provide for calling forth the Militia to execute the Laws of the Union, suppress Insurrections and repel Invasions;

To provide for organizing, arming, and disciplining, the Militia, and for governing such Part of them as may be employed in the Service of the United States, reserving to the States respectively, the Appointment of the Officers, and the Authority of training the Militia according to the discipline prescribed by Congress;

To exercise exclusive Legislation in all Cases whatsoever, over such District (not exceeding ten Miles square) as may, by Cession of particular States, and the Acceptance of Congress, become the Seat of the Government of the United States, and to exercise like Authority over all Places purchased by the Consent of the Legislature of the State in which the Same shall be, for the Erection of Forts, Magazines, Arsenals, dock-Yards, and other needful Buildings;—And

To make all Laws which shall be necessary and proper for carrying into Execution the foregoing Powers, and all other Powers vested by this Constitution in the Government of the United States, or in any Department or Officer thereof.

Section 9. The Migration or Importation of such Persons as any of the States now existing shall think proper to admit, shall not be prohibited by the Congress prior to the Year one thousand eight hundred and eight, but a Tax or duty may be imposed on such Importation, not exceeding ten dollars for each Person.

The Privilege of the Writ of Habeas Corpus shall not be suspended, unless when in Cases of Rebellion or Invasion the public Safety may require it.

No Bill of Attainder or ex post facto Law shall be passed.

No Capitation, or other direct, Tax shall be laid, unless in Proportion to the Census or Enumeration herein before directed to be taken.[5]

No Tax or Duty shall be laid on Articles exported from any State.

No Preference shall be given by any Regulation of Commerce or Revenue to the Ports of one State over those of another; nor shall Vessels bound to, or from, one State, be obliged to enter, clear, or pay Duties in another.

No Money shall be drawn from the Treasury, but in Consequence of Appropriations made by Law; and a regular Statement and Account of the Receipts and Expenditures of all public Money shall be published from time to time.

No Title of Nobility shall be granted by the United States: And no Person holding any Office of Profit or Trust under them, shall, without the Consent of the Congress, accept of any present, Emolument, Office, or Title, of any kind whatever, from any King, Prince, or foreign State.

Section 10. No State shall enter into any Treaty, Alliance, or Confederation; grant Letters of Marque and Reprisal; coin Money; emit Bills of Credit; make any Thing but gold and silver Coin a Tender in Payment of Debts; pass any Bill of Attainder, ex post facto Law, or Law impairing the Obligation of Contracts, or grant any Title of Nobility.

No State shall, without the Consent of the Congress, lay any Imposts or Duties on Imports or Exports, except what may be absolutely necessary for executing its inspection Laws: and the net Produce of all Duties and Imposts, laid by any State on Imports or Exports, shall be for the Use of the Treasury of the United States; and all such Laws shall be subject to the Revision and Controul of the Congress.

No State shall, without the Consent of Congress, lay any Duty of Tonnage, keep Troops, or Ships of War in time of Peace, enter into any Agreement or Compact with another State, or with a foreign Power, or engage in War, unless actually invaded, or in such imminent Danger as will not admit of delay.

ARTICLE II

Section 1. The executive Power shall be vested in a President of the United States of America. He shall hold his Office during the Term of four Years, and, together with the Vice President, chosen for the same Term, be elected, as follows:

Each State shall appoint, in such Manner as the Legislature thereof may direct, a Number of Electors, equal to the whole Number of Senators and Representatives to which the State may be entitled in the Congress: but no Senator or Representative, or Person holding an Office of Trust or Profit under the United States, shall be appointed an Elector.

[The Electors shall meet in their respective States, and vote by Ballot for two Persons, of whom one at least shall not be an Inhabitant of the same State with themselves. And they shall make a List of all the Persons voted for, and of the Number of Votes for each; which List they shall sign and certify, and transmit sealed to the Seat of the Government of the United States, directed to the President of the Senate. The President of the Senate shall, in the Presence of the Senate and House of Representatives, open all the Certificates, and the Votes shall then be counted. The Person having the greatest Number of Votes shall be the President, if such Number be a Majority of the whole Number of Electors appointed; and if there be more than one who have such Majority, and have an equal Number of Votes, then the House of Representatives shall immediately chuse by Ballot one of them for President; and if no Person have a Majority, then from the five highest on the list the said House shall in like Manner chuse the President. But in chusing the President, the Votes shall be taken by States, the Representation from each State having one Vote; A quorum for this Purpose shall consist of a Member or Members from two thirds of the States, and a Majority of all the States shall be necessary to a Choice. In every Case, after the Choice of the President, the Person having the greatest Number of Votes of the Electors shall be the Vice President. But if there should remain two or more who have equal Votes, the Senate shall chuse from them by Ballot the Vice President.][6]

The Congress may determine the Time of chusing the Electors, and the Day on which they shall give their Votes; which Day shall be the same throughout the United States.

No Person except a natural born Citizen, or a Citizen of the United States, at the time of the Adoption of this Constitution, shall be eligible to the Office of President; neither shall any Person be eligible to that Office who shall not have attained to the Age of thirty five Years, and been fourteen Years a Resident within the United States.

In Case of the Removal of the President from Office, or of his Death, Resignation, or Inability to discharge the Powers and Duties of the said Office,[7] the Same shall devolve on the Vice President, and the Congress may by Law provide for the Case of Removal, Death, Resignation or Inability, both of the President and Vice President, declaring what Officer shall then act as President, and such Officer shall act accordingly, until the Disability be removed, or a President shall be elected.

The President shall, at stated Times, receive for his Services, a Compensation, which shall neither be encreased nor diminished during the Period for which he shall have been elected, and he shall not receive within that Period any other Emolument from the United States, or any of them.

Before he enter on the Execution of his Office, he shall take the following Oath or Affirmation:—"I do solemnly swear (or affirm) that I will faithfully execute the Office of President of the United States, and will to the best of my Ability, preserve, protect and defend the Constitution of the United States."

Section 2. The President shall be Commander in Chief of the Army and Navy of the United States, and of the Militia of the several States, when called into the actual Service of the United States; he may require the Opinion, in writing, of the principal Officer in each of the executive Departments, upon any Subject relating to the Duties of their respective Offices, and he shall have Power to grant Reprieves and Pardons for Offences against the United States, except in Cases of Impeachment.

He shall have Power, by and with the Advice and Consent of the Senate, to make Treaties, provided two thirds of the Senators present concur; and he shall nominate, and by and with the Advice and Consent of the Senate, shall appoint Ambassadors, other public Ministers and Consuls, Judges of the supreme Court, and all other Officers of the United States, whose Appointments are not herein otherwise provided for, and which shall be established by Law: but the Congress may by Law vest the Appointment of such inferior Officers, as they think proper, in the President alone, in the Courts of Law, or in the Heads of Departments.

The President shall have Power to fill up all Vacancies that may happen during the Recess of the Senate, by granting Commissions which shall expire at the End of their next Session.

Section 3. He shall from time to time give to the Congress Information of the State of the Union, and recommend to their Consideration such Measures as he shall judge necessary and expedient; he may, on extraordinary Occasions, convene both Houses, or either of them, and in Case of Disagreement between them, with Respect to the Time of Adjournment, he may adjourn them to such Time as he shall think proper; he shall receive Ambassadors and other public Ministers; he shall take Care that the Laws be faithfully executed, and shall Commission all the Officers of the United States.

Section 4. The President, Vice President and all civil Officers of the United States, shall be removed from Office on Impeachment for, and Conviction of, Treason, Bribery, or other high Crimes and Misdemeanors.

ARTICLE III

Section 1. The judicial Power of the United States, shall be vested in one supreme Court, and in such inferior Courts as the Congress may from time to time ordain and establish. The Judges, both of the supreme and inferior Courts, shall hold their Offices during good Behaviour, and shall, at stated Times, receive for their Services, a Compensation, which shall not be diminished during their Continuance in Office.

Section 2. The judicial Power shall extend to all Cases, in Law and Equity, arising under this Constitution, the Laws of the United States, and Treaties made, or which shall be made, under their Authority; —to all Cases affecting Ambassadors, other public Ministers and Consuls; —to all Cases of admiralty and maritime Jurisdiction; —to Controversies to which the United States shall be a Party; —to Controversies between two or more States; —between a State and Citizens of another State;[8] —between Citizens of different States; —between Citizens of the same State claiming Lands under Grants of different States, and between a State, or the Citizens thereof, and foreign States, Citizens or Subjects.[8]

In all Cases affecting Ambassadors, other public Ministers and Consuls, and those in which a State shall be Party, the supreme Court shall have original Jurisdiction. In all the other Cases before mentioned, the supreme Court shall have appellate Jurisdiction, both as to Law and Fact, with such Exceptions, and under such Regulations as the Congress shall make.

The Trial of all Crimes, except in Cases of Impeachment, shall be by Jury; and such Trial shall be held in the State where the said Crimes shall have been committed; but when not committed within any State, the Trial shall be at such Place or Places as the Congress may by Law have directed.

Section 3. Treason against the United States, shall consist only in levying War against them, or in adhering to their Enemies, giving them Aid and Comfort. No Person shall be convicted of Treason unless on the Testimony of two Witnesses to the same overt Act, or on Confession in open Court.

The Congress shall have Power to declare the Punishment of Treason, but no Attainder of Treason shall work Corruption of Blood, or Forfeiture except during the Life of the Person attainted.

ARTICLE IV

Section 1. Full Faith and Credit shall be given in each State to the public Acts, Records, and judicial Proceedings of every other State. And the Congress may by general Laws prescribe the Manner in which such Acts, Records and Proceedings shall be proved, and the Effect thereof.

Section 2. The Citizens of each State shall be entitled to all Privileges and Immunities of Citizens in the several States.

A Person charged in any State with Treason, Felony, or other Crime, who shall flee from Justice, and be found in another State, shall on Demand of the executive Authority of the State from which he fled, be delivered up, to be removed to the State having Jurisdiction of the Crime.

[No Person held to Service or Labour in one State, under the Laws thereof, escaping into another, shall, in Consequence of any Law or Regulation therein, be discharged from such Service or Labour, but shall be delivered up on Claim of the Party to whom such Service or Labour may be due.][9]

Section 3. New States may be admitted by the Congress into this Union; but no new State shall be formed or erected within the Jurisdiction of any other State; nor any State be formed by the Junction of two or more States, or Parts of States, without the Consent of the Legislatures of the States concerned as well as of the Congress.

The Congress shall have Power to dispose of and make all needful Rules and Regulations respecting the Territory or other Property belonging to the United States; and nothing in this Constitution shall be so construed as to Prejudice any Claims of the United States, or of any particular State.

Section 4. The United States shall guarantee to every State in this Union a Republican Form of Government, and shall protect each of them against Invasion; and on Application of the Legislature, or of the Executive (when the Legislature cannot be convened) against domestic Violence.

ARTICLE V

The Congress, whenever two thirds of both Houses shall deem it necessary, shall propose Amendments to this Constitution, or, on the Application of the Legislatures of two thirds of the several States, shall call a Convention for proposing Amendments, which, in either Case, shall be valid to all Intents and Purposes, as Part of this Constitution, when ratified by the Legislatures of three fourths of the several States, or by Conventions in three fourths thereof, as the one or the other Mode of Ratification may be proposed by the Congress; Provided [that no Amendment which may be made prior to the Year One thousand eight hundred and eight shall in any Manner affect the first and fourth Clauses in the Ninth Section of the first Article; and][10] that no State, without its Consent, shall be deprived of its equal Suffrage in the Senate.

ARTICLE VI

All Debts contracted and Engagements entered into, before the Adoption of this Constitution, shall be as valid against the United States under this Constitution, as under the Confederation.

This Constitution, and the Laws of the United States which shall be made in Pursuance thereof; and all Treaties made, or which shall be made, under the Authority of the United States, shall be the supreme Law of the Land; and the Judges in every State shall be bound thereby, any Thing in the Constitution or Laws of any State to the Contrary notwithstanding.

The Senators and Representatives before mentioned, and the Members of the several State Legislatures, and all executive and judicial Officers, both of the United States and of the several States, shall be bound by Oath or Affirmation, to support this Constitution; but no religious Test shall ever be required as a Qualification to any Office or public Trust under the United States.

ARTICLE VII

The Ratification of the Conventions of nine States, shall be sufficient for the Establishment of this Constitution between the States so ratifying the Same.

Done in Convention by the Unanimous Consent of the States present the Seventeenth Day of September in the Year of our Lord one thousand seven hundred and Eighty seven and of the Independence of the United States of America the Twelfth. IN WITNESS whereof We have hereunto subscribed our Names,

George Washington, President and deputy from Virginia, and thirty-eight other delegates.

[The language of the original Constitution, not including the Amendments, was adopted by a convention of the states on September 17, 1787, and was subsequently ratified by the states on the following dates: Delaware, December 7, 1787; Pennsylvania, December 12, 1787; New Jersey, December 18, 1787; Georgia, January 2,

1788; Connecticut, January 9, 1788; Massachusetts, February 6, 1788; Maryland, April 28, 1788; South Carolina, May 23, 1788; New Hampshire, June 21, 1788.

Ratification was completed on June 21, 1788.

The Constitution subsequently was ratified by Virginia, June 25, 1788; New York, July 26, 1788; North Carolina, November 21, 1789; Rhode Island, May 29, 1790; and Vermont, January 10, 1791.]

AMENDMENTS

AMENDMENT I

(First ten amendments ratified December 15, 1791.)

Congress shall make no law respecting an establishment of religion, or prohibiting the free exercise thereof; or abridging the freedom of speech, or of the press; or the right of the people peaceably to assemble, and to petition the Government for a redress of grievances.

AMENDMENT II

A well regulated Militia, being necessary to the security of a free State, the right of the people to keep and bear Arms, shall not be infringed.

AMENDMENT III

No Soldier shall, in time of peace be quartered in any house, without the consent of the Owner, nor in time of war, but in a manner to be prescribed by law.

AMENDMENT IV

The right of the people to be secure in their persons, houses, papers, and effects, against unreasonable searches and seizures, shall not be violated, and no Warrants shall issue, but upon probable cause, supported by Oath or affirmation, and particularly describing the place to be searched, and the persons or things to be seized.

AMENDMENT V

No person shall be held to answer for a capital, or otherwise infamous crime, unless on a presentment or indictment of a Grand Jury, except in cases arising in the land or naval forces, or in the Militia, when in actual service in time of War or public danger; nor shall any person be subject for the same offence to be twice put in jeopardy of life or limb; nor shall be compelled in any criminal case to be a witness against himself, nor be deprived of life, liberty, or property, without due process of law; nor shall private property be taken for public use, without just compensation.

AMENDMENT VI

In all criminal prosecutions, the accused shall enjoy the right to a speedy and public trial, by an impartial jury of the State and district wherein the crime shall have been committed, which district shall have been previously ascertained by law, and to be informed of the nature and cause of the accusation; to be confronted with the witnesses against him; to have compulsory process for obtaining witnesses in his favor, and to have the Assistance of Counsel for his defence.

AMENDMENT VII

In Suits at common law, where the value in controversy shall exceed twenty dollars, the right of trial by jury shall be preserved, and no fact tried by a jury, shall be otherwise re-examined in any Court of the United States, than according to the rules of the common law.

AMENDMENT VIII

Excessive bail shall not be required, nor excessive fines imposed, nor cruel and unusual punishments inflicted.

AMENDMENT IX

The enumeration in the Constitution, of certain rights, shall not be construed to deny or disparage others retained by the people.

AMENDMENT X

The powers not delegated to the United States by the Constitution, nor prohibited by it to the States, are reserved to the States respectively, or to the people.

AMENDMENT XI *(Ratified February 7, 1795)*

The Judicial power of the United States shall not be construed to extend to any suit in law or equity, commenced or prosecuted against one of the United States by Citizens of another State, or by Citizens or Subjects of any Foreign State.

AMENDMENT XII *(Ratified June 15, 1804)*

The Electors shall meet in their respective states and vote by ballot for President and Vice-President, one of whom, at least, shall not be an inhabitant of the same state with themselves; they shall name in their ballots the person voted for as President, and in distinct ballots the person voted for as Vice-President, and they shall make distinct lists of all persons voted for as President, and of all persons voted for as Vice-President, and of the number of votes for each, which lists they shall sign and certify, and transmit sealed to the seat of the government of the United States, directed to the President of the Senate; — The President of the Senate shall, in the presence of the Senate and House of Representatives, open all the certificates and the votes shall then be counted; — The person having the greatest number of votes for President, shall be the President, if such number be a majority of the whole number of Electors appointed; and if no person have such majority, then from the persons having the highest numbers not exceeding three on the list of those voted for as President, the House of Representatives shall choose immediately, by ballot, the President. But in choosing the President, the votes shall be taken by states, the representation from each state having one vote; a quorum for this purpose shall consist of a member or members from two-thirds of the states, and a majority of all the states shall be necessary to a choice. [And if the House of Representatives shall not choose a President whenever the right of choice shall devolve upon them, before the fourth day of March next following, then the Vice-President shall act as President, as in the case of the death or other constitutional disability of the President. —][11] The person having the greatest number of votes as Vice-President, shall be the Vice-President, if such number be a majority of the whole number of Electors appointed, and if no person have a majority, then from the two highest numbers on the list, the Senate shall choose the Vice-President; a quorum for the purpose shall consist of two-thirds of the whole number of Senators, and a majority of the whole number shall be necessary to a choice. But no person constitutionally ineligible to the office of President shall be eligible to that of Vice-President of the United States.

AMENDMENT XIII *(Ratified December 6, 1865)*

Section 1. Neither slavery nor involuntary servitude, except as a punishment for crime whereof the party shall have been duly convicted, shall exist within the United States, or any place subject to their jurisdiction.

Section 2. Congress shall have power to enforce this article by appropriate legislation.

AMENDMENT XIV (RATIFIED JULY 9, 1868)

Section 1. All persons born or naturalized in the United States, and subject to the jurisdiction thereof, are citizens of the United States and of the State wherein they reside. No State shall make or enforce any law which shall abridge the privileges or immunities of citizens of the United States; nor shall any State deprive any person of life, liberty, or property, without due process of law; nor deny to any person within its jurisdiction the equal protection of the laws.

Section 2. Representatives shall be apportioned among the several States according to their respective numbers, counting the whole number of persons in each State, excluding Indians not taxed. But when the right to vote at any election for the choice of electors for President and Vice President of the United States, Representatives in Congress, the Executive and Judicial officers of a State, or the members of the Legislature thereof, is denied to any of the male inhabitants of such State, being twenty-one years of age,[12] and citizens of the United States, or in any way abridged, except for participation in rebellion, or other crime, the basis of representation therein shall be reduced in the proportion which the number of such male citizens shall bear to the whole number of male citizens twenty-one years of age in such State.

Section 3. No person shall be a Senator or Representative in Congress, or elector of President and Vice President, or hold any Office, civil or military, under the United States, or under any State, who, having previously taken an oath, as a member of Congress, or as an officer of the United States, or as a member of any State legislature, or as an executive or judicial officer of any State, to support the Constitution of the United States, shall have engaged in insurrection or rebellion against the same, or given aid or comfort to the enemies thereof. But Congress may by a vote of two-thirds of each House, remove such disability.

Section 4. The validity of the public debt of the United States, authorized by law, including debts incurred for payment of pensions and bounties for services in suppressing insurrection or rebellion, shall not be questioned. But neither the United States nor any State shall assume or pay any debt or obligation incurred in aid of insurrection or rebellion against the United States, or any claim for the loss or emancipation of any slave; but all such debts, obligations and claims shall be held illegal and void.

Section 5. The Congress shall have power to enforce, by appropriate legislation, the provisions of this article.

AMENDMENT XV *(Ratified February 3, 1870)*

Section 1. The right of citizens of the United States to vote shall not be denied or abridged by the United States or by any State on account of race, color, or previous condition of servitude.

Section 2. The Congress shall have power to enforce this article by appropriate legislation.

AMENDMENT XVI *(Ratified February 3, 1913)*

The Congress shall have power to lay and collect taxes on incomes, from whatever source derived, without apportionment among the several States, and without regard to any census or enumeration.

AMENDMENT XVII *(Ratified April 8, 1913)*

The Senate of the United States shall be composed of two Senators from each State, elected by the people thereof, for six years; and each Senator shall have one vote. The electors in each State shall have the qualifications requisite for electors of the most numerous branch of the State legislatures.

When vacancies happen in the representation of any State in the Senate, the executive authority of such State shall issue writs of election to fill such vacancies: Provided, That the legislature of any State may empower the executive thereof to make temporary appointments until the people fill the vacancies by election as the legislature may direct.

This amendment shall not be so construed as to affect the election or term of any Senator chosen before it becomes valid as part of the Constitution.

AMENDMENT XVIII *(Ratified January 16, 1919)*

Section 1. After one year from the ratification of this article the manufacture, sale, or transportation of intoxicating liquors within, the importation thereof into, or the exportation thereof from the United States and all territory subject to the jurisdiction thereof for beverage purposes is hereby prohibited.

Section 2. The Congress and the several States shall have concurrent power to enforce this article by appropriate legislation.

Section 3. This article shall be inoperative unless it shall have been ratified as an amendment to the Constitution by the legislatures of the several States, as provided in the Constitution, within seven years from the date of the submission hereof to the States by the Congress.[13]

AMENDMENT XIX *(Ratified August 18, 1920)*

The right of citizens of the United States to vote shall not be denied or abridged by the United States or by any State on account of sex.

Congress shall have power to enforce this article by appropriate legislation.

AMENDMENT XX *(Ratified January 23, 1933)*

Section 1. The terms of the President and Vice President shall end at noon on the 20th day of January, and the terms of Senators and Representatives at noon on the 3d day of January, of the years in which such terms would have ended if this article had not been ratified; and the terms of their successors shall then begin.

Section 2. The Congress shall assemble at least once in every year, and such meeting shall begin at noon on the 3d day of January, unless they shall by law appoint a different day.

Section 3.[14] If, at the time fixed for the beginning of the term of the President, the President elect shall have died, the Vice President elect shall become President. If a President shall not have been chosen before the time fixed for the beginning of his term, or if the President elect shall have failed to qualify, then the Vice President elect shall act as President until a President shall have qualified; and the Congress may by law provide for the case wherein neither a President elect nor a Vice President elect shall have qualified, declaring who shall then act as President, or the manner in which one who is to act shall be selected, and such person shall act accordingly until a President or Vice President shall have qualified.

Section 4. The Congress may by law provide for the case of the death of any of the persons from whom the House of Representatives may choose a President whenever the right of choice shall have devolved upon them, and for the case of the death of any of the persons from whom the Senate may choose a Vice President whenever the right of choice shall have devolved upon them.

Section 5. Sections 1 and 2 shall take effect on the 15th day of October following the ratification of this article.

Section 6. This article shall be inoperative unless it shall have been ratified as an amendment to the Constitution by the legislatures of three-fourths of the several States within seven years from the date of its submission.

AMENDMENT XXI *(Ratified December 5, 1933)*

Section 1. The eighteenth article of amendment to the Constitution of the United States is hereby repealed.

Section 2. The transportation or importation into any State, Territory, or possession of the United States for delivery or use therein of intoxicating liquors, in violation of the laws thereof, is hereby prohibited.

Section 3. This article shall be inoperative unless it shall have been ratified as an amendment to the Constitution by conventions in the several States, as provided in the Constitution, within seven years from the date of the submission hereof to the States by the Congress.

AMENDMENT XXII *(Ratified February 27, 1951)*

Section 1. No person shall be elected to the office of the President more than twice, and no person who has held the office of President, or acted as President, for more than two years of a term to which some other person was elected President shall be elected to the office of the President more than once. But this Article shall not apply to any person holding the office of President when this Article was proposed by the Congress, and shall not prevent any person who may be holding the office of President, or acting as President, during the term within which this Article becomes operative from holding the office of President or acting as President during the remainder of such term.

Section 2. This article shall be inoperative unless it shall have been ratified as an amendment to the Constitution by the legislatures of three-fourths of the several States within seven years from the date of its submission to the States by the Congress.

AMENDMENT XXIII *(Ratified March 29, 1961)*

Section 1. The District constituting the seat of Government of the United States shall appoint in such manner as the Congress may direct:

A number of electors of President and Vice President equal to the whole number of Senators and Representatives in Congress to which the District would be entitled if it were a State, but in no event more than the least populous State; they shall be in addition to those appointed by the States, but they shall be considered, for the purposes of the election of President and Vice President, to be electors appointed by a State; and they shall meet in the District and perform such duties as provided by the twelfth article of amendment.

Section 2. The Congress shall have power to enforce this article by appropriate legislation.

AMENDMENT XXIV *(Ratified January 23, 1964)*

Section 1. The right of citizens of the United States to vote in any primary or other election for President or Vice President, for electors for President or Vice President, or for Senator or Representative in Congress, shall not be denied or abridged by the United States or any State by reason of failure to pay any poll tax or other tax.

Section 2. The Congress shall have power to enforce this article by appropriate legislation.

AMENDMENT XXV *(Ratified February 10, 1967)*

Section 1. In case of the removal of the President from office or of his death or resignation, the Vice President shall become President.

Section 2. Whenever there is a vacancy in the offie of the Vice President, the President shall nominate a Vice President who shall take office upon confirmation by a majority vote of both Houses of Congress.

Section 3. Whenever the President transmits to the President pro tempore of the Senate and the Speaker of the House of Representatives his written declaration that he is unable to discharge the powers and duties of his office, and until he transmits to them a written declaration to the contrary, such powers and duties shall be discharged by the Vice President as Acting President.

Section 4. Whenever the Vice President and a majority of either the principal officers of the executive departments or of such other body as Congress may by law provide, transmit to the President pro tempore of the Senate and the Speaker of the House of Representatives their written declaration that the President is unable to discharge the powers and duties of his office, the Vice President shall immediately assume the powers and duties of the office as Acting President.

Thereafter, when the President transmits to the President pro tempore of the Senate and the Speaker of the House of Representatives his written declaration that no inability exists, he shall resume the powers and duties of his office unless the Vice President and a majority of either the principal officers of the executive departments or of such other body as Congress may by law provide, transmit within four days to the President pro tempore of the Senate and the Speaker of the House of Representatives their written declaration that the President is unable to discharge the powers and duties of his office. Thereupon Congress shall decide the issue, assembling within forty-eight hours for that purpose if not in session. If the Congress, within twenty-one days after receipt of the latter written declaration, or, if Congress is not in session, within twenty-one days after Congress is required to assemble, determines by two-thirds vote of both Houses that the President is unable to discharge the powers and duties of his office, the Vice President shall continue to discharge the same as Acting President; otherwise, the President shall resume the powers and duties of his office.

AMENDMENT XXVI *(Ratified July 1, 1971)*

Section 1. The right of citizens of the United States, who are eighteen years of age or older, to vote shall not be denied or abridged by the United States or by any State on account of age.

Section 2. The Congress shall have power to enforce this article by appropriate legislation.

AMENDMENT XXVII *(Ratified May 7, 1992)*

No law varying the compensation for the services of the Senators and Representatives shall take effect, until an election of Representatives shall have intervened.

Source: U.S. Congress, House, Committee on the Judiciary, The Constitution of the United States of America, as Amended, 100th Cong., 1st sess., 1987, H Doc 100–94.

Notes:

1. The part in brackets was changed by section 2 of the Fourteenth Amendment.
2. The part in brackets was changed by the first paragraph of the Seventeenth Amendment.
3. The part in brackets was changed by the second paragraph of the Seventeenth Amendment.
4. The part in brackets was changed by section 2 of the Twentieth Amendment.
5. The Sixteenth Amendment gave Congress the power to tax incomes.
6. The material in brackets was superseded by the Twelfth Amendment.
7. This provision was affected by the Twenty-fifth Amendment.
8. These clauses were affected by the Eleventh Amendment.
9. This paragraph was superseded by the Thirteenth Amendment.
10. Obsolete.
11. The part in brackets was superseded by section 3 of the Twentieth Amendment.
12. See the Nineteenth and Twenty-sixth Amendments.
13. This amendment was repealed by section 1 of the Twenty-first Amendment.
14. See the Twenty-fifth Amendment.

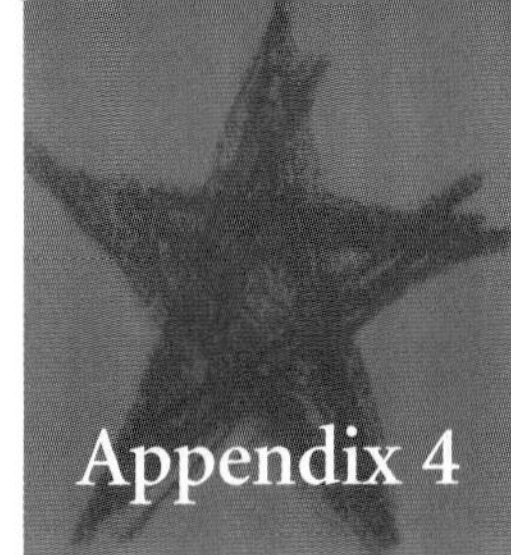

FEDERALIST NO. 10

The Same Subject Continued: The Union as a Safeguard Against Domestic Faction and Insurrection.

From the New York Packet
Friday, November 23, 1787.
Author: James Madison

To the People of the State of New York:

AMONG the numerous advantages promised by a well-constructed Union, none deserves to be more accurately developed than its tendency to break and control the violence of faction. The friend of popular governments never finds himself so much alarmed for their character and fate, as when he contemplates their propensity to this dangerous vice. He will not fail, therefore, to set a due value on any plan which, without violating the principles to which he is attached, provides a proper cure for it. The instability, injustice, and confusion introduced into the public councils, have, in truth, been the mortal diseases under which popular governments have everywhere perished; as they continue to be the favorite and fruitful topics from which the adversaries to liberty derive their most specious declamations. The valuable improvements made by the American constitutions on the popular models, both ancient and modern, cannot certainly be too much admired; but it would be an unwarrantable partiality, to contend that they have as effectually obviated the danger on this side, as was wished and expected. Complaints are everywhere heard from our most considerate and virtuous citizens, equally the friends of public and private faith, and of public and personal liberty, that our governments are too unstable, that the public good is disregarded in the conflicts of rival parties, and that measures are too often decided, not according to the rules of justice and the rights of the minor party, but by the superior force of an interested and overbearing majority. However anxiously we may wish that these complaints had no foundation, the evidence, of known facts will not permit us to deny that they are in some degree true. It will be found, indeed, on a candid review of our situation, that some of the distresses under which we labor have been erroneously charged on the operation of our governments; but it will be found, at the same time, that other causes will not alone account for many of our heaviest misfortunes; and, particularly, for that prevailing and increasing distrust of public engagements, and alarm for private rights, which are echoed from one end of the continent to the other. These must be chiefly, if not wholly, effects of the unsteadiness and injustice with which a factious spirit has tainted our public administrations.

By a faction, I understand a number of citizens, whether amounting to a majority or a minority of the whole, who are united and actuated by some common impulse of passion, or of interest, adversed to the rights of other citizens, or to the permanent and aggregate interests of the community.

There are two methods of curing the mischiefs of faction: the one, by removing its causes; the other, by controlling its effects.

There are again two methods of removing the causes of faction: the one, by destroying the liberty which is essential to its existence; the other, by giving to every citizen the same opinions, the same passions, and the same interests.

It could never be more truly said than of the first remedy, that it was worse than the disease. Liberty is to faction what air is to fire, an aliment without which it instantly expires. But it could not be less folly to abolish liberty, which is essential to political life, because it nourishes faction, than it would be to wish the annihilation of air, which is essential to animal life, because it imparts to fire its destructive agency.

The second expedient is as impracticable as the first would be unwise. As long as the reason of man continues fallible, and he is at liberty to exercise it, different opinions will be formed. As long as the connection subsists between his reason and his self-love, his opinions and his passions will have a reciprocal influence on each other; and the former will be objects to which the latter will attach themselves. The diversity in the faculties of men, from which the rights of property originate, is not less an insuperable obstacle to a uniformity of interests. The protection of these faculties is the first object of government. From the protection of different and unequal faculties of acquiring property, the possession of different degrees and kinds of property immediately results; and from the influence of these on the sentiments and views of the respective proprietors, ensues a division of the society into different interests and parties.

The latent causes of faction are thus sown in the nature of man; and we see them everywhere brought into different degrees of activity, according to the different circumstances of civil society. A zeal for different opinions concerning religion, concerning government, and many other points, as well of speculation as of practice; an attachment to different leaders ambitiously contending for pre-eminence and power; or to persons of other descriptions whose fortunes have been interesting to the human passions, have, in turn, divided mankind into parties, inflamed them with mutual animosity, and rendered them much more disposed to vex and oppress each other than to co-operate for their common good. So strong is this propensity of mankind to fall into mutual animosities, that where no substantial occasion presents itself, the most frivolous and fanciful distinctions have been sufficient to kindle their unfriendly passions and excite their most violent conflicts. But the most common and durable source of factions has been the various and unequal distribution of property. Those who hold and those who are without property have ever formed distinct interests in society. Those who are creditors, and those who are debtors, fall under a like discrimination. A landed interest, a manufacturing interest, a mercantile interest, a moneyed interest, with many lesser interests, grow up of necessity in civilized nations, and divide them into different classes, actuated by different sentiments and views. The regulation of these various and interfering interests forms the principal task of modern legislation, and involves the spirit of party and faction in the necessary and ordinary operations of the government.

No man is allowed to be a judge in his own cause, because his interest would certainly bias his judgment, and, not improbably, corrupt his integrity. With equal, nay with greater reason, a body of men are unfit to be both judges and parties at the same time; yet what are many of the most important acts of legislation, but so many judicial determinations, not indeed concerning the rights of single persons, but concerning the rights of large bodies of citizens? And what are the different classes of legislators but advocates and parties to the causes which they determine? Is a law proposed concerning private debts? It is a question to which the creditors are parties on one side and the debtors on the other. Justice ought to hold the balance between them. Yet the parties are, and must be, themselves the judges; and the most numerous party, or, in other words, the most powerful faction must be expected to prevail. Shall domestic manufactures be encouraged, and in what degree, by restrictions on foreign manufactures? are questions which would be differently decided by the landed and the manufacturing classes, and probably by neither with a sole regard to justice and the public good. The apportionment of taxes on the various descriptions of property is an act which seems to require the most exact impartiality; yet there is, perhaps, no legislative act in which greater opportunity and temptation are given to a predominant party to trample on the rules of justice. Every shilling with which they overburden the inferior number, is a shilling saved to their own pockets.

It is in vain to say that enlightened statesmen will be able to adjust these clashing interests, and render them all subservient to the public good. Enlightened statesmen will not always be at the helm. Nor, in many cases, can such an adjustment be made at all without taking into view indirect and remote considerations, which will rarely prevail over the immediate interest which one party may find in disregarding the rights of another or the good of the whole.

The inference to which we are brought is, that the CAUSES of faction cannot be removed, and that relief is only to be sought in the means of controlling its EFFECTS.

If a faction consists of less than a majority, relief is supplied by the republican principle, which enables the majority to defeat its sinister views by regular vote. It may clog the administration, it may convulse the society; but it will be unable to execute and mask its violence under the forms of the Constitution. When a majority is included in a faction, the form of popular government, on the other hand, enables it to sacrifice to its ruling passion or interest both the public good and the rights of other citizens. To secure the public good and private rights against the danger of such a faction, and at the same time to preserve the spirit and the form of popular government, is then the great object to which our inquiries are directed. Let me add that it is the great desideratum by which this form of government can be rescued from the opprobrium under which it has so long labored, and be recommended to the esteem and adoption of mankind.

By what means is this object attainable? Evidently by one of two only. Either the existence of the same passion or interest in a majority at the same time must be prevented, or the majority, having such coexistent passion or interest, must be rendered, by their number and local situation, unable to concert and carry into effect schemes of oppression. If the impulse and the opportunity be suffered to coincide, we well know that neither moral nor religious motives can be relied on as an adequate control. They are not found to be such on the injustice and violence of individuals, and lose their efficacy in proportion to the number combined together, that is, in proportion as their efficacy becomes needful.

From this view of the subject it may be concluded that a pure democracy, by which I mean a society consisting of a small number of citizens, who assemble and administer the government in person, can admit of no cure for the mischiefs of faction. A common passion or interest will, in almost every case, be felt by a majority of the whole; a communication and concert result from the form of government itself; and there is nothing to check the inducements to sacrifice the weaker party or an obnoxious individual. Hence it is that such democracies have ever been spectacles of turbulence and contention; have ever been found incompatible with personal security or the rights of property; and have in general been as short in their lives as they have been violent in their deaths. Theoretic politicians, who have patronized this species of government, have erroneously supposed that by reducing mankind to a perfect equality in their political rights, they would, at the same time, be perfectly equalized and assimilated in their possessions, their opinions, and their passions.

A republic, by which I mean a government in which the scheme of representation takes place, opens a different prospect, and promises the cure for which we are seeking. Let us examine the points in which it varies from pure democracy, and we shall comprehend both the nature of the cure and the efficacy which it must derive from the Union.

The two great points of difference between a democracy and a republic are: first, the delegation of the government, in the latter, to a small number of citizens elected by the rest; secondly, the greater number of citizens, and greater sphere of country, over which the latter may be extended.

The effect of the first difference is, on the one hand, to refine and enlarge the public views, by passing them through the medium of a chosen body of citizens, whose wisdom may best discern the true interest of their country, and whose patriotism and love of justice will be least likely to sacrifice it to temporary or partial considerations. Under such a regulation, it may well happen that the public voice, pronounced by the representatives of the people, will be more consonant to the public good than if pronounced by the people themselves, convened for the purpose. On the other hand, the effect may be inverted. Men of factious tempers, of local prejudices, or of sinister designs, may, by intrigue, by corruption, or by other means, first obtain the suffrages, and then betray the interests, of the people. The question resulting is, whether small or extensive republics are more favorable to the election of proper guardians of the public weal; and it is clearly decided in favor of the latter by two obvious considerations:

In the first place, it is to be remarked that, however small the republic may be, the representatives must be raised to a certain number, in order to guard against the cabals of a few; and that, however large it may be, they must be limited to a certain number, in order to guard against the confusion of a multitude. Hence, the number of representatives in the two cases not being in proportion to that of the two constituents, and being proportionally greater in the small republic, it follows that, if the proportion of fit characters be not less in the large than in the small republic, the former will present a greater option, and consequently a greater probability of a fit choice.

In the next place, as each representative will be chosen by a greater number of citizens in the large than in the small republic, it will be more difficult for unworthy candidates to practice with success the vicious arts by which elections are too often carried; and the suffrages of the people being more free, will be more likely to centre in men who possess the most attractive merit and the most diffusive and established characters.

It must be confessed that in this, as in most other cases, there is a mean, on both sides of which inconveniences will be found to lie. By enlarging too much the number of electors, you render the representatives too little acquainted with all their local circumstances and lesser interests; as by reducing it too much, you render him unduly attached to these, and too little fit to comprehend and pursue great and national objects. The federal Constitution forms a happy combination in this respect; the great and aggregate interests being referred to the national, the local and particular to the State legislatures.

The other point of difference is, the greater number of citizens and extent of territory which may be brought within the compass of republican than of democratic government; and it is this circumstance principally which renders factious combinations less to be dreaded in the former than in the latter. The smaller the society, the fewer probably will be the distinct parties and interests composing it; the fewer the distinct parties and interests, the more frequently will a majority be found of the same party; and the smaller the number of individuals composing a majority, and the smaller the compass within which they are placed, the more easily will they concert and execute their plans of oppression. Extend the sphere, and you take in a greater variety of parties and interests; you make it less probable that a majority of the whole will have a common motive to invade the rights of other

citizens; or if such a common motive exists, it will be more difficult for all who feel it to discover their own strength, and to act in unison with each other. Besides other impediments, it may be remarked that, where there is a consciousness of unjust or dishonorable purposes, communication is always checked by distrust in proportion to the number whose concurrence is necessary.

Hence, it clearly appears, that the same advantage which a republic has over a democracy, in controlling the effects of faction, is enjoyed by a large over a small republic,—is enjoyed by the Union over the States composing it. Does the advantage consist in the substitution of representatives whose enlightened views and virtuous sentiments render them superior to local prejudices and schemes of injustice? It will not be denied that the representation of the Union will be most likely to possess these requisite endowments. Does it consist in the greater security afforded by a greater variety of parties, against the event of any one party being able to outnumber and oppress the rest? In an equal degree does the increased variety of parties comprised within the Union, increase this security. Does it, in fine, consist in the greater obstacles opposed to the concert and accomplishment of the secret wishes of an unjust and interested majority? Here, again, the extent of the Union gives it the most palpable advantage.

The influence of factious leaders may kindle a flame within their particular States, but will be unable to spread a general conflagration through the other States. A religious sect may degenerate into a political faction in a part of the Confederacy; but the variety of sects dispersed over the entire face of it must secure the national councils against any danger from that source. A rage for paper money, for an abolition of debts, for an equal division of property, or for any other improper or wicked project, will be less apt to pervade the whole body of the Union than a particular member of it; in the same proportion as such a malady is more likely to taint a particular county or district, than an entire State.

In the extent and proper structure of the Union, therefore, we behold a republican remedy for the diseases most incident to republican government. And according to the degree of pleasure and pride we feel in being republicans, ought to be our zeal in cherishing the spirit and supporting the character of Federalists.

PUBLIUS.

FEDERALIST NO. 51

The Structure of the Government Must Furnish the Proper Checks and Balances Between the Different Departments

From the New York Packet.
Friday, February 8, 1788.
Author: James Madison

To the People of the State of New York:
TO WHAT expedient, then, shall we finally resort, for maintaining in practice the necessary partition of power among the several departments, as laid down in the Constitution? The only answer that can be given is, that as all these exterior provisions are found to be inadequate, the defect must be supplied, by so contriving the interior structure of the government as that its several constituent parts may, by their mutual relations, be the means of keeping each other in their proper places. Without presuming to undertake a full development of this important idea, I will hazard a few general observations, which may perhaps place it in a clearer light, and enable us to form a more correct judgment of the principles and structure of the government planned by the convention.

In order to lay a due foundation for that separate and distinct exercise of the different powers of government, which to a certain extent is admitted on all hands to be essential to the preservation of liberty, it is evident that each department should have a will of its own; and consequently should be so constituted that the members of each should have as little agency as possible in the appointment of the members of the others. Were this principle rigorously adhered to, it would require that all the appointments for the supreme executive, legislative, and judiciary magistracies should be drawn from the same fountain of authority, the people, through channels having no communication whatever with one another. Perhaps such a plan of constructing the several departments would be less difficult in practice than it may in contemplation appear. Some difficulties, however, and some additional expense would attend the execution of it. Some deviations, therefore, from the principle must be admitted. In the constitution of the judiciary department in particular, it might be inexpedient to insist rigorously on the principle: first, because peculiar qualifications being essential in the members, the primary consideration ought to be to select that mode of choice which best secures these qualifications; secondly, because the permanent tenure by which the appointments are held in that department, must soon destroy all sense of dependence on the authority conferring them.

It is equally evident, that the members of each department should be as little dependent as possible on those of the others, for the emoluments annexed to their offices. Were the executive magistrate, or the judges, not independent of the legislature in this particular, their independence in every other would be merely nominal. But the great security against a gradual concentration of the several powers in the same department, consists in giving to those who administer each department the necessary constitutional means and personal motives to resist encroachments of the others. The provision for defense must in this, as in all other cases, be made commensurate to the danger of attack. Ambition must be made to counteract ambition. The interest of the man must be connected with the constitutional rights of the place. It may be a reflection on human nature, that such devices should be necessary to control the abuses of government. But what is government itself, but the greatest of all reflections on human nature? If men were angels, no government would be necessary. If angels were to govern men, neither external nor internal controls on government would be necessary. In framing a government which is to be administered by men over men, the great difficulty lies in this: you must first enable the government to control the governed; and in the next place oblige it to control itself.

A dependence on the people is, no doubt, the primary control on the government; but experience has taught mankind the necessity of auxiliary precautions. This policy of supplying, by opposite and rival interests, the defect of better motives, might be traced through the whole system of human affairs, private as well as public. We see it particularly displayed in all the subordinate distributions of power, where the constant aim is to divide and arrange the several offices in such a manner as that each may be a check on the other that the private interest of every individual may be a sentinel over the public rights. These inventions of prudence cannot be less requisite in the distribution of the supreme powers of the State. But it is not possible to give to each department an equal power of self-defense. In republican government, the legislative authority necessarily predominates. The remedy for this inconveniency is to divide the legislature into different branches; and to render them, by different modes of election and different principles of action, as little connected with each other as the nature of their common functions and their common dependence on the society will admit. It may even be necessary to guard against dangerous encroachments by still further precautions. As the weight of the legislative authority requires that it should be thus divided, the weakness of the executive may require, on the other hand, that it should be fortified.

An absolute negative on the legislature appears, at first view, to be the natural defense with which the executive magistrate should be armed. But perhaps it would be neither altogether safe nor alone sufficient. On ordinary occasions it might not be exerted with the requisite firmness, and on extraordinary occasions it might be perfidiously abused. May not this defect of an absolute negative be supplied by some qualified connection between this weaker department and the weaker branch of the stronger department, by which the latter may be led to support the constitutional rights of the former, without being too much detached from the rights of its own department? If the principles on which these observations are founded be just, as I persuade myself they are, and they be applied as a criterion to the several State constitutions, and to the federal Constitution it will be found that if the latter does not perfectly correspond with them, the former are infinitely less able to bear such a test.

There are, moreover, two considerations particularly applicable to the federal system of America, which place that system in a very interesting point of view. First. In a single republic, all the power surrendered by the people is submitted to the administration of a single government; and the usurpations are guarded against by a division of the government into distinct and separate departments. In the compound republic of America, the power surrendered by the people is first divided between two distinct governments, and then the portion allotted to each subdivided among distinct and separate departments. Hence a double security arises to the rights of the people. The different governments will control each other, at the same time that each will be controlled by itself. Second. It is of great importance in a republic not only to guard the society against the oppression of its rulers, but to guard one part of the society against the injustice of the other part. Different interests necessarily exist in different classes of citizens. If a majority be united by a common interest, the rights of the minority will be insecure.

There are but two methods of providing against this evil: the one by creating a will in the community independent of the majority that is, of the society itself; the other, by comprehending in the society so many separate descriptions of citizens as will render an unjust combination of a majority of the whole very improbable, if not impracticable. The first method prevails in all governments possessing an hereditary or self-appointed authority. This, at best, is but a precarious security; because a power independent of the society may as well espouse the unjust views of the major, as the rightful interests of the minor party, and may possibly be turned against both parties. The second method will be exemplified in the federal republic of the United States. Whilst all authority in it will be derived from and dependent on the society, the society itself will be broken into so many parts, interests, and classes of citizens, that the rights of individuals, or of the minority, will be in little danger from interested combinations of the majority.

In a free government the security for civil rights must be the same as that for religious rights. It consists in the one case in the multiplicity of interests, and in the other in the multiplicity of sects. The degree of security in both cases will depend on the number of interests and sects; and this may be presumed to depend on the extent of country and number of people comprehended under the same government. This view of the subject must particularly recommend a proper federal system to all the sincere and considerate friends of republican government, since it shows that in exact proportion as the territory of the Union may be formed into more circumscribed Confederacies, or States oppressive combinations of a majority will be facilitated: the best security, under the republican forms, for the rights of every class of citizens, will be diminished: and consequently the stability and independence of some member of the government, the only other security, must be proportionately increased. Justice is the end of government. It is the end of civil society. It ever has been and ever will be pursued until it be obtained, or until liberty be lost in the pursuit. In a society under the forms of which the stronger faction can readily unite and oppress the weaker, anarchy may as truly be said to reign as in a state of nature, where the weaker individual is not secured against the violence of the stronger; and as, in the latter state, even the stronger individuals are prompted, by the uncertainty of their condition, to submit to a government which may protect the weak as well as themselves; so, in the former state, will the more powerful factions or parties be gradually induced, by a like motive, to wish for a government which will protect all parties, the weaker as well as the more powerful.

It can be little doubted that if the State of Rhode Island was separated from the Confederacy and left to itself, the insecurity of rights under the popular form of government within such narrow limits would be displayed by such reiterated oppressions of factious majorities that some power altogether independent of the people would soon be called for by the voice of the very factions whose misrule had proved the necessity of it. In the extended republic of the United States, and among the great variety of interests, parties, and sects which it embraces, a coalition of a majority of the whole society could seldom take place on any other principles than those of justice and the general good; whilst there being thus less danger to a minor from the will of a major party, there must be less pretext, also, to provide for the security of the former, by introducing into the government a will not dependent on the latter, or, in other words, a will independent of the society itself. It is no less certain than it is important, notwithstanding the contrary opinions which have been entertained, that the larger the society, provided it lie within a practical sphere, the more duly capable it will be of self-government. And happily for the REPUBLICAN CAUSE, the practicable sphere may be carried to a very great extent, by a judicious modification and mixture of the FEDERAL PRINCIPLE.

PUBLIUS.

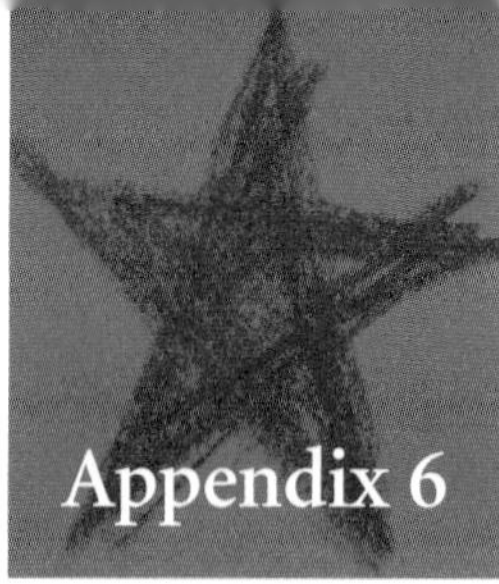

Appendix 6

PRESIDENTS, VICE PRESIDENTS, SPEAKERS, AND CHIEF JUSTICES, 1789–2005

PRESIDENT/VICE PRESIDENT	TERM	CONGRESS	SPEAKER OF THE HOUSE	CHIEF JUSTICE OF THE UNITED STATES
George Washington[1]	(1789–1797)	1st	Frederick A.C. Muhlenberg, Pa.	John Jay (1789–1795)
John Adams		2nd	Jonathan Trumbull, F-Conn.	John Rutledge (1795)
		3rd	Muhlenberg	Oliver Ellsworth (1796–1800)
		4th	Jonathan Dayton, F-N.J.	
John Adams, F	(1797–1801)	5th	Dayton	Ellsworth
Thomas Jefferson, D-R		6th	Theodore Sedgwick, F-Mass.	John Marshall (1801–1835)
Thomas Jefferson, D-R	(1801–1809)	7th	Nathaniel Macon, D-N.C.	Marshall
Aaron Burr (1801–1805)		8th	Macon	
George Clinton (1805–1809)		9th	Macon	
		10th	Joseph B. Varnum, Mass.	
James Madison, D-R	(1809–1817)	11th	Varnum	Marshall
George Clinton[2] (1809–1812)		12th	Henry Clay, R-Ky.	
Elbridge Gerry[2] (1813–1814)		13th	Clay/Langdon Cheves, D-S.C.	
		14th	Clay	
James Monroe, D-R	(1817–1825)	15th	Clay	Marshall
Daniel D. Tompkins		16th	Clay/John W. Taylor, D-N.Y.	
		17th	Philip P. Barbour, D-Va.	
		18th	Clay	
John Quincy Adams, D-R	(1825–1829)	19th	Taylor	Marshall
John C. Calhoun		20th	Andrew Stevenson, D-Va.	
Andrew Jackson, D	(1829–1837)	21st	Stevenson	Marshall
John C. Calhoun[3] (1829–1832)		22nd	Stevenson	Roger B. Taney (1836–1864)
Martin Van Buren (1833–1837)		23rd	Stevenson/John Bell, W-Tenn.	
		24th	James K. Polk, D-Tenn.	
Martin Van Buren, D	(1837–1841)	25th	Polk	Taney
Richard M. Johnson		26th	Robert M.T. Hunter, D-Va.	
William Henry Harrison,[2] W	(1841)			Taney
John Tyler				
John Tyler, W	(1841–1845)	27th	John White, W-Ky.	Taney
		28th	John W. Jones, D-Va.	
James K. Polk, D	(1845–1849)	29th	John W. Davis, D-Ind.	Taney
George M. Dallas		30th	Robert C. Winthrop, W-Mass.	
Zachary Taylor,[2] W	(1849–1850)	31st	Howell Cobb, D-Ga.	Taney
Millard Fillmore				
Millard Fillmore, W	(1850–1853)	31st	Cobb	Taney
		32nd	Linn Boyd, D-Ky.	

PRESIDENT/VICE PRESIDENT	TERM	CONGRESS	SPEAKER OF THE HOUSE	CHIEF JUSTICE OF THE UNITED STATES
Franklin Pierce, D William R. King[2] (1853)	(1853–1857)	33rd 34th	Boyd Nathaniel P. Banks, R-Mass.	Taney
James Buchanan, D John C. Breckinridge	(1857–1861)	35th 36th	James L. Orr, D-S.C. William Pennington, R-N.J.	Taney
Abraham Lincoln,[2] R Hannibal Hamlin (1861–1865) Andrew Johnson,[4] D (1865)	(1861–1865)	37th 38th	Galusha A. Grow, R-Pa. Schuyler Colfax, R-Ind.	Taney Salmon P. Chase (1864–1873)
Andrew Johnson, D	(1865–1869)	39th 40th	Colfax Colfax/Theodore M. Pomeroy, R-N.Y.	Chase
Ulysses S. Grant, R Schuyler Colfax (1869–1873) Henry Wilson[2] (1873–1875)	(1869–1877)	41st 42nd 43rd 44th	James G. Blaine, R-Maine Blaine Blaine Michael C. Kerr, D-Ind./ Samuel J. Randall, D-Pa.	Chase Morrison R. Waite (1874–1888)
Rutherford B. Hayes, R William A. Wheeler	(1877–1881)	45th 46th	Randall Randall	Waite
James A. Garfield,[2] R Chester A. Arthur	(1881)			Waite
Chester A. Arthur, R	(1881–1885)	47th 48th	Joseph Warren Keifer, R-Ohio John G. Carlisle, D-Ky.	Waite
Grover Cleveland, D Thomas A. Hendricks[2] (1885)	(1885–1889)	49th 50th	Carlisle Carlisle	Waite Melville W. Fuller (1888–1910)
Benjamin Harrison, R Levi P. Morton	(1889–1893)	51st 52nd	Thomas Brackett Reed, R-Maine Charles F. Crisp, D-Ga.	Fuller
Grover Cleveland, D Adlai E. Stevenson	(1893–1897)	53rd 54th	Crisp Reed	Fuller
William McKinley,[2] R Garret A. Hobart[2] (1897–1899) Theodore Roosevelt (1901)	(1897–1901)	55th 56th	Reed David B. Henderson, R-Iowa	Fuller
Theodore Roosevelt, R Charles W. Fairbanks (1905–1909)	(1901–1909)	57th 58th 59th 60th	Henderson Joseph G. Cannon, R-Ill. Cannon Cannon	Fuller
William Howard Taft, R James S. Sherman[2] (1909–1912)	(1909–1913)	61st 62nd	Cannon James B. "Champ" Clark, D-Mo.	Fuller Edward D. White (1910–1921)
Woodrow Wilson, D Thomas R. Marshall	(1913–1921)	63rd 64th 65th 66th	Clark Clark Clark Frederick H. Gillett, R-Mass.	White
Warren G. Harding,[2] R Calvin Coolidge	(1921–1923)	67th	Gillett	William Howard Taft (1921–1930)
Calvin Coolidge, R Charles G. Dawes (1925–1929)	(1923–1929)	68th 69th 70th	Gillett Nicholas Longworth, R-Ohio Longworth	Taft
Herbert C. Hoover, R Charles Curtis	(1929–1933)	71st 72nd	Longworth John Nance Garner, D-Texas	Taft Charles Evans Hughes (1930–1941)

continued

PRESIDENT/VICE PRESIDENT	TERM	CONGRESS	SPEAKER OF THE HOUSE	CHIEF JUSTICE OF THE UNITED STATES
Franklin D. Roosevelt,[2] D	(1933–1945)	73rd	Henry T. Rainey, D-Ill.	Hughes
John Nance Garner (1933–1941)		74th	Joseph W. Byrns, D-Tenn./ William B. Bankhead, D-Ala.	Harlan F. Stone (1941–1946)
Henry A. Wallace (1941–1945)			Bankhead	
Harry S. Truman (1945)		75th		
		76th	Bankhead/Sam Rayburn, D-Texas	
		77th	Rayburn	
		78th	Rayburn	
		79th	Rayburn	
Harry S. Truman, D	(1945–1953)	79th	Rayburn	Stone
Alben W. Barkley (1949–1953)		80th	Joseph W. Martin Jr., R-Mass.	Frederick M. Vinson (1946–1953)
		81st	Rayburn	
		82nd	Rayburn	
Dwight D. Eisenhower, R	(1953–1961)	83rd	Martin	Vinson
Richard Nixon		84th	Rayburn	Earl Warren (1953–1969)
		85th	Rayburn	
		86th	Rayburn	
John F. Kennedy,[2] D	(1961–1963)	87th	Rayburn/John W. McCormack, D-Mass.	Warren
Lyndon B. Johnson		88th	McCormack	
Lyndon B. Johnson, D	(1963–1969)	88th	McCormack	Warren
Hubert H. Humphrey (1965–1969)		89th	McCormack	
		90th	McCormack	
Richard Nixon,[3] R	(1969–1974)	91st	McCormack	Warren
Spiro T. Agnew[3] (1969–1973)		92nd	Carl Albert, D-Okla.	Warren E. Burger (1969–1986)
Gerald R. Ford[5](1973–1974)		93rd	Albert	
Gerald R. Ford, R	(1974–1977)	93rd	Albert	Burger
Nelson A. Rockefeller[5]		94th	Albert	
Jimmy Carter, D	(1977–1981)	95th	Thomas P. O'Neill Jr., D-Mass.	Burger
Walter F. Mondale		96th	O'Neill	
Ronald Reagan, R	(1981–1989)	97th	O'Neill	Burger
George Bush		98th	O'Neill	William Rehnquist (1986–2005)
		99th	O'Neill	
		100th	Jim Wright, D-Texas	
George H.W. Bush, R	(1989–1993)	101st	Wright/Thomas S. Foley, D-Wash.	Rehnquist
Dan Quayle		102nd	Foley	
Bill Clinton, D	(1993–2001)	103rd	Foley	Rehnquist
Al Gore		104th	Newt Gingrich, R-Ga.	
		105th	Gingrich	
		106th	J. Dennis Hastert, R-Ill.	
George W. Bush, R	(2001–)	107th	J. Dennis Hastert, R-Ill.	Rehnquist
Richard B. Cheney		108th		John Roberts (2005–)
		109th		

Notes: The vice president's term or party is noted when it differs from that of the president. Key to abbreviations: D—Democrat; D-R—Democratic-Republican; F—Federalist; R—Republican; W—Whig.

1. Washington belonged to no formal party.
2. Died in office.
3. Resigned from office.
4. Democrat Johnson and Republican Lincoln ran under the Union Party banner in 1864.
5. Appointed to office.

POLITICAL PARTY AFFILIATIONS IN CONGRESS AND THE PRESIDENCY, 1789–2005

YEAR	CONGRESS	HOUSE		SENATE		PRESIDENT
		MAJORITY PARTY	PRINCIPAL MINORITY PARTY	MAJORITY PARTY	PRINCIPAL MINORITY MINORITY PARTY	
1789–1791	1st	AD-38	Op-26	AD-17	Op-9	F (Washington)
1791–1793	2nd	F-37	DR-33	F-16	DR-13	F (Washington)
1793–1795	3rd	DR-57	F-48	F-17	DR-13	F (Washington)
1795–1797	4th	F-54	DR-52	F-19	DR-13	F (Washington)
1797–1799	5th	F-58	DR-48	F-20	DR-12	F (John Adams)
1799–1801	6th	F-64	DR-42	F-19	DR-13	F (John Adams)
1801–1803	7th	DR-69	F-36	DR-18	F-13	DR (Jefferson)
1803–1805	8th	DR-102	F-39	DR-25	F-9	DR (Jefferson)
1805–1807	9th	DR-116	F-25	DR-27	F-7	DR (Jefferson)
1807–1809	10th	DR-118	F-24	DR-28	F-6	DR (Jefferson)
1809–1811	11th	DR-94	F-48	DR-28	F-6	DR (Madison)
1811–1813	12th	DR-108	F-36	DR-30	F-6	DR (Madison)
1813–1815	13th	DR-112	F-68	DR-27	F-9	DR (Madison)
1815–1817	14th	DR-117	F-65	DR-25	F-11	DR (Madison)
1817–1819	15th	DR-141	F-42	DR-34	F-10	DR (Monroe)
1819–1821	16th	DR-156	F-27	DR-35	F-7	DR (Monroe)
1821–1823	17th	DR-158	F-25	DR-44	F-4	DR (Monroe)
1823–1825	18th	DR-187	F-26	DR-44	F-4	DR (Monroe)
1825–1827	19th	AD-105	J-97	AD-26	J-20	DR (John Q. Adams)
1827–1829	20th	J-119	AD-94	J-28	AD-20	DR (John Q. Adams)
1829–1831	21st	D-139	NR-74	D-26	NR-22	DR (Jackson)
1831–1833	22nd	D-141	NR-58	D-25	NR-21	D (Jackson)
1833–1835	23rd	D-147	AM-53	D-20	NR-20	D (Jackson)
1835–1837	24th	D-145	W-98	D-27	W-25	D (Jackson)
1837–1839	25th	D-108	W-107	D-30	W-18	D (Van Buren)
1839–1841	26th	D-124	W-118	D-28	W-22	D (Van Buren)
1841–1843	27th	W-133	D-102	W-28	D-22	W (W. Harrison) W (Tyler)
1843–1845	28th	D-142	W-79	W-28	D-25	W (Tyler)
1845–1847	29th	D-143	W-77	D-31	W-25	D (Polk)

continued

YEAR	CONGRESS	HOUSE		SENATE		PRESIDENT
		MAJORITY PARTY	PRINCIPAL MINORITY PARTY	MAJORITY PARTY	PRINCIPAL MINORITY MINORITY PARTY	
1847–1849	30th	W-115	D-108	D-36	W-21	D (Polk)
1849–1851	31st	D-112	W-109	D-35	W-25	W (Taylor) W (Fillmore)
1851–1853	32nd	D–140	W–88	D–35	W24	W (Fillmore)
1853–1855	33rd	D-159	W-71	D-38	W-22	D (Pierce)
1855–1857	34th	R-108	D-83	D-40	R-15	D (Pierce)
1857–1859	35th	D-118	R-92	D-36	R-20	D (Buchanan)
1859–1861	36th	R-114	D-92	D-36	R-26	D (Buchanan)
1861–1863	37th	R-105	D-43	R-31	D-10	R (Lincoln)
1863–1865	38th	R-102	D-75	R-36	D-9	R (Lincoln)
1865–18671	39th	U-149	D-42	U-42	D-10	U (Lincoln) U (A. Johnson)
1867–1869	40th	R-143	D-49	R-42	D-11	R (A. Johnson)
1869–1871	41st	R-149	D-63	R-56	D-11	R (Grant)
1871–1873	42nd	R-134	D-104	R-52	D-17	R (Grant)
1873–1875	43rd	R-194	D-92	R-49	D-19	R (Grant)
1875–1877	44th	D-169	R-109	R-45	D-29	R (Grant)
1877–1879	45th	D-153	R-140	R-39	D-36	R (Hayes)
1879–1881	46th	D-149	R-130	D-42	R-33	R (Hayes)
1881–1883	47th	R-147	D-135	R-37	D-37	R (Garfield) R (Arthur)
1883–1885	48th	D-197	R-118	R-38	D-36	R (Arthur)
1885–1887	49th	D-183	R-140	R-43	D-34	D (Cleveland)
1887–1889	50th	D-169	R-152	R-39	D-37	D (Cleveland)
1889–1891	51st	R-166	D-159	R-39	D-37	R (B. Harrison)
1891–1893	52nd	D-235	R-88	R-47	D-39	R (B. Harrison)
1893–1895	53rd	D-218	R-127	D-44	R-38	D (Cleveland)
1895–1897	54th	R-244	D-105	R-43	D-39	D (Cleveland)
1897–1899	55th	R-204	D-113	R-47	D-34	R (McKinley)
1899–1901	56th	R-185	D-163	R-53	D-26	R (McKinley)
1901–1903	57th	R-197	D-151	R-55	D-31	R (McKinley) R (T. Roosevelt)
1903–1905	58th	R-208	D-178	R-57	D-33	R (T. Roosevelt)
1905–1907	59th	R-250	D-136	R-57	D-33	R (T. Roosevelt)
1907–1909	60th	R-222	D-164	R-61	D-31	R (T. Roosevelt)
1909–1911	61st	R-219	D-172	R-61	D-32	R (Taft)
1911–1913	62nd	D-228	R-161	R-51	D-41	R (Taft)
1913–1915	63rd	D-291	R-127	D-51	R-44	D (Wilson)
1915–1917	64th	D-230	R-196	D-56	R-40	D (Wilson)
1917–1919	65th	D-216	R-210	D-53	R-42	D (Wilson)

		HOUSE		SENATE		
YEAR	CONGRESS	MAJORITY PARTY	PRINCIPAL MINORITY PARTY	MAJORITY PARTY	PRINCIPAL MINORITY MINORITY PARTY	PRESIDENT
1919–1921	66th	R-240	D-190	R-49	D-47	D (Wilson)
1921–1923	67th	R-301	D-131	R-59	D-37	R (Harding)
1923–1925	68th	R-225	D-205	R-51	D-43	R (Coolidge)
1925–1927	69th	R-247	D-183	R-56	D-39	R (Coolidge)
1927–1929	70th	R-237	D-195	R-49	D-46	R (Coolidge)
1929–1931	71st	R-267	D-167	R-56	D-39	R (Hoover)
1931–1933	72nd	D-220	R-214	R-48	D-47	R (Hoover)
1933–1935	73rd	D-310	R-117	D-60	R-35	D (F. Roosevelt)
1935–1937	74th	D-319	R-103	D-69	R-25	D (F. Roosevelt)
1937–1939	75th	D-331	R-89	D-76	R-16	D (F. Roosevelt)
1939–1941	76th	D-261	R-164	D-69	R-23	D (F. Roosevelt)
1941–1943	77th	D-268	R-162	D-66	R-28	D (F. Roosevelt)
1943–1945	78th	D-218	R-208	D-58	R-37	D (F. Roosevelt)
1945–1947	79th	D-242	R-190	D-56	R-38	D (F. Roosevelt) D (Truman)
1947–1949	80th	R-245	D-188	R-51	D-45	D (Truman)
1949–1951	81st	D-263	R-171	D-54	R-42	D (Truman)
1951–1953	82nd	D-234	R-199	D-49	R-47	D (Truman)
1953–1955	83rd	R-221	D-211	R-48	D-47	R (Eisenhower)
1955–1957	84th	D-232	R-203	D-48	R-47	R (Eisenhower)
1957–1959	85th	D-233	R-200	D-49	R-47	R (Eisenhower)
1959–1961	86th	D-283	R-153	D-64	R-34	R (Eisenhower)
1961–1963	87th	D-263	R-174	D-65	R-35	D (Kennedy)
1963–1965	88th	D-258	R-177	D-67	R-33	D (Kennedy) D (L. Johnson)
1965–1967	89th	D-295	R-140	D-68	R-32	D (L. Johnson)
1967–1969	90th	D-247	R-187	D-64	R-36	D (L. Johnson)
1969–1971	91st	D-243	R-192	D-57	R-43	R (Nixon)
1971–1973	92nd	D-254	R-180	D-54	R-44	R (Nixon)
1973–1975	93rd	D-239	R-192	D-56	R-42	R (Nixon) R (Ford)
1975–1977	94th	D-291	R-144	D-60	R-37	R (Ford)
1977–1979	95th	D-292	R-143	D-61	R-38	D (Carter)
1979–1981	96th	D-276	R-157	D-58	R-41	D (Carter)
1981–1983	97th	D-243	R-192	R-53	D-46	R (Reagan)
1983–1985	98th	D-269	R-165	R-54	D-46	R (Reagan)
1985–1987	99th	D-252	R-182	R-53	D-47	R (Reagan)
1987–1989	100th	D-258	R-177	D-55	R-45	R (Reagan)
1989–1991	101st	D-259	R-174	D-55	R-45	R (G.H.W. Bush)

continued

YEAR	CONGRESS	HOUSE MAJORITY PARTY	HOUSE PRINCIPAL MINORITY PARTY	SENATE MAJORITY PARTY	SENATE PRINCIPAL MINORITY MINORITY PARTY	PRESIDENT
1991–1993	102nd	D-267	R-167	D-56	R-44	R (G.H.W. Bush)
1993–1995	103rd	D-258	R-176	D-57	R-43	D (Clinton)
1995–1997	104th	R-230	D-204	R-53	D-47	D (Clinton)
1997–1999	105th	R-227	D-207	R-55	D-45	D (Clinton)
1999–2001	106th	R-222	D-211	R-55	D-45	D (Clinton)
2001–2003	107th	R-222	D-211	D-50	R-49	R (G.W. Bush)
2003–2005	108th	R-229	D-205	D-48	R-51	R (G. W. Bush)
2005–	109th	R-232	D-202	D-44	R-55	R (G. W. Bush)

Sources: U.S. Bureau of the Census, Historical Statistics of the United States, Colonial Times to 1970 (Washington, D.C.: Government Printing Office, 1975); and U.S. Congress, Joint Committee on Printing, Official Congressional Directory (Washington, D.C.: Government Printing Office, 1967–); CQ Weekly, selected issues.

Note: Figures are for the beginning of the first session of each Congress. Key to abbreviations: AD—Administration; AM—Anti-Masonic; D—Democratic; DR—Democratic-Republican; F—Federalist; J—Jacksonian; NR—National Republican; Op—Opposition; R—Republican; U—Unionist; W—Whig.

1. The Republican Party ran under the Union Party banner in 1864.

SUMMARY OF PRESIDENTIAL ELECTIONS, 1789–2004

YEAR	NO. OF STATES	CANDIDATES		ELECTORAL VOTE		POPULAR VOTE	
1789[a]	10	Fed. George Washington		Fed. 69		—[b]	
1792[a]	15	Fed. George Washington		Fed. 132		—[b]	
1796[a]	16	Dem.-Rep. Thomas Jefferson	Fed. John Adams	Dem.-Rep. 68	Fed. 71	—[b]	
1800[a]	16	Dem.-Rep. Thomas Jefferson Aaron Burr	Fed. John Adams Charles Cotesworth Pinckney	Dem.-Rep 73	Fed. 65	—[b]	
1804	17	Dem.-Rep. Thomas Jefferson George Clinton	Fed. Charles Cotesworth Pinckney Rufus King	Dem.-Rep 162	Fed. 14	—[b]	
1808	17	Dem.-Rep. James Madison George Clinton	Fed. Charles Cotesworth Pinckney Rufus King	Dem.-Rep 122	Fed. 47	—[b]	
1812	18	Dem.-Rep. James Madison Elbridge Gerry	Fed. George Clinton Jared Ingersoll	Dem.-Rep 128	Fed. 89	—[b]	
1816	19	Dem.-Rep. James Monroe Daniel D. Tompkins	Fed. Rufus King John Howard	Dem.-Rep 183	Fed. 34	—[b]	
1820	24	Dem.-Rep James Monroe Daniel D. Tompkins	—[c]	Dem.-Rep 231	—[c]	—[b]	
1824[d]	24	Dem.-Rep Andrew Jackson John C. Calhoun	Dem.-Rep John Q. Adams Nathan Sanford	Dem.-Rep 99	Dem.-Rep. 84	Dem.-Rep 151,271 41.3%	Dem.-Rep 113,122 30.9%
1828	24	Dem.-Rep. Andrew Jackson John C. Calhoun	Nat.-Rep. John Q. Adams Richard Rush	Dem.-Rep. 178	Nat.-Rep. 83	Dem.-Rep. 642,553 56.0%	Nat.-Rep. 500,897 43.6%
1832[e]	24	Dem. Andrew Jackson Martin Van Buren	Nat.-Rep. Henry Clay John Sergeant	Dem. 219	Nat.-Rep. 49 54.2%	Dem. 701,780	Nat.-Rep. 484,205 37.4%
1836[f]	26	Dem. Martin Van Buren Richard M. Johnson	Whig William H. Harrison Francis Granger	Dem. 170	Whig 73	Dem. 764,176 50.8%	Whig 550,816 36.6%
1840	26	Dem. Martin Van Buren Richard M. Johnson	Whig William H. Harrison John Tyler	Dem. 60	Whig 234	Dem. 1,128,854 46.8%	Whig 1,275,390 52.9%

continued

YEAR	NO. OF STATES	CANDIDATES		ELECTORAL VOTE		POPULAR VOTE	
1844	26	Dem. James Polk George M. Dallas	Whig Henry Clay Theodore Frelinghuysen	Dem. 170	Whig 105	Dem. 1,339,494 49.5%	Whig 1,300,004 48.1%
1848	30	Dem. Lewis Cass William O. Butler	Whig Zachary Taylor Millard Fillmore	Dem. 127	Whig 163	Dem. 1,233,460 42.5%	Whig 1,361,393 47.3%
1852	31	Dem. Franklin Pierce William R. King	Whig Winfield Scott William A. Graham	Dem. 254	Whig 42	Dem. 1,607,510 50.8%	Whig 1,386,942 43.9%

YEAR	NO. OF STATES	CANDIDATES DEM.	REP.	ELECTORAL VOTE DEM.	REP.	POPULAR VOTE DEM.	REP.
1856[g]	31	James Buchanan John C. Breckinridge	John C. Fremont William L. Dayton	174	114	1,836,072 45.3%	1,342,345 33.1%
1860[h]	33	Stephen A. Douglas Herschel V. Johnson	Abraham Lincoln Hannibal Hamlin	12	180	1,380,202 29.5%	1,865,908 39.8%
1864[i]	36	George B. McClellan George H. Pendleton	Abraham Lincoln Andrew Johnson	21	212	1,812,807 45.0%	2,218,388 55.0%
1868[j]	37	Horatio Seymour Francis P. Blair, Jr.	Ulysses S. Grant Schuyler Colfax	80	214	2,708,744 47.3%	3,013,650 52.7%
1872[k]	37	Horace Greeley Benjamin Gratz Brown	Ulysses S. Grant Henry Wilson		286	2,834,761 43.8%	3,598,235 55.6%
1876	38	Samuel J. Tilden Thomas A. Hendricks	Rutherford B. Hayes William A. Wheeler	184	185	4,288,546 51.0%	4,034,311 47.9%
1880	38	Winfield S. Hancock William H. English	James A. Garfield Chester A. Arthur	155	214	4,444,260 48.2%	4,446,158 48.3%
1884	38	Grover Cleveland Thomas A. Hendricks	James G. Blaine John A. Logan	219	182	4,874,621 48.5%	4,848,936 48.2%
1888	38	Grover Cleveland Allen G. Thurman	Benjamin Harrison Levi P. Morton	168	233	5,534,488 48.6%	5,443,892 47.8%
1892[l]	44	Grover Cleveland Adlai E. Stevenson	Benjamin Harrison Whitelaw Reid	277	145	5,551,883 46.1%	5,179,244 43.0%
1896	45	William J. Bryan Arthur Sewall	William McKinley Garret A. Hobart	176	271	6,511,495 46.7%	7,108,480 51.0%
1900	45	William J. Bryan Adlai E. Stevenson	William McKinley Theodore Roosevelt	155	292	6,358,345 45.5%	7,218,039 51.7%
1904	45	Alton B. Parker Henry G. Davis	Theodore Roosevelt Charles W. Fairbanks	140	336	5,028,898 37.6%	7,626,593 56.4%
1908	46	William J. Bryan John W. Kern	William H. Taft James S. Sherman	162	321	6,406,801 43.0%	7,676,258 51.6%
1912[m]	48	Woodrow Wilson Thomas R. Marshall	William H. Taft James S. Sherman	435	8	6,293,152 41.8%	3,486,333 23.2%
1916	48	Woodrow Wilson Thomas R. Marshall	Charles E. Hughes Charles W. Fairbanks	277	254	9,126,300 49.2%	8,546,789 46.1%
1920	48	James M. Cox Franklin D. Roosevelt	Warren G. Harding Calvin Coolidge	127	404	9,140,884 34.2%	16,133,314 60.3%
1924[n]	48	John W. Davis Charles W. Bryant	Calvin Coolidge Charles G. Dawes	136	382	8,386,169 28.8%	15,717,553 54.1%
1928	48	Alfred E. Smith Joseph T. Robinson	Herbert C. Hoover Charles Curtis	87	444	15,000,185 40.8%	21,411,991 58.2%

YEAR	NO. OF STATES	CANDIDATES DEM.	CANDIDATES REP.	ELECTORAL VOTE DEM.	ELECTORAL VOTE REP.	POPULAR VOTE DEM.	POPULAR VOTE REP.
1932	48	Franklin D. Roosevelt John N. Garner	Herbert C. Hoover Charles Curtis	472	59	22,825,016 57.4%	15,758,397 39.6%
1936	48	Franklin D. Roosevelt John N. Garner	Alfred M. Landon Frank Knox	523	8	27,747,636 60.8%	16,679,543 36.5%
1940	48	Franklin D. Roosevelt Henry A. Wallace	Wendell L. Willkie Charles L. McNary	449	82	27,263,448 54.7%	22,336,260 44.8%
1944	48	Franklin D. Roosevelt Harry S. Truman	Thomas E. Dewey John W. Bricker	432	99	25,611,936 53.4%	22,013,372 45.9%
1948[o]	48	Harry S. Truman Alben W. Barkley	Thomas E. Dewey Earl Warren	303	189	24,105,587 49.5%	21,970,017 45.1%
1952	48	Adlai E. Stevenson II John J. Sparkman	Dwight D. Eisenhower Richard M. Nixon	89	442	27,314,649 44.4%	33,936,137 55.1%
1956[p]	48	Adlai E. Stevenson II Estes Kefauver	Dwight D. Eisenhower Richard M. Nixon	73	457	26,030,172 42.0%	35,585,245 57.4%
1960[q]	50	John F. Kennedy Lyndon B. Johnson	Richard M. Nixon Henry Cabot Lodge	303	219	34,221,344 49.7%	34,106,671 49.5%
1964	50*	Lyndon B. Johnson Hubert H. Humphrey	Barry Goldwater William E. Miller	486	52	43,126,584 61.1%	27,177,838 38.5%
1968[r]	50*	Hubert H. Humphrey Edmund S. Muskie	Richard M. Nixon Spiro T. Agnew	191	301	31,274,503 42.7%	31,785,148 43.4%
1972[s]	50*	George McGovern Sargent Shriver	Richard M. Nixon Spiro T. Agnew	17	520	29,171,791 37.5%	47,170,179 60.7%
1976[t]	50*	Jimmy Carter Walter F. Mondale	Gerald R. Ford Robert Dole	297	240	40,830,763 50.1%	39,147,793 48.0%
1980	50*	Jimmy Carter Walter F. Mondale	Ronald Reagan George H.W. Bush	49	489	35,483,883 41.0%	43,904,153 50.7%
1984	50*	Walter F. Mondale Geraldine Ferraro	Ronald Reagan George H.W. Bush	13	525	37,577,185 40.6%	54,455,075 58.8%
1988[u]	50*	Michael S. Dukakis Lloyd Bentsen	George H.W. Bush Dan Quayle	111	426	41,809,083 45.6%	48,886,097 53.4%
1992	50*	William J. Clinton Albert Gore	George H.W. Bush Dan Quayle	370	168	43,728,275 43.2%	38,167,416 37.7%
1996	50*	William J. Clinton Albert Gore	Robert J. Dole Jack F. Kemp	379	159	47,401,054 49.2%	39,197,350 40.7%
2000	50	Albert Gore Joseph I. Lieberman	George W. Bush Richard B. Cheney	266	271	50,996,039 48.4%	50,456,141 47.9%
2004	50*	John Kerry John Edwards	George W. Bush Richard B. Cheney	252	286	55,437,243 48.1%	59,019,598 51.0%

Sources: Harold W. Stanley and Richard G. Niemi, Vital Statistics on American Politics, 2005–2006 (Washington, D.C.: CQ Press, 2006); Guide to U.S. Elections, 4th ed. (Washington, D.C.: CQ Press, 2006); Federal Election Commission.

Note: Dem.-Rep.—Democratic-Republican; Fed.—Federalist; Nat.-Rep.—National-Republican; Dem.—Democratic; Rep.—Republican.

a. Elections from 1789 through 1800 were held under rules that did not allow separate voting for president and vice president.

b. Popular vote returns are not shown before 1824 because consistent, reliable data are not available.

c. 1820: One electoral vote was cast for John Adams and Richard Stockton, who were not candidates.

d. 1824: All four candidates represented Democratic-Republican factions. William H. Crawford received 41 electoral votes and Henry Clay received 37 votes. Because no candidate received a majority, the election was decided (in Adams's favor) by the House of Representatives.

e. 1832: Two electoral votes were not cast.

f. 1836: Other Whig candidates receiving electoral votes were Hugh L. White, who received 26 votes, and Daniel Webster, who received 14 votes.

g. 1856: Millard Fillmore, Whig-American, received 8 electoral votes.

h. 1860: John C. Breckinridge, southern Democrat, received 72 electoral votes. John Bell, Constitutional Union, received 39 electoral votes.

i. 1864: Eighty-one electoral votes were not cast.

j. 1868: Twenty-three electoral votes were not cast.

k. 1872: Horace Greeley, Democrat, died after the election. In the electoral college, Democratic electoral votes went to Thomas Hendricks, 42 votes; Benjamin Gratz Brown, 18 votes; Charles J. Jenkins, 2 votes; and David Davis, 1 vote. Seventeen electoral votes were not cast.

l. 1892: James B. Weaver, People's party, received 22 electoral votes.

m. 1912: Theodore Roosevelt, Progressive party, received 88 electoral votes.

n. 1924: Robert M. La Follette, Progressive party, received 13 electoral votes.

o. 1948: J. Strom Thurmond, States' Rights party, received 39 electoral votes.

p. 1956: Walter B. Jones, Democrat, received 1 electoral vote.

q. 1960: Harry Flood Byrd, Democrat, received 15 electoral votes.

r. 1968: George C. Wallace, American Independent party, received 46 electoral votes.

s. 1972: John Hospers, Libertarian party, received 1 electoral vote.

t. 1976: Ronald Reagan, Republican, received 1 electoral vote.

u. 1988: Lloyd Bentsen, the Democratic vice-presidential nominee, received 1 electoral vote for president.

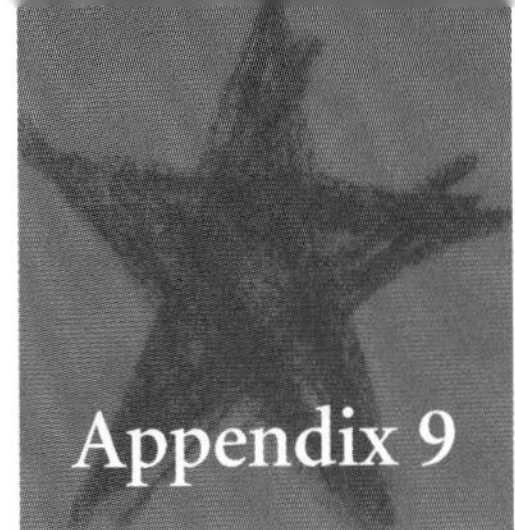

THE AMERICAN ECONOMY

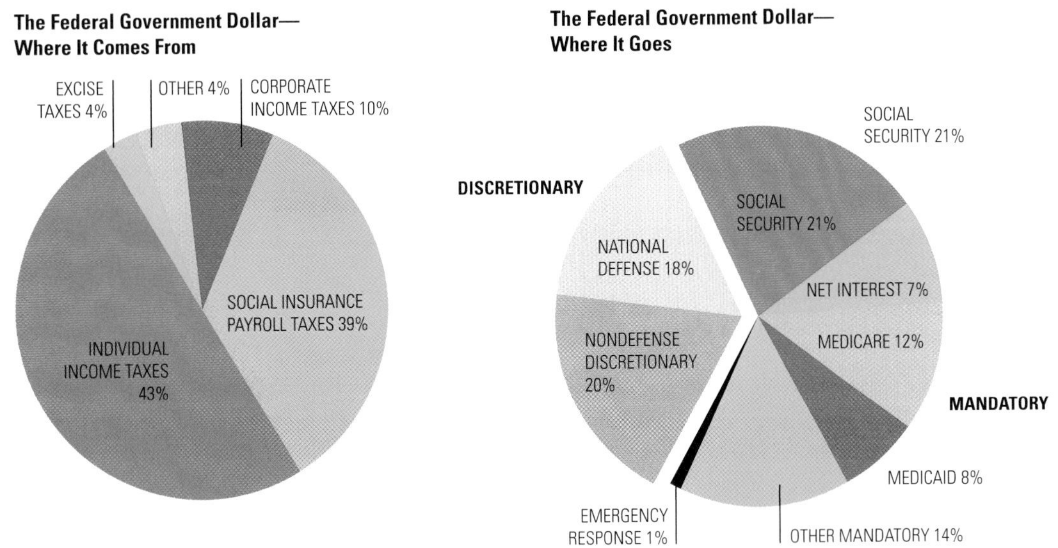

Source: Office of Management and Budget, Budget of the United States Government, Fiscal Year 2006 (Washington, D.C.: U.S. Government Printing Office, 2005).

YEAR	GDP (IN CONSTANT 2000 DOLLARS)	FEDERAL GOVERNMENT SPENDING (BILLIONS) (IN CONSTANT 2000 DOLLARS)			NATIONAL DEBT (CURRENT DOLLARS)	
		NATIONAL DEFENSE	NON-DEFENSE	TOTAL	DEBT HELD BY THE PUBLIC (MILLIONS)	AS A PERCENTAGE OF GDP
1940	1,034.1	$19.9	$88.9	$108.8	42,772	44.2
1941	1,211.1	64.7	82.4	147.1	48,223	42.3
1942	1,435.4	216.3	125.2	341.8	67,753	47.0
1943	1,670.9	526.0	173.8	700.1	127,766	70.9
1944	1,806.5	684.0	176.5	860.5	184,796	88.4
1945	1,786.3	774.6	115.6	890.6	235,182	106.3
1946	1,589.4	405.7	110.1	515.7	241,861	108.6
1947	1,574.5	112.6	184.3	296.9	224,339	95.6
1948	1,643.2	86.5	147.2	233.8	216,270	84.3
1949	1,634.6	123.8	187.9	311.7	214,322	78.9
1950	1,777.3	129.6	201.1	330.7	219,023	80.1
1951	1,915.0	211.7	144.1	355.9	214,326	66.8
1952	1,988.3	396.6	132.3	528.8	214,758	61.6
1953	2,079.5	416.1	140.3	556.3	218,383	58.5
1954	2,065.4	381.9	121.0	502.9	224,499	59.4

continued

YEAR	GDP (IN CONSTANT 2000 DOLLARS)	FEDERAL GOVERNMENT SPENDING (BILLIONS) (IN CONSTANT 2000 DOLLARS)			NATIONAL DEBT (CURRENT DOLLARS)	
		NATIONAL DEFENSE	NON-DEFENSE	TOTAL	DEBT HELD BY THE PUBLIC (MILLIONS)	AS A PERCENTAGE OF GDP
1955	2,212.8	320.1	150.5	470.4	226,616	57.3
1956	2,255.8	298.4	164.4	462.9	222,156	51.9
1957	2,301.1	303.5	175.0	478.3	219,320	48.7
1958	2,279.2	299.7	188.8	488.5	226,336	49.1
1959	2,441.3	297.6	229.8	527.5	234,701	47.7
1960	2,501.8	300.2	226.5	526.8	236,840	45.6
1961	2,560.0	301.5	242.9	544.4	238,357	44.8
1962	2,715.2	315.9	276.4	592.5	248,010	43.6
1963	2,834.0	309.4	284.7	594.3	253,978	42.4
1964	2,998.6	314.9	309.0	623.8	256,849	40.1
1965	3,191.1	291.8	321.6	613.2	260,778	37.9
1966	3,399.1	322.8	358.6	681.5	263,714	35.0
1967	3,484.6	383.3	393.8	777.2	266,626	32.8
1968	3,652.7	420.1	426.8	847.0	289,545	33.3
1969	3,765.4	400.1	423.2	823.5	278,108	29.3
1970	3,771.9	375.1	453.1	828.0	283,198	28.0
1971	3,898.6	340.8	493.4	834.3	303,037	28.0
1972	4,105.0	310.4	547.2	857.6	322,377	27.3
1973	4,341.5	278.6	588.5	867.3	340,910	26.1
1974	4,319.6	267.4	609.8	877.4	343,699	23.8
1975	4,311.2	262.7	719.2	982.1	394,700	25.3
1976	4,540.9	252.7	768.9	1,021.4	477,404	27.5
TQ[1]	n/a	61.0	194.7	255.8	495,509	27.1
1977	4,750.5	250.6	789.6	1,040.2	549,104	27.8
1978	5,015.0	251.1	842.7	1,093.6	607,126	27.4
1979	5,173.4	257.4	850.0	1,107.3	640,306	25.6
1980	5,161.7	267.1	907.9	1,175.1	711,923	26.1
1981	5,291.7	282.2	937.2	1,219.4	789,410	25.8
1982	5,189.3	307.0	944.8	1,251.7	924,575	28.6
1983	5,423.8	330.7	963.7	1,294.4	1,137,268	33.1
1984	5,813.6	334.0	965.6	1,299.5	1,306,975	34.0
1985	6,053.7	356.5	1,039.0	1,395.7	1,507,260	36.4
1986	6,263.6	380.7	1,045.1	1,425.7	1,740,623	39.4
1987	6,475.1	387.1	1,018.5	1,405.7	1,889,753	40.7
1988	6,742.7	393.1	1,053.4	1,446.5	2,051,616	41.0
1989	6,981.4	398.9	1,100.0	1,498.9	2,190,716	40.6
1990	7,112.5	382.7	1,207.0	1,589.8	2,411,558	42.0
1991	7,100.5	333.7	1,276.1	1,609.9	2,688,999	45.3
1992	7,336.6	354.3	1,269.8	1,623.9	2,999,737	48.1
1993	7,532.7	340.3	1,275.3	1,615.5	3,248,396	49.4
1994	7,835.5	322.8	1,319.3	1,642.2	3,433,065	49.3
1995	8,031.7	305.9	1,356.2	1,662.1	3,604,378	49.2
1996	8,328.9	289.2	1,383.9	1,673.0	3,734,073	48.5
1997	8,703.5	288.4	1,395.8	1,684.1	3,772,344	46.1
1998	9,066.9	282.6	1,438.4	1,720.9	3,721,099	43.1
1999	9,470.3	283.7	1,462.3	1,745.9	3,632,363	39.8
2000	9,817.0	294.5	1,494.6	1,789.1	3,409,804	35.1
2001	9,890.7	297.2	1,523.3	1,820.6	3,319,615	33.0
2002	10,074.8	330.3	1,599.9	1,930.1	3,540,427	34.1
2003	10,381.3	366.6	1,655.7	2,022.4	3,913,443	36.1
2004	10,837.2	403.6	1,696.0	2,098.3	4,295,544	37.2
2005 est.	n/a	404.6	1,808.9	2,212.6	4,721,225	38.6
2006 est.	n/a	382.0	1,864.6	2,245.4	5,120,821	39.7
2007 est.	n/a	360.1	1,892.5	2,250.3	5,454,047	40.1
2008 est.	n/a	366.2	1,920.2	2,284.1	5,726,675	39.9
2009 est.	n/a	375.4	1,960.7	2,333.8	5,981,768	39.6
2010 est.	n/a	380.5	2,017.6	2,395.9	6,211,545	39.1

[1] Transitional quarter when fiscal year start was shifted from July 1 to October 1.

Source: Office of Management and Budget, Budget of the United States Government, Fiscal Year 2006, Historical Tables (Washington, D.C.: U.S. Government Printing Office, 2005), 110–117.

NOTES

Chapter 1

1. Email correspondence with Todd Barnhouse Walters, December 8, 2004.
2. Andrew Kohut for America Online, "Young People Up to Speed in Terrorism News," Pew Research Center for the People and the Press, January 15, 2002, www.people-press.org.
3. E. J. Dionne Jr., *Why Americans Hate Politics* (New York: Simon & Schuster, 1991), 355.
4. Harold D. Lasswell, *Politics: Who Gets What, When, How* (New York: McGraw-Hill, 1938).
5. Joseph A. Schumpeter, *Capitalism, Socialism, and Democracy,* 3d ed. (New York: Harper Colophon Books, 1950), 269–296.
6. Robert A. Dahl, *Pluralist Democracy in the United States* (Chicago: Rand McNally, 1967).
7. Carole Pateman, *Participation and Democratic Theory* (New York: Cambridge University Press, 1970).
8. For an explanation of this view, see, for example, Russell L. Hanson, *The Democratic Imagination in America: Conversation with Our Past* (Princeton: Princeton University Press, 1985), 55–91; and Gordon Wood, *The Creation of the American Republic, 1776–1787* (New York: Norton, 1969).
9. Dionne, 354, 355.
10. Daniel M. Shea, Director of Allegheny College's Center for Political Participation in Meadville, Pa., cited in Bryan Bender, "Turnout Was Strong, But Maintaining Interest Is Key, *Boston Globe,* November 5, 2004, A6.
11. Mark Carreau, "America Responds," *Houston Chronicle,* September 22, 2001, A26; Bronwen Maddox, "America Feels the Draft," *Times* (London), October 4, 2001; Chuck Haga, "Rules for Draft Changed Since Vietnam," *Minneapolis Star Tribune,* September 19, 2001, 11A.
12. "GOP Warns Rock the Vote About 'Malicious' Draft-Themed Campaign," *Chicago Sun-Times,* November 4, 2004, 50.

Chapter 2

1. *Graham v. Richardson,* 403 U.S. 532 (1971).
2. See, for instance, Nicole Cusano, "Amherst Mulls Giving Non-Citizens Right to Vote," *Boston Globe,* October 26, 1998, B1; "Casual Citizenship?" editorial, *Boston Globe,* October 31, 1998, A18.
3. Thomas A. Bailey et al., *The American Pageant,* 11th ed. (Boston: Houghton Mifflin, 1998), 749.
4. Benjamin R. Barber, "Foreword," in Grant Reeher and Joseph Cammarano, eds., *Education for Citizenship: Ideas and Innovations in Political Learning* (New York: Rowman & Littlefield, 1997), ix.

Chapter 3

1. Toni Lucy, "Anti-Government Forces Still Struggle to Recover from Oklahoma City Fallout," *USA Today,* May 9, 2000, 9A.
2. There are many good illustrations of this point of view. See, for example, Gordon Wood, *The Creation of the American Republic, 1776–1787* (New York: Norton, 1969); Lawrence Henry Gipson, *The Coming of the Revolution, 1763–1775* (New York: Harper Torchbooks, 1962); Bernard Bailyn, *The Ideological Origins of the American Revolution* (Cambridge, Mass.: Belknap, 1967); and Jack P. Greene, ed., *The Reinterpretation of the American Revolution, 1763–1789* (New York: Harper & Row, 1968).
3. Albert Edward McKinley, *The Suffrage Franchise in the Thirteen English Colonies in America* (Philadelphia: University of Pennsylvania Press, 1905), 313, 324–325.
4. Robert Darcy, Susan Welch, and Janet Clark, *Women, Elections, and Representation* (Lincoln: University of Nebraska Press, 1994), 5–6.
5. Donald R. Wright, *African Americans in the Colonial Era* (Arlington Heights, Ill.: Harlan Davidson, 1990), 52.
6. Ibid., 56.
7. Ibid., 57–58.
8. Lawrence Henry Gipson, "The American Revolution as an Aftermath of the Great War for the Empire, 1754–1765," in Edmund S. Morgan, ed., *The American Revolution* (Englewood Cliffs, N.J.: Prentice-Hall, 1965), 160.
9. Bailyn, 160–229.
10. Gipson, "The American Revolution," 163.
11. Thomas Paine, *Common Sense and Other Political Writings* (Indianapolis, Ind.: Bobbs-Merrill, 1953).
12. Cited in John L. Moore, *Speaking of Washington* (Washington, D.C.: Congressional Quarterly, 1993), 102–103.
13. John Locke, *Second Treatise of Government,* C. B. Macpherson, ed. (Indianapolis: Hackett, 1980), 31.
14. Garry Wills, *Inventing America* (New York: Doubleday, 1978), 377.

15. Wright, 122.
16. Ibid., 152.
17. Mary Beth Norton et al., *A People and a Nation* (Boston: Houghton Mifflin, 1994), 159.
18. Darcy, Welch, and Clark, 8.
19. See, for example, Sally Smith Booth, *The Women of '76* (New York: Hastings House, 1973); and Charles E. Claghorn, *Women Patriots of the American Revolution: A Biographical Dictionary* (Metuchen, N.J.: Scarecrow Press, 1991).
20. Carl Holliday, *Woman's Life in Colonial Days* (Boston: Cornhill, 1922), 143.
21. Wood, 398–399.
22. Ibid., 404.
23. Alexander Hamilton, James Madison, and John Jay, *The Federalist Papers,* Clinton Rossiter, ed. (New York: New American Library, 1961), 84.
24. Adrienne Koch, "Introduction," in James Madison, *Notes of Debates in the Federal Convention of 1787* (New York: Norton, 1969), xiii.
25. Moore, 9.
26. James Madison, *Notes of Debates in the Federal Convention of 1787 Reported by James Madison,* reissue ed. (New York: Norton, 1987).
27. There are many collections of Anti-Federalist writings. See, for example, W. B. Allen and Gordon Lloyd, eds., *The Essential Antifederalist* (Lanham, Md.: University Press of America, 1985); Cecilia Kenyon, ed., *The Antifederalists* (Indianapolis: Bobbs Merrill, 1966); and Ralph Ketcham, *The Anti-Federalist Papers and the Constitutional Convention Debates* (New York: New American Library, 1986).
28. Hamilton, Madison, and Jay, 322.
29. Ketcham, 14.
30. James H. Kettner, *The Development of American Citizenship, 1608–1870* (Chapel Hill: University of North Carolina Press, 1978), 4–10.

Chapter 4

1. Alexander Hamilton, James Madison, and John Jay, *The Federalist Papers,* Clinton Rossiter, ed. (New York: New American Library, 1961), 82.
2. James Madison, *Notes of Debates in the Federal Convention of 1787,* reissue ed. (New York: Norton, 1987), 86.
3. David M. Olson, *The Legislative Process* (Cambridge, Mass.: Harper & Row, 1980), 21–23.
4. Richard F. Fenno Jr., *The United States Senate: A Bicameral Perspective* (Washington, D.C.: American Enterprise Institute for Public Policy Research, 1982), 5.
5. Madison, 136, 158.
6. Hamilton, Madison, and Jay, 465.
7. Lawrence S. Graham et al., *Politics and Government: A Brief Introduction,* 3d ed. (Chatham, N.J.: Chatham House Publishers, 1994), 172–173.
8. Baron de Montesquieu, *The Spirit of the Laws,* Thomas Nugent, trans. (New York: Hafner Press, 1949), 152.
9. Hamilton, Madison, and Jay, 322.
10. Ibid., 84.
11. Ibid., 322.
12. Ibid., 321–322.
13. James C. McKinley Jr., "Agreement on Tougher Drunken-Driving Standard," *New York Times,* May 10, 2001, B5.
14. For a full explanation of the bakery metaphors, see Morton Grodzins, *The American System* (Chicago: Rand McNally, 1966). A more updated discussion of federalism can be found in Joseph Zimmerman, *Contemporary American Federalism: The Growth of National Power* (New York: Praeger, 1992).
15. Paul E. Peterson, *City Limits.* (Chicago: University of Chicago Press, 1981).
16. Charles Mahtesian, "Romancing the Smokestack," *Governing* (November 1994): 36–40.
17. Harold Wolman, "Local Economic Development Policy: What Explains the Divergence Between Policy Analysis and Political Behavior?" *Journal of Urban Affairs* 10 (1988): 19–28; Martin Saiz and Susan Clarke, "Economic Development and Infrastructure Policy," in Virginia Gray and Russell Hanson, eds., *Politics in the American States,* 8th ed. (Washington, D.C.: CQ Press, 2004).
18. Christopher Swope, "Mississippi Signs on the Assembly Line" *Governing* (January 2001): 62; Jonathan Walters, "Gone With the Windfall," *Governing* (January 2004): 12.
19. Kierstan Gordan, "Scholars, Dollars and Sense," *Governing* (May 2000): 44.
20. The National Organization for the Reform of Marijuana Laws, "State By State Laws," February 22, 2005, www.norml.org/index.cfm?Group_ID=4516.
21. James Dao, "Red, Blue and Angry All Over," *New York Times,* January 16, 2005.
22. *McCulloch v. Maryland,* 4 Wheat. 316 (1819).
23. *Gibbons v. Ogden,* 9 Wheat. 1 (1824).
24. *Cooley v. Board of Wardens of Port of Philadelphia,* 53 U.S. (12 How.) 299 (1851).
25. *Dred Scott v. Sanford,* 60 U.S. 393 (1857).
26. *Pollock v. Farmer's Loan and Trust Company,* 1157 U.S. 429 (1895).
27. *Lochner v. New York,* 198 U.S. 45 (1905).
28. *Hammer v. Dagenhart,* 247 U.S. 251 (1918).
29. *United States v. Lopez,* 514 U.S. 549 (1995).
30. *Printz v. United States,* 521 U.S. 898 (1997).
31. Linda Greenhouse, "Supreme Court Shields States From Lawsuits on Age Bias," *New York Times,* January 11, 2000; Mark R. Kilenbeck, "In(re)Dignity: The New Federalism in Practice," *Arkansas Law Review* 57 (2004): 1.
32. Theodore Lowi, *The End of Liberalism* (New York: Norton, 1969).
33. Morris Fiorina, *Congress: Keystone of the Washington Establishment,* 2d ed. (New Haven: Yale University Press, 1989); John E. Chubb, "Federalism and the Bias for Centralization," in John E. Chubb and Paul E. Peterson, eds., *The New Directions in American Politics* (Washington, D.C.: Brookings Institution, 1985), 273–306.
34. Harold W. Stanley and Richard G. Niemi, *Vital Statistics on American Politics,* 2005–2006 ed. (Washington, D.C.: CQ Press, 2005), table 8-12.
35. David Walker, *The Rebirth of Federalism* (Chatham, N.J.: Chatham House, 1995), 139, 224.
36. Quote from Rochelle L. Stanfield,

"Holding the Bag," *National Journal,* September 9, 1995, 2206.

37. Walker, 232–234.
38. Martha Derthick, "Madison's Middle Ground in the 1980s," *Public Administration Review* (January–February 1987): 66–74.
39. Advisory Commission on Intergovernmental Relations, *Federal Mandate Relief for State, Local, and Tribal Governments* (Washington, D.C.: U.S. Government Printing Office, January 1995), 18.
40. *South Dakota v. Dole,* 483 U.S. 203 (1987).
41. Donald F. Kettl, "Mandates Forever," *Governing* (August 2003): 12; Tom Diemer, "Unfunded Mandate Bill Working Well," *Cleveland Plain Dealer,* February 8, 1998, 20A; Jonathan Walters, "The Accidental Tyranny of Congress," *Governing* (April 1997): 14.
42. "Funding Left Behind: Federal Education Law Piles Extra Expenses on Cash-Strapped States," *Columbus Dispatch,* March 15, 2004, 10A; Chris L. Jenkins, "Bill Imperiling U.S. School Aid Killed by Va. Panel," *Washington Post,* November 11, 2004, B06.
43. *Printz v. United States,* 117 S. Ct. 2365 (1997).
44. Charles R. Wise, "Judicial Federalism: The Resurgence of the Supreme Court's Role in the Protection of State Sovereignty," *Public Administration Review* 58 (March–April 1998): 95–98.
45. Hamilton, Madison, and Jay, 278.
46. "Unnatural Act: Foreign-Born Citizens Don't Need to Become President," *Pittsburgh Post-Gazette,* October 11, 2004, A-10.
47. Michael McGough, "Guns and the Governator," *Pittsburgh Post-Gazette,* January 3, 2005, A-15.

Chapter 5

1. Darren K. Carlson, "Far Enough? Public Wary of Restricted Liberties," *Gallup Poll,* January 20, 2004.
2. *West Virginia Board of Education v. Barnette,* 319 U.S. 624 (1943).
3. *Hamdi v. Rumsfeld,* 124 S. Ct. 2633 (2004); *Rasul v. Bush,* 124 S. Ct. 2686 (2004).
4. *Korematsu v. United States,* 323 U.S. 214 (1944).
5. Associated Press, *The Cold War at Home and Abroad 1945–1953* (New York: Grollier, 1995), 145.
6. Robert Frederick Burk, *The Eisenhower Administration and Black Civil Rights* (Knoxville: University of Tennessee Press, 1984), 204.
7. Jack N. Rakove, "James Madison and the Bill of Rights," in *This Constitution: From Ratification to the Bill of Rights,* American Political Science Association and American Historical Association (Washington, D.C.: Congressional Quarterly, 1988), 165.
8. David M. O'Brien, *Constitutional Law and Politics,* vol. 2 (New York: Norton, 1995), 300.
9. Ann Bowman and Richard Kearney, *State and Local Government,* 3d ed. (Boston: Houghton Mifflin, 1996), 39.
10. *Barron v. The Mayor and City Council of Baltimore,* 7 Peters 243 (1833).
11. *Chicago, Burlington & Quincy Railroad Co. v. Chicago,* 166 U.S. 226 (1897).
12. *Gitlow v. New York* 268 U.S. 652 (1920), cited in David M. O'Brien, *Constitutional Law and Politics,* vol. 2 (New York: Norton, 1995), 304.
13. Peter Irons, *Brennan vs. Rehnquist: The Battle for the Constitution* (New York: Knopf, 1994), 116.
14. O'Brien, 646.
15. Ibid., 647.
16. Ibid., 645; Henry J. Abraham and Barbara A. Perry, *Freedom and the Court* (New York: Oxford University Press, 1994), 223.
17. Ibid., 648.
18. Irons, 137.
19. *Abington School District v. Schempp,* 374 U.S. 203, 83 S. Ct. 1560 (1963).
20. Ibid.; *Murray v. Curlett,* 374 U.S. 203 (1963).
21. *Engel v. Vitale,* 370 U.S. 421, 82 S. Ct. 1261 (1962).
22. *Epperson v. Arkansas,* 393 U.S. 97 (1968).
23. *Lemon v. Kurtzman,* 403 U.S. 602, 91 S. Ct. 2105 (1971).
24. O'Brien, 661.
25. *Lynch v. Donnelly,* 465 U.S. 668 (1984).
26. *Wallace v. Jaffree,* 472 U.S. 38 (1985).
27. *Edwards v. Aguillard,* 482 U.S. 578 (1987).
28. *Board of Education of Westside Community Schools v. Mergens,* 496 U.S. 226 (1990).
29. *Lee v. Weisman,* 112 S. Ct. 2649 (1992).
30. *Santa Fe Independent School District v. Doe,* 530 U.S. 290 (2000).
31. *Locke v. Davey,* 124 S. Ct. 1307 (2004).
32. *Cantwell v. Connecticut,* 310 U.S. 296 (1940).
33. *Minersville School District v. Gobitis,* 310 U.S. 586 (1940).
34. *West Virginia State Board of Education v. Barnette,* 319 U.S. 624 (1943).
35. *McGowan v. Maryland,* 36 U.S. 420; *Two Guys From Harrison-Allentown, Inc., v. McGinley,* 366 U.S. 582; *Gallagher v. Crown Kosher Super Market of Massachusetts,* 366 U.S. 617; *Braunfield v. Brown,* 366 U.S. 599 (1961).
36. *Sherbert v. Verner,* 374 U.S. 398 (1963).
37. *Employment Division, Department of Human Resources v. Smith,* 494 U.S. 872 (1990).
38. *City of Boerne v. Flores,* 521 U.S. 507, 1997.
39. *Reynolds v. U.S.,* 98 U.S. 145 (1878).
40. *Welsh v. United States,* 398 U.S. 333 (1970).
41. John L. Sullivan, James Piereson, and George Marcus, *Political Tolerance and American Democracy* (Chicago: University of Chicago Press, 1982), 203.
42. O'Brien, 373; Samuel Walker, *In Defense of American Liberties: A History of the ACLU* (New York: Oxford University Press, 1990), 29.
43. Cited in Walker, 14.
44. *Schenck v. United States,* 249 U.S. 47 (1919); *Debs v. United States,* 249 U.S. 211 (1919); *Frowerk v. United States,* 249 U.S. 204 (1919); *Abrams v. United States,* 250 U.S. 616 (1919).
45. *Whitney v. California,* 274 U.S. 357 (1927).
46. *Brandenburg v. Ohio,* 395 U.S. 444 (1969).
47. *United States v. O'Brien,* 391 U.S. 367 (1968).
48. *Tinker v. Des Moines,* 393 U.S. 503 (1969).
49. *Street v. New York,* 394 U.S. 576 (1969).
50. *Texas v. Johnson,* 491 U.S. 397 (1989).

51. *United States v. Eichman,* 110 S. Ct. 2404 (1990).
52. *Virginia v. Black,* 538 U.S. 343 (2003).
53. *National Association for the Advancement of Colored People v. Alabama,* 357 U.S. 449 (1958).
54. *Sheldon v. Tucker,* 364 U.S. 516 (1960).
55. *Heart of Atlanta Motel v. United States,* 379 U.S. 241 (1964).
56. *Roberts v. United States Jaycees,* 468 U.S. 609 (1984).
57. *Jacobellis v. Ohio,* 378 U.S. 476 (1964).
58. *Miller v. California,* 413 U.S. 15 (1973).
59. *Cohen v. California,* 403 U.S. 15 (1971).
60. *Chaplinsky v. New Hampshire,* 315 U.S. 568 (1942).
61. *Terminello v. Chicago,* 337 U.S. 1 (1949).
62. *Cohen v. California,* 403 U.S. 15 (1971).
63. *Doe v. University of Michigan,* 721 F. Supp. 852 (E. D. Mich. 1989); *UMW Post v. Board of Regents of the University of Wisconsin,* 774 F. Supp. 1163, 1167, 1179 (E. D. Wis. 1991).
64. *R.A.V. v. City of St. Paul,* 60 LW 4667 (1992).
65. *Near v. Minnesota,* 283 U.S. 697 (1930).
66. *New York Times Company v. United States,* 403 U.S. 670 (1971).
67. Anthony Lewis, *Make No Law: The Sullivan Case and the First Amendment* (New York: Vintage Books/Random House, 1991).
68. *New York Times v. Sullivan,* 376 U.S. 254 (1964).
69. *Sheppard v. Maxwell,* 385 U.S. 333 (1966).
70. *Nebraska Press Association v. Stuart,* 427 U.S. 539 (1976).
71. *Reno v. ACLU,* 521 U.S. 1113 (1997).
72. *Ashcroft v. ACLU,* 124 S. Ct. 2783 (2004).
73. *United States v. American Library Association, Inc.,* 539 U.S. 194 (2003).
74. Pamela LiCalzi O'Connell, "Compressed Data: Law Newsletter Has to Sneak Past Filters," *New York Times,* April 2, 2001, C4.
75. Jeffery Seligno, "Student Writers Try to Duck the Censors by Going On-line," *New York Times,* June 7, 2001, G6.
76. *United States v. Lopez,* 514 U.S. 549 (1995); *Printz v. United States,* 521 U.S. 898 (1997).
77. Robert J. Spitzer, *The Politics of Gun Control* (Chatham, N.J.: Chatham House, 1995), 49.
78. Ibid., 47.
79. *United States v. Cruikshank,* 92 U.S. 542 (1876); *Presser v. Illinois,* 116 U.S. 252 (1886); *Miller v. Texas,* 153 U.S. 535 (1894); *United States v. Miller,* 307 U.S. 174 (1939).
80. *Printz v. United States,* 521 U.S. 898 (1997).
81. *Olmstead v. United States,* 277 U.S. 438 (1928).
82. *Katz v. United States,* 389 U.S. 347 (1967).
83. *Berger v. State of New York,* 388 U.S. 41 (1967).
84. *Skinner v. Railway Labor Executive Association,* 489 U.S. 602 (1989).
85. *Veronia School District v. Acton,* 515 U.S. 646 (1995).
86. *Weeks v. United States,* 232 U.S. 383 (1914).
87. *Wolf v. Colorado,* 338 U.S. 25 (1949).
88. *Mapp v. Ohio,* 367 U.S. 643 (1961).
89. *United States v. Calandra,* 414 U.S. 338 (1974).
90. *United States v. Janis,* 428 U.S. 433 (1976).
91. *Massachusetts v. Sheppard,* 468 U.S. 981 (1984); *United States v. Leon,* 468 U.S. 897 (1984); *Illinois v. Krull,* 480 U.S. 340 (1987).
92. *Miranda v. Arizona,* 382 U.S. 925 (1965); *Dickerson v. United States,* 530 U.S. 428, 120 S. Ct. 2326; 2000 U.S. LEXIS 4305.
93. *Johnson v. Zerbst,* 304 U.S. 458 (1938).
94. *Gideon v. Wainwright,* 372 U.S. 335 (1963).
95. *Ross v. Mofitt,* 417 U.S. 600 (1974); *Murray v. Giarratano,* 492 U.S. 1 (1989).
96. Henry Weinstein, "Many Denied Right to Counsel, Group Says," *Los Angeles Times,* July 13, 2004, A10.
97. *In re Kemmler,* 136 U.S. 436 (1890).
98. *Atkins v. Virginia,* 536 U.S. 304 (2002).
99. *Furman v. Georgia, Jackson v. Georgia, Branch v. Texas,* 408 U.S. 238 (1972).
100. *Gregg v. Georgia,* 428 U.S. 153 (1976); *Woodson v. North Carolina,* 428 U.S. 280 (1976); *Roberts v. Louisiana,* 428 U.S. 325 (1976).
101. *McClesky v. Kemp,* 481 U.S. 279 (1987).
102. *McClesky v. Zant,* 111 S. Ct. 1454 (1991).
103. Gallup poll, cited in William Saletan, "Calculating the Risk," *Mother Jones,* July–August 2000.
104. Jack Hitt, "The Moratorium Gambit," *New York Times Magazine,* December 9, 2001, 82.
105. Samuel D. Warren and Louis D. Brandeis, "The Right to Privacy," *Harvard Law Review* 4 (1890).
106. *Griswold v. Connecticut,* 391 U.S. 145 (1965).
107. *Eisenstadt v. Baird,* 405 U.S. 438 (1972).
108. *Roe v. Wade,* 410 U.S. 113 (1973).
109. *Harris v. McRae,* 448 U.S. 297 (1980).
110. See, for example, *Webster v. Reproductive Health Services,* 492 U.S. 4090 (1989) and *Rust v. Sullivan,* 111 S. Ct. 1759 (1991).
111. *Bowers v. Hardwick,* 478 U.S. 186 (1986).
112. *Commonwealth of Kentucky v. Wasson,* 842 S.W.2d 487 (1992).
113. *Lawrence v. Texas,* 539 U.S. 558 (2003).
114. *Romer v. Evans,* 517 U.S. 620 (1996).
115. *Cruzan by Cruzan v. Director, Missouri Department of Health,* 497 U.S. 261 (1990).
116. Frank Newport, "The Terri Schiavo Case in Review: Support for Her Being Allowed to Die Consistent," April 1, 2005, www.gallup.com.
117. *Washington v. Glucksberg,* 521 U.S. 702 (1997); *Vacco v. Quill,* 521 U.S. 793 (1997).
118. Stephen Adler and Wade Lambert, "Just About Everyone Violates Some Laws, Even Model Citizens," *Wall Street Journal,* March 12, 1993, 1.
119. Thomas Janoski, *Citizenship and Civil Society: A Framework of Rights and Obligations in Liberal, Traditional and Social Democratic Regimes* (Cambridge, U.K.: Cambridge University Press, 1998), 53–54.

Chapter 6

1. Ken Ellingwood and Nicholas Ricardi, "After the Attack: Racial Profiling," *Los Angeles Times,* September 20, 2001; Blaine Harden and Somini Sengupta, "A Nation Challenged: Commercial

Flights," *New York Times*, September 22, 2001, B8.

2. Sam Howe Verhovek, "A Nation Challenged: Civil Liberties: Americans Give In to Racial Profiling," *New York Times*, September 23, 2001; Robert Franklin, commentator on National Public Radio, *All Things Considered*, September 25, 2001.
3. Kathy Kiely, "These Are America's Governors. No Blacks. No Hispanics," *USA Today*, January 21, 2002, 1A.
4. David O'Brien, *Constitutional Law and Politics*, Vol. 2 (New York: Norton, 1991), 1265.
5. Roberto Suro, "Felonies to Bar 1.4 Million Black Men From Voting, Study Says," *Washington Post*, October 23, 1998, A12.
6. *Dred Scott v. Sanford*, 19 How. (60 U.S.) 393 (1857).
7. Scholars are divided about Lincoln's motives in issuing the Emancipation Proclamation; whether he genuinely desired to end slavery or merely used political means to shorten the war is hard to tell at this distance. Donald G. Nieman, *Promises to Keep: African-Americans and the Constitutional Order, 1776 to the Present* (New York: Oxford University Press, 1991), 55.
8. Bernard A. Weisberger, *Many Papers, One Nation* (Boston: Houghton Mifflin Company, 1987), 200.
9. Nieman, 107.
10. *The Civil Rights Cases*, 109 U.S. 3 (1883).
11. *Plessy v. Ferguson*, 163 U.S. 537 (1896).
12. Weisberger, 205–206.
13. *Guinn v. United States*, 238 U.S. 347 (1915).
14. *Missouri ex rel Gaines v. Canada*, 305 U.S. 337 (1938).
15. *Sweatt v. Painter*, 339 U.S. 629 (1950).
16. *Korematsu v. United States*, 323 U.S. 214 (1944).
17. *Brown v. Board of Education of Topeka (I)*, 347 U.S. 483 (1954).
18. *Brown v. Board of Education of Topeka (II)*, 349 U.S. 294 (1955).
19. *Gayle v. Browder*, 352 U.S. 903 (1956).
20. *Heart of Atlanta Motel, Inc. v. United States*, 379 U.S. 241 (1964); *Katzenbach v. McClung*, 379 U.S. 294 (1964); *Harper v. Virginia Board of Elections*, 383 U.S. 663 (1966).
21. Nieman, 179.
22. Ibid., 180.
23. *Swann v. Charlotte-Mecklenberg Board of Education*, 402 U.S. 1 (1971).
24. *Milliken v. Bradley*, 418 U.S. 717 (1974).
25. "*Brown v. Board*'s Goals Unrealized," *Atlanta Journal-Constitution*, May 16, 2004, 6C; Gary Orfield and Chungmei Lee, "*Brown* at 50: King's Dream or *Plessy*'s Nightmare?" Report conducted by the Harvard Civil Rights Project, 2004, www.civilrightsproject.harvard.edu/research/reseg04/brown50.pdf.
26. *Regents of the University of California v. Bakke*, 438 U.S. 265 (1978).
27. See, for example, *United Steelworkers of America v. Weber*, 443 U.S. 193 (1979); *Fullilove v. Klutznick*, 448 U.S. 448 (1980); *Firefighters Local Union No. 1784 v. Stotts*, 467 U.S. 561 (1984); and *Wygant v. Jackson Board of Education*, 476 U.S. 267 (1986).
28. *Patterson v. McLean Credit Union*, 491 U.S. 164 (1989).
29. *Wards Cove Packing, Inc. v. Atonio*, 490 U.S. 642 (1989).
30. *City of Richmond v. J. A. Croson*, 488 U.S. 469 (1989).
31. Darryl Fears, "A Diverse—and Divided—Black Community," *Washington Post*, February 24, 2002, A1.
32. Jonathan D. Glater, "Racial Gap in Pay Gets a Degree Sharper, a Study Finds," *Washington Post*, November 2, 1995, 13.
33. Joel Dresang, "Black Professional Men Paid Less Than White Peers," *Milwaukee Journal Sentinel*, August 16, 2001, 1D.
34. Ford Fessenden, "Examining the Vote: The Patterns," *New York Times*, November 12, 2001, A17.
35. Mireya Navarro and Somini Sengupta, "Arriving at Florida Voting Places, Some Blacks Found Frustration," *New York Times Online*, November 30, 2000.
36. Katherine Q. Seeyle, "Divided Civil Rights Panel Approves Election Report," *New York Times*, June 9, 2001, A8.
37. John Mintz and Dan Keating, "A Racial Gap in Voided Votes," *Washington Post*, December 27, 2000, A1.
38. Ruth A. Wooden, "Forty Years After Civil Rights Act, We Haven't Crossed the Finish Line," *USA Today*, July 1, 2004, 15A.
39. Kathy Kiely, "National Elite Political Circles Lack Minorities," *USA Today Online*, January 21, 2002.
40. Joe Klein, "The End of Affirmative Action," *Newsweek*, February 13, 1995; Ann Scales, "Affirmative Action: An American Dilemma, Part 2. Talking Across Divides," *Boston Globe*, May 22, 1995, 1; Jonathan Tilove, "Gap in Perceptions of Racism Growing," *Times-Picayune*, July 11, 2001, 1.
41. Jodi Wilgoren, "U.S. Court Bars Race as Factor in School Entry," *New York Times*, March 28, 2001, A1.
42. Jacques Steinberg, "Redefining Diversity," *New York Times*, August 29, 2001, A14.
43. *Gratz v. Bollinger*, 539 U.S. 244 (2003).
44. *Grutter v. Bollinger*, 539 U.S. 306 (2003).
45. Ward Connerly, "Up From Affirmative Action," *New York Times*, April 29, 1996.
46. David K. Shipler, "My Equal Opportunity, Your Free Lunch," *New York Times*, March 5, 1995.
47. *Cherokee Nation v. Georgia*, 30 U.S. (5 Pet.) 1, 20 (1831).
48. Vine Delori Jr., and Clifford M. Lytle, *The Nations Within: The Past and Future of American Indian Sovereignty* (New York: Pantheon, 1984), 17.
49. *Lyng v. Northwest Indian Cemetery Protective Association*, 485 U.S. 439 (1988).
50. *Employment Division v. Oregon*, 494 U.S. 872 (1990).
51. U.S. Census Bureau, Historical Poverty Tables, "Table 24. Number in Poverty and Poverty Rate by Race and Hispanic Origin Using 3-Year Averages: 1987 to 2003," August 26, 2004, www.census.gov/hhes/poverty/histpov/hstpov24.html.
52. Christopher B. Swanson, "Projections of 2003–2004 High School Graduates," 2004, www.urban.org/uploadedpdf/411019_2003_04_hs_graduates.pdf.

53. "Despite Prayers, a Navajo-Mormon Culture Clash," *New York Times,* July 24, 1996, A8.
54. *Seminole Tribe of Florida v. Butterworth* 658 F.2d 310 (1981), cert. denied, 455 U.S. 1020 (1982); *State of California v. Cabazon Band of Mission Indians* 480 U.S. 202 (1987).
55. National Indian Gaming Commission, "Tribal Gaming Revenues (in thousands) by Region Fiscal Year 2003 and 2002," n.d., www.nigc.gov/nigc/tribes/tribaldata2003/gamerevenue.jsp.
56. Mark Falcoff, "Our Language Needs No Law," *New York Times,* August 5, 1996.
57. Rene Sanchez, "Both Parties Courting Latinos Vigorously," *Washington Post Online,* October 26, 1998, 2.
58. CNN.com, National Exit Polls, November 10, 2004, www.cnn.com/ELECTION/2004/pages/results/states/US/P/00/epolls.0.html. An exit poll of Hispanic voters conducted by the Willie C. Velazquez Institute put Bush's percentage of the Hispanic vote at only 31 percent; Brian DeBose, "Bush Share of Hispanic Vote Rose to 44 percent," *Washington Times,* November 8, 2004, www.washingtontimes.com/national/20041108-125405-9126r.htm.
59. Christine Nifong, "Hispanics and Asians Change the Face of the South," *Christian Science Monitor,* August 6, 1996.
60. Ronald Takaki, *Strangers From a Different Shore* (Boston: Little, Brown, 1989), 363–364.
61. *Hirabayashi v. United States,* 320 U.S. 81 (1943); *Korematsu v. United States,* 323 U.S. 214 (1944).
62. Robert Franek, *The Best 345 Colleges by the Princeton Review* (New York: Random House, 2003).
63. Ibid., 479.
64. Norimitsu Onishi, "Affirmative Action: Choosing Sides," *New York Times* Education Life Supplement, March 31, 1996, 27.
65. Lena H. Sun, "Getting Out the Ethnic Vote," *Washington Post,* October 7, 1996, B5; K. Connie Kang, "Asian Americans Slow to Flex Their Political Muscle," *Los Angeles Times,* October 31, 1996, A18.
66. Sun, B5; Kang, A18.
67. William Booth, "California Race Could Signal New Cohesion for Asian Voters," *Washington Post,* November 3, 1998, 1.
68. "Asian Americans' Political Mark," *Los Angeles Times,* November 25, 1996, B4.
69. CNN.com, National Exit Polls, November 10, 2004, www.cnn.com/ELECTION/2004/pages/results/states/US/P/00/epolls.0.html. See polls for each state.
70. Sun, B5.
71. Paul Van Slambrouck, "Asian-Americans' Politics Evolving," *Christian Science Monitor,* September 8, 1998, 2.
72. CNN.com, National Exit Polls, November 11, 2004, www.cnn.com/ELECTION/2004/pages/results/states/US/P/00/epolls.0.html.
73. See Paula D. McClain and Joseph Stewart Jr., *Can We All Get Along?* 3d ed. (Boulder: Westview, 2003), 78.
74. Eleanor Flexner, *Century of Struggle: The Woman's Rights Movement in the United States* (New York: Atheneum, 1973), 148–149.
75. Nancy E. McGlen and Karen O'Connor, *Women's Rights: The Struggle for Equality in the 19th and 20th Centuries* (New York: Praeger, 1983), 272–273.
76. *Bradwell v. Illinois,* 16 Wall. 130 (1873).
77. Quoted in Flexner, 178.
78. Flexner, 296.
79. McGlen and O'Connor, 83.
80. Jane Mansbridge, *Why We Lost the ERA* (Chicago: Chicago University Press, 1986), 13.
81. *Reed v. Reed,* 404 U.S. 71 (1971); *Craig v. Boren,* 429 U.S. 190 (1976).
82. *Weinberger v. Wiesenfeld,* 420 U.S. 636 (1975); *Califano v. Goldfarb,* 430 U.S. 199 (1977); *Califano v. Westcott,* 443 U.S. 76 (1979); *Orr v. Orr,* 440 U.S. 268 (1979).
83. Shelley Donald Coolidge, "Flat Tire on the Road to Pay Equity," *Christian Science Monitor,* April 11, 1997, 9.
84. *Johnson v. Transportation Agency, Santa Clara, California,* 480 U.S. 616 (1987).
85. Barbara Noble, "At Work: And Now the Sticky Floor," *New York Times,* November 22, 1992, 23.
86. Kenneth Gray, "The Gender Gap in Yearly Earnings: Can Vocational Education Help?" Office of Special Populations' Brief, vol. 5, no. 2. National Center for Research in Vocational Education, University of California, Berkeley, Office of Special Populations, University of California, Berkeley.
87. Stephanie Armour, "Pregnant Workers Report Growing Discrimination," *USA Today,* February 16, 2005.
88. Binnie Fisher, "Gender Equity Laws: A Push for Fair Prices for the Fair Sex," *Christian Science Monitor,* March 7, 1996.
89. Ibid.
90. Center for American Women and Politics, "Women in Elective Office 2005," www.cawp.rutgers.edu.
91. Barbara Burrell, "Campaign Finance: Women's Experience in the Modern Era," in Sue Thomas and Clyde Wilcox, eds., *Women and Elective Office: Past, Present, and Future* (New York: Oxford University Press, 1998), 27.
92. Gary F. Moncrief, Peverill Squire, and Malcolm E. Jewell, *Who Runs for the Legislature?* (Upper Saddle River, N.J.: Prentice Hall, 2001), 98–99.
93. Siena Research Institute, "Do you think the United States is ready for a woman president in 2008?" February 22, 2005, www.siena.edu/sri/firstwomanpresident/fwp_release_final_sans.pdf.
94. Moncrief, Squire, and Jewell, 98–99.
95. Nancy E. McGlen, Karen O'Connor, Laura van Assendelft, and Wendy Gunther-Canada, *Women, Politics, and American Society,* 4th ed. (New York: Pearson Longman, 2005), 88.
96. Kristin Eliasberg, "Making a Case for the Right to Be Different," *New York Times,* June 16, 2001, B11.
97. *Bowers v. Hardwick,* 478 U.S. 186 (1986).
98. *John J. Hurley, and South Boston Allied War Veterans Council v. Irish-American Gay, Lesbian, and Bisexual Group of Boston,* 115 S. Ct. 714 (1995).
99. *Romer v. Evans,* 115 S. Ct. 1092 (1996).
100. Linda Greenhouse, "The Supreme Court: The New Jersey Case; Supreme Court Backs Boy Scouts in Ban of

Gays from Membership," *New York Times,* June 29, 2000, A1.

101. *Lawrence v. Texas,* 539 U.S. 558 (2003).

102. *Goodridge v. Dept. of Pub. Health,* 440 Mass. 309 (2003).

103. David W. Dunlap, "Gay Survey Raises a New Question," *New York Times,* October 18, 1994, B8.

104. National Gay and Lesbian Task Force, "The Gay, Lesbian, and Bisexual Vote: As Much as 5% of Presidential and Congressional Voters," 2004, www.thetaskforce.org/theissues/issue.cfm?issueID=32.

105. Center for Responsive Politics, "Human Rights: Top Contributors to Federal Candidates and Parties," www.opensecrets.org/industries/contrib.asp?Ind=Q09, May 31, 2005.

106. "Military misguidance," *Chicago Sun Times,* November 20, 2002, 51.

107. Philip Shenon, "Homosexuality Still Questioned by the Military," *New York Times,* February 27, 1996.

108. *Los Angeles Times* poll, "Gay Issues," March 27–30, 2004.

109. *Massachusetts Board of Retirement v. Murgia,* 427 U.S. 307 (1976).

110. *Massachusetts Board of Retirement v. Murgia,* 427 U.S. 307 (1976); *Vance v. Bradley,* 440 U.S. 93 (1979); *Gregory v. Ashcroft,* 501 U.S. 452 (1991).

111. *Alabama v. Garrett,* 531 U.S. 356 (2001).

112. *Graham v. Richardson,* 403 U.S. 365 (1971).

113. *Pyler v. Doe,* 457 U.S. 202 (1982).

114. Robert J. Samuelson, "Immigration and Poverty," *Newsweek,* July 15, 1996, 43.

115. Sanford J. Ungar, "Enough of the Immigrant Bashing," *USA Today,* October 11, 1995, 11A.

116. Theda Skocpol, "Advocates Without Members: The Recent Transformation of American Civil Life," in Theda Skocpol and Morris P. Fiorina, eds., *Civic Engagement in American Democracy* (Washington, D.C., and New York: Brookings Institution and the Russell Sage Foundation, 1999), 470–472.

117. William Glaberson, "Racial Profiling May Get Wider Approval by Courts," *New York Times,* September 21, 2001, A16.

118. Ibid.

119. Michael Kinsley, "When Is Racial Profiling Okay?" *Washington Post,* September 30, 2001, B7.

120. Ronald D. White, "U.S. Strikes Back: Workplace," *Los Angeles Times,* October 16, 2001, Part 3, 1.

Chapter 7

1. Nick Madigan, "On the Lam, Texas Democrats Rough It," *New York Times,* August 1, 2003, 11.
2. John R. Hibbing and Elizabeth Theiss-Morse, *Congress as Public Enemy* (New York: Cambridge University Press, 1995), chs. 2, 3.
3. Glenn R. Parker and Roger H. Davidson, "Why Do Americans Love Their Congressmen So Much More Than Their Congress?" *Legislative Studies Quarterly* (February 1979): 52–61.
4. Heinz Eulau and Paul D. Karps, "The Puzzle of Representation: Specifying Components of Responsiveness," *Legislative Studies Quarterly* 2 (1977): 233–254.
5. Richard Fenno, *Homestyle* (Boston: Little, Brown, 1978), ch. 3.
6. Gary Jacobson, *The Politics of Congressional Elections,* 4th ed. (New York: Longman, 1997), ch. 8.
7. Ross K. Baker, *House and Senate* (New York: Norton, 1989).
8. David M. O'Brien, "Ironies and Disappointments: Bush and Federal Judgeships," in Colin Campbell and Bert Rockman, eds., *The George W. Bush Presidency* (Washington, D.C.: CQ Press, 2004), 139–143.
9. "Shortage of Judges Not Fault of the Senate, Hatch Asserts," *Chicago Tribune,* January 2, 1998, 3.
10. Neil A. Lewis, "Panel Rejects Bush Nominee in Judgeship," *New York Times,* March 15, 2002, Web version.
11. Charles Cameron, Albert Cover, and Jeffrey Segal, "Senate Voting on Supreme Court Nominations," *American Political Science Review* 84 (1990): 525–534.
12. David Mayhew, *Congress: The Electoral Connection* (New Haven: Yale University Press, 1974).
13. *Baker v. Carr,* 396 U.S. 186 (1962); *Westberry v. Sanders,* 376 U.S. 1 (1964).
14. Karen Mills, "Census 2000 Brief: Congressional Apportionment," (Washington, D.C.: U.S. Census Bureau, July 2001), www.census.gov/prod/2001pubs/c2kbr01-7.pdf.
15. Roger H. Davidson and Walter J. Oleszek, *Congress and Its Members,* 9th ed. (Washington, D.C.: CQ Press, 2004), 48.
16. Charles Cameron, David Epstein, and Sharyn O'Halloran, "Do Majority–Minority Districts Maximize Substantive Black Representation in Congress?" *American Political Science Review* 90 (December 1996): 794–812; Kevin Hill, "Does the Creation of Majority Black Districts Aid Republicans? An Analysis of the 1992 Congressional Election in Eight Southern States," *Journal of Politics* 57 (May 1995): 384–401.
17. Holly Idelson, "Court Takes a Hard Line on Minority Voting Blocs," *CQ Weekly Report,* July 1, 1995, 4, 5.
18. *Shaw v. Reno,* 509 U.S. 630 (1993); *Miller v. Johnson,* 115 S. Ct. 2475 (1995).
19. *Shaw v. Hunt,* 116 S. Ct. 1894 (1996); *Bush v. Vera,* 116 S. Ct. 1941 (1996); *Hunt v. Cromartie et al.,* 532 U.S. 534 (2001).
20. Peter Urban, "Congress Gets Lavish Benefits," *Connecticut Post,* January 16, 2005; Debra J. Saunders, "Perks of Office" (editorial), *San Francisco Chronicle,* November 19, 2000, 9.
21. Commission on the Executive, Legislative and Judicial Salaries, *Fairness for Public Servants* (Washington, D.C.: U.S. Government Printing Office, 1988), 23.
22. Eric Uslaner, *The Decline of Comity in Congress* (Ann Arbor: University of Michigan Press, 1993).
23. Gary Jacobson, *The Politics of Congressional Elections,* 3d ed. (New York: HarperCollins, 1992); Peverill Squire, "Challengers in Senate Elections," *Legislative Studies Quarterly* 14 (1989): 531–547; David Cannon, *Actors, Athletes and Astronauts: Political Amateurs in the United States Congress* (Chicago: University of Chicago Press, 1990).
24. Norman J. Ornstein, Thomas E. Mann, and Michael J. Malbin, *Vital Statistics on Congress, 2001–2002* (Washington,

D.C.: AEI Press, 2002), 69; Roger H. Davidson and Walter J. Oleszek, *Congress and Its Members,* 9th ed. (Washington, D.C.: CQ Press, 2004), 60; Peter E. Harrell, "A Slightly Redder Hue," *CQ Weekly,* November 6, 2004, 2621–2625.

25. Calculated by the authors from Tables 2 and 4 of Campaign Finance Institute press release, "House Winners Average $1 Million for First Time; Senate Winners Up 47%," November 5, 2004, www.cfinst.org/pr/110504a.html.
26. Figure derived from Table 2 category of "incumbent beat challenger with less than 60 percent" of the vote; cited in Campaign Finance Institute press release, "House Winners Average $1 Million for First Time; Senate Winners Up 47%," November 5, 2004, www.cfinst.org/pr/110504a.html.
27. Harold Stanley and Richard Niemi, *Vital Statistics on American Politics,* 5th ed. (Washington, D.C.: Congressional Quarterly Press, 1995).
28. Edward R. Tufte, *Political Control of the Economy* (Princeton: Princeton University Press, 1978); Robert S. Erikson, "The Puzzle of the Midterm Loss," *Journal of Politics* 50 (November 1988): 1011–1029; Robert S. Erikson and Gerald C. Wright, "Voters, Candidates, and Issues in Congressional Elections," in Lawrence Dodd and Bruce Oppenheimer, eds., *Congress Reconsidered,* 6th ed. (Washington, D.C.: Congressional Quarterly Press, 1997), 132–140.
29. John Adams, "Thoughts on Government," cited in Gordon S. Wood, *The Creation of the American Republic, 1776–1787* (New York: Norton, 1969), 165.
30. Davidson and Oleszek.
31. Mildred L. Amer, "Membership of the 109th Congress: A Profile," *Congressional Research Service,* December 20, 2004.
32. Alexander Bolton and Tom Sullivan, "Not All Lawmakers Are Millionaires—Shock! More Than 1 in 4 in House Have 7-Figure Assets," *The Hill,* June 17, 2004, 1.
33. Richard E. Cohen, "Is It an Earthquake, or Only a Tremor?" *National Journal,* July 8, 1995, 1786.
34. Richette L. Haywood, "CBC Legislative Conference Celebrates 25 Years as 'Conscience of Congress,' " *Jet,* October 16, 1995, 5.
35. Glenn Parker, *Characteristics of Congress: Patterns in Congressional Behavior* (Englewood Cliffs, N.J.: Prentice Hall, 1989), 17–18, ch. 9.
36. Davidson and Oleszek, 155–156.
37. Leroy Rieselbach, *Congressional Reform in the Seventies* (Morristown, N.J.: General Learning Press, 1977); Leroy Rieselbach, *Congressional Reform* (Washington, D.C.: Congressional Quarterly Press, 1986).
38. Ed Gillespie and Bob Schellhas, eds., *Contract With America: The Bold Plan by Rep. Newt Gingrich, Rep. Dick Armey and the House Republicans to Change the Nation* (New York: Random House, 1994); James G. Gimpel, *Legislating the Revolution* (Boston: Allyn & Bacon, 1996).
39. Sheryl Gay Stolberg, "Quietly but Firmly, Hastert Asserts His Power," *New York Times,* January 3, 2003, A1; Lawrence C. Dodd and Bruce I. Oppenheimer, "A Decade of Republican Control: The House of Representatives, 1995–2005," in Lawrence Dodd and Bruce Oppenheimer, eds., *Congress Reconsidered,* 8th ed. (Washington, D.C.: CQ Press, 2005), 47–49.
40. Davidson and Oleszek, 193.
41. Matthew McCubbins and Thomas Schwartz, "Congressional Oversight Overlooked: Police Patrols Versus Fire Alarms," *American Journal of Political Science* (February 1984): 165–179.
42. Barbara Sinclair, "Party Leaders and the New Legislative Process," in Lawrence Dodd and Bruce Oppenheimer, eds., *Congress Reconsidered,* 6th ed. (Washington, D.C.: Congressional Quarterly Press, 1997), 229–245.
43. Richard Fenno, *Congressmen in Committees* (Boston: Little, Brown, 1973); Glenn R. Parker, *Characteristics of Congress* (Englewood Cliffs, N.J.: Prentice Hall, 1989).
44. Davidson and Oleszek, 204.
45. Steven Smith and Eric Lawrence, "Party Control of Committees in the Republican Congress," in Lawrence Dodd and Bruce Oppenheimer, eds., *Congress Reconsidered,* 6th ed. (Washington, D.C.: Congressional Quarterly Press, 1997), 163–192.
46. Davidson and Oleszek, 219–220.
47. These reports are GAO/HEHS-98-30 and T-NSIAD-98-44. Copies of these and hundreds of other GAO reports are available online at www.gao.gov.
48. Barbara Sinclair, *The Transformation of the U.S. Senate* (Baltimore: Johns Hopkins University Press, 1989).
49. John Stewart, "A Chronology of the Civil Rights Act of 1964," in Robert Loevy, ed., *The Civil Rights Act of 1964: The Passage of the Law That Ended Racial Segregation* (Albany: SUNY Press, 1997), 358.
50. Ibid., 358–360.
51. Barbara Sinclair, "The New World of U.S. Senators," in Lawrence C. Dodd and Bruce I. Oppenheimer, eds., *Congress Reconsidered,* 8th ed. (Washington, D.C.: CQ Press, 2005), 11; Richard Beth and Stanley Bach, "Filibusters and Cloture in the Senate," Congressional Research Service, March 28, 2003, www.senate.gov/reference/resources/pdf/RL30360.pdf.
52. Donald R. Matthews and James A. Stimson, *Yeas and Nays* (New York: Wiley, 1975).
53. Richard Smith, "Interest Group Influence in the U.S. Congress," *Legislative Studies Quarterly* 20 (February 1995): 89–140.
54. Richard S. Dunham, "Power to the President—Courtesy of the GOP," *Business Week,* October 20, 1997, 51.
55. Stephen C. Craig, *The Malevolent Leaders: Popular Discontent in America* (Boulder: Westview Press, 1993); David Easton, "A Reassessment of the Concept of Political Support," *British Journal of Political Science* 5 (1975): 435–457; Glenn Parker, "Some Themes in Congressional Unpopularity," *American Journal of Political Science* 21 (1977): 93–110; E. J. Dionne, Jr., *Why Americans Hate Politics* (New York: Simon & Schuster, 1991).
56. Seymour M. Lipset and William Schneider, *The Confidence Gap: Business, Labor, and Government in the Public Mind* (Baltimore: Johns Hopkins University Press, 1987).

57. Parker and Davidson; Richard F. Fenno Jr., "If, as Ralph Nader Says, Congress Is 'the Broken Branch,' How Come We Love Our Congressmen So Much?" in Norman J. Ornstein, ed., *Congress in Change* (New York: Praeger, 1975), 277–287.
58. John R. Hibbing and Elizabeth Theiss-Morse, *Congress as Public Enemy* (New York: Cambridge University Press, 1995).
59. John R. Hibbing and Elizabeth Theiss-Morse, "Civics Is Not Enough: Teaching Barbarics in K-12," *Political Science and Politics* 29 (1996): 157.
60. Gary Jacobson, *Money in Congressional Elections* (New Haven: Yale University Press, 1980).
61. Madigan.
62. R. G. Ratcliffe, "Federal Panel Upholds Plan for Redistricting; Texas Districts Stay Same Unless Supreme Court Decides to Step In," *Houston Chronicle*, June 10, 2005, B1.

Chapter 8

1. Peter Baker, "Privilege at Stake with Nominees," *Washington Post*, August 2, 2005, A06.
2. Tom Curry, "Executive Privilege Again at Issue," MSNBC News Web site, February 1, 2002, www.msnbc.com/news/695487.asp.
3. Katharine Q. Seelye, "Ideas and Trends; The Presidency Has Its Privileges," *New York Times*, September 19, 1999, 4:3.
4. Bruce Miroff, "Monopolizing the Public Space: The President as a Problem for Democratic Politics," in Bruce Miroff, Raymond Seidelman, and Todd Swanstrom, eds., *Debating Democracy* (Boston: Houghton Mifflin, 1997), 294–303.
5. Max Farrand, *The Framing of the Constitution of the United States* (New Haven: Yale University Press, 1913), 163.
6. Skip Thurman, "One Man's Impeachment Crusade," *Christian Science Monitor*, November 18, 1997, 4.
7. Robert DiClerico, *The American President*, 4th ed. (Englewood Cliffs, N.J.: Prentice Hall, 1995), 374.
8. Joseph A. Pika and John Anthony Maltese, *The Politics of the Modern Presidency*, 6th ed. (Washington, D.C.: CQ Press, 2004), 3; Jeffrey K. Tulis, "The Two Constitutional Presidencies," in Michael Nelson, ed., *The Presidency and the Political System* (Washington, D.C.: Congressional Quarterly Press, 1995), 91–123.
9. Pika and Maltese, 374.
10. Authors' calculations from Pika and Maltese, "Table 10-3: International Agreements, 1969–2002," 374–375.
11. Lawrence Margolis, *Executive Agreements and Presidential Power in Foreign Policy* (New York: Praeger, 1985).
12. D. Roderick Kiewiet and Mathew D. McCubbins, "Presidential Influence on Congressional Appropriations Decisions," *American Political Science Review* 32 (1988): 713–736.
13. Joseph J. Schatz, "With a Deft and Light Touch, Bush Finds Ways to Win," *CQ Weekly*, December 11, 2004, 2900–2904.
14. Kenneth R. Mayer, *With the Stroke of a Pen: Executive Orders and Presidential Power* (Princeton: Princeton University Press, 2002), 88–89.
15. Robert A. Carp, Ronald Stidham, and Kenneth L. Manning, *Judicial Process in America*, 6th ed. (Washington, D.C.: CQ Press, 2004), 168.
16. Quoted in Henry Abramson, *Justices and Presidents: A Political History of Appointments to the Supreme Court*, 2d ed. (New York: Oxford University Press, 1985), 263.
17. Gerald Boyd, "White House Hunts for a Justice, Hoping to Tip Ideological Scales," *New York Times*, June 30, 1987; Alan I. Abramowitz and Jeffrey A. Segal, *Senate Elections* (Ann Arbor: University of Michigan Press, 1992), 1–6.
18. David Plotz, "Advise and Consent (Also, Obstruct, Delay, and Stymie): What's Still Wrong With the Appointments Process," *Slate Magazine*, March 19, 1999, www.slate.com/StrangeBedfellow/99-03-19/StrangeBedfellow.asp.
19. Carl Hulse, "Bipartisan Group in Senate Averts Judge Showdown," *New York Times*, May 24, 2005, A1.
20. "Clinton Knows Better Than to Lean on a Judge," Greensboro, N.C., *News and Record*, March 25, 1996, A6.
21. Rebecca Mae Salokar, *The Solicitor General: The Politics of Law* (Philadelphia: Temple University Press, 1992), 29.
22. Bob Woodward, *Shadow: Five Presidents and the Legacy of Watergate* (New York: Simon & Schuster, 1999), 212–217.
23. Cited in David O'Brien, *Constitutional Law and Politics* (New York: Norton, 1991), vol. 1, 218.
24. *In re Neagle*, 135 U.S. 546 (1890); *In re Debs*, 158 U.S. 564 (1895); *United States v. Curtiss-Wright Export Corp.*, [299]U.S. 304, 57 S. Ct. 216 (1936); *Youngstown Sheet & Tube v. Sawyer*, 343 U.S. 579 (1952).
25. Lyn Ragsdale, *Presidential Politics* (Boston: Houghton Mifflin, 1993), 55.
26. *Historical Statistics of the United States: Colonial Times to 1970* (Washington, D.C.: U.S. Government Printing Office, 1975).
27. *Inaugural Addresses of the United States* (Washington, D.C.: U.S. Government Printing Office, 1982), quoted in Ragsdale, 71.
28. *United States v. Curtiss-Wright Export Corp.*, 299 U.S. 304, 57 S. Ct. 216 (1936).
29. *Youngstown Sheet & Tube v. Sawyer*, 343 U.S. 579 (1952).
30. Roger H. Davidson and Walter J. Oleszek, *Congress and Its Members*, 9th ed. (Washington, D.C.: CQ Press, 2004), 407.
31. *Clinton v. Jones*, 520 U.S. 681 (1997).
32. Dana Milbank, "Cheney Refuses Records' Release; Energy Showdown With GAO Looms," *Washington Post*, January 28, 2002, A1.
33. Jeffrey Tulis, *The Rhetorical Presidency* (Princeton: Princeton University Press, 1987).
34. Richard E. Neustadt, *Presidential Power and the Modern Presidents* (New York: Free Press, 1990), 10.
35. Ibid.
36. Samuel Kernell, *Going Public: New Strategies of Presidential Leadership*, 2d ed. (Washington, D.C.: Congressional Quarterly Press, 1996).
37. Barbara Hinckley, *The Symbolic Presidency* (London: Routledge, 1990), ch. 2.

38. David E. Rosenbaum, "Few See Gains From Social Security Tour," *New York Times,* April 3, 2005, 24.
39. Michael A. Fletcher and Jim VandeHei, "Bush Warns Democrats About Opposing Accounts," *Washington Post,* March 23, 2005, A3; Maeve Reston, "Battle Royale Over Social Security Moves to the Hustings," *Pittsburgh Post-Gazette,* March 20, 2005, A1.
40. See Hedrick Smith, *The Power Game: How Washington Works* (New York: Random House, 1988), 405–406, for similar reports on the Nixon and Reagan administrations.
41. Lee Sigelman, "Gauging the Public Response to Presidential Leadership," *Presidential Studies Quarterly* 10 (Summer 1980): 427–433; James A. Stimson, "Public Support for American Presidents: A Cyclical Model," *Public Opinion Quarterly* 40 (Spring 1976): 1–21; Michael MacKuen, "Political Drama, Economic Conditions, and the Dynamics of Presidential Popularity," *American Journal of Political Science* 27 (February 1983): 165–192.
42. Gerald Pomper, "The Presidential Election," in Gerald Pomper, ed., *The Election of 1992* (Chatham, N.J.: Chatham House, 1993), 144–150; Richard L. Berke, "Poll Finds Most Give Clinton Credit for Strong Economy," *New York Times,* September 6, 1996, A1.
43. John Hibbing and Elizabeth Theiss-Morse, in *Congress as Public Enemy* (New York: Cambridge University Press, 1995). Hibbing and Theiss-Morse demonstrate the public intolerance for controversy in Congress; the same reaction is undoubtedly true for the presidency.
44. Paul Brace and Barbara Hinckley, *Follow the Leader: Opinion Polls and the Modern Presidents* (New York: Basic Books, 1992), ch. 4., Appendix B.
45. Ibid., ch. 5.
46. Ibid., ch. 6.
47. Neustadt, 50–72.
48. Mark A. Peterson, *Legislating Together: The White House and Capitol Hill From Eisenhower to Reagan* (Cambridge, Mass.: Harvard University Press, 1990); George Edwards, *At the Margins: Presidential Leadership of Congress* (New Haven: Yale University Press, 1989), ch. 9.
49. James L. Sundquist, "Needed: A Political Theory for a New Era of Coalition Government in the United States," *Political Science Quarterly* 103 (Winter 1988–1989): 613–635.
50. *Congressional Quarterly Weekly Report,* December 21, 1996, 3455.
51. David Mayhew, *Divided We Govern: Party Control, Lawmaking, and Investigations, 1946–1990* (New Haven: Yale University Press, 1991).
52. Ragsdale, 1–4.
53. Terry Moe, "Presidents, Institutions, and Theory," in George C. Edwards III, John H. Kessel, and Bert A. Rockman, eds., *Researching the Presidency: Vital Questions, New Approaches* (Pittsburgh: University of Pittsburgh Press, 1993), 370.
54. Ibid.
55. The President's Committee on Administrative Management, *Report of the Committee* (Washington, D.C.: U.S. Government Printing Office, 1937).
56. Jane Meyer and Doyle MacManus, *Landslide: The Unmaking of the President, 1984–1988* (Boston: Houghton Mifflin, 1988).
57. U.S. Office of Personnel Management, "Federal Civilian Employment and Payroll," March 2004, Table 9, www.opm.gov/feddata/html/2004/march/table9.asp.
58. James P. Pfiffner, *The Modern Presidency,* 2d ed. (New York: St. Martin's, 1998), 91.
59. Harold Relyea, "Growth and Development of the President's Office," in David Kozak and Kenneth Ciboski, eds., *The American Presidency* (Chicago: Nelson Hall, 1985), 135; Pfiffner, 122.
60. Sid Frank and Arden Davis Melick, *The Presidents: Tidbits and Trivia* (Maplewood, N.J.: Hammond, 1986), 103.
61. Timothy Walch, ed., *At the President's Side: The Vice-Presidency in the Twentieth Century* (Columbia: University of Missouri Press, 1997), 45.
62. Ann Devroy and Stephen Barr, "Reinventing the Vice Presidency: Defying History, Al Gore Has Emerged as Bill Clinton's Closest Political Advisor," *Washington Post National Weekly Edition,* February 27–March 5, 1995, 6–7.
63. Barbara Bush, *Barbara Bush: A Memoir* (New York: Scribner's, 1994).
64. Robert K. Murray and Tim H. Blessing, "The Presidential Performance Study: A Progress Report," *Journal of American History* 70 (December 1983): 535–555.
65. Jon R. Bond and Richard Fleisher, *The President in the Legislative Arena* (Chicago: University of Chicago Press, 1990); George C. Edwards III, *Presidential Influence in Congress* (San Francisco: Freeman, 1980).
66. James David Barber, *The Presidential Character,* 4th ed. (Englewood Cliffs, N.J.: Prentice Hall, 1992).
67. See Michael Nelson, "James David Barber and the Psychological Presidency," in David Pederson, ed., *The "Barberian" Presidency: Theoretical and Empirical Readings* (New York: Peter Lang, 1989), 93–110; Alexander George, "Assessing Presidential Character," *World Politics* (January 1974): 234–283; Jeffrey Tulis, "On Presidential Character," in Jeffrey Tulis and Joseph Bessette, eds., *Presidency and the Constitutional Order* (Baton Rouge: Louisiana State University Press, 1981).
68. Joseph Califano, *A Presidential Nation* (New York: Norton, 1975), 184–188.
69. Elizabeth Bumiller, "A President Leaves No Doubt About Being Fit to Run the Country," *New York Times,* April 1, 2002, A17.
70. Gallup poll, December 19, 1998, http://institution.gallup.com/documents/topics.aspx.

Chapter 9

1. "Organic Standards Regrown: New USDA Guidelines," *Better Homes and Gardens,* August 1998, 80.
2. Dann Denny, "Defining 'Organic', " *Bloomington Herald Times,* April 16, 1998, D1.
3. Marian Burros, "Eating Well: U.S. Proposal on Organic Food Gets a Grass-Roots Review," *New York Times,* March 25, 1998, F10.
4. Gene Kahn, "National Organic Standard Will Aid Consumers," *Frozen Food Age* 47 (September 1998): 18.

5. Burros, F10.
6. H. H. Gerth and C. Wright Mills, eds., *From Max Weber* (New York: Oxford University Press, 1946), 196–199.
7. Herbert Kaufman, "Emerging Conflicts in the Doctrines of Public Administration," *American Political Science Review* 50 (December 1956): 1057–1073.
8. Morris P. Fiorina, *Congress: Keystone of the Washington Establishment* (New Haven: Yale University Press, 1977).
9. Office of Personnel Management, "Federal Civilian Workforce Statistics: Employment and Trends, Table 1—Federal Civilian Personnel Summary," May 2004, www.opm.gov/feddata/html/2004/may/table1.asp.
10. Kenneth J. Meier, *Politics and the Bureaucracy,* 4th ed. (Fort Worth, Texas: Harcourt-Brace, 2000), 17.
11. Ibid., 18–19.
12. "U.S. National Debt Clock," www.brillig.com/debt_clock, accessed May 2005.
13. Dennis D. Riley, *Controlling the Federal Bureaucracy* (Philadelphia: Temple University Press, 1987), 139–142.
14. Meier, 72.
15. *U.S. News and World Report,* February 11, 1980, 64.
16. Meier, 177–181.
17. Quoted in Donald F. Kettl, *System Under Stress: Homeland Security and American Politics* (Washington, D.C.: CQ Press, 2004), 48.
18. "The 9/11 Commission Report: Final Report of the National Commission on Terrorist Attacks Upon the United States, Executive Summary," www.c-span.org/pdf/911finalreportexecsum.pdf.
19. Quoted in Kettl, 53.
20. Dana Milbank, "Bush Seeks to Rule the Bureaucracy; Appointments Aim at White House Control," *Washington Post,* November 22, 2004, A4.
21. Terry Moe, "The President's Cabinet," in James Pfiffer and Roger J. Davidson, eds., *Understanding the Presidency,* 3d ed. (New York: Longman, 2003), 208.
22. Office of Personnel Management, *Federal Workforce Statistics: The Fact Book 2003 Edition* (Washington, D.C.: OPM, 2003), 10, www.opm.gov/feddata/03factbk.pdf.
23. Francis E. Rourke, *Bureaucracy, Politics and Public Policy,* 3d ed. (Boston: Little, Brown, 1984), 106.
24. Albert B. Crenshaw, "Cash Flow," *Washington Post,* June 28, 1998, H1.
25. Anthony E. Brown, *The Politics of Airline Regulation* (Knoxville: University of Tennessee Press, 1987).
26. Milbank, A4.
27. Walter Pincus, "CIA Director Cuts Meetings on Terrorism; Coordinating Sessions Reduced to 3 a Week," *Washington Post,* January 10, 2005, A15; Walter Pincus, "Changing of the Guard at the CIA; Goss's Shake-Ups Leave Some Questioning Agency's Role," *Washington Post,* January 6, 2005, A3.
28. Riley, ch. 2.
29. Harold Seidman and Robert Gilmour, *Politics, Position, and Power: From the Positive to the Regulatory State,* 4th ed. (New York: Oxford University Press, 1986), 3.
30. Stephen Barr, "Gore's Team Turns to Making Reinvention Deliver; At 5-Year Point, 32 Agencies' Goals Are Readjusted," *Washington Post,* March 3, 1998, A15; Elaine Kamarck, "Q: Has the White House delivered on promises to reinvent government? Yes: Reinventing efforts have made Uncle Sam slimmer, more efficient and customer-friendly," *Insight on the News,* June 15, 1998, 24.
31. Quoted in Riley, 43.
32. As an example, Representative Walden received contributions from eleven forestry and forest products political action committees in 2003–2004, totaling almost $40,000 (see www.opensecrets.org).
33. Hugh Heclo, "Issue Networks and the Executive Establishment," in Anthony King, ed., *The New American Political System* (Washington, D.C.: American Enterprise Institute, 1978), 87–124.
34. Many examples of environmental groups' efforts to challenge the traditional iron triangles of congressional committees, agencies, and industry can be found in the news sections of the groups' Web sites (see, for example, www.wilderness.org/newsroom/index.cfm and www.sierraclub.org/pressroom).
35. Kenneth Shepsle and Barry Weingast, "The Institutional Foundations of Committee Power," *American Political Science Review* 81 (1987): 85–104.
36. Matthew Crenson and Francis E. Rourke, "By Way of Conclusion: American Bureaucracy Since World War II," in Louis Galambois, ed., *The New American State: Bureaucracies and Policies Since World War II* (Baltimore: Johns Hopkins University Press, 1987), 137–177.
37. Martha Derthick, *Policymaking for Social Security* (Washington, D.C.: Brookings Institution, 1979), reprinted in "The Art of Cooptation: Advisory Councils in Social Security," in Francis E. Rourke, ed., *Bureaucratic Power in National Policy Making,* 3d ed. (Boston: Little, Brown, 1986), 109.
38. Charles T. Goodsell, *The Case for Bureaucracy* (Chatham, N.J.: Chatham House, 1993), ch. 3; Robert L. Kahn, Barbara A. Gutek, Eugenia Barton, and Daniel Katz, "Americans Love Their Bureaucrats," in Francis E. Rourke, ed., *Bureaucracy, Politics, and Public Policy,* 4th ed. (Boston: Little, Brown, 1988).
39. Meier, 210–211.

Chapter 10

1. This list is based loosely on the discussion of the functions of law in James V. Calvi and Susan Coleman, *American Law and Legal Systems* (Upper Saddle River, N.J.: Prentice Hall, 1997), 2–4; Steven Vago, *Law and Society* (Upper Saddle River, N.J.: Prentice Hall, 1997), 16–20; and Lawrence Baum, *American Courts: Process and Policy,* 4th ed. (Boston: Houghton Mifflin, 1998), 4–5.
2. Christopher E. Smith, *Courts, Politics, and the Judicial Process* (Chicago: Nelson-Hall, 1993), 179.
3. Henry Abraham, *The Judicial Process* (New York: Oxford University Press, 1993), 97.
4. Ibid., 96–97.
5. Smith, 329.
6. Jethro K. Lieberman, *The Litigious Society* (New York: Basic Books, 1981), 6.
7. Smith, 324.

8. Ibid., 324, 327.
9. Lieberman, 168–190.
10. Walter K. Olson, *The Litigation Explosion: What Happened When America Unleashed the Lawsuit* (New York: Truman Talley Books, 1991), 1–11.
11. Lawrence Friedman, *Total Justice: What Americans Want From the Legal System and Why* (Boston: Beacon Press, 1985), 31–32, cited in Smith, 323.
12. "Prison Suits," *Reader's Digest,* August 1994, 96.
13. Alexander Hamilton, James Madison, and John Jay, *The Federalist Papers,* ed. Clinton Rossiter (New York: New American Library, 1961).
14. Robert A. Carp and Ronald Stidham, *The Federal Courts* (Washington, D.C.: Congressional Quarterly Press, 1991), 4.
15. Lawrence Baum, *The Supreme Court,* 5th ed. (Washington, D.C.: Congressional Quarterly Press, 1995), 13.
16. *Marbury v. Madison,* 5 U.S. (1 Cranch) 137 (1803).
17. *Dred Scott v. Sanford,* 60 U.S. (19 How.) 393.
18. Lawrence Baum, *The Supreme Court,* 8th ed. (Washington, D.C.: CQ Press: 2004), 170, 173.
19. Baum, *The Supreme Court,* 5th ed., 1995, 22–24.
20. Matthew J. Streb, "Just Like Any Other Election? The Politics of Judicial Elections," in Matthew J. Streb, ed., *Law and Election Politics: The Rules of the Game* (Boulder: Lynne Rienner, 2005).
21. Joan Biskupic, "Making a Mark on the Bench," *Washington Post National Weekly Edition,* December 2–8, 1996, 31.
22. Ibid.
23. Ibid.
24. Harold W. Stanley and Richard G. Niemi, *Vital Statistics on American Politics, 2003–2004* (Washington D.C.: CQ Press, 2003), 282.
25. David G. Savage, "Judge Battles Transcends Numbers," *Los Angeles Times,* April 17, 2005, Web version.
26. Tom Brune, "Will Filibuster Deal Hold?" *Newsday,* May 25, 2005, A23; "A Near Miss: The Filibuster Question Is Off the Table, For Now, But the Really Big Nomination Questions Still Await," *Plain Dealer,* May 25, 2005, B8.
27. David M. O'Brien, "Ironies and Disappointments: Bush and Federal Judgeships," in Colin Campbell and Bert Rockman, eds., *The George W. Bush Presidency* (Washington, D.C.: CQ Press, 2004), 139–143.
28. Greg Gordon, "Federal Courts, Winner Will Make a Mark on the Bench," *Minneapolis Star Tribune,* September 27, 2004, 1A.
29. The Gallup Organization, *Polls, Topics & Trends: Trust in Government,* various dates through 2004, www.gallup.com/poll/content/?ci=5392&pg=1; Linda Greenhouse, "The Nation: Vote Count Omits a Verdict on the Court," *New York Times,* November 18, 2001, sec. 4, 4.
30. Cited in Robert Marquand, "Why America Puts Its Supreme Court on a Lofty Pedestal," *Christian Science Monitor,* June 25, 1997, 14.
31. Although the president has no official "list" of criteria, scholars are mostly agreed on these factors. See, for instance, Henry J. Abraham, *The Judiciary* (New York: New York University Press, 1996), 65–69; Lawrence Baum, *American Courts: Process and Policy,* 4th ed., (Boston: Houghton Mifflin, 1998), 105–106; Philip Cooper and Howard Ball, *The United States Supreme Court: From the Inside Out* (Upper Saddle River, N.J.: Prentice Hall, 1996), 49–60; and Thomas G. Walker and Lee Epstein, *The Supreme Court of the United States* (New York: St. Martin's Press, 1993), 34–40.
32. Baum, *American Courts,* 105.
33. From the filmstrip, *This Honorable Court* (Washington, D.C.: Greater Washington Educational Telecommunications Association, 1988), program 1.
34. Ibid.
35. Baum, *American Courts,* 105.
36. Walker and Epstein, 40.
37. Carl Hulse and Adam Nagourney, "Senators Clash on Questioning a Court Nominee," *New York Times,* July 4, 2005, Web version; Alan Cooperman, "Evangelical Groups Plan Aggressive Drive for Nominee," *Washington Post,* July 4, 2005, A6.
38. Baum, *The Supreme Court,* 8th ed., 2004, 103.
39. U.S. Supreme Court, "2004 Year-End Report on the Federal Judiciary." Retrieved from www.supremecourtus.gov/publicinfo/year-end/2004year-endreport.pdf.
40. Philip Cooper and Howard Ball, *The United States Supreme Court: From the Inside Out* (Upper Saddle River, N.J.: Prentice Hall, 1996), 104.
41. Ibid., 134.
42. Walker and Epstein, 90.
43. Ibid., 91–92.
44. David O'Brien, *Storm Center* (New York: Norton, 1990), 272.
45. Walker and Epstein, 129–130.
46. Adam Cohen, "Psst . . . Justice Scalia . . . You Know, You're an Activist Too," *New York Times,* April 19, 2005, Web version.
47. Walker and Epstein, 126–130.
48. What follows is drawn from the excellent discussion in ibid., 131–139.
49. Baum, *The Supreme Court,* 8th ed., 2004, 82.
50. *Gratz v. Bollinger,* 539 U.S. 244 (2003); *Grutter v. Bollinger,* 539 U.S. 306 (2003).
51. Max Lerner, *Nine Scorpions in a Bottle: Great Judges and Cases of the Supreme Court* (New York: Arcade Publishing, 1994).
52. Philip J. Cooper, *Battles on the Bench: Conflict Inside the Supreme Court* (Lawrence: University Press of Kansas, 1995), 42–46.
53. For a provocative argument that the Court does not, in fact, successfully produce significant social reform and actually damaged the civil rights struggles in this country, see Gerald N. Rosenberg, *The Hollow Hope: Can Courts Bring About Social Change?* (Chicago: University of Chicago Press, 1991).
54. *Marbury v. Madison,* 1 Cr. 137 (1803).
55. *Martin v. Hunter's Lessee,* 14 U.S. 304 (1816).
56. *McCulloch v. Maryland,* 4 Wheat. 316 (1819).
57. *Gibbons v. Ogden,* 9 Wheat. 1 (1824).

58. *Lochner v. New York,* 198 U.S. 45 (1905).
59. *Hammer v. Dagenhart,* 247 U.S. 251 (1918).
60. *Adkins v. Children's Hospital,* 261 U.S. 525 (1923).
61. *Dred Scott v. Sanford,* 19 How. 393 (1857).
62. *Plessy v. Ferguson,* 163 U.S. 537 (1896).
63. *Brown v. Board of Education,* 347 U.S. 483 (1954).
64. For example, *Mapp v. Ohio,* 367 U.S. 643 (1961); *Gideon v. Wainwright,* 372 U.S. 335 (1963); and *Miranda v. Arizona,* 382 U.S. 925 (1965).
65. *Baker v. Carr,* 396 U.S. 186 (1962).
66. *Roe v. Wade,* 410 U.S. 113 (1973).
67. Maria Puente, "Poll: Blacks' Confidence in Police Plummets," *USA Today,* March 21, 1995, 3A.
68. Michael Tonry, "Racial Politics, Racial Disparities, and the War on Crime," *Crime and Delinquency* (1994): 475–494.
69. John H. Langbein, "Money Talks, Clients Walk," *Newsweek,* April 17, 1995, 32.
70. Legal Services Corporation, "Annual Report 2000–2001." Retrieved from www.lsc.gov/foia/lscar01.pdf.
71. Consortium on Legal Services and the Public, *Agenda for Success: The American People and Civil Justice* (Chicago: American Bar Association, 1996); see also Legal Services Corporation, "Serving the Civil Legal Needs of Low-Income Americans," April 30, 2000. Retrieved from www.lsc.gov/pressr/exsum.pdf.
72. Linda Greenhouse, "Bush v. Gore: A Special Report," *New York Times,* February 20, 2001.

Chapter 11

1. Mike Gravel, "Philadelphia II: National Initiatives," *Campaigns and Elections* (Dec. 1995/Jan. 1996): 2.
2. According to a September 1994 Roper poll, 76 percent favor a national referendum.
3. Survey by Fox News and Opinion Dynamics, May 24–May 25, 2000. Retrieved from the iPOLL database, The Roper Center for Public Opinion Research, University of Connecticut, www.ropercenter.uconn.edu/ipoll.html.
4. "Exchange With Reporters in Waco, Texas, August 7, 2001," Public Papers of the Presidents: George W. Bush—2001, vol. 2, p. 945. U.S. Government Printing Office via GPO Access.
5. Joshua Green, "The Other War Room," *Washington Monthly,* April 2002, 16.
6. Matt Bai, "Rove's Way," *New York Times Magazine,* October 20, 2002, 56.
7. V. O. Key Jr., *Public Opinion and American Democracy* (New York: Knopf, 1961), 7.
8. John Kingdon, *Congressmen's Voting Decisions,* 2d ed. (New York: Harper & Row, 1981), ch. 2.
9. Susan Herbst, *Numbered Voices: How Opinion Polling Has Shaped American Politics* (Chicago: University of Chicago Press, 1993), ch. 4.
10. William Safire, *Safire's New Political Dictionary: The Definitive Guide to the New Language of Politics* (New York: Random House, 1993), 764.
11. Robert S. Erikson and Kent Tedin, *American Public Opinion,* 5th ed. (Boston: Allyn & Bacon, 1995), 29–31.
12. Richard Morin, "Don't Ask Me: As Fewer Cooperate on Polls, Criticism and Questions Mount," *Washington Post,* October 28, 2004, C1.
13. The Pew Research Center for the People and the Press, "Opinion Poll Experiment Reveals Conservative Opinions Not Underestimated, But Racial Hostility Missed," March 27, 1998. Retrieved from www.people-press.org/content.htm; Andrew Rosenthal, "The 1989 Elections: Predicting the Outcome; Broad Disparities in Votes and Polls Raising Questions," *New York Times,* November 9, 1989, A1; Adam Clymer, "Election Day Shows What the Opinion Polls Can't Do," *New York Times,* November 12, 1989, sec. 4, 4; George Flemming and Kimberly Parker, "Race and Reluctant Respondents: Possible Consequences of Non-Response for Pre-Election Survey," May 16, 1998. Retrieved from www.people-press.org/content.htm.
14. George F. Bishop et al., "Pseudo-Opinions on Public Affairs," *Public Opinion Quarterly* 44 (Summer 1980): 198–209.
15. Howard Schuman and Stanley Presser, *Questions and Answers in Attitude Surveys* (New York: Academic Press, 1981), 148–160.
16. This was a Roper Starch Worldwide poll conducted in November 1992 for the American Jewish Committee, and it was reported in conjunction with the dedication of the Holocaust Memorial Museum.
17. Debra J. Saunders, "Poll Shows Americans in Deep Dumbo," *San Francisco Chronicle,* April 23, 1993, A30; Leonard Larsen, "What's on Americans' Mind? Not Much, History Poll Finds," *Sacramento Bee,* June 2, 1993, B7, cited in David W. Moore and Frank Newport, "Misreading the Public: The Case of the Holocaust Poll," *Public Perspective* (March–April 1994), 28.
18. Moore and Newport, 29.
19. Here are some Web addresses that you may find helpful. ABC News: abcnews.go.com/US/PollVault/; CBS News: www.cbsnews.com/sections/opinion/polls/main500160.shtml; *Washington Post*: www.washingtonpost.com/wp-dyn/politics/polls; *New York Times* (click on "Poll Watch" to see recent polls): www.nytimes.com/pages/politics/index.html; *Los Angles Times*: www.latimes.com/news/custom/timespoll; Pew Research Center: www.people-press.org; The Gallup Poll: www.gallup.com/poll; and for an excellent roundup of political polls, see www.pollingreport.com.
20. Adam Lisberg, "Exit Polls Out of Whack: Early Numbers Told Wrong Story," New York *Daily News,* November 4, 2002, 11; "Evaluation of Edison/Mitofsky Election System 2004," prepared by Edison Media Research and Mitofsky International for the National Election Pool (NEP), January 19, 2005.
21. Quoted in "Planting Lies With 'Push Polls,'" *St. Petersburg Times,* June 7, 1995, 10A.
22. Quoted in Betsy Rothstein, "Push Polls Utilized in Final Weeks," *The Hill,* October 28, 1998, 3.
23. "Pollsters Seek AAPC Action," *Campaigns and Elections* (July 1996): 55.

24. Erikson and Tedin, 5th ed., 42–47.
25. Many works repeat this theme of the uninformed and ignorant citizen. See, for example, Bernard Berelson, Paul F. Lazarsfeld, and William N. McPhee, *Voting: A Study of Opinion Formation in a Presidential Campaign* (Chicago: University of Chicago Press, 1954); Angus Campbell, Philip E. Converse, Warren E. Miller, and Donald E. Stokes, *The American Voter* (New York: Wiley, 1960); W. Russell Neuman, *The Paradox of Mass Politics* (Cambridge: Harvard University Press, 1986); and Michael X. Delli Carpini and Scott Keeter, *What Americans Know About Politics and Why It Matters* (New Haven: Yale University Press, 1996).
26. These data come from Delli Carpini and Keeter, 70–75.
27. Philip Converse, "The Nature of Belief Systems in Mass Publics," in David Apter, ed., *Ideology and Discontent* (Glencoe, Ill.: Free Press, 1964) 206–261.
28. Authors' analysis of CBS News/*New York Times* polls covering the period from 1997 to 2004.
29. Converse, 206–261; Erikson and Tedin, 5th ed., 74–77.
30. John Marzulli and Michael Saul, "A Disturbing Wave of Hatred Anti-Muslim, Anti-Arab Incidents in City, Nation," *New York Daily News,* September 19, 2001.
31. Herbert McClosky and Alida Brill, *Dimensions of Tolerance* (New York: Russell Sage Foundation, 1983), 50.
32. McClosky and Brill, 250.
33. Sidney Verba, Norman Nie, and J. O. Kim, *Modes of Democratic Participation* (Beverly Hills, Calif.: Sage, 1971); Russell Dalton, *Citizen Politics: Public Opinion and Political Parties in Advanced Industrial Democracies,* 2d ed. (Chatham, N.J.: Chatham House, 1996), 57–58; Raymond Wolfinger and Steven Rosenstone, *Who Votes?* (New Haven: Yale University Press, 1980).
34. Carol A. Cassel, "Overreporting and Electoral Participation Research," *American Politics Research* 31 (January 2003): 81–92; Robert Bernstein, A. Chadha, and Robert Montjoy, "Overreporting Voting—Why It Happens and Why It Matters," *Public Opinion Quarterly* 65 (Spring 2001): 22–44; Michael W. Traugott and John P. Katosh, "Response Validity in Surveys of Voting Behavior," *Public Opinion Quarterly* 43 (1979): 359–377.
35. Erikson and Tedin, 5th ed., 127–128.
36. M. Kent Jennings and Richard G. Niemi, *The Political Character of Adolescence* (Princeton: Princeton University Press, 1974); Robert C. Luskin, John P. McIver, and Edward Carmines, "Issues and the Transmission of Partisanship," *American Journal of Political Science* 33 (May 1989): 440–458.
37. Shirley Engle and Anna Ochoa, *Education for Democratic Citizenship: Decision Making in the Social Studies* (New York: Teachers College of Columbia University, 1988).
38. Robert D. Hess and Judith V. Torney, *The Development of Political Attitudes in Children* (Chicago: Aldine, 1967).
39. Kenneth D. Wald, Dennis E. Owen, and Samuel S. Jill Jr., "Political Cohesion in Churches," *Journal of Politics* 52 (1990): 197–215; Robert Huckfeldt, Paul Allen Beck, Russell J. Dalton, and Jeffrey Levine, "Political Environments, Cohesive Social Groups, and the Communication of Public Opinion," *American Journal of Political Science* 39 (1995): 1025–1054; David C. Leege, Kenneth D. Wald, Brian S. Krueger, and Paul D. Mueller, *The Politics of Cultural Differences: Social Change and Voter Mobilization in the Post-New Deal Period* (Princeton: Princeton University Press, 2002).
40. Elisabeth Noelle-Neumann, *The Spiral of Silence: Public Opinion, Our Social Skin* (Chicago: University of Chicago Press, 1984).
41. Paul R. Abramson and Ada W. Finifter, "On the Meaning of Political Trust: New Evidence From Items Introduced in 1978," *American Journal of Political Science* 25 (May 1981): 295–306; Arthur H. Miller, "Is Confidence Rebounding?" *Public Opinion* (June/July 1983); Robert S. Erikson and Kent L. Tedin, *American Public Opinion,* 7th ed. (New York: Pearson-Longman, 2005), 162–166.
42. Norman H. Nie, Jane Junn, and Kenneth Stehlik-Barry, *Education and Democratic Citizenship in America* (Chicago: University of Chicago Press, 1996).
43. For more on the effects of education, see Delli Carpini and Keeter, 188–189; Erikson and Tedin, 7th ed., 152–159; and Herbert H. Hyman, Charles R. Wright, and John Shelton Reed, *The Enduring Effects of Education* (Chicago: University of Chicago Press, 1975). But for a dissenting view that formal education is just a mask for intelligence and native cognitive ability, see Robert Luskin, "Explaining Political Sophistication," *Political Behavior* 12 (1990): 3298–3409.
44. Christine L. Day, *What Older Americans Think: Interest Groups and Aging Policy* (Princeton: Princeton University Press, 1990).
45. Warren E. Miller and J. Merrill Shanks, *The New American Voter* (Cambridge: Harvard University Press, 1996), ch. 7.
46. Figure calculated by the authors from National Election Studies data.
47. Erikson and Tedin, 5th ed., 208–212.
48. Based on authors' analysis of the 1996 and 2000 Voter News Service election day exit polls
49. Lee Sigelman and Susan Welch, *Black Americans' Views of Racial Equality—The Dream Deferred* (Cambridge: Cambridge University Press, 1991).
50. Katherine Tate, "Black Political Participation in the 1984 and 1988 Presidential Elections," *American Political Science Review* 85 (December 1991): 1159–1176.
51. Wendy K. Tam Cho, "Asians—a Monolithic Voting Bloc?" *Political Behavior* 17 (1995): 223–249; Rodolfo O. De La Garza, *Latino Voices: Mexican, Puerto Rican, and Cuban Perspectives on American Politics* (Boulder: Westview Press, 1992).
52. Robert S. Erikson, Gerald C. Wright, and John P. McIver, *Statehouse Democracy* (New York: Cambridge University Press, 1993), 18.
53. Research suggests that use of information shortcuts does allow the electorate to make decisions that are more in line with their values than if they did not have such shortcuts; see Samuel Popkin, *The Reasoning Voter* (Chicago: University of Chicago Press, 1991); and Paul Sniderman, Richard

Brody, and Philip Tetlock, *Reasoning and Choice: Exploration in Political Psychology* (New York: Cambridge University Press, 1991). However, this is not the same as saying that if fully informed, everyone would make the same decision as they do without information. Indeed, information really does count; see Larry Bartels, "Uninformed Votes: Information Effects in Presidential Elections," *American Journal of Political Science* 40 (February 1996): 194–230; and Scott Althaus, "Information Effects in Collective Preferences" *American Political Science Review* 92 (September 1998): 545–558.

54. Milton Lodge, Kathleen McGraw, and Patrick Stroh, "An Impression-Driven Model of Candidate Evaluation," *American Political Science Review* 82 (June 1989): 399–419.
55. Berelson, Lazarsfeld, and McPhee, 109–115.
56. Gerald C. Wright, "Level of Analysis Effects on Explanations of Voting," *British Journal of Political Science* 18 (July 1989): 381–398; Samuel Popkin, *The Reasoning Voter* (Chicago: University of Chicago Press, 1991); Benjamin Page and Robert Shapiro, *The Rational Public* (Chicago: University of Chicago Press, 1993).
57. Erikson, Wright, and McIver.
58. Michael B. MacKuen, Robert S. Erikson, and James A. Stimson, "Macropartisanship," *American Political Science Review* 89 (December 1989): 1125–1142.
59. Jean Bethke Elshtain, "A Parody of True Democracy," *Christian Science Monitor,* August 13, 1992, 18.

Chapter 12

1. Ronnie Dugger, "Ralph, Don't Run," *Nation,* December 2, 2002. Retrieved from www.thenation.com/doc.mhtml%3Fi=20021202&s=dugger.
2. Michael Brus, "Nader: Spoiler or Savior," *Slate,* June 26, 2000. Retrieved from slate.msn.com/?id=1005569.
3. Scott Martelle, "Campaign 2000: Nader Vote May Cast His Name in History," *Los Angeles Times,* November 3, 2000, A1.
4. Jack Dennis, "Trends in Public Support for the American Party System," *British Journal of Political Science* 5 (April 1975): 204; "Changing Public Support for the American Party System," in William J. Crotty, ed., *Paths to Political Reform* (Lexington, Mass.: D. C. Heath, 1980), 38–39.
5. See, for example, James Bryce, *The American Commonwealth* (Chicago: Sergel, 1891), vol. 2, pt. 3.
6. E. E. Schattschneider, *Party Government* (New York: Holt, Rinehart, and Winston, 1942), 1.
7. This division and the following discussion are based on Frank Sorauf, *Party Politics in America* (Boston: Little, Brown, 1964), ch. 1; and V. O. Key, *Politics, Parties, and Pressure Groups,* 5th ed. (New York: Corwell, 1964).
8. Richard G. Niemi and M. Kent Jennings, "Issues of Inheritance in the Formation of Party Identification," *American Journal of Political Science* 35 (1991): 970–988.
9. The discussion of the responsible party model is based on Austin Ranney, *The Doctrine of the Responsible Party Government* (Urbana: University of Illinois Press, 1962), chs. 1, 2.
10. Morris P. Fiorina, "The Decline of Collective Responsibility in American Politics," *Daedalus* 109 (Summer 1980): 25–45; John H. Aldrich, *Why Parties: The Origin and Transformation of Party Politics in America* (Chicago: University of Chicago Press, 1995), 3.
11. Frank J. Sorauf and Paul Allen Beck, *Party Politics in America,* 6th ed. (Glenview, Ill.: Scott, Foresman, 1988), 454.
12. American National Election Studies cumulative data file, 1948–2002. (Ann Arbor: University of Michigan, Center for Political Studies).
13. Alan I. Abramowitz and Kyle L. Saunder, "Ideological Realignment in the U.S. Electorate," *Journal of Politics* 60 (1998): 634–652; Geoffrey C. Layman and Thomas M. Carsey, "Party Polarization and 'Conflict Extension' in the American Electorate," *American Journal of Political Science* 46 (2002): 786–802.
14. Edward G. Carmines and Geoffrey C. Layman, "Issue Evolution in Postwar American Politics: Old Certainties and Fresh Tensions," in Byron E. Shafer, ed., *Present Discontents: American Politics in the Very Late Twentieth Century* (Chatham, N.J.: Chatham House, 1997), 89–134.
15. Benjamin Ginsberg, *Consequences of Consent* (New York: Random House, 1982), 128–133.
16. Anthony Downs, *An Economic Theory of Democracy* (New York: Harper & Row, 1957).
17. Kevin A. Hassett and Maya MacGuineas, "Hung up on Words," *National Review,* March 18, 2005; Mike Allen, "Semantics Shape Social Security Debate; Democrats Assail 'Crisis' While GOP Gives 'Privatization' a 'Personal' Twist," *Washington Post,* January 23, 2005, A4.
18. Karen DeYoung and Glenn Kessler, "Cheney Says Tax Cuts Eased Recession; Democrats Assail Speech to Foreign Relations Group as 'Revisionism,'" *Washington Post,* February 16, 2002, A5.
19. James L. Gibson and Susan E. Scarrow, "State Organizations in American Politics," in Eric M. Uslaner, ed., *American Political Parties: A Reader* (Itasca, Ill.: F. E. Peacock, 1993), 234.
20. James Q. Wilson, *The Amateur Democrat: Club Politics in Three Cities* (Chicago: University of Chicago Press, 1965).
21. Joseph A. Aistrup, *The Southern Strategy Revisited: Republican Top-Down Advancement in the South* (Lexington: University of Kentucky Press, 1996), 148–151; Robert S. Erikson, Gerald C. Wright, and John P. McIver, *Statehouse Democracy: Public Opinion and Policy in the American States* (Cambridge: Cambridge University Press, 1993), ch. 5.
22. Aldrich, 186–192.
23. Leslie Wayne, "A Back Door for the Conservative Donor," *New York Times,* May 22, 1997, 1.
24. Gerald C. Wright and Michael B. Berkman, "Candidates and Policy in U.S. Senatorial Elections," *American Political Science Review* 80 (June 1986): 576–590.

25. Aldrich.
26. Ibid., 5.
27. This discussion of the Jacksonian Democrats and machine politics and patronage is based on Aldrich, ch. 4; Leon D. Epstein, *Political Parties in the American Mold* (Madison: University of Wisconsin Press, 1986), 134–143; and Sorauf and Beck, 83–91.
28. James L. Sundquist, *Dynamics of the Party System: Alignment and Realignment in Political Parties in the United States,* rev. ed. (Washington, D.C.: Brookings Institution Press, 1983), 156.
29. Marjorie Randon Hershey, *Party Politics in America,* 11th ed. (New York: Longman, 2004), 130–135.
30. William H. Flanigan and Nancy H. Zingale, *Political Behavior of the American Electorate,* 9th ed. (Washington, D.C.: CQ Press, 1998).
31. Ibid., 59–66; Martin Wattenberg, *The Decline of American Political Parties: 1952–1994* (Cambridge: Harvard University Press, 1996).
32. Gerald C. Wright, John P. McIver, Robert S. Erikson, and David B. Holian, "Stability and Change in State Electorates, Carter Through Clinton" (paper presented at the Midwest Political Science Association Meetings, Chicago, 2000); Larry Bartels, "Partisanship and Voting Behavior, 1952–1996," *American Journal of Political Science* 44 (January 2000): 35–50.
33. Gary C. Jacobson, *The Electoral Origins of Divided Government* (Boulder: Westview Press, 1990), and *The Politics of Congressional Elections,* 6th ed. (New York: Longman, 2003).
34. Xandra Kayden and Eddie Mahe Jr., "Back From the Depths: Party Resurgence," in Uslaner, 192, 196; Aistrup, ch. 4.
35. Sarah McCally Morehouse and Malcolm E. Jewell, *State Politics, Parties, & Policy,* 2d ed. (Lanham, Md.: Rowman & Littlefield, 2003), 127–133.
36. David E. Price, *Bring Back the Parties* (Washington, D.C.: Congressional Quarterly Press, 1984), 130–132.
37. Sorauf and Beck, 218–233.
38. Ginsberg.
39. C. P. Cotter, J. L. Gibson, J. F. Bibby, and R. J. Huckshorn, *Party Organizations in American Politics* (New York: Praeger, 1984); John J. Coleman, "Resurgent or Just Busy? Party Organizations in Contemporary America," in John Green and Daniel Shea, eds., *The State of the Parties* (Lanham, Md.: Rowman & Littlefield, 1996), ch. 22.
40. Jill Abramson, "Democrats and Republicans Step Up Pursuit of 'Soft Money,'" *New York Times,* May 13, 1998, 2; Jill Abramson, "Cost of '96 Campaign Sets Record at $2.2 Billion," *New York Times,* November 25, 1997, 1.
41. Hershey, ch. 12.
42. Aistrup, 76; Paul S. Herrnson, *Congressional Elections: Campaigning at Home and in Washington,* 2d ed. (Washington, D.C.: Congressional Quarterly Press, 1998), ch. 4.
43. Pam Belluck, "The First Lady Finding a Full Democratic Dance Card," *New York Times,* November 1, 1998, 27.
44. Katharine Q. Seelye, "The 2002 Election: The Voters East and West Explain the Bush Effect," *New York Times,* November 9, 2002, A1; R. W. Apple Jr., "The 2002 Elections: New Analysis Victory and Challenges," *New York Times,* November 7, 2002, A1.
45. Sorauf and Beck.
46. Gerald Pomper with Susan Lederman, *Elections in America* (New York: Longman, 1980), 145–150, 167–173.
47. Samuel Huntington, "The Visions of the Democratic Party," *Public Interest* (Spring 1985): 64.
48. This section is based on Alan Ware, *Political Parties and Party Systems* (New York: Oxford University Press, 1996).
49. L. Sandy Maisel, *Parties and Elections in America,* 2d ed. (New York: McGraw-Hill, 1993), ch. 10; Epstein; Price, 284.
50. Nelson Polsby, *The Consequences to Party Reform* (New York: Oxford University Press, 1983), 83.
51. Anthony Gierzynski, *Legislative Party Campaign Committees in the American States* (Lexington: University Press of Kentucky, 1992).
52. Andrew M. Appleton and Daniel S. Ward, eds., *State Party Profiles: A Fifty-State Guide to Development, Organization, and Resources* (Washington, D.C.: Congressional Quarterly Press, 1996), xix–xxvii, appendix.
53. "Analysts Say Condit's Run May Hurt Democrats in '02," *New York Times,* December 9, 2001.
54. Joseph Cooper and David W. Brady, "Institutional Context and Leadership Style: The House From Cannon to Rayburn," *American Political Science Review* 75 (1981): 411–425; John H. Aldrich and David W. Rohde, "The Logic of Conditional Party Government: Revisiting the Electoral Connection," in Lawrence Dodd and Bruce Oppenheimer, eds., *Congress Reconsidered,* 7th ed. (Washington, D.C.: CQ Press, 2001).
55. Morris Fiorina, *Divided Government* (New York: Macmillan, 1992).
56. See, for example, ibid.; and John R. Hibbing and Elizabeth Theiss-Morse, *Congress as Public Enemy: Public Attitudes Toward American Political Institutions* (Cambridge: Cambridge University Press, 1995).
57. Ibid., 157.
58. Terry Collins, "Nader, Ventura Air Their Third Party Views," *Minneapolis Star Tribune,* November 1, 2000, 7A.
59. Robin Toner, "Public Lives: An Unrepentant Nader Sees a Positive Side of Bush Policy," *New York Times,* April 23, 2001, A11.
60. Michael Powell, "Seared But Unwilted: Democrats See Red But Green Party Faithful Say They Made Their Point," *Washington Post,* December 27, 2000, C1.
61. David Leonhardt, "The Election: Was Buchanan the Real Nader?" *New York Times,* December 10, 2000, sec. 4, 4.
62. April Witt, "Florida Green Party Is on the Map," *Washington Post,* November 13, 2000, A12.

Chapter 13

1. Center for Responsive Politics, "Swift Vets Top Contributors, 2004 Cycle," 2005, www.opensecrets.org/527s/527cmtedetail.asp?ein=201041228&cycle=2004&format=&tname=Swift+Vets+&+POWs+for+Truth; Lois Romano and Jim VandeHei, "Kerry Says Group Is a Front for Bush,"

Washington Post, August 20, 2004, A1; "Election Ad," *USA Today,* August 20, 2004, 8A.

2. Lois Romano and Jim VandeHei, "'That's It': A Two Year Quest Ends," *Washington Post,* November 4, 2004, A27.
3. Richard Willing and Jim Drinkard, "Political Finance Limits Survive," *USA Today,* December 11, 2003, 1A; Warren Richey, "Court Upholds 'Soft Money' Ban," *Christian Science Monitor,* December 11, 2003, 1.
4. Alexis de Tocqueville, *Democracy in America,* Richard D. Heffner, ed. (New York: New American Library, 1956), 198.
5. James Madison, "*Federalist* No. 10," in Roy P. Fairfield, ed. *The Federalist Papers,* 2d ed. (Baltimore: Johns Hopkins University Press, 1981), 16.
6. This definition is based on Jeffrey M. Berry, *The Interest Group Society,* 3d ed. (New York: Longman, 1997), and David Truman, *The Governmental Process: Political Interest and Public Opinion,* 2d ed. (New York: Knopf, 1971).
7. Berry; Truman; Allan J. Cigler and Burdett A. Loomis, eds., *Interest Group Politics,* 6th ed. (Washington, D.C.: CQ Press, 2002).
8. Burdett A. Loomis and Allan J. Cigler, "Introduction: The Changing Nature of Interest Group Politics," in Cigler and Loomis, 2002, 2–5, 21–22.
9. Jonathan Rauch, *Demosclerosis: The Silent Killer of American Government* (New York: Crown, 1994), 39.
10. M. Margaret Conway, Joanne Connor Green, and Marian Currinder, "Groups in the Electoral Process," in Cigler and Loomis, 2002, 121.
11. On this last point, see Rauch.
12. Berry, 6–8; John W. Kingdon, *Agendas, Alternatives, and Public Policy* (Boston: Little, Brown, 1984).
13. Kingdon.
14. Children's Defense Fund, 2005, www.childrensdefense.org.
15. Truman, 66–108.
16. Berry, 66.
17. Jeffrey Berry, Kent E. Portney, and Ken Thomson, *The Rebirth of Urban Democracy* (Washington, D.C.: Brookings Institution, 1993).
18. Robert Salisbury, "An Exchange Theory of Interest Groups," *Midwest Journal of Political Science* 13 (1969): 1–32.
19. For a full description of these incentives, see Peter B. Clark and James Q. Wilson, "Incentive Systems: A Theory of Organizations," *Administrative Science Quarterly* 6 (1961): 129–166.
20. Mancur Olson Jr., *The Logic of Collective Action* (New York: Schocken, 1971).
21. The idea of selective incentives is Olson's (1971, 51). This discussion comes from the work of Clark and Wilson (1961), 129–166, as interpreted in Salisbury. Clark and Wilson use the terms "material, solidary, and purposive" benefits, while Salisbury prefers "material, solidary, and expressive." We follow Salisbury's interpretation and usage here.
22. John P. Heinz et al., *The Hollow Core* (Cambridge: Harvard University Press, 1993), 1–3.
23. Ronald G. Shaiko, "Making the Connection: Organized Interests, Political Representation, and the Changing Rules of the Game in Washington Politics," in Paul S. Herrnson, Ronald G. Shaiko, and Clyde Wilcox, eds., *The Interest Group Connection* (Washington, D.C.: CQ Press, 2005), 6.
24. Foundation for Public Affairs, *Public Interest Group Profiles, 2004–2005* (Washington, D.C.: CQ Press, 2004), 486–488.
25. Ibid., 674–676.
26. Ibid.
27. "Labor Pains," *Houston Chronicle,* July 28, 2005, B10; Amanda Paulson, "Union Split: Sign of Decline or Revival," *Christian Science Monitor,* July 27, 2005, 2.
28. International Brotherhood of Teamsters, 2005, www.teamsters.org; United Auto Workers, 2005, www.uaw.org; United Mine Workers at Answers.com, 2005, www.answers.com/topic/united-mine-workers.
29. Steve Lohr, "Bush's Next Target: Malpractice Lawyers," *New York Times,* February 27, 2005, sect. 3, 1.
30. American Farm Bureau, "We Are Farm Bureau," 2005, www.fb.org/about/thisis/wearefarmbureau.pdf; American Agriculture Movement, 2005, www.aaminc.org; National Farmers Union, 2005, www.nfu.org.
31. AARP, 2005, "AARP History," www.aarp.org/about_aarp/aarp_overview/a2003-01-13-aarphistory.html.
32. Children's Defense Fund, 2005, www.childrensdefense.org.
33. Foundation for Public Affairs, 483–485; NAACP, 2005, www.naacp.org.
34. League of United Latin American Citizens, 2005, www.lulac.org.
35. Foundation for Public Affairs, 460–462
36. American Indian Movement, 2005, www.aimovement.org.
37. Southeast Asia Resource Action Center, 2005, www.searac.org.
38. Foundation for Public Affairs, 545–547.
39. Eagle Forum, 2005, www.eagleforum.org.
40. American Coalition for Fathers and Children, 2005, www.acfc.org; National Congress for Fathers and Children, 2005, www.ncfc.net.
41. Log Cabin Republicans, "About Log Cabin," 2005, online.logcabin.org/about.
42. Allan J. Cigler and Anthony J. Nowns, "Public Interest Entrepreneurs and Group Patrons," in Allan J. Cigler and Burdett A. Loomis, eds., *Interest Group Politics,* 4th ed. (Washington, D.C.: Congressional Quarterly Press, 1995), 77–78.
43. Christopher J. Bosso, "The Color of Money," in Cigler and Loomis, 1995, 104.
44. William Booth, "Logging Protester Killed by Falling Redwood Tree," *Washington Post,* September 19, 1998, A2; Ed Henry, "Earth First! Activists Invade Rigg's California Office. In Aftermath, Congressman Considers Bill to Strengthen Penalty for Assaulting Congressional Staffers," *Roll Call,* October 27, 1997.
45. For a discussion of coalition politics involving Ralph Nader, see Loree Bykerk and Ardith Maney, "Consumer

Groups and Coalition Politics on Capitol Hill," in Cigler and Loomis, 1995, 259–279.

46. Consumers Union, 2005, www.consumersunion.org.
47. Foundation for Public Affairs, 197–199.
48. See James Guth et al., "Onward Christian Soldiers: Religious Activist Groups in American Politics," in Cigler and Loomis, 1995, 55–75; Guth et al., "A Distant Thunder?" in Cigler and Loomis, 2002, 162–165.
49. Joseph A. Aistrup, *Southern Strategy Revisited* (Lexington: University Press of Kentucky, 1996), 56–61.
50. Adam Clymer, "Decision in the Senate: The Overview; Crime Bill Approved 61–38, but Senate Is Going Home Without Acting on Health Care," *New York Times,* August 26, 1994, 1.
51. Sheryl Gay Stolberg, "Effort to Renew Weapons Ban Falters on Hill," *New York Times,* September 9, 2004, A1; Edward Epstein, "Supporters of Gun Ban Lament Its Expiration," *San Francisco Chronicle,* September 10, 2004, A1.
52. Jon Jeter, "Jury Says Abortion Opponents Are Liable; Efforts to Close Clinics Violate Racketeering Law," *Washington Post,* April 21, 1998, A1; "Operation Rescue Founder Files for Bankruptcy Due to Lawsuits," *Washington Post,* November 8, 1998, A29.
53. American Civil Liberties Union, "About Us," 2005, www.aclu.org/about/aboutmain.cfm.
54. Foundation for Public Affairs, 76–78; Amnesty International, "Current Campaigns," 2005, www.amnesty.org/campaign.
55. Loomis and Cigler, 22–23; People for the Ethical Treatment of Animals, 2005, www.peta.org.
56. Animal Rights Law Project, 2005, www.animal-law.org; Animal Liberation Front, 2005, animalliberationfront.us; "Deaths of More Baby Rats on Shuttle Prompt Protests," *Los Angeles Times,* April 29, 1998, A14; Daniel B. Wood, "Animal Activists vs. Furriers: Now It's All in the Label," *Christian Science Monitor,* November 27, 1998, 2; Brad Knickerbocker, "Activists Step Up War to 'Liberate' Nature," *Christian Science Monitor,* January 20, 1999, 4.
57. Ronald J. Hrebenar and Clive S. Thomas, "The Japanese Lobby in Washington: How Different Is It?" in Cigler and Loomis, 1995, 349–368.
58. Judy Sarasohn, "For Lobbyists, the $65 Million List," *Washington Post,* March 17, 2005, A23; *Congressional Quarterly Weekly Report,* December 12, 1992, 3792; Allison Mitchell, "A New Form of Lobbying Puts Public Face on Private Interests," *New York Times,* September 30, 1998, Web version.
59. Beverly A. Cigler, "Not Just Another Special Interest: Intergovernmental Representation," in Cigler and Loomis, 1995, 134–135.
60. William Safire, *Safire's New Political Dictionary* (New York: Random House, 1993), 417–418.
61. John Mintz, "Clinton Reverses 5-Year Ban on Lobbying by Appointees," *Washington Post,* December 29, 2000, A31.
62. James Dao, "No Apologies as Solomon Takes Eagerly to Lobbying," *New York Times,* June 1, 1999, Web version.
63. Jeffrey H. Birnbaum, "The Road to Riches Is Called K Street," *Washington Post,* June 22, 2005, A1.
64. Ibid.
65. See Diana M. Evans, "Lobbying the Committee: Interest Groups and the House Public Works and Transportation Committee," in Allan J. Cigler and Burdett A. Loomis, eds., *Interest Group Politics,* 3d ed. (Washington, D.C.: Congressional Quarterly Press, 1991), 264–265. For a graphic example of this practice, see Michael Weisskopf and David Maraniss, "Forging an Alliance for Deregulation; Rep. DeLay Makes Companies Full Partners in the Movement," *Washington Post,* March 12, 1995, A1.
66. Carl Hulse, "Tough Going as Negotiators Hammer Out Energy Bill," *New York Times,* September 30, 2003, A20.
67. Ibid.
68. Mike Soraghan, "Measure Stresses Drilling in Rockies; Energy Bill Gets OK, May Go to House Today," *Denver Post,* November 18, 2003, A1.
69. Adam Clymer, "Congress Passes Bill to Disclose Lobbyists' Roles," *New York Times,* November 30, 1995, 1.
70. Adam Clymer, "Senate, 98–0, Sets Tough Restriction on Lobbyist Gifts," *New York Times,* July 29, 1995, 1; "House Approves Rule to Prohibit Lobbyists' Gifts," *New York Times,* November 17, 1995, 1.
71. Jim VandeHei and Juliet Eilperinl, "House GOP Erodes Its Gift Ban; New Rules Let Lobbyists Offer More Meals, Tickets and Trips, *Washington Post,* January 21, 2003, A1.
72. Damon Chappie, "DeLay Foundation Exploits New Rules," *Roll Call,* January 20, 2003, Web version.
73. U.S. House of Representatives, "Gifts Highlights," 2005, www.house.gov/ethics/Gifts_and_Travel_Chapter.htm#_Toc476623563; U.S. Senate, "Standing Rules of the Senate, Rule XXXV, Gifts," 2005, rules.senate.gov/senaterules/rule35.htm.
74. David S. Cloud, "Three-Month-Old Gift Ban Having Ripple Effect," *CQ Weekly,* March 23, 1996, 777–778.
75. Larry Margasak, "Special Interests' Combine Lobbying, Travel, Contributions," *CNN Interactive* Web page, May 31, 1999.
76. VandeHei and Eilperinl.
77. Carl Hulse and Philip Shenon, "G.O.P. Seeks End to Ethics Clash; DeLay Is at Issue," *New York Times,* April 25, 2005, A1.
78. Jeffrey H. Birnbaum, *The Lobbyists: How Influence Peddlers Work Their Way in Washington* (New York: Random House, 1992), vi, viii.
79. See Douglas Yates, *Bureaucratic Democracy* (Cambridge: Harvard University Press, 1982), ch. 4.
80. Cindy Skrzcki, "OSHA Set to Propose Ergonomics Standards; Long-Studied Rules Repeatedly Blocked," *Washington Post,* February 19, 1999.
81. Samuel Kernell, *Going Public: New Strategies of Presidential Leadership* (Washington, D.C.: Congressional Quarterly Press, 1986), 34.
82. Berry, 121–122.
83. The Tax Foundation, "Tax Freedom Day to Arrive April 17 in 2005," 2005, www.taxfoundation.org/taxfreedomday.html.

84. Richard Willing and Jim Drinkard, "Political Finance Limits Survive," *USA Today,* December 11, 2003, 1A; Warren Richey, "Court Upholds 'Soft Money' Ban," *Christian Science Monitor,* December 11, 2003, 1.
85. Center for Responsive Politics, "Types of Advocacy Groups," 2005, www.opensecrets.org/527s/types.asp.
86. John Green, "John Green Discusses Differences Between 527 Groups and Political Action Committees" (interview), *All Things Considered,* National Public Radio, August 19, 2004.
87. Glen Justice, "Concern Grows About Role of Interest Groups in Elections," *New York Times,* March 9, 2005, 20.
88. William B. Browne, "Organized Interests, Grassroots Confidants, and Congress," in Cigler and Loomis, 1995, 288; John W. Kingdon, *Congressmen's Voting Decisions,* 2d ed. (New York: Harper & Row, 1981).
89. Evans, 269.
90. Muriel Dobbin, "White House Played Smart, Won Big Prize. But It Was Bush's Fervor That Won Back the Senate and Added 5 to GOP House Roll," *Sacramento Bee,* November 7, 2002, A14.
91. Alan Cooperman and Thomas P. Edsall, "Evangelicals Say They Led Charge for the GOP," *Washington Post,* November 8, 2004, A1.
92. *Censure and Move On* (news release), October 15, 1998, www.moveon.org.
93. Linda Greenhouse, "Supreme Court Roundup; Justices Extend Decision on Gay Rights and Equality," *New York Times,* June 28, 2003, A10.
94. Susan Dodge and Becky Beaupre, "Internet Blamed in Spread of Hate," *Chicago Sun Times,* July 6, 1999, 3; Jennifer Oldham, "Wiesenthal Center Compiles List of Hate-Based Web Sites," *Los Angeles Times,* December 18, 1999, A1; Victor Volland, "Group Warns of Hate on Internet," *St. Louis Post Dispatch,* October 22, 1997, 8A; Becky Beaupre, "Internet Pumps Up the Volume of Hatred," *USA Today,* February 18, 1997, 6A.
95. Colleen O'Connor, "Prayer Wars Civil Disobedience Is an Increasingly Popular Cross to Bear," *Denver Post,* December 23, 2004, F1; Anna Badkhen, "Protesters Drawn to Schiavo's Hospice; Christian Conservatives Sponsor Some, Others Say They're Following Their Hearts," *San Francisco Chronicle,* March 24, 2005, A1; Dennis Mahoney, "Christian Group Plans Rallies, Protests; Gay Rights, Abortion Focus of Weeklong Visit to Columbus," *Columbus Dispatch,* June 7, 2004, 5D.
96. James Cox, "Anti-Globalization Activists: Divided, They Make a Stand," *USA Today,* September 27, 2002, 1B; Dan Eggen, "Policing Is Aggressive at Bush Events; To Some, Protesters' Arrests Recall Vietnam War Era," *Washington Post,* October 28, 2004, A7.
97. Mark Brunswick, "Prescription Politics; Drug Lobby Intensifies Fight on Price Controls and Imports," Minneapolis *Star Tribune,* November 16, 2003, 1A; Jim VandeHei and Juliet Eilperin, "Drug Firms Gain Church Group's Aid; Claim About Import Measure Stirs Anger," *Washington Post,* July 23 2003, A1.
98. Adam Clymer, Robert Pear, and Robin Toner, "The Health Care Debate: What Went Wrong? How the Health Care Campaign Collapsed—A Special Report," *New York Times,* August 29, 1994, A1.
99. Robert Pear, "Getting Even With Harry and Louise, or, Republicans Get a Taste of Their Own Medicine," *New York Times,* July 10, 1994, sec. 4, 2.
100. J. A. Savage, "Astroturf Lobbying Replaces Grassroots Organizing: Corporations Mask Their Interests by Supporting Supposed Grassroots Organizations," *Business and Society Review,* September 22, 1995, 8.
101. Kirk Victor, "Astroturf Lobbying Takes a Hit," *National Journal,* September 23, 1995, 2359.
102. John Stauber, director of the Center for Media & Democracy, quoted in Savage, 8.
103. Mike Murphy in Mitchell, A1.
104. Bill McAllister, "Rainmakers Making a Splash," *Washington Post,* December 4, 1997, A21.
105. Federal Election Commission, "PAC Activity Increases for 2004 Election," April 13, 2005, www.fec.gov/press/press2005/20050412pac/PACFinal2004.html.
106. Federal Election Commission, "PAC's Grouped by Total Spent," April 13, 2005, www.fec.gov/press/press2005/20050412pac/groupbyspending2004.pdf; Richard L. Hall and Frank W. Wayman, "Buying Time: Money Interests and the Mobilization of Bias in Congressional Committees," *American Political Science Review* 84 (1990): 797–820.
107. Federal Election Commission, "PAC Activity Increases for 2004 Election."
108. Andrew Bard Schmookler, "When Money Talks, Is It Free Speech?" *Christian Science Monitor,* November 11, 1997, 15; Nelson W. Polsby, "Money Gains Access. So What?" *New York Times,* August 13, 1997, A19.
109. Sara Fritz, "Citizen Lobby's Call to Arms," *International Herald-Tribune,* January 4–5, 1997; Katharine Q. Seelye, "G.O.P.'s Reward for Top Donors: 3 Days With Party Leaders," *New York Times,* February 20, 1997, A6.
110. Leslie Wayne, "Lobbyists' Gifts to Politicians Reap Benefits, Study Shows," *New York Times,* January 23, 1997, B10.
111. See John R. Wright, *Interest Groups and Congress* (Boston: Allyn & Bacon, 1996), 136–145; and "Contributions, Lobbying, and Committee Voting in the U.S. House of Representatives," *American Political Science Review* 84 (1990): 417–438; Richard L. Hall and Frank W. Wayman, "Buying Time: Money Interests and the Mobilization of Bias in Congressional Committees," *American Political Science Review* 84 (1990): 797–820.
112. Katharine Q. Seelye, "An Ailing Gun Lobby Faces a Bitter Struggle for Power," *New York Times,* January 1, 1997, A1, A9; and "Close Votes Inside N.R.A. Quashes Hope for New Unity," *New York Times,* June 5, 1997, A14.
113. Kelly D. Patterson and Matthew M. Singer, "The National Rifle Association in the Face of the Clinton Challenge," in Cigler and Loomis, 2002, 62–63.
114. Jeffrey Birnbaum and Russell Newell, "Fat & Happy in D.C.," *Fortune,* May 28, 2001, 94; Patterson and Singer.
115. Patterson and Singer.
116. A. Lee Fritscheler and James M. Hoefler, *Smoking and Politics,* 5th ed.

(Upper Saddle River, N.J.: Prentice Hall, 1996), 20–35.

117. Truman, 519.

118. See C. Wright Mills, *The Power Elite* (New York: Oxford University Press, 1956); G. William Domhoff, *The Powers That Be* (New York: Vintage, 1979).

119. David S. Hilzenrath, "Health Care Factions Clashing on Medicare Battlefield," *Washington Post,* July 19, 1997, C1; Ruth Marcus, "Some Swat Home Runs, Others Strike Out on Budget Deal," *Washington Post,* August 3, 1997, A1; Jennifer Mattos, "Clinton Proposes Medicare Cuts," *Time Daily,* January 14, 1997.

120. The problem is that there are a relatively small number of groups with large memberships. Labor unions, some environmental groups like the Sierra Club, some social movements revolving around abortion and women's rights, and the NRA currently have large memberships spread across a number of congressional districts.

121. Linda Greenhouse, "Justices to Rule on Tobacco," *New York Times,* May 2, 1999, sec. 4, 2; David E. Rosenbaum, "The Tobacco Bill: The Overview," *New York Times,* June 18, 1999, 1.

122. Katie Hafner, "Screen Grab: Mobilizing on Line for Gun Control," *New York Times,* May 20, 1999, G5; Francis X. Clines, "Guns and Schools: In Congress—Sketchbook," *New York Times,* June 17, 1999, 30.

123. *Buckley v. Valeo,* 424 U.S. 1 (1976).

Chapter 14

1. Gerald Pomper, *Elections in America* (New York: Dodd, Mead, 1970), 1.
2. John Stuart Mill, *Considerations on Representative Government* (New York: Liberal Arts Press, 1958), 114.
3. David W. Brady, *Critical Elections and Congressional Policy Making* (Palo Alto, Calif.: Stanford University Press, 1988); Barbara Sinclair, "Party Realignment and the Transformation of the Political Agenda: The House of Representatives, 1925–1938," *American Political Science Review* 71 (September 1977): 940–954.
4. Robert S. Erikson, Gerald C. Wright, and John P. McIver, *Statehouse Democracy* (New York: Cambridge University Press, 1993).
5. Robert Erikson and Gerald Wright, "Voters, Candidates, and Issues in Congressional Elections," in Lawrence Dodd and Bruce Oppenheimer, *Congress Reconsidered,* 6th ed. (Washington, D.C.: Congressional Quarterly Press, 1997); Gerald C. Wright and Michael Berkman, "Candidates and Policy Position in U.S. Senate Elections," *American Political Science Review* 80 (June 1986): 576–590.
6. Gerald Pomper with Susan Lederman, *Elections in America,* 2d ed. (New York: Longman, 1980), chs. 7 and 8; Benjamin Ginsberg, *The Consequences of Consent* (Reading, Mass.: Addison Wesley Longman), 1982; Ian Budge and Richard I. Hofferbert, "Mandates and Policy Outputs: U.S. Party Platforms and Federal Expenditures, 1950–1985," *American Political Science Review* 84 (March 1990): 248–261.
7. Robert S. Erikson, Michael MacKuen, and James A. Stimson, *The Macro Polity* (New York: Cambridge University Press, 2002).
8. Carole Pateman, *Participation and Democratic Theory* (Cambridge: Cambridge University Press, 1970).
9. Sidney Verba and Norman H. Nie, *Participation in America* (New York: Harper, 1972).
10. Thomas E. Patterson and Robert D. McClure, *The Unseeing Eye* (New York: Putnam, 1976); Andrew Gelman and Gary King, "Why Are American Presidential Polls So Variable When Votes Are So Predictable?" *British Journal of Political Science* 23 (October 1993): 409–451.
11. Ginsberg.
12. Roper Center for Public Opinion Research, Community Consensus Survey, February 12–14, 1999.
13. Steven J. Rosenstone and John Mark Hansen, *Mobilization, Participation, and Democracy in America* (New York: Macmillan, 1993); Ruy A. Teixeira, *The Disappearing American Voter* (Washington, D.C.: Brookings Institution, 1992); Raymond E. Wolfinger and Steven J. Rosenstone, *Who Votes?* (New Haven: Yale University Press, 1980); Richard J. Timpone, "Structure, Behavior, and Voter Turnout in the United States," *American Political Science Review* 92 (March 1998): 145–158.
14. Percentages calculated by the authors from the National Election Study, 2004 Pre-Post Study, Version 20050131 (Advanced Release), January 31, 2005. In surveys such as this one, "reported turnout" always runs higher than actual turnout for two reasons: the homeless and institutionalized are not sampled and seldom vote, and some nonvoters give what they see as the socially desirable response and say they voted. The reported voting in the National Election Study, 2004 Pre-Post Study was 78.5 percent, about 18 percent above the official participation.
15. Ibid.
16. Ibid.
17. Ibid.
18. Calculated by the authors from the National Election Study, 2004 Pre-Post Study, Version 20050131 (Advanced Release), January 31, 2005.
19. Richard Brody, "The Puzzle of Political Participation in America," in Anthony King, ed., *The New American Political System* (Washington, D.C.: American Enterprise Institute, 1978), 287–324.
20. Stephen Knack, "Drivers Wanted: Motor Voter and the Election of 1996," *PS: Political Science & Politics* (June 1999): 237–243.
21. G. Bingham Powell, "American Voter Turnout in Comparative Perspective," *American Political Science Review* 80: 17–43; Russell Dalton, *Citizen Politics,* 3d ed. (New York: Chatham House, 2002), 37.
22. International Institute for Democracy and Electoral Assistance, "Turnout in the World, Country by Country Performance," 2005, www.idea.int/vt/survey/voter_turnout_pop2.cfm.
23. Knack, 237–243.
24. Mark N. Franklin, "Electoral Participation," in Laurence LeDuc, Richard G. Niemi, and Pippa Norris, eds., *Comparing Democracies: Elections and Voting in Global Perspective* (Thousand Oaks, Calif.: Sage, 1996), 226–230.

25. Tomoko Hosaka, "Voters, Unwittingly, Tested Limits of Vote-by-Mail System," *Oregonian,* November 12, 2000, A1; Harry Esteve, "Election Anxiety Extends to Voting by Mail," *Oregonian,* November 1, 2004, A1.
26. The Oregon analysis is by Michael Traugott and Robert Mason and is reported in David Broder, "What Works," *Washington Post Magazine,* October 11, 1998, W9. The general analysis is reported in Franklin.
27. Teixeira, ch. 2; Paul R. Abramson, John H. Aldrich, and David W. Rohde, *Change and Continuity in the 1998 Elections* (Washington, D.C.: Congressional Quarterly Press, 1999).
28. Rosenstone and Hansen.
29. Stephen Ansolabehere and Shanto Iyengar, *Going Negative: How Political Ads Shrink and Polarize the Electorate* (New York: Free Press, 1995).
30. Jeff Mapes, "National Parties Try Personal Touch" *Oregonian,* December 23, 2003, A1; Sharon Schmickle and Greg Gordon, "Vying for Voters," Minneapolis *Star Tribune,* October 31, 2004, 13A; Thomas B. Edsall, "Labor Targets Nonunion Voters; $20 Million Turnout Effort Expands Effort to Regain Influence," *Washington Post,* February 27, 2003, A4.
31. Gerald Pomper, "The Presidential Election: The Ills of American Politics After 9/11," in Michael Nelson, ed., *The Elections of 2004* (Washington, D.C.: CQ Press, 2005), 46.
32. Teixeira, 36–50; Robert Putnam, *Bowling Alone: The Collapse and Revival of American Community* (New York: Simon & Shuster, 2000), 31–47.
33. Warren E. Miller and Merrill J. Shanks, *The New American Voter* (Cambridge: Harvard University Press, 1996); Kevin Chen, *Political Alienation and Voting Turnout in the United States, 1969–1988* (Pittsburgh: Mellon Research University Press, 1992).
34. Anthony Downs, *An Economic Theory of Democracy* (New York: Harper & Row, 1957), 260–276.
35. John Petrocik, "Voter Turnout and Electoral Preference: The Anomalous Reagan Elections," in Kay Lehman Schlozman, ed., *Elections in America* (Boston: Allen & Unwin, 1987), 239–260.
36. Petrocik, 243–251; Stephen Earl Bennett and David Resnick, "The Implications of Nonvoting for Democracy in the United States," *American Journal of Political Science* 34 (August 1990): 795.
37. Calculated by the authors from the National Election Study, 2004 Pre-Post Study, Version 20050131 (Advanced Release), January 31, 2005.
38. V. O. Key, Jr., *The Responsible Electorate: Rationality in Presidential Voting, 1936–1960* (Cambridge: Harvard University Press, 1966); Miller and Shanks.
39. Calculated by the authors from the National Election Study, 2004 Pre-Post Study, Version 20050131 (Advanced Release), January 31, 2005.
40. Angus Campbell, Phillip Converse, Warren Miller, and Donald Stokes. *The American Voter* (New York: Wiley, 1960).
41. CNN, Election Results, 2005, www.cnn.com/ELECTION/2004/pages/results/states/US/P/00/epolls.0.html.
42. Downs.
43. Edward Carmines and James Stimson, "Two Faces of Issue Voting," *American Political Science Review* 74 (March 1980): 78–91.
44. James Fallows, "Why Americans Hate the Media," *Atlantic Monthly,* February 1996, 45–64.
45. Morris P. Fiorina, *Retrospective Voting in American National Elections* (New Haven: Yale University Press, 1981).
46. "The Candidates' Confrontation: Excerpts From the Debate," *Washington Post,* October 30, 1980, A14.
47. Peter Baker, "Clinton Reads Reagan's Script; President's Reelection Bid Takes Cues From Last Successful One," *Washington Post,* November 3, 1996, A31.
48. Fiorina; Benjamin I. Page, *Choice and Echoes in Presidential Elections* (Chicago: University of Chicago Press, 1978).
49. Pew Research Center for the People and the Press Survey Reports, "Race Tightens Again, Kerry's Image Improves," 2005, people-press.org/reports/display.php3?ReportID=229.
50. Jill Abramson, "Unregulated Cash Flows Into Hands of P.A.C.s for 2000," *New York Times,* November 29, 1998, Web version.
51. Federal Election Commission, "FEC Presidential Pre-Nomination Campaign Receipts Through December 31, 2003," 2005, www.fec.gov/press/bkgnd/pres_cf/atm1231/presreceiptsye2003.pdf.
52. Julie Mason, "2004 Election; Caucuses in the Heartland," *Houston Chronicle,* January 20, 2004, A1.
53. Barry Burden, "The Nominations: Technology, Money, and Transferable Momentum," in Nelson, 21–22.
54. Rhodes Cook, "Steps to the Nomination: Earlier Voting in 1996 Forecasts Fast and Furious Campaigns," *Congressional Quarterly Weekly Report,* August 19, 1995, 24487.
55. Burden, 21.
56. Jack Germond and Jules W. Witcover, "Front-Loading Folly: A Dash to Decision, at a Cost in Deliberation," *Baltimore Sun,* March 22, 1996.
57. Pomper, 55.
58. Sholomo Slonim, "The Electoral College at Philadelphia," *Journal of American History* 73 (June 1986): 35.
59. Robin Kolodny and Angela Logan, "Political Consultants and the Extension of Party Goals," *PS: Political Science & Politics* (June 1998): 155–159.
60. Patrick Sellers, "Strategy and Background in Congressional Campaigns," *American Political Science Review* 92 (March 1998): 159–172.
61. Ruth Shalit, "The Oppo Boom," *New Republic,* January 3, 1994, 16–21; Adam Nagourney, "Researching the Enemy: An Old Political Tool Resurfaces in a New Election," *New York Times,* April 3, 1996, D20.
62. John Petrocik, "Issue Ownership in Presidential Elections, With a 1980 Case Study," *American Journal of Political Science* 40 (August 1996): 825–850.
63. David B. Holian, "He's Stealing My Issues! Clinton's Crime Rhetoric and the Dynamics of Issue Ownership," *Political Behavior* 26 (2004): 95–124.
64. American Museum of the Moving Image, "The Living Room Candidate: Presidential Campaign

Commercials 1952–2004," 2005, livingroomcandidate.movingimage.us/index.php.

65. Darrell M. West, *Air Wars: Television Advertising in Election Campaigns, 1952–2004* (Washington, D.C.: CQ Press, 2005).

66. Kathleen Hall Jamieson, "Shooting to Win; Do Attack Ads Work? You Bet—and That's Not All Bad," *Washington Post,* September 26, 2004, B1.

67. Jim Rutenberg and Kate Zernike, "Going Negative: When It Works," *New York Times,* August 22, 2004, sect. 4, 1; Pomper, 57.

68. Thomas Patterson, *Out of Order* (New York: Knopf, 1993); Fallows, 45–64.

69. Elihu Katz and Jacob Feldman, "The Debates in Light of Research," in Sidney Kraus, ed., *The Great Debates* (Bloomington: Indiana University Press, 1962), 173–223.

70. Thomas Holbrook, "Campaigns, National Conditions, and U.S. Presidential Elections," *American Journal of Political Science* 38 (November 1994): 986–992; John Geer, "The Effects of Presidential Debates on the Electorate's Preferences for Candidates," *American Politics Quarterly* 16 (1988): 486–501; David Lanoue, "The 'Turning Point': Viewers' Reactions to the Second 1988 Presidential Debate," *American Politics Quarterly* 19 (1991): 80–89.

71. David Lanoue, "One That Made a Difference: Cognitive Consistency, Political Knowledge, and the 1980 Presidential Debate," *Public Opinion Quarterly* 56 (Summer 1992): 168–184; Carol Winkler and Catherine Black, "Assessing the 1992 Presidential and Vice Presidential Debates: The Public Rationale," *Argumentation and Advocacy* 30 (Fall 1993): 77–87; Lori McKinnon, John Tedesco, and Lynda Kaid, "The Third 1992 Presidential Debate: Channel and Commentary Effects," *Argumentation and Advocacy* 30 (Fall 1993): 106–118; Mike Yawn, Kevin Ellsworth, and Kim Fridkin Kahn, "How a Presidential Primary Debate Changed Attitudes of Audience Members," *Political Behavior* 20 (July 1998): 155–164; Annenberg Public Policy Center, "Voters Learned Positions on Issues Since Presidential Debates," NAES04 National Annenberg Election Survey, 2005, www.naes04.org.

72. Scott Keeter, "Public Opinion and the Election," in Gerald Pomper, ed., *The Election of 1996* (Chatham, N.J.: Chatham House, 1997), 127. Drawn from polls done by the Pew Research Center and the Times Mirror Center.

73. The $13.60 figure is calculated by the authors from $4 billion reported in Marian Currinder, "Campaign Finance: Funding the Presidential and Congressional Elections," in Nelson, 108.

74. Federal Election Commission, "Chapter Two: Presidential Public Funding," 2005, www.fec.gov/info/arch2.htm.

75. Susan Glasser, "Court's Ruling in Colorado Case May Reshape Campaign Finance; Limits on Political Parties' 'Hard Money' Spending Nullified," *Washington Post,* March 28, 1999, A6; *FEC v. Colorado Republican Federal Campaign Committee,* 121 S. Ct. 2351, 2371 (2001).

76. Dan Balz and David S. Broder, "Close Election Turns on Voter Turnout," *Washington Post,* November 1, 2002, A1.

77. Ibid.

78. Ibid.

79. Les Blumenthal, "Down to the Wire; Canvassers Set a Frenetic Pace to Get Out the Vote," *Sacramento Bee,* October 25, 2004, A1.

80. Craig Gilbert, "Personal Touch in Political Race; Bush, Kerry Sides Try to Rally Support Like Never Before," Milwaukee *Journal Sentinel,* June 28, 2004, 1A.

81. Blumenthal.

82. "Voters Liked Campaign 2004, But Too Much 'Mud-Slinging,' " Pew Research Center for the People and the Press Survey Reports, November 11, 2004, online version, 2005, people-press.org/reports/display.php3?ReportID=233.

83. Blumenthal.

84. Marjorie Hershey, "The Constructed Explanation: Interpreting Election Results in the 1984 Presidential Race," *Journal of Politics* 54 (November 1992): 943–976.

85. Bernard Berelson, Paul Lazarsfeld, and William N. McPhee, *Voting* (Chicago: University of Chicago Press, 1954), ch. 10.

86. Erikson, MacKuen, and Stimson; James A. Stimson, Michael B. MacKuen, and Robert S. Erikson, "Dynamic Representation," *American Political Science Review* 89 (September 1995): 543.

87. Erikson, Wright, and McIver.

Chapter 15

1. The Committee to Protect Journalists, "Journalists Killed in 2004," www.cpj.org/killed/Ten_Year_Killed/2004_list.html.

2. Frank Rich, "Freedom From the Press," *New York Times,* March 2, 2002, Web version.

3. Neil Hickey, "Access Denied: The Pentagon's War Reporting Rules Are the Toughest Ever," *Columbia Journalism Review* (March–April 2002), www.cjr.org/year/02/1/hickey.asp.

4. Michael Scherer, "In Review: Framing the Flag," *Columbia Journalism Review* (March–April 2002), www.cjr.org/year/02/2/Scherer.asp.

5. Pew Research Center for the People and the Press, "Internet Sapping Broadcast News Audience," June 11, 2000, www.people-press.org.

6. Greg Mitchell, "Gallup: Online News Hasn't Beaten Old Media—Yet," *Editor and Publisher,* December 21, 2004.

7. Pew Research Center, "Trends 2005" (Washington, D.C.: Pew Research Center, 2005), 47.

8. Pew Research Center for the People and the Press, "The Times Mirror News Interest Index: 1989–1995," www.people-press.org.

9. Ben H. Bagdikian, *The Media Monopoly,* 5th ed. (Boston: Beacon Press, 1997), 203.

10. Richard Davis, *The Press and American Politics: The New Mediator* (Upper Saddle River, N.J.: Prentice Hall, 1996), 60.

11. Ibid., 63.

12. Ibid., 67.

13. Harold W. Stanley and Richard G. Niemi, *Vital Statistics on American*

Politics (Washington, D.C.: Congressional Quarterly Press, 1998), 47.

14. Nielsen Media Research, *1998 Report on Television* (New York: Nielsen Media Research, 1998).
15. "Universe Collapses: Well, TV's Anyway," July 1, 2004, www.mediapost.com.
16. For an in-depth study of the negative effects of this sort of advertising on national community, see Joseph Turow, *Breaking Up America: Advertisers and the New Media World* (Chicago: University of Chicago Press, 1997).
17. Pew Research Center, "Trends 2005," 58.
18. Robert Marquand, "Hate Groups Market to the Mainstream," *Christian Science Monitor,* March 6, 1998, 4.
19. Davis, 27.
20. Michael Emery and Edwin Emery, *The Press and America* (Upper Saddle River, N.J.: Prentice Hall, 1988), 115.
21. David Broder, *Behind the Front Page* (New York: Simon & Schuster, 1987), 134–135.
22. Bagdikian, xv.
23. Bagdikian, ix.
24. Robert Entman, *Democracy Without Citizens* (New York: Oxford University Press, 1989), 110–111.
25. Walter Goodman, "Where's Edward R. Murrow When You Need Him?" *New York Times,* December 30, 1997, E2.
26. Mark Crispin Miller, "Free the Media," *Nation,* June 3, 1996, 9.
27. Bagdikian, xxii.
28. Ibid., 217.
29. Miller, 2.
30. David Armstrong, "Alternative, Inc.," *In These Times,* August 21, 1995, 14–18.
31. Jeff Gremillion, "Showdown at Generation Gap," *Columbia Journalism Review* (July–August 1995): 34–38.
32. Lydia Saad, "Blogs Not Yet in the Media Big Leagues," The Gallup News Service, March 11, 2005, www.gallup.com; Mark Blumenthal, "Gallup Poll on Blogs," March 11, 2005, www.mysterypollster.com.
33. Doris Graber, *Mass Media and American Politics,* 5th ed. (Washington, D.C.: Congressional Quarterly Press, 1997), 62.
34. David H. Weaver and G. Cleveland Wilhoit, *The American Journalist in the 1990s* (Mahwah, N.J.: Erlbaum Associates, 1996), 133–141.
35. Cited in Broder, 138.
36. Graber, 95–96.
37. William Schneider and I. A. Lewis, "Views on the News," *Public Opinion* (August–September 1985): 6.
38. Data in Weaver and Wilhoit, 15–19.
39. Mark Hertsgaard, *On Bended Knee: The Press and the Reagan Presidency* (New York: Farrar, Straus & Giroux, 1988), 3.
40. Gerald M. Pomper, "The Presidential Election: The Ills of American Politics After 9/11," in Michael Nelson, ed., *The Elections of 2004* (Washington, D.C.: CQ Press, 2005), 57.
41. Pew Research Center, "Trends 2005," 52–53.
42. Broder, 126.
43. Ibid., 148.
44. Dom Bonafede, "Crossing Over," *National Journal,* January 14, 1989, 102; Michael Kelly, "David Gergen, Master of the Game," *New York Times Magazine,* October 31, 1993, 64ff.; Jonathan Alter, "Lost in the Big Blur," *Newsweek,* June 9, 1997, 43.
45. Shanto Iyengar, *Is Anyone Responsible?* (Chicago: University of Chicago Press, 1991), 2.
46. Shanto Iyengar and Donald R. Kinder, *News That Matters* (Chicago: University of Chicago Press, 1987).
47. Stephen Hess, *News and Newsmaking* (Washington, D.C.: Brookings Institution, 1996), 91–92.
48. Iyengar and Kinder, 72.
49. Benjamin I. Page, Robert Y. Shapiro, and Glenn R. Dempsey, "What Moves Public Opinion?" *American Political Science Review* (March 1987): 23–43. The term "professional communicator" is used by Benjamin Page, *Who Deliberates? Mass Media in Modern Democracy* (Chicago: University of Chicago Press, 1996), 106–109.
50. Iyengar and Kinder, 93.
51. W. Russell Neuman, Marion R. Just, and Ann N. Crigler, *Common Knowledge: News and the Construction of Political Meaning* (Chicago: University of Chicago Press, 1996), 106–119.
52. Steven Kull, "Misperceptions, the Media, and the Iraq War," the PIPA/Knowledge Networks Poll, Program on International Policy Attitudes, October 2, 2003, 13–16, www.pipa.org/OnlineReports/Iraq/Media_10_02_03_Report.pdf.
53. James Fallows, "Why Americans Hate the Media," *Atlantic Monthly,* February 1996, 16.
54. Ibid., 5–6.
55. Center for Media and Democracy, "Sound Bites Get Shorter," O'Dwyer's PR Newsletter, November 11, 2000, www.prwatch.org/node/384.
56. Thomas E. Patterson, *Out of Order* (New York: Vintage Books, 1994), 74.
57. Goodman, E2.
58. Larry J. Sabato, *Feeding Frenzy: How Attack Journalism Has Transformed American Politics* (New York: Free Press, 1991), 6.
59. Patterson, 243.
60. Ibid., 245.
61. Ibid., 23.
62. Judith Valente, "Do You Believe What Newspeople Tell You?" *Parade Magazine,* March 2, 1997, 4.
63. Joseph N. Cappella and Kathleen Hall Jamieson, *Spiral of Cynicism: The Press and the Public Good* (New York: Oxford University Press, 1997), 9–10.
64. S. Robert Lichter and Richard E. Noyes, *Good Intentions Make Bad News: Why Americans Hate Campaign Journalism* (Lanham, Md.: Rowman & Littlefield, 1995), xix.
65. Walter Cronkite, "Reporting Political Campaigns: A Reporter's View," in Doris Graber, Denis McQuail, and Pippa Norris, eds., *The Politics of News, The News of Politics* (Washington, D.C.: Congressional Quarterly Press, 1998), 57–69.
66. Kelly, 7.
67. Ibid., 7–10.
68. Kenneth T. Walsh, *Feeding the Beast: The White House Versus the Press* (New York: Random House, 1996).
69. Hess, 68–90.
70. Hertsgaard, 6.
71. Dana Milbank, "Bush Courts Regional Media," *Washington Post,* October 14, 2003, A04.

72. Anne Kornblut, "Administration Is Warned About Its Publicity Videos," *New York Times,* February 19, 2005, 11.
73. David Barstow and Robin Stein, "Under Bush, a New Age of Prepackaged News," *New York Times,* March 13, 2005, 1.
74. Anne E. Kornblut and David Barstow, "Debate Rekindles Over Government-Produced News," *New York Times,* April 15, 2005, 17.
75. Johanna Neuman, "An Identity Crisis Unfolds in a Not-So-Elite Press Corps," *Los Angeles Times,* February 25, 2005, 18.
76. Mark Sauer, "Bush Team Press Policy Raises Many Concerns," *San Diego Times Union,* March 21, 2005, D-1.
77. Jack Shafer, "The Propaganda President: George W. Bush Does His Best Kim Jong-il," *Slate,* February 3, 2005, slate.msn.com/id/2113052.
78. Michael Kinsley, "Filter Tips," October 16, 2003, slate.msn.com/id/2089915.
79. Stephen Ansolabehere, Roy Beyr, and Shanto Iyengar, *The Media Game: American Politics in the Television Age* (New York: Macmillan, 1993); Iyengar, *Is Anyone Responsible?*
80. Pew Center for Civic Journalism, "Community Impact, Journalism Shifts Cited in New Civic Journalism Study," November 4, 2002, www.pewcenter.org/doingcj/spotlight/index.php.
81. Jay Rosen, *Getting the Connections Right: Public Journalism and the Troubles in the Press* (New York: Twentieth Century Fund, 1996), 12.
82. Hickey, 10.

GLOSSARY

accommodationists supporters of government nonpreferential accommodation of religions (5)

accountability the principle that bureaucratic employees should be answerable for their performance to supervisors, all the way up the chain of command (9)

administrative law law established by the bureaucracy, on behalf of Congress (10)

adversarial system trial procedures designed to resolve conflict through the clash of opposing sides, moderated by a neutral, passive judge who applies the law (10)

affirmative action a policy of creating opportunities for members of certain groups as a substantive remedy for past discrimination (6)

allocative representation congressional work to secure projects, services, and funds for the represented district (7)

amendability the provision for the Constitution to be changed, so as to adapt to new circumstances (4)

amicus curiae briefs "friend of the court" documents filed by interested parties to encourage the court to grant or deny certiorari or to urge it to decide a case in a particular way (10)

analysis understanding how something works by breaking it down into its component parts (1)

anarchy the absence of government and laws (1)

Anti-Federalists advocates of states' rights who opposed the Constitution (3)

appeal a rehearing of a case because the losing party in the original trial argues that a point of law was not applied properly (10)

appellate jurisdiction the authority of a court to review decisions made by lower courts (10)

Articles of Confederation the first constitution of the United States (1777), creating an association of states with a weak central government (3)

astroturf lobbying indirect lobbying efforts that manipulate or create public sentiment, "astroturf" being artificial grassroots (13)

asylum protection or sanctuary, especially from political persecution (2)

authoritarian government a system in which the state holds all power (1)

authority power that is recognized as legitimate (1)

bad tendency test rule used by the courts that allows speech to be punished if it leads to punishable actions (5)

benchmark poll initial poll on a candidate and issues on which campaign strategy is based and against which later polls are compared (11)

bicameral legislature legislature with two chambers (4, 7)

Bill of Rights a summary of citizen rights guaranteed and protected by a government; added to the Constitution as its first ten amendments in order to achieve ratification (3)

bills of attainder laws under which specific persons or groups are detained and sentenced without trial (5)

black codes a series of laws in the post–Civil War South designed to restrict the rights of former slaves before the passage of the Fourteenth and Fifteenth Amendments (6)

block grants federal funds provided for a broad purpose, unrestricted by detailed requirements and regulations (4)

blogs Web logs, or on-line journals that can cover any topic, including political analysis (15)

boycott refusal to buy certain goods or services as a way to protest policy or force political reform (6)

Brown v. Board of Education Supreme Court case that rejected the idea that separate could be equal in education; catalyst for civil rights movement (6)

bureaucracy an organization characterized by hierarchical structure, worker specialization, explicit rules, and advancement by merit (9)

bureaucratese the often unintelligible language used by bureaucrats to avoid controversy and lend weight to their words (9)

bureaucratic culture the accepted values and procedures of an organization (9)

bureaucratic discretion top bureaucrats' authority to use their own judgment in interpreting and carrying out the laws of Congress (9)

busing achieving racial balance by transporting students to schools across neighborhood boundaries (6)

cabinet a presidential advisory group selected by the president, made up of the vice president, the heads of the federal executive departments, and other high officials to whom the president elects to give cabinet status (8)

capitalist economy an economic system in which the market determines production, distribution, and price decisions and property is privately owned (1)

casework legislative work on behalf of individual constituents to solve their problems with government agencies and programs (7)

categorical grants federal funds provided for a specific purpose, restricted by detailed instructions, regulations, and compliance standards (4)

checks and balances the principle that allows each branch of government to exercise some form of control over the others (4)

chief administrator the president's executive role as the head of federal agencies and the person responsible for the implementation of national policy (8)

chief foreign policy maker the president's executive role as the primary shaper of relations with other nations (8)

chief of staff the person who oversees the operations of all White House staff and controls access to the president (8)

citizen advisory council a citizen group that considers the policy decisions of an agency; a way to make the bureaucracy responsive to the general public (9)

citizens members of a political community having both rights and responsibilities (1)

civic journalism a movement among journalists to be responsive to citizen input in determining what news stories to cover (15)

civil laws laws regulating interactions between individuals; violation of a civil law is called a tort (10)

civil law tradition a legal system based on a detailed comprehensive legal code, usually created by the legislature (10)

civil liberties individual freedoms guaranteed to the people primarily by the Bill of Rights (5)

civil rights citizenship rights guaranteed to the people (primarily in the Thirteenth, Fourteenth, Fifteenth, Nineteenth, and Twentieth Amendments) and protected by government (5, 6)

civil service nonmilitary employees of the government who are appointed through the merit system (9)

clear and present danger test rule used by the courts that allows language to be regulated only if it presents an immediate and urgent danger (5)

clientele groups groups of citizens whose interests are affected by an agency or department and who work to influence its policies (9)

closed primaries primary elections in which only registered party members may vote (12, 14)

cloture a vote to end a Senate filibuster; requires a three-fifths majority, or sixty votes (7)

coattail effect the added votes received by congressional candidates of a winning presidential party (7)

collective good a good or service that, by its very nature, cannot be denied to anyone who wants to consume it (13)

commander-in-chief the president's role as the top officer of the country's military establishment (8)

commercial bias the tendency of the media to make coverage and programming decisions based on what will attract a large audience and maximize profits (15)

common law tradition a legal system based on the accumulated rulings of judges over time, applied uniformly—judgemade law (10)

"Common Sense" 1776 pamphlet by Thomas Paine that persuaded many Americans to support the Revolutionary cause (3)

communitarians those who favor a strong substantive government role in the economy and the social order in order to realize their vision of a community of equals (2)

compelling state interest a fundamental state purpose, which must be shown before the law can limit some freedoms or treat some groups of people differently (5)

concurrent powers powers that are shared by both the federal and state governments (4)

concurring opinions documents written by justices expressing agreement with the majority ruling but describing different or additional reasons for the ruling (10)

confederal systems governments in which local units hold all the power (4)

confederation a government in which independent states unite for common purpose, but retain their own sovereignty (3)

conference committees temporary committees formed to reconcile differences in House and Senate versions of a bill (7)

conservatives people who generally favor limited government and are cautious about change (2)

constituency the voters in a state or district (7)

constitution the rules that establish a government (3)

Constitutional Convention the assembly of fifty-five delegates in the summer of 1787 to recast the Articles of Confederation; the result was the U.S. Constitution (3)

constitutional law law stated in the Constitution or in the body of judicial decisions about the meaning of the Constitution handed down in the courts (10)

cooperative federalism the federal system under which the national and state governments share responsibility for most domestic policy areas (4)

Council of Economic Advisers organization within the EOP that advises the president on economic matters (8)

courts institutions that sit as neutral third parties to resolve conflicts according to the law (10)

criminal laws laws prohibiting behavior the government has determined to be harmful to society; violation of a criminal law is called a crime (10)

critical election an election signaling significant change in popular allegiance from one party to another (12)

critical thinking analysis and evaluation of ideas and arguments based on reason and evidence (1)

cycle effect the predictable rise and fall of a president's popularity at different stages of a term in office (8)

dealignment a trend among voters to identify themselves as independents rather than as members of a major party (12)

Declaration of Independence the political document that dissolved the colonial ties between the United States and Britain (3)

de facto discrimination discrimination that is the result not of law but rather of tradition and habit (6)

de jure discrimination discrimination arising from or supported by the law (6)

democracy government that vests power in the people (1)

department one of the major subdivisions of the federal government, represented in the president's cabinet (9)

descriptive representation the idea that an elected body should mirror demographically the population it represents (7)

devolution the transfer of powers and responsibilities from the federal government to the states (4)

direct lobbying direct interaction with public officials for the purpose of influencing policy decisions (13)

dissenting opinions documents written by justices expressing disagreement with the majority ruling (10)

divided government political rule split between two parties: one controlling the White House and the other controlling one or both houses of Congress (8)

divine right of kings the principle that earthly rulers receive their authority from God (1)

dual federalism the federal system under which the national and state governments were responsible for separate policy areas (4)

due process of law guarantee that laws will be fair and reasonable and that citizens suspected of breaking the law will be treated fairly (5)

economic conservatives those who favor a strictly procedural government role in the economy and the social order (2)

economic interest groups groups that organize to influence government policy for the economic benefit of their members (13)

economic liberals those who favor an expanded government role in the economy but a limited role in the social order (2)

economics production and distribution of a society's material resources and services (1)

electioneering the process of getting a person elected to public office (12)

electoral college an intermediary body that elects the president (4)

electoral mandate the perception that an election victory signals broad support for the winner's proposed policies (14)

elite democracy a theory of democracy that limits the citizens' role to choosing among competing leaders (1)

English-only movements efforts to make English the official language of the United States (6)

Enlightenment a philosophical movement (1600s–1700s) that emphasized human reason, scientific examination, and industrial progress (1)

enumerated powers of Congress congressional powers specifically named in the Constitution (Article I, Section 8) (4)

equal opportunity interest groups groups that organize to promote the civil and economic rights of underrepresented or disadvantaged groups (13)

Equal Rights Amendment constitutional amendment passed by Congress but *never ratified* that would have banned discrimination on the basis of gender (6)

establishment clause the First Amendment guarantee that the government will not create and support an official state church (5)

evaluation assessing how well something works or performs according to a particular standard or yardstick (1)

exclusionary rule rule created by the Supreme Court that says that evidence illegally seized may not be used to obtain a conviction (5)

executive the branch of government responsible for putting laws into effect (4)

executive agreement a presidential arrangement with another country that creates foreign policy without the need for Senate approval (8)

Executive Office of the President, or EOP collection of nine organizations that help the president with policy and political objectives (8)

executive orders clarifications of congressional policy issued by the president and having the full force of law (8, 10)

exit polls election-related questions asked of voters right after they vote (11)

ex post facto laws laws that criminalize an action *after* it occurs (5)

expressive benefits selective incentives that derive from the opportunity to express values and beliefs and to be committed to a greater cause (13)

factions groups of citizens united by some common passion or interest and opposed to the rights of other citizens or to the interests of the whole community (3, 13)

fascist government an authoritarian government in which policy is made for the ultimate glory of the state (1)

federalism a political system in which power is divided between the central and regional units (3)

The Federalist Papers a series of essays written in support of the Constitution to build support for its ratification (3)

Federalists supporters of the Constitution, who favored a strong central government (3)

Federal Register publication containing all federal regulations and notifications of regulatory agency hearings (9)

feeding frenzy excessive press coverage of an embarrassing or scandalous subject (15)

feudalism a hierarchical political and economic system based on the ownership of land by the few (3)

fighting words speech intended to incite violence (5)

filibuster a practice of unlimited debate in the Senate in order to prevent or delay a vote on a bill (7)

527 groups groups that mobilize voters with issue advocacy advertisements on television and radio but may not directly advocate the election or defeat of a particular candidate (13)

framing process through which the media emphasize particular aspects of a news story, thereby influencing the public's perception of the story (15)

franking the privilege of free mail service provided to members of Congress (7)

freedom of assembly the right of people to gather peacefully and to petition government (5)

Freedom of Information Act a 1966 law that allows citizens to obtain copies of most public records (9)

free exercise clause the First Amendment guarantee that citizens may freely engage in the religious activities of their choice (5)

free rider problem the difficulty groups face in recruiting when potential members can gain the benefits of the group's actions whether they join or not (13)

French and Indian War a war fought between France and England, and allied Indians, from 1754 to 1763; resulted in France's expulsion from New World (3)

front-loading the process of scheduling presidential primaries early in the primary season (14)

front-runner the leading candidate and expected winner of a nomination or an election (14)

fusion of powers an alternative to separation of powers, combining or blending branches of government (4)

gatekeepers journalists and media elite who determine which news stories are covered and which are not (15)

gender gap the tendency of men and women to differ in their political views on some issues (11)

gerrymandering redistricting to benefit a particular group (7)

get-out-the-vote (GOTV) drives efforts by political parties, interest groups, and the candidate's staff to maximize voter turnout among supporters (14)

Gibbons v. Ogden Supreme Court ruling (1824) establishing national authority over interstate business (4)

going public a president's strategy of appealing to the public on an issue, expecting that public pressure will be brought to bear on other political actors (8)

governing activities directed toward controlling the distribution of political resources by providing executive and legislative leadership, enacting agendas, mobilizing support, and building coalitions (12)

government a system or organization for exercising authority over a body of people (1)

government corporation a company created by Congress to provide a good or service to the public that private enterprise cannot or will not profitably provide (9)

government matching funds money given by the federal government to qualified presidential candidates in the primary and general election campaigns (14)

grandfather clauses provisions exempting from voting restrictions the descendants of those able to vote in 1867 (6)

grassroots lobbying indirect lobbying efforts that spring from wide-spread public concern (13)

Great Compromise the constitutional solution to congressional representation: equal votes in the Senate, votes by population in the House (3)

habeas corpus the right of an accused person to be brought before a judge and informed of the charges and evidence against him or her (5)

hard money campaign funds donated directly to candidates; amounts are limited by federal election laws (14)

Hatch Act 1939 law limiting the political involvement of civil servants in order to protect them from political pressure and keep politics out of the bureaucracy (9)

head of government the political role of the president as leader of a political party and chief arbiter of who gets what resources (8)

head of state the apolitical, unifying role of the president as symbolic representative of the whole country (8)

honeymoon period the time following an election when a president's popularity is high and congressional relations are likely to be productive (8)

horse-race journalism the media's focus on the competitive aspects of politics rather than on actual policy proposals and political decisions (15)

House Rules Committee the committee that determines how and when debate on a bill will take place (7)

ideologies belief systems about politics, the economy, and society that help people make sense of their world (2)

immigrants citizens or subjects of other countries who come to the United States to live or work (2)

imminent lawless action test rule used by the courts that restricts speech only if it is aimed at producing or is likely to produce imminent lawless action (5)

incorporation Supreme Court action making the protections of the Bill of Rights applicable to the states (5)

incumbency advantage the electoral edge afforded to those already in office (7)

independent agency a government organization independent of the departments but with a narrower policy focus (9)

independent regulatory boards and commissions government organizations that regulate various businesses, industries, or economic sectors (9)

indirect lobbying attempts to influence government policymakers by encouraging the general public to put pressure on them (13)

individualism belief that what is good for society is based on what is good for individuals (2)

inherent powers presidential powers implied but not explicitly stated in the Constitution (8)

initiative a citizen petition to place a proposal or constitutional amendment on the ballot, to be adopted or rejected by majority vote, bypassing the legislature (4)

inquisitorial systems trial procedures designed to determine the truth through the intervention of an active judge who seeks evidence and questions witnesses (10)

institutions organizations where governmental power is exercised (1)

interest group an organization of individuals who share a common political goal and unite for the purpose of influencing government decisions (13)

interest group entrepreneurs effective group leaders who are likely to have organized the group and can effectively promote its interests among members and the public (13)

intermediate standard of review standard of review used by the Court to evaluate laws that make a quasisuspect classification (6)

iron triangle the phenomenon of a clientele group, congressional committee, and bureaucratic agency cooperating to make mutually beneficial policy (9)

issue advocacy ads advertisements that support issues or candidates without telling constituents how to vote (13); advertisements paid for by soft money, and thus not regulated, that promote certain issue positions but do not endorse specific candidates (14)

issue network a complex system of relationships between groups that influence policy, including elected leaders, interest groups, specialists, consultants, and research institutes (9)

issue ownership the tendency of one party to be seen as more competent in a specific policy area (14)

Jim Crow laws Southern laws designed to circumvent the Thirteenth, Fourteenth, and Fifteenth Amendments and to deny blacks rights on bases other than race (6)

joint committees combined House-Senate committees formed to coordinate activities and expedite legislation in a certain area (7)

judicial activism view that the courts should be lawmaking, policymaking bodies (10)

judicial interpretivism a judicial approach holding that the Constitution is a living document and that judges should interpret it according to changing times and values (10)

judicial power the power to interpret laws and judge whether a law has been broken (4)

judicial restraint view that the courts should reject any active lawmaking functions and stick to judicial interpretations of the past (10)

judicial review power of the Supreme Court to rule on the constitutionality of laws (4, 10)

jurisdiction a court's authority to hear certain cases (10)

laissez-faire capitalism an economic system in which the market makes all decisions and the government plays no role (1)

leaks confidential information secretly revealed to the press (15)

legislative agenda the slate of proposals and issues that representatives think it worthwhile to consider and act on (7)

legislative liaison executive personnel who work with members of Congress to secure their support in getting a president's legislation passed (8)

legislative oversight a committee's investigation of government agencies to ensure they are acting as Congress intends (7)

legislative supremacy an alternative to judicial review, the acceptance of legislative acts as the final law of the land (4)

legislature the body of government that makes laws (4)

legitimate accepted as "right" or proper (1)

***Lemon* test** three-pronged rule used by the courts to determine whether the establishment clause is violated (5)

libel written defamation of character (5)

liberals people who generally favor government action and view change as progress (2)

libertarians those who favor a minimal government role in any sphere (2)

literacy tests tests requiring reading or comprehension skills as a qualification for voting (6)

lobbying interest group activities aimed at persuading policymakers to support the group's positions (13)

majority party the party with the most seats in a house of Congress (7)

Marbury v. Madison the landmark case that established the U.S. Supreme Court's power of judicial review (10)

marriage gap the tendency for married people to hold political opinions that differ from those of people who have never married (11)

mass media means of conveying information to large public audiences cheaply and efficiently (15)

material benefits selective incentives in the form of a tangible reward (13)

McCulloch v. Maryland Supreme Court ruling (1819) confirming the supremacy of national over state government (4)

midterm loss the tendency for the presidential party to lose congressional seats in off-year elections (7)

***Miller* test** rule used by the courts in which the definition of *obscenity* must be based on local standards (5)

minimum rationality test standard of review used by the Court to evaluate laws that make a nonsuspect classification (6)

momentum the widely held public perception that a candidate is gaining electoral strength (14)

monarchy an authoritarian government with power vested in a king or queen (1)

Motor Voter Bill legislation allowing citizens to register to vote at the same time they apply for a driver's license or other state benefit (14)

muckrakers investigative reporters who search for and expose misconduct in corporate activity or public officials (15)

narrowcasting the targeting of specialized audiences by the media (15)

National Association for the Advancement of Colored People (NAACP) an interest group founded in 1910 to promote civil rights for African Americans (6)

national lawmaking the creation of policy to address the problems and needs of the entire nation (7)

National Security Council organization within the EOP that provides foreign policy advice to the president (8)

naturalization the legal process of acquiring citizenship for someone who has not acquired it by birth (2)

necessary and proper clause constitutional authorization for Congress to make any law required to carry out its powers (4)

negative advertising campaign advertising that emphasizes the negative characteristics of opponents rather than one's own strengths (14)

neutral competence the principle that bureaucracy should be depoliticized by making it more professional (9)

New Jersey Plan a proposal at the Constitutional Convention that congressional representation be equal, thus favoring the small states (3)

news management the efforts of a politician's staff to control news about the politician (15)

nominating convention formal party gathering to choose candidates (12)

norms informal rules that govern behavior in Congress (7)

nullification declaration by a state that a federal law is void within its borders (4)

Office of Management and Budget organization within the EOP that oversees the budgets of departments and agencies (8)

oligarchy rule by a small group of elites (1)

on-line processing the ability to receive and evaluate information as events happen, allowing us to remember our evaluation even if we have forgotten the specific events that caused it (11)

open primaries primary elections in which eligible voters do not need to be registered party members (12, 14)

opinion the written decision of the court that states the judgment of the majority (10)

opinion leaders people who know more about certain topics than we do and whose advice we trust, seek out, and follow (11)

oppo research investigation of an opponent's background for the purpose of exploiting weaknesses or undermining credibility (14)

original jurisdiction the authority of a court to hear a case first (10)

pardoning power a president's authority to release or excuse a person from the legal penalties of a crime (8)

parliamentary system government in which the executive is chosen by the legislature from among its members and the two branches are merged (4)

participatory democracy a theory of democracy that holds that citizens should actively and directly control all aspects of their lives (1)

partisanship loyalty to a political cause or party (12)

party activists the "party faithful"; the rank-and-file members who actually carry out the party's electioneering efforts (12)

party base members of a political party who consistently vote for that party's candidates (12)

party bosses party leaders, usually in an urban district, who exercised tight control over electioneering and patronage (12)

party caucus local gathering of party members to choose convention delegates (14)

party discipline ability of party leaders to bring party members in the legislature into line with the party program (12)

party eras extended periods of relative political stability in which one party tends to control both the presidency and Congress (12)

party identification voter affiliation with a political party (12)

party-in-government members of the party who have been elected to serve in government (12)

party-in-the-electorate ordinary citizens who identify with the party (12)

party machines mass-based party systems in which parties provided services and resources to voters in exchange for votes (12)

party organization the official structure that conducts the political business of parties (12)

party platform list of policy positions a party endorses and pledges its elected officials to enact (12)

party primary nomination of party candidates by registered party members rather than party bosses (12)

patronage system in which successful party candidates reward supporters with jobs or favors (9, 12)

Pendleton Act 1883 civil service reform that required the hiring and promoting of civil servants to be based on merit, not patronage (9)

Plessy v. Ferguson Supreme Court case that established the constitutionality of the principle "separate but equal" (6)

pluralist democracy a theory of democracy that holds that citizen membership in groups is the key to political power (1)

pocket veto presidential authority to kill a bill submitted within ten days of the end of a legislative session by not signing it (7)

police power the ability of a government to protect its citizens and maintain social order (5)

policy entrepreneurship practice of legislators becoming experts and taking leadership roles in specific policy areas (7)

policy representation congressional work to advance the issues and ideological preferences of constituents (7)

political accountability the democratic principle that political leaders must answer to the public for their actions (15)

political action committee (PAC) the fundraising arm of an interest group (13)

political correctness the idea that language shapes behavior and therefore should be regulated to control its social effects (5)

political culture the shared values and beliefs about the nature of the political world that give people a common language in which to discuss and debate political ideas (2)

political generations groups of citizens whose political views have been shaped by the common events of their youth (11)

political gridlock the stalemate that occurs when political rivals, especially parties, refuse to budge from their positions to achieve a compromise in the public interest (12)

political party a group of citizens united by ideology and seeking control of government in order to promote their ideas and policies (12)

political socialization the process by which we learn our political orientations and allegiances (11)

politics who gets what, when, and how; a process of determining how power and resources are distributed in a society without recourse to violence (1)

poll taxes taxes levied as a qualification for voting (6)

popular sovereignty the concept that the citizens are the ultimate source of political power (1, 3)

popular tyranny the unrestrained power of the people (3)

pork barrel public works projects and grants for specific districts paid for by general revenues (7)

position issues issues on which the parties differ in their perspectives and proposed solutions (14)

power the ability to get other people to do what you want (1)

power to persuade a president's ability to convince Congress, other political actors, and the public to cooperate with the administration's agenda (8)

precedent a previous decision or ruling that, in common law tradition, is binding on subsequent decisions (10)

presidential primary an election by which voters choose convention delegates committed to voting for a certain candidate (14)

presidential style image projected by the president that represents how he would like to be perceived at home and abroad (8)

presidential system government in which the executive is chosen independently of the legislature and the two branches are separate (4)

presidential veto a president's authority to reject a bill passed by Congress; may only be overridden by a two-thirds majority in each house (8)

priming the way in which the media's emphasis on particular characteristics of people, events, or issues influences the public's perception of those people, events, or issues (15)

prior restraint censorship of or punishment for the expression of ideas before the ideas are printed or spoken (5)

Privacy Act of 1974 a law that gives citizens access to the government's files on them (9)

procedural due process procedural laws that protect the rights of individuals who must deal with the legal system (10)

procedural guarantees government assurance that the rules will work smoothly and treat everyone fairly, with no promise of particular outcomes (1, 2)

procedural laws laws that establish how laws are applied and enforced—how legal proceedings take place (10)

prospective voting basing voting decisions on well-informed opinions and consideration of the future consequences of a given vote (14)

Protestant Reformation the break (1500s) from the Roman Catholic Church by those who believed in direct access to God and salvation by faith (1)

public interest group group that organizes to influence government to produce collective goods or services that benefit the general public (13)

public opinion the collective attitudes and beliefs of individuals on one or more issues (11)

public opinion polls scientific efforts to estimate what an entire group thinks about an issue by asking a smaller sample of the group for its opinion (11)

pundit a professional observer and commentator on politics (15)

Puritans a Protestant religious sect that sought to reform the Church of England in the sixteenth and seventeenth centuries (3)

push polls polls that ask for reactions to hypothetical, often false, information in order to manipulate public opinion (11)

racial gerrymandering redistricting to enhance or reduce the chances that a racial or ethnic group will elect members to the legislature (7)

racism institutionalized power inequalities in society based on the perception of racial differences (6)

random samples samples chosen in such a way that any member of the population being polled has an equal chance of being selected (11)

ratification the process through which a proposal is formally approved and adopted by vote (3)

rational ignorance the state of being uninformed about politics because of the cost in time and energy (11)

realignment substantial and long-term shift in party allegiance by individuals and groups, usually resulting in a change in policy direction (12)

reapportionment a reallocation of congressional seats among the states every ten years, following the census (7)

recall election a vote to remove an elected official from office (4)

Reconstruction the period following the Civil War during which the federal government took action to rebuild the South (6)

redistricting process of dividing states into legislative districts (7)

red tape the complex procedures and regulations surrounding bureaucratic activity (9)

referendum an election in which a bill passed by the state legislature is submitted to voters for approval (4)

refugees individuals who flee an area or country because of persecution on the basis of race, nationality, religion, group membership, or political opinion (2)

regulated capitalism a market system in which the government intervenes to protect rights and make procedural guarantees (1)

regulations limitations or restrictions on the activities of a business or individual (9)

representation the efforts of elected officials to look out for the interests of those who elect them (7)

republic a government in which decisions are made through representatives of the people (1, 4)

responsible party model party government when four conditions are met: clear choice of ideologies, candidates pledged to implement ideas, party held accountable by voters, and party control over members (12)

retrospective voting basing voting decisions on reactions to past performance; approving the status quo or signaling a desire for change (14)

revolving door the tendency of public officials, journalists, and lobbyists to move between public and private sector (media, lobbying) jobs (13, 15)

roll call voting publicly recorded votes on bills and amendments on the floor of the House or Senate (7)

Rule of Four the unwritten requirement that four Supreme Court justices must agree to grant a case certiorari in order for the case to be heard (10)

rules directives that specify how resources will be distributed or what procedures govern collective activity (1)

sample the portion of the population that is selected to participate in a poll (11)

sample bias the effect of having a sample that does not represent all segments of the population (11)

sampling error a number that indicates within what range the results of a poll are accurate (11)

sedition speech that criticizes the government (5)

segregation the practice and policy of separating races (6)

select committee a committee appointed to deal with an issue or problem not suited to a standing committee (7)

selective incentives benefits that are available only to group members as an inducement to get them to join (13)

selective incorporation incorporation of rights on a case-by-case basis (5)

selective perception the phenomenon of filtering incoming information through personal values and interests (15)

senatorial courtesy tradition of granting senior senators of the president's party considerable power over federal judicial appointments in their home states (8, 10)

seniority system the accumulation of power and authority in conjunction with the length of time spent in office (7)

separationists supporters of a "wall of separation" between church and state (5)

separation of powers the institutional arrangement that assigns judicial, executive, and legislative powers to different persons or groups, thereby limiting the powers of each (4)

sexual harassment unwelcome sexual speech or behavior that creates a hostile work environment (6)

Shays's Rebellion a grassroots uprising (1787) by armed Massachusetts farmers protesting foreclosures (3)

slavery the ownership, for forced labor, of one people by another (3)

social connectedness citizens' involvement in groups and their relationships to their communities and families (14)

social conservatives those who endorse limited government control of the economy but considerable government intervention to realize a traditional social order; based on religious values and hierarchy rather than equality (2)

social contract the notion that society is based on an agreement between government and the governed in which people agree to give up some rights in exchange for the protection of others (1)

social democracy a hybrid system combining a capitalist economy and a government that supports equality (1)

socialist economy an economic system in which the state determines production, distribution, and price decisions and property is government owned (1)

social liberals those who favor greater government control of the economy and the social order to bring about greater equality and to regulate the effects of progress (2)

social order a particular view of how we ought to organize and live our collective lives; who should get what (1)

social protest public activities designed to bring attention to political causes, usually generated by those without access to conventional means of expressing their views (13)

soft money unregulated campaign contributions by individuals, groups, or parties that promote general election activities but do not directly support individual candidates (14)

solicitor general the Justice Department officer who argues the government's cases before the Supreme Court (8, 10)

solidarity benefits selective incentives related to the interaction and bonding among group members (13)

Speaker of the House the leader of the majority party who serves as the presiding officer of the House of Representatives (7)

spin an interpretation of a politician's words or actions, designed to present a favorable image (15)

spiral of silence the process by which a majority opinion becomes exaggerated because minorities do not feel comfortable speaking out in opposition (11)

spoils system the nineteenth-century practice of rewarding political supporters with public office (9)

standing committees permanent committees responsible for legislation in particular policy areas (7)

State of the Union address a speech given annually by the president to a joint session of Congress and to the nation announcing the president's agenda (8)

statutory laws laws passed by a state or the federal legislature (10)

strategic politician an office-seeker who bases the decision to run on a rational calculation that he or she will be successful (7)

straw polls polls that attempt to determine who is ahead in a political race (11)

strict constructionism a judicial approach holding that the Constitution should be read literally, with the framers' intentions uppermost in mind (10)

strict scrutiny a heightened standard of review used by the Supreme Court to assess the constitutionality of laws that limit some freedoms or that make a suspect classification (6)

subjects individuals who are obliged to submit to a government authority against which they have no rights (1)

substantive guarantees government assurance of particular outcomes or results (1)

substantive laws laws whose content, or substance, define what we can or cannot do (10)

sunshine laws legislation opening the process of bureaucratic policymaking to the public (9)

supremacy clause constitutional declaration (Article VI) that the Constitution and laws made under its provisions are the supreme law of the land (4)

suspect classifications classifications, such as race, for which any discriminatory law must be justified by a compelling state interest (6)

swing voters the approximately one-third of the electorate who are undecided at the start of a campaign (14)

symbolic representations efforts of members of Congress to stand for American ideals or identify with common constituency values (7)

theocracy an authoritarian government that claims to draw its power from divine or religious authority (1)

Three-fifths Compromise the formula for counting five slaves as three people for purposes of representation that reconciled northern and southern factions at the Constitutional Convention (3)

totalitarian government a system in which absolute power is exercised over every aspect of life (1)

tracking polls ongoing series of surveys that follow changes in public opinion over time (11)

treaties formal agreements with other countries; negotiated by the president and requiring approval by two-thirds of the Senate (8)

trial balloon an official leak of a proposal to determine public reaction to it without risk (15)

two-step flow of information the process by which citizens take their political cues from more well-informed opinion leaders (11)

unfunded mandate a federal order under which states operate and pay for a program created at the national level (4)

unicameral legislature a legislature with one chamber (4)

unitary system government in which all power is centralized (4)

valence issues issues on which most voters and candidates share the same position (14)

values central ideas, principles, or standards that most people agree are important (2)

veto override reversal of a presidential veto by a two-thirds vote in both houses of Congress (7)

Virginia Plan a proposal at the Constitutional Convention that congressional representation be based on population, thus favoring the large states (3)

voter mobilization a party's efforts to inform potential voters about issues and candidates and persuade them to vote (14)

wedge issue a controversial issue that one party uses to split the voters in the other party (14)

whistle blowers individuals who publicize instances of fraud, corruption, or other wrongdoing in the bureaucracy (9)

White House Office the approximately four hundred employees within the EOP who work most closely and directly with the president (8)

writ of certiorari formal request by the U.S. Supreme Court to call up the lower court case it decides to hear on appeal (10)

INDEX

Note: Page numbers in **boldface** indicate page on which key term is defined; in *italics* indicate photos or illustrations; followed by *f* or *t* indicate figures and tables respectively.

B

D

E

F

G

H

J

N

Q

R

T

U

V

IMAGE CREDITS

Chapter 1, Politics: Who Gets What, and How?

2 Kevin Guckes/*Kenyon Collegian*
Inset: AP/Wide World Photos
7 Reuters
11 Mary Marin/iStockphoto
16 AP/Wide World Photos
17 Courtesy of Christine Barbour
22 AP/Wide World Photos

Chapter 2, American Citizens and Political Culture

32 AP/Wide World Photos
Inset: AP/Wide World Photos
37 © Steve Kelly/*San Diego Union Tribune*
41 AP/Wide World Photos
54 AP/Wide World Photos
58 Photo by Frank Cantor

Chapter 3, Politics of the American Founding

66 The Granger Collection, New York
Inset: AP/Wide World Photos
71 FOR BETTER OR FOR WORSE © 1996 Lynn Johnston Productions. Dist. by UNIVERSAL PRESS SYNDICATE. Reprinted with permission.
76 The Granger Collection, New York
77 The Granger Collection, New York
79 Library of Congress
83 (left) The Granger Collection, New York
(right) The Granger Collection, New York
88 The Granger Collection, New York
96 Photo by Anne McDonough
99 © Sidney Harris, ScienceCartoonsPlus.com

Chapter 4, Federalism and the U.S. Constitution

104 Reuters
Inset: J. D. Crowe/Artizans
107 CALVIN AND HOBBES © 1990 Watterson. Dist. by UNIVERSAL PRESS SYNDICATE. Reprinted with permission. All rights reserved.
110 AP/Wide World Photos
114 Reuters
130 Reuters
132 The Granger Collection, New York
138 AP/Wide World Photos
142 Tom Williams/*Roll Call* Photos
143 David Ulmer/Stock Boston

Chapter 5, Fundamental American Liberties

152 Courtesy of Christine Barbour
Inset: AP/Wide World Photos
158 Landov
160 CORBIS
161 AP/Wide World Photos
168 Doug Potter/*Austin Chronicle*
173 Image Works
175 Photo by Darla Khazei/Wenn/Landov
178 Robert Ginn/PhotoEdit
191 AP/Wide World Photos
193 The Collection of the Supreme Court of the United States
199 Clay Bennett © *The Christian Science Monitor* (www.csmonitor.com). All rights reserved.

Chapter 6, The Struggle for Equal Rights

206 AP/Wide World Photos
Inset: Reuters
215 CORBIS
219 (left) CORBIS
(right) Will Count estate and Indiana University
227 AP/Wide World Photos
231 AP/Wide World Photos
234 AP/Wide World Photos
237 AP/Wide World Photos
248 © From the collection of Christine Barbour
249 AP/Wide World Photos
252 Clay Bennett © *The Christian Science Monitor* (www.csmonitor.com). All rights reserved.
256 AP/Wide World Photos

Chapter 7, Congress

266 Reuters
Inset: AP/Wide World Photos
271 AP/Wide World Photos
272 © 1989 Jeff MacNelly Tribune Media Services, Inc. All rights reserved. Reprinted with permission.
277 AP/Wide World Photos
280 Library of Congress
284 Reuters
289 AP/Wide World Photos
297 George Tames/*The New York Times*
309 AP/Wide World Photos
313 THE BOONDOCKS © 2002 Aaron McGruder. Dist. by UNIVERSAL PRESS SYNDICATE. Reprinted with permission. All rights reserved.

Chapter 8, The Presidency

318 Reuters
Inset: AP/Wide World Photos
322 TOLES © *The Buffalo News*. Reprinted with permission of UNIVERSAL PRESS SYNDICATE. All rights reserved.
324 (top) Reuters
(bottom) AP/Wide World Photos
327 © 2005 Steve Sack Tribune Media Services, Inc. All rights reserved. Reprinted with permission.
333 Reuters
334 AP/Wide World Photos
339 AP/Wide World Photos
343 AP/Wide World Photos
350 Reuters
352 Getty Images
356 AP/Wide World Photos
361 Reuters
363 Courtesy Ronald Reagan Library
367 © 2004, The Washington Post Writers Group, reprinted with permission.

Chapter 9, The Bureaucracy

372 AP/Wide World Photos
Inset: AP/Wide World Photos
378 © Sidney Harris, ScienceCartoonsPlus.com
380 Library of Congress
385 Landov
387 Copyright John Trevor and Cagle Cartoons 2005. All rights reserved.
391 Getty Images
395 Courtesy of Christine Barbour
397 AP/Wide World Photos
401 Reuters
405 AP/Wide World Photos

Chapter 10, The American Legal System and the Courts

412 Getty Images
Inset: Reuters
418 Reuters
419 Courtesy of Michael Kerns
426 Library of Congress
435 Getty Images
436 HISTORICAL FIGURES from *Herblock: A Cartoonist's Life* (Times Books, 1998).
437 King Features Syndicate
440 Photo by Scott Ferrell/Congressional Quarterly Inc.
445 AP/Wide World Photos
449 AP/Wide World Photos

Chapter 11, Public Opinion

456 AP/Wide World Photos
Inset: AP/Wide World Photos
460 Courtesy of Loretta Sanchez
463 Library of Congress
465 DOONESBURY © 1989 G. B. Trudeau. Reprinted with permission of UNIVERSAL PRESS SYNDICATE. All rights reserved.
468 The Pew Research Center for the People and the Press
470 © 1989 Jeff MacNelly Tribune Media Services, Inc. All rights reserved. Reprinted with permission.
474 AP/Wide World Photos
478 Courtesy of Ann West

Chapter 12, Political Parties

496 AP/Wide World Photos
Inset: AP/Wide World Photos
503 Reuters
511 AP/Wide World Photos
515 The Granger Collection, New York
518 The Granger Collection, New York
521 AP/Wide World Photos
522 Landov
525 Reuters
526 Photo by Andy Nelson/*The Christian Science Monitor* via Getty Images
532 Landov
534 Copyright Mike Lane and Cagle Cartoons 2005. All rights reserved.

Chapter 13, Interest Groups

542 Landov
Inset: AP/Wide World Photos
549 Suchat Pederson/*The New York Times*
551 AP/Wide World Photos
554 AP/Wide World Photos
559 AP/Wide World Photos

562 Courtesy of the Humane Society of the United States
566 AP/Wide World Photos
571 AP/Wide World Photos
572 Phil Schermeister/CORBIS
578 AP/Wide World Photos

Chapter 14, Voting, Campaigns, and Elections

586 Reuters
Inset: AP/Wide World Photos
590 CORBIS
594 Kirk Anderson, www.kirktoons.com
597 AP/Wide World Photos
600 Reuters
605 Copyright M. e. Cohen and Cagle Cartoons 2005. All rights reserved.
606 Getty Images
607 Getty Images
615 Getty Images
616 Photo by Alex Wong/Getty Images
621 CORBIS
623 Reuters
630 Bruce MacKinnon/Artizans.com

Chapter 15, The Media

634 Getty Images
Inset: AP/Wide World Photos
638 CORBIS
638 AP/Wide World Photos
641 Reuters
654 CORBIS
658 © 2005 Ed Koren from cartoonbank.com. All rights reserved.
666 Clay Bennett © *The Christian Science Monitor* (www.csmonitor.com). All rights reserved.
668 AP/Wide World Photos
671 Clay Bennett © *The Christian Science Monitor* (www.csmonitor.com). All rights reserved.
672 Photo by Paul Delahanty